America Votes™ 33

Sara Miller McCune founded SAGE Publishing in 1965 to support the dissemination of usable knowledge and educate a global community. SAGE publishes more than 1000 journals and over 800 new books each year, spanning a wide range of subject areas. Our growing selection of library products includes archives, data, case studies and video. SAGE remains majority owned by our founder and after her lifetime will become owned by a charitable trust that secures the company's continued independence.

Los Angeles | London | New Delhi | Singapore | Washington DC | Melbourne

America Votes™ 33

ELECTION RETURNS BY STATE

RHODES COOK

2017–2018

SAGE reference | CQPRESS

Los Angeles | London | New Delhi
Singapore | Washington DC | Melbourne

FOR INFORMATION:

CQ Press
An Imprint of SAGE Publications, Inc.
2455 Teller Road
Thousand Oaks, California 91320
E-mail: order@sagepub.com

SAGE Publications Ltd.
1 Oliver's Yard
55 City Road
London, EC1Y 1SP
United Kingdom

SAGE Publications India Pvt. Ltd.
B 1/I 1 Mohan Cooperative Industrial Area
Mathura Road, New Delhi 110 044
India

SAGE Publications Asia-Pacific Pte. Ltd.
18 Cross Street #10-10/11/12
China Square Central
Singapore 048423

SAGE Editor: Laura Notton
Assistant Editor: Tamara Tanso
Researchers: Luana Shafer, Alexis Bates
Database Lead: Nora Varbedian
Database Team: Sal Hewavita, Andre Messier
Production Editor: Tracy Buyan
Typesetter: Hurix Systems Pvt. Ltd., India
Proofreader: Laura Webb
Cover Designer: Candice Harman
Marketing Manager: Carmel Schrire

ACKNOWLEDGMENT: Richard M. Scammon
The publishers of *America Votes* wish to recognize the creator and long-time editor of *America Votes*, the late Richard M. Scammon. He brought his keen perceptions of the American electorate and his in-depth knowledge of U.S. voting patterns to his more than 40 years of work on the *America Votes* series. Scammon founded and directed the nonprofit Elections Research Center and was widely considered the most prominent American elections expert during his long career as a government official, advisor to presidents, and analyst of voting trends and developments. His love of elections was rooted in his lifelong commitment to democracy and his belief that the voice of one is always bested by the voice of the many.

Printed in the United States of America.

ISSN: 0065-678X
ISBN: 978-1-5443-5444-6

19 20 21 22 23 10 9 8 7 6 5 4 3 2 1

Contents

List of Maps vi
Introduction vii
Errata xvii

Summary Tables
- Voter Turnout 2018 1
- Gubernatorial Elections 2017 and 2018 2
- Senate Elections 2017 and 2018 3
- House of Representatives Elections 2018 4

Special Elections and Postelections Changes 2017–2018
- Summary of House and Senate Special Elections 2017–2018 5
  - Special Elections and Postelections Changes to the 115th Congress 5
  - Changes following the 2018 Election 9

U.S. Presidential Elections
- Popular Vote for President 1920–2016 10
- Electoral College Vote 1920–2016 10

County and District Results by State
- Alabama 11
- Alaska 18
- Arizona 25
- Arkansas 33
- California 39
- Colorado 59
- Connecticut 67
- Delaware 75
- Florida 80
- Georgia 92
- Hawaii 102
- Idaho 107
- Illinois 113
- Indiana 123
- Iowa 131
- Kansas 138
- Kentucky 145
- Louisiana 150
- Maine 155
- Maryland 163
- Massachusetts 171
- Michigan 182
- Minnesota 193
- Mississippi 205
- Missouri 214
- Montana 222
- Nebraska 227
- Nevada 235
- New Hampshire 242
- New Jersey 249
- New Mexico 257
- New York 263
- North Carolina 275
- North Dakota 281
- Ohio 287
- Oklahoma 299
- Oregon 306
- Pennsylvania 312
- Rhode Island 322
- South Carolina 329
- South Dakota 336
- Tennessee 342
- Texas 352
- Utah 377
- Vermont 383
- Virginia 391
- Washington 402
- West Virginia 410
- Wisconsin 416
- Wyoming 425
- District of Columbia 431

List of Maps

Alabama 11
Alaska 19
Arizona 25
Greater Phoenix Area 26
Arkansas 33
California 39
Greater Los Angeles, San Diego Areas 40
Greater San Francisco Bay Area 41
Colorado 59
Denver Area 60
Connecticut 67
Delaware 75
Florida 80
Greater Miami, Fort Lauderdale Areas 81
Georgia 92
Atlanta Area 93
Hawaii 102
Idaho 107
Illinois 113
Chicago Area 114
Indiana 123
Iowa 131
Kansas 138
Kentucky 145
Louisiana 150
Maine 155
Maryland 163
Baltimore, Washington, D.C., Areas 164
Massachusetts 171
Boston Area 172
Michigan 182
Detroit Area 183
Minnesota 193
Minneapolis–St. Paul Area 194
Mississippi 205
Missouri 214
Montana 222
Nebraska 227
Nevada 235
Greater Las Vegas Area 236
New Hampshire 242
New Jersey 249
Northern New Jersey Gateway Area 250
New Mexico 257
New York 263
New York City Area 264
North Carolina 275
North Dakota 281
Ohio 287
Cleveland Area 288
Columbus Area 288
Oklahoma 299
Oregon 306
Pennsylvania 312
Rhode Island 322
South Carolina 329
South Dakota 336
Tennessee 342
Texas 352
Greater Dallas–Forth Worth Area 353
Greater Houston Area 354
Greater San Antonio, Austin Areas 355
Utah 377
Vermont 383
Virginia 391
Washington 402
Seattle Area 403
West Virginia 410
Wisconsin 416
Wyoming 425
District of Columbia 431

Introduction

The 2018 midterm elections provided the first nationwide voter feedback to the tempestuous personality and controversial presidency of Donald J. Trump. By and large, the results were good news for the Democrats. They took over the House of Representatives, the first time the party had won House control in a decade. They also picked up a slew of governorships and state legislative seats. Republicans did manage to hold onto the Senate, albeit on a playing field that strongly favored the GOP.

On election night, many political commentators referred to the result as a "split decision," largely equating the Democrats' House breakthrough with the GOP's expansion of their Senate majority to 53 seats from 51.

2018: Democratic Tide

Democrats gained a number of high-profile victories in the 2018 midterm elections, flipping the House of Representatives in their favor and making inroads in the states among the governorships and state legislatures. But Republicans could take solace in their expanded Senate majority and their continued control of most of the nation's governorships and state legislatures. The table below reflects partisan seat totals for Congress and the governorships immediately before and after the 2018 general election. The pre-election House totals include five Republican and two Democratic vacancies, which are each credited to the party that held them before they became vacant. The post-election House total adds to 434, because the results from a North Carolina district were not certified because of evidence of absentee vote fraud by Republican operatives. The seat was not filled until September 2019 when Republicans won a special "do over" election. Meanwhile, two independent senators who caucus with the Democrats, Angus King of Maine and Bernie Sanders of Vermont, are listed in the "Other" column in the table below. Heading into the 2018 election, there was one independent governor, Bill Walker of Alaska, who abandoned his re-election bid before the November balloting.

	Pre-election			Post-election		
	Rep.	Dem.	Other	Rep.	Dem.	Other
Governor	33	16	1	27	23	0
Senate	51	47	2	53	45	2
House	240	195	0	199	235	0

But as the days went by and more congressional races fell to the Democrats, the consensus viewpoint shifted to describing the 2018 midterms as a Democratic victory. The party picked up a net of 40 House seats, their most in a midterm since the Watergate election of 1974. Democrats also netted seven governorships and hundreds of state legislative seats, important gains as the states gear up for the next round of congressional and state legislative redistricting after the 2020 census.

But was this really the "blue wave" that was a major topic of speculation throughout 2018? Along with the Senate, Republicans after the election still held a majority of governorships (27 to the Democrats' 23), and controlled fully 60 percent of state legislatures. Taking the results in their entirety, it would seem more appropriate to call the 2018 election results a "Democratic tide."

The legacy of 2018 also included the phenomenally large turnout that featured a record number of ballots cast in a midterm election. The nationwide House vote surpassed 113 million, a figure that dwarfed the previous record of ballots counted in a midterm congressional election of 86.5 million votes set in 2010. (The House vote is used here in comparing midterm turnouts because it is the only office that is contested in midterm years in all 50 states.)

There is no denying that in 2018, the turnout was pro-Democratic. Four years earlier, the nationwide House vote was 40.0 million for Republican candidates, 35.6 million for their Democratic counterparts. That translated into a convincing 247–188 GOP majority in House seats heading into 2015.

Altogether, there were 4.4 million more congressional votes cast for Republican than Democratic candidates in 2014. In 2018, the vote for Democratic House candidates exceeded that for Republicans by almost 10 million votes, with the Democratic total surging upward by about 25 million votes from the 2014 midterm compared to the Republicans additional 11 million. As a result, Democrats emerged from the 2018 midterms with a 235–199 House majority. (One seat in North Carolina remained uncertified and unfilled until Republicans won it in a "do-over" election in September 2019.)

It has been shown over the years that people vote when they feel that they have something to vote for. In that regard, the huge 2018 turnout was a testament to the

Counting the 2018 Vote

Democrats dominated the vote in 2018 for the House, the Senate and the governorships. They amassed a 17.6-million vote advantage in Senate races, a nearly 9.7-million vote edge in House contests, and a lead approaching 3.4 million in gubernatorial elections. The House vote was based on results from all 50 states. The Senate vote reflected returns from 36 Senate races, 34 of which were held on November 6, 2018 (33 regularly scheduled elections and one special election in Minnesota). In addition, one special Senate contest was held in December 2017 in Alabama and another was decided in late November 2018 in Mississippi. The gubernatorial vote was from 38 races, 36 conducted in November 2018 and two in November 2017 (New Jersey and Virginia). The Democrats' large advantage in the Senate vote was due in no small part to the Republicans' inability in California to advance a Senate candidate to the general election. There, under the state's unique election rules, two Democrats competed in the Senate election in 2018 and divided the 11.1 million votes cast between them. The results from all races in the 2017-18 election cycle were official. No blank or void ballots were included.

						Percentage of Total Vote		
Office	Total Vote	Republican	Democratic	Other	Rep.-Dem. Plurality	Rep.	Dem.	Other
Governor	96,662,826	45,552,196	48,911,266	2,199,364	3,359,070 D	47.1%	50.6%	2.3%
Senate	90,868,337	35,642,679	53,238,099	1,987,559	17,595,420 D	39.2%	58.6%	2.2%
House	113,696,207	50,982,902	60,651,350	2,061,955	9,668,448 D	44.8%	53.3%	1.8%

varying voter responses to President Trump and the conflicting emotions that he generates. Trump had been a source of partisan controversy like no other president in memory. His sharp edges and "stroke the base" positions made him a hero to many Republicans. But he was the devil incarnate to many Democrats and independents, who viewed his tit for tat style of dealing with critics and his unpredictability in governing a threat to basic democratic institutions.

It has been the norm for presidents to limit their campaigning during midterm elections, preferring to focus on governing rather than barnstorming for their party's candidates. But Trump took the opposite approach, spending much of the fall crisscrossing the "red" part of the country to stump at large rallies for GOP candidates and to sing the praises of his presidency. Trump was not shy about positioning himself front and center as the focal point of the election and encouraged Republicans to vote as if he were on the ballot.

Yet it turned out to be a questionable strategy. Trump had a favorable economy on which to campaign in 2018, with the lowest midterm-eve unemployment rate in decades. But he chose instead to accent more peripheral (albeit visceral) issues, such as guarding the nation's southern border from a slow-moving "caravan" of would-be Latin migrants. He clearly felt the issue was more likely than the economy to arouse his base, yet polls in 2018 often showed anti-Trump voters far more intense in their opposition to the president than pro-Trump voters were in their support.

It has been a rule of thumb that midterm turnouts are smaller, whiter, and older than those in presidential years. Yet the 2018 voter turnout was closer in size to the last presidential election (136.7 million votes were cast in the Trump–Hillary Rodham Clinton contest in 2016) than the previous midterm election in 2014, when fewer than 80 million voters cast congressional ballots.

As a consequence, the composition of the 2018 vote was racially more diverse than the last midterm. According to exit polls from both years, the white share of the vote stayed predominately Republican but dropped from 75 percent of the 2014 vote to 72 percent in 2018. Meanwhile, the minority share of the vote rose to 28 percent, with African Americans voting 90 percent Democratic, Asians 77 percent Democratic, and Hispanics 69 percent Democratic.

Altogether, more self-described Democrats than Republicans voted in the 2018 elections (37 percent to 33 percent), a change from the GOP-dominated midterms of 2010 and 2014 when adherents of the two parties cast equal proportions of the vote. Self-described Independents, which comprised 30 percent of the 2018 vote, favored the Democrats after breaking for the Republicans in 2010 and 2014.

In many ways, 2018 was the "year of the woman," or maybe more accurately, the "year of the woman, part two." The first such election to draw that title accompanied Bill Clinton's initial presidential election in 1992, and featured Democratic Senate victories by Barbara

Boxer and Dianne Feinstein in California, Carol Moseley Braun in Illinois, and Patty Murray in Washington.

But the showing by women candidates in 1992 looked like a modest preamble compared to 2018. Altogether, an all-time high of more than 250 women won major party nominations for seats in Congress, 197 Democrats and 56 Republicans. A record 127 were elected to Senate and House seats in 2018, 106 Democrats and 21 Republicans.

Much of the huge increase in female candidates was attributed to the shock of Trump's election, the rise of the #MeToo movement aimed at exposing male sexual harassment, and the general feeling that in a male-dominated culture, women candidates offered the best chance for political change.

In 2018 Senate races, major parties in six states both nominated women—Arizona, Minnesota, Nebraska, New York, Washington, and Wisconsin. In Michigan, women won every major statewide contest—senator, governor, state attorney general, and secretary of state. In Virginia, a trio of female Democratic House candidates ousted three Republican incumbents, flipping the Old Dominion's House delegation from 7–4 Republican to 7–4 Democratic.

It was also a "year of diversity," again primarily on the Democratic side. In two major Southern states, Florida and Georgia, Democrats selected African Americans to run for governor. In the latter state, Stacey Abrams was bidding to become the nation's first female African-American governor. In Idaho, Democrats nominated Paulette Jordan, who was vying to become the nation's first Native American governor.

And Democratic voters nominated a pair of Muslims to run for the House: Rashida Tlaib in the Detroit-area district long represented by Democrat John Conyers; Ilhan Omar in the Minneapolis-based district formerly represented by Keith Ellison, a Muslim who left Congress to run successfully for Minnesota attorney general. Omar and Tlaib were both elected in November. Abrams and Jordan both lost, although Abrams' defeat was narrow and her campaign made her a national figure.

2017: A Harbinger of Things to Come

Through much of American history, even-numbered years have been for elections and odd-numbered years have been for governing. What few elections that are held in the latter rarely rise to a level of national prominence.

However, that was not the case in 2017, the first year of both the midterm election cycle and the controversial presidency of Donald Trump. The latter's long shadow

2016: Close House Races

The 2018 midterm election produced a far larger number of highly competitive House races than two years earlier. Then, barely 20 House seats were won with less than 52% of the total vote. In 2018, the number of sub-52% winners topped 50. By and large, the group featured a combination of embattled Republican incumbents and barely successful Democratic challengers and open seat candidates. The list below does not include the result in the North Carolina 9th District, where Republican Mark Harris led the November 2018 balloting with 49.3% of the vote. However, the vote in his district was not certified because it was deemed there had been absentee vote fraud by operatives for his campaign. The GOP won a "do over" election in September 2019 with a new candidate. An asterisk (*) indicates an incumbent. A pound sign (#) denotes that Democrat Jared Golden's election was the result of Maine's newly created "ranked choice" or "instant runoff" system. To the chagrin of Republicans, GOP Rep. Bruce L. Poliquin led the initial vote in the Maine 2nd District, but fell short of a majority. That triggered a redistribution of votes under the "instant runoff" system that resulted in Golden's election.

Republicans (29)	2018 Winning Percentage	Democrats (22)	2018 Winning Percentage
Steve Watkins, Kan. 2	47.6%	Cindy Axne, Iowa 3	49.3%
Chris Collins, N.Y. 27*	49.1%	Andy Kim, N.J. 3	50.0%
Will Hurd, Texas 23*	49.2%	Ben McAdams, Utah 4	50.1%
Rob Woodall, Ga. 7*	50.1%	Abigail Spanberger, Va. 7	50.3%
James "Jim" Hagedorn, Minn. 1	50.1%	T.J. Cox, Calif. 21	50.4%
Fred Upton, Mich. 6*	50.2%	Jared Golden, Maine 2#	50.4%
Chip Roy, Texas 21	50.2%	Lucy Kay McBath, Ga. 6	50.5%
Steve King, Iowa 4*	50.3%	Elissa Slotkin, Mich. 8	50.6%
Rodney L. Davis, Ill. 13*	50.4%	Joe Cunningham, S.C. 1	50.6%
Kenny Marchant, Texas 24*	50.6%	Kendra Horn, Okla. 5	50.7%
John Carter, Texas 31*	50.6%	Anthony Brindisi, N.Y. 22	50.8%
Pete Stauber, Minn. 8	50.7%	Debbe Mucarsel-Powell, Fla. 26	50.9%
Greg Gianforte, Mont. AL*	50.9%	Xochitl Torres Small, N.M. 2	50.9%
Garland "Andy" Barr, Ky. 6*	51.0%	Abby Finkenauer, Iowa 1	51.0%
Don Bacon, Neb. 2*	51.0%	Elaine Luria, Va. 2	51.1%
Michael T. McCaul, Texas 10*	51.1%	Antonio Delgado, N.Y. 19	51.3%
Ann Wagner, Mo. 2*	51.2%	Gil Cisneros, Calif. 39	51.6%
George Holding, N.C. 2*	51.3%	Tom Malinowski, N.J. 7	51.7%
Steve Chabot, Ohio 1*	51.3%	Donna Shalala, Fla. 27	51.8%
Brian Fitzpatrick, Pa. 1	51.3%	Haley Stevens, Mich. 11	51.8%
Scott Perry, Pa. 10*	51.3%	Susie Lee, Nev. 3	51.9%
Troy Balderson, Ohio 12*	51.4%	Steven A. Horsford, Nev. 4	51.9%
Pete Olson, Texas 22*	51.4%		
Scott Tipton, Colo. 3*	51.5%		
Lee Zeldin, N.Y. 1*	51.5%		
Ted Budd, N.C. 13*	51.5%		
Mike Bost, Ill. 12*	51.6%		
Mike Kelly, Pa. 16*	51.6%		
Duncan D. Hunter, Calif. 50*	51.7%		

helped to create a series of high-profile races from special congressional contests beginning in the spring through the fall's regularly scheduled gubernatorial elections in New Jersey and Virginia. The year concluded with a high-profile special Senate election in Alabama. From start to finish, the contests were seen at least in part as a referendum on Trump. And as such, they drew national attention.

Unlike many presidents who largely stayed clear of off-year elections, Trump threw himself head first into the 2017 action on behalf of Republican candidates. He recorded robo-calls, raised money, and tweeted. In Alabama, he also very publicly endorsed the Republican candidate.

But by and large throughout 2017 (and 2018 as well), anti-Trump voters were much more passionate and motivated than those who supported the president. The result: a series of narrower than expected Republican victories in the year's special congressional elections and stinging GOP defeats in the statewide races.

The special House contests in Kansas, Georgia, Montana, and South Carolina were for seats vacated by GOP representatives who took positions in the Trump administration. All but one of the districts was carried by Trump in 2016 by at least 18 percentage points, and the Republican House members that had formerly held the seats triumphed in 2016 by margins much wider than that.

Yet Democrats were able to score a series of moral victories, as none of the GOP House candidates in 2017 won by more than 6 percentage points. Democrats might actually have picked off a seat or two in Kansas, Montana, or South Carolina if they had played with more gusto and invested more money in these races. However, they concentrated their effort on a suburban Georgia district north of Atlanta, which Republican standard-bearer Mitt Romney swept by 24 percentage points in 2012. Trump, though, had won it by barely 1 percentage point four years later, giving Democrats hope. They saw it as a prime target of opportunity—the type of district, loaded with well-heeled and well-educated voters, that they believed could help them produce a House majority in 2018.

Money poured in from across the country for the Georgia special election, much of it for the Democrat Jon Ossoff, a young, photogenic former congressional aide. His campaign spent more than $20 million, dwarfing the $3.5 million spent by the Democratic candidates in Kansas, Montana, and South Carolina combined.

Ossoff came close to winning the needed majority in the first round of voting in April, taking 48 percent of the vote in a field crowded with Republicans. But that near miss was as close as Ossoff would get. Republican money poured in for the two-way runoff in June and the GOP proclivities of the district took hold. Republican Karen Handel, a former Georgia secretary of state, won the seat by 4 percentage points. By the time of the runoff, it was—according to *The New York Times*—the most expensive House election in history, with candidates and outside groups spending about $55 million.

After the Georgia loss, only the most optimistic of Democrats would have predicted the extent of the party's electoral victories in the final weeks of 2017. Gubernatorial wins in bright blue New Jersey (expected) and the swing state of Virginia (more decisive than was expected) were followed by a noteworthy special Senate victory in bright red Alabama on December 12. In the process, Democrats picked up a governorship in New Jersey and a Senate seat in Alabama, while leaving Republicans on the defensive entering 2018.

The Democratic victories had some common threads. In all three races, women, the young, the well-educated, and minorities voted strongly Democratic. The party's candidates also rolled up the vote in populous metro areas, from the cities and suburbs of northern New Jersey through suburban Northern Virginia to Jefferson County (Birmingham), Alabama. And in all three states, exit polling showed that the Democratic Party was viewed more favorably than its Republican counterpart.

As it was, Virginia provided Democrats with their most sweeping triumph of 2017, as Democratic candidates in the Old Dominion romped to victories up and down the ballot. Democratic gubernatorial candidate Ralph Northam, the state's lieutenant governor, defeated his GOP opponent, former Republican National Committee Chairman Ed Gillespie, by 9 percentage points in a race that was regarded as virtually even heading into Election Day. Northam's margin of victory exceeded that of any Democratic gubernatorial winner in Virginia since 1985, a nationally prominent group that included Douglas Wilder, Mark Warner, Tim Kaine, and the outgoing governor, Terry McAuliffe.

Like Democrats in other bluish states, Northam was not shy about taking pot shots at Trump. In the Democratic primary, he referred to the president as a "narcissistic maniac." It was not only an effective applause line, but helped make Northam acceptable to Democrats of all stripes, including those who had supported his Bernie Sanders-backed challenger.

Meanwhile, even in Republican Alabama, Trump's involvement in 2017 did not produce the White House's desired result. First, he lined up behind Luther Strange, an establishment favorite who was appointed to fill the

The House since 1990: A Political Weathervane

Republicans lost 40 seats in the House of Representatives in the 2018 election, relegating the GOP to minority status in the nation's lower chamber for the first time since the middle of Barack Obama's first term. Nationwide, Democrats won 54% of House seats in 2018 to the Republicans' 46%. Yet in three of the four regions, one party dominated. Republicans won nearly two-thirds of all House seats in the South. Democrats swept roughly three-fourths of the seats in both the East and West. One House seat in North Carolina was not filled by the 2018 election because of charges of vote fraud against the GOP campaign. Republicans finally won the seat in September 2019 when a special "do over" election was held. That result is not included in the regional tallies below.

	South				West			Midwest			East				Total House			
	R	D	I		R	D		R	D		R	D	I		R	D	I	
1990	44	85	0	D	37	48	D	45	68	D	41	66	1	D	167	267	1	D
1992	52	85	0	D	38	55	D	44	61	D	42	57	1	D	176	258	1	D
1994	73	64	0	R	53	40	R	59	46	R	45	54	1	D	230	204	1	R
1996	82	55	0	R	51	42	R	55	50	R	39	60	1	D	227	207	1	R
1998	82	55	0	R	49	44	R	54	51	R	38	61	1	D	223	211	1	R
2000	81	55	1	R	43	50	D	57	48	R	40	59	1	D	221	212	2	R
2002	85	57	0	R	46	52	D	61	39	R	37	57	1	D	229	205	1	R
2004	91	51	0	R	45	53	D	60	40	R	36	58	1	D	232	202	1	R
2006	85	57	0	R	41	57	D	51	49	R	25	70	0	D	202	233	0	D
2008	80	62	0	R	35	63	D	45	55	D	18	77	0	D	178	257	0	D
2010	102	40	0	R	43	55	D	65	35	R	32	63	0	D	242	193	0	R
2012	108	41	0	R	39	63	D	59	35	R	28	62	0	D	234	201	0	R
2014	111	38	0	R	41	61	D	61	33	R	34	56	0	D	247	188	0	R
2016	109	40	0	R	39	63	D	61	33	R	32	58	0	D	241	194	0	R
2018	98	50	0	R	27	75	D	54	40	R	20	70	0	D	199	235	0	D
Net Change in GOP Seats, 1994-2018	+25				−26			−5			−25				−31			

EAST - Connecticut, Delaware, Maine, Maryland, Massachusetts, New Hampshire, New Jersey, New York, Pennsylvania, Rhode Island, Vermont, West Virginia.

MIDWEST - Illinois, Indiana, Iowa, Kansas, Michigan, Minnesota, Missouri, Nebraska, North Dakota, Ohio, South Dakota, Wisconsin.

SOUTH - Alabama, Arkansas, Florida, Georgia, Kentucky, Louisiana, Mississippi, North Carolina, Oklahoma, South Carolina, Tennessee, Texas, Virginia.

WEST - Alaska, Arizona, California, Colorado, Hawaii, Idaho, Montana, Nevada, New Mexico, Oregon, Utah, Washington, Wyoming.

Senate seat vacated by Trump's attorney general selection, Jeff Sessions. After Strange lost a Republican primary runoff in September to Roy Moore, Trump switched his support to Moore, a controversial former chief justice of the Alabama Supreme Court. In the process, the president went 0 for 2 in one of the most Republican states in the country, as Democrat Doug Jones, a former federal prosecutor, narrowly won the special Senate election.

The 2018 Primaries

It is safe to say that no president in the nation's history threw himself into a midterm election as fully and forcefully as Donald Trump did in 2018, and nowhere was that more apparent than in the 2018 Republican primaries. It was during the primary season, with virtually unanimous support from GOP voters, that he was able to use his political capital most effectively.

Tweets, campaign rallies, recorded telephone messages were all used to promote Republican candidates he favored and defame those he opposed. His involvement contrasted with previous occupants of the White House, who basically kept out of their party's primaries in midterm years. They preferred not to be seen as a divisive force in their party, and any pre-Trump presidential involvement in the primaries was generally limited.

The one conspicuous exception was Franklin D. Roosevelt. After his landslide re-election victory in 1936, FDR felt emboldened to attack Democratic opposition within Congress, who resisted aspects of his New Deal agenda as well as his controversial 1937 effort to enlarge the Supreme Court. Roosevelt decided to seek the defeat

2018: Defeated Incumbents

The 2017–2018 election cycle was difficult for Republican incumbents, although the primary season was comparatively quiet. The GOP lost an incumbent governor and incumbent senator in primaries, the latter as part of a special Senate election held in Alabama in 2017. Two Republican and two Democratic representatives were also defeated in primaries in 2018. Yet there were far more incumbent casualties in the 2018 general election, with Republicans losing 30 sitting House members (to none for the Democrats), one of five senators (the other four were Democrats), and two of three governors (the other was an independent). The chart below lists the gubernatorial, Senate, and House incumbents defeated in the 2018 primaries and general election (plus the Alabama special Senate election), including the full term in which they were serving at the time of their loss in 2018, the percentage of the total vote they had received in the previous general election (2012 for senators, 2014 for governors, and 2016 for House members), and their percentage of the total vote in the 2018 general election (for those who were not sidelined by the primaries). A "@" sign indicates that the incumbent had assumed office since the last general election. A dash (–) indicates an incumbent did not participate in the previous general election or was not a candidate in the 2018 general election. Alaska Gov. Bill Walker, an independent, abandoned his re-election bid before the November voting, although his name remained on the ballot.

	Number of Full Terms	Previous Election Percentage	2018 Election Percentage
GOVERNORS			
Primaries (1)			
(1 Republican)			
Jeff Colyer, R-Kan.	@	–	–
General Election (3)			
(2 Republicans, 1 Independent)			
Bruce Rauner, R-Ill.	1	50.3%	38.8%
Bill Walker, Ind.-Alaska	1	48.1%	2.0%
Scott Walker, R-Wis.	2	52.3%	48.4%
SENATORS			
Primaries (1)			
(1 Republican)			
Luther Strange, R-Ala.	@	–	–
General Election (5)			
(4 Democrats, 1 Republican)			
Joe Donnelly, D-Ind.	1	50.0%	44.8%
Heidi Heitkamp, D-N.D.	1	50.2%	44.3%
Dean Heller, R-Nev.	1	45.9%	45.4%
Claire McKaskill, D-Mo.	2	54.8%	45.6%
Bill Nelson, D-Fla.	3	55.2%	49.9%
REPRESENTATIVES			
Primaries (4)			
(2 Democrats, 2 Republicans)			
Michael Capuano, D-Mass. 7	10	98.6%	–
Joseph Crowley, D-N.Y. 14	10	82.8%	–
Robert Pittenger, R-N.C. 9	3	58.2%	–
Mark Sanford, R-S.C. 1	5	58.6%	–
General Election (30)			
(30 Republicans)			
Mike Bishop, R-Mich. 8	2	56.0%	46.8%
Rod Blum, R-Iowa 1	2	53.7%	45.9%
David Brat, R-Va. 7	2	57.5%	48.4%
Mike Coffman, R-Colo. 6	5	50.9%	42.9%
Barbara Comstock, R-Va. 10	2	52.7%	43.7%
John Culberson, R-Texas 7	9	56.2%	47.5%
Carlos Curbelo, R-Fla. 26	2	53.0%	49.1%
Daniel Donovan, R-N.Y. 11	1	61.5%	46.5%
Jeff Denham, R-Calif. 10	4	51.7%	47.7%
John Faso, R-N.Y. 19	1	54.0%	46.1%
Karen Handel, R-Ga. 6	@	–	49.5%
Randy M. Hultgren, R-Ill. 14	4	59.3%	47.5%
Steve Knight, R-Calif. 25	2	53.1%	45.6%
Leonard Lance, R-N.J. 7	5	54.1%	46.7%
Jason Mark Lewis, R-Minn. 2	1	47.0%	47.1%
Mia B. Love, R-Utah 4	2	53.8%	49.9%
Tom MacArthur, R-N.J. 3	2	59.3%	48.7%
Erik Paulsen, R-Minn. 3	5	56.7%	44.2%
Bruce L. Poliquin, R-Maine 2	2	54.8%	49.4%
Dana Rohrabacher, R-Calif. 48	15	58.3%	46.4%
Peter J. Roskam, R-Ill. 6	6	59.2%	46.4%
Keith Rothfus, R-Pa. 17	3	61.8%	43.7%
Steve D. Russell, R-Okla. 5	2	57.1%	49.3%
Pete Sessions, R-Texas 32	11	71.1%	45.8%
Scott W. Taylor, R-Va. 2	1	61.3%	48.8%
Claudia Tenney, R-N.Y. 22	1	46.5%	49.1%
David Valadao, R-Calif. 21	3	56.7%	49.6%
Mimi Walters, R-Calif. 45	2	58.6%	47.9%
Kevin Yoder, R-Kan. 3	4	51.3%	43.9%
David Young, R-Iowa 3	2	53.4%	47.1%

of unfriendly Democrats in both houses in the midterm election of 1938.

Nine senators and three representatives were targeted by FDR for purging, but only one was defeated in the Democratic primaries. Such a poor track record served as a powerful warning to Roosevelt's successors not to get too engaged in congressional or gubernatorial primaries.

That is, until Trump. He exhibited a hands-on role in the 2018 primaries, endorsing Republican candidates across the country and up and down the ballot—at the Senate, House, and gubernatorial levels as well as for some lesser elective offices. Sometimes, Trump forcefully opposed a candidate who he viewed as either unfriendly or unelectable. Much more often he directly backed a candidate who he saw as both friendly to himself and electable in November. By and large, his efforts were crowned with success.

After his ill-starred endorsements in the 2017 Alabama special Senate election, Trump had one success after another in the 2018 Republican primaries with rarely a setback. Meanwhile, two high-riding candidates he forcefully opposed were both primary losers. The first, controversial former coal baron Don Blankenship advertised himself in the West Virginia GOP Senate primary as "Trumpier than Trump." But Blankenship was dismissed by the president as unelectable with two words, "Remember Alabama," and finished a distant third.

Another candidate that ended up on Trump's bad side, Rep. Mark Sanford of South Carolina, was the victim of a hostile tweet by Trump just hours before the polls closed for the Republican primary for his Charleston-area seat. The tweet disparaged Sanford and elevated his opponent, state legislator Katie Arrington, who won the primary.

And then there were the Trump primary endorsements that appeared to have a guileful quality to them. In Utah, Trump threw his backing behind one-time critic, Mitt Romney, the 2012 GOP presidential nominee, after he entered the Senate race to succeed the retiring Orrin Hatch. Back in 2016, Romney had intimated that Trump was unfit for office, saying, "Think of Donald Trump's personal qualities, the bullying, the greed, the showing off, the misogyny, the absurd third-grade theatrics."

And in Alabama, Trump endorsed another critic from two years earlier, Rep. Martha Roby, before her Republican runoff. In 2016, she had lambasted Trump after release of the Access Hollywood tapes, saying that his language was "unacceptable" and that she could not vote for him. "I cannot look my children in the eye and justify my vote for a man who promotes and boasts about sexually assaulting women."

Yet after the 2016 election, both Roby and Romney toned down their criticism of Trump, with Romney even being publicly considered for secretary of state in the Trump administration. Romney's warmer relationship with the president did not last; following the former's 2018 election he resumed his role as Trump critic. Nonetheless, both Romney and Roby won their nominating contests in 2018 with ease, and were elected by decisive margins in the fall.

These results tended to reinforce a basic theme of the 2018 Republican primaries: support Trump and win, oppose him and run the risk of losing. Another option for Trump critics was to simply retire, the alternative chosen by Sens. Bob Corker of Tennessee and Jeff Flake of Arizona.

Altogether, four House members, one senator (Strange) and one governor (Jeff Colyer of Kansas, an unelected successor to GOP Governor Sam Brownback, who left to take a job in the Trump administration), were beaten in the 2017–2018 primaries. It was about the average number of incumbent defeats for the three sets of offices in recent election cycles.

Two veteran male Democratic representatives lost to women of color. Boston City Council member Ayanna Pressley (who is African American) defeated veteran House member Michael Capuano. Alexandria Ocasio-Cortez of New York City, a twenty-something Latina who began her campaign as a political unknown, ousted incumbent Joseph Crowley, the chair of the House Democratic caucus. Fewer than 30,000 votes were cast in the primary, but Ocasio-Cortez skillfully combined social media with endorsements from progressive groups and emerged from her primary not only victorious but as a new star of the Democratic left.

A New Electoral Concept: Maine's "Instant Runoff"

One of the most famous political adages in American history is: "As Maine goes, so goes the nation." It is a reference to the time when Maine held its state elections in September, acting as a harbinger of sorts for the November presidential election to follow.

Humorists, though, changed the adage after the presidential election of 1936 to say: "As Maine goes, so goes Vermont"—the only two states that FDR lost in his landslide victory that year.

But Maine returned to the public eye in 2018, not for its prescience in predicting elections, but for the way it conducts elections. 2018 was the first year that any state used the "instant runoff" or "ranked-choice" system of voting in congressional or major statewide races, and the Maine primary was the first time it was used.

Rather than cast a single vote in each race as the rest of the country does, voters in Maine's primary were allowed to rank order all the candidates in races with more than two entrants for Congress, the governorship, and state legislature. In contests where no candidate won a majority of the vote in the initial count, the candidate with the fewest votes was eliminated and their vote redistributed among the remaining candidates to reflect their second-choice preference. The process proceeded until one candidate won a majority of the vote.

Case in point: Maine's Democratic primary for governor. There were seven candidates on the ballot and a write-in line. Maine Attorney General Janet Mills led Adam

Cote, a renewable energy entrepreneur, in the initial count, 33 percent to 28 percent. She inched closer to a majority on subsequent rounds as her opponents fell by the wayside. Mills took 35 percent on the second round and 41 percent on the third. She won on the fourth round, defeating Cote, 54 percent to 46 percent.

The race for the Democratic nomination in Maine's 2nd congressional district also went to "overtime," with the eventual nominee winning in the second round. As in the Democratic primary for governor, the leader on the first round in the 2nd District, assistant state House leader Jared Golden, went on to win the nomination. There were no instant runoffs in the Republican primary.

On the one hand, proponents of the instant runoff said that by requiring a majority of the vote, the system helps create consensus and lessens the odds of a fringe candidate winning, without necessitating the need for a runoff election several weeks later. The latter is the case in many Southern states, where runoffs can be expensive and fray party harmony if they turn nasty.

On the other hand, critics of the instant runoff say that it is too complicated and confusing, and it takes too long to tally the vote. While the winner of the GOP gubernatorial primary took more than 50 percent of the vote and was known on Primary Election Night, the outcome of the Maine Democratic gubernatorial primary took a week to determine.

A few cities with a progressive heritage, such as San Francisco, Santa Fe, and Cambridge, Massachusetts, predated Maine in using the instant runoff system. But Maine was the first state to adopt it—a surprise of sorts, since Maine does not have the same sort of progressive reputation that some other states do.

Still, several factors made Maine favorable terrain for the instant runoff. First, the state's largest city, Portland, had been using the instant runoff in recent elections and had acted as an in-state model for the system. Second, Maine has had a long history of independent candidates, particularly for governor, who often have kept the vote for the winning candidate well below 50 percent. Only once since 1982 has a candidate for governor won with a majority of the vote, and that was Independent Angus King in 1998. (He is now an independent U.S. senator.)

Maine twice voted in favor of the instant runoff, the first time to adopt the system in 2016; the second time to reaffirm it in June 2018 in response to efforts by the legislature to delay or cancel its implementation.

Neither time, though, did the vote for the instant runoff exceed 54 percent, with the 2018 referendum showing how highly partisan the system can be, at least in Maine. Basically, Democrats like it, while Republicans are more skeptical. Seven of the eight counties that backed the instant runoff in the 2018 referendum lay along the Atlantic coast and were carried by Hillary Clinton in the presidential election two years earlier. All eight counties that opposed the instant runoff in 2018 were won by Trump, most of them in the rural interior of the state.

Republican concerns about the instant runoff system were born out in the November general election, when GOP Rep. Bruce Poliquin of Maine's 2nd District led Democrat Golden by fully 2,000 votes in the initial tally. But he was short of a majority, triggering the instant runoff. Once the second-choice votes of independent candidates were redistributed, Golden had procured a 3,500-vote victory with 50.6 percent of the vote. Poliquin sued to have the results overturned, but a U.S. District Court judge ruled that the new system fell "short of constitutional impropriety."

The 2018 General Elections

In the November general elections, Democrats gained a net of 40 House seats (jumping to 235 from 195), seven governorships (increasing their total to 23 from 16), and increased their total of states with complete Democratic legislative control by four (hiking their number to 18 from 14). Republicans added two Senate seats (expanding their majority to 53 from 51).

Democrats needed to gain only two seats in 2018 to win Senate control. Yet that deficit might as well have been 20 seats, given how difficult a goal it was for the Democrats to accomplish. Not only were they defending 26 of the 35 seats up (including two seats held by independents who caucused with the Democrats), but 10 were in states carried by Trump in 2016. On the other hand, only one Republican Senate seat was at stake in a state (Nevada) won by Clinton that year.

Democrats won the Nevada seat, ousting Republican Sen. Dean Heller, as well as taking the Arizona seat vacated by GOP incumbent Jeff Flake. However, Republicans were able to extend their Senate majority by defeating four Democratic incumbents in states won by Trump in 2016. Three were in the Midwest—Joe Donnelly of Indiana, Claire McCaskill of Missouri, and Heidi Heitkamp of North Dakota. The other was in Florida, where Bill Nelson was narrowly beaten.

While Democrats had to play defense in Senate races in 2018, they were able to go on offense on the House side. The playing field for the latter was well larded with open seats created by Republican retirements, along with a plethora of well-funded women candidates running in suburban districts.

The cornerstone of the new Democratic House majority was on the two coasts, as the party emerged from the 2018 midterms holding in the vicinity of three-quarters of House seats in both the Northeast (78 percent) and West (74 percent). But it was significant Democratic inroads in the more Republican South and Midwest that gave them a comfortable majority in the 116th Congress.

In short, the Democratic congressional victory was nationwide in scope, as they scored a net gain of seven House seats in the Midwest, 10 in the South, 11 in the Northeast, and 12 in the West. In California alone, Democrats gained seven House seats, pushing their advantage over the Republicans in the nation's most populous state to 46 to 7. In New Jersey, Democrats picked up four congressional seats to bring them possession of a nearly unanimous 11 of 12 in the Garden State. In addition, Democrats in 2018 gained seats in unlikely places, including Kansas, Oklahoma, South Carolina, and Utah.

In state-level politics, Democrats had spent most of the previous decade wandering in the political wilderness. But in 2018, they made dramatic gains, particularly in the governorships. Four of the Democrats' seven gubernatorial pick-ups were in the Midwest, including two states critical to Trump's election in 2016, Michigan and Wisconsin. The Democrats also gained Midwestern governorships in Illinois and bright red Kansas, took two governorships in the Mountain West (Nevada and New Mexico), and captured the top spot in Maine. The lone Republican gubernatorial pick up in 2018 came in Alaska, which previously had an independent governor.

Trump threw himself into the fall campaign with gusto, traveling around the country to rally Republican voters. In his quiver, he had favorable economic news in the form of an unemployment rate (3.7 percent) that tied for the lowest for October of a midterm election year since 1966. Yet that was trumped by the president's consistently low job approval ratings, which on the eve of the 2018 midterm election stood in the long-running Gallup Poll at 40 percent. Historically, the farther the president's approval rating falls below 50 percent, the more difficult it is for his party's more endangered incumbents to survive.

Methodology

The thirty-third edition of *America Votes* follows the same format of recent editions in this series. The introductory text and a variety of summary tables that accompany it seek to tie together basic aspects of the 2018 election cycle. The section that follows presents national tables on voter turnout as well as the aggregate vote for gubernatorial, Senate and House elections by state in 2018.

The turnout table uses voter registration and "citizen" voting-age population figures compiled by the Census Bureau. In the latter, the millions and millions of noncitizens in the United States age 18 years and older are excluded, giving a truer sense of the voter turnout rate than if all persons of voting age were included.

The overview material also features a summary of special elections held between the general elections of 2016 and 2018 that filled vacancies in the 115th Congress. There is also a list of changes in the congressional membership in the 116th Congress that occurred between the 2018 general election and August 2019. The heart of the volume, 50 chapters—one for each state—follows the introductory material.

Each state chapter begins with a list of the current governor, senators and representatives, followed by tables with the statewide vote for president, governor and senator from the end of World War II (1945) to the present. A map of the state shows its counties, major population centers, and congressional districts for members of the House in the 116th Congress. Other maps are included in states with one or more particularly large population centers that feature a number of congressional districts. County-by-county tables of gubernatorial and Senate elections follow the maps. All these tables are from the 2018 general election, with the exception of gubernatorial contests in New Jersey and Virginia and a special Senate election in Alabama, all of which were held in 2017.

In most cases, the county tables for gubernatorial and Senate elections feature three columns of votes (Republican, Democratic, Other). Exceptions occur where an independent or third-party candidate has received at least 10 percent of the statewide vote, in which case a column for their vote is also included. All the county tables include 2010 population figures from the Census Bureau.

Following the gubernatorial and Senate tables, a listing of votes cast for the House of Representatives is arranged by congressional district. The implementation of the 2010 Census for redistricting purposes led to changes before the 2012 election in district boundaries in all states with more than one House member. House results for elections before 2012 are not included for any state except those with a single House seat. Meanwhile, a few states redrew their congressional district lines before the 2018 election. Notes are included where the districts cannot be compared to those in earlier elections.

The conclusion of each state chapter consists of two parts. The first is a notes section containing a breakdown of votes cast in the general election for third party, independent, and write-in candidates. The total of scattered write-in votes is listed in states where they were included in the official returns. For those major party candidates who also ran on a third party ballot line, most notably the case in New York, votes are aggregated as Democratic or Republican.

The end of each state chapter deals with primary elections. There is an explanation of who could vote in the state's primary as well as voter registration totals at the time of the primary election. The latter is broken down by party in the 30 or so states in which voters register by party. This material is followed by Democratic and Republican primary results for governor, senator, and House held in the 2018 election cycle, as well as the results for runoff elections in states, mainly in the South, that held them.

In the six New England states, tables list the vote for governor and senator by larger cities and towns as well as by counties. In Rhode Island, the results are listed for all cities and towns.

The *America Votes* series is compiled from official results obtained from election authorities in each state. Although complete accuracy is always the goal, it can sometimes prove elusive in a work such as this. On occasion, states may belatedly report changes in their vote totals that occur after publication of this volume. And human nature being what it is, there is always an example or two (or three) of self-inflicted errors. The goal is always to keep these to a minimum. In light of the desire to make these reference volumes as useful as possible to readers and researchers, corrections of data are always welcome as are suggestions for new material.

The creation of each edition in this series has always taken a small army. Laura Notton, the editor at CQ Press, efficiently spearheaded this edition with patience and expertise. She was ably assisted by Tamara Tanso, who worked tirelessly to help database election returns, verify election results, and provide other valuable assistance during the creation of this book. A tip of the cap is also in order to Nora Varbedian and her team of technical experts, Sal Hewavita and Andre Messier, for their database expertise and heroic work in creating the tables that you see in this book. And no list of acknowledgments is complete without mention of the book's production editor, Tracy Buyan, who was instrumental in turning this mass of tables and data into a book that readers will hopefully find quite usable.

Rhodes Cook
September 2019

Errata

America Votes 32

The following corrections should be noted for the previous edition, *America Votes* 32, covering the 2015–2016 election cycle.

Page viii. In the "Counting the 2016 Vote" table, the Republican plurality should be "1,223,730."

Page 4. In the "House of Representatives Elections 2016" table, the Rep.-Dem. Plurality in the Total line should be "1,223,730 R."

Page 51. In the "Presidential Primaries 2016" chart, the New Hampshire Republican section should include the vote of Jeb Bush, which is missing. Bush finished fourth in the New Hampshire GOP primary with 31,341 votes.

Page 67. In the Alaska Senators listing, Republican Lisa Murkowski was re-elected to a six-year term in 2016. She was previously elected in 2010 (as a write-in candidate) and 2004.

Page 126. In the Delaware "President 2016" table, "2017" should be deleted from the title.

Page 151. In the Georgia "House of Representatives" table, the 14th District information in the Rep.-Dem. Plurality column for 2016 and 2014 is incomplete. It should be "216,743 R" and "118,782 R," respectively.

Page 230. The Note section for the Maine "Postwar Vote for President" table should mention that Republican Donald J. Trump received one electoral vote from Maine in 2016, by virtue of winning Maine's northeastern district (the 2nd). Maine and Nebraska award an electoral vote to the winner in each of the state's congressional districts, and two electoral votes to the statewide winner.

Page 231. In the Maine "Postwar Vote for Governor" table, the Rep.-Dem. Plurality in 1998 should have a pound sign after it to indicate that the ultimate winner that year was an independent.

Page 296. The Note section for the Nebraska "Postwar Vote for President" table should mention that Democrat Barack Obama received one electoral vote from Nebraska in 2008, for winning the vote in the Omaha-based 2nd District.

Page 392. In the Representatives listing for Pennsylvania, the 8th District House member should be Republican Brian Fitzpatrick (not Republican Michael G. Fitzpatrick).

Page 406. In the Senators listing for South Carolina, Republican Tim Scott was re-elected in 2016 (not 2014) to a six-year term. He was previously elected in 2014.

Page 453. In the Governor listing for Vermont, Republican Phil Scott won re-election in 2016 to a two-year term (not four years).

Page 501. In the District of Columbia "Postwar Vote for President" table, the vote for 1964 is missing. It should be as follows: Total Vote – 198,597; Republican – 28,801 (14.5%); Democratic – 169,796 (85.5%); Rep.-Dem. Plurality – 140,995 D.

UNITED STATES

VOTER TURNOUT 2018

State	2018 Est. Voting Age Population	2018 Est. Registration General Election	Percent Voting Age Registered	House	Senate	Governor	High Race	High Race Vote	High Race Vote as Percentage of 2018 Voting Age Population	High Race Vote as Percentage of 2018 Registration General Election
Alabama	3,609,000	2,490,000	69.0%	1,659,895	1,348,720	1,719,589	G	1,719,589	47.6%	69.1%
Alaska	497,000	337,000	67.8%	282,166	—	283,134	G	283,134	57.0%	84.0%
Arizona	4,757,000	3,262,000	68.6%	2,341,270	2,384,308	2,376,441	S	2,384,308	50.1%	73.1%
Arkansas	2,158,000	1,262,000	58.5%	889,298	—	891,509	G	891,509	41.3%	70.6%
California	25,525,000	15,690,000	61.5%	12,184,522	11,113,364	12,464,235	G	12,464,235	48.8%	79.4%
Colorado	4,029,000	2,645,000	65.6%	2,513,907	—	2,525,062	G	2,525,062	62.7%	95.5%
Connecticut	2,539,000	1,726,000	68.0%	1,379,808	1,386,840	1,406,803	G	1,406,803	55.4%	81.5%
Delaware	713,000	472,000	66.2%	353,814	362,606	—	S	362,606	50.9%	76.8%
Florida	15,047,000	9,435,000	62.7%	7,021,476	8,190,005	8,220,561	G	8,220,561	54.6%	87.1%
Georgia	7,311,000	4,840,000	66.2%	3,802,343	—	3,939,409	G	3,939,409	53.9%	81.4%
Hawaii	971,000	523,000	53.9%	382,332	388,351	390,843	G	390,843	40.3%	74.7%
Idaho	1,226,000	743,000	60.6%	595,724	—	605,131	G	605,131	49.4%	81.4%
Illinois	8,947,000	6,068,000	67.8%	4,539,704	—	4,547,657	G	4,547,657	50.8%	74.9%
Indiana	4,792,000	3,131,000	65.3%	2,256,149	2,282,565	—	S	2,282,565	47.6%	72.9%
Iowa	2,239,000	1,658,000	74.1%	1,316,648	—	1,327,638	G	1,327,638	59.3%	80.1%
Kansas	2,026,000	1,449,000	71.5%	1,050,322	—	1,055,060	G	1,055,060	52.1%	72.8%
Kentucky	3,249,000	2,389,000	73.5%	1,569,798	—	—	H	1,569,798	48.3%	65.7%
Louisiana	3,326,000	2,263,000	68.0%	1,460,593	—	—	H	1,460,593	43.9%	64.5%
Maine	1,056,000	828,000	78.4%	623,424	634,409	630,667	S	634,409	60.1%	76.6%
Maryland	4,281,000	3,095,000	72.3%	2,286,284	2,299,889	2,304,512	G	2,304,512	53.8%	74.5%
Massachusetts	4,919,000	3,345,000	68.0%	2,485,081	2,707,090	2,674,615	S	2,707,090	55.0%	80.9%
Michigan	7,430,000	5,453,000	73.4%	4,154,703	4,237,271	4,250,585	G	4,250,585	57.2%	77.9%
Minnesota	4,006,000	3,000,000	74.9%	2,576,996	2,596,879	2,587,287	S	2,596,879	64.8%	86.6%
Mississippi	2,178,000	1,599,000	73.4%	938,903	936,215	—	H	938,903	43.1%	58.7%
Missouri	4,564,000	3,299,000	72.3%	2,418,413	2,442,289	—	S	2,442,289	53.5%	74.0%
Montana	812,000	579,000	71.3%	504,421	504,384	—	H	504,421	62.1%	87.1%
Nebraska	1,332,000	883,000	66.3%	696,570	698,883	697,981	S	698,883	52.5%	79.1%
Nevada	2,067,000	1,277,000	61.8%	960,774	972,132	971,799	S	972,132	47.0%	76.1%
New Hampshire	1,025,000	726,000	70.8%	570,744	—	573,602	G	573,602	56.0%	79.0%
New Jersey	6,267,000	4,297,000	68.6%	3,098,743	3,169,310	2,147,415	S	3,169,310	50.6%	73.8%
New Mexico	1,485,000	916,000	61.7%	693,311	697,012	696,459	S	697,012	46.9%	76.1%
New York	13,684,000	8,553,000	62.5%	5,948,673	6,059,023	6,104,477	G	6,104,477	44.6%	71.4%
North Carolina	7,444,000	5,160,000	69.3%	3,663,326	—	—	H	3,663,326	49.2%	71.0%
North Dakota	541,000	397,000[1]	73.4%	321,532	326,138	—	S	326,138	60.3%	82.2%
Ohio	8,640,000	6,062,000	70.2%	4,406,358	4,410,898	4,429,582	G	4,429,582	51.3%	73.1%
Oklahoma	2,732,000	1,777,000	65.0%	1,178,836	—	1,186,385	G	1,186,385	43.4%	66.8%
Oregon	3,138,000	2,274,000	72.5%	1,847,646	—	1,866,997	G	1,866,997	59.5%	82.1%
Pennsylvania	9,475,000	6,469,000	68.3%	4,929,875	5,009,400	5,012,555	G	5,012,555	52.9%	77.5%
Rhode Island	782,000	532,000	68.0%	373,280	376,738	376,401	S	376,738	48.2%	70.8%
South Carolina	3,769,000	2,430,000	64.5%	1,709,292	—	1,707,569	H	1,709,292	45.4%	70.3%
South Dakota	637,000	429,000	67.3%	335,965	—	339,214	G	339,214	53.3%	79.1%
Tennessee	5,016,000	3,183,000	63.5%	2,159,825	2,243,740	2,243,294	S	2,243,740	44.7%	70.5%
Texas	18,374,000	11,634,000	63.3%	8,202,708	8,371,655	8,343,443	S	8,371,655	45.6%	72.0%
Utah	2,109,000	1,443,000	68.4%	1,052,506	1,062,897	—	S	1,062,897	50.4%	73.7%
Vermont	497,000	343,000	69.0%	272,451	272,624	274,087	G	274,087	55.1%	79.9%
Virginia	5,773,000	4,159,000	72.0%	3,312,956	3,351,373	2,614,282	S	3,351,373	58.1%	80.6%
Washington	5,228,000	3,852,000	73.7%	3,021,951	3,086,168	—	S	3,086,168	59.0%	80.1%
West Virginia	1,384,000	892,000	64.5%	577,991	586,034	—	S	586,034	42.3%	65.7%
Wisconsin	4,296,000	3,129,000	72.8%	2,571,655	2,660,763	2,673,308	G	2,673,308	62.2%	85.4%
Wyoming	422,000	268,000	63.5%	201,245	203,420	203,238	S	203,420	48.2%	75.9%
Total	*228,324,000*	*152,666,000*	*66.9%*	*113,696,207*	*87,373,393*	*96,662,826*	—	*116,793,914*	*51.2%*	*76.5%*

Source: Registration and voting age population (VAP) figures were provided by the U.S. Census Bureau. VAP figures are based on estimated numbers of citizens of voting age in each state (and nationally) at the time of the November 2018 general election. Figures do not account for felony or other forms of disenfranchisement. They also do not account for those living outside the United States and those naturalized in 2018, both of which are enfranchised but not counted in the Census enumeration of age-eligible citizens.

Notes: Does not include special elections or elections for non-voting delegates. The gubernatorial vote includes 2017 elections in New Jersey and Virginia. The Senate vote includes a December 2017 runoff in Alabama. In states with two Senate elections in 2018, Minnesota and Mississippi, the race with the highest number of votes is used. In each case, that was the state's regularly scheduled Senate election. North Dakota does not require voter registration.

GUBERNATORIAL ELECTIONS 2017 AND 2018

State	Total Vote	Republican Vote	Republican Candidate	Democratic Vote	Democratic Candidate	Other Vote	Rep.-Dem. Plurality	Percentage Total Vote Rep.	Percentage Total Vote Dem.	Percentage Major Vote Rep.	Percentage Major Vote Dem.
Alabama	1,719,589	1,022,457	Ivey, Kay	694,495	Maddox, Walter	2,637	327,962 R	59.5%	40.4%	59.6%	40.4%
Alaska	283,134	145,631	Dunleavy, Mike J.	125,739	Begich, Mark	11,764	19,892 R	51.4%	44.4%	53.7%	46.3%
Arizona	2,376,441	1,330,863	Ducey, Doug	994,341	Garcia, David	51,237	336,522 R	56.0%	41.8%	57.2%	42.8%
Arkansas	891,509	582,406	Hutchinson, Asa	283,218	Henderson, Jared K.	25,885	299,188 R	65.3%	31.8%	67.3%	32.7%
California	12,464,235	4,742,825	Cox, John H.	7,721,410	Newsom, Gavin		2,978,585 D	38.1%	61.9%	38.1%	61.9%
Colorado	2,525,062	1,080,801	Stapleton, Walker	1,348,888	Polis, Jared	95,373	268,087 D	42.8%	53.4%	44.5%	55.5%
Connecticut	1,406,803	650,138	Stefanowski, Bob	694,510	Lamont, Ned	62,155	44,372 D	46.2%	49.4%	48.4%	51.6%
Florida	8,220,561	4,076,186	DeSantis, Ron	4,043,723	Gillum, Andrew	100,652	32,463 R	49.6%	49.2%	50.2%	49.8%
Georgia	3,939,409	1,978,408	Kemp, Brian	1,923,685	Abrams, Stacey	37,316	54,723 R	50.2%	48.8%	50.7%	49.3%
Hawaii	390,843	131,719	Tupola, Andria	244,934	Ige, David Yutaka	14,190	113,215 D	33.7%	62.7%	35.0%	65.0%
Idaho	605,131	361,661	Little, Brad	231,081	Jordan, Paulette	12,389	130,580 R	59.8%	38.2%	61.0%	39.0%
Illinois	4,547,657	1,765,751	Rauner, Bruce	2,479,746	Pritzker, Jay	302,160	713,995 D	38.8%	54.5%	41.6%	58.4%
Iowa	1,327,638	667,275	Reynolds, Kim	630,986	Hubbell , Fred	29,377	36,289 R	50.3%	47.5%	51.4%	48.6%
Kansas	1,055,060	453,030	Kobach, Kris W.	506,509	Kelly, Laura	95,521	53,479 D	42.9%	48.0%	47.2%	52.8%
Maine	630,667	272,311	Moody, Shawn H.	320,962	Mills, Janet T.	37,394	48,651 D	43.2%	50.9%	45.9%	54.1%
Maryland	2,304,512	1,275,644	Hogan, Larry	1,002,639	Jealous, Ben	26,229	273,005 R	55.4%	43.5%	56.0%	44.0%
Massachusetts	2,674,615	1,781,341	Baker, Charles D.	885,770	Gonzalez, Jay	7,504	895,571 R	66.6%	33.1%	66.8%	33.2%
Michigan	4,250,585	1,859,534	Schuette, Bill	2,266,193	Whitmer, Gretchen	124,858	406,659 D	43.7%	53.3%	45.1%	54.9%
Minnesota	2,587,287	1,097,705	Johnson, Jeff	1,393,096	Walz, Timothy J.	96,486	295,391 D	42.4%	53.8%	44.1%	55.9%
Nebraska	697,981	411,812	Ricketts, Pete	286,169	Krist, Bob		125,643 R	59.0%	41.0%	59.0%	41.0%
Nevada	971,799	440,320	Laxalt, Adam	480,007	Sisolak, Steve	51,472	39,687 D	45.3%	49.4%	47.8%	52.2%
New Hampshire	573,602	302,764	Sununu, Chris	262,359	Kelly, Molly	8,479	40,405 R	52.8%	45.7%	53.6%	46.4%
New Jersey (2017)	2,147,415	899,583	Guadagno, Kim	1,203,110	Murphy, Philip	44,722	303,527 D	41.9%	56.0%	42.8%	57.2%
New Mexico	696,459	298,091	Pearce, Steve	398,368	Grisham, Michelle Lujan		100,277 D	42.8%	57.2%	42.8%	57.2%
New York	6,104,477	2,207,602	Molinaro, Marcus	3,635,340	Cuomo, Andrew	261,535	1,427,738 D	36.2%	59.6%	37.8%	62.2%
Ohio	4,429,582	2,231,917	DeWine, Michael	2,067,847	Cordray, Richard	129,818	164,070 R	50.4%	46.7%	51.9%	48.1%
Oklahoma	1,186,385	644,579	Stitt, Kevin	500,973	Edmondson, Drew	40,833	143,606 R	54.3%	42.2%	56.3%	43.7%
Oregon	1,866,997	814,988	Buehler, Knute	934,498	Brown, Kate	117,511	119,510 D	43.7%	50.1%	46.6%	53.4%
Pennsylvania	5,012,555	2,039,882	Wagner, Scott	2,895,652	Wolf, Thomas W.	77,021	855,770 D	40.7%	57.8%	41.3%	58.7%
Rhode Island	376,401	139,932	Fung, Allan	198,122	Raimondo, Gina	38,347	58,190 D	37.2%	52.6%	41.4%	58.6%
South Carolina	1,707,569	921,342	McMaster, Henry D.	784,182	Smith, James	2,045	137,160 R	54.0%	45.9%	54.0%	46.0%
South Dakota	339,214	172,912	Noem, Kristi	161,454	Sutton, Billie	4,848	11,458 R	51.0%	47.6%	51.7%	48.3%
Tennessee	2,243,294	1,336,106	Lee, Bill	864,863	Dean, Karl	42,325	471,243 R	59.6%	38.6%	60.7%	39.3%
Texas	8,343,443	4,656,196	Abbott, Greg	3,546,615	Valdez, Lupe	140,632	1,109,581 R	55.8%	42.5%	56.8%	43.2%
Vermont	274,087	151,261	Scott, Phil	110,335	Hallquist, Christine	12,491	40,926 R	55.2%	40.3%	57.8%	42.2%
Virginia (2017)	2,614,282	1,175,731	Gillespie, Edward W.	1,409,175	Northam, Ralph S.	29,376	233,444 D	45.0%	53.9%	45.5%	54.5%
Wisconsin	2,673,308	1,295,080	Walker, Scott	1,324,307	Evers, Tony	53,921	29,227 D	48.4%	49.5%	49.4%	50.6%
Wyoming	203,238	136,412	Gordon, Mark	55,965	Throne, Mary A.	10,861	80,447 R	67.1%	27.5%	70.9%	29.1%
Total	*96,662,826*	*45,552,196*		*48,911,266*		*2,199,364*	*3,359,070 D*	*47.1%*	*50.6%*	*48.2%*	*51.8%*

Note: The gubernatorial vote includes 2017 elections in New Jersey and Virginia.

SENATE ELECTIONS 2017 AND 2018

State	Total Vote	Republican Vote	Republican Candidate	Democratic Vote	Democratic Candidate	Other Vote	Rep.-Dem. Plurality	Percentage Total Vote Rep.	Percentage Total Vote Dem.	Percentage Major Vote Rep.	Percentage Major Vote Dem.
Alabama (2017) S*	1,348,720	651,972	Moore, Roy	673,896	Jones, Doug	22,852	21,924 D	48.3%	50.0%	49.2%	50.8%
Arizona	2,384,308	1,135,200	McSally, Martha	1,191,100	Sinema, Kyrsten	58,008	55,900 D	47.6%	50.0%	48.8%	51.2%
California**	11,113,364			11,113,364	Feinstein, Dianne/DeLeon, Kevin		11,113,364 D		100.0%		100.0%
Connecticut	1,386,840	545,717	Corey, Matthew M.	825,579	Murphy, Christopher	15,544	279,862 D	39.3%	59.5%	39.8%	60.2%
Delaware	362,606	137,127	Arlett, Robert	217,385	Carper, Thomas R.	8,094	80,258 D	37.8%	60.0%	38.7%	61.3%
Florida	8,190,005	4,099,505	Scott, Rick	4,089,472	Nelson, Bill	1,028	10,033 R	50.1%	49.9%	50.1%	49.9%
Hawaii	388,351	112,035	Curtis, Ron	276,316	Hirono, Mazie K.		164,281 D	28.8%	71.2%	28.8%	71.2%
Indiana	2,282,565	1,158,000	Braun, Mike	1,023,553	Donnelly, Joseph S.	101,012	134,447 R	50.7%	44.8%	53.1%	46.9%
Maine***	634,409	223,502	Brakey, Eric	66,268	Ringelstein, Zak	344,639	121,073 I	35.2%	10.4%	77.1%	22.9%
Maryland	2,299,889	697,017	Campbell, Tony	1,491,614	Cardin, Benjamin L.	111,258	794,597 D	30.3%	64.9%	31.8%	68.2%
Massachusetts	2,707,090	979,210	Diehl, Geoff	1,633,371	Warren, Elizabeth	94,509	654,161 D	36.2%	60.3%	37.5%	62.5%
Michigan	4,237,271	1,938,818	James, John	2,214,478	Stabenow, Debbie	83,975	275,660 D	45.8%	52.3%	46.7%	53.3%
Minnesota	2,596,879	940,437	Newberger, James	1,566,174	Klobuchar, Amy	90,268	625,737 D	36.2%	60.3%	37.5%	62.5%
Minnesota S*	2,587,356	1,095,777	Housely, Karin	1,370,540	Smith, Tina	121,039	274,763 D	42.4%	53.0%	44.4%	55.6%
Mississippi	936,215	547,619	Wicker, Roger F.	369,567	Baria, David	19,029	178,052 R	58.5%	39.5%	59.7%	40.3%
Mississippi S*	907,588	486,769	Hyde-Smith, Cindy	420,819	Espy, Mike		65,950 R	53.6%	46.4%	53.6%	46.4%
Missouri	2,442,289	1,254,927	Hawley, Josh	1,112,935	McCaskill, Claire	74,427	141,992 R	51.4%	45.6%	53.0%	47.0%
Montana	504,384	235,963	Rosendale, Matt	253,876	Tester, Jon	14,545	17,913 D	46.8%	50.3%	48.2%	51.8%
Nebraska	698,883	403,151	Fischer, Deb	269,917	Raybould, Jane	25,815	133,234 R	57.7%	38.6%	59.9%	40.1%
Nevada	972,132	441,202	Heller, Dean	490,071	Rosen, Jacky	40,859	48,869 D	45.4%	50.4%	47.4%	52.6%
New Jersey	3,169,310	1,357,355	Hugin, Robert	1,711,654	Menendez, Robert	100,301	354,299 D	42.8%	54.0%	44.2%	55.8%
New Mexico	697,012	212,813	Rich, Mick	376,998	Heinrich, Martin	107,201	164,185 D	30.5%	54.1%	36.1%	63.9%
New York	6,059,023	1,998,220	Farley, Chele C.	4,056,931	Gillibrand, Kirsten E.	3,872	2,058,711 D	33.0%	67.0%	33.0%	67.0%
North Dakota	326,138	179,720	Cramer, Kevin	144,376	Heitkamp, Heidi	2,042	35,344 R	55.1%	44.3%	55.5%	44.5%
Ohio	4,410,898	2,053,963	Renacci, Jim	2,355,923	Brown, Sherrod	1,012	301,960 D	46.6%	53.4%	46.6%	53.4%
Pennsylvania	5,009,400	2,134,848	Barletta, Lou	2,792,437	Casey, Bob Jr.	82,115	657,589 D	42.6%	55.7%	43.3%	56.7%
Rhode Island	376,738	144,421	Flanders , Robert Jr.	231,477	Whitehouse, Sheldon	840	87,056 D	38.3%	61.4%	38.4%	61.6%
Tennessee	2,243,740	1,227,483	Blackburn, Marsha	985,450	Bredesen, Phil	30,807	242,033 R	54.7%	43.9%	55.5%	44.5%
Texas	8,371,655	4,260,553	Cruz, Ted	4,045,632	O'Rourke, Beto	65,470	214,921 R	50.9%	48.3%	51.3%	48.7%
Utah	1,062,897	665,215	Romney, Mitt	328,541	Wilson, Jenny	69,141	336,674 R	62.6%	30.9%	66.9%	33.1%
Vermont***	272,624	74,815	Zupan, Lawrence			197,809	108,834 I	27.4%		100.0%	
Virginia	3,351,373	1,374,313	Stewart, Corey A.	1,910,370	Kaine, Tim	66,690	536,057 D	41.0%	57.0%	41.8%	58.2%
Washington	3,086,168	1,282,804	Hutchison, Susan	1,803,364	Cantwell, Maria		520,560 D	41.6%	58.4%	41.6%	58.4%
West Virginia	586,034	271,113	Morrisey, Patrick	290,510	Manchin, Joe III	24,411	19,397 D	46.3%	49.6%	48.3%	51.7%
Wisconsin	2,660,763	1,184,885	Vukmir, Leah	1,472,914	Baldwin, Tammy	2,964	288,029 D	44.5%	55.4%	44.6%	55.4%
Wyoming	203,420	136,210	Barrasso, John	61,227	Trauner, Gary	5,983	74,983 R	67.0%	30.1%	69.0%	31.0%
Total	*90,868,337*	*35,642,679*		*53,238,099*		*1,987,559*	*17,595,420 D*	*39.2%*	*58.6%*	*40.1%*	*59.9%*

Notes: The compilation of 2017–18 Senate elections includes a special election in Alabama held in December 2017, plus two Senate elections in Minnesota and Mississippi—one regularly scheduled, the other for a short term caused by the resignation of an incumbent. The plurality is the difference between the top two vote recipients, regardless of party or independent status. *S indicates a special election for a short term to fill a vacancy. The Mississippi special election results here are from the late November 2018 runoff.

** In California's jungle primary, the top two vote recipients, Dianne Feinstein and Kevin DeLeon, were both Democrats. Feinstein received 6,019,422 votes to DeLeon's 5,093,942 (or 54.2% to 45.8%), producing a Feinstein plurality of 925,480 votes.

*** In Maine's general election, independent Angus King was the highest vote recipient with 344,575 votes (54.3%). In Vermont's general election, independent Bernard Sanders was the highest vote recipient with 183,649 votes (67.4%).

HOUSE OF REPRESENTATIVES ELECTIONS 2018

	Seats Won							Percentage			
								Total Vote		Major Vote	
State	Republican	Democratic	Total Vote	Republican	Democratic	Other	Rep.-Dem. Plurality	Rep.	Dem.	Rep.	Dem.
Alabama	6	1	1,659,895	975,737	678,687	5,471	297,050 R	58.8%	40.9%	59.0%	41.0%
Alaska	1	0	282,166	149,779	131,199	1,188	18,580 R	53.1%	46.5%	53.3%	46.7%
Arizona	4	5	2,341,270	1,139,251	1,179,193	22,826	39,942 D	48.7%	50.4%	49.1%	50.9%
Arkansas	4	0	889,298	556,339	312,978	19,981	243,361 R	62.6%	35.2%	64.0%	36.0%
California	7	46	12,184,522	3,973,396	8,010,445	200,681	4,037,049 D	32.6%	65.7%	33.2%	66.8%
Colorado	3	4	2,513,907	1,079,772	1,343,211	90,924	263,439 D	43.0%	53.4%	44.6%	55.4%
Connecticut	0	5	1,379,808	520,521	849,341	9,946	328,820 D	37.7%	61.6%	38.0%	62.0%
Delaware	0	1	353,814	125,384	227,353	1,077	101,969 D	35.4%	64.3%	35.5%	64.5%
Florida	14	13	7,021,476	3,675,417	3,307,228	38,831	368,189 R	52.3%	47.1%	52.6%	47.4%
Georgia	9	5	3,802,343	1,987,191	1,814,469	683	172,722 R	52.3%	47.7%	52.3%	47.7%
Hawaii	0	2	382,332	87,348	287,921	7,063	200,573 D	22.8%	75.3%	23.3%	76.7%
Idaho	2	0	595,724	367,993	207,303	20,428	160,690 R	61.8%	34.8%	64.0%	36.0%
Illinois	5	13	4,539,704	1,754,449	2,757,540	27,715	1,003,091 D	38.6%	60.7%	38.9%	61.1%
Indiana	7	2	2,256,149	1,247,978	1,000,104	8,067	247,874 R	55.3%	44.3%	55.5%	44.5%
Iowa	1	3	1,316,648	612,338	664,676	39,634	52,338 D	46.5%	50.5%	48.0%	52.0%
Kansas	3	1	1,050,322	563,190	464,380	22,752	98,810 R	53.6%	44.2%	54.8%	45.2%
Kentucky	5	1	1,569,798	935,304	612,977	21,517	322,327 R	59.6%	39.0%	60.4%	39.6%
Louisiana	5	1	1,460,593	835,715	553,184	71,694	282,531 R	57.2%	37.9%	60.2%	39.8%
Maine	0	2	623,424	250,119	343,635	29,670	93,516 D	40.1%	55.1%	42.1%	57.9%
Maryland	1	7	2,286,284	737,906	1,493,047	55,331	755,141 D	32.3%	65.3%	33.1%	66.9%
Massachusetts	0	9	2,485,081	497,953	1,943,597	43,531	1,445,644 D	20.0%	78.2%	20.4%	79.6%
Michigan	7	7	4,154,703	1,853,459	2,175,003	126,241	321,544 D	44.6%	52.4%	46.0%	54.0%
Minnesota	3	5	2,576,996	1,125,533	1,420,769	30,694	295,236 D	43.7%	55.1%	44.2%	55.8%
Mississippi	3	1	938,903	471,162	398,770	68,971	72,392 R	50.2%	42.5%	54.2%	45.8%
Missouri	6	2	2,418,413	1,330,975	1,027,969	59,469	303,006 R	55.0%	42.5%	56.4%	43.6%
Montana	1	0	504,421	256,661	233,284	14,476	23,377 R	50.9%	46.2%	52.4%	47.6%
Nebraska	3	0	696,570	432,077	264,493		167,584 R	62.0%	38.0%	62.0%	38.0%
Nevada	1	3	960,774	439,727	491,272	29,775	51,545 D	45.8%	51.1%	47.2%	52.8%
New Hampshire	0	2	570,744	248,986	311,242	10,516	62,256 D	43.6%	54.5%	44.4%	55.6%
New Jersey	1	11	3,098,743	1,198,664	1,856,819	43,260	658,155 D	38.7%	59.9%	39.2%	60.8%
New Mexico	0	3	693,311	264,701	404,026	24,584	139,325 D	38.2%	58.3%	39.6%	60.4%
New York	6	21	5,948,673	1,859,074	3,990,483	99,116	2,131,409 D	31.3%	67.1%	31.8%	68.2%
North Carolina	9	3	3,663,326	1,846,041	1,771,061	46,224	74,980 R	50.4%	48.3%	51.0%	49.0%
North Dakota	1	0	321,532	193,568	114,377	13,587	79,191 R	60.2%	35.6%	62.9%	37.1%
Ohio	12	4	4,406,358	2,291,333	2,082,684	32,341	208,649 R	52.0%	47.3%	52.4%	47.6%
Oklahoma	4	1	1,178,836	730,531	428,452	19,853	302,079 R	62.0%	36.3%	63.0%	37.0%
Oregon	1	4	1,847,646	702,531	1,061,412	83,703	358,881 D	38.0%	57.4%	39.8%	60.2%
Pennsylvania	9	9	4,929,875	2,206,260	2,712,665	10,950	506,405 D	44.8%	55.0%	44.9%	55.1%
Rhode Island	0	2	373,280	129,838	242,575	867	112,737 D	34.8%	65.0%	34.9%	65.1%
South Carolina	5	2	1,709,292	927,494	758,340	23,458	169,154 R	54.3%	44.4%	55.0%	45.0%
South Dakota	1	0	335,965	202,695	121,033	12,237	81,662 R	60.3%	36.0%	62.6%	37.4%
Tennessee	7	2	2,159,825	1,279,655	846,450	33,720	433,205 R	59.2%	39.2%	60.2%	39.8%
Texas	23	13	8,202,708	4,135,359	3,852,752	214,597	282,607 R	50.4%	47.0%	51.8%	48.2%
Utah	3	1	1,052,506	617,307	374,009	61,190	243,298 R	58.7%	35.5%	62.3%	37.7%
Vermont	0	1	272,451	70,705	188,547	13,199	117,842 D	26.0%	69.2%	27.3%	72.7%
Virginia	4	7	3,312,956	1,408,701	1,867,061	37,194	458,360 D	42.5%	56.4%	43.0%	57.0%
Washington	3	7	3,021,951	1,048,712	1,811,371	161,868	762,659 D	34.7%	59.9%	36.7%	63.3%
West Virginia	3	0	577,991	337,146	234,568	6,277	102,578 R	58.3%	40.6%	59.0%	41.0%
Wisconsin	5	3	2,571,655	1,172,964	1,367,492	31,199	194,528 D	45.6%	53.2%	46.2%	53.8%
Wyoming	1	0	201,245	127,963	59,903	13,379	68,060 R	63.6%	29.8%	68.1%	31.9%
Total	*199*	*235*	*113,696,207*	*50,982,902*	*60,651,350*	*2,061,955*	*9,668,448 D*	*44.8%*	*53.3%*	*45.7%*	*54.3%*

Notes: Does not include special elections. The following states allow cross-endorsement, that is, where third parties could endorse candidates of the major parties, and all such votes are credited to the major party with which the candidates indentified: Connecticut, Delaware, Idaho, Mississippi, New York, Oregon, South Carolina, and Vermont. California and Washington hold jungle primaries, and the top two vote recipients, regardless of party, advance to the November general election. Where two candidates of the same party ran against each other, the vote totals for all Republicans and Democrats are included in the state total for each party. Maine's new ranked-choice voting system requires winning candidates to receive a majority vote. Candidates with the fewest ranked votes are eliminated, and their votes are transferred to the candidates ranked second on each voter's ballot. This process continues until a candidate receives a majority. Balloting in Maine's District 2 resulted in round 2 counting, and that final counting is presented here, not the initial vote. North Carolina's 9th District results were not certified, following allegations of absentee ballot election fraud by Republican operatives. However, since a vote was taken, the district results are included here as part of the North Carolina and nationwide House vote tallies.

UNITED STATES

SUMMARY OF HOUSE AND SENATE SPECIAL ELECTIONS, 2017–2018

REPRESENTATIVES

State	Former Member	New Member	Date Elected	Winning Percentage	Total Vote
Kansas 4th	Mike Pompeo (R)	Ron Estes (R)	April 11, 2017	52.2%	122,594
Montana At Large	Ryan Zinke (R)	Greg Gianforte (R)	May 25, 2017	50.0%	381,416
California 34th	Xavier Bacerra (D)	Jimmy Gomez (D)	June 6, 2017	59.2%	43,179
Georgia 6th	Tom Price (R)	Karen Handel (R)	June 20, 2017	51.8%	260,316
South Carolina 5th	Mick Mulvaney (R)	Ralph Norman (R)	June 20, 2017	51.0%	88,316
Utah 3rd	Jason Chaffetz (R)	John Curtis (R)	November 7, 2017	58.0%	147,796
Pennsylvania 18th	Tim Murphy (R)	Conor Lamb (D)	March 13, 2018	49.9%	228,830
Arizona 8th	Trent Franks (R)	Debbie Lesko (R)	April 24, 2018	52.4%	183,343
Texas 27th	Blake Farenthold (R)	Michael Cloud (R)	June 30, 2018	59.8%	36,291
Ohio 12th	Patrick Tiberi (R)	Troy Balderson (R)	August 7, 2018	50.1%	208,141
Michigan 13th	John Conyers Jr. (D)	Brenda Jones (D)	November 6, 2018	86.8%	194,993
New York 25th	Louise Slaughter (D)	Joseph Morelle (D)	November 6, 2018	58.6%	255,710
Pennsylvania 7th	Patrick Meehan (R)	Mary Gay Scanlon (D)	November 6, 2018	52.3%	331,459
Pennsylvania 15th	Charlie Dent (R)	Susan Wild (D)	November 6, 2018	48.5%	268,526

SENATORS

State	Former Member	New Member	Date Elected	Winning Percentage	Total Vote
Alabama	Jeff Sessions (R)	Doug Jones (D)	December 12, 2017	50.0%	1,348,720
Minnesota	Al Franken (D)	Tina Smith (D)	November 6, 2018	53.0%	2,587,356
Mississippi	Thad Cochran (R)	Cindy Hyde-Smith (R)	November 27, 2018	53.6%	907,588

SPECIAL ELECTIONS AND POSTELECTIONS CHANGES TO THE 115TH CONGRESS

From the beginning of 2017 through the general election of 2018, 14 special elections were held in the House to fill unexpired terms in the 115th Congress. There were three special elections in the Senate in this timeframe, and there were no party switches.

REPRESENTATIVES

ARIZONA 8TH CD

Trent Franks (R) resigned December 8, 2017, following sexual harassment allegations by female staffers. A special general election was held on April 24, 2018, and Debbie Lesko (R) was elected to fill the remainder of the term of the 115th Congress.

April 24, 2018 Special General Election

96,012 Debbie Lesko (R); 87,331 Hiral Tipirneni (D).

CALIFORNIA 34TH CD

Xavier Becerra (D) left office following his appointment as state attorney general. Candidates ran together on a single ballot, and the top two vote recipients, both Democrats, proceeded to a general election on June 6, 2017. Jimmy Gomez (D) was elected to fill the remainder of the term of the 115th Congress.

April 4, 2017 Special All Party Primary

10,728 Jimmy Gomez (D); 9,415 Robert Lee Ahn (D); 4,259 Maria Cabildo (D); 2,358 Sara Hernandez (D); 2,205 Arturo Carmona (D); 2,195 Wendy Carrillo (D); 1,964 Kenneth Mejia (Green); 1,368 Yolie Flores (D); 1,360 William "Rodriguez" Morrison (R); 1,042 Tracy Van Houten (D); 1,001 Alejandra Campoverdi (D); 853 Vanessa L. Aramayo (D); 674 Sandra Mendoza (D); 663 Steven Mac (D); 509 Raymond Meza (D); 427 Mark Edward Padilla (No Party Preference); 331 Ricardo "Ricky" De La Fuente (D); 319 Angela E. McArdle (Libertarian); 182 Adrienne Nicole Edwards (D); 155 Richard Joseph Sullivan (D); 118 Armando Sotomayor (D); 103 Tenaya Wallace (D); 79 Melissa "Sharkie" Garza (D).

June 6, 2017 Special General Election

25,569 Jimmy Gomez (D); 17,610 Robert Lee Ahn (D).

UNITED STATES

SUMMARY OF HOUSE AND SENATE SPECIAL ELECTIONS, 2017–2018

GEORGIA 6TH CD

Tom Price (R) resigned February 10, 2017, following his appointment as U.S. Health and Human Services Secretary. No candidate received a majority of the vote in the April 18, 2017, special general election, and the two highest vote recipients advanced to a runoff on June 20, 2017. Karen Handel (R) was elected to fill the remainder of the term of the 115th Congress.

April 18, 2017 Special General Election

92,673 Jon Ossoff (D); 38,071 Karen Handel (R); 20,802 Bob Gray (R); 17,028 Dan Moody (R); 16,870 Judson Hill (R); 1,820 Kurt Wilson (R); 1,639 David Abroms (R); 504 Ragin Edwards (D); 491 Ron Slotin (D); 455 Bruce Levell (R); 415 Mohammad Ali Bhuiyan (R); 415 Keith Grawert (R); 351 Amy Kremer (R); 326 William Llop (R); 304 Rebecca Quigg (D); 229 Richard Keatley (D); 121 Alexander Hernandez (Independent); 55 Andre Pollard (Independent).

June 20, 2017 Special Runoff Election

134,799 Karen Handel (R); 125,517 Jon Ossoff (D).

KANSAS 4TH CD

Mike Pompeo (R) resigned January 23, 2017, following his appointment as director of the Central Intelligence Agency. Each party chose a nominee for the April 11, 2017, special general election.

April 11, 2017 Special General Election

64,044 Ron Estes (R); 56,435 James Thompson (D).

MICHIGAN 13TH CD

John Conyers Jr. (D) resigned December 5, 2017, after sexual harassment allegations by female staff members. A special election was held November 6, 2018, concurrent with the general election to the 116th Congress. Brenda Jones was elected to fill the remainder of the term of the 115th Congress.

August 7, 2018 Special Republican Primary Election

277 David Anthony Dudenhoefer (Write-in).

August 7, 2018 Special Democratic Primary Election

32,769 Brenda Jones; 31,121 Rashida Tlaib; 13,174 Bill Wild; 9,749 Ian Conyers; 2 Clyde Darnell Lynch (Write-in); 1 Royce Kinniebrew (Write-in).

November 6, 2018 Special General Election

169,330 Brenda Jones (D); 17,303 Marc Joseph Sosnowski (U.S. Taxpayers); 8,319 D. Etta Wilcoxon (Green); 36 David Anthony Dudenhoefer (Write-in); 5 Jonathan Lee Pommerville (Write-in); 1 DaNetta L. Simpson (Write-in).

MONTANA AT LARGE

Ryan Zinke (R) resigned March 1, 2017, following his appointment as U.S. Interior Secretary. Each party chose a nominee for the May 25, 2017, special general election.

May 25, 2017 Special General Election

190,520 Greg Gianforte (R); 169,214 Rob Quist (D); 21,682 Mark Wicks (Libertarian).

NEW YORK 25TH CD

Louise Slaughter (D) passed away March 16, 2018, after suffering a concussion following a fall. This special election was distinct from the November 6, 2018, general election to the 116th Congress, although the same candidate—Joseph Morelle (D)—won both. Morelle was elected November 6, 2018, to fill the remainder of the term of the 115th Congress.

November 6, 2018 Special General Election

149,937 Joseph Morelle (D); 105,621 Jim Maxwell (R).

UNITED STATES

SUMMARY OF HOUSE AND SENATE SPECIAL ELECTIONS, 2017–2018

OHIO 12TH CD

Patrick Tiberi (R) resigned January 15, 2018, to lead the Ohio Business Roundtable. Each party chose a nominee for the June 7, 2016 special general election. Troy Balderson (R) was elected August 7, 2018, to fill the remainder of the term of the 115th Congress.

May 8, 2018 Special Republican Primary

20,101 Troy Balderson; 19,437 Melanie Leneghan; 11,743 Tim Kaine; 9,819 Kevin Bacon; 4,406 Carol O'Brien; 998 Jon Halverstadt; 807 Lawrence Cohen; 750 Mick Shoemaker Jr.; 741 Pat Manley.

May 8, 2018 Special Democratic Primary

18,422 Danny O'Connor; 7,544 Zach Scott; 7,515 John Russel; 6,111 Jackie Patton; 3,638 Ed Albertson; 1,771 Doug Wilson.

August 7, 2018 Special General Election

104,328 Troy Balderson (R); 102,648 Danny O'Connor (D); 1,165 Joe Manchik (Green).

PENNSYLVANIA 7TH CD

Patrick Meehan (R) resigned April 27, 2018, following sexual misconduct allegations. The Pennsylvania Supreme Court adopted a new congressional map after the original map was found to be unconstitutionally partisan gerrymandered. The special election used the original map for CD 7, and the general election used the new map. This special election was distinct from the November 6, 2016, general election to the 115th Congress, and the same candidate—Mary Gay Scanlon (D)—won two separate races. Scanlon won the CD 7 special election to fill the remainder of the term of the 115th Congress, and also the general election to represent CD 5 in the 116th Congress.

November 6, 2018 Special General Election

173,268 Mary Gay Scanlon (D); 152,503 Pearl Kim (R); 3,177 Sandra Salas (Libertarian); 2,511 Brianna Johnston (Green).

PENNSYLVANIA 15TH CD

Charlie Dent (R) resigned May 12, 2018, citing personal matters. The Pennsylvania Supreme Court adopted a new congressional map after the original map was found to be unconstitutionally partisan gerrymandered. The special election used the original map for CD 15, and the general election used the new map. This special election was distinct from the November 6, 2018, general election to the 116th Congress, and the same candidate—Susan Wild (D)—won two separate races. Wild won the CD 15 special election to fill the remainder of the term of the 115th Congress, and also the general election to represent CD 7 in the 116th Congress.

March 13, 2018 Special General Election

130,353 Susan Wild (D); 129,594 Marty Nothstein (R); 8,579 Tim Silfies (Libertarian).

PENNSYLVANIA 18TH CD

Tim Murphy (R) resigned October 21, 2017, following reports that he asked a woman with whom he had an extramarital affair to get an abortion. The Pennsylvania Supreme Court adopted a new congressional map after the original map was found to be unconstitutionally partisan gerrymandered. The special election held on March 13, 2018, used the original map for CD 18, and the general election used the new map. Conor Lamb (D) was elected in the special election to fill the remainder of the term of the 115th Congress, and also in the general election on November 6, 2018, to represent CD 17 in the 116th Congress.

March 13, 2018 Special General Election

114,102 Conor Lamb (D); 113,347 Richard Saccone (R); 1,381 Drew Gray Miller (Libertarian).

SOUTH CAROLINA 5TH CD

Mick Mulvaney (R) resigned February 16, 2017, following his appointment as director of the U.S. Office of Management and Budget. Ralph Norman (R) was elected June 20, 2017, to fill the remainder of the term of the 115th Congress.

May 2, 2017 Special Democratic Primary

13,333 Archie Parnell; 4,030 Alexis Frank; 1,346 Les Murphy.

UNITED STATES

SUMMARY OF HOUSE AND SENATE SPECIAL ELECTIONS, 2017–2018

May 2, 2017 Special Republican Primary

11,943 Tommy Pope; 11,808 Ralph Norman; 7,759 Tom Mullikin; 5,546 Chad Connelly; 1,930 Sheri Few; 197 Kris Wampler; 87 Ray Craig.

May 16, 2017 Special Republican Runoff

17,823 Ralph Norman; 17,602 Tommy Pope.

June 20, 2017 Special General Election

45,076 Ralph Norman (R); 42,341 Archie Parnell (D); 319 Josh Thornton (American); 273 Victor Kocher (Libertarian); 242 David Kulma (Green); 65 (Write-in).

TEXAS 27TH CD

Blake Farenthold (R) resigned April 6, 2018, amid sexual misconduct allegations. Michael Cloud (R) was elected June 30, 2018, to fill the remainder of the term of the 115th Congress.

June 30, 2018 Special General Election

19,872 Michael Cloud (R); 11,599 Eric Holguin (D); 1,748 Raul "Roy" Barrera (D); 1,571 Bech Bruun (R); 858 Michael Westergren (D); 144 Daniel Tinus (Libertarian); 276 Marty Perez (R); 172 Judith Cutright (Independent); 51 Christopher Suprun (Independent).

UTAH 3RD CD

Jason Chaffetz (R) resigned June 30, 2017, to return to the private sector. The Republican Party held a special primary on August 15, 2017, and the Democratic candidate was selected by the party nominating convention. John Curtis (R) was elected November 7, 2017, to fill the remainder of the term of the 115th Congress.

August 15, 2017 Special Republican Primary

31,481 John Curtis; 23,686 Christopher Niles Herrod; 17,565 Tanner Ainge.

November 7, 2017 Special General Election

85,739 John Curtis (R); 37,778 Kathie Allen (D); 13,745 Jim Bennett (United Utah); 4,550 Sean Whalen (Independent); 3,643 Joe Buchman (Libertarian); 2,286 Jason Christensen (Independent American).

SENATORS

ALABAMA

Jeff Sessions (R) resigned February 9, 2017, following his confirmation as U.S. Attorney General. Doug Jones (D) was elected December 12, 2017, to fill the remainder of the term ending in 2021.

August 15, 2017 Special Democratic Primary

109,105 Doug Jones; 29,215 Robert Kennedy; 11,105 Michael Hansen; 8,010 Will Boyd; 3,478 Jason Fisher; 1,450 Brian McGee; 1,404 Charles Nana; 1,239 Vann Caldwell.

August 15, 2017 Special Republican Primary

164,524 Roy Moore; 138,971 Luther Strange; 83,287 Mo Brooks; 29,124 Trip Pittman; 2,621 Randy Brinson; 1,579 Bryan Peeples; 1,543 Mary Maxwell; 1,078 James Beretta; 303 Dom Gentile; 252 Joseph Breault.

September 26, 2017 Special Republican Runoff

262,641 Roy Moore; 218,505 Luther Strange.

December 12, 2017 Special General Election

673,896 Doug Jones (D); 651,972 Roy Moore (R); 22,852 Write-in.

UNITED STATES

SUMMARY OF HOUSE AND SENATE SPECIAL ELECTIONS, 2017–2018

MINNESOTA

Al Franken (D) resigned January 2, 2018, following sexual misconduct allegations. Governor Mark Dayton appointed Tina Smith (D) to fill the seat temporarily, and Smith went on to be elected in the special election on November 6, 2018, which was held concurrent to the general election, to fill the remainder of the term ending in 2021.

August 14, 2018 Special Democratic Primary

433,705 Tina Smith; 78,193 Richard W. Painter; 18,897 Ali Chehem Ali; 17,825 Gregg A. Iverson; 16,529 Nick Leonard; 5,041 Christopher Lovell Seymore Sr.

August 14, 2018 Special Republican Primary

186,384 Karin Housley; 107,102 Bob Anderson; 7,375 Nikolay Nikolayevich Bey.

November 6, 2018 Special General Election

1,370,540 Tina Smith (D); 1,095,777 Karin Housley (R); 95,614 Sarah Wellington (Legal Marijuana Now); 24,324 Jerry Trooien (Unaffiliated); 1,101 Write-in.

MISSISSIPPI

Thad Cochran (R) resigned April 1, 2018, due to health issues. In the special election on November 6, 2018, all candidates ran together on a single ballot. No candidate received a majority of the vote, and the two highest vote recipients advanced to the runoff on November 27, 2018. Cindy Hyde-Smith (R) was elected to fill the remainder of the term ending in 2021.

November 6, 2018 Special All Party Election

389,995 Cindy Hyde-Smith (R); 386,742 Mike Espy (D); 154,878 Chris McDaniel (R); 13,852 Tobey Bartee (D).

November 27, 2018 Special Election Runoff

486,769 Cindy Hyde-Smith (R); 420,819 Mike Espy (D).

CHANGES FOLLOWING THE 2018 ELECTION

Following the 2018 general election, and through August 22, 2018, the following changes took place in the membership of the 116th Congress.

REPRESENTATIVES

North Carolina 3rd District—Walter Jones (R) passed away February 10, 2019. A special election was held September 10, 2019, to replace him.

North Carolina 9th District—The results of the 2018 general election were not certified due to alleged absentee ballot election fraud committed by Republican operatives. A new election was held September 10, 2019.

Pennsylvania 12th District—Tom Marino (R) resigned January 23, 2019, to return to the private sector. Fred Keller (R) won a special election May 21, 2019, to replace him.

SENATOR

Arizona—John McCain (R) passed away August 25, 2018, from cancer. Former U.S. Sen. Jon Kyl (R) was appointed by Governor Doug Ducey to replace him through 2018. Governor Ducey then appointed Martha McSally (R) to replace Kyl until the special election scheduled for November 3, 2020.

UNITED STATES

POPULAR VOTE FOR PRESIDENT 1920 TO 2016

		Republican		Democratic				Percentage			
								Total Vote		Major Vote	
Year	Total Vote	Vote	Candidate	Vote	Candidate	Other	Rep.-Dem. Plurality	Rep.	Dem.	Rep.	Dem.
2016	136,562,629	62,984,804	Trump, Donald J.	65,853,508	Clinton, Hillary	7,724,317	2,868,704 D	46.1%	48.2%	48.9%	51.1%
2012	129,085,474	60,933,500	Romney, W. Mitt	65,915,796	Obama, Barack	2,236,178	4,982,296 D	47.2%	51.1%	48.0%	52.0%
2008	131,313,820	59,948,323	McCain, John S. III	69,498,516	Obama, Barack	1,866,981	9,550,193 D	45.7%	52.9%	46.3%	53.7%
2004	122,295,345	62,040,610	Bush, George W.	59,028,439	Kerry, John	1,226,296	3,012,171 R	50.7%	48.3%	51.2%	48.8%
2000	105,396,627	50,455,156	Bush, George W.	50,992,335	Gore, Albert Jr.	3,949,136	537,179 D	47.9%	48.4%	49.7%	50.3%
1996	96,277,872	39,198,755	Dole, Bob	47,402,357	Clinton, Bill	9,676,760	8,203,602 D	40.7%	49.2%	45.3%	54.7%
1992	104,425,014	39,103,882	Bush, George H.	44,909,326	Clinton, Bill	20,411,806	5,805,444 D	37.4%	43.0%	46.5%	53.5%
1988	91,597,809	48,886,097	Bush, George H.	41,812,075	Dukakis, Michael S.	899,637	7,074,022 R	53.4%	45.6%	53.9%	46.1%
1984	92,652,842	54,455,075	Reagan, Ronald	37,577,185	Mondale, Walter F.	620,582	16,877,890 R	58.8%	40.6%	59.2%	40.8%
1980	86,515,221	43,904,153	Reagan, Ronald	35,483,883	Carter, Jimmy	7,127,185	8,420,270 R	50.7%	41.0%	55.3%	44.7%
1976	81,554,989	39,141,091	Ford, Gerald R.	40,829,763	Carter, Jimmy	1,584,135	1,688,672 D	48.0%	50.1%	48.9%	51.1%
1972	77,718,554	47,169,911	Nixon, Richard M.	29,170,383	McGovern, George S.	1,378,260	17,999,528 R	60.7%	37.5%	61.8%	38.2%
1968	73,211,875	31,785,480	Nixon, Richard M.	31,275,166	Humphrey, Hubert H.	10,151,229	510,314 R	43.4%	42.7%	50.4%	49.6%
1964	70,644,592	27,178,188	Goldwater, Barry M.	43,129,566	Johnson, Lyndon B.	336,838	15,951,378 D	38.5%	61.1%	38.7%	61.3%
1960	68,838,219	34,108,157	Nixon, Richard M.	34,226,731	Kennedy, John F.	503,331	118,574 D	49.5%	49.7%	49.9%	50.1%
1956	62,026,908	35,590,472	Eisenhower, Dwight D.	26,022,752	Stevenson, Adlai E.	413,684	9,567,720 R	57.4%	42.0%	57.8%	42.2%
1952	61,550,918	33,936,234	Eisenhower, Dwight D.	27,314,992	Stevenson, Adlai E.	299,692	6,621,242 R	55.1%	44.4%	55.4%	44.6%
1948	48,793,826	21,991,291	Dewey, Thomas E.	24,179,345	Truman, Harry S.	2,623,190	2,188,054 D	45.1%	49.6%	47.6%	52.4%
1944	47,976,670	22,017,617	Dewey, Thomas E.	25,612,610	Roosevelt, Franklin D.	346,443	3,594,993 D	45.9%	53.4%	46.2%	53.8%
1940	49,900,774	22,348,836	Willkie, Wendell	27,313,041	Roosevelt, Franklin D.	238,897	4,964,205 D	44.8%	54.7%	45.0%	55.0%
1936	45,654,763	16,684,231	Landon, Alfred M.	27,757,333	Roosevelt, Franklin D.	1,213,199	11,073,102 D	36.5%	60.8%	37.5%	62.5%
1932	39,761,034	15,760,684	Hoover, Herbert C.	22,829,501	Roosevelt, Franklin D.	1,170,849	7,068,817 D	39.6%	57.4%	40.8%	59.2%
1928	36,805,951	21,437,277	Hoover, Herbert C.	15,007,698	Smith, Alfred E.	360,976	6,429,579 R	58.2%	40.8%	58.8%	41.2%
1924	29,095,023	15,719,921	Coolidge, Calvin	8,386,704	Davis, John W.	4,988,398	7,333,217 R	54.0%	28.8%	65.2%	34.8%
1920	26,768,150	16,153,115	Harding, Warren G.	9,133,092	Cox, James M.	1,481,943	7,020,023 R	60.3%	34.1%	63.9%	36.1%

Republican Donald J. Trump lost the popular vote in 2016, but won the electoral vote and was elected president. Republican George W. Bush lost the popular vote in 2000, but won the electoral vote and was elected president. In past elections, the other vote included: 2016 - 4,489,325 Libertarian (Gary Johnson); 2000 - 2,882,738 Green (Ralph Nader); 1996 - 8,085,402 Reform (Ross Perot); 1992 - 19,741,657 Independent (Ross Perot); 1980 - 5,720,060 Independent (John Anderson); 1968 - 9,906,473 American Independent (George Wallace); 1948 - 1,176,125 States' Rights (Strom Thurmond); 1948 - 1,157,326 Progressive (Henry Wallace); 1924 - 4,832,532 Progressive (Robert La Follette).

ELECTORAL COLLEGE VOTE 1920 TO 2016

Year	Total	Republican	Democratic	Other	Other Candidate	Other Party
2016	538	304	227	7	See Note*	See Note
2012	538	206	332	0		
2008	538	173	365	0		
2004	538	286	251	1	John Edwards*	Democrat
2000	538	271	266	1	Abstained*	
1996	538	159	379	0		
1992	538	168	370	0		
1988	538	426	111	1	Lloyd Bentsen*	Democrat
1984	538	525	13	0		
1980	538	489	49	0		
1976	538	240	297	1	Ronald Reagan*	Republican
1972	538	520	17	1	John Hospers*	Libertarian
1968	538	301	191	46	George Wallace	American Independent
1964	538	52	486	0		
1960	537	219	303	15	Harry Byrd	Democrat
1956	531	457	73	1	Walter Jones*	Democrat
1952	531	442	89	0		
1948	531	189	303	39	Strom Thurmond	States' Rights
1944	531	99	432	0		
1940	531	82	449	0		
1936	531	8	523	0		
1932	531	59	472	0		
1928	531	444	87	0		
1924	531	382	136	13	Robert M. La Follette	Progressive
1920	531	404	127	0		

Note: An asterisk (*) indicates "faithless" electors who did not vote for the presidential candidates to which they were pledged. One of the electoral votes for Strom Thurmond in 1948, Harry Byrd in 1960, and George Wallace in 1968 was cast by a faithless elector. The rest of Byrd's support in 1960 came from unpledged electors. Due to faithless electors in the 2016 election, the following individuals received electoral votes: Bernie Sanders (1), Ron Paul (1), John Kasich (1), Colin Powell (3), and Faith Spotted Eagle (1).

ALABAMA

Congressional districts first established for elections held in 2012

7 members

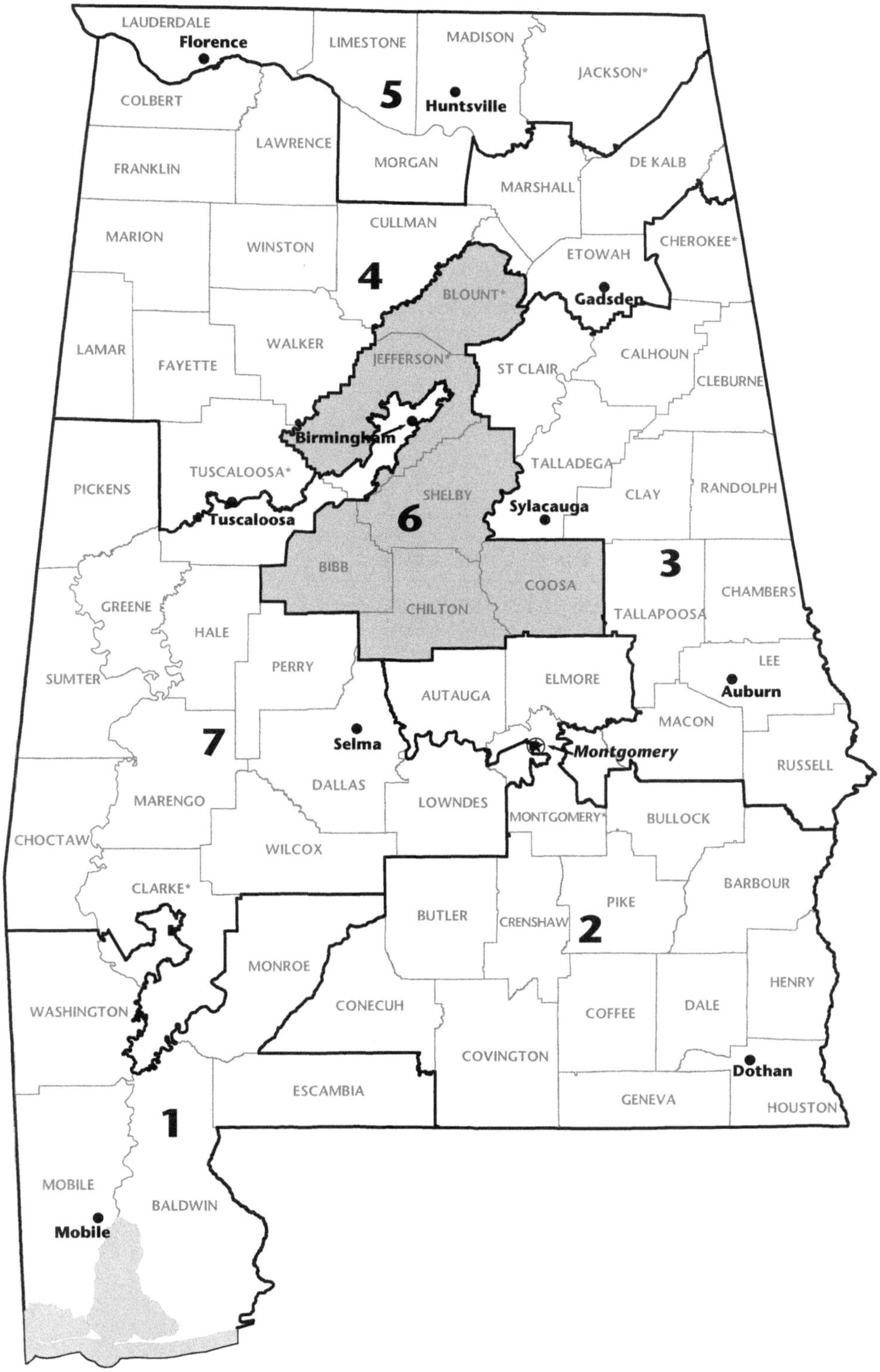

* Asterisk indicates a county whose boundaries include parts of two or more congressional districts.

ALABAMA

GOVERNOR

Kay Ivey (R). Assumed office April 10, 2017, to complete the remainder of the term vacated by the resignation of Robert Bentley (R).

SENATORS (1 Democrat, 1 Republican)

Doug Jones (D). Elected December 12, 2017, in a special election to complete the remainder of the term vacated by the appointment of Jeff Sessions (R) to U.S. Attorney General.

Richard C. Shelby (R). Re-elected 2016 to a six-year term. Previously elected 2010, 2004, 1998, 1992, 1986. Changed party affiliation from Democratic to Republican after the 1994 election.

REPRESENTATIVES (6 Republicans, 1 Democrat)

1. Bradley Byrne (R)
2. Martha Roby (R)
3. Mike Rogers (R)
4. Robert B. Aderholt (R)
5. Mo Brooks (R)
6. Gary J. Palmer (R)
7. Terri A. Sewell (D)

POSTWAR VOTE FOR PRESIDENT

		Republican		Democratic				Percentage			
								Total Vote		Major Vote	
Year	Total Vote	Vote	Candidate	Vote	Candidate	Other Vote	Rep.-Dem. Plurality	Rep.	Dem.	Rep.	Dem.
2016**	2,123,372	1,318,255	Trump, Donald J.	729,547	Clinton, Hillary Rodham	75,570	588,708 R	62.1%	34.4%	64.4%	35.6%
2012	2,074,338	1,255,925	Romney, W. Mitt	795,696	Obama, Barack H.*	22,717	460,229 R	60.5%	38.4%	61.2%	38.8%
2008	2,099,819	1,266,546	McCain, John S. III	813,479	Obama, Barack H.	19,794	453,067 R	60.3%	38.7%	60.9%	39.1%
2004	1,883,449	1,176,394	Bush, George W.*	693,933	Kerry, John F.	13,122	482,461 R	62.5%	36.8%	62.9%	37.1%
2000**	1,666,272	941,173	Bush, George W.	692,611	Gore, Albert Jr.	32,488	248,562 R	56.5%	41.6%	57.6%	42.4%
1996**	1,534,349	769,044	Dole, Robert "Bob"	662,165	Clinton, Bill*	103,140	106,879 R	50.1%	43.2%	53.7%	46.3%
1992**	1,688,060	804,283	Bush, George H.*	690,080	Clinton, Bill	193,697	114,203 R	47.6%	40.9%	53.8%	46.2%
1988	1,378,476	815,576	Bush, George H.	549,506	Dukakis, Michael S.	13,394	266,070 R	59.2%	39.9%	59.7%	40.3%
1984	1,441,713	872,849	Reagan, Ronald*	551,899	Mondale, Walter F.	16,965	320,950 R	60.5%	38.3%	61.3%	38.7%
1980**	1,341,929	654,192	Reagan, Ronald	636,730	Carter, Jimmy*	51,007	17,462 R	48.8%	47.4%	50.7%	49.3%
1976	1,182,850	504,070	Ford, Gerald R.*	659,170	Carter, Jimmy	19,610	155,100 D	42.6%	55.7%	43.3%	56.7%
1972	1,006,111	728,701	Nixon, Richard M.*	256,923	McGovern, George S.	20,487	471,778 R	72.4%	25.5%	73.9%	26.1%
1968**	1,049,922	146,923	Nixon, Richard M.	196,579	Humphrey, Hubert Horatio Jr.	706,420	49,656 D#	14.0%	18.7%	42.8%	57.2%
1964**	689,818	479,085	Goldwater, Barry M. Sr.		Johnson, Lyndon B.*	210,733	479,085 R	69.5%		100.0%	
1960	570,225	237,981	Nixon, Richard M.	324,050	Kennedy, John F.	8,194	86,069 D	41.7%	56.8%	42.3%	57.7%
1956	496,861	195,694	Eisenhower, Dwight D.*	280,844	Stevenson, Adlai E. II	20,323	85,150 D	39.4%	56.5%	41.1%	58.9%
1952	426,120	149,231	Eisenhower, Dwight D.	275,075	Stevenson, Adlai E. II	1,814	125,844 D	35.0%	64.6%	35.2%	64.8%
1948**	214,980	40,930	Dewey, Thomas E.		Truman, Harry S.*	174,050	40,930 R#	19.0%		100.0%	

Note: An asterisk (*) denotes incumbent. A pound sign (#) in the plurality column indicates that the winner in 1948 and 1968 did not run under the banner of either major party. **In past elections, the other vote included: 2016 - 44,467 Libertarian (Gary Johnson); 2000 - 18,323 Green (Ralph Nader); 1996 - 92,149 Reform (Ross Perot); 1992 - 183,109 Independent (Perot); 1980 - 16,481 Independent (John Anderson); 1968 - 691,425 American Independent (George Wallace); 1964 - 210,732 Unpledged Democratic; 1948 - 171,443 States' Rights (Strom Thurmond). In 1964 and 1948, the Democratic presidential candidates were not listed on the ballot. Wallace carried Alabama in 1968 with 65.9 percent of the total vote. Thurmond won the state in 1948 with 79.7 percent.

ALABAMA

POSTWAR VOTE FOR GOVERNOR

		Republican		Democratic				Percentage			
								Total Vote		Major Vote	
Year	Total Vote	Vote	Candidate	Vote	Candidate	Other Vote	Rep.-Dem. Plurality	Rep.	Dem.	Rep.	Dem.
2018	1,719,589	1,022,457	Ivey, Kay*	694,495	Maddox, Walter	2,637	327,962 R	59.5%	40.4%	59.6%	40.4%
2014	1,180,413	750,231	Bentley, Robert*	427,787	Griffith, Parker	2,395	322,444 R	63.6%	36.2%	63.7%	36.3%
2010	1,494,273	860,472	Bentley, Robert	625,710	Sparks, Ron	8,091	234,762 R	57.6%	41.9%	57.9%	42.1%
2006	1,250,401	718,327	Riley, Robert*	519,827	Baxley, Lucy	12,247	198,500 R	57.4%	41.6%	58.0%	42.0%
2002	1,367,053	672,225	Riley, Robert	669,105	Siegelman, Don*	25,723	3,120 R	49.2%	48.9%	50.1%	49.9%
1998	1,317,842	554,746	James, Forrest H. "Fob" Jr.*	760,155	Siegelman, Don	2,941	205,409 D	42.1%	57.7%	42.2%	57.8%
1994	1,201,969	604,926	James, Forrest H. "Fob" Jr.	594,169	Folsom, James E. Jr.*	2,874	10,757 R	50.3%	49.4%	50.4%	49.6%
1990	1,216,250	633,519	Hunt, Guy*	582,106	Hubbert, Paul R.	625	51,413 R	52.1%	47.9%	52.1%	47.9%
1986	1,236,230	696,203	Hunt, Guy	537,163	Baxley, Bill	2,864	159,040 R	56.3%	43.5%	56.4%	43.6%
1982	1,128,725	440,815	Folmar, Emory	650,538	Wallace, George C.	37,372	209,723 D	39.1%	57.6%	40.4%	59.6%
1978	760,474	196,963	Hunt, Guy	551,886	James, Forrest H. "Fob" Jr.	11,625	354,923 D	25.9%	72.6%	26.3%	73.7%
1974	598,305	88,381	McCary, Elvin	497,574	Wallace, George C.*	12,350	409,193 D	14.8%	83.2%	15.1%	84.9%
1970**	854,952			637,046	Wallace, George C.	217,906	637,046 D		74.5%		100.0%
1966	848,101	262,943	Martin, James D.	537,505	Wallace, Lurleen B.	47,653	274,562 D	31.0%	63.4%	32.8%	67.2%
1962	315,776			303,987	Wallace, George C.	11,789	303,987 D		96.3%		100.0%
1958	270,952	30,415	Longshore, William L. Jr.	239,633	Patterson, John	904	209,218 D	11.2%	88.4%	11.3%	88.7%
1954	333,090	88,688	Abernethy, Tom	244,401	Folsom, James E.	1	155,713 D	26.6%	73.4%	26.6%	73.4%
1950	170,591	15,177	Crowder, John S.	155,414	Persons, Gordon		140,237 D	8.9%	91.1%	8.9%	91.1%
1946	197,321	22,362	Ward, Lyman	174,959	Folsom, James E.		152,597 D	11.3%	88.7%	11.3%	88.7%

Note: An asterisk (*) denotes incumbent. **In past elections, the other vote included: 1970 - 125,491 National Democratic Party of Alabama (John Logan Cashin), who finished second. The Republican Party did not run a candidate in the 1962 and 1970 gubernatorial elections.

POSTWAR VOTE FOR SENATOR

		Republican		Democratic				Percentage			
								Total Vote		Major Vote	
Year	Total Vote	Vote	Candidate	Vote	Candidate	Other Vote	Rep.-Dem. Plurality	Rep.	Dem.	Rep.	Dem.
2017S**	1,348,720	651,972	Moore, Roy	673,896	Jones, Doug	22,852	21,924 D	48.3%	50.0%	49.2%	50.8%
2016	2,087,444	1,335,104	Shelby, Richard C.*	748,709	Crumpton, Ron	3,631	586,395 R	64.0%	35.9%	64.1%	35.9%
2014	818,090	795,606	Sessions, Jeff*			22,484	795,606 R	97.3%		100.0%	
2010	1,485,499	968,181	Shelby, Richard C.*	515,619	Barnes, William G.	1,699	452,562 R	65.2%	34.7%	65.3%	34.7%
2008	2,060,191	1,305,383	Sessions, Jeff*	752,391	Figures, Vivian Davis	2,417	552,992 R	63.4%	36.5%	63.4%	36.6%
2004	1,839,066	1,242,200	Shelby, Richard C.*	595,018	Sowell, Wayne	1,848	647,182 R	67.5%	32.4%	67.6%	32.4%
2002	1,353,023	792,561	Sessions, Jeff*	538,878	Parker, Susan	21,584	253,683 R	58.6%	39.8%	59.5%	40.5%
1998	1,293,405	817,973	Shelby, Richard C.*	474,568	Suddith, Clayton	864	343,405 R	63.2%	36.7%	63.3%	36.7%
1996	1,499,393	786,436	Sessions, Jeff	681,651	Bedford, Roger	31,306	104,785 R	52.5%	45.5%	53.6%	46.4%
1992	1,577,899	522,015	Sellers, Richard	1,022,698	Shelby, Richard C.	33,186	500,683 D	33.1%	64.8%	33.8%	66.2%
1990	1,185,563	467,190	Cabaniss, Bill	717,814	Heflin, Howell*	559	250,624 D	39.4%	60.5%	39.4%	60.6%
1986	1,211,953	602,537	Denton, Jeremiah*	609,360	Shelby, Richard C.	56	6,823 D	49.7%	50.3%	49.7%	50.3%
1984	1,371,238	498,508	Smith, Albert Lee Jr.	860,535	Heflin, Howell*	12,195	362,027 D	36.4%	62.8%	36.7%	63.3%
1980	1,296,757	650,362	Denton, Jeremiah	610,175	Folsom, James E. Jr.	36,220	40,187 R	50.2%	47.1%	51.6%	48.4%
1978	582,025			547,054	Heflin, Howell	34,971	547,054 D		94.0%		100.0%
1978S**	731,610	316,170	Martin, James D.	401,852	Stewart, Donald W.	13,588	85,682 D	43.2%	54.9%	44.0%	56.0%
1974	523,290			501,541	Allen, James B.*	21,749	501,541 D		95.8%		100.0%
1972	1,051,099	347,523	Blount, Winton M.	654,491	Sparkman, Richard D.*	49,085	306,968 D	33.1%	62.3%	34.7%	65.3%
1968	912,708	201,227	Hooper, Perry	638,774	Allen, James B.	72,707	437,547 D	22.0%	70.0%	24.0%	76.0%
1966	802,608	313,018	Grenier, John	482,138	Sparkman, John J.*	7,452	169,120 D	39.0%	60.1%	39.4%	60.6%
1962	397,079	195,134	Martin, James D.	201,937	Hill, Lister*	8	6,803 D	49.1%	50.9%	49.1%	50.9%
1960	554,081	164,868	Elgin, Julian	389,196	Sparkman, John J.*	17	224,328 D	29.8%	70.2%	29.8%	70.2%
1956	330,191			330,182	Hill, Lister*	9	330,182 D		100.0%		100.0%
1954	314,459	55,110	Guin, J. Foy Jr.	259,348	Sparkman, John J.*	1	204,238 D	17.5%	82.5%	17.5%	82.5%
1950	164,011			125,534	Hill, Lister*	38,477	125,534 D		76.5%		100.0%
1948	220,875	35,341	Parsons, Paul G.	185,534	Sparkman, John J.*		150,193 D	16.0%	84.0%	16.0%	84.0%
1946S**	163,217			163,217	Sparkman, John J.*		163,217 D		100.0%		100.0%

Note: An asterisk (*) denotes incumbent. **The 1946 election, one of the 1978 elections, and the 2017 election were for short terms to fill vacancies. The Republican Party did not run a candidate in Senate elections in 1946, 1950, 1956, 1974, and 1978.

ALABAMA

GOVERNOR 2018

2010 Census Population	County	Total Vote	Republican (Ivey)	Democratic (Maddox)	Other	Rep.-Dem. Plurality	Percentage Total Vote Rep.	Percentage Total Vote Dem.	Percentage Major Vote Rep.	Percentage Major Vote Dem.
54,571	AUTAUGA	19,749	13,994	5,734	21	8,260 R	70.9%	29.0%	70.9%	29.1%
182,265	BALDWIN	77,997	57,415	20,464	118	36,951 R	73.6%	26.2%	73.7%	26.3%
27,457	BARBOUR	8,390	4,336	4,043	11	293 R	51.7%	48.2%	51.7%	48.3%
22,915	BIBB	6,896	5,082	1,799	15	3,283 R	73.7%	26.1%	73.9%	26.1%
57,322	BLOUNT	19,503	16,984	2,479	40	14,505 R	87.1%	12.7%	87.3%	12.7%
10,914	BULLOCK	3,682	949	2,729	4	1,780 D	25.8%	74.1%	25.8%	74.2%
20,947	BUTLER	8,178	4,812	3,363	3	1,449 R	58.8%	41.1%	58.9%	41.1%
118,572	CALHOUN	37,039	24,460	12,487	92	11,973 R	66.0%	33.7%	66.2%	33.8%
34,215	CHAMBERS	11,332	6,687	4,625	20	2,062 R	59.0%	40.8%	59.1%	40.9%
25,989	CHEROKEE	8,541	6,974	1,552	15	5,422 R	81.7%	18.2%	81.8%	18.2%
43,643	CHILTON	13,802	11,291	2,501	10	8,790 R	81.8%	18.1%	81.9%	18.1%
13,859	CHOCTAW	6,131	3,475	2,649	7	826 R	56.7%	43.2%	56.7%	43.3%
25,833	CLARKE	11,240	6,344	4,889	7	1,455 R	56.4%	43.5%	56.5%	43.5%
13,932	CLAY	5,414	4,164	1,241	9	2,923 R	76.9%	22.9%	77.0%	23.0%
14,972	CLEBURNE	4,424	3,902	508	14	3,394 R	88.2%	11.5%	88.5%	11.5%
49,948	COFFEE	15,972	12,117	3,782	73	8,335 R	75.9%	23.7%	76.2%	23.8%
54,428	COLBERT	20,906	13,180	7,692	34	5,488 R	63.0%	36.8%	63.1%	36.9%
13,228	CONECUH	4,924	2,473	2,444	7	29 R	50.2%	49.6%	50.3%	49.7%
11,539	COOSA	4,314	2,785	1,522	7	1,263 R	64.6%	35.3%	64.7%	35.3%
37,765	COVINGTON	12,042	9,852	2,168	22	7,684 R	81.8%	18.0%	82.0%	18.0%
13,906	CRENSHAW	5,401	3,873	1,522	6	2,351 R	71.7%	28.2%	71.8%	28.2%
80,406	CULLMAN	28,713	24,361	4,309	43	20,052 R	84.8%	15.0%	85.0%	15.0%
50,251	DALE	14,306	10,528	3,731	47	6,797 R	73.6%	26.1%	73.8%	26.2%
43,820	DALLAS	15,220	4,917	10,295	8	5,378 D	32.3%	67.6%	32.3%	67.7%
71,109	DEKALB	21,490	17,316	4,087	87	13,229 R	80.6%	19.0%	80.9%	19.1%
79,303	ELMORE	29,505	21,752	7,722	31	14,030 R	73.7%	26.2%	73.8%	26.2%
38,319	ESCAMBIA	12,152	8,098	4,035	19	4,063 R	66.6%	33.2%	66.7%	33.3%
104,430	ETOWAH	34,646	24,041	10,513	92	13,528 R	69.4%	30.3%	69.6%	30.4%
17,241	FAYETTE	7,489	5,455	2,025	9	3,430 R	72.8%	27.0%	72.9%	27.1%
31,704	FRANKLIN	8,823	6,465	2,336	22	4,129 R	73.3%	26.5%	73.5%	26.5%
26,790	GENEVA	9,019	7,784	1,220	15	6,564 R	86.3%	13.5%	86.5%	13.5%
9,045	GREENE	4,168	661	3,506	1	2,845 D	15.9%	84.1%	15.9%	84.1%
15,760	HALE	6,572	2,361	4,206	5	1,845 D	35.9%	64.0%	36.0%	64.0%
17,302	HENRY	6,714	4,655	2,045	14	2,610 R	69.3%	30.5%	69.5%	30.5%
101,547	HOUSTON	32,227	23,112	9,062	53	14,050 R	71.7%	28.1%	71.8%	28.2%
53,227	JACKSON	15,682	12,074	3,569	39	8,505 R	77.0%	22.8%	77.2%	22.8%
658,466	JEFFERSON	258,068	105,661	152,103	304	46,442 D	40.9%	58.9%	41.0%	59.0%
14,564	LAMAR	5,377	4,399	974	4	3,425 R	81.8%	18.1%	81.9%	18.1%
92,709	LAUDERDALE	30,965	20,692	10,222	51	10,470 R	66.8%	33.0%	66.9%	33.1%
34,339	LAWRENCE	12,002	8,181	3,796	25	4,385 R	68.2%	31.6%	68.3%	31.7%
140,247	LEE	49,333	29,238	20,021	74	9,217 R	59.3%	40.6%	59.4%	40.6%
82,782	LIMESTONE	33,687	23,213	10,421	53	12,792 R	68.9%	30.9%	69.0%	31.0%
11,299	LOWNDES	5,046	1,555	3,487	4	1,932 D	30.8%	69.1%	30.8%	69.2%
21,452	MACON	7,260	1,376	5,882	2	4,506 D	19.0%	81.0%	19.0%	81.0%
334,811	MADISON	141,640	75,874	65,522	244	10,352 R	53.6%	46.3%	53.7%	46.3%
21,027	MARENGO	8,769	4,029	4,735	5	706 D	45.9%	54.0%	46.0%	54.0%
30,776	MARION	9,915	8,021	1,877	17	6,144 R	80.9%	18.9%	81.0%	19.0%
93,019	MARSHALL	27,294	22,031	5,193	70	16,838 R	80.7%	19.0%	80.9%	19.1%
412,992	MOBILE	133,485	69,671	63,656	158	6,015 R	52.2%	47.7%	52.3%	47.7%
23,068	MONROE	8,924	5,038	3,881	5	1,157 R	56.5%	43.5%	56.5%	43.5%
229,363	MONTGOMERY	77,275	28,491	48,722	62	20,231 D	36.9%	63.1%	36.9%	63.1%
119,490	MORGAN	39,563	28,415	11,091	57	17,324 R	71.8%	28.0%	71.9%	28.1%
10,591	PERRY	4,246	1,061	3,182	3	2,121 D	25.0%	74.9%	25.0%	75.0%
19,746	PICKENS	8,316	4,636	3,672	8	964 R	55.7%	44.2%	55.8%	44.2%
32,899	PIKE	10,413	6,226	4,176	11	2,050 R	59.8%	40.1%	59.9%	40.1%
22,913	RANDOLPH	7,600	5,729	1,859	12	3,870 R	75.4%	24.5%	75.5%	24.5%
52,947	RUSSELL	15,049	7,168	7,864	17	696 D	47.6%	52.3%	47.7%	52.3%
195,085	SHELBY	84,042	56,989	26,928	125	30,061 R	67.8%	32.0%	67.9%	32.1%
83,593	ST. CLAIR	29,973	23,529	6,389	55	17,140 R	78.5%	21.3%	78.6%	21.4%
13,763	SUMTER	5,443	1,289	4,151	3	2,862 D	23.7%	76.3%	23.7%	76.3%

ALABAMA

GOVERNOR 2018

2010 Census Population	County	Total Vote	Republican (Ivey)	Democratic (Maddox)	Other	Rep.-Dem. Plurality	Percentage: Total Vote		Percentage: Major Vote	
							Rep.	Dem.	Rep.	Dem.
82,291	TALLADEGA	26,254	15,621	10,606	27	5,015 R	59.5%	40.4%	59.6%	40.4%
41,616	TALLAPOOSA	15,743	10,703	5,015	25	5,688 R	68.0%	31.9%	68.1%	31.9%
194,656	TUSCALOOSA	68,793	34,335	34,336	122	1 D	49.9%	49.9%	50.0%	50.0%
67,023	WALKER	23,177	17,671	5,468	38	12,203 R	76.2%	23.6%	76.4%	23.6%
17,581	WASHINGTON	6,908	4,729	2,172	7	2,557 R	68.5%	31.4%	68.5%	31.5%
11,670	WILCOX	4,719	1,577	3,138	4	1,561 D	33.4%	66.5%	33.4%	66.6%
24,484	WINSTON	7,707	6,580	1,102	25	5,478 R	85.4%	14.3%	85.7%	14.3%
4,779,736	*TOTAL*	*1,719,589*	*1,022,457*	*694,495*	*2,637*	*327,962 R*	*59.5%*	*40.4%*	*59.6%*	*40.4%*

ALABAMA

SENATOR SPECIAL 2017

2010 Census Population	County	Total Vote	Republican (Moore)	Democratic (Jones)	Other	Rep.-Dem. Plurality	Percentage: Total Vote		Percentage: Major Vote	
							Rep.	Dem.	Rep.	Dem.
54,571	AUTAUGA	14,630	8,762	5,615	253	3,147 R	59.9%	38.4%	60.9%	39.1%
182,265	BALDWIN	62,530	38,566	22,261	1,703	16,305 R	61.7%	35.6%	63.4%	36.6%
27,457	BARBOUR	6,459	2,702	3,716	41	1,014 D	41.8%	57.5%	42.1%	57.9%
22,915	BIBB	5,232	3,599	1,567	66	2,032 R	68.8%	30.0%	69.7%	30.3%
57,322	BLOUNT	14,219	11,631	2,408	180	9,223 R	81.8%	16.9%	82.8%	17.2%
10,914	BULLOCK	3,378	656	2,715	7	2,059 D	19.4%	80.4%	19.5%	80.5%
20,947	BUTLER	5,714	2,758	2,915	41	157 D	48.3%	51.0%	48.6%	51.4%
118,572	CALHOUN	27,998	15,238	12,331	429	2,907 R	54.4%	44.0%	55.3%	44.7%
34,215	CHAMBERS	7,636	3,312	4,257	67	945 D	43.4%	55.7%	43.8%	56.2%
25,989	CHEROKEE	5,644	4,006	1,529	109	2,477 R	71.0%	27.1%	72.4%	27.6%
43,643	CHILTON	10,001	7,563	2,306	132	5,257 R	75.6%	23.1%	76.6%	23.4%
13,859	CHOCTAW	4,243	1,949	2,277	17	328 D	45.9%	53.7%	46.1%	53.9%
25,833	CLARKE	8,401	3,995	4,363	43	368 D	47.6%	51.9%	47.8%	52.2%
13,932	CLAY	3,598	2,589	990	19	1,599 R	72.0%	27.5%	72.3%	27.7%
14,972	CLEBURNE	3,098	2,468	600	30	1,868 R	79.7%	19.4%	80.4%	19.6%
49,948	COFFEE	11,995	8,063	3,730	202	4,333 R	67.2%	31.1%	68.4%	31.6%
54,428	COLBERT	14,823	7,771	6,881	171	890 R	52.4%	46.4%	53.0%	47.0%
13,228	CONECUH	4,092	1,815	2,259	18	444 D	44.4%	55.2%	44.6%	55.4%
11,539	COOSA	3,312	1,867	1,415	30	452 R	56.4%	42.7%	56.9%	43.1%
37,765	COVINGTON	9,030	6,835	2,107	88	4,728 R	75.7%	23.3%	76.4%	23.6%
13,906	CRENSHAW	3,723	2,347	1,320	56	1,027 R	63.0%	35.5%	64.0%	36.0%
80,406	CULLMAN	21,094	16,609	4,161	324	12,448 R	78.7%	19.7%	80.0%	20.0%
50,251	DALE	10,971	6,991	3,844	136	3,147 R	63.7%	35.0%	64.5%	35.5%
43,820	DALLAS	14,050	3,487	10,503	60	7,016 D	24.8%	74.8%	24.9%	75.1%
71,109	DEKALB	13,890	10,097	3,559	234	6,538 R	72.7%	25.6%	73.9%	26.1%
79,303	ELMORE	22,464	14,415	7,711	338	6,704 R	64.2%	34.3%	65.1%	34.9%
38,319	ESCAMBIA	8,716	4,987	3,642	87	1,345 R	57.2%	41.8%	57.8%	42.2%
104,430	ETOWAH	26,918	15,730	10,568	620	5,162 R	58.4%	39.3%	59.8%	40.2%
17,241	FAYETTE	4,684	3,491	1,143	50	2,348 R	74.5%	24.4%	75.3%	24.7%
31,704	FRANKLIN	6,035	4,216	1,771	48	2,445 R	69.9%	29.3%	70.4%	29.6%
26,790	GENEVA	6,816	5,433	1,290	93	4,143 R	79.7%	18.9%	80.8%	19.2%
9,045	GREENE	3,816	462	3,345	9	2,883 D	12.1%	87.7%	12.1%	87.9%
15,760	HALE	5,625	1,691	3,902	32	2,211 D	30.1%	69.4%	30.2%	69.8%
17,302	HENRY	4,952	3,015	1,899	38	1,116 R	60.9%	38.3%	61.4%	38.6%
101,547	HOUSTON	24,329	14,846	9,198	285	5,648 R	61.0%	37.8%	61.7%	38.3%
53,227	JACKSON	10,801	7,317	3,330	154	3,987 R	67.7%	30.8%	68.7%	31.3%
658,466	JEFFERSON	219,825	66,350	149,759	3,716	83,409 D	30.2%	68.1%	30.7%	69.3%
14,564	LAMAR	3,655	2,847	779	29	2,068 R	77.9%	21.3%	78.5%	21.5%
92,709	LAUDERDALE	23,176	12,818	9,970	388	2,848 R	55.3%	43.0%	56.2%	43.8%
34,339	LAWRENCE	8,415	5,321	3,033	61	2,288 R	63.2%	36.0%	63.7%	36.3%

ALABAMA

SENATOR SPECIAL 2017

2010 Census Population	County	Total Vote	Republican (Moore)	Democratic (Jones)	Other	Rep.-Dem. Plurality	Total Vote Rep.	Total Vote Dem.	Major Vote Rep.	Major Vote Dem.
140,247	LEE	34,619	14,059	19,886	674	5,827 D	40.6%	57.4%	41.4%	58.6%
82,782	LIMESTONE	24,514	14,339	9,660	515	4,679 R	58.5%	39.4%	59.7%	40.3%
11,299	LOWNDES	4,784	988	3,783	13	2,795 D	20.7%	79.1%	20.7%	79.3%
21,452	MACON	6,562	759	5,783	20	5,024 D	11.6%	88.1%	11.6%	88.4%
334,811	MADISON	115,825	46,381	65,997	3,447	19,616 D	40.0%	57.0%	41.3%	58.7%
21,027	MARENGO	7,365	2,805	4,498	62	1,693 D	38.1%	61.1%	38.4%	61.6%
30,776	MARION	6,648	5,269	1,311	68	3,958 R	79.3%	19.7%	80.1%	19.9%
93,019	MARSHALL	19,437	13,842	5,145	450	8,697 R	71.2%	26.5%	72.9%	27.1%
412,992	MOBILE	111,090	46,828	62,716	1,546	15,888 D	42.2%	56.5%	42.7%	57.3%
23,068	MONROE	6,586	3,280	3,266	40	14 R	49.8%	49.6%	50.1%	49.9%
229,363	MONTGOMERY	66,858	17,739	48,374	745	30,635 D	26.5%	72.4%	26.8%	73.2%
119,490	MORGAN	30,821	19,215	10,935	671	8,280 R	62.3%	35.5%	63.7%	36.3%
10,591	PERRY	3,972	821	3,140	11	2,319 D	20.7%	79.1%	20.7%	79.3%
19,746	PICKENS	6,075	2,965	3,064	46	99 D	48.8%	50.4%	49.2%	50.8%
32,899	PIKE	8,277	4,165	4,015	97	150 R	50.3%	48.5%	50.9%	49.1%
22,913	RANDOLPH	4,949	3,231	1,695	23	1,536 R	65.3%	34.2%	65.6%	34.4%
52,947	RUSSELL	10,438	3,622	6,761	55	3,139 D	34.7%	64.8%	34.9%	65.1%
195,085	SHELBY	65,484	36,455	27,311	1,718	9,144 R	55.7%	41.7%	57.2%	42.8%
83,593	ST. CLAIR	22,560	15,889	6,212	459	9,677 R	70.4%	27.5%	71.9%	28.1%
13,763	SUMTER	4,365	814	3,533	18	2,719 D	18.6%	80.9%	18.7%	81.3%
82,291	TALLADEGA	19,901	9,701	9,977	223	276 D	48.7%	50.1%	49.3%	50.7%
41,616	TALLAPOOSA	11,934	7,179	4,605	150	2,574 R	60.2%	38.6%	60.9%	39.1%
194,656	TUSCALOOSA	53,943	22,067	30,869	1,007	8,802 D	40.9%	57.2%	41.7%	58.3%
67,023	WALKER	16,527	11,938	4,330	259	7,608 R	72.2%	26.2%	73.4%	26.6%
17,581	WASHINGTON	5,178	3,325	1,805	48	1,520 R	64.2%	34.9%	64.8%	35.2%
11,670	WILCOX	4,361	1,000	3,345	16	2,345 D	22.9%	76.7%	23.0%	77.0%
24,484	WINSTON	5,659	4,681	911	67	3,770 R	82.7%	16.1%	83.7%	16.3%
4,779,736	*TOTAL*	*1,348,720*	*651,972*	*673,896*	*22,852*	*21,924 D*	*48.3%*	*50.0%*	*49.2%*	*50.8%*

ALABAMA

HOUSE OF REPRESENTATIVES

CD	Year	Total Vote	Republican Vote	Republican Candidate	Democratic Vote	Democratic Candidate	Other Vote	Rep.-Dem. Plurality	Total Vote Rep.	Total Vote Dem.	Major Vote Rep.	Major Vote Dem.
1	2018	242,617	153,228	BYRNE, BRADLEY*	89,226	KENNEDY, ROBERT JR.	163	64,002 R	63.2%	36.8%	63.2%	36.8%
1	2016	215,893	208,083	BYRNE, BRADLEY*			7,810	208,083 R	96.4%		100.0%	
1	2014	152,234	103,758	BYRNE, BRADLEY*	48,278	LEFLORE, BURTON R.	198	55,480 R	68.2%	31.7%	68.2%	31.8%
1	2012	200,676	196,374	BONNER, JOSIAH ROBBINS "JO" JR.*			4,302	196,374 R	97.9%		100.0%	
2	2018	226,230	138,879	ROBY, MARTHA*	86,931	ISNER, TABITHA	420	51,948 R	61.4%	38.4%	61.5%	38.5%
2	2016	276,584	134,886	ROBY, MARTHA*	112,089	MATHIS, NATHAN	29,609	22,797 R	48.8%	40.5%	54.6%	45.4%
2	2014	167,952	113,103	ROBY, MARTHA*	54,692	WRIGHT, ERICK	157	58,411 R	67.3%	32.6%	67.4%	32.6%
2	2012	283,953	180,591	ROBY, MARTHA*	103,092	FORD, THERESE	270	77,499 R	63.6%	36.3%	63.7%	36.3%
3	2018	231,915	147,770	ROGERS, MIKE D.*	83,996	HAGAN, MALLORY	149	63,774 R	63.7%	36.2%	63.8%	36.2%
3	2016	287,104	192,164	ROGERS, MIKE D.*	94,549	SMITH, JESSE TREMAIN	391	97,615 R	66.9%	32.9%	67.0%	33.0%
3	2014	156,620	103,558	ROGERS, MIKE D.*	52,816	SMITH, JESSE TREMAIN	246	50,742 R	66.1%	33.7%	66.2%	33.8%
3	2012	273,930	175,306	ROGERS, MIKE D.*	98,141	HARRIS, JOHN ANDREW	483	77,165 R	64.0%	35.8%	64.1%	35.9%
4	2018	230,969	184,255	ADERHOLT, ROBERT*	46,492	AUMAN, LEE	222	137,763 R	79.8%	20.1%	79.9%	20.1%
4	2016	239,444	235,925	ADERHOLT, ROBERT*			3,519	235,925 R	98.5%		100.0%	
4	2014	134,752	132,831	ADERHOLT, ROBERT*			1,921	132,831 R	98.6%		100.0%	
4	2012	269,118	199,071	ADERHOLT, ROBERT*	69,706	BOMAN, DANIEL H.	341	129,365 R	74.0%	25.9%	74.1%	25.9%

ALABAMA

HOUSE OF REPRESENTATIVES

			Republican		Democratic				Percentage			
									Total Vote		Major Vote	
CD	Year	Total Vote	Vote	Candidate	Vote	Candidate	Other Vote	Rep.-Dem. Plurality	Rep.	Dem.	Rep.	Dem.
5	2018	260,673	159,063	BROOKS, MO*	101,388	JOFFRION, PETER	222	57,675 R	61.0%	38.9%	61.1%	38.9%
5	2016	308,326	205,647	BROOKS, MO*	102,234	BOYD, WILL	445	103,413 R	66.7%	33.2%	66.8%	33.2%
5	2014	154,974	115,338	BROOKS, MO*			39,636	115,338 R	74.4%		100.0%	
5	2012	291,293	189,185	BROOKS, MO*	101,772	HOLLEY, CHARLIE L.	336	87,413 R	64.9%	34.9%	65.0%	35.0%
6	2018	278,328	192,542	PALMER, GARY*	85,644	KLINE, DANNER	142	106,898 R	69.2%	30.8%	69.2%	30.8%
6	2016	329,306	245,313	PALMER, GARY*	83,709	PUTMAN, DAVID	284	161,604 R	74.5%	25.4%	74.6%	25.4%
6	2014	178,449	135,945	PALMER, GARY	42,291	LESTER, MARK	213	93,654 R	76.2%	23.7%	76.3%	23.7%
6	2012	308,102	219,262	BACHUS, SPENCER*	88,267	BAILEY, PENNY "COLONEL"	573	130,995 R	71.2%	28.6%	71.3%	28.7%
7	2018	189,163			185,010	SEWELL, TERRI A.*	4,153	185,010 D		97.8%		100.0%
7	2016	233,028			229,330	SEWELL, TERRI A.*	3,698	229,330 D		98.4%		100.0%
7	2014	135,899			133,687	SEWELL, TERRI A.*	2,212	133,687 D		98.4%		100.0%
7	2012	306,558	73,835	CHAMBERLAIN, DON	232,520	SEWELL, TERRI A.*	203	158,685 D	24.1%	75.8%	24.1%	75.9%
TOTAL	*2018*	*1,659,895*	*975,737*		*678,687*		*5,471*	*297,050 R*	*58.8%*	*40.9%*	*59.0%*	*41.0%*
TOTAL	*2016*	*1,889,685*	*1,222,018*		*621,911*		*45,756*	*600,107 R*	*64.7%*	*32.9%*	*66.3%*	*33.7%*
TOTAL	*2014*	*1,080,880*	*704,533*		*331,764*		*44,583*	*372,769 R*	*65.2%*	*30.7%*	*68.0%*	*32.0%*
TOTAL	*2012*	*1,933,630*	*1,233,624*		*693,498*		*6,508*	*540,126 R*	*63.8%*	*35.9%*	*64.0%*	*36.0%*

Note: An asterisk (*) denotes incumbent.

ALABAMA

GENERAL AND PRIMARY ELECTIONS

2018 GENERAL ELECTIONS: OTHER VOTES

Governor Other vote was 2,637 Write-in (Write-in)

Senate (2017) Other vote was 22,852 Write-in (Write-in)

House Other vote was:

CD 1 163 Write-in (Write-in)
CD 2 420 Write-in (Write-in)
CD 3 149 Write-in (Write-in)
CD 4 222 Write-in (Write-in)
CD 5 222 Write-in (Write-in)
CD 6 142 Write-in (Write-in)
CD 7 4,153 Write-in (Write-in)

2018 PRIMARY ELECTIONS: SUPPLEMENTARY INFORMATION

Primary June 5, 2018 **Registration** (as of June 5, 2018 – includes 315,403 inactive registrants) 3,377,902 No Party Registration

Primary Runoff July 17, 2018

Primary Type Open—Any registered voter could vote in either the Democratic or the Republican primary. Democratic primary voters could participate in a Republican runoff. However, Republican primary voters could not cast a ballot in a Democratic runoff.

ALABAMA

GENERAL AND PRIMARY ELECTIONS

	REPUBLICAN PRIMARIES			DEMOCRATIC PRIMARIES		
Senator (2017 Special)	Moore, Roy	164,524	38.9%	Jones, Doug	109,105	66.1%
	Strange, Luther*	138,971	32.8%	Kennedy, Robert Jr.	29,215	17.7%
	Brooks, Mo	83,287	19.7%	Hansen, Michael	11,105	6.7%
	Pittman, Trip	29,124	6.9%	Boyd, Will	8,010	4.9%
	Brinson, Randy	2,621	0.6%	Fisher, Jason	3,478	2.1%
	Peeples, Bryan	1,579	0.4%	McGee, Brian	1,450	0.9%
	Maxwell, Mary	1,543	0.4%	Nana, Charles	1,404	0.9%
	Beretta, James	1,078	0.3%	Caldwell, Vann	1,239	0.8%
	Gentile, Dom	303	0.1%			
	Breault, Joseph	252	0.1%			
	TOTAL	*423,282*		*TOTAL*	*165,006*	
	PRIMARY RUNOFF					
	Moore, Roy	262,641	54.6%			
	Strange, Luther*	218,505	45.4%			
	TOTAL	*481,146*				
Governor	Ivey, Kay*	331,739	56.1%	Maddox, Walter	154,850	54.6%
	Battle, Tommy	147,207	24.9%	Cobb, Sue Bell	82,236	29.0%
	Dawson, Scott	79,546	13.5%	Fields, James	22,683	8.0%
	Hightower, Bill	29,367	5.0%	White, Anthony	9,719	3.4%
	McAllister, Michael	3,340	0.6%	Smith, Doug "New Blue"	9,274	3.3%
				Countryman, Chris	4,943	1.7%
	TOTAL	*591,199*		*TOTAL*	*283,705*	
Congressional District 1	Byrne, Bradley*	Unopposed		Kennedy, Robert Jr.	27,651	80.7%
				McConnell, Lizzetta Hill	6,592	19.3%
				TOTAL	*34,243*	
Congressional District 2	Roby, Martha*	36,708	39.0%	Isner, Tabitha	20,351	60.4%
	Bright, Bobby	26,481	28.1%	Williams, Audri	13,315	39.6%
	Moore, Barry	18,177	19.3%			
	Hobson, Rich	7,052	7.5%			
	Amason, Thomas	5,763	6.1%			
	TOTAL	*94,181*		*TOTAL*	*33,666*	
	PRIMARY RUNOFF					
	Roby, Martha*	48,331	68.0%			
	Bright, Bobby	22,795	32.0%			
	TOTAL	*71,126*				
Congressional District 3	Rogers, Mike D.*	Unopposed		Hagan, Mallory	21,410	65.7%
				Winfrey, Adia McClellan	11,157	34.3%
				TOTAL	*32,567*	
Congressional District 4	Aderholt, Robert*	93,959	81.5%	Auman, Lee	8,609	54.1%
	Blackmon, Anthony	21,366	18.5%	Neighbors, Rick	7,297	45.9%
	TOTAL	*115,325*		*TOTAL*	*15,906*	
Congressional District 5	Brooks, Mo*	54,928	61.3%	Joffrion, Peter	Unopposed	
	Hinchman, Clayton Robert	34,739	38.7%			
	TOTAL	*89,667*				
Congressional District 6	Palmer, Gary*	Unopposed		Kline, Danner	Unopposed	
Congressional District 7				Sewell, Terri A.*	Unopposed	

Note: An asterisk (*) denotes incumbent.

ALASKA

One member At Large

Alaska reports election results by legislative district. The districts indicated were first effective for the 2014 elections.

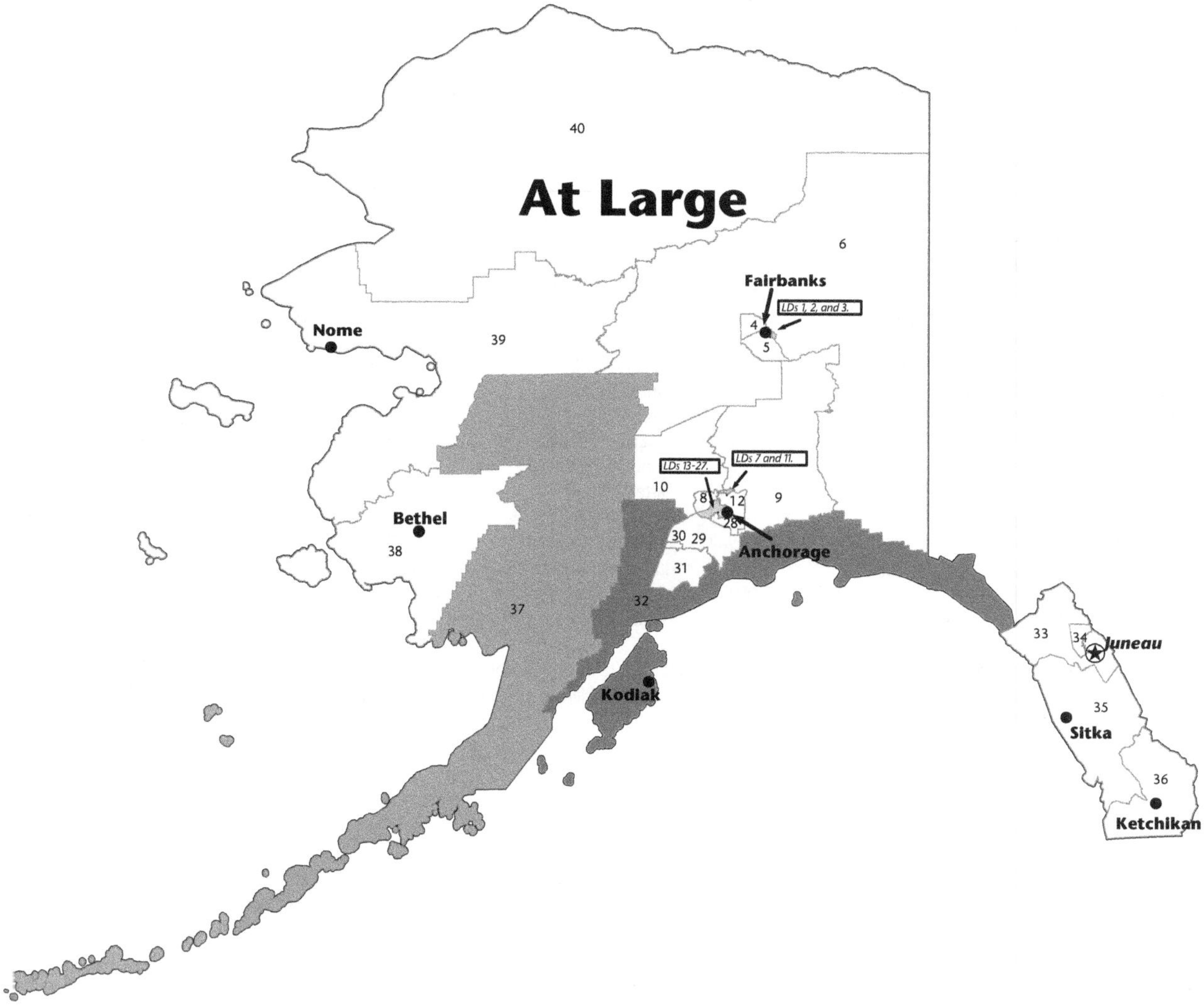

Alaska includes more islands to the west of those that are illustrated on this map.

ALASKA

GOVERNOR

Mike Dunleavy (R). Elected 2018 to a four-year term.

SENATORS (2 Republicans)

Lisa Murkowski (R). Re-elected 2016 to a six-year term. Previously elected 2004, and elected 2010 as a write-in candidate. Had been appointed December 20, 2002, to fill the vacancy created by the resignation of her father, Frank H. Murkowski (R), to become governor of Alaska.

Daniel Sullivan (R). Elected 2014 to a six-year term.

REPRESENTATIVE (1 Republican)

At Large. Don Young (R)

POSTWAR VOTE FOR PRESIDENT

		Republican		Democratic				Percentage			
								Total Vote		Major Vote	
Year	Total Vote	Vote	Candidate	Vote	Candidate	Other Vote	Rep.-Dem. Plurality	Rep.	Dem.	Rep.	Dem.
2016**	318,608	163,387	Trump, Donald J.	116,454	Clinton, Hillary Rodham	38,767	46,933 R	51.3%	36.6%	58.4%	41.6%
2012	300,495	164,676	Romney, W. Mitt	122,640	Obama, Barack H.*	13,179	42,036 R	54.8%	40.8%	57.3%	42.7%
2008	326,197	193,841	McCain, John S. III	123,594	Obama, Barack H.	8,762	70,247 R	59.4%	37.9%	61.1%	38.9%
2004	312,598	190,889	Bush, George W.*	111,025	Kerry, John F.	10,684	79,864 R	61.1%	35.5%	63.2%	36.8%
2000**	285,560	167,398	Bush, George W.	79,004	Gore, Albert Jr.	39,158	88,394 R	58.6%	27.7%	67.9%	32.1%
1996**	241,620	122,746	Dole, Robert "Bob"	80,380	Clinton, Bill*	38,494	42,366 R	50.8%	33.3%	60.4%	39.6%
1992**	258,506	102,000	Bush, George H.*	78,294	Clinton, Bill	78,212	23,706 R	39.5%	30.3%	56.6%	43.4%
1988	200,116	119,251	Bush, George H.	72,584	Dukakis, Michael S.	8,281	46,667 R	59.6%	36.3%	62.2%	37.8%
1984	207,605	138,377	Reagan, Ronald*	62,007	Mondale, Walter F.	7,221	76,370 R	66.7%	29.9%	69.1%	30.9%
1980**	158,445	86,112	Reagan, Ronald	41,842	Carter, Jimmy*	30,491	44,270 R	54.3%	26.4%	67.3%	32.7%
1976	123,574	71,555	Ford, Gerald R.*	44,058	Carter, Jimmy	7,961	27,497 R	57.9%	35.7%	61.9%	38.1%
1972	95,219	55,349	Nixon, Richard M.*	32,967	McGovern, George S.	6,903	22,382 R	58.1%	34.6%	62.7%	37.3%
1968**	83,035	37,600	Nixon, Richard M.	35,411	Humphrey, Hubert Horatio Jr.	10,024	2,189 R	45.3%	42.6%	51.5%	48.5%
1964	67,259	22,930	Goldwater, Barry M. Sr.	44,329	Johnson, Lyndon B.*		21,399 D	34.1%	65.9%	34.1%	65.9%
1960	60,762	30,953	Nixon, Richard M.	29,809	Kennedy, John F.		1,144 R	50.9%	49.1%	50.9%	49.1%

Note: An asterisk (*) denotes incumbent. **In past elections, the other vote included: 2016 - 18,725 Libertarian (Gary Johnson); 2000 - 28,747 Green (Ralph Nader); 1996 - 26,333 Reform (Ross Perot); 1992 - 73,481 Independent (Perot); 1980 - 18,479 Libertarian (Ed Clark) and 11,155 Independent (John Anderson); 1968 - 10,024 American Independent (George Wallace). Alaska was formally admitted as a state in January 1959.

ALASKA

POSTWAR VOTE FOR GOVERNOR

		Republican		Democratic				Percentage			
								Total Vote		Major Vote	
Year	Total Vote	Vote	Candidate	Vote	Candidate	Other Vote	Rep.-Dem. Plurality	Rep.	Dem.	Rep.	Dem.
2018	283,134	145,631	Dunleavy, Mike J.	125,739	Begich, Mark	11,764	19,892 R	51.4%	44.4%	53.7%	46.3%
2014**	279,958	128,435	Parnell, Sean R.*			151,523	128,435 R#	45.9%		100.0%	
2010	256,192	151,318	Parnell, Sean R.*	96,519	Berkowitz, Ethan A.	8,355	54,799 R	59.1%	37.7%	61.1%	38.9%
2006	237,322	114,697	Palin, Sarah H.	97,238	Knowles, Tony	25,387	17,459 R	48.3%	41.0%	54.1%	45.9%
2002	231,484	129,279	Murkowski, Frank H.	94,216	Ulmer, Fran	7,989	35,063 R	55.8%	40.7%	57.8%	42.2%
1998**	220,177	39,331	Lindauer, John	112,879	Knowles, Tony*	67,967	73,548 D	17.9%	51.3%	25.8%	74.2%
1994**	213,435	87,157	Campbell, James O.	87,693	Knowles, Tony*	38,585	536 D	40.8%	41.1%	49.8%	50.2%
1990**	194,750	50,991	Sturgulewski, Arliss	60,201	Knowles, Tony	83,558	9,210 D#	26.2%	30.9%	45.9%	54.1%
1986	179,555	76,515	Sturgulewski, Arliss	84,943	Cowper, Steve	18,097	8,428 D	42.6%	47.3%	47.4%	52.6%
1982**	194,885	72,291	Fink, Tom	89,918	Sheffield, Bill	32,676	17,627 D	37.1%	46.1%	44.6%	55.4%
1978**	126,910	49,580	Hammond, Jay S.*	25,656	Croft, Chancy	51,674	23,924 R	39.1%	20.2%	65.9%	34.1%
1974	96,163	45,840	Hammond, Jay S.	45,553	Egan, William A.*	4,770	287 R	47.7%	47.4%	50.2%	49.8%
1970	80,779	37,264	Miller, Keith	42,309	Egan, William A.	1,206	5,045 D	46.1%	52.4%	46.8%	53.2%
1966	66,294	33,145	Hickel, Walter J.	32,065	Egan, William A.*	1,084	1,080 R	50.0%	48.4%	50.8%	49.2%
1962	56,681	27,054	Stepovich, Mike	29,627	Egan, William A.*		2,573 D	47.7%	52.3%	47.7%	52.3%
1958	48,968	19,299	Butrovich, John Jr.	29,189	Egan, William A.	480	9,890 D	39.4%	59.6%	39.8%	60.2%

Note: An asterisk (*) denotes incumbent. A pound sign (#) in the plurality column indicates that the winners in 1990 and 2014 were independents. **In past elections, the other vote included: 2014 - 134,658 Independent (Bill Walker); 1998 - 40,209 write-in (Robin Taylor), who finished second; 1994 - 27,838 Alaskan Independence (John B. "Jack" Coghill); 1990 - 75,721 Alaskan Independence (Walter J. Hickel); 1982 - 29,067 Libertarian (Richard L. Randolph); 1978 - 33,555 write-in (Hickel) and 15,656 Alaskans for Kelly (Tom Kelly). Walker won the 2014 election with 48.1 percent of the total vote and a plurality over the runner-up of 6,223 votes. Hickel won the 1990 election with 38.9 percent of the total vote and a plurality of 15,520 votes over the runner-up.

POSTWAR VOTE FOR SENATOR

		Republican		Democratic				Percentage			
								Total Vote		Major Vote	
Year	Total Vote	Vote	Candidate	Vote	Candidate	Other Vote	Rep.-Dem. Plurality	Rep.	Dem.	Rep.	Dem.
2016**	311,441	138,149	Murkowski, Lisa A.*	36,200	Metcalfe, Ray	137,092	101,949 R	44.4%	11.6%	79.2%	20.8%
2014	282,400	135,445	Sullivan, Dan S.	129,431	Begich, Mark*	17,524	6,014 R	48.0%	45.8%	51.1%	48.9%
2010**	255,474	90,839	Miller, Joe	60,045	McAdams, Scott T.	104,590	30,794 R#	35.6%	23.5%	60.2%	39.8%
2008	317,723	147,814	Stevens, Ted*	151,767	Begich, Mark	18,142	3,953 D	46.5%	47.8%	49.3%	50.7%
2004	308,315	149,773	Murkowski, Lisa A.*	140,424	Knowles, Tony	18,118	9,349 R	48.6%	45.5%	51.6%	48.4%
2002	229,548	179,438	Stevens, Ted*	24,133	Vondersaar, Frank	25,977	155,305 R	78.2%	10.5%	88.1%	11.9%
1998	221,807	165,227	Murkowski, Frank H.*	43,743	Sonneman, Joseph	12,837	121,484 R	74.5%	19.7%	79.1%	20.9%
1996**	231,916	177,893	Stevens, Ted*	23,977	Obermeyer, Theresa N.	30,046	153,916 R	76.7%	10.3%	88.1%	11.9%
1992	239,714	127,163	Murkowski, Frank H.*	92,065	Smith, Tony	20,486	35,098 R	53.0%	38.4%	58.0%	42.0%
1990	189,957	125,806	Stevens, Ted*	61,152	Beasley, Michael	2,999	64,654 R	66.2%	32.2%	67.3%	32.7%
1986	180,801	97,674	Murkowski, Frank H.*	79,727	Olds, Glenn	3,400	17,947 R	54.0%	44.1%	55.1%	44.9%
1984	206,438	146,919	Stevens, Ted*	58,804	Havelock, John E.	715	88,115 R	71.2%	28.5%	71.4%	28.6%
1980	156,762	84,159	Murkowski, Frank H.	72,007	Gruening, Clark S.	596	12,152 R	53.7%	45.9%	53.9%	46.1%
1978	122,741	92,783	Stevens, Ted*	29,574	Hobbs, Donald W.	384	63,209 R	75.6%	24.1%	75.8%	24.2%
1974	93,275	38,914	Lewis, C. R.	54,361	Gravel, Mike*		15,447 D	41.7%	58.3%	41.7%	58.3%
1972	96,007	74,216	Stevens, Ted*	21,791	Guess, Gene		52,425 R	77.3%	22.7%	77.3%	22.7%
1970S**	80,364	47,908	Stevens, Ted*	32,456	Kay, Wendell P.		15,452 R	59.6%	40.4%	59.6%	40.4%
1968	80,931	30,286	Rasmuson, Elmer	36,527	Gravel, Mike	14,118	6,241 D	37.4%	45.1%	45.3%	54.7%
1966	65,250	15,961	McKinley, Lee L.	49,289	Bartlett, E. L.*		33,328 D	24.5%	75.5%	24.5%	75.5%
1962	58,181	24,354	Stevens, Ted	33,827	Gruening, Ernest*		9,473 D	41.9%	58.1%	41.9%	58.1%
1960	59,978	21,937	McKinley, Lee L.	38,041	Bartlett, E. L.*		16,104 D	36.6%	63.4%	36.6%	63.4%
1958**	48,837	7,299	Robertson, R. E.	40,939	Bartlett, E. L.	599	33,640 D	14.9%	83.8%	15.1%	84.9%
1958**	49,525	23,462	Stepovich, Mike	26,063	Gruening, Ernest		2,601 D	47.4%	52.6%	47.4%	52.6%

Note: An asterisk (*) denotes incumbent. A pound sign (#) in the plurality column indicates that the winner in 2010 was Republican Senator Lisa A. Murkowski, who ran as a write-in candidate. **In past elections, the other vote included: 2016 - 90,825 Libertarian (Joe Miller), who finished second, 47,324 votes behind Murkowski, 41,194 Non-Affiliated (Margaret Stock), who finished third; 2010 - 101,091 Republican write-in (Lisa Murkowski), who won re-election with 39.6 percent of the total vote and a plurality of 10,252 votes over the runner-up; 1996 - 29,037 Green (Jed Whittaker), who finished second. The 1970 election was for a short term to fill a vacancy. The two 1958 elections were held to indeterminate terms and the Senate later determined by lot that Senator Gruening would serve four years, Senator Bartlett two. The plurality for 2010 shows the difference between the official Republican and Democratic candidates.

ALASKA

GOVERNOR 2018

2010 Census Population	Election District County	Total Vote	Republican (Dunleavy)	Democratic (Begich)	Other	Rep.-Dem. Plurality	Percentage Total Vote Rep.	Percentage Total Vote Dem.	Percentage Major Vote Rep.	Percentage Major Vote Dem.
17,726	Election District 1	5,611	2,568	2,768	275	200 D	45.8%	49.3%	48.1%	51.9%
17,738	Election District 2	3,775	2,184	1,406	185	778 R	57.9%	37.2%	60.8%	39.2%
17,673	Election District 3	5,999	4,395	1,341	263	3,054 R	73.3%	22.4%	76.6%	23.4%
17,786	Election District 4	8,714	3,659	4,692	363	1,033 D	42.0%	53.8%	43.8%	56.2%
17,837	Election District 5	6,979	3,160	3,532	287	372 D	45.3%	50.6%	47.2%	52.8%
17,807	Election District 6	7,122	4,085	2,687	350	1,398 R	57.4%	37.7%	60.3%	39.7%
17,703	Election District 7	7,334	5,391	1,735	208	3,656 R	73.5%	23.7%	75.7%	24.3%
17,830	Election District 8	7,441	5,743	1,472	226	4,271 R	77.2%	19.8%	79.6%	20.4%
17,739	Election District 9	8,163	5,484	2,346	333	3,138 R	67.2%	28.7%	70.0%	30.0%
17,827	Election District 10	8,318	5,916	2,142	260	3,774 R	71.1%	25.8%	73.4%	26.6%
17,716	Election District 11	8,499	5,733	2,482	284	3,251 R	67.5%	29.2%	69.8%	30.2%
17,671	Election District 12	8,510	6,019	2,270	221	3,749 R	70.7%	26.7%	72.6%	27.4%
17,678	Election District 13	5,006	3,212	1,605	189	1,607 R	64.2%	32.1%	66.7%	33.3%
17,818	Election District 14	8,672	5,229	3,142	301	2,087 R	60.3%	36.2%	62.5%	37.5%
17,672	Election District 15	3,621	1,716	1,729	176	13 D	47.4%	47.7%	49.8%	50.2%
17,806	Election District 16	6,307	2,780	3,298	229	518 D	44.1%	52.3%	45.7%	54.3%
17,797	Election District 17	5,810	2,287	3,309	214	1,022 D	39.4%	57.0%	40.9%	59.1%
17,925	Election District 18	6,462	2,322	3,898	242	1,576 D	35.9%	60.3%	37.3%	62.7%
17,692	Election District 19	4,158	1,435	2,556	167	1,121 D	34.5%	61.5%	36.0%	64.0%
17,718	Election District 20	6,279	1,955	4,051	273	2,096 D	31.1%	64.5%	32.6%	67.4%
17,642	Election District 21	7,812	3,146	4,398	268	1,252 D	40.3%	56.3%	41.7%	58.3%
17,755	Election District 22	7,721	3,998	3,469	254	529 R	51.8%	44.9%	53.5%	46.5%
17,809	Election District 23	5,988	2,927	2,841	220	86 R	48.9%	47.4%	50.7%	49.3%
17,702	Election District 24	8,525	4,478	3,772	275	706 R	52.5%	44.2%	54.3%	45.7%
17,924	Election District 25	7,391	3,522	3,638	231	116 D	47.7%	49.2%	49.2%	50.8%
17,693	Election District 26	8,208	4,453	3,509	246	944 R	54.3%	42.8%	55.9%	44.1%
17,678	Election District 27	7,924	3,779	3,900	245	121 D	47.7%	49.2%	49.2%	50.8%
17,778	Election District 28	10,541	5,290	4,930	321	360 R	50.2%	46.8%	51.8%	48.2%
18,026	Election District 29	8,515	5,684	2,472	359	3,212 R	66.8%	29.0%	69.7%	30.3%
18,021	Election District 30	7,913	5,383	2,169	361	3,214 R	68.0%	27.4%	71.3%	28.7%
17,971	Election District 31	9,794	5,114	4,251	429	863 R	52.2%	43.4%	54.6%	45.4%
18,077	Election District 32	6,360	2,700	3,280	380	580 D	42.5%	51.6%	45.2%	54.8%
17,635	Election District 33	9,444	2,750	6,301	393	3,551 D	29.1%	66.7%	30.4%	69.6%
17,668	Election District 34	8,983	3,977	4,643	363	666 D	44.3%	51.7%	46.1%	53.9%
17,825	Election District 35	8,053	3,355	4,212	486	857 D	41.7%	52.3%	44.3%	55.7%
17,874	Election District 36	7,336	4,050	2,902	384	1,148 R	55.2%	39.6%	58.3%	41.7%
17,448	Election District 37	4,709	1,520	2,893	296	1,373 D	32.3%	61.4%	34.4%	65.6%
17,546	Election District 38	5,304	1,323	3,600	381	2,277 D	24.9%	67.9%	26.9%	73.1%
17,677	Election District 39	5,667	1,459	3,739	469	2,280 D	25.7%	66.0%	28.1%	71.9%
17,323	Election District 40	4,166	1,450	2,359	357	909 D	34.8%	56.6%	38.1%	61.9%
710,231	*TOTAL*	*283,134*	*145,631*	*125,739*	*11,764*	*19,892 R*	*51.4%*	*44.4%*	*53.7%*	*46.3%*

ALASKA

HOUSE OF REPRESENTATIVES

			Republican		Democratic				Percentage			
									Total Vote		Major Vote	
CD	Year	Total Vote	Vote	Candidate	Vote	Candidate	Other Vote	Rep.-Dem. Plurality	Rep.	Dem.	Rep.	Dem.
At Large	2018	282,166	149,779	YOUNG, DON*	131,199	GALVIN, ALYSE S.	1,188	18,580 R	53.1%	46.5%	53.3%	46.7%
At Large	2016	308,198	155,088	YOUNG, DON*	111,019	LINDBECK, STEVE	42,091	44,069 R	50.3%	36.0%	58.3%	41.7%
At Large	2014	279,741	142,572	YOUNG, DON*	114,602	DUNBAR, FORREST	22,567	27,970 R	51.0%	41.0%	55.4%	44.6%
At Large	2012	289,804	185,296	YOUNG, DON*	82,927	CISSNA, SHARON M.	21,581	102,369 R	63.9%	28.6%	69.1%	30.9%
At Large	2010	254,335	175,384	YOUNG, DON*	77,606	CRAWFORD, HARRY T.	1,345	97,778 R	69.0%	30.5%	69.3%	30.7%
At Large	2008	316,978	158,939	YOUNG, DON*	142,560	BERKOWITZ, ETHAN A.	15,479	16,379 R	50.1%	45.0%	52.7%	47.3%
At Large	2006	234,645	132,743	YOUNG, DON*	93,879	BENSON, DIANE E.	8,023	38,864 R	56.6%	40.0%	58.6%	41.4%
At Large	2004	299,996	213,216	YOUNG, DON*	67,074	HIGGINS, THOMAS M.	19,706	146,142 R	71.1%	22.4%	76.1%	23.9%
At Large	2002	227,725	169,685	YOUNG, DON*	39,357	GREENE, CLIFFORD	18,683	130,328 R	74.5%	17.3%	81.2%	18.8%
At Large	2000	274,393	190,862	YOUNG, DON*	45,372	GREENE, CLIFFORD	38,159	145,490 R	69.6%	16.5%	80.8%	19.2%
At Large	1998	223,300	139,676	YOUNG, DON*	77,232	DUNCAN, JIM	6,392	62,444 R	62.6%	34.6%	64.4%	35.6%
At Large	1996	233,700	138,834	YOUNG, DON*	85,114	LINCOLN, GEORGIANNA	9,752	53,720 R	59.4%	36.4%	62.0%	38.0%
At Large	1994	208,240	118,537	YOUNG, DON*	68,172	SMITH, TONY	21,531	50,365 R	56.9%	32.7%	63.5%	36.5%
At Large	1992	239,116	111,849	YOUNG, DON*	102,378	DEVENS, JOHN S.	24,889	9,471 R	46.8%	42.8%	52.2%	47.8%
At Large	1990	191,647	99,003	YOUNG, DON*	91,677	DEVENS, JOHN S.	967	7,326 R	51.7%	47.8%	51.9%	48.1%
At Large	1988	192,955	120,595	YOUNG, DON*	71,881	GRUENSTEIN, PETER	479	48,714 R	62.5%	37.3%	62.7%	37.3%
At Large	1986	180,277	101,799	YOUNG, DON*	74,053	BEGICH, PEGGE	4,425	27,746 R	56.5%	41.1%	57.9%	42.1%
At Large	1984	206,437	113,582	YOUNG, DON*	86,052	BEGICH, PEGGE	6,803	27,530 R	55.0%	41.7%	56.9%	43.1%
At Large	1982	181,084	128,274	YOUNG, DON*	52,011	CARLSON, DAVE	799	76,263 R	70.8%	28.7%	71.2%	28.8%
At Large	1980	154,618	114,089	YOUNG, DON*	39,922	PARNELL, KEVIN	607	74,167 R	73.8%	25.8%	74.1%	25.9%
At Large	1978	124,187	68,811	YOUNG, DON*	55,176	RODEY, PATRICK	200	13,635 R	55.4%	44.4%	55.5%	44.5%
At Large	1976	118,208	83,722	YOUNG, DON*	34,194	HOPSON, EBEN	292	49,528 R	70.8%	28.9%	71.0%	29.0%
At Large	1974	95,921	51,641	YOUNG, DON*	44,280	HENSLEY, WILLIAM L.		7,361 R	53.8%	46.2%	53.8%	46.2%
At Large	1972	95,401	41,750	YOUNG, DON	53,651	BEGICH, NICHOLAS J.*		11,901 D	43.8%	56.2%	43.8%	56.2%
At Large	1970	80,084	35,947	MURKOWSKI, FRANK H.	44,137	BEGICH, NICHOLAS J.		8,190 D	44.9%	55.1%	44.9%	55.1%
At Large	1968	80,362	43,577	POLLOCK, HOWARD W.*	36,785	BEGICH, NICHOLAS J.		6,792 R	54.2%	45.8%	54.2%	45.8%
At Large	1966	65,907	34,040	POLLOCK, HOWARD W.	31,867	RIVERS, RALPH J.*		2,173 R	51.6%	48.4%	51.6%	48.4%
At Large	1964	67,156	32,566	THOMAS, LOWELL	34,590	RIVERS, RALPH J.*		2,024 D	48.5%	51.5%	48.5%	51.5%
At Large	1962	58,591	26,638	THOMAS, LOWELL	31,953	RIVERS, RALPH J.*		5,315 D	45.5%	54.5%	45.5%	54.5%
At Large	1960	59,063	25,517	RETTIG, R. L.	33,546	RIVERS, RALPH J.*		8,029 D	43.2%	56.8%	43.2%	56.8%
At Large	1958	48,644	20,699	BENSON, HENRY A.	27,945	RIVERS, RALPH J.		7,246 D	42.6%	57.4%	42.6%	57.4%

Note: An asterisk (*) denotes incumbent.

ALASKA

GENERAL AND PRIMARY ELECTIONS

2018 GENERAL ELECTIONS: OTHER VOTES

Governor Other vote was 5,757 Non-affiliated (Bill Walker), 5,402 Libertarian (William S. "Billy" Toien), 605 Write-in (Write-in)

House Other vote was:

At Large 1,188 Write-in (Write-in)

ALASKA

GENERAL AND PRIMARY ELECTIONS

2018 PRIMARY ELECTIONS: SUPPLEMENTARY INFORMATION

Primary	August 21, 2018	**Registration** (as of August 3, 2018)	567,403	Republican	140,060
				Democratic	74,964
				Alaskan Independence	17,298
				Libertarian	7,497
				Green	1,692
				Veterans	1,146
				Constitution	443
				Nonpartisan	84,482
				Undeclared	239,631
				Other	190

Primary Type Semi-closed—Any registered voter could participate in the Democratic primary for Congress. The Republican primary was restricted to registered Republican, undeclared, and nonpartisan voters. Democratic candidates were listed on the primary ballot together with candidates of the Alaskan Independence and Libertarian parties. The highest vote-getter of each party went on to the general election ballot. Republican candidates were listed on a primary ballot of their own.

	REPUBLICAN PRIMARIES			DEMOCRATIC PRIMARIES		
Governor	Dunleavy, Mike J.	43,802	61.5%	Begich, Mark	33,451	100.0%
	Treadwell, Mead	22,780	32.0%			
	Sheldon, Michael D.	1,640	2.3%			
	Hlatcu, Merica	1,064	1.5%			
	Gordon, Thomas A.	994	1.4%			
	Heikes, Gerald L.	499	0.7%			
	Colbry, Darin A.	416	0.6%			
	TOTAL	*71,195*		*TOTAL*	*33,451*	
Congressional At Large	Young, Don*	49,667	70.8%	Galvin, Alyse S.	21,742	53.6%
	Nelson, Thomas	10,913	15.6%	Shein, Dimitri	9,434	23.3%
	Whittaker, Jed	9,525	13.6%	Hafner, Carol	6,071	15.0%
				Cumings, Christopher	3,304	8.1%
	TOTAL	*70,105*		*TOTAL*	*40,551*	

Note: An asterisk (*) denotes incumbent.

ARIZONA

Congressional districts first established for elections held in 2012

9 members

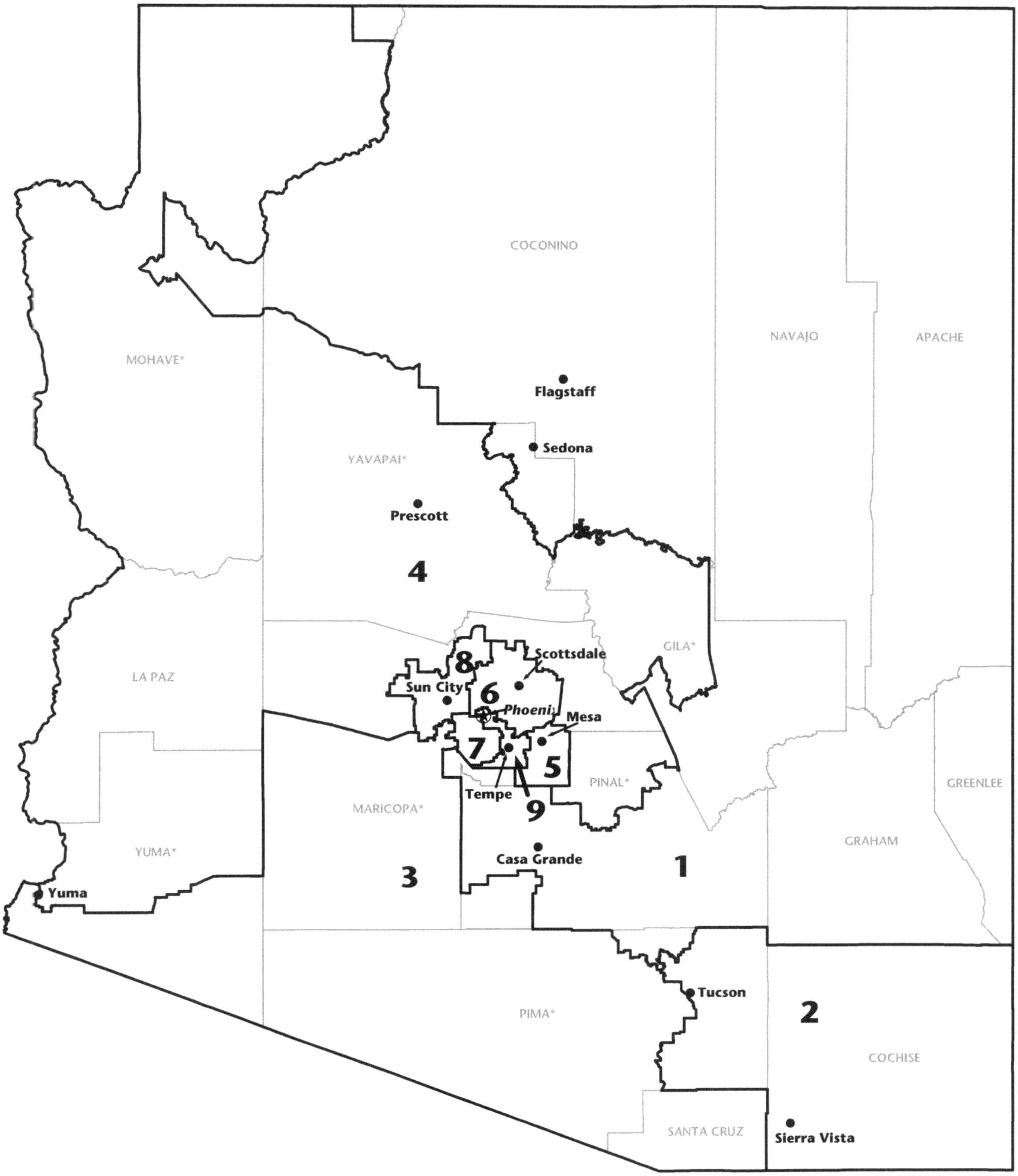

* Asterisk indicates a county whose boundaries include parts of two or more congressional districts.

ARIZONA

Greater Phoenix Area

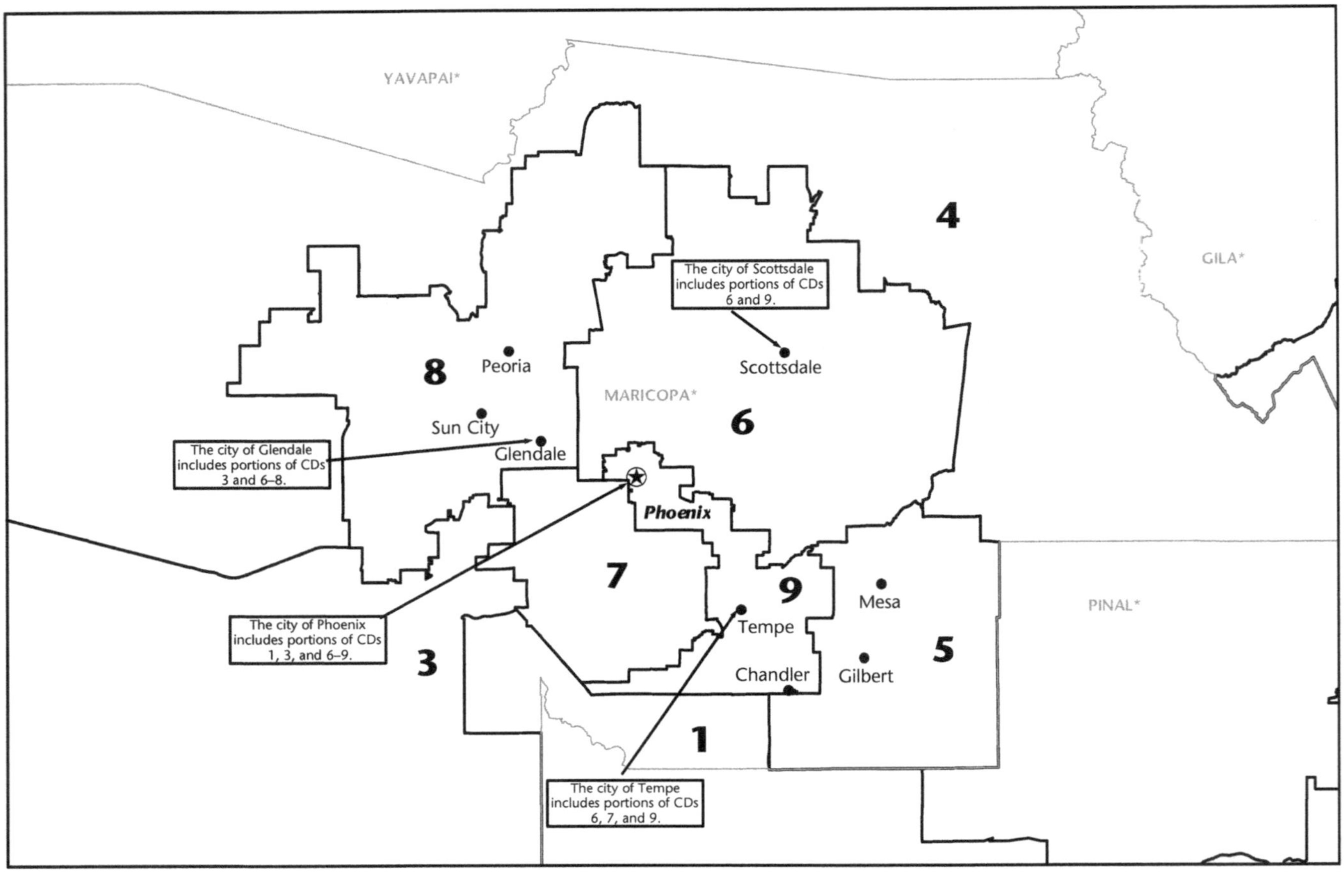

ARIZONA

GOVERNOR

Doug Ducey (R). Re-elected 2018 to a four-year term. Previously elected 2014.

SENATORS (2 Republicans)

Kyrsten Sinema (D). Elected 2018 to a six-year term.

Martha McSally (R). Appointed December 18, 2018, by the governor to complete the term of John Kyl (R). Kyl was appointed to the seat following the death of John McCain (R), and resigned December 12, 2018.

REPRESENTATIVES (4 Republicans, 5 Democrats)

1. Tom O'Halleran (D)
2. Ann Kirkpatrick (D)
3. Raúl M. Grijalva (D)
4. Paul A. Gosar (R)
5. Andy Biggs (R)
6. David Schweikert (R)
7. Ruben Gallego (D)
8. Debbie Lesko (R)
9. Greg Stanton (D)

POSTWAR VOTE FOR PRESIDENT

		Republican		Democratic				Percentage			
								Total Vote		Major Vote	
Year	Total Vote	Vote	Candidate	Vote	Candidate	Other Vote	Rep.-Dem. Plurality	Rep.	Dem.	Rep.	Dem.
2016**	2,573,165	1,252,401	Trump, Donald J.	1,161,167	Clinton, Hillary Rodham	159,597	91,234 R	48.7%	45.1%	51.9%	48.1%
2012	2,299,254	1,233,654	Romney, W. Mitt	1,025,232	Obama, Barack H.*	40,368	208,422 R	53.7%	44.6%	54.6%	45.4%
2008	2,293,475	1,230,111	McCain, John S. III	1,034,707	Obama, Barack H.	28,657	195,404 R	53.6%	45.1%	54.3%	45.7%
2004	2,012,585	1,104,294	Bush, George W.*	893,524	Kerry, John F.	14,767	210,770 R	54.9%	44.4%	55.3%	44.7%
2000**	1,532,016	781,652	Bush, George W.	685,341	Gore, Albert Jr.	65,023	96,311 R	51.0%	44.7%	53.3%	46.7%
1996**	1,404,405	622,073	Dole, Robert "Bob"	653,288	Clinton, Bill*	129,044	31,215 D	44.3%	46.5%	48.8%	51.2%
1992**	1,486,975	572,086	Bush, George H.*	543,050	Clinton, Bill	371,839	29,036 R	38.5%	36.5%	51.3%	48.7%
1988	1,171,873	702,541	Bush, George H.	454,029	Dukakis, Michael S.	15,303	248,512 R	60.0%	38.7%	60.7%	39.3%
1984	1,025,897	681,416	Reagan, Ronald*	333,854	Mondale, Walter F.	10,627	347,562 R	66.4%	32.5%	67.1%	32.9%
1980**	873,945	529,688	Reagan, Ronald	246,843	Carter, Jimmy*	97,414	282,845 R	60.6%	28.2%	68.2%	31.8%
1976	742,719	418,642	Ford, Gerald R.*	295,602	Carter, Jimmy	28,475	123,040 R	56.4%	39.8%	58.6%	41.4%
1972	622,926	402,812	Nixon, Richard M.*	198,540	McGovern, George S.	21,574	204,272 R	64.7%	31.9%	67.0%	33.0%
1968**	486,936	266,721	Nixon, Richard M.	170,514	Humphrey, Hubert Horatio Jr.	49,701	96,207 R	54.8%	35.0%	61.0%	39.0%
1964	480,770	242,535	Goldwater, Barry M. Sr.	237,753	Johnson, Lyndon B.*	482	4,782 R	50.4%	49.5%	50.5%	49.5%
1960	398,491	221,241	Nixon, Richard M.	176,781	Kennedy, John F.	469	44,460 R	55.5%	44.4%	55.6%	44.4%
1956	290,173	176,990	Eisenhower, Dwight D.*	112,880	Stevenson, Adlai E. II	303	64,110 R	61.0%	38.9%	61.1%	38.9%
1952	260,570	152,042	Eisenhower, Dwight D.	108,528	Stevenson, Adlai E. II		43,514 R	58.3%	41.7%	58.3%	41.7%
1948	177,065	77,597	Dewey, Thomas E.	95,251	Truman, Harry S.*	4,217	17,654 D	43.8%	53.8%	44.9%	55.1%

Note: An asterisk (*) denotes incumbent. **In past elections, the other vote included: 2016 - Libertarian 106,327 (Gary Johnson); 2000 - 45,645 Green (Ralph Nader); 1996 - 112,072 Reform (Ross Perot); 1992 - 353,741 Independent (Perot); 1980 - 76,952 Independent (John Anderson); 1968 - 46,573 American Independent (George Wallace).

ARIZONA

POSTWAR VOTE FOR GOVERNOR

Year	Total Vote	Republican Vote	Republican Candidate	Democratic Vote	Democratic Candidate	Other Vote	Rep.-Dem. Plurality	Percentage Total Vote Rep.	Percentage Total Vote Dem.	Percentage Major Vote Rep.	Percentage Major Vote Dem.
2018	2,376,441	1,330,863	Ducey, Doug*	994,341	Garcia, David	51,237	336,522 R	56.0%	41.8%	57.2%	42.8%
2014	1,506,416	805,062	Ducey, Doug	626,921	Duval, Fred	74,433	178,141 R	53.4%	41.6%	56.2%	43.8%
2010	1,728,081	938,934	Brewer, Jan*	733,935	Goddard, Terry	55,212	204,999 R	54.3%	42.5%	56.1%	43.9%
2006	1,533,645	543,528	Munsil, Len	959,830	Napolitano, Janet*	30,287	416,302 D	35.4%	62.6%	36.2%	63.8%
2002	1,226,111	554,465	Salmon, Matt	566,284	Napolitano, Janet	105,362	11,819 D	45.2%	46.2%	49.5%	50.5%
1998	1,017,616	620,188	Hull, Jane Dee*	361,552	Johnson, Paul	35,876	258,636 R	60.9%	35.5%	63.2%	36.8%
1994	1,129,607	593,492	Symington, Fife*	500,702	Basha, Eddie	35,413	92,790 R	52.5%	44.3%	54.2%	45.8%
1991S**	940,737	492,569	Symington, Fife	448,168	Goddard, Terry		44,401 R	52.4%	47.6%	52.4%	47.6%
1986**	866,984	343,913	Mecham, Evan	298,986	Warner, Carolyn	224,085	44,927 R	39.7%	34.5%	53.5%	46.5%
1982	726,364	235,877	Corbet, Leo	453,795	Babbitt, Bruce*	36,692	217,918 D	32.5%	62.5%	34.2%	65.8%
1978	538,556	241,093	Mecham, Evan	282,605	Babbitt, Bruce*	14,858	41,512 D	44.8%	52.5%	46.0%	54.0%
1974	552,202	273,674	Williams, Jack R.*	278,375	Castro, Raul H.	153	4,701 D	49.6%	50.4%	49.6%	50.4%
1970**	411,409	209,522	Williams, Jack R.*	201,887	Castro, Raul H.		7,635 R	50.9%	49.1%	50.9%	49.1%
1968	483,998	279,923	Williams, Jack R.*	204,075	Goddard, Sam		75,848 R	57.8%	42.2%	57.8%	42.2%
1966	378,342	203,438	Williams, Jack R.	174,904	Goddard, Sam*		28,534 R	53.8%	46.2%	53.8%	46.2%
1964	473,502	221,404	Kleindienst, Richard	252,098	Goddard, Sam		30,694 D	46.8%	53.2%	46.8%	53.2%
1962	365,841	200,578	Fannin, Paul*	165,263	Goddard, Sam		35,315 R	54.8%	45.2%	54.8%	45.2%
1960	397,107	235,502	Fannin, Paul*	161,605	Ackerman, Lee		73,897 R	59.3%	40.7%	59.3%	40.7%
1958	290,465	160,136	Fannin, Paul	130,329	Morrison, Robert		29,807 R	55.1%	44.9%	55.1%	44.9%
1956	288,592	116,744	Griffen, Horace B.	171,848	McFarland, Ernest W.*		55,104 D	40.5%	59.5%	40.5%	59.5%
1954	243,970	115,866	Pyle, Howard*	128,104	McFarland, Ernest W.		12,238 D	47.5%	52.5%	47.5%	52.5%
1952	260,285	156,592	Pyle, Howard*	103,693	Haldiman, Joe C.		52,899 R	60.2%	39.8%	60.2%	39.8%
1950	195,227	99,109	Pyle, Howard	96,118	Frohmiller, Ana		2,991 R	50.8%	49.2%	50.8%	49.2%
1948	175,767	70,419	Brockett, Bruce D.	104,008	Garvey, Dan E.	1,340	33,589 D	40.1%	59.2%	40.4%	59.6%
1946	122,462	48,867	Brockett, Bruce D.	73,595	Osborn, Sidney P.*		24,728 D	39.9%	60.1%	39.9%	60.1%

Note: An asterisk (*) denotes incumbent. **In 1990 neither major party candidate won an absolute majority, therefore a runoff election was held February 26, 1991; the vote above is for the February runoff. In the November 1990 election, a total of 1,055,406 votes were cast as follows: 523,984 (49.6%) Republican (Fife Symington); 519,691 (49.2%) Democratic (Terry Goddard); 11,731 (1.1%) Other. In past elections, the other vote included: 1986 - 224,085 Independent (Bill Schulz). The term of office for Arizona's Governor was increased from two to four years effective with the 1970 election.

POSTWAR VOTE FOR SENATOR

Year	Total Vote	Republican Vote	Republican Candidate	Democratic Vote	Democratic Candidate	Other Vote	Rep.-Dem. Plurality	Percentage Total Vote Rep.	Percentage Total Vote Dem.	Percentage Major Vote Rep.	Percentage Major Vote Dem.
2018	2,384,308	1,135,200	McSally, Martha	1,191,100	Sinema, Kyrsten	58,008	55,900 D	47.6%	50.0%	48.8%	51.2%
2016	2,530,730	1,359,267	McCain, John S. III*	1,031,245	Kirkpatrick, Ann	140,218	328,022 R	53.7%	40.7%	56.9%	43.1%
2012	2,243,422	1,104,457	Flake, Jeff	1,036,542	Carmona, Richard	102,423	67,915 R	49.2%	46.2%	51.6%	48.4%
2010	1,708,484	1,005,615	McCain, John S. III*	592,011	Glassman, Rodney	110,858	413,604 R	58.9%	34.7%	62.9%	37.1%
2006	1,526,782	814,398	Kyl, Jon*	664,141	Pederson, Jim	48,243	150,257 R	53.3%	43.5%	55.1%	44.9%
2004	1,961,677	1,505,372	McCain, John S. III*	404,507	Starky, Stuart Marc	51,798	1,100,865 R	76.7%	20.6%	78.8%	21.2%
2000	1,397,076	1,108,196	Kyl, Jon*			288,880	1,108,196 R	79.3%		100.0%	
1998	1,013,280	696,577	McCain, John S. III*	275,224	Ranger, Ed	41,479	421,353 R	68.7%	27.2%	71.7%	28.3%
1994	1,119,060	600,999	Kyl, Jon	442,510	Coppersmith, Sam G.	75,551	158,489 R	53.7%	39.5%	57.6%	42.4%
1992**	1,382,051	771,395	McCain, John S. III*	436,321	Sargent, Claire	174,335	335,074 R	55.8%	31.6%	63.9%	36.1%
1988	1,164,539	478,060	DeGreen, Keith	660,403	DeConcini, Dennis*	26,076	182,343 D	41.1%	56.7%	42.0%	58.0%
1986	862,921	521,850	McCain, John S. III	340,965	Kimball, Richard	106	180,885 R	60.5%	39.5%	60.5%	39.5%
1982	723,885	291,749	Dunn, Pete	411,970	DeConcini, Dennis*	20,166	120,221 D	40.3%	56.9%	41.5%	58.5%
1980	874,178	432,371	Goldwater, Barry M. Sr.*	422,972	Schulz, Bill	18,835	9,399 R	49.5%	48.4%	50.5%	49.5%
1976	741,210	321,236	Steiger, Sam	400,334	DeConcini, Dennis	19,640	79,098 D	43.3%	54.0%	44.5%	55.5%
1974	549,919	320,396	Goldwater, Barry M. Sr.*	229,523	Marshall, Jonathan		90,873 R	58.3%	41.7%	58.3%	41.7%
1970	407,796	228,284	Fannin, Paul*	179,512	Grossman, Sam		48,772 R	56.0%	44.0%	56.0%	44.0%
1968	479,945	274,607	Goldwater, Barry M. Sr.	205,338	Elson, Roy L.		69,269 R	57.2%	42.8%	57.2%	42.8%
1964	468,788	241,084	Fannin, Paul	227,704	Elson, Roy L.		13,380 R	51.4%	48.6%	51.4%	48.6%
1962	362,605	163,388	Mecham, Evan	199,217	Hayden, Carl*		35,829 D	45.1%	54.9%	45.1%	54.9%
1958	293,623	164,593	Goldwater, Barry M. Sr.*	129,030	McFarland, Ernest W.		35,563 R	56.1%	43.9%	56.1%	43.9%
1956	278,263	107,447	Jones, Ross F.	170,816	Hayden, Carl*		63,369 D	38.6%	61.4%	38.6%	61.4%
1952	257,401	132,063	Goldwater, Barry M. Sr.	125,338	McFarland, Ernest W.*		6,725 R	51.3%	48.7%	51.3%	48.7%
1950	185,092	68,846	Brockett, Bruce	116,246	Hayden, Carl*		47,400 D	37.2%	62.8%	37.2%	62.8%
1946	116,239	35,022	Powers, Ward S.	80,415	McFarland, Ernest W.*	802	45,393 D	30.1%	69.2%	30.3%	69.7%

Note: An asterisk (*) denotes incumbent. **In past elections, the other vote included: 1992 - 145,361 Independent (Evan Mecham). The Democratic Party did not run a candidate in the 2000 Senate election.

ARIZONA

GOVERNOR 2018

2010 Census Population	County	Total Vote	Republican (Ducey)	Democratic (Garcia)	Other	Rep.-Dem. Plurality	Percentage Total Vote Rep.	Percentage Total Vote Dem.	Percentage Major Vote Rep.	Percentage Major Vote Dem.
71,518	APACHE	25,049	9,175	14,955	919	5,780 D	36.6%	59.7%	38.0%	62.0%
131,346	COCHISE	45,424	29,638	14,576	1,210	15,062 R	65.2%	32.1%	67.0%	33.0%
134,421	COCONINO	54,946	22,778	30,712	1,456	7,934 D	41.5%	55.9%	42.6%	57.4%
53,597	GILA	20,535	14,444	5,623	468	8,821 R	70.3%	27.4%	72.0%	28.0%
37,220	GRAHAM	10,624	7,776	2,569	279	5,207 R	73.2%	24.2%	75.2%	24.8%
8,437	GREENLEE	2,549	1,637	832	80	805 R	64.2%	32.6%	66.3%	33.7%
20,489	LA PAZ	5,103	3,852	1,122	129	2,730 R	75.5%	22.0%	77.4%	22.6%
3,817,117	MARICOPA	1,432,938	800,210	603,055	29,673	197,155 R	55.8%	42.1%	57.0%	43.0%
200,186	MOHAVE	71,593	56,682	13,580	1,331	43,102 R	79.2%	19.0%	80.7%	19.3%
107,449	NAVAJO	36,585	21,880	13,646	1,059	8,234 R	59.8%	37.3%	61.6%	38.4%
980,263	PIMA	388,554	184,621	195,227	8,706	10,606 D	47.5%	50.2%	48.6%	51.4%
375,770	PINAL	116,853	75,272	38,801	2,780	36,471 R	64.4%	33.2%	66.0%	34.0%
47,420	SANTA CRUZ	13,460	4,792	8,407	261	3,615 D	35.6%	62.5%	36.3%	63.7%
211,033	YAVAPAI	108,344	74,148	32,159	2,037	41,989 R	68.4%	29.7%	69.7%	30.3%
195,751	YUMA	43,884	23,958	19,077	849	4,881 R	54.6%	43.5%	55.7%	44.3%
6,392,017	*TOTAL*	*2,376,441*	*1,330,863*	*994,341*	*51,237*	*336,522 R*	*56.0%*	*41.8%*	*57.2%*	*42.8%*

ARIZONA

SENATOR 2018

2010 Census Population	County	Total Vote	Republican (McSally)	Democratic (Sinema)	Other	Rep.-Dem. Plurality	Percentage Total Vote Rep.	Percentage Total Vote Dem.	Percentage Major Vote Rep.	Percentage Major Vote Dem.
71,518	APACHE	25,087	7,810	16,298	979	8,488 D	31.1%	65.0%	32.4%	67.6%
131,346	COCHISE	45,549	26,929	17,383	1,237	9,546 R	59.1%	38.2%	60.8%	39.2%
134,421	COCONINO	55,280	19,249	34,240	1,791	14,991 D	34.8%	61.9%	36.0%	64.0%
53,597	GILA	20,499	12,180	7,643	676	4,537 R	59.4%	37.3%	61.4%	38.6%
37,220	GRAHAM	10,606	6,870	3,368	368	3,502 R	64.8%	31.8%	67.1%	32.9%
8,437	GREENLEE	2,567	1,416	1,042	109	374 R	55.2%	40.6%	57.6%	42.4%
20,489	LA PAZ	5,073	3,265	1,609	199	1,656 R	64.4%	31.7%	67.0%	33.0%
3,817,117	MARICOPA	1,437,952	672,505	732,761	32,686	60,256 D	46.8%	51.0%	47.9%	52.1%
200,186	MOHAVE	71,469	50,209	19,214	2,046	30,995 R	70.3%	26.9%	72.3%	27.7%
107,449	NAVAJO	36,640	18,767	16,624	1,249	2,143 R	51.2%	45.4%	53.0%	47.0%
980,263	PIMA	390,568	160,550	221,242	8,776	60,692 D	41.1%	56.6%	42.1%	57.9%
375,770	PINAL	117,395	63,782	50,395	3,218	13,387 R	54.3%	42.9%	55.9%	44.1%
47,420	SANTA CRUZ	13,488	3,828	9,241	419	5,413 D	28.4%	68.5%	29.3%	70.7%
211,033	YAVAPAI	108,368	65,308	40,160	2,900	25,148 R	60.3%	37.1%	61.9%	38.1%
195,751	YUMA	43,767	22,532	19,880	1,355	2,652 R	51.5%	45.4%	53.1%	46.9%
6,392,017	*TOTAL*	*2,384,308*	*1,135,200*	*1,191,100*	*58,008*	*55,900 D*	*47.6%*	*50.0%*	*48.8%*	*51.2%*

ARIZONA

HOUSE OF REPRESENTATIVES

			Republican		Democratic				Percentage			
									Total Vote		Major Vote	
CD	Year	Total Vote	Vote	Candidate	Vote	Candidate	Other Vote	Rep.-Dem. Plurality	Rep.	Dem.	Rep.	Dem.
1	2018	266,089	122,784	ROGERS, WENDY	143,240	O'HALLERAN, TOM*	65	20,456 D	46.1%	53.8%	46.2%	53.8%
1	2016	280,710	121,745	BABEU, PAUL	142,219	O'HALLERAN, TOM	16,746	20,474 D	43.4%	50.7%	46.1%	53.9%
1	2014	185,114	87,723	TOBIN, ANDY	97,391	KIRKPATRICK, ANN*		9,668 D	47.4%	52.6%	47.4%	52.6%
1	2012	251,595	113,594	PATON, JONATHAN	122,774	KIRKPATRICK, ANN	15,227	9,180 D	45.1%	48.8%	48.1%	51.9%
2	2018	294,152	133,083	PETERSON, LEA MARQUEZ	161,000	KIRKPATRICK, ANN	69	27,917 D	45.2%	54.7%	45.3%	54.7%
2	2016	315,679	179,806	MCSALLY, MARTHA*	135,873	HEINZ, MATT		43,933 R	57.0%	43.0%	57.0%	43.0%
2	2014	219,351	109,704	MCSALLY, MARTHA	109,543	BARBER, RON*	104	161 R	50.0%	49.9%	50.0%	50.0%
2	2012	292,279	144,884	MCSALLY, MARTHA	147,338	BARBER, RON*	57	2,454 D	49.6%	50.4%	49.6%	50.4%
3	2018	179,518	64,868	PIERSON, NICHOLAS "NICK"	114,650	GRIJALVA, RAÚL M.*		49,782 D	36.1%	63.9%	36.1%	63.9%
3	2016	151,035			148,973	GRIJALVA, RAÚL M.*	2,062	148,973 D		98.6%		100.0%
3	2014	104,428	46,185	SAUCEDO MERCER, GABRIELLA	58,192	GRIJALVA, RAÚL M.*	51	12,007 D	44.2%	55.7%	44.2%	55.8%
3	2012	168,698	62,663	SAUCEDO MERCER, GABRIELLA	98,468	GRIJALVA, RAÚL M.*	7,567	35,805 D	37.1%	58.4%	38.9%	61.1%
4	2018	277,035	188,842	GOSAR, PAUL*	84,521	BRILL, DAVID	3,672	104,321 R	68.2%	30.5%	69.1%	30.9%
4	2016	284,783	203,487	GOSAR, PAUL*	81,296	WEISSER, MIKEL		122,191 R	71.5%	28.5%	71.5%	28.5%
4	2014	175,179	122,560	GOSAR, PAUL*	45,179	WEISSER, MIKEL	7,440	77,381 R	70.0%	25.8%	73.1%	26.9%
4	2012	243,760	162,907	GOSAR, PAUL*	69,154	ROBINSON, JOHNNIE	11,699	93,753 R	66.8%	28.4%	70.2%	29.8%
5	2018	313,064	186,037	BIGGS, ANDY*	127,027	GREENE, JOAN		59,010 R	59.4%	40.6%	59.4%	40.6%
5	2016	320,124	205,184	BIGGS, ANDY	114,940	FUENTES, TALIA		90,244 R	64.1%	35.9%	64.1%	35.9%
5	2014	179,463	124,867	SALMON, MATT*	54,596	WOODS, JAMES ISSAC		70,271 R	69.6%	30.4%	69.6%	30.4%
5	2012	273,059	183,470	SALMON, MATT	89,589	MORGAN, SPENCER		93,881 R	67.2%	32.8%	67.2%	32.8%
6	2018	313,699	173,140	SCHWEIKERT, DAVID*	140,559	MALIK, ANITA		32,581 R	55.2%	44.8%	55.2%	44.8%
6	2016	324,444	201,578	SCHWEIKERT, DAVID*	122,866	WILLIAMSON, W. JOHN		78,712 R	62.1%	37.9%	62.1%	37.9%
6	2014	199,776	129,578	SCHWEIKERT, DAVID*	70,198	WILLIAMSON, W. JOHN		59,380 R	64.9%	35.1%	64.9%	35.1%
6	2012	293,177	179,706	SCHWEIKERT, DAVID*	97,666	JETTE, MATTHEW	15,805	82,040 R	61.3%	33.3%	64.8%	35.2%
7	2018	132,051			113,044	GALLEGO, RUBEN*	19,007	113,044 D		85.6%		100.0%
7	2016	158,811	39,286	NUNEZ, EVE	119,465	GALLEGO, RUBEN*	60	80,179 D	24.7%	75.2%	24.7%	75.3%
7	2014	72,452			54,235	GALLEGO, RUBEN	18,217	54,235 D		74.9%		100.0%
7	2012	127,827			104,489	PASTOR, ED*	23,338	104,489 D		81.7%		100.0%
8	2018	304,417	168,835	LESKO, DEBBIE*	135,569	TIPIRNENI, HIRAL	13	33,266 R	55.5%	44.5%	55.5%	44.5%
8	2016	298,971	204,942	FRANKS, TRENT*			94,029	204,942 R	68.5%		100.0%	
8	2014	169,776	128,710	FRANKS, TRENT*			41,066	128,710 R	75.8%		100.0%	
8	2012	272,791	172,809	FRANKS, TRENT*	95,635	SCHARER, GENE	4,347	77,174 R	63.3%	35.1%	64.4%	35.6%
9	2018	261,245	101,662	FERRARA, STEPHEN L.	159,583	STANTON, GREG		57,921 D	38.9%	61.1%	38.9%	61.1%
9	2016	277,507	108,350	GILES, DAVE	169,055	SINEMA, KYRSTEN*	102	60,705 D	39.0%	60.9%	39.1%	60.9%
9	2014	162,062	67,841	ROGERS, WENDY	88,609	SINEMA, KYRSTEN*	5,612	20,768 D	41.9%	54.7%	43.4%	56.6%
9	2012	250,131	111,630	PARKER, VERNON B.	121,881	SINEMA, KYRSTEN	16,620	10,251 D	44.6%	48.7%	47.8%	52.2%
TOTAL	*2018*	*2,341,270*	*1,139,251*		*1,179,193*		*22,826*	*39,942 D*	*48.7%*	*50.4%*	*49.1%*	*50.9%*
TOTAL	*2016*	*2,412,064*	*1,264,378*		*1,034,687*		*112,999*	*229,691 R*	*52.4%*	*42.9%*	*55.0%*	*45.0%*
TOTAL	*2014*	*1,467,601*	*817,168*		*577,943*		*72,490*	*239,225 R*	*55.7%*	*39.4%*	*58.6%*	*41.4%*
TOTAL	*2012*	*2,173,317*	*1,131,663*		*946,994*		*94,660*	*184,669 R*	*52.1%*	*43.6%*	*54.4%*	*45.6%*

Note: An asterisk (*) denotes incumbent.

ARIZONA

GENERAL AND PRIMARY ELECTIONS

2018 GENERAL ELECTIONS: OTHER VOTES

Governor Other vote was 50,962 Green (Angel Torres), 177 Write-in (Patrick Masoya), 66 Write-in (Christian Komor), 13 Write-in (Cary Dolego), 12 Write-in (Arthur Arvizu), 7 Write-in (James Gibson)

Senate Other vote was 57,442 Green (Angela Green), 365 Write-in (Barry Hess), 46 Write-in (Jonathan Ringham), 45 Write-in (Michael DeCarlo), 42 Write-in (Shelia Bilyeu), 37 Write-in (Robert Kay), 29 Write-in (Jeff Pearce), 2 Write-in (Edward Davida)

House Other vote was:

CD 1	65 Write-in (David Shock)
CD 2	50 Write-in (Jordan Flayer), 19 Write-in (Melissa Grable)
CD 4	3,672 Green (Haryaksha Knauer)
CD 7	18,706 Green (Gary Swing), 301 Write-in (James Bond)
CD 8	13 Write-in (Steven Hummel)

2018 PRIMARY ELECTIONS: SUPPLEMENTARY INFORMATION

Primary	August 28, 2018	**Registration** (as of August 28, 2018 — includes 540,017 inactive registrants)	3,631,552	Republican	1,264,199
				Democratic	1,111,334
				Libertarian	31,175
				Green	6,565
				Other	1,218,279

Primary Type Semi-open—Registered Democrats and Republicans could vote only in their party's primary. But voters not registered with any political party could participate in either the Democratic or Republican primary.

	REPUBLICAN PRIMARIES			DEMOCRATIC PRIMARIES		
Senator	McSally, Martha	357,626	54.6%	Sinema, Kyrsten	404,170	79.3%
	Ward, Kelli	180,926	27.6%	Abboud, Deedra	105,800	20.7%
	Arpaio, Joe	116,555	17.8%			
	Glenn, Nicholas N. (Write-in)	121				
	Gonzales, William	70				
	TOTAL	*655,298*		*TOTAL*	*509,970*	
Governor	Ducey, Doug*	463,672	70.7%	Garcia, David	255,555	50.6%
	Bennett, Ken	191,775	29.3%	Farley, Steve	163,072	32.3%
	Weber, Robert (Write-in)	91		Fryer, Kelly	86,810	17.2%
				Baig, Mirza Fareed (Write-in)	44	
	TOTAL	*655,538*		*TOTAL*	*505,481*	
Congressional District 1	Rogers, Wendy	30,180	43.7%	O'Halleran, Tom*	64,114	100.0%
	Smith, Steve	25,552	37.0%			
	Shedd, Tiffany	13,260	19.2%			
	TOTAL	*68,992*		*TOTAL*	*64,114*	
Congressional District 2	Peterson, Lea Marquez	23,571	34.2%	Kirkpatrick, Ann	33,938	41.9%
	Martin, Brandon	19,809	28.7%	Heinz, Matt	23,992	29.6%
	Welch, Casey	14,499	21.0%	Matiella, Maria "Mary"	7,606	9.4%
	Morales, Daniel Romero Jr.	11,135	16.1%	Wheeler, Bruce	6,814	8.4%
				Kovacs, Billy	5,350	6.6%
				Sherry, Barbara	2,074	2.6%
				Yuksel, Yahya	1,319	1.6%
	TOTAL	*69,014*		*TOTAL*	*81,093*	

ARIZONA

GENERAL AND PRIMARY ELECTIONS

	REPUBLICAN PRIMARIES			DEMOCRATIC PRIMARIES		
Congressional District 3	Pierson, Nicholas "Nick"	13,090	49.9%	Grijalva, Raúl M.*	45,186	99.8%
	Arellano, Sergio	7,400	28.2%	Garcia, Joshua (Write-in)	81	0.2%
	San Miguel, Edna	5,756	21.9%			
	TOTAL	*26,246*		*TOTAL*	*45,267*	
Congressional District 4	Gosar, Paul*	94,092	100.0%	Brill, David	19,048	52.4%
				DiSanto, Delina	17,256	47.5%
				Perez, Ana Maria (Write-in)	49	0.1%
	TOTAL	*94,092*		*TOTAL*	*36,353*	
Congressional District 5	Biggs, Andy*	86,418	100.0%	Greene, Joan	27,222	59.3%
				Torres, Jose	18,671	40.7%
	TOTAL	*86,418*		*TOTAL*	*45,893*	
Congressional District 6	Schweikert, David*	83,406	100.0%	Malik, Anita	22,666	42.2%
				Ross, Heather	20,203	37.6%
				McFadden, Garrick	10,825	20.2%
	TOTAL	*83,406*		*TOTAL*	*53,694*	
Congressional District 7				Gallego, Ruben*	32,231	74.8%
				Miranda, Catherine	10,856	25.2%
				TOTAL	*43,087*	
Congressional District 8	Lesko, Debbie*	73,776	77.2%	Tipirneni, Hiral	52,215	100.0%
	Dowling, Sandra E.	21,825	22.8%			
	TOTAL	*95,601*		*TOTAL*	*52,215*	
Congressional District 9	Ferrara, Stephen L.	31,006	59.9%	Stanton, Greg	59,066	100.0%
	Giles, Dave	16,722	32.3%			
	Baroness von Behr, Irina	4,020	7.8%			
	TOTAL	*51,748*		*TOTAL*	*59,066*	

Note: An asterisk (*) denotes incumbent.

ARKANSAS

Congressional districts first established for elections held in 2012

4 members

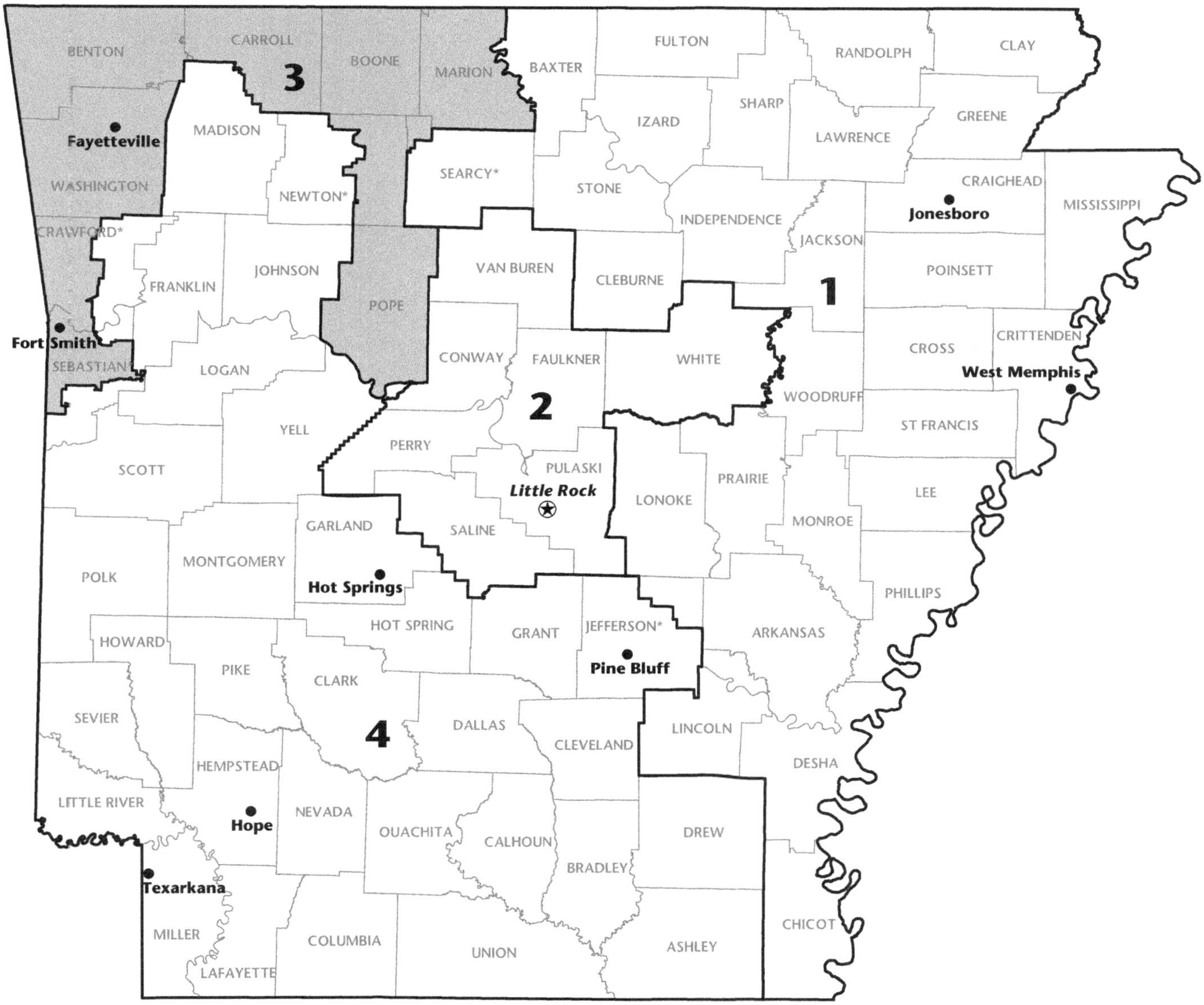

* Asterisk indicates a county whose boundaries include parts of two or more congressional districts.

ARKANSAS

GOVERNOR

Asa Hutchinson (R). Re-elected 2018 to a four-year term. Previously elected 2014.

SENATORS (2 Republicans)

John Boozman (R). Re-elected 2016 to a six-year term. Previously elected 2010.

Tom Cotton (R). Elected 2014 to a six-year term.

REPRESENTATIVES (4 Republicans)

1. Rick Crawford (R)
2. French Hill (R)
3. Steve Womack (R)
4. Bruce Westerman (R)

POSTWAR VOTE FOR PRESIDENT

		Republican		Democratic				Percentage			
								Total Vote		Major Vote	
Year	Total Vote	Vote	Candidate	Vote	Candidate	Other Vote	Rep.-Dem. Plurality	Rep.	Dem.	Rep.	Dem.
2016**	1,130,676	684,872	Trump, Donald J.	380,494	Clinton, Hillary Rodham	65,310	304,378 R	60.6%	33.7%	64.3%	35.7%
2012	1,069,468	647,744	Romney, W. Mitt	394,409	Obama, Barack H.*	27,315	253,335 R	60.6%	36.9%	62.2%	37.8%
2008	1,086,617	638,017	McCain, John S. III	422,310	Obama, Barack H.	26,290	215,707 R	58.7%	38.9%	60.2%	39.8%
2004	1,054,945	572,898	Bush, George W.*	469,953	Kerry, John F.	12,094	102,945 R	54.3%	44.5%	54.9%	45.1%
2000**	921,781	472,940	Bush, George W.	422,768	Gore, Albert Jr.	26,073	50,172 R	51.3%	45.9%	52.8%	47.2%
1996**	884,262	325,416	Dole, Robert "Bob"	475,171	Clinton, Bill*	83,675	149,755 D	36.8%	53.7%	40.6%	59.4%
1992**	950,653	337,324	Bush, George H.*	505,823	Clinton, Bill	107,506	168,499 D	35.5%	53.2%	40.0%	60.0%
1988	827,738	466,578	Bush, George H.	349,237	Dukakis, Michael S.	11,923	117,341 R	56.4%	42.2%	57.2%	42.8%
1984	884,406	534,774	Reagan, Ronald*	338,646	Mondale, Walter F.	10,986	196,128 R	60.5%	38.3%	61.2%	38.8%
1980**	837,582	403,164	Reagan, Ronald	398,041	Carter, Jimmy*	36,377	5,123 R	48.1%	47.5%	50.3%	49.7%
1976	767,535	267,903	Ford, Gerald R.*	498,604	Carter, Jimmy	1,028	230,701 D	34.9%	65.0%	35.0%	65.0%
1972	651,320	448,541	Nixon, Richard M.*	199,892	McGovern, George S.	2,887	248,649 R	68.9%	30.7%	69.2%	30.8%
1968**	619,969	190,759	Nixon, Richard M.	188,228	Humphrey, Hubert Horatio Jr.	240,982	2,531 R#	30.8%	30.4%	50.3%	49.7%
1964	560,426	243,264	Goldwater, Barry M. Sr.	314,197	Johnson, Lyndon B.*	2,965	70,933 D	43.4%	56.1%	43.6%	56.4%
1960	428,509	184,508	Nixon, Richard M.	215,049	Kennedy, John F.	28,952	30,541 D	43.1%	50.2%	46.2%	53.8%
1956	406,572	186,287	Eisenhower, Dwight D.*	213,277	Stevenson, Adlai E. II	7,008	26,990 D	45.8%	52.5%	46.6%	53.4%
1952	404,800	177,155	Eisenhower, Dwight D.	226,300	Stevenson, Adlai E. II	1,345	49,145 D	43.8%	55.9%	43.9%	56.1%
1948**	242,475	50,959	Dewey, Thomas E.	149,659	Truman, Harry S.*	41,857	98,700 D	21.0%	61.7%	25.4%	74.6%

Note: An asterisk (*) denotes incumbent. A pound sign (#) in the plurality column indicates that the winner in 1968 did not run under the banner of either major party. **In past elections, the other vote included: 2016 - 29,949 Libertarian (Gary Johnson); 2000 - 13,421 Green (Ralph Nader); 1996 - 69,884 Reform (Ross Perot); 1992 - 99,132 Independent (Perot); 1980 - 22,468 Independent (John Anderson); 1968 - 240,982 American Independent (Wallace); 1948 - 40,068 States' Rights (Strom Thurmond). Wallace carried Arkansas in 1968 with 38.9 percent of the vote.

ARKANSAS

POSTWAR VOTE FOR GOVERNOR

		Republican		Democratic				Percentage			
								Total Vote		Major Vote	
Year	Total Vote	Vote	Candidate	Vote	Candidate	Other Vote	Rep.-Dem. Plurality	Rep.	Dem.	Rep.	Dem.
2018	891,509	582,406	Hutchinson, Asa*	283,218	Henderson, Jared K.	25,885	299,188 R	65.3%	31.8%	67.3%	32.7%
2014	848,592	470,429	Hutchinson, Asa	352,115	Ross, Mike	26,048	118,314 R	55.4%	41.5%	57.2%	42.8%
2010	781,333	262,784	Keet, Jim	503,336	Beebe, Mike D.*	15,213	240,552 D	33.6%	64.4%	34.3%	65.7%
2006	774,680	315,040	Hutchinson, Asa	430,765	Beebe, Mike D.	28,875	115,725 D	40.7%	55.6%	42.2%	57.8%
2002	805,696	427,082	Huckabee, Mike*	378,250	Fisher, Jimmie Lou	364	48,832 R	53.0%	46.9%	53.0%	47.0%
1998	728,619	430,919	Huckabee, Mike*	278,155	King, James	19,545	152,764 R	59.1%	38.2%	60.8%	39.2%
1994	716,840	287,904	Nelson, Sheffield	428,936	Tucker, Jim Guy*		141,032 D	40.2%	59.8%	40.2%	59.8%
1990	696,412	295,925	Nelson, Sheffield	400,386	Clinton, Bill*	101	104,461 D	42.5%	57.5%	42.5%	57.5%
1986**	688,551	248,427	White, Frank D.	439,882	Clinton, Bill*	242	191,455 D	36.1%	63.9%	36.1%	63.9%
1984	886,548	331,987	Freeman, Woody	554,561	Clinton, Bill*		222,574 D	37.4%	62.6%	37.4%	62.6%
1982	789,351	357,496	White, Frank D.*	431,855	Clinton, Bill		74,359 D	45.3%	54.7%	45.3%	54.7%
1980	838,925	435,684	White, Frank D.	403,241	Clinton, Bill*		32,443 R	51.9%	48.1%	51.9%	48.1%
1978	528,912	193,746	Lowe, A. Lynn	335,101	Clinton, Bill	65	141,355 D	36.6%	63.4%	36.6%	63.4%
1976	726,949	121,716	Griffith, Leon	605,083	Pryor, David H.*	150	483,367 D	16.7%	83.2%	16.7%	83.3%
1974	545,974	187,872	Coon, Ken	358,018	Pryor, David H.	84	170,146 D	34.4%	65.6%	34.4%	65.6%
1972	648,069	159,177	Blaylock, Len E.	488,892	Bumpers, Dale*		329,715 D	24.6%	75.4%	24.6%	75.4%
1970	608,198	196,418	Rockefeller, Winthrop*	375,648	Bumpers, Dale	36,132	179,230 D	32.3%	61.8%	34.3%	65.7%
1968	615,590	322,777	Rockefeller, Winthrop*	292,813	Crank, Marion		29,964 R	52.4%	47.6%	52.4%	47.6%
1966	563,527	306,324	Rockefeller, Winthrop	257,203	Johnson, James Douglas		49,121 R	54.4%	45.6%	54.4%	45.6%
1964	592,113	254,561	Rockefeller, Winthrop	337,489	Faubus, Orval E.*	63	82,928 D	43.0%	57.0%	43.0%	57.0%
1962	308,092	82,349	Ricketts, Willis	225,743	Faubus, Orval E.*		143,394 D	26.7%	73.3%	26.7%	73.3%
1960	421,985	129,921	Britt, Henry M.	292,064	Faubus, Orval E.*		162,143 D	30.8%	69.2%	30.8%	69.2%
1958	286,886	50,288	Johnson, George W.	236,598	Faubus, Orval E.*		186,310 D	17.5%	82.5%	17.5%	82.5%
1956	399,012	77,215	Mitchell, Roy	321,797	Faubus, Orval E.*		244,582 D	19.4%	80.6%	19.4%	80.6%
1954	335,176	127,004	Remmel, Pratt C.	208,121	Faubus, Orval E.	51	81,117 D	37.9%	62.1%	37.9%	62.1%
1952	391,592	49,292	Speck, Jefferson W.	342,292	Cherry, Francis	8	293,000 D	12.6%	87.4%	12.6%	87.4%
1950	317,081	50,303	Speck, Jefferson W.	266,778	McMath, Sidney S.*		216,475 D	15.9%	84.1%	15.9%	84.1%
1948	244,271	26,500	Black, Charles R.	217,771	McMath, Sidney S.		191,271 D	10.8%	89.2%	10.8%	89.2%
1946	152,162	24,133	Mills, W. T.	128,029	Laney, Ben*		103,896 D	15.9%	84.1%	15.9%	84.1%

Note: An asterisk (*) denotes incumbent. **The term of office for Arkansas Governor was increased from two to four years effective with the 1986 election.

POSTWAR VOTE FOR SENATOR

		Republican		Democratic				Percentage			
								Total Vote		Major Vote	
Year	Total Vote	Vote	Candidate	Vote	Candidate	Other Vote	Rep.-Dem. Plurality	Rep.	Dem.	Rep.	Dem.
2016	1,107,522	661,984	Boozman, John*	400,602	Eldridge, Conner	44,936	261,382 R	59.8%	36.2%	62.3%	37.7%
2014	847,505	478,819	Cotton, Tom	334,174	Pryor, Mark*	34,512	144,645 R	56.5%	39.4%	58.9%	41.1%
2010	779,957	451,618	Boozman, John	288,156	Lincoln, Blanche L.*	40,183	163,462 R	57.9%	36.9%	61.0%	39.0%
2008**	1,011,754			804,678	Pryor, Mark*	207,076	804,678 D		79.5%		100.0%
2004	1,039,349	458,036	Holt, Jim L.	580,973	Lincoln, Blanche L.*	340	122,937 D	44.1%	55.9%	44.1%	55.9%
2002	803,959	370,653	Hutchinson, Tim*	433,306	Pryor, Mark		62,653 D	46.1%	53.9%	46.1%	53.9%
1998	700,644	295,870	Boozman, Fay	385,878	Lincoln, Blanche L.	18,896	90,008 D	42.2%	55.1%	43.4%	56.6%
1996	846,183	445,942	Hutchinson, Tim	400,241	Bryant, Winston		45,701 R	52.7%	47.3%	52.7%	47.3%
1992	920,008	366,373	Huckabee, Mike	553,635	Bumpers, Dale*		187,262 D	39.8%	60.2%	39.8%	60.2%
1990**	494,735			493,910	Pryor, David H.*	825	493,910 D		99.8%		100.0%
1986	695,487	262,313	Hutchinson, Asa	433,122	Bumpers, Dale*	52	170,809 D	37.7%	62.3%	37.7%	62.3%
1984	875,956	373,615	Bethune, Ed	502,341	Pryor, David H.*		128,726 D	42.7%	57.3%	42.7%	57.3%
1980	808,812	330,576	Clark, Bill	477,905	Bumpers, Dale*	331	147,329 D	40.9%	59.1%	40.9%	59.1%
1978	522,239	84,722	Kelly, Tom	399,916	Pryor, David H.	37,601	315,194 D	16.2%	76.6%	17.5%	82.5%
1974	543,082	82,026	Jones, John Harris	461,056	Bumpers, Dale		379,030 D	15.1%	84.9%	15.1%	84.9%
1972	634,636	248,238	Babbitt, Wayne H.	386,398	McClellan, John L.*		138,160 D	39.1%	60.9%	39.1%	60.9%
1968	591,704	241,739	Bernard, Charles T.	349,965	Fulbright, J. William*		108,226 D	40.9%	59.1%	40.9%	59.1%
1966**					McClellan, John L.*		D				
1962	312,880	98,013	Jones, Kenneth	214,867	Fulbright, J. William*		116,854 D	31.3%	68.7%	31.3%	68.7%
1960**					McClellan, John L.*		D				
1956	399,695	68,016	Henley, Ben C.	331,679	Fulbright, J. William*		263,663 D	17.0%	83.0%	17.0%	83.0%
1954	291,058			291,058	McClellan, John L.*		291,058 D		100.0%		100.0%
1950	302,582			302,582	Fulbright, J. William*		302,582 D		100.0%		100.0%
1948	231,922			216,401	McClellan, John L.*	15,521	216,401 D		93.3%		100.0%

Note: An asterisk (*) denotes incumbent. **In past elections, the other vote included: 2008 - 207,076 Green (Rebekah Kennedy), who finished second. In 1990 the vote for Senator David H. Pryor was not canvassed in seven counties because he was unopposed. Senator John L. McClellan was re-elected in 1960 and in 1966, but his vote was not canvassed in many counties. The Republican Party did not run a candidate in the 1948, 1950, 1954, 1960, 1966, 1990, and 2008 Senate elections.

ARKANSAS

GOVERNOR 2018

2010 Census Population	County	Total Vote	Republican (Hutchinson)	Democratic (Henderson)	Other	Rep.-Dem. Plurality	Percentage: Total Vote Rep.	Percentage: Total Vote Dem.	Percentage: Major Vote Rep.	Percentage: Major Vote Dem.
19,019	ARKANSAS	4,962	3,530	1,355	77	2,175 R	71.1%	27.3%	72.3%	27.7%
21,853	ASHLEY	6,155	4,278	1,751	126	2,527 R	69.5%	28.4%	71.0%	29.0%
41,513	BAXTER	14,351	10,694	2,978	679	7,716 R	74.5%	20.8%	78.2%	21.8%
221,339	BENTON	77,534	53,185	22,316	2,033	30,869 R	68.6%	28.8%	70.4%	29.6%
36,903	BOONE	11,623	9,028	2,208	387	6,820 R	77.7%	19.0%	80.3%	19.7%
11,508	BRADLEY	2,854	1,906	868	80	1,038 R	66.8%	30.4%	68.7%	31.3%
5,368	CALHOUN	1,791	1,335	423	33	912 R	74.5%	23.6%	75.9%	24.1%
27,446	CARROLL	8,968	5,796	2,968	204	2,828 R	64.6%	33.1%	66.1%	33.9%
11,800	CHICOT	3,551	1,638	1,857	56	219 D	46.1%	52.3%	46.9%	53.1%
22,995	CLARK	6,731	3,988	2,611	132	1,377 R	59.2%	38.8%	60.4%	39.6%
16,083	CLAY	4,132	3,218	782	132	2,436 R	77.9%	18.9%	80.4%	19.6%
25,970	CLEBURNE	9,624	7,856	1,495	273	6,361 R	81.6%	15.5%	84.0%	16.0%
8,689	CLEVELAND	2,589	2,020	513	56	1,507 R	78.0%	19.8%	79.7%	20.3%
24,552	COLUMBIA	6,342	4,199	2,044	99	2,155 R	66.2%	32.2%	67.3%	32.7%
21,273	CONWAY	6,465	4,339	1,966	160	2,373 R	67.1%	30.4%	68.8%	31.2%
96,443	CRAIGHEAD	26,078	17,313	7,407	1,358	9,906 R	66.4%	28.4%	70.0%	30.0%
61,948	CRAWFORD	16,860	13,200	3,120	540	10,080 R	78.3%	18.5%	80.9%	19.1%
50,902	CRITTENDEN	11,918	5,775	5,833	310	58 D	48.5%	48.9%	49.8%	50.2%
17,870	CROSS	5,794	4,108	1,498	188	2,610 R	70.9%	25.9%	73.3%	26.7%
8,116	DALLAS	2,115	1,316	773	26	543 R	62.2%	36.5%	63.0%	37.0%
13,008	DESHA	3,469	1,833	1,560	76	273 R	52.8%	45.0%	54.0%	46.0%
18,509	DREW	5,397	3,658	1,606	133	2,052 R	67.8%	29.8%	69.5%	30.5%
113,237	FAULKNER	38,559	25,643	11,689	1,227	13,954 R	66.5%	30.3%	68.7%	31.3%
18,125	FRANKLIN	5,295	4,204	916	175	3,288 R	79.4%	17.3%	82.1%	17.9%
12,245	FULTON	3,832	2,829	900	103	1,929 R	73.8%	23.5%	75.9%	24.1%
96,024	GARLAND	31,767	21,969	8,865	933	13,104 R	69.2%	27.9%	71.2%	28.8%
17,853	GRANT	5,549	4,524	898	127	3,626 R	81.5%	16.2%	83.4%	16.6%
42,090	GREENE	10,953	8,275	2,088	590	6,187 R	75.6%	19.1%	79.9%	20.1%
22,609	HEMPSTEAD	4,971	3,312	1,554	105	1,758 R	66.6%	31.3%	68.1%	31.9%
32,923	HOT SPRING	8,739	6,368	2,113	258	4,255 R	72.9%	24.2%	75.1%	24.9%
13,789	HOWARD	3,519	2,489	974	56	1,515 R	70.7%	27.7%	71.9%	28.1%
36,647	INDEPENDENCE	10,145	7,733	1,928	484	5,805 R	76.2%	19.0%	80.0%	20.0%
13,696	IZARD	4,471	3,423	869	179	2,554 R	76.6%	19.4%	79.8%	20.2%
17,997	JACKSON	4,171	2,998	1,067	106	1,931 R	71.9%	25.6%	73.8%	26.2%
77,435	JEFFERSON	19,820	9,005	10,406	409	1,401 D	45.4%	52.5%	46.4%	53.6%
25,540	JOHNSON	7,477	5,546	1,672	259	3,874 R	74.2%	22.4%	76.8%	23.2%
7,645	LAFAYETTE	2,131	1,395	693	43	702 R	65.5%	32.5%	66.8%	33.2%
17,415	LAWRENCE	4,669	3,584	908	177	2,676 R	76.8%	19.4%	79.8%	20.2%
10,424	LEE	2,119	947	1,130	42	183 D	44.7%	53.3%	45.6%	54.4%
14,134	LINCOLN	3,039	2,227	771	41	1,456 R	73.3%	25.4%	74.3%	25.7%
13,171	LITTLE RIVER	3,925	2,820	1,014	91	1,806 R	71.8%	25.8%	73.6%	26.4%
22,353	LOGAN	5,528	4,303	1,041	184	3,262 R	77.8%	18.8%	80.5%	19.5%
68,356	LONOKE	20,613	15,791	4,171	651	11,620 R	76.6%	20.2%	79.1%	20.9%
15,717	MADISON	5,576	4,151	1,283	142	2,868 R	74.4%	23.0%	76.4%	23.6%
16,653	MARION	5,163	3,959	1,027	177	2,932 R	76.7%	19.9%	79.4%	20.6%
43,462	MILLER	11,431	8,393	2,841	197	5,552 R	73.4%	24.9%	74.7%	25.3%
46,480	MISSISSIPPI	10,455	6,429	3,660	366	2,769 R	61.5%	35.0%	63.7%	36.3%
8,149	MONROE	2,640	1,493	1,104	43	389 R	56.6%	41.8%	57.5%	42.5%
9,487	MONTGOMERY	2,831	2,204	558	69	1,646 R	77.9%	19.7%	79.8%	20.2%
8,997	NEVADA	2,516	1,628	842	46	786 R	64.7%	33.5%	65.9%	34.1%
8,330	NEWTON	3,091	2,203	695	193	1,508 R	71.3%	22.5%	76.0%	24.0%
26,120	OUACHITA	7,386	4,227	3,031	128	1,196 R	57.2%	41.0%	58.2%	41.8%
10,445	PERRY	3,701	2,731	838	132	1,893 R	73.8%	22.6%	76.5%	23.5%
21,757	PHILLIPS	5,444	2,401	2,923	120	522 D	44.1%	53.7%	45.1%	54.9%
11,291	PIKE	3,358	2,708	563	87	2,145 R	80.6%	16.8%	82.8%	17.2%
24,583	POINSETT	6,109	4,690	1,194	225	3,496 R	76.8%	19.5%	79.7%	20.3%
20,662	POLK	6,056	4,903	904	249	3,999 R	81.0%	14.9%	84.4%	15.6%
61,754	POPE	17,956	13,437	3,756	763	9,681 R	74.8%	20.9%	78.2%	21.8%
8,715	PRAIRIE	2,860	2,256	560	44	1,696 R	78.9%	19.6%	80.1%	19.9%
382,748	PULASKI	134,667	62,510	69,265	2,892	6,755 D	46.4%	51.4%	47.4%	52.6%

ARKANSAS

GOVERNOR 2018

2010 Census Population	County	Total Vote	Republican (Hutchinson)	Democratic (Henderson)	Other	Rep.-Dem. Plurality	Percentage Total Vote Rep.	Percentage Total Vote Dem.	Percentage Major Vote Rep.	Percentage Major Vote Dem.
17,969	RANDOLPH	5,662	4,285	1,063	314	3,222 R	75.7%	18.8%	80.1%	19.9%
107,118	SALINE	41,578	30,756	9,676	1,146	21,080 R	74.0%	23.3%	76.1%	23.9%
11,233	SCOTT	2,879	2,331	390	158	1,941 R	81.0%	13.5%	85.7%	14.3%
8,195	SEARCY	3,194	2,512	524	158	1,988 R	78.6%	16.4%	82.7%	17.3%
125,744	SEBASTIAN	33,165	23,785	8,316	1,064	15,469 R	71.7%	25.1%	74.1%	25.9%
17,058	SEVIER	3,202	2,412	682	108	1,730 R	75.3%	21.3%	78.0%	22.0%
17,264	SHARP	5,670	4,430	1,038	202	3,392 R	78.1%	18.3%	81.0%	19.0%
28,258	ST. FRANCIS	5,811	2,660	3,019	132	359 D	45.8%	52.0%	46.8%	53.2%
12,394	STONE	4,442	3,302	956	184	2,346 R	74.3%	21.5%	77.5%	22.5%
41,639	UNION	12,502	8,225	4,036	241	4,189 R	65.8%	32.3%	67.1%	32.9%
17,295	VAN BUREN	6,296	4,937	1,157	202	3,780 R	78.4%	18.4%	81.0%	19.0%
203,065	WASHINGTON	65,863	35,967	28,051	1,845	7,916 R	54.6%	42.6%	56.2%	43.8%
77,076	WHITE	21,993	17,610	3,799	584	13,811 R	80.1%	17.3%	82.3%	17.7%
7,260	WOODRUFF	2,086	1,271	760	55	511 R	60.9%	36.4%	62.6%	37.4%
22,185	YELL	5,331	4,002	1,108	221	2,894 R	75.1%	20.8%	78.3%	21.7%
2,915,918	*TOTAL*	*891,509*	*582,406*	*283,218*	*25,885*	*299,188 R*	*65.3%*	*31.8%*	*67.3%*	*32.7%*

ARKANSAS

HOUSE OF REPRESENTATIVES

CD	Year	Total Vote	Republican Vote	Republican Candidate	Democratic Vote	Democratic Candidate	Other Vote	Rep.-Dem. Plurality	Percentage Total Vote Rep.	Percentage Total Vote Dem.	Percentage Major Vote Rep.	Percentage Major Vote Dem.
1	2018	201,245	138,757	CRAWFORD, RICK*	57,907	DESAI, CHINTAN	4,581	80,850 R	68.9%	28.8%	70.6%	29.4%
1	2016	241,047	183,866	CRAWFORD, RICK*			57,181	183,866 R	76.3%		100.0%	
1	2014	196,256	124,139	CRAWFORD, RICK*	63,555	MCPHERSON, JACKIE	8,562	60,584 R	63.3%	32.4%	66.1%	33.9%
1	2012	246,843	138,800	CRAWFORD, RICK*	96,601	ELLINGTON, SCOTT	11,442	42,199 R	56.2%	39.1%	59.0%	41.0%
2	2018	253,453	132,125	HILL, FRENCH*	116,135	TUCKER, CLARKE	5,193	15,990 R	52.1%	45.8%	53.2%	46.8%
2	2016	302,464	176,472	HILL, FRENCH*	111,347	CURRY, DIANNE	14,645	65,125 R	58.3%	36.8%	61.3%	38.7%
2	2014	237,330	123,073	HILL, FRENCH	103,477	HAYS, PATRICK	10,780	19,596 R	51.9%	43.6%	54.3%	45.7%
2	2012	286,598	158,175	GRIFFIN, TIM*	113,156	RULE, HERB	15,267	45,019 R	55.2%	39.5%	58.3%	41.7%
3	2018	229,708	148,717	WOMACK, STEVE*	74,952	MAHONY, JOSHUA	6,039	73,765 R	64.7%	32.6%	66.5%	33.5%
3	2016	280,907	217,192	WOMACK, STEVE*			63,715	217,192 R	77.3%		100.0%	
3	2014	190,935	151,630	WOMACK, STEVE*			39,305	151,630 R	79.4%		100.0%	
3	2012	245,660	186,467	WOMACK, STEVE*			59,193	186,467 R	75.9%		100.0%	
4	2018	204,892	136,740	WESTERMAN, BRUCE*	63,984	SHAMEL, HAYDEN	4,168	72,756 R	66.7%	31.2%	68.1%	31.9%
4	2016	244,159	182,885	WESTERMAN, BRUCE*			61,274	182,885 R	74.9%		100.0%	
4	2014	206,131	110,789	WESTERMAN, BRUCE	87,742	WITT, JAMES LEE	7,600	23,047 R	53.7%	42.6%	55.8%	44.2%
4	2012	258,953	154,149	COTTON, TOM	95,013	JEFFRESS, GENE	9,791	59,136 R	59.5%	36.7%	61.9%	38.1%
TOTAL	*2018*	*889,298*	*556,339*		*312,978*		*19,981*	*243,361 R*	*62.6%*	*35.2%*	*64.0%*	*36.0%*
TOTAL	*2016*	*1,068,577*	*760,415*		*111,347*		*196,815*	*649,068 R*	*71.2%*	*10.4%*	*87.2%*	*12.8%*
TOTAL	*2014*	*830,652*	*509,631*		*254,774*		*66,247*	*254,857 R*	*61.4%*	*30.7%*	*66.7%*	*33.3%*
TOTAL	*2012*	*1,038,054*	*637,591*		*304,770*		*95,693*	*332,821 R*	*61.4%*	*29.4%*	*67.7%*	*32.3%*

Note: An asterisk (*) denotes incumbent.

ARKANSAS

GENERAL AND PRIMARY ELECTIONS

2018 GENERAL ELECTIONS: OTHER VOTES

Governor	Other vote was 25,885 Libertarian (Mark West)
House	Other vote was:
CD 1	4,581 Libertarian (Elvis Presley)
CD 2	5,193 Libertarian (Joe Swafford)
CD 3	5,899 Libertarian (Michael Kalagias), 140 Write-in (Write-in)
CD 4	3,952 Libertarian (Tom Canada), 216 Write-in (Write-in)

2018 PRIMARY ELECTIONS: SUPPLEMENTARY INFORMATION

Primary	May 22, 2018	**Registration** (as of June 1, 2017)	1,670,119	No Party Registration
Primary Runoff	June 19, 2018			

Primary Type Open—Any registered voter could participate in either the Democratic or the Republican primary. However, if they participated in one party's primary they could not vote in the runoff of the other party.

	REPUBLICAN PRIMARIES			DEMOCRATIC PRIMARIES		
Governor	Hutchinson, Asa*	143,648	69.6%	Henderson, Jared K.	67,046	63.3%
	Morgan, Jan	62,757	30.4%	Sanders, Leticia	38,873	36.7%
	TOTAL	*206,405*		*TOTAL*	*105,919*	
Congressional District 1	Crawford, Rick*	Unopposed		Desai, Chintan	Unopposed	
Congressional District 2	Hill, French*	Unopposed		Tucker, Clarke	23,325	57.8%
				Combs, Gwen	8,188	20.3%
				Spencer, Paul J.	5,063	12.5%
				Dunkley, Jonathan	3,768	9.3%
				TOTAL	*40,344*	
Congressional District 3	Womack, Steve*	47,757	84.2%	Mahony, Joshua	Unopposed	
	Ryerse, Robb	8,988	15.8%			
	TOTAL	*56,745*				
Congressional District 4	Westerman, Bruce*	40,201	79.8%	Shamel, Hayden	Unopposed	
	Caldwell, Randy	10,151	20.2%			
	TOTAL	*50,352*				

Note: An asterisk (*) denotes incumbent.

CALIFORNIA

Congressional districts first established for elections held in 2012

53 members

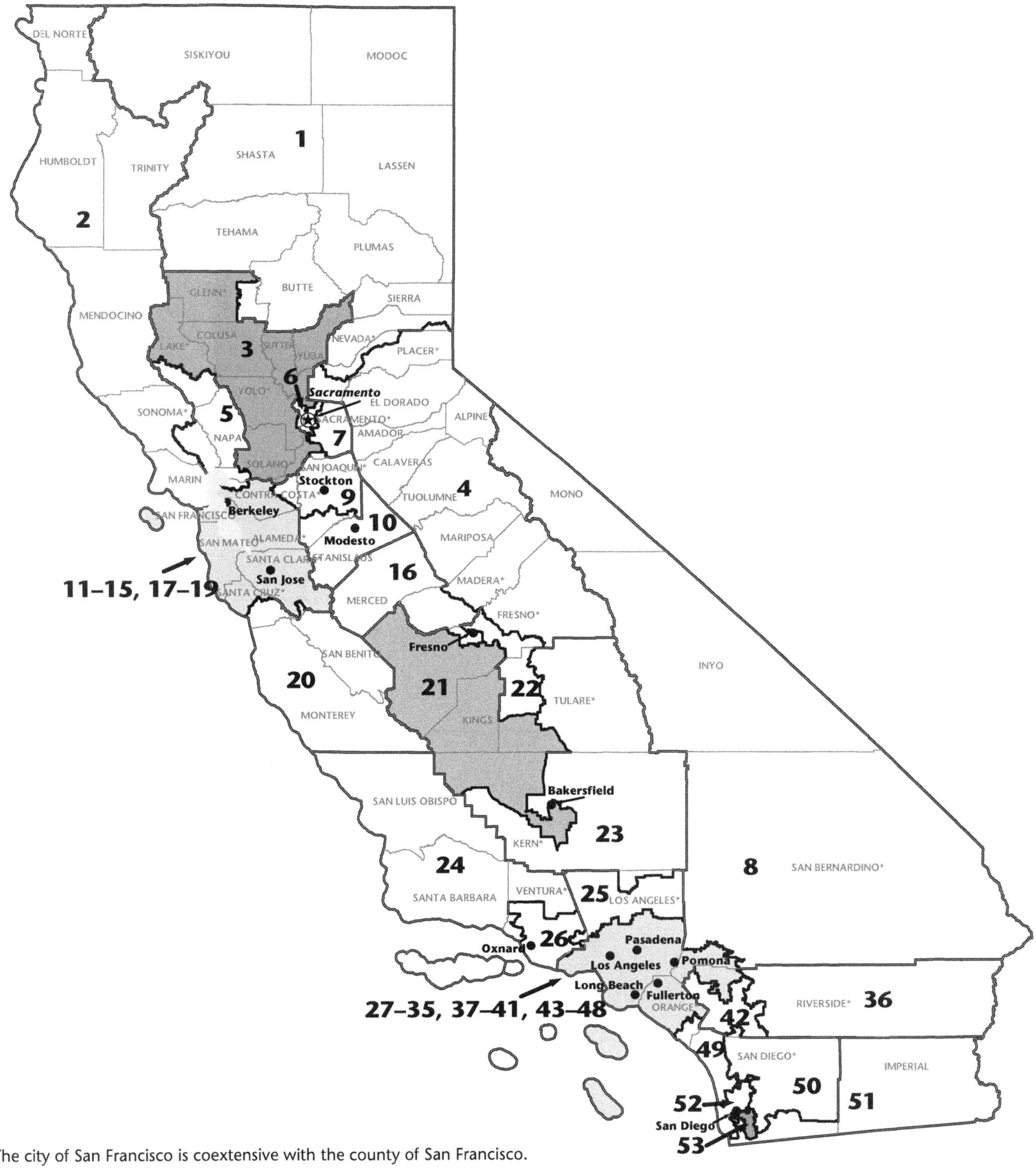

The city of San Francisco is coextensive with the county of San Francisco.

* Asterisk indicates a county whose boundaries include parts of two or more congressional districts.

CALIFORNIA

Greater Los Angeles, San Diego Areas

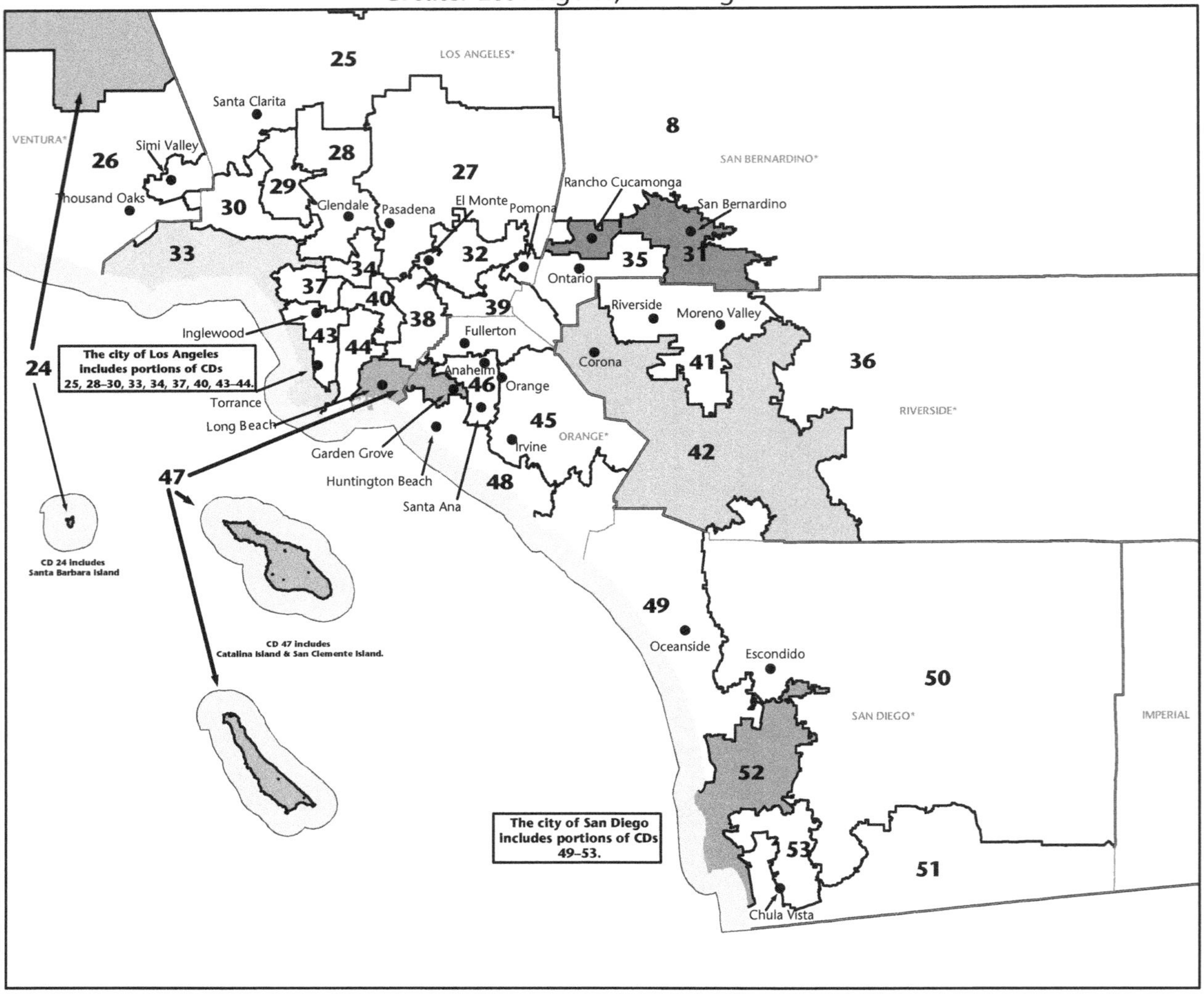

* Asterisk indicates a county whose boundaries include parts of two or more congressional districts.

CALIFORNIA

Greater San Francisco Bay Area

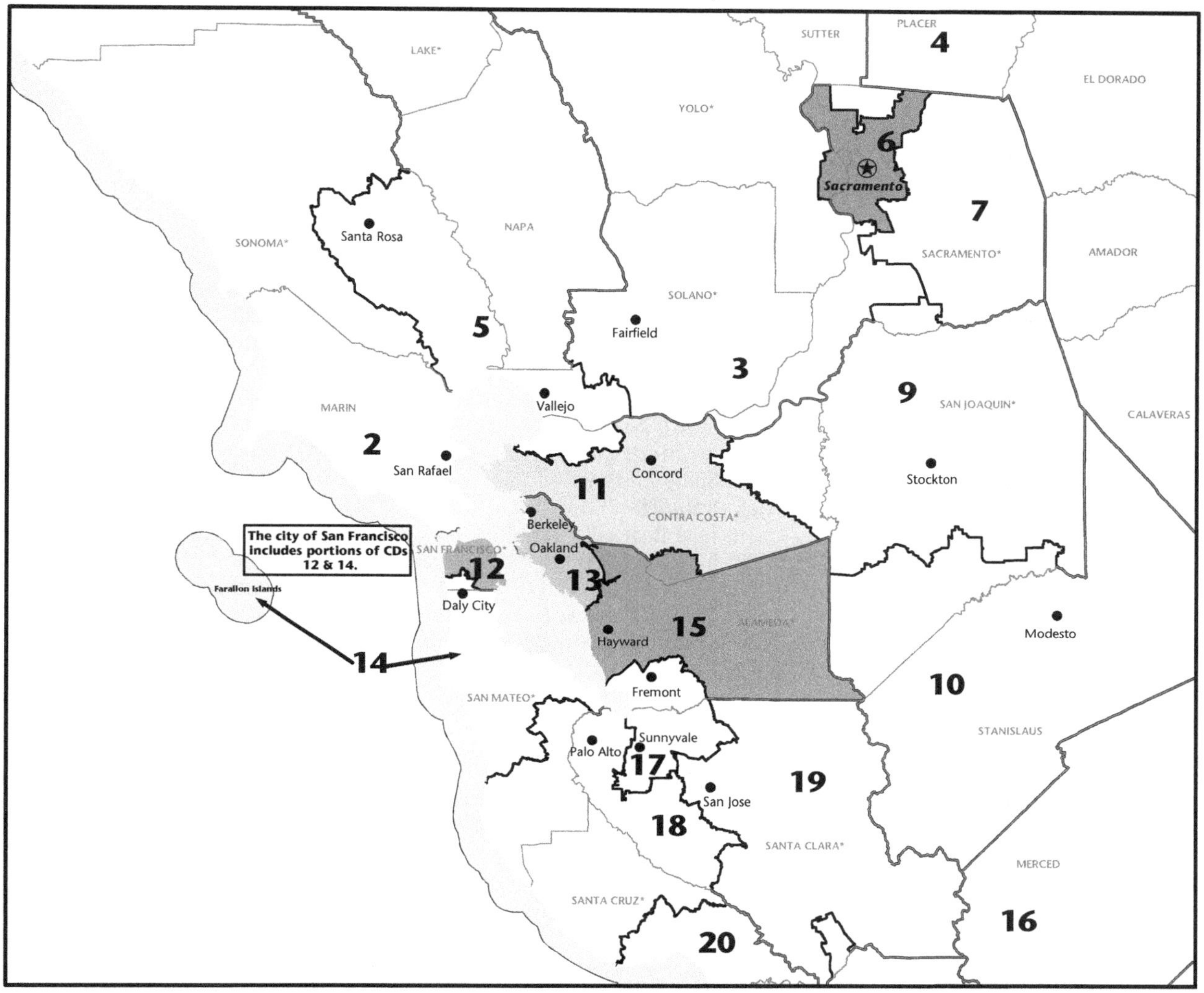

* Asterisk indicates a county whose boundaries include parts of two or more congressional districts.

CALIFORNIA

GOVERNOR

Gavin Newsom (D). Elected 2018 to a four-year term.

SENATORS (2 Democrats)

Dianne Feinstein (D). Re-elected 2018 to a six-year term. Previously elected 2012, 2006, 2000, 1994, and 1992 to fill the remaining two years of the term vacated when Senator Pete Wilson (R) was elected governor in November 1990.

Kamala D. Harris (D). Elected 2016 to a six-year term.

REPRESENTATIVES (7 Republicans, 46 Democrats)

1. Doug LaMalfa (R)
2. Jared Huffman (D)
3. John Garamendi (D)
4. Tom McClintock (R)
5. Mike Thompson (D)
6. Doris Matsui (D)
7. Ami Bera (D)
8. Paul Cook (R)
9. Jerry McNerney (D)
10. Josh Harder (D)
11. Mark DeSaulnier (D)
12. Nancy Pelosi (D)
13. Barbara Lee (D)
14. Jackie Speier (D)
15. Eric Swalwell (D)
16. Jim Costa (D)
17. Ro Khanna (D)
18. Anna G. Eshoo (D)
19. Zoe Lofgren (D)
20. Jimmy Panetta (D)
21. T.J. Cox (D)
22. Devin Nunes (R)
23. Kevin McCarthy (R)
24. Salud Carbajal (D)
25. Katie Hill (D)
26. Julia Brownley (D)
27. Judy Chu (D)
28. Adam B. Schiff (D)
29. Tony Cardenas (D)
30. Brad Sherman (D)
31. Pete Aguilar (D)
32. Grace Flores Napolitano (D)
33. Ted Lieu (D)
34. Jimmy Gomez (D)
35. Norma J. Torres (D)
36. Raul Ruiz (D)
37. Karen Bass (D)
38. Linda J. Sánchez (D)
39. Gil Cisneros (D)
40. Lucille Roybal-Allard (D)
41. Mark A. Takano (D)
42. Ken Calvert (R)
43. Maxine Waters (D)
44. Nanette Diaz Barragan (D)
45. Katie Porter (D)
46. Lou Correa (D)
47. Alan Lowenthal (D)
48. Harley Rouda Jr. (D)
49. Mike Levin (D)
50. Duncan D. Hunter (R)
51. Juan Vargas (D)
52. Scott Peters (D)
53. Susan A. Davis (D)

POSTWAR VOTE FOR PRESIDENT

		Republican		Democratic					Percentage		
								Total Vote		Major Vote	
Year	Total Vote	Vote	Candidate	Vote	Candidate	Other Vote	Rep.-Dem. Plurality	Rep.	Dem.	Rep.	Dem.
2016**	14,181,595	4,483,810	Trump, Donald J.	8,753,788	Clinton, Hillary Rodham	943,997	4,269,978 D	31.6%	61.7%	33.9%	66.1%
2012	13,038,547	4,839,958	Romney, W. Mitt	7,854,285	Obama, Barack H.*	344,304	3,014,327 D	37.1%	60.2%	38.1%	61.9%
2008	13,561,900	5,011,781	McCain, John S. III	8,274,473	Obama, Barack H.	275,646	3,262,692 D	37.0%	61.0%	37.7%	62.3%
2004	12,421,852	5,509,826	Bush, George W.*	6,745,485	Kerry, John F.	166,541	1,235,659 D	44.4%	54.3%	45.0%	55.0%
2000**	10,965,856	4,567,429	Bush, George W.	5,861,203	Gore, Albert Jr.	537,224	1,293,774 D	41.7%	53.4%	43.8%	56.2%
1996**	10,019,484	3,828,380	Dole, Robert "Bob"	5,119,835	Clinton, Bill*	1,071,269	1,291,455 D	38.2%	51.1%	42.8%	57.2%
1992**	11,131,721	3,630,574	Bush, George H.*	5,121,325	Clinton, Bill	2,379,822	1,490,751 D	32.6%	46.0%	41.5%	58.5%
1988	9,887,065	5,054,917	Bush, George H.	4,702,233	Dukakis, Michael S.	129,915	352,684 R	51.1%	47.6%	51.8%	48.2%
1984	9,505,423	5,467,009	Reagan, Ronald*	3,922,519	Mondale, Walter F.	115,895	1,544,490 R	57.5%	41.3%	58.2%	41.8%
1980**	8,587,063	4,524,858	Reagan, Ronald	3,083,661	Carter, Jimmy*	978,544	1,441,197 R	52.7%	35.9%	59.5%	40.5%
1976	7,867,117	3,882,244	Ford, Gerald R.*	3,742,284	Carter, Jimmy	242,589	139,960 R	49.3%	47.6%	50.9%	49.1%
1972	8,367,862	4,602,096	Nixon, Richard M.*	3,475,847	McGovern, George S.	289,919	1,126,249 R	55.0%	41.5%	57.0%	43.0%
1968**	7,251,587	3,467,664	Nixon, Richard M.	3,244,318	Humphrey, Hubert Horatio Jr.	539,605	223,346 R	47.8%	44.7%	51.7%	48.3%
1964	7,057,586	2,879,108	Goldwater, Barry M. Sr.	4,171,877	Johnson, Lyndon B.*	6,601	1,292,769 D	40.8%	59.1%	40.8%	59.2%
1960	6,506,578	3,259,722	Nixon, Richard M.	3,224,099	Kennedy, John F.	22,757	35,623 R	50.1%	49.6%	50.3%	49.7%
1956	5,466,355	3,027,668	Eisenhower, Dwight D.*	2,420,135	Stevenson, Adlai E. II	18,552	607,533 R	55.4%	44.3%	55.6%	44.4%
1952	5,141,849	2,897,310	Eisenhower, Dwight D.	2,197,548	Stevenson, Adlai E. II	46,991	699,762 R	56.3%	42.7%	56.9%	43.1%
1948	4,021,538	1,895,269	Dewey, Thomas E.	1,913,134	Truman, Harry S.*	213,135	17,865 D	47.1%	47.6%	49.8%	50.2%

Note: An asterisk (*) denotes incumbent. **In past elections, the other vote included: 2016 - 478,500 Libertarian (Gary Johnson); 2000 - 418,707 Green (Ralph Nader); 1996 - 697,847 Reform (Ross Perot); 1992 - 2,296,006 Independent (Perot); 1980 - 739,833 Independent (John Anderson); 1968 - 487,270 American Independent (George Wallace).

CALIFORNIA

POSTWAR VOTE FOR GOVERNOR

		Republican		Democratic				Percentage			
								Total Vote		Major Vote	
Year	Total Vote	Vote	Candidate	Vote	Candidate	Other Vote	Rep.-Dem. Plurality	Rep.	Dem.	Rep.	Dem.
2018	12,464,235	4,742,825	Cox, John H.	7,721,410	Newsom, Gavin		2,978,585 D	38.1%	61.9%	38.1%	61.9%
2014	7,317,581	2,929,213	Kashkari, Neel	4,388,368	Brown, Edmund G. Jr.*		1,459,155 D	40.0%	60.0%	40.0%	60.0%
2010	10,095,185	4,127,391	Whitman, Meg	5,428,149	Brown, Edmund G. Jr.	539,645	1,300,758 D	40.9%	53.8%	43.2%	56.8%
2006	8,679,416	4,850,157	Schwarzenegger, Arnold*	3,376,732	Angelides, Phil	452,527	1,473,425 R	55.9%	38.9%	59.0%	41.0%
2003S**	8,657,915	4,206,284	Schwarzenegger, Arnold	2,724,874	Bustamante, Cruz	1,726,757	1,481,410 R	48.6%	31.5%	60.7%	39.3%
2002	7,476,311	3,169,801	Simon, Bill	3,533,490	Davis, Gray*	773,020	363,689 D	42.4%	47.3%	47.3%	52.7%
1998	8,385,196	3,218,030	Lungren, Dan	4,860,702	Davis, Gray	306,464	1,642,672 D	38.4%	58.0%	39.8%	60.2%
1994	8,665,375	4,781,766	Wilson, Pete*	3,519,799	Brown, Kathleen	363,810	1,261,967 R	55.2%	40.6%	57.6%	42.4%
1990	7,699,467	3,791,904	Wilson, Pete	3,525,197	Feinstein, Dianne	382,366	266,707 R	49.2%	45.8%	51.8%	48.2%
1986	7,443,551	4,506,601	Deukmejian, George*	2,781,714	Bradley, Tom	155,236	1,724,887 R	60.5%	37.4%	61.8%	38.2%
1982	7,876,698	3,881,014	Deukmejian, George	3,787,669	Bradley, Tom	208,015	93,345 R	49.3%	48.1%	50.6%	49.4%
1978	6,922,378	2,526,534	Younger, Evelle J.	3,878,812	Brown, Edmund G. Jr.*	517,032	1,352,278 D	36.5%	56.0%	39.4%	60.6%
1974	6,248,070	2,952,954	Flournoy, Houston I.	3,131,648	Brown, Edmund G. Jr.	163,468	178,694 D	47.3%	50.1%	48.5%	51.5%
1970	6,510,272	3,439,664	Reagan, Ronald*	2,938,807	Unruh, Jess	131,801	500,857 R	52.8%	45.1%	53.9%	46.1%
1966	6,503,445	3,742,913	Reagan, Ronald	2,749,174	Brown, Edmund G.*	11,358	993,739 R	57.6%	42.3%	57.7%	42.3%
1962	5,853,270	2,740,351	Nixon, Richard M.	3,037,109	Brown, Edmund G.*	75,810	296,758 D	46.8%	51.9%	47.4%	52.6%
1958	5,255,777	2,110,911	Knowland, William F.	3,140,076	Brown, Edmund G.	4,790	1,029,165 D	40.2%	59.7%	40.2%	59.8%
1954	4,030,368	2,290,519	Knight, Goodwin J.*	1,739,368	Graves, Richard Perrin	481	551,151 R	56.8%	43.2%	56.8%	43.2%
1950	3,796,090	2,461,754	Warren, Earl*	1,333,856	Roosevelt, James	480	1,127,898 R	64.8%	35.1%	64.9%	35.1%
1946**	2,738,978	2,344,542	Warren, Earl*			394,436	2,344,542 R	85.6%		100.0%	

Note: An asterisk (*) denotes incumbent. **The 2003 election was for a short term to fill a vacancy created by voter approval of a measure to remove Governor Gray Davis (D) from office. The measure passed by a vote of 4,976,274 votes (55.4 percent) for recall to 4,007,783 (44.6 percent) against recall. In the same election, more than 100 candidates ran for the right to succeed Davis. No primary election was held to cull the field. All candidates, regardless of party, ran together on the same ballot. The winner, Arnold Schwarzenegger, is listed as the Republican candidate. The leading Democratic vote-getter, Cruz Bustamante, is listed as the Democratic candidate. The percentages given are for Schwarzenegger and Bustamante. The leading "Other" candidate was Republican Tom McClintock, who received 1,161,287 votes (13.4 percent of the total). The percentage columns are for Schwarzenegger and Bustamante and do not include additional candidates. In 1946 the Republican candidate won both major party nominations.

POSTWAR VOTE FOR SENATOR

		Republican		Democratic				Percentage			
								Total Vote		Major Vote	
Year	Total Vote	Vote	Candidate	Vote	Candidate	Other Vote	Rep.-Dem. Plurality	Rep.	Dem.	Rep.	Dem.
2018**	11,113,364			6,019,422	Feinstein, Dianne*		11,113,364 D		54.2%		100.0%
2016**	12,244,170			7,542,753	Harris, Kamala D.		12,244,170 D		61.6%		100.0%
2012	12,578,511	4,713,887	Emken, Elizabeth	7,864,624	Feinstein, Dianne*		3,150,737 D	37.5%	62.5%	37.5%	62.5%
2010	9,999,860	4,217,386	Fiorina, Carly	5,218,137	Boxer, Barbara*	564,337	1,000,751 D	42.2%	52.2%	44.7%	55.3%
2006	8,541,476	2,990,822	Mountjoy, Dick	5,076,289	Feinstein, Dianne*	474,365	2,085,467 D	35.0%	59.4%	37.1%	62.9%
2004	12,053,295	4,555,922	Jones, Bill	6,955,728	Boxer, Barbara*	541,645	2,399,806 D	37.8%	57.7%	39.6%	60.4%
2000	10,623,614	3,886,853	Campbell, Tom	5,932,522	Feinstein, Dianne*	804,239	2,045,669 D	36.6%	55.8%	39.6%	60.4%
1998	8,314,953	3,576,351	Fong, Matt	4,411,705	Boxer, Barbara*	326,897	835,354 D	43.0%	53.1%	44.8%	55.2%
1994	8,514,089	3,817,025	Huffington, Michael	3,979,152	Feinstein, Dianne*	717,912	162,127 D	44.8%	46.7%	49.0%	51.0%
1992**	10,799,703	4,644,182	Sargent, Claire	5,173,467	Boxer, Barbara	982,054	529,285 D	43.0%	47.9%	47.3%	52.7%
1992S	10,782,743	4,093,501	Seymour, John*	5,853,651	Feinstein, Dianne	835,591	1,760,150 D	38.0%	54.3%	41.2%	58.8%
1988	9,743,598	5,143,409	Wilson, Pete*	4,287,253	McCarthy, Leo T.	312,936	856,156 R	52.8%	44.0%	54.5%	45.5%
1986	7,398,522	3,541,804	Zschau, Ed	3,646,672	Cranston, Alan*	210,046	104,868 D	47.9%	49.3%	49.3%	50.7%
1982	7,805,538	4,022,565	Wilson, Pete	3,494,968	Brown, Edmund G. Jr.	288,005	527,597 R	51.5%	44.8%	53.5%	46.5%
1980	8,327,481	3,093,426	Gann, Paul	4,705,399	Cranston, Alan*	528,656	1,611,973 D	37.1%	56.5%	39.7%	60.3%
1976	7,472,268	3,748,973	Hayakawa, S. I.	3,502,862	Tunney, John V.*	220,433	246,111 R	50.2%	46.9%	51.7%	48.3%
1974	6,102,432	2,210,267	Richardson, H. L.	3,693,160	Cranston, Alan*	199,005	1,482,893 D	36.2%	60.5%	37.4%	62.6%
1970	6,492,157	2,877,617	Murphy, George*	3,496,558	Tunney, John V.	117,982	618,941 D	44.3%	53.9%	45.1%	54.9%
1968	7,102,465	3,329,148	Rafferty, Max	3,680,352	Cranston, Alan	92,965	351,204 D	46.9%	51.8%	47.5%	52.5%
1964	7,041,821	3,628,555	Murphy, George	3,411,912	Salinger, Pierre*	1,354	216,643 R	51.5%	48.5%	51.5%	48.5%
1962	5,647,952	3,180,483	Kuchel, Thomas H.*	2,452,839	Richards, Richard	14,630	727,644 R	56.3%	43.4%	56.5%	43.5%
1958	5,135,221	2,204,337	Knight, Goodwin J.	2,927,693	Engle, Clair	3,191	723,356 D	42.9%	57.0%	43.0%	57.0%
1956	5,361,467	2,892,918	Kuchel, Thomas H.*	2,445,816	Richards, Richard	22,733	447,102 R	54.0%	45.6%	54.2%	45.8%
1954S**	3,929,668	2,090,836	Kuchel, Thomas H.*	1,788,071	Yorty, Samuel W.	50,761	302,765 R	53.2%	45.5%	53.9%	46.1%
1952**	4,542,548	3,982,448	Knowland, William F.*			560,100	3,982,448 R	87.7%		100.0%	
1950	3,686,315	2,183,454	Nixon, Richard M.	1,502,507	Douglas, Helen Gahagan	354	680,947 R	59.2%	40.8%	59.2%	40.8%
1946	2,639,465	1,428,067	Knowland, William F.*	1,167,161	Rogers, Will Jr.	44,237	260,906 R	54.1%	44.2%	55.0%	45.0%

Note: An asterisk (*) denotes incumbent. **In 2018, California's jungle primary sent two Democrats to the general election, with the results as follows: 6,019,422 Dianne Feinstein (54.2%); 5,093,942 Kevin DeLeon (45.8%). Feinstein won by a plurality of 925,480 votes. In 2016, California's jungle primary sent two Democrats to the general election, with the results as follows: 7,542,753 Kamala D. Harris (61.6%); 4,701,417 Loretta Sanchez (38.4%). Harris won by a plurality of 2,841,336 votes. In past elections, the other vote included: 1952 - 542,270 Progressive (Reuben W. Borough), who finished second. The Republican candidate that year (William F. Knowland) won both major party nominations. The 1954 election was for a short term to fill a vacancy, as was one of the 1992 elections.

CALIFORNIA

GOVERNOR 2018

							Percentage			
							Total Vote		Major Vote	
2010 Census Population	County	Total Vote	Republican (Cox)	Democratic (Newsom)	Other	Rep.-Dem. Plurality	Rep.	Dem.	Rep.	Dem.
1,510,271	ALAMEDA	574,235	111,677	462,558		350,881 D	19.4%	80.6%	19.4%	80.6%
1,175	ALPINE	615	229	386		157 D	37.2%	62.8%	37.2%	62.8%
38,091	AMADOR	17,593	11,356	6,237		5,119 R	64.5%	35.5%	64.5%	35.5%
220,000	BUTTE	88,726	47,226	41,500		5,726 R	53.2%	46.8%	53.2%	46.8%
45,578	CALAVERAS	21,610	13,845	7,765		6,080 R	64.1%	35.9%	64.1%	35.9%
21,419	COLUSA	5,763	3,764	1,999		1,765 R	65.3%	34.7%	65.3%	34.7%
1,049,025	CONTRA COSTA	416,150	132,345	283,805		151,460 D	31.8%	68.2%	31.8%	68.2%
28,610	DEL NORTE	8,328	4,887	3,441		1,446 R	58.7%	41.3%	58.7%	41.3%
181,058	EL DORADO	89,437	53,140	36,297		16,843 R	59.4%	40.6%	59.4%	40.6%
930,450	FRESNO	253,306	128,974	124,332		4,642 R	50.9%	49.1%	50.9%	49.1%
28,122	GLENN	8,332	5,908	2,424		3,484 R	70.9%	29.1%	70.9%	29.1%
134,623	HUMBOLDT	51,873	18,418	33,455		15,037 D	35.5%	64.5%	35.5%	64.5%
174,528	IMPERIAL	33,358	12,785	20,573		7,788 D	38.3%	61.7%	38.3%	61.7%
18,546	INYO	7,262	4,018	3,244		774 R	55.3%	44.7%	55.3%	44.7%
839,631	KERN	203,377	119,870	83,507		36,363 R	58.9%	41.1%	58.9%	41.1%

CALIFORNIA

GOVERNOR 2018

2010 Census Population	County	Total Vote	Republican (Cox)	Democratic (Newsom)	Other	Rep.-Dem. Plurality	Percentage Total Vote Rep.	Total Vote Dem.	Major Vote Rep.	Major Vote Dem.
152,982	KINGS	30,251	17,976	12,275		5,701 R	59.4%	40.6%	59.4%	40.6%
64,665	LAKE	21,149	10,280	10,869		589 D	48.6%	51.4%	48.6%	51.4%
34,895	LASSEN	9,016	6,973	2,043		4,930 R	77.3%	22.7%	77.3%	22.7%
9,818,605	LOS ANGELES	2,941,101	826,402	2,114,699		1,288,297 D	28.1%	71.9%	28.1%	71.9%
150,865	MADERA	38,525	23,488	15,037		8,451 R	61.0%	39.0%	61.0%	39.0%
252,409	MARIN	130,421	26,750	103,671		76,921 D	20.5%	79.5%	20.5%	79.5%
18,251	MARIPOSA	8,226	5,043	3,183		1,860 R	61.3%	38.7%	61.3%	38.7%
87,841	MENDOCINO	33,407	11,255	22,152		10,897 D	33.7%	66.3%	33.7%	66.3%
255,793	MERCED	59,207	28,424	30,783		2,359 D	48.0%	52.0%	48.0%	52.0%
9,686	MODOC	3,448	2,628	820		1,808 R	76.2%	23.8%	76.2%	23.8%
14,202	MONO	4,853	2,147	2,706		559 D	44.2%	55.8%	44.2%	55.8%
415,057	MONTEREY	116,164	39,516	76,648		37,132 D	34.0%	66.0%	34.0%	66.0%
136,484	NAPA	56,347	19,834	36,513		16,679 D	35.2%	64.8%	35.2%	64.8%
98,764	NEVADA	52,867	24,882	27,985		3,103 D	47.1%	52.9%	47.1%	52.9%
3,010,232	ORANGE	1,082,998	539,951	543,047		3,096 D	49.9%	50.1%	49.9%	50.1%
348,432	PLACER	175,427	103,157	72,270		30,887 R	58.8%	41.2%	58.8%	41.2%
20,007	PLUMAS	9,240	5,807	3,433		2,374 R	62.8%	37.2%	62.8%	37.2%
2,189,641	RIVERSIDE	642,088	322,243	319,845		2,398 R	50.2%	49.8%	50.2%	49.8%
1,418,788	SACRAMENTO	514,706	212,010	302,696		90,686 D	41.2%	58.8%	41.2%	58.8%
55,269	SAN BENITO	20,089	8,815	11,274		2,459 D	43.9%	56.1%	43.9%	56.1%
2,035,210	SAN BERNARDINO	537,253	260,379	276,874		16,495 D	48.5%	51.5%	48.5%	51.5%
3,095,313	SAN DIEGO	1,157,878	499,532	658,346		158,814 D	43.1%	56.9%	43.1%	56.9%
805,235	SAN FRANCISCO	361,362	49,181	312,181		263,000 D	13.6%	86.4%	13.6%	86.4%
685,306	SAN JOAQUIN	194,440	92,966	101,474		8,508 D	47.8%	52.2%	47.8%	52.2%
269,637	SAN LUIS OBISPO	126,254	61,137	65,117		3,980 D	48.4%	51.6%	48.4%	51.6%
718,451	SAN MATEO	283,524	70,242	213,282		143,040 D	24.8%	75.2%	24.8%	75.2%
423,895	SANTA BARBARA	155,141	61,300	93,841		32,541 D	39.5%	60.5%	39.5%	60.5%
1,781,642	SANTA CLARA	614,549	175,791	438,758		262,967 D	28.6%	71.4%	28.6%	71.4%
262,382	SANTA CRUZ	119,188	27,665	91,523		63,858 D	23.2%	76.8%	23.2%	76.8%
177,223	SHASTA	70,081	49,825	20,256		29,569 R	71.1%	28.9%	71.1%	28.9%
3,240	SIERRA	1,667	1,068	599		469 R	64.1%	35.9%	64.1%	35.9%
44,900	SISKIYOU	18,164	10,946	7,218		3,728 R	60.3%	39.7%	60.3%	39.7%
413,344	SOLANO	146,321	56,627	89,694		33,067 D	38.7%	61.3%	38.7%	61.3%
483,878	SONOMA	210,378	58,338	152,040		93,702 D	27.7%	72.3%	27.7%	72.3%
514,453	STANISLAUS	156,971	79,751	77,220		2,531 R	50.8%	49.2%	50.8%	49.2%
94,737	SUTTER	30,075	18,953	11,122		7,831 R	63.0%	37.0%	63.0%	37.0%
63,463	TEHAMA	20,893	15,137	5,756		9,381 R	72.5%	27.5%	72.5%	27.5%
13,786	TRINITY	5,325	3,075	2,250		825 R	57.7%	42.3%	57.7%	42.3%
442,179	TULARE	99,714	57,012	42,702		14,310 R	57.2%	42.8%	57.2%	42.8%
55,365	TUOLUMNE	23,874	14,580	9,294		5,286 R	61.1%	38.9%	61.1%	38.9%
823,318	VENTURA	309,122	137,393	171,729		34,336 D	44.4%	55.6%	44.4%	55.6%
200,849	YOLO	73,370	23,611	49,759		26,148 D	32.2%	67.8%	32.2%	67.8%
72,155	YUBA	19,196	12,293	6,903		5,390 R	64.0%	36.0%	64.0%	36.0%
37,253,956	*TOTAL*	*12,464,235*	*4,742,825*	*7,721,410*		*2,978,585 D*	*38.1%*	*61.9%*	*38.1%*	*61.9%*

CALIFORNIA

SENATOR 2018

2010 Census Population	County	Total Vote	Democratic (Feinstein)	Democratic (DeLeon)	Plurality	Percentage Feinstein	Percentage DeLeon
1,510,271	ALAMEDA	545,327	318,377	226,950	91,427 F	58.4%	41.6%
1,175	ALPINE	547	267	280	13 D	48.8%	51.2%
38,091	AMADOR	14,079	5,835	8,244	2,409 D	41.4%	58.6%
220,000	BUTTE	75,526	32,418	43,108	10,690 D	42.9%	57.1%
45,578	CALAVERAS	17,388	7,031	10,357	3,326 D	40.4%	59.6%
21,419	COLUSA	4,682	1,643	3,039	1,396 D	35.1%	64.9%
1,049,025	CONTRA COSTA	381,097	222,349	158,748	63,601 F	58.3%	41.7%
28,610	DEL NORTE	6,844	2,590	4,254	1,664 D	37.8%	62.2%
181,058	EL DORADO	72,563	33,772	38,791	5,019 D	46.5%	53.5%
930,450	FRESNO	217,048	103,491	113,557	10,066 D	47.7%	52.3%
28,122	GLENN	6,729	2,341	4,388	2,047 D	34.8%	65.2%
134,623	HUMBOLDT	47,655	21,336	26,319	4,983 D	44.8%	55.2%
174,528	IMPERIAL	30,271	13,121	17,150	4,029 D	43.3%	56.7%
18,546	INYO	5,876	2,344	3,532	1,188 D	39.9%	60.1%
839,631	KERN	166,609	66,628	99,981	33,353 D	40.0%	60.0%
152,982	KINGS	25,347	9,599	15,748	6,149 D	37.9%	62.1%
64,665	LAKE	18,459	8,142	10,317	2,175 D	44.1%	55.9%
34,895	LASSEN	6,818	2,030	4,788	2,758 D	29.8%	70.2%
9,818,605	LOS ANGELES	2,711,211	1,565,167	1,146,044	419,123 F	57.7%	42.3%
150,865	MADERA	32,316	13,284	19,032	5,748 D	41.1%	58.9%
252,409	MARIN	122,957	80,319	42,638	37,681 F	65.3%	34.7%
18,251	MARIPOSA	6,688	2,749	3,939	1,190 D	41.1%	58.9%
87,841	MENDOCINO	30,642	15,113	15,529	416 D	49.3%	50.7%
255,793	MERCED	51,644	23,659	27,985	4,326 D	45.8%	54.2%
9,686	MODOC	2,618	751	1,867	1,116 D	28.7%	71.3%
14,202	MONO	4,198	2,001	2,197	196 D	47.7%	52.3%
415,057	MONTEREY	106,882	56,320	50,562	5,758 F	52.7%	47.3%
136,484	NAPA	51,194	27,904	23,290	4,614 F	54.5%	45.5%
98,764	NEVADA	46,109	22,198	23,911	1,713 D	48.1%	51.9%
3,010,232	ORANGE	922,492	501,678	420,814	80,864 F	54.4%	45.6%
348,432	PLACER	143,311	66,578	76,733	10,155 D	46.5%	53.5%
20,007	PLUMAS	7,243	2,815	4,428	1,613 D	38.9%	61.1%
2,189,641	RIVERSIDE	547,976	269,567	278,409	8,842 D	49.2%	50.8%
1,418,788	SACRAMENTO	455,520	241,571	213,949	27,622 F	53.0%	47.0%
55,269	SAN BENITO	17,978	8,607	9,371	764 D	47.9%	52.1%
2,035,210	SAN BERNARDINO	466,463	233,103	233,360	257 D	50.0%	50.0%
3,095,313	SAN DIEGO	995,192	526,628	468,564	58,064 F	52.9%	47.1%
805,235	SAN FRANCISCO	352,121	226,167	125,954	100,213 F	64.2%	35.8%
685,306	SAN JOAQUIN	171,439	79,088	92,351	13,263 D	46.1%	53.9%
269,637	SAN LUIS OBISPO	107,269	53,242	54,027	785 D	49.6%	50.4%
718,451	SAN MATEO	267,815	168,679	99,136	69,543 F	63.0%	37.0%
423,895	SANTA BARBARA	136,491	75,274	61,217	14,057 F	55.1%	44.9%
1,781,642	SANTA CLARA	568,508	339,866	228,642	111,224 F	59.8%	40.2%
262,382	SANTA CRUZ	111,594	64,178	47,416	16,762 F	57.5%	42.5%
177,223	SHASTA	55,624	19,397	36,227	16,830 D	34.9%	65.1%
3,240	SIERRA	1,314	506	808	302 D	38.5%	61.5%
44,900	SISKIYOU	14,702	5,772	8,930	3,158 D	39.3%	60.7%
413,344	SOLANO	132,680	70,174	62,506	7,668 F	52.9%	47.1%
483,878	SONOMA	193,692	108,472	85,220	23,252 F	56.0%	44.0%
514,453	STANISLAUS	136,099	58,375	77,724	19,349 D	42.9%	57.1%
94,737	SUTTER	24,667	10,501	14,166	3,665 D	42.6%	57.4%
63,463	TEHAMA	16,688	5,435	11,253	5,818 D	32.6%	67.4%
13,786	TRINITY	4,584	1,746	2,838	1,092 D	38.1%	61.9%
442,179	TULARE	82,770	33,005	49,765	16,760 D	39.9%	60.1%
55,365	TUOLUMNE	19,054	7,783	11,271	3,488 D	40.8%	59.2%
823,318	VENTURA	267,242	137,141	130,101	7,040 F	51.3%	48.7%
200,849	YOLO	67,622	35,071	32,551	2,520 F	51.9%	48.1%
72,155	YUBA	15,890	6,224	9,666	3,442 D	39.2%	60.8%
37,253,956	*TOTAL*	*11,113,364*	*6,019,422*	*5,093,942*	*925,480 F*	*54.2%*	*45.8%*

Note: In California's jungle primary, the top two vote recipients, Dianne Feinstein and Kevin DeLeon, were both Democrats.

CALIFORNIA

HOUSE OF REPRESENTATIVES

CD	Year	Total Vote	Republican Vote	Republican Candidate	Democratic Vote	Democratic Candidate	Other Vote	Rep.-Dem. Plurality	Percentage Total Vote Rep.	Percentage Total Vote Dem.	Percentage Major Vote Rep.	Percentage Major Vote Dem.
1	2018	291,594	160,046	LAMALFA, DOUG*	131,548	DENNEY, AUDREY		28,498 R	54.9%	45.1%	54.9%	45.1%
1	2016	314,036	185,448	LAMALFA, DOUG*	128,588	REED, JIM		56,860 R	59.1%	40.9%	59.1%	40.9%
1	2014	216,372	132,052	LAMALFA, DOUG*	84,320	HALL, HEIDI		47,732 R	61.0%	39.0%	61.0%	39.0%
1	2012	294,213	168,827	LAMALFA, DOUG	125,386	REED, JIM		43,441 R	57.4%	42.6%	57.4%	42.6%
2	2018	315,657	72,576	MENSING, DALE K.	243,081	HUFFMAN, JARED*		170,505 D	23.0%	77.0%	23.0%	77.0%
2	2016	330,766	76,572	MENSING, DALE K.	254,194	HUFFMAN, JARED*		177,622 D	23.1%	76.9%	23.1%	76.9%
2	2014	217,524	54,400	MENSING, DALE K.	163,124	HUFFMAN, JARED*		108,724 D	25.0%	75.0%	25.0%	75.0%
2	2012	317,526	91,310	ROBERTS, DANIEL W.	226,216	HUFFMAN, JARED		134,906 D	28.8%	71.2%	28.8%	71.2%
3	2018	232,251	97,376	SCHAUPP, CHARLES	134,875	GARAMENDI, JOHN*		37,499 D	41.9%	58.1%	41.9%	58.1%
3	2016	256,966	104,453	CLEEK, N. EUGENE	152,513	GARAMENDI, JOHN*		48,060 D	40.6%	59.4%	40.6%	59.4%
3	2014	150,260	71,036	LOGUE, DAN	79,224	GARAMENDI, JOHN*		8,188 D	47.3%	52.7%	47.3%	52.7%
3	2012	233,968	107,086	VANN, KIM	126,882	GARAMENDI, JOHN*		19,796 D	45.8%	54.2%	45.8%	54.2%
4	2018	340,654	184,401	MCCLINTOCK, TOM*	156,253	MORSE, JESSICA		28,148 R	54.1%	45.9%	54.1%	45.9%
4	2016	350,978	220,133	MCCLINTOCK, TOM*	130,845	DERLET, ROBERT W.		89,288 R	62.7%	37.3%	62.7%	37.3%
4	2014	211,134	126,784	MCCLINTOCK, TOM*			84,350	126,784 R	60.0%		100.0%	
4	2012	323,688	197,803	MCCLINTOCK, TOM*	125,885	UPPAL, JACK		71,918 R	61.1%	38.9%	61.1%	38.9%
5	2018	261,018			205,860	THOMPSON, MIKE*	55,158	205,860 D		78.9%		100.0%
5	2016	292,091	67,565	SANTAMARIA, CARLOS	224,526	THOMPSON, MIKE*		156,961 D	23.1%	76.9%	23.1%	76.9%
5	2014	171,148			129,613	THOMPSON, MIKE*	41,535	129,613 D		75.7%		100.0%
5	2012	272,417	69,545	LOFTIN, RANDY	202,872	THOMPSON, MIKE*		133,327 D	25.5%	74.5%	25.5%	74.5%
6**	2018	201,939			162,411	MATSUI, DORIS*	39,528	162,411 D		80.4%		100.0%
6	2016	235,413	57,848	EVANS, ROBERT H. JR.	177,565	MATSUI, DORIS*		119,717 D	24.6%	75.4%	24.6%	75.4%
6	2014	133,456	36,448	MCCRAY, JOSEPH SR.	97,008	MATSUI, DORIS*		60,560 D	27.3%	72.7%	27.3%	72.7%
6	2012	214,073	53,406	MCCRAY, JOSEPH SR.	160,667	MATSUI, DORIS*		107,261 D	24.9%	75.1%	24.9%	75.1%
7	2018	281,617	126,601	GRANT, ANDREW	155,016	BERA, AMI*		28,415 D	45.0%	55.0%	45.0%	55.0%
7	2016	297,301	145,168	JONES, SCOTT R.	152,133	BERA, AMI*		6,965 D	48.8%	51.2%	48.8%	51.2%
7	2014	183,587	91,066	OSE, DOUG	92,521	BERA, AMI*		1,455 D	49.6%	50.4%	49.6%	50.4%
7	2012	273,291	132,050	LUNGREN, DAN*	141,241	BERA, AMI		9,191 D	48.3%	51.7%	48.3%	51.7%
8**	2018	170,785	102,415	COOK, PAUL*			68,370	102,415 R	60.0%		100.0%	
8	2016	220,007	136,972	COOK, PAUL*	83,035	RAMIREZ, RITA		53,937 R	62.3%	37.7%	62.3%	37.7%
8	2014	114,536	77,480	COOK, PAUL*	37,056	CONAWAY, ROBERT DEAN "BOB"		40,424 R	67.6%	32.4%	67.6%	32.4%
8	2012	179,644	103,093	COOK, PAUL			76,551	103,093 R	57.4%		100.0%	
9	2018	200,763	87,349	LIVENGOOD, MARLA	113,414	MCNERNEY, JERRY*		26,065 D	43.5%	56.5%	43.5%	56.5%
9	2016	232,155	98,992	AMADOR, ANTONIO C. "TONY"	133,163	MCNERNEY, JERRY*		34,171 D	42.6%	57.4%	42.6%	57.4%
9	2014	121,204	57,729	AMADOR, ANTONIO C. "TONY"	63,475	MCNERNEY, JERRY*		5,746 D	47.6%	52.4%	47.6%	52.4%
9	2012	213,077	94,704	GILL, RICKY	118,373	MCNERNEY, JERRY*		23,669 D	44.4%	55.6%	44.4%	55.6%
10	2018	221,900	105,955	DENHAM, JEFF*	115,945	HARDER, JOSH		9,990 D	47.7%	52.3%	47.7%	52.3%
10	2016	241,141	124,671	DENHAM, JEFF*	116,470	EGGMAN, MICHAEL		8,201 R	51.7%	48.3%	51.7%	48.3%
10	2014	125,705	70,582	DENHAM, JEFF*	55,123	EGGMAN, MICHAEL		15,459 R	56.1%	43.9%	56.1%	43.9%
10	2012	209,199	110,265	DENHAM, JEFF*	98,934	HERNANDEZ, JOSE		11,331 R	52.7%	47.3%	52.7%	47.3%
11	2018	275,681	71,312	FITZGERALD, JOHN	204,369	DESAULNIER, MARK*		133,057 D	25.9%	74.1%	25.9%	74.1%
11	2016	298,209	83,341	PETERSEN, ROGER ALLEN	214,868	DESAULNIER, MARK*		131,527 D	27.9%	72.1%	27.9%	72.1%
11	2014	174,662	57,160	PHAN-QUANG, TUE	117,502	DESAULNIER, MARK		60,342 D	32.7%	67.3%	32.7%	67.3%
11	2012	287,879	87,136	FULLER, VIRGINIA	200,743	MILLER, GEORGE*		113,607 D	30.3%	69.7%	30.3%	69.7%
12	2018	317,072	41,780	REMMER, LISA	275,292	PELOSI, NANCY*		233,512 D	13.2%	86.8%	13.2%	86.8%
12	2016	338,845			274,035	PELOSI, NANCY*	64,810	274,035 D		80.9%		100.0%
12	2014	192,264	32,197	DENNIS, JOHN	160,067	PELOSI, NANCY*		127,870 D	16.7%	83.3%	16.7%	83.3%
12	2012	298,187	44,478	DENNIS, JOHN	253,709	PELOSI, NANCY*		209,231 D	14.9%	85.1%	14.9%	85.1%
13	2018	294,837			260,580	LEE, BARBARA*	34,257	260,580 D		88.4%		100.0%
13	2016	322,871	29,754	CARO, SUE	293,117	LEE, BARBARA*		263,363 D	9.2%	90.8%	9.2%	90.8%
13	2014	190,431	21,940	SUNDEEN, DAKIN	168,491	LEE, BARBARA*		146,551 D	11.5%	88.5%	11.5%	88.5%
13	2012	288,582			250,436	LEE, BARBARA*	38,146	250,436 D		86.8%		100.0%
14	2018	266,823	55,439	OSMENA, CRISTINA	211,384	SPEIER, JACKIE*		155,945 D	20.8%	79.2%	20.8%	79.2%
14	2016	286,447	54,817	CARDENAS, ANGEL	231,630	SPEIER, JACKIE*		176,813 D	19.1%	80.9%	19.1%	80.9%
14	2014	149,146	34,757	CHEW, ROBIN	114,389	SPEIER, JACKIE*		79,632 D	23.3%	76.7%	23.3%	76.7%
14	2012	258,283	54,455	BACIGALUPI, DEBORAH "DEBBIE"	203,828	SPEIER, JACKIE*		149,373 D	21.1%	78.9%	21.1%	78.9%
15	2018	243,929	65,940	PETERS, RUDY JR.	177,989	SWALWELL, ERIC*		112,049 D	27.0%	73.0%	27.0%	73.0%
15	2016	269,197	70,619	TURNER, DANNY R.	198,578	SWALWELL, ERIC*		127,959 D	26.2%	73.8%	26.2%	73.8%
15	2014	142,906	43,150	BUSSELL, HUGH	99,756	SWALWELL, ERIC*		56,606 D	30.2%	69.8%	30.2%	69.8%
15	2012	231,034			120,388	SWALWELL, ERIC	110,646	120,388 D		52.1%		100.0%

CALIFORNIA

HOUSE OF REPRESENTATIVES

			Republican		Democratic				Percentage			
									Total Vote		Major Vote	
CD	Year	Total Vote	Vote	Candidate	Vote	Candidate	Other Vote	Rep.-Dem. Plurality	Rep.	Dem.	Rep.	Dem.
16	2018	142,959	60,693	HENG, ELIZABETH	82,266	COSTA, JIM*		21,573 D	42.5%	57.5%	42.5%	57.5%
16	2016	167,956	70,483	TACHERRA, JOHNNY M.	97,473	COSTA, JIM*		26,990 D	42.0%	58.0%	42.0%	58.0%
16	2014	91,220	44,943	TACHERRA, JOHNNY M.	46,277	COSTA, JIM*		1,334 D	49.3%	50.7%	49.3%	50.7%
16	2012	147,450	62,801	WHELAN, BRIAN DANIEL	84,649	COSTA, JIM*		21,848 D	42.6%	57.4%	42.6%	57.4%
17	2018	211,162	52,057	COHEN, RONALD “RON”	159,105	KHANNA, RO*		107,048 D	24.7%	75.3%	24.7%	75.3%
17	2016	233,192			142,268	KHANNA, RO	90,924	142,268 D		61.0%		100.0%
17	2014	134,408			69,561	HONDA, MIKE M.*	64,847	69,561 D		51.8%		100.0%
17	2012	216,728	57,336	LI, EVELYN	159,392	HONDA, MIKE M.*		102,056 D	26.5%	73.5%	26.5%	73.5%
18	2018	302,238	77,096	RUSSELL, CHRISTINE	225,142	ESHOO, ANNA G.*		148,046 D	25.5%	74.5%	25.5%	74.5%
18	2016	323,930	93,470	FOX, RICHARD B.	230,460	ESHOO, ANNA G.*		136,990 D	28.9%	71.1%	28.9%	71.1%
18	2014	196,386	63,326	FOX, RICHARD B.	133,060	ESHOO, ANNA G.*		69,734 D	32.2%	67.8%	32.2%	67.8%
18	2012	301,934	89,103	CHAPMAN, DAVE	212,831	ESHOO, ANNA G.*		123,728 D	29.5%	70.5%	29.5%	70.5%
19	2018	220,319	57,823	AGUILERA, JUSTIN JAMES	162,496	LOFGREN, ZOE*		104,673 D	26.2%	73.8%	26.2%	73.8%
19	2016	245,863	64,061	LANCASTER, G. BURT	181,802	LOFGREN, ZOE*		117,741 D	26.1%	73.9%	26.1%	73.9%
19	2014	127,788			85,888	LOFGREN, ZOE*	41,900	85,888 D		67.2%		100.0%
19	2012	221,613	59,313	MURRAY, ROBERT	162,300	LOFGREN, ZOE*		102,987 D	26.8%	73.2%	26.8%	73.2%
20	2018	225,721			183,677	PANETTA, JIMMY*	42,044	183,677 D		81.4%		100.0%
20	2016	255,791	74,811	LUCIUS, CASEY	180,980	PANETTA, JIMMY		106,169 D	29.2%	70.8%	29.2%	70.8%
20	2014	141,044			106,034	FARR, SAM*	35,010	106,034 D		75.2%		100.0%
20	2012	233,562	60,566	TAYLOR, JEFF	172,996	FARR, SAM*		112,430 D	25.9%	74.1%	25.9%	74.1%
21	2018	113,616	56,377	VALADAO, DAVID*	57,239	COX, T.J.		862 D	49.6%	50.4%	49.6%	50.4%
21	2016	132,408	75,126	VALADAO, DAVID*	57,282	HUERTA, EMILIO JESUS		17,844 R	56.7%	43.3%	56.7%	43.3%
21	2014	79,377	45,907	VALADAO, DAVID*	33,470	RENTERIA, AMANDA		12,437 R	57.8%	42.2%	57.8%	42.2%
21	2012	116,283	67,164	VALADAO, DAVID	49,119	HERNANDEZ, JOHN		18,045 R	57.8%	42.2%	57.8%	42.2%
22	2018	222,379	117,243	NUNES, DEVIN*	105,136	JANZ, ANDREW		12,107 R	52.7%	47.3%	52.7%	47.3%
22	2016	234,966	158,755	NUNES, DEVIN*	76,211	CAMPOS, LOUIE J.		82,544 R	67.6%	32.4%	67.6%	32.4%
22	2014	133,342	96,053	NUNES, DEVIN*	37,289	AGUILERA-MARRERO, SUZANNA “SAM”		58,764 R	72.0%	28.0%	72.0%	28.0%
22	2012	213,941	132,386	NUNES, DEVIN*	81,555	LEE, OTTO		50,831 R	61.9%	38.1%	61.9%	38.1%
23	2018	205,774	131,113	MCCARTHY, KEVIN*	74,661	MATTA, TATIANA		56,452 R	63.7%	36.3%	63.7%	36.3%
23	2016	241,584	167,116	MCCARTHY, KEVIN*	74,468	REED, WENDY		92,648 R	69.2%	30.8%	69.2%	30.8%
23	2014	134,043	100,317	MCCARTHY, KEVIN*	33,726	GARCIA, RAUL		66,591 R	74.8%	25.2%	74.8%	25.2%
23	2012	216,003	158,161	MCCARTHY, KEVIN*			57,842	158,161 R	73.2%		100.0%	
24	2018	284,431	117,881	FAREED, JUSTIN	166,550	CARBAJAL, SALUD*		48,669 D	41.4%	58.6%	41.4%	58.6%
24	2016	310,814	144,780	FAREED, JUSTIN	166,034	CARBAJAL, SALUD		21,254 D	46.6%	53.4%	46.6%	53.4%
24	2014	198,794	95,566	MITCHUM, CHRIS	103,228	CAPPS, LOIS*		7,662 D	48.1%	51.9%	48.1%	51.9%
24	2012	284,495	127,746	MALDONADO, ABEL	156,749	CAPPS, LOIS*		29,003 D	44.9%	55.1%	44.9%	55.1%
25	2018	245,022	111,813	KNIGHT, STEVE*	133,209	HILL, KATIE		21,396 D	45.6%	54.4%	45.6%	54.4%
25	2016	261,161	138,755	KNIGHT, STEVE*	122,406	CAFORIO, BRYAN		16,349 R	53.1%	46.9%	53.1%	46.9%
25	2014	114,072	60,847	KNIGHT, STEVE			53,225	60,847 R	53.3%		100.0%	
25	2012	236,575	129,593	MCKEON, HOWARD P. “BUCK”*	106,982	ROGERS, LEE C.		22,611 R	54.8%	45.2%	54.8%	45.2%
26	2018	255,426	97,210	SABATO, ANTONIO JR.	158,216	BROWNLEY, JULIA*		61,006 D	38.1%	61.9%	38.1%	61.9%
26	2016	280,307	111,059	DAGNESSES, RAFAEL	169,248	BROWNLEY, JULIA*		58,189 D	39.6%	60.4%	39.6%	60.4%
26	2014	169,829	82,653	GORELL, JEFF	87,176	BROWNLEY, JULIA*		4,523 D	48.7%	51.3%	48.7%	51.3%
26	2012	263,935	124,863	STRICKLAND, TONY	139,072	BROWNLEY, JULIA		14,209 D	47.3%	52.7%	47.3%	52.7%
27**	2018	202,636			160,504	CHU, JUDY*	42,132	160,504 D		79.2%		100.0%
27	2016	250,632	81,655	ORSWELL, JACK	168,977	CHU, JUDY*		87,322 D	32.6%	67.4%	32.6%	67.4%
27	2014	127,580	51,852	ORSWELL, JACK	75,728	CHU, JUDY*		23,876 D	40.6%	59.4%	40.6%	59.4%
27	2012	241,008	86,817	ORSWELL, JACK	154,191	CHU, JUDY*		67,374 D	36.0%	64.0%	36.0%	64.0%
28	2018	250,934	54,272	NALBANDIAN, JOHNNY	196,662	SCHIFF, ADAM B.*		142,390 D	21.6%	78.4%	21.6%	78.4%
28	2016	270,409	59,526	SOLIS, LENORE	210,883	SCHIFF, ADAM B.*		151,357 D	22.0%	78.0%	22.0%	78.0%
28	2014	120,264			91,996	SCHIFF, ADAM B.*	28,268	91,996 D		76.5%		100.0%
28	2012	246,711	58,008	JENNERJAHN, PHIL	188,703	SCHIFF, ADAM B.*		130,695 D	23.5%	76.5%	23.5%	76.5%
29	2018	154,692	29,995	BERNAL, BENITO BENNY	124,697	CARDENAS, TONY*		94,702 D	19.4%	80.6%	19.4%	80.6%
29	2016	171,824			128,407	CARDENAS, TONY*	43,417	128,407 D		74.7%		100.0%
29	2014	67,141	17,045	LEADER, WILLIAM O'CALLGHAN	50,096	CARDENAS, TONY*		33,051 D	25.4%	74.6%	25.4%	74.6%
29	2012	150,281			111,287	CARDENAS, TONY	38,994	111,287 D		74.1%		100.0%
30	2018	260,993	69,420	REED, MARK	191,573	SHERMAN, BRAD*		122,153 D	26.6%	73.4%	26.6%	73.4%
30	2016	282,604	77,325	REED, MARK	205,279	SHERMAN, BRAD*		127,954 D	27.4%	72.6%	27.4%	72.6%
30	2014	131,883	45,315	REED, MARK	86,568	SHERMAN, BRAD*		41,253 D	34.4%	65.6%	34.4%	65.6%
30	2012	247,851			149,456	SHERMAN, BRAD*	98,395	149,456 D		60.3%		100.0%

CALIFORNIA

HOUSE OF REPRESENTATIVES

			Republican		Democratic				Percentage			
									Total Vote		Major Vote	
CD	Year	Total Vote	Vote	Candidate	Vote	Candidate	Other Vote	Rep.-Dem. Plurality	Rep.	Dem.	Rep.	Dem.
31	2018	187,495	77,352	FLYNN, SEAN	110,143	AGUILAR, PETE*		32,791 D	41.3%	58.7%	41.3%	58.7%
31	2016	215,936	94,866	CHABOT, PAUL	121,070	AGUILAR, PETE*		26,204 D	43.9%	56.1%	43.9%	56.1%
31	2014	99,784	48,162	CHABOT, PAUL	51,622	AGUILAR, PETE		3,460 D	48.3%	51.7%	48.3%	51.7%
31	2012	161,219	88,964	MILLER, GARY G.*			72,255	88,964 R	55.2%		100.0%	
32	2018	177,031	55,272	SCOTT, JOSHUA M.	121,759	NAPOLITANO, GRACE FLORES*		66,487 D	31.2%	68.8%	31.2%	68.8%
32	2016	186,646			114,926	NAPOLITANO, GRACE FLORES*	71,720	114,926 D		61.6%		100.0%
32	2014	84,406	34,053	ALAS, ARTURO "ART"	50,353	NAPOLITANO, GRACE FLORES*		16,300 D	40.3%	59.7%	40.3%	59.7%
32	2012	190,111	65,208	MILLER, DAVID L	124,903	NAPOLITANO, GRACE FLORES*		59,695 D	34.3%	65.7%	34.3%	65.7%
33	2018	312,860	93,769	WRIGHT, KENNETH W.	219,091	LIEU, TED W.*		125,322 D	30.0%	70.0%	30.0%	70.0%
33	2016	330,219	110,822	WRIGHT, KENNETH W.	219,397	LIEU, TED W.*		108,575 D	33.6%	66.4%	33.6%	66.4%
33	2014	183,031	74,700	CARR, ELAN S.	108,331	LIEU, TED W.		33,631 D	40.8%	59.2%	40.8%	59.2%
33	2012	318,520			171,860	WAXMAN, HENRY A.*	146,660	171,860 D		54.0%		100.0%
34	2018	151,906			110,195	GOMEZ, JIMMY*	41,711	110,195 D		72.5%		100.0%
34	2016	159,156			122,842	BECERRA, XAVIER*	36,314	122,842 D		77.2%		100.0%
34	2014	61,621			44,697	BECERRA, XAVIER*	16,924	44,697 D		72.5%		100.0%
34	2012	140,590	20,223	SMITH, STEPHEN	120,367	BECERRA, XAVIER*		100,144 D	14.4%	85.6%	14.4%	85.6%
35	2018	149,024	45,604	VALIENTE, CHRISTIAN LEONEL	103,420	TORRES, NORMA*		57,816 D	30.6%	69.4%	30.6%	69.4%
35	2016	171,353	47,309	FISCHELLA, TYLER	124,044	TORRES, NORMA*		76,735 D	27.6%	72.4%	27.6%	72.4%
35	2014	62,475			39,502	TORRES, NORMA	22,973	39,502 D		63.2%		100.0%
35	2012	142,680			79,698	MCLEOD, GLORIA NEGRETE	62,982	79,698 D		55.9%		100.0%
36	2018	207,008	84,839	PELZER, KIMBERLIN	122,169	RUIZ, RAUL*		37,330 D	41.0%	59.0%	41.0%	59.0%
36	2016	232,617	88,269	STONE, JEFF	144,348	RUIZ, RAUL*		56,079 D	37.9%	62.1%	37.9%	62.1%
36	2014	134,139	61,457	NESTANDE, BRIAN	72,682	RUIZ, RAUL*		11,225 D	45.8%	54.2%	45.8%	54.2%
36	2012	208,142	97,953	BONO MACK, MARY*	110,189	RUIZ, RAUL		12,236 D	47.1%	52.9%	47.1%	52.9%
37	2018	236,378	25,823	BASSILIAN, RON	210,555	BASS, KAREN*		184,732 D	10.9%	89.1%	10.9%	89.1%
37	2016	237,272			192,490	BASS, KAREN*	44,782	192,490 D		81.1%		100.0%
37	2014	114,838	18,051	KING, R. ADAM	96,787	BASS, KAREN*		78,736 D	15.7%	84.3%	15.7%	84.3%
37	2012	239,580	32,541	OSBORNE, MORGAN	207,039	BASS, KAREN*		174,498 D	13.6%	86.4%	13.6%	86.4%
38	2018	202,156	62,968	DOWNING, RYAN	139,188	SANCHEZ, LINDA*		76,220 D	31.1%	68.9%	31.1%	68.9%
38	2016	232,114	68,524	DOWNING, RYAN	163,590	SANCHEZ, LINDA*		95,066 D	29.5%	70.5%	29.5%	70.5%
38	2014	98,480	40,288	CAMPOS, BENJAMIN	58,192	SANCHEZ, LINDA*		17,904 D	40.9%	59.1%	40.9%	59.1%
38	2012	215,087	69,807	CAMPOS, BENJAMIN	145,280	SANCHEZ, LINDA*		75,473 D	32.5%	67.5%	32.5%	67.5%
39	2018	244,393	118,391	KIM, YOUNG	126,002	CISNEROS, GIL		7,611 D	48.4%	51.6%	48.4%	51.6%
39	2016	263,456	150,777	ROYCE, ED*	112,679	MURDOCK, BRETT		38,098 R	57.2%	42.8%	57.2%	42.8%
39	2014	133,225	91,319	ROYCE, ED*	41,906	ANDERSON, PETER		49,413 R	68.5%	31.5%	68.5%	31.5%
39	2012	251,967	145,607	ROYCE, ED*	106,360	CHEN, JAY		39,247 R	57.8%	42.2%	57.8%	42.2%
40	2018	121,449			93,938	ROYBAL-ALLARD, LUCILLE*	27,511	93,938 D		77.3%		100.0%
40	2016	149,297			106,554	ROYBAL-ALLARD, LUCILLE*	42,743	106,554 D		71.4%		100.0%
40	2014	49,379			30,208	ROYBAL-ALLARD, LUCILLE*	19,171	30,208 D		61.2%		100.0%
40	2012	125,553			73,940	ROYBAL-ALLARD, LUCILLE*	51,613	73,940 D		58.9%		100.0%
41	2018	166,248	58,021	SMITH, AJA	108,227	TAKANO, MARK A.*		50,206 D	34.9%	65.1%	34.9%	65.1%
41	2016	197,323	69,159	SHEPHERD, DOUG	128,164	TAKANO, MARK A.*		59,005 D	35.0%	65.0%	35.0%	65.0%
41	2014	82,884	35,936	ADAMS, STEVE	46,948	TAKANO, MARK A.*		11,012 D	43.4%	56.6%	43.4%	56.6%
41	2012	175,652	72,074	TAVAGLIONE, JOHN	103,578	TAKANO, MARK A.		31,504 D	41.0%	59.0%	41.0%	59.0%
42	2018	231,932	131,040	CALVERT, KEN*	100,892	PEACOCK, JULIA		30,148 R	56.5%	43.5%	56.5%	43.5%
42	2016	254,236	149,547	CALVERT, KEN*	104,689	SHERIDAN, TIM		44,858 R	58.8%	41.2%	58.8%	41.2%
42	2014	113,390	74,540	CALVERT, KEN*	38,850	SHERIDAN, TIM		35,690 R	65.7%	34.3%	65.7%	34.3%
42	2012	214,947	130,245	CALVERT, KEN*	84,702	WILLIAMSON, MICHAEL		45,543 R	60.6%	39.4%	60.6%	39.4%
43	2018	196,052	43,780	NAVARRO, OMAR	152,272	WATERS, MAXINE*		108,492 D	22.3%	77.7%	22.3%	77.7%
43	2016	219,516	52,499	NAVARRO, OMAR	167,017	WATERS, MAXINE*		114,518 D	23.9%	76.1%	23.9%	76.1%
43	2014	98,202	28,521	WOOD JR., JOHN	69,681	WATERS, MAXINE*		41,160 D	29.0%	71.0%	29.0%	71.0%
43	2012	200,894			143,123	WATERS, MAXINE*	57,771	143,123 D		71.2%		100.0%
44**	2018	143,322			97,944	BARRAGAN, NANETTE DIAZ*	45,378	97,944 D		68.3%		100.0%
44	2016	178,413			93,124	BARRAGAN, NANETTE DIAZ	85,289	93,124 D		52.2%		100.0%
44	2014	68,862			59,670	HAHN, JANICE*	9,192	59,670 D		86.7%		100.0%
44	2012	165,898			99,909	HAHN, JANICE*	65,989	99,909 D		60.2%		100.0%
45	2018	305,289	146,383	WALTERS, MIMI*	158,906	PORTER, KATIE		12,523 D	47.9%	52.1%	47.9%	52.1%
45	2016	311,849	182,618	WALTERS, MIMI*	129,231	VARASTEH, RON		53,387 R	58.6%	41.4%	58.6%	41.4%
45	2014	162,902	106,083	WALTERS, MIMI	56,819	LEAVENS, DREW		49,264 R	65.1%	34.9%	65.1%	34.9%
45	2012	293,231	171,417	CAMPBELL, JOHN*	121,814	KANG, SUKHEE		49,603 R	58.5%	41.5%	58.5%	41.5%

CALIFORNIA

HOUSE OF REPRESENTATIVES

CD	Year	Total Vote	Republican Vote	Republican Candidate	Democratic Vote	Democratic Candidate	Other Vote	Rep.-Dem. Plurality	Percentage: Total Vote Rep.	Percentage: Total Vote Dem.	Percentage: Major Vote Rep.	Percentage: Major Vote Dem.
46	2018	147,916	45,638	LAMBERT, RUSSELL	102,278	CORREA, LOU*		56,640 D	30.9%	69.1%	30.9%	69.1%
46	2016	164,593			115,248	CORREA, LOU	49,345	115,248 D		70.0%		100.0%
46	2014	83,315	33,577	NICK, ADAM	49,738	SANCHEZ, LORETTA*		16,161 D	40.3%	59.7%	40.3%	59.7%
46	2012	149,815	54,121	HAYDEN, JERRY	95,694	SANCHEZ, LORETTA*		41,573 D	36.1%	63.9%	36.1%	63.9%
47	2018	221,036	77,682	BRISCOE, JOHN	143,354	LOWENTHAL, ALAN*		65,672 D	35.1%	64.9%	35.1%	64.9%
47	2016	242,868	88,109	WHALLON, ANDY	154,759	LOWENTHAL, ALAN*		66,650 D	36.3%	63.7%	36.3%	63.7%
47	2014	123,400	54,309	WHALLON, ANDY	69,091	LOWENTHAL, ALAN*		14,782 D	44.0%	56.0%	44.0%	56.0%
47	2012	230,012	99,919	DELONG, GARY	130,093	LOWENTHAL, ALAN		30,174 D	43.4%	56.6%	43.4%	56.6%
48	2018	294,736	136,899	ROHRABACHER, DANA*	157,837	ROUDA, HARLEY JR.		20,938 D	46.4%	53.6%	46.4%	53.6%
48	2016	306,416	178,701	ROHRABACHER, DANA*	127,715	SAVARY, SUE		50,986 R	58.3%	41.7%	58.3%	41.7%
48	2014	174,795	112,082	ROHRABACHER, DANA*	62,713	SAVARY, SUE		49,369 R	64.1%	35.9%	64.1%	35.9%
48	2012	290,502	177,144	ROHRABACHER, DANA*	113,358	VARASTEH, RON		63,786 R	61.0%	39.0%	61.0%	39.0%
49	2018	295,030	128,577	HARKEY, DIANE	166,453	LEVIN, MIKE		37,876 D	43.6%	56.4%	43.6%	56.4%
49	2016	310,155	155,888	ISSA, DARRELL*	154,267	APPLEGATE, DOUG		1,621 R	50.3%	49.7%	50.3%	49.7%
49	2014	163,142	98,161	ISSA, DARRELL*	64,981	PEISER, DAVE		33,180 R	60.2%	39.8%	60.2%	39.8%
49	2012	274,618	159,725	ISSA, DARRELL*	114,893	TETALMAN, JERRY		44,832 R	58.2%	41.8%	58.2%	41.8%
50	2018	259,810	134,362	HUNTER, DUNCAN D.*	125,448	CAMPA-NAJJAR, AMMAR		8,914 R	51.7%	48.3%	51.7%	48.3%
50	2016	283,583	179,937	HUNTER, DUNCAN D.*	103,646	MALLOY, PATRICK		76,291 R	63.5%	36.5%	63.5%	36.5%
50	2014	157,299	111,997	HUNTER, DUNCAN D.*	45,302	KIMBER, JAMES H.		66,695 R	71.2%	28.8%	71.2%	28.8%
50	2012	258,293	174,838	HUNTER, DUNCAN D.*	83,455	SECOR, DAVID B.		91,383 R	67.7%	32.3%	67.7%	32.3%
51	2018	153,828	44,301	HIDALGO, JUAN M. JR.	109,527	VARGAS, JUAN*		65,226 D	28.8%	71.2%	28.8%	71.2%
51	2016	199,524	54,362	HIDALGO, JUAN M. JR.	145,162	VARGAS, JUAN*		90,800 D	27.2%	72.8%	27.2%	72.8%
51	2014	81,950	25,577	MEADE, STEPHEN	56,373	VARGAS, JUAN*		30,796 D	31.2%	68.8%	31.2%	68.8%
51	2012	159,398	45,464	CRIMMINS, MICHAEL	113,934	VARGAS, JUAN		68,470 D	28.5%	71.5%	28.5%	71.5%
52	2018	296,007	107,015	QUDRAT, OMAR	188,992	PETERS, SCOTT*		81,977 D	36.2%	63.8%	36.2%	63.8%
52	2016	320,656	139,403	GITSHAM, DENISE	181,253	PETERS, SCOTT*		41,850 D	43.5%	56.5%	43.5%	56.5%
52	2014	191,572	92,746	DEMAIO, CARL	98,826	PETERS, SCOTT*		6,080 D	48.4%	51.6%	48.4%	51.6%
52	2012	295,910	144,459	BILBRAY, BRIAN P.*	151,451	PETERS, SCOTT		6,992 D	48.8%	51.2%	48.8%	51.2%
53	2018	268,794	83,127	MURTAUGH, MORGAN	185,667	DAVIS, SUSAN A.*		102,540 D	30.9%	69.1%	30.9%	69.1%
53	2016	296,956	97,968	VELTMEYER, JAMES	198,988	DAVIS, SUSAN A.*		101,020 D	33.0%	67.0%	33.0%	67.0%
53	2014	148,044	60,940	WILSKE, LARRY	87,104	DAVIS, SUSAN A.*		26,164 D	41.2%	58.8%	41.2%	58.8%
53	2012	268,307	103,482	POPADITCH, NICK	164,825	DAVIS, SUSAN A.*		61,343 D	38.6%	61.4%	38.6%	61.4%
TOTAL	*2018*	*12,184,522*	*3,905,026*		*7,883,407*		*396,089*	*3,978,381 D*	*32.0%*	*64.7%*	*33.1%*	*66.9%*
TOTAL	*2016*	*13,414,018*	*4,682,033*		*8,151,297*		*580,688*	*3,469,264 D*	*34.9%*	*60.8%*	*36.5%*	*63.5%*
TOTAL	*2014*	*7,132,641*	*2,813,104*		*3,902,142*		*417,395*	*1,089,038 D*	*39.4%*	*54.7%*	*41.9%*	*58.1%*
TOTAL	*2012*	*12,204,357*	*4,381,206*		*6,945,307*		*877,844*	*2,564,101 D*	*35.9%*	*56.9%*	*38.7%*	*61.3%*

Note: An asterisk (*) denotes incumbent. **Due to California's all-party primary, which qualifies the top two vote recipients for the general election, the 2018 general election in four districts pitted either two Republicans or two Democrats against each other: 6th District, second place was Jrmar Jefferson (D), who received 39,528 votes (19.6 percent); 8th District, second place was Tim Donnelly (R), who received 68,370 votes (40.0 percent); 27th District, second place was Bryan Witt (D), who received 42,132 votes (20.8 percent); and 44th District, second place was Aja Brown (D), who received 45,378 votes (31.7 percent). When this happened, the second-place same-party candidate is included in the other vote in the table above. However, when the votes of all Democratic and Republican candidates (first and second place) are aggregated, the totals are as follows: Democratic 8,010,445; Republican 3,973,396; Other 200,681, with a Democratic plurality of 4,037,049 votes. Meanwhile, in each district, only the top vote recipient from the party is used to calculate the plurality, total vote, and major vote. Because there are two candidates only in the general election, the other vote is exactly the total of the second place finisher. For notes on the 2012, 2014, and 2016 elections with candidates of the same party running on the general election ballot, consult America Votes 30, 31, and 32 respectively.

CALIFORNIA

GENERAL AND PRIMARY ELECTIONS

2018 GENERAL ELECTIONS: OTHER VOTES

Senate	Other vote was 5,093,942 Democrat (Kevin De Leon)
House	Other vote was:
CD 5	55,158 No Party Preference (Anthony Mills)
CD 6	39,528 Democrat (Jrmar Jefferson)
CD 8	68,370 Republican (Tim Donnelly)
CD 13	34,257 Green (Laura Wells)
CD 20	42,044 No Party Preference (Ronald Kabat)
CD 27	42,132 Democrat (Bryan Witt)
CD 34	41,711 Green (Kenneth Mejia)
CD 40	27,511 Green (Rodolfo Cortes Barragan)
CD 44	45,378 Democrat (Aja Brown)

2018 PRIMARY ELECTIONS: SUPPLEMENTARY INFORMATION

Primary	June 5, 2018	**Registration** (as of May 21, 2018)	19,023,417	Democratic	8,438,268
				No Party Preference	4,852,817
				Republican	4,769,299
				Other	963,033

Primary Type Open—Any registered voter could participate in the "top two" primary, in which candidates of all parties (and independents) run together on the same ballot and the top two finishers in each primary race advanced to the general election.

ALL-PARTY PRIMARIES

Senator	Feinstein, Dianne* (Democrat)#	2,947,039	44.2%
	De Leon, Kevin (Democrat)#	805,446	12.1%
	Bradley, James (Republican)	556,252	8.3%
	Bhumitra, Arun (Republican)	350,815	5.3%
	Taylor, Paul (Republican)	323,534	4.9%
	Cruz, Erin (Republican)	267,494	4.0%
	Palzer, Tom (Republican)	205,183	3.1%
	Hartson, Alison (Democrat)	147,061	2.2%
	De La Fuente, Roque "Rocky" (Republican)	135,279	2.0%
	Harris, Patterson "Pat" (Democrat)	126,947	1.9%
	Crew, John "Jack" (Republican)	93,808	1.4%
	Little, Patrick (Republican)	89,867	1.3%
	Mottus, Kevin N. (Republican)	87,646	1.3%
	Laws, Jerry J. (Republican)	67,140	1.0%
	Reid, Derrick Michael (Libertarian)	60,000	0.9%
	Edwards, Adrienne Nicole (Democrat)	56,172	0.8%
	Pierce, Douglas (Democrat)	42,671	0.6%
	Nabliba, Mario (Republican)	39,209	0.6%
	Hildebrand, David (Democrat)	30,305	0.5%
	Turner, Donnie (Democrat)	30,101	0.5%
	Peters, Herbert (Democrat)	27,468	0.4%
	Moore, David (No Party Preference)	24,614	0.4%
	Shi, Ling Ling (No Party Preference)	23,506	0.4%
	Parker, John Thompson (Peace and Freedom)	22,825	0.3%
	Olson, Lee (No Party Preference)	20,393	0.3%
	Plummer, Gerald (Democrat)	18,234	0.3%
	Hanania, Jason (No Party Preference)	18,171	0.3%

CALIFORNIA

GENERAL AND PRIMARY ELECTIONS

ALL-PARTY PRIMARIES

	Grundmann, Don J. (No Party Preference)	15,125	0.2%
	Fernald, Colleen (No Party Preference)	13,536	0.2%
	Ghosh, Rash Bihari (No Party Preference)	12,557	0.2%
	Gildersleeve, Tim (No Party Preference)	8,482	0.1%
	Girgis, Michael Fahmy (No Party Preference)	2,986	
	Ziesing, Michael V. (Write-in)	842	
	Schilling, Ursula M. (Write-in)	17	
	Reddy, Seelam Prabhakar (Write-in)	4	
	TOTAL	*6,670,729*	
Governor	Newsom, Gavin (Democrat)#	2,343,792	33.7%
	Cox, John H. (Republican)#	1,766,488	25.4%
	Villaraigosa, Antonio (Democrat)	926,394	13.3%
	Allen, Travis (Republican)	658,798	9.5%
	Chiang, John (Democrat)	655,920	9.4%
	Eastin, Delaine (Democrat)	234,869	3.4%
	Renteria, Amanda (Democrat)	93,446	1.3%
	Newman, Robert C. II (Republican)	44,674	0.6%
	Shellenberger, Michael (Democrat)	31,692	0.5%
	Liu, Peter Yuan (Republican)	27,336	0.4%
	Girard, Yvonne Terrell (Republican)	21,840	0.3%
	La Riva, Gloria (Peace and Freedom)	19,075	0.3%
	Bribiesca, Juan (Democrat)	17,586	0.3%
	Jones, Josh (Green)	16,131	0.2%
	Istvan, Zoltan (Libertarian)	14,462	0.2%
	Mezzetti, Albert (Democrat)	12,026	0.2%
	Wildstar, Nickolas (Libertarian)	11,566	0.2%
	Griffis, Robert (Democrat)	11,103	0.2%
	Agbede, Akinyemi (Democrat)	9,380	0.1%
	Cares, Thomas Jefferson (Democrat)	8,937	0.1%
	Carlson, Christopher N. (Green)	7,302	0.1%
	Tinaj, Klement (Democrat)	5,368	0.1%
	Mikado, Hakan "Hawk" (No Party Preference)	5,346	0.1%
	Wattenburg, Johnny (No Party Preference)	4,973	0.1%
	Silveira, Desmond (No Party Preference)	4,633	0.1%
	Goel, Shubnam (No Party Preference)	4,020	0.1%
	Taylor, Jeffrey Edward (No Party Preference)	3,973	0.1%
	Fimbres, Veronika (Write-in)	62	
	Soltani, Arman (Write-in)	32	
	Valentino, Peter Crawford (Write-in)	21	
	Pearce, K. (Write-in)	8	
	Arreola, Armando M. (Write-in)	1	
	TOTAL	*6,961,254*	
Congressional District 1	LaMalfa, Doug* (Republican)#	98,354	51.7%
	Denney, Audrey (Democrat)#	34,121	17.9%
	Holcombe, Jessica Jones (Democrat)	22,306	11.7%
	Walters, Martha "Marty" (Democrat)	16,032	8.4%
	Cheadle, Gregory (Republican)	11,660	6.1%
	Peterson, David (Democrat)	5,707	3.0%
	Elbinger, Lewis (Green)	2,191	1.2%
	TOTAL	*190,371*	
Congressional District 2	Huffman, Jared* (Democrat)#	144,005	72.5%
	Mensing, Dale K. (Republican)#	41,608	20.9%
	Caffrey, Andy (Democrat)	13,072	6.6%
	TOTAL	*198,685*	
Congressional District 3	Garamendi, John* (Democrat)#	74,552	53.6%
	Schaupp, Charles (Republican)#	58,598	42.1%
	Puett, Kevin (Democrat)	5,971	4.3%
	TOTAL	*139,121*	

CALIFORNIA

GENERAL AND PRIMARY ELECTIONS

ALL-PARTY PRIMARIES

Congressional District 4	McClintock, Tom* (Republican)#	109,679	51.8%
	Morse, Jessica (Democrat)#	42,942	20.3%
	Bateson, Regina (Democrat)	26,303	12.4%
	White, Mitchell (Republican)	14,433	6.8%
	Calderon, Roza (Democrat)	13,621	6.4%
	Lawton, Robert (Democrat)	4,593	2.2%
	TOTAL	*211,571*	
Congressional District 5	Thompson, Mike* (Democrat)#	121,428	79.3%
	Mills, Anthony (No Party Preference)#	13,538	8.8%
	Palsson, Nils (No Party Preference)	12,652	8.3%
	Kishineff, Jason (Green)	5,458	3.6%
	TOTAL	*153,076*	
Congressional District 6	Matsui, Doris* (Democrat)#	99,789	87.9%
	Jefferson, Jrmar (Democrat)#	13,786	12.1%
	Nwobi, Ralph (Write-in)	9	
	TOTAL	*113,584*	
Congressional District 7	Bera, Ami* (Democrat)#	84,776	51.7%
	Grant, Andrew (Republican)#	51,221	31.2%
	Barash, Yona (Republican)	22,845	13.9%
	Richardson, Robert Christian "Chris" (Green)	3,183	1.9%
	Claytor, Reginald H. (No Party Preference)	2,095	1.3%
	TOTAL	*164,120*	
Congressional District 8	Cook, Paul* (Republican)#	44,482	40.8%
	Donnelly, Tim (Republican)#	24,933	22.8%
	Doyle, Marjorie "Marge" (Democrat)	23,675	21.7%
	Ramirez, Rita (Democrat)	10,990	10.1%
	O'Donnell, Ronald (Democrat)	5,049	4.6%
	Napolitano, Joseph D. (Write-in)		
	TOTAL	*109,129*	
Congressional District 9	McNerney, Jerry* (Democrat)#	55,923	53.2%
	Livengood, Marla (Republican)#	43,242	41.1%
	Tsarnas, Mike A. (American Independent)	6,038	5.7%
	TOTAL	*105,203*	
Congressional District 10	Denham, Jeff* (Republican)#	45,719	37.5%
	Harder, Josh (Democrat)#	20,742	17.0%
	Howze, Ted II (Republican)	17,723	14.6%
	Eggman, Michael (Democrat)	12,446	10.2%
	Madueno, Virginia (Democrat)	11,178	9.2%
	Zwahlen, Sue (Democrat)	9,945	8.2%
	Barkley, Michael J. "Mike" (Democrat)	2,904	2.4%
	Nygard, Dorothy "Dotty" (Democrat)	1,100	0.9%
	TOTAL	*121,757*	
Congressional District 11	DeSaulnier, Mark* (Democrat)#	107,115	68.3%
	Fitzgerald, John (Republican)#	36,279	23.1%
	Lytton, Dennis (Democrat)	8,695	5.5%
	Wood, Chris (No Party Preference)	4,789	3.1%
	TOTAL	*156,878*	
Congressional District 12	Pelosi, Nancy* (Democrat)#	141,365	68.5%
	Remmer, Lisa (Republican)#	18,771	9.1%
	Buttar, Shahid (Democrat)	17,597	8.5%
	Jaffe, Stephen (Democrat)	12,114	5.9%
	Khojasteh, Ryan (Democrat)	9,498	4.6%
	Hermanson, Barry (Green)	4,217	2.0%
	Goldstein, Michael (No Party Preference)	2,820	1.4%
	TOTAL	*206,382*	

CALIFORNIA

GENERAL AND PRIMARY ELECTIONS

ALL-PARTY PRIMARIES

Congressional District 13	Lee, Barbara* (Democrat)#	159,751	99.3%
	Wells, Laura (Write-in)#	832	0.5%
	Solnordal, Jeanne Marie (Write-in)	178	0.1%
	Eyer, James M. "Jim" (Write-in)	39	
	Joiner, Lanenna (Write-in)	26	
	May, Vincent (Write-in)	3	
	TOTAL	*160,829*	
Congressional District 14	Speier, Jackie* (Democrat)#	123,900	79.4%
	Osmena, Cristina (Republican)#	32,054	20.6%
	TOTAL	*155,954*	
Congressional District 15	Swalwell, Eric* (Democrat)#	90,971	70.5%
	Peters, Rudy Jr. (Republican)#	33,771	26.2%
	St. John, Brendan (No Party Preference)	4,322	3.3%
	TOTAL	*129,064*	
Congressional District 16	Costa, Jim* (Democrat)#	39,527	53.0%
	Heng, Elizabeth (Republican)#	35,080	47.0%
	TOTAL	*74,607*	
Congressional District 17	Khanna, Ro* (Democrat)#	72,676	62.0%
	Cohen, Ronald "Ron" (Republican)#	26,865	22.9%
	Tran, Khanh (Democrat)	8,455	7.2%
	Forbes, Stephen (Democrat)	6,259	5.3%
	Watson, Kennita (Libertarian)	2,997	2.6%
	TOTAL	*117,252*	
Congressional District 18	Eshoo, Anna G.* (Democrat)#	133,993	73.4%
	Russell, Christine (Republican)#	42,692	23.4%
	Fredrich, John Karl (No Party Preference)	5,803	3.2%
	TOTAL	*182,488*	
Congressional District 19	Lofgren, Zoe* (Democrat)#	97,096	99.0%
	Aguilera, Justin James (Write-in)#	792	0.8%
	Ryan, Karl (Write-in)	160	0.2%
	Ornelas, Robert (Write-in)	7	
	TOTAL	*98,055*	
Congressional District 20	Panetta, Jimmy* (Democrat)#	102,828	80.7%
	Kabat, Ronald Paul (No Party Preference)#	19,657	15.4%
	Deitch, Douglas (Democrat)	4,956	3.9%
	Clark, Casey K. (Write-in)	20	
	TOTAL	*127,461*	
Congressional District 21	Valadao, David* (Republican)#	34,290	62.8%
	Cox, T.J. (Democrat)#	20,293	37.2%
	TOTAL	*54,583*	
Congressional District 22	Nunes, Devin* (Republican)#	70,112	57.6%
	Janz, Andrew (Democrat)#	38,596	31.7%
	Bliatout, Bobby (Democrat)	6,002	4.9%
	Franco, Ricardo "Rico" (Democrat)	4,365	3.6%
	Carroll, Brian T. (No Party Preference)	1,591	1.3%
	Merryman, Bill (Libertarian)	1,137	0.9%
	TOTAL	*121,803*	
Congressional District 23	McCarthy, Kevin* (Republican)#	81,633	68.8%
	Matta, Tatiana (Democrat)#	14,935	12.6%
	Reed, Wendy (Democrat)	11,974	10.1%
	Barro, Mary (Democrat)	6,363	5.4%
	Davis, James (No Party Preference)	2,076	1.7%
	Wilson, Kurtis (Democrat)	1,691	1.4%
	TOTAL	*118,672*	

CALIFORNIA

GENERAL AND PRIMARY ELECTIONS

ALL-PARTY PRIMARIES

Congressional District 24	Carbajal, Salud* (Democrat)#	94,558	53.6%
	Fareed, Justin (Republican)#	64,177	36.4%
	Woody, Michael Erin (Republican)	17,715	10.0%
	TOTAL	*176,450*	
Congressional District 25	Knight, Steve* (Republican)#	61,411	51.8%
	Hill, Katie (Democrat)#	24,507	20.7%
	Caforio, Bryan (Democrat)	21,821	18.4%
	Phoenix, Jess Pelaez (Democrat)	7,549	6.4%
	Pallant, Mary (Democrat)	3,157	2.7%
	TOTAL	*118,445*	
Congressional District 26	Brownley, Julia* (Democrat)#	72,764	54.1%
	Sabato, Antonio Jr. (Republican)#	30,107	22.4%
	Burum, Jeffrey (Republican)	26,656	19.8%
	Nelson, John (Democrat)	4,959	3.7%
	TOTAL	*134,486*	
Congressional District 27	Chu, Judy* (Democrat)#	86,932	83.5%
	Witt, Bryan (Democrat)#	17,186	16.5%
	TOTAL	*104,118*	
Congressional District 28	Schiff, Adam B.* (Democrat)#	94,249	73.5%
	Nalbandian, Johnny (Republican)#	26,566	20.7%
	Genovese, Sal (Democrat)	7,406	5.8%
	TOTAL	*128,221*	
Congressional District 29	Cardenas, Tony* (Democrat)#	43,579	66.7%
	Bernal, Benito Benny (Republican)#	11,353	17.4%
	Shammas, Joseph "Joe" (Democrat)	5,278	8.1%
	Duenas, Angelica Maria (Green)	4,164	6.4%
	Rey, Juan (No Party Preference)	944	1.4%
	TOTAL	*65,318*	
Congressional District 30	Sherman, Brad* (Democrat)#	80,038	62.3%
	Reed, Mark (Republican)#	35,046	27.3%
	Rab, A. "Raji" (Democrat)	6,753	5.3%
	Pelzer, Jonathan "Jon" (Democrat)	6,642	5.2%
	TOTAL	*128,479*	
Congressional District 31	Aguilar, Pete* (Democrat)#	41,337	45.9%
	Flynn, Sean (Republican)#	40,622	45.1%
	Ahmed, Kaisar (Democrat)	8,108	9.0%
	TOTAL	*90,067*	
Congressional District 32	Napolitano, Grace Flores* (Democrat#)	56,674	99.9%
	Scott, Joshua M. (Write-in)#	42	0.1%
	De La Fuente, Ricardo (Write-in)	1	
	TOTAL	*56,717*	
Congressional District 33	Lieu, Ted W.* (Democrat)#	100,581	61.7%
	Wright, Kenneth W. (Republican)#	48,985	30.1%
	Rodgers, Emory (Democrat)	13,435	8.2%
	TOTAL	*163,001*	
Congressional District 34	Gomez, Jimmy* (Democrat)#	54,661	78.7%
	Mejia, Kenneth (Green)#	8,987	12.9%
	McArdle, Angela Elise (Libertarian)	5,804	8.4%
	TOTAL	*69,452*	
Congressional District 35	Torres, Norma* (Democrat)#	32,474	51.2%
	Valiente, Christian Leonel (Republican)#	21,572	34.0%
	Baca, Joe (Democrat)	9,417	14.8%
	TOTAL	*63,463*	

CALIFORNIA

GENERAL AND PRIMARY ELECTIONS

ALL-PARTY PRIMARIES

Congressional District 36	Ruiz, Raul* (Democrat)#	65,554	55.0%
	Pelzer, Kimberlin (Republican)#	27,648	23.2%
	Ball, Dan (Republican)	9,312	7.8%
	Hassett, Douglas (Republican)	6,001	5.0%
	Wolkowicz, Stephan J. (Republican)	5,576	4.7%
	Bentley, Robert (Republican)	5,030	4.2%
	TOTAL	*119,121*	
Congressional District 37	Bass, Karen* (Democrat)#	99,118	89.2%
	Bassilian, Ron (Republican)#	12,020	10.8%
	TOTAL	*111,138*	
Congressional District 38	Sanchez, Linda* (Democrat)#	54,691	62.7%
	Downing, Ryan (Republican)#	32,584	37.3%
	TOTAL	*87,275*	
Congressional District 39	Kim, Young (Republican)#	30,019	21.2%
	Cisneros, Gil (Democrat)#	27,469	19.4%
	Liberatore, Phil (Republican)	20,257	14.3%
	Thorburn, Andy (Democrat)	12,990	9.2%
	Nelson, Shawn (Republican)	9,750	6.9%
	Huff, Bob (Republican)	8,699	6.2%
	Jammal, Sam (Democrat)	7,613	5.4%
	Tran, Mai-Khanh (Democrat)	7,430	5.3%
	Lee, Herbert (Democrat)	5,988	4.2%
	Vargas, Steven C. (Republican)	4,144	2.9%
	Leggett, Suzi (Democrat)	2,058	1.5%
	Cullum, John J. (Republican)	1,747	1.2%
	Schatzle, Karen Lee (No Party Preference)	903	0.6%
	Cox, Steve (No Party Preference)	856	0.6%
	Sarega, Andrew (Republican)	823	0.6%
	Alexander, Sophia J. (American Independent)	523	0.4%
	Alemayhu, Ted M. (American Independent)	176	0.1%
	TOTAL	*141,445*	
Congressional District 40	Roybal-Allard, Lucille* (Democrat)#	35,636	80.3%
	Cortes Barragan, Rodolfo (Green)#	8,741	19.7%
	TOTAL	*44,377*	
Congressional District 41	Takano, Mark A.* (Democrat)#	45,585	58.5%
	Smith, Aja (Republican)#	32,360	41.5%
	TOTAL	*77,945*	
Congressional District 42	Calvert, Ken* (Republican)#	70,289	60.8%
	Peacock, Julia (Democrat)#	30,237	26.1%
	Quintero, Norman (Democrat)	9,540	8.2%
	Woody, Matt (No Party Preference)	5,587	4.8%
	TOTAL	*115,653*	
Congressional District 43	Waters, Maxine* (Democrat)#	63,908	72.3%
	Navarro, Omar (Republican)#	12,522	14.2%
	DeMartini, Frank (Republican)	6,156	7.0%
	Duterte, Edwin (Republican)	3,673	4.2%
	Zuniga, Miguel Angel (Green)	2,074	2.3%
	TOTAL	*88,333*	
Congressional District 44	Barragan, Nanette Diaz* (Democrat)#	39,453	65.5%
	Brown, Aja (Democrat)#	10,257	17.0%
	Saavedra, Jazmina (Republican)	6,153	10.2%
	Dash, Stacey (Republican)	4,361	7.2%
	TOTAL	*60,224*	

CALIFORNIA

GENERAL AND PRIMARY ELECTIONS

ALL-PARTY PRIMARIES

Congressional District 45	Walters, Mimi* (Republican)#	86,764	51.7%
	Porter, Katie (Democrat)#	34,078	20.3%
	Min, Dave (Democrat)	29,979	17.8%
	Forde, Brian (Democrat)	10,107	6.0%
	Graham, John (No Party Preference)	3,817	2.3%
	Hamadanchy, Kia (Democrat)	3,212	1.9%
	TOTAL	*167,957*	
Congressional District 46	Correa, Lou* (Democrat)#	43,700	62.2%
	Lambert, Russell (Republican)#	22,770	32.4%
	Rushman, Ed (No Party Preference)	2,313	3.3%
	Johnson, Will (No Party Preference)	1,425	2.0%
	TOTAL	*70,208*	
Congressional District 47	Lowenthal, Alan* (Democrat)#	70,539	60.6%
	Briscoe, John (Republican)#	25,122	21.6%
	Clifford, David (Republican)	20,687	17.8%
	TOTAL	*116,348*	
Congressional District 48	Rohrabacher, Dana* (Republican)#	52,737	30.3%
	Rouda, Harley Jr. (Democrat)#	30,099	17.3%
	Keirstead, Hans (Democrat)	29,974	17.2%
	Baugh, Scott (Republican)	27,514	15.8%
	Siddiqui, Omar (Democrat)	8,658	5.0%
	Gabbard, John (Republican)	5,664	3.3%
	Payne, Rachel (Democrat)	3,598	2.1%
	Martin, Paul (Republican)	2,893	1.7%
	Sandman, Shastina (Republican)	2,762	1.6%
	Kotick, Michael (Democrat)	2,606	1.5%
	Oatman, Laura (Democrat)	2,412	1.4%
	Schaarsmith, Deanie (Democrat)	1,433	0.8%
	Zarkades, Tony (Democrat)	1,281	0.7%
	Reiser, Brandon (Libertarian)	964	0.6%
	Onufrei, Stelian (Republican)	739	0.4%
	Kensinger, Kevin (No Party Preference)	690	0.4%
	TOTAL	*174,024*	
Congressional District 49	Harkey, Diane (Republican)#	46,468	25.5%
	Levin, Mike (Democrat)#	31,850	17.5%
	Jacobs, Sara (Democrat)	28,778	15.8%
	Applegate, Doug (Democrat)	23,850	13.1%
	Gaspar, Kristin (Republican)	15,467	8.5%
	Chavez, Rocky (Republican)	13,739	7.5%
	Kerr, Paul (Democrat)	8,099	4.4%
	Maryott, Brian (Republican)	5,496	3.0%
	Schmitt, Michael D. "Mike" (Republican)	2,379	1.3%
	Schoonover, Joshua (Republican)	1,362	0.7%
	Nordal, Craig (Republican)	1,156	0.6%
	Medway, David (Republican)	1,066	0.6%
	Pendleton, Robert (No Party Preference)	905	0.5%
	St. John, Danielle (Green)	690	0.4%
	Hancock, Joshua L. (Libertarian)	552	0.3%
	Mills, Jordan P. (Peace and Freedom)	233	0.1%
	TOTAL	*182,090*	
Congressional District 50	Hunter, Duncan D.* (Republican)#	69,563	47.4%
	Campa-Najjar, Ammar (Democrat)#	25,799	17.6%
	Wells, Bill (Republican)	18,951	12.9%
	Butner, Josh (Democrat)	18,944	12.9%
	Malloy, Patrick (Democrat)	8,607	5.9%
	Sayed, Shamus (Republican)	3,079	2.1%
	Kahle, Richard (No Party Preference)	1,714	1.2%
	TOTAL	*146,657*	

CALIFORNIA

GENERAL AND PRIMARY ELECTIONS

ALL-PARTY PRIMARIES

Congressional District 51	Vargas, Juan* (Democrat)#	50,132	64.0%
	Hidalgo, Juan M. Jr. (Republican)#	11,979	15.3%
	Renison, John R. Jr. (Republican)	10,972	14.0%
	Mercado, Juan Carlos "Charlie" (No Party Preference)	2,452	3.1%
	Mitchell, Kevin (No Party Preference)	1,473	1.9%
	Fuentes, Louis (Republican)	1,310	1.7%
	TOTAL	*78,318*	
Congressional District 52	Peters, Scott* (Democrat)#	98,744	59.0%
	Qudrat, Omar (Republican)#	25,530	15.3%
	Veltmeyer, James (Republican)	19,040	11.4%
	Casara, Danny (Republican)	7,680	4.6%
	Allman, Michael (Republican)	6,561	3.9%
	Horst, John (Republican)	5,654	3.4%
	Cullen, Jeffrey (Republican)	4,027	2.4%
	TOTAL	*167,236*	
Congressional District 53	Davis, Susan A.* (Democrat)#	93,051	64.1%
	Murtaugh, Morgan (Republican)#	20,827	14.3%
	Mendoza, Matthew "Matt" (Republican)	19,710	13.6%
	Kane, Shawn Gino (Republican)	5,319	3.7%
	Kim, Bryan (No Party Preference)	3,460	2.4%
	Goda, Brett (Republican)	2,898	2.0%
	TOTAL	*145,265*	

Note: An asterisk (*) denotes incumbent. A pound sign (#) next to the top two candidates in each primary indicates that they qualified for the general election.

COLORADO

Congressional districts first established for elections held in 2012
7 members

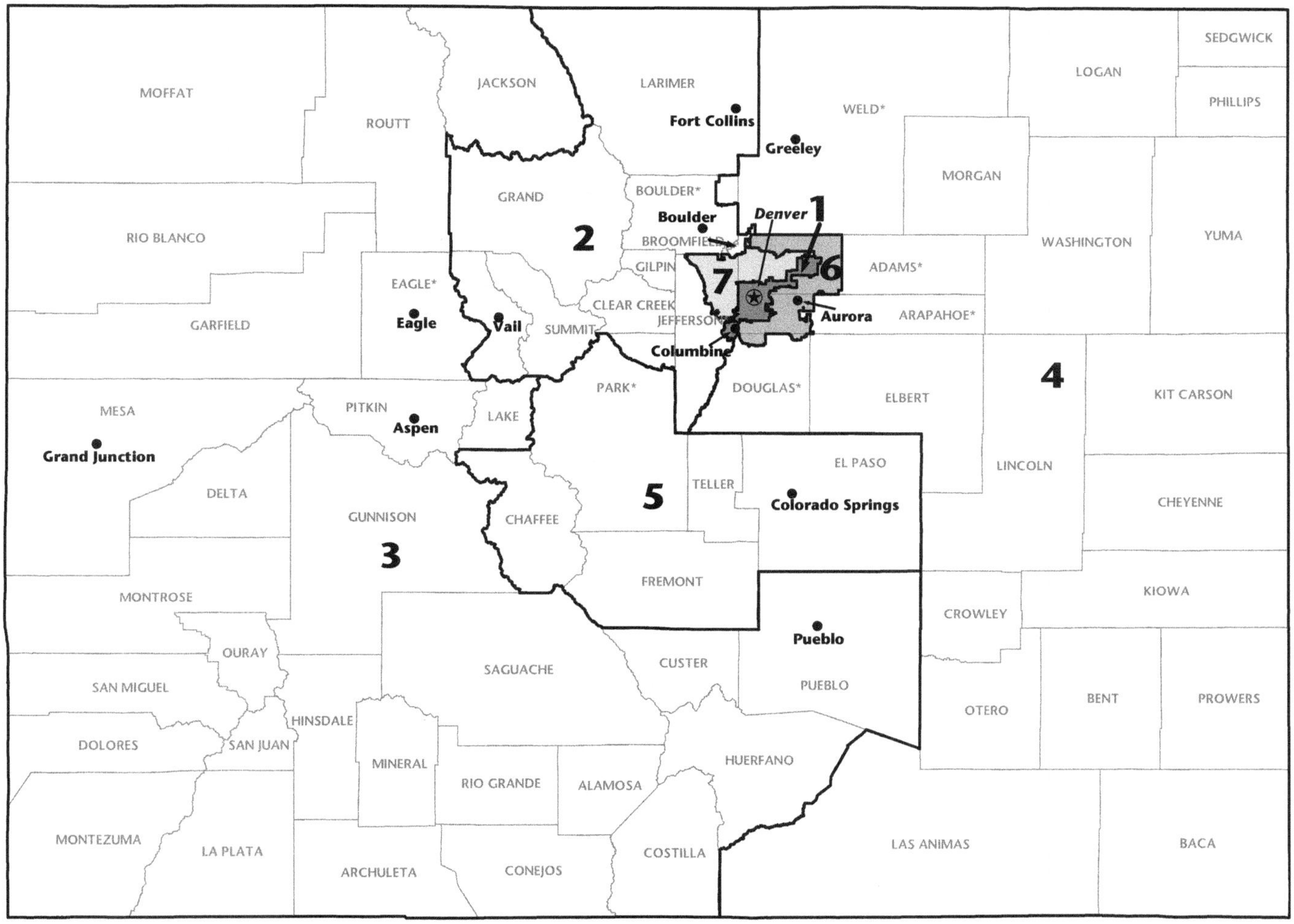

* Asterisk indicates a county whose boundaries include parts of two or more congressional districts.

COLORADO

Denver Area

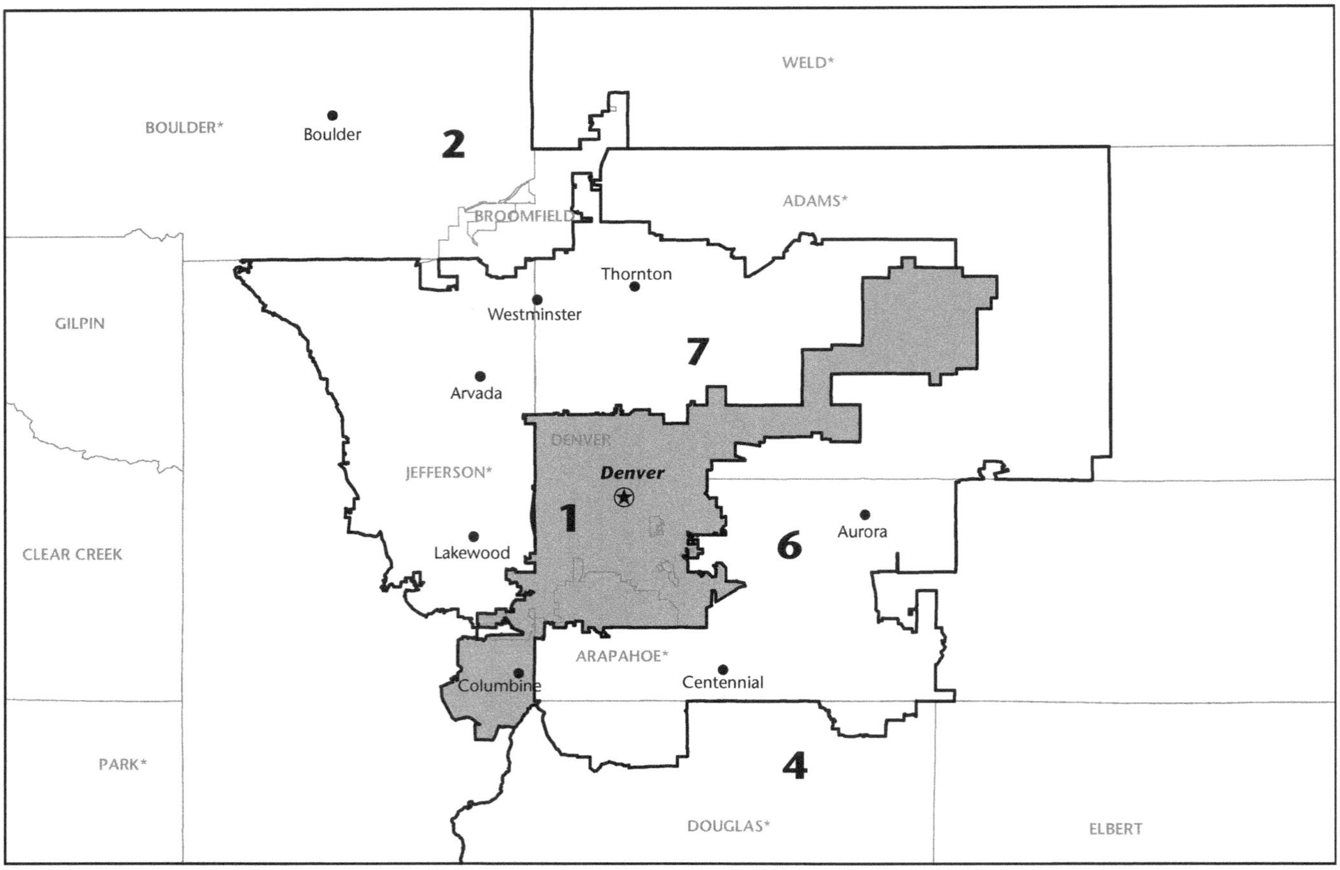

* Asterisk indicates a county whose boundaries include parts of two or more congressional districts.

COLORADO

GOVERNOR

Jared Polis (D). Elected 2018 to a four-year term.

SENATORS (1 Democrat, 1 Republican)

Michael F. Bennet (D). Re-elected 2016 to a six-year term. Sworn in as senator January 22, 2009, to fill the vacancy created by the resignation of Ken Salazar (D) to become U.S. secretary of interior, and elected 2010.

Cory Gardner (R). Elected 2014 to a six-year term.

REPRESENTATIVES (3 Republicans, 4 Democrats)

1. Diana L. DeGette (D)
2. Joseph "Joe" Neguse (D)
3. Scott R. Tipton (R)
4. Ken Buck (R)
5. Doug Lamborn (R)
6. Jason Crow (D)
7. Ed Perlmutter (D)

POSTWAR VOTE FOR PRESIDENT

		Republican		Democratic				Percentage			
								Total Vote		Major Vote	
Year	Total Vote	Vote	Candidate	Vote	Candidate	Other Vote	Rep.-Dem. Plurality	Rep.	Dem.	Rep.	Dem.
2016**	2,780,247	1,202,484	Trump, Donald J.	1,338,870	Clinton, Hillary Rodham	238,893	136,386 D	43.3%	48.2%	47.3%	52.7%
2012	2,569,522	1,185,243	Romney, W. Mitt	1,323,102	Obama, Barack H.*	61,177	137,859 D	46.1%	51.5%	47.3%	52.7%
2008	2,401,462	1,073,629	McCain, John S. III	1,288,633	Obama, Barack H.	39,200	215,004 D	44.7%	53.7%	45.4%	54.6%
2004	2,130,330	1,101,255	Bush, George W.*	1,001,732	Kerry, John F.	27,343	99,523 R	51.7%	47.0%	52.4%	47.6%
2000**	1,741,368	883,748	Bush, George W.	738,227	Gore, Albert Jr.	119,393	145,521 R	50.8%	42.4%	54.5%	45.5%
1996**	1,510,704	691,848	Dole, Robert "Bob"	671,152	Clinton, Bill*	147,704	20,696 R	45.8%	44.4%	50.8%	49.2%
1992**	1,569,180	562,850	Bush, George H.*	629,681	Clinton, Bill	376,649	66,831 D	35.9%	40.1%	47.2%	52.8%
1988	1,372,394	728,177	Bush, George H.	621,453	Dukakis, Michael S.	22,764	106,724 R	53.1%	45.3%	54.0%	46.0%
1984	1,295,380	821,817	Reagan, Ronald*	454,975	Mondale, Walter F.	18,588	366,842 R	63.4%	35.1%	64.4%	35.6%
1980**	1,184,415	652,264	Reagan, Ronald	367,973	Carter, Jimmy*	164,178	284,291 R	55.1%	31.1%	63.9%	36.1%
1976	1,081,554	584,367	Ford, Gerald R.*	460,353	Carter, Jimmy	36,834	124,014 R	54.0%	42.6%	55.9%	44.1%
1972	953,884	597,189	Nixon, Richard M.*	329,980	McGovern, George S.	26,715	267,209 R	62.6%	34.6%	64.4%	35.6%
1968**	811,199	409,345	Nixon, Richard M.	335,174	Humphrey, Hubert Horatio Jr.	66,680	74,171 R	50.5%	41.3%	55.0%	45.0%
1964	776,986	296,767	Goldwater, Barry M. Sr.	476,024	Johnson, Lyndon B.*	4,195	179,257 D	38.2%	61.3%	38.4%	61.6%
1960	736,236	402,242	Nixon, Richard M.	330,629	Kennedy, John F.	3,365	71,613 R	54.6%	44.9%	54.9%	45.1%
1956	657,074	394,479	Eisenhower, Dwight D.*	257,997	Stevenson, Adlai E. II	4,598	136,482 R	60.0%	39.3%	60.5%	39.5%
1952	630,103	379,782	Eisenhower, Dwight D.	245,504	Stevenson, Adlai E. II	4,817	134,278 R	60.3%	39.0%	60.7%	39.3%
1948	515,237	239,714	Dewey, Thomas E.	267,288	Truman, Harry S.*	8,235	27,574 D	46.5%	51.9%	47.3%	52.7%

Note: An asterisk (*) denotes incumbent. **In past elections, the other vote included: 2016 - 144,121 Libertarian (Gary Johnson); 2000 - 91,434 Green (Ralph Nader); 1996 - 99,629 Reform (Ross Perot); 1992 - 366,010 Independent (Perot); 1980 - 130,633 Independent (John Anderson); 1968 - 60,813 American Independent (George Wallace).

COLORADO

POSTWAR VOTE FOR GOVERNOR

		Republican		Democratic				Percentage			
								Total Vote		Major Vote	
Year	Total Vote	Vote	Candidate	Vote	Candidate	Other Vote	Rep.-Dem. Plurality	Rep.	Dem.	Rep.	Dem.
2018	2,525,062	1,080,801	Stapleton, Walker	1,348,888	Polis, Jared	95,373	268,087 D	42.8%	53.4%	44.5%	55.5%
2014	2,041,607	938,195	Beauprez, Bob	1,006,433	Hickenlooper, John*	96,979	68,238 D	46.0%	49.3%	48.2%	51.8%
2010**	1,788,001	199,062	Maes, Dan	912,189	Hickenlooper, John	676,750	713,127 D	11.1%	51.0%	17.9%	82.1%
2006	1,558,387	625,886	Beauprez, Bob	888,096	Ritter, Bill Jr.	44,405	262,210 D	40.2%	57.0%	41.3%	58.7%
2002	1,412,602	884,583	Owens, Bill*	475,373	Heath, Rollie	52,646	409,210 R	62.6%	33.7%	65.0%	35.0%
1998	1,323,530	649,688	Owens, Bill	639,358	Schoettler, Gail	34,484	10,330 R	49.1%	48.3%	50.4%	49.6%
1994	1,116,307	432,042	Benson, Bruce	619,205	Romer, Roy*	65,060	187,163 D	38.7%	55.5%	41.1%	58.9%
1990	1,011,272	358,403	Andrews, John	626,032	Romer, Roy*	26,837	267,629 D	35.4%	61.9%	36.4%	63.6%
1986	1,058,928	434,420	Strickland, Ted	616,325	Romer, Roy	8,183	181,905 D	41.0%	58.2%	41.3%	58.7%
1982	956,021	302,740	Fuhr, John D.	627,960	Lamm, Richard D.*	25,321	325,220 D	31.7%	65.7%	32.5%	67.5%
1978	823,807	317,292	Strickland, Ted	483,985	Lamm, Richard D.*	22,530	166,693 D	38.5%	58.7%	39.6%	60.4%
1974	828,968	378,907	Vanderhoof, John D.*	441,199	Lamm, Richard D.	8,862	62,292 D	45.7%	53.2%	46.2%	53.8%
1970	668,496	350,690	Love, John A.*	302,432	Hogan, Mark	15,374	48,258 R	52.5%	45.2%	53.7%	46.3%
1966	660,063	356,730	Love, John A.*	287,132	Knous, Robert L.	16,201	69,598 R	54.0%	43.5%	55.4%	44.6%
1962	616,481	349,342	Love, John A.	262,890	McNichols, Stephen L.R.*	4,249	86,452 R	56.7%	42.6%	57.1%	42.9%
1958**	549,808	228,643	Burch, Palmer L.	321,165	McNichols, Stephen L.R.*		92,522 D	41.6%	58.4%	41.6%	58.4%
1956	645,233	313,950	Brotzman, Donald G.	331,283	McNichols, Stephen L.R.		17,333 D	48.7%	51.3%	48.7%	51.3%
1954	489,540	227,335	Brotzman, Donald G.	262,205	Johnson, Edwin C.		34,870 D	46.4%	53.6%	46.4%	53.6%
1952	613,034	349,924	Thornton, Dan*	260,044	Metzger, John W.	3,066	89,880 R	57.1%	42.4%	57.4%	42.6%
1950	450,994	236,472	Thornton, Dan	212,976	Johnson, Walter W.	1,546	23,496 R	52.4%	47.2%	52.6%	47.4%
1948	501,680	168,928	Hamil, David A.	332,752	Knous, William Lee*		163,824 D	33.7%	66.3%	33.7%	66.3%
1946	335,087	160,483	Lavington, Leon E.	174,604	Knous, William Lee		14,121 D	47.9%	52.1%	47.9%	52.1%

Note: An asterisk (*) denotes incumbent. **In past elections, the other vote included: 2010 - 651,232 American Constitution (Tom Tancredo), who finished second. The term of office of Colorado's Governor was increased from two to four years effective with the 1958 election.

POSTWAR VOTE FOR SENATOR

		Republican		Democratic				Percentage			
								Total Vote		Major Vote	
Year	Total Vote	Vote	Candidate	Vote	Candidate	Other Vote	Rep.-Dem. Plurality	Rep.	Dem.	Rep.	Dem.
2016	2,743,029	1,215,318	Glenn, Darryl	1,370,710	Bennet, Michael F.*	157,001	155,392 D	44.3%	50.0%	47.0%	53.0%
2014	2,041,058	983,891	Gardner, Cory	944,203	Udall, Mark*	112,964	39,688 R	48.2%	46.3%	51.0%	49.0%
2010	1,777,464	824,789	Buck, Ken	854,685	Bennet, Michael F.*	97,990	29,896 D	46.4%	48.1%	49.1%	50.9%
2008	2,331,712	990,784	Schaffer, Bob	1,231,049	Udall, Mark	109,879	240,265 D	42.5%	52.8%	44.6%	55.4%
2004	2,107,554	980,668	Coors, Pete	1,081,188	Salazar, Ken	45,698	100,520 D	46.5%	51.3%	47.6%	52.4%
2002	1,416,082	717,893	Allard, Wayne*	648,130	Strickland, Tom	50,059	69,763 R	50.7%	45.8%	52.6%	47.4%
1998	1,327,235	829,370	Campbell, Ben Nighthorse*	464,754	Lamm, Dottie	33,111	364,616 R	62.5%	35.0%	64.1%	35.9%
1996	1,469,611	750,325	Allard, Wayne	677,600	Strickland, Tom	41,686	72,725 R	51.1%	46.1%	52.5%	47.5%
1992	1,552,289	662,893	Considine, Terry	803,725	Campbell, Ben Nighthorse	85,671	140,832 D	42.7%	51.8%	45.2%	54.8%
1990	1,022,027	569,048	Brown, Hank	425,746	Heath, Josie	27,233	143,302 R	55.7%	41.7%	57.2%	42.8%
1986	1,060,765	512,994	Kramer, Ken	529,449	Wirth, Timothy E.	18,322	16,455 D	48.4%	49.9%	49.2%	50.8%
1984	1,297,809	833,821	Armstrong, William L.*	449,327	Dick, Nancy	14,661	384,494 R	64.2%	34.6%	65.0%	35.0%
1980	1,173,646	571,295	Buchanan, Mary E.	590,501	Hart, Gary W.*	11,850	19,206 D	48.7%	50.3%	49.2%	50.8%
1978	819,150	480,596	Armstrong, William L.	330,247	Haskell, Floyd K.*	8,307	150,349 R	58.7%	40.3%	59.3%	40.7%
1974	824,166	325,508	Dominick, Peter H.*	471,691	Hart, Gary W.	26,967	146,183 D	39.5%	57.2%	40.8%	59.2%
1972	926,093	447,957	Alott, Gordon Llewellyn*	457,545	Haskell, Floyd K.	20,591	9,588 D	48.4%	49.4%	49.5%	50.5%
1968	785,536	459,952	Dominick, Peter H.*	325,584	McNichols, Stephen L.R.		134,368 R	58.6%	41.4%	58.6%	41.4%
1966	634,837	368,307	Alott, Gordon Llewellyn*	266,198	Romer, Roy	332	102,109 R	58.0%	41.9%	58.0%	42.0%
1962	613,444	328,655	Dominick, Peter H.	279,586	Carroll, John Albert*	5,203	49,069 R	53.6%	45.6%	54.0%	46.0%
1960	727,633	389,428	Alott, Gordon Llewellyn*	334,854	Knous, Robert L.	3,351	54,574 R	53.5%	46.0%	53.8%	46.2%
1956	636,974	317,102	Thornton, Dan	319,872	Carroll, John Albert		2,770 D	49.8%	50.2%	49.8%	50.2%
1954	484,188	248,502	Alott, Gordon Llewellyn	235,686	Carroll, John Albert		12,816 R	51.3%	48.7%	51.3%	48.7%
1950	450,176	239,734	Millikin, Eugene D.*	210,442	Carroll, John Albert		29,292 R	53.3%	46.7%	53.3%	46.7%
1948	510,121	165,069	Nicholson, Will F.	340,719	Johnson, Edwin C.*	4,333	175,650 D	32.4%	66.8%	32.6%	67.4%

Note: An asterisk (*) denotes incumbent.

COLORADO

GOVERNOR 2018

2010 Census Population	County	Total Vote	Republican (Stapleton)	Democratic (Polis)	Other	Rep.-Dem. Plurality	Percentage Total Vote Rep.	Percentage Total Vote Dem.	Percentage Major Vote Rep.	Percentage Major Vote Dem.
441,603	ADAMS	171,235	69,465	93,449	8,321	23,984 D	40.6%	54.6%	42.6%	57.4%
15,445	ALAMOSA	6,040	2,696	3,039	305	343 D	44.6%	50.3%	47.0%	53.0%
572,003	ARAPAHOE	271,140	106,833	155,056	9,251	48,223 D	39.4%	57.2%	40.8%	59.2%
12,084	ARCHULETA	6,776	3,736	2,800	240	936 R	55.1%	41.3%	57.2%	42.8%
3,788	BACA	1,873	1,454	331	88	1,123 R	77.6%	17.7%	81.5%	18.5%
6,499	BENT	1,871	1,094	638	139	456 R	58.5%	34.1%	63.2%	36.8%
294,567	BOULDER	176,262	38,423	133,116	4,723	94,693 D	21.8%	75.5%	22.4%	77.6%
55,889	BROOMFIELD	36,148	13,582	21,405	1,161	7,823 D	37.6%	59.2%	38.8%	61.2%
17,809	CHAFFEE	10,933	5,018	5,461	454	443 D	45.9%	49.9%	47.9%	52.1%
1,836	CHEYENNE	980	809	138	33	671 R	82.6%	14.1%	85.4%	14.6%
9,088	CLEAR CREEK	5,376	2,215	2,932	229	717 D	41.2%	54.5%	43.0%	57.0%
8,256	CONEJOS	3,541	1,756	1,652	133	104 R	49.6%	46.7%	51.5%	48.5%
3,524	COSTILLA	1,609	510	1,012	87	502 D	31.7%	62.9%	33.5%	66.5%
5,823	CROWLEY	1,388	888	400	100	488 R	64.0%	28.8%	68.9%	31.1%
4,255	CUSTER	2,863	1,869	895	99	974 R	65.3%	31.3%	67.6%	32.4%
30,952	DELTA	15,126	9,699	4,817	610	4,882 R	64.1%	31.8%	66.8%	33.2%
600,158	DENVER	308,518	60,151	238,762	9,605	178,611 D	19.5%	77.4%	20.1%	79.9%
2,064	DOLORES	1,184	868	270	46	598 R	73.3%	22.8%	76.3%	23.7%
285,465	DOUGLAS	176,641	99,123	71,573	5,945	27,550 R	56.1%	40.5%	58.1%	41.9%
52,197	EAGLE	22,326	7,804	13,802	720	5,998 D	35.0%	61.8%	36.1%	63.9%
622,263	EL PASO	276,292	155,006	109,154	12,132	45,852 R	56.1%	39.5%	58.7%	41.3%
23,086	ELBERT	14,618	10,859	3,242	517	7,617 R	74.3%	22.2%	77.0%	23.0%
46,824	FREMONT	19,581	12,574	6,022	985	6,552 R	64.2%	30.8%	67.6%	32.4%
56,389	GARFIELD	24,058	11,436	11,791	831	355 D	47.5%	49.0%	49.2%	50.8%
5,441	GILPIN	3,368	1,407	1,809	152	402 D	41.8%	53.7%	43.8%	56.2%
14,843	GRAND	7,745	3,837	3,596	312	241 R	49.5%	46.4%	51.6%	48.4%
15,324	GUNNISON	8,785	2,927	5,526	332	2,599 D	33.3%	62.9%	34.6%	65.4%
843	HINSDALE	556	318	218	20	100 R	57.2%	39.2%	59.3%	40.7%
6,711	HUERFANO	3,611	1,647	1,798	166	151 D	45.6%	49.8%	47.8%	52.2%
1,394	JACKSON	778	564	176	38	388 R	72.5%	22.6%	76.2%	23.8%
534,543	JEFFERSON	305,997	127,038	166,455	12,504	39,417 D	41.5%	54.4%	43.3%	56.7%
1,398	KIOWA	767	638	94	35	544 R	83.2%	12.3%	87.2%	12.8%
8,270	KIT CARSON	3,089	2,417	547	125	1,870 R	78.2%	17.7%	81.5%	18.5%
51,334	LA PLATA	28,384	11,727	15,859	798	4,132 D	41.3%	55.9%	42.5%	57.5%
7,310	LAKE	2,870	998	1,678	194	680 D	34.8%	58.5%	37.3%	62.7%
299,630	LARIMER	179,636	75,002	98,361	6,273	23,359 D	41.8%	54.8%	43.3%	56.7%
15,507	LAS ANIMAS	6,239	3,008	2,949	282	59 R	48.2%	47.3%	50.5%	49.5%
5,467	LINCOLN	2,074	1,619	358	97	1,261 R	78.1%	17.3%	81.9%	18.1%
22,709	LOGAN	8,588	6,349	1,867	372	4,482 R	73.9%	21.7%	77.3%	22.7%
146,723	MESA	67,566	41,193	23,873	2,500	17,320 R	61.0%	35.3%	63.3%	36.7%
712	MINERAL	602	319	259	24	60 R	53.0%	43.0%	55.2%	44.8%
13,795	MOFFAT	5,377	4,228	946	203	3,282 R	78.6%	17.6%	81.7%	18.3%
25,535	MONTEZUMA	11,714	6,933	4,403	378	2,530 R	59.2%	37.6%	61.2%	38.8%
41,276	MONTROSE	18,937	12,466	5,855	616	6,611 R	65.8%	30.9%	68.0%	32.0%
28,159	MORGAN	10,633	7,329	2,844	460	4,485 R	68.9%	26.7%	72.0%	28.0%
18,831	OTERO	7,438	4,076	2,913	449	1,163 R	54.8%	39.2%	58.3%	41.7%
4,436	OURAY	3,192	1,237	1,868	87	631 D	38.8%	58.5%	39.8%	60.2%
16,206	PARK	9,522	5,452	3,645	425	1,807 R	57.3%	38.3%	59.9%	40.1%
4,442	PHILLIPS	2,056	1,583	397	76	1,186 R	77.0%	19.3%	79.9%	20.1%
17,148	PITKIN	9,830	2,354	7,244	232	4,890 D	23.9%	73.7%	24.5%	75.5%
12,551	PROWERS	4,150	2,898	1,090	162	1,808 R	69.8%	26.3%	72.7%	27.3%
159,063	PUEBLO	66,456	29,545	33,674	3,237	4,129 D	44.5%	50.7%	46.7%	53.3%
6,666	RIO BLANCO	3,053	2,473	488	92	1,985 R	81.0%	16.0%	83.5%	16.5%
11,982	RIO GRANDE	4,931	2,795	1,912	224	883 R	56.7%	38.8%	59.4%	40.6%
23,509	ROUTT	13,357	4,787	8,163	407	3,376 D	35.8%	61.1%	37.0%	63.0%
6,108	SAGUACHE	2,670	1,014	1,529	127	515 D	38.0%	57.3%	39.9%	60.1%
699	SAN JUAN	450	167	271	12	104 D	37.1%	60.2%	38.1%	61.9%
7,359	SAN MIGUEL	4,085	923	3,047	115	2,124 D	22.6%	74.6%	23.2%	76.8%
2,379	SEDGWICK	1,209	859	290	60	569 R	71.1%	24.0%	74.8%	25.2%
27,994	SUMMIT	14,229	4,243	9,499	487	5,256 D	29.8%	66.8%	30.9%	69.1%

COLORADO

GOVERNOR 2018

2010 Census Population	County	Total Vote	Republican (Stapleton)	Democratic (Polis)	Other	Rep.-Dem. Plurality	Percentage Total Vote Rep.	Percentage Total Vote Dem.	Percentage Major Vote Rep.	Percentage Major Vote Dem.
23,350	TELLER	12,876	8,409	3,986	481	4,423 R	65.3%	31.0%	67.8%	32.2%
4,814	WASHINGTON	2,389	2,004	294	91	1,710 R	83.9%	12.3%	87.2%	12.8%
252,825	WELD	125,372	72,886	46,653	5,833	26,233 R	58.1%	37.2%	61.0%	39.0%
10,043	YUMA	4,102	3,264	697	141	2,567 R	79.6%	17.0%	82.4%	17.6%
5,029,196	*TOTAL*	*2,525,062*	*1,080,801*	*1,348,888*	*95,373*	*268,087 D*	*42.8%*	*53.4%*	*44.5%*	*55.5%*

COLORADO

HOUSE OF REPRESENTATIVES

CD	Year	Total Vote	Republican Vote	Republican Candidate	Democratic Vote	Democratic Candidate	Other Vote	Rep.-Dem. Plurality	Percentage Total Vote Rep.	Percentage Total Vote Dem.	Percentage Major Vote Rep.	Percentage Major Vote Dem.
1	2018	369,715	85,207	STOCKHAM, CHARLES "CASPER"	272,886	DEGETTE, DIANA L.*	11,622	187,679 D	23.0%	73.8%	23.8%	76.2%
1	2016	379,036	105,030	STOCKHAM, CHARLES "CASPER"	257,254	DEGETTE, DIANA L.*	16,752	152,224 D	27.7%	67.9%	29.0%	71.0%
1	2014	278,494	80,682	WALSH, MARTIN H.	183,281	DEGETTE, DIANA L.*	14,531	102,599 D	29.0%	65.8%	30.6%	69.4%
1	2012	348,228	93,217	STROUD, DANNY	237,579	DEGETTE, DIANA L.*	17,432	144,362 D	26.8%	68.2%	28.2%	71.8%
2	2018	430,765	144,901	YU, PETER	259,608	NEGUSE, JOSEPH "JOE"	26,256	114,707 D	33.6%	60.3%	35.8%	64.2%
2	2016	457,312	170,001	MORSE, NICHOLAS	260,175	POLIS, JARED*	27,136	90,174 D	37.2%	56.9%	39.5%	60.5%
2	2014	345,945	149,645	LEING, GEORGE	196,300	POLIS, JARED*		46,655 D	43.3%	56.7%	43.3%	56.7%
2	2012	421,580	162,639	LUNDBERG, KEVIN	234,758	POLIS, JARED*	24,183	72,119 D	38.6%	55.7%	40.9%	59.1%
3	2018	336,201	173,205	TIPTON, SCOTT R.*	146,426	BUSH, DIANE MITSCH	16,570	26,779 R	51.5%	43.6%	54.2%	45.8%
3	2016	374,037	204,220	TIPTON, SCOTT R.*	150,914	SCHWARTZ, GAIL	18,903	53,306 R	54.6%	40.3%	57.5%	42.5%
3	2014	281,141	163,011	TIPTON, SCOTT R.*	100,364	TAPIA, ABEL	17,766	62,647 R	58.0%	35.7%	61.9%	38.1%
3	2012	347,574	185,291	TIPTON, SCOTT R.*	142,920	PACE, SAL	19,363	42,371 R	53.3%	41.1%	56.5%	43.5%
4	2018	369,621	224,038	BUCK, KEN*	145,544	MCCORMICK, KAREN	39	78,494 R	60.6%	39.4%	60.6%	39.4%
4	2016	390,635	248,230	BUCK, KEN*	123,642	SEAY, BOB	18,763	124,588 R	63.5%	31.7%	66.8%	33.2%
4	2014	286,507	185,292	BUCK, KEN	83,727	MEYERS, VIC	17,488	101,565 R	64.7%	29.2%	68.9%	31.1%
4	2012	342,336	200,006	GARDNER, CORY*	125,800	SHAFFER, BRANDON	16,530	74,206 R	58.4%	36.7%	61.4%	38.6%
5	2018	322,716	184,002	LAMBORN, DOUG*	126,848	SPAULDING, STEPHANY ROSE	11,866	57,154 R	57.0%	39.3%	59.2%	40.8%
5	2016	362,114	225,445	LAMBORN, DOUG*	111,676	PLOWRIGHT, MISTY	24,993	113,769 R	62.3%	30.8%	66.9%	33.1%
5	2014	262,855	157,182	LAMBORN, DOUG*	105,673	HALTER JR., IRVING LESLIE "IRV"		51,509 R	59.8%	40.2%	59.8%	40.2%
5	2012	307,237	199,639	LAMBORN, DOUG*			107,598	199,639 R	65.0%		100.0%	
6	2018	346,822	148,685	COFFMAN, MIKE*	187,639	CROW, JASON	10,498	38,954 D	42.9%	54.1%	44.2%	55.8%
6	2016	376,417	191,626	COFFMAN, MIKE*	160,372	CARROLL, MORGAN	24,419	31,254 R	50.9%	42.6%	54.4%	45.6%
6	2014	276,440	143,467	COFFMAN, MIKE*	118,847	ROMANOFF, ANDREW	14,126	24,620 R	51.9%	43.0%	54.7%	45.3%
6	2012	342,914	163,938	COFFMAN, MIKE*	156,937	MIKLOSI, JOE	22,039	7,001 R	47.8%	45.8%	51.1%	48.9%
7	2018	338,067	119,734	BARRINGTON, MARK	204,260	PERLMUTTER, ED*	14,073	84,526 D	35.4%	60.4%	37.0%	63.0%
7	2016	362,010	144,066	ATHANASOPOULOS, GEORGE	199,758	PERLMUTTER, ED*	18,186	55,692 D	39.8%	55.2%	41.9%	58.1%
7	2014	269,143	120,918	YTTERBERG, DON	148,225	PERLMUTTER, ED*		27,307 D	44.9%	55.1%	44.9%	55.1%
7	2012	340,970	139,066	COORS, JOE	182,460	PERLMUTTER, ED*	19,444	43,394 D	40.8%	53.5%	43.3%	56.7%
TOTAL	*2018*	*2,513,907*	*1,079,772*		*1,343,211*		*90,924*	*263,439 D*	*43.0%*	*53.4%*	*44.6%*	*55.4%*
TOTAL	*2016*	*2,701,561*	*1,288,618*		*1,263,791*		*149,152*	*24,827 R*	*47.7%*	*46.8%*	*50.5%*	*49.5%*
TOTAL	*2014*	*2,000,525*	*1,000,197*		*936,417*		*63,911*	*63,780 R*	*50.0%*	*46.8%*	*51.6%*	*48.4%*
TOTAL	*2012*	*2,450,839*	*1,143,796*		*1,080,454*		*226,589*	*63,342 R*	*46.7%*	*44.1%*	*51.4%*	*48.6%*

Note: An asterisk (*) denotes incumbent.

COLORADO

GENERAL AND PRIMARY ELECTIONS

2018 GENERAL ELECTIONS: OTHER VOTES

Governor	Other vote was 69,519 Libertarian (Scott Helker), 25,854 Unity Party of Colorado (Bill Hammons)
House	Other vote was:
CD 1	11,600 Libertarian (Raymon Doane), 22 Write-in (Miguel Lopez)
CD 2	16,356 Independent (Nick Thomas), 9,749 Libertarian (Roger Barris), 151 Write-in (Kevin Alumbaugh)
CD 3	10,831 Independent (Mary Malarsie), 5,727 Libertarian (Gaylon Kent), 9 Write-in (Gary Swing), 3 Write-in (Bruce Lohmiller)
CD 4	26 Write-in (John Vigil), 13 Write-in (Richard Weil)
CD 5	11,795 Libertarian (Douglas Randall), 55 Write-in (Lori Furstenberg), 16 Write-in (John Croom)
CD 6	5,886 Libertarian (Kat Martin), 4,607 Unaffiliated (Dan Chapin), 5 Write-in (Christopher Allen)
CD 7	14,012 Libertarian (Jennifer Nackerud), 45 Write-in (Steve Zorn), 16 Write-in (Michael Haughey)

2018 PRIMARY ELECTIONS: SUPPLEMENTARY INFORMATION

Primary	June 26, 2018	**Registration** (as of June 1, 2016 – includes 514,882 inactive registrants)	3,822,942	Democratic	1,160,497
				Republican	1,130,810
				Libertarian	46,226
				Green	12,832
				American Constitution	12,305
				Unity	1,223
				Unaffiliated	1,459,049

Primary Type Semi-open—Registered Democrats and Republicans could vote only in their party's primary. Any other registered voter could participate in either the Democratic or Republican primary but in the process had to declare his or her affiliation with that party.

	REPUBLICAN PRIMARIES			DEMOCRATIC PRIMARIES		
Governor	Stapleton, Walker	239,861	47.7%	Polis, Jared	283,340	44.5%
	Mitchell, Victor	151,585	30.1%	Kennedy, Cary	157,396	24.7%
	Lopez, Greg	66,432	13.2%	Johnston, Michael	149,884	23.5%
	Robinson, Doug	45,327	9.0%	Lynne, Donna	46,382	7.3%
	TOTAL	*503,205*		*TOTAL*	*637,002*	
Congressional District 1	Stockham, Charles "Casper"	29,933	100.0%	DeGette, Diana L.*	91,102	68.2%
				Rao, Saira	42,398	31.8%
	TOTAL	*29,933*		*TOTAL*	*133,500*	
Congressional District 2	Yu, Peter	45,970	100.0%	Neguse, Joseph "Joe"	76,829	65.7%
				Williams, Mark	40,044	34.3%
	TOTAL	*45,970*		*TOTAL*	*116,873*	
Congressional District 3	Tipton, Scott R.*	66,854	100.0%	Bush, Diane Mitsch	44,809	64.1%
				Hanlon, Karl	19,368	27.7%
				Menconi, Arnold "Arn"	5,754	8.2%
	TOTAL	*66,854*		*TOTAL*	*69,931*	
Congressional District 4	Buck, Ken*	85,290	100.0%	McCormick, Karen	37,120	64.7%
				Kohne, Chase	20,269	35.3%
	TOTAL	*85,290*		*TOTAL*	*57,389*	

COLORADO

GENERAL AND PRIMARY ELECTIONS

	REPUBLICAN PRIMARIES			DEMOCRATIC PRIMARIES		
Congressional District 5	Lamborn, Doug*	54,974	52.2%	Spaulding, Stephany Rose	45,466	99.9%
	Glenn, Darryl	21,479	20.4%	Murphy, Marcus	38	0.1%
	Hill, Owen	19,141	18.2%			
	Rhea, Bill	6,167	5.9%			
	Stevens, Tyler	3,643	3.5%			
	TOTAL	*105,404*		*TOTAL*	*45,504*	
Congressional District 6	Coffman, Mike*	56,703	100.0%	Crow, Jason	49,851	65.9%
				Tillemann, Levi	25,757	34.1%
	TOTAL	*56,703*		*TOTAL*	*75,608*	
Congressional District 7	Barrington, Mark	46,028	100.0%	Perlmutter, Ed*	81,991	100.0%
	TOTAL	*46,028*		*TOTAL*	*81,991*	

Note: An asterisk (*) denotes incumbent.

CONNECTICUT

Congressional districts first established for elections held in 2012
5 members

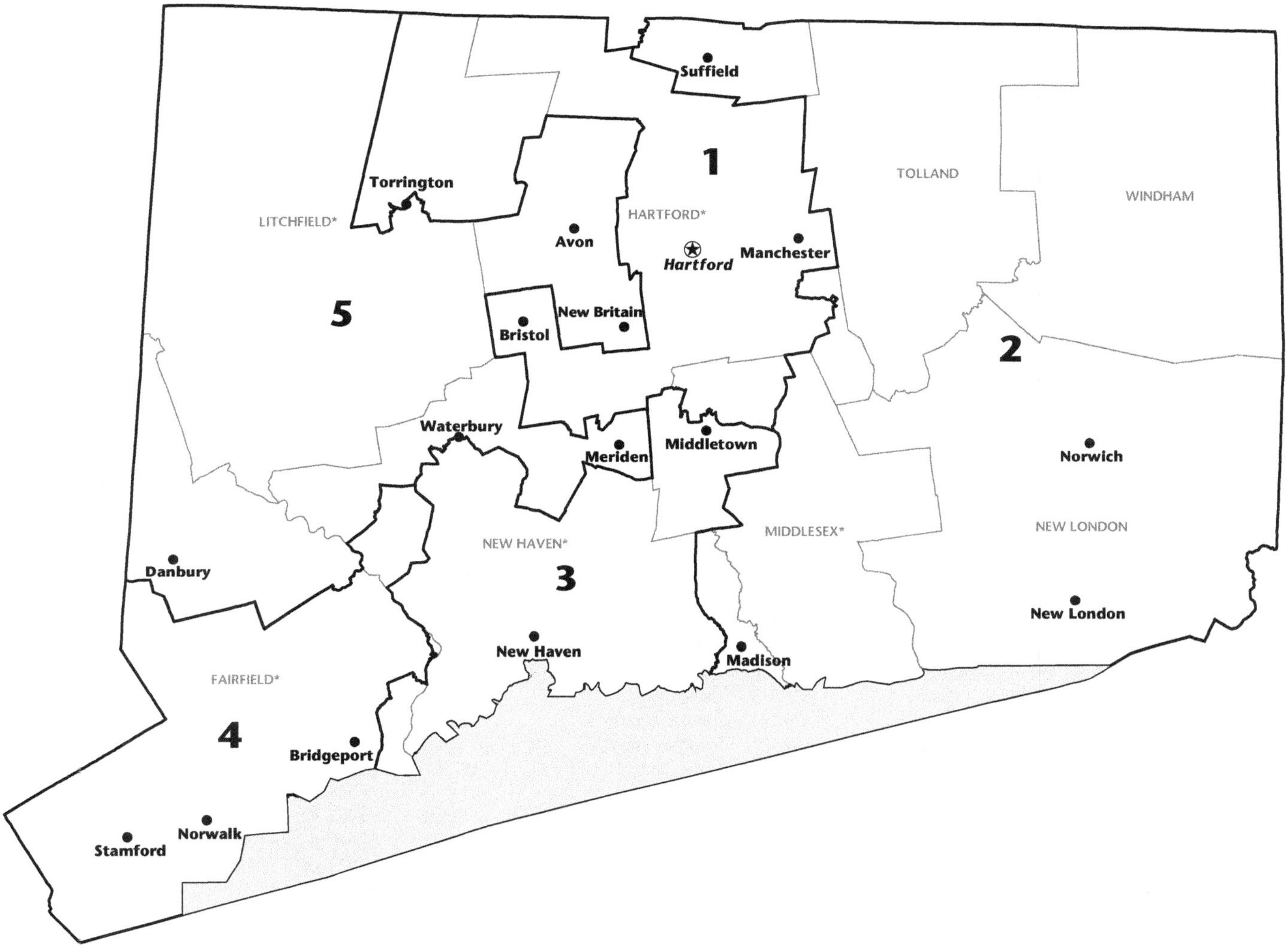

*Asterisk indicates a county whose boundaries include parts of two or more congressional districts.

CONNECTICUT

GOVERNOR

Ned Lamont (D). Elected 2018 to a four-year term.

SENATORS (2 Democrats)

Richard Blumenthal (D). Re-elected 2016 to a six-year term. Previously elected 2010.

Christopher Murphy (D). Re-elected 2018 to a six-year term. Previously elected 2012.

REPRESENTATIVES (5 Democrats)

1. John B. Larson (D)
2. Joe Courtney (D)
3. Rosa L. DeLauro (D)
4. Jim Himes (D)
5. Jahana Hayes (D)

POSTWAR VOTE FOR PRESIDENT

		Republican		Democratic				Percentage			
								Total Vote		Major Vote	
Year	Total Vote	Vote	Candidate	Vote	Candidate	Other Vote	Rep.-Dem. Plurality	Rep.	Dem.	Rep.	Dem.
2016**	1,644,920	673,215	Trump, Donald J.	897,572	Clinton, Hillary Rodham	74,133	224,357 D	40.9%	54.6%	42.9%	57.1%
2012	1,558,960	634,892	Romney, W. Mitt	905,083	Obama, Barack H.*	18,985	270,191 D	40.7%	58.1%	41.2%	58.8%
2008	1,646,792	629,428	McCain, John S. III	997,772	Obama, Barack H.	19,592	368,344 D	38.2%	60.6%	38.7%	61.3%
2004	1,578,769	693,826	Bush, George W.*	857,488	Kerry, John F.	27,455	163,662 D	43.9%	54.3%	44.7%	55.3%
2000**	1,459,525	561,094	Bush, George W.	816,015	Gore, Albert Jr.	82,416	254,921 D	38.4%	55.9%	40.7%	59.3%
1996**	1,392,614	483,109	Dole, Robert "Bob"	735,740	Clinton, Bill*	173,765	252,631 D	34.7%	52.8%	39.6%	60.4%
1992**	1,616,332	578,313	Bush, George H.*	682,318	Clinton, Bill	355,701	104,005 D	35.8%	42.2%	45.9%	54.1%
1988	1,443,394	750,241	Bush, George H.	676,584	Dukakis, Michael S.	16,569	73,657 R	52.0%	46.9%	52.6%	47.4%
1984	1,466,900	890,877	Reagan, Ronald*	569,597	Mondale, Walter F.	6,426	321,280 R	60.7%	38.8%	61.0%	39.0%
1980**	1,406,285	677,210	Reagan, Ronald	541,732	Carter, Jimmy*	187,343	135,478 R	48.2%	38.5%	55.6%	44.4%
1976	1,381,526	719,261	Ford, Gerald R.*	647,895	Carter, Jimmy	14,370	71,366 R	52.1%	46.9%	52.6%	47.4%
1972	1,384,277	810,763	Nixon, Richard M.*	555,498	McGovern, George S.	18,016	255,265 R	58.6%	40.1%	59.3%	40.7%
1968**	1,256,232	556,721	Nixon, Richard M.	621,561	Humphrey, Hubert Horatio Jr.	77,950	64,840 D	44.3%	49.5%	47.2%	52.8%
1964	1,218,578	390,996	Goldwater, Barry M. Sr.	826,269	Johnson, Lyndon B.*	1,313	435,273 D	32.1%	67.8%	32.1%	67.9%
1960	1,222,883	565,813	Nixon, Richard M.	657,055	Kennedy, John F.	15	91,242 D	46.3%	53.7%	46.3%	53.7%
1956	1,117,121	711,837	Eisenhower, Dwight D.*	405,079	Stevenson, Adlai E. II	205	306,758 R	63.7%	36.3%	63.7%	36.3%
1952	1,096,911	611,012	Eisenhower, Dwight D.	481,649	Stevenson, Adlai E. II	4,250	129,363 R	55.7%	43.9%	55.9%	44.1%
1948	883,518	437,754	Dewey, Thomas E.	423,297	Truman, Harry S.*	22,467	14,457 R	49.5%	47.9%	50.8%	49.2%

Note: An asterisk (*) denotes incumbent. **In past elections, the other vote included: 2016 - 48,676 Libertarian (Gary Johnson); 2000 - 64,452 Green (Ralph Nader); 1996 - 139,523 Reform (Ross Perot); 1992 - 348,771 Independent (Perot); 1980 - 171,807 Independent (John Anderson); 1968 - 76,650 American Independent (George Wallace).

CONNECTICUT

POSTWAR VOTE FOR GOVERNOR

		Republican		Democratic				Percentage			
								Total Vote		Major Vote	
Year	Total Vote	Vote	Candidate	Vote	Candidate	Other Vote	Rep.-Dem. Plurality	Rep.	Dem.	Rep.	Dem.
2018	1,406,803	650,138	Stefanowski, Bob	694,510	Lamont, Ned	62,155	44,372 D	46.2%	49.4%	48.4%	51.6%
2014	1,092,773	526,295	Foley, Tom C.	554,314	Malloy, Dan*	12,164	28,019 D	48.2%	50.7%	48.7%	51.3%
2010	1,145,799	560,874	Foley, Tom C.	567,278	Malloy, Dan	17,647	6,404 D	49.0%	49.5%	49.7%	50.3%
2006	1,123,466	710,048	Rell, M. Jodi*	398,220	DeStefano, John Jr.	15,198	311,828 R	63.2%	35.4%	64.1%	35.9%
2002	1,022,998	573,958	Rowland, John G.*	448,984	Curry, Bill	56	124,974 R	56.1%	43.9%	56.1%	43.9%
1998	999,537	628,707	Rowland, John G.*	354,187	Kennelly, Barbara B.	16,643	274,520 R	62.9%	35.4%	64.0%	36.0%
1994**	1,147,084	415,201	Rowland, John G.	375,133	Curry, Bill	356,750	40,068 R	36.2%	32.7%	52.5%	47.5%
1990**	1,142,101	427,840	Rowland, John G.	237,641	Morrison, Bruce A.	476,620	190,199 R#	37.5%	20.8%	64.3%	35.7%
1986	993,692	408,489	Belaga, Julie D.	575,638	O'Neill, William A.*	9,565	167,149 D	41.1%	57.9%	41.5%	58.5%
1982	1,083,876	497,773	Rome, Lewis B.	578,264	O'Neill, William A.*	7,839	80,491 D	45.9%	53.4%	46.3%	53.7%
1978	1,036,608	422,316	Sarasin, Ronald A.	613,109	Grasso, Ella T.*	1,183	190,793 D	40.7%	59.1%	40.8%	59.2%
1974	1,102,773	440,169	Steele, Robert H.	643,490	Grasso, Ella T.	19,114	203,321 D	39.9%	58.4%	40.6%	59.4%
1970	1,082,797	582,160	Meskill, Thomas J.	500,561	Daddario, Emilio Q.	76	81,599 R	53.8%	46.2%	53.8%	46.2%
1966	1,008,557	446,536	Gengras, E. Clayton	561,599	Dempsey, John N.*	422	115,063 D	44.3%	55.7%	44.3%	55.7%
1962	1,031,902	482,852	Alsop, John	549,027	Dempsey, John N.*	23	66,175 D	46.8%	53.2%	46.8%	53.2%
1958	974,509	360,644	Zeller, Fred R.	607,012	Ribicoff, Abraham A.*	6,853	246,368 D	37.0%	62.3%	37.3%	62.7%
1954	936,753	460,528	Lodge, John D.*	463,643	Ribicoff, Abraham A.	12,582	3,115 D	49.2%	49.5%	49.8%	50.2%
1950**	878,735	436,418	Lodge, John D.	419,404	Bowles, Chester*	22,913	17,014 R	49.7%	47.7%	51.0%	49.0%
1948	875,620	429,071	Shannon, James C.*	431,746	Bowles, Chester	14,803	2,675 D	49.0%	49.3%	49.8%	50.2%
1946	683,831	371,852	McConaughy, James L.	276,335	Snow, Wilbert*	35,644	95,517 R	54.4%	40.4%	57.4%	42.6%

Note: An asterisk (*) denotes incumbent. A pound sign (#) in the plurality column indicates that the winner in 1990 did not run under the banner of either major party. **In past elections, the other vote included: 1994 - 216,585 A Connecticut Party (Elaine Strong Groark); 130,128 Independent (Tom Scott); 1990 - 460,576 A Connecticut Party (Lowell P. Weicker Jr.). Weicker won the 1990 election with 40.4 percent of the total vote and a plurality of 32,736 votes. The term of office for Connecticut's Governor was increased from two to four years effective with the 1950 election.

CONNECTICUT

POSTWAR VOTE FOR SENATOR

		Republican		Democratic				Percentage			
								Total Vote		Major Vote	
Year	Total Vote	Vote	Candidate	Vote	Candidate	Other Vote	Rep.-Dem. Plurality	Rep.	Dem.	Rep.	Dem.
2018	1,386,840	545,717	Corey, Matthew M.	825,579	Murphy, Christopher S.*	15,544	279,862 D	39.3%	59.5%	39.8%	60.2%
2016	1,596,276	552,621	Carter, Dan	1,008,714	Blumenthal, Richard*	34,941	456,093 D	34.6%	63.2%	35.4%	64.6%
2012	1,511,764	651,089	McMahon, Linda E.	828,761	Murphy, Christopher S.	31,914	177,672 D	43.1%	54.8%	44.0%	56.0%
2010	1,153,115	498,341	McMahon, Linda E.	636,040	Blumenthal, Richard	18,734	137,699 D	43.2%	55.2%	43.9%	56.1%
2006**	1,134,780	109,198	Achlesinger, Alan	450,844	Lamont, Ned	574,738	341,646 D#	9.6%	39.7%	19.5%	80.5%
2004	1,424,726	457,749	Orchulli, Jack	945,347	Dodd, Christopher J.*	21,630	487,598 D	32.1%	66.4%	32.6%	67.4%
2000	1,311,261	448,077	Giordano, Phil	828,902	Lieberman, Joseph I.*	34,282	380,825 D	34.2%	63.2%	35.1%	64.9%
1998	964,457	312,177	Franks, Gary A.	628,306	Dodd, Christopher J.*	23,974	316,129 D	32.4%	65.1%	33.2%	66.8%
1994	1,079,767	334,833	Labriola, Jerry Jr.	723,842	Lieberman, Joseph I.*	21,092	389,009 D	31.0%	67.0%	31.6%	68.4%
1992	1,500,709	572,036	Johnson, Brook	882,569	Dodd, Christopher J.*	46,104	310,533 D	38.1%	58.8%	39.3%	60.7%
1988	1,383,526	678,454	Weicker, Lowell P. Jr.*	688,499	Lieberman, Joseph I.	16,573	10,045 D	49.0%	49.8%	49.6%	50.4%
1986	976,933	340,438	Eddy, Roger W.	632,695	Dodd, Christopher J.*	3,800	292,257 D	34.8%	64.8%	35.0%	65.0%
1982	1,083,613	545,987	Weicker, Lowell P. Jr.*	499,146	Moffett, Anthony T.	38,480	46,841 R	50.4%	46.1%	52.2%	47.8%
1980	1,356,075	581,884	Buckley, James L.	763,969	Dodd, Christopher J.	10,222	182,085 D	42.9%	56.3%	43.2%	56.8%
1976	1,361,666	785,683	Weicker, Lowell P. Jr.*	561,018	Schaffer, Gloria	14,965	224,665 R	57.7%	41.2%	58.3%	41.7%
1974	1,084,918	372,055	Brannen, James H.	690,820	Ribicoff, Abraham A.*	22,043	318,765 D	34.3%	63.7%	35.0%	65.0%
1970**	1,089,353	454,721	Weicker, Lowell P. Jr.	368,111	Duffey, Joseph D.	266,521	86,610 R	41.7%	33.8%	55.3%	44.7%
1968	1,206,537	551,455	May, Edwin H. Jr.	655,043	Ribicoff, Abraham A.*	39	103,588 D	45.7%	54.3%	45.7%	54.3%
1964	1,208,163	426,939	Lodge, Henry Cabot Jr.	781,008	Dodd, Thomas J.*	216	354,069 D	35.3%	64.6%	35.3%	64.7%
1962	1,029,301	501,694	Seely-Brown, Horace Jr.	527,522	Ribicoff, Abraham A.	85	25,828 D	48.7%	51.3%	48.7%	51.3%
1958	965,463	410,622	Purtell, William A.*	554,841	Dodd, Thomas J.		144,219 D	42.5%	57.5%	42.5%	57.5%
1956	1,113,819	610,829	Bush, Prescott S.*	479,460	Dodd, Thomas J.	23,530	131,369 R	54.8%	43.0%	56.0%	44.0%
1952	1,093,467	573,854	Purtell, William A.	485,066	Benton, William*	34,547	88,788 R	52.5%	44.4%	54.2%	45.8%
1952S**	1,093,268	559,465	Bush, Prescott S.	530,505	Ribicoff, Abraham A.	3,298	28,960 R	51.2%	48.5%	51.3%	48.7%
1950	877,827	409,053	Talbot, Joseph E.	453,646	McMahon, Brien*	15,128	44,593 D	46.6%	51.7%	47.4%	52.6%
1950S**	877,135	430,311	Bush, Prescott S.	431,413	Benton, William	15,411	1,102 D	49.1%	49.2%	49.9%	50.1%
1946	682,921	381,328	Baldwin, Raymond E.*	276,424	Tone, Joseph M.	25,169	104,904 R	55.8%	40.5%	58.0%	42.0%

Note: An asterisk (*) denotes incumbent. A pound sign (#) in the plurality column indicates that the winner in 2006 did not run under the banner of either major party. **In past elections, the other vote included: 2006 - 564,095 Connecticut For Lieberman (Joseph I. Lieberman); 1970 - 266,497 Independent (Thomas J. Dodd). Lieberman won the 2006 election with 49.7 percent of the vote and a plurality of 113,251 votes. One each of the 1950 and 1952 elections were for short terms to fill a vacancy.

CONNECTICUT

GOVERNOR 2018

							Percentage			
							Total Vote		Major Vote	
2010 Census Population	County	Total Vote	Republican (Stefanowski)	Democratic (Lamont)	Other	Rep.-Dem. Plurality	Rep.	Dem.	Rep.	Dem.
916,829	FAIRFIELD	355,277	160,641	188,334	6,302	27,693 D	45.2%	53.0%	46.0%	54.0%
894,014	HARTFORD	346,348	144,218	179,182	22,948	34,964 D	41.6%	51.7%	44.6%	55.4%
189,927	LITCHFIELD	85,421	49,280	32,125	4,016	17,155 R	57.7%	37.6%	60.5%	39.5%
165,676	MIDDLESEX	79,687	38,678	36,483	4,526	2,195 R	48.5%	45.8%	51.5%	48.5%
862,477	NEW HAVEN	324,785	153,865	160,406	10,514	6,541 D	47.4%	49.4%	49.0%	51.0%
274,055	NEW LONDON	106,411	49,364	50,417	6,630	1,053 D	46.4%	47.4%	49.5%	50.5%
152,691	TOLLAND	66,450	31,882	29,992	4,576	1,890 R	48.0%	45.1%	51.5%	48.5%
118,428	WINDHAM	42,424	22,210	17,571	2,643	4,639 R	52.4%	41.4%	55.8%	44.2%
3,574,097	*TOTAL*	*1,406,803*	*650,138*	*694,510*	*62,155*	*44,372 D*	*46.2%*	*49.4%*	*48.4%*	*51.6%*

Note: Candidates in Connecticut can appear on the ballot line of more than one party. In the 2018 Gubernatorial election, Ned Lamont received the following votes per party: 676,649 (Democrat), 17,861 (Working Families).

CONNECTICUT

GOVERNOR 2018

							Percentage			
							Total Vote		Major Vote	
2010 Census Population	City/Town	Total Vote	Republican (Stefanowski)	Democratic (Lamont)	Other	Rep.-Dem. Plurality	Rep.	Dem.	Rep.	Dem.
19,249	ANSONIA	6,245	3,300	2,703	242	597 R	52.8%	43.3%	55.0%	45.0%
20,486	BLOOMFIELD	10,459	1,850	8,068	541	6,218 D	17.7%	77.1%	18.7%	81.3%
28,026	BRANFORD	14,230	6,752	7,062	416	310 D	47.4%	49.6%	48.9%	51.1%
144,229	BRIDGEPORT	29,071	5,337	23,383	351	18,046 D	18.4%	80.4%	18.6%	81.4%
60,477	BRISTOL	21,660	11,447	8,988	1,225	2,459 R	52.8%	41.5%	56.0%	44.0%
29,261	CHESHIRE	13,994	7,397	5,932	665	1,465 R	52.9%	42.4%	55.5%	44.5%
80,893	DANBURY	21,579	9,404	11,729	446	2,325 D	43.6%	54.4%	44.5%	55.5%
20,732	DARIEN	9,761	6,098	3,548	115	2,550 R	62.5%	36.3%	63.2%	36.8%
51,252	EAST HARTFORD	14,982	4,675	9,511	796	4,836 D	31.2%	63.5%	33.0%	67.0%
29,257	EAST HAVEN	10,379	5,999	4,099	281	1,900 R	57.8%	39.5%	59.4%	40.6%
44,654	ENFIELD	15,690	8,136	6,527	1,027	1,609 R	51.9%	41.6%	55.5%	44.5%
59,404	FAIRFIELD	27,760	13,062	14,171	527	1,109 D	47.1%	51.0%	48.0%	52.0%
25,340	FARMINGTON	12,752	6,028	5,810	914	218 R	47.3%	45.6%	50.9%	49.1%
34,427	GLASTONBURY	17,912	8,146	8,167	1,599	21 D	45.5%	45.6%	49.9%	50.1%
61,171	GREENWICH	27,329	14,258	12,822	249	1,436 R	52.2%	46.9%	52.7%	47.3%
40,115	GROTON	25,743	5,545	19,384	814	13,839 D	21.5%	75.3%	22.2%	77.8%
22,375	GUILFORD	12,481	5,447	6,674	360	1,227 D	43.6%	53.5%	44.9%	55.1%
60,960	HAMDEN	24,143	7,517	15,924	702	8,407 D	31.1%	66.0%	32.1%	67.9%
124,775	HARTFORD	23,026	2,252	20,102	672	17,850 D	9.8%	87.3%	10.1%	89.9%
58,241	MANCHESTER	21,253	7,900	11,832	1,521	3,932 D	37.2%	55.7%	40.0%	60.0%
26,543	MANSFIELD	8,830	2,035	6,359	436	4,324 D	23.0%	72.0%	24.2%	75.8%
60,868	MERIDEN	18,751	8,304	9,545	902	1,241 D	44.3%	50.9%	46.5%	53.5%
47,648	MIDDLETOWN	18,177	6,830	10,388	959	3,558 D	37.6%	57.1%	39.7%	60.3%
52,759	MILFORD	24,818	13,095	11,002	721	2,093 R	52.8%	44.3%	54.3%	45.7%
31,862	NAUGATUCK	10,843	6,610	3,806	427	2,804 R	61.0%	35.1%	63.5%	36.5%
73,206	NEW BRITAIN	16,940	5,439	10,727	774	5,288 D	32.1%	63.3%	33.6%	66.4%
129,779	NEW HAVEN	33,189	4,617	27,983	589	23,366 D	13.9%	84.3%	14.2%	85.8%
27,620	NEW LONDON	6,875	1,623	4,937	315	3,314 D	23.6%	71.8%	24.7%	75.3%
28,142	NEW MILFORD	11,823	6,270	5,104	449	1,166 R	53.0%	43.2%	55.1%	44.9%
30,562	NEWINGTON	13,678	6,174	6,537	967	363 D	45.1%	47.8%	48.6%	51.4%
27,560	NEWTOWN	13,540	6,790	6,176	574	614 R	50.1%	45.6%	52.4%	47.6%
24,093	NORTH HAVEN	12,183	7,280	4,539	364	2,741 R	59.8%	37.3%	61.6%	38.4%
85,603	NORWALK	32,280	11,923	19,803	554	7,880 D	36.9%	61.3%	37.6%	62.4%
40,493	NORWICH	10,958	4,490	5,806	662	1,316 D	41.0%	53.0%	43.6%	56.4%
24,638	RIDGEFIELD	12,791	6,167	6,385	239	218 D	48.2%	49.9%	49.1%	50.9%
39,559	SHELTON	17,857	11,311	6,119	427	5,192 R	63.3%	34.3%	64.9%	35.1%
23,511	SIMSBURY	12,983	5,816	5,940	1,227	124 D	44.8%	45.8%	49.5%	50.5%
25,709	SOUTH WINDSOR	12,301	5,489	5,841	971	352 D	44.6%	47.5%	48.4%	51.6%
43,069	SOUTHINGTON	20,555	12,036	7,431	1,088	4,605 R	58.6%	36.2%	61.8%	38.2%
122,643	STAMFORD	43,525	15,478	27,447	600	11,969 D	35.6%	63.1%	36.1%	63.9%
51,384	STRATFORD	21,281	9,482	11,303	496	1,821 D	44.6%	53.1%	45.6%	54.4%
36,383	TORRINGTON	12,921	7,818	4,336	767	3,482 R	60.5%	33.6%	64.3%	35.7%
36,018	TRUMBULL	17,062	9,450	7,285	327	2,165 R	55.4%	42.7%	56.5%	43.5%
29,179	VERNON	6,844	5,268	718	858	4,489 R	77.0%	10.5%	88.0%	12.0%
45,135	WALLINGFORD	19,758	10,806	8,175	777	2,631 R	54.7%	41.4%	56.9%	43.1%
110,366	WATERBURY	26,362	11,206	14,355	801	3,149 D	42.5%	54.5%	43.8%	56.2%
22,514	WATERTOWN	10,160	6,957	2,782	421	4,175 R	68.5%	27.4%	71.4%	28.6%
63,268	WEST HARTFORD	30,187	9,080	18,417	2690	9,337 D	30.1%	61.0%	33.0%	67.0%
55,564	WEST HAVEN	17,249	7,110	9,582	557	2,472 D	41.2%	55.6%	42.6%	57.4%
26,391	WESTPORT	14,088	5,653	8,283	152	2,630 D	40.1%	58.8%	40.6%	59.4%
26,668	WETHERSFIELD	12,843	5,871	5,997	975	126 D	45.7%	46.7%	49.5%	50.5%
25,268	WINDHAM	6,756	2,191	4,176	389	1,985 D	32.4%	61.8%	34.4%	65.6%
29,044	WINDSOR	14,089	4,121	9,211	757	5,090 D	29.2%	65.4%	30.9%	69.1%

CONNECTICUT

SENATOR 2018

2010 Census Population	County	Total Vote	Republican (Corey)	Democratic (Murphy)	Other	Rep.-Dem. Plurality	Percentage Total Vote Rep.	Percentage Total Vote Dem.	Percentage Major Vote Rep.	Percentage Major Vote Dem.
916,829	FAIRFIELD	352,005	131,321	217,601	3,083	86,280 D	37.3%	61.8%	37.6%	62.4%
894,014	HARTFORD	340,866	123,864	213,157	3,845	89,293 D	36.3%	62.5%	36.8%	63.2%
189,927	LITCHFIELD	84,294	43,621	39,593	1,080	4,028 R	51.7%	47.0%	52.4%	47.6%
165,676	MIDDLESEX	78,667	32,836	44,886	945	12,050 D	41.7%	57.1%	42.2%	57.8%
862,477	NEW HAVEN	318,686	126,004	189,456	3,226	63,452 D	39.5%	59.4%	39.9%	60.1%
274,055	NEW LONDON	104,787	40,993	62,115	1,679	21,122 D	39.1%	59.3%	39.8%	60.2%
152,691	TOLLAND	65,729	28,046	36,713	970	8,667 D	42.7%	55.9%	43.3%	56.7%
118,428	WINDHAM	41,806	19,032	22,058	716	3,026 D	45.5%	52.8%	46.3%	53.7%
3,574,097	*TOTAL*	*1,386,840*	*545,717*	*825,579*	*15,544*	*279,862 D*	*39.3%*	*59.5%*	*39.8%*	*60.2%*

Note: Candidates in Connecticut can appear on the ballot line of more than one party. In the 2018 Senate election, Christopher S. Murphy received the following votes per party: 787,685 (Democrat), 37,894 (Working Families).

2010 Census Population	City/Town	Total Vote	Republican (Corey)	Democratic (Murphy)	Other	Rep.-Dem. Plurality	Percentage Total Vote Rep.	Percentage Total Vote Dem.	Percentage Major Vote Rep.	Percentage Major Vote Dem.
19,249	ANSONIA	6,108	2,653	3,384	71	731 D	43.4%	55.4%	43.9%	56.1%
20,486	BLOOMFIELD	10,326	1,543	8,689	94	7,146 D	14.9%	84.1%	15.1%	84.9%
28,026	BRANFORD	14,040	5,359	8,549	132	3,190 D	38.2%	60.9%	38.5%	61.5%
144,229	BRIDGEPORT	28,680	4,147	24,298	235	20,151 D	14.5%	84.7%	14.6%	85.4%
60,477	BRISTOL	21,102	9,652	11,171	279	1,519 D	45.7%	52.9%	46.4%	53.6%
29,261	CHESHIRE	13,893	6,184	7,587	122	1,403 D	44.5%	54.6%	44.9%	55.1%
80,893	DANBURY	21,160	7,713	13,193	254	5,480 D	36.5%	62.3%	36.9%	63.1%
20,732	DARIEN	9,672	4,855	4,753	64	102 R	50.2%	49.1%	50.5%	49.5%
51,252	EAST HARTFORD	14,543	3,866	10,477	200	6,611 D	26.6%	72.0%	27.0%	73.0%
29,257	EAST HAVEN	10,010	4,761	5,149	100	388 D	47.6%	51.4%	48.0%	52.0%
44,654	ENFIELD	15,414	6,847	8,344	223	1,497 D	44.4%	54.1%	45.1%	54.9%
59,404	FAIRFIELD	27,526	10,397	16,897	232	6,500 D	37.8%	61.4%	38.1%	61.9%
25,340	FARMINGTON	12,591	5,164	7,315	112	2,151 D	41.0%	58.1%	41.4%	58.6%
34,427	GLASTONBURY	17,788	7,244	10,349	195	3,105 D	40.7%	58.2%	41.2%	58.8%
61,171	GREENWICH	27,306	11,683	15,447	176	3,764 D	42.8%	56.6%	43.1%	56.9%
40,115	GROTON	12,703	4,496	8,010	197	3,514 D	35.4%	63.1%	36.0%	64.0%
22,375	GUILFORD	12,343	4,312	7,937	94	3,625 D	34.9%	64.3%	35.2%	64.8%
60,960	HAMDEN	23,872	5,912	17,731	229	11,819 D	24.8%	74.3%	25.0%	75.0%
124,775	HARTFORD	22,105	1,716	20,178	211	18,462 D	7.8%	91.3%	7.8%	92.2%
58,241	MANCHESTER	21,015	7,114	13,581	320	6,467 D	33.9%	64.6%	34.4%	65.6%
26,543	MANSFIELD	8,787	1,712	6,928	147	5,216 D	19.5%	78.8%	19.8%	80.2%
60,868	MERIDEN	18,363	6,631	11,475	257	4,844 D	36.1%	62.5%	36.6%	63.4%
47,648	MIDDLETOWN	17,945	5,762	11,939	244	6,177 D	32.1%	66.5%	32.6%	67.4%
52,759	MILFORD	24,470	10,570	13,658	242	3,088 D	43.2%	55.8%	43.6%	56.4%
31,862	NAUGATUCK	10,602	5,537	4,922	143	615 R	52.2%	46.4%	52.9%	47.1%
73,206	NEW BRITAIN	16,396	4,349	11,859	188	7,510 D	26.5%	72.3%	26.8%	73.2%
129,779	NEW HAVEN	32,496	3,333	28,861	302	25,528 D	10.3%	88.8%	10.4%	89.6%
27,620	NEW LONDON	6,717	1,215	5,359	143	4,144 D	18.1%	79.8%	18.5%	81.5%
28,142	NEW MILFORD	11,660	5,347	6,142	171	795 D	45.9%	52.7%	46.5%	53.5%
30,562	NEWINGTON	13,492	5,329	8,018	145	2,689 D	39.5%	59.4%	39.9%	60.1%
27,560	NEWTOWN	13,422	5,779	7,507	136	1,728 D	43.1%	55.9%	43.5%	56.5%
24,093	NORTH HAVEN	11,899	5,857	5,960	82	103 D	49.2%	50.1%	49.6%	50.4%
85,603	NORWALK	32,006	9,721	21,970	315	12,249 D	30.4%	68.6%	30.7%	69.3%
40,493	NORWICH	10,773	3,672	6,900	201	3,228 D	34.1%	64.0%	34.7%	65.3%
24,638	RIDGEFIELD	12,704	4,990	7,621	93	2,631 D	39.3%	60.0%	39.6%	60.4%
39,559	SHELTON	17,605	9,564	7,871	170	1,693 R	54.3%	44.7%	54.9%	45.1%

CONNECTICUT

SENATOR 2018

2010 Census Population	City/Town	Total Vote	Republican (Corey)	Democratic (Murphy)	Other	Rep.-Dem. Plurality	Percentage Total Vote Rep.	Percentage Total Vote Dem.	Percentage Major Vote Rep.	Percentage Major Vote Dem.
23,511	SIMSBURY	12,893	5,125	7,635	133	2,510 D	39.8%	59.2%	40.2%	59.8%
25,709	SOUTH WINDSOR	12,177	4,716	7,319	142	2,603 D	38.7%	60.1%	39.2%	60.8%
43,069	SOUTHINGTON	20,298	10,342	9,724	232	618 R	51.0%	47.9%	51.5%	48.5%
122,643	STAMFORD	43,056	12,651	29,953	452	17,302 D	29.4%	69.6%	29.7%	70.3%
51,384	STRATFORD	21,011	7,723	13,099	189	5,376 D	36.8%	62.3%	37.1%	62.9%
36,383	TORRINGTON	12,688	6,837	5,661	190	1,176 R	53.9%	44.6%	54.7%	45.3%
36,018	TRUMBULL	16,883	7,863	8,891	129	1,028 D	46.6%	52.7%	46.9%	53.1%
29,179	VERNON	11,521	4,518	6,853	150	2,335 D	39.2%	59.5%	39.7%	60.3%
45,135	WALLINGFORD	19,234	8,806	10,178	250	1,372 D	45.8%	52.9%	46.4%	53.6%
110,366	WATERBURY	25,632	9,423	15,911	298	6,488 D	36.8%	62.1%	37.2%	62.8%
22,514	WATERTOWN	9,994	6,237	3,645	112	2,592 R	62.4%	36.5%	63.1%	36.9%
63,268	WEST HARTFORD	29,990	7,652	22,033	305	14,381 D	25.5%	73.5%	25.8%	74.2%
55,564	WEST HAVEN	16,859	5,699	10,971	189	5,272 D	33.8%	65.1%	34.2%	65.8%
26,391	WESTPORT	14,058	4,118	9,864	76	5,746 D	29.3%	70.2%	29.5%	70.5%
26,668	WETHERSFIELD	12,601	5,054	7,420	127	2,366 D	40.1%	58.9%	40.5%	59.5%
25,268	WINDHAM	6,647	1,778	4,746	123	2,968 D	26.7%	71.4%	27.3%	72.7%
29,044	WINDSOR	13,971	3,484	10,343	144	6,859 D	24.9%	74.0%	25.2%	74.8%

CONNECTICUT

HOUSE OF REPRESENTATIVES

CD	Year	Total Vote	Republican Vote	Republican Candidate	Democratic Vote	Democratic Candidate	Other Vote	Rep.-Dem. Plurality	Percentage Total Vote Rep.	Percentage Total Vote Dem.	Percentage Major Vote Rep.	Percentage Major Vote Dem.
1	2018	274,140	96,024	NYE, JENNIFER	175,087	LARSON, JOHN B.*	3,029	79,063 D	35.0%	63.9%	35.4%	64.6%
1	2016	312,925	105,674	COREY, MATTHEW M.	200,686	LARSON, JOHN B.*	6,565	95,012 D	33.8%	64.1%	34.5%	65.5%
1	2014	217,881	78,609	COREY, MATTHEW M.	135,825	LARSON, JOHN B.*	3,447	57,216 D	36.1%	62.3%	36.7%	63.3%
1	2012	297,061	82,321	DECKER, JOHN HENRY	206,973	LARSON, JOHN B.*	7,767	124,652 D	27.7%	69.7%	28.5%	71.5%
2	2018	289,114	102,483	POSTEMSKI, DANNY	179,731	COURTNEY, JOE*	6,900	77,248 D	35.4%	62.2%	36.3%	63.7%
2	2016	330,257	111,149	NOVAK, DARIA	208,818	COURTNEY, JOE*	10,290	97,669 D	33.7%	63.2%	34.7%	65.3%
2	2014	227,936	80,837	HOPKINS-CAVANAGH, LORI	141,948	COURTNEY, JOE*	5,151	61,111 D	35.5%	62.3%	36.3%	63.7%
2	2012	299,960	88,103	FORMICA, PAUL	204,708	COURTNEY, JOE*	7,149	116,605 D	29.4%	68.2%	30.1%	69.9%
3	2018	270,239	95,667	CADENA, ANGEL LUIS JR.	174,572	DELAURO, ROSA L.*		78,905 D	35.4%	64.6%	35.4%	64.6%
3	2016	309,379	95,786	CADENA, ANGEL LUIS JR.	213,572	DELAURO, ROSA L.*	21	117,786 D	31.0%	69.0%	31.0%	69.0%
3	2014	209,939	69,454	BROWN, JAMES E.	140,485	DELAURO, ROSA L.*		71,031 D	33.1%	66.9%	33.1%	66.9%
3	2012	291,301	73,726	WINSLEY, WAYNE	217,573	DELAURO, ROSA L.*	2	143,847 D	25.3%	74.7%	25.3%	74.7%
4	2018	275,651	106,921	ARORA, HARRY	168,726	HIMES, JIM*	4	61,805 D	38.8%	61.2%	38.8%	61.2%
4	2016	313,540	125,724	SHABAN, JOHN	187,811	HIMES, JIM*	5	62,087 D	40.1%	59.9%	40.1%	59.9%
4	2014	198,800	91,922	DEBICELLA, DAN	106,873	HIMES, JIM*	5	14,951 D	46.2%	53.8%	46.2%	53.8%
4	2012	293,432	117,503	OBSITNIK, STEVE	175,929	HIMES, JIM*		58,426 D	40.0%	60.0%	40.0%	60.0%
5	2018	270,664	119,426	SANTOS, MANNY	151,225	HAYES, JAHANA	13	31,799 D	44.1%	55.9%	44.1%	55.9%
5	2016	309,082	129,801	COPE, CLAY	179,252	ESTY, ELIZABETH*	29	49,451 D	42.0%	58.0%	42.0%	58.0%
5	2014	213,301	97,767	GREENBERG, MARK	113,564	ESTY, ELIZABETH*	1,970	15,797 D	45.8%	53.2%	46.3%	53.7%
5	2012	284,757	138,637	RORABACK, ANDREW	146,098	ESTY, ELIZABETH	22	7,461 D	48.7%	51.3%	48.7%	51.3%
TOTAL	*2018*	*1,379,808*	*520,521*		*849,341*		*9,946*	*328,820 D*	*37.7%*	*61.6%*	*38.0%*	*62.0%*
TOTAL	*2016*	*1,575,183*	*568,134*		*990,139*		*16,910*	*422,005 D*	*36.1%*	*62.9%*	*36.5%*	*63.5%*
TOTAL	*2014*	*1,067,857*	*418,589*		*638,695*		*10,573*	*220,106 D*	*39.2%*	*59.8%*	*39.6%*	*60.4%*
TOTAL	*2012*	*1,466,511*	*500,290*		*951,281*		*14,940*	*450,991 D*	*34.1%*	*64.9%*	*34.5%*	*65.5%*

Note: An asterisk (*) denotes incumbent. Votes received by each Democratic and Republican candidate on the ballot lines of other parties are included in their totals above. All Democratic Party candidates except Jim Himes received Working Families Party votes in 2018. Republicans Harry Arora (4th district) and Manny Santos (5th district) received Independent Party votes.

CONNECTICUT

GENERAL AND PRIMARY ELECTIONS

2018 GENERAL ELECTIONS: OTHER VOTES

Governor Other vote was 54,741 Griebel Frank for CT (Oz Griebel), 6,086 Libertarian (Rodney Hanscomb), 1,254 Amigo Constitution Liberty (Mark Greenstein), 74 Write-in (Lee Whitnum)

Senate Other vote was 8,838 Libertarian (Richard Lion), 6,618 Green (Jeffery Russell), 70 Write-in (Fred Linck), 18 Write-in (Kristi Talmadge)

House Other vote was:

CD 1	3,029 Green (Thomas McCormick)
CD 2	3,595 Green (Michelle Bicking), 3,305 Libertarian (Daniel Reale)
CD 4	4 Write-in (Yusheng Peng)
CD 5	13 Write-in (John Pistone)

2018 PRIMARY ELECTIONS: SUPPLEMENTARY INFORMATION

Primary	August 8, 2018	**Registration** (as of November 1, 2017 – includes 201,780 inactive registrants)	2,318,251	Democratic	848,493
				Republican	481,336
				Other	31,959
				Unaffiliated	956,463

Primary Type Closed—Only registered Democrats and Republicans could vote in their party's primary.

	REPUBLICAN PRIMARIES			DEMOCRATIC PRIMARIES		
Senator	Corey, Matthew M.	99,899	76.5%	Murphy, Christopher S.*	Unopposed	
	Rapini, Dominic	30,624	23.5%			
	TOTAL	*130,523*				
Governor	Stefanowski, Bob	42,041	29.4%	Lamont, Ned	172,567	81.2%
	Boughton, Mark	30,475	21.3%	Ganim, Joseph	39,976	18.8%
	Stemerman, David	26,177	18.3%			
	Herbst, Tim	25,063	17.5%			
	Obsitnik, Steve	19,102	13.4%			
	TOTAL	*142,858*		*TOTAL*	*212,543*	
Congressional District 1	Nye, Jennifer	Unopposed		Larson, John B.*	Unopposed	
Congressional District 2	Postemski, Danny	Unopposed		Courtney, Joe*	Unopposed	
Congressional District 3	Cadena, Angel Luis Jr.	Unopposed		DeLauro, Rosa L.*	Unopposed	
Congressional District 4	Arora, Harry	Unopposed		Himes, Jim*	Unopposed	
Congressional District 5	Santos, Manny	16,816	52.4%	Hayes, Jahana	24,693	62.3%
	Corby-O'Neill, Ruby	8,419	26.2%	Glassman, Mary	14,964	37.7%
	DuPont, Richard	6,863	21.4%			
	TOTAL	*32,098*		*TOTAL*	*39,657*	

Note: An asterisk (*) denotes incumbent.

DELAWARE

One member At Large

DELAWARE

GOVERNOR

John C. Carney Jr. (D). Elected 2016 to a four-year term.

SENATORS (2 Democrats)

Thomas R. Carper (D). Re-elected 2018 to a six-year term. Previously elected 2012, 2006, and 2000.

Christopher A. Coons (D). Re-elected 2014 to a six-year term. Previously elected 2010 in a special election.

REPRESENTATIVE (1 Democrat)

At Large. Lisa Blunt Rochester (D)

POSTWAR VOTE FOR PRESIDENT

		Republican		Democratic				Percentage			
								Total Vote		Major Vote	
Year	Total Vote	Vote	Candidate	Vote	Candidate	Other Vote	Rep.-Dem. Plurality	Rep.	Dem.	Rep.	Dem.
2016**	443,814	185,127	Trump, Donald J.	235,603	Clinton, Hillary Rodham	23,084	50,476 D	41.7%	53.1%	44.0%	56.0%
2012	413,921	165,484	Romney, W. Mitt	242,584	Obama, Barack H.*	5,853	77,100 D	40.0%	58.6%	40.6%	59.4%
2008	412,412	152,374	McCain, John S. III	255,459	Obama, Barack H.	4,579	103,085 D	36.9%	61.9%	37.4%	62.6%
2004	375,190	171,660	Bush, George W.*	200,152	Kerry, John F.	3,378	28,492 D	45.8%	53.3%	46.2%	53.8%
2000**	327,622	137,288	Bush, George W.	180,068	Gore, Albert Jr.	10,266	42,780 D	41.9%	55.0%	43.3%	56.7%
1996**	271,084	99,062	Dole, Robert "Bob"	140,355	Clinton, Bill*	31,667	41,293 D	36.5%	51.8%	41.4%	58.6%
1992**	289,735	102,313	Bush, George H.*	126,054	Clinton, Bill	61,368	23,741 D	35.3%	43.5%	44.8%	55.2%
1988	249,891	139,639	Bush, George H.	108,647	Dukakis, Michael S.	1,605	30,992 R	55.9%	43.5%	56.2%	43.8%
1984	254,572	152,190	Reagan, Ronald*	101,656	Mondale, Walter F.	726	50,534 R	59.8%	39.9%	60.0%	40.0%
1980**	235,900	111,252	Reagan, Ronald	105,754	Carter, Jimmy*	18,894	5,498 R	47.2%	44.8%	51.3%	48.7%
1976	235,834	109,831	Ford, Gerald R.*	122,596	Carter, Jimmy	3,407	12,765 D	46.6%	52.0%	47.3%	52.7%
1972	235,516	140,357	Nixon, Richard M.*	92,283	McGovern, George S.	2,876	48,074 R	59.6%	39.2%	60.3%	39.7%
1968**	214,367	96,714	Nixon, Richard M.	89,194	Humphrey, Hubert Horatio Jr.	28,459	7,520 R	45.1%	41.6%	52.0%	48.0%
1964	201,320	78,078	Goldwater, Barry M. Sr.	122,704	Johnson, Lyndon B.*	538	44,626 D	38.8%	60.9%	38.9%	61.1%
1960	196,683	96,373	Nixon, Richard M.	99,590	Kennedy, John F.	720	3,217 D	49.0%	50.6%	49.2%	50.8%
1956	177,988	98,057	Eisenhower, Dwight D.*	79,421	Stevenson, Adlai E. II	510	18,636 R	55.1%	44.6%	55.3%	44.7%
1952	174,025	90,059	Eisenhower, Dwight D.	83,315	Stevenson, Adlai E. II	651	6,744 R	51.8%	47.9%	51.9%	48.1%
1948	139,073	69,588	Dewey, Thomas E.	67,813	Truman, Harry S.*	1,672	1,775 R	50.0%	48.8%	50.6%	49.4%

Note: An asterisk (*) denotes incumbent. **In past elections, the other vote included: 2016 - 14,757 Libertarian (Gary Johnson); 2000 - 8,307 Green (Ralph Nader); 1996 - 28,719 Reform (Ross Perot); 1992 - 59,213 Independent (Perot); 1980 - 16,288 Independent (John Anderson); 1968 - 28,459 American Independent (George Wallace).

DELAWARE

POSTWAR VOTE FOR GOVERNOR

		Republican		Democratic				Percentage			
								Total Vote		Major Vote	
Year	Total Vote	Vote	Candidate	Vote	Candidate	Other Vote	Rep.-Dem. Plurality	Rep.	Dem.	Rep.	Dem.
2016	425,812	166,852	Bonini, Colin	248,404	Carney, John C. Jr.	10,556	81,552 D	39.2%	58.3%	40.2%	59.8%
2012	398,033	113,793	Cragg, Jeffrey	275,993	Markell, Jack*	8,247	162,200 D	28.6%	69.3%	29.2%	70.8%
2008	395,204	126,662	Lee, William Swain	266,861	Markell, Jack	1,681	140,199 D	32.0%	67.5%	32.2%	67.8%
2004	365,008	167,115	Lee, William Swain	185,687	Minner, Ruth Ann*	12,206	18,572 D	45.8%	50.9%	47.4%	52.6%
2000	323,688	128,603	Burris, John M.	191,695	Minner, Ruth Ann	3,390	63,092 D	39.7%	59.2%	40.2%	59.8%
1996	271,122	82,654	Rzewnicki, Janet C.	188,300	Carper, Thomas R.*	168	105,646 D	30.5%	69.5%	30.5%	69.5%
1992	277,058	90,725	Scott, B. Gary	179,365	Carper, Thomas R.	6,968	88,640 D	32.7%	64.7%	33.6%	66.4%
1988	239,969	169,733	Castle, Michael N.*	70,236	Kreshtoll, Jacob		99,497 R	70.7%	29.3%	70.7%	29.3%
1984	243,565	135,250	Castle, Michael N.	108,315	Quillen, William T.		26,935 R	55.5%	44.5%	55.5%	44.5%
1980	225,081	159,004	du Pont, Pierre S. IV*	64,217	Gordy, William J.	1,860	94,787 R	70.6%	28.5%	71.2%	28.8%
1976	229,563	130,531	du Pont, Pierre S. IV	97,480	Tribbitt, Sherman W.*	1,552	33,051 R	56.9%	42.5%	57.2%	42.8%
1972	228,722	109,583	Peterson, Russell W.*	117,274	Tribbitt, Sherman W.	1,865	7,691 D	47.9%	51.3%	48.3%	51.7%
1968	206,834	104,474	Peterson, Russell W.	102,360	Terry, Charles L. Jr.*		2,114 R	50.5%	49.5%	50.5%	49.5%
1964	200,171	97,374	Buckson, David P.	102,797	Terry, Charles L. Jr.		5,423 D	48.6%	51.4%	48.6%	51.4%
1960	194,835	94,043	Rollins, John W.	100,792	Carvel, Elbert N.		6,749 D	48.3%	51.7%	48.3%	51.7%
1956	177,012	91,965	Boggs, James Caleb*	85,047	McConnell, J. H. Tyler		6,918 R	52.0%	48.0%	52.0%	48.0%
1952	170,749	88,977	Boggs, James Caleb	81,772	Carvel, Elbert N.*		7,205 R	52.1%	47.9%	52.1%	47.9%
1948	140,335	64,996	George, Hyland P.	75,339	Carvel, Elbert N.		10,343 D	46.3%	53.7%	46.3%	53.7%

Note: An asterisk (*) denotes incumbent.

POSTWAR VOTE FOR SENATOR

		Republican		Democratic				Percentage			
								Total Vote		Major Vote	
Year	Total Vote	Vote	Candidate	Vote	Candidate	Other Vote	Rep.-Dem. Plurality	Rep.	Dem.	Rep.	Dem.
2018	362,606	137,127	Arlett, Robert	217,385	Carper, Thomas R.*	8,094	80,258 D	37.8%	60.0%	38.7%	61.3%
2014	234,038	98,823	Wade, Kevin	130,655	Coons, Christopher A.*	4,560	31,832 D	42.2%	55.8%	43.1%	56.9%
2012	399,607	115,700	Wade, Kevin	265,415	Carper, Thomas R.*	18,492	149,715 D	29.0%	66.4%	30.4%	69.6%
2010S**	307,402	123,053	O'Donnell, Christine	174,012	Coons, Christopher A.	10,337	50,959 D	40.0%	56.6%	41.4%	58.6%
2008	398,134	140,595	O'Donnell, Christine	257,539	Biden, Joseph R. Jr.*		116,944 D	35.3%	64.7%	35.3%	64.7%
2006	254,099	69,734	Ting, Jan	170,567	Carper, Thomas R.*	13,798	100,833 D	27.4%	67.1%	29.0%	71.0%
2002	232,314	94,793	Clatworthy, Raymond J.	135,253	Biden, Joseph R. Jr.*	2,268	40,460 D	40.8%	58.2%	41.2%	58.8%
2000	327,017	142,891	Roth, William V.*	181,566	Carper, Thomas R.	2,560	38,675 D	43.7%	55.5%	44.0%	56.0%
1996	275,591	105,088	Clatworthy, Raymond J.	165,465	Biden, Joseph R. Jr.*	5,038	60,377 D	38.1%	60.0%	38.8%	61.2%
1994	199,029	111,088	Roth, William V.*	84,554	Oberly, Charles M.	3,387	26,534 R	55.8%	42.5%	56.8%	43.2%
1990	180,152	64,554	Brady, M. Jane	112,918	Biden, Joseph R. Jr.*	2,680	48,364 D	35.8%	62.7%	36.4%	63.6%
1988	243,493	151,115	Roth, William V.*	92,378	Woo, S. B.		58,737 R	62.1%	37.9%	62.1%	37.9%
1984	245,932	98,101	Burris, John M.	147,831	Biden, Joseph R. Jr.*		49,730 D	39.9%	60.1%	39.9%	60.1%
1982	190,960	105,357	Roth, William V.*	84,413	Levinson, David N.	1,190	20,944 R	55.2%	44.2%	55.5%	44.5%
1978	162,072	66,479	Baxter, James H.	93,930	Biden, Joseph R. Jr.*	1,663	27,451 D	41.0%	58.0%	41.4%	58.6%
1976	224,859	125,502	Roth, William V.*	98,055	Maloney, Thomas C.	1,302	27,447 R	55.8%	43.6%	56.1%	43.9%
1972	229,828	112,844	Boggs, James Caleb*	116,006	Biden, Joseph R. Jr.	978	3,162 D	49.1%	50.5%	49.3%	50.7%
1970	161,439	94,979	Roth, William V.	64,740	Zimmerman, Jacob	1,720	30,239 R	58.8%	40.1%	59.5%	40.5%
1966	164,531	97,268	Boggs, James Caleb*	67,263	Tunnell, James M. Jr.		30,005 R	59.1%	40.9%	59.1%	40.9%
1964	200,703	103,782	Williams, John J.*	96,850	Carvel, Elbert N.	71	6,932 R	51.7%	48.3%	51.7%	48.3%
1960	194,964	98,874	Boggs, James Caleb	96,090	Frear, J. Allen Jr.*		2,784 R	50.7%	49.3%	50.7%	49.3%
1958	154,432	82,280	Williams, John J.*	72,152	Carvel, Elbert N.		10,128 R	53.3%	46.7%	53.3%	46.7%
1954	144,900	62,389	Warburton, Herbert B.	82,511	Frear, J. Allen Jr.*		20,122 D	43.1%	56.9%	43.1%	56.9%
1952	170,705	93,020	Williams, John J.*	77,685	du Pont Bayard, Alexis I.		15,335 R	54.5%	45.5%	54.5%	45.5%
1948	141,362	68,246	Buck, Clayton Douglass*	71,888	Frear, J. Allen Jr.	1,228	3,642 D	48.3%	50.9%	48.7%	51.3%
1946	113,513	62,603	Williams, John J.	50,910	Tunnell, James M.*		11,693 R	55.2%	44.8%	55.2%	44.8%

Note: An asterisk (*) denotes incumbent. **The 2010 election was for a short term to fill a vacancy.

DELAWARE

SENATOR 2018

2010 Census Population	County	Total Vote	Republican (Arlett)	Democratic (Carper)	Other	Rep.-Dem. Plurality	Percentage: Total Vote Rep.	Total Vote Dem.	Major Vote Rep.	Major Vote Dem.
162,310	KENT	59,753	27,210	31,282	1,261	4,072 D	45.5%	52.4%	46.5%	53.5%
538,479	NEW CASTLE	210,323	59,526	145,428	5,369	85,902 D	28.3%	69.1%	29.0%	71.0%
197,145	SUSSEX	92,530	50,391	40,675	1,464	9,716 R	54.5%	44.0%	55.3%	44.7%
897,934	*TOTAL*	*362,606*	*137,127*	*217,385*	*8,094*	*80,258 D*	*37.8%*	*60.0%*	*38.7%*	*61.3%*

DELAWARE

HOUSE OF REPRESENTATIVES

CD	Year	Total Vote	Republican Vote	Republican Candidate	Democratic Vote	Democratic Candidate	Other Vote	Rep.-Dem. Plurality	Percentage: Total Vote Rep.	Total Vote Dem.	Major Vote Rep.	Major Vote Dem.
At Large	2018	353,814	125,384	WALKER, SCOTT	227,353	ROCHESTER, LISA BLUNT*	1,077	101,969 D	35.4%	64.3%	35.5%	64.5%
At Large	2016	420,682	172,301	REIGLE, HANS	233,554	ROCHESTER, LISA BLUNT	14,827	61,253 D	41.0%	55.5%	42.5%	57.5%
At Large	2014	231,617	85,146	IZZO, ROSE	137,251	CARNEY, JOHN C. JR.*	9,220	52,105 D	36.8%	59.3%	38.3%	61.7%
At Large	2012	388,059	129,757	KOVACH, THOMAS H.	249,933	CARNEY, JOHN C. JR.*	8,369	120,176 D	33.4%	64.4%	34.2%	65.8%
At Large	2010	305,636	125,442	URQUHART, GLEN	173,543	CARNEY, JOHN C. JR.	6,651	48,101 D	41.0%	56.8%	42.0%	58.0%
At Large	2008	385,457	235,437	CASTLE, MICHAEL N.*	146,434	HARTLEY-NAGLE, KAREN	3,586	89,003 R	61.1%	38.0%	61.7%	38.3%
At Large	2006	251,694	143,897	CASTLE, MICHAEL N.*	97,565	SPIVACK, DENNIS	10,232	46,332 R	57.2%	38.8%	59.6%	40.4%
At Large	2004	356,045	245,978	CASTLE, MICHAEL N.*	105,716	DONNELLY, PAUL	4,351	140,262 R	69.1%	29.7%	69.9%	30.1%
At Large	2002	228,405	164,605	CASTLE, MICHAEL N.*	61,011	MILLER, MICHAEL C.	2,789	103,594 R	72.1%	26.7%	73.0%	27.0%
At Large	2000	313,171	211,797	CASTLE, MICHAEL N.*	96,488	MILLER, MICHAEL C.	4,886	115,309 R	67.6%	30.8%	68.7%	31.3%
At Large	1998	180,527	119,811	CASTLE, MICHAEL N.*	57,446	WILLIAMS, DENNIS E.	3,270	62,365 R	66.4%	31.8%	67.6%	32.4%
At Large	1996	266,836	185,576	CASTLE, MICHAEL N.*	73,253	WILLIAMS, DENNIS E.	8,007	112,323 R	69.5%	27.5%	71.7%	28.3%
At Large	1994	195,037	137,960	CASTLE, MICHAEL N.*	51,803	DESANTIS, CAROL ANN	5,274	86,157 R	70.7%	26.6%	72.7%	27.3%
At Large	1992	276,157	153,037	CASTLE, MICHAEL N.	117,426	WOO, S. B.	5,694	35,611 R	55.4%	42.5%	56.6%	43.4%
At Large	1990	177,432	58,037	WILLIAMS, RALPH O.	116,274	CARPER, THOMAS R.*	3,121	58,237 D	32.7%	65.5%	33.3%	66.7%
At Large	1988	234,517	76,179	KRAPF, JAMES P.	158,338	CARPER, THOMAS R.*		82,159 D	32.5%	67.5%	32.5%	67.5%
At Large	1986	160,757	53,767	NEUBERGER, THOMAS S.	106,351	CARPER, THOMAS R.*	639	52,584 D	33.4%	66.2%	33.6%	66.4%
At Large	1984	243,014	100,650	DUPONT, ELISE	142,070	CARPER, THOMAS R.*	294	41,420 D	41.4%	58.5%	41.5%	58.5%
At Large	1982	188,064	87,153	EVANS, THOMAS B.*	98,533	CARPER, THOMAS R.	2,378	11,380 D	46.3%	52.4%	46.9%	53.1%
At Large	1980	216,629	133,842	EVANS, THOMAS B.*	81,227	MAXWELL, ROBERT L.	1,560	52,615 R	61.8%	37.5%	62.2%	37.8%
At Large	1978	157,566	91,689	EVANS, THOMAS B.*	64,863	HINDES, GARY E.	1,014	26,826 R	58.2%	41.2%	58.6%	41.4%
At Large	1976	214,799	110,677	EVANS, THOMAS B.	102,431	SHIPLEY, SAMUEL L.	1,691	8,246 R	51.5%	47.7%	51.9%	48.1%
At Large	1974	160,328	93,826	DU PONT, PIERRE S. IV*	63,490	SOLES, JAMES	3,012	30,336 R	58.5%	39.6%	59.6%	40.4%
At Large	1972	225,851	141,237	DU PONT, PIERRE S. IV*	83,230	HANDLOFF, NORMA	1,384	58,007 R	62.5%	36.9%	62.9%	37.1%
At Large	1970	160,313	86,125	DU PONT, PIERRE S. IV	71,429	DANIELLO, JOHN D.	2,759	14,696 R	53.7%	44.6%	54.7%	45.3%
At Large	1968	200,820	117,827	ROTH, WILLIAM V.*	82,993	MCDOWELL, HARRIS B. JR.		34,834 R	58.7%	41.3%	58.7%	41.3%
At Large	1966	163,093	90,961	ROTH, WILLIAM V.	72,132	MCDOWELL, HARRIS B. JR.*		18,829 R	55.8%	44.2%	55.8%	44.2%
At Large	1964	198,691	86,254	SNOWDEN, JAMES H.	112,361	MCDOWELL, HARRIS B. JR.*	76	26,107 D	43.4%	56.6%	43.4%	56.6%
At Large	1962	153,356	71,934	WILLIAMS, WILMER F.	81,166	MCDOWELL, HARRIS B. JR.*	256	9,232 D	46.9%	52.9%	47.0%	53.0%
At Large	1960	194,564	96,337	MCKINSTRY, JAMES T.	98,227	MCDOWELL, HARRIS B. JR.*		1,890 D	49.5%	50.5%	49.5%	50.5%
At Large	1958	152,896	76,099	HASKELL, HARRY G. JR.*	76,797	MCDOWELL, HARRIS B. JR.*		698 D	49.8%	50.2%	49.8%	50.2%
At Large	1956	176,182	91,538	HASKELL, HARRY G. JR.	84,644	MCDOWELL, HARRIS B. JR.*		6,894 R	52.0%	48.0%	52.0%	48.0%
At Large	1954	144,236	65,035	MARTIN, LILLIAN I.	79,201	MCDOWELL, HARRIS B. JR.		14,166 D	45.1%	54.9%	45.1%	54.9%
At Large	1952	170,015	88,285	WARBURTON, H. B.	81,730	SCANNELL, JOSEPH S.		6,555 R	51.9%	48.1%	51.9%	48.1%
At Large	1950	129,404	73,313	BOGGS, JAMES CALEB*	56,091	WINCHESTER, H. M.		17,222 R	56.7%	43.3%	56.7%	43.3%
At Large	1948	140,535	71,127	BOGGS, JAMES CALEB*	68,909	MCGUIGAN, J. CARL	499	2,218 R	50.6%	49.0%	50.8%	49.2%
At Large	1946	112,621	63,516	BOGGS, JAMES CALEB	49,105	TRAYNOR, PHILIP A.*		14,411 R	56.4%	43.6%	56.4%	43.6%

Note: An asterisk (*) denotes incumbent.

DELAWARE

GENERAL AND PRIMARY ELECTIONS

2018 GENERAL ELECTIONS: OTHER VOTES

Senate Other vote was 4,170 Green (Demitri Theodoropoulos), 3,910 Libertarian (Nadine Frost), 7 Write-in (Peter Farina), 4 Write-in (Matthew Stout), 3 Write-in (Barry Eveland)

House Other vote was:

At Large 637 Write-in (Paul Johnston), 417 Write-in (Andrew Webb), 23 Write-in (Marvin Davis)

2018 PRIMARY ELECTIONS: SUPPLEMENTARY INFORMATION

Primary September 6, 2018

Registration (as of September 1, 2018) 692,449

Democratic	327,149
Republican	192,570
Independent	6,068
Libertarian	1,676
Green	780
Other	3,533
Nonpartisan	791
Unaffiliated	159,882

Primary Type Closed—Only registered Democrats and Republicans could vote in their party's primary.

	REPUBLICAN PRIMARIES			DEMOCRATIC PRIMARIES		
Senator	Arlett, Robert	25,284	66.8%	Carper, Thomas R.*	53,635	64.6%
	Truono, Eugene J. Jr.	10,588	28.0%	Harris, Kerri Evelyn	29,407	35.4%
	De La Fuente, Roque "Rocky"	1,998	5.3%			
	TOTAL	*37,870*		*TOTAL*	*83,042*	
Congressional At Large	Walker, Scott	19,573	53.0%	Rochester, Lisa Blunt*	Unopposed	
	Murphy, Lee H.	17,359	47.0%			
	TOTAL	*36,932*				

Note: An asterisk (*) denotes incumbent.

FLORIDA

Congressional districts first established for elections held in 2016

27 members

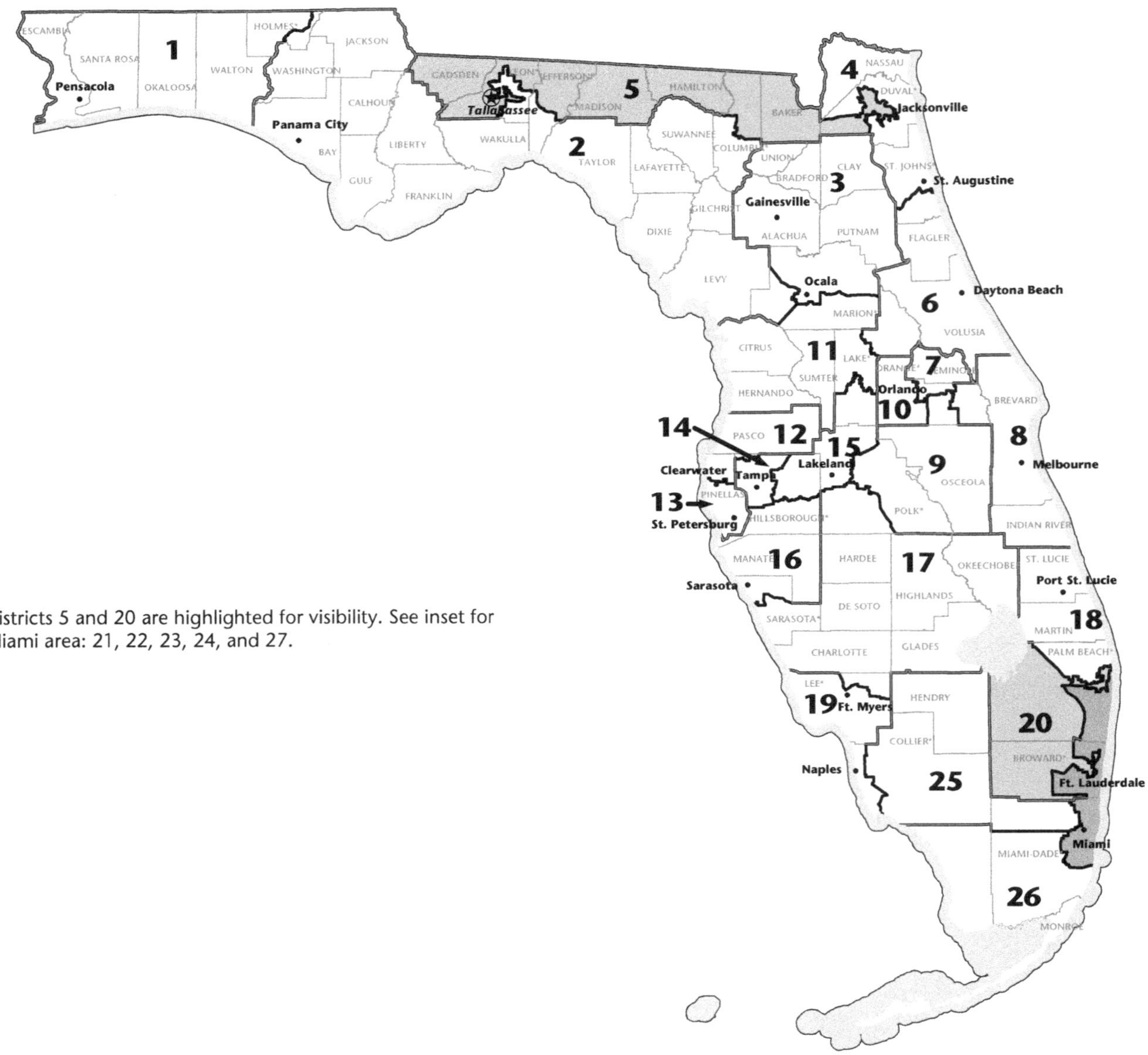

Districts 5 and 20 are highlighted for visibility. See inset for Miami area: 21, 22, 23, 24, and 27.

* Asterisk indicates a county whose boundaries include parts of two or more congressional districts.

FLORIDA

Greater Miami, Fort Lauderdale Areas

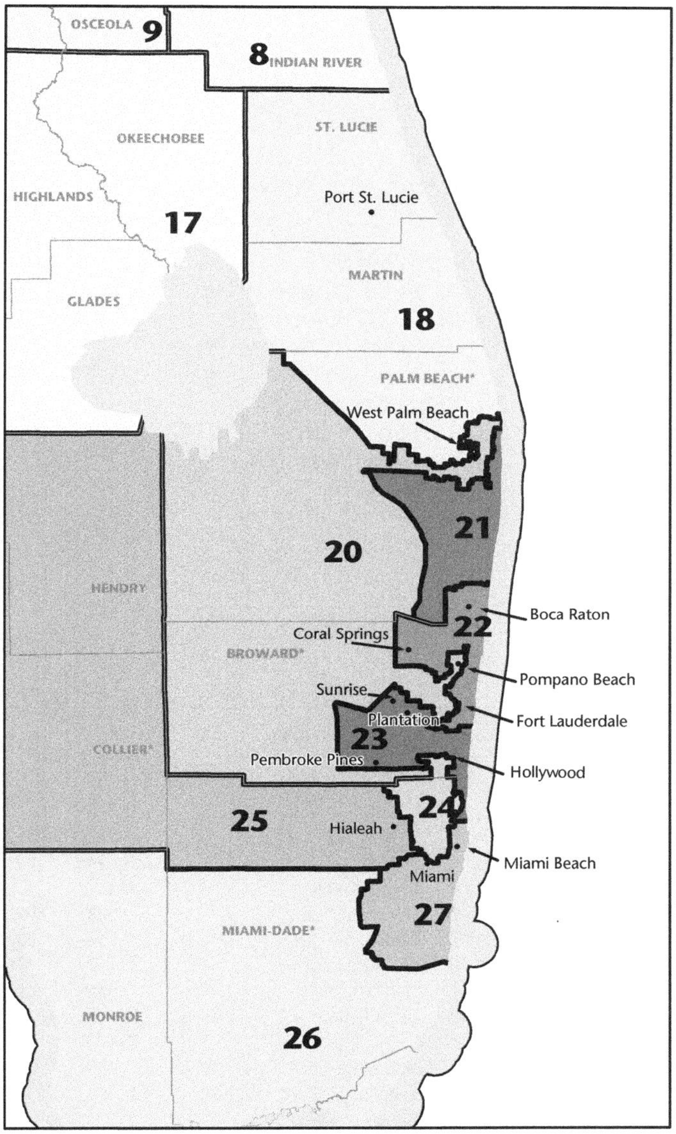

*Asterisk indicates a county whose boundaries include parts of two or more congressional districts.

FLORIDA

GOVERNOR

Ron DeSantis (R). Elected 2018 to a four-year term.

SENATORS (2 Republicans)

Rick Scott (R). Elected 2018 to a six-year term.

Marco Rubio (R). Re-elected 2016 to a six-year term. Previously elected 2010.

REPRESENTATIVES (14 Republicans, 13 Democrats)

1. Matt Gaetz (R)
2. Neal Dunn (R)
3. Ted Yoho (R)
4. John Rutherford (R)
5. Al Lawson (D)
6. Michael Waltz (R)
7. Stephanie Murphy (D)
8. Bill Posey (R)
9. Darren Soto (D)
10. Val A. Demings (D)
11. Daniel A. Webster (R)
12. Gus Michael Bilirakis (R)
13. Charlie Crist (D)
14. Kathy Castor (D)
15. Ross Spano (R)
16. Vern Buchanan (R)
17. Greg Steube (R)
18. Brian Mast (R)
19. Francis Rooney (R)
20. Alcee L. Hastings (D)
21. Lois Frankel (D)
22. Ted Deutch (D)
23. Debbie Wasserman-Schultz (D)
24. Frederica S. Wilson (D)
25. Mario Diaz-Balart (R)
26. Debbie Mucarsel-Powell (D)
27. Donna Shalala (D)

POSTWAR VOTE FOR PRESIDENT

									Percentage			
		Republican		Democratic					Total Vote		Major Vote	
Year	Total Vote	Vote	Candidate	Vote	Candidate	Other Vote	Rep.-Dem. Plurality		Rep.	Dem.	Rep.	Dem.
2016**	9,420,039	4,617,886	Trump, Donald J.	4,504,975	Clinton, Hillary Rodham	297,178	112,911	R	49.0%	47.8%	50.6%	49.4%
2012	8,474,179	4,163,447	Romney, W. Mitt	4,237,756	Obama, Barack H.*	72,976	74,309	D	49.1%	50.0%	49.6%	50.4%
2008	8,390,744	4,045,624	McCain, John S. III	4,282,074	Obama, Barack H.	63,046	236,450	D	48.2%	51.0%	48.6%	51.4%
2004	7,609,810	3,964,522	Bush, George W.*	3,583,544	Kerry, John F.	61,744	380,978	R	52.1%	47.1%	52.5%	47.5%
2000**	5,963,110	2,912,790	Bush, George W.	2,912,253	Gore, Albert Jr.	138,067	537	R	48.8%	48.8%	50.0%	50.0%
1996**	5,303,794	2,244,536	Dole, Robert "Bob"	2,546,870	Clinton, Bill*	512,388	302,334	D	42.3%	48.0%	46.8%	53.2%
1992**	5,314,392	2,173,310	Bush, George H.*	2,072,698	Clinton, Bill	1,068,384	100,612	R	40.9%	39.0%	51.2%	48.8%
1988	4,302,313	2,618,885	Bush, George H.	1,656,701	Dukakis, Michael S.	26,727	962,184	R	60.9%	38.5%	61.3%	38.7%
1984	4,180,051	2,730,350	Reagan, Ronald*	1,448,816	Mondale, Walter F.	885	1,281,534	R	65.3%	34.7%	65.3%	34.7%
1980**	3,686,930	2,046,951	Reagan, Ronald	1,419,475	Carter, Jimmy*	220,504	627,476	R	55.5%	38.5%	59.1%	40.9%
1976	3,150,631	1,469,531	Ford, Gerald R.*	1,636,000	Carter, Jimmy	45,100	166,469	D	46.6%	51.9%	47.3%	52.7%
1972	2,583,283	1,857,759	Nixon, Richard M.*	718,117	McGovern, George S.	7,407	1,139,642	R	71.9%	27.8%	72.1%	27.9%
1968**	2,187,805	886,804	Nixon, Richard M.	676,794	Humphrey, Hubert Horatio Jr.	624,207	210,010	R	40.5%	30.9%	56.7%	43.3%
1964	1,854,481	905,941	Goldwater, Barry M. Sr.	948,540	Johnson, Lyndon B.*		42,599	D	48.9%	51.1%	48.9%	51.1%
1960	1,544,176	795,476	Nixon, Richard M.	748,700	Kennedy, John F.		46,776	R	51.5%	48.5%	51.5%	48.5%
1956	1,125,762	643,849	Eisenhower, Dwight D.*	480,371	Stevenson, Adlai E. II	1,542	163,478	R	57.2%	42.7%	57.3%	42.7%
1952	989,337	544,036	Eisenhower, Dwight D.	444,950	Stevenson, Adlai E. II	351	99,086	R	55.0%	45.0%	55.0%	45.0%
1948**	577,643	194,280	Dewey, Thomas E.	281,988	Truman, Harry S.*	101,375	87,708	D	33.6%	48.8%	40.8%	59.2%

Note: An asterisk (*) denotes incumbent. **In past elections, the other vote included: 2016 - 207,043 (Gary Johnson); 2000 - 97,488 Green (Ralph Nader); 1996 - 483,870 Reform (Ross Perot); 1992 - 1,053,067 Independent (Perot); 1980 - 189,692 Independent (John Anderson); 1968 - 624,207 American Independent (George Wallace); 1948 - 89,755 States' Rights (Strom Thurmond).

FLORIDA

POSTWAR VOTE FOR GOVERNOR

		Republican		Democratic				Percentage			
								Total Vote		Major Vote	
Year	Total Vote	Vote	Candidate	Vote	Candidate	Other Vote	Rep.-Dem. Plurality	Rep.	Dem.	Rep.	Dem.
2018	8,220,561	4,076,186	DeSantis, Ron	4,043,723	Gillum, Andrew	100,652	32,463 R	49.6%	49.2%	50.2%	49.8%
2014	5,951,561	2,865,343	Scott, Rick*	2,801,198	Crist, Charlie	285,020	64,145 R	48.1%	47.1%	50.6%	49.4%
2010	5,359,735	2,619,335	Scott, Rick	2,557,785	Sink, Alex	182,615	61,550 R	48.9%	47.7%	50.6%	49.4%
2006	4,829,270	2,519,845	Crist, Charlie	2,178,289	Davis, Jim	131,136	341,556 R	52.2%	45.1%	53.6%	46.4%
2002	5,100,581	2,856,845	Bush, Jeb*	2,201,427	McBride, Bill	42,309	655,418 R	56.0%	43.2%	56.5%	43.5%
1998	3,964,441	2,191,105	Bush, Jeb	1,773,054	MacKay, Buddy	282	418,051 R	55.3%	44.7%	55.3%	44.7%
1994	4,206,659	2,071,068	Bush, Jeb	2,135,008	Chiles, Lawton*	583	63,940 D	49.2%	50.8%	49.2%	50.8%
1990	3,530,871	1,535,068	Martinez, Bob*	1,995,206	Chiles, Lawton	597	460,138 D	43.5%	56.5%	43.5%	56.5%
1986	3,386,171	1,847,525	Martinez, Bob	1,538,620	Pajcic, Steve	26	308,905 R	54.6%	45.4%	54.6%	45.4%
1982	2,688,566	949,013	Bafalis, L. A.	1,739,553	Graham, Bob*		790,540 D	35.3%	64.7%	35.3%	64.7%
1978	2,530,468	1,123,888	Eckerd, Jack M.	1,406,580	Graham, Bob		282,692 D	44.4%	55.6%	44.4%	55.6%
1974	1,828,392	709,438	Thomas, Jerry	1,118,954	Askew, Reubin*		409,516 D	38.8%	61.2%	38.8%	61.2%
1970	1,730,813	746,243	Kirk, Claude R. Jr.*	984,305	Askew, Reubin	265	238,062 D	43.1%	56.9%	43.1%	56.9%
1966	1,489,661	821,190	Kirk, Claude R. Jr.	668,233	High, Robert King	238	152,957 R	55.1%	44.9%	55.1%	44.9%
1964**	1,663,481	686,297	Holley, Charles R.	933,554	Burns, Haydon	43,630	247,257 D	41.3%	56.1%	42.4%	57.6%
1960	1,419,343	569,936	Petersen, George C.	849,407	Bryant, Farris		279,471 D	40.2%	59.8%	40.2%	59.8%
1956	1,014,733	266,980	Washburn, William A. Jr.	747,753	Collins, Leroy*		480,773 D	26.3%	73.7%	26.3%	73.7%
1954S**	357,783	69,852	Watson, J. Tom	287,769	Collins, Leroy	162	217,917 D	19.5%	80.4%	19.5%	80.5%
1952	834,518	210,009	Swan, Harry S.	624,463	McCarty, Daniel T.	46	414,454 D	25.2%	74.8%	25.2%	74.8%
1948	457,638	76,153	Acker, Bert L.	381,459	Warren, Fuller	26	305,306 D	16.6%	83.4%	16.6%	83.4%

Note: An asterisk (*) denotes incumbent. **The 1964 election was for a two-year term to permit shifting the vote for governor to non-presidential years. The 1954 election was for a short term to fill a vacancy.

POSTWAR VOTE FOR SENATOR

		Republican		Democratic				Percentage			
								Total Vote		Major Vote	
Year	Total Vote	Vote	Candidate	Vote	Candidate	Other Vote	Rep.-Dem. Plurality	Rep.	Dem.	Rep.	Dem.
2018	8,190,005	4,099,505	Scott, Rick	4,089,472	Nelson, Bill*	1,028	10,033 R	50.1%	49.9%	50.1%	49.9%
2016	9,301,820	4,835,191	Rubio, Marco*	4,122,088	Murphy, Patrick	344,541	713,103 R	52.0%	44.3%	54.0%	46.0%
2012	8,189,946	3,458,267	Mack, Connie IV	4,523,451	Nelson, Bill*	208,228	1,065,184 D	42.2%	55.2%	43.3%	56.7%
2010**	5,411,106	2,645,743	Rubio, Marco	1,092,936	Meek, Kendrick B.	1,672,427	1,552,807 R	48.9%	20.2%	70.8%	29.2%
2006	4,793,534	1,826,127	Harris, Katherine	2,890,548	Nelson, "Bill"*	76,859	1,064,421 D	38.1%	60.3%	38.7%	61.3%
2004	7,429,894	3,672,864	Martinez, Mel	3,590,201	Castor, Betty	166,829	82,663 R	49.4%	48.3%	50.6%	49.4%
2000	5,856,731	2,705,348	McCollum, Bill	2,989,487	Nelson, "Bill"	161,896	284,139 D	46.2%	51.0%	47.5%	52.5%
1998	3,900,162	1,463,755	Crist, Charlie	2,436,407	Graham, Bob*		972,652 D	37.5%	62.5%	37.5%	62.5%
1994	4,106,176	2,894,726	Mack, Connie III*	1,210,412	Rodham, Hugh E.	1,038	1,684,314 R	70.5%	29.5%	70.5%	29.5%
1992	4,962,290	1,716,505	Grant, Bill	3,245,565	Graham, Bob*	220	1,529,060 D	34.6%	65.4%	34.6%	65.4%
1988	4,068,209	2,051,071	Mack, Connie III	2,016,553	MacKay, Buddy	585	34,518 R	50.4%	49.6%	50.4%	49.6%
1986	3,429,996	1,552,376	Hawkins, Paula*	1,877,543	Graham, Bob	77	325,167 D	45.3%	54.7%	45.3%	54.7%
1982	2,653,419	1,015,330	Poole, Van B.	1,637,667	Chiles, Lawton*	422	622,337 D	38.3%	61.7%	38.3%	61.7%
1980	3,528,028	1,822,460	Hawkins, Paula	1,705,409	Gunter, Bill	159	117,051 R	51.7%	48.3%	51.7%	48.3%
1976	2,857,534	1,057,886	Grady, John	1,799,518	Chiles, Lawton*	130	741,632 D	37.0%	63.0%	37.0%	63.0%
1974**	1,800,539	736,674	Eckerd, Jack M.	781,031	Stone, Richard	282,834	44,357 D	40.9%	43.4%	48.5%	51.5%
1970	1,675,378	772,817	Cramer, William C.	902,438	Chiles, Lawton	123	129,621 D	46.1%	53.9%	46.1%	53.9%
1968	2,024,136	1,131,499	Gurney, Edward J.	892,637	Collins, Leroy		238,862 R	55.9%	44.1%	55.9%	44.1%
1964	1,560,337	562,212	Kirk, Claude R. Jr.	997,585	Holland, Spessard L.*	540	435,373 D	36.0%	63.9%	36.0%	64.0%
1962	939,207	281,381	Rupert, Emerson H.	657,633	Smathers, George A.*	193	376,252 D	30.0%	70.0%	30.0%	70.0%
1958	542,069	155,956	Hyzer, Leland	386,113	Holland, Spessard L.*		230,157 D	28.8%	71.2%	28.8%	71.2%
1956	655,418			655,418	Smathers, George A.*		655,418 D		100.0%		100.0%
1952	617,800			616,665	Holland, Spessard L.*	1,135	616,665 D		99.8%		100.0%
1950	313,487	74,228	Booth, John P.	238,987	Smathers, George A.	272	164,759 D	23.7%	76.2%	23.7%	76.3%
1946	198,645	42,413	Schad, J. Harry	156,232	Holland, Spessard L.		113,819 D	21.4%	78.6%	21.4%	78.6%

Note: An asterisk (*) denotes incumbent. **In past elections, the other vote included: 2010 - 1,607,549 Independent (Charlie Crist), who placed second; 1974 - 282,659 American (John Grady). The Republican Party did not run a candidate in the 1952 and 1956 Senate elections.

FLORIDA

GOVERNOR 2018

2010 Census Population	County	Total Vote	Republican (DeSantis)	Democratic (Gillum)	Other	Rep.-Dem. Plurality	Percentage			
							Total Vote		Major Vote	
							Rep.	Dem.	Rep.	Dem.
247,336	ALACHUA	115,194	41,278	72,711	1,205	31,433 D	35.8%	63.1%	36.2%	63.8%
27,115	BAKER	10,542	8,687	1,760	95	6,927 R	82.4%	16.7%	83.2%	16.8%
168,852	BAY	63,331	45,709	16,757	865	28,952 R	72.2%	26.5%	73.2%	26.8%
28,520	BRADFORD	10,505	7,698	2,671	136	5,027 R	73.3%	25.4%	74.2%	25.8%
543,376	BREVARD	281,588	162,213	114,921	4,454	47,292 R	57.6%	40.8%	58.5%	41.5%
1,748,066	BROWARD	709,179	222,012	482,152	5,015	260,140 D	31.3%	68.0%	31.5%	68.5%
14,625	CALHOUN	4,609	3,576	923	110	2,653 R	77.6%	20.0%	79.5%	20.5%
159,978	CHARLOTTE	86,896	54,102	31,248	1,546	22,854 R	62.3%	36.0%	63.4%	36.6%
141,236	CITRUS	70,898	47,729	21,197	1,972	26,532 R	67.3%	29.9%	69.2%	30.8%
190,865	CLAY	93,482	64,401	28,150	931	36,251 R	68.9%	30.1%	69.6%	30.4%
321,520	COLLIER	155,453	100,303	53,594	1,556	46,709 R	64.5%	34.5%	65.2%	34.8%
67,531	COLUMBIA	24,843	17,426	7,105	312	10,321 R	70.1%	28.6%	71.0%	29.0%
34,862	DESOTO	8,902	5,663	3,059	180	2,604 R	63.6%	34.4%	64.9%	35.1%
16,422	DIXIE	5,801	4,663	1,008	130	3,655 R	80.4%	17.4%	82.2%	17.8%
864,263	DUVAL	379,948	179,902	196,612	3,434	16,710 D	47.3%	51.7%	47.8%	52.2%
297,619	ESCAMBIA	129,367	74,719	52,835	1,813	21,884 R	57.8%	40.8%	58.6%	41.4%
95,696	FLAGLER	52,816	30,951	21,183	682	9,768 R	58.6%	40.1%	59.4%	40.6%
11,549	FRANKLIN	5,420	3,508	1,790	122	1,718 R	64.7%	33.0%	66.2%	33.8%
46,389	GADSDEN	20,058	6,200	13,712	146	7,512 D	30.9%	68.4%	31.1%	68.9%
16,939	GILCHRIST	7,366	5,975	1,282	109	4,693 R	81.1%	17.4%	82.3%	17.7%
12,884	GLADES	3,830	2,647	1,095	88	1,552 R	69.1%	28.6%	70.7%	29.3%
15,863	GULF	5,896	4,265	1,511	120	2,754 R	72.3%	25.6%	73.8%	26.2%
14,799	HAMILTON	4,552	2,908	1,591	53	1,317 R	63.9%	35.0%	64.6%	35.4%
27,731	HARDEE	6,398	4,486	1,802	110	2,684 R	70.1%	28.2%	71.3%	28.7%
39,140	HENDRY	8,873	5,177	3,516	180	1,661 R	58.3%	39.6%	59.6%	40.4%
172,778	HERNANDO	80,614	49,671	29,426	1,517	20,245 R	61.6%	36.5%	62.8%	37.2%
98,786	HIGHLANDS	39,757	26,285	12,783	689	13,502 R	66.1%	32.2%	67.3%	32.7%
1,229,226	HILLSBOROUGH	522,863	234,835	281,598	6,430	46,763 D	44.9%	53.9%	45.5%	54.5%
19,927	HOLMES	6,773	5,940	737	96	5,203 R	87.7%	10.9%	89.0%	11.0%
138,028	INDIAN RIVER	74,252	44,925	28,460	867	16,465 R	60.5%	38.3%	61.2%	38.8%
49,746	JACKSON	15,977	10,771	5,019	187	5,752 R	67.4%	31.4%	68.2%	31.8%
14,761	JEFFERSON	7,359	3,877	3,375	107	502 R	52.7%	45.9%	53.5%	46.5%
8,870	LAFAYETTE	2,825	2,364	419	42	1,945 R	83.7%	14.8%	84.9%	15.1%
297,052	LAKE	155,138	92,633	60,289	2,216	32,344 R	59.7%	38.9%	60.6%	39.4%
618,754	LEE	289,577	174,085	111,172	4,320	62,913 R	60.1%	38.4%	61.0%	39.0%
275,487	LEON	140,034	49,942	88,764	1,328	38,822 D	35.7%	63.4%	36.0%	64.0%
40,801	LEVY	17,089	12,084	4,718	287	7,366 R	70.7%	27.6%	71.9%	28.1%
8,365	LIBERTY	2,682	2,060	527	95	1,533 R	76.8%	19.6%	79.6%	20.4%
19,224	MADISON	7,625	4,345	3,235	45	1,110 R	57.0%	42.4%	57.3%	42.7%
322,833	MANATEE	163,349	93,246	67,629	2,474	25,617 R	57.1%	41.4%	58.0%	42.0%
331,298	MARION	154,861	94,901	57,392	2,568	37,509 R	61.3%	37.1%	62.3%	37.7%
146,318	MARTIN	77,723	47,820	29,133	770	18,687 R	61.5%	37.5%	62.1%	37.9%
2,496,435	MIAMI-DADE	799,024	311,581	478,958	8,485	167,377 D	39.0%	59.9%	39.4%	60.6%
73,090	MONROE	36,133	18,509	17,176	448	1,333 R	51.2%	47.5%	51.9%	48.1%
73,314	NASSAU	43,566	31,704	11,472	390	20,232 R	72.8%	26.3%	73.4%	26.6%
180,822	OKALOOSA	83,882	59,940	22,408	1,534	37,532 R	71.5%	26.7%	72.8%	27.2%
39,996	OKEECHOBEE	11,239	7,730	3,306	203	4,424 R	68.8%	29.4%	70.0%	30.0%
1,145,956	ORANGE	475,719	174,228	296,257	5,234	122,029 D	36.6%	62.3%	37.0%	63.0%
268,685	OSCEOLA	115,021	44,627	68,707	1,687	24,080 D	38.8%	59.7%	39.4%	60.6%
1,320,134	PALM BEACH	586,724	241,016	341,409	4,299	100,393 D	41.1%	58.2%	41.4%	58.6%
464,697	PASCO	210,941	120,753	86,384	3,804	34,369 R	57.2%	41.0%	58.3%	41.7%
916,542	PINELLAS	435,294	207,677	220,818	6,799	13,141 D	47.7%	50.7%	48.5%	51.5%
602,095	POLK	244,413	136,711	104,057	3,645	32,654 R	55.9%	42.6%	56.8%	43.2%
74,364	PUTNAM	28,124	18,721	9,011	392	9,710 R	66.6%	32.0%	67.5%	32.5%
151,372	SANTA ROSA	75,567	56,148	18,207	1,212	37,941 R	74.3%	24.1%	75.5%	24.5%
379,448	SARASOTA	210,948	113,211	94,986	2,751	18,225 R	53.7%	45.0%	54.4%	45.6%
422,718	SEMINOLE	199,216	96,622	100,197	2,397	3,575 D	48.5%	50.3%	49.1%	50.9%
190,039	ST. JOHNS	130,997	83,658	46,206	1,133	37,452 R	63.9%	35.3%	64.4%	35.6%
277,789	ST. LUCIE	124,038	58,990	63,605	1,443	4,615 D	47.6%	51.3%	48.1%	51.9%
93,420	SUMTER	74,396	51,798	21,843	755	29,955 R	69.6%	29.4%	70.3%	29.7%

FLORIDA

GOVERNOR 2018

2010 Census Population	County	Total Vote	Republican (DeSantis)	Democratic (Gillum)	Other	Rep.-Dem. Plurality	Percentage: Total Vote Rep.	Total Vote Dem.	Major Vote Rep.	Major Vote Dem.
41,551	SUWANNEE	15,906	12,234	3,450	222	8,784 R	76.9%	21.7%	78.0%	22.0%
22,570	TAYLOR	7,941	5,942	1,877	122	4,065 R	74.8%	23.6%	76.0%	24.0%
15,535	UNION	4,868	3,841	972	55	2,869 R	78.9%	20.0%	79.8%	20.2%
494,593	VOLUSIA	228,760	124,819	100,478	3,463	24,341 R	54.6%	43.9%	55.4%	44.6%
30,776	WAKULLA	14,220	9,802	4,194	224	5,608 R	68.9%	29.5%	70.0%	30.0%
55,043	WALTON	30,331	22,925	7,019	387	15,906 R	75.6%	23.1%	76.6%	23.4%
24,896	WASHINGTON	9,048	7,017	1,865	166	5,152 R	77.6%	20.6%	79.0%	21.0%
18,801,310	*TOTAL*	*8,220,561*	*4,076,186*	*4,043,723*	*100,652*	*32,463 R*	*49.6%*	*49.2%*	*50.2%*	*49.8%*

FLORIDA

SENATOR 2018

2010 Census Population	County	Total Vote	Republican (Scott)	Democratic (Nelson)	Other	Rep.-Dem. Plurality	Percentage: Total Vote Rep.	Total Vote Dem.	Major Vote Rep.	Major Vote Dem.
247,336	ALACHUA	115,112	40,599	74,493	20	33,894 D	35.3%	64.7%	35.3%	64.7%
27,115	BAKER	10,525	8,579	1,945	1	6,634 R	81.5%	18.5%	81.5%	18.5%
168,852	BAY	63,411	46,681	16,723	7	29,958 R	73.6%	26.4%	73.6%	26.4%
28,520	BRADFORD	10,456	7,576	2,879	1	4,697 R	72.5%	27.5%	72.5%	27.5%
543,376	BREVARD	281,473	160,305	121,112	56	39,193 R	57.0%	43.0%	57.0%	43.0%
1,748,066	BROWARD	683,636	211,397	472,239		260,842 D	30.9%	69.1%	30.9%	69.1%
14,625	CALHOUN	4,619	3,586	1,033		2,553 R	77.6%	22.4%	77.6%	22.4%
159,978	CHARLOTTE	86,457	52,916	33,525	16	19,391 R	61.2%	38.8%	61.2%	38.8%
141,236	CITRUS	70,683	48,008	22,660	15	25,348 R	67.9%	32.1%	67.9%	32.1%
190,865	CLAY	93,368	65,639	27,718	11	37,921 R	70.3%	29.7%	70.3%	29.7%
321,520	COLLIER	155,662	101,266	54,390	6	46,876 R	65.1%	34.9%	65.1%	34.9%
67,531	COLUMBIA	24,745	17,234	7,505	6	9,729 R	69.6%	30.3%	69.7%	30.3%
34,862	DESOTO	8,831	5,503	3,328		2,175 R	62.3%	37.7%	62.3%	37.7%
16,422	DIXIE	5,764	4,442	1,322		3,120 R	77.1%	22.9%	77.1%	22.9%
864,263	DUVAL	378,330	185,904	192,381	45	6,477 D	49.1%	50.9%	49.1%	50.9%
297,619	ESCAMBIA	128,855	75,947	52,891	17	23,056 R	58.9%	41.0%	58.9%	41.1%
95,696	FLAGLER	52,897	31,467	21,419	11	10,048 R	59.5%	40.5%	59.5%	40.5%
11,549	FRANKLIN	5,415	3,404	2,011		1,393 R	62.9%	37.1%	62.9%	37.1%
46,389	GADSDEN	19,997	6,051	13,945	1	7,894 D	30.3%	69.7%	30.3%	69.7%
16,939	GILCHRIST	7,336	5,703	1,633		4,070 R	77.7%	22.3%	77.7%	22.3%
12,884	GLADES	3,823	2,666	1,156	1	1,510 R	69.7%	30.2%	69.8%	30.2%
15,863	GULF	5,901	4,321	1,580		2,741 R	73.2%	26.8%	73.2%	26.8%
14,799	HAMILTON	4,527	2,856	1,671		1,185 R	63.1%	36.9%	63.1%	36.9%
27,731	HARDEE	6,371	4,455	1,916		2,539 R	69.9%	30.1%	69.9%	30.1%
39,140	HENDRY	8,846	5,304	3,542		1,762 R	60.0%	40.0%	60.0%	40.0%
172,778	HERNANDO	80,313	49,501	30,798	14	18,703 R	61.6%	38.3%	61.6%	38.4%
98,786	HIGHLANDS	39,686	26,282	13,398	6	12,884 R	66.2%	33.8%	66.2%	33.8%
1,229,226	HILLSBOROUGH	521,374	239,641	281,661	72	42,020 D	46.0%	54.0%	46.0%	54.0%
19,927	HOLMES	6,775	5,919	856		5,063 R	87.4%	12.6%	87.4%	12.6%
138,028	INDIAN RIVER	74,004	44,798	29,195	11	15,603 R	60.5%	39.5%	60.5%	39.5%
49,746	JACKSON	15,974	10,791	5,182	1	5,609 R	67.6%	32.4%	67.6%	32.4%
14,761	JEFFERSON	7,327	3,699	3,626	2	73 R	50.5%	49.5%	50.5%	49.5%
8,870	LAFAYETTE	2,818	2,195	623		1,572 R	77.9%	22.1%	77.9%	22.1%
297,052	LAKE	154,954	93,537	61,402	15	32,135 R	60.4%	39.6%	60.4%	39.6%
618,754	LEE	289,214	174,316	114,857	41	59,459 R	60.3%	39.7%	60.3%	39.7%

FLORIDA

SENATOR 2018

2010 Census Population	County	Total Vote	Republican (Scott)	Democratic (Nelson)	Other	Rep.-Dem. Plurality	Percentage Total Vote Rep.	Total Vote Dem.	Major Vote Rep.	Major Vote Dem.
275,487	LEON	139,898	48,767	91,097	34	42,330 D	34.9%	65.1%	34.9%	65.1%
40,801	LEVY	16,980	11,658	5,319	3	6,339 R	68.7%	31.3%	68.7%	31.3%
8,365	LIBERTY	2,708	2,076	632		1,444 R	76.7%	23.3%	76.7%	23.3%
19,224	MADISON	7,609	4,184	3,425		759 R	55.0%	45.0%	55.0%	45.0%
322,833	MANATEE	163,295	94,390	68,877	28	25,513 R	57.8%	42.2%	57.8%	42.2%
331,298	MARION	154,661	95,592	59,025	44	36,567 R	61.8%	38.2%	61.8%	38.2%
146,318	MARTIN	77,436	46,733	30,691	12	16,042 R	60.4%	39.6%	60.4%	39.6%
2,496,435	MIAMI-DADE	801,547	316,020	485,496	31	169,476 D	39.4%	60.6%	39.4%	60.6%
73,090	MONROE	36,090	18,035	18,051	4	16 D	50.0%	50.0%	50.0%	50.0%
73,314	NASSAU	43,501	31,795	11,703	3	20,092 R	73.1%	26.9%	73.1%	26.9%
180,822	OKALOOSA	83,845	60,924	22,902	19	38,022 R	72.7%	27.3%	72.7%	27.3%
39,996	OKEECHOBEE	11,224	7,727	3,496	1	4,231 R	68.8%	31.1%	68.8%	31.2%
1,145,956	ORANGE	475,141	180,763	294,308	70	113,545 D	38.0%	61.9%	38.0%	62.0%
268,685	OSCEOLA	115,029	47,898	67,123	8	19,225 D	41.6%	58.4%	41.6%	58.4%
1,320,134	PALM BEACH	588,894	244,850	344,008	36	99,158 D	41.6%	58.4%	41.6%	58.4%
464,697	PASCO	210,710	121,212	89,447	51	31,765 R	57.5%	42.5%	57.5%	42.5%
916,542	PINELLAS	434,774	205,935	228,712	127	22,777 D	47.4%	52.6%	47.4%	52.6%
602,095	POLK	244,544	138,751	105,748	45	33,003 R	56.7%	43.2%	56.7%	43.3%
74,364	PUTNAM	28,038	18,689	9,344	5	9,345 R	66.7%	33.3%	66.7%	33.3%
151,372	SANTA ROSA	75,431	56,374	19,047	10	37,327 R	74.7%	25.3%	74.7%	25.3%
379,448	SARASOTA	210,593	113,585	96,973	35	16,612 R	53.9%	46.0%	53.9%	46.1%
422,718	SEMINOLE	198,992	97,457	101,504	31	4,047 D	49.0%	51.0%	49.0%	51.0%
190,039	ST. JOHNS	130,681	85,031	45,638	12	39,393 R	65.1%	34.9%	65.1%	34.9%
277,789	ST. LUCIE	123,624	59,612	63,978	34	4,366 D	48.2%	51.8%	48.2%	51.8%
93,420	SUMTER	74,549	52,868	21,678	3	31,190 R	70.9%	29.1%	70.9%	29.1%
41,551	SUWANNEE	15,888	11,842	4,044	2	7,798 R	74.5%	25.5%	74.5%	25.5%
22,570	TAYLOR	7,901	5,638	2,263		3,375 R	71.4%	28.6%	71.4%	28.6%
15,535	UNION	4,847	3,650	1,197		2,453 R	75.3%	24.7%	75.3%	24.7%
494,593	VOLUSIA	228,581	125,762	102,819		22,943 R	55.0%	45.0%	55.0%	45.0%
30,776	WAKULLA	14,190	9,322	4,868		4,454 R	65.7%	34.3%	65.7%	34.3%
55,043	WALTON	30,265	22,776	7,485	4	15,291 R	75.3%	24.7%	75.3%	24.7%
24,896	WASHINGTON	9,060	7,101	1,959		5,142 R	78.4%	21.6%	78.4%	21.6%
18,801,310	*TOTAL*	*8,190,005*	*4,099,505*	*4,089,472*	*1,028*	*10,033 R*	*50.1%*	*49.9%*	*50.1%*	*49.9%*

FLORIDA

HOUSE OF REPRESENTATIVES

CD	Year	Total Vote	Republican Vote	Republican Candidate	Democratic Vote	Democratic Candidate	Other Vote	Rep.-Dem. Plurality	Percentage Total Vote Rep.	Total Vote Dem.	Major Vote Rep.	Major Vote Dem.
1	2018	322,388	216,189	GAETZ, MATT*	106,199	ZIMMERMAN, JENNIFER M.		109,990 R	67.1%	32.9%	67.1%	32.9%
1	2016	369,186	255,107	GAETZ, MATT	114,079	SPECHT, STEVEN		141,028 R	69.1%	30.9%	69.1%	30.9%
1	2014	235,343	165,086	MILLER, JEFF*	54,976	BRYAN, JAMES "JIM"	15,281	110,110 R	70.1%	23.4%	75.0%	25.0%
1	2012	342,594	238,440	MILLER, JEFF*	92,961	BRYAN, JAMES "JIM"	11,193	145,479 R	69.6%	27.1%	71.9%	28.1%
2**	2018	295,568	199,335	DUNN, NEAL*	96,233	RACKLEFF, BOB		103,102 R	67.4%	32.6%	67.4%	32.6%
2**	2016	343,362	231,163	DUNN, NEAL	102,801	DARTLAND, WALTER	9,398	128,362 R	67.3%	29.9%	69.2%	30.8%
2	2014	249,780	123,262	SOUTHERLAND, STEVE*	126,096	GRAHAM, GWEN	422	2,834 D	49.3%	50.5%	49.4%	50.6%
2	2012	333,718	175,856	SOUTHERLAND, STEVE*	157,634	LAWSON, AL	228	18,222 R	52.7%	47.2%	52.7%	47.3%
3**	2018	306,496	176,616	YOHO, TED*	129,880	HAYES HINSON, YVONNE		46,736 R	57.6%	42.4%	57.6%	42.4%
3**	2016	342,700	193,843	YOHO, TED*	136,338	MCGURN, KENNETH "KEN"	12,519	57,505 R	56.6%	39.8%	58.7%	41.3%
3	2014	228,809	148,691	YOHO, TED*	73,910	WHEELER, MARIHELEN HADDOCK	6,208	74,781 R	65.0%	32.3%	66.8%	33.2%
3	2012	315,669	204,331	YOHO, TED	102,468	GAILLOT, J.R.	8,870	101,863 R	64.7%	32.5%	66.6%	33.4%

FLORIDA

HOUSE OF REPRESENTATIVES

			Republican		Democratic				Percentage			
									Total Vote		Major Vote	
CD	Year	Total Vote	Vote	Candidate	Vote	Candidate	Other Vote	Rep.-Dem. Plurality	Rep.	Dem.	Rep.	Dem.
4**	2018	381,249	248,420	RUTHERFORD, JOHN*	123,351	SELMONT, GEORGE "GES"	9,478	125,069 R	65.2%	32.4%	66.8%	33.2%
4**	2016	409,662	287,509	RUTHERFORD, JOHN	113,088	BRUDERLY, DAVID E.	9,065	174,421 R	70.2%	27.6%	71.8%	28.2%
4	2014	227,253	177,887	CRENSHAW, ANDER*			49,366	177,887 R	78.3%		100.0%	
4	2012	315,470	239,988	CRENSHAW, ANDER*			75,482	239,988 R	76.1%		100.0%	
5**	2018	270,326	89,799	FULLER, VIRGINIA	180,527	LAWSON, AL*		90,728 D	33.2%	66.8%	33.2%	66.8%
5**	2016	302,874	108,325	SCURRY-SMITH, GLOREATHA "GLO"	194,549	LAWSON, AL		86,224 D	35.8%	64.2%	35.8%	64.2%
5	2014	171,577	59,237	SCURRY-SMITH, GLOREATHA "GLO"	112,340	BROWN, CORRINE*		53,103 D	34.5%	65.5%	34.5%	65.5%
5	2012	269,153	70,700	KOLB, LEANNE	190,472	BROWN, CORRINE*	7,981	119,772 D	26.3%	70.8%	27.1%	72.9%
6**	2018	333,649	187,891	WALTZ, MICHAEL	145,758	SODERBERG, NANCY		42,133 R	56.3%	43.7%	56.3%	43.7%
6**	2016	364,570	213,519	DESANTIS, RON*	151,051	MCCULLOUGH, WILLIAM "BILL"		62,468 R	58.6%	41.4%	58.6%	41.4%
6	2014	265,817	166,254	DESANTIS, RON*	99,563	COX, DAVID		66,691 R	62.5%	37.5%	62.5%	37.5%
6	2012	342,451	195,962	DESANTIS, RON	146,489	BEAVEN, HEATHER		49,473 R	57.2%	42.8%	57.2%	42.8%
7**	2018	317,398	134,285	MILLER, MIKE	183,113	MURPHY, STEPHANIE*		48,828 D	42.3%	57.7%	42.3%	57.7%
7**	2016	353,655	171,583	MICA, JOHN L.*	182,039	MURPHY, STEPHANIE	33	10,456 D	48.5%	51.5%	48.5%	51.5%
7	2014	227,164	144,474	MICA, JOHN L.*	73,011	NEUMAN, WESLEY RYAN "WES"	9,679	71,463 R	63.6%	32.1%	66.4%	33.6%
7	2012	316,010	185,518	MICA, JOHN L.*	130,479	KENDALL, JASON H.	13	55,039 R	58.7%	41.3%	58.7%	41.3%
8	2018	360,527	218,112	POSEY, BILL*	142,415	PATEL, SANJAY		75,697 R	60.5%	39.5%	60.5%	39.5%
8	2016	390,561	246,483	POSEY, BILL*	127,127	WESTBROOK, CORRY	16,951	119,356 R	63.1%	32.5%	66.0%	34.0%
8	2014	274,513	180,728	POSEY, BILL*	93,724	ROTHBLATT, GABRIEL	61	87,004 R	65.8%	34.1%	65.9%	34.1%
8	2012	348,909	205,432	POSEY, BILL*	130,870	ROBERTS, SHANNON	12,607	74,562 R	58.9%	37.5%	61.1%	38.9%
9**	2018	296,737	124,565	LIEBNITZKY, WAYNE	172,172	SOTO, DARREN*		47,607 D	42.0%	58.0%	42.0%	58.0%
9**	2016	339,761	144,450	LIEBNITZKY, WAYNE	195,311	SOTO, DARREN		50,861 D	42.5%	57.5%	42.5%	57.5%
9	2014	173,878	74,963	PLATT, CAROL	93,850	GRAYSON, ALAN*	5,065	18,887 D	43.1%	54.0%	44.4%	55.6%
9	2012	263,747	98,856	LONG, TODD	164,891	GRAYSON, ALAN		66,035 D	37.5%	62.5%	37.5%	62.5%
10**	2018				Unopposed	DEMINGS, VAL B.*		D				
10**	2016	305,989	107,498	LOWE, THUY "TWEE"	198,491	DEMINGS, VAL B.		90,993 D	35.1%	64.9%	35.1%	64.9%
10	2014	232,574	143,128	WEBSTER, DANIEL A.*	89,426	MCKENNA, MICHAEL PATRICK	20	53,702 R	61.5%	38.5%	61.5%	38.5%
10	2012	318,269	164,649	WEBSTER, DANIEL A.*	153,574	DEMINGS, VAL B.	46	11,075 R	51.7%	48.3%	51.7%	48.3%
11**	2018	367,506	239,395	WEBSTER, DANIEL A.*	128,053	COTTRELL, DANA	58	111,342 R	65.1%	34.8%	65.2%	34.8%
11**	2016	394,719	258,016	WEBSTER, DANIEL A.	124,713	KOLLER, DAVID C.	11,990	133,303 R	65.4%	31.6%	67.4%	32.6%
11	2014	272,294	181,508	NUGENT, RICHARD B.*	90,786	KOLLER, DAVID C.		90,722 R	66.7%	33.3%	66.7%	33.3%
11	2012	338,663	218,360	NUGENT, RICHARD B.*	120,303	WERDER, H. DAVID		98,057 R	64.5%	35.5%	64.5%	35.5%
12**	2018	334,918	194,564	BILIRAKIS, GUS MICHAEL*	132,844	HUNTER, CHRIS	7,510	61,720 R	58.1%	39.7%	59.4%	40.6%
12**	2016	369,669	253,559	BILIRAKIS, GUS MICHAEL*	116,110	TAGER, ROBERT MATTHEW		137,449 R	68.6%	31.4%	68.6%	31.4%
12	2014		Unopposed	BILIRAKIS, GUS MICHAEL*				R				
12	2012	330,167	209,604	BILIRAKIS, GUS MICHAEL*	108,770	SNOW, JONATHAN MICHAEL	11,793	100,834 R	63.5%	32.9%	65.8%	34.2%
13**	2018	316,971	134,254	BUCK, GEORGE	182,717	CRIST, CHARLIE*		48,463 D	42.4%	57.6%	42.4%	57.6%
13**	2016	355,842	171,149	JOLLY, DAVID W.*	184,693	CRIST, CHARLIE		13,544 D	48.1%	51.9%	48.1%	51.9%
13	2014	223,576	168,172	JOLLY, DAVID W.*			55,404	168,172 R	75.2%		100.0%	
13	2012	329,347	189,605	YOUNG, C.W. BILL*	139,742	EHRLICH, JESSICA		49,863 R	57.6%	42.4%	57.6%	42.4%
14**	2018				Unopposed	CASTOR, KATHY*		D				
14**	2016	316,877	121,088	QUINN, CHRISTINE	195,789	CASTOR, KATHY*		74,701 D	38.2%	61.8%	38.2%	61.8%
14	2014				Unopposed	CASTOR, KATHY*		D				
14	2012	280,601	83,480	OTERO, EVELIO "EJ"	197,121	CASTOR, KATHY*		113,641 D	29.8%	70.2%	29.8%	70.2%
15**	2018	285,532	151,380	SPANO, ROSS	134,132	CARLSON, KRISTEN	20	17,248 R	53.0%	47.0%	53.0%	47.0%
15**	2016	318,474	182,999	ROSS, DENNIS A.*	135,475	LANGE, JIM		47,524 R	57.5%	42.5%	57.5%	42.5%
15	2014	213,582	128,750	ROSS, DENNIS A.*	84,832	COHN, ALAN MICHAEL		43,918 R	60.3%	39.7%	60.3%	39.7%
15	2012		Unopposed	ROSS, DENNIS A.				R				
16**	2018	361,946	197,483	BUCHANAN, VERN*	164,463	SHAPIRO, DAVID		33,020 R	54.6%	45.4%	54.6%	45.4%
16**	2016	385,916	230,654	BUCHANAN, VERN*	155,262	SCHNEIDER, JAN		75,392 R	59.8%	40.2%	59.8%	40.2%
16	2014	274,829	169,126	BUCHANAN, VERN*	105,483	LAWRENCE, HENRY	220	63,643 R	61.5%	38.4%	61.6%	38.4%
16	2012	349,076	187,147	BUCHANAN, VERN*	161,929	FITZGERALD, KEITH		25,218 R	53.6%	46.4%	53.6%	46.4%
17**	2018	310,520	193,326	STEUBE, GREG	117,194	ELLISON, ALLEN		76,132 R	62.3%	37.7%	62.3%	37.7%
17**	2016	338,675	209,348	ROONEY, TOM*	115,974	FREEMAN, APRIL	13,353	93,374 R	61.8%	34.2%	64.4%	35.6%
17	2014	223,756	141,493	ROONEY, TOM*	82,263	BRONSON, WILLIAM		59,230 R	63.2%	36.8%	63.2%	36.8%
17	2012	282,271	165,488	ROONEY, TOM*	116,766	BRONSON, WILLIAM	17	48,722 R	58.6%	41.4%	58.6%	41.4%

FLORIDA

HOUSE OF REPRESENTATIVES

CD	Year	Total Vote	Republican Vote	Republican Candidate	Democratic Vote	Democratic Candidate	Other Vote	Rep.-Dem. Plurality	Percentage Total Vote Rep.	Percentage Total Vote Dem.	Percentage Major Vote Rep.	Percentage Major Vote Dem.
18**	2018	342,359	185,905	MAST, BRIAN*	156,454	BAER, LAUREN		29,451 R	54.3%	45.7%	54.3%	45.7%
18**	2016	375,918	201,488	MAST, BRIAN	161,918	PERKINS, RANDY	12,512	39,570 R	53.6%	43.1%	55.4%	44.6%
18	2014	253,374	101,896	DOMINO, CARL J.	151,478	MURPHY, PATRICK*		49,582 D	40.2%	59.8%	40.2%	59.8%
18	2012	330,665	164,353	WEST, ALLEN*	166,257	MURPHY, PATRICK	55	1,904 D	49.7%	50.3%	49.7%	50.3%
19	2018	339,607	211,465	ROONEY, FRANCIS*	128,106	HOLDEN, DAVID	36	83,359 R	62.3%	37.7%	62.3%	37.7%
19	2016	363,166	239,225	ROONEY, FRANCIS	123,812	NEELD, ROBERT M.	129	115,413 R	65.9%	34.1%	65.9%	34.1%
19	2014	246,861	159,354	CLAWSON, CURT J.*	80,824	FREEMAN, APRIL	6,683	78,530 R	64.6%	32.7%	66.3%	33.7%
19	2012	306,216	189,833	RADEL, TREY	109,746	ROACH, JIM	6,637	80,087 R	62.0%	35.8%	63.4%	36.6%
20**	2018	202,824			202,659	HASTINGS, ALCEE L.*	165	202,659 D		99.9%		100.0%
20**	2016	277,560	54,646	STEIN, GARY	222,914	HASTINGS, ALCEE L.*		168,268 D	19.7%	80.3%	19.7%	80.3%
20	2014	157,466	28,968	BONNER, JAY	128,498	HASTINGS, ALCEE L.*		99,530 D	18.4%	81.6%	18.4%	81.6%
20	2012	244,285			214,727	HASTINGS, ALCEE L.*	29,558	214,727 D		87.9%		100.0%
21**	2018				Unopposed	FRANKEL, LOIS*		D				
21**	2016	335,861	118,038	SPAIN, PAUL DOUGLAS	210,606	FRANKEL, LOIS*	7,217	92,568 D	35.1%	62.7%	35.9%	64.1%
21	2014	153,970			153,395	DEUTCH, TED*	575	153,395 D		99.6%		100.0%
21	2012	284,400			221,263	DEUTCH, TED*	63,137	221,263 D		77.8%		100.0%
22**	2018	297,683	113,049	KIMAZ, NICHOLAS	184,634	DEUTCH, TED*		71,585 D	38.0%	62.0%	38.0%	62.0%
22**	2016	337,850	138,737	MCGEE, ANDREA LEIGH	199,113	DEUTCH, TED*		60,376 D	41.1%	58.9%	41.1%	58.9%
22	2014	216,096	90,685	SPAIN, PAUL DOUGLAS	125,404	FRANKEL, LOIS*	7	34,719 D	42.0%	58.0%	42.0%	58.0%
22	2012	313,071	142,050	HASNER, ADAM	171,021	FRANKEL, LOIS		28,971 D	45.4%	54.6%	45.4%	54.6%
23**	2018	276,366	99,446	KAUFMAN, JOSEPH "JOE"	161,611	WASSERMAN-SCHULTZ, DEBBIE*	15,309	62,165 D	36.0%	58.5%	38.1%	61.9%
23**	2016	323,120	130,818	KAUFMAN, JOSEPH "JOE"	183,225	WASSERMAN-SCHULTZ, DEBBIE*	9,077	52,407 D	40.5%	56.7%	41.7%	58.3%
23	2014	164,788	61,519	KAUFMAN, JOSEPH "JOE"	103,269	WASSERMAN-SCHULTZ, DEBBIE*		41,750 D	37.3%	62.7%	37.3%	62.7%
23	2012	275,430	98,096	HARRINGTON, KAREN	174,205	WASSERMAN-SCHULTZ, DEBBIE*	3,129	76,109 D	35.6%	63.2%	36.0%	64.0%
24**	2018				Unopposed	WILSON, FREDERICA S.*		D				
24**	2016				Unopposed	WILSON, FREDERICA S.*		D				
24	2014	149,918	15,239	NEREE, DUFIRSTSON	129,192	WILSON, FREDERICA S.*	5,487	113,953 D	10.2%	86.2%	10.6%	89.4%
24	2012				Unopposed	WILSON, FREDERICA S.		D				
25**	2018	212,845	128,672	DIAZ-BALART, MARIO*	84,173	BARZEE FLORES, MARY		44,499 R	60.5%	39.5%	60.5%	39.5%
25**	2016	253,240	157,921	DIAZ-BALART, MARIO*	95,319	VALDES, ALINA		62,602 R	62.4%	37.6%	62.4%	37.6%
25	2014		Unopposed	DIAZ-BALART, MARIO*								
25	2012	200,229	151,466	DIAZ-BALART, MARIO*			48,763	151,466 R	75.6%		100.0%	
26**	2018	235,475	115,678	CURBELO, CARLOS*	119,797	MUCARSEL-POWELL, DEBBIE		4,119 D	49.1%	50.9%	49.1%	50.9%
26**	2016	280,542	148,547	CURBELO, CARLOS*	115,493	GARCIA, JOE	16,502	33,054 R	53.0%	41.2%	56.3%	43.7%
26	2014	161,337	83,031	CURBELO, CARLOS	78,306	GARCIA, JOE*		4,725 R	51.5%	48.5%	51.5%	48.5%
26	2012	252,957	108,820	RIVERA, DAVID*	135,694	GARCIA, JOE	8,443	26,874 D	43.0%	53.6%	44.5%	55.5%
27**	2018	252,586	115,588	SALAZAR, MARIA ELVIRA	130,743	SHALALA, DONNA	6,255	15,155 D	45.8%	51.8%	46.9%	53.1%
27**	2016	287,677	157,917	ROS-LEHTINEN, ILEANA*	129,760	FUHRMAN, SCOTT		28,157 R	54.9%	45.1%	54.9%	45.1%
27	2014		Unopposed	ROS-LEHTINEN, ILEANA*				R				
27	2012	230,171	138,488	ROS-LEHTINEN, ILEANA*	85,020	YEVANCEY, MANNY	6,663	53,468 R	60.2%	36.9%	62.0%	38.0%
TOTAL	*2018*	*7,021,476*	*3,675,417*		*3,307,228*		*38,831*	*368,189 R*	*52.3%*	*47.1%*	*52.6%*	*47.4%*
TOTAL	*2016*	*8,837,426*	*4,733,630*		*3,985,050*		*118,746*	*748,580 R*	*53.6%*	*45.1%*	*54.3%*	*45.7%*
TOTAL	*2014*	*4,998,555*	*2,713,451*		*2,130,626*		*154,478*	*582,825 R*	*54.3%*	*42.6%*	*56.0%*	*44.0%*
TOTAL	*2012*	*7,513,539*	*3,826,522*		*3,392,402*		*294,615*	*434,120 R*	*50.9%*	*45.2%*	*53.0%*	*47.0%*

Note: An asterisk (*) denotes incumbent. **Due to mid-decade redistricting, boundaries for all districts except CD 1, 8, and 19 are not comparable to those used in the 2012 and 2014 races.

FLORIDA

GENERAL AND PRIMARY ELECTIONS

2018 GENERAL ELECTIONS: OTHER VOTES

Governor Other vote was 47,140 Reform (Darcy Richardson), 24,310 No Party Affiliation (Kyle Gibson), 14,630 No Party Affiliation (Ryan Foley), 14,505 No Party Affiliation (Bruce Stanley), 61 Write-in (Hal Johnson), 6 Write-in (Piotr Blass)

Senate Other vote was 467 Write-in (Lateresa Jones), 220 Write-in (David Weeks), 121 Write-in (Charles Tolbert), 113 Write-in (Howard Knepper), 107 Write-in (Michael Levinson)

House Other vote was:

CD 4	7,155 No Party Affiliation (Joceline Berrios), 2,321 No Party Affiliation (Jason Michael Bulger), 2 Write-in (Gary Koniz)
CD 11	58 Write-in (Luis Saldana)
CD 12	7,510 No Party Affiliation (Angelika Purkis)
CD 15	15 Write-in (Dave Johnson), 3 Write-in (Jeffrey Rabinowitz), 2 Write-in (Alek Bynzar)
CD 19	36 Write-in (Pete Pollard)
CD 20	165 Write-in (Jay Bonner)
CD 23	13,697 No Party Affiliation (Tim Canova), 1,612 No Party Affiliation (Don Endriss)
CD 27	6,255 No Party Affiliation (Mayra Joli)

2018 PRIMARY ELECTIONS: SUPPLEMENTARY INFORMATION

Primary	August 28, 2018	**Registration** (as of August 31, 2018)	13,093,881	Democratic	4,875,282
				Republican	4,626,815
				Other Parties	91,742
				No Party Affiliation	3,500,042

Primary Type Closed—Only registered Democrats and Republicans could vote in their party's primary, with the exception of races where there were to be no other candidates (including write-ins) on the general election ballot. Then, the contested primary would be open to all voters.

	REPUBLICAN PRIMARIES			DEMOCRATIC PRIMARIES		
Senator	Scott, Rick	1,456,187	88.6%	Nelson, Bill*	Unopposed	
	De La Fuente, Roque "Rocky"	187,209	11.4%			
	TOTAL	*1,643,396*				
Governor	DeSantis, Ron	916,298	56.5%	Gillum, Andrew	522,164	34.4%
	Putnam, Adam H.	592,518	36.5%	Graham, Gwen	474,875	31.3%
	White, Bob	32,710	2.0%	Levine, Philip	308,801	20.3%
	Devine, Timothy M.	21,380	1.3%	Greene, Jeff	152,955	10.1%
	Langford, Bob	19,842	1.2%	King, Chris	37,616	2.5%
	Nathan, Bruce	14,556	0.9%	Wetherbee, John	14,426	0.9%
	Baldauf, Don	13,173	0.8%	Lundmark, Alex "Lundy"	8,655	0.6%
	Mercadante, John Joseph	11,647	0.7%			
	TOTAL	*1,622,124*		*TOTAL*	*1,519,492*	
Congressional District 1	Gaetz, Matt*	65,203	64.8%	Zimmerman, Jennifer M.	22,422	60.5%
	Dosev, Cris	30,433	30.2%	Ehr, Phil	14,650	39.5%
	Mills, John	4,992	5.0%			
	TOTAL	*100,628*		*TOTAL*	*37,072*	
Congressional District 2	Dunn, Neal*	Unopposed		Rackleff, Bob	29,395	50.8%
				Peters, Brandon	28,483	49.2%
				TOTAL	*57,878*	

FLORIDA

GENERAL AND PRIMARY ELECTIONS

	REPUBLICAN PRIMARIES			DEMOCRATIC PRIMARIES		
Congressional District 3	Yoho, Ted*	54,848	76.3%	Hayes Hinson, Yvonne	31,655	59.5%
	Sapp, Judson	17,068	23.7%	Wells, Tom	17,663	33.2%
				Jethagir Gosai, Dushyant	3,883	7.3%
	TOTAL	*71,916*		*TOTAL*	*53,201*	
Congressional District 4	Rutherford, John*	Unopposed		Selmont, George "Ges"	Unopposed	
Congressional District 5	Fuller, Virginia	Unopposed		Lawson, Al*	53,990	60.3%
				Brown, Alvin	35,584	39.7%
				TOTAL	*89,574*	
Congressional District 6	Waltz, Michael	32,916	42.4%	Soderberg, Nancy	32,174	55.6%
	Ward, John	23,593	30.4%	Upchurch, John	13,088	22.6%
	Costello, Fred	21,074	27.2%	Sevigny, Stephen	12,633	21.8%
	TOTAL	*77,583*		*TOTAL*	*57,895*	
Congressional District 7	Miller, Mike	30,629	53.9%	Murphy, Stephanie*	49,060	86.2%
	Sturgill, Scott	17,253	30.4%	Richardson, Chardo	7,846	13.8%
	Francois, Vennia	8,950	15.7%			
	TOTAL	*56,832*		*TOTAL*	*56,906*	
Congressional District 8	Posey, Bill*	Unopposed		Patel, Sanjay	Unopposed	
Congressional District 9	Liebnitzky, Wayne	Unopposed		Soto, Darren*	36,586	66.4%
				Grayson, Alan	18,528	33.6%
				TOTAL	*55,114*	
Congressional District 10				Demings, Val B.*	73,601	75.0%
				Darius, Wade	24,534	25.0%
				TOTAL	*98,135*	
Congressional District 11	Webster, Daniel A.*	Unopposed		Cottrell, Dana	Unopposed	
Congressional District 12	Bilirakis, Gus Michael*	Unopposed		Hunter, Chris	31,771	65.3%
				Perenich, Stephen M.	9,308	19.1%
				Tager, Robert Matthew	7,604	15.6%
				TOTAL	*48,683*	
Congressional District 13	Buck, George	30,567	56.0%	Crist, Charlie*	Unopposed	
	Sostack, Brad	24,020	44.0%			
	TOTAL	*54,587*				
Congressional District 14				Castor, Kathy*	Unopposed	
Congressional District 15	Spano, Ross	26,904	44.1%	Carlson, Kristen	24,498	53.4%
	Combee, Neil	20,590	33.8%	Learned, Andrew P.	14,509	31.6%
	Harper, Sean	6,018	9.9%	Peña, Raymond "Ray"	6,912	15.1%
	Kushmer, Danny	4,067	6.7%			
	Shoemaker, Ed	3,379	5.5%			
	TOTAL	*60,958*		*TOTAL*	*45,919*	
Congressional District 16	Buchanan, Vern*	Unopposed		Shapiro, David	34,807	54.7%
				Schneider, Jan	28,834	45.3%
				TOTAL	*63,641*	
Congressional District 17	Steube, Greg	48,983	62.4%	Freeman, April	33,410	77.0%
	Akins, Bill	15,142	19.3%	Pollard, Bill	9,990	23.0%
	Gonzalez, Julio	14,409	18.3%			
	TOTAL	*78,534*		*TOTAL*	*43,400*	

FLORIDA

GENERAL AND PRIMARY ELECTIONS

	REPUBLICAN PRIMARIES			DEMOCRATIC PRIMARIES		
Congressional District 18	Mast, Brian*	55,527	77.6%	Baer, Lauren	35,028	60.3%
	Freeman, Mark	8,096	11.3%	Keith, Pam	23,064	39.7%
	Cummings, Dave	7,888	11.0%			
	TOTAL	*71,511*		*TOTAL*	*58,092*	
Congressional District 19	Rooney, Francis*	Unopposed		Holden, David	24,405	67.9%
				Truax, Todd James	11,517	32.1%
				TOTAL	*35,922*	
Congressional District 20				Hastings, Alcee L.*	52,628	73.8%
				Cherfilus-McCormick, Sheila	18,697	26.2%
				TOTAL	*71,325*	
Congressional District 21				Frankel, Lois*	Unopposed	
Congressional District 22	Kimaz, Nicholas	14,245	40.8%	Deutch, Ted*	54,236	86.5%
	Manjarres, Javier "Javi"	11,925	34.2%	Fandl, Jeff	8,441	13.5%
	Walters, Eddison	8,749	25.1%			
	TOTAL	*34,919*		*TOTAL*	*62,677*	
Congressional District 23	Kaufman, Joseph "Joe"	11,659	44.7%	Wasserman-Schultz, Debbie*	Unopposed	
	Reyes, Carlos J.	8,794	33.7%			
	Spalding, Carla	5,627	21.6%			
	TOTAL	*26,080*				
Congressional District 24				Wilson, Frederica S.*	66,202	83.7%
				De La Fuente, Ricardo	12,924	16.3%
				TOTAL	*79,126*	
Congressional District 25	Diaz-Balart, Mario*	Unopposed		Barzee Flores, Mary	Unopposed	
Congressional District 26	Curbelo, Carlos*	29,508	84.0%	Mucarsel-Powell, Debbie	21,002	63.5%
	Faas, Souraya	5,629	16.0%	Grimes, Demetries Andrew	12,098	36.5%
	TOTAL	*35,137*		*TOTAL*	*33,100*	
Congressional District 27	Salazar, Maria Elvira	15,817	40.5%	Shalala, Donna	14,158	31.9%
	Barreiro, Bruno A.	10,029	25.7%	Richardson, David	12,192	27.5%
	Peiro, Maria	3,121	8.0%	Rosen Gonzalez, Kristen	7,783	17.5%
	Marks, Stephen	2,733	7.0%	Haggman, Matt	7,511	16.9%
	Chirino, Angie	2,678	6.9%	Hepburn, Michael A.	2,723	6.1%
	Rodriguez Aguilera, Bettina	1,684	4.3%			
	Ohevzion, Michael	1,467	3.8%			
	Adadi, Elizabeth	775	2.0%			
	Sosa, Gina	760	1.9%			
	TOTAL	*39,064*		*TOTAL*	*44,367*	

Note: An asterisk (*) denotes incumbent.

GEORGIA

Congressional districts first established for elections held in 2012

14 members

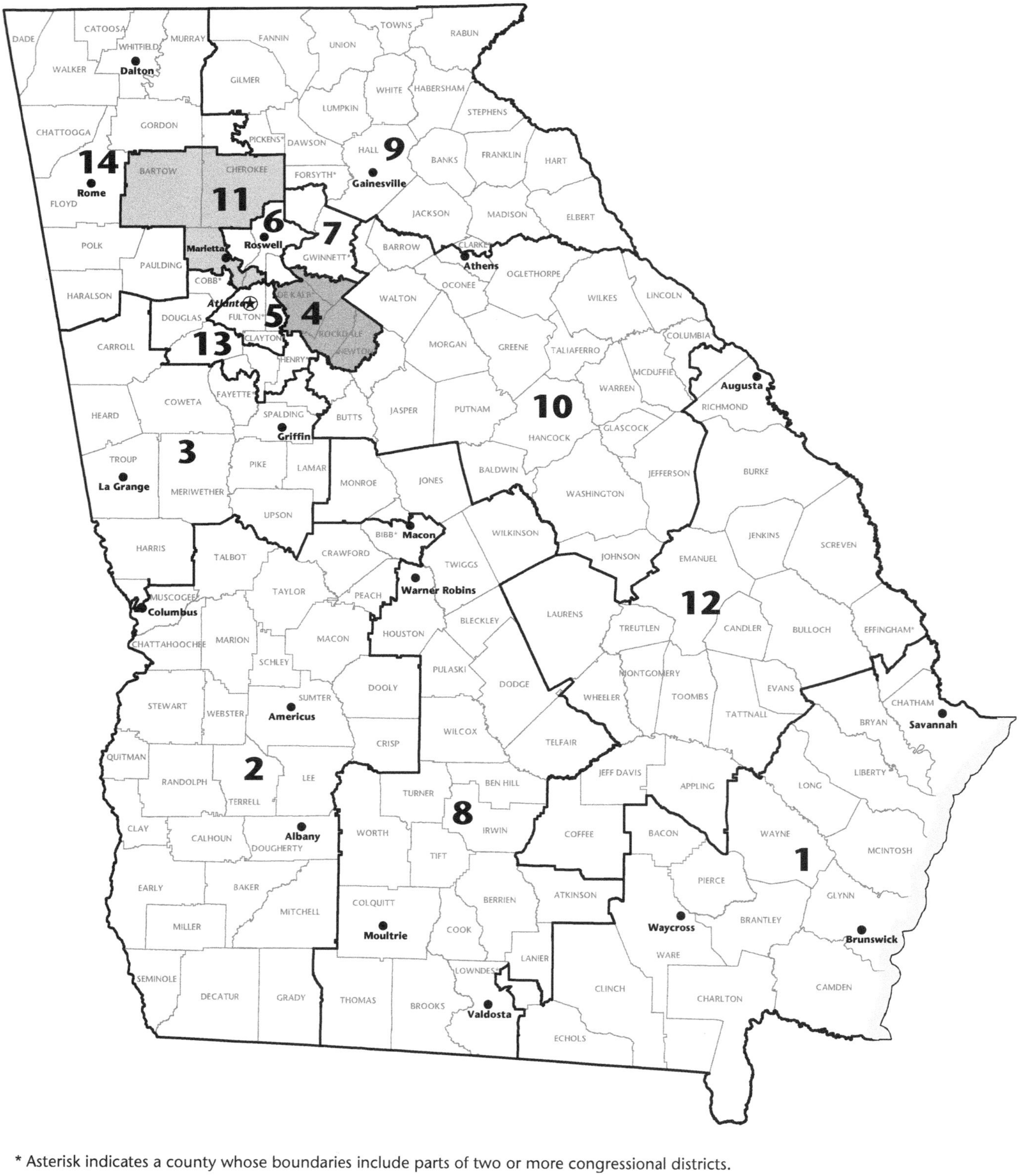

* Asterisk indicates a county whose boundaries include parts of two or more congressional districts.

GEORGIA

Atlanta Area

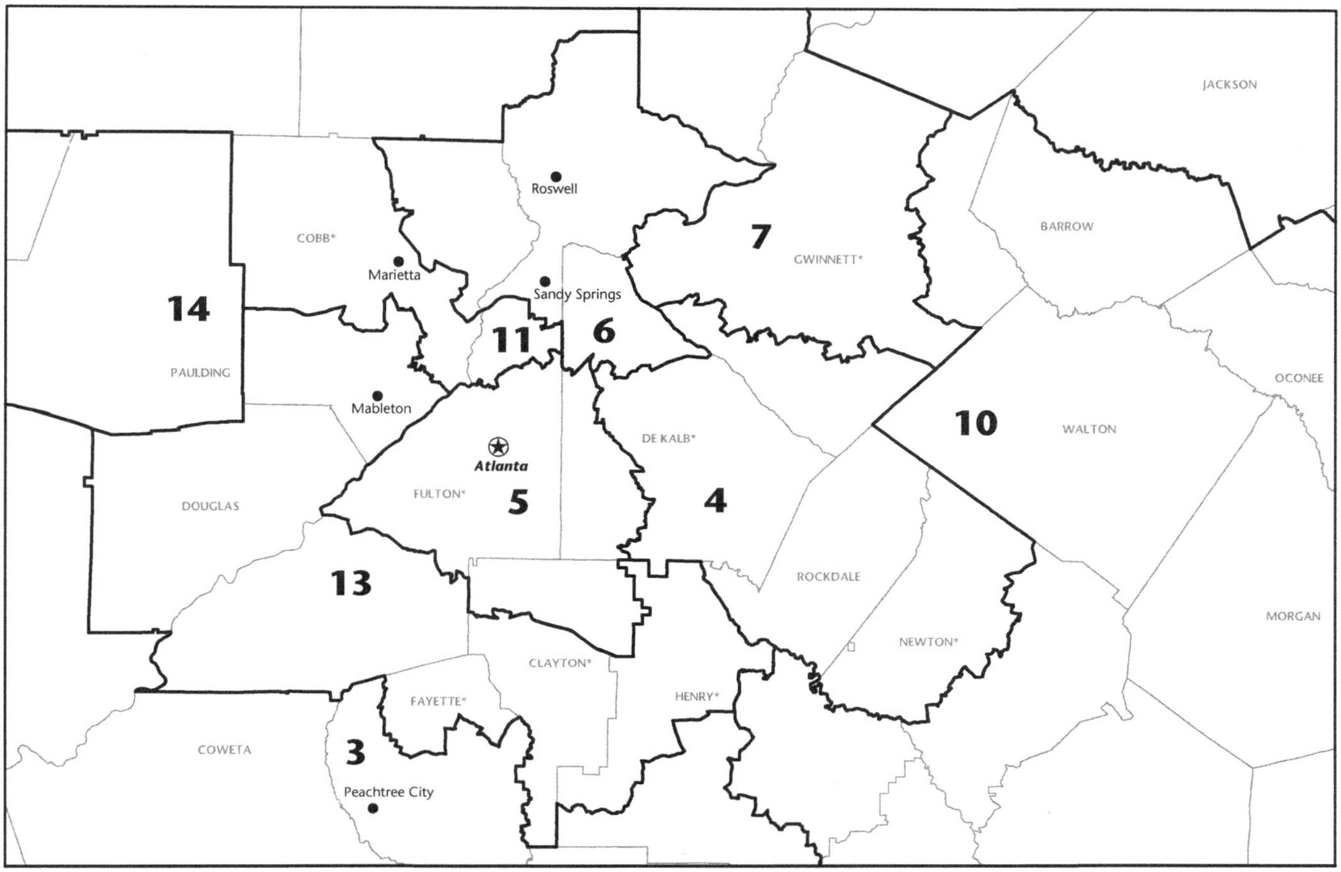

* Asterisk indicates a county whose boundaries include parts of two or more congressional districts.

GEORGIA

GOVERNOR

Brian Kemp (R). Elected 2018 to a four-year term.

SENATORS (2 Republicans)

Johnny Isakson (R). Re-elected 2016 to a six-year term. Previously elected 2010, 2004.

David A. Perdue (R). Elected 2014 to a six-year term.

REPRESENTATIVES (9 Republicans, 5 Democrats)

1. Earl Leroy "Buddy" Carter (R)
2. Sanford Bishop (D)
3. Drew Ferguson (R)
4. Henry C. "Hank" Johnson (D)
5. John Lewis (D)
6. Lucy McBath (D)
7. Rob Woodall (R)
8. Austin Scott (R)
9. Doug Collins (R)
10. Jody Hice (R)
11. Barry Loudermilk (R)
12. Rick W. Allen (R)
13. David Scott (D)
14. Tom Graves (R)

POSTWAR VOTE FOR PRESIDENT

		Republican		Democratic				Percentage			
								Total Vote		Major Vote	
Year	Total Vote	Vote	Candidate	Vote	Candidate	Other Vote	Rep.-Dem. Plurality	Rep.	Dem.	Rep.	Dem.
2016**	4,114,732	2,089,104	Trump, Donald J.	1,877,963	Clinton, Hillary Rodham	147,665	211,141 R	50.8%	45.6%	52.7%	47.3%
2012	3,900,050	2,078,688	Romney, W. Mitt	1,773,827	Obama, Barack H.*	47,535	304,861 R	53.3%	45.5%	54.0%	46.0%
2008	3,924,486	2,048,759	McCain, John S. III	1,844,123	Obama, Barack H.	31,604	204,636 R	52.2%	47.0%	52.6%	47.4%
2004	3,301,875	1,914,254	Bush, George W.*	1,366,149	Kerry, John F.	21,472	548,105 R	58.0%	41.4%	58.4%	41.6%
2000**	2,596,645	1,419,720	Bush, George W.	1,116,230	Gore, Albert Jr.	60,695	303,490 R	54.7%	43.0%	56.0%	44.0%
1996**	2,299,071	1,080,843	Dole, Robert "Bob"	1,053,849	Clinton, Bill*	164,379	26,994 R	47.0%	45.8%	50.6%	49.4%
1992**	2,321,125	995,252	Bush, George H.*	1,008,966	Clinton, Bill	316,907	13,714 D	42.9%	43.5%	49.7%	50.3%
1988	1,812,672	1,081,331	Bush, George H.	717,792	Dukakis, Michael S.	13,549	363,539 R	59.7%	39.6%	60.1%	39.9%
1984	1,776,120	1,068,722	Reagan, Ronald*	706,628	Mondale, Walter F.	770	362,094 R	60.2%	39.8%	60.2%	39.8%
1980**	1,596,695	654,168	Reagan, Ronald	890,733	Carter, Jimmy*	51,794	236,565 D	41.0%	55.8%	42.3%	57.7%
1976	1,467,458	483,743	Ford, Gerald R.*	979,409	Carter, Jimmy	4,306	495,666 D	33.0%	66.7%	33.1%	66.9%
1972	1,174,772	881,496	Nixon, Richard M.*	289,529	McGovern, George S.	3,747	591,967 R	75.0%	24.6%	75.3%	24.7%
1968**	1,250,266	380,111	Nixon, Richard M.	334,440	Humphrey, Hubert Horatio Jr.	535,715	45,671 R#	30.4%	26.7%	53.2%	46.8%
1964	1,139,335	616,584	Goldwater, Barry M. Sr.	522,556	Johnson, Lyndon B.*	195	94,028 R	54.1%	45.9%	54.1%	45.9%
1960	733,349	274,472	Nixon, Richard M.	458,638	Kennedy, John F.	239	184,166 D	37.4%	62.5%	37.4%	62.6%
1956	669,655	222,778	Eisenhower, Dwight D.*	444,688	Stevenson, Adlai E. II	2,189	221,910 D	33.3%	66.4%	33.4%	66.6%
1952	655,785	198,961	Eisenhower, Dwight D.	456,823	Stevenson, Adlai E. II	1	257,862 D	30.3%	69.7%	30.3%	69.7%
1948**	418,844	76,691	Dewey, Thomas E.	254,646	Truman, Harry S.*	87,507	177,955 D	18.3%	60.8%	23.1%	76.9%

Note: An asterisk (*) denotes incumbent. A pound sign (#) in the plurality column indicates that the winner in 1968 did not run under the banner of either major party. **In past elections, the other vote included: 2016 - 125,306 Libertarian (Gary Johnson); 2000 - 13,273 Green (Ralph Nader); 1996 - 146,337 Reform (Ross Perot); 1992 - 309,657 Independent (Perot); 1980 - 36,055 Independent (John Anderson); 1968 - 535,550 American Independent (George Wallace); 1948 - 85,135 States' Rights (Strom Thurmond, who placed second statewide). Wallace carried Georgia in 1968 with 42.8 percent of the vote.

GEORGIA

POSTWAR VOTE FOR GOVERNOR

		Republican		Democratic				Percentage			
								Total Vote		Major Vote	
Year	Total Vote	Vote	Candidate	Vote	Candidate	Other Vote	Rep.-Dem. Plurality	Rep.	Dem.	Rep.	Dem.
2018	3,939,409	1,978,408	Kemp, Brian	1,923,685	Abrams, Stacey	37,316	54,723 R	50.2%	48.8%	50.7%	49.3%
2014	2,550,648	1,345,237	Deal, Nathan*	1,144,794	Carter, Jason J.	60,617	200,443 R	52.7%	44.9%	54.0%	46.0%
2010	2,576,161	1,365,832	Deal, Nathan	1,107,011	Barnes, Roy E.	103,318	258,821 R	53.0%	43.0%	55.2%	44.8%
2006	2,122,258	1,229,724	Perdue, Sonny*	811,049	Taylor, Mark	81,485	418,675 R	57.9%	38.2%	60.3%	39.7%
2002	2,027,177	1,041,700	Perdue, Sonny	937,070	Barnes, Roy E.*	48,407	104,630 R	51.4%	46.2%	52.6%	47.4%
1998	1,792,808	790,201	Millner, Guy	941,076	Barnes, Roy E.	61,531	150,875 D	44.1%	52.5%	45.6%	54.4%
1994	1,545,328	756,371	Millner, Guy	788,926	Miller, Zell*	31	32,555 D	48.9%	51.1%	48.9%	51.1%
1990	1,449,682	645,625	Isakson, Johnny	766,662	Miller, Zell	37,395	121,037 D	44.5%	52.9%	45.7%	54.3%
1986	1,175,114	346,512	Davis, Guy	828,465	Harris, Joe Frank*	137	481,953 D	29.5%	70.5%	29.5%	70.5%
1982	1,169,043	434,496	Bell, Robert H.	734,092	Harris, Joe Frank	455	299,596 D	37.2%	62.8%	37.2%	62.8%
1978	662,862	128,139	Cook, Rodney M.	534,572	Busbee, George*	151	406,433 D	19.3%	80.6%	19.3%	80.7%
1974	936,438	289,113	Thompson, Ronnie	646,777	Busbee, George	548	357,664 D	30.9%	69.1%	30.9%	69.1%
1970	1,046,663	424,983	Suit, Hal	620,419	Carter, Jimmy	1,261	195,436 D	40.6%	59.3%	40.7%	59.3%
1966**	975,019	453,665	Callaway, Howard H.	450,626	Maddox, Lester	70,728	3,039 R	46.5%	46.2%	50.2%	49.8%
1962	311,691			311,524	Sanders, Carl E.	167	311,524 D		99.9%		100.0%
1958	168,497			168,414	Vandiver, S. Ernest	83	168,414 D		100.0%		100.0%
1954	331,966			331,899	Griffin, S. Marvin	67	331,899 D		100.0%		100.0%
1950	234,430			230,771	Talmadge, Herman E.*	3,659	230,771 D		98.4%		100.0%
1948S**	363,764			354,712	Talmadge, Herman E.	9,052	354,712 D		97.5%		100.0%
1946	146,191			144,067	Talmadge, Eugene	2,124	144,067 D		98.5%		100.0%

Note: An asterisk (*) denotes incumbent. **In 1966 in the absence of a majority for any candidate, the State Legislature elected Democrat Lester Maddox to a four-year term. The 1948 election was for a short term to fill a vacancy. The Republican Party did not run a candidate in the 1946, 1948, 1950, 1954, 1958, and 1962 gubernatorial elections.

POSTWAR VOTE FOR SENATOR

		Republican		Democratic				Percentage			
								Total Vote		Major Vote	
Year	Total Vote	Vote	Candidate	Vote	Candidate	Other Vote	Rep.-Dem. Plurality	Rep.	Dem.	Rep.	Dem.
2016	3,898,605	2,135,806	Isakson, Johnny*	1,599,726	Barksdale, Jim	163,073	536,080 R	54.8%	41.0%	57.2%	42.8%
2014	2,567,805	1,358,088	Perdue, David A.	1,160,811	Nunn, Michelle	48,906	197,277 R	52.9%	45.2%	53.9%	46.1%
2010	2,555,258	1,489,904	Isakson, Johnny*	996,516	Thurmond, Michael	68,838	493,388 R	58.3%	39.0%	59.9%	40.1%
2008**	3,752,485	1,867,097	Chambliss, Saxby*	1,757,393	Martin, Jim	127,995	109,704 R	49.8%	46.8%	51.5%	48.5%
2008**	2,137,956	1,228,033	Chambliss, Saxby*	909,923	Martin, Jim		318,110 R	57.4%	42.6%	57.4%	42.6%
2004	3,220,981	1,864,202	Isakson, Johnny	1,287,690	Majette, Denise L.	69,089	576,512 R	57.9%	40.0%	59.1%	40.9%
2002	2,030,608	1,071,464	Chambliss, Saxby	932,156	Cleland, Max*	26,988	139,308 R	52.8%	45.9%	53.5%	46.5%
2000S**	2,428,510	920,478	Mattingly, Mack F.	1,413,224	Miller, Zell*	94,808	492,746 D	37.9%	58.2%	39.4%	60.6%
1998	1,753,911	918,540	Coverdell, Paul*	791,904	Coles, Michael	43,467	126,636 R	52.4%	45.2%	53.7%	46.3%
1996	2,259,232	1,073,969	Millner, Guy	1,103,993	Cleland, Max	81,270	30,024 D	47.5%	48.9%	49.3%	50.7%
1992**	2,251,587	1,073,282	Coverdell, Paul	1,108,416	Fowler, Wyche Jr.*	69,889	35,134 D	47.7%	49.2%	49.2%	50.8%
1992**	1,253,991	635,114	Coverdell, Paul	618,877	Fowler, Wyche Jr.*		16,237 R	50.6%	49.4%	50.6%	49.4%
1990	1,033,517			1,033,439	Nunn, Sam*	78	1,033,439 D		100.0%		100.0%
1986	1,225,008	601,241	Mattingly, Mack F.*	623,707	Fowler, Wyche Jr.	60	22,466 D	49.1%	50.9%	49.1%	50.9%
1984	1,681,344	337,196	Hicks, John Michael	1,344,104	Nunn, Sam*	44	1,006,908 D	20.1%	79.9%	20.1%	79.9%
1980	1,580,340	803,686	Mattingly, Mack F.	776,143	Talmadge, Herman E.*	511	27,543 R	50.9%	49.1%	50.9%	49.1%
1978	645,164	108,808	Stokes, John W.	536,320	Nunn, Sam*	36	427,512 D	16.9%	83.1%	16.9%	83.1%
1974	874,555	246,866	Johnson, Jerry R.	627,376	Talmadge, Herman E.*	313	380,510 D	28.2%	71.7%	28.2%	71.8%
1972	1,178,708	542,331	Thompson, S. Fletcher	635,970	Nunn, Sam	407	93,639 D	46.0%	54.0%	46.0%	54.0%
1968	1,141,889	256,796	Patton, E. Earl	885,093	Talmadge, Herman E.*		628,297 D	22.5%	77.5%	22.5%	77.5%
1966	631,330			631,002	Russell, Richard Brevard Jr.*	328	631,002 D		99.9%		100.0%
1962	306,250			306,250	Talmadge, Herman E.*		306,250 D		100.0%		100.0%
1960	576,495			576,140	Russell, Richard Brevard Jr.*	355	576,140 D		99.9%		100.0%
1956	541,267			541,094	Talmadge, Herman E.	173	576,140 D		100.0%		100.0%
1954	333,936			333,917	Russell, Richard Brevard Jr.*	19	333,917 D		100.0%		100.0%
1950	261,293			261,290	George, Walter F.*	3	261,290 D		100.0%		100.0%
1948	362,504			362,104	Russell, Richard Brevard Jr.*	400	362,104 D		99.9%		100.0%

Note: An asterisk (*) denotes incumbent. **The 2000 election was for a short term to fill a vacancy. In 1992 and 2008, no candidate drew a majority of the general election vote required by state law, forcing runoff elections. In each case, the general election vote is presented first and the runoff vote second. The 2008 runoff was held December 2; the 1992 runoff took place on November 24. The Republican Party did not run a candidate in the 1948, 1950, 1954, 1956, 1960, 1962, 1966, and 1990 Senate elections.

GEORGIA

GOVERNOR 2018

2010 Census Population	County	Total Vote	Republican (Kemp)	Democratic (Abrams)	Other	Rep.-Dem. Plurality	Percentage: Total Vote		Percentage: Major Vote	
							Rep.	Dem.	Rep.	Dem.
18,236	APPLING	6,809	5,428	1,358	23	4,070 R	79.7%	19.9%	80.0%	20.0%
8,375	ATKINSON	2,522	1,876	637	9	1,239 R	74.4%	25.3%	74.7%	25.3%
11,096	BACON	3,830	3,321	489	20	2,832 R	86.7%	12.8%	87.2%	12.8%
3,451	BAKER	1,293	753	535	5	218 R	58.2%	41.4%	58.5%	41.5%
45,720	BALDWIN	15,636	7,735	7,793	108	58 D	49.5%	49.8%	49.8%	50.2%
18,395	BANKS	6,852	6,150	645	57	5,505 R	89.8%	9.4%	90.5%	9.5%
69,367	BARROW	27,405	20,162	6,900	343	13,262 R	73.6%	25.2%	74.5%	25.5%
100,157	BARTOW	37,359	28,425	8,524	410	19,901 R	76.1%	22.8%	76.9%	23.1%
17,634	BEN HILL	5,547	3,539	1,983	25	1,556 R	63.8%	35.7%	64.1%	35.9%
19,286	BERRIEN	6,252	5,314	900	38	4,414 R	85.0%	14.4%	85.5%	14.5%
155,547	BIBB	60,692	23,225	37,066	401	13,841 D	38.3%	61.1%	38.5%	61.5%
13,063	BLECKLEY	4,860	3,816	1,002	42	2,814 R	78.5%	20.6%	79.2%	20.8%
18,411	BRANTLEY	5,694	5,198	461	35	4,737 R	91.3%	8.1%	91.9%	8.1%
16,243	BROOKS	5,722	3,511	2,188	23	1,323 R	61.4%	38.2%	61.6%	38.4%
30,233	BRYAN	14,985	10,507	4,313	165	6,194 R	70.1%	28.8%	70.9%	29.1%
70,217	BULLOCH	23,683	14,848	8,630	205	6,218 R	62.7%	36.4%	63.2%	36.8%
23,316	BURKE	8,721	4,410	4,269	42	141 R	50.6%	49.0%	50.8%	49.2%
23,655	BUTTS	8,863	6,358	2,451	54	3,907 R	71.7%	27.7%	72.2%	27.8%
6,694	CALHOUN	1,899	810	1,084	5	274 D	42.7%	57.1%	42.8%	57.2%
50,513	CAMDEN	17,061	11,139	5,727	195	5,412 R	65.3%	33.6%	66.0%	34.0%
10,998	CANDLER	3,539	2,560	963	16	1,597 R	72.3%	27.2%	72.7%	27.3%
110,527	CARROLL	41,843	29,204	12,180	459	17,024 R	69.8%	29.1%	70.6%	29.4%
63,942	CATOOSA	23,758	18,881	4,590	287	14,291 R	79.5%	19.3%	80.4%	19.6%
12,171	CHARLTON	3,375	2,534	822	19	1,712 R	75.1%	24.4%	75.5%	24.5%
265,128	CHATHAM	103,543	41,425	61,059	1,059	19,634 D	40.0%	59.0%	40.4%	59.6%
11,267	CHATTAHOOCHEE	1,105	603	494	8	109 R	54.6%	44.7%	55.0%	45.0%
26,015	CHATTOOGA	7,434	5,936	1,445	53	4,491 R	79.8%	19.4%	80.4%	19.6%
214,346	CHEROKEE	106,411	76,700	28,047	1,664	48,653 R	72.1%	26.4%	73.2%	26.8%
116,714	CLARKE	43,302	12,365	30,427	510	18,062 D	28.6%	70.3%	28.9%	71.1%
3,183	CLAY	1,186	536	642	8	106 D	45.2%	54.1%	45.5%	54.5%
259,424	CLAYTON	92,212	10,868	80,971	373	70,103 D	11.8%	87.8%	11.8%	88.2%
6,798	CLINCH	2,258	1,717	534	7	1,183 R	76.0%	23.6%	76.3%	23.7%
688,078	COBB	311,814	138,852	168,767	4,195	29,915 D	44.5%	54.1%	45.1%	54.9%
42,356	COFFEE	12,615	8,929	3,630	56	5,299 R	70.8%	28.8%	71.1%	28.9%
45,498	COLQUITT	12,963	9,830	3,054	79	6,776 R	75.8%	23.6%	76.3%	23.7%
124,053	COLUMBIA	61,634	40,947	20,023	664	20,924 R	66.4%	32.5%	67.2%	32.8%
17,212	COOK	5,803	4,116	1,667	20	2,449 R	70.9%	28.7%	71.2%	28.8%
127,317	COWETA	58,071	40,471	16,908	692	23,563 R	69.7%	29.1%	70.5%	29.5%
12,630	CRAWFORD	4,934	3,595	1,302	37	2,293 R	72.9%	26.4%	73.4%	26.6%
23,439	CRISP	7,050	4,445	2,577	28	1,868 R	63.0%	36.6%	63.3%	36.7%
16,633	DADE	5,462	4,508	884	70	3,624 R	82.5%	16.2%	83.6%	16.4%
22,330	DAWSON	11,581	9,953	1,519	109	8,434 R	85.9%	13.1%	86.8%	13.2%
27,842	DECATUR	9,146	5,492	3,615	39	1,877 R	60.0%	39.5%	60.3%	39.7%
691,893	DEKALB	312,741	48,923	261,042	2,776	212,119 D	15.6%	83.5%	15.8%	84.2%
21,796	DODGE	7,061	5,220	1,817	24	3,403 R	73.9%	25.7%	74.2%	25.8%
14,918	DOOLY	3,795	2,001	1,782	12	219 R	52.7%	47.0%	52.9%	47.1%
94,565	DOUGHERTY	31,425	9,330	21,980	115	12,650 D	29.7%	69.9%	29.8%	70.2%
132,403	DOUGLAS	55,255	21,744	33,053	458	11,309 D	39.4%	59.8%	39.7%	60.3%
11,008	EARLY	4,135	2,285	1,840	10	445 R	55.3%	44.5%	55.4%	44.6%
4,034	ECHOLS	1,143	1,008	126	9	882 R	88.2%	11.0%	88.9%	11.1%
52,250	EFFINGHAM	23,371	17,969	5,145	257	12,824 R	76.9%	22.0%	77.7%	22.3%
20,166	ELBERT	7,388	5,152	2,194	42	2,958 R	69.7%	29.7%	70.1%	29.9%
22,598	EMANUEL	7,716	5,400	2,278	38	3,122 R	70.0%	29.5%	70.3%	29.7%
11,000	EVANS	3,447	2,392	1,040	15	1,352 R	69.4%	30.2%	69.7%	30.3%
23,682	FANNIN	11,218	9,306	1,809	103	7,497 R	83.0%	16.1%	83.7%	16.3%
106,567	FAYETTE	57,998	32,497	24,796	705	7,701 R	56.0%	42.8%	56.7%	43.3%
96,317	FLOYD	30,338	21,569	8,445	324	13,124 R	71.1%	27.8%	71.9%	28.1%
175,511	FORSYTH	93,298	65,845	26,092	1,361	39,753 R	70.6%	28.0%	71.6%	28.4%
22,084	FRANKLIN	8,148	7,051	1,036	61	6,015 R	86.5%	12.7%	87.2%	12.8%
920,581	FULTON	423,788	112,991	306,589	4,208	193,598 D	26.7%	72.3%	26.9%	73.1%

GEORGIA

GOVERNOR 2018

2010 Census Population	County	Total Vote	Republican (Kemp)	Democratic (Abrams)	Other	Rep.-Dem. Plurality	Percentage Total Vote Rep.	Percentage Total Vote Dem.	Percentage Major Vote Rep.	Percentage Major Vote Dem.
28,292	GILMER	12,510	10,471	1,917	122	8,554 R	83.7%	15.3%	84.5%	15.5%
3,082	GLASCOCK	1,301	1,189	107	5	1,082 R	91.4%	8.2%	91.7%	8.3%
79,626	GLYNN	32,648	20,743	11,636	269	9,107 R	63.5%	35.6%	64.1%	35.9%
55,186	GORDON	17,804	14,586	3,046	172	11,540 R	81.9%	17.1%	82.7%	17.3%
25,011	GRADY	8,370	5,633	2,704	33	2,929 R	67.3%	32.3%	67.6%	32.4%
15,994	GREENE	8,995	5,856	3,093	46	2,763 R	65.1%	34.4%	65.4%	34.6%
805,321	GWINNETT	314,918	132,998	178,097	3,823	45,099 D	42.2%	56.6%	42.8%	57.2%
43,041	HABERSHAM	15,500	12,944	2,417	139	10,527 R	83.5%	15.6%	84.3%	15.7%
179,684	HALL	67,406	49,442	17,187	777	32,255 R	73.3%	25.5%	74.2%	25.8%
9,429	HANCOCK	3,548	872	2,666	10	1,794 D	24.6%	75.1%	24.6%	75.4%
28,780	HARALSON	10,585	9,278	1,219	88	8,059 R	87.7%	11.5%	88.4%	11.6%
32,024	HARRIS	15,986	11,834	4,021	131	7,813 R	74.0%	25.2%	74.6%	25.4%
25,213	HART	9,622	7,370	2,178	74	5,192 R	76.6%	22.6%	77.2%	22.8%
11,834	HEARD	4,055	3,374	654	27	2,720 R	83.2%	16.1%	83.8%	16.2%
203,922	HENRY	98,558	41,364	56,485	709	15,121 D	42.0%	57.3%	42.3%	57.7%
139,900	HOUSTON	59,232	34,314	24,358	560	9,956 R	57.9%	41.1%	58.5%	41.5%
9,538	IRWIN	3,562	2,701	851	10	1,850 R	75.8%	23.9%	76.0%	24.0%
60,485	JACKSON	26,899	21,950	4,674	275	17,276 R	81.6%	17.4%	82.4%	17.6%
13,900	JASPER	5,945	4,430	1,484	31	2,946 R	74.5%	25.0%	74.9%	25.1%
15,068	JEFF DAVIS	4,815	3,979	814	22	3,165 R	82.6%	16.9%	83.0%	17.0%
16,930	JEFFERSON	6,767	3,177	3,564	26	387 D	46.9%	52.7%	47.1%	52.9%
8,340	JENKINS	2,872	1,857	1,004	11	853 R	64.7%	35.0%	64.9%	35.1%
9,980	JOHNSON	3,483	2,524	948	11	1,576 R	72.5%	27.2%	72.7%	27.3%
28,669	JONES	12,441	8,438	3,938	65	4,500 R	67.8%	31.7%	68.2%	31.8%
18,317	LAMAR	7,357	5,105	2,195	57	2,910 R	69.4%	29.8%	69.9%	30.1%
10,078	LANIER	2,681	1,910	762	9	1,148 R	71.2%	28.4%	71.5%	28.5%
48,434	LAURENS	18,952	12,484	6,375	93	6,109 R	65.9%	33.6%	66.2%	33.8%
28,298	LEE	13,555	10,120	3,356	79	6,764 R	74.7%	24.8%	75.1%	24.9%
63,453	LIBERTY	15,368	5,557	9,696	115	4,139 D	36.2%	63.1%	36.4%	63.6%
7,996	LINCOLN	3,969	2,756	1,188	25	1,568 R	69.4%	29.9%	69.9%	30.1%
14,464	LONG	3,998	2,591	1,371	36	1,220 R	64.8%	34.3%	65.4%	34.6%
109,233	LOWNDES	35,753	20,488	15,024	241	5,464 R	57.3%	42.0%	57.7%	42.3%
29,966	LUMPKIN	11,558	9,157	2,228	173	6,929 R	79.2%	19.3%	80.4%	19.6%
14,740	MACON	4,217	1,556	2,652	9	1,096 D	36.9%	62.9%	37.0%	63.0%
28,120	MADISON	11,699	9,181	2,418	100	6,763 R	78.5%	20.7%	79.2%	20.8%
8,742	MARION	2,931	1,872	1,037	22	835 R	63.9%	35.4%	64.4%	35.6%
21,875	MCDUFFIE	8,792	5,323	3,427	42	1,896 R	60.5%	39.0%	60.8%	39.2%
14,333	MCINTOSH	5,408	3,218	2,161	29	1,057 R	59.5%	40.0%	59.8%	40.2%
21,992	MERIWETHER	8,650	5,093	3,501	56	1,592 R	58.9%	40.5%	59.3%	40.7%
6,125	MILLER	2,315	1,803	502	10	1,301 R	77.9%	21.7%	78.2%	21.8%
23,498	MITCHELL	7,455	4,187	3,245	23	942 R	56.2%	43.5%	56.3%	43.7%
26,424	MONROE	12,938	9,308	3,516	114	5,792 R	71.9%	27.2%	72.6%	27.4%
9,123	MONTGOMERY	3,528	2,686	821	21	1,865 R	76.1%	23.3%	76.6%	23.4%
17,868	MORGAN	9,558	6,807	2,675	76	4,132 R	71.2%	28.0%	71.8%	28.2%
39,628	MURRAY	11,091	9,512	1,489	90	8,023 R	85.8%	13.4%	86.5%	13.5%
189,885	MUSCOGEE	63,272	24,348	38,462	462	14,114 D	38.5%	60.8%	38.8%	61.2%
99,958	NEWTON	43,141	19,449	23,412	280	3,963 D	45.1%	54.3%	45.4%	54.6%
32,808	OCONEE	20,744	14,480	6,015	249	8,465 R	69.8%	29.0%	70.7%	29.3%
14,899	OGLETHORPE	6,485	4,568	1,847	70	2,721 R	70.4%	28.5%	71.2%	28.8%
142,324	PAULDING	61,305	40,784	19,959	562	20,825 R	66.5%	32.6%	67.1%	32.9%
27,695	PEACH	10,445	5,432	4,966	47	466 R	52.0%	47.5%	52.2%	47.8%
29,431	PICKENS	13,362	11,331	1,901	130	9,430 R	84.8%	14.2%	85.6%	14.4%
18,758	PIERCE	6,884	6,123	738	23	5,385 R	88.9%	10.7%	89.2%	10.8%
17,869	PIKE	8,543	7,322	1,164	57	6,158 R	85.7%	13.6%	86.3%	13.7%
41,475	POLK	12,861	10,177	2,588	96	7,589 R	79.1%	20.1%	79.7%	20.3%
12,010	PULASKI	3,622	2,527	1,079	16	1,448 R	69.8%	29.8%	70.1%	29.9%
21,218	PUTNAM	9,335	6,704	2,579	52	4,125 R	71.8%	27.6%	72.2%	27.8%
2,513	QUITMAN	940	522	410	8	112 R	55.5%	43.6%	56.0%	44.0%
16,276	RABUN	7,578	6,063	1,428	87	4,635 R	80.0%	18.8%	80.9%	19.1%
7,719	RANDOLPH	2,789	1,257	1,518	14	261 D	45.1%	54.4%	45.3%	54.7%

GEORGIA

GOVERNOR 2018

2010 Census Population	County	Total Vote	Republican (Kemp)	Democratic (Abrams)	Other	Rep.-Dem. Plurality	Percentage Total Vote Rep.	Total Vote Dem.	Major Vote Rep.	Major Vote Dem.
200,549	RICHMOND	70,155	22,076	47,531	548	25,455 D	31.5%	67.8%	31.7%	68.3%
85,215	ROCKDALE	36,655	11,703	24,725	227	13,022 D	31.9%	67.5%	32.1%	67.9%
5,010	SCHLEY	1,933	1,565	353	15	1,212 R	81.0%	18.3%	81.6%	18.4%
14,593	SCREVEN	5,414	3,268	2,131	15	1,137 R	60.4%	39.4%	60.5%	39.5%
8,729	SEMINOLE	3,227	2,149	1,061	17	1,088 R	66.6%	32.9%	66.9%	33.1%
64,073	SPALDING	24,417	14,937	9,258	222	5,679 R	61.2%	37.9%	61.7%	38.3%
26,175	STEPHENS	9,087	7,326	1,692	69	5,634 R	80.6%	18.6%	81.2%	18.8%
6,058	STEWART	1,819	760	1,053	6	293 D	41.8%	57.9%	41.9%	58.1%
32,819	SUMTER	10,556	5,149	5,360	47	211 D	48.8%	50.8%	49.0%	51.0%
6,865	TALBOT	2,954	1,167	1,765	22	598 D	39.5%	59.7%	39.8%	60.2%
1,717	TALIAFERRO	921	350	568	3	218 D	38.0%	61.7%	38.1%	61.9%
25,520	TATTNALL	6,647	5,073	1,537	37	3,536 R	76.3%	23.1%	76.7%	23.3%
8,906	TAYLOR	3,294	2,069	1,205	20	864 R	62.8%	36.6%	63.2%	36.8%
16,500	TELFAIR	3,632	2,425	1,191	16	1,234 R	66.8%	32.8%	67.1%	32.9%
9,315	TERRELL	3,939	1,800	2,125	14	325 D	45.7%	53.9%	45.9%	54.1%
44,720	THOMAS	17,244	10,557	6,602	85	3,955 R	61.2%	38.3%	61.5%	38.5%
40,118	TIFT	13,673	9,523	4,070	80	5,453 R	69.6%	29.8%	70.1%	29.9%
27,223	TOOMBS	8,860	6,623	2,201	36	4,422 R	74.8%	24.8%	75.1%	24.9%
10,471	TOWNS	6,132	5,009	1,065	58	3,944 R	81.7%	17.4%	82.5%	17.5%
6,885	TREUTLEN	2,614	1,800	806	8	994 R	68.9%	30.8%	69.1%	30.9%
67,044	TROUP	23,913	14,533	9,218	162	5,315 R	60.8%	38.5%	61.2%	38.8%
8,930	TURNER	3,274	2,062	1,200	12	862 R	63.0%	36.7%	63.2%	36.8%
9,023	TWIGGS	3,792	1,999	1,776	17	223 R	52.7%	46.8%	53.0%	47.0%
21,356	UNION	11,865	9,899	1,852	114	8,047 R	83.4%	15.6%	84.2%	15.8%
27,153	UPSON	10,568	7,063	3,443	62	3,620 R	66.8%	32.6%	67.2%	32.8%
68,756	WALKER	21,490	17,400	3,838	252	13,562 R	81.0%	17.9%	81.9%	18.1%
83,768	WALTON	38,686	29,742	8,679	265	21,063 R	76.9%	22.4%	77.4%	22.6%
36,312	WARE	11,016	7,894	3,067	55	4,827 R	71.7%	27.8%	72.0%	28.0%
5,834	WARREN	2,261	1,053	1,200	8	147 D	46.6%	53.1%	46.7%	53.3%
21,187	WASHINGTON	8,169	4,128	4,012	29	116 R	50.5%	49.1%	50.7%	49.3%
30,099	WAYNE	10,131	8,120	1,940	71	6,180 R	80.2%	19.1%	80.7%	19.3%
2,799	WEBSTER	1,100	659	440	1	219 R	59.9%	40.0%	60.0%	40.0%
7,421	WHEELER	1,931	1,372	555	4	817 R	71.1%	28.7%	71.2%	28.8%
27,144	WHITE	11,439	9,667	1,647	125	8,020 R	84.5%	14.4%	85.4%	14.6%
102,599	WHITFIELD	27,327	19,758	7,323	246	12,435 R	72.3%	26.8%	73.0%	27.0%
9,255	WILCOX	2,815	2,064	745	6	1,319 R	73.3%	26.5%	73.5%	26.5%
10,593	WILKES	4,377	2,578	1,774	25	804 R	58.9%	40.5%	59.2%	40.8%
9,563	WILKINSON	4,265	2,373	1,877	15	496 R	55.6%	44.0%	55.8%	44.2%
21,679	WORTH	7,846	5,915	1,894	37	4,021 R	75.4%	24.1%	75.7%	24.3%
9,687,653	*TOTAL*	*3,939,409*	*1,978,408*	*1,923,685*	*37,316*	*54,723 R*	*50.2%*	*48.8%*	*50.7%*	*49.3%*

GEORGIA

HOUSE OF REPRESENTATIVES

CD	Year	Total Vote	Republican Vote	Republican Candidate	Democratic Vote	Democratic Candidate	Other Vote	Rep.-Dem. Plurality	Percentage Total Vote Rep.	Total Vote Dem.	Major Vote Rep.	Major Vote Dem.
1	2018	250,683	144,741	CARTER, EARL LEROY "BUDDY"*	105,942	RING, LISA		38,799 R	57.7%	42.3%	57.7%	42.3%
1	2016	211,112	210,243	CARTER, EARL LEROY "BUDDY"*			869	210,243 R	99.6%		100.0%	
1	2014	156,512	95,337	CARTER, EARL LEROY "BUDDY"	61,175	REESE, BRIAN CORWIN		34,162 R	60.9%	39.1%	60.9%	39.1%
1	2012	249,580	157,181	KINGSTON, JACK*	92,399	MESSINGER, LESLI		64,782 R	63.0%	37.0%	63.0%	37.0%

GEORGIA

HOUSE OF REPRESENTATIVES

			Republican		Democratic				Percentage			
									Total Vote		Major Vote	
CD	Year	Total Vote	Vote	Candidate	Vote	Candidate	Other Vote	Rep.-Dem. Plurality	Rep.	Dem.	Rep.	Dem.
2	2018	229,171	92,472	WEST, HERMAN JR.	136,699	BISHOP, SANFORD*		44,227 D	40.4%	59.6%	40.4%	59.6%
2	2016	242,599	94,056	DUKE, GREG	148,543	BISHOP, SANFORD*		54,487 D	38.8%	61.2%	38.8%	61.2%
2	2014	162,900	66,537	DUKE, GREG	96,363	BISHOP, SANFORD*		29,826 D	40.8%	59.2%	40.8%	59.2%
2	2012	255,161	92,410	HOUSE, JOHN	162,751	BISHOP, SANFORD*		70,341 D	36.2%	63.8%	36.2%	63.8%
3	2018	293,006	191,996	FERGUSON, DREW*	101,010	ENDERLIN, CHUCK		90,986 R	65.5%	34.5%	65.5%	34.5%
3	2016	303,187	207,218	FERGUSON, DREW	95,969	PENDLEY, ANGELA		111,249 R	68.3%	31.7%	68.3%	31.7%
3	2014	156,277	156,277	WESTMORELAND, LYNN A.*				156,277 R	100.0%		100.0%	
3	2012	232,485	232,380	WESTMORELAND, LYNN A.*			105	232,380 R	100.0%		100.0%	
4	2018	288,809	61,092	PROFIT, JOE	227,717	JOHNSON, HENRY C. "HANK"*		166,625 D	21.2%	78.8%	21.2%	78.8%
4	2016	290,739	70,593	ARMENDARIZ, VICTOR	220,146	JOHNSON, HENRY C. "HANK"*		149,553 D	24.3%	75.7%	24.3%	75.7%
4	2014	161,320			161,211	JOHNSON, HENRY C. "HANK"*	109	161,211 D		99.9%		100.0%
4	2012	283,962	75,041	VAUGHN, J. CHRIS	208,861	JOHNSON, HENRY C. "HANK"*	60	133,820 D	26.4%	73.6%	26.4%	73.6%
5	2018	275,406			275,406	LEWIS, JOHN*		275,406 D		100.0%		100.0%
5	2016	300,549	46,768	BELL, DOUGLAS	253,781	LEWIS, JOHN*		207,013 D	15.6%	84.4%	15.6%	84.4%
5	2014	170,326			170,326	LEWIS, JOHN*		170,326 D		100.0%		100.0%
5	2012	277,689	43,335	STOPECK, HOWARD	234,330	LEWIS, JOHN*	24	190,995 D	15.6%	84.4%	15.6%	84.4%
6	2018	317,032	156,875	HANDEL, KAREN*	160,139	MCBATH, LUCY KAY	18	3,264 D	49.5%	50.5%	49.5%	50.5%
6	2016	326,005	201,088	PRICE, THOMAS E.*	124,917	STOOKSBURY, RODNEY		76,171 R	61.7%	38.3%	61.7%	38.3%
6	2014	210,504	139,018	PRICE, THOMAS E.*	71,486	MONTIGEL, ROBERT		67,532 R	66.0%	34.0%	66.0%	34.0%
6	2012	294,034	189,669	PRICE, THOMAS E.*	104,365	KAZANOW, JEFF		85,304 R	64.5%	35.5%	64.5%	35.5%
7	2018	280,441	140,430	WOODALL, ROB*	140,011	BOURDEAUX, CAROLYN		419 R	50.1%	49.9%	50.1%	49.9%
7	2016	288,301	174,081	WOODALL, ROB*	114,220	MALIK, RASHID		59,861 R	60.4%	39.6%	60.4%	39.6%
7	2014	173,669	113,557	WOODALL, ROB*	60,112	WIGHT, THOMAS D.		53,445 R	65.4%	34.6%	65.4%	34.6%
7	2012	252,066	156,689	WOODALL, ROB*	95,377	REILLY, STEVE		61,312 R	62.2%	37.8%	62.2%	37.8%
8	2018	198,716	198,152	SCOTT, AUSTIN*			564	198,152 R	99.7%		100.0%	
8	2016	257,208	173,983	SCOTT, AUSTIN*	83,225	HARRIS, JAMES NEAL		90,758 R	67.6%	32.4%	67.6%	32.4%
8	2014	130,057	129,938	SCOTT, AUSTIN*			119	129,938 R	99.9%		100.0%	
8	2012	197,789	197,789	SCOTT, AUSTIN*				197,789 R	100.0%		100.0%	
9	2018	282,578	224,661	COLLINS, DOUG*	57,912	MCCALL, JOSHUA BRAXTON	5	166,749 R	79.5%	20.5%	79.5%	20.5%
9	2016	256,535	256,535	COLLINS, DOUG*				256,535 R	100.0%		100.0%	
9	2014	181,047	146,059	COLLINS, DOUG*	34,988	VOGEL, DAVID D.		111,071 R	80.7%	19.3%	80.7%	19.3%
9	2012	252,153	192,101	COLLINS, DOUG	60,052	COOLEY, JODY		132,049 R	76.2%	23.8%	76.2%	23.8%
10	2018	302,735	190,396	HICE, JODY*	112,339	JOHNSON-GREEN, TABITHA A.		78,057 R	62.9%	37.1%	62.9%	37.1%
10	2016	244,821	243,725	HICE, JODY*			1,096	243,725 R	99.6%		100.0%	
10	2014	196,480	130,703	HICE, JODY	65,777	DIOUS, IVORY KENNETH "KEN"		64,926 R	66.5%	33.5%	66.5%	33.5%
10	2012	211,466	211,065	BROUN, PAUL*			401	211,065 R	99.8%		100.0%	
11	2018	310,540	191,887	LOUDERMILK, BARRY*	118,653	BROADY, FLYNN D. JR.		73,234 R	61.8%	38.2%	61.8%	38.2%
11	2016	323,318	217,935	LOUDERMILK, BARRY*	105,383	WILSON, DON		112,552 R	67.4%	32.6%	67.4%	32.6%
11	2014	161,532	161,532	LOUDERMILK, BARRY				161,532 R	100.0%		100.0%	
11	2012	287,351	196,968	GINGREY, PHIL*	90,353	THOMPSON, PATRICK	30	106,615 R	68.5%	31.4%	68.6%	31.4%
12	2018	250,492	148,986	ALLEN, RICK*	101,503	JOHNSON, FRANCYS	3	47,483 R	59.5%	40.5%	59.5%	40.5%
12	2016	258,912	159,492	ALLEN, RICK*	99,420	MCCRACKEN, PATRICIA "TRICIA"		60,072 R	61.6%	38.4%	61.6%	38.4%
12	2014	166,814	91,336	ALLEN, RICK	75,478	BARROW, JOHN*		15,858 R	54.8%	45.2%	54.8%	45.2%
12	2012	259,121	119,973	ANDERSON, LEE	139,148	BARROW, JOHN*		19,175 D	46.3%	53.7%	46.3%	53.7%
13	2018	293,010	69,760	CALLAHAN, DAVID	223,157	SCOTT, DAVID*	93	153,397 D	23.8%	76.2%	23.8%	76.2%
13	2016	252,833			252,833	SCOTT, DAVID*		252,833 D		100.0%		100.0%
13	2014	159,445			159,445	SCOTT, DAVID*		159,445 D		100.0%		100.0%
13	2012	281,538	79,550	MALIK, S.	201,988	SCOTT, DAVID*		122,438 D	28.3%	71.7%	28.3%	71.7%
14	2018	229,724	175,743	GRAVES, TOM*	53,981	FOSTER, STEVE LAMAR		121,762 R	76.5%	23.5%	76.5%	23.5%
14	2016	216,743	216,743	GRAVES, TOM*				216,743 R	100.0%		100.0%	
14	2014	118,782	118,782	GRAVES, TOM*				118,782 R	100.0%		100.0%	
14	2012	219,192	159,947	GRAVES, TOM*	59,245	GRANT, DANIEL "DANNY"		100,702 R	73.0%	27.0%	73.0%	27.0%
TOTAL	*2018*	*3,802,343*	*1,987,191*		*1,814,469*		*683*	*172,722 R*	*52.3%*	*47.7%*	*52.3%*	*47.7%*
TOTAL	*2016*	*3,772,862*	*2,272,460*		*1,498,437*		*1,965*	*774,023 R*	*60.2%*	*39.7%*	*60.3%*	*39.7%*
TOTAL	*2014*	*2,305,665*	*1,349,076*		*956,361*		*228*	*392,715 R*	*58.5%*	*41.5%*	*58.5%*	*41.5%*
TOTAL	*2012*	*3,553,587*	*2,104,098*		*1,448,869*		*620*	*655,229 R*	*59.2%*	*40.8%*	*59.2%*	*40.8%*

Note: An asterisk (*) denotes incumbent.

GEORGIA

GENERAL AND PRIMARY ELECTIONS

2018 GENERAL ELECTIONS: OTHER VOTES

Governor	Other vote was 37,235 Libertarian (Ted Metz), 24 Write-in (Bobby Williams), 24 Write-in (Rod Mack), 21 Write-in (Bobby Waldrep), 12 Write-in (David Byrne)
House	Other vote was:
CD 6	18 Write-in (Jeremy Stubbs)
CD 8	564 Write-in (James Cooper)
CD 9	5 Write-in (Clifford Baxter)
CD 12	3 Write-in (Brian Brown)
CD 13	93 Write-in (Martin Cowen)

2018 PRIMARY ELECTIONS: SUPPLEMENTARY INFORMATION

Primary	May 22, 2018	**Registration** (as of May 22, 2018 — includes 551,212 inactive registrants)	6,694,441	No Party Registration
Primary Runoff	July 24, 2018			

Primary Type Open—Any registered voter could participate in either the Democratic or the Republican primary, although if voters cast a ballot in one party's primary they could not participate in a primary runoff of the other party. Voters who did not participate in the primary could vote in either party's runoff.

	REPUBLICAN PRIMARIES			DEMOCRATIC PRIMARIES		
Governor	Cagle, Casey	236,987	39.0%	Abrams, Stacey	424,305	76.4%
	Kemp, Brian	155,189	25.5%	Evans, Stacey	130,784	23.6%
	Hill, Hunter	111,464	18.3%			
	Tippins, Clay	74,182	12.2%			
	Williams, Michael	29,619	4.9%			
	TOTAL	*607,441*		*TOTAL*	*555,089*	
	PRIMARY RUNOFF					
	Kemp, Brian	408,595	69.5%			
	Cagle, Casey	179,712	30.5%			
	TOTAL	*588,307*				
Congressional District 1	Carter, Earl Leroy "Buddy"*	35,552	100.0%	Ring, Lisa	20,543	67.5%
				Seidman, Barbara	9,871	32.5%
	TOTAL	*35,552*		*TOTAL*	*30,414*	
Congressional District 2	West, Herman Jr.	23,147	100.0%	Bishop, Sanford*	42,855	100.0%
	TOTAL	*23,147*		*TOTAL*	*42,855*	
Congressional District 3	Ferguson, Drew*	43,381	74.4%	Enderlin, Chuck	13,614	59.9%
	Singleton, Philip	14,948	25.6%	Oliver, Melvin Russell "Rusty"	9,126	40.1%
	TOTAL	*58,329*		*TOTAL*	*22,740*	
Congressional District 4	Profit, Joe	15,367	100.0%	Johnson, Henry C. "Hank"*	55,060	79.8%
				Parks, Juan	13,966	20.2%
	TOTAL	*15,367*		*TOTAL*	*69,026*	

GEORGIA

GENERAL AND PRIMARY ELECTIONS

	REPUBLICAN PRIMARIES			DEMOCRATIC PRIMARIES		
Congressional District 5				Lewis, John*	80,860	100.0%
				TOTAL	*80,860*	
Congressional District 6	Handel, Karen*	40,410	100.0%	McBath, Lucy Kay	15,138	36.3%
				Abel, Kevin	12,747	30.5%
				Kaple, Bobby	10,956	26.2%
				Griffin, Steven Knight	2,901	6.9%
	TOTAL	*40,410*		*TOTAL*	*41,742*	
				PRIMARY RUNOFF		
				McBath, Lucy Kay	14,504	53.8%
				Abel, Kevin	12,431	46.2%
				TOTAL	*26,935*	
Congressional District 7	Woodall, Rob*	30,450	71.9%	Bourdeaux, Carolyn	8,662	27.3%
	Hazel, Shane	11,883	28.1%	Kim, David	8,249	26.0%
				Pham, Ethan	5,666	17.8%
				Davis, Melissa	4,340	13.7%
				Allen, Kathleen	3,500	11.0%
				Reilly, Steve	1,335	4.2%
	TOTAL	*42,333*		*TOTAL*	*31,752*	
				PRIMARY RUNOFF		
				Bourdeaux, Carolyn	8,114	51.8%
				Kim, David	7,545	48.2%
				TOTAL	*15,659*	
Congressional District 8	Scott, Austin*	41,467	100.0%			
	TOTAL	*41,467*				
Congressional District 9	Collins, Doug*	63,646	100.0%	McCall, Joshua Braxton	6,949	52.7%
				Cooper, Dave	6,230	47.3%
	TOTAL	*63,646*		*TOTAL*	*13,179*	
Congressional District 10	Hice, Jody*	42,960	78.9%	Johnson-Green, Tabitha A.	17,020	50.2%
	Griffin, Bradley	5,846	10.7%	Montgomery, Chalis	8,971	26.5%
	Hunt, Joseph "Joe"	5,644	10.4%	Winfield, Richard Dien	7,911	23.3%
	TOTAL	*54,450*		*TOTAL*	*33,902*	
Congressional District 11	Loudermilk, Barry*	43,309	100.0%	Broady, Flynn D. Jr.	21,621	100.0%
	TOTAL	*43,309*		*TOTAL*	*21,621*	
Congressional District 12	Allen, Rick*	37,776	76.0%	Johnson, Francys	16,991	52.9%
	Yu, Eugene	11,938	24.0%	Ingham, Robert	10,011	31.1%
				Nesmith, Michael "Trent"	5,139	16.0%
	TOTAL	*49,714*		*TOTAL*	*32,141*	
Congressional District 13	Callahan, David	17,475	93.0%	Scott, David*	56,216	100.0%
	Akinkugbe, Femi	1,315	7.0%			
	TOTAL	*18,790*		*TOTAL*	*56,216*	
Congressional District 14	Graves, Tom*	38,270	100.0%	Foster, Steve Lamar	10,627	100.0%
	TOTAL	*38,270*		*TOTAL*	*10,627*	

Note: An asterisk (*) denotes incumbent.

HAWAII

Congressional districts first established for elections held in 2012

2 members

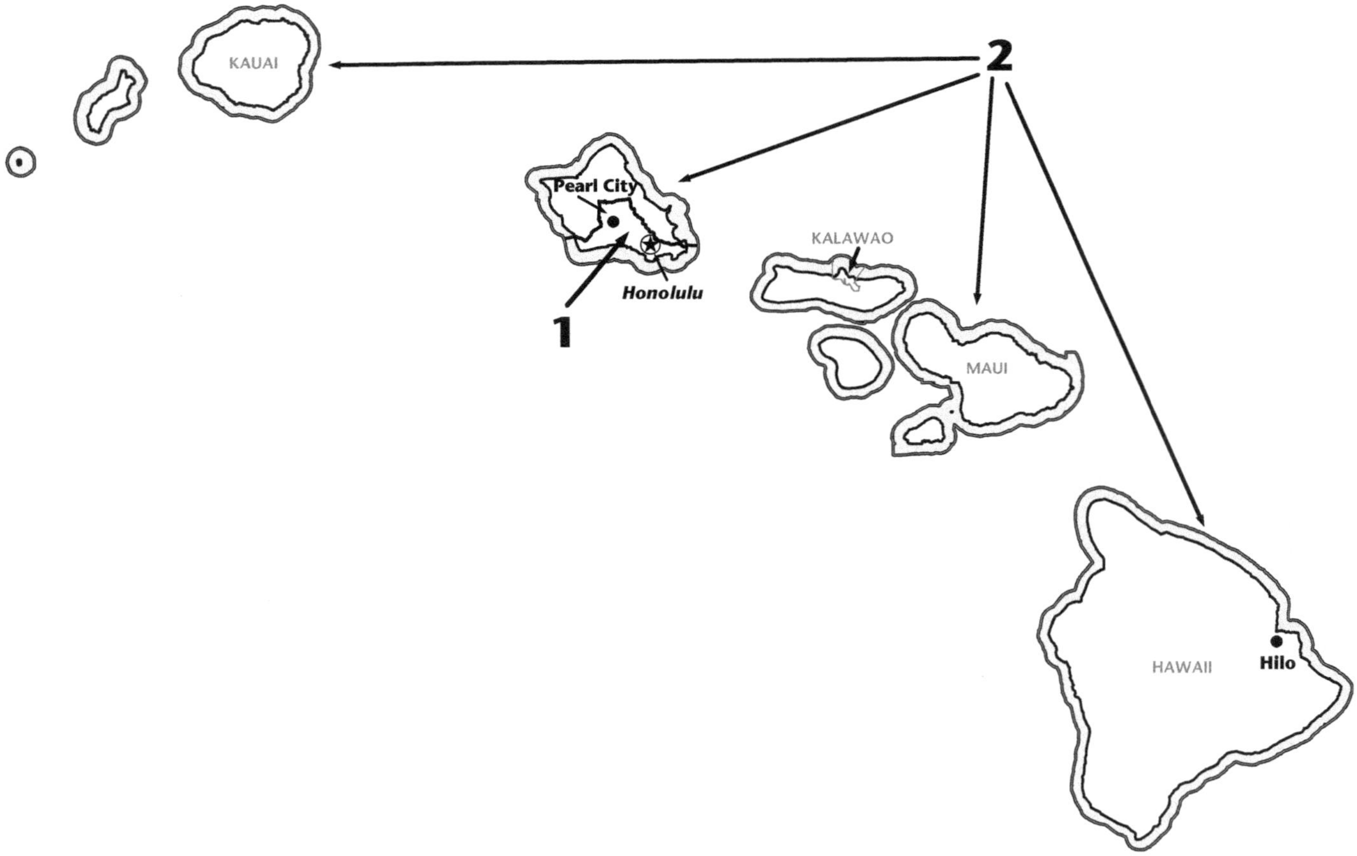

Hawaii includes more islands to the west of those that are illustrated on this map.

HAWAII

GOVERNOR

David Yutaka Ige (D). Re-elected 2018 to a four-year term. Previously elected 2014.

SENATORS (2 Democrats)

Mazie K. Hirono (D). Re-elected 2018 to a six-year term. Previously elected 2012.

Brian Schatz (D). Re-elected 2016 to a six-year term. Elected November 4, 2014, in a special election following the death of Senator Daniel K. Inouye. Schatz was initially appointed December 27, 2012, to fill the vacancy.

REPRESENTATIVES (2 Democrats)

1. Ed Case (D)
2. Tulsi Gabbard (D)

POSTWAR VOTE FOR PRESIDENT

		Republican		Democratic				Percentage			
								Total Vote		Major Vote	
Year	Total Vote	Vote	Candidate	Vote	Candidate	Other Vote	Rep.-Dem. Plurality	Rep.	Dem.	Rep.	Dem.
2016**	428,937	128,847	Trump, Donald J.	266,891	Clinton, Hillary Rodham	33,199	138,044 D	30.0%	62.2%	32.6%	67.4%
2012	434,697	121,015	Romney, W. Mitt	306,658	Obama, Barack H.*	7,024	185,643 D	27.8%	70.5%	28.3%	71.7%
2008	453,568	120,566	McCain, John S. III	325,871	Obama, Barack H.	7,131	205,305 D	26.6%	71.8%	27.0%	73.0%
2004	429,013	194,191	Bush, George W.*	231,708	Kerry, John F.	3,114	37,517 D	45.3%	54.0%	45.6%	54.4%
2000**	367,951	137,845	Bush, George W.	205,286	Gore, Albert Jr.	24,820	67,441 D	37.5%	55.8%	40.2%	59.8%
1996**	360,120	113,943	Dole, Robert "Bob"	205,012	Clinton, Bill*	41,165	91,069 D	31.6%	56.9%	35.7%	64.3%
1992**	372,842	136,822	Bush, George H.*	179,310	Clinton, Bill	56,710	42,488 D	36.7%	48.1%	43.3%	56.7%
1988	354,461	158,625	Bush, George H.	192,364	Dukakis, Michael S.	3,472	33,739 D	44.8%	54.3%	45.2%	54.8%
1984	335,846	185,050	Reagan, Ronald*	147,154	Mondale, Walter F.	3,642	37,896 R	55.1%	43.8%	55.7%	44.3%
1980**	303,287	130,112	Reagan, Ronald	135,879	Carter, Jimmy*	37,296	5,767 D	42.9%	44.8%	48.9%	51.1%
1976	291,301	140,003	Ford, Gerald R.*	147,375	Carter, Jimmy	3,923	7,372 D	48.1%	50.6%	48.7%	51.3%
1972	270,274	168,865	Nixon, Richard M.*	101,409	McGovern, George S.		67,456 R	62.5%	37.5%	62.5%	37.5%
1968**	236,218	91,425	Nixon, Richard M.	141,324	Humphrey, Hubert Horatio Jr.	3,469	49,899 D	38.7%	59.8%	39.3%	60.7%
1964	207,271	44,022	Goldwater, Barry M. Sr.	163,249	Johnson, Lyndon B.*		119,227 D	21.2%	78.8%	21.2%	78.8%
1960	184,705	92,295	Nixon, Richard M.	92,410	Kennedy, John F.		115 D	50.0%	50.0%	50.0%	50.0%

Note: An asterisk (*) denotes incumbent. **In past elections, the other vote included: 2016 - 15,954 Libertarian (Gary Johnson); 2000 - 21,623 Green (Ralph Nader); 1996 - 27,358 Reform (Ross Perot); 1992 - 53,003 Independent (Perot); 1980 - 32,021 Independent (John Anderson); 1968 - 3,469 American Independent (George Wallace). Hawaii was formally admitted as a state in August 1959.

HAWAII

POSTWAR VOTE FOR GOVERNOR

								Percentage			
		Republican		Democratic				Total Vote		Major Vote	
Year	Total Vote	Vote	Candidate	Vote	Candidate	Other Vote	Rep.-Dem. Plurality	Rep.	Dem.	Rep.	Dem.
2018	390,843	131,719	Tupola, Andria	244,934	Ige, David Yutaka*	14,190	113,215 D	33.7%	62.7%	35.0%	65.0%
2014	366,210	135,775	Aiona, Duke	181,106	Ige, David Yutaka	49,329	45,331 D	37.1%	49.5%	42.8%	57.2%
2010	382,563	157,311	Aiona, Duke	222,724	Abercrombie, Neil	2,528	65,413 D	41.1%	58.2%	41.4%	58.6%
2006	344,315	215,313	Lingle, Linda*	121,717	Iwase, Randy	7,285	93,596 R	62.5%	35.4%	63.9%	36.1%
2002	382,110	197,009	Lingle, Linda	179,647	Hirono, Mazie K.	5,454	17,362 R	51.6%	47.0%	52.3%	47.7%
1998	407,556	198,952	Lingle, Linda	204,206	Cayetano, Benjamin J.*	4,398	5,254 D	48.8%	50.1%	49.3%	50.7%
1994**	369,013	107,908	Saiki, Patricia	134,978	Cayetano, Benjamin J.	126,127	27,070 D	29.2%	36.6%	44.4%	55.6%
1990	340,132	131,310	Hemmings, Fred	203,491	Waihee, John*	5,331	72,181 D	38.6%	59.8%	39.2%	60.8%
1986	334,115	160,460	Anderson, D. G.	173,655	Waihee, John		13,195 D	48.0%	52.0%	48.0%	52.0%
1982**	311,853	81,507	Anderson, D. G.	141,043	Ariyoshi, George R.*	89,303	59,536 D	26.1%	45.2%	36.6%	63.4%
1978	281,587	124,610	Leopold, John	153,394	Ariyoshi, George R.*	3,583	28,784 D	44.3%	54.5%	44.8%	55.2%
1974	249,650	113,388	Crossley, Randolph	136,262	Ariyoshi, George R.		22,874 D	45.4%	54.6%	45.4%	54.6%
1970	239,061	101,249	King, Samuel P.	137,812	Burns, John A.*		36,563 D	42.4%	57.6%	42.4%	57.6%
1966	213,164	104,324	Crossley, Randolph	108,840	Burns, John A.*		4,516 D	48.9%	51.1%	48.9%	51.1%
1962	196,015	81,707	Quinn, Willam F.*	114,308	Burns, John A.		32,601 D	41.7%	58.3%	41.7%	58.3%
1959**	168,662	86,213	Quinn, Willam F.	82,074	Burns, John A.	375	4,139 R	51.1%	48.7%	51.2%	48.8%

Note: An asterisk (*) denotes incumbent. **In past elections, the other vote included: 1994 - 113,158 Best Party (Frank F. Fasi); 1982 - 89,303 Independent Democrat (Fasi). In both 1982 and 1994, Fasi finished second. The 1959 election was for a short term pending the regular vote in 1962.

POSTWAR VOTE FOR SENATOR

								Percentage			
		Republican		Democratic				Total Vote		Major Vote	
Year	Total Vote	Vote	Candidate	Vote	Candidate	Other Vote	Rep.-Dem. Plurality	Rep.	Dem.	Rep.	Dem.
2018	388,351	112,035	Curtis, Ron	276,316	Hirono, Mazie K.*		164,281 D	28.8%	71.2%	28.8%	71.2%
2016	416,562	92,653	Carroll, John S.	306,604	Schatz, Brian*	17,305	213,951 D	22.2%	73.6%	23.2%	76.8%
2014S**	353,774	98,006	Cavasso, Cam	246,827	Schatz, Brian*	8,941	148,821 D	27.7%	69.8%	28.4%	71.6%
2012	430,910	161,091	Lingle, Linda	269,819	Hirono, Mazie K.		108,728 D	37.4%	62.6%	37.4%	62.6%
2010	370,660	79,954	Cavasso, Cam	277,289	Inouye, Daniel K.*	13,417	197,335 D	21.6%	74.8%	22.4%	77.6%
2006	342,842	126,097	Thielen, Cynthia	210,330	Akaka, Daniel K.*	6,415	84,233 D	36.8%	61.3%	37.5%	62.5%
2004	415,347	87,172	Cavasso, Cam	313,629	Inouye, Daniel K.*	14,546	226,457 D	21.0%	75.5%	21.7%	78.3%
2000	345,623	84,701	Carroll, John	251,215	Akaka, Daniel K.*	9,707	166,514 D	24.5%	72.7%	25.2%	74.8%
1998	398,124	70,964	Young, Crystal	315,252	Inouye, Daniel K.*	11,908	244,288 D	17.8%	79.2%	18.4%	81.6%
1994	356,902	86,320	Hustace, Maria M.	256,189	Akaka, Daniel K.*	14,393	169,869 D	24.2%	71.8%	25.2%	74.8%
1992**	363,662	97,928	Reed, Rick	208,266	Inouye, Daniel K.*	57,468	110,338 D	26.9%	57.3%	32.0%	68.0%
1990S**	349,666	155,978	Saiki, Patricia	188,901	Akaka, Daniel K.	4,787	32,923 D	44.6%	54.0%	45.2%	54.8%
1988	323,876	66,987	Hustace, Maria M.	247,941	Matsunaga, Spark M.*	8,948	180,954 D	20.7%	76.6%	21.3%	78.7%
1986	328,797	86,910	Hutchinson, Frank	241,887	Inouye, Daniel K.*		154,977 D	26.4%	73.6%	26.4%	73.6%
1982	306,410	52,071	Brown, Clarence J.	245,386	Matsunaga, Spark M.*	8,953	193,315 D	17.0%	80.1%	17.5%	82.5%
1980	288,006	53,068	Brown, Cooper	224,485	Inouye, Daniel K.*	10,453	171,417 D	18.4%	77.9%	19.1%	80.9%
1976	302,092	122,724	Quinn, Willam F.	162,305	Matsunaga, Spark M.	17,063	39,581 D	40.6%	53.7%	43.1%	56.9%
1974**	250,221			207,454	Inouye, Daniel K.*	42,767	207,454 D		82.9%		100.0%
1970	240,760	124,163	Fong, Hiram L.*	116,597	Heftel, Cecil		7,566 R	51.6%	48.4%	51.6%	48.4%
1968	226,927	34,008	Thiessen, Wayne C.	189,248	Inouye, Daniel K.*	3,671	155,240 D	15.0%	83.4%	15.2%	84.8%
1964	208,814	110,747	Fong, Hiram L.*	96,789	Gill, Thomas P.	1,278	13,958 R	53.0%	46.4%	53.4%	46.6%
1962	196,361	60,067	Dillingham, Ben	136,294	Inouye, Daniel K.		76,227 D	30.6%	69.4%	30.6%	69.4%
1959**	163,875	79,123	Tsukiyama, Wilfred C.	83,700	Long, Oren E.	1,052	4,577 D	48.3%	51.1%	48.6%	51.4%
1959	164,808	87,161	Fong, Hiram L.	77,647	Fasi, Frank F.		9,514 R	52.9%	47.1%	52.9%	47.1%

Note: An asterisk (*) denotes incumbent. **In past elections, the other vote was: 1992 - 49,921 Green (Linda B. Martin); 1974 - 42,767 Peoples (James D. Kimmel), who finished second. The 1990 and 2014 elections were for a short term to fill a vacancy. The two 1959 elections were held to indeterminate terms and the Senate later determined by lot that Senator Long would serve a short term, Senator Fong a long term. The Republican Party did not run a Senate candidate in the 1974 election.

HAWAII

GOVERNOR 2018

2010 Census Population	County	Total Vote	Republican (Tupola)	Democratic (Ige)	Other	Rep.-Dem. Plurality	Percentage Total Vote Rep.	Total Vote Dem.	Major Vote Rep.	Major Vote Dem.
185,079	HAWAII	58,617	17,953	38,301	2,363	20,348 D	30.6%	65.3%	31.9%	68.1%
953,207	HONOLULU	258,080	90,929	158,623	8,528	67,694 D	35.2%	61.5%	36.4%	63.6%
67,091	KAUAI	24,833	8,135	15,868	830	7,733 D	32.8%	63.9%	33.9%	66.1%
154,834	MAUI	49,313	14,702	32,142	2,469	17,440 D	29.8%	65.2%	31.4%	68.6%
1,360,211	*TOTAL*	*390,843*	*131,719*	*244,934*	*14,190*	*113,215 D*	*33.7%*	*62.7%*	*35.0%*	*65.0%*

HAWAII

SENATOR 2018

2010 Census Population	County	Total Vote	Republican (Curtis)	Democratic (Hirono)	Other	Rep.-Dem. Plurality	Percentage Total Vote Rep.	Total Vote Dem.	Major Vote Rep.	Major Vote Dem.
185,079	HAWAII	58,379	15,031	43,348		28,317 D	25.7%	74.3%	25.7%	74.3%
953,207	HONOLULU	256,208	79,503	176,705		97,202 D	31.0%	69.0%	31.0%	69.0%
67,091	KAUAI	24,630	6,120	18,510		12,390 D	24.8%	75.2%	24.8%	75.2%
154,834	MAUI	49,134	11,381	37,753		26,372 D	23.2%	76.8%	23.2%	76.8%
1,360,211	*TOTAL*	*388,351*	*112,035*	*276,316*		*164,281 D*	*28.8%*	*71.2%*	*28.8%*	*71.2%*

HAWAII

HOUSE OF REPRESENTATIVES

CD	Year	Total Vote	Republican Vote	Republican Candidate	Democratic Vote	Democratic Candidate	Other Vote	Rep.-Dem. Plurality	Percentage Total Vote Rep.	Total Vote Dem.	Major Vote Rep.	Major Vote Dem.
1	2018	184,211	42,498	CAVASSO, CAM	134,650	CASE, EDWARD E.	7,063	92,152 D	23.1%	73.1%	24.0%	76.0%
1	2016	202,357	45,958	OSTROV, SHIRLENE D. "SHIRL"	145,417	HANABUSA, COLLEEN	10,982	99,459 D	22.7%	71.9%	24.0%	76.0%
1	2014	179,844	86,454	DJOU, CHARLES	93,390	TAKAI, MARK		6,936 D	48.1%	51.9%	48.1%	51.9%
1	2012	213,329	96,824	DJOU, CHARLES	116,505	HANABUSA, COLLEEN*		19,681 D	45.4%	54.6%	45.4%	54.6%
2	2018	198,121	44,850	EVANS, BRIAN	153,271	GABBARD, TULSI*		108,421 D	22.6%	77.4%	22.6%	77.4%
2	2016	210,516	39,668	KAAIHUE, ANGELA AULANI	170,848	GABBARD, TULSI*		131,180 D	18.8%	81.2%	18.8%	81.2%
2	2014	180,333	33,630	CROWLEY, KAWIKA	142,010	GABBARD, TULSI*	4,693	108,380 D	18.6%	78.7%	19.1%	80.9%
2	2012	209,210	40,707	CROWLEY, KAWIKA	168,503	GABBARD, TULSI		127,796 D	19.5%	80.5%	19.5%	80.5%
TOTAL	*2018*	*382,332*	*87,348*		*287,921*		*7,063*	*200,573 D*	*22.8%*	*75.3%*	*23.3%*	*76.7%*
TOTAL	*2016*	*412,873*	*85,626*		*316,265*		*10,982*	*230,639 D*	*20.7%*	*76.6%*	*21.3%*	*78.7%*
TOTAL	*2014*	*360,177*	*120,084*		*235,400*		*4,693*	*115,316 D*	*33.3%*	*65.4%*	*33.8%*	*66.2%*
TOTAL	*2012*	*422,539*	*137,531*		*285,008*			*147,477 D*	*32.5%*	*67.5%*	*32.5%*	*67.5%*

Note: An asterisk (*) denotes incumbent.

HAWAII

GENERAL AND PRIMARY ELECTIONS

2018 GENERAL ELECTIONS: OTHER VOTES

Governor	Other vote was 10,123 Green (Jim Brewer), 4,067 Nonpartisan (Terrence Teruya)
House	Other vote was:
CD 1	3,498 Libertarian (Michelle Tippens), 2,214 Green (Zachary Burd), 1,351 Nonpartisan (Calvin Griffin)

2018 PRIMARY ELECTIONS: SUPPLEMENTARY INFORMATION

Primary	August 11, 2018	**Registration** (as of August 11, 2018)	741,007	No Party Registration

Primary Type Open—Any registered voter could participate in the party primary of his or her choice.

	REPUBLICAN PRIMARIES			DEMOCRATIC PRIMARIES		
Senator	Curtis, Ron	6,370	23.7%	Hirono, Mazie K.*	201,679	100.0%
	Anderson, Consuelo	5,172	19.3%			
	Helsham, Robert C. Sr.	3,988	14.9%			
	White, Thomas E.	3,661	13.6%			
	De La Fuente, Roque "Rocky"	3,065	11.4%			
	Berish, George L.	1,658	6.2%			
	Hodgkiss, Michael R.	1,576	5.9%			
	Pirkowski, Eddie	1,358	5.1%			
	TOTAL	*26,848*		*TOTAL*	*201,679*	
Governor	Tupola, Andria	17,297	55.5%	Ige, David Yutaka*	124,572	51.4%
	Carroll, John	10,974	35.2%	Hanabusa, Colleen	107,631	44.4%
	L'Heureux, Ray	2,885	9.3%	Caravalho, Ernest	5,662	2.3%
				Ka'Ehu'Ae'A, Wendell	2,298	0.9%
				Kim, Richard Y.	1,576	0.6%
				Tanabe, Van "Tanaban"	775	0.3%
	TOTAL	*31,156*		*TOTAL*	*242,514*	
Congressional District 1	Cavasso, Cam	10,564	81.9%	Case, Edward E.	47,491	40.0%
	Vinole, Raymond Rene	2,342	18.1%	Chin, Doug	30,290	25.5%
				Kim, Donna Mercado	21,563	18.2%
				Ing, Kaniela	7,539	6.4%
				Fukumoto, Beth	7,476	6.3%
				Martin, Ernie	3,827	3.2%
				Puletasi, Sam	519	0.4%
	TOTAL	*12,906*		*TOTAL*	*118,705*	
Congressional District 2	Evans, Brian	12,337	100.0%	Gabbard, Tulsi*	94,665	83.5%
				Alu Campagna, Sheryl	13,947	12.3%
				Austin, Anthony Tony	4,692	4.1%
	TOTAL	*12,337*		*TOTAL*	*113,304*	

Note: An asterisk (*) denotes incumbent.

IDAHO

Congressional districts first established for elections held in 2012

2 members

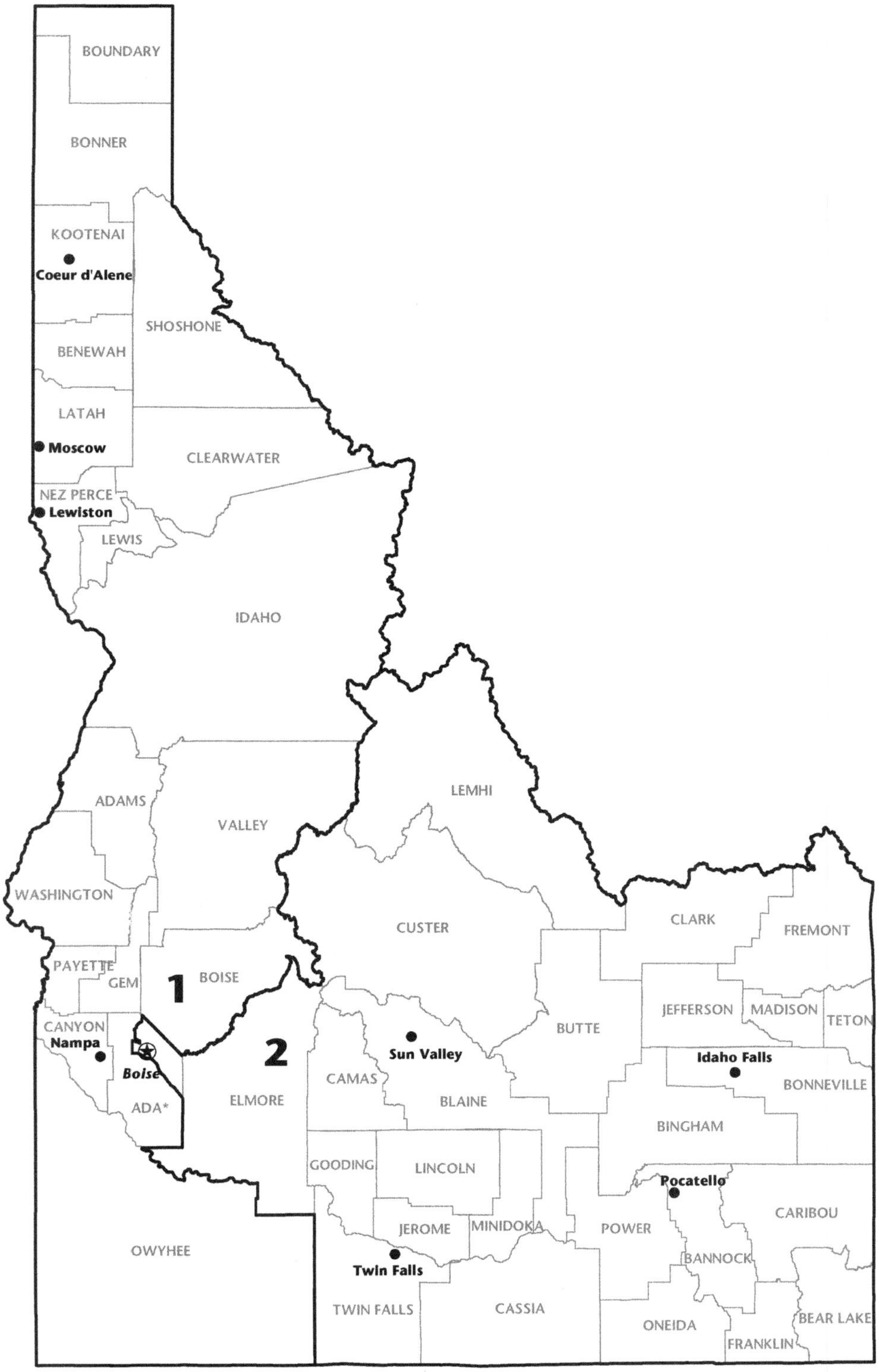

* Asterisk indicates a county whose boundaries include parts of two or more congressional districts.

IDAHO

GOVERNOR

Brad Little (R). Elected 2018 to a four-year term.

SENATORS (2 Republicans)

Michael D. Crapo (R). Re-elected 2016 to a six-year term. Previously elected 2010, 2004, 1998.

Jim Risch (R). Re-elected 2014 to a six-year term. Previously elected 2008.

REPRESENTATIVES (2 Republicans)

1. Russ M. Fulcher (R)
2. Michael K. Simpson (R)

POSTWAR VOTE FOR PRESIDENT

		Republican		Democratic				Percentage			
								Total Vote		Major Vote	
Year	Total Vote	Vote	Candidate	Vote	Candidate	Other Vote	Rep.-Dem. Plurality	Rep.	Dem.	Rep.	Dem.
2016**	690,255	409,055	Trump, Donald J.	189,765	Clinton, Hillary Rodham	91,435	219,290 R	59.3%	27.5%	68.3%	31.7%
2012	652,346	420,911	Romney, W. Mitt	212,787	Obama, Barack H.*	18,648	208,124 R	64.5%	32.6%	66.4%	33.6%
2008	655,122	403,012	McCain, John S. III	236,440	Obama, Barack H.	15,670	166,572 R	61.5%	36.1%	63.0%	37.0%
2004	598,447	409,235	Bush, George W.*	181,098	Kerry, John F.	8,114	228,137 R	68.4%	30.3%	69.3%	30.7%
2000**	501,621	336,937	Bush, George W.	138,637	Gore, Albert Jr.	26,047	198,300 R	67.2%	27.6%	70.8%	29.2%
1996**	491,719	256,595	Dole, Robert "Bob"	165,443	Clinton, Bill*	69,681	91,152 R	52.2%	33.6%	60.8%	39.2%
1992**	482,142	202,645	Bush, George H.*	137,013	Clinton, Bill	142,484	65,632 R	42.0%	28.4%	59.7%	40.3%
1988	408,968	253,881	Bush, George H.	147,272	Dukakis, Michael S.	7,815	106,609 R	62.1%	36.0%	63.3%	36.7%
1984	411,144	297,523	Reagan, Ronald*	108,510	Mondale, Walter F.	5,111	189,013 R	72.4%	26.4%	73.3%	26.7%
1980**	437,431	290,699	Reagan, Ronald	110,192	Carter, Jimmy*	36,540	180,507 R	66.5%	25.2%	72.5%	27.5%
1976	344,071	204,151	Ford, Gerald R.*	126,549	Carter, Jimmy	13,371	77,602 R	59.3%	36.8%	61.7%	38.3%
1972	310,379	199,384	Nixon, Richard M.*	80,826	McGovern, George S.	30,169	118,558 R	64.2%	26.0%	71.2%	28.8%
1968**	291,183	165,369	Nixon, Richard M.	89,273	Humphrey, Hubert Horatio Jr.	36,541	76,096 R	56.8%	30.7%	64.9%	35.1%
1964	292,477	143,557	Goldwater, Barry M. Sr.	148,920	Johnson, Lyndon B.*		5,363 D	49.1%	50.9%	49.1%	50.9%
1960	300,450	161,597	Nixon, Richard M.	138,853	Kennedy, John F.		22,744 R	53.8%	46.2%	53.8%	46.2%
1956	272,989	166,979	Eisenhower, Dwight D.*	105,868	Stevenson, Adlai E. II	142	61,111 R	61.2%	38.8%	61.2%	38.8%
1952	276,254	180,707	Eisenhower, Dwight D.	95,081	Stevenson, Adlai E. II	466	85,626 R	65.4%	34.4%	65.5%	34.5%
1948	214,816	101,514	Dewey, Thomas E.	107,370	Truman, Harry S.*	5,932	5,856 D	47.3%	50.0%	48.6%	51.4%

Note: An asterisk (*) denotes incumbent. **In past elections, the other vote included: 2016 - 46,476 Independent (Evan McMullin); 28,331 Libertarian (Johnson); 2000 - 12,292 Green (Ralph Nader); 1996 - 62,518 Reform (Ross Perot); 1992 - 130,395 Independent (Perot); 1980 - 27,058 Independent (John Anderson); 1968 - 36,541 American Independent (George Wallace).

IDAHO

POSTWAR VOTE FOR GOVERNOR

		Republican		Democratic				Percentage			
								Total Vote		Major Vote	
Year	Total Vote	Vote	Candidate	Vote	Candidate	Other Vote	Rep.-Dem. Plurality	Rep.	Dem.	Rep.	Dem.
2018	605,131	361,661	Little, Brad	231,081	Jordan, Paulette	12,389	130,580 R	59.8%	38.2%	61.0%	39.0%
2014	439,830	235,405	Otter, C. L. "Butch"*	169,556	Balukoff, A.J.	34,869	65,849 R	53.5%	38.6%	58.1%	41.9%
2010	452,535	267,483	Otter, C. L. "Butch"*	148,680	Allred, Keith	36,372	118,803 R	59.1%	32.9%	64.3%	35.7%
2006	450,850	237,437	Otter, C. L. "Butch"	198,845	Brady, Jerry M.	14,568	38,592 R	52.7%	44.1%	54.4%	45.6%
2002	411,477	231,566	Kempthorne, Dirk*	171,711	Brady, Jerry M.	8,200	59,855 R	56.3%	41.7%	57.4%	42.6%
1998	381,248	258,095	Kempthorne, Dirk	110,815	Huntley, Robert C.	12,338	147,280 R	67.7%	29.1%	70.0%	30.0%
1994	413,346	216,123	Batt, Phil	181,363	Echohawk, Larry	15,860	34,760 R	52.3%	43.9%	54.4%	45.6%
1990	320,610	101,937	Fairchild, Roger	218,673	Andrus, Cecil D.*		116,736 D	31.8%	68.2%	31.8%	68.2%
1986	387,426	189,794	Leroy, David H.	193,429	Andrus, Cecil D.	4,203	3,635 D	49.0%	49.9%	49.5%	50.5%
1982	326,522	161,157	Batt, Phil	165,365	Evans, John V.*		4,208 D	49.4%	50.6%	49.4%	50.6%
1978	288,566	114,149	Larsen, Allan	169,540	Evans, John V.*	4,877	55,391 D	39.6%	58.8%	40.2%	59.8%
1974	259,632	68,731	Murphy, Jack M.	184,142	Andrus, Cecil D.*	6,759	115,411 D	26.5%	70.9%	27.2%	72.8%
1970	245,112	117,108	Samuelson, Don*	128,004	Andrus, Cecil D.		10,896 D	47.8%	52.2%	47.8%	52.2%
1966**	252,593	104,586	Samuelson, Don	93,744	Andrus, Cecil D.	54,263	10,842 R	41.4%	37.1%	52.7%	47.3%
1962	255,454	139,578	Smylie, Robert E.*	115,876	Smith, Vernon K.		23,702 R	54.6%	45.4%	54.6%	45.4%
1958	239,046	121,810	Smylie, Robert E.*	117,236	Derr, A. M.		4,574 R	51.0%	49.0%	51.0%	49.0%
1954	228,685	124,038	Smylie, Robert E.	104,647	Hamilton, Clark		19,391 R	54.2%	45.8%	54.2%	45.8%
1950	204,792	107,642	Jordan, Len B.	97,150	Wright, Calvin E.		10,492 R	52.6%	47.4%	52.6%	47.4%
1946	181,364	102,233	Robins, Charles A.	79,131	Williams, Arnold*		23,102 R	56.4%	43.6%	56.4%	43.6%

Note: An asterisk (*) denotes incumbent. **In past elections, the other vote included: 1966 - 30,913 Independent (Perry Swisher).

POSTWAR VOTE FOR SENATOR

		Republican		Democratic				Percentage			
								Total Vote		Major Vote	
Year	Total Vote	Vote	Candidate	Vote	Candidate	Other Vote	Rep.-Dem. Plurality	Rep.	Dem.	Rep.	Dem.
2016	678,943	449,017	Crapo, Michael D.*	188,249	Sturgill, Jerry	41,677	260,768 R	66.1%	27.7%	70.5%	29.5%
2014	437,170	285,596	Risch, Jim*	151,574	Mitchell, Nels		134,022 R	65.3%	34.7%	65.3%	34.7%
2010	449,530	319,953	Crapo, Michael D.*	112,057	Sullivan, P. Tom	17,520	207,896 R	71.2%	24.9%	74.1%	25.9%
2008	644,780	371,744	Risch, Jim	219,903	Larocco, Larry	53,133	151,841 R	57.7%	34.1%	62.8%	37.2%
2004**	503,932	499,796	Crapo, Michael D.*			4,136	499,796 R	99.2%		100.0%	
2002	408,544	266,215	Craig, Larry E.*	132,975	Blinken, Alan	9,354	133,240 R	65.2%	32.5%	66.7%	33.3%
1998	378,174	262,966	Crapo, Michael D.	107,375	Mauk, Bill	7,833	155,591 R	69.5%	28.4%	71.0%	29.0%
1996	497,233	283,532	Craig, Larry E.*	198,422	Minnick, Walt	15,279	85,110 R	57.0%	39.9%	58.8%	41.2%
1992	478,504	270,468	Kempthorne, Dirk	208,036	Stallings, Richard		62,432 R	56.5%	43.5%	56.5%	43.5%
1990	315,936	193,641	Craig, Larry E.	122,295	Twilegar, Ron J.		71,346 R	61.3%	38.7%	61.3%	38.7%
1986	382,024	196,958	Symms, Steven D.*	185,066	Evans, John V.		11,892 R	51.6%	48.4%	51.6%	48.4%
1984	406,168	293,193	McClure, James A.*	105,591	Busch, Peter M.	7,384	187,602 R	72.2%	26.0%	73.5%	26.5%
1980	439,647	218,701	Symms, Steven D.	214,439	Church, Frank*	6,507	4,262 R	49.7%	48.8%	50.5%	49.5%
1978	284,047	194,412	McClure, James A.*	89,635	Jensen, Dwight		104,777 R	68.4%	31.6%	68.4%	31.6%
1974	258,847	109,072	Smith, Robert L.	145,140	Church, Frank*	4,635	36,068 D	42.1%	56.1%	42.9%	57.1%
1972	309,602	161,804	McClure, James A.	140,913	Davis, William E. Bud	6,885	20,891 R	52.3%	45.5%	53.5%	46.5%
1968	287,876	114,394	Hansen, George V.	173,482	Church, Frank*		59,088 D	39.7%	60.3%	39.7%	60.3%
1966	252,456	139,819	Jordan, Len B.*	112,637	Harding, Ralph R.		27,182 R	55.4%	44.6%	55.4%	44.6%
1962	258,786	117,129	Hawley, Jack	141,657	Church, Frank*		24,528 D	45.3%	54.7%	45.3%	54.7%
1962S**	257,677	131,279	Jordan, Len B.*	126,398	Pfost, Gracie B.		4,881 R	50.9%	49.1%	50.9%	49.1%
1960	292,096	152,648	Dworshak, Henry C.*	139,448	McLaughlin, R. F.		13,200 R	52.3%	47.7%	52.3%	47.7%
1956	265,292	102,781	Welker, Herman*	149,096	Church, Frank	13,415	46,315 D	38.7%	56.2%	40.8%	59.2%
1954	226,408	142,269	Dworshak, Henry C.*	84,139	Taylor, Glen H.		58,130 R	62.8%	37.2%	62.8%	37.2%
1950	201,417	124,237	Welker, Herman	77,180	Clark, D. Worth		47,057 R	61.7%	38.3%	61.7%	38.3%
1950S**	201,700	104,608	Dworshak, Henry C.	97,092	Burtenshaw, Claude		7,516 R	51.9%	48.1%	51.9%	48.1%
1948	214,188	103,868	Dworshak, Henry C.*	107,000	Miller, Bert H.	3,320	3,132 D	48.5%	50.0%	49.3%	50.7%
1946S**	180,152	105,523	Dworshak, Henry C.	74,629	Donart, George E.		30,894 R	58.6%	41.4%	58.6%	41.4%

Note: An asterisk (*) denotes incumbent. **In 2004 there was no candidate on the Democratic line. A write-in candidate, who was a Democrat, received 4,136 votes, which are listed in the Other Vote column. The 1946 election and one each of the 1950 and 1962 elections were for short terms to fill vacancies.

IDAHO

GOVERNOR 2018

2010 Census Population	County	Total Vote	Republican (Little)	Democratic (Jordan)	Other	Rep.-Dem. Plurality	Percentage: Total Vote		Percentage: Major Vote	
							Rep.	Dem.	Rep.	Dem.
392,365	ADA	190,502	92,684	94,772	3,046	2,088 D	48.7%	49.7%	49.4%	50.6%
3,976	ADAMS	1,906	1,288	579	39	709 R	67.6%	30.4%	69.0%	31.0%
82,839	BANNOCK	29,086	14,975	13,386	725	1,589 R	51.5%	46.0%	52.8%	47.2%
5,986	BEAR LAKE	2,151	1,780	307	64	1,473 R	82.8%	14.3%	85.3%	14.7%
9,285	BENEWAH	3,763	2,672	1,004	87	1,668 R	71.0%	26.7%	72.7%	27.3%
45,607	BINGHAM	13,250	9,337	3,515	398	5,822 R	70.5%	26.5%	72.7%	27.3%
21,376	BLAINE	10,487	3,063	7,267	157	4,204 D	29.2%	69.3%	29.7%	70.3%
7,028	BOISE	3,510	2,374	1,051	85	1,323 R	67.6%	29.9%	69.3%	30.7%
40,877	BONNER	18,590	11,477	6,749	364	4,728 R	61.7%	36.3%	63.0%	37.0%
104,234	BONNEVILLE	35,261	23,497	10,699	1,065	12,798 R	66.6%	30.3%	68.7%	31.3%
10,972	BOUNDARY	4,271	3,101	1,075	95	2,026 R	72.6%	25.2%	74.3%	25.7%
2,891	BUTTE	1,031	788	214	29	574 R	76.4%	20.8%	78.6%	21.4%
1,117	CAMAS	538	371	157	10	214 R	69.0%	29.2%	70.3%	29.7%
188,923	CANYON	63,593	40,636	21,839	1,118	18,797 R	63.9%	34.3%	65.0%	35.0%
6,963	CARIBOU	2,267	1,824	371	72	1,453 R	80.5%	16.4%	83.1%	16.9%
22,952	CASSIA	6,180	4,888	1,111	181	3,777 R	79.1%	18.0%	81.5%	18.5%
982	CLARK	253	195	47	11	148 R	77.1%	18.6%	80.6%	19.4%
8,761	CLEARWATER	3,156	2,310	779	67	1,531 R	73.2%	24.7%	74.8%	25.2%
4,368	CUSTER	2,124	1,518	545	61	973 R	71.5%	25.7%	73.6%	26.4%
27,038	ELMORE	7,031	4,582	2,253	196	2,329 R	65.2%	32.0%	67.0%	33.0%
12,786	FRANKLIN	3,833	3,228	416	189	2,812 R	84.2%	10.9%	88.6%	11.4%
13,242	FREMONT	4,784	3,798	841	145	2,957 R	79.4%	17.6%	81.9%	18.1%
16,719	GEM	7,141	5,438	1,572	131	3,866 R	76.2%	22.0%	77.6%	22.4%
15,464	GOODING	4,422	3,209	1,110	103	2,099 R	72.6%	25.1%	74.3%	25.7%
16,267	IDAHO	7,027	5,478	1,372	177	4,106 R	78.0%	19.5%	80.0%	20.0%
26,140	JEFFERSON	8,709	7,125	1,307	277	5,818 R	81.8%	15.0%	84.5%	15.5%
22,374	JEROME	5,384	3,808	1,440	136	2,368 R	70.7%	26.7%	72.6%	27.4%
138,494	KOOTENAI	56,746	38,173	17,620	953	20,553 R	67.3%	31.1%	68.4%	31.6%
37,244	LATAH	15,997	6,803	8,981	213	2,178 D	42.5%	56.1%	43.1%	56.9%
7,936	LEMHI	3,435	2,470	883	82	1,587 R	71.9%	25.7%	73.7%	26.3%
3,821	LEWIS	1,397	1,051	326	20	725 R	75.2%	23.3%	76.3%	23.7%
5,208	LINCOLN	1,488	1,022	419	47	603 R	68.7%	28.2%	70.9%	29.1%
37,536	MADISON	8,773	6,887	1,520	366	5,367 R	78.5%	17.3%	81.9%	18.1%
20,069	MINIDOKA	5,155	3,849	1,179	127	2,670 R	74.7%	22.9%	76.6%	23.4%
39,265	NEZ PERCE	14,450	8,845	5,385	220	3,460 R	61.2%	37.3%	62.2%	37.8%
4,286	ONEIDA	1,516	1,249	200	67	1,049 R	82.4%	13.2%	86.2%	13.8%
11,526	OWYHEE	3,467	2,613	772	82	1,841 R	75.4%	22.3%	77.2%	22.8%
22,623	PAYETTE	7,595	5,553	1,890	152	3,663 R	73.1%	24.9%	74.6%	25.4%
7,817	POWER	2,194	1,456	681	57	775 R	66.4%	31.0%	68.1%	31.9%
12,765	SHOSHONE	4,263	2,564	1,623	76	941 R	60.1%	38.1%	61.2%	38.8%
10,170	TETON	4,800	2,055	2,636	109	581 D	42.8%	54.9%	43.8%	56.2%
77,230	TWIN FALLS	24,492	16,102	7,742	648	8,360 R	65.7%	31.6%	67.5%	32.5%
9,862	VALLEY	5,199	2,676	2,442	81	234 R	51.5%	47.0%	52.3%	47.7%
10,198	WASHINGTON	3,914	2,849	1,004	61	1,845 R	72.8%	25.7%	73.9%	26.1%
1,567,582	*TOTAL*	*605,131*	*361,661*	*231,081*	*12,389*	*130,580 R*	*59.8%*	*38.2%*	*61.0%*	*39.0%*

IDAHO

HOUSE OF REPRESENTATIVES

			Republican		Democratic				Percentage			
									Total Vote		Major Vote	
CD	Year	Total Vote	Vote	Candidate	Vote	Candidate	Other Vote	Rep.-Dem. Plurality	Rep.	Dem.	Rep.	Dem.
1	2018	315,069	197,719	FULCHER, RUSSELL M.	96,922	MCNEIL, CRISTINA	20,428	100,797 R	62.8%	30.8%	67.1%	32.9%
1	2016	355,357	242,252	LABRADOR, RAUL R.*	113,052	PIOTROWSKI, JAMES	53	129,200 R	68.2%	31.8%	68.2%	31.8%
1	2014	220,864	143,580	LABRADOR, RAUL R.*	77,277	RINGO, SHIRLEY G.	7	66,303 R	65.0%	35.0%	65.0%	35.0%
1	2012	316,724	199,402	LABRADOR, RAUL R.*	97,450	FARRIS, JIMMY	19,872	101,952 R	63.0%	30.8%	67.2%	32.8%
2	2018	280,655	170,274	SIMPSON, MICHAEL K.*	110,381	SWISHER, AARON		59,893 R	60.7%	39.3%	60.7%	39.3%
2	2016	326,237	205,292	SIMPSON, MICHAEL K.*	95,940	MARTINEZ, JENNIFER	25,005	109,352 R	62.9%	29.4%	68.2%	31.8%
2	2014	214,293	131,492	SIMPSON, MICHAEL K.*	82,801	STALLINGS, RICHARD		48,691 R	61.4%	38.6%	61.4%	38.6%
2	2012	318,494	207,412	SIMPSON, MICHAEL K.*	110,847	LEFAVOUR, NICOLE	235	96,565 R	65.1%	34.8%	65.2%	34.8%
TOTAL	*2018*	*595,724*	*367,993*		*207,303*		*20,428*	*160,690 R*	*61.8%*	*34.8%*	*64.0%*	*36.0%*
TOTAL	*2016*	*681,594*	*447,544*		*208,992*		*25,058*	*238,552 R*	*65.7%*	*30.7%*	*68.2%*	*31.8%*
TOTAL	*2014*	*435,157*	*275,072*		*160,078*		*7*	*114,994 R*	*63.2%*	*36.8%*	*63.2%*	*36.8%*
TOTAL	*2012*	*635,218*	*406,814*		*208,297*		*20,107*	*198,517 R*	*64.0%*	*32.8%*	*66.1%*	*33.9%*

Note: An asterisk (*) denotes incumbent.

IDAHO

GENERAL AND PRIMARY ELECTIONS

2018 GENERAL ELECTIONS: OTHER VOTES

Governor Other vote was 6,551 Libertarian (Bev Boeck), 5,787 Constitution (Walter Bayes), 51 Write-in (Lisa Marie)

House Other vote was:

CD 1 6,188 Independent (Natalie Fleming), 5,435 Libertarian (William Howard), 4,479 Independent (Paul Farmer), 3,181 Constitution (Marvin Richardson), 1,054 Independent (Gordon Counsil), 91 Write-in (Michael Rath)

2018 PRIMARY ELECTIONS: SUPPLEMENTARY INFORMATION

Primary May 15, 2018

Registration (as of May 3, 2018) 809,720

Republican	403,771
Democratic	90,230
Libertarian	6,733
Constitution	3,006
Unaffiliated	305,980

Primary Type Semi-Open—Registered Democrats and unaffiliated voters could participate in the Democratic primary. Only registered Republicans could vote in the Republican primary.

IDAHO

GENERAL AND PRIMARY ELECTIONS

	REPUBLICAN PRIMARIES			DEMOCRATIC PRIMARIES		
Governor	Little, Brad	72,548	37.3%	Jordan, Paulette	38,505	58.4%
	Labrador, Raul R.	63,478	32.6%	Balukoff, A.J.	26,423	40.1%
	Ahlquist, Tommy	51,008	26.2%	Dill, Peter	954	1.4%
	Marie, Lisa	3,397	1.7%			
	Pankey, Steven D.	2,704	1.4%			
	Brown, Harley D.	874	0.4%			
	Cannady, Dalton Ben	527	0.3%			
	TOTAL	*194,536*		*TOTAL*	*65,882*	
Congressional District 1	Fulcher, Russell M.	42,790	43.1%	McNeil, Cristina	19,073	69.7%
	Leroy, David H.	15,414	15.5%	Vandermaas, James	4,337	15.8%
	Malek, Lucas	14,152	14.3%	Smith, Michael W.	3,964	14.5%
	Perry, Christy	11,108	11.2%			
	Snyder, Michael	10,288	10.4%			
	Gallegos, Alex	3,478	3.5%			
	Henderson, Nicholas	2,003	2.0%			
	TOTAL	*99,233*		*TOTAL*	*27,374*	
Congressional District 2	Simpson, Michael K.*	72,243	100.0%	Swisher, Aaron	18,709	67.6%
				Rickards, Peter	8,987	32.4%
	TOTAL	*72,243*		*TOTAL*	*27,696*	

Note: An asterisk (*) denotes incumbent.

ILLINOIS

Congressional districts first established for elections held in 2012

18 members

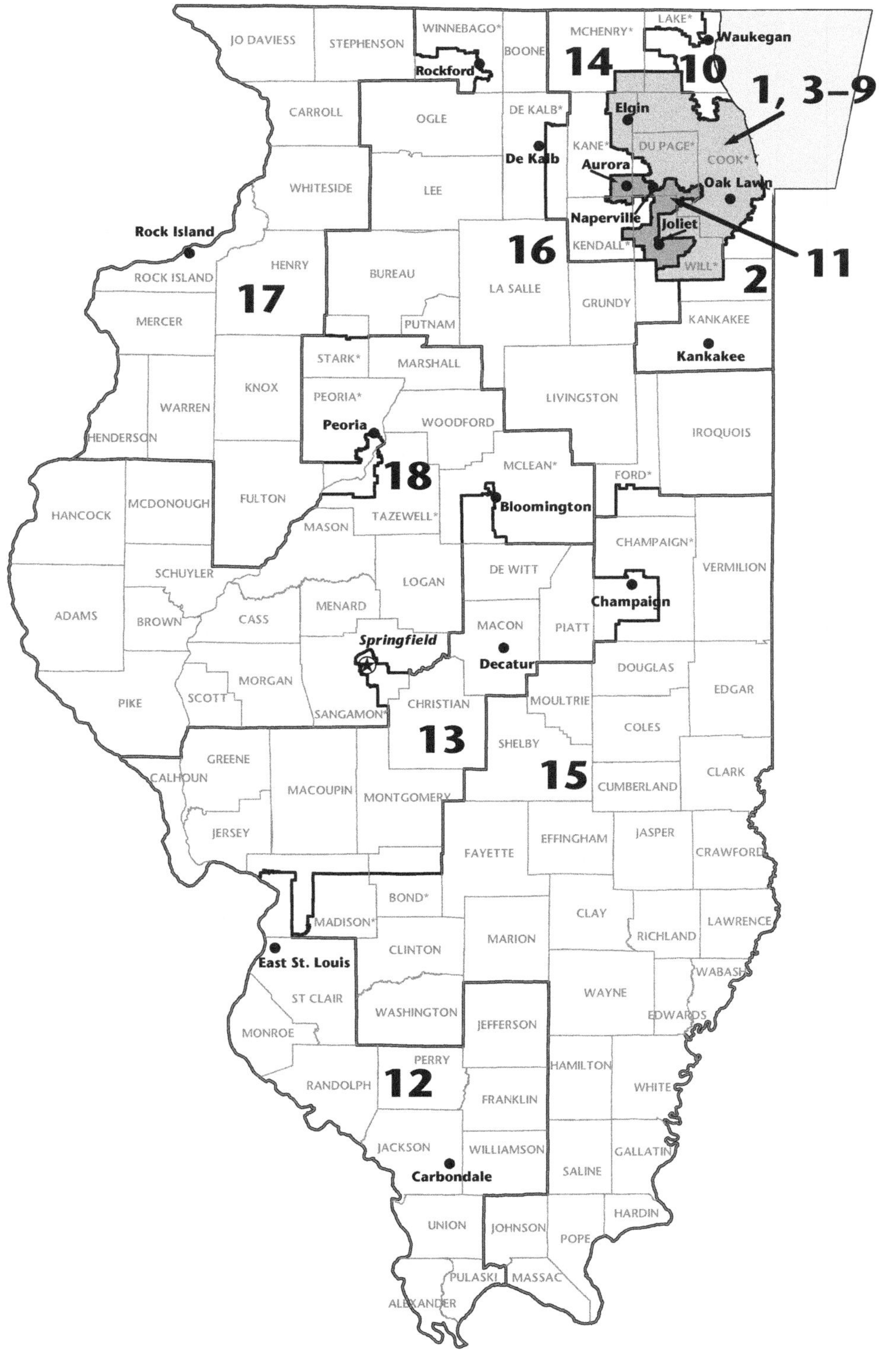

* Asterisk indicates a county whose boundaries include parts of two or more congressional districts.

ILLINOIS

Chicago Area

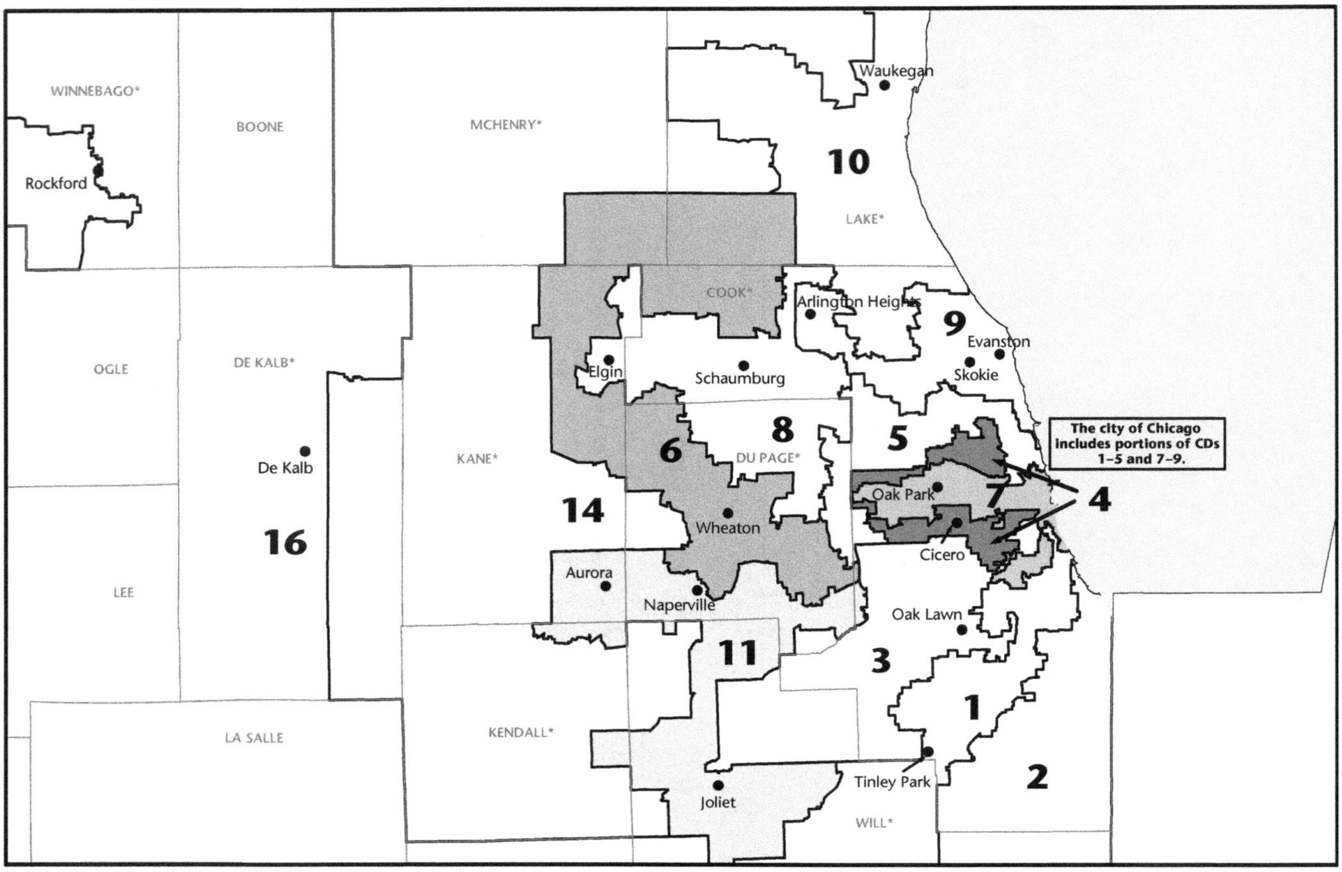

* Asterisk indicates a county whose boundaries include parts of two or more congressional districts.

ILLINOIS

GOVERNOR

Jay "J. B." Pritzker (D). Elected 2018 to a four-year term.

SENATORS (1 Republican, 1 Democrat)

Richard J. Durbin (D). Re-elected 2014 to a six-year term. Previously elected 2008, 2002, 1996.

Tammy Duckworth (D). Elected 2016 to a six-year term.

REPRESENTATIVES (5 Republicans, 13 Democrats)

1. Bobby L. Rush (D)
2. Robin L. Kelly (D)
3. Daniel William Lipinski (D)
4. Jesus "Chuy" Garcia (D)
5. Mike Quigley (D)
6. Sean Casten (D)
7. Danny K. Davis (D)
8. Raja Krishnamoorthi (D)
9. Janice D. "Jan" Schakowsky (D)
10. Brad Schneider (D)
11. Bill Foster (D)
12. Mike Bost (R)
13. Rodney L. Davis (R)
14. Lauren Underwood (D)
15. John M. Shimkus (R)
16. Adam Kinzinger (R)
17. Cheri Bustos (D)
18. Darin LaHood (R)

POSTWAR VOTE FOR PRESIDENT

		Republican		Democratic				Percentage			
								Total Vote		Major Vote	
Year	Total Vote	Vote	Candidate	Vote	Candidate	Other Vote	Rep.-Dem. Plurality	Rep.	Dem.	Rep.	Dem.
2016**	5,536,424	2,146,015	Trump, Donald J.	3,090,729	Clinton, Hillary Rodham	299,680	944,714 D	38.8%	55.8%	41.0%	59.0%
2012	5,242,014	2,135,216	Romney, W. Mitt	3,019,512	Obama, Barack H.*	87,286	884,296 D	40.7%	57.6%	41.4%	58.6%
2008	5,522,371	2,031,179	McCain, John S. III	3,419,348	Obama, Barack H.	71,844	1,388,169 D	36.8%	61.9%	37.3%	62.7%
2004	5,274,322	2,345,946	Bush, George W.*	2,891,550	Kerry, John F.	36,826	545,604 D	44.5%	54.8%	44.8%	55.2%
2000**	4,742,123	2,019,421	Bush, George W.	2,589,026	Gore, Albert Jr.	133,676	569,605 D	42.6%	54.6%	43.8%	56.2%
1996**	4,311,391	1,587,021	Dole, Robert "Bob"	2,341,744	Clinton, Bill*	382,626	754,723 D	36.8%	54.3%	40.4%	59.6%
1992**	5,050,157	1,734,096	Bush, George H.*	2,453,350	Clinton, Bill	862,711	719,254 D	34.3%	48.6%	41.4%	58.6%
1988	4,559,120	2,310,939	Bush, George H.	2,215,940	Dukakis, Michael S.	32,241	94,999 R	50.7%	48.6%	51.0%	49.0%
1984	4,819,088	2,707,103	Reagan, Ronald*	2,086,499	Mondale, Walter F.	25,486	620,604 R	56.2%	43.3%	56.5%	43.5%
1980**	4,749,721	2,358,049	Reagan, Ronald	1,981,413	Carter, Jimmy*	410,259	376,636 R	49.6%	41.7%	54.3%	45.7%
1976	4,718,914	2,364,269	Ford, Gerald R.*	2,271,295	Carter, Jimmy	83,350	92,974 R	50.1%	48.1%	51.0%	49.0%
1972	4,723,236	2,788,179	Nixon, Richard M.*	1,913,472	McGovern, George S.	21,585	874,707 R	59.0%	40.5%	59.3%	40.7%
1968**	4,619,749	2,174,774	Nixon, Richard M.	2,039,814	Humphrey, Hubert Horatio Jr.	405,161	134,960 R	47.1%	44.2%	51.6%	48.4%
1964	4,702,841	1,905,946	Goldwater, Barry M. Sr.	2,796,833	Johnson, Lyndon B.*	62	890,887 D	40.5%	59.5%	40.5%	59.5%
1960	4,757,409	2,368,988	Nixon, Richard M.	2,377,846	Kennedy, John F.	10,575	8,858 D	49.8%	50.0%	49.9%	50.1%
1956	4,407,407	2,623,327	Eisenhower, Dwight D.*	1,775,682	Stevenson, Adlai E. II	8,398	847,645 R	59.5%	40.3%	59.6%	40.4%
1952	4,481,058	2,457,327	Eisenhower, Dwight D.	2,013,920	Stevenson, Adlai E. II	9,811	443,407 R	54.8%	44.9%	55.0%	45.0%
1948	3,984,046	1,961,103	Dewey, Thomas E.	1,994,715	Truman, Harry S.*	28,228	33,612 D	49.2%	50.1%	49.6%	50.4%

Note: An asterisk (*) denotes incumbent. **In past elections, the other vote included: 2016 - 209,596 Libertarian (Gary Johnson); 2000 - 103,759 Green (Ralph Nader); 1996 - 346,408 Reform (Ross Perot); 1992 - 840,515 Independent (Perot); 1980 - 346,754 Independent (John Anderson); 1968 - 390,958 American Independent (George Wallace).

ILLINOIS

POSTWAR VOTE FOR GOVERNOR

		Republican		Democratic				Percentage			
								Total Vote		Major Vote	
Year	Total Vote	Vote	Candidate	Vote	Candidate	Other Vote	Rep.-Dem. Plurality	Rep.	Dem.	Rep.	Dem.
2018	4,547,657	1,765,751	Rauner, Bruce	2,479,746	Pritzker, Jay "J.B."	302,160	713,995 D	38.8%	54.5%	41.6%	58.4%
2014	3,627,690	1,823,627	Rauner, Bruce	1,681,343	Quinn, Pat*	122,720	142,284 R	50.3%	46.3%	52.0%	48.0%
2010	3,729,989	1,713,385	Brady, Bill	1,745,219	Quinn, Pat*	271,385	31,834 D	45.9%	46.8%	49.5%	50.5%
2006**	3,487,989	1,369,315	Topinka, Judy Baar	1,736,731	Blagojevich, Rod R.*	381,943	367,416 D	39.3%	49.8%	44.1%	55.9%
2002	3,538,891	1,594,960	Ryan, Jim	1,847,040	Blagojevich, Rod R.	96,891	252,080 D	45.1%	52.2%	46.3%	53.7%
1998	3,358,705	1,714,094	Ryan, George H.	1,594,191	Poshard, Glenn	50,420	119,903 R	51.0%	47.5%	51.8%	48.2%
1994	3,106,566	1,984,318	Edgar, Jim*	1,069,850	Netsch, Dawn C.	52,398	914,468 R	63.9%	34.4%	65.0%	35.0%
1990	3,257,410	1,653,126	Edgar, Jim	1,569,217	Hartigan, Neil F.	35,067	83,909 R	50.7%	48.2%	51.3%	48.7%
1986**	3,143,978	1,655,849	Thompson, James R.*	208,830	(See note)	1,279,299	1,447,019 R	52.7%	6.6%	88.8%	11.2%
1982	3,673,681	1,816,101	Thompson, James R.*	1,811,027	Stevenson, Adlai E. II	46,553	5,074 R	49.4%	49.3%	50.1%	49.9%
1978	3,150,095	1,859,684	Thompson, James R.*	1,263,134	Bakalis, Michael	27,277	596,550 R	59.0%	40.1%	59.6%	40.4%
1976**	4,635,728	3,000,395	Thompson, James R.	1,606,989	Howlett, Michael J.	28,344	1,393,406 R	64.7%	34.7%	65.1%	34.9%
1972	4,678,802	2,293,809	Ogilvie, Richard B.*	2,371,301	Walker, Daniel	13,692	77,492 D	49.0%	50.7%	49.2%	50.8%
1968	4,506,000	2,307,295	Ogilvie, Richard B.	2,179,501	Shapiro, Samuel H.	19,204	127,794 R	51.2%	48.4%	51.4%	48.6%
1964	4,657,500	2,239,095	Percy, Charles H.	2,418,394	Kerner, Otto*	11	179,299 D	48.1%	51.9%	48.1%	51.9%
1960	4,674,187	2,070,479	Stratton, William G.*	2,594,731	Kerner, Otto	8,977	524,252 D	44.3%	55.5%	44.4%	55.6%
1956	4,314,611	2,171,786	Stratton, William G.*	2,134,909	Austin, Richard B.	7,916	36,877 R	50.3%	49.5%	50.4%	49.6%
1952	4,415,864	2,317,363	Stratton, William G.	2,089,721	Dixon, Sherwood	8,780	227,642 R	52.5%	47.3%	52.6%	47.4%
1948	3,940,257	1,678,007	Green, Dwight H.*	2,250,074	Stevenson, Adlai E. II	12,176	572,067 D	42.6%	57.1%	42.7%	57.3%

Note: An asterisk (*) denotes incumbent. **In past elections, the other vote included: 2006 - 361,336 Green (Rich Whitney); 1986 - 1,256,626 Illinois Solidarity (Adlai E. Stevenson III). In 1986 there was no Democratic candidate for Governor on the ballot. Mark Fairchild, a supporter of Lyndon H. LaRouche Jr., was the "paired" Democratic candidate for Lt. Governor and the Democratic vote was cast for this ticket of "no name" and Fairchild. Running on the Illinois Solidarity line, Stevenson finished second with 40.0 percent of the vote. The 1976 vote was for a two-year term to permit shifting the election for Governor to non-presidential years.

POSTWAR VOTE FOR SENATOR

		Republican		Democratic				Percentage			
								Total Vote		Major Vote	
Year	Total Vote	Vote	Candidate	Vote	Candidate	Other Vote	Rep.-Dem. Plurality	Rep.	Dem.	Rep.	Dem.
2016	5,491,878	2,184,692	Kirk, Mark Steven*	3,012,940	Duckworth, Tammy	294,246	828,248 D	39.8%	54.9%	42.0%	58.0%
2014	3,603,519	1,538,522	Oberweis, James D.	1,929,637	Durbin, Richard J.*	135,360	391,115 D	42.7%	53.5%	44.4%	55.6%
2010	3,704,473	1,778,698	Kirk, Mark Steven	1,719,478	Giannoulias, Alexander	206,297	59,220 R	48.0%	46.4%	50.8%	49.2%
2010S	3,545,984	1,677,729	Kirk, Mark Steven	1,641,486	Giannoulias, Alexander	226,769	36,243 R	47.3%	46.3%	50.5%	49.5%
2008	5,329,884	1,520,621	Sauerberg, Steve	3,615,844	Durbin, Richard J.*	193,419	2,095,223 D	28.5%	67.8%	29.6%	70.4%
2004	5,141,520	1,390,690	Keyes, Alan	3,597,456	Obama, Barack H.	153,374	2,206,766 D	27.0%	70.0%	27.9%	72.1%
2002	3,486,851	1,325,703	Durkin, Jim	2,103,766	Durbin, Richard J.*	57,382	778,063 D	38.0%	60.3%	38.7%	61.3%
1998	3,395,033	1,709,041	Fitzgerald, Peter G.	1,610,496	Moseley-Braun, Carol*	75,496	98,545 R	50.3%	47.4%	51.5%	48.5%
1996	4,250,722	1,728,824	Salvi, Al	2,384,028	Durbin, Richard J.	137,870	655,204 D	40.7%	56.1%	42.0%	58.0%
1992	4,939,558	2,126,833	Williamson, Richard S.	2,631,229	Moseley-Braun, Carol	181,496	504,396 D	43.1%	53.3%	44.7%	55.3%
1990	3,251,005	1,135,628	Martin, Lynn	2,115,377	Simon, Paul*		979,749 D	34.9%	65.1%	34.9%	65.1%
1986	3,122,883	1,053,734	Koehler, Judy	2,033,783	Dixon, Alan J.*	35,366	980,049 D	33.7%	65.1%	34.1%	65.9%
1984	4,787,473	2,308,039	Percy, Charles H.*	2,397,303	Simon, Paul	82,131	89,264 D	48.2%	50.1%	49.1%	50.9%
1980	4,580,029	1,946,296	O'Neal, David C.	2,565,302	Dixon, Alan J.	68,431	619,006 D	42.5%	56.0%	43.1%	56.9%
1978	3,184,764	1,698,711	Percy, Charles H.*	1,448,187	Seith, Alex	37,866	250,524 R	53.3%	45.5%	54.0%	46.0%
1974	2,914,666	1,084,884	Burditt, George M.	1,811,496	Stevenson, Adlai E. II*	18,286	726,612 D	37.2%	62.2%	37.5%	62.5%
1972	4,608,380	2,867,078	Percy, Charles H.*	1,721,031	Pucinski, Roman C.	20,271	1,146,047 R	62.2%	37.3%	62.5%	37.5%
1970S**	3,599,272	1,519,718	Smith, Ralph T.*	2,065,054	Stevenson, Adlai E. II	14,500	545,336 D	42.2%	57.4%	42.4%	57.6%
1968	4,449,757	2,358,947	Dirksen, Everett McKinley*	2,073,242	Clark, William G.	17,568	285,705 R	53.0%	46.6%	53.2%	46.8%
1966	3,822,725	2,100,449	Percy, Charles H.	1,678,147	Douglas, Paul H.*	44,129	422,302 R	54.9%	43.9%	55.6%	44.4%
1962	3,709,216	1,961,202	Dirksen, Everett McKinley*	1,748,007	Yates, Sidney R.	7	213,195 R	52.9%	47.1%	52.9%	47.1%
1960	4,632,796	2,093,846	Witwer, Samuel W.	2,530,943	Douglas, Paul H.*	8,007	437,097 D	45.2%	54.6%	45.3%	54.7%
1956	4,264,830	2,307,352	Dirksen, Everett McKinley*	1,949,883	Stengel, Richard	7,595	357,469 R	54.1%	45.7%	54.2%	45.8%
1954	3,368,025	1,563,683	Meek, Joseph T.	1,804,338	Douglas, Paul H.*	4	240,655 D	46.4%	53.6%	46.4%	53.6%
1950	3,622,673	1,951,984	Dirksen, Everett McKinley	1,657,630	Lucas, Scott W.*	13,059	294,354 R	53.9%	45.8%	54.1%	45.9%
1948	3,900,285	1,740,026	Brooks, C. Wayland*	2,147,754	Douglas, Paul H.	12,505	407,728 D	44.6%	55.1%	44.8%	55.2%

Note: An asterisk (*) denotes incumbent. **The 1970 election and one of the 2010 elections were for a short term to fill a vacancy.

ILLINOIS

GOVERNOR 2018

2010 Census Population	County	Total Vote	Republican (Rauner)	Democratic (Pritzker)	Other	Rep.-Dem. Plurality	Percentage Total Vote Rep.	Total Vote Dem.	Major Vote Rep.	Major Vote Dem.
67,103	ADAMS	24,358	15,898	6,176	2,284	9,722 R	65.3%	25.4%	72.0%	28.0%
8,238	ALEXANDER	2,174	878	1,154	142	276 D	40.4%	53.1%	43.2%	56.8%
17,768	BOND	6,561	3,388	2,370	803	1,018 R	51.6%	36.1%	58.8%	41.2%
54,165	BOONE	17,861	8,792	6,970	2,099	1,822 R	49.2%	39.0%	55.8%	44.2%
6,937	BROWN	1,882	972	402	508	570 R	51.6%	21.4%	70.7%	29.3%
34,978	BUREAU	13,468	6,902	5,290	1,276	1,612 R	51.2%	39.3%	56.6%	43.4%
5,089	CALHOUN	2,282	898	795	589	103 R	39.4%	34.8%	53.0%	47.0%
15,387	CARROLL	5,945	3,658	1,804	483	1,854 R	61.5%	30.3%	67.0%	33.0%
13,642	CASS	4,509	2,191	1,483	835	708 R	48.6%	32.9%	59.6%	40.4%
201,081	CHAMPAIGN	78,394	29,690	43,257	5,447	13,567 D	37.9%	55.2%	40.7%	59.3%
34,800	CHRISTIAN	12,717	6,701	3,702	2,314	2,999 R	52.7%	29.1%	64.4%	35.6%
16,335	CLARK	6,084	3,742	1,823	519	1,919 R	61.5%	30.0%	67.2%	32.8%
13,815	CLAY	4,791	3,314	1,104	373	2,210 R	69.2%	23.0%	75.0%	25.0%
37,762	CLINTON	14,079	9,112	3,874	1,093	5,238 R	64.7%	27.5%	70.2%	29.8%
53,873	COLES	17,000	9,159	5,964	1,877	3,195 R	53.9%	35.1%	60.6%	39.4%
5,194,675	COOK	1,756,583	426,196	1,262,334	68,053	836,138 D	24.3%	71.9%	25.2%	74.8%
19,817	CRAWFORD	6,853	3,996	2,105	752	1,891 R	58.3%	30.7%	65.5%	34.5%
11,048	CUMBERLAND	4,321	2,809	969	543	1,840 R	65.0%	22.4%	74.4%	25.6%
16,561	DE WITT	6,161	3,981	1,539	641	2,442 R	64.6%	25.0%	72.1%	27.9%
105,160	DEKALB	36,206	16,181	17,016	3,009	835 D	44.7%	47.0%	48.7%	51.3%
19,980	DOUGLAS	6,361	4,223	1,416	722	2,807 R	66.4%	22.3%	74.9%	25.1%
916,924	DU PAGE	365,034	168,347	176,556	20,131	8,209 D	46.1%	48.4%	48.8%	51.2%
18,576	EDGAR	6,087	3,820	1,637	630	2,183 R	62.8%	26.9%	70.0%	30.0%
6,721	EDWARDS	2,387	1,745	453	189	1,292 R	73.1%	19.0%	79.4%	20.6%
34,242	EFFINGHAM	14,238	9,767	2,840	1,631	6,927 R	68.6%	19.9%	77.5%	22.5%
22,140	FAYETTE	7,815	4,407	1,951	1,457	2,456 R	56.4%	25.0%	69.3%	30.7%
14,081	FORD	4,979	3,495	971	513	2,524 R	70.2%	19.5%	78.3%	21.7%
39,561	FRANKLIN	15,234	7,922	5,227	2,085	2,695 R	52.0%	34.3%	60.2%	39.8%
37,069	FULTON	12,551	5,070	5,650	1,831	580 D	40.4%	45.0%	47.3%	52.7%
5,589	GALLATIN	2,065	1,046	779	240	267 R	50.7%	37.7%	57.3%	42.7%
13,886	GREENE	4,366	1,844	1,026	1,496	818 R	42.2%	23.5%	64.3%	35.7%
50,063	GRUNDY	19,308	10,184	7,319	1,805	2,865 R	52.7%	37.9%	58.2%	41.8%
8,457	HAMILTON	3,431	2,076	881	474	1,195 R	60.5%	25.7%	70.2%	29.8%
19,104	HANCOCK	6,930	4,255	1,950	725	2,305 R	61.4%	28.1%	68.6%	31.4%
4,320	HARDIN	1,622	835	558	229	277 R	51.5%	34.4%	59.9%	40.1%
7,331	HENDERSON	2,652	1,488	940	224	548 R	56.1%	35.4%	61.3%	38.7%
50,486	HENRY	19,323	10,794	6,997	1,532	3,797 R	55.9%	36.2%	60.7%	39.3%
29,718	IROQUOIS	10,228	7,419	1,858	951	5,561 R	72.5%	18.2%	80.0%	20.0%
60,218	JACKSON	20,220	7,921	10,597	1,702	2,676 D	39.2%	52.4%	42.8%	57.2%
9,698	JASPER	4,392	2,828	1,170	394	1,658 R	64.4%	26.6%	70.7%	29.3%
38,827	JEFFERSON	13,767	7,848	4,408	1,511	3,440 R	57.0%	32.0%	64.0%	36.0%
22,985	JERSEY	8,607	4,200	2,569	1,838	1,631 R	48.8%	29.8%	62.0%	38.0%
22,678	JO DAVIESS	9,113	4,900	3,602	611	1,298 R	53.8%	39.5%	57.6%	42.4%
12,582	JOHNSON	5,187	3,013	1,427	747	1,586 R	58.1%	27.5%	67.9%	32.1%
515,269	KANE	169,709	77,289	81,310	11,110	4,021 D	45.5%	47.9%	48.7%	51.3%
113,449	KANKAKEE	36,667	19,249	14,595	2,823	4,654 R	52.5%	39.8%	56.9%	43.1%
114,736	KENDALL	44,801	20,442	20,990	3,369	548 D	45.6%	46.9%	49.3%	50.7%
52,919	KNOX	17,700	7,831	8,292	1,577	461 D	44.2%	46.8%	48.6%	51.4%
113,924	LA SALLE	39,601	19,034	17,397	3,170	1,637 R	48.1%	43.9%	52.2%	47.8%
703,462	LAKE	250,739	109,287	128,603	12,849	19,316 D	43.6%	51.3%	45.9%	54.1%
16,833	LAWRENCE	4,268	2,589	1,380	299	1,209 R	60.7%	32.3%	65.2%	34.8%
36,031	LEE	12,524	6,056	4,995	1,473	1,061 R	48.4%	39.9%	54.8%	45.2%
38,950	LIVINGSTON	12,004	7,431	3,345	1,228	4,086 R	61.9%	27.9%	69.0%	31.0%
30,305	LOGAN	10,008	5,840	2,546	1,622	3,294 R	58.4%	25.4%	69.6%	30.4%
110,768	MACON	38,923	20,316	14,961	3,646	5,355 R	52.2%	38.4%	57.6%	42.4%
47,765	MACOUPIN	18,118	7,872	6,469	3,777	1,403 R	43.4%	35.7%	54.9%	45.1%
269,282	MADISON	103,315	48,138	46,374	8,803	1,764 R	46.6%	44.9%	50.9%	49.1%
39,437	MARION	12,603	7,358	4,194	1,051	3,164 R	58.4%	33.3%	63.7%	36.3%
12,640	MARSHALL	4,667	2,763	1,428	476	1,335 R	59.2%	30.6%	65.9%	34.1%
14,666	MASON	5,194	2,599	1,790	805	809 R	50.0%	34.5%	59.2%	40.8%

ILLINOIS

GOVERNOR 2018

2010 Census Population	County	Total Vote	Republican (Rauner)	Democratic (Pritzker)	Other	Rep.-Dem. Plurality	Percentage Total Vote Rep.	Total Vote Dem.	Major Vote Rep.	Major Vote Dem.
15,429	MASSAC	5,352	3,363	1,527	462	1,836 R	62.8%	28.5%	68.8%	31.2%
32,612	MCDONOUGH	10,156	4,798	4,196	1,162	602 R	47.2%	41.3%	53.3%	46.7%
308,760	MCHENRY	116,214	60,646	48,633	6,935	12,013 R	52.2%	41.8%	55.5%	44.5%
169,572	MCLEAN	67,276	32,501	29,364	5,411	3,137 R	48.3%	43.6%	52.5%	47.5%
12,705	MENARD	5,379	3,049	1,619	711	1,430 R	56.7%	30.1%	65.3%	34.7%
16,434	MERCER	6,904	3,658	2,546	700	1,112 R	53.0%	36.9%	59.0%	41.0%
32,957	MONROE	15,570	9,348	5,291	931	4,057 R	60.0%	34.0%	63.9%	36.1%
30,104	MONTGOMERY	11,458	4,669	3,940	2,849	729 R	40.7%	34.4%	54.2%	45.8%
35,547	MORGAN	11,698	5,382	3,207	3,109	2,175 R	46.0%	27.4%	62.7%	37.3%
14,846	MOULTRIE	5,090	3,271	1,181	638	2,090 R	64.3%	23.2%	73.5%	26.5%
53,497	OGLE	19,010	10,198	6,384	2,428	3,814 R	53.6%	33.6%	61.5%	38.5%
186,494	PEORIA	64,748	28,254	31,238	5,256	2,984 D	43.6%	48.2%	47.5%	52.5%
22,350	PERRY	8,474	4,309	3,077	1,088	1,232 R	50.8%	36.3%	58.3%	41.7%
16,729	PIATT	7,590	4,698	2,180	712	2,518 R	61.9%	28.7%	68.3%	31.7%
16,430	PIKE	6,547	2,633	1,232	2,682	1,401 R	40.2%	18.8%	68.1%	31.9%
4,470	POPE	1,721	1,091	433	197	658 R	63.4%	25.2%	71.6%	28.4%
6,161	PULASKI	2,355	1,094	1,005	256	89 R	46.5%	42.7%	52.1%	47.9%
6,006	PUTNAM	2,538	1,217	1,088	233	129 R	48.0%	42.9%	52.8%	47.2%
33,476	RANDOLPH	12,165	5,939	4,955	1,271	984 R	48.8%	40.7%	54.5%	45.5%
16,233	RICHLAND	6,036	3,692	1,800	544	1,892 R	61.2%	29.8%	67.2%	32.8%
147,546	ROCK ISLAND	50,699	21,434	25,774	3,491	4,340 D	42.3%	50.8%	45.4%	54.6%
24,913	SALINE	9,336	4,608	3,332	1,396	1,276 R	49.4%	35.7%	58.0%	42.0%
197,465	SANGAMON	85,663	39,099	36,538	10,026	2,561 R	45.6%	42.7%	51.7%	48.3%
7,544	SCHUYLER	3,077	1,525	973	579	552 R	49.6%	31.6%	61.0%	39.0%
5,355	SCOTT	2,065	882	388	795	494 R	42.7%	18.8%	69.4%	30.6%
22,363	SHELBY	9,146	5,694	1,975	1,477	3,719 R	62.3%	21.6%	74.2%	25.8%
270,056	ST. CLAIR	98,431	40,524	52,603	5,304	12,079 D	41.2%	53.4%	43.5%	56.5%
5,994	STARK	2,035	1,219	586	230	633 R	59.9%	28.8%	67.5%	32.5%
47,711	STEPHENSON	16,194	8,560	5,760	1,874	2,800 R	52.9%	35.6%	59.8%	40.2%
135,394	TAZEWELL	51,432	27,986	17,859	5,587	10,127 R	54.4%	34.7%	61.0%	39.0%
17,808	UNION	7,498	3,794	2,875	829	919 R	50.6%	38.3%	56.9%	43.1%
81,625	VERMILION	22,977	12,402	7,573	3,002	4,829 R	54.0%	33.0%	62.1%	37.9%
11,947	WABASH	3,940	2,528	1,093	319	1,435 R	64.2%	27.7%	69.8%	30.2%
17,707	WARREN	6,069	3,261	2,268	540	993 R	53.7%	37.4%	59.0%	41.0%
14,716	WASHINGTON	6,065	4,031	1,536	498	2,495 R	66.5%	25.3%	72.4%	27.6%
16,760	WAYNE	5,926	4,340	1,015	571	3,325 R	73.2%	17.1%	81.0%	19.0%
14,665	WHITE	5,817	3,891	1,480	446	2,411 R	66.9%	25.4%	72.4%	27.6%
58,498	WHITESIDE	21,362	10,221	9,371	1,770	850 R	47.8%	43.9%	52.2%	47.8%
677,560	WILL	246,670	107,859	123,292	15,519	15,433 D	43.7%	50.0%	46.7%	53.3%
66,357	WILLIAMSON	26,890	14,471	9,440	2,979	5,031 R	53.8%	35.1%	60.5%	39.5%
295,266	WINNEBAGO	95,017	41,156	43,440	10,421	2,284 D	43.3%	45.7%	48.7%	51.3%
38,664	WOODFORD	16,100	10,457	4,097	1,546	6,360 R	65.0%	25.4%	71.8%	28.2%
12,830,632	*TOTAL*	*4,547,657*	*1,765,751*	*2,479,746*	*302,160*	*713,995 D*	*38.8%*	*54.5%*	*41.6%*	*58.4%*

ILLINOIS

HOUSE OF REPRESENTATIVES

			Republican		Democratic				Percentage			
									Total Vote		Major Vote	
CD	Year	Total Vote	Vote	Candidate	Vote	Candidate	Other Vote	Rep.-Dem. Plurality	Rep.	Dem.	Rep.	Dem.
1	2018	257,885	50,960	TILLMAN, JIMMY LEE II	189,560	RUSH, BOBBY L.*	17,365	138,600 D	19.8%	73.5%	21.2%	78.8%
1	2016	315,862	81,817	DEUSER, AUGUST (O'NEILL)	234,037	RUSH, BOBBY L.*	8	152,220 D	25.9%	74.1%	25.9%	74.1%
1	2014	222,017	59,749	TILLMAN, JIMMY LEE II	162,268	RUSH, BOBBY L.*		102,519 D	26.9%	73.1%	26.9%	73.1%
1	2012	320,844	83,989	PELOQUIN, DONALD E.	236,854	RUSH, BOBBY L.*	1	152,865 D	26.2%	73.8%	26.2%	73.8%
2	2018	235,251	44,567	MERKLE, DAVID	190,684	KELLY, ROBIN L.*		146,117 D	18.9%	81.1%	18.9%	81.1%
2	2016	294,522	59,471	MORROW, JOHN F.	235,051	KELLY, ROBIN L.*		175,580 D	20.2%	79.8%	20.2%	79.8%
2	2014	204,266	43,799	WALLACE, ERIC M.	160,337	KELLY, ROBIN L.*	130	116,538 D	21.4%	78.5%	21.5%	78.5%
2	2012	297,712	69,115	WOODWORTH, BRIAN	188,303	JACKSON, JESSE L. JR.*	40,294	119,188 D	23.2%	63.3%	26.8%	73.2%
3	2018	223,334	57,885	JONES, ARTHUR J.	163,053	LIPINSKI, DANIEL WILLIAM*	2,396	105,168 D	25.9%	73.0%	26.2%	73.8%
3	2016	225,411			225,320	LIPINSKI, DANIEL WILLIAM*	91	225,320 D		100.0%		100.0%
3	2014	180,855	64,091	BRANNIGAN, SHARON M.	116,764	LIPINSKI, DANIEL WILLIAM*		52,673 D	35.4%	64.6%	35.4%	64.6%
3	2012	246,398	77,653	GRABOWSKI, RICHARD	168,738	LIPINSKI, DANIEL WILLIAM*	7	91,085 D	31.5%	68.5%	31.5%	68.5%
4	2018	166,189	22,294	LORCH, MARK WAYNE	143,895	GARCIA, JESUS "CHUY"		121,601 D	13.4%	86.6%	13.4%	86.6%
4	2016	171,297			171,297	GUTIERREZ, LUIS V.*		171,297 D		100.0%		100.0%
4	2014	101,944	22,278	CONCEPCION, HECTOR	79,666	GUTIERREZ, LUIS V.*		57,388 D	21.9%	78.1%	21.9%	78.1%
4	2012	160,509	27,279	CONCEPCION, HECTOR	133,226	GUTIERREZ, LUIS V.*	4	105,947 D	17.0%	83.0%	17.0%	83.0%
5	2018	279,131	65,134	HANSON, TOM	213,992	QUIGLEY, MIKE*	5	148,858 D	23.3%	76.7%	23.3%	76.7%
5	2016	313,724	86,222	KOLBER, VINCENT A. "VINCE"	212,842	QUIGLEY, MIKE*	14,660	126,620 D	27.5%	67.8%	28.8%	71.2%
5	2014	184,019	56,350	KOLBER, VINCENT A. "VINCE"	116,364	QUIGLEY, MIKE*	11,305	60,014 D	30.6%	63.2%	32.6%	67.4%
5	2012	270,377	77,289	SCHMITT, DAN	177,729	QUIGLEY, MIKE*	15,359	100,440 D	28.6%	65.7%	30.3%	69.7%
6	2018	315,446	146,445	ROSKAM, PETER J.*	169,001	CASTEN, SEAN		22,556 D	46.4%	53.6%	46.4%	53.6%
6	2016	352,146	208,555	ROSKAM, PETER J.*	143,591	HOWLAND, AMANDA		64,964 R	59.2%	40.8%	59.2%	40.8%
6	2014	238,752	160,287	ROSKAM, PETER J.*	78,465	MASON, MICHAEL		81,822 R	67.1%	32.9%	67.1%	32.9%
6	2012	326,129	193,138	ROSKAM, PETER J.*	132,991	COOLIDGE, LESLIE		60,147 R	59.2%	40.8%	59.2%	40.8%
7	2018	246,243	30,497	CAMERON, CRAIG	215,746	DAVIS, DANNY K.*		185,249 D	12.4%	87.6%	12.4%	87.6%
7	2016	297,466	46,882	LEEF, JEFFREY A	250,584	DAVIS, DANNY K.*		203,702 D	15.8%	84.2%	15.8%	84.2%
7	2014	182,278	27,168	BUMPERS, ROBERT L.	155,110	DAVIS, DANNY K.*		127,942 D	14.9%	85.1%	14.9%	85.1%
7	2012	286,435	31,466	ZAK, RITA	242,439	DAVIS, DANNY K.*	12,530	210,973 D	11.0%	84.6%	11.5%	88.5%
8	2018	197,127	67,073	DIGANVKER, JITENDRA "JD"	130,054	KRISHNAMOORTHI, RAJA*		62,981 D	34.0%	66.0%	34.0%	66.0%
8	2016	248,571	103,617	DICIANNI, PETER "PETE"	144,954	KRISHNAMOORTHI, RAJA		41,337 D	41.7%	58.3%	41.7%	58.3%
8	2014	151,056	66,878	KAIFESH, LAWRENCE JOSEPH "LARRY"	84,178	DUCKWORTH, TAMMY*		17,300 D	44.3%	55.7%	44.3%	55.7%
8	2012	225,066	101,860	WALSH, JOE*	123,206	DUCKWORTH, TAMMY		21,346 D	45.3%	54.7%	45.3%	54.7%
9	2018	290,351	76,983	ELLESON, JOHN D.	213,368	SCHAKOWSKY, JANICE D. "JAN"*		136,385 D	26.5%	73.5%	26.5%	73.5%
9	2016	326,948	109,550	LASONDE, JOAN MCCARTHY	217,306	SCHAKOWSKY, JANICE D. "JAN"*	92	107,756 D	33.5%	66.5%	33.5%	66.5%
9	2014	213,450	72,384	ATANUS, SUSANNE	141,000	SCHAKOWSKY, JANICE D. "JAN"*	66	68,616 D	33.9%	66.1%	33.9%	66.1%
9	2012	293,807	98,924	WOLFE, TIMOTHY	194,869	SCHAKOWSKY, JANICE D. "JAN"*	14	95,945 D	33.7%	66.3%	33.7%	66.3%
10	2018	238,664	82,124	BENNETT, DOUGLAS R.	156,540	SCHNEIDER, BRAD*		74,416 D	34.4%	65.6%	34.4%	65.6%
10	2016	285,996	135,535	DOLD, ROBERT*	150,435	SCHNEIDER, BRAD	26	14,900 D	47.4%	52.6%	47.4%	52.6%
10	2014	187,128	95,992	DOLD, ROBERT	91,136	SCHNEIDER, BRAD*		4,856 R	51.3%	48.7%	51.3%	48.7%
10	2012	264,454	130,564	DOLD, ROBERT*	133,890	SCHNEIDER, BRAD		3,326 D	49.4%	50.6%	49.4%	50.6%
11	2018	227,765	82,358	STELLA, DOMINICK J. "NICK"	145,407	FOSTER, BILL*		63,049 D	36.2%	63.8%	36.2%	63.8%
11	2016	275,573	108,995	KHOURI, TONIA	166,578	FOSTER, BILL*		57,583 D	39.6%	60.4%	39.6%	60.4%
11	2014	174,772	81,335	SENGER, DARLENE	93,436	FOSTER, BILL*	1	12,101 D	46.5%	53.5%	46.5%	53.5%
11	2012	254,295	105,348	BIGGERT, JUDY*	148,928	FOSTER, BILL	19	43,580 D	41.4%	58.6%	41.4%	58.6%
12	2018	261,543	134,884	BOST, MIKE*	118,724	KELLY, BRENDAN	7,935	16,160 R	51.6%	45.4%	53.2%	46.8%
12	2016	313,002	169,976	BOST, MIKE*	124,246	BARICEVIC, CHARLES "C.J."	18,780	45,730 R	54.3%	39.7%	57.8%	42.2%
12	2014	209,738	110,038	BOST, MIKE	87,860	ENYART, WILLIAM*	11,840	22,178 R	52.5%	41.9%	55.6%	44.4%
12	2012	303,949	129,902	PLUMMER, JASON	157,000	ENYART, WILLIAM	17,047	27,098 D	42.7%	51.7%	45.3%	54.7%
13	2018	270,981	136,516	DAVIS, RODNEY L.*	134,458	DIRKSEN LONDRIGAN, BETSY	7	2,058 R	50.4%	49.6%	50.4%	49.6%
13	2016	314,394	187,583	DAVIS, RODNEY L.*	126,811	WICKLUND, MARK D.		60,772 R	59.7%	40.3%	59.7%	40.3%
13	2014	210,272	123,337	DAVIS, RODNEY L.*	86,935	CALLIS, ANN E.		36,402 R	58.7%	41.3%	58.7%	41.3%
13	2012	294,385	137,034	DAVIS, RODNEY L.	136,032	GILL, DAVID M.	21,319	1,002 R	46.5%	46.2%	50.2%	49.8%
14	2018	297,199	141,164	HULTGREN, RANDY M.*	156,035	UNDERWOOD, LAUREN		14,871 D	47.5%	52.5%	47.5%	52.5%
14	2016	338,097	200,508	HULTGREN, RANDY M.*	137,589	WALZ, JIM		62,919 R	59.3%	40.7%	59.3%	40.7%
14	2014	222,230	145,369	HULTGREN, RANDY M.*	76,861	ANDERSON, DENNIS		68,508 R	65.4%	34.6%	65.4%	34.6%
14	2012	301,954	177,603	HULTGREN, RANDY M.*	124,351	ANDERSON, DENNIS		53,252 R	58.8%	41.2%	58.8%	41.2%

ILLINOIS

HOUSE OF REPRESENTATIVES

			Republican		Democratic				Percentage			
									Total Vote		Major Vote	
CD	Year	Total Vote	Vote	Candidate	Vote	Candidate	Other Vote	Rep.-Dem. Plurality	Rep.	Dem.	Rep.	Dem.
15	2018	255,608	181,294	SHIMKUS, JOHN M.*	74,309	GAITHER, KEVIN	5	106,985 R	70.9%	29.1%	70.9%	29.1%
15	2016	274,554	274,554	SHIMKUS, JOHN M.*				274,554 R	100.0%		100.0%	
15	2014	221,926	166,274	SHIMKUS, JOHN M.*	55,652	THORSLAND, ERIC		110,622 R	74.9%	25.1%	74.9%	25.1%
15	2012	299,937	205,775	SHIMKUS, JOHN M.*	94,162	MICHAEL, ANGELA		111,613 R	68.6%	31.4%	68.6%	31.4%
16	2018	255,825	151,254	KINZINGER, ADAM*	104,569	DADY, SARA	2	46,685 R	59.1%	40.9%	59.1%	40.9%
16	2016	259,853	259,722	KINZINGER, ADAM*			131	259,722 R	99.9%		100.0%	
16	2014	217,198	153,388	KINZINGER, ADAM*	63,810	OLSEN, RANDALL WAYNE		89,578 R	70.6%	29.4%	70.6%	29.4%
16	2012	294,090	181,789	KINZINGER, ADAM*	112,301	ROHL, WANDA		69,488 R	61.8%	38.2%	61.8%	38.2%
17	2018	229,749	87,090	FAWELL, BILL	142,659	BUSTOS, CHERI*		55,569 D	37.9%	62.1%	37.9%	62.1%
17	2016	287,068	113,943	HARLAN, PATRICK	173,125	BUSTOS, CHERI*		59,182 D	39.7%	60.3%	39.7%	60.3%
17	2014	199,361	88,785	SCHILLING, BOBBY	110,560	BUSTOS, CHERI*	16	21,775 D	44.5%	55.5%	44.5%	55.5%
17	2012	288,161	134,623	SCHILLING, BOBBY*	153,519	BUSTOS, CHERI	19	18,896 D	46.7%	53.3%	46.7%	53.3%
18	2018	291,413	195,927	LAHOOD, DARIN*	95,486	RODRIGUEZ, JUNIUS		100,441 R	67.2%	32.8%	67.2%	32.8%
18	2016	347,283	250,506	LAHOOD, DARIN*	96,770	RODRIGUEZ, JUNIUS	7	153,736 R	72.1%	27.9%	72.1%	27.9%
18	2014	246,740	184,363	SCHOCK, AARON*	62,377	MILLER, DARREL ERVIN		121,986 R	74.7%	25.3%	74.7%	25.3%
18	2012	329,631	244,467	SCHOCK, AARON*	85,164	WATERWORTH, STEVE		159,303 R	74.2%	25.8%	74.2%	25.8%
TOTAL	*2018*	*4,539,704*	*1,754,449*		*2,757,540*		*27,715*	*1,003,091 D*	*38.6%*	*60.7%*	*38.9%*	*61.1%*
TOTAL	*2016*	*5,241,767*	*2,397,436*		*2,810,536*		*33,795*	*413,100 D*	*45.7%*	*53.6%*	*46.0%*	*54.0%*
TOTAL	*2014*	*3,568,002*	*1,721,865*		*1,822,779*		*23,358*	*100,914 D*	*48.3%*	*51.1%*	*48.6%*	*51.4%*
TOTAL	*2012*	*5,058,133*	*2,207,818*		*2,743,702*		*106,613*	*535,884 D*	*43.6%*	*54.2%*	*44.6%*	*55.4%*

Note: An asterisk (*) denotes incumbent.

ILLINOIS

GENERAL AND PRIMARY ELECTIONS

2018 GENERAL ELECTIONS: OTHER VOTES

Governor Other vote was 192,527 Conservative (William McCann), 109,518 Libertarian (Grayson Jackson), 32 Write-in (Nancy Foster), 20 Write-in (Kevin Ryan), 16 Write-in (JO 753), 15 Write-in (Michael Scruggs), 13 Write-in (Greg Moore), 12 Write-in (Robert Canfield), 4 Write-in (Thomas Kuna), 3 Write-in (David Tholin)

House Other vote was:

CD 1 17,365 Independent (Thomas Rudbeck)
CD 3 1,353 Write-in (Justin Hanson), 1,039 Write-in (Kenneth Yerkes), 4 Write-in (Richard Mayers)
CD 5 5 Write-in (Frank Rowder)
CD 12 7,935 Green (Randy Auxier)
CD 13 7 Write-in (Thomas Kuna)
CD 15 5 Write-in (Tim Buckner)
CD 16 2 Write-in (John Stassi)

2018 PRIMARY ELECTIONS: SUPPLEMENTARY INFORMATION

Primary March 20, 2018 **Registration** (as of March 20, 2018) 7,945,074 No Party Registration

Primary Type Open—Any registered voter could participate in the primary of either party.

ILLINOIS

GENERAL AND PRIMARY ELECTIONS

	REPUBLICAN PRIMARIES			DEMOCRATIC PRIMARIES		
Governor	Rauner, Bruce*	372,124	51.5%	Pritzker, Jay "J.B."	597,756	45.1%
	Ives, Jeanne	350,038	48.5%	Biss, Daniel	353,625	26.7%
				Kennedy, Chris	322,730	24.4%
				Hardiman, Tio	21,075	1.6%
				Daiber, Bob	15,009	1.1%
				Marshall, Robert	14,353	1.1%
	TOTAL	*722,162*		*TOTAL*	*1,324,548*	
Congressional District 1	Tillman, Jimmy Lee II	15,389	100.0%	Rush, Bobby L.*	104,114	100.0%
	TOTAL	*15,389*		*TOTAL*	*104,114*	
Congressional District 2	Merkle, David	4,963	36.6%	Kelly, Robin L.*	80,659	82.1%
	Harmon, Patrick	4,810	35.5%	Lewis, Marcus	17,640	17.9%
	Morrow, John F.	3,790	27.9%			
	TOTAL	*13,563*		*TOTAL*	*98,299*	
Congressional District 3	Jones, Arthur J.	20,681	100.0%	Lipinski, Daniel William*	48,675	51.1%
				Newman, Marie	46,530	48.9%
	TOTAL	*20,681*		*TOTAL*	*95,205*	
Congressional District 4	Lorch, Mark Wayne	5,805	100.0%	Garcia, Jesus "Chuy"	49,631	66.2%
				Flores, Sol A.	16,398	21.9%
				Gonzalez, Richard	8,921	11.9%
	TOTAL	*5,805*		*TOTAL*	*74,950*	
Congressional District 5	Hanson, Tom	18,837	100.0%	Quigley, Mike*	66,254	62.5%
				Mustafa, Sameena	25,591	24.1%
				Wolf, Benjamin Thomas	10,032	9.5%
				Schwartzberg, Steven J.	4,196	4.0%
	TOTAL	*18,837*		*TOTAL*	*106,073*	
Congressional District 6	Roskam, Peter J.*	56,544	100.0%	Casten, Sean	19,774	29.5%
				Mazeski, Kelly	17,984	26.8%
				Cheney, Carole	11,663	17.4%
				Howland, Amanda	8,483	12.7%
				Anderson Wilkins, Becky	4,001	6.0%
				Zordani, Jennifer	2,743	4.1%
				Huffman, Ryan	2,365	3.5%
	TOTAL	*56,544*		*TOTAL*	*67,013*	
Congressional District 7	Cameron, Craig	3,706	56.3%	Davis, Danny K.*	81,570	73.9%
	Leef, Jeffrey A	2,873	43.7%	Clark, Anthony V.	28,867	26.1%
	TOTAL	*6,579*		*TOTAL*	*110,437*	
Congressional District 8	Diganvker, Jitendra "JD"	25,448	100.0%	Krishnamoorthi, Raja*	44,042	100.0%
	TOTAL	*25,448*		*TOTAL*	*44,042*	
Congressional District 9	Elleson, John D.	10,476	40.4%	Schakowsky, Janice D. "Jan"*	108,417	100.0%
	Sangari, Sargis	7,954	30.7%			
	Thomas, D. Vincent Jr.	4,886	18.8%			
	Rice, Maxwell	2,634	10.2%			
	TOTAL	*25,950*		*TOTAL*	*108,417*	
Congressional District 10	Bennett, Douglas R.	11,026	36.2%	Schneider, Brad*	58,195	100.0%
	Wynes, Jeremy	10,556	34.7%			
	Shah, Sapan	8,841	29.1%			
	Rutagwibira, Aloys (Write-in)	10				
	TOTAL	*30,433*		*TOTAL*	*58,195*	
Congressional District 11	Stella, Dominick J. "Nick"	23,992	79.3%	Foster, Bill*	49,762	100.0%
	Vlakancic, Constant G. "Connor"	6,253	20.7%			
	TOTAL	*30,245*		*TOTAL*	*49,762*	

ILLINOIS

GENERAL AND PRIMARY ELECTIONS

	REPUBLICAN PRIMARIES			DEMOCRATIC PRIMARIES		
Congressional District 12	Bost, Mike*	31,658	83.5%	Kelly, Brendan	40,555	81.0%
	Nelson, Preston	6,258	16.5%	Bequette, David	9,526	19.0%
	TOTAL	*37,916*		*TOTAL*	*50,081*	
Congressional District 13	Davis, Rodney L.*	44,512	100.0%	Dirksen Londrigan, Betsy	24,515	45.7%
				Jones, Erik	12,024	22.4%
				Gill, David M.	7,757	14.4%
				Ebel, Jon	7,167	13.3%
				Sides, Angel	2,237	4.2%
	TOTAL	*44,512*		*TOTAL*	*53,700*	
Congressional District 14	Hultgren, Randy M.*	51,672	100.0%	Underwood, Lauren	29,391	57.3%
				Brolley, Matthew	6,845	13.4%
				Walz, Jim	5,100	10.0%
				Swanson, Victor	3,597	7.0%
				Hosta, John J.	2,578	5.0%
				Weber, George	2,570	5.0%
				Roldan-Johnson, Daniel	1,170	2.3%
	TOTAL	*51,672*		*TOTAL*	*51,251*	
Congressional District 15	Shimkus, John M.*	73,825	100.0%	Gaither, Kevin	17,300	62.1%
				Spoerer, Carl	10,573	37.9%
	TOTAL	*73,825*		*TOTAL*	*27,873*	
Congressional District 16	Kinzinger, Adam*	44,878	67.9%	Dady, Sara	17,173	40.3%
	Marter, James T.	21,242	32.1%	Mohammad, Neill	11,599	27.2%
				Briel, Amy "Murri"	8,291	19.5%
				Vercolio-Osmund, Beth	5,526	13.0%
	TOTAL	*66,120*		*TOTAL*	*42,589*	
Congressional District 17	Fawell, Bill	38,411	100.0%	Bustos, Cheri*	42,964	100.0%
	TOTAL	*38,411*		*TOTAL*	*42,964*	
Congressional District 18	LaHood, Darin*	61,722	78.9%	Rodriguez, Junius	14,990	41.7%
	Rients, Donald Ray	16,535	21.1%	Deters, Brian J.	14,189	39.5%
				Miller, Darrel Ervin	6,757	18.8%
	TOTAL	*78,257*		*TOTAL*	*35,936*	

Note: An asterisk (*) denotes incumbent.

INDIANA

Congressional districts first established for elections held in 2012

9 members

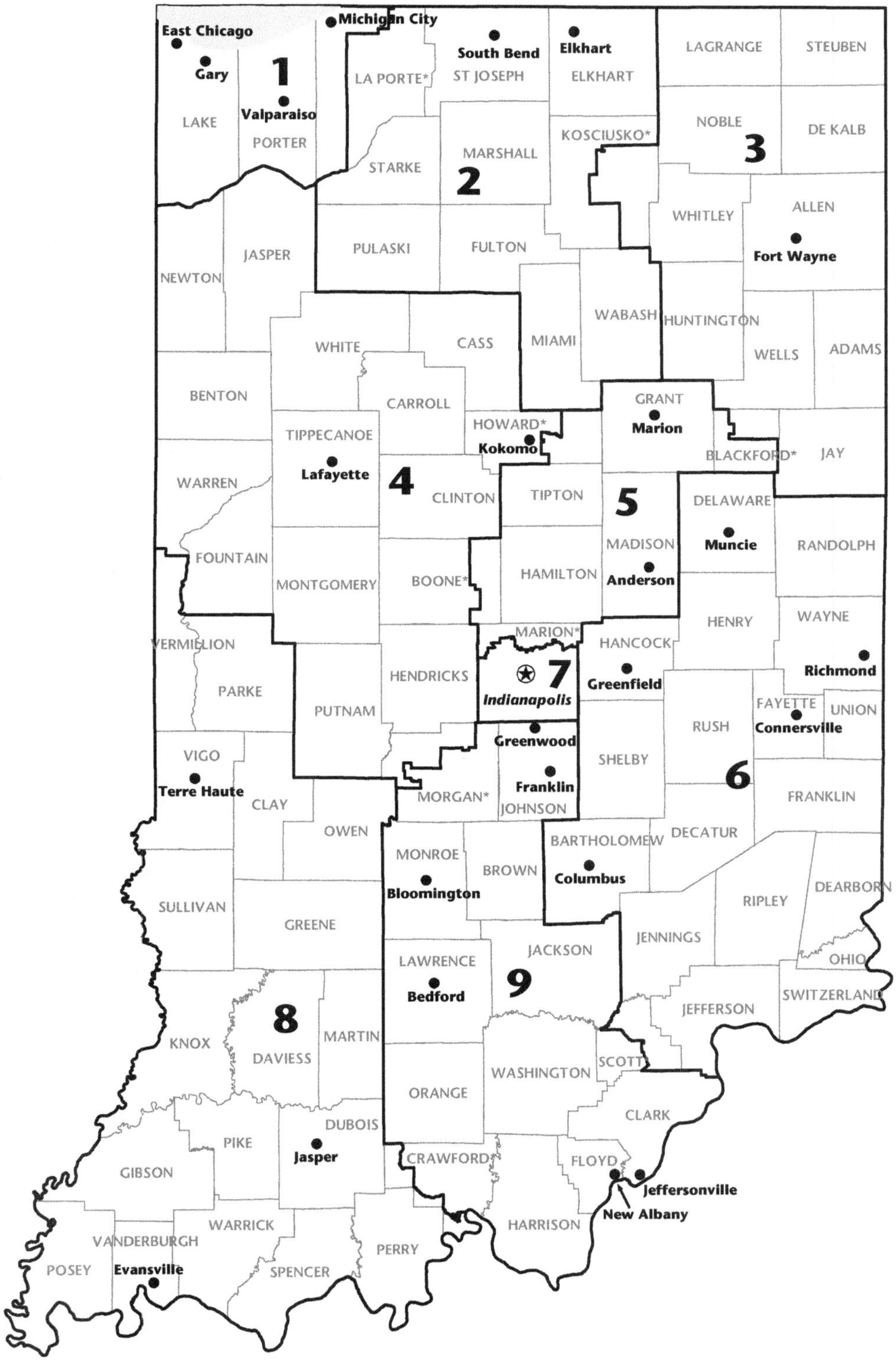

* Asterisk indicates a county whose boundaries include parts of two or more congressional districts.

INDIANA

GOVERNOR

Eric Holcomb (R). Elected 2016 to a four-year term.

SENATORS (2 Republicans)

Mike Braun (R). Elected 2018 to a six-year term.

Todd Young (R). Elected 2016 to a six-year term.

REPRESENTATIVES (7 Republicans, 2 Democrats)

1. Peter J. Visclosky (D)
2. Jackie Walorski (R)
3. James "Jim" Banks (R)
4. James "Jim" Baird (R)
5. Susan Brooks (R)
6. Gregory "Greg" Pence (R)
7. Andre D. Carson (D)
8. Larry D. Bucshon (R)
9. Trey Hollingsworth (R)

POSTWAR VOTE FOR PRESIDENT

		Republican		Democratic				Percentage			
								Total Vote		Major Vote	
Year	Total Vote	Vote	Candidate	Vote	Candidate	Other Vote	Rep.-Dem. Plurality	Rep.	Dem.	Rep.	Dem.
2016**	2,734,958	1,557,286	Trump, Donald J.	1,033,126	Clinton, Hillary Rodham	144,546	524,160 R	56.9%	37.8%	60.1%	39.9%
2012	2,624,534	1,420,543	Romney, W. Mitt	1,152,887	Obama, Barack H.*	51,104	267,656 R	54.1%	43.9%	55.2%	44.8%
2008	2,751,054	1,345,648	McCain, John S. III	1,374,039	Obama, Barack H.	31,367	28,391 D	48.9%	49.9%	49.5%	50.5%
2004	2,468,002	1,479,438	Bush, George W.*	969,011	Kerry, John F.	19,553	510,427 R	59.9%	39.3%	60.4%	39.6%
2000**	2,199,305	1,245,836	Bush, George W.	901,980	Gore, Albert Jr.	51,489	343,856 R	56.6%	41.0%	58.0%	42.0%
1996**	2,135,842	1,006,693	Dole, Robert "Bob"	887,424	Clinton, Bill*	241,725	119,269 R	47.1%	41.5%	53.1%	46.9%
1992**	2,305,871	989,375	Bush, George H.*	848,420	Clinton, Bill	468,076	140,955 R	42.9%	36.8%	53.8%	46.2%
1988	2,168,621	1,297,763	Bush, George H.	860,643	Dukakis, Michael S.	10,215	437,120 R	59.8%	39.7%	60.1%	39.9%
1984	2,233,069	1,377,230	Reagan, Ronald*	841,481	Mondale, Walter F.	14,358	535,749 R	61.7%	37.7%	62.1%	37.9%
1980**	2,242,033	1,255,656	Reagan, Ronald	844,197	Carter, Jimmy*	142,180	411,459 R	56.0%	37.7%	59.8%	40.2%
1976	2,220,362	1,183,958	Ford, Gerald R.*	1,014,714	Carter, Jimmy	21,690	169,244 R	53.3%	45.7%	53.8%	46.2%
1972	2,125,529	1,405,154	Nixon, Richard M.*	708,568	McGovern, George S.	11,807	696,586 R	66.1%	33.3%	66.5%	33.5%
1968**	2,123,597	1,067,885	Nixon, Richard M.	806,659	Humphrey, Hubert Horatio Jr.	249,053	261,226 R	50.3%	38.0%	57.0%	43.0%
1964	2,091,606	911,118	Goldwater, Barry M. Sr.	1,170,848	Johnson, Lyndon B.*	9,640	259,730 D	43.6%	56.0%	43.8%	56.2%
1960	2,135,360	1,175,120	Nixon, Richard M.	952,358	Kennedy, John F.	7,882	222,762 R	55.0%	44.6%	55.2%	44.8%
1956	1,974,607	1,182,811	Eisenhower, Dwight D.*	783,908	Stevenson, Adlai E. II	7,888	398,903 R	59.9%	39.7%	60.1%	39.9%
1952	1,955,049	1,136,259	Eisenhower, Dwight D.	801,530	Stevenson, Adlai E. II	17,260	334,729 R	58.1%	41.0%	58.6%	41.4%
1948	1,656,212	821,079	Dewey, Thomas E.	807,831	Truman, Harry S.*	27,302	13,248 R	49.6%	48.8%	50.4%	49.6%

Note: An asterisk (*) denotes incumbent. **In past elections, the other vote included: 2016 - 133,993 Libertarian (Gary Johnson); 2000 - 18,531 Green (Ralph Nader); 1996 - 224,299 Reform (Ross Perot); 1992 - 455,934 Independent (Perot); 1980 - 111,639 Independent (John Anderson); 1968 - 243,108 American Independent (George Wallace).

INDIANA

POSTWAR VOTE FOR GOVERNOR

		Republican		Democratic				Percentage			
								Total Vote		Major Vote	
Year	Total Vote	Vote	Candidate	Vote	Candidate	Other Vote	Rep.-Dem. Plurality	Rep.	Dem.	Rep.	Dem.
2016	2,719,968	1,397,396	Holcomb, Eric	1,235,503	Gregg, John R.	87,069	161,893 R	51.4%	45.4%	53.1%	46.9%
2012	2,577,329	1,275,424	Pence, Mike	1,200,016	Gregg, John R.	101,889	75,408 R	49.5%	46.6%	51.5%	48.5%
2008	2,703,752	1,563,885	Daniels, Mitch*	1,082,463	Thompson, Jill Long	57,404	481,422 R	57.8%	40.0%	59.1%	40.9%
2004	2,448,498	1,302,912	Daniels, Mitch	1,113,900	Kernan, Joseph E.	31,686	189,012 R	53.2%	45.5%	53.9%	46.1%
2000	2,179,413	908,285	McIntosh, David M.	1,232,525	O'Bannon, Frank*	38,603	324,240 D	41.7%	56.6%	42.4%	57.6%
1996	2,110,047	986,982	Goldsmith, Stephen	1,087,128	O'Bannon, Frank	35,937	100,146 D	46.8%	51.5%	47.6%	52.4%
1992	2,229,116	822,533	Pearson, Linley E.	1,382,151	Bayh, Evan*	24,432	559,618 D	36.9%	62.0%	37.3%	62.7%
1988	2,140,781	1,002,207	Mutz, John M.	1,138,574	Bayh, Evan		136,367 D	46.8%	53.2%	46.8%	53.2%
1984	2,197,988	1,146,497	Orr, Robert D.*	1,036,922	Townsend, W. Wayne	14,569	109,575 R	52.2%	47.2%	52.5%	47.5%
1980	2,178,403	1,257,383	Orr, Robert D.	913,116	Hillenbrand, John A.	7,904	344,267 R	57.7%	41.9%	57.9%	42.1%
1976	2,175,324	1,236,555	Bowen, Otis R.*	927,243	Conrad, Larry A.	11,526	309,312 R	56.8%	42.6%	57.1%	42.9%
1972	2,120,847	1,203,903	Bowen, Otis R.	900,489	Welsh, Matthew E.	16,455	303,414 R	56.8%	42.5%	57.2%	42.8%
1968	2,049,063	1,080,262	Whitcomb, Edgar D.	965,816	Rock, Robert L.	2,985	114,446 R	52.7%	47.1%	52.8%	47.2%
1964	2,073,058	901,342	Ristine, Richard O.	1,164,763	Branigin, Roger D.	6,953	263,421 D	43.5%	56.2%	43.6%	56.4%
1960	2,128,965	1,049,540	Parker, Crawford F.	1,072,717	Welsh, Matthew E.	6,708	23,177 D	49.3%	50.4%	49.5%	50.5%
1956	1,954,290	1,086,868	Handley, Harold W.	859,393	Tucker, Ralph	8,029	227,475 R	55.6%	44.0%	55.8%	44.2%
1952	1,931,869	1,075,685	Craig, George N.	841,984	Watkins, John A.	14,200	233,701 R	55.7%	43.6%	56.1%	43.9%
1948	1,652,321	745,892	Creighton, Hobart	884,995	Schricker, Henry F.	21,434	139,103 D	45.1%	53.6%	45.7%	54.3%

Note: An asterisk (*) denotes incumbent.

POSTWAR VOTE FOR SENATOR

		Republican		Democratic				Percentage			
								Total Vote		Major Vote	
Year	Total Vote	Vote	Candidate	Vote	Candidate	Other Vote	Rep.-Dem. Plurality	Rep.	Dem.	Rep.	Dem.
2018	2,282,565	1,158,000	Braun, Mike	1,023,553	Donnelly, Joseph S.*	101,012	134,447 R	50.7%	44.8%	53.1%	46.9%
2016	2,732,546	1,423,991	Young, Todd	1,158,947	Bayh, Evan	149,608	265,044 R	52.1%	42.4%	55.1%	44.9%
2012	2,560,102	1,133,621	Mourdock, Richard E.	1,281,181	Donnelly, Joseph S.	145,300	147,560 D	44.3%	50.0%	46.9%	53.1%
2010	1,744,481	952,116	Coats, Daniel R.	697,775	Ellsworth, Brad	94,590	254,341 R	54.6%	40.0%	57.7%	42.3%
2006**	1,341,111	1,171,553	Lugar, Richard G.*			169,558	1,171,553 R	87.4%		100.0%	
2004	2,428,233	903,913	Scott, Marvin B.	1,496,976	Bayh, Evan*	27,344	593,063 D	37.2%	61.6%	37.6%	62.4%
2000	2,145,209	1,427,944	Lugar, Richard G.*	683,273	Johnson, David L.	33,992	744,671 R	66.6%	31.9%	67.6%	32.4%
1998	1,588,617	552,732	Helmke, Paul	1,012,244	Bayh, Evan	23,641	459,512 D	34.8%	63.7%	35.3%	64.7%
1994	1,543,568	1,039,625	Lugar, Richard G.*	470,799	Jontz, Jim	33,144	568,826 R	67.4%	30.5%	68.8%	31.2%
1992	2,211,426	1,267,972	Coats, Daniel R.*	900,148	Hogsett, Joseph H.	43,306	367,824 R	57.3%	40.7%	58.5%	41.5%
1990S**	1,504,302	806,048	Coats, Daniel R.	696,639	Hill, Baron P.	1,615	109,409 R	53.6%	46.3%	53.6%	46.4%
1988	2,099,303	1,430,525	Lugar, Richard G.*	668,778	Wickes, Jack		761,747 R	68.1%	31.9%	68.1%	31.9%
1986	1,545,563	936,143	Quayle, John Danforth*	595,192	Long, Jill Lynette	14,228	340,951 R	60.6%	38.5%	61.1%	38.9%
1982	1,817,287	978,301	Lugar, Richard G.*	828,400	Fithian, Floyd	10,586	149,901 R	53.8%	45.6%	54.1%	45.9%
1980	2,198,376	1,182,414	Quayle, John Danforth	1,015,962	Bayh, Birch Evan*		166,452 R	53.8%	46.2%	53.8%	46.2%
1976	2,171,187	1,275,833	Lugar, Richard G.	878,522	Hartke, R. Vance*	16,832	397,311 R	58.8%	40.5%	59.2%	40.8%
1974	1,752,978	814,117	Lugar, Richard G.	889,269	Bayh, Birch Evan*	49,592	75,152 D	46.4%	50.7%	47.8%	52.2%
1970	1,737,697	866,707	Roudebush, Richard	870,990	Hartke, R. Vance*		4,283 D	49.9%	50.1%	49.9%	50.1%
1968	2,053,118	988,571	Ruckelshaus, William	1,060,456	Bayh, Birch Evan*	4,091	71,885 D	48.1%	51.7%	48.2%	51.8%
1964	2,076,963	941,519	Bontrager, D. Russell	1,128,505	Hartke, R. Vance*	6,939	186,986 D	45.3%	54.3%	45.5%	54.5%
1962	1,800,038	894,547	Capehart, Homer E.*	905,491	Bayh, Birch Evan		10,944 D	49.7%	50.3%	49.7%	50.3%
1958	1,724,598	731,635	Handley, Harold W.	973,636	Hartke, R. Vance	19,327	242,001 D	42.4%	56.5%	42.9%	57.1%
1956	1,963,986	1,084,262	Capehart, Homer E.*	871,781	Wickard, Claude R.	7,943	212,481 R	55.2%	44.4%	55.4%	44.6%
1952	1,946,118	1,020,605	Jenner, William E.*	911,169	Schricker, Henry F.	14,344	109,436 R	52.4%	46.8%	52.8%	47.2%
1950	1,598,724	844,303	Capehart, Homer E.*	741,025	Campbell, Alex M.	13,396	103,278 R	52.8%	46.4%	53.3%	46.7%
1946	1,347,434	739,809	Jenner, William E.	584,288	Townsend, M. Clifford	23,337	155,521 R	54.9%	43.4%	55.9%	44.1%

Note: An asterisk (*) denotes incumbent. **In past elections, the other vote included: 2006 - 168,820 Libertarian (Steve Osborn), who finished second. The 1990 election was for a short term to fill a vacancy. The Democratic Party did not run a candidate in the 2006 Senate election.

INDIANA

SENATOR 2018

2010 Census Population	County	Total Vote	Republican (Braun)	Democratic (Donnelly)	Other	Rep.-Dem. Plurality	Percentage: Total Vote Rep.	Total Vote Dem.	Major Vote Rep.	Major Vote Dem.
34,387	ADAMS	11,146	7,511	3,146	489	4,365 R	67.4%	28.2%	70.5%	29.5%
355,329	ALLEN	125,917	65,927	55,903	4,087	10,024 R	52.4%	44.4%	54.1%	45.9%
76,794	BARTHOLOMEW	26,520	15,222	10,071	1,227	5,151 R	57.4%	38.0%	60.2%	39.8%
8,854	BENTON	2,964	1,926	847	191	1,079 R	65.0%	28.6%	69.5%	30.5%
12,766	BLACKFORD	3,878	2,303	1,275	300	1,028 R	59.4%	32.9%	64.4%	35.6%
56,640	BOONE	27,540	15,540	10,981	1,019	4,559 R	56.4%	39.9%	58.6%	41.4%
15,242	BROWN	7,189	4,103	2,768	318	1,335 R	57.1%	38.5%	59.7%	40.3%
20,155	CARROLL	6,914	4,518	2,071	325	2,447 R	65.3%	30.0%	68.6%	31.4%
38,966	CASS	11,450	6,617	4,061	772	2,556 R	57.8%	35.5%	62.0%	38.0%
110,232	CLARK	43,284	22,766	18,551	1,967	4,215 R	52.6%	42.9%	55.1%	44.9%
26,890	CLAY	9,277	6,207	2,601	469	3,606 R	66.9%	28.0%	70.5%	29.5%
33,224	CLINTON	9,207	5,967	2,755	485	3,212 R	64.8%	29.9%	68.4%	31.6%
10,713	CRAWFORD	3,963	2,252	1,504	207	748 R	56.8%	38.0%	60.0%	40.0%
31,648	DAVIESS	8,739	6,555	1,901	283	4,654 R	75.0%	21.8%	77.5%	22.5%
50,047	DEARBORN	18,256	13,287	4,481	488	8,806 R	72.8%	24.5%	74.8%	25.2%
25,740	DECATUR	9,006	6,246	2,287	473	3,959 R	69.4%	25.4%	73.2%	26.8%
42,223	DEKALB	13,932	9,167	4,204	561	4,963 R	65.8%	30.2%	68.6%	31.4%
117,671	DELAWARE	37,710	17,447	18,159	2,104	712 D	46.3%	48.2%	49.0%	51.0%
41,889	DUBOIS	17,126	11,204	5,264	658	5,940 R	65.4%	30.7%	68.0%	32.0%
197,559	ELKHART	53,887	31,164	21,062	1,661	10,102 R	57.8%	39.1%	59.7%	40.3%
24,277	FAYETTE	7,464	4,704	2,295	465	2,409 R	63.0%	30.7%	67.2%	32.8%
74,578	FLOYD	31,826	16,588	14,070	1,168	2,518 R	52.1%	44.2%	54.1%	45.9%
17,240	FOUNTAIN	5,869	4,060	1,496	313	2,564 R	69.2%	25.5%	73.1%	26.9%
23,087	FRANKLIN	7,432	5,614	1,619	199	3,995 R	75.5%	21.8%	77.6%	22.4%
20,836	FULTON	7,008	4,154	2,539	315	1,615 R	59.3%	36.2%	62.1%	37.9%
33,503	GIBSON	12,513	8,040	4,001	472	4,039 R	64.3%	32.0%	66.8%	33.2%
70,061	GRANT	20,067	12,393	6,745	929	5,648 R	61.8%	33.6%	64.8%	35.2%
33,165	GREENE	10,773	6,949	3,313	511	3,636 R	64.5%	30.8%	67.7%	32.3%
274,569	HAMILTON	138,075	72,325	61,337	4,413	10,988 R	52.4%	44.4%	54.1%	45.9%
70,002	HANCOCK	30,267	19,097	9,770	1,400	9,327 R	63.1%	32.3%	66.2%	33.8%
39,364	HARRISON	15,617	9,847	5,131	639	4,716 R	63.1%	32.9%	65.7%	34.3%
145,448	HENDRICKS	62,812	36,966	23,599	2,247	13,367 R	58.9%	37.6%	61.0%	39.0%
49,462	HENRY	15,693	9,569	5,171	953	4,398 R	61.0%	33.0%	64.9%	35.1%
82,752	HOWARD	41,664	16,736	11,159	13,769	5,577 R	40.2%	26.8%	60.0%	40.0%
37,124	HUNTINGTON	13,209	8,879	3,699	631	5,180 R	67.2%	28.0%	70.6%	29.4%
42,376	JACKSON	14,414	9,431	4,198	785	5,233 R	65.4%	29.1%	69.2%	30.8%
33,478	JASPER	10,586	6,987	3,278	321	3,709 R	66.0%	31.0%	68.1%	31.9%
21,253	JAY	6,291	3,990	1,933	368	2,057 R	63.4%	30.7%	67.4%	32.6%
32,428	JEFFERSON	11,242	6,345	4,313	584	2,032 R	56.4%	38.4%	59.5%	40.5%
28,525	JENNINGS	9,149	5,921	2,686	542	3,235 R	64.7%	29.4%	68.8%	31.2%
139,654	JOHNSON	51,902	32,540	17,479	1,883	15,061 R	62.7%	33.7%	65.1%	34.9%
38,440	KNOX	12,625	7,876	3,977	772	3,899 R	62.4%	31.5%	66.4%	33.6%
77,358	KOSCIUSKO	26,382	18,558	6,801	1,023	11,757 R	70.3%	25.8%	73.2%	26.8%
111,467	LA PORTE	37,247	16,008	20,014	1,225	4,006 D	43.0%	53.7%	44.4%	55.6%
37,128	LAGRANGE	7,680	5,183	2,217	280	2,966 R	67.5%	28.9%	70.0%	30.0%
496,005	LAKE	162,298	54,564	104,390	3,344	49,826 D	33.6%	64.3%	34.3%	65.7%
46,134	LAWRENCE	15,496	10,274	4,434	788	5,840 R	66.3%	28.6%	69.9%	30.1%
131,636	MADISON	44,069	22,841	18,701	2,527	4,140 R	51.8%	42.4%	55.0%	45.0%
903,393	MARION	307,130	98,385	197,880	10,865	99,495 D	32.0%	64.4%	33.2%	66.8%
47,051	MARSHALL	14,899	8,747	5,619	533	3,128 R	58.7%	37.7%	60.9%	39.1%
10,334	MARTIN	4,324	2,997	1,127	200	1,870 R	69.3%	26.1%	72.7%	27.3%
36,903	MIAMI	10,364	6,975	2,862	527	4,113 R	67.3%	27.6%	70.9%	29.1%
137,974	MONROE	51,912	15,540	34,193	2,179	18,653 D	29.9%	65.9%	31.2%	68.8%
38,124	MONTGOMERY	12,539	8,362	3,518	659	4,844 R	66.7%	28.1%	70.4%	29.6%
68,894	MORGAN	25,159	17,539	6,471	1,149	11,068 R	69.7%	25.7%	73.0%	27.0%
14,244	NEWTON	4,563	2,966	1,402	195	1,564 R	65.0%	30.7%	67.9%	32.1%
47,536	NOBLE	13,689	8,993	4,132	564	4,861 R	65.7%	30.2%	68.5%	31.5%
6,128	OHIO	2,395	1,586	747	62	839 R	66.2%	31.2%	68.0%	32.0%
19,840	ORANGE	6,772	4,353	2,135	284	2,218 R	64.3%	31.5%	67.1%	32.9%
21,575	OWEN	7,194	4,601	2,210	383	2,391 R	64.0%	30.7%	67.6%	32.4%

INDIANA

SENATOR 2018

2010 Census Population	County	Total Vote	Republican (Braun)	Democratic (Donnelly)	Other	Rep.-Dem. Plurality	Percentage Total Vote Rep.	Total Vote Dem.	Major Vote Rep.	Major Vote Dem.
17,339	PARKE	5,342	3,532	1,499	311	2,033 R	66.1%	28.1%	70.2%	29.8%
19,338	PERRY	7,151	3,450	3,364	337	86 R	48.2%	47.0%	50.6%	49.4%
12,845	PIKE	5,159	3,235	1,679	245	1,556 R	62.7%	32.5%	65.8%	34.2%
164,343	PORTER	64,795	29,368	33,390	2,037	4,022 D	45.3%	51.5%	46.8%	53.2%
25,910	POSEY	10,640	6,324	3,881	435	2,443 R	59.4%	36.5%	62.0%	38.0%
13,402	PULASKI	4,359	2,583	1,617	159	966 R	59.3%	37.1%	61.5%	38.5%
37,963	PUTNAM	11,899	7,814	3,512	573	4,302 R	65.7%	29.5%	69.0%	31.0%
26,171	RANDOLPH	8,110	5,138	2,467	505	2,671 R	63.4%	30.4%	67.6%	32.4%
28,818	RIPLEY	9,469	6,880	2,350	239	4,530 R	72.7%	24.8%	74.5%	25.5%
17,392	RUSH	6,083	3,991	1,690	402	2,301 R	65.6%	27.8%	70.3%	29.7%
24,181	SCOTT	7,663	4,241	3,113	309	1,128 R	55.3%	40.6%	57.7%	42.3%
44,436	SHELBY	14,418	9,340	4,333	745	5,007 R	64.8%	30.1%	68.3%	31.7%
20,952	SPENCER	8,875	5,202	3,218	455	1,984 R	58.6%	36.3%	61.8%	38.2%
266,931	ST. JOSEPH	93,288	36,456	53,758	3,074	17,302 D	39.1%	57.6%	40.4%	59.6%
23,363	STARKE	7,584	4,149	3,119	316	1,030 R	54.7%	41.1%	57.1%	42.9%
34,185	STEUBEN	12,175	7,839	3,864	472	3,975 R	64.4%	31.7%	67.0%	33.0%
21,475	SULLIVAN	7,398	4,340	2,663	395	1,677 R	58.7%	36.0%	62.0%	38.0%
10,613	SWITZERLAND	2,925	1,874	936	115	938 R	64.1%	32.0%	66.7%	33.3%
172,780	TIPPECANOE	51,457	22,649	26,376	2,432	3,727 D	44.0%	51.3%	46.2%	53.8%
15,936	TIPTON	6,127	4,062	1,734	331	2,328 R	66.3%	28.3%	70.1%	29.9%
7,516	UNION	2,504	1,749	682	73	1,067 R	69.8%	27.2%	71.9%	28.1%
179,703	VANDERBURGH	58,522	29,375	27,183	1,964	2,192 R	50.2%	46.4%	51.9%	48.1%
16,212	VERMILLION	5,593	3,002	2,198	393	804 R	53.7%	39.3%	57.7%	42.3%
107,848	VIGO	31,659	14,813	15,171	1,675	358 D	46.8%	47.9%	49.4%	50.6%
32,888	WABASH	11,299	7,658	3,159	482	4,499 R	67.8%	28.0%	70.8%	29.2%
8,508	WARREN	3,279	2,208	914	157	1,294 R	67.3%	27.9%	70.7%	29.3%
59,689	WARRICK	24,366	14,010	9,594	762	4,416 R	57.5%	39.4%	59.4%	40.6%
28,262	WASHINGTON	9,382	6,127	2,806	449	3,321 R	65.3%	29.9%	68.6%	31.4%
68,917	WAYNE	19,763	11,241	7,482	1,040	3,759 R	56.9%	37.9%	60.0%	40.0%
27,636	WELLS	10,892	7,819	2,694	379	5,125 R	71.8%	24.7%	74.4%	25.6%
24,643	WHITE	8,490	5,100	2,736	654	2,364 R	60.1%	32.2%	65.1%	34.9%
33,292	WHITLEY	13,384	9,019	3,818	547	5,201 R	67.4%	28.5%	70.3%	29.7%
6,483,802	*TOTAL*	*2,282,565*	*1,158,000*	*1,023,553*	*101,012*	*134,447 R*	*50.7%*	*44.8%*	*53.1%*	*46.9%*

INDIANA

HOUSE OF REPRESENTATIVES

CD	Year	Total Vote	Republican Vote	Republican Candidate	Democratic Vote	Democratic Candidate	Other Vote	Rep.-Dem. Plurality	Percentage Total Vote Rep.	Total Vote Dem.	Major Vote Rep.	Major Vote Dem.
1	2018	245,209	85,594	LEYVA, MARK J.	159,611	VISCLOSKY, PETER J.*	4	74,017 D	34.9%	65.1%	34.9%	65.1%
1	2016	254,583			207,515	VISCLOSKY, PETER J.*	47,068	207,515 D		81.5%		100.0%
1	2014	142,293	51,000	LEYVA, MARK J.	86,579	VISCLOSKY, PETER J.*	4,714	35,579 D	35.8%	60.8%	37.1%	62.9%
1	2012	279,034	91,291	PHELPS, JOEL	187,743	VISCLOSKY, PETER J.*		96,452 D	32.7%	67.3%	32.7%	67.3%
2	2018	228,889	125,499	WALORSKI, JACKIE*	103,363	HALL, MEL	27	22,136 R	54.8%	45.2%	54.8%	45.2%
2	2016	277,357	164,355	WALORSKI, JACKIE*	102,401	COLEMAN, LYNN C.	10,601	61,954 R	59.3%	36.9%	61.6%	38.4%
2	2014	145,200	85,583	WALORSKI, JACKIE*	55,590	BOCK, JOE	4,027	29,993 R	58.9%	38.3%	60.6%	39.4%
2	2012	273,475	134,033	WALORSKI, JACKIE	130,113	MULLEN, BRENDAN	9,329	3,920 R	49.0%	47.6%	50.7%	49.3%
3	2018	245,537	158,927	BANKS, JAMES "JIM"*	86,610	TRITCH, COURTNEY		72,317 R	64.7%	35.3%	64.7%	35.3%
3	2016	287,247	201,396	BANKS, JAMES "JIM"	66,023	SCHRADER, THOMAS ALLEN	19,828	135,373 R	70.1%	23.0%	75.3%	24.7%
3	2014	148,793	102,889	STUTZMAN, MARLIN A.*	39,771	KUHNLE, JUSTIN	6,133	63,118 R	69.1%	26.7%	72.1%	27.9%
3	2012	280,235	187,872	STUTZMAN, MARLIN A.*	92,363	BOYD, KEVIN		95,509 R	67.0%	33.0%	67.0%	33.0%

INDIANA

HOUSE OF REPRESENTATIVES

			Republican		Democratic				Percentage			
									Total Vote		Major Vote	
CD	Year	Total Vote	Vote	Candidate	Vote	Candidate	Other Vote	Rep.-Dem. Plurality	Rep.	Dem.	Rep.	Dem.
4	2018	244,363	156,539	BAIRD, JAMES "JIM"	87,824	BECK, TOBI		68,715 R	64.1%	35.9%	64.1%	35.9%
4	2016	299,434	193,412	ROKITA, TODD*	91,256	DALE, JOHN	14,766	102,156 R	64.6%	30.5%	67.9%	32.1%
4	2014	142,054	94,998	ROKITA, TODD*	47,056	DALE, JOHN		47,942 R	66.9%	33.1%	66.9%	33.1%
4	2012	272,268	168,688	ROKITA, TODD*	93,015	NELSON, TARA E.	10,565	75,673 R	62.0%	34.2%	64.5%	35.5%
5	2018	317,177	180,035	BROOKS, SUSAN*	137,142	THORNTON, DIERDRE "DEE"		42,893 R	56.8%	43.2%	56.8%	43.2%
5	2016	361,135	221,957	BROOKS, SUSAN*	123,849	DEMAREE, ANGELA	15,329	98,108 R	61.5%	34.3%	64.2%	35.8%
5	2014	161,440	105,277	BROOKS, SUSAN*	49,756	DENNEY, SHAWN A.	6,407	55,521 R	65.2%	30.8%	67.9%	32.1%
5	2012	333,359	194,570	BROOKS, SUSAN	125,347	RESKE, SCOTT	13,442	69,223 R	58.4%	37.6%	60.8%	39.2%
6	2018	241,726	154,260	PENCE, GREGORY "GREG"	79,430	LAKE, JEANNINE	8,036	74,830 R	63.8%	32.9%	66.0%	34.0%
6	2016	296,385	204,920	MESSER, LUKE*	79,135	WELSH, BARRY A.	12,330	125,785 R	69.1%	26.7%	72.1%	27.9%
6	2014	155,071	102,187	MESSER, LUKE*	45,509	HEITZMAN, SUSAN HALL	7,375	56,678 R	65.9%	29.3%	69.2%	30.8%
6	2012	275,253	162,613	MESSER, LUKE	96,678	BOOKOUT, BRAD	15,962	65,935 R	59.1%	35.1%	62.7%	37.3%
7	2018	217,596	76,457	HARMON, WAYNE E. "GUNNY"	141,139	CARSON, ANDRE D.*		64,682 D	35.1%	64.9%	35.1%	64.9%
7	2016	264,670	94,456	PING, CATHERINE "CAT"	158,739	CARSON, ANDRE D.*	11,475	64,283 D	35.7%	60.0%	37.3%	62.7%
7	2014	112,261	46,887	PING, CATHERINE "CAT"	61,443	CARSON, ANDRE D.*	3,931	14,556 D	41.8%	54.7%	43.3%	56.7%
7	2012	257,950	95,828	MAY, CARLOS	162,122	CARSON, ANDRE D.*		66,294 D	37.1%	62.9%	37.1%	62.9%
8	2018	244,291	157,396	BUCSHON, LARRY D.*	86,895	TANOOS, WILLIAM		70,501 R	64.4%	35.6%	64.4%	35.6%
8	2016	294,713	187,702	BUCSHON, LARRY D.*	93,356	DRAKE, RON	13,655	94,346 R	63.7%	31.7%	66.8%	33.2%
8	2014	171,315	103,344	BUCSHON, LARRY D.	61,384	SPANGLER, TOM	6,587	41,960 R	60.3%	35.8%	62.7%	37.3%
8	2012	283,992	151,533	BUCSHON, LARRY D.*	122,325	CROOKS, DAVE	10,134	29,208 R	53.4%	43.1%	55.3%	44.7%
9	2018	271,361	153,271	HOLLINGSWORTH, TREY*	118,090	WATSON, LIZ		35,181 R	56.5%	43.5%	56.5%	43.5%
9	2016	322,843	174,791	HOLLINGSWORTH, TREY	130,627	YODER, SHELLI	17,425	44,164 R	54.1%	40.5%	57.2%	42.8%
9	2014	162,387	101,594	YOUNG, TODD*	55,016	BAILEY, BILL	5,777	46,578 R	62.6%	33.9%	64.9%	35.1%
9	2012	298,180	165,332	YOUNG, TODD*	132,848	YODER, SHELLI		32,484 R	55.4%	44.6%	55.4%	44.6%
TOTAL	*2018*	*2,256,149*	*1,247,978*		*1,000,104*		*8,067*	*247,874 R*	*55.3%*	*44.3%*	*55.5%*	*44.5%*
TOTAL	*2016*	*2,658,367*	*1,442,989*		*1,052,901*		*162,477*	*390,088 R*	*54.3%*	*39.6%*	*57.8%*	*42.2%*
TOTAL	*2014*	*1,340,814*	*793,759*		*502,104*		*44,951*	*291,655 R*	*59.2%*	*37.4%*	*61.3%*	*38.7%*
TOTAL	*2012*	*2,553,746*	*1,351,760*		*1,142,554*		*59,432*	*209,206 R*	*52.9%*	*44.7%*	*54.2%*	*45.8%*

Note: An asterisk (*) denotes incumbent.

INDIANA

GENERAL AND PRIMARY ELECTIONS

2018 GENERAL ELECTIONS: OTHER VOTES

Senate Other vote was 100,942 Libertarian (Lucy Brenton), 52 Write-in (Nathan Altman), 12 Write-in (Christopher Fischer), 6 Write-in (James Johnson)

House Other vote was:

CD 1 4 Write-in (Jonathan Kleinman)

CD 2 27 Write-in (Richard Wolf)

CD 6 8,030 Libertarian (Tom Ferkinhoff), 5 Write-in (John Miller), 1 Write-in (Heather Meloy)

INDIANA

GENERAL AND PRIMARY ELECTIONS

2018 PRIMARY ELECTIONS: SUPPLEMENTARY INFORMATION

Primary	May 8, 2018	**Registration** (as of May 8, 2018)	4,406,549	No Party Registration

Primary Type Open—Any registered voter could participate in the primary of either party, although he or she could be challenged based on party affiliation. When a voter is challenged, they must execute a statement saying that they voted for a majority of the party's candidates in the previous general election. If they did not vote in the previous general election, they must indicate that they will vote for a majority of the party's candidates in the next general election.

	REPUBLICAN PRIMARIES			DEMOCRATIC PRIMARIES		
Senator	Braun, Mike	208,602	41.2%	Donnelly, Joseph S.*	284,621	100.0%
	Rokita, Todd	151,967	30.0%			
	Messer, Luke	146,131	28.8%			
	TOTAL	*506,700*		*TOTAL*	*284,621*	
Congressional District 1	Leyva, Mark J.	5,960	27.0%	Visclosky, Peter J.*	42,269	80.5%
	Meyer, John	4,328	19.6%	Daggett, Antonio "Tony" Sr.	5,813	11.1%
	Ivanovich, Roseann	4,318	19.6%	Chubb, Larry	4,406	8.4%
	Pappas, Nicholas	4,311	19.5%			
	Dopp, David	1,680	7.6%			
	Belko, Jeremy	1,486	6.7%			
	TOTAL	*22,083*		*TOTAL*	*52,488*	
Congressional District 2	Walorski, Jackie*	43,016	78.6%	Hall, Mel	15,402	41.7%
	Summe, Mark	11,684	21.4%	Hackett, Patricia "Pat"	10,429	28.2%
				Joshi, Yatish	8,165	22.1%
				Carpenter, Douglas M.	1,949	5.3%
				Petroff, John	570	1.5%
				Leech, Roland	451	1.2%
	TOTAL	*54,700*		*TOTAL*	*36,966*	
Congressional District 3	Banks, James "Jim"*	58,745	100.0%	Tritch, Courtney	16,376	79.1%
				Schrader, Thomas Allen	2,224	10.7%
				Roberson, John Forrest	2,116	10.2%
	TOTAL	*58,745*		*TOTAL*	*20,716*	
Congressional District 4	Baird, James "Jim"	29,319	36.6%	Beck, Tobi	6,467	34.6%
	Braun, Steve	23,602	29.5%	Ziol, Veronikka	3,938	21.1%
	Morales, Diego	11,997	15.0%	Mackey, Joseph "Joe"	3,013	16.1%
	Thomas, Jared	8,435	10.5%	Day, Roger D.	2,324	12.4%
	Grant, Kevin Jay	3,667	4.6%	Ellis, Roland	1,712	9.2%
	Nease, James	2,097	2.6%	Griesey, Darin Patrick	1,249	6.7%
	Radice, Timothy "Tim"	1,013	1.3%			
	TOTAL	*80,130*		*TOTAL*	*18,703*	
Congressional District 5	Brooks, Susan*	63,904	100.0%	Thornton, Dierdre "Dee"	18,073	53.0%
				Moore, Kyle	8,077	23.7%
				Douglas, Dion	3,521	10.3%
				Faraggi, Eshel	2,583	7.6%
				Dugdale, Sean	1,860	5.5%
	TOTAL	*63,904*		*TOTAL*	*34,114*	
Congressional District 6	Pence, Gregory "Greg"	47,962	64.5%	Lake, Jeannine	8,890	38.3%
	Lamb, Jonathan	17,526	23.6%	Pruett, James	5,984	25.8%
	MacKenzie, Stephen M.	3,400	4.6%	Siekman, Lane	3,612	15.6%
	Campbell, Mike	3,231	4.3%	Holland, George Thomas	2,570	11.1%
	Smith, Jeff	2,258	3.0%	Williamson, Joshua	1,695	7.3%
				Lave, Kenneth "K"	446	1.9%
	TOTAL	*74,377*		*TOTAL*	*23,197*	

INDIANA

GENERAL AND PRIMARY ELECTIONS

	REPUBLICAN PRIMARIES			DEMOCRATIC PRIMARIES		
Congressional District 7	Harmon, Wayne E. "Gunny"	6,547	28.8%	Carson, Andre D.*	37,662	88.0%
	Eason, Donald	4,354	19.2%	Spicer, Sue	3,499	8.2%
	Couch, John	3,464	15.2%	Godfrey, Curtis	725	1.7%
	Miniear, J.D.	3,087	13.6%	Kern, Bob	704	1.6%
	Davis, J. Jason	2,703	11.9%	Pullins, Pierre Quincy	226	0.5%
	Van Pelt, Tony "Big Dog"	2,568	11.3%			
	TOTAL	*22,723*		*TOTAL*	*42,816*	
Congressional District 8	Bucshon, Larry D.*	34,516	63.0%	Tanoos, William	26,232	100.0%
	Moss, Richard	13,831	25.2%			
	Covington, Rachel	6,451	11.8%			
	TOTAL	*54,798*		*TOTAL*	*26,232*	
Congressional District 9	Hollingsworth, Trey*	46,892	77.7%	Watson, Liz	24,989	66.4%
	Alspach, James Dean	13,449	22.3%	Canon, Daniel	11,558	30.7%
				Chatlos, Rob	1,100	2.9%
	TOTAL	*60,341*		*TOTAL*	*37,647*	

Note: An asterisk (*) denotes incumbent.

IOWA

Congressional districts first established for elections held in 2012

4 members

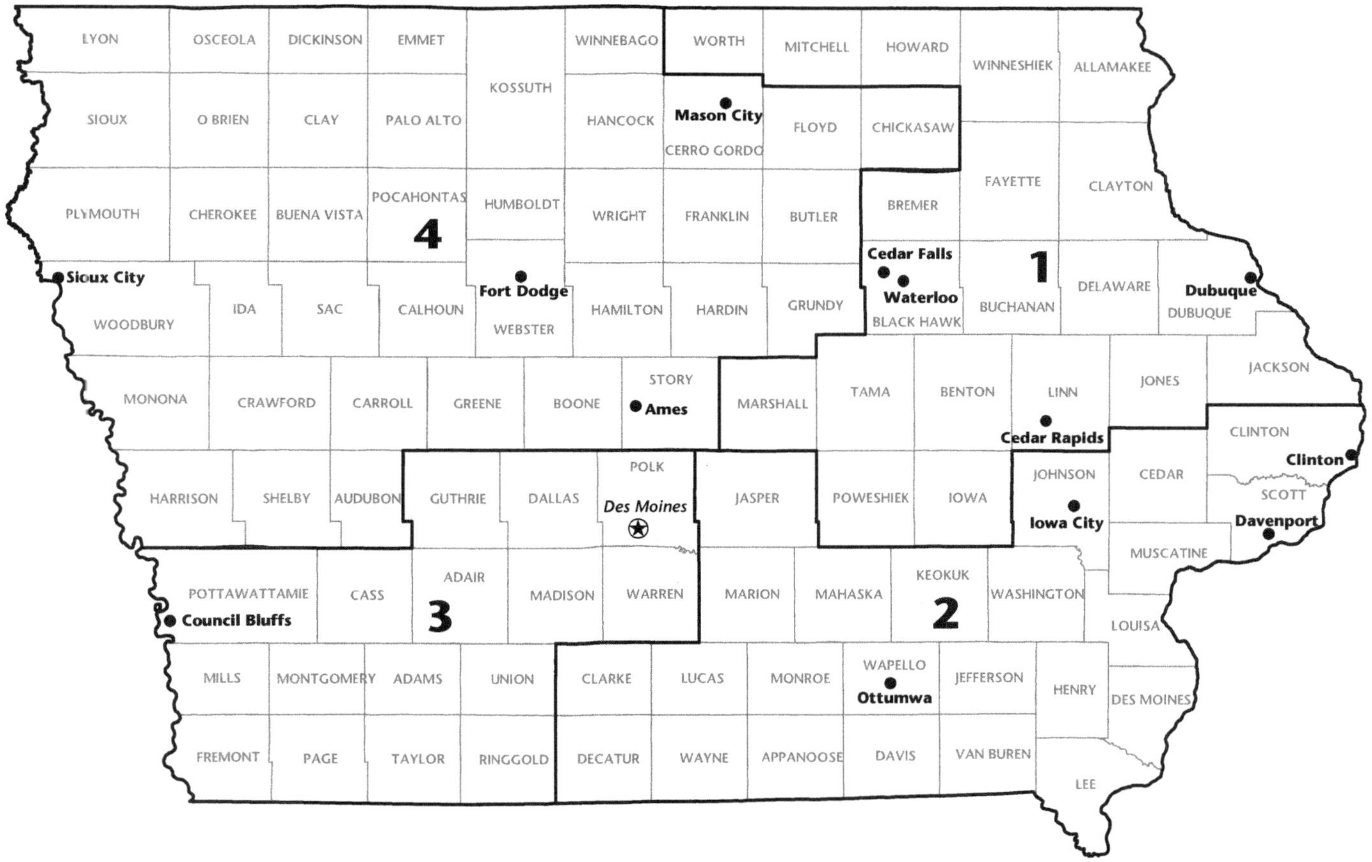

IOWA

GOVERNOR

Kim Reynolds (R). Assumed office May 24, 2017, to serve the remainder of the term vacated by the resignation of Terry E. Branstad to become the U.S. ambassador to China.

SENATORS (2 Republicans)

Joni Ernst (R). Elected 2014 to a six-year term.

Chuck E. Grassley (R). Re-elected 2016 to a six-year term. Previously elected 2010, 2004, 1998, 1992, 1986, 1980.

REPRESENTATIVES (1 Republican, 3 Democrats)

1. Abby Finkenauer (D)
2. David Loebsack (D)
3. Cindy Axne (D)
4. Steve King (R)

POSTWAR VOTE FOR PRESIDENT

								Percentage			
		Republican		Democratic				Total Vote		Major Vote	
Year	Total Vote	Vote	Candidate	Vote	Candidate	Other Vote	Rep.-Dem. Plurality	Rep.	Dem.	Rep.	Dem.
2016**	1,566,031	800,983	Trump, Donald J.	653,669	Clinton, Hillary Rodham	111,379	147,314 R	51.1%	41.7%	55.1%	44.9%
2012	1,582,180	730,617	Romney, W. Mitt	822,544	Obama, Barack H.*	29,019	91,927 D	46.2%	52.0%	47.0%	53.0%
2008	1,537,123	682,379	McCain, John S. III	828,940	Obama, Barack H.	25,804	146,561 D	44.4%	53.9%	45.2%	54.8%
2004	1,506,908	751,957	Bush, George W.*	741,898	Kerry, John F.	13,053	10,059 R	49.9%	49.2%	50.3%	49.7%
2000**	1,315,563	634,373	Bush, George W.	638,517	Gore, Albert Jr.	42,673	4,144 D	48.2%	48.5%	49.8%	50.2%
1996**	1,234,075	492,644	Dole, Robert "Bob"	620,258	Clinton, Bill*	121,173	127,614 D	39.9%	50.3%	44.3%	55.7%
1992**	1,354,607	504,891	Bush, George H.*	586,353	Clinton, Bill	263,363	81,462 D	37.3%	43.3%	46.3%	53.7%
1988	1,225,614	545,355	Bush, George H.	670,557	Dukakis, Michael S.	9,702	125,202 D	44.5%	54.7%	44.9%	55.1%
1984	1,319,805	703,088	Reagan, Ronald*	605,620	Mondale, Walter F.	11,097	97,468 R	53.3%	45.9%	53.7%	46.3%
1980**	1,317,661	676,026	Reagan, Ronald	508,672	Carter, Jimmy*	132,963	167,354 R	51.3%	38.6%	57.1%	42.9%
1976	1,279,306	632,863	Ford, Gerald R.*	619,931	Carter, Jimmy	26,512	12,932 R	49.5%	48.5%	50.5%	49.5%
1972	1,225,944	706,207	Nixon, Richard M.*	496,206	McGovern, George S.	23,531	210,001 R	57.6%	40.5%	58.7%	41.3%
1968**	1,167,931	619,106	Nixon, Richard M.	476,699	Humphrey, Hubert Horatio Jr.	72,126	142,407 R	53.0%	40.8%	56.5%	43.5%
1964	1,184,539	449,148	Goldwater, Barry M. Sr.	733,030	Johnson, Lyndon B.*	2,361	283,882 D	37.9%	61.9%	38.0%	62.0%
1960	1,273,810	722,381	Nixon, Richard M.	550,565	Kennedy, John F.	864	171,816 R	56.7%	43.2%	56.7%	43.3%
1956	1,234,564	729,187	Eisenhower, Dwight D.*	501,858	Stevenson, Adlai E. II	3,519	227,329 R	59.1%	40.7%	59.2%	40.8%
1952	1,268,773	808,906	Eisenhower, Dwight D.	451,513	Stevenson, Adlai E. II	8,354	357,393 R	63.8%	35.6%	64.2%	35.8%
1948	1,038,264	494,018	Dewey, Thomas E.	522,380	Truman, Harry S.*	21,866	28,362 D	47.6%	50.3%	48.6%	51.4%

Note: An asterisk (*) denotes incumbent. **In past elections, the other vote included: 2016 - 59,186 Libertarian (Gary Johnson); 2000 - 29,374 Green (Ralph Nader); 1996 - 105,159 Reform (Ross Perot); 1992 - 253,468 Independent (Perot); 1980 - 115,633 Independent (John Anderson); 1968 - 66,422 American Independent (George Wallace).

IOWA

POSTWAR VOTE FOR GOVERNOR

		Republican		Democratic				Percentage			
								Total Vote		Major Vote	
Year	Total Vote	Vote	Candidate	Vote	Candidate	Other Vote	Rep.-Dem. Plurality	Rep.	Dem.	Rep.	Dem.
2018	1,327,638	667,275	Reynolds, Kim*	630,986	Hubbell, Fred	29,377	36,289 R	50.3%	47.5%	51.4%	48.6%
2014	1,129,057	666,032	Branstad, Terry E.*	420,787	Hatch, Jack	42,238	245,245 R	59.0%	37.3%	61.3%	38.7%
2010	1,122,013	592,494	Branstad, Terry E.	484,798	Culver, Chet*	44,721	107,696 R	52.8%	43.2%	55.0%	45.0%
2006	1,053,255	467,425	Nussle, Jim	569,021	Culver, Chet	16,809	101,596 D	44.4%	54.0%	45.1%	54.9%
2002	1,025,802	456,612	Gross, Doug	540,449	Vilsack, Tom*	28,741	83,837 D	44.5%	52.7%	45.8%	54.2%
1998	956,418	444,787	Lightfoot, Jim Ross	500,231	Vilsack, Tom	11,400	55,444 D	46.5%	52.3%	47.1%	52.9%
1994	997,248	566,395	Branstad, Terry E.*	414,453	Campbell, Bonnie J.	16,400	151,942 R	56.8%	41.6%	57.7%	42.3%
1990	976,483	591,852	Branstad, Terry E.*	379,372	Avenson, Donald D.	5,259	212,480 R	60.6%	38.9%	60.9%	39.1%
1986	910,623	472,712	Branstad, Terry E.*	436,987	Junkins, Lowell L.	924	35,725 R	51.9%	48.0%	52.0%	48.0%
1982	1,038,229	548,313	Branstad, Terry E.	483,291	Conlin, Roxanne	6,625	65,022 R	52.8%	46.5%	53.2%	46.8%
1978	843,190	491,713	Ray, Robert E.*	345,519	Fitzgerald, Jerome D.	5,958	146,194 R	58.3%	41.0%	58.7%	41.3%
1974**	920,458	534,518	Ray, Robert E.*	377,553	Schaben, James F.	8,387	156,965 R	58.1%	41.0%	58.6%	41.4%
1972	1,210,222	707,177	Ray, Robert E.*	487,282	Franzenburg, Paul	15,763	219,895 R	58.4%	40.3%	59.2%	40.8%
1970	791,241	403,394	Ray, Robert E.*	368,911	Fulton, Robert	18,936	34,483 R	51.0%	46.6%	52.2%	47.8%
1968	1,135,988	613,827	Ray, Robert E.	521,216	Franzenburg, Paul	945	92,611 R	54.0%	45.9%	54.1%	45.9%
1966	893,175	394,518	Murray, William G.	494,259	Hughes, Harold E.*	4,398	99,741 D	44.2%	55.3%	44.4%	55.6%
1964	1,167,734	365,131	Hultman, Evan	794,610	Hughes, Harold E.*	7,993	429,479 D	31.3%	68.0%	31.5%	68.5%
1962	819,854	388,955	Erbe, Norman A.*	430,899	Hughes, Harold E.		41,944 D	47.4%	52.6%	47.4%	52.6%
1960	1,237,089	645,026	Erbe, Norman A.	592,063	McManus, E. J.		52,963 R	52.1%	47.9%	52.1%	47.9%
1958	859,095	394,071	Murray, William G.	465,024	Loveless, Herschel C.*		70,953 D	45.9%	54.1%	45.9%	54.1%
1956	1,204,235	587,383	Hoegh, Leo A.*	616,852	Loveless, Herschel C.		29,469 D	48.8%	51.2%	48.8%	51.2%
1954	848,592	435,944	Hoegh, Leo A.	410,255	Herring, Clyde E.	2,393	25,689 R	51.4%	48.3%	51.5%	48.5%
1952	1,230,045	638,388	Beardsley, William*	587,671	Loveless, Herschel C.	3,986	50,717 R	51.9%	47.8%	52.1%	47.9%
1950	857,213	506,642	Beardsley, William*	347,176	Gillette, Lester S.	3,395	159,466 R	59.1%	40.5%	59.3%	40.7%
1948	994,833	553,900	Beardsley, William	434,432	Switzer, Carroll O.	6,501	119,468 R	55.7%	43.7%	56.0%	44.0%
1946	631,681	362,592	Blue, Robert D.	266,190	Miles, Frank	2,899	96,402 R	57.4%	42.1%	57.7%	42.3%

Note: An asterisk (*) denotes incumbent. **The term of office of Iowa's Governor was increased from two to four years effective with the 1974 election.

POSTWAR VOTE FOR SENATOR

		Republican		Democratic				Percentage			
								Total Vote		Major Vote	
Year	Total Vote	Vote	Candidate	Vote	Candidate	Other Vote	Rep.-Dem. Plurality	Rep.	Dem.	Rep.	Dem.
2016	1,541,036	926,007	Grassley, Charles E.*	549,460	Judge, Patty	65,569	376,547 R	60.1%	35.7%	62.8%	37.2%
2014	1,129,700	588,575	Ernst, Joni	494,370	Braley, Bruce	46,755	94,205 R	52.1%	43.8%	54.3%	45.7%
2010	1,116,063	718,215	Grassley, Charles E.*	371,686	Conlin, Roxanne	26,162	346,529 R	64.4%	33.3%	65.9%	34.1%
2008	1,502,918	560,006	Reed, Christopher	941,665	Harkin, Tom*	1,247	381,659 D	37.3%	62.7%	37.3%	62.7%
2004	1,479,228	1,038,175	Grassley, Charles E.*	412,365	Small, Arthur A.	28,688	625,810 R	70.2%	27.9%	71.6%	28.4%
2002	1,023,075	447,892	Ganske, Greg	554,278	Harkin, Tom*	20,905	106,386 D	43.8%	54.2%	44.7%	55.3%
1998	947,907	648,480	Grassley, Charles E.*	289,049	Osterberg, David	10,378	359,431 R	68.4%	30.5%	69.2%	30.8%
1996	1,224,054	571,807	Lightfoot, Jim Ross	634,166	Harkin, Tom*	18,081	62,359 D	46.7%	51.8%	47.4%	52.6%
1992	1,292,494	899,761	Grassley, Charles E.*	351,561	Lloyd-Jones, Jean	41,172	548,200 R	69.6%	27.2%	71.9%	28.1%
1990	983,933	446,869	Tauke, Tom	535,975	Harkin, Tom*	1,089	89,106 D	45.4%	54.5%	45.5%	54.5%
1986	891,762	588,880	Grassley, Charles E.*	299,406	Roehrick, John P.	3,476	289,474 R	66.0%	33.6%	66.3%	33.7%
1984	1,292,700	564,381	Jepsen, Roger W.*	716,883	Harkin, Tom	11,436	152,502 D	43.7%	55.5%	44.0%	56.0%
1980	1,277,034	683,014	Grassley, Charles E.	581,545	Culver, John C.*	12,475	101,469 R	53.5%	45.5%	54.0%	46.0%
1978	824,654	421,598	Jepsen, Roger W.	395,066	Clark, Richard*	7,990	26,532 R	51.1%	47.9%	51.6%	48.4%
1974	889,561	420,546	Stanley, David M.	462,947	Culver, John C.	6,068	42,401 D	47.3%	52.0%	47.6%	52.4%
1972	1,203,333	530,525	Miller, Jack*	662,637	Clark, Richard	10,171	132,112 D	44.1%	55.1%	44.5%	55.5%
1968	1,144,086	568,469	Stanley, David M.	574,884	Hughes, Harold E.	733	6,415 D	49.7%	50.2%	49.7%	50.3%
1966	857,496	522,339	Miller, Jack*	324,114	Smith, E. B.	11,043	198,225 R	60.9%	37.8%	61.7%	38.3%
1962	807,972	431,364	Hickenlooper, Bourke B.*	376,602	Smith, E. B.	6	54,762 R	53.4%	46.6%	53.4%	46.6%
1960	1,237,582	642,463	Miller, Jack	595,119	Loveless, Herschel C.		47,344 R	51.9%	48.1%	51.9%	48.1%
1956	1,178,655	635,499	Hickenlooper, Bourke B.*	543,156	Evans, R. M.		92,343 R	53.9%	46.1%	53.9%	46.1%
1954	847,355	442,409	Martin, Thomas E.	402,712	Gillette, Guy M.*	2,234	39,697 R	52.2%	47.5%	52.3%	47.7%
1950	858,523	470,613	Hickenlooper, Bourke B.*	383,766	Loveland, Albert J.	4,144	86,847 R	54.8%	44.7%	55.1%	44.9%
1948	1,000,412	415,778	Wilson, George*	578,226	Gillette, Guy M.	6,408	162,448 D	41.6%	57.8%	41.8%	58.2%

Note: An asterisk (*) denotes incumbent.

IOWA

GOVERNOR 2018

2010 Census Population	County	Total Vote	Republican (Reynolds)	Democratic (Hubbell)	Other	Rep.-Dem. Plurality	Percentage Total Vote		Percentage Major Vote	
							Rep.	Dem.	Rep.	Dem.
7,682	ADAIR	3,444	2,213	1,167	64	1,046 R	64.3%	33.9%	65.5%	34.5%
4,029	ADAMS	1,747	1,160	549	38	611 R	66.4%	31.4%	67.9%	32.1%
14,330	ALLAMAKEE	5,680	3,326	2,165	189	1,161 R	58.6%	38.1%	60.6%	39.4%
12,887	APPANOOSE	5,049	3,101	1,834	114	1,267 R	61.4%	36.3%	62.8%	37.2%
6,119	AUDUBON	2,694	1,658	990	46	668 R	61.5%	36.7%	62.6%	37.4%
26,076	BENTON	11,629	6,845	4,482	302	2,363 R	58.9%	38.5%	60.4%	39.6%
131,090	BLACK HAWK	53,258	22,786	29,259	1,213	6,473 D	42.8%	54.9%	43.8%	56.2%
26,306	BOONE	12,201	6,107	5,810	284	297 R	50.1%	47.6%	51.2%	48.8%
24,276	BREMER	11,450	6,220	4,999	231	1,221 R	54.3%	43.7%	55.4%	44.6%
20,958	BUCHANAN	8,493	4,400	3,865	228	535 R	51.8%	45.5%	53.2%	46.8%
20,260	BUENA VISTA	6,565	3,771	2,649	145	1,122 R	57.4%	40.4%	58.7%	41.3%
14,867	BUTLER	6,156	3,952	2,064	140	1,888 R	64.2%	33.5%	65.7%	34.3%
9,670	CALHOUN	4,310	2,710	1,464	136	1,246 R	62.9%	34.0%	64.9%	35.1%
20,816	CARROLL	9,027	5,676	3,186	165	2,490 R	62.9%	35.3%	64.0%	36.0%
13,956	CASS	5,815	3,813	1,886	116	1,927 R	65.6%	32.4%	66.9%	33.1%
18,499	CEDAR	8,118	4,409	3,518	191	891 R	54.3%	43.3%	55.6%	44.4%
44,151	CERRO GORDO	19,040	9,651	9,011	378	640 R	50.7%	47.3%	51.7%	48.3%
12,072	CHEROKEE	5,156	3,327	1,715	114	1,612 R	64.5%	33.3%	66.0%	34.0%
12,439	CHICKASAW	5,249	3,021	2,103	125	918 R	57.6%	40.1%	59.0%	41.0%
9,286	CLARKE	3,706	2,341	1,280	85	1,061 R	63.2%	34.5%	64.7%	35.3%
16,667	CLAY	6,915	4,364	2,417	134	1,947 R	63.1%	35.0%	64.4%	35.6%
18,129	CLAYTON	7,922	4,512	2,978	432	1,534 R	57.0%	37.6%	60.2%	39.8%
49,116	CLINTON	18,224	8,847	9,047	330	200 D	48.5%	49.6%	49.4%	50.6%
17,096	CRAWFORD	5,422	3,579	1,735	108	1,844 R	66.0%	32.0%	67.4%	32.6%
66,135	DALLAS	41,744	21,189	19,804	751	1,385 R	50.8%	47.4%	51.7%	48.3%
8,753	DAVIS	3,141	2,070	1,002	69	1,068 R	65.9%	31.9%	67.4%	32.6%
8,457	DECATUR	2,956	1,872	1,008	76	864 R	63.3%	34.1%	65.0%	35.0%
17,764	DELAWARE	7,673	4,779	2,667	227	2,112 R	62.3%	34.8%	64.2%	35.8%
40,325	DES MOINES	15,152	6,827	8,038	287	1,211 D	45.1%	53.0%	45.9%	54.1%
16,667	DICKINSON	8,843	5,564	3,134	145	2,430 R	62.9%	35.4%	64.0%	36.0%
93,653	DUBUQUE	42,760	20,532	21,108	1,120	576 D	48.0%	49.4%	49.3%	50.7%
10,302	EMMET	3,769	2,298	1,383	88	915 R	61.0%	36.7%	62.4%	37.6%
20,880	FAYETTE	8,231	4,528	3,446	257	1,082 R	55.0%	41.9%	56.8%	43.2%
16,303	FLOYD	6,318	3,366	2,812	140	554 R	53.3%	44.5%	54.5%	45.5%
10,680	FRANKLIN	4,109	2,647	1,379	83	1,268 R	64.4%	33.6%	65.7%	34.3%
7,441	FREMONT	3,012	1,956	992	64	964 R	64.9%	32.9%	66.4%	33.6%
9,336	GREENE	4,098	2,326	1,675	97	651 R	56.8%	40.9%	58.1%	41.9%
12,453	GRUNDY	5,764	3,785	1,875	104	1,910 R	65.7%	32.5%	66.9%	33.1%
10,954	GUTHRIE	5,037	3,169	1,738	130	1,431 R	62.9%	34.5%	64.6%	35.4%
15,673	HAMILTON	6,386	3,703	2,560	123	1,143 R	58.0%	40.1%	59.1%	40.9%
11,341	HANCOCK	4,823	3,257	1,464	102	1,793 R	67.5%	30.4%	69.0%	31.0%
17,534	HARDIN	7,250	4,407	2,689	154	1,718 R	60.8%	37.1%	62.1%	37.9%
14,928	HARRISON	6,000	3,931	1,912	157	2,019 R	65.5%	31.9%	67.3%	32.7%
20,145	HENRY	7,446	4,284	2,996	166	1,288 R	57.5%	40.2%	58.8%	41.2%
9,566	HOWARD	3,622	2,050	1,422	150	628 R	56.6%	39.3%	59.0%	41.0%
9,815	HUMBOLDT	4,086	2,797	1,200	89	1,597 R	68.5%	29.4%	70.0%	30.0%
7,089	IDA	2,948	2,196	713	39	1,483 R	74.5%	24.2%	75.5%	24.5%
16,355	IOWA	7,648	4,499	2,966	183	1,533 R	58.8%	38.8%	60.3%	39.7%
19,848	JACKSON	8,589	4,744	3,582	263	1,162 R	55.2%	41.7%	57.0%	43.0%
36,842	JASPER	15,935	8,377	7,234	324	1,143 R	52.6%	45.4%	53.7%	46.3%
16,843	JEFFERSON	7,076	3,146	3,750	180	604 D	44.5%	53.0%	45.6%	54.4%
130,882	JOHNSON	68,107	18,119	48,758	1,230	30,639 D	26.6%	71.6%	27.1%	72.9%
20,638	JONES	8,603	4,752	3,650	201	1,102 R	55.2%	42.4%	56.6%	43.4%
10,511	KEOKUK	4,085	2,716	1,294	75	1,422 R	66.5%	31.7%	67.7%	32.3%
15,543	KOSSUTH	7,365	4,642	2,588	135	2,054 R	63.0%	35.1%	64.2%	35.8%
35,862	LEE	12,638	5,973	6,387	278	414 D	47.3%	50.5%	48.3%	51.7%
211,226	LINN	102,102	42,449	56,767	2,886	14,318 D	41.6%	55.6%	42.8%	57.2%
11,387	LOUISA	3,828	2,288	1,469	71	819 R	59.8%	38.4%	60.9%	39.1%
8,898	LUCAS	3,582	2,335	1,172	75	1,163 R	65.2%	32.7%	66.6%	33.4%
11,581	LYON	5,187	4,281	853	53	3,428 R	82.5%	16.4%	83.4%	16.6%

IOWA

GOVERNOR 2018

2010 Census Population	County	Total Vote	Republican (Reynolds)	Democratic (Hubbell)	Other	Rep.-Dem. Plurality	Percentage Total Vote Rep.	Total Vote Dem.	Major Vote Rep.	Major Vote Dem.
15,679	MADISON	7,658	4,754	2,739	165	2,015 R	62.1%	35.8%	63.4%	36.6%
22,381	MAHASKA	8,596	6,007	2,409	180	3,598 R	69.9%	28.0%	71.4%	28.6%
33,309	MARION	15,051	9,479	5,249	323	4,230 R	63.0%	34.9%	64.4%	35.6%
40,648	MARSHALL	14,652	7,243	7,095	314	148 R	49.4%	48.4%	50.5%	49.5%
15,059	MILLS	6,325	3,945	2,191	189	1,754 R	62.4%	34.6%	64.3%	35.7%
10,776	MITCHELL	4,527	2,711	1,704	112	1,007 R	59.9%	37.6%	61.4%	38.6%
9,243	MONONA	3,797	2,556	1,171	70	1,385 R	67.3%	30.8%	68.6%	31.4%
7,970	MONROE	3,161	2,053	1,061	47	992 R	64.9%	33.6%	65.9%	34.1%
10,740	MONTGOMERY	3,966	2,648	1,220	98	1,428 R	66.8%	30.8%	68.5%	31.5%
42,745	MUSCATINE	14,981	7,535	7,081	365	454 R	50.3%	47.3%	51.6%	48.4%
14,398	O'BRIEN	5,851	4,472	1,296	83	3,176 R	76.4%	22.2%	77.5%	22.5%
6,462	OSCEOLA	2,431	1,922	481	28	1,441 R	79.1%	19.8%	80.0%	20.0%
15,932	PAGE	5,635	3,702	1,839	94	1,863 R	65.7%	32.6%	66.8%	33.2%
9,421	PALO ALTO	3,788	2,320	1,398	70	922 R	61.2%	36.9%	62.4%	37.6%
24,986	PLYMOUTH	10,829	7,941	2,717	171	5,224 R	73.3%	25.1%	74.5%	25.5%
7,310	POCAHONTAS	3,125	2,091	962	72	1,129 R	66.9%	30.8%	68.5%	31.5%
430,640	POLK	206,881	82,473	120,257	4,151	37,784 D	39.9%	58.1%	40.7%	59.3%
93,158	POTTAWATTAMIE	34,129	19,036	14,234	859	4,802 R	55.8%	41.7%	57.2%	42.8%
18,914	POWESHIEK	8,315	4,160	3,998	157	162 R	50.0%	48.1%	51.0%	49.0%
5,131	RINGGOLD	2,316	1,476	804	36	672 R	63.7%	34.7%	64.7%	35.3%
10,350	SAC	4,310	2,965	1,253	92	1,712 R	68.8%	29.1%	70.3%	29.7%
165,224	SCOTT	69,255	32,750	35,147	1,358	2,397 D	47.3%	50.8%	48.2%	51.8%
12,167	SHELBY	5,069	3,537	1,450	82	2,087 R	69.8%	28.6%	70.9%	29.1%
33,704	SIOUX	14,942	12,840	1,955	147	10,885 R	85.9%	13.1%	86.8%	13.2%
89,542	STORY	42,824	16,535	25,155	1,134	8,620 D	38.6%	58.7%	39.7%	60.3%
17,767	TAMA	7,328	3,931	3,238	159	693 R	53.6%	44.2%	54.8%	45.2%
6,317	TAYLOR	2,445	1,632	759	54	873 R	66.7%	31.0%	68.3%	31.7%
12,534	UNION	4,896	2,949	1,835	112	1,114 R	60.2%	37.5%	61.6%	38.4%
7,570	VAN BUREN	2,922	2,026	839	57	1,187 R	69.3%	28.7%	70.7%	29.3%
35,625	WAPELLO	12,058	6,313	5,480	265	833 R	52.4%	45.4%	53.5%	46.5%
46,225	WARREN	24,261	12,801	10,942	518	1,859 R	52.8%	45.1%	53.9%	46.1%
21,704	WASHINGTON	9,162	5,189	3,746	227	1,443 R	56.6%	40.9%	58.1%	41.9%
6,403	WAYNE	2,405	1,624	722	59	902 R	67.5%	30.0%	69.2%	30.8%
38,013	WEBSTER	14,149	7,727	6,132	290	1,595 R	54.6%	43.3%	55.8%	44.2%
10,866	WINNEBAGO	4,632	2,726	1,788	118	938 R	58.9%	38.6%	60.4%	39.6%
21,056	WINNESHIEK	9,873	4,841	4,785	247	56 R	49.0%	48.5%	50.3%	49.7%
102,172	WOODBURY	35,430	19,630	15,024	776	4,606 R	55.4%	42.4%	56.6%	43.4%
7,598	WORTH	3,533	2,043	1,382	108	661 R	57.8%	39.1%	59.6%	40.4%
13,229	WRIGHT	4,947	3,049	1,788	110	1,261 R	61.6%	36.1%	63.0%	37.0%
3,046,355	*TOTAL*	*1,327,638*	*667,275*	*630,986*	*29,377*	*36,289 R*	*50.3%*	*47.5%*	*51.4%*	*48.6%*

IOWA

HOUSE OF REPRESENTATIVES

CD	Year	Total Vote	Republican Vote	Republican Candidate	Democratic Vote	Democratic Candidate	Other Vote	Rep.-Dem. Plurality	Percentage Total Vote Rep.	Total Vote Dem.	Major Vote Rep.	Major Vote Dem.
1	2018	334,243	153,442	BLUM, ROD*	170,342	FINKENAUER, ABBY	10,459	16,900 D	45.9%	51.0%	47.4%	52.6%
1	2016	384,977	206,903	BLUM, ROD*	177,403	VERNON, MONICA	671	29,500 R	53.7%	46.1%	53.8%	46.2%
1	2014	289,306	147,762	BLUM, ROD	141,145	MURPHY, PAT	399	6,617 R	51.1%	48.8%	51.1%	48.9%
1	2012	390,849	162,465	LANGE, BENJAMIN M.	222,422	BRALEY, BRUCE*	5,962	59,957 D	41.6%	56.9%	42.2%	57.8%

IOWA

HOUSE OF REPRESENTATIVES

			Republican		Democratic				Percentage			
									Total Vote		Major Vote	
CD	Year	Total Vote	Vote	Candidate	Vote	Candidate	Other Vote	Rep.-Dem. Plurality	Rep.	Dem.	Rep.	Dem.
2	2018	312,913	133,287	PETERS, CHRISTOPHER	171,446	LOEBSACK, DAVID*	8,180	38,159 D	42.6%	54.8%	43.7%	56.3%
2	2016	370,032	170,933	PETERS, CHRISTOPHER	198,571	LOEBSACK, DAVID*	528	27,638 D	46.2%	53.7%	46.3%	53.7%
2	2014	273,329	129,455	MILLER-MEEKS, MARIANNETTE	143,431	LOEBSACK, DAVID*	443	13,976 D	47.4%	52.5%	47.4%	52.6%
2	2012	381,275	161,977	ARCHER, JOHN	211,863	LOEBSACK, DAVID*	7,435	49,886 D	42.5%	55.6%	43.3%	56.7%
3	2018	356,241	167,933	YOUNG, DAVID*	175,642	AXNE, CINDY	12,666	7,709 D	47.1%	49.3%	48.9%	51.1%
3	2016	390,287	208,598	YOUNG, DAVID*	155,002	MOWRER, JIM	26,687	53,596 R	53.4%	39.7%	57.4%	42.6%
3	2014	282,066	148,814	YOUNG, DAVID	119,109	APPEL, STACI	14,143	29,705 R	52.8%	42.2%	55.5%	44.5%
3	2012	386,842	202,000	LATHAM, TOM*	168,632	BOSWELL, LEONARD L.	16,210	33,368 R	52.2%	43.6%	54.5%	45.5%
4	2018	313,251	157,676	KING, STEVE*	147,246	SCHOLTEN, JAMES	8,329	10,430 R	50.3%	47.0%	51.7%	48.3%
4	2016	370,259	226,719	KING, STEVE*	142,993	WEAVER, KIM	547	83,726 R	61.2%	38.6%	61.3%	38.7%
4	2014	275,633	169,834	KING, STEVE*	105,504	MOWRER, JIM	295	64,330 R	61.6%	38.3%	61.7%	38.3%
4	2012	377,883	200,063	KING, STEVE*	169,470	VILSACK, CHRISTIE	8,350	30,593 R	52.9%	44.8%	54.1%	45.9%
TOTAL	*2018*	*1,316,648*	*612,338*		*664,676*		*39,634*	*52,338 D*	*46.5%*	*50.5%*	*48.0%*	*52.0%*
TOTAL	*2016*	*1,515,555*	*813,153*		*673,969*		*28,433*	*139,184 R*	*53.7%*	*44.5%*	*54.7%*	*45.3%*
TOTAL	*2014*	*1,120,334*	*595,865*		*509,189*		*15,280*	*86,676 R*	*53.2%*	*45.4%*	*53.9%*	*46.1%*
TOTAL	*2012*	*1,536,849*	*726,505*		*772,387*		*37,957*	*45,882 D*	*47.3%*	*50.3%*	*48.5%*	*51.5%*

Note: An asterisk (*) denotes incumbent.

IOWA

GENERAL AND PRIMARY ELECTIONS

2018 GENERAL ELECTIONS: OTHER VOTES

Governor Other vote was 21,426 Libertarian (Jake Porter), 7,463 Clear Water Party of Iowa (Gary Siegwarth), 488 Write-in (Write-In)

House Other vote was:

CD 1 10,285 Libertarian (Troy Hageman), 174 Write-in (Write-In)

CD 2 6,181 Libertarian (Mark Strauss), 1,837 No Party (Daniel Clark), 162 Write-in (Write-In)

CD 3 7,267 Libertarian (Bryan Holder), 2,015 Legal Medical Now (Mark Elworth), 1,888 Green (Paul Knupp), 1,301 No Party (Joe Grandanette), 195 Write-in (Write-In)

CD 4 6,161 Libertarian (Charles Aldrich), 1,962 No Party (Edward Peterson), 206 Write-in (Write-In)

2018 PRIMARY ELECTIONS: SUPPLEMENTARY INFORMATION

Primary June 5, 2018

Registration (as of June 1, 2018 — includes 166,329 inactive registrants) 2,130,851

Republican	639,348
Democratic	594,198
Libertarian	10,129
No Party	717,995
Other	2,852

Primary Type Semi-open—Registered Democrats and Republicans could vote only in their party's primary, although any registered voter (including those not affiliated with either party) could participate in either party's primary by changing his or her registration to that party on primary day.

IOWA

GENERAL AND PRIMARY ELECTIONS

	REPUBLICAN PRIMARIES			DEMOCRATIC PRIMARIES		
Governor	Reynolds, Kim*	94,118	98.6%	Hubbell, Fred	99,245	55.4%
	Write-In	1,307	1.4%	Glasson, Cathy	36,815	20.6%
				Norris, John	20,498	11.4%
				McGuire, Andrea "Andy"	9,404	5.2%
				Boulton, Nate	9,082	5.1%
				Wilburn, Ross	3,880	2.2%
				Write-In	200	0.1%
	TOTAL	*95,425*		*TOTAL*	*179,124*	
Congressional District 1	Blum, Rod*	14,737	98.9%	Finkenauer, Abby	29,745	66.8%
	Write-In	167	1.1%	Heckroth, Thomas	8,516	19.1%
				Rowe, Courtney	3,381	7.6%
				Ramsey, George	2,837	6.4%
				Write-In	50	0.1%
	TOTAL	*14,904*		*TOTAL*	*44,529*	
Congressional District 2	Peters, Christopher	18,056	87.5%	Loebsack, David*	42,378	99.3%
	Caligiuri, Ginny	2,389	11.6%	Write-In	314	0.7%
	Write-In	181	0.9%			
	TOTAL	*20,626*		*TOTAL*	*42,692*	
Congressional District 3	Young, David*	21,712	98.9%	Axne, Cindy	32,910	57.8%
	Write-In	234	1.1%	Mauro, Eddie	15,006	26.4%
				D'Alessandro, Pete	8,874	15.6%
				Write-In	150	0.3%
	TOTAL	*21,946*		*TOTAL*	*56,940*	
Congressional District 4	King, Steve*	28,053	74.7%	Scholten, James	14,733	51.3%
	Hanson, Cyndi	9,437	25.1%	Jacobsen, Leann	9,176	31.9%
	Write-In	44	0.1%	Paschen, John	4,806	16.7%
				Write-In	29	0.1%
	TOTAL	*37,534*		*TOTAL*	*28,744*	

Note: An asterisk (*) denotes incumbent.

KANSAS

Congressional districts first established for elections held in 2012
4 members

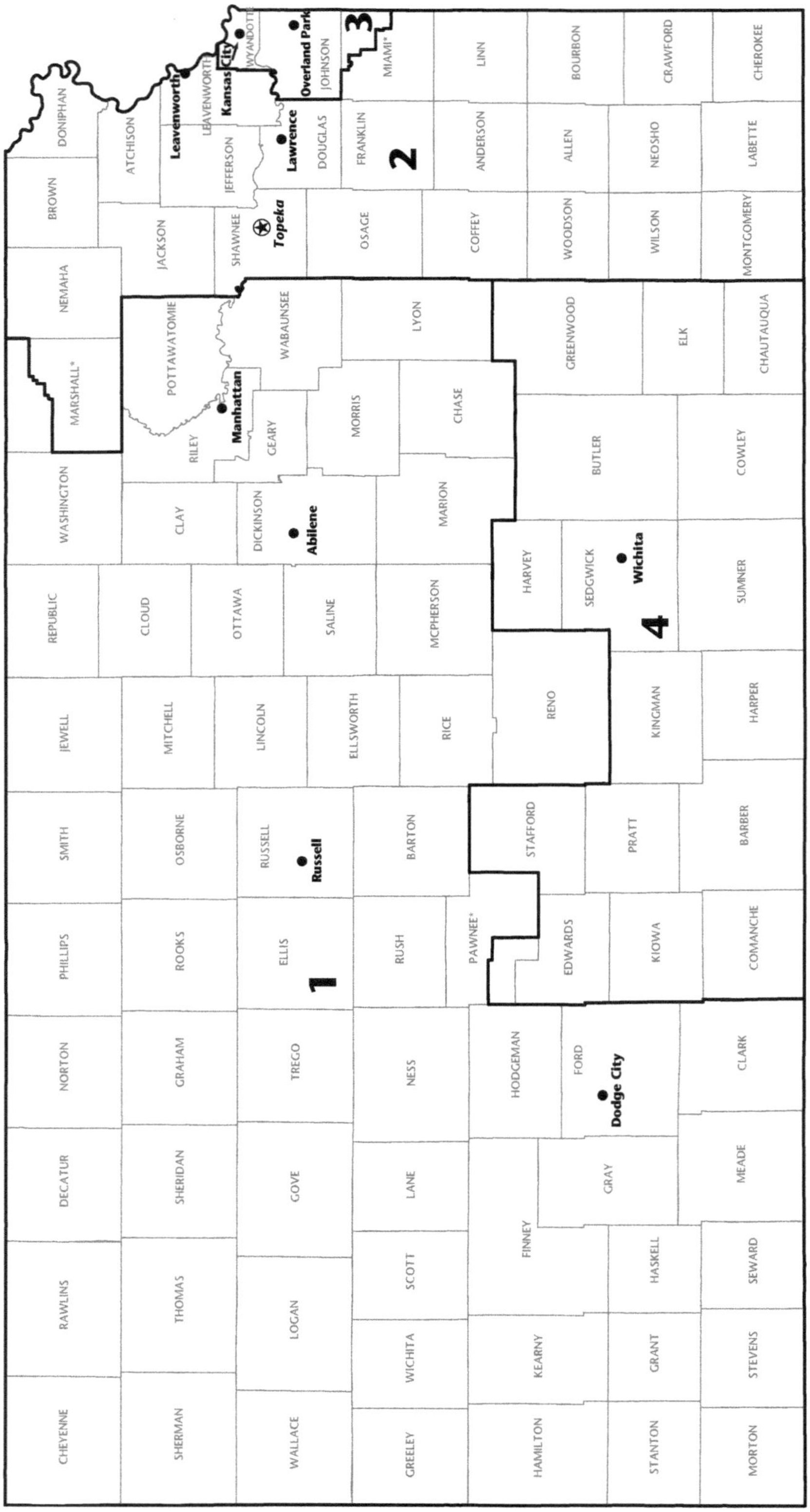

* Asterisk indicates a county whose boundaries include parts of two or more congressional districts.

KANSAS

GOVERNOR

Laura Kelly (D). Elected 2018 to a four-year term.

SENATORS (2 Republicans)

Jerry Moran (R). Re-elected 2016 to a six-year term. Previously elected 2010.

Pat Roberts (R). Re-elected 2014 to a six-year term. Previously elected 2008, 2002, 1996.

REPRESENTATIVES (3 Republicans, 1 Democrat)

1. Roger Marshall (R)
2. Steve Watkins (R)
3. Sharice Davids (D)
4. Ron Estes (R)

POSTWAR VOTE FOR PRESIDENT

		Republican		Democratic				Percentage			
								Total Vote		Major Vote	
Year	Total Vote	Vote	Candidate	Vote	Candidate	Other Vote	Rep.-Dem. Plurality	Rep.	Dem.	Rep.	Dem.
2016**	1,184,402	671,018	Trump, Donald J.	427,005	Clinton, Hillary Rodham	86,379	244,013 R	56.7%	36.1%	61.1%	38.9%
2012	1,159,971	692,634	Romney, W. Mitt	440,726	Obama, Barack H.*	26,611	251,908 R	59.7%	38.0%	61.1%	38.9%
2008	1,235,872	699,655	McCain, John S. III	514,765	Obama, Barack H.	21,452	184,890 R	56.6%	41.7%	57.6%	42.4%
2004	1,187,756	736,456	Bush, George W.*	434,993	Kerry, John F.	16,307	301,463 R	62.0%	36.6%	62.9%	37.1%
2000**	1,072,218	622,332	Bush, George W.	399,276	Gore, Albert Jr.	50,610	223,056 R	58.0%	37.2%	60.9%	39.1%
1996**	1,074,300	583,245	Dole, Robert "Bob"	387,659	Clinton, Bill*	103,396	195,586 R	54.3%	36.1%	60.1%	39.9%
1992**	1,157,335	449,951	Bush, George H.*	390,434	Clinton, Bill	316,950	59,517 R	38.9%	33.7%	53.5%	46.5%
1988	993,044	554,049	Bush, George H.	422,636	Dukakis, Michael S.	16,359	131,413 R	55.8%	42.6%	56.7%	43.3%
1984	1,021,991	677,296	Reagan, Ronald*	333,149	Mondale, Walter F.	11,546	344,147 R	66.3%	32.6%	67.0%	33.0%
1980**	979,795	566,812	Reagan, Ronald	326,150	Carter, Jimmy*	86,833	240,662 R	57.9%	33.3%	63.5%	36.5%
1976	957,845	502,752	Ford, Gerald R.*	430,421	Carter, Jimmy	24,672	72,331 R	52.5%	44.9%	53.9%	46.1%
1972	916,095	619,812	Nixon, Richard M.*	270,287	McGovern, George S.	25,996	349,525 R	67.7%	29.5%	69.6%	30.4%
1968**	872,783	478,674	Nixon, Richard M.	302,996	Humphrey, Hubert Horatio Jr.	91,113	175,678 R	54.8%	34.7%	61.2%	38.8%
1964	857,901	386,579	Goldwater, Barry M. Sr.	464,028	Johnson, Lyndon B.*	7,294	77,449 D	45.1%	54.1%	45.4%	54.6%
1960	928,825	561,474	Nixon, Richard M.	363,213	Kennedy, John F.	4,138	198,261 R	60.4%	39.1%	60.7%	39.3%
1956	866,243	566,878	Eisenhower, Dwight D.*	296,317	Stevenson, Adlai E. II	3,048	270,561 R	65.4%	34.2%	65.7%	34.3%
1952	896,166	616,302	Eisenhower, Dwight D.	273,296	Stevenson, Adlai E. II	6,568	343,006 R	68.8%	30.5%	69.3%	30.7%
1948	788,819	423,039	Dewey, Thomas E.	351,902	Truman, Harry S.*	13,878	71,137 R	53.6%	44.6%	54.6%	45.4%

Note: An asterisk (*) denotes incumbent. **In past elections, the other vote included: 2016 - 55,406 Libertarian (Gary Johnson); 2000 - 36,086 Green (Ralph Nader); 1996 - 92,639 Reform (Ross Perot); 1992 - 312,358 Independent (Perot); 1980 - 68,231 Independent (John Anderson); 1968 - 88,921 American Independent (George Wallace).

KANSAS

POSTWAR VOTE FOR GOVERNOR

		Republican		Democratic				Percentage			
								Total Vote		Major Vote	
Year	Total Vote	Vote	Candidate	Vote	Candidate	Other Vote	Rep.-Dem. Plurality	Rep.	Dem.	Rep.	Dem.
2018	1,055,060	453,030	Kobach, Kris W.	506,509	Kelly, Laura	95,521	53,479 D	42.9%	48.0%	47.2%	52.8%
2014	869,502	433,196	Brownback, Sam*	401,100	Davis, Paul	35,206	32,096 R	49.8%	46.1%	51.9%	48.1%
2010	838,790	530,760	Brownback, Sam	270,166	Holland, Tom	37,864	260,594 R	63.3%	32.2%	66.3%	33.7%
2006	849,700	343,586	Barnett, Jim	491,993	Sebelius, Kathleen*	14,121	148,407 D	40.4%	57.9%	41.1%	58.9%
2002	835,692	376,830	Shallenburger, Tim	441,858	Sebelius, Kathleen	17,004	65,028 D	45.1%	52.9%	46.0%	54.0%
1998	742,665	544,882	Graves, Bill*	168,243	Sawyer, Tom	29,540	376,639 R	73.4%	22.7%	76.4%	23.6%
1994	821,030	526,113	Graves, Bill	294,733	Slattery, Jim	184	231,380 R	64.1%	35.9%	64.1%	35.9%
1990	783,325	333,589	Hayden, Mike*	380,609	Finney, Joan	69,127	47,020 D	42.6%	48.6%	46.7%	53.3%
1986	840,605	436,267	Hayden, Mike	404,338	Docking, Thomas R.		31,929 R	51.9%	48.1%	51.9%	48.1%
1982	763,263	339,356	Hardage, Sam	405,772	Carlin, John*	18,135	66,416 D	44.5%	53.2%	45.5%	54.5%
1978	736,246	348,015	Bennett, Robert F.*	363,835	Carlin, John	24,396	15,820 D	47.3%	49.4%	48.9%	51.1%
1974**	783,875	387,792	Bennett, Robert F.	384,115	Miller, Vern	11,968	3,677 R	49.5%	49.0%	50.2%	49.8%
1972	921,550	341,438	Kay, Morris	571,256	Docking, Robert*	8,856	229,818 D	37.1%	62.0%	37.4%	62.6%
1970	745,196	333,227	Frizzell, Kent	404,611	Docking, Robert*	7,358	71,384 D	44.7%	54.3%	45.2%	54.8%
1968	862,473	410,673	Harman, Rick	447,269	Docking, Robert*	4,531	36,596 D	47.6%	51.9%	47.9%	52.1%
1966	692,955	304,325	Avery, William H.*	380,030	Docking, Robert	8,600	75,705 D	43.9%	54.8%	44.5%	55.5%
1964	850,414	432,667	Avery, William H.	400,264	Wiles, Harry G.	17,483	32,403 R	50.9%	47.1%	51.9%	48.1%
1962	638,798	341,257	Anderson, John Jr.*	291,285	Saffels, Dale E.	6,256	49,972 R	53.4%	45.6%	54.0%	46.0%
1960	922,522	511,534	Anderson, John Jr.	402,261	Docking, George*	8,727	109,273 R	55.4%	43.6%	56.0%	44.0%
1958	735,939	313,036	Reed, Clyde M.	415,506	Docking, George*	7,397	102,470 D	42.5%	56.5%	43.0%	57.0%
1956	864,935	364,340	Shaw, Warren W.	479,701	Docking, George	20,894	115,361 D	42.1%	55.5%	43.2%	56.8%
1954	622,633	329,868	Hall, Fred	286,218	Docking, George	6,547	43,650 R	53.0%	46.0%	53.5%	46.5%
1952	872,139	491,338	Arn, Edward F.*	363,482	Rooney, Charles	17,319	127,856 R	56.3%	41.7%	57.5%	42.5%
1950	619,310	333,001	Arn, Edward F.	275,494	Anderson, Kenneth T.	10,815	57,507 R	53.8%	44.5%	54.7%	45.3%
1948	760,407	433,396	Carlson, Frank*	307,485	Carpenter, Randolph	19,526	125,911 R	57.0%	40.4%	58.5%	41.5%
1946	577,694	309,064	Carlson, Frank	254,283	Woodring, Harry H.	14,347	54,781 R	53.5%	44.0%	54.9%	45.1%

Note: An asterisk (*) denotes incumbent. **The term of office of Kansas's governor was increased from two to four years effective with the 1974 election.

POSTWAR VOTE FOR SENATOR

		Republican		Democratic				Percentage			
								Total Vote		Major Vote	
Year	Total Vote	Vote	Candidate	Vote	Candidate	Other Vote	Rep.-Dem. Plurality	Rep.	Dem.	Rep.	Dem.
2016	1,177,922	732,376	Moran, Jerry*	379,740	Wiesner, Patrick	65,806	352,636 R	62.2%	32.2%	65.9%	34.1%
2014**	866,191	460,350	Roberts, Pat*			405,841	460,350 R	53.1%		100.0%	
2010	837,692	587,175	Moran, Jerry	220,971	Johnston, Lisa	29,546	366,204 R	70.1%	26.4%	72.7%	27.3%
2008	1,210,690	727,121	Roberts, Pat*	441,399	Slattery, Jim	42,170	285,722 R	60.1%	36.5%	62.2%	37.8%
2004	1,129,022	780,863	Brownback, Sam*	310,337	Jones, Lee	37,822	470,526 R	69.2%	27.5%	71.6%	28.4%
2002	776,850	641,075	Roberts, Pat*			135,775	641,075 R	82.5%		100.0%	
1998	727,236	474,639	Brownback, Sam*	229,718	Feleciano, Paul Jr.	22,879	244,921 R	65.3%	31.6%	67.4%	32.6%
1996	1,052,300	652,677	Roberts, Pat	362,380	Thompson, Sally	37,243	290,297 R	62.0%	34.4%	64.3%	35.7%
1996S**	1,064,716	574,021	Brownback, Sam	461,344	Docking, Jill	29,351	112,677 R	53.9%	43.3%	55.4%	44.6%
1992	1,126,447	706,246	Dole, Robert "Bob"*	349,525	O'Dell, Gloria	70,676	356,721 R	62.7%	31.0%	66.9%	33.1%
1990	786,235	578,605	Kassebaum, Nancy Landon*	207,491	Williams, Dick	139	371,114 R	73.6%	26.4%	73.6%	26.4%
1986	823,566	576,902	Dole, Robert "Bob"*	246,664	MacDonald, Guy		330,238 R	70.0%	30.0%	70.0%	30.0%
1984	996,729	757,402	Kassebaum, Nancy Landon*	211,664	Maher, James R.	27,663	545,738 R	76.0%	21.2%	78.2%	21.8%
1980	938,957	598,686	Dole, Robert "Bob"*	340,271	Simpson, John		258,415 R	63.8%	36.2%	63.8%	36.2%
1978	748,839	403,354	Kassebaum, Nancy Landon	317,602	Roy, William R.	27,883	85,752 R	53.9%	42.4%	55.9%	44.1%
1974	794,437	403,983	Dole, Robert "Bob"*	390,451	Roy, William R.	3	13,532 R	50.9%	49.1%	50.9%	49.1%
1972	871,702	622,591	Pearson, James B.*	200,764	Tetzlaff, Arch O.	48,347	421,827 R	71.4%	23.0%	75.6%	24.4%
1968	817,096	490,911	Dole, Robert "Bob"	315,911	Robinson, William I.	10,274	175,000 R	60.1%	38.7%	60.8%	39.2%
1966	671,345	350,077	Pearson, James B.*	303,223	Breeding, J. Floyd	18,045	46,854 R	52.1%	45.2%	53.6%	46.4%
1962	622,232	388,500	Carlson, Frank*	223,630	Smith, K. L.	10,102	164,870 R	62.4%	35.9%	63.5%	36.5%
1962S**	613,250	344,689	Pearson, James B.*	260,756	Aylward, Paul L.	7,805	83,933 R	56.2%	42.5%	56.9%	43.1%
1960	888,592	485,499	Schoeppel, Andrew F.*	388,895	Theis, Frank	14,198	96,604 R	54.6%	43.8%	55.5%	44.5%
1956	825,280	477,822	Carlson, Frank*	333,939	Hart, George	13,519	143,883 R	57.9%	40.5%	58.9%	41.1%
1954	618,063	348,144	Schoeppel, Andrew F.*	258,575	McGill, George	11,344	89,569 R	56.3%	41.8%	57.4%	42.6%
1950	619,104	335,880	Carlson, Frank*	271,365	Aiken, Paul	11,859	64,515 R	54.3%	43.8%	55.3%	44.7%
1948	716,342	393,412	Schoeppel, Andrew F.	305,987	McGill, George	16,943	87,425 R	54.9%	42.7%	56.3%	43.7%

Note: An asterisk (*) denotes incumbent. **In past elections, the other vote included: 2014 - 368,372 Independent (Greg Orman). One of the 1996 and 1962 elections was for a short term to fill a vacancy. The Democratic Party did not run a candidate in the 2002 and 2014 Senate elections.

KANSAS

GOVERNOR 2018

2010 Census Population	County	Total Vote	Republican (Kobach)	Democratic (Kelly)	Other	Rep.-Dem. Plurality	Percentage: Total Vote Rep.	Total Vote Dem.	Major Vote Rep.	Major Vote Dem.
13,371	ALLEN	4,436	2,292	1,795	349	497 R	51.7%	40.5%	56.1%	43.9%
8,102	ANDERSON	2,765	1,596	957	212	639 R	57.7%	34.6%	62.5%	37.5%
16,924	ATCHISON	5,472	2,558	2,447	467	111 R	46.7%	44.7%	51.1%	48.9%
4,861	BARBER	1,757	1,155	396	206	759 R	65.7%	22.5%	74.5%	25.5%
27,674	BARTON	8,587	4,841	2,645	1,101	2,196 R	56.4%	30.8%	64.7%	35.3%
15,173	BOURBON	4,933	2,970	1,576	387	1,394 R	60.2%	31.9%	65.3%	34.7%
9,984	BROWN	3,388	1,836	1,133	419	703 R	54.2%	33.4%	61.8%	38.2%
65,880	BUTLER	23,967	12,822	8,651	2,494	4,171 R	53.5%	36.1%	59.7%	40.3%
2,790	CHASE	1,218	653	440	125	213 R	53.6%	36.1%	59.7%	40.3%
3,669	CHAUTAUQUA	1,135	808	252	75	556 R	71.2%	22.2%	76.2%	23.8%
21,603	CHEROKEE	6,991	4,284	2,314	393	1,970 R	61.3%	33.1%	64.9%	35.1%
2,726	CHEYENNE	1,087	733	248	106	485 R	67.4%	22.8%	74.7%	25.3%
2,215	CLARK	849	521	181	147	340 R	61.4%	21.3%	74.2%	25.8%
8,535	CLAY	3,176	1,743	1,040	393	703 R	54.9%	32.7%	62.6%	37.4%
9,533	CLOUD	3,243	1,744	1,092	407	652 R	53.8%	33.7%	61.5%	38.5%
8,601	COFFEY	3,475	1,926	1,082	467	844 R	55.4%	31.1%	64.0%	36.0%
1,891	COMANCHE	715	453	170	92	283 R	63.4%	23.8%	72.7%	27.3%
36,311	COWLEY	10,529	5,165	4,221	1,143	944 R	49.1%	40.1%	55.0%	45.0%
39,134	CRAWFORD	12,878	5,662	6,294	922	632 D	44.0%	48.9%	47.4%	52.6%
2,961	DECATUR	1,129	736	287	106	449 R	65.2%	25.4%	71.9%	28.1%
19,754	DICKINSON	6,762	3,790	2,265	707	1,525 R	56.0%	33.5%	62.6%	37.4%
7,945	DONIPHAN	2,599	1,699	749	151	950 R	65.4%	28.8%	69.4%	30.6%
110,826	DOUGLAS	49,518	10,154	36,678	2,686	26,524 D	20.5%	74.1%	21.7%	78.3%
3,037	EDWARDS	1,142	692	307	143	385 R	60.6%	26.9%	69.3%	30.7%
2,882	ELK	1,057	669	277	111	392 R	63.3%	26.2%	70.7%	29.3%
28,452	ELLIS	10,447	5,138	4,243	1,066	895 R	49.2%	40.6%	54.8%	45.2%
6,497	ELLSWORTH	2,301	1,168	840	293	328 R	50.8%	36.5%	58.2%	41.8%
36,776	FINNEY	8,680	3,891	3,192	1,597	699 R	44.8%	36.8%	54.9%	45.1%
33,848	FORD	7,115	3,574	2,582	959	992 R	50.2%	36.3%	58.1%	41.9%
25,992	FRANKLIN	9,376	4,742	3,806	828	936 R	50.6%	40.6%	55.5%	44.5%
34,362	GEARY	6,169	2,769	2,703	697	66 R	44.9%	43.8%	50.6%	49.4%
2,695	GOVE	1,096	720	256	120	464 R	65.7%	23.4%	73.8%	26.2%
2,597	GRAHAM	1,080	671	284	125	387 R	62.1%	26.3%	70.3%	29.7%
7,829	GRANT	1,835	1,096	451	288	645 R	59.7%	24.6%	70.8%	29.2%
6,006	GRAY	1,791	1,138	347	306	791 R	63.5%	19.4%	76.6%	23.4%
1,247	GREELEY	498	313	118	67	195 R	62.9%	23.7%	72.6%	27.4%
6,689	GREENWOOD	2,135	1,214	653	268	561 R	56.9%	30.6%	65.0%	35.0%
2,690	HAMILTON	630	373	166	91	207 R	59.2%	26.3%	69.2%	30.8%
6,034	HARPER	2,046	1,243	570	233	673 R	60.8%	27.9%	68.6%	31.4%
34,684	HARVEY	13,722	5,872	6,450	1,400	578 D	42.8%	47.0%	47.7%	52.3%
4,256	HASKELL	1,134	681	287	166	394 R	60.1%	25.3%	70.4%	29.6%
1,916	HODGEMAN	883	597	167	119	430 R	67.6%	18.9%	78.1%	21.9%
13,462	JACKSON	5,309	2,565	2,088	656	477 R	48.3%	39.3%	55.1%	44.9%
19,126	JEFFERSON	7,562	3,485	3,306	771	179 R	46.1%	43.7%	51.3%	48.7%
3,077	JEWELL	1,183	765	294	124	471 R	64.7%	24.9%	72.2%	27.8%
544,179	JOHNSON	271,017	102,813	148,082	20,122	45,269 D	37.9%	54.6%	41.0%	59.0%
3,977	KEARNY	1,095	687	286	122	401 R	62.7%	26.1%	70.6%	29.4%
7,858	KINGMAN	2,993	1,764	891	338	873 R	58.9%	29.8%	66.4%	33.6%
2,553	KIOWA	944	615	218	111	397 R	65.1%	23.1%	73.8%	26.2%
21,607	LABETTE	6,341	3,273	2,646	422	627 R	51.6%	41.7%	55.3%	44.7%
1,750	LANE	719	437	174	108	263 R	60.8%	24.2%	71.5%	28.5%
76,227	LEAVENWORTH	26,340	12,379	11,802	2,159	577 R	47.0%	44.8%	51.2%	48.8%
3,241	LINCOLN	1,252	769	383	100	386 R	61.4%	30.6%	66.8%	33.2%
9,656	LINN	3,767	2,401	1,091	275	1,310 R	63.7%	29.0%	68.8%	31.2%
2,756	LOGAN	1,162	785	255	122	530 R	67.6%	21.9%	75.5%	24.5%
33,690	LYON	10,899	3,920	5,679	1,300	1,759 D	36.0%	52.1%	40.8%	59.2%
12,660	MARION	4,862	2,564	1,785	513	779 R	52.7%	36.7%	59.0%	41.0%
10,117	MARSHALL	3,488	1,581	1,449	458	132 R	45.3%	41.5%	52.2%	47.8%
29,180	MCPHERSON	11,349	5,832	4,440	1,077	1,392 R	51.4%	39.1%	56.8%	43.2%
4,575	MEADE	1,394	914	311	169	603 R	65.6%	22.3%	74.6%	25.4%

KANSAS

GOVERNOR 2018

2010 Census Population	County	Total Vote	Republican (Kobach)	Democratic (Kelly)	Other	Rep.-Dem. Plurality	Percentage Total Vote Rep.	Percentage Total Vote Dem.	Percentage Major Vote Rep.	Percentage Major Vote Dem.
32,787	MIAMI	13,100	7,160	4,842	1,098	2,318 R	54.7%	37.0%	59.7%	40.3%
6,373	MITCHELL	2,499	1,375	876	248	499 R	55.0%	35.1%	61.1%	38.9%
35,471	MONTGOMERY	9,786	6,133	2,931	722	3,202 R	62.7%	30.0%	67.7%	32.3%
5,923	MORRIS	2,250	1,106	898	246	208 R	49.2%	39.9%	55.2%	44.8%
3,233	MORTON	907	626	184	97	442 R	69.0%	20.3%	77.3%	22.7%
10,178	NEMAHA	4,580	2,605	1,415	560	1,190 R	56.9%	30.9%	64.8%	35.2%
16,512	NEOSHO	5,440	2,930	2,069	441	861 R	53.9%	38.0%	58.6%	41.4%
3,107	NESS	1,178	808	250	120	558 R	68.6%	21.2%	76.4%	23.6%
5,671	NORTON	1,891	1,187	511	193	676 R	62.8%	27.0%	69.9%	30.1%
16,295	OSAGE	6,306	2,964	2,525	817	439 R	47.0%	40.0%	54.0%	46.0%
3,858	OSBORNE	1,498	907	413	178	494 R	60.5%	27.6%	68.7%	31.3%
6,091	OTTAWA	2,438	1,497	669	272	828 R	61.4%	27.4%	69.1%	30.9%
6,973	PAWNEE	2,242	1,145	837	260	308 R	51.1%	37.3%	57.8%	42.2%
5,642	PHILLIPS	2,170	1,419	518	233	901 R	65.4%	23.9%	73.3%	26.7%
21,604	POTTAWATOMIE	9,821	5,384	3,344	1,093	2,040 R	54.8%	34.0%	61.7%	38.3%
9,656	PRATT	3,269	1,701	1,221	347	480 R	52.0%	37.4%	58.2%	41.8%
2,519	RAWLINS	1,216	771	333	112	438 R	63.4%	27.4%	69.8%	30.2%
64,511	RENO	21,022	9,892	8,799	2,331	1,093 R	47.1%	41.9%	52.9%	47.1%
4,980	REPUBLIC	2,025	1,245	592	188	653 R	61.5%	29.2%	67.8%	32.2%
10,083	RICE	3,088	1,729	963	396	766 R	56.0%	31.2%	64.2%	35.8%
71,115	RILEY	19,862	6,514	11,280	2,068	4,766 D	32.8%	56.8%	36.6%	63.4%
5,181	ROOKS	2,151	1,409	506	236	903 R	65.5%	23.5%	73.6%	26.4%
3,307	RUSH	1,304	754	403	147	351 R	57.8%	30.9%	65.2%	34.8%
6,970	RUSSELL	2,687	1,564	783	340	781 R	58.2%	29.1%	66.6%	33.4%
55,606	SALINE	18,379	8,384	8,181	1,814	203 R	45.6%	44.5%	50.6%	49.4%
4,936	SCOTT	1,864	1,244	324	296	920 R	66.7%	17.4%	79.3%	20.7%
498,365	SEDGWICK	168,074	70,879	81,011	16,184	10,132 D	42.2%	48.2%	46.7%	53.3%
22,952	SEWARD	3,815	2,009	1,394	412	615 R	52.7%	36.5%	59.0%	41.0%
177,934	SHAWNEE	70,741	23,933	40,936	5,872	17,003 D	33.8%	57.9%	36.9%	63.1%
2,556	SHERIDAN	1,138	795	219	124	576 R	69.9%	19.2%	78.4%	21.6%
6,010	SHERMAN	2,103	1,376	510	217	866 R	65.4%	24.3%	73.0%	27.0%
3,853	SMITH	1,614	1,074	418	122	656 R	66.5%	25.9%	72.0%	28.0%
4,437	STAFFORD	1,620	950	458	212	492 R	58.6%	28.3%	67.5%	32.5%
2,235	STANTON	598	376	148	74	228 R	62.9%	24.7%	71.8%	28.2%
5,724	STEVENS	1,517	1,042	274	201	768 R	68.7%	18.1%	79.2%	20.8%
24,132	SUMNER	7,994	4,203	2,827	964	1,376 R	52.6%	35.4%	59.8%	40.2%
7,900	THOMAS	3,027	1,856	813	358	1,043 R	61.3%	26.9%	69.5%	30.5%
3,001	TREGO	1,269	755	348	166	407 R	59.5%	27.4%	68.4%	31.6%
7,053	WABAUNSEE	3,148	1,582	1,233	333	349 R	50.3%	39.2%	56.2%	43.8%
1,485	WALLACE	661	506	106	49	400 R	76.6%	16.0%	82.7%	17.3%
5,799	WASHINGTON	2,267	1,342	626	299	716 R	59.2%	27.6%	68.2%	31.8%
2,234	WICHITA	758	560	129	69	431 R	73.9%	17.0%	81.3%	18.7%
9,409	WILSON	2,981	1,869	921	191	948 R	62.7%	30.9%	67.0%	33.0%
3,309	WOODSON	1,180	693	394	93	299 R	58.7%	33.4%	63.8%	36.2%
157,505	WYANDOTTE	42,160	10,526	28,285	3,349	17,759 D	25.0%	67.1%	27.1%	72.9%
2,853,118	*TOTAL*	*1,055,060*	*453,030*	*506,509*	*95,521*	*53,479 D*	*42.9%*	*48.0%*	*47.2%*	*52.8%*

KANSAS

HOUSE OF REPRESENTATIVES

CD	Year	Total Vote	Republican Vote	Republican Candidate	Democratic Vote	Democratic Candidate	Other Vote	Rep.-Dem. Plurality	Percentage Total Vote Rep.	Percentage Total Vote Dem.	Percentage Major Vote Rep.	Percentage Major Vote Dem.
1	2018	224,640	153,082	MARSHALL, ROGER*	71,558	LAPOLICE, ALAN		81,524 R	68.1%	31.9%	68.1%	31.9%
1	2016	257,971	169,992	MARSHALL, ROGER			87,979	169,992 R	65.9%		100.0%	
1	2014	204,161	138,764	HUELSKAMP, TIM*	65,397	SHEROW, JAMES E.		73,367 R	68.0%	32.0%	68.0%	32.0%
1	2012	211,337	211,337	HUELSKAMP, TIM*				211,337 R	100.0%		100.0%	
2	2018	264,688	126,098	WATKINS, STEVE	123,859	DAVIS, PAUL	14,731	2,239 R	47.6%	46.8%	50.4%	49.6%
2	2016	297,401	181,228	JENKINS, LYNN*	96,840	POTTER, BRITANI	19,333	84,388 R	60.9%	32.6%	65.2%	34.8%
2	2014	225,686	128,742	JENKINS, LYNN*	87,153	WAKEFIELD, MARGIE	9,791	41,589 R	57.0%	38.6%	59.6%	40.4%
2	2012	293,718	167,463	JENKINS, LYNN*	113,735	SCHLINGENSIEPEN, TOBIAS	12,520	53,728 R	57.0%	38.7%	59.6%	40.4%
3	2018	318,301	139,762	YODER, KEVIN*	170,518	DAVIDS, SHARICE	8,021	30,756 D	43.9%	53.6%	45.0%	55.0%
3	2016	343,113	176,022	YODER, KEVIN*	139,300	SIDIE, JAY	27,791	36,722 R	51.3%	40.6%	55.8%	44.2%
3	2014	224,077	134,493	YODER, KEVIN*	89,584	KULTALA, KELLY		44,909 R	60.0%	40.0%	60.0%	40.0%
3	2012	293,762	201,087	YODER, KEVIN*			92,675	201,087 R	68.5%		100.0%	
4	2018	242,693	144,248	ESTES, RON*	98,445	THOMPSON, JAMES A.		45,803 R	59.4%	40.6%	59.4%	40.6%
4	2016	275,251	166,998	POMPEO, MIKE*	81,495	GIROUX, DANIEL B.	26,758	85,503 R	60.7%	29.6%	67.2%	32.8%
4	2014	208,153	138,757	POMPEO, MIKE*	69,396	SCHUCKMAN, PERRY		69,361 R	66.7%	33.3%	66.7%	33.3%
4	2012	258,922	161,094	POMPEO, MIKE*	81,770	TILLMAN, ROBERT	16,058	79,324 R	62.2%	31.6%	66.3%	33.7%
TOTAL	*2018*	*1,050,322*	*563,190*		*464,380*		*22,752*	*98,810 R*	*53.6%*	*44.2%*	*54.8%*	*45.2%*
TOTAL	*2016*	*1,173,736*	*694,240*		*317,635*		*161,861*	*376,605 R*	*59.1%*	*27.1%*	*68.6%*	*31.4%*
TOTAL	*2014*	*862,077*	*540,756*		*311,530*		*9,791*	*229,226 R*	*62.7%*	*36.1%*	*63.4%*	*36.6%*
TOTAL	*2012*	*1,057,739*	*740,981*		*195,505*		*121,253*	*545,476 R*	*70.1%*	*18.5%*	*79.1%*	*20.9%*

Note: An asterisk (*) denotes incumbent.

KANSAS

GENERAL AND PRIMARY ELECTIONS

2018 GENERAL ELECTIONS: OTHER VOTES

Governor Other vote was 68,498 Independent (Greg Orman), 20,009 Libertarian (Jeff Caldwell), 6,576 Independent (Rick Kloos), 438 Write-in (Write-In)

House Other vote was:

CD 2 14,731 Libertarian (Kelly Standley)
CD 3 8,021 Libertarian (Christopher Clemmons)

2018 PRIMARY ELECTIONS: SUPPLEMENTARY INFORMATION

Primary August 7, 2018

Registration (as of July 31, 2018) 1,801,023

Republican	789,764
Democratic	436,040
Libertarian	16,769
Unaffiliated	558,450

Primary Type Semi-open—Registered Democrats and Republicans could vote only in their party's primary. "Unaffiliated" voters could participate in either primary, although they had to change their registration to that party on primary day.

KANSAS

GENERAL AND PRIMARY ELECTIONS

	REPUBLICAN PRIMARIES			DEMOCRATIC PRIMARIES		
Governor	Kobach, Kris W.	128,832	40.6%	Kelly, Laura	80,377	51.4%
	Coyler, Jeff*	128,489	40.5%	Brewer, Carl	31,493	20.2%
	Barnett, Jim	27,994	8.8%	Svaty, Joshua	27,292	17.5%
	Selzer, Ken	24,804	7.8%	Andersen, Arden	13,161	8.4%
	Kucera, Patrick "PK"	3,212	1.0%	Bergeson, Jack	3,950	2.5%
	Ruzich, Tyler	2,275	0.7%			
	Tutera, Joseph	1,559	0.5%			
	TOTAL	*317,165*		*TOTAL*	*156,273*	
Congressional District 1	Marshall, Roger*	64,843	78.7%	LaPolice, Alan	17,195	100.0%
	Reinecker, Nick	17,593	21.3%			
	TOTAL	*82,436*		*TOTAL*	*17,195*	
Congressional District 2	Watkins, Steve	20,052	26.5%	Davis, Paul	38,846	100.0%
	Tyson, Caryn	17,749	23.5%			
	Jones, Kevin	11,201	14.8%			
	Fitzgerald, Stephen	9,227	12.2%			
	Pyle, Dennis	9,126	12.1%			
	Mays, Doug	6,221	8.2%			
	Fields, Vernon	1,987	2.6%			
	TOTAL	*75,563*		*TOTAL*	*38,846*	
Congressional District 3	Yoder, Kevin*	53,130	68.1%	Davids, Sharice	23,379	37.3%
	Keegan, Trevor	14,574	18.7%	Welder, Brent	21,190	33.8%
	Myers, Joe	10,268	13.2%	Niermann, Tom	8,939	14.3%
				Mccamon, Mike	4,354	7.0%
				Williams, Sylvia	2,955	4.7%
				Sidie, Jay	1,790	2.9%
	TOTAL	*77,972*		*TOTAL*	*62,607*	
Congressional District 4	Estes, Ron*	57,522	81.4%	Thompson, James A.	20,261	65.2%
	Estes, Ron M.	13,159	18.6%	Lombard, Laura	10,797	34.8%
	TOTAL	*70,681*		*TOTAL*	*31,058*	

Note: An asterisk (*) denotes incumbent.

KENTUCKY

Congressional districts first established for elections held in 2012
6 members

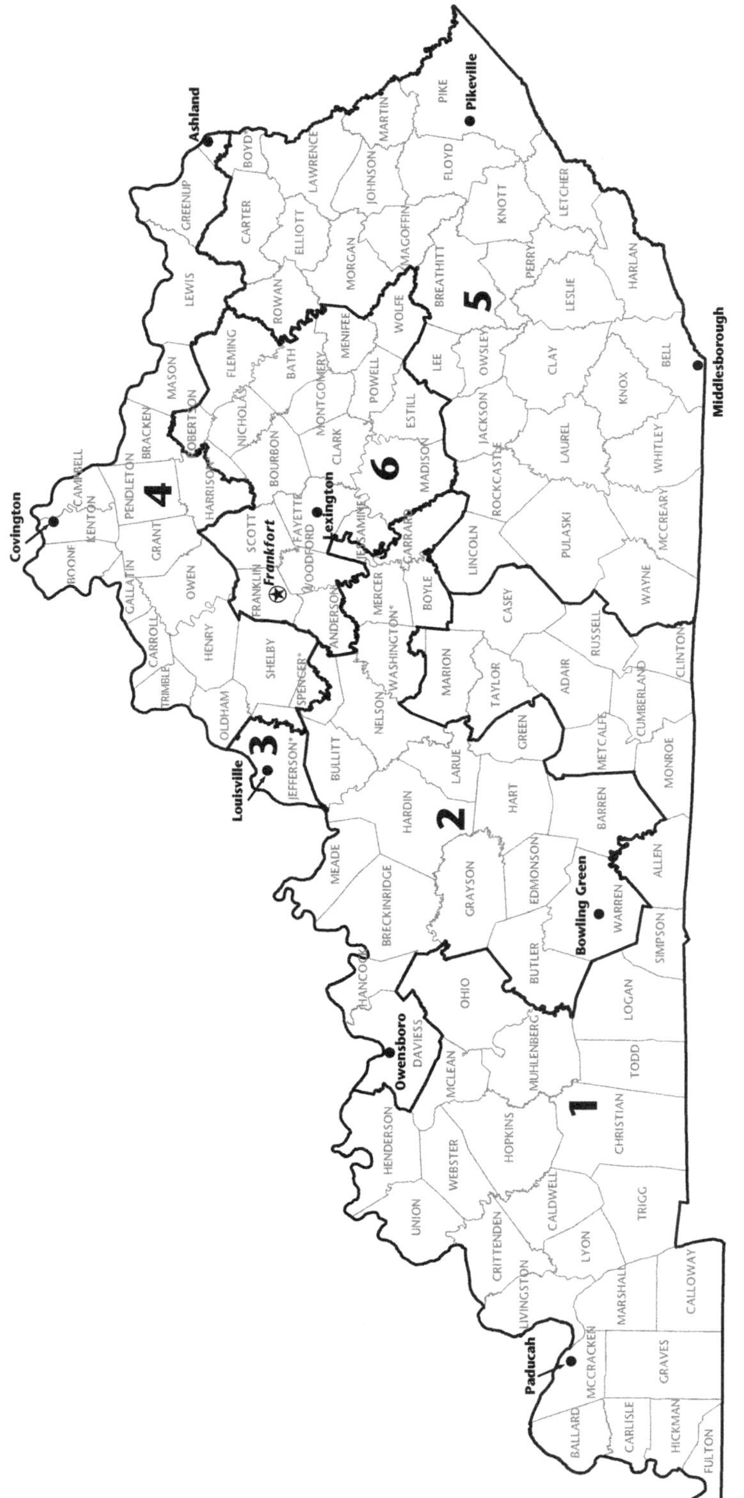

* Asterisk indicates a county whose boundaries include parts of two or more congressional districts.

KENTUCKY

GOVERNOR

Matt Bevin (R). Elected 2015 to a four-year term.

SENATORS (2 Republicans)

Mitch McConnell (R). Re-elected 2014 to a six-year term. Previously elected 2008, 2002, 1996, 1990, 1984.

Rand Paul (R). Re-elected 2016 to a six-year term. Previously elected 2010.

REPRESENTATIVES (5 Republicans, 1 Democrat)

1. James R. Comer (R)
2. Brett Guthrie (R)
3. John Yarmuth (D)
4. Thomas Massie (R)
5. Harold "Hal" Rogers (R)
6. Garland "Andy" Barr (R)

POSTWAR VOTE FOR PRESIDENT

		Republican		Democratic				Percentage			
								Total Vote		Major Vote	
Year	Total Vote	Vote	Candidate	Vote	Candidate	Other Vote	Rep.-Dem. Plurality	Rep.	Dem.	Rep.	Dem.
2016**	1,924,149	1,202,971	Trump, Donald J.	628,854	Clinton, Hillary Rodham	92,324	574,117 R	62.5%	32.7%	65.7%	34.3%
2012	1,797,212	1,087,190	Romney, W. Mitt	679,370	Obama, Barack H.*	30,652	407,820 R	60.5%	37.8%	61.5%	38.5%
2008	1,826,620	1,048,462	McCain, John S. III	751,985	Obama, Barack H.	26,173	296,477 R	57.4%	41.2%	58.2%	41.8%
2004	1,795,882	1,069,439	Bush, George W.*	712,733	Kerry, John F.	13,710	356,706 R	59.5%	39.7%	60.0%	40.0%
2000**	1,544,187	872,492	Bush, George W.	638,898	Gore, Albert Jr.	32,797	233,594 R	56.5%	41.4%	57.7%	42.3%
1996**	1,388,708	623,283	Dole, Robert "Bob"	636,614	Clinton, Bill*	128,811	13,331 D	44.9%	45.8%	49.5%	50.5%
1992**	1,492,900	617,178	Bush, George H.*	665,104	Clinton, Bill	210,618	47,926 D	41.3%	44.6%	48.1%	51.9%
1988	1,322,517	734,281	Bush, George H.	580,368	Dukakis, Michael S.	7,868	153,913 R	55.5%	43.9%	55.9%	44.1%
1984	1,369,345	821,702	Reagan, Ronald*	539,539	Mondale, Walter F.	8,104	282,163 R	60.0%	39.4%	60.4%	39.6%
1980**	1,294,627	635,274	Reagan, Ronald	616,417	Carter, Jimmy*	42,936	18,857 R	49.1%	47.6%	50.8%	49.2%
1976	1,167,142	531,852	Ford, Gerald R.*	615,717	Carter, Jimmy	19,573	83,865 D	45.6%	52.8%	46.3%	53.7%
1972	1,067,499	676,446	Nixon, Richard M.*	371,159	McGovern, George S.	19,894	305,287 R	63.4%	34.8%	64.6%	35.4%
1968**	1,055,893	462,411	Nixon, Richard M.	397,541	Humphrey, Hubert Horatio Jr.	195,941	64,870 R	43.8%	37.6%	53.8%	46.2%
1964	1,046,105	372,977	Goldwater, Barry M. Sr.	669,659	Johnson, Lyndon B.*	3,469	296,682 D	35.7%	64.0%	35.8%	64.2%
1960	1,124,462	602,607	Nixon, Richard M.	521,855	Kennedy, John F.		80,752 R	53.6%	46.4%	53.6%	46.4%
1956	1,053,805	572,192	Eisenhower, Dwight D.*	476,453	Stevenson, Adlai E. II	5,160	95,739 R	54.3%	45.2%	54.6%	45.4%
1952	993,148	495,029	Eisenhower, Dwight D.	495,729	Stevenson, Adlai E. II	2,390	700 D	49.8%	49.9%	50.0%	50.0%
1948	822,658	341,210	Dewey, Thomas E.	466,756	Truman, Harry S.*	14,692	125,546 D	41.5%	56.7%	42.2%	57.8%

Note: An asterisk (*) denotes incumbent. **In past elections, the other vote included: 2016 - 53,752 Independent (Gary Johnson); 2000 - 23,192 Green (Ralph Nader); 1996 - 120,396 Reform (Ross Perot); 1992 - 203,944 Independent (Perot); 1980 - 31,127 Independent (John Anderson); 1968 - 193,098 American Independent (George Wallace).

KENTUCKY

POSTWAR VOTE FOR GOVERNOR

		Republican		Democratic				Percentage			
								Total Vote		Major Vote	
Year	Total Vote	Vote	Candidate	Vote	Candidate	Other Vote	Rep.-Dem. Plurality	Rep.	Dem.	Rep.	Dem.
2015	973,692	511,374	Bevin, Matt G.	426,620	Conway, Jack	35,698	84,754 R	52.5%	43.8%	54.5%	45.5%
2011	833,139	294,034	Williams, David Lynn	464,245	Beshear, Steven L.*	74,860	170,211 D	35.3%	55.7%	38.8%	61.2%
2007	1,055,325	435,773	Fletcher, Ernest*	619,552	Beshear, Steven L.		183,779 D	41.3%	58.7%	41.3%	58.7%
2003	1,083,443	596,284	Fletcher, Ernest	487,159	Chandler, Ben		109,125 R	55.0%	45.0%	55.0%	45.0%
1999**	580,074	128,788	Martin, Peppy	352,099	Patton, Paul E.*	99,187	223,311 D	22.2%	60.7%	26.8%	73.2%
1995	983,979	479,227	Forgy, Larry	500,787	Patton, Paul E.	3,965	21,560 D	48.7%	50.9%	48.9%	51.1%
1991	834,920	294,452	Harper, John	540,468	Jones, Brereton C.		246,016 D	35.3%	64.7%	35.3%	64.7%
1987	777,815	273,141	Harper, John	504,674	Wilkinson, Wallace G.		231,533 D	35.1%	64.9%	35.1%	64.9%
1983	1,030,628	454,650	Bunning, Jim	561,674	Collins, Martha Layne	14,304	107,024 D	44.1%	54.5%	44.7%	55.3%
1979	939,366	381,278	Nunn, Louie B.	558,088	Brown, J. Y. Jr.		176,810 D	40.6%	59.4%	40.6%	59.4%
1975	748,157	277,998	Gable, Robert E.	470,159	Carroll, Julian*		192,161 D	37.2%	62.8%	37.2%	62.8%
1971	930,792	412,653	Emberton, Thomas	470,722	Ford, Wendell H.	47,417	58,069 D	44.3%	50.6%	46.7%	53.3%
1967	886,146	453,323	Nunn, Louie B.	425,674	Ward, Henry	7,149	27,649 R	51.2%	48.0%	51.6%	48.4%
1963	886,047	436,496	Nunn, Louie B.	449,551	Breathitt, Edward T.		13,055 D	49.3%	50.7%	49.3%	50.7%
1959	853,005	336,456	Robsion, John M. Jr.	516,549	Combs, Bert T.		180,093 D	39.4%	60.6%	39.4%	60.6%
1955	778,488	322,671	Denney, Edwin R.	451,647	Chandler, Happy	4,170	128,976 D	41.4%	58.0%	41.7%	58.3%
1951	634,359	288,014	Siler, Eugene	346,345	Wetherby, Lawrence W.		58,331 D	45.4%	54.6%	45.4%	54.6%
1947	675,551	287,756	Dummit, Eldon S.	387,795	Clements, Earle C.		100,039 D	42.6%	57.4%	42.6%	57.4%

Note: An asterisk (*) denotes incumbent. **In past elections, the other vote included: 1999 - 88,930 Reform (Gatewood Galbraith).

POSTWAR VOTE FOR SENATOR

		Republican		Democratic				Percentage			
								Total Vote		Major Vote	
Year	Total Vote	Vote	Candidate	Vote	Candidate	Other Vote	Rep.-Dem. Plurality	Rep.	Dem.	Rep.	Dem.
2016	1,903,465	1,090,177	Paul, Rand*	813,246	Gray, Jim	42	276,931 R	57.3%	42.7%	57.3%	42.7%
2014	1,435,868	806,787	McConnell, Mitch*	584,698	Grimes, Alison Lundergan	44,383	222,089 R	56.2%	40.7%	58.0%	42.0%
2010	1,356,468	755,411	Paul, Rand	599,843	Conway, Jack	1,214	155,568 R	55.7%	44.2%	55.7%	44.3%
2008	1,800,821	953,816	McConnell, Mitch*	847,005	Lunsford, Bruce		106,811 R	53.0%	47.0%	53.0%	47.0%
2004	1,724,362	873,507	Bunning, Jim*	850,855	Mongiardo, Frank Daniel		22,652 R	50.7%	49.3%	50.7%	49.3%
2002	1,131,475	731,679	McConnell, Mitch*	399,634	Weinberg, Lois Combs	162	332,045 R	64.7%	35.3%	64.7%	35.3%
1998	1,145,414	569,817	Bunning, Jim	563,051	Baesler, Scott	12,546	6,766 R	49.7%	49.2%	50.3%	49.7%
1996	1,307,046	724,794	McConnell, Mitch*	560,012	Beshear, Steven L.	22,240	164,782 R	55.5%	42.8%	56.4%	43.6%
1992	1,330,858	476,604	Williams, David Lynn	836,888	Ford, Wendell H.*	17,366	360,284 D	35.8%	62.9%	36.3%	63.7%
1990	916,010	478,034	McConnell, Mitch*	437,976	Sloane, Harvey		40,058 R	52.2%	47.8%	52.2%	47.8%
1986	677,280	173,330	Andrews, Jackson M.	503,775	Ford, Wendell H.*	175	330,445 D	25.6%	74.4%	25.6%	74.4%
1984	1,292,407	644,990	McConnell, Mitch	639,721	Huddleston, Walter*	7,696	5,269 R	49.9%	49.5%	50.2%	49.8%
1980	1,106,890	386,029	Foust, Mary Louise	720,861	Ford, Wendell H.*		334,832 D	34.9%	65.1%	34.9%	65.1%
1978	476,783	175,766	Guenthner, Louie	290,730	Huddleston, Walter*	10,287	114,964 D	36.9%	61.0%	37.7%	62.3%
1974	745,994	328,982	Cook, Marlow W.*	399,406	Ford, Wendell H.	17,606	70,424 D	44.1%	53.5%	45.2%	54.8%
1972	1,037,861	494,337	Nunn, Louie B.	528,550	Huddleston, Walter	14,974	34,213 D	47.6%	50.9%	48.3%	51.7%
1968	942,865	484,260	Cook, Marlow W.	448,960	Peden, Katherine	9,645	35,300 R	51.4%	47.6%	51.9%	48.1%
1966	749,884	483,805	Cooper, John Sherman*	266,079	Brown, John Young		217,726 R	64.5%	35.5%	64.5%	35.5%
1962	820,088	432,648	Morton, Thruston B.*	387,440	Wyatt, Wilson W.		45,208 R	52.8%	47.2%	52.8%	47.2%
1960	1,088,377	644,087	Cooper, John Sherman*	444,290	Johnson, Keen		199,797 R	59.2%	40.8%	59.2%	40.8%
1956	1,006,825	506,903	Morton, Thruston B.	499,922	Clements, Earle C.*		6,981 R	50.3%	49.7%	50.3%	49.7%
1956S**	1,011,645	538,505	Cooper, John Sherman	473,140	Wetherby, Lawrence W.		65,365 R	53.2%	46.8%	53.2%	46.8%
1954	797,057	362,948	Cooper, John Sherman*	434,109	Barkley, Alben W.		71,161 D	45.5%	54.5%	45.5%	54.5%
1952S**	960,228	494,576	Cooper, John Sherman	465,652	Underwood, Thomas R.		28,924 R	51.5%	48.5%	51.5%	48.5%
1950	612,617	278,368	Dawson, Charles I.	334,249	Clements, Earle C.		55,881 D	45.4%	54.6%	45.4%	54.6%
1948	794,469	383,776	Cooper, John Sherman*	408,256	Chapman, Virgil	2,437	24,480 D	48.3%	51.4%	48.5%	51.5%
1946S**	615,119	327,652	Cooper, John Sherman	285,829	Brown, John Young	1,638	41,823 R	53.3%	46.5%	53.4%	46.6%

Note: An asterisk (*) denotes incumbent. **The elections in 1946 and 1952 as well as one in 1956 were for short terms to fill vacancies.

KENTUCKY

HOUSE OF REPRESENTATIVES

			Republican		Democratic				Percentage			
									Total Vote		Major Vote	
CD	Year	Total Vote	Vote	Candidate	Vote	Candidate	Other Vote	Rep.-Dem. Plurality	Rep.	Dem.	Rep.	Dem.
1	2018	251,016	172,167	COMER, JAMES R.*	78,849	WALKER, PAUL		93,318 R	68.6%	31.4%	68.6%	31.4%
1	2016	299,001	216,959	COMER, JAMES R.	81,710	GASKINS, SAM	332	135,249 R	72.6%	27.3%	72.6%	27.4%
1	2014	236,618	173,022	WHITFIELD, EDWARD*	63,596	HATCHETT, CHARLES KENDALL		109,426 R	73.1%	26.9%	73.1%	26.9%
1	2012	287,155	199,956	WHITFIELD, EDWARD*	87,199	HATCHETT, CHARLES KENDALL		112,757 R	69.6%	30.4%	69.6%	30.4%
2	2018	257,345	171,700	GUTHRIE, BRETT*	79,964	LINDERMAN, HANK	5,681	91,736 R	66.7%	31.1%	68.2%	31.8%
2	2016	251,825	251,825	GUTHRIE, BRETT*				251,825 R	100.0%		100.0%	
2	2014	226,834	156,936	GUTHRIE, BRETT*	69,898	LEACH, RON		87,038 R	69.2%	30.8%	69.2%	30.8%
2	2012	282,267	181,508	GUTHRIE, BRETT*	89,541	WILLIAMS, DAVID LYNN	11,218	91,967 R	64.3%	31.7%	67.0%	33.0%
3	2018	278,720	101,930	GLISSON, VICKIE	173,002	YARMUTH, JOHN*	3,788	71,072 D	36.6%	62.1%	37.1%	62.9%
3	2016	334,494	122,093	BRATCHER, HAROLD	212,401	YARMUTH, JOHN*		90,308 D	36.5%	63.5%	36.5%	63.5%
3	2014	247,355	87,981	MACFARLANE, MICHAEL	157,056	YARMUTH, JOHN*	2,318	69,075 D	35.6%	63.5%	35.9%	64.1%
3	2012	322,656	111,452	WICKER, BROOKS	206,385	YARMUTH, JOHN*	4,819	94,933 D	34.5%	64.0%	35.1%	64.9%
4	2018	261,812	162,946	MASSIE, THOMAS*	90,536	HALL, SETH	8,330	72,410 R	62.2%	34.6%	64.3%	35.7%
4	2016	327,987	233,922	MASSIE, THOMAS*	94,065	SIDLE, CALVIN		139,857 R	71.3%	28.7%	71.3%	28.7%
4	2014	222,158	150,464	MASSIE, THOMAS*	71,694	NEWBERRY, PETER		78,770 R	67.7%	32.3%	67.7%	32.3%
4	2012	299,444	186,036	MASSIE, THOMAS*	104,734	ADKINS, WILLIAM R. "BILL"	8,674	81,302 R	62.1%	35.0%	64.0%	36.0%
5	2018	218,017	172,093	ROGERS, HAROLD "HAL"*	45,890	STEPP, KENNETH	34	126,203 R	78.9%	21.0%	78.9%	21.1%
5	2016	221,242	221,242	ROGERS, HAROLD "HAL"*				221,242 R	100.0%		100.0%	
5	2014	218,967	171,350	ROGERS, HAROLD "HAL"*	47,617	STEPP, KENNETH		123,733 R	78.3%	21.7%	78.3%	21.7%
5	2012	250,855	195,408	ROGERS, HAROLD "HAL"*	55,447	STEPP, KENNETH		139,961 R	77.9%	22.1%	77.9%	22.1%
6	2018	302,888	154,468	BARR, GARLAND "ANDY"*	144,736	MCGRATH, AMY	3,684	9,732 R	51.0%	47.8%	51.6%	48.4%
6	2016	330,827	202,099	BARR, GARLAND "ANDY"*	128,728	KEMPER, NANCY JO		73,371 R	61.1%	38.9%	61.1%	38.9%
6	2014	245,694	147,404	BARR, GARLAND "ANDY"*	98,290	JENSEN, ELISABETH		49,114 R	60.0%	40.0%	60.0%	40.0%
6	2012	303,000	153,222	BARR, GARLAND "ANDY"	141,438	CHANDLER, BEN*	8,340	11,784 R	50.6%	46.7%	52.0%	48.0%
TOTAL	*2018*	*1,569,798*	*935,304*		*612,977*		*21,517*	*322,327 R*	*59.6%*	*39.0%*	*60.4%*	*39.6%*
TOTAL	*2016*	*1,765,376*	*1,248,140*		*516,904*		*332*	*731,236 R*	*70.7%*	*29.3%*	*70.7%*	*29.3%*
TOTAL	*2014*	*1,397,626*	*887,157*		*508,151*		*2,318*	*379,006 R*	*63.5%*	*36.4%*	*63.6%*	*36.4%*
TOTAL	*2012*	*1,745,377*	*1,027,582*		*684,744*		*33,051*	*342,838 R*	*58.9%*	*39.2%*	*60.0%*	*40.0%*

Note: An asterisk (*) denotes incumbent.

KENTUCKY

GENERAL AND PRIMARY ELECTIONS

2018 GENERAL ELECTIONS: OTHER VOTES

House	Other vote was:
CD 2	5,681 Independent (Thomas Loecken)
CD 3	3,788 Libertarian (Gregory Boles)
CD 4	8,318 Independent (Mike Moffett), 12 Write-in (David Goodwin)
CD 5	34 Write-in (Billy Wilson)
CD 6	2,150 Libertarian (Frank Harris), 1,011 Independent (Rikka Wallin), 523 Independent (James Germalic)

2018 PRIMARY ELECTIONS: SUPPLEMENTARY INFORMATION

Primary	May 22, 2018	**Registration** (as of May 22, 2018)	3,368,107	Democratic	1,684,899
				Republican	1,393,898
				Other	289,310

Primary Type Closed—Only registered Democrats and Republicans could vote in their party's primary.

KENTUCKY

GENERAL AND PRIMARY ELECTIONS

	REPUBLICAN PRIMARIES			DEMOCRATIC PRIMARIES		
Congressional District 1	Comer, James R.*	Unopposed		Walker, Paul	51,094	74.6%
				Pennington, Alonzo	17,398	25.4%
				TOTAL	*68,492*	
Congressional District 2	Guthrie, Brett*	Unopposed		Linderman, Hank	14,517	30.0%
				Pedigo, Brian	13,866	28.7%
				Sessions, Rane	10,501	21.7%
				Short, Grant T.	9,470	19.6%
				TOTAL	*48,354*	
Congressional District 3	Glisson, Vickie	11,240	49.1%	Yarmuth, John*	Unopposed	
	Craven, Mike	6,163	26.9%			
	Palazzo, Rhonda	5,510	24.0%			
	TOTAL	*22,913*				
Congressional District 4	Massie, Thomas*	Unopposed		Hall, Seth	17,862	40.8%
				Piatt, Patti	16,442	37.5%
				Lord, Christina	9,510	21.7%
				TOTAL	*43,814*	
Congressional District 5	Rogers, Harold "Hal"*	75,601	84.2%	Stepp, Kenneth	33,602	58.7%
	Serrano, Gerardo	14,216	15.8%	Sykes, Scott	23,644	41.3%
	TOTAL	*89,817*		*TOTAL*	*57,246*	
Congressional District 6	Barr, Garland "Andy"*	40,514	83.8%	McGrath, Amy	48,860	48.7%
	Eddy, Chuck	7,858	16.2%	Gray, Jim	40,684	40.5%
				Thomas, Reggie	7,226	7.2%
				Young, Geoffrey M. "Geoff"	1,574	1.6%
				Kemph, Daniel	1,240	1.2%
				Green, Theodore	835	0.8%
	TOTAL	*48,372*		*TOTAL*	*100,419*	

Note: An asterisk (*) denotes incumbent.

LOUISIANA

Congressional districts first established for elections held in 2012

6 members

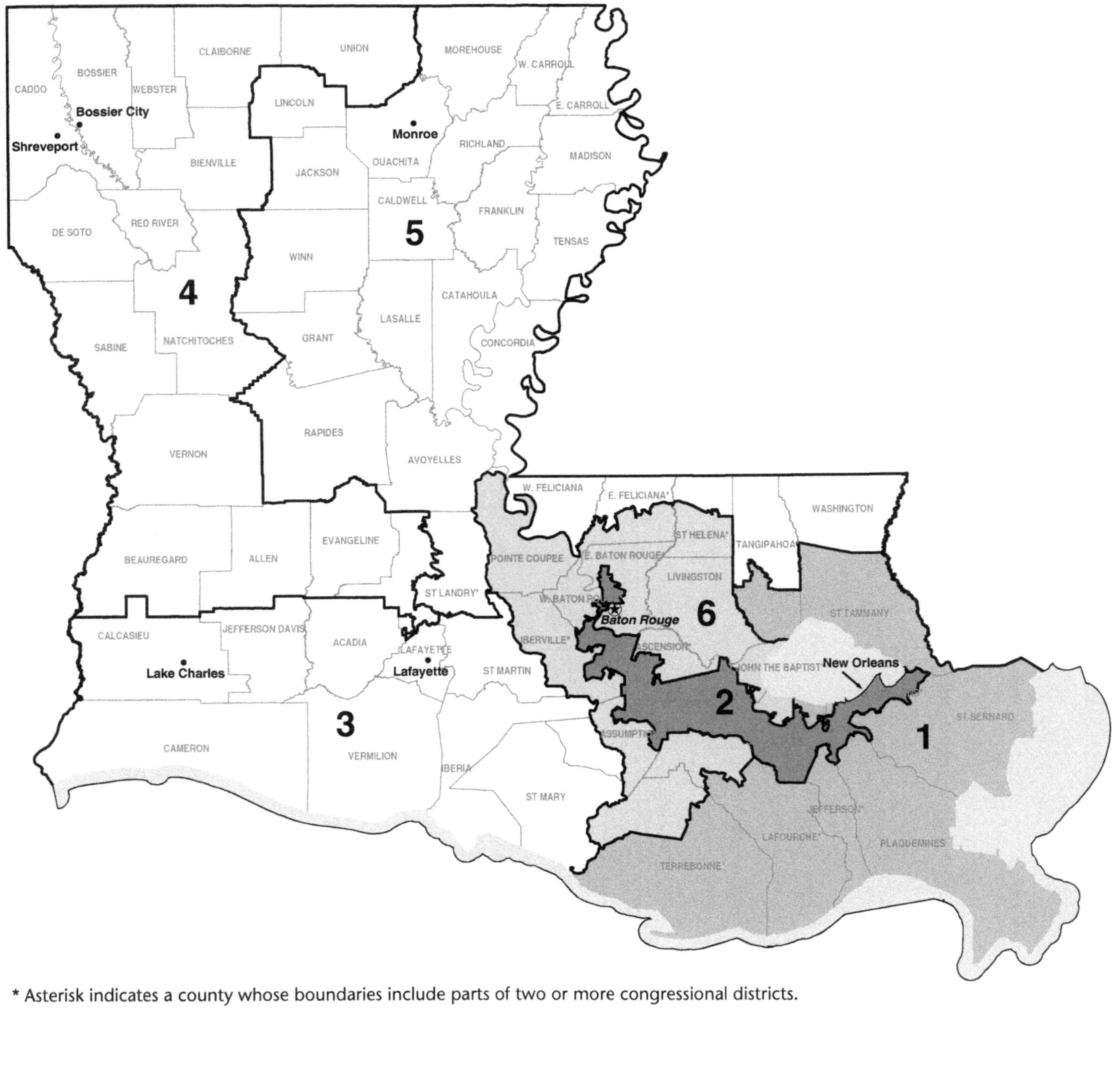

* Asterisk indicates a county whose boundaries include parts of two or more congressional districts.

LOUISIANA

GOVERNOR

John Bel Edwards (D). Elected 2015 to a four-year term.

SENATORS (2 Republicans)

Bill Cassidy (R). Elected 2014 to a six-year term.

John Neely Kennedy (R). Elected 2016 to a six-year term.

REPRESENTATIVES (5 Republicans, 1 Democrat)

1. Steve Scalise (R)
2. Cedric Richmond (D)
3. Clay Higgins (R)
4. Mike Johnson (R)
5. Ralph Lee Abraham (R)
6. Garret Graves (R)

POSTWAR VOTE FOR PRESIDENT

		Republican		Democratic				Percentage			
								Total Vote		Major Vote	
Year	Total Vote	Vote	Candidate	Vote	Candidate	Other Vote	Rep.-Dem. Plurality	Rep.	Dem.	Rep.	Dem.
2016**	2,029,032	1,178,638	Trump, Donald J.	780,154	Clinton, Hillary Rodham	70,240	398,484 R	58.1%	38.4%	60.2%	39.8%
2012	1,994,065	1,152,262	Romney, W. Mitt	809,141	Obama, Barack H.*	32,662	343,121 R	57.8%	40.6%	58.7%	41.3%
2008	1,960,761	1,148,275	McCain, John S. III	782,989	Obama, Barack H.	29,497	365,286 R	58.6%	39.9%	59.5%	40.5%
2004	1,943,106	1,102,169	Bush, George W.*	820,299	Kerry, John F.	20,638	281,870 R	56.7%	42.2%	57.3%	42.7%
2000**	1,765,656	927,871	Bush, George W.	792,344	Gore, Albert Jr.	45,441	135,527 R	52.6%	44.9%	53.9%	46.1%
1996**	1,783,959	712,586	Dole, Robert "Bob"	927,837	Clinton, Bill*	143,536	215,251 D	39.9%	52.0%	43.4%	56.6%
1992**	1,790,017	733,386	Bush, George H.*	815,971	Clinton, Bill	240,660	82,585 D	41.0%	45.6%	47.3%	52.7%
1988	1,628,202	883,702	Bush, George H.	717,460	Dukakis, Michael S.	27,040	166,242 R	54.3%	44.1%	55.2%	44.8%
1984	1,706,822	1,037,299	Reagan, Ronald*	651,586	Mondale, Walter F.	17,937	385,713 R	60.8%	38.2%	61.4%	38.6%
1980**	1,548,591	792,853	Reagan, Ronald	708,453	Carter, Jimmy*	47,285	84,400 R	51.2%	45.7%	52.8%	47.2%
1976	1,278,539	587,446	Ford, Gerald R.*	661,365	Carter, Jimmy	29,728	73,919 D	45.9%	51.7%	47.0%	53.0%
1972	1,051,491	686,852	Nixon, Richard M.*	298,142	McGovern, George S.	66,497	388,710 R	65.3%	28.4%	69.7%	30.3%
1968**	1,097,450	257,535	Nixon, Richard M.	309,615	Humphrey, Hubert Horatio Jr.	530,300	52,080 D#	23.5%	28.2%	45.4%	54.6%
1964	896,293	509,225	Goldwater, Barry M. Sr.	387,068	Johnson, Lyndon B.*		122,157 R	56.8%	43.2%	56.8%	43.2%
1960**	807,891	230,980	Nixon, Richard M.	407,339	Kennedy, John F.	169,572	176,359 D	28.6%	50.4%	36.2%	63.8%
1956	617,544	329,047	Eisenhower, Dwight D.*	243,977	Stevenson, Adlai E. II	44,520	85,070 R	53.3%	39.5%	57.4%	42.6%
1952	651,952	306,925	Eisenhower, Dwight D.	345,027	Stevenson, Adlai E. II		38,102 D	47.1%	52.9%	47.1%	52.9%
1948**	416,336	72,657	Dewey, Thomas E.	136,344	Truman, Harry S.*	207,335	63,687 D#	17.5%	32.7%	34.8%	65.2%

Note: An asterisk (*) denotes incumbent. A pound sign (#) in the plurality column indicates that the winner in 1948 and 1968 did not run under the banner of either major party. **In past elections, the other vote included: 2016 - 37,978 Libertarian (Gary Johnson); 2000 - 20,473 Green (Ralph Nader); 1996 - 123,293 Reform (Ross Perot); 1992 - 211,478 Independent (Perot); 1980 - 26,345 Independent (John Anderson); 1968 - 530,300 American Independent (George Wallace); 1960 - 169,572 Unpledged Independent Electors; 1948 - 204,290 States' Rights (Strom Thurmond). Wallace carried Louisiana in 1968 with 48.3 percent of the vote. Thurmond won the state in 1948 with 49.1 percent.

LOUISIANA

POSTWAR VOTE FOR GOVERNOR

		Republican		Democratic				Percentage			
								Total Vote		Major Vote	
Year	Total Vote	Vote	Candidate	Vote	Candidate	Other Vote	Rep.-Dem. Plurality	Rep.	Dem.	Rep.	Dem.
2015**	1,152,864	505,940	Vitter, David B.	646,924	Edwards, John Bel		140,984 D	43.9%	56.1%	43.9%	56.1%
2011	1,023,163	673,239	Jindal, Bobby*	182,925	Hollis, Tara	166,999	490,314 R	65.8%	17.9%	78.6%	21.4%
2007**	1,297,840	699,275	Jindal, Bobby	226,476	Boasso, Walter J.	372,089	472,799 R	53.9%	17.5%	75.5%	24.5%
2003**	1,407,842	676,484	Jindal, Bobby	731,358	Kathleen, Babineaux		54,874 D	48.1%	51.9%	48.1%	51.9%
1999	1,295,205	805,203	Foster, Mike*	382,445	Jefferson, William J.	107,557	422,758 R	62.2%	29.5%	67.8%	32.2%
1995**	1,550,360	984,499	Foster, Mike	565,861	Fields, Cleo		418,638 R	63.5%	36.5%	63.5%	36.5%
1991**	1,728,040	671,009	Duke, David E.	1,057,031	Edwards, Edwin W.		386,022 D	38.8%	61.2%	38.8%	61.2%
1987**	1,558,730	287,780	Livingston, Bob	516,078	Roemer, Charles	754,872	228,298 D	18.5%	33.1%	35.8%	64.2%
1983	1,615,905	588,508	Treen, David Conner*	1,006,561	Edwards, Edwin W.	20,836	418,053 D	36.4%	62.3%	36.9%	63.1%
1979**	1,371,825	690,691	Treen, David Conner	681,134	Lambert, Louis		9,557 R	50.3%	49.7%	50.3%	49.7%
1975	430,095			430,095	Edwards, Edwin W.*		430,095 D		100.0%		100.0%
1972	1,121,570	480,424	Treen, David Conner	641,146	Edwards, Edwin W.		160,722 D	42.8%	57.2%	42.8%	57.2%
1968	372,762		430,095 R	372,762	McKeithen, John J.*		372,762 D		100.0%		100.0%
1964	773,390	297,753	Lyons, Charlton H. Sr.	469,589	McKeithen, John J.	6,048	171,836 D	38.5%	60.7%	38.8%	61.2%
1960	506,562	86,135	Grevemberg, F. C.	407,907	Davis, Jimmie H.	12,520	321,772 D	17.0%	80.5%	17.4%	82.6%
1956	172,291			172,291	Long, Earl K.		172,291 D		100.0%		100.0%
1952	118,723			118,723	Kennon, Robert F.		118,723 D		100.0%		100.0%
1948	76,566			76,566	Long, Earl K.		76,566 D		100.0%		100.0%

Note: An asterisk (*) denotes incumbent. **Since the 1970s, Louisiana has had a two-tier election system for governor in which all candidates, regardless of party, run together in an open election. A candidate who wins a majority of the vote is elected. If no candidate receives 50 percent, a runoff is held between the top two finishers. The results of the runoff are listed in this chart for 1979, 1991, 1995, 2003, and 2015. In elections that did not require a runoff, the leading Democratic and Republican candidates are listed with their votes from the first-round, open election. The votes for other candidates are listed in the "Other Vote" column, regardless of whether they were Democratic, Republican, or independent. In past elections, the other vote included: 2007 - 186,682 No Party (John Georges), 161,665 Democrat (Foster Campbell); 1987 - 437,801 Democrat (Edwin W. Edwards). In 1987, Edwards withdrew after finishing second in the initial round of voting. Democrat Charles Roemer finished first with 33.1 percent and with Edwards's withdrawal, no runoff was held. The major party vote percentages are calculated for the top vote-getter for each party only; it does not include additional members of the same party. The Republican Party did not run a candidate in the 1948, 1952, 1956, 1968, and 1975 gubernatorial elections.

LOUISIANA

POSTWAR VOTE FOR SENATOR

		Republican		Democratic				Percentage			
								Total Vote		Major Vote	
Year	Total Vote	Vote	Candidate	Vote	Candidate	Other Vote	Rep.-Dem. Plurality	Rep.	Dem.	Rep.	Dem.
2016**	884,007	536,191	Kennedy, John Neely	347,816	Campbell, Foster		188,375 R	60.7%	39.3%	60.7%	39.3%
2014**	1,273,589	712,379	Cassidy, Bill	561,210	Landrieu, Mary L.*		151,169 R	55.9%	44.1%	55.9%	44.1%
2010	1,264,994	715,415	Vitter, David B.*	476,572	Melancon, Charlie R.	73,007	238,843 R	56.6%	37.7%	60.0%	40.0%
2008	1,896,574	867,177	Kennedy, John	988,298	Landrieu, Mary L.*	41,099	121,121 D	45.7%	52.1%	46.7%	53.3%
2004**	1,848,056	943,014	Vitter, David B.	542,150	John, Chris	362,892	400,864 R	51.0%	29.3%	63.5%	36.5%
2002**	1,235,296	596,642	Terrell, Suzanne Haik	638,654	Landrieu, Mary L.*		42,012 D	48.3%	51.7%	48.3%	51.7%
1998	969,165	306,616	Donelon, Jim	620,502	Breaux, John B.*	42,047	313,886 D	31.6%	64.0%	33.1%	66.9%
1996**	1,700,102	847,157	Jenkins, Louis E. "Woody" Jr.	852,945	Landrieu, Mary L.		5,788 D	49.8%	50.2%	49.8%	50.2%
1992	843,037	69,986	Stockstill, Lyle	616,021	Breaux, John B.*	157,030	546,035 D	8.3%	73.1%	10.2%	89.8%
1990	1,396,113	607,391	Duke, David E.	752,902	Johnston, J. Bennett*	35,820	145,511 D	43.5%	53.9%	44.7%	55.3%
1986**	1,369,897	646,311	Moore, W. Henson	723,586	Breaux, John B.		77,275 D	47.2%	52.8%	47.2%	52.8%
1984	977,473	86,546	Ross, Robert M.	838,181	Johnston, J. Bennett*	52,746	751,635 D	8.9%	85.7%	9.4%	90.6%
1980**	843,362	13,739	Bardwell, Jerry C.	484,770	Long, Russell B.*	342,504	471,031 D	1.6%	57.6%		100.0%
1978**	839,669			498,773	Johnston, J. Bennett*	340,896	498,773 D		59.4%		100.0%
1974	434,643			434,643	Long, Russell B.*		434,643 D		100.0%		100.0%
1972**	1,084,904	206,846	Toledano, Ben C.	598,987	Johnston, J. Bennett	279,071	392,141 D	19.1%	55.2%	25.7%	74.3%
1968	518,586			518,586	Long, Russell B.*		518,586 D		100.0%		100.0%
1966	437,695			437,695	Ellender, Allen J.*		437,695 D		100.0%		100.0%
1962	421,904	103,066	O'Hearn, Taylor Walters	318,838	Long, Russell B.*		215,772 D	24.4%	75.6%	24.4%	75.6%
1960	541,928	109,698	Reese, George W. Jr.	432,228	Ellender, Allen J.*	2	322,530 D	20.2%	79.8%	20.2%	79.8%
1956	335,564			335,564	Long, Russell B.*		335,564 D		100.0%		100.0%
1954	207,115			207,115	Ellender, Allen J.*		207,115 D		100.0%		100.0%
1950	251,838	30,931	Gerth, Charles S.	220,907	Long, Russell B.*		189,976 D	12.3%	87.7%	12.3%	87.7%
1948	330,324			330,315	Ellender, Allen J.	9	330,315 D		100.0%		100.0%
1948S**	407,685	102,339	Clarke, Clem S.	305,346	Long, Russell B.		203,007 D	25.1%	74.9%	25.1%	74.9%

Note: An asterisk (*) denotes incumbent. **In 2008 and 2010, Louisiana used the more typical system of party primaries followed by a general election to fill seats in Congress. Since 1978, all other Senate seats were decided in open elections in which candidates of all parties ran together on the same ballot. If no candidate won a majority of the vote in the first round, a runoff was held between the top two vote-getters, regardless of party. The Senate elections in 1986, 1996, 2002, 2014, and 2016 were decided by a runoff, with the results of the runoff listed in this chart. In elections that did not require a runoff, the leading Democratic and Republican candidates are listed with their votes in the first-round, open election. The votes for other candidates are listed in the "Other Vote" column, regardless of whether they were Democratic, Republican, or independent. In past elections, the other vote included: 2004 - 275,821 Democrat (John Kennedy); 1980 - 325,922 Democrat (Louis Jenkins), who finished second; 1978 - 340,896 Democrat (Louis Jenkins), who finished second; 1972 - 250,161 Independent (John J. McKeithen), who finished second. One of the 1948 elections was for a short term to fill a vacancy. The major party vote percentages are calculated for the top vote-getter for each party only; it does not include additional members of the same party. The Republican Party did not run a candidate in Senate elections in 1948, 1954, 1956, 1966, 1968, 1974, and 1978.

LOUISIANA

HOUSE OF REPRESENTATIVES

			Republican		Democratic				Percentage			
									Total Vote		Major Vote	
CD	Year	Total Vote	Vote	Candidate	Vote	Candidate	Other Vote	Rep.-Dem. Plurality	Rep.	Dem.	Rep.	Dem.
1	2018	269,325	192,555	SCALISE, STEVE*	44,273	SAVOIE, TAMMY	32,497	148,282 R	71.5%	16.4%	81.3%	18.7%
1	2016	326,788	243,645	SCALISE, STEVE*	41,840	DUGAS, LEE ANN	41,303	201,805 R	74.6%	12.8%	85.3%	14.7%
1	2014	244,004	189,250	SCALISE, STEVE*	24,761	MENDOZA, M.V. VINNY	29,993	164,489 R	77.6%	10.1%	88.4%	11.6%
1	2012	290,410	193,496	SCALISE, STEVE*	61,703	MENDOZA, M.V. VINNY	35,211	131,793 R	66.6%	21.2%	75.8%	24.2%
2	2018	235,982			190,182	RICHMOND, CEDRIC*	45,800	190,182 D		80.6%		100.0%
2	2016	284,269			198,289	RICHMOND, CEDRIC*	85,980	198,289 D		69.8%		100.0%
2	2014	221,570			152,201	RICHMOND, CEDRIC*	69,369	152,201 D		68.7%		100.0%
2	2012	287,354	38,801	BAILEY, DWAYNE	158,501	RICHMOND, CEDRIC*	90,052	119,700 D	13.5%	55.2%	19.7%	80.3%
3	2018	245,943	136,876	HIGGINS, CLAY*	43,729	METHVIN, MILDRED "MIMI"	65,338	93,147 R	55.7%	17.8%	75.8%	24.2%
3**	2016	138,433	77,671	HIGGINS, CLAY			60,762	77,671 R	56.1%		100.0%	
3	2014	236,268	185,867	BOUSTANY, CHARLES W. JR.*			50,401	185,867 R	78.7%		100.0%	
3	2012	311,393	139,123	BOUSTANY, CHARLES W. JR.*	67,070	RICHARD, RON	105,200	72,053 R	44.7%	21.5%	67.5%	32.5%

LOUISIANA

HOUSE OF REPRESENTATIVES

CD	Year	Total Vote	Republican Vote	Republican Candidate	Democratic Vote	Democratic Candidate	Other Vote	Rep.-Dem. Plurality	Percentage: Total Vote Rep.	Total Vote Dem.	Major Vote Rep.	Major Vote Dem.
4	2018	216,872	139,326	JOHNSON, MIKE*	72,934	TRUNDLE, RYAN	4,612	66,392 R	64.2%	33.6%	65.6%	34.4%
4**	2016	133,949	87,370	JOHNSON, MIKE	46,579	JONES, MARSHALL		40,791 R	65.2%	34.8%	65.2%	34.8%
4	2014	207,919	152,683	FLEMING, JOHN*			55,236	152,683 R	73.4%		100.0%	
4	2012	249,531	187,894	FLEMING, JOHN*			61,637	187,894 R	75.3%		100.0%	
5	2018	223,946	149,018	ABRAHAM, RALPH LEE*	67,118	FLEENOR, JESSEE CARLTON	7,810	81,900 R	66.5%	30.0%	68.9%	31.1%
5	2016	255,662	208,545	ABRAHAM, RALPH LEE*			47,117	208,545 R	81.6%		100.0%	
5**	2014	209,622	134,616	ABRAHAM, RALPH LEE	75,006	MAYO, JAMIE		59,610 R	64.2%	35.8%	64.2%	35.8%
5	2012	260,216	202,536	ALEXANDER, RODNEY*			57,680	202,536 R	77.8%		100.0%	
6	2018	268,525	186,553	GRAVES, GARRET*	55,089	DEWITT, JUSTIN	26,883	131,464 R	69.5%	20.5%	77.2%	22.8%
6	2016	331,098	207,483	GRAVES, GARRET*	49,380	LIEBERMAN, RICHARD	74,235	158,103 R	62.7%	14.9%	80.8%	19.2%
6**	2014	22,990	139,209	GRAVES, GARRET	83,781	EDWARDS, EDWIN W.		55,428 R	62.4%	37.6%	62.4%	37.6%
6	2012	306,713	243,553	CASSIDY, BILL*			63,160	243,553 R	79.4%		100.0%	
TOTAL	*2018*	*1,460,593*	*804,328*		*473,325*		*182,940*	*331,003 R*	*55.1%*	*32.4%*	*63.0%*	*37.0%*
TOTAL	*2016*	*1,362,091*	*756,440*		*370,489*		*309,397*	*385,951 R*	*55.5%*	*27.2%*	*67.1%*	*32.8%*
TOTAL	*2014*	*1,342,373*	*823,684*		*394,840*		*123,849*	*428,844 R*	*61.4%*	*29.4%*	*67.6%*	*32.4%*
TOTAL	*2012*	*1,705,617*	*1,005,403*		*287,274*		*412,940*	*718,129 R*	*58.9%*	*16.8%*	*77.8%*	*22.2%*

Note: An asterisk (*) denotes incumbent. **Indicates results of a runoff. Louisiana has a unique two-tier electoral system for House seats, with a first round of voting that featured candidates from all parties running together on the same ballot. A candidate who won a majority of the vote in the first round was elected. Otherwise, the top two finishers participated in a runoff. In elections that did not require a runoff, the leading Democratic and Republican candidates are listed with their votes in the first-round, open election. The votes for other candidates are listed in the "Other Vote" column regardless of whether they were Democratic, Republican, or unaffiliated with either major party. The major vote and total vote percentages are calculated only for the top candidate for each party in the district. However, when the votes of all Democratic and Republican candidates are aggregated, the totals for 2018 are as follows: Republican 835,715; Democratic 553,184; Other 71,694, with a Republican plurality of 282,531.

LOUISIANA

GENERAL AND PRIMARY ELECTIONS

2018 GENERAL ELECTIONS: OTHER VOTES

House Other vote was:

- CD 1: 18,560 Democrat (Lee Dugas), 8,688 Democrat (Jim Francis), 2,443 Independent (Frederick Jones), 2,443 Libertarian (Howard Kearney)
- CD 2: 20,465 Libertarian (Jesse Schmidt), 17,260 Independent (Belden Batiste), 8,075 No Party (Shawndra Rodriguez)
- CD 3: 31,387 Republican (Joshua Guillory), 13,477 Democrat (Rob Anderson), 9,692 Democrat (Larry Rader), 7,815 Democrat (Verone Thomas), 2,967 Libertarian (Aaron Andrus)
- CD 4: 4,612 No Party (Mark Halverson)
- CD 5: 4,799 Independent (Billy Burkette), 3,011 Libertarian (Kyle Randol)
- CD 6: 21,627 Democrat (Andie Saizan), 5,256 Independent (Devin Graham)

2018 FIRST ROUND: SUPPLEMENTARY INFORMATION

Primary November 6, 2018

Registration (as of November 1, 2018) 2,958,984

Democratic	1,285,219
Republican	897,611
Other Parties	776,154

Primary Type Open—For governor and other federal offices, Louisiana has a two-tier electoral system open to all voters, with a first round of voting (sometimes called an open or "jungle" primary) that features candidates from all parties running together on the same ballot. A candidate who wins a majority of the vote in the first round is elected. Otherwise, there is a runoff held several weeks later between the top two finishers.

MAINE

Congressional districts first established for elections held in 2012

2 members

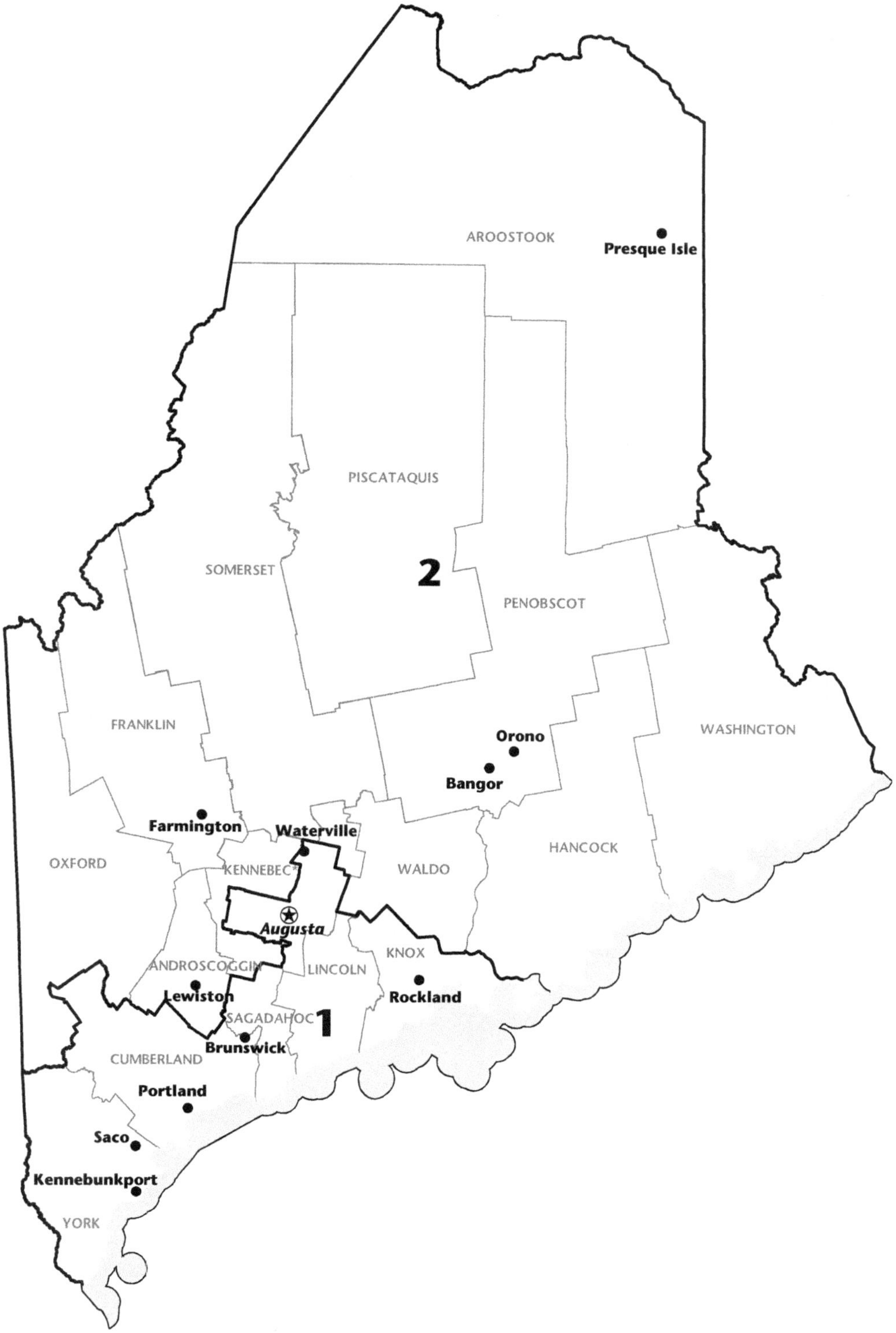

* Asterisk indicates a county whose boundaries include parts of two or more congressional districts.

MAINE

GOVERNOR

Janet T. Mills (D). Elected 2018 to a four-year term.

SENATORS (1 Republican, 1 Independent)

Susan M. Collins (R). Re-elected 2014 to a six-year term. Previously elected 2008, 2002, 1996.

Angus S. King Jr. (Ind.). Re-elected 2018 to a six-year term. Previously elected 2012.

REPRESENTATIVES (2 Democrats)

1. Chellie Pingree (D)
2. Jared Golden (D)

POSTWAR VOTE FOR PRESIDENT

		Republican		Democratic				Percentage			
								Total Vote		Major Vote	
Year	Total Vote	Vote	Candidate	Vote	Candidate	Other Vote	Rep.-Dem. Plurality	Rep.	Dem.	Rep.	Dem.
2016**	747,927	335,593	Trump, Donald J.	357,735	Clinton, Hillary Rodham	54,599	22,142 D	44.9%	47.8%	48.4%	51.6%
2012	713,180	292,276	Romney, W. Mitt	401,306	Obama, Barack H.*	19,598	109,030 D	41.0%	56.3%	42.1%	57.9%
2008	731,163	295,273	McCain, John S. III	421,923	Obama, Barack H.	13,967	126,650 D	40.4%	57.7%	41.2%	58.8%
2004	740,752	330,201	Bush, George W.*	396,842	Kerry, John F.	13,709	66,641 D	44.6%	53.6%	45.4%	54.6%
2000**	651,817	286,616	Bush, George W.	319,951	Gore, Albert Jr.	45,250	33,335 D	44.0%	49.1%	47.3%	52.7%
1996**	605,897	186,378	Dole, Robert "Bob"	312,788	Clinton, Bill*	106,731	126,410 D	30.8%	51.6%	37.3%	62.7%
1992**	679,499	206,504	Bush, George H.*	263,420	Clinton, Bill	209,575	56,916 D	30.4%	38.8%	43.9%	56.1%
1988	555,035	307,131	Bush, George H.	243,569	Dukakis, Michael S.	4,335	63,562 R	55.3%	43.9%	55.8%	44.2%
1984	553,144	336,500	Reagan, Ronald*	214,515	Mondale, Walter F.	2,129	121,985 R	60.8%	38.8%	61.1%	38.9%
1980**	523,011	238,522	Reagan, Ronald	220,974	Carter, Jimmy*	63,515	17,548 R	45.6%	42.3%	51.9%	48.1%
1976	483,216	236,320	Ford, Gerald R.*	232,279	Carter, Jimmy	14,617	4,041 R	48.9%	48.1%	50.4%	49.6%
1972	417,042	256,458	Nixon, Richard M.*	160,584	McGovern, George S.		95,874 R	61.5%	38.5%	61.5%	38.5%
1968**	392,936	169,254	Nixon, Richard M.	217,312	Humphrey, Hubert Horatio Jr.	6,370	48,058 D	43.1%	55.3%	43.8%	56.2%
1964	380,965	118,701	Goldwater, Barry M. Sr.	262,264	Johnson, Lyndon B.*		143,563 D	31.2%	68.8%	31.2%	68.8%
1960	421,767	240,608	Nixon, Richard M.	181,159	Kennedy, John F.		59,449 R	57.0%	43.0%	57.0%	43.0%
1956	351,706	249,238	Eisenhower, Dwight D.*	102,468	Stevenson, Adlai E. II		146,770 R	70.9%	29.1%	70.9%	29.1%
1952	351,786	232,353	Eisenhower, Dwight D.	118,806	Stevenson, Adlai E. II	627	113,547 R	66.0%	33.8%	66.2%	33.8%
1948	264,787	150,234	Dewey, Thomas E.	111,916	Truman, Harry S.*	2,637	38,318 R	56.7%	42.3%	57.3%	42.7%

Note: An asterisk (*) denotes incumbent. **In past elections, the other vote included: 2016 - 38,105 Libertarian (Gary Johnson); 2000 - 37,127 Green (Ralph Nader); 1996 - 85,970 Reform (Ross Perot); 1992 - 206,820 Independent (Perot), who placed second; 1980 - 53,327 Independent (John Anderson); 1968 - 6,370 American Independent (George Wallace). Under Maine's unique system of distributing electoral votes, Republican Donald J. Trump won a single electoral vote in 2016 to Hillary Rodham Clinton's three.

MAINE

POSTWAR VOTE FOR GOVERNOR

Year	Total Vote	Republican		Democratic		Other Vote	Rep.-Dem. Plurality	Percentage			
								Total Vote		Major Vote	
		Vote	Candidate	Vote	Candidate			Rep.	Dem.	Rep.	Dem.
2018	630,667	272,311	Moody, Shawn H.	320,962	Mills, Janet T.	37,394	48,651 D	43.2%	50.9%	45.9%	54.1%
2014	611,227	294,519	LePage, Paul R.*	265,114	Michaud, Michael H.	51,594	29,405 R	48.2%	43.4%	52.6%	47.4%
2010**	572,766	218,065	LePage, Paul R.	109,387	Mitchell, Elizabeth H. "Libby"	245,314	108,678 R	38.1%	19.1%	66.6%	33.4%
2006**	550,865	166,425	Woodcock, Chandler E.	209,927	Baldacci, John*	174,513	43,502 D	30.2%	38.1%	44.2%	55.8%
2002	505,190	209,496	Cianchette, Peter E.	238,179	Baldacci, John	57,515	28,683 D	41.5%	47.1%	46.8%	53.2%
1998**	421,009	79,716	Longley, James B. Jr.	50,506	Connolly, Thomas J.	290,787	29,210 R#	18.9%	12.0%	61.2%	38.8%
1994**	511,308	117,990	Collins, Susan M.	172,951	Brennan, Joseph E.	220,367	54,961 D#	23.1%	33.8%	40.6%	59.4%
1990	522,492	243,766	McKernan, John R.*	230,038	Brennan, Joseph E.	48,688	13,728 R	46.7%	44.0%	51.4%	48.6%
1986**	426,861	170,312	McKernan, John R.	128,744	Tierney, James	127,805	41,568 R	39.9%	30.2%	56.9%	43.1%
1982	460,295	172,949	Cragin, Charles L.	281,066	Brennan, Joseph E.*	6,280	108,117 D	37.6%	61.1%	38.1%	61.9%
1978**	370,258	126,862	Palmer, Linwood E.	176,493	Brennan, Joseph E.	66,903	49,631 D	34.3%	47.7%	41.8%	58.2%
1974**	363,945	84,176	Erwin, James S.	132,219	Mitchell, George J.	147,550	48,043 D#	23.1%	36.3%	38.9%	61.1%
1970	325,386	162,248	Erwin, James S.	163,138	Curtis, Kenneth M.*		890 D	49.9%	50.1%	49.9%	50.1%
1966	323,838	151,802	Reed, John H.*	172,036	Curtis, Kenneth M.		20,234 D	46.9%	53.1%	46.9%	53.1%
1962	292,725	146,604	Reed, John H.*	146,121	Dolloff, Maynard C.		483 R	50.1%	49.9%	50.1%	49.9%
1960S**	417,215	219,768	Reed, John H.	197,447	Coffin, Frank M.		22,321 R	52.7%	47.3%	52.7%	47.3%
1958**	280,245	134,572	Hildreth, Horace A.	145,673	Clauson, Clinton A.		11,101 D	48.0%	52.0%	48.0%	52.0%
1956	304,649	124,395	Trafton, Willis A. Jr.	180,254	Muskie, Edmund S.*		55,859 D	40.8%	59.2%	40.8%	59.2%
1954	248,971	113,298	Cross, Burton M.*	135,673	Muskie, Edmund S.		22,375 D	45.5%	54.5%	45.5%	54.5%
1952	248,441	128,532	Cross, Burton M.	82,538	Oliver, James C.	37,371	45,994 R	51.7%	33.2%	60.9%	39.1%
1950	241,177	145,823	Payne, Frederick G.*	94,304	Grant, Earle S.	1,050	51,519 R	60.5%	39.1%	60.7%	39.3%
1948	222,500	145,956	Payne, Frederick G.	76,544	Lausier, Louis B.		69,412 R	65.6%	34.4%	65.6%	34.4%
1946	179,951	110,327	Hildreth, Horace A.	69,624	Clark, F. Davis		40,703 R	61.3%	38.7%	61.3%	38.7%

Note: An asterisk (*) denotes incumbent. A pound sign (#) in the plurality column indicates that the winners in 1974, 1994, and 1998 were independents. **In past elections, the other vote included: 2010 - 208,270 Independent (Eliot R. Cutler), who placed second; 2006 - 118,715 Independent Maine Course (Barbara Merrill); 1998 - 246,772 Independent (Angus King), who was re-elected with 58.6 percent of the total vote; 1994 - 180,829 Independent (King), who was elected with 35.4 percent of the total vote; 1986 - 64,317 Independent (Sherry F. Huber), 63,474 Independent (John E. Menario); 1978 - 65,889 Independent (Herman C. Frankland); 1974 - 142,464 Independent (James B. Longley), who was elected with 39.1 percent of the total vote. The 1960 election was for a short term to fill a vacancy. The term of office of Maine's Governor was increased from two to four years effective with the 1958 election.

POSTWAR VOTE FOR SENATOR

Year	Total Vote	Republican		Democratic		Other Vote	Rep.-Dem. Plurality	Percentage			
								Total Vote		Major Vote	
		Vote	Candidate	Vote	Candidate			Rep.	Dem.	Rep.	Dem.
2018	634,409	223,502	Brakey, Eric	66,268	Ringelstein, Zak	344,639	157,234 R#	35.2%	10.4%	77.1%	22.9%
2014	604,008	413,495	Collins, Susan M.*	190,244	Bellows, Shenna	269	223,251 R	68.5%	31.5%	68.5%	31.5%
2012**	700,599	215,399	Summers, Charles E.	92,900	Dill, Cynthia Ann	392,300	122,499 R#	30.7%	13.3%	69.9%	30.1%
2008	724,430	444,300	Collins, Susan M.*	279,510	Allen, Tom	620	164,790 R	61.3%	38.6%	61.4%	38.6%
2006	543,981	402,598	Snowe, Olympia J.*	111,984	Bright, Jean Hay	29,399	290,614 R	74.0%	20.6%	78.2%	21.8%
2002	504,899	295,041	Collins, Susan M.*	209,858	Pingree, Chellie		85,183 R	58.4%	41.6%	58.4%	41.6%
2000	634,872	437,689	Snowe, Olympia J.*	197,183	Lawrence, Mark W.		240,506 R	68.9%	31.1%	68.9%	31.1%
1996	606,777	298,422	Collins, Susan M.	266,226	Brennan, Joseph E.	42,129	32,196 R	49.2%	43.9%	52.9%	47.1%
1994	511,733	308,244	Snowe, Olympia J.	186,042	Andrews, Thomas H.	17,447	122,202 R	60.2%	36.4%	62.4%	37.6%
1990	520,320	319,167	Cohen, William S.*	201,053	Rolde, Neil	100	118,114 R	61.3%	38.6%	61.4%	38.6%
1988	557,375	104,758	Wyman, Jasper S.	452,590	Mitchell, George J.*	27	347,832 D	18.8%	81.2%	18.8%	81.2%
1984	551,406	404,414	Cohen, William S.*	142,626	Mitchell, Elizabeth H. "Libby"	4,366	261,788 R	73.3%	25.9%	73.9%	26.1%
1982	459,715	179,882	Emery, David F.	279,819	Mitchell, George J.	14	99,937 D	39.1%	60.9%	39.1%	60.9%
1978	375,172	212,294	Cohen, William S.	127,327	Hathaway, William D.*	35,551	84,967 R	56.6%	33.9%	62.5%	37.5%
1976	486,254	193,489	Monks, Robert A.G.	292,704	Muskie, Edmund S.*	61	99,215 D	39.8%	60.2%	39.8%	60.2%
1972	421,310	197,040	Smith, Margaret Chase*	224,270	Hathaway, William D.		27,230 D	46.8%	53.2%	46.8%	53.2%
1970	323,860	123,906	Bishop, Neil S.	199,954	Muskie, Edmund S.*		76,048 D	38.3%	61.7%	38.3%	61.7%
1966	319,535	188,291	Smith, Margaret Chase*	131,136	Violette, Elmer H.	108	57,155 R	58.9%	41.0%	58.9%	41.1%
1964	380,551	127,040	McIntire, Clifford G.	253,511	Muskie, Edmund S.*		126,471 D	33.4%	66.6%	33.4%	66.6%
1960	416,699	256,890	Smith, Margaret Chase*	159,809	Cormier, Lucia M.		97,081 R	61.6%	38.4%	61.6%	38.4%
1958	284,364	111,522	Payne, Frederick G.*	172,842	Muskie, Edmund S.		61,320 D	39.2%	60.8%	39.2%	60.8%
1954	246,605	144,530	Smith, Margaret Chase*	102,075	Fullam, Paul A.		42,455 R	58.6%	41.4%	58.6%	41.4%
1952	237,164	139,205	Payne, Frederick G.	82,665	Dube, Roger P.	15,294	56,540 R	58.7%	34.9%	62.7%	37.3%
1948	223,256	159,182	Smith, Margaret Chase	64,074	Scolten, Adrian H.		95,108 R	71.3%	28.7%	71.3%	28.7%
1946	175,014	111,215	Brewster, Ralph O.*	63,799	MacDonald, Peter M.		47,416 R	63.5%	36.5%	63.5%	36.5%

Note: An asterisk (*) denotes incumbent. A pound sign (#) in the plurality column indicates that the winner in 2012 and 2018 was an independent. **In past elections, the other vote included: 2018 - 344,575 Independent (Angus King), who received 54.3 percent of the total vote and was elected with a plurality of 121,073 votes; 2012 - 370,580 Independent (King), who received 52.9 percent of the total vote and was elected with a plurality of 155,181 votes.

MAINE

GOVERNOR 2018

2010 Census Population	County	Total Vote	Republican (Moody)	Democratic (Mills)	Other	Rep.-Dem. Plurality	Percentage Total Vote Rep.	Total Vote Dem.	Major Vote Rep.	Major Vote Dem.
107,702	ANDROSCOGGIN	45,071	21,903	19,801	3,367	2,102 R	48.6%	43.9%	52.5%	47.5%
71,870	AROOSTOOK	27,072	14,486	10,347	2,239	4,139 R	53.5%	38.2%	58.3%	41.7%
281,674	CUMBERLAND	153,484	52,811	93,368	7,305	40,557 D	34.4%	60.8%	36.1%	63.9%
30,768	FRANKLIN	14,083	6,257	7,085	741	828 D	44.4%	50.3%	46.9%	53.1%
54,418	HANCOCK	28,115	11,345	15,221	1,549	3,876 D	40.4%	54.1%	42.7%	57.3%
122,151	KENNEBEC	55,954	25,752	26,777	3,425	1,025 D	46.0%	47.9%	49.0%	51.0%
39,736	KNOX	20,401	7,694	11,691	1,016	3,997 D	37.7%	57.3%	39.7%	60.3%
34,457	LINCOLN	19,024	8,324	9,676	1,024	1,352 D	43.8%	50.9%	46.2%	53.8%
57,833	OXFORD	25,592	12,339	10,508	2,745	1,831 R	48.2%	41.1%	54.0%	46.0%
153,923	PENOBSCOT	64,306	31,621	29,039	3,646	2,582 R	49.2%	45.2%	52.1%	47.9%
17,535	PISCATAQUIS	7,405	4,074	2,868	463	1,206 R	55.0%	38.7%	58.7%	41.3%
35,293	SAGADAHOC	19,095	7,714	10,152	1,229	2,438 D	40.4%	53.2%	43.2%	56.8%
52,228	SOMERSET	20,782	11,048	8,524	1,210	2,524 R	53.2%	41.0%	56.4%	43.6%
38,786	WALDO	19,594	8,397	10,109	1,088	1,712 D	42.9%	51.6%	45.4%	54.6%
32,856	WASHINGTON	13,057	6,542	5,740	775	802 R	50.1%	44.0%	53.3%	46.7%
197,131	YORK	95,303	41,727	48,078	5,498	6,351 D	43.8%	50.4%	46.5%	53.5%
	Votes Not Reported by County	2,329	277	1,978	74	1,701 D	11.9%	84.9%	12.3%	87.7%
1,328,361	*TOTAL*	*630,667*	*272,311*	*320,962*	*37,394*	*48,651 D*	*43.2%*	*50.9%*	*45.9%*	*54.1%*

2010 Census Population	City/Town	Total Vote	Republican (Moody)	Democratic (Mills)	Other	Rep.-Dem. Plurality	Percentage Total Vote Rep.	Total Vote Dem.	Major Vote Rep.	Major Vote Dem.
23,055	AUBURN	9,526	4,235	4,578	713	343 D	44.5%	48.1%	48.1%	51.9%
19,136	AUGUSTA	7,556	3,098	4,018	440	920 D	41.0%	53.2%	43.5%	56.5%
33,039	BANGOR	12,308	4,464	7,116	728	2,652 D	36.3%	57.8%	38.5%	61.5%
8,514	BATH	4,118	1,213	2,633	272	1,420 D	29.5%	63.9%	31.5%	68.5%
6,668	BELFAST	3,519	1,006	2,342	171	1,336 D	28.6%	66.6%	30.0%	70.0%
7,246	BERWICK	2,995	1,516	1,294	185	222 R	50.6%	43.2%	54.0%	46.0%
21,277	BIDDEFORD	8,053	3,010	4,559	484	1,549 D	37.4%	56.6%	39.8%	60.2%
9,482	BREWER	3,991	1,893	1,881	217	12 R	47.4%	47.1%	50.2%	49.8%
20,278	BRUNSWICK	11,165	3,024	7,578	563	4,554 D	27.1%	67.9%	28.5%	71.5%
8,034	BUXTON	4,086	2,334	1,580	172	754 R	57.1%	38.7%	59.6%	40.4%
4,850	CAMDEN	3,195	746	2,339	110	1,593 D	23.3%	73.2%	24.2%	75.8%
9,015	CAPE ELIZABETH	5,649	1,514	3,943	192	2,429 D	26.8%	69.8%	27.7%	72.3%
8,189	CARIBOU	3,016	1,594	1,141	281	453 R	52.9%	37.8%	58.3%	41.7%
7,211	CUMBERLAND TOWN	5,083	1,909	2,967	207	1,058 D	37.6%	58.4%	39.2%	60.8%
6,204	ELIOT	3,637	1,398	2,044	195	646 D	38.4%	56.2%	40.6%	59.4%
7,741	ELLSWORTH	3,668	1,698	1,747	223	49 D	46.3%	47.6%	49.3%	50.7%
6,735	FAIRFIELD	2,566	1,238	1,178	150	60 R	48.2%	45.9%	51.2%	48.8%
11,185	FALMOUTH	7,511	2,791	4,413	307	1,622 D	37.2%	58.8%	38.7%	61.3%
7,760	FARMINGTON	3,214	1,137	2,019	58	882 D	35.4%	62.8%	36.0%	64.0%
7,879	FREEPORT	5,047	1,525	3,289	233	1,764 D	30.2%	65.2%	31.7%	68.3%
5,800	GARDINER	2,574	1,036	1,362	176	326 D	40.2%	52.9%	43.2%	56.8%
16,381	GORHAM	8,853	4,424	4,039	390	385 R	50.0%	45.6%	52.3%	47.7%
7,761	GRAY	4,160	2,135	1,794	231	341 R	51.3%	43.1%	54.3%	45.7%
7,257	HAMPDEN	3,509	1,687	1,655	167	32 R	48.1%	47.2%	50.5%	49.5%
4,740	HARPSWELL	3,147	1,210	1,788	149	578 D	38.4%	56.8%	40.4%	59.6%
6,123	HOULTON	2,012	1,099	729	184	370 R	54.6%	36.2%	60.1%	39.9%
4,851	JAY	2,112	949	1,032	131	83 D	44.9%	48.9%	47.9%	52.1%
10,798	KENNEBUNK	6,523	2,423	3,792	308	1,369 D	37.1%	58.1%	39.0%	61.0%
9,490	KITTERY	4,815	1,381	3,163	271	1,782 D	28.7%	65.7%	30.4%	69.6%
36,592	LEWISTON	13,528	5,497	7,056	975	1,559 D	40.6%	52.2%	43.8%	56.2%

MAINE

GOVERNOR 2018

2010 Census Population	City/Town	Total Vote	Republican (Moody)	Democratic (Mills)	Other	Rep.-Dem. Plurality	Percentage Total Vote Rep.	Total Vote Dem.	Major Vote Rep.	Major Vote Dem.
2,314	LIMESTONE	628	339	218	71	121 R	54.0%	34.7%	60.9%	39.1%
5,085	LINCOLN TOWN	1,890	1,114	660	116	454 R	58.9%	34.9%	62.8%	37.2%
9,009	LISBON	3,921	2,060	1,536	325	524 R	52.5%	39.2%	57.3%	42.7%
4,506	MILLINOCKET	1,828	853	840	135	13 R	46.7%	46.0%	50.4%	49.6%
6,240	OAKLAND	2,846	1,366	1,267	213	99 R	48.0%	44.5%	51.9%	48.1%
8,624	OLD ORCHARD BEACH	4,658	1,769	2,603	286	834 D	38.0%	55.9%	40.5%	59.5%
7,840	OLD TOWN	3,103	1,187	1,733	183	546 D	38.3%	55.8%	40.7%	59.3%
10,362	ORONO	4,246	1,029	2,969	248	1,940 D	24.2%	69.9%	25.7%	74.3%
66,194	PORTLAND	33,276	5,675	26,237	1,364	20,562 D	17.1%	78.8%	17.8%	82.2%
9,692	PRESQUE ISLE	3,203	1,656	1,250	297	406 R	51.7%	39.0%	57.0%	43.0%
7,297	ROCKLAND	2,986	943	1,895	148	952 D	31.6%	63.5%	33.2%	66.8%
5,841	RUMFORD	2,201	995	991	215	4 R	45.2%	45.0%	50.1%	49.9%
18,482	SACO	9,112	3,492	5,127	493	1,635 D	38.3%	56.3%	40.5%	59.5%
20,798	SANFORD	7,331	3,464	3,374	493	90 R	47.3%	46.0%	50.7%	49.3%
18,919	SCARBOROUGH	11,572	4,917	6,110	545	1,193 D	42.5%	52.8%	44.6%	55.4%
8,589	SKOWHEGAN	3,177	1,483	1,548	146	65 D	46.7%	48.7%	48.9%	51.1%
7,220	SOUTH BERWICK	3,300	1,237	1,873	190	636 D	37.5%	56.8%	39.8%	60.2%
25,002	SOUTH PORTLAND	13,027	3,308	9,072	647	5,764 D	25.4%	69.6%	26.7%	73.3%
9,874	STANDISH	4,588	2,528	1,818	242	710 R	55.1%	39.6%	58.2%	41.8%
8,784	TOPSHAM	5,106	1,881	2,860	365	979 D	36.8%	56.0%	39.7%	60.3%
15,722	WATERVILLE	5,889	1,839	3,705	345	1,866 D	31.2%	62.9%	33.2%	66.8%
9,589	WELLS	5,849	2,546	2,969	334	423 D	43.5%	50.8%	46.2%	53.8%
17,494	WESTBROOK	8,426	3,015	4,941	470	1,926 D	35.8%	58.6%	37.9%	62.1%
17,001	WINDHAM	8,309	4,178	3,662	469	516 R	50.3%	44.1%	53.3%	46.7%
7,794	WINSLOW	3,585	1,729	1,659	197	70 R	48.2%	46.3%	51.0%	49.0%
6,092	WINTHROP	2,950	1,276	1,495	179	219 D	43.3%	50.7%	46.0%	54.0%
8,349	YARMOUTH	5,219	1,570	3,425	224	1,855 D	30.1%	65.6%	31.4%	68.6%
12,529	YORK TOWN	7,622	2,729	4,456	437	1,727 D	35.8%	58.5%	38.0%	62.0%

MAINE

SENATOR 2018

2010 Census Population	County	Total Vote	Republican (Brakey)	Democratic (Ringelstein)	Independent (King)	Other	Plurality	Percentage Total Vote Rep.	Total Vote Dem.	Major Vote Rep.	Major Vote Dem.
107,702	ANDROSCOGGIN	45,409	18,931	4,316	22,150	12	3,219 I	41.7%	9.5%	81.4%	18.6%
71,870	AROOSTOOK	27,334	10,767	1,822	14,742	3	3,975 I	39.4%	6.7%	85.5%	14.5%
281,674	CUMBERLAND	154,180	40,053	20,262	93,860	5	53,807 I	26.0%	13.1%	66.4%	33.6%
30,768	FRANKLIN	14,128	5,194	1,383	7,546	5	2,352 I	36.8%	9.8%	79.0%	21.0%
54,418	HANCOCK	28,277	9,837	2,969	15,463	8	5,626 I	34.8%	10.5%	76.8%	23.2%
122,151	KENNEBEC	56,088	21,608	4,837	29,640	3	8,032 I	38.5%	8.6%	81.7%	18.3%
39,736	KNOX	20,516	6,270	2,234	12,009	3	5,739 I	30.6%	10.9%	73.7%	26.3%
34,457	LINCOLN	19,169	6,814	1,592	10,763		3,949 I	35.5%	8.3%	81.1%	18.9%
57,833	OXFORD	25,605	10,510	2,141	12,954		2,444 I	41.0%	8.4%	83.1%	16.9%
153,923	PENOBSCOT	64,847	27,692	5,856	31,290	9	3,598 I	42.7%	9.0%	82.5%	17.5%
17,535	PISCATAQUIS	7,494	3,578	534	3,379	3	199 R	47.7%	7.1%	87.0%	13.0%
35,293	SAGADAHOC	19,264	6,284	1,507	11,473		5,189 I	32.6%	7.8%	80.7%	19.3%
52,228	SOMERSET	20,961	9,831	1,493	9,631	6	200 R	46.9%	7.1%	86.8%	13.2%
38,786	WALDO	19,747	7,265	1,976	10,503	3	3,238 I	36.8%	10.0%	78.6%	21.4%
32,856	WASHINGTON	13,181	5,770	1,097	6,310	4	540 I	43.8%	8.3%	84.0%	16.0%
197,131	YORK	95,787	32,849	11,551	51,387		18,538 I	34.3%	12.1%	74.0%	26.0%
	Votes Not Reported by County	2,422	249	698	1,475		777 I	10.3%	28.8%	26.3%	73.7%
1,328,361	*TOTAL*	*634,409*	*223,502*	*66,268*	*344,575*	*64*	*121,073 I*	*35.2%*	*10.4%*	*77.1%*	*22.9%*

MAINE

SENATOR 2018

2010 Census Population	City/Town	Total Vote	Republican (Brakey)	Democratic (Ringelstein)	Independent (King)	Other	Plurality	Percentage Total Vote Rep.	Total Vote Dem.	Major Vote Rep.	Major Vote Dem.
23,055	AUBURN	9,620	3,813	862	4,945		1,132 I	39.6%	9.0%	81.6%	18.4%
19,136	AUGUSTA	7,589	2,539	711	4,339		1,800 I	33.5%	9.4%	78.1%	21.9%
33,039	BANGOR	12,420	3,844	1,527	7,049		3,205 I	31.0%	12.3%	71.6%	28.4%
8,514	BATH	4,159	960	462	2,737		1,777 I	23.1%	11.1%	67.5%	32.5%
6,668	BELFAST	3,546	865	429	2,251	1	1,386 I	24.4%	12.1%	66.8%	33.2%
7,246	BERWICK	3,032	1,274	434	1,324		50 I	42.0%	14.3%	74.6%	25.4%
21,277	BIDDEFORD	8,117	2,187	1,117	4,813		2,626 I	26.9%	13.8%	66.2%	33.8%
9,482	BREWER	4,019	1,647	328	2,044		397 I	41.0%	8.2%	83.4%	16.6%
20,278	BRUNSWICK	11,326	2,386	1,081	7,859		5,473 I	21.1%	9.5%	68.8%	31.2%
8,034	BUXTON	4,097	1,705	325	2,067		362 I	41.6%	7.9%	84.0%	16.0%
4,850	CAMDEN	3,253	583	352	2,318		1,735 I	17.9%	10.8%	62.4%	37.6%
9,015	CAPE ELIZABETH	5,657	1,124	552	3,981		2,857 I	19.9%	9.8%	67.1%	32.9%
8,189	CARIBOU	3,065	1,135	177	1,753		618 I	37.0%	5.8%	86.5%	13.5%
7,211	CUMBERLAND TOWN	5,123	1,426	409	3,288		1,862 I	27.8%	8.0%	77.7%	22.3%
6,204	ELIOT	3,691	1,168	628	1,895		727 I	31.6%	17.0%	65.0%	35.0%
7,741	ELLSWORTH	3,686	1,475	349	1,862		387 I	40.0%	9.5%	80.9%	19.1%
6,735	FAIRFIELD	2,582	1,126	213	1,243		117 I	43.6%	8.2%	84.1%	15.9%
11,185	FALMOUTH	7,435	2,034	693	4,708		2,674 I	27.4%	9.3%	74.6%	25.4%
7,760	FARMINGTON	3,286	948	509	1,829		881 I	28.8%	15.5%	65.1%	34.9%
7,879	FREEPORT	5,140	1,180	545	3,415		2,235 I	23.0%	10.6%	68.4%	31.6%
5,800	GARDINER	2,581	874	243	1,464		590 I	33.9%	9.4%	78.2%	21.8%
16,381	GORHAM	8,883	2,969	981	4,930	3	1,961 I	33.4%	11.0%	75.2%	24.8%
7,761	GRAY	4,193	1,743	358	2,092		349 I	41.6%	8.5%	83.0%	17.0%
7,257	HAMPDEN	3,614	1,488	261	1,865		377 I	41.2%	7.2%	85.1%	14.9%
4,740	HARPSWELL	3,211	975	188	2,048		1,073 I	30.4%	5.9%	83.8%	16.2%
6,123	HOULTON	2,037	863	121	1,053		190 I	42.4%	5.9%	87.7%	12.3%
4,851	JAY	2,127	785	183	1,159		374 I	36.9%	8.6%	81.1%	18.9%
10,798	KENNEBUNK	6,564	1,924	727	3,913		1,989 I	29.3%	11.1%	72.6%	27.4%
9,490	KITTERY	4,938	1,201	963	2,774		1,573 I	24.3%	19.5%	55.5%	44.5%
36,592	LEWISTON	13,577	4,639	1,942	6,993	3	2,354 I	34.2%	14.3%	70.5%	29.5%
2,314	LIMESTONE	626	233	40	353		120 I	37.2%	6.4%	85.3%	14.7%
5,085	LINCOLN TOWN	1,909	1,012	133	764		248 R	53.0%	7.0%	88.4%	11.6%
9,009	LISBON	3,978	1,745	312	1,921		176 I	43.9%	7.8%	84.8%	15.2%
4,506	MILLINOCKET	1,839	706	101	1,032		326 I	38.4%	5.5%	87.5%	12.5%
6,240	OAKLAND	2,892	1,126	212	1,554		428 I	38.9%	7.3%	84.2%	15.8%
8,624	OLD ORCHARD BEACH	4,672	1,348	535	2,789		1,441 I	28.9%	11.5%	71.6%	28.4%
7,840	OLD TOWN	3,141	1,017	368	1,756		739 I	32.4%	11.7%	73.4%	26.6%
10,362	ORONO	4,350	804	974	2,572		1,598 I	18.5%	22.4%	45.2%	54.8%
66,194	PORTLAND	33,482	4,201	7,479	21,802		14,323 I	12.5%	22.3%	36.0%	64.0%
9,692	PRESQUE ISLE	3,267	1,194	226	1,847		653 I	36.5%	6.9%	84.1%	15.9%
7,297	ROCKLAND	2,980	768	455	1,757		989 I	25.8%	15.3%	62.8%	37.2%
5,841	RUMFORD	2,198	832	189	1,177		345 I	37.9%	8.6%	81.5%	18.5%
18,482	SACO	9,079	2,639	965	5,475		2,836 I	29.1%	10.6%	73.2%	26.8%
20,798	SANFORD	7,308	2,655	861	3,792		1,137 I	36.3%	11.8%	75.5%	24.5%
18,919	SCARBOROUGH	11,571	3,621	1,088	6,862		3,241 I	31.3%	9.4%	76.9%	23.1%
8,589	SKOWHEGAN	3,226	1,259	243	1,724		465 I	39.0%	7.5%	83.8%	16.2%
7,220	SOUTH BERWICK	3,292	1,024	609	1,659		635 I	31.1%	18.5%	62.7%	37.3%
25,002	SOUTH PORTLAND	13,035	2,495	2,155	8,385		5,890 I	19.1%	16.5%	53.7%	46.3%
9,874	STANDISH	4,566	1,938	411	2,217		279 I	42.4%	9.0%	82.5%	17.5%
8,784	TOPSHAM	5,138	1,537	381	3,220		1,683 I	29.9%	7.4%	80.1%	19.9%
15,722	WATERVILLE	5,993	1,569	1,021	3,403		1,834 I	26.2%	17.0%	60.6%	39.4%
9,589	WELLS	5,857	2,069	721	3,067		998 I	35.3%	12.3%	74.2%	25.8%
17,494	WESTBROOK	8,442	2,196	1,280	4,966		2,770 I	26.0%	15.2%	63.2%	36.8%
17,001	WINDHAM	8,352	3,127	768	4,457		1,330 I	37.4%	9.2%	80.3%	19.7%
7,794	WINSLOW	3,592	1,481	284	1,827		346 I	41.2%	7.9%	83.9%	16.1%
6,092	WINTHROP	2,946	1,035	261	1,650		615 I	35.1%	8.9%	79.9%	20.1%
8,349	YARMOUTH	5,331	1,136	622	3,573		2,437 I	21.3%	11.7%	64.6%	35.4%
12,529	YORK TOWN	7,707	2,251	1,058	4,398		2,147 I	29.2%	13.7%	68.0%	32.0%

MAINE

HOUSE OF REPRESENTATIVES

			Republican		Democratic				Percentage			
									Total Vote		Major Vote	
CD	Year	Total Vote	Vote	Candidate	Vote	Candidate	Other Vote	Rep.-Dem. Plurality	Rep.	Dem.	Rep.	Dem.
1	2018	342,053	111,188	HOLBROOK, MARK I.	201,195	PINGREE, CHELLIE*	29,670	90,007 D	32.5%	58.8%	35.6%	64.4%
1	2016	392,391	164,569	HOLBROOK, MARK I.	227,546	PINGREE, CHELLIE*	276	62,977 D	41.9%	58.0%	42.0%	58.0%
1	2014	308,898	94,751	MISIUK, ISAAC J.	186,674	PINGREE, CHELLIE*	27,473	91,923 D	30.7%	60.4%	33.7%	66.3%
1	2012	364,803	128,440	COURTNEY, JONATHAN T.E.	236,363	PINGREE, CHELLIE*		107,923 D	35.2%	64.8%	35.2%	64.8%
2**	2018	281,371	138,931	POLIQUIN, BRUCE L.*	142,440	GOLDEN, JARED		3,509 D	49.4%	50.4%	49.4%	50.4%
2	2016	352,183	192,878	POLIQUIN, BRUCE L.*	159,081	CAIN, EMILY ANN	224	33,797 R	54.8%	45.2%	54.8%	45.2%
2	2014	283,448	133,308	POLIQUIN, BRUCE L.	118,556	CAIN, EMILY ANN	31,584	14,752 R	47.0%	41.8%	52.9%	47.1%
2	2012	328,998	137,542	RAYE, KEVIN L.	191,456	MICHAUD, MICHAEL H.*		53,914 D	41.8%	58.2%	41.8%	58.2%
TOTAL	*2018*	*623,424*	*250,119*		*343,635*		*29,670*	*93,516 D*	*40.1%*	*55.1%*	*42.1%*	*57.9%*
TOTAL	*2016*	*744,574*	*357,447*		*386,627*		*500*	*29,180 D*	*48.0%*	*51.9%*	*48.0%*	*52.0%*
TOTAL	*2014*	*592,346*	*228,059*		*305,230*		*59,057*	*77,171 D*	*38.5%*	*51.5%*	*42.8%*	*57.2%*
TOTAL	*2012*	*693,801*	*265,982*		*427,819*			*161,837 D*	*38.3%*	*61.7%*	*38.3%*	*61.7%*

Note: An asterisk (*) denotes incumbent. **Maine's new ranked-choice voting system requires winning candidates to receive a majority vote. Candidates with the fewest ranked votes are eliminated, and their votes are transferred to the candidates ranked second on each voter's ballot. Balloting in District 2 resulted in Round 2 counting, and is presented here. In Round 1 counting, the vote was Bruce L. Poliquin with 134,184 votes (46.3%), Jared F. Golden with 132,013 votes (45.6%), Tiffany L. Bond with 16,552 votes (5.7%), and William R.S. Hoar with 6,875 votes (2.4%). In Round 2 counting, 4,747 votes were transferred to Bruce L. Poliquin's vote total, and 10,427 votes were transferred to Jared F. Golden's vote total.

MAINE

GENERAL AND PRIMARY ELECTIONS

2018 GENERAL ELECTIONS: OTHER VOTES

Governor Other vote was 37,268 Independent (Teresea Hayes), 126 Write-in (Others)

Senate Other vote was 64 Write-in (Others)

House Other vote was:

CD 1 29,670 Independent (Martin Grohman)

CD 2 16,552 Independent (Tiffany L. Bond), 6,875 Independent (William R.S. Hoar). Other vote in District 2 from initial count.

2018 PRIMARY ELECTIONS: SUPPLEMENTARY INFORMATION

Primary	June 12, 2018	**Registration** (as of January 27, 2018)	1,036,264	Democratic	329,965
				Republican	277,963
				Green Independent	43,940
				Libertarian	5,573
				Unenrolled	378,823

Primary Type Semi-open—Registered voters in a political party could participate only in their party's primary. "Unenrolled" and new voters could vote in either party's primary by enrolling in that party on primary day.

	REPUBLICAN PRIMARIES			DEMOCRATIC PRIMARIES		
Senator	Brakey, Eric	59,853	58.9%	Ringelstein, Zak	89,841	100.0%
	Linn, Max	41,732	41.1%			
	TOTAL	*101,585*		*TOTAL*	*89,841*	

MAINE

GENERAL AND PRIMARY ELECTIONS

	REPUBLICAN PRIMARIES			DEMOCRATIC PRIMARIES		
Governor**	Moody, Shawn H.	53,436	56.6%	Mills, Janet T.	41,735	33.1%
	Mason, Garrett	21,571	22.9%	Cote, Adam Roland	35,478	28.1%
	Mayhew, Mary	14,034	14.9%	Sweet, Elizabeth A.	20,767	16.5%
	Fredette, Kenneth	5,341	5.7%	Eves, Mark W.	17,887	14.2%
				Dion, Mark N.	5,200	4.1%
				Russell, Diane Marie	2,728	2.2%
				Dion, Donna J.	1,596	1.3%
				Write-In	748	0.6%
	TOTAL	*94,382*		*TOTAL*	*126,139*	
				PRIMARY RUNOFF (ranked-choice)		
				Mills, Janet T.	63,384	54.1%
				Cote, Adam Roland	53,866	46.9%
				TOTAL	*117,250*	
Congressional District 1	Holbrook, Mark I.	40,679	100.0%	Pingree, Chellie*	74,376	100.0%
	TOTAL	*40,679*		*TOTAL*	*74,376*	
Congressional District 2**	Poliquin, Bruce L.*	43,047	100.0%	Golden, Jared	20,987	46.4%
				St. Clair, Lucas	17,742	39.2%
				Olson, Craig	3,993	8.8%
				Fulford, Jonathan	2,489	5.5%
	TOTAL	*43,047*		*TOTAL*	*45,211*	
				PRIMARY RUNOFF (ranked-choice)		
				Golden, Jared	23,611	54.3%
				St. Clair, Lucas	19,853	45.7%
				TOTAL	*43,464*	

Note: An asterisk (*) denotes incumbent. **Maine's new ranked-choice voting system requires winning candidates to receive a majority vote. Candidates with the fewest ranked votes are eliminated, and their votes are transferred to the candidates ranked second on each voter's ballot. This process continues until a candidate receives a majority. Balloting in the Democratic gubernatorial race resulted in Round 4 balloting. The results of Round 1 gubernatorial counting are presented as the primary. In Round 2 counting, 2,307 votes were transferred to Janet T. Mills for a total of 44,042 votes (35.5%), 2,065 votes were transferred to Adam Roland Cote for a total of 37,543 votes (30.3%), 2,220 votes were transferred to Elizabeth A. Sweet for a total of 22,987 votes (18.5%), and 1,634 votes were transferred to Mark W. Eves for a total of 19,521 votes (15.7%). In Round 3 counting, 5,903 votes were transferred to Janet T. Mills for a total of 49,945 votes (40.8%), 5,080 votes were transferred to Adam Roland Cote for a total of 42,623 votes (34.8%), and 5,957 votes were transferred to Elizabeth A. Sweet for a total of 29,944 votes (24.4%). The final round, Round 4, is presented as a runoff. Democratic balloting in District 2 resulted in Round 2 counting, and is presented here as a runoff. In Round 2 counting, 2,624 votes were transferred to Jared Golden, and 2,111 votes were transferred to Lucas St. Clair.

MARYLAND

Congressional districts first established for elections held in 2012
8 members

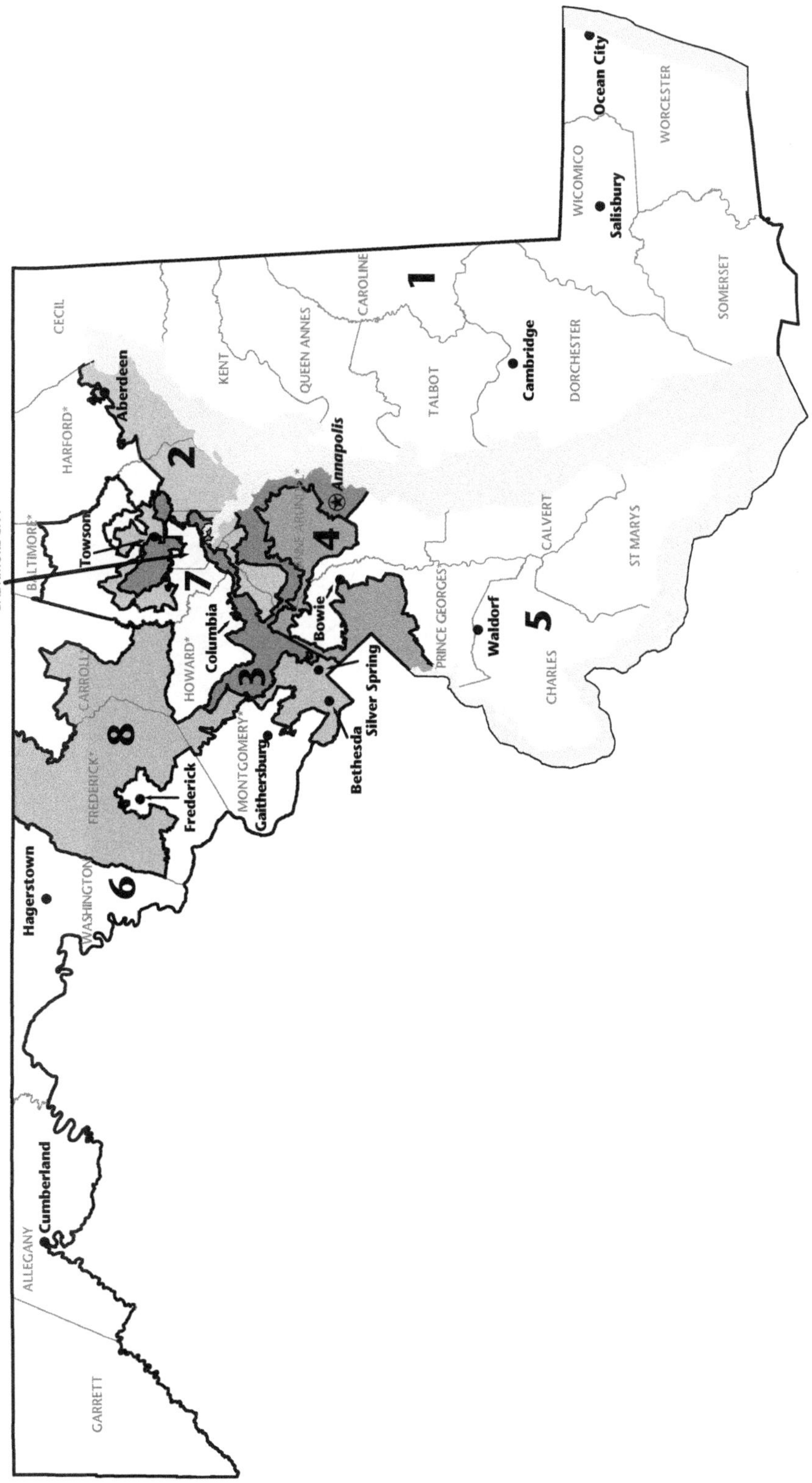

The city of Baltimore City is an independent city that is treated as a county equivalent.

*Asterisk indicates a county whose boundaries include parts of two or more congressional districts.

MARYLAND

Baltimore, Washington, D.C., Areas

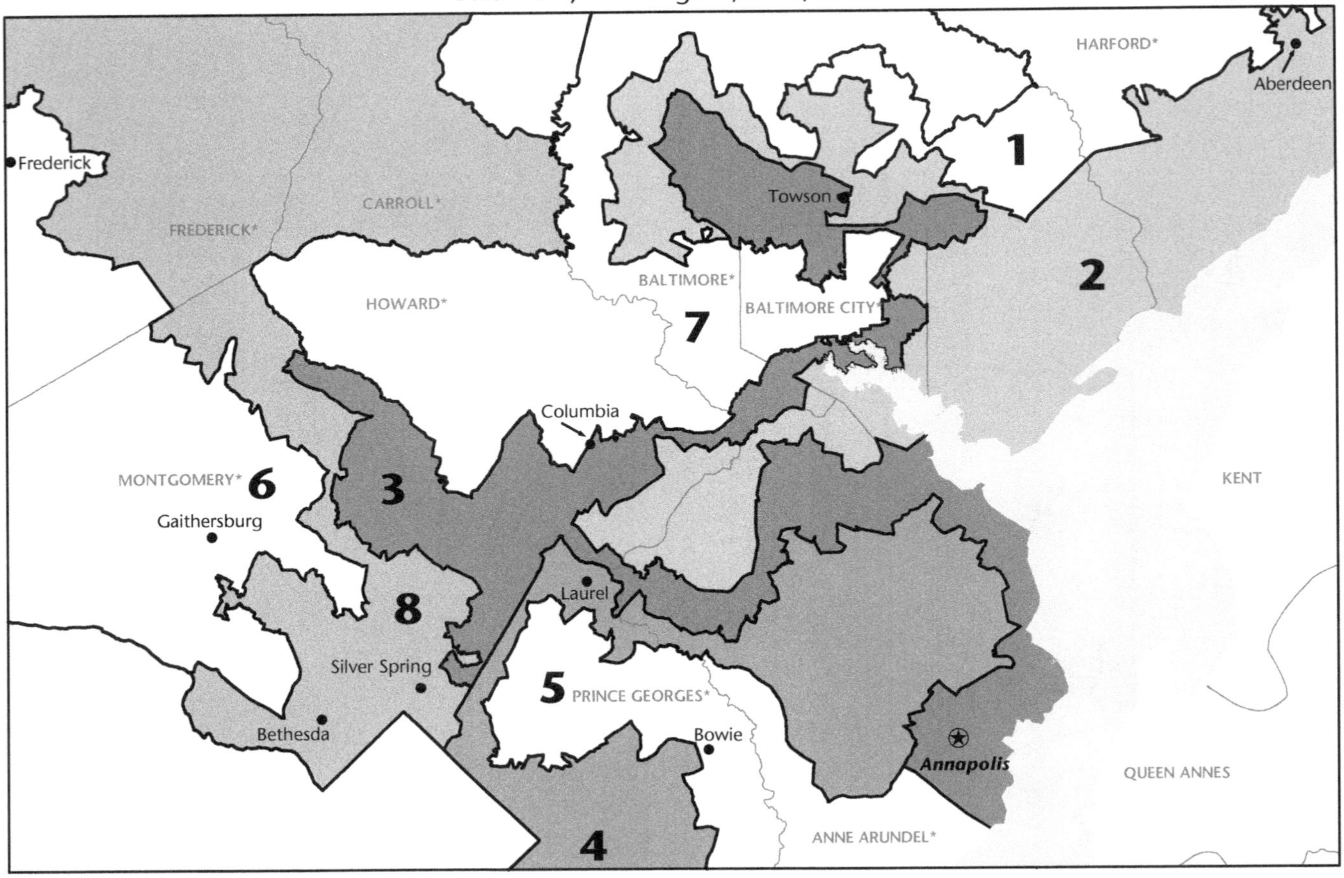

* Asterisk indicates a county whose boundaries include parts of two or more congressional districts.

MARYLAND

GOVERNOR

Larry Hogan (R). Re-elected 2018 to a four-year term. Previously elected 2014.

SENATORS (2 Democrats)

Benjamin L. Cardin (D). Re-elected 2018 to a six-year term. Previously elected 2012, 2006.

Chris Van Hollen Jr. (D). Elected 2016 to a six-year term.

REPRESENTATIVES (1 Republican, 7 Democrats)

1. Andy Harris (R)
2. C. A. Dutch Ruppersberger (D)
3. John P. Sarbanes (D)
4. Anthony G. Brown (D)
5. Steny H. Hoyer (D)
6. David Trone (D)
7. Elijah E. Cummings (D)
8. Jamie Raskin (D)

POSTWAR VOTE FOR PRESIDENT

		Republican		Democratic				Percentage			
								Total Vote		Major Vote	
Year	Total Vote	Vote	Candidate	Vote	Candidate	Other Vote	Rep.-Dem. Plurality	Rep.	Dem.	Rep.	Dem.
2016**	2,781,446	943,169	Trump, Donald J.	1,677,928	Clinton, Hillary Rodham	160,349	734,759 D	33.9%	60.3%	36.0%	64.0%
2012	2,707,327	971,869	Romney, W. Mitt	1,677,844	Obama, Barack H.*	57,614	705,975 D	35.9%	62.0%	36.7%	63.3%
2008	2,631,596	959,862	McCain, John S. III	1,629,467	Obama, Barack H.	42,267	669,605 D	36.5%	61.9%	37.1%	62.9%
2004	2,386,678	1,024,703	Bush, George W.*	1,334,493	Kerry, John F.	27,482	309,790 D	42.9%	55.9%	43.4%	56.6%
2000**	2,020,480	813,797	Bush, George W.	1,140,782	Gore, Albert Jr.	65,901	326,985 D	40.3%	56.5%	41.6%	58.4%
1996**	1,780,870	681,530	Dole, Robert "Bob"	966,207	Clinton, Bill*	133,133	284,677 D	38.3%	54.3%	41.4%	58.6%
1992**	1,985,046	707,094	Bush, George H.*	988,571	Clinton, Bill	289,381	281,477 D	35.6%	49.8%	41.7%	58.3%
1988	1,714,358	876,167	Bush, George H.	826,304	Dukakis, Michael S.	11,887	49,863 R	51.1%	48.2%	51.5%	48.5%
1984	1,675,873	879,918	Reagan, Ronald*	787,935	Mondale, Walter F.	8,020	91,983 R	52.5%	47.0%	52.8%	47.2%
1980**	1,540,496	680,606	Reagan, Ronald	726,161	Carter, Jimmy*	133,729	45,555 D	44.2%	47.1%	48.4%	51.6%
1976	1,439,897	672,661	Ford, Gerald R.*	759,612	Carter, Jimmy	7,624	86,951 D	46.7%	52.8%	47.0%	53.0%
1972	1,353,812	829,305	Nixon, Richard M.*	505,781	McGovern, George S.	18,726	323,524 R	61.3%	37.4%	62.1%	37.9%
1968**	1,235,039	517,995	Nixon, Richard M.	538,310	Humphrey, Hubert Horatio Jr.	178,734	20,315 D	41.9%	43.6%	49.0%	51.0%
1964	1,116,457	385,495	Goldwater, Barry M. Sr.	730,912	Johnson, Lyndon B.*	50	345,417 D	34.5%	65.5%	34.5%	65.5%
1960	1,055,349	489,538	Nixon, Richard M.	565,808	Kennedy, John F.	3	76,270 D	46.4%	53.6%	46.4%	53.6%
1956	932,827	559,738	Eisenhower, Dwight D.*	372,613	Stevenson, Adlai E. II	476	187,125 R	60.0%	39.9%	60.0%	40.0%
1952	902,074	499,424	Eisenhower, Dwight D.	395,337	Stevenson, Adlai E. II	7,313	104,087 R	55.4%	43.8%	55.8%	44.2%
1948	596,748	294,814	Dewey, Thomas E.	286,521	Truman, Harry S.*	15,413	8,293 R	49.4%	48.0%	50.7%	49.3%

Note: An asterisk (*) denotes incumbent. **In past elections, the other vote included: 2016 - 79,605 Libertarian (Gary Johnson); 2000 - 53,768 Green (Ralph Nader); 1996 - 115,812 Reform (Ross Perot); 1992 - 281,414 Independent (Perot); 1980 - 119,537 Independent (John Anderson); 1968 - 178,734 American Independent (George Wallace).

MARYLAND

POSTWAR VOTE FOR GOVERNOR

		Republican		Democratic				Percentage			
								Total Vote		Major Vote	
Year	Total Vote	Vote	Candidate	Vote	Candidate	Other Vote	Rep.-Dem. Plurality	Rep.	Dem.	Rep.	Dem.
2018	2,304,512	1,275,644	Hogan, Larry*	1,002,639	Jealous, Ben	26,229	273,005 R	55.4%	43.5%	56.0%	44.0%
2014	1,733,177	884,400	Hogan, Larry	818,890	Brown, Anthony G.	29,887	65,510 R	51.0%	47.2%	51.9%	48.1%
2010	1,857,880	776,319	Ehrlich, Robert L. "Bob" Jr.	1,044,961	O'Malley, Martin*	36,600	268,642 D	41.8%	56.2%	42.6%	57.4%
2006	1,788,316	825,464	Ehrlich, Robert L. "Bob" Jr.*	942,279	O'Malley, Martin	20,573	116,815 D	46.2%	52.7%	46.7%	53.3%
2002	1,706,179	879,592	Ehrlich, Robert L. "Bob" Jr.	813,422	Townsend, Kathleen Kennedy	13,165	66,170 R	51.6%	47.7%	52.0%	48.0%
1998	1,535,978	688,357	Sauerbrey, Ellen R.	846,972	Glendening, Parris N.*	649	158,615 D	44.8%	55.1%	44.8%	55.2%
1994	1,410,300	702,101	Sauerbrey, Ellen R.	708,094	Glendening, Parris N.	105	5,993 D	49.8%	50.2%	49.8%	50.2%
1990	1,111,088	446,980	Shepard, William S.	664,015	Schaefer, William D.*	93	217,035 D	40.2%	59.8%	40.2%	59.8%
1986	1,101,476	194,185	Mooney, Thomas J.	907,291	Schaefer, William D.		713,106 D	17.6%	82.4%	17.6%	82.4%
1982	1,139,149	432,826	Pascal, Robert A.	705,910	Hughes, Harry R.*	413	273,084 D	38.0%	62.0%	38.0%	62.0%
1978	1,011,963	293,635	Beall, John Glenn Jr.	718,328	Hughes, Harry R.		424,693 D	29.0%	71.0%	29.0%	71.0%
1974	949,097	346,449	Gore, Louise	602,648	Mandel, Marvin*		256,199 D	36.5%	63.5%	36.5%	63.5%
1970	973,099	314,336	Blair, C. Stanley	639,579	Mandel, Marvin*	19,184	325,243 D	32.3%	65.7%	33.0%	67.0%
1966	919,760	455,318	Agnew, Spiro T.	373,543	Mahoney, George P.	90,899	81,775 R	49.5%	40.6%	54.9%	45.1%
1962	769,347	341,271	Small, Frank Jr.	428,071	Tawes, J. Millard*	5	86,800 D	44.4%	55.6%	44.4%	55.6%
1958	763,234	278,173	Devereux, James Patrick	485,061	Tawes, J. Millard		206,888 D	36.4%	63.6%	36.4%	63.6%
1954	700,484	381,451	McKeldin, Theodore R.*	319,033	Byrd, Harry Clifton		62,418 R	54.5%	45.5%	54.5%	45.5%
1950	645,631	369,807	McKeldin, Theodore R.	275,824	Lane, William Preston*		93,983 R	57.3%	42.7%	57.3%	42.7%
1946	489,836	221,752	McKeldin, Theodore R.	268,084	Lane, William Preston		46,332 D	45.3%	54.7%	45.3%	54.7%

Note: An asterisk (*) denotes incumbent.

POSTWAR VOTE FOR SENATOR

		Republican		Democratic				Percentage			
								Total Vote		Major Vote	
Year	Total Vote	Vote	Candidate	Vote	Candidate	Other Vote	Rep.-Dem. Plurality	Rep.	Dem.	Rep.	Dem.
2018	2,299,889	697,017	Campbell, Tony	1,491,614	Cardin, Benjamin L.*	111,258	794,597 D	30.3%	64.9%	31.8%	68.2%
2016	2,726,170	972,557	Szeliga, Kathy	1,659,907	Van Hollen, Chris Jr.	93,706	687,350 D	35.7%	60.9%	36.9%	63.1%
2012**	2,633,234	693,291	Bongino, Daniel John	1,474,028	Cardin, Benjamin L.*	465,915	780,737 D	26.3%	56.0%	32.0%	68.0%
2010	1,833,858	655,666	Wartotz, Eric	1,140,531	Mikulski, Barbara A.*	37,661	484,865 D	35.8%	62.2%	36.5%	63.5%
2006	1,781,139	787,182	Steele, Michael	965,477	Cardin, Benjamin L.	28,480	178,295 D	44.2%	54.2%	44.9%	55.1%
2004	2,323,183	783,055	Pipkin, Edward J.	1,504,691	Mikulski, Barbara A.*	35,437	721,636 D	33.7%	64.8%	34.2%	65.8%
2000	1,946,898	715,178	Rappaport, Paul H.	1,230,013	Sarbanes, Paul S.*	1,707	514,835 D	36.7%	63.2%	36.8%	63.2%
1998	1,507,447	444,637	Pierpont, Ross Z.	1,062,810	Mikulski, Barbara A.*		618,173 D	29.5%	70.5%	29.5%	70.5%
1994	1,369,104	559,908	Brock, William E.	809,125	Sarbanes, Paul S.*	71	249,217 D	40.9%	59.1%	40.9%	59.1%
1992	1,841,735	533,688	Keyes, Alan	1,307,610	Mikulski, Barbara A.*	437	773,922 D	29.0%	71.0%	29.0%	71.0%
1988	1,617,065	617,537	Keyes, Alan	999,166	Sarbanes, Paul S.*	362	381,629 D	38.2%	61.8%	38.2%	61.8%
1986	1,112,637	437,411	Chavez, Linda	675,225	Mikulski, Barbara A.	1	237,814 D	39.3%	60.7%	39.3%	60.7%
1982	1,114,690	407,334	Hogan, Lawrence J.	707,356	Sarbanes, Paul S.*		300,022 D	36.5%	63.5%	36.5%	63.5%
1980	1,286,088	850,970	Mathias, Charles McCurdy Jr.*	435,118	Conroy, Edward T.		415,852 R	66.2%	33.8%	66.2%	33.8%
1976	1,365,568	530,439	Beall, John Glenn Jr.*	772,101	Sarbanes, Paul S.	63,028	241,662 D	38.8%	56.5%	40.7%	59.3%
1974	877,786	503,223	Mathias, Charles McCurdy Jr.*	374,563	Mikulski, Barbara A.		128,660 R	57.3%	42.7%	57.3%	42.7%
1970	956,370	484,960	Beall, John Glenn Jr.	460,422	Tydings, Joseph D.*	10,988	24,538 R	50.7%	48.1%	51.3%	48.7%
1968**	1,133,727	541,893	Mathias, Charles McCurdy Jr.	443,367	Brewster, Daniel B.*	148,467	98,526 R	47.8%	39.1%	55.0%	45.0%
1964	1,081,049	402,393	Beall, James Glenn*	678,649	Tydings, Joseph D.	7	276,256 D	37.2%	62.8%	37.2%	62.8%
1962	708,855	269,131	Miller, Edward T.	439,723	Brewster, Daniel B.	1	170,592 D	38.0%	62.0%	38.0%	62.0%
1958	749,291	382,021	Beall, James Glenn*	367,270	D'Alesandro, Thomas Jr.		14,751 R	51.0%	49.0%	51.0%	49.0%
1956	892,167	473,059	Butler, John Marshall*	419,108	Mahoney, George P.		53,951 R	53.0%	47.0%	53.0%	47.0%
1952	856,193	449,823	Beall, James Glenn	406,370	Mahoney, George P.		43,453 R	52.5%	47.5%	52.5%	47.5%
1950	615,614	326,291	Butler, John Marshall	283,180	Tydings, Millard E.*	6,143	43,111 R	53.0%	46.0%	53.5%	46.5%
1946	472,232	235,000	Markey, David John	237,232	O'Conor, Herbert R.		2,232 D	49.8%	50.2%	49.8%	50.2%

Note: An asterisk (*) denotes incumbent. **In past elections, the other vote included: 2012 - 430,934 Independent (S. Rob Sobhani); 1968 - 148,467 Independent (George P. Mahoney).

MARYLAND

GOVERNOR 2018

2010 Census Population	County	Total Vote	Republican (Hogan)	Democratic (Jealous)	Other	Rep.-Dem. Plurality	Percentage Total Vote Rep.	Total Vote Dem.	Major Vote Rep.	Major Vote Dem.
75,087	ALLEGANY	23,530	19,224	3,985	321	15,239 R	81.7%	16.9%	82.8%	17.2%
537,656	ANNE ARUNDEL	229,206	157,202	69,399	2,605	87,803 R	68.6%	30.3%	69.4%	30.6%
805,029	BALTIMORE	324,276	198,122	122,773	3,381	75,349 R	61.1%	37.9%	61.7%	38.3%
620,961	BALTIMORE CITY	184,691	58,360	123,609	2,722	65,249 D	31.6%	66.9%	32.1%	67.9%
88,737	CALVERT	39,284	29,610	9,216	458	20,394 R	75.4%	23.5%	76.3%	23.7%
33,066	CAROLINE	11,505	9,489	1,900	116	7,589 R	82.5%	16.5%	83.3%	16.7%
167,134	CARROLL	75,051	62,445	11,767	839	50,678 R	83.2%	15.7%	84.1%	15.9%
101,108	CECIL	34,939	27,063	7,354	522	19,709 R	77.5%	21.0%	78.6%	21.4%
146,551	CHARLES	64,360	31,756	32,100	504	344 D	49.3%	49.9%	49.7%	50.3%
32,618	DORCHESTER	12,367	9,205	3,043	119	6,162 R	74.4%	24.6%	75.2%	24.8%
233,385	FREDERICK	107,219	72,560	33,355	1,304	39,205 R	67.7%	31.1%	68.5%	31.5%
30,097	GARRETT	11,008	9,472	1,395	141	8,077 R	86.0%	12.7%	87.2%	12.8%
244,826	HARFORD	110,579	85,259	24,012	1,308	61,247 R	77.1%	21.7%	78.0%	22.0%
287,085	HOWARD	143,383	80,574	61,146	1,663	19,428 R	56.2%	42.6%	56.9%	43.1%
20,197	KENT	8,694	6,370	2,222	102	4,148 R	73.3%	25.6%	74.1%	25.9%
971,777	MONTGOMERY	408,428	180,018	224,029	4,381	44,011 D	44.1%	54.9%	44.6%	55.4%
863,420	PRINCE GEORGES	318,985	89,925	225,889	3,171	135,964 D	28.2%	70.8%	28.5%	71.5%
47,798	QUEEN ANNES	22,971	19,503	3,268	200	16,235 R	84.9%	14.2%	85.6%	14.4%
26,470	SOMERSET	7,713	5,203	2,379	131	2,824 R	67.5%	30.8%	68.6%	31.4%
105,151	ST. MARYS	40,383	30,703	9,084	596	21,619 R	76.0%	22.5%	77.2%	22.8%
37,782	TALBOT	18,190	14,081	3,957	152	10,124 R	77.4%	21.8%	78.1%	21.9%
147,430	WASHINGTON	50,461	38,765	10,894	802	27,871 R	76.8%	21.6%	78.1%	21.9%
98,733	WICOMICO	33,534	22,659	10,426	449	12,233 R	67.6%	31.1%	68.5%	31.5%
51,454	WORCESTER	23,755	18,076	5,437	242	12,639 R	76.1%	22.9%	76.9%	23.1%
5,773,552	*TOTAL*	*2,304,512*	*1,275,644*	*1,002,639*	*26,229*	*273,005 R*	*55.4%*	*43.5%*	*56.0%*	*44.0%*

MARYLAND

SENATOR 2018

2010 Census Population	County	Total Vote	Republican (Campbell)	Democratic (Cardin)	Other	Rep.-Dem. Plurality	Percentage Total Vote Rep.	Total Vote Dem.	Major Vote Rep.	Major Vote Dem.
75,087	ALLEGANY	23,349	13,790	8,597	962	5,193 R	59.1%	36.8%	61.6%	38.4%
537,656	ANNE ARUNDEL	228,703	92,401	122,910	13,392	30,509 D	40.4%	53.7%	42.9%	57.1%
805,029	BALTIMORE	324,600	106,275	197,530	20,795	91,255 D	32.7%	60.9%	35.0%	65.0%
620,961	BALTIMORE CITY	184,442	16,184	160,370	7,888	144,186 D	8.8%	86.9%	9.2%	90.8%
88,737	CALVERT	39,031	19,901	17,372	1,758	2,529 R	51.0%	44.5%	53.4%	46.6%
33,066	CAROLINE	11,304	6,474	4,265	565	2,209 R	57.3%	37.7%	60.3%	39.7%
167,134	CARROLL	74,489	42,479	25,986	6,024	16,493 R	57.0%	34.9%	62.0%	38.0%
101,108	CECIL	34,791	19,851	13,237	1,703	6,614 R	57.1%	38.0%	60.0%	40.0%
146,551	CHARLES	64,533	17,872	44,874	1,787	27,002 D	27.7%	69.5%	28.5%	71.5%
32,618	DORCHESTER	12,292	5,864	5,928	500	64 D	47.7%	48.2%	49.7%	50.3%
233,385	FREDERICK	106,933	47,038	55,256	4,639	8,218 D	44.0%	51.7%	46.0%	54.0%
30,097	GARRETT	10,939	7,801	2,817	321	4,984 R	71.3%	25.8%	73.5%	26.5%
244,826	HARFORD	110,307	56,749	45,921	7,637	10,828 R	51.4%	41.6%	55.3%	44.7%
287,085	HOWARD	143,448	38,797	96,067	8,584	57,270 D	27.0%	67.0%	28.8%	71.2%
20,197	KENT	8,578	3,490	4,588	500	1,098 D	40.7%	53.5%	43.2%	56.8%
971,777	MONTGOMERY	406,997	74,924	314,568	17,505	239,644 D	18.4%	77.3%	19.2%	80.8%
863,420	PRINCE GEORGES	318,523	24,140	286,975	7,408	262,835 D	7.6%	90.1%	7.8%	92.2%
47,798	QUEEN ANNES	22,744	12,813	8,463	1,468	4,350 R	56.3%	37.2%	60.2%	39.8%
26,470	SOMERSET	7,767	3,882	3,652	233	230 R	50.0%	47.0%	51.5%	48.5%
105,151	ST. MARYS	40,168	21,393	16,849	1,926	4,544 R	53.3%	41.9%	55.9%	44.1%

MARYLAND

SENATOR 2018

2010 Census Population	County	Total Vote	Republican (Campbell)	Democratic (Cardin)	Other	Rep.-Dem. Plurality	Percentage: Total Vote Rep.	Total Vote Dem.	Major Vote Rep.	Major Vote Dem.
37,782	TALBOT	18,066	8,050	9,054	962	1,004 D	44.6%	50.1%	47.1%	52.9%
147,430	WASHINGTON	50,406	28,319	19,956	2,131	8,363 R	56.2%	39.6%	58.7%	41.3%
98,733	WICOMICO	33,691	15,644	16,539	1,508	895 D	46.4%	49.1%	48.6%	51.4%
51,454	WORCESTER	23,788	12,886	9,840	1,062	3,046 R	54.2%	41.4%	56.7%	43.3%
5,773,552	*TOTAL*	*2,299,889*	*697,017*	*1,491,614*	*111,258*	*794,597 D*	*30.3%*	*64.9%*	*31.8%*	*68.2%*

MARYLAND

HOUSE OF REPRESENTATIVES

CD	Year	Total Vote	Republican Vote	Republican Candidate	Democratic Vote	Democratic Candidate	Other Vote	Rep.-Dem. Plurality	Percentage: Total Vote Rep.	Total Vote Dem.	Major Vote Rep.	Major Vote Dem.
1	2018	306,186	183,662	HARRIS, ANDY*	116,631	COLVIN, JESSE	5,893	67,031 R	60.0%	38.1%	61.2%	38.8%
1	2016	362,097	242,574	HARRIS, ANDY*	103,622	WERNER, JOSEPH	15,901	138,952 R	67.0%	28.6%	70.1%	29.9%
1	2014	250,418	176,342	HARRIS, ANDY*	73,843	TILGHMAN, BILL	233	102,499 R	70.4%	29.5%	70.5%	29.5%
1	2012	337,760	214,204	HARRIS, ANDY*	92,812	ROSEN, WENDY	30,744	121,392 R	63.4%	27.5%	69.8%	30.2%
2	2018	253,302	77,782	MATORY, LIZ	167,201	RUPPERSBERGER, C.A. DUTCH*	8,319	89,419 D	30.7%	66.0%	31.7%	68.3%
2	2016	309,480	102,577	MCDONOUGH, PATRICK L.	192,183	RUPPERSBERGER, C.A. DUTCH*	14,720	89,606 D	33.1%	62.1%	34.8%	65.2%
2	2014	196,354	70,411	BANACH, DAVID	120,412	RUPPERSBERGER, C.A. DUTCH*	5,531	50,001 D	35.9%	61.3%	36.9%	63.1%
2	2012	295,940	92,071	JACOBS, NANCY C.	194,088	RUPPERSBERGER, C.A. DUTCH*	9,781	102,017 D	31.1%	65.6%	32.2%	67.8%
3	2018	292,880	82,774	ANTHONY, CHARLES	202,407	SARBANES, JOHN P.*	7,699	119,633 D	28.3%	69.1%	29.0%	71.0%
3	2016	339,675	115,048	PLASTER, MARK	214,640	SARBANES, JOHN P.*	9,987	99,592 D	33.9%	63.2%	34.9%	65.1%
3	2014	215,946	87,029	LONG, CHARLES A.	128,594	SARBANES, JOHN P.*	323	41,565 D	40.3%	59.5%	40.4%	59.6%
3	2012	319,859	94,549	KNOWLES, ERIC DELANO	213,747	SARBANES, JOHN P.*	11,563	119,198 D	29.6%	66.8%	30.7%	69.3%
4	2018	268,583	53,327	MCDERMOTT, GEORGE E.	209,642	BROWN, ANTHONY G.*	5,614	156,315 D	19.9%	78.1%	20.3%	79.7%
4	2016	320,650	68,670	MCDERMOTT, GEORGE E.	237,501	BROWN, ANTHONY G.	14,479	168,831 D	21.4%	74.1%	22.4%	77.6%
4	2014	191,837	54,217	HOYT, NANCY	134,628	EDWARDS, DONNA*	2,992	80,411 D	28.3%	70.2%	28.7%	71.3%
4	2012	311,512	64,560	LOUDON, FAITH M.	240,385	EDWARDS, DONNA*	6,567	175,825 D	20.7%	77.2%	21.2%	78.8%
5	2018	304,209	82,361	DEVINE, WILLIAM A. III	213,796	HOYER, STENY H.*	8,052	131,435 D	27.1%	70.3%	27.8%	72.2%
5	2016	360,634	105,931	ARNESS, MARK KENNETH	242,989	HOYER, STENY H.*	11,714	137,058 D	29.4%	67.4%	30.4%	69.6%
5	2014	226,040	80,752	CHAFFEE, CHRIS	144,725	HOYER, STENY H.*	563	63,973 D	35.7%	64.0%	35.8%	64.2%
5	2012	343,820	95,271	O'DONNELL, TONY	238,618	HOYER, STENY H.*	9,931	143,347 D	27.7%	69.4%	28.5%	71.5%
6	2018	277,084	105,209	HOEBER, AMIE	163,346	TRONE, DAVID	8,529	58,137 D	38.0%	59.0%	39.2%	60.8%
6	2016	331,973	133,081	HOEBER, AMIE	185,770	DELANEY, JOHN*	13,122	52,689 D	40.1%	56.0%	41.7%	58.3%
6	2014	190,536	91,930	BONGINO, DANIEL JOHN	94,704	DELANEY, JOHN*	3,902	2,774 D	48.2%	49.7%	49.3%	50.7%
6	2012	309,549	117,313	BARTLETT, ROSCOE G.*	181,921	DELANEY, JOHN	10,315	64,608 D	37.9%	58.8%	39.2%	60.8%
7	2018	264,710	56,266	DAVIS, RICHMOND	202,345	CUMMINGS, ELIJAH E.*	6,099	146,079 D	21.3%	76.4%	21.8%	78.2%
7	2016	318,912	69,556	VAUGHN, CORROGAN R.	238,838	CUMMINGS, ELIJAH E.*	10,518	169,282 D	21.8%	74.9%	22.6%	77.4%
7	2014	206,809	55,860	VAUGHN, CORROGAN R.	144,639	CUMMINGS, ELIJAH E.*	6,310	88,779 D	27.0%	69.9%	27.9%	72.1%
7	2012	323,818	67,405	MIRABILE, FRANK C.	247,770	CUMMINGS, ELIJAH E.*	8,643	180,365 D	20.8%	76.5%	21.4%	78.6%
8	2018	319,330	96,525	WALSH, JOHN	217,679	RASKIN, JAMIE*	5,126	121,154 D	30.2%	68.2%	30.7%	69.3%
8	2016	364,324	124,651	COX, DAN	220,657	RASKIN, JAMIE	19,016	96,006 D	34.2%	60.6%	36.1%	63.9%
8	2014	225,097	87,859	WALLACE, DAVE	136,722	VAN HOLLEN, CHRIS JR.*	516	48,863 D	39.0%	60.7%	39.1%	60.9%
8	2012	343,256	113,033	TIMMERMAN, KENNETH R.	217,531	VAN HOLLEN, CHRIS JR.*	12,692	104,498 D	32.9%	63.4%	34.2%	65.8%
TOTAL	*2018*	*2,286,284*	*737,906*		*1,493,047*		*55,331*	*755,141 D*	*32.3%*	*65.3%*	*33.1%*	*66.9%*
TOTAL	*2016*	*2,707,745*	*962,088*		*1,636,200*		*109,457*	*674,112 D*	*35.5%*	*60.4%*	*37.0%*	*63.0%*
TOTAL	*2014*	*1,703,037*	*704,400*		*978,267*		*20,370*	*273,867 D*	*41.4%*	*57.4%*	*41.9%*	*58.1%*
TOTAL	*2012*	*2,585,514*	*858,406*		*1,626,872*		*100,236*	*768,466 D*	*33.2%*	*62.9%*	*34.5%*	*65.5%*

Note: An asterisk (*) denotes incumbent.

MARYLAND

GENERAL AND PRIMARY ELECTIONS

2018 GENERAL ELECTIONS: OTHER VOTES

Governor Other vote was 13,241 Libertarian (Shawn Quinn), 11,175 Green (Ian Schlakman), 1,813 Write-in (Write-in)

Senate Other vote was 85,964 Independent (Neal Simon), 2,2943 Libertarian (Arvin Vohra), 1,650 Write-in (Write-in), 364 Write-in (Lih Young), 247 Write-in (Michael Puskar), 90 Write-in (Edward Shlikas)

House Other vote was:

CD 1	5,744 Libertarian (Jenica Martin), 149 Write-in (Write-In)
CD 2	5,215 Libertarian (Michael Carney), 2,904 Green (Guy Mimoun), 200 Write-in (Write-in)
CD 3	7,476 Libertarian (David Lashar), 223 Write-in (Write-in)
CD 4	5,326 Libertarian (David Bishop), 288 Write-in (Write-in)
CD 5	4,082 Green (Patrick Elder), 3,592 Libertarian (Jacob Pulcher), 279 Write-in (Write-in), 99 Write-in (Johnny Rice)
CD 6	4,972 Libertarian (Kevin Caldwell), 3,275 Green (George Gluck), 282 Write-in (Write-in)
CD 7	5,827 Libertarian (David Griggs), 272 Write-in (Write-in)
CD 8	4,853 Libertarian (Jasen Wunder), 273 Write-in (Write-in)

2018 PRIMARY ELECTIONS: SUPPLEMENTARY INFORMATION

Primary	June 26, 2018	**Registration** (as of June 26, 2018)	3,597,135	Democratic	2,143,288
				Republican	1,003,153
				Libertarian	11,726
				Green	5,078
				Other	17,242
				Unaffiliated	416,648

Primary Type Closed—Only registered Democrats and Republicans could vote in their party's primary.

	REPUBLICAN PRIMARIES			DEMOCRATIC PRIMARIES		
Senator	Campbell, Tony	51,426	29.2%	Cardin, Benjamin L.*	477,441	80.3%
	Chaffee, Chris	42,328	24.1%	Manning, Chelsea	34,611	5.8%
	Grigorian, Christina J.	30,756	17.5%	Segal, Jerome "Jerry"	20,027	3.4%
	Graziani, John R.	15,435	8.8%	Wilson, Debbie "Rica"	18,953	3.2%
	Taylor, Blaine	8,848	5.0%	Morgan, Marcia H.	16,047	2.7%
	Smith, Gerald I. Jr.	7,564	4.3%	Young, Lih	9,874	1.7%
	Vaeth, Brian Charles	5,411	3.1%	Vaughn, Richard "Rikki"	9,480	1.6%
	Cronhardt, Evan M.	4,445	2.5%	Jetmir, Erik	8,259	1.4%
	Krehnbrink, Bill	3,606	2.0%			
	Eze, Nnabu	3,442	2.0%			
	Howard, Albert Binyahmin	2,720	1.5%			
	TOTAL	*175,981*		*TOTAL*	*594,692*	
Governor	Hogan, Larry*	210,935	100.0%	Jealous, Ben	231,895	39.6%
				Baker, Rushern L. III	171,697	29.3%
				Shea, Jim	48,647	8.3%
				Vignarajah, Krish O'Mara	48,042	8.2%
				Madaleno, Rich	34,184	5.8%
				Ervin, Valerie	18,851	3.2%
				Ross, Alec	13,780	2.4%
				Jaffe, Ralph	9,405	1.6%
				Jones, James Hugh II	9,188	1.6%
	TOTAL	*210,935*		*TOTAL*	*585,689*	

MARYLAND

GENERAL AND PRIMARY ELECTIONS

	REPUBLICAN PRIMARIES			DEMOCRATIC PRIMARIES		
Congressional District 1	Harris, Andy*	48,944	85.8%	Colvin, Jesse	14,075	37.8%
	Elborn, Martin	5,606	9.8%	Galbraith, Allison	10,440	28.1%
	Taylor, Lamont	2,496	4.4%	Brown, Michael	5,600	15.1%
				Pullen, Michael	4,819	13.0%
				Worton, Steve	1,442	3.9%
				Lane, Erik	815	2.2%
	TOTAL	*57,046*		*TOTAL*	*37,191*	
Congressional District 2	Matory, Liz	7,426	42.0%	Ruppersberger, C.A. Dutch*	47,776	78.1%
	Shell, Mark Gerard	4,171	23.6%	Pretot, Jake	13,405	21.9%
	Toland, Mitchell Jr.	3,061	17.3%			
	Owens, Hubert Jr.	3,017	17.1%			
	TOTAL	*17,675*		*TOTAL*	*61,181*	
Congressional District 3	Anthony, Charles	6,935	43.6%	Sarbanes, John P.*	64,567	82.3%
	Harris, Thomas E. "Pinkston"	5,722	36.0%	DeMarco, Adam D.	6,778	8.6%
	Seyfferth, Rob	3,254	20.5%	Rosas, Eduardo	4,847	6.2%
				Rea, John	2,300	2.9%
	TOTAL	*15,911*		*TOTAL*	*78,492*	
Congressional District 4	McDermott, George E.	12,485	100.0%	Brown, Anthony G.*	80,699	100.0%
	TOTAL	*12,485*		*TOTAL*	*80,699*	
Congressional District 5	Devine, William A. III	11,372	57.6%	Hoyer, Steny H.*	72,493	84.1%
	Rice, Johnny	8,385	42.4%	Fritz, Dennis L.	13,681	15.9%
	TOTAL	*19,757*		*TOTAL*	*86,174*	
Congressional District 6	Hoeber, Amie	19,571	67.8%	Trone, David	24,103	40.0%
	Lloyd, Lisa	5,144	17.8%	Miller, Aruna	18,524	30.7%
	Elsasser, Kurt	2,526	8.7%	Hashimi, Nadia	6,304	10.5%
	Rohrs, Bradley St.	1,641	5.7%	Manno, Roger	6,257	10.4%
				Duck, Andrew	2,949	4.9%
				Graves, Chris	982	1.6%
				English, George	650	1.1%
				Hearsey, Christopher	531	0.9%
	TOTAL	*28,882*		*TOTAL*	*60,300*	
Congressional District 7	Davis, Richmond	3,554	31.3%	Cummings, Elijah E.*	81,679	91.5%
	Pearson, Michael T.	3,392	29.9%	Moser, John	2,289	2.6%
	Newton, William T.	2,536	22.3%	Carter, Anthony Sr.	2,267	2.5%
	Bly, Raymond J.	1,877	16.5%	Stokes, Charles	2,247	2.5%
				Smith, Charles U.	833	0.9%
	TOTAL	*11,359*		*TOTAL*	*89,315*	
Congressional District 8	Walsh, John	9,095	44.9%	Raskin, Jamie*	81,071	90.5%
	Cooper, Bridgette L.	6,341	31.3%	Spring, Summer	5,239	5.8%
	Williams, Victor	4,835	23.9%	Paul, Utam	3,272	3.7%
	TOTAL	*20,271*		*TOTAL*	*89,582*	

Note: An asterisk (*) denotes incumbent.

MASSACHUSETTS

Congressional districts first established for elections held in 2012

9 members

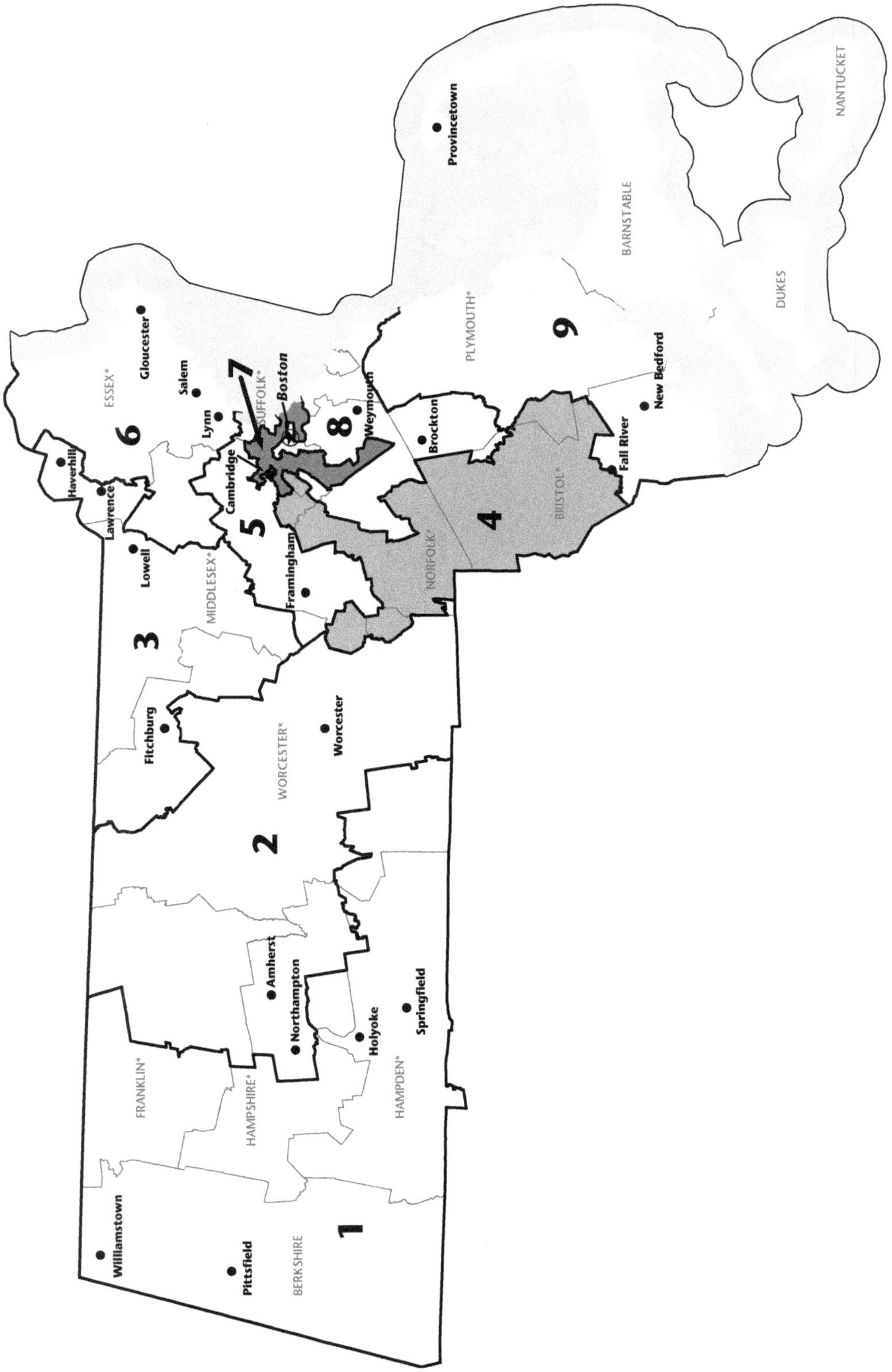

* Asterisk indicates a county whose boundaries include parts of two or more congressional districts.

MASSACHUSETTS

Boston Area

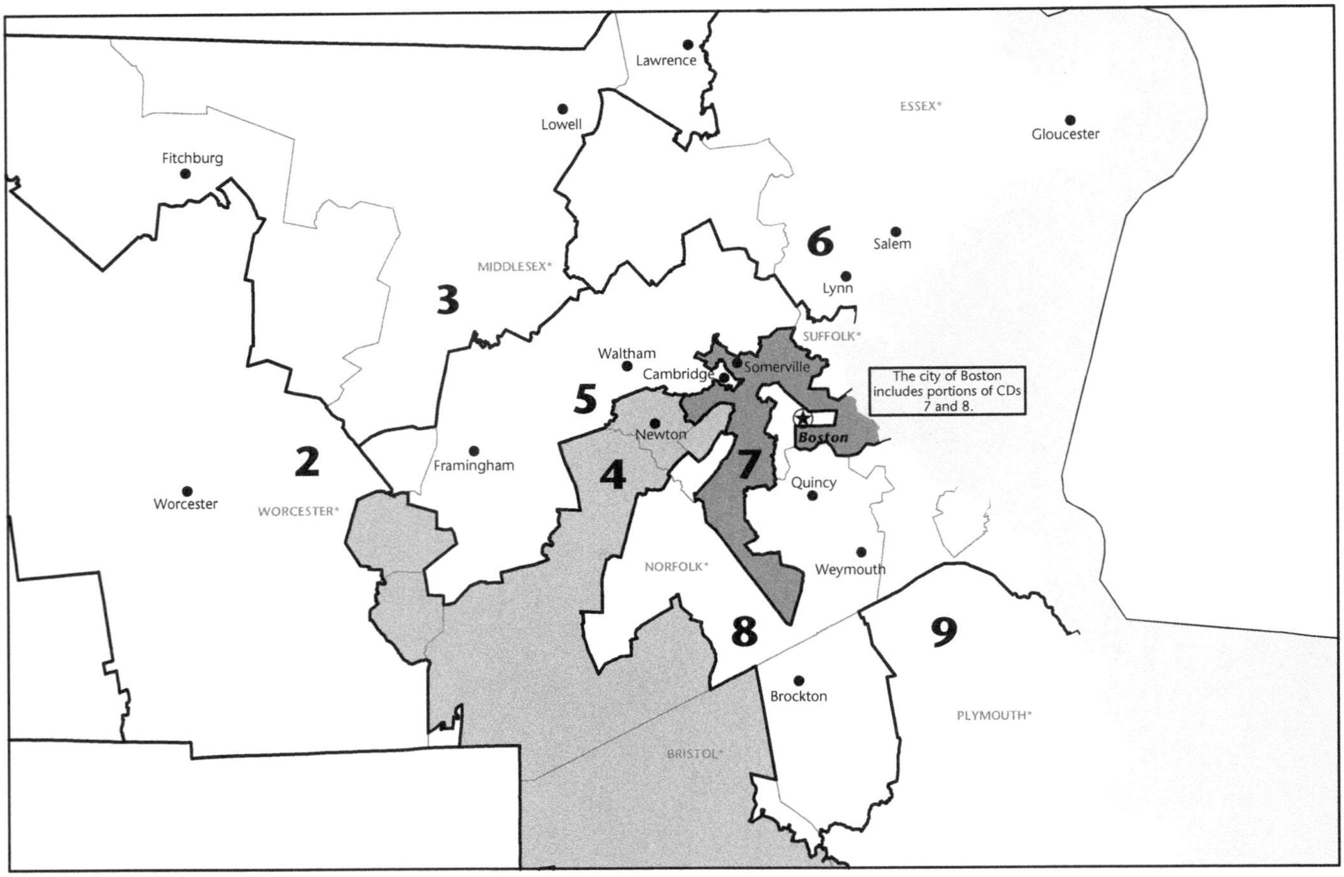

* Asterisk indicates a county whose boundaries include parts of two or more congressional districts.

MASSACHUSETTS

GOVERNOR

Charles D. Baker (R). Re-elected 2018 to a four-year term. Previously elected 2014.

SENATORS (2 Democrats)

Edward J. Markey (D). Re-elected 2014 to a full six-year term. Previously elected June 25, 2013, to serve the remainder of the term vacated by the January 2013 resignation of John Kerry to become secretary of state. William "Mo" Cowan (D) had been appointed on January 30, 2013, to fill the vacant seat until the June 2013 special election.

Elizabeth Warren (D). Re-elected 2018 to a six-year term. Previously elected 2012.

REPRESENTATIVES (9 Democrats)

1. Richard E. Neal (D)
2. James McGovern (D)
3. Lori Trahan (D)
4. Joseph Patrick Kennedy III (D)
5. Katherine M. Clark (D)
6. Seth Moulton (D)
7. Ayanna Pressley (D)
8. Stephen F. Lynch (D)
9. William Richard Keating (D)

POSTWAR VOTE FOR PRESIDENT

								Percentage			
		Republican		Democratic				Total Vote		Major Vote	
Year	Total Vote	Vote	Candidate	Vote	Candidate	Other Vote	Rep.-Dem. Plurality	Rep.	Dem.	Rep.	Dem.
2016**	3,325,046	1,090,893	Trump, Donald J.	1,995,196	Clinton, Hillary Rodham	238,957	904,303 D	32.8%	60.0%	35.3%	64.7%
2012	3,167,767	1,188,314	Romney, W. Mitt	1,921,290	Obama, Barack H.*	58,163	732,976 D	37.5%	60.7%	38.2%	61.8%
2008	3,080,985	1,108,854	McCain, John S. III	1,904,097	Obama, Barack H.	68,034	795,243 D	36.0%	61.8%	36.8%	63.2%
2004	2,912,388	1,071,109	Bush, George W.*	1,803,800	Kerry, John F.	37,479	732,691 D	36.8%	61.9%	37.3%	62.7%
2000**	2,702,984	878,502	Bush, George W.	1,616,487	Gore, Albert Jr.	207,995	737,985 D	32.5%	59.8%	35.2%	64.8%
1996**	2,556,785	718,107	Dole, Robert "Bob"	1,571,763	Clinton, Bill*	266,915	853,656 D	28.1%	61.5%	31.4%	68.6%
1992**	2,773,700	805,049	Bush, George H.*	1,318,662	Clinton, Bill	649,989	513,613 D	29.0%	47.5%	37.9%	62.1%
1988	2,632,805	1,194,635	Bush, George H.	1,401,415	Dukakis, Michael S.	36,755	206,780 D	45.4%	53.2%	46.0%	54.0%
1984	2,559,453	1,310,936	Reagan, Ronald*	1,239,606	Mondale, Walter F.	8,911	71,330 R	51.2%	48.4%	51.4%	48.6%
1980**	2,524,298	1,057,631	Reagan, Ronald	1,053,802	Carter, Jimmy*	412,865	3,829 R	41.9%	41.7%	50.1%	49.9%
1976	2,547,558	1,030,276	Ford, Gerald R.*	1,429,475	Carter, Jimmy	87,807	399,199 D	40.4%	56.1%	41.9%	58.1%
1972	2,458,756	1,112,078	Nixon, Richard M.*	1,332,540	McGovern, George S.	14,138	220,462 D	45.2%	54.2%	45.5%	54.5%
1968**	2,331,752	766,844	Nixon, Richard M.	1,469,218	Humphrey, Hubert Horatio Jr.	95,690	702,374 D	32.9%	63.0%	34.3%	65.7%
1964	2,344,798	549,727	Goldwater, Barry M. Sr.	1,786,422	Johnson, Lyndon B.*	8,649	1,236,695 D	23.4%	76.2%	23.5%	76.5%
1960	2,469,480	976,750	Nixon, Richard M.	1,487,174	Kennedy, John F.	5,556	510,424 D	39.6%	60.2%	39.6%	60.4%
1956	2,348,506	1,393,197	Eisenhower, Dwight D.*	948,190	Stevenson, Adlai E. II	7,119	445,007 R	59.3%	40.4%	59.5%	40.5%
1952	2,383,398	1,292,325	Eisenhower, Dwight D.	1,083,525	Stevenson, Adlai E. II	7,548	208,800 R	54.2%	45.5%	54.4%	45.6%
1948	2,107,146	909,370	Dewey, Thomas E.	1,151,788	Truman, Harry S.*	45,988	242,418 D	43.2%	54.7%	44.1%	55.9%

Note: An asterisk (*) denotes incumbent. **In past elections, the other vote included: 2016 - 138,018 Libertarian (Gary Johnson); 2000 - 173,564 - Green (Ralph Nader); 1996 - 227,217 Reform (Ross Perot); 1992 - 630,731 Independent (Perot); 1980 - 382,539 Independent (John Anderson); 1968 - 87,088 American Independent (George Wallace).

MASSACHUSETTS

POSTWAR VOTE FOR GOVERNOR

		Republican		Democratic				Percentage			
								Total Vote		Major Vote	
Year	Total Vote	Vote	Candidate	Vote	Candidate	Other Vote	Rep.-Dem. Plurality	Rep.	Dem.	Rep.	Dem.
2018	2,674,615	1,781,341	Baker, Charles D.*	885,770	Gonzalez, Jay	7,504	895,571 R	66.6%	33.1%	66.8%	33.2%
2014	2,158,326	1,044,573	Baker, Charles D.	1,004,408	Coakley, Martha	109,345	40,165 R	48.4%	46.5%	51.0%	49.0%
2010	2,297,039	964,866	Baker, Charles D.	1,112,283	Patrick, Deval*	219,890	147,417 D	42.0%	48.4%	46.5%	53.5%
2006	2,219,779	784,342	Healey, Kerry	1,234,984	Patrick, Deval	200,453	450,642 D	35.3%	55.6%	38.8%	61.2%
2002	2,194,179	1,091,988	Romney, W. Mitt	985,981	O'Brien, Shannon P.	116,210	106,007 R	49.8%	44.9%	52.6%	47.4%
1998	1,903,336	967,160	Cellucci, Argeo Paul*	901,843	Harshbarger, Scott	34,333	65,317 R	50.8%	47.4%	51.7%	48.3%
1994	2,255,150	1,599,141	Weld, William F.*	636,138	Roosevelt, Mark	19,871	963,003 R	70.9%	28.2%	71.5%	28.5%
1990	2,342,927	1,175,817	Weld, William F.	1,099,878	Silber, John	67,232	75,939 R	50.2%	46.9%	51.7%	48.3%
1986	1,684,079	525,364	Kariotis, George	1,157,786	Dukakis, Michael S.*	929	632,422 D	31.2%	68.7%	31.2%	68.8%
1982	2,050,254	749,679	Sears, John W.	1,219,109	Dukakis, Michael S.	81,466	469,430 D	36.6%	59.5%	38.1%	61.9%
1978	1,962,251	926,072	Hatch, Francis W.	1,030,294	King, Edward J.	5,885	104,222 D	47.2%	52.5%	47.3%	52.7%
1974	1,854,798	784,353	Sargent, Francis W.*	992,284	Dukakis, Michael S.	78,161	207,931 D	42.3%	53.5%	44.1%	55.9%
1970	1,867,906	1,058,623	Sargent, Francis W.*	799,269	White, Kevin H.	10,014	259,354 R	56.7%	42.8%	57.0%	43.0%
1966**	2,041,177	1,277,358	Volpe, John A.*	752,720	McCormack, Edward J.	11,099	524,638 R	62.6%	36.9%	62.9%	37.1%
1964	2,340,130	1,176,462	Volpe, John A.	1,153,416	Bellotti, Francis X.	10,252	23,046 R	50.3%	49.3%	50.5%	49.5%
1962	2,109,089	1,047,891	Volpe, John A.*	1,053,322	Peabody, Endicott	7,876	5,431 D	49.7%	49.9%	49.9%	50.1%
1960	2,417,133	1,269,295	Volpe, John A.	1,130,810	Ward, Joseph D.	17,028	138,485 R	52.5%	46.8%	52.9%	47.1%
1958	1,899,117	818,463	Gibbons, Charles	1,067,020	Furcolo, Foster*	13,634	248,557 D	43.1%	56.2%	43.4%	56.6%
1956	2,339,884	1,096,759	Whittier, Sumner G.	1,234,618	Furcolo, Foster	8,507	137,859 D	46.9%	52.8%	47.0%	53.0%
1954	1,903,774	985,339	Herter, Christian A.*	910,087	Murphy, Robert F.	8,348	75,252 R	51.8%	47.8%	52.0%	48.0%
1952	2,356,298	1,175,955	Herter, Christian A.	1,161,499	Dever, Paul A.*	18,844	14,456 R	49.9%	49.3%	50.3%	49.7%
1950	1,910,180	824,069	Coolidge, Arthur W.	1,074,570	Dever, Paul A.*	11,541	250,501 D	43.1%	56.3%	43.4%	56.6%
1948	2,099,250	849,895	Bradford, Robert F.*	1,239,247	Dever, Paul A.	10,108	389,352 D	40.5%	59.0%	40.7%	59.3%
1946	1,683,452	911,152	Bradford, Robert F.	762,743	Tobin, Maurice J.*	9,557	148,409 R	54.1%	45.3%	54.4%	45.6%

Note: An asterisk (*) denotes incumbent. **The term of office of Massachusetts's governor was increased from two to four years effective with the 1966 election.

POSTWAR VOTE FOR SENATOR

		Republican		Democratic				Percentage			
								Total Vote		Major Vote	
Year	Total Vote	Vote	Candidate	Vote	Candidate	Other Vote	Rep.-Dem. Plurality	Rep.	Dem.	Rep.	Dem.
2018	2,707,090	979,210	Diehl, Geoff	1,633,371	Warren, Elizabeth*	94,509	654,161 D	36.2%	60.3%	37.5%	62.5%
2014	2,084,972	791,950	Herr, Brian J.	1,289,944	Markey, Edward J.*	3,078	497,994 D	38.0%	61.9%	38.0%	62.0%
2013S**	1,177,790	525,307	Gomez, Gabriel E.	645,429	Markey, Edward J.	7,054	120,122 D	44.6%	54.8%	44.9%	55.1%
2012	3,156,553	1,458,048	Brown, Scott P.*	1,696,346	Warren, Elizabeth	2,159	238,298 D	46.2%	53.7%	46.2%	53.8%
2010S**	2,252,582	1,168,178	Brown, Scott P.	1,060,861	Coakley, Martha	23,543	107,317 R	51.9%	47.1%	52.4%	47.6%
2008	2,994,247	926,044	Beatty, Jeffrey K.	1,971,974	Kerry, John F.*	96,229	1,045,930 D	30.9%	65.9%	32.0%	68.0%
2006	2,165,490	661,532	Chase, Kenneth G.	1,500,738	Kennedy, Edward M.*	3,220	839,206 D	30.5%	69.3%	30.6%	69.4%
2002**	2,006,758			1,605,976	Kerry, John F.*	400,782	1,605,976 D		80.0%		100.0%
2000**	2,599,420	334,341	Robinson, Jack E. III	1,889,494	Kennedy, Edward M.*	375,585	1,555,153 D	12.9%	72.7%	15.0%	85.0%
1996	2,555,886	1,142,837	Weld, William F.	1,334,345	Kerry, John F.*	78,704	191,508 D	44.7%	52.2%	46.1%	53.9%
1994	2,179,964	894,005	Romney, W. Mitt	1,266,011	Kennedy, Edward M.*	19,948	372,006 D	41.0%	58.1%	41.4%	58.6%
1990	2,316,212	992,917	Rappaport, Jim	1,321,712	Kerry, John F.*	1,583	328,795 D	42.9%	57.1%	42.9%	57.1%
1988	2,606,225	884,267	Malone, Joseph D.	1,693,344	Kennedy, Edward M.*	28,614	809,077 D	33.9%	65.0%	34.3%	65.7%
1984	2,530,195	1,136,806	Shamie, Raymond	1,392,981	Kerry, John F.	408	256,175 D	44.9%	55.1%	44.9%	55.1%
1982	2,050,769	784,602	Shamie, Raymond	1,247,084	Kennedy, Edward M.*	19,083	462,482 D	38.3%	60.8%	38.6%	61.4%
1978	1,985,700	890,584	Brooke, Edward W. III*	1,093,283	Tsongas, Paul E.	1,833	202,699 D	44.8%	55.1%	44.9%	55.1%
1976	2,491,255	722,641	Robertson, Michael	1,726,657	Kennedy, Edward M.*	41,957	1,004,016 D	29.0%	69.3%	29.5%	70.5%
1972	2,370,676	1,505,932	Brooke, Edward W. III*	823,278	Droney, John J.	41,466	682,654 R	63.5%	34.7%	64.7%	35.3%
1970	1,935,607	715,978	Spaulding, Josiah A.	1,202,856	Kennedy, Edward M.*	16,773	486,878 D	37.0%	62.1%	37.3%	62.7%
1966	1,999,949	1,213,473	Brooke, Edward W. III	774,761	Peabody, Endicott	11,715	438,712 R	60.7%	38.7%	61.0%	39.0%
1964	2,312,028	587,663	Whitmore, Howard Jr.	1,716,907	Kennedy, Edward M.*	7,458	1,129,244 D	25.4%	74.3%	25.5%	74.5%
1962S**	2,097,085	877,669	Lodge, George C.	1,162,611	Kennedy, Edward M.	56,805	284,942 D	41.9%	55.4%	43.0%	57.0%
1960	2,417,813	1,358,556	Saltonstall, Leverett*	1,050,725	O'Connor, Thomas J. Jr.	8,532	307,831 R	56.2%	43.5%	56.4%	43.6%
1958	1,862,041	488,318	Celeste, Vincent J.	1,362,926	Kennedy, John F.*	10,797	874,608 D	26.2%	73.2%	26.4%	73.6%
1954	1,892,710	956,605	Saltonstall, Leverett*	927,899	Furcolo, Foster	8,206	28,706 R	50.5%	49.0%	50.8%	49.2%
1952	2,360,425	1,141,247	Lodge, Henry Cabot Jr.*	1,211,984	Kennedy, John F.	7,194	70,737 D	48.3%	51.3%	48.5%	51.5%
1948	2,055,798	1,088,475	Saltonstall, Leverett*	954,398	Fitzgerald, John I.	12,925	134,077 R	52.9%	46.4%	53.3%	46.7%
1946	1,662,063	989,736	Lodge, Henry Cabot Jr.	660,200	Walsh, David I.*	12,127	329,536 R	59.5%	39.7%	60.0%	40.0%

Note: An asterisk (*) denotes incumbent. **In past elections, the other vote included: 2002 - 369,807 Libertarian (Michael E. Cloud); 2000 - 308,748 Libertarian (Carla Howell). The Republican Party did not run a candidate in the 2002 Senate election. The 1962, 2010, and 2013 elections were for short terms to fill a vacancy; the 2010 election was held in January 2010.

MASSACHUSETTS

GOVERNOR 2018

2010 Census Population	County	Total Vote	Republican (Baker)	Democratic (Gonzalez)	Other	Rep.-Dem. Plurality	Percentage Total Vote Rep.	Total Vote Dem.	Major Vote Rep.	Major Vote Dem.
215,888	BARNSTABLE	116,254	85,726	30,169	359	55,557 R	73.7%	26.0%	74.0%	26.0%
131,219	BERKSHIRE	53,428	28,331	25,030	67	3,301 R	53.0%	46.8%	53.1%	46.9%
548,285	BRISTOL	187,074	132,371	54,280	423	78,091 R	70.8%	29.0%	70.9%	29.1%
16,535	DUKES	10,033	5,556	4,470	7	1,086 R	55.4%	44.6%	55.4%	44.6%
743,159	ESSEX	307,269	219,522	86,893	854	132,629 R	71.4%	28.3%	71.6%	28.4%
71,372	FRANKLIN	32,805	18,263	14,507	35	3,756 R	55.7%	44.2%	55.7%	44.3%
463,490	HAMPDEN	154,279	109,952	43,806	521	66,146 R	71.3%	28.4%	71.5%	28.5%
158,080	HAMPSHIRE	70,036	37,272	32,667	97	4,605 R	53.2%	46.6%	53.3%	46.7%
1,503,085	MIDDLESEX	659,505	411,687	246,197	1,621	165,490 R	62.4%	37.3%	62.6%	37.4%
10,172	NANTUCKET	4,148	2,388	1,750	10	638 R	57.6%	42.2%	57.7%	42.3%
670,850	NORFOLK	303,045	209,318	92,709	1,018	116,609 R	69.1%	30.6%	69.3%	30.7%
494,919	PLYMOUTH	219,486	164,438	54,303	745	110,135 R	74.9%	24.7%	75.2%	24.8%
722,023	SUFFOLK	248,259	125,247	122,249	763	2,998 R	50.5%	49.2%	50.6%	49.4%
798,552	WORCESTER	308,994	231,270	76,740	984	154,530 R	74.8%	24.8%	75.1%	24.9%
6,547,629	*TOTAL*	*2,674,615*	*1,781,341*	*885,770*	*7,504*	*895,571 R*	*66.6%*	*33.1%*	*66.8%*	*33.2%*

2010 Census Population	City/Town	Total Vote	Republican (Baker)	Democratic (Gonzalez)	Other	Rep.-Dem. Plurality	Percentage Total Vote Rep.	Total Vote Dem.	Major Vote Rep.	Major Vote Dem.
21,924	ACTON	10,937	6,774	4,141	22	2,633 R	61.9%	37.9%	62.1%	37.9%
28,438	AGAWAM	11,721	9,536	2,135	50	7,401 R	81.4%	18.2%	81.7%	18.3%
37,819	AMHERST	10,890	3,554	7,322	14	3,768 D	32.6%	67.2%	32.7%	67.3%
33,201	ANDOVER	16,133	11,893	4,186	54	7,707 R	73.7%	25.9%	74.0%	26.0%
42,844	ARLINGTON	23,698	11,516	12,142	40	626 D	48.6%	51.2%	48.7%	51.3%
43,593	ATTLEBORO	15,659	11,067	4,579	13	6,488 R	70.7%	29.2%	70.7%	29.3%
45,193	BARNSTABLE	21,664	16,424	5,193	47	11,231 R	75.8%	24.0%	76.0%	24.0%
24,729	BELMONT	12,647	7,217	5,399	31	1,818 R	57.1%	42.7%	57.2%	42.8%
39,502	BEVERLY	18,409	12,935	5,458	16	7,477 R	70.3%	29.6%	70.3%	29.7%
40,243	BILLERICA	17,423	13,310	4,012	101	9,298 R	76.4%	23.0%	76.8%	23.2%
617,594	BOSTON	220,835	108,134	112,031	670	3,897 D	49.0%	50.7%	49.1%	50.9%
35,744	BRAINTREE	16,367	12,094	4,189	84	7,905 R	73.9%	25.6%	74.3%	25.7%
93,810	BROCKTON	25,969	14,109	11,824	36	2,285 R	54.3%	45.5%	54.4%	45.6%
58,732	BROOKLINE	25,011	11,489	13,497	25	2,008 D	45.9%	54.0%	46.0%	54.0%
24,498	BURLINGTON	11,086	8,228	2,816	42	5,412 R	74.2%	25.4%	74.5%	25.5%
105,162	CAMBRIDGE	45,449	15,422	29,966	61	14,544 D	33.9%	65.9%	34.0%	66.0%
21,561	CANTON	10,701	7,838	2,840	23	4,998 R	73.2%	26.5%	73.4%	26.6%
33,802	CHELMSFORD	16,547	12,599	3,896	52	8,703 R	76.1%	23.5%	76.4%	23.6%
55,298	CHICOPEE	17,939	13,145	4,707	87	8,438 R	73.3%	26.2%	73.6%	26.4%
17,668	CONCORD	9,963	6,193	3,758	12	2,435 R	62.2%	37.7%	62.2%	37.8%
26,493	DANVERS	12,259	9,622	2,567	70	7,055 R	78.5%	20.9%	78.9%	21.1%
34,032	DARTMOUTH	12,539	8,766	3,748	25	5,018 R	69.9%	29.9%	70.0%	30.0%
24,729	DEDHAM	12,018	8,264	3,711	43	4,553 R	68.8%	30.9%	69.0%	31.0%
29,457	DRACUT	12,740	10,298	2,442	0	7,856 R	80.8%	19.2%	80.8%	19.2%
23,112	EASTON	10,300	7,764	2,502	34	5,262 R	75.4%	24.3%	75.6%	24.4%
41,667	EVERETT	10,037	5,764	4,240	33	1,524 R	57.4%	42.2%	57.6%	42.4%
88,857	FALL RIVER	19,371	12,801	6,540	30	6,261 R	66.1%	33.8%	66.2%	33.8%
31,531	FALMOUTH	17,203	12,205	4,942	56	7,263 R	70.9%	28.7%	71.2%	28.8%
40,318	FITCHBURG	11,333	8,152	3,141	40	5,011 R	71.9%	27.7%	72.2%	27.8%
68,318	FRAMINGHAM	23,887	15,214	8,613	60	6,601 R	63.7%	36.1%	63.9%	36.1%
31,635	FRANKLIN	14,814	11,414	3,339	61	8,075 R	77.0%	22.5%	77.4%	22.6%
28,789	GLOUCESTER	13,541	9,521	3,976	44	5,545 R	70.3%	29.4%	70.5%	29.5%
60,879	HAVERHILL	22,571	16,237	6,252	82	9,985 R	71.9%	27.7%	72.2%	27.8%
22,157	HINGHAM	12,221	9,267	2,926	28	6,341 R	75.8%	23.9%	76.0%	24.0%
39,880	HOLYOKE	12,063	6,989	5,057	17	1,932 R	57.9%	41.9%	58.0%	42.0%

MASSACHUSETTS

GOVERNOR 2018

2010 Census Population	City/Town	Total Vote	Republican (Baker)	Democratic (Gonzalez)	Other	Rep.-Dem. Plurality	Percentage Total Vote Rep.	Percentage Total Vote Dem.	Percentage Major Vote Rep.	Percentage Major Vote Dem.
76,377	LAWRENCE	15,114	7,477	7,593	44	116 D	49.5%	50.2%	49.6%	50.4%
40,759	LEOMINSTER	15,062	11,404	3,593	65	7,811 R	75.7%	23.9%	76.0%	24.0%
31,394	LEXINGTON	15,686	8,851	6,823	12	2,028 R	56.4%	43.5%	56.5%	43.5%
106,519	LOWELL	25,811	16,738	9,073	0	7,665 R	64.8%	35.2%	64.8%	35.2%
90,329	LYNN	23,972	14,616	9,264	92	5,352 R	61.0%	38.6%	61.2%	38.8%
59,450	MALDEN	17,277	9,468	7,741	68	1,727 R	54.8%	44.8%	55.0%	45.0%
19,808	MARBLEHEAD	11,336	8,450	2,875	11	5,575 R	74.5%	25.4%	74.6%	25.4%
38,499	MARLBOROUGH	14,205	10,229	3,955	21	6,274 R	72.0%	27.8%	72.1%	27.9%
25,132	MARSHFIELD	12,848	10,094	2,754	0	7,340 R	78.6%	21.4%	78.6%	21.4%
56,173	MEDFORD	24,918	13,763	11,072	83	2,691 R	55.2%	44.4%	55.4%	44.6%
26,983	MELROSE	14,250	9,329	4,861	60	4,468 R	65.5%	34.1%	65.7%	34.3%
47,255	METHUEN	17,242	12,919	4,236	87	8,683 R	74.9%	24.6%	75.3%	24.7%
27,999	MILFORD	10,288	7,830	2,429	29	5,401 R	76.1%	23.6%	76.3%	23.7%
27,003	MILTON	13,608	9,035	4,540	33	4,495 R	66.4%	33.4%	66.6%	33.4%
33,006	NATICK	16,960	11,382	5,556	22	5,826 R	67.1%	32.8%	67.2%	32.8%
28,886	NEEDHAM	16,119	10,722	5,369	28	5,353 R	66.5%	33.3%	66.6%	33.4%
95,072	NEW BEDFORD	22,945	12,973	9,893	79	3,080 R	56.5%	43.1%	56.7%	43.3%
85,146	NEWTON	40,673	22,689	17,888	96	4,801 R	55.8%	44.0%	55.9%	44.1%
28,352	NORTH ANDOVER	12,987	10,063	2,924	0	7,139 R	77.5%	22.5%	77.5%	22.5%
28,712	NORTH ATTLEBOROUGH	11,710	8,931	2,762	17	6,169 R	76.3%	23.6%	76.4%	23.6%
28,549	NORTHAMPTON	14,958	5,224	9,721	13	4,497 D	34.9%	65.0%	35.0%	65.0%
28,602	NORWOOD	12,727	9,047	3,617	63	5,430 R	71.1%	28.4%	71.4%	28.6%
51,251	PEABODY	21,839	16,761	4,964	114	11,797 R	76.7%	22.7%	77.2%	22.8%
44,737	PITTSFIELD	16,289	8,755	7,517	17	1,238 R	53.7%	46.1%	53.8%	46.2%
56,468	PLYMOUTH	27,283	20,963	6,208	112	14,755 R	76.8%	22.8%	77.2%	22.8%
92,271	QUINCY	32,899	21,583	11,162	154	10,421 R	65.6%	33.9%	65.9%	34.1%
32,112	RANDOLPH	11,784	6,433	5,317	34	1,116 R	54.6%	45.1%	54.7%	45.3%
24,747	READING	13,029	9,722	3,264	43	6,458 R	74.6%	25.1%	74.9%	25.1%
51,755	REVERE	13,535	8,604	4,871	60	3,733 R	63.6%	36.0%	63.9%	36.1%
41,340	SALEM	18,437	10,733	7,660	44	3,073 R	58.2%	41.5%	58.4%	41.6%
26,628	SAUGUS	10,790	8,374	2,416	0	5,958 R	77.6%	22.4%	77.6%	22.4%
18,133	SCITUATE	10,317	7,865	2,419	33	5,446 R	76.2%	23.4%	76.5%	23.5%
35,608	SHREWSBURY	15,995	12,393	3,593	9	8,800 R	77.5%	22.5%	77.5%	22.5%
75,754	SOMERVILLE	34,954	12,222	22,642	90	10,420 D	35.0%	64.8%	35.1%	64.9%
153,060	SPRINGFIELD	36,871	20,672	16,068	131	4,604 R	56.1%	43.6%	56.3%	43.7%
21,437	STONEHAM	10,692	7,937	2,755	0	5,182 R	74.2%	25.8%	74.2%	25.8%
26,962	STOUGHTON	10,858	7,638	3,194	26	4,444 R	70.3%	29.4%	70.5%	29.5%
55,874	TAUNTON	17,421	12,445	4,903	73	7,542 R	71.4%	28.1%	71.7%	28.3%
28,961	TEWKSBURY	13,793	10,876	2,824	93	8,052 R	78.9%	20.5%	79.4%	20.6%
24,932	WAKEFIELD	12,450	9,087	3,302	61	5,785 R	73.0%	26.5%	73.3%	26.7%
24,070	WALPOLE	11,897	9,279	2,580	38	6,699 R	78.0%	21.7%	78.2%	21.8%
60,632	WALTHAM	21,789	13,447	8,279	63	5,168 R	61.7%	38.0%	61.9%	38.1%
31,915	WATERTOWN	15,632	8,019	7,555	58	464 R	51.3%	48.3%	51.5%	48.5%
27,982	WELLESLEY	12,956	8,919	4,017	20	4,902 R	68.8%	31.0%	68.9%	31.1%
28,391	WEST SPRINGFIELD	9,282	7,178	2,088	16	5,090 R	77.3%	22.5%	77.5%	22.5%
41,094	WESTFIELD	14,589	11,415	3,132	42	8,283 R	78.2%	21.5%	78.5%	21.5%
53,743	WEYMOUTH	23,982	17,306	6,533	143	10,773 R	72.2%	27.2%	72.6%	27.4%
21,374	WINCHESTER	10,979	7,718	3,261	0	4,457 R	70.3%	29.7%	70.3%	29.7%
38,120	WOBURN	16,284	11,828	4,412	44	7,416 R	72.6%	27.1%	72.8%	27.2%
181,045	WORCESTER	48,674	29,609	18,933	132	10,676 R	60.8%	38.9%	61.0%	39.0%
23,793	YARMOUTH	11,975	9,138	2,783	54	6,355 R	76.3%	23.2%	76.7%	23.3%

MASSACHUSETTS

SENATOR 2018

2010 Census Population	County	Total Vote	Republican (Diehl)	Democratic (Warren)	Other	Rep.-Dem. Plurality	Percentage Total Vote Rep.	Percentage Total Vote Dem.	Percentage Major Vote Rep.	Percentage Major Vote Dem.
215,888	BARNSTABLE	118,171	51,810	62,670	3,691	10,860 D	43.8%	53.0%	45.3%	54.7%
131,219	BERKSHIRE	53,867	13,501	38,792	1,574	25,291 D	25.1%	72.0%	25.8%	74.2%
548,285	BRISTOL	189,625	83,919	98,921	6,785	15,002 D	44.3%	52.2%	45.9%	54.1%
16,535	DUKES	10,138	2,338	7,414	386	5,076 D	23.1%	73.1%	24.0%	76.0%
743,159	ESSEX	311,443	121,067	178,343	12,033	57,276 D	38.9%	57.3%	40.4%	59.6%
71,372	FRANKLIN	32,976	8,790	22,912	1,274	14,122 D	26.7%	69.5%	27.7%	72.3%
463,490	HAMPDEN	156,064	63,152	86,861	6,051	23,709 D	40.5%	55.7%	42.1%	57.9%
158,080	HAMPSHIRE	70,771	18,217	49,943	2,611	31,726 D	25.7%	70.6%	26.7%	73.3%
1,503,085	MIDDLESEX	667,183	202,871	440,901	23,411	238,030 D	30.4%	66.1%	31.5%	68.5%
10,172	NANTUCKET	4,159	1,351	2,662	146	1,311 D	32.5%	64.0%	33.7%	66.3%
670,850	NORFOLK	307,095	117,202	179,853	10,040	62,651 D	38.2%	58.6%	39.5%	60.5%
494,919	PLYMOUTH	224,201	109,995	107,595	6,611	2,400 R	49.1%	48.0%	50.6%	49.4%
722,023	SUFFOLK	250,010	46,502	196,623	6,885	150,121 D	18.6%	78.6%	19.1%	80.9%
798,552	WORCESTER	311,387	138,495	159,881	13,011	21,386 D	44.5%	51.3%	46.4%	53.6%
6,547,629	*TOTAL*	*2,707,090*	*979,210*	*1,633,371*	*94,509*	*654,161 D*	*36.2%*	*60.3%*	*37.5%*	*62.5%*

2010 Census Population	City/Town	Total Vote	Republican (Diehl)	Democratic (Warren)	Other	Rep.-Dem. Plurality	Percentage Total Vote Rep.	Percentage Total Vote Dem.	Percentage Major Vote Rep.	Percentage Major Vote Dem.
21,924	ACTON	11,024	2,611	7,983	430	5,372 D	23.7%	72.4%	24.6%	75.4%
28,438	AGAWAM	11,859	6,127	5,303	429	824 R	51.7%	44.7%	53.6%	46.4%
37,819	AMHERST	10,985	891	9,782	312	8,891 D	8.1%	89.0%	8.3%	91.7%
33,201	ANDOVER	16,328	6,275	9,257	796	2,982 D	38.4%	56.7%	40.4%	59.6%
42,844	ARLINGTON	24,038	4,405	18,922	711	14,517 D	18.3%	78.7%	18.9%	81.1%
43,593	ATTLEBORO	15,775	6,799	8,343	633	1,544 D	43.1%	52.9%	44.9%	55.1%
45,193	BARNSTABLE	22,049	10,501	10,874	674	373 D	47.6%	49.3%	49.1%	50.9%
24,729	BELMONT	12,783	3,073	9,141	569	6,068 D	24.0%	71.5%	25.2%	74.8%
39,502	BEVERLY	18,655	6,534	11,331	790	4,797 D	35.0%	60.7%	36.6%	63.4%
40,243	BILLERICA	17,772	8,795	8,193	784	602 R	49.5%	46.1%	51.8%	48.2%
617,594	BOSTON	222,217	37,305	178,895	6,017	141,590 D	16.8%	80.5%	17.3%	82.7%
35,744	BRAINTREE	16,756	8,090	8,182	484	92 D	48.3%	48.8%	49.7%	50.3%
93,810	BROCKTON	26,348	7,087	18,622	639	11,535 D	26.9%	70.7%	27.6%	72.4%
58,732	BROOKLINE	25,088	3,316	21,086	686	17,770 D	13.2%	84.0%	13.6%	86.4%
24,498	BURLINGTON	11,304	4,851	6,010	443	1,159 D	42.9%	53.2%	44.7%	55.3%
105,162	CAMBRIDGE	45,910	3,343	41,589	978	38,246 D	7.3%	90.6%	7.4%	92.6%
21,561	CANTON	10,912	4,641	5,915	356	1,274 D	42.5%	54.2%	44.0%	56.0%
33,802	CHELMSFORD	16,753	7,086	9,006	661	1,920 D	42.3%	53.8%	44.0%	56.0%
55,298	CHICOPEE	18,112	7,371	9,878	863	2,507 D	40.7%	54.5%	42.7%	57.3%
17,668	CONCORD	10,033	2,303	7,427	303	5,124 D	23.0%	74.0%	23.7%	76.3%
26,493	DANVERS	12,475	5,761	6,189	525	428 D	46.2%	49.6%	48.2%	51.8%
34,032	DARTMOUTH	12,759	5,583	6,775	401	1,192 D	43.8%	53.1%	45.2%	54.8%
24,729	DEDHAM	12,214	4,665	7,157	392	2,492 D	38.2%	58.6%	39.5%	60.5%
29,457	DRACUT	13,014	6,928	5,409	677	1,519 R	53.2%	41.6%	56.2%	43.8%
23,112	EASTON	10,483	4,757	5,384	342	627 D	45.4%	51.4%	46.9%	53.1%
41,667	EVERETT	10,107	2,776	7,000	331	4,224 D	27.5%	69.3%	28.4%	71.6%
88,857	FALL RIVER	19,519	7,162	11,662	695	4,500 D	36.7%	59.7%	38.0%	62.0%
31,531	FALMOUTH	17,442	7,021	9,833	588	2,812 D	40.3%	56.4%	41.7%	58.3%
40,318	FITCHBURG	11,491	4,694	6,333	464	1,639 D	40.8%	55.1%	42.6%	57.4%
68,318	FRAMINGHAM	24,073	6,782	16,568	723	9,786 D	28.2%	68.8%	29.0%	71.0%

MASSACHUSETTS

SENATOR 2018

2010 Census Population	City/Town	Total Vote	Republican (Diehl)	Democratic (Warren)	Other	Rep.-Dem. Plurality	Percentage Total Vote Rep.	Total Vote Dem.	Major Vote Rep.	Major Vote Dem.
31,635	FRANKLIN	14,926	6,778	7,667	481	889 D	45.4%	51.4%	46.9%	53.1%
28,789	GLOUCESTER	13,631	4,736	8,405	490	3,669 D	34.7%	61.7%	36.0%	64.0%
60,879	HAVERHILL	22,949	9,732	12,241	976	2,509 D	42.4%	53.3%	44.3%	55.7%
22,157	HINGHAM	12,390	5,324	6,700	366	1,376 D	43.0%	54.1%	44.3%	55.7%
39,880	HOLYOKE	12,197	3,281	8,488	428	5,207 D	26.9%	69.6%	27.9%	72.1%
76,377	LAWRENCE	15,219	2,495	12,336	388	9,841 D	16.4%	81.1%	16.8%	83.2%
40,759	LEOMINSTER	15,267	6,951	7,676	640	725 D	45.5%	50.3%	47.5%	52.5%
31,394	LEXINGTON	15,866	3,379	11,978	509	8,599 D	21.3%	75.5%	22.0%	78.0%
106,519	LOWELL	26,171	8,092	17,039	1,040	8,947 D	30.9%	65.1%	32.2%	67.8%
90,329	LYNN	24,209	7,173	16,262	774	9,089 D	29.6%	67.2%	30.6%	69.4%
59,450	MALDEN	17,469	4,404	12,529	536	8,125 D	25.2%	71.7%	26.0%	74.0%
19,808	MARBLEHEAD	11,397	4,090	6,903	404	2,813 D	35.9%	60.6%	37.2%	62.8%
38,499	MARLBOROUGH	14,331	5,355	8,391	585	3,036 D	37.4%	58.6%	39.0%	61.0%
25,132	MARSHFIELD	13,257	6,953	5,951	353	1,002 R	52.4%	44.9%	53.9%	46.1%
56,173	MEDFORD	25,184	6,437	17,896	851	11,459 D	25.6%	71.1%	26.5%	73.5%
26,983	MELROSE	14,444	4,681	9,262	501	4,581 D	32.4%	64.1%	33.6%	66.4%
47,255	METHUEN	17,458	7,977	8,765	716	788 D	45.7%	50.2%	47.6%	52.4%
27,999	MILFORD	10,362	4,526	5,447	389	921 D	43.7%	52.6%	45.4%	54.6%
27,003	MILTON	13,806	4,527	8,842	437	4,315 D	32.8%	64.0%	33.9%	66.1%
33,006	NATICK	17,083	5,004	11,538	541	6,534 D	29.3%	67.5%	30.3%	69.7%
28,886	NEEDHAM	16,143	4,657	10,954	532	6,297 D	28.8%	67.9%	29.8%	70.2%
95,072	NEW BEDFORD	23,327	7,593	14,784	950	7,191 D	32.6%	63.4%	33.9%	66.1%
85,146	NEWTON	40,824	8,355	31,088	1,381	22,733 D	20.5%	76.2%	21.2%	78.8%
28,352	NORTH ANDOVER	13,173	5,852	6,773	548	921 D	44.4%	51.4%	46.4%	53.6%
28,712	NORTH ATTLEBOROUGH	11,825	5,455	5,826	544	371 D	46.1%	49.3%	48.4%	51.6%
28,549	NORTHAMPTON	15,072	1,718	12,967	387	11,249 D	11.4%	86.0%	11.7%	88.3%
28,602	NORWOOD	12,925	5,265	7,228	432	1,963 D	40.7%	55.9%	42.1%	57.9%
51,251	PEABODY	22,214	10,238	11,133	843	895 D	46.1%	50.1%	47.9%	52.1%
44,737	PITTSFIELD	16,444	3,978	11,970	496	7,992 D	24.2%	72.8%	24.9%	75.1%
56,468	PLYMOUTH	27,793	13,661	13,292	840	369 R	49.2%	47.8%	50.7%	49.3%
92,271	QUINCY	33,519	12,380	20,067	1,072	7,687 D	36.9%	59.9%	38.2%	61.8%
32,112	RANDOLPH	11,913	2,603	9,048	262	6,445 D	21.9%	76.0%	22.3%	77.7%
24,747	READING	13,183	5,271	7,404	508	2,133 D	40.0%	56.2%	41.6%	58.4%
51,755	REVERE	13,661	4,824	8,416	421	3,592 D	35.3%	61.6%	36.4%	63.6%
41,340	SALEM	18,618	4,763	13,162	693	8,399 D	25.6%	70.7%	26.6%	73.4%
26,628	SAUGUS	11,106	5,894	4,845	367	1,049 R	53.1%	43.6%	54.9%	45.1%
18,133	SCITUATE	10,499	4,769	5,413	317	644 D	45.4%	51.6%	46.8%	53.2%
35,608	SHREWSBURY	15,935	6,531	8,838	566	2,307 D	41.0%	55.5%	42.5%	57.5%
75,754	SOMERVILLE	35,218	3,647	30,686	885	27,039 D	10.4%	87.1%	10.6%	89.4%
153,060	SPRINGFIELD	37,070	8,174	27,708	1,188	19,534 D	22.1%	74.7%	22.8%	77.2%
21,437	STONEHAM	10,904	4,689	5,782	433	1,093 D	43.0%	53.0%	44.8%	55.2%
26,962	STOUGHTON	11,052	4,360	6,345	347	1,985 D	39.4%	57.4%	40.7%	59.3%
55,874	TAUNTON	17,685	8,018	9,029	638	1,011 D	45.3%	51.1%	47.0%	53.0%
28,961	TEWKSBURY	14,055	7,233	6,118	704	1,115 R	51.5%	43.5%	54.2%	45.8%
24,932	WAKEFIELD	12,652	5,471	6,699	482	1,228 D	43.2%	52.9%	45.0%	55.0%
24,070	WALPOLE	12,110	5,884	5,766	460	118 R	48.6%	47.6%	50.5%	49.5%
60,632	WALTHAM	21,994	6,652	14,502	840	7,850 D	30.2%	65.9%	31.4%	68.6%
31,915	WATERTOWN	15,816	3,421	11,817	578	8,396 D	21.6%	74.7%	22.5%	77.5%
27,982	WELLESLEY	12,940	4,103	8,334	503	4,231 D	31.7%	64.4%	33.0%	67.0%
28,391	WEST SPRINGFIELD	9,400	4,399	4,646	355	247 D	46.8%	49.4%	48.6%	51.4%
41,094	WESTFIELD	14,851	7,570	6,720	561	850 R	51.0%	45.2%	53.0%	47.0%
53,743	WEYMOUTH	24,532	11,365	12,430	737	1,065 D	46.3%	50.7%	47.8%	52.2%
21,374	WINCHESTER	11,103	3,927	6,750	426	2,823 D	35.4%	60.8%	36.8%	63.2%
38,120	WOBURN	16,572	7,163	8,724	685	1,561 D	43.2%	52.6%	45.1%	54.9%
181,045	WORCESTER	48,771	14,377	32,573	1,821	18,196 D	29.5%	66.8%	30.6%	69.4%
23,793	YARMOUTH	12,146	5,551	6,197	398	646 D	45.7%	51.0%	47.3%	52.7%

MASSACHUSETTS

HOUSE OF REPRESENTATIVES

			Republican		Democratic				Percentage			
									Total Vote		Major Vote	
CD	Year	Total Vote	Vote	Candidate	Vote	Candidate	Other Vote	Rep.-Dem. Plurality	Rep.	Dem.	Rep.	Dem.
1	2018	216,900			211,790	NEAL, RICHARD E.*	5,110	211,790 D		97.6%		100.0%
1	2016	321,539			235,803	NEAL, RICHARD E.*	85,736	235,803 D		73.3%		100.0%
1	2014	171,110			167,612	NEAL, RICHARD E.*	3,498	167,612 D		98.0%		100.0%
1	2012	266,133			261,936	NEAL, RICHARD E.*	4,197	261,936 D		98.4%		100.0%
2	2018	284,893	93,391	LOVVORN, TRACY LYN	191,332	MCGOVERN, JAMES*	170	97,941 D	32.8%	67.2%	32.8%	67.2%
2	2016	280,411			275,487	MCGOVERN, JAMES*	4,924	275,487 D		98.2%		100.0%
2	2014	172,745			169,640	MCGOVERN, JAMES*	3,105	169,640 D		98.2%		100.0%
2	2012	263,335			259,257	MCGOVERN, JAMES*	4,078	259,257 D		98.5%		100.0%
3	2018	279,327	93,445	GREEN, RICK	173,175	TRAHAN, LORI	12,707	79,730 D	33.5%	62.0%	35.0%	65.0%
3	2016	344,592	107,519	WOFFORD, ROSEANN EHRHARD	236,713	TSONGAS, NICOLA S.*	360	129,194 D	31.2%	68.7%	31.2%	68.8%
3	2014	220,946	81,638	WOFFORD, ROSEANN EHRHARD	139,104	TSONGAS, NICOLA S.*	204	57,466 D	36.9%	63.0%	37.0%	63.0%
3	2012	321,753	109,372	GOLNIK, JONATHAN A.	212,119	TSONGAS, NICOLA S.*	262	102,747 D	34.0%	65.9%	34.0%	66.0%
4	2018	251,016			245,289	KENNEDY, JOSEPH PATRICK III*	5,727	245,289 D		97.7%		100.0%
4	2016	379,213	113,055	ROSA, DAVID A.	265,823	KENNEDY, JOSEPH PATRICK III*	335	152,768 D	29.8%	70.1%	29.8%	70.2%
4	2014	188,098			184,158	KENNEDY, JOSEPH PATRICK III*	3,940	184,158 D		97.9%		100.0%
4	2012	362,245	129,936	BIELAT, SEAN	221,303	KENNEDY, JOSEPH PATRICK III	11,006	91,367 D	35.9%	61.1%	37.0%	63.0%
5	2018	311,324	74,856	HUGO, JOHN	236,243	CLARK, KATHERINE M.*	225	161,387 D	24.0%	75.9%	24.1%	75.9%
5	2016	289,807			285,606	CLARK, KATHERINE M.*	4,201	285,606 D		98.6%		100.0%
5	2014	185,260			182,100	CLARK, KATHERINE M.*	3,160	182,100 D		98.3%		100.0%
5	2012	341,109	82,944	TIERNEY, TOM	257,490	MARKEY, EDWARD J.*	675	174,546 D	24.3%	75.5%	24.4%	75.6%
6	2018	333,975	104,798	SCHNEIDER, JOSEPH S.	217,703	MOULTON, SETH*	11,474	112,905 D	31.4%	65.2%	32.5%	67.5%
6	2016	314,055			308,923	MOULTON, SETH*	5,132	308,923 D		98.4%		100.0%
6	2014	272,219	111,989	TISEI, RICHARD	149,638	MOULTON, SETH	10,592	37,649 D	41.1%	55.0%	42.8%	57.2%
6	2012	374,807	176,612	TISEI, RICHARD	180,942	TIERNEY, JOHN F.*	17,253	4,330 D	47.1%	48.3%	49.4%	50.6%
7	2018	220,411			216,559	PRESSLEY, AYANNA	3,852	216,559 D		98.3%		100.0%
7	2016	256,911			253,354	CAPUANO, MICHAEL E.*	3,557	253,354 D		98.6%		100.0%
7	2014	144,546			142,133	CAPUANO, MICHAEL E.*	2,413	142,133 D		98.3%		100.0%
7	2012	252,836			210,794	CAPUANO, MICHAEL E.*	42,042	210,794 D		83.4%		100.0%
8	2018	263,307			259,159	LYNCH, STEPHEN F.*	4,148	259,159 D		98.4%		100.0%
8	2016	374,265	102,744	BURKE, WILLIAM	271,019	LYNCH, STEPHEN F.*	502	168,275 D	27.5%	72.4%	27.5%	72.5%
8	2014	203,351			200,644	LYNCH, STEPHEN F.*	2,707	200,644 D		98.7%		100.0%
8	2012	346,811	82,242	SELVAGGI, JOE	263,999	LYNCH, STEPHEN F.*	570	181,757 D	23.7%	76.1%	23.8%	76.2%
9	2018	323,928	131,463	TEDESCHI, PETER D.	192,347	KEATING, WILLIAM RICHARD*	118	60,884 D	40.6%	59.4%	40.6%	59.4%
9	2016	379,895	127,803	ALLIEGRO, MARK C.	211,790	KEATING, WILLIAM RICHARD*	40,302	83,987 D	33.6%	55.7%	37.6%	62.4%
9	2014	255,541	114,971	CHAPMAN, JOHN C.	140,413	KEATING, WILLIAM RICHARD*	157	25,442 D	45.0%	54.9%	45.0%	55.0%
9	2012	362,405	116,531	SHELDON, CHRISTOPHER	212,754	KEATING, WILLIAM RICHARD*	33,120	96,223 D	32.2%	58.7%	35.4%	64.6%
TOTAL	*2018*	*2,485,081*	*497,953*		*1,943,597*		*43,531*	*1,445,644 D*	*20.0%*	*78.2%*	*20.4%*	*79.6%*
TOTAL	*2016*	*2,940,688*	*451,121*		*2,344,518*		*145,049*	*1,893,397 D*	*15.3%*	*79.7%*	*16.1%*	*83.9%*
TOTAL	*2014*	*1,813,816*	*308,598*		*1,475,442*		*29,776*	*1,166,844 D*	*17.0%*	*81.3%*	*17.3%*	*82.7%*
TOTAL	*2012*	*2,891,434*	*697,637*		*2,080,594*		*113,203*	*1,382,957 D*	*24.1%*	*72.0%*	*25.1%*	*74.9%*

Note: An asterisk (*) denotes incumbent.

MASSACHUSETTS

GENERAL AND PRIMARY ELECTIONS

2018 GENERAL ELECTIONS: OTHER VOTES

Governor	7,504 Write-in (All Others)
Senate	91,710 U.S. Marijuana (Shiva Ayyadurai), 2,799 Write-in (All Others)
House	Other vote was:
CD 1	5,110 Write-in (All Others)
CD 2	170 Write-in (All Others)
CD 3	12,572 Independent (Michael Mullen), 135 Write-in (All Others)
CD 4	5,727 Write-in (All Others)
CD 5	225 Write-in (All Others)
CD 6	11,309 Independent (Mary Charbonneau), 165 Write-in (All Others)
CD 7	3,852 Write-in (All Others)
CD 8	4,148 Write-in (All Others)
CD 9	118 Write-in (All Others)

2018 PRIMARY ELECTIONS: SUPPLEMENTARY INFORMATION

Primary	September 18, 2018	**Registration** (as of August 15, 2018)	4,493,007	Democratic	1,492,399
				Republican	465,952
				Libertarian	14,271
				Other	45,850
				Unenrolled (Independent)	2,474,535

Primary Type Semi-open—Registered Democrats and Republicans could vote only in their party's primary. "Unenrolled" voters could participate in either party's primary.

	REPUBLICAN PRIMARIES			DEMOCRATIC PRIMARIES		
Senator	Diehl, Geoff	144,043	55.2%	Warren, Elizabeth*	590,835	98.1%
	Kingston, John	69,636	26.7%	All Others (Write-in)	11,558	1.9%
	Lindstrom, Beth	46,693	17.9%			
	All Others (Write-in)	798	0.3%			
	TOTAL	*261,170*		*TOTAL*	*602,393*	
Governor	Baker, Charles D.*	174,126	63.8%	Gonzalez, Jay	348,353	63.2%
	Lively, Scott	98,421	36.1%	Massie, Robert	192,375	34.9%
	All Others (Write-in)	464	0.2%	All Others (Write-in)	10,742	1.9%
	TOTAL	*273,011*		*TOTAL*	*551,470*	
Congressional District 1				Neal, Richard E.*	49,696	70.6%
				Amatul-Wadud, Tahirah	20,565	29.2%
				All Others (Write-in)	93	0.1%
				TOTAL	*70,354*	
Congressional District 2	Lovvorn, Tracy Lyn	15,792	60.6%	McGovern, James*	53,848	99.2%
	Powers, Kevin William	10,170	39.0%	All Others (Write-in)	448	0.8%
	All Others (Write-in)	105	0.4%			
	TOTAL	*26,067*		*TOTAL*	*54,296*	

MASSACHUSETTS

GENERAL AND PRIMARY ELECTIONS

	REPUBLICAN PRIMARIES			DEMOCRATIC PRIMARIES		
Congressional District 3	Green, Rick	24,047	98.9%	Trahan, Lori	18,580	21.7%
	All Others (Write-in)	273	1.1%	Koh, Dan Arrigg	18,435	21.5%
				L'Italien, Barbara	13,018	15.2%
				Matias, Juana	12,993	15.2%
				Gifford, Rufus	12,873	15.0%
				Chandler, Alexandra	4,846	5.7%
				Das, Beej	1,492	1.7%
				Ballinger, Jeff	1,381	1.6%
				Malone, Bopha T.	1,365	1.6%
				Golder, Leonard	584	0.7%
				All Others (Write-in)	102	0.1%
	TOTAL	*24,320*		*TOTAL*	*85,669*	
Congressional District 4				Kennedy, Joseph Patrick III*	60,214	93.4%
				Rucinski, Gary	4,240	6.6%
				All Others (Write-in)	38	0.1%
				TOTAL	*64,492*	
Congressional District 5	Hugo, John	11,859	63.2%	Clark, Katherine M.*	78,156	99.3%
	Kuchnir, Louis	6,763	36.0%	All Others (Write-in)	574	0.7%
	All Others (Write-in)	151	0.8%			
	TOTAL	*18,773*		*TOTAL*	*78,730*	
Congressional District 6	Schneider, Joseph S.	26,579	98.9%	Moulton, Seth*	59,326	99.0%
	All Others (Write-in)	233	0.9%	All Others (Write-in)	608	1.0%
	Hernandez, Carlos Armando (Write-in)	51	0.2%			
	TOTAL	*26,863*		*TOTAL*	*59,934*	
Congressional District 7				Pressley, Ayanna	60,046	58.5%
				Capuano, Michael E.*	42,430	41.3%
				All Others (Write-in)	172	0.2%
				TOTAL	*102,648*	
Congressional District 8				Lynch, Stephen F.*	52,269	70.9%
				Wu, Brianna	16,878	22.9%
				Voehl, Christopher	4,435	6.0%
				All Others (Write-in)	161	0.2%
				TOTAL	*73,743*	
Congressional District 9	Tedeschi, Peter D.	35,911	99.6%	Keating, William Richard*	50,015	85.3%
	All Others (Write-in)	136	0.4%	Cimbrelo, William E. "Bill"	8,530	14.5%
				All Others (Write-in)	109	0.2%
	TOTAL	*36,047*		*TOTAL*	*58,654*	

Note: An asterisk (*) denotes incumbent.

MICHIGAN

Congressional districts first established for elections held in 2012

14 members

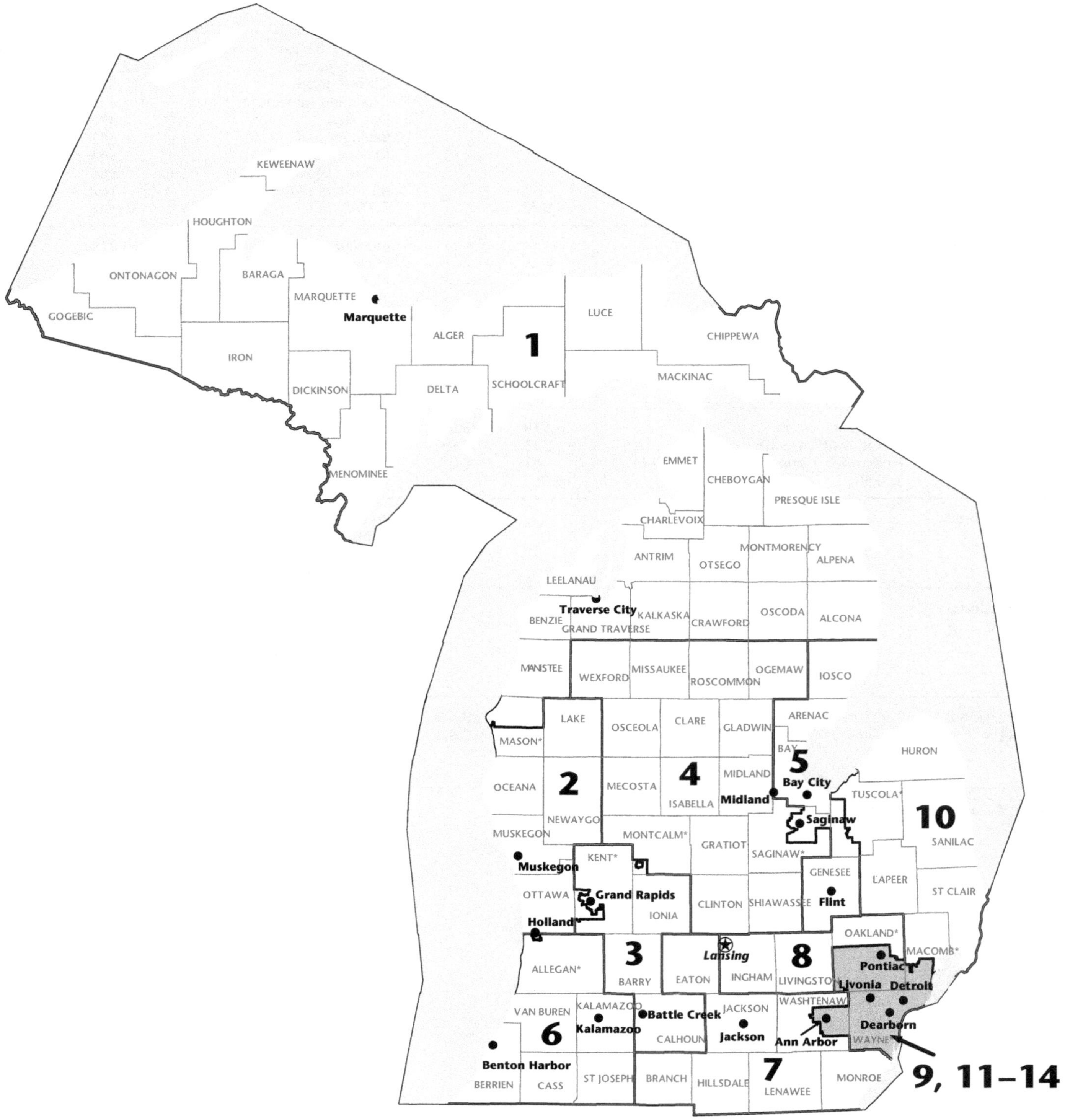

* Asterisk indicates a county whose boundaries include parts of two or more congressional districts.

MICHIGAN

Detroit Area

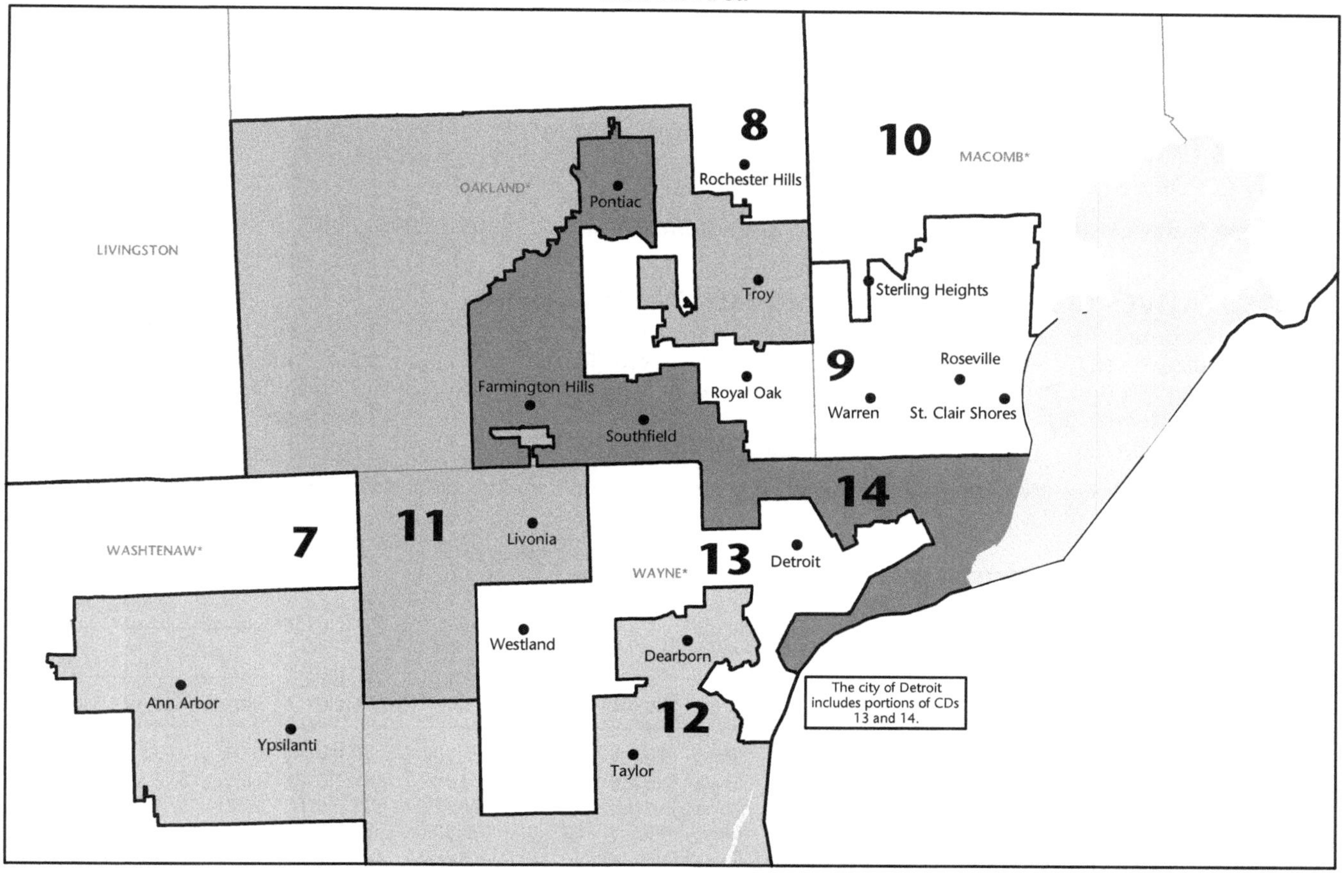

* Asterisk indicates a county whose boundaries include parts of two or more congressional districts.

MICHIGAN

GOVERNOR

Gretchen Whitmer (D). Elected 2018 to a four-year term.

SENATORS (2 Democrats)

Gary C. Peters (D). Elected 2014 to a six-year term.

Debbie Stabenow (D). Re-elected 2018 to a six-year term. Previously elected 2012, 2006, 2000.

REPRESENTATIVES (6 Republicans, 7 Democrats, 1 Independent)

1. Jack Bergman (R)
2. Bill Huizenga (R)
3. Justin Amash (Ind.)*
4. John Moolenaar (R)
5. Daniel Kildee (D)
6. Fred Upton (R)
7. Timothy Walberg (R)
8. Elissa Slotkin (D)
9. Andy Levin (D)
10. Paul Mitchell (R)
11. Haley Stevens (D)
12. Debbie Dingell (D)
13. Rashida Tlaib (D)
14. Brenda Lawrence (D)

Note: An asterisk (*) indicates that Justin Amash changed his partisan affiliation from Republican to Independent on July 4, 2019.

POSTWAR VOTE FOR PRESIDENT

		Republican		Democratic				Percentage			
								Total Vote		Major Vote	
Year	Total Vote	Vote	Candidate	Vote	Candidate	Other Vote	Rep.-Dem. Plurality	Rep.	Dem.	Rep.	Dem.
2016**	4,799,284	2,279,543	Trump, Donald J.	2,268,839	Clinton, Hillary Rodham	250,902	10,704 R	47.5%	47.3%	50.1%	49.9%
2012	4,730,961	2,115,256	Romney, W. Mitt	2,564,569	Obama, Barack H.*	51,136	449,313 D	44.7%	54.2%	45.2%	54.8%
2008	5,001,766	2,048,639	McCain, John S. III	2,872,579	Obama, Barack H.	80,548	823,940 D	41.0%	57.4%	41.6%	58.4%
2004	4,839,252	2,313,746	Bush, George W.*	2,479,183	Kerry, John F.	46,323	165,437 D	47.8%	51.2%	48.3%	51.7%
2000**	4,232,711	1,953,139	Bush, George W.	2,170,418	Gore, Albert Jr.	109,154	217,279 D	46.1%	51.3%	47.4%	52.6%
1996**	3,848,844	1,481,212	Dole, Robert "Bob"	1,989,653	Clinton, Bill*	377,979	508,441 D	38.5%	51.7%	42.7%	57.3%
1992**	4,274,673	1,554,940	Bush, George H.*	1,871,182	Clinton, Bill	848,551	316,242 D	36.4%	43.8%	45.4%	54.6%
1988	3,669,163	1,965,486	Bush, George H.	1,675,783	Dukakis, Michael S.	27,894	289,703 R	53.6%	45.7%	54.0%	46.0%
1984	3,801,658	2,251,571	Reagan, Ronald*	1,529,638	Mondale, Walter F.	20,449	721,933 R	59.2%	40.2%	59.5%	40.5%
1980**	3,909,725	1,915,225	Reagan, Ronald	1,661,532	Carter, Jimmy*	332,968	253,693 R	49.0%	42.5%	53.5%	46.5%
1976	3,653,749	1,893,742	Ford, Gerald R.*	1,696,714	Carter, Jimmy	63,293	197,028 R	51.8%	46.4%	52.7%	47.3%
1972	3,489,727	1,961,721	Nixon, Richard M.*	1,459,435	McGovern, George S.	68,571	502,286 R	56.2%	41.8%	57.3%	42.7%
1968**	3,306,250	1,370,665	Nixon, Richard M.	1,593,082	Humphrey, Hubert Horatio Jr.	342,503	222,417 D	41.5%	48.2%	46.2%	53.8%
1964	3,203,102	1,060,152	Goldwater, Barry M. Sr.	2,136,615	Johnson, Lyndon B.*	6,335	1,076,463 D	33.1%	66.7%	33.2%	66.8%
1960	3,318,097	1,620,428	Nixon, Richard M.	1,687,269	Kennedy, John F.	10,400	66,841 D	48.8%	50.9%	49.0%	51.0%
1956	3,080,468	1,713,647	Eisenhower, Dwight D.*	1,359,898	Stevenson, Adlai E. II	6,923	353,749 R	55.6%	44.1%	55.8%	44.2%
1952	2,798,592	1,551,529	Eisenhower, Dwight D.	1,230,657	Stevenson, Adlai E. II	16,406	320,872 R	55.4%	44.0%	55.8%	44.2%
1948	2,109,609	1,038,595	Dewey, Thomas E.	1,003,448	Truman, Harry S.*	67,566	35,147 R	49.2%	47.6%	50.9%	49.1%

Note: An asterisk (*) denotes incumbent. **In past elections, the other vote included: 2016 - 172,136 Libertarian (Gary Johnson); 2000 - 84,165 Green (Ralph Nader); 1996 - 336,670 Reform (Ross Perot); 1992 - 824,813 Independent (Perot); 1980 - 275,223 Independent (John Anderson); 1968 - 331,968 American Independent (George Wallace).

MICHIGAN

POSTWAR VOTE FOR GOVERNOR

		Republican		Democratic				Percentage			
								Total Vote		Major Vote	
Year	Total Vote	Vote	Candidate	Vote	Candidate	Other Vote	Rep.-Dem. Plurality	Rep.	Dem.	Rep.	Dem.
2018	4,250,585	1,859,534	Schuette, Bill	2,266,193	Whitmer, Gretchen	124,858	406,659 D	43.7%	53.3%	45.1%	54.9%
2014	3,156,531	1,607,399	Snyder, Rick*	1,479,057	Schauer, Mark H.	70,075	128,342 R	50.9%	46.9%	52.1%	47.9%
2010	3,226,088	1,874,834	Snyder, Rick	1,287,320	Bernero, Virg	63,934	587,514 R	58.1%	39.9%	59.3%	40.7%
2006	3,801,256	1,608,086	DeVos, Dick	2,142,513	Granholm, Jennifer M.*	50,657	534,427 D	42.3%	56.4%	42.9%	57.1%
2002	3,177,565	1,506,104	Posthumus, Dick	1,633,796	Granholm, Jennifer M.	37,665	127,692 D	47.4%	51.4%	48.0%	52.0%
1998	3,027,104	1,883,005	Engler, John*	1,143,574	Fieger, Geoffrey	525	739,431 R	62.2%	37.8%	62.2%	37.8%
1994	3,089,077	1,899,101	Engler, John*	1,188,438	Wolpe, Howard	1,538	710,663 R	61.5%	38.5%	61.5%	38.5%
1990	2,564,563	1,276,134	Engler, John	1,258,539	Blanchard, James J.*	29,890	17,595 R	49.8%	49.1%	50.3%	49.7%
1986	2,396,564	753,647	Lucas, William	1,632,138	Blanchard, James J.*	10,779	878,491 D	31.4%	68.1%	31.6%	68.4%
1982	3,040,008	1,369,582	Headlee, Richard H.	1,561,291	Blanchard, James J.	109,135	191,709 D	45.1%	51.4%	46.7%	53.3%
1978	2,867,212	1,628,485	Milliken, William G.*	1,237,256	Fitzgerald, William	1,471	391,229 R	56.8%	43.2%	56.8%	43.2%
1974	2,657,020	1,356,865	Milliken, William G.*	1,242,250	Levin, Sander M.	57,905	114,615 R	51.1%	46.8%	52.2%	47.8%
1970	2,656,093	1,338,711	Milliken, William G.*	1,294,600	Levin, Sander M.	22,782	44,111 R	50.4%	48.7%	50.8%	49.2%
1966**	2,461,909	1,490,430	Romney, George W.*	963,383	Ferency, Zoltan A.	8,096	527,047 R	60.5%	39.1%	60.7%	39.3%
1964	3,158,102	1,764,355	Romney, George W.*	1,381,442	Staebler, Neil	12,305	382,913 R	55.9%	43.7%	56.1%	43.9%
1962	2,764,839	1,420,086	Romney, George W.	1,339,513	Swainson, John B.*	5,240	80,573 R	51.4%	48.4%	51.5%	48.5%
1960	3,255,991	1,602,022	Bagwell, Paul D.	1,643,634	Swainson, John B.	10,335	41,612 D	49.2%	50.5%	49.4%	50.6%
1958	2,312,184	1,078,089	Bagwell, Paul D.	1,225,533	Williams, G. Mennen*	8,562	147,444 D	46.6%	53.0%	46.8%	53.2%
1956	3,049,651	1,376,376	Cobo, Albert E.	1,666,689	Williams, G. Mennen*	6,586	290,313 D	45.1%	54.7%	45.2%	54.8%
1954	2,187,027	963,300	Leonard, Donald S.	1,216,308	Williams, G. Mennen*	7,419	253,008 D	44.0%	55.6%	44.2%	55.8%
1952	2,865,980	1,423,275	Alger, Fred M. Jr.	1,431,893	Williams, G. Mennen*	10,812	8,618 D	49.7%	50.0%	49.8%	50.2%
1950	1,879,382	933,998	Kelly, Harry F.	935,152	Williams, G. Mennen*	10,232	1,154 D	49.7%	49.8%	50.0%	50.0%
1948	2,113,122	964,810	Sigler, Kim*	1,128,664	Williams, G. Mennen	19,648	163,854 D	45.7%	53.4%	46.1%	53.9%
1946	1,665,475	1,003,878	Sigler, Kim	644,540	Van Wagoner, Murray D.	17,057	359,338 R	60.3%	38.7%	60.9%	39.1%

Note: An asterisk (*) denotes incumbent. **The term of office of Michigan's Governor was increased from two to four years effective with the 1966 election.

POSTWAR VOTE FOR SENATOR

		Republican		Democratic				Percentage			
								Total Vote		Major Vote	
Year	Total Vote	Vote	Candidate	Vote	Candidate	Other Vote	Rep.-Dem. Plurality	Rep.	Dem.	Rep.	Dem.
2018	4,237,271	1,938,818	James, John	2,214,478	Stabenow, Debbie*	83,975	275,660 D	45.8%	52.3%	46.7%	53.3%
2014	3,121,775	1,290,199	Land, Terri Lynn	1,704,936	Peters, Gary C.	126,640	414,737 D	41.3%	54.6%	43.1%	56.9%
2012	4,652,918	1,767,386	Hoekstra, Peter	2,735,826	Stabenow, Debbie*	149,706	968,440 D	38.0%	58.8%	39.2%	60.8%
2008	4,848,620	1,641,070	Hoogendyk, Jack Jr.	3,038,386	Levin, Carl*	169,164	1,397,316 D	33.8%	62.7%	35.1%	64.9%
2006	3,780,142	1,559,597	Bouchard, Michael	2,151,278	Stabenow, Debbie*	69,267	591,681 D	41.3%	56.9%	42.0%	58.0%
2002	3,129,287	1,185,545	Raczkowski, Andrew	1,896,614	Levin, Carl*	47,128	711,069 D	37.9%	60.6%	38.5%	61.5%
2000	4,167,685	1,994,693	Abraham, Spencer*	2,061,952	Stabenow, Debbie	111,040	67,259 D	47.9%	49.5%	49.2%	50.8%
1996	3,762,575	1,500,106	Romney, Ronna	2,195,738	Levin, Carl*	66,731	695,632 D	39.9%	58.4%	40.6%	59.4%
1994	3,043,385	1,578,770	Abraham, Spencer	1,300,960	Carr, M. Robert	163,655	277,810 R	51.9%	42.7%	54.8%	45.2%
1990	2,560,494	1,055,695	Schuette, Bill	1,471,753	Levin, Carl*	33,046	416,058 D	41.2%	57.5%	41.8%	58.2%
1988	3,505,985	1,348,219	Dunn, Jim	2,116,865	Riegle, Donald Wayne Jr.*	40,901	768,646 D	38.5%	60.4%	38.9%	61.1%
1984	3,700,938	1,745,302	Lousma, Jack	1,915,831	Levin, Carl*	39,805	170,529 D	47.2%	51.8%	47.7%	52.3%
1982	2,994,334	1,223,288	Ruppe, Philip E.	1,728,793	Riegle, Donald Wayne Jr.*	42,253	505,505 D	40.9%	57.7%	41.4%	58.6%
1978	2,846,630	1,362,165	Griffin, Robert P.*	1,484,193	Levin, Carl	272	122,028 D	47.9%	52.1%	47.9%	52.1%
1976	3,484,664	1,635,087	Esch, Marvin L.	1,831,031	Riegle, Donald Wayne Jr.	18,546	195,944 D	46.9%	52.5%	47.2%	52.8%
1972	3,406,906	1,781,065	Griffin, Robert P.*	1,577,178	Kelley, Frank J.	48,663	203,887 R	52.3%	46.3%	53.0%	47.0%
1970	2,610,763	858,438	Romney, Lenore	1,744,672	Hart, Philip A.*	7,653	886,234 D	32.9%	66.8%	33.0%	67.0%
1966	2,439,365	1,363,530	Griffin, Robert P.*	1,069,484	Williams, G. Mennen	6,351	294,046 R	55.9%	43.8%	56.0%	44.0%
1964	3,101,667	1,096,272	Peterson, Elly M.	1,996,912	Hart, Philip A.*	8,483	900,640 D	35.3%	64.4%	35.4%	64.6%
1960	3,226,647	1,548,873	Bentley, Alvin M.	1,669,179	McNamara, Patrick V.*	8,595	120,306 D	48.0%	51.7%	48.1%	51.9%
1958	2,271,644	1,046,963	Potter, Charles E.*	1,216,966	Hart, Philip A.	7,715	170,003 D	46.1%	53.6%	46.2%	53.8%
1954	2,144,840	1,049,420	Ferguson, Homer*	1,088,550	McNamara, Patrick V.	6,870	39,130 D	48.9%	50.8%	49.1%	50.9%
1952	2,821,133	1,428,352	Potter, Charles E.	1,383,416	Moody, Blair	9,365	44,936 R	50.6%	49.0%	50.8%	49.2%
1948	2,062,097	1,045,156	Ferguson, Homer*	1,000,329	Hook, Frank E.	16,612	44,827 R	50.7%	48.5%	51.1%	48.9%
1946	1,618,720	1,085,570	Vandenberg, Arthur H.*	517,923	Lee, James H.	15,227	567,647 R	67.1%	32.0%	67.7%	32.3%

Note: An asterisk (*) denotes incumbent.

MICHIGAN

GOVERNOR 2018

2010 Census Population	County	Total Vote	Republican (Schuette)	Democratic (Whitmer)	Other	Rep.-Dem. Plurality	Percentage: Total Vote		Percentage: Major Vote	
							Rep.	Dem.	Rep.	Dem.
10,942	ALCONA	5,534	3,408	1,982	144	1,426 R	61.6%	35.8%	63.2%	36.8%
9,601	ALGER	4,159	2,097	1,950	112	147 R	50.4%	46.9%	51.8%	48.2%
111,408	ALLEGAN	49,853	28,648	19,497	1,708	9,151 R	57.5%	39.1%	59.5%	40.5%
29,598	ALPENA	13,072	7,031	5,595	446	1,436 R	53.8%	42.8%	55.7%	44.3%
23,580	ANTRIM	12,900	7,480	5,025	395	2,455 R	58.0%	39.0%	59.8%	40.2%
15,899	ARENAC	6,758	3,881	2,631	246	1,250 R	57.4%	38.9%	59.6%	40.4%
8,860	BARAGA	3,237	1,789	1,356	92	433 R	55.3%	41.9%	56.9%	43.1%
59,173	BARRY	26,858	15,573	10,272	1,013	5,301 R	58.0%	38.2%	60.3%	39.7%
107,771	BAY	46,531	21,847	23,159	1,525	1,312 D	47.0%	49.8%	48.5%	51.5%
17,525	BENZIE	9,793	4,963	4,551	279	412 R	50.7%	46.5%	52.2%	47.8%
156,813	BERRIEN	62,036	32,161	27,861	2,014	4,300 R	51.8%	44.9%	53.6%	46.4%
45,248	BRANCH	15,212	9,381	5,324	507	4,057 R	61.7%	35.0%	63.8%	36.2%
136,146	CALHOUN	50,044	24,711	23,484	1,849	1,227 R	49.4%	46.9%	51.3%	48.7%
52,293	CASS	19,457	11,538	7,255	664	4,283 R	59.3%	37.3%	61.4%	38.6%
25,949	CHARLEVOIX	13,677	7,556	5,720	401	1,836 R	55.2%	41.8%	56.9%	43.1%
26,152	CHEBOYGAN	12,555	7,249	4,838	468	2,411 R	57.7%	38.5%	60.0%	40.0%
38,520	CHIPPEWA	13,978	7,381	6,187	410	1,194 R	52.8%	44.3%	54.4%	45.6%
30,926	CLARE	11,836	6,955	4,424	457	2,531 R	58.8%	37.4%	61.1%	38.9%
75,382	CLINTON	37,157	17,649	18,495	1,013	846 D	47.5%	49.8%	48.8%	51.2%
14,074	CRAWFORD	6,259	3,613	2,367	279	1,246 R	57.7%	37.8%	60.4%	39.6%
37,069	DELTA	16,430	9,061	6,991	378	2,070 R	55.1%	42.6%	56.4%	43.6%
26,168	DICKINSON	11,333	6,914	4,119	300	2,795 R	61.0%	36.3%	62.7%	37.3%
107,759	EATON	51,106	22,438	27,003	1,665	4,565 D	43.9%	52.8%	45.4%	54.6%
32,694	EMMET	17,882	9,539	7,788	555	1,751 R	53.3%	43.6%	55.1%	44.9%
425,790	GENESEE	168,545	63,537	100,073	4,935	36,536 D	37.7%	59.4%	38.8%	61.2%
25,692	GLADWIN	11,005	6,512	4,155	338	2,357 R	59.2%	37.8%	61.0%	39.0%
16,427	GOGEBIC	6,507	3,003	3,312	192	309 D	46.2%	50.9%	47.6%	52.4%
86,986	GRAND TRAVERSE	48,801	24,031	23,220	1,550	811 R	49.2%	47.6%	50.9%	49.1%
42,476	GRATIOT	14,353	7,690	6,170	493	1,520 R	53.6%	43.0%	55.5%	44.5%
46,688	HILLSDALE	16,821	11,088	5,166	567	5,922 R	65.9%	30.7%	68.2%	31.8%
36,628	HOUGHTON	14,311	7,372	6,539	400	833 R	51.5%	45.7%	53.0%	47.0%
33,118	HURON	13,732	8,519	4,828	385	3,691 R	62.0%	35.2%	63.8%	36.2%
280,895	INGHAM	119,230	35,579	80,292	3,359	44,713 D	29.8%	67.3%	30.7%	69.3%
63,905	IONIA	23,830	13,007	9,929	894	3,078 R	54.6%	41.7%	56.7%	43.3%
25,887	IOSCO	11,690	6,534	4,772	384	1,762 R	55.9%	40.8%	57.8%	42.2%
11,817	IRON	5,403	2,970	2,269	164	701 R	55.0%	42.0%	56.7%	43.3%
70,311	ISABELLA	22,485	10,097	11,656	732	1,559 D	44.9%	51.8%	46.4%	53.6%
160,248	JACKSON	60,852	32,021	26,704	2,127	5,317 R	52.6%	43.9%	54.5%	45.5%
250,331	KALAMAZOO	114,862	44,183	67,023	3,656	22,840 D	38.5%	58.4%	39.7%	60.3%
17,153	KALKASKA	8,357	5,190	2,782	385	2,408 R	62.1%	33.3%	65.1%	34.9%
602,622	KENT	280,291	129,988	141,629	8,674	11,641 D	46.4%	50.5%	47.9%	52.1%
2,156	KEWEENAW	1,316	707	571	38	136 R	53.7%	43.4%	55.3%	44.7%
11,539	LAKE	4,700	2,602	1,904	194	698 R	55.4%	40.5%	57.7%	42.3%
88,319	LAPEER	39,372	23,209	14,798	1,365	8,411 R	58.9%	37.6%	61.1%	38.9%
21,708	LEELANAU	14,202	6,630	7,264	308	634 D	46.7%	51.1%	47.7%	52.3%
99,892	LENAWEE	40,052	21,225	17,624	1,203	3,601 R	53.0%	44.0%	54.6%	45.4%
180,967	LIVINGSTON	97,578	55,842	39,187	2,549	16,655 R	57.2%	40.2%	58.8%	41.2%
6,631	LUCE	2,420	1,469	851	100	618 R	60.7%	35.2%	63.3%	36.7%
11,113	MACKINAC	5,716	3,229	2,345	142	884 R	56.5%	41.0%	57.9%	42.1%
840,978	MACOMB	360,226	169,073	181,603	9,550	12,530 D	46.9%	50.4%	48.2%	51.8%
24,733	MANISTEE	11,717	5,928	5,420	369	508 R	50.6%	46.3%	52.2%	47.8%
67,077	MARQUETTE	30,002	11,963	17,173	866	5,210 D	39.9%	57.2%	41.1%	58.9%
28,705	MASON	13,710	7,420	5,823	467	1,597 R	54.1%	42.5%	56.0%	44.0%
42,798	MECOSTA	15,654	8,686	6,408	560	2,278 R	55.5%	40.9%	57.5%	42.5%
24,029	MENOMINEE	8,784	5,030	3,528	226	1,502 R	57.3%	40.2%	58.8%	41.2%
83,629	MIDLAND	38,505	21,215	16,238	1,052	4,977 R	55.1%	42.2%	56.6%	43.4%
14,849	MISSAUKEE	6,566	4,641	1,759	166	2,882 R	70.7%	26.8%	72.5%	27.5%
152,021	MONROE	61,539	32,336	27,413	1,790	4,923 R	52.5%	44.5%	54.1%	45.9%
63,342	MONTCALM	23,357	13,408	9,003	946	4,405 R	57.4%	38.5%	59.8%	40.2%
9,765	MONTMORENCY	4,625	2,976	1,508	141	1,468 R	64.3%	32.6%	66.4%	33.6%

MICHIGAN

GOVERNOR 2018

2010 Census Population	County	Total Vote	Republican (Schuette)	Democratic (Whitmer)	Other	Rep.-Dem. Plurality	Percentage Total Vote Rep.	Total Vote Dem.	Major Vote Rep.	Major Vote Dem.
172,188	MUSKEGON	73,660	29,655	37,029	6,976	7,374 D	40.3%	50.3%	44.5%	55.5%
48,460	NEWAYGO	20,327	12,621	6,944	762	5,677 R	62.1%	34.2%	64.5%	35.5%
1,202,362	OAKLAND	605,267	244,417	347,080	13,770	102,663 D	40.4%	57.3%	41.3%	58.7%
26,570	OCEANA	10,757	6,151	4,260	346	1,891 R	57.2%	39.6%	59.1%	40.9%
21,699	OGEMAW	9,134	5,471	3,335	328	2,136 R	59.9%	36.5%	62.1%	37.9%
6,780	ONTONAGON	3,140	1,741	1,293	106	448 R	55.4%	41.2%	57.4%	42.6%
23,528	OSCEOLA	9,391	6,098	2,901	392	3,197 R	64.9%	30.9%	67.8%	32.2%
8,640	OSCODA	3,732	2,379	1,226	127	1,153 R	63.7%	32.9%	66.0%	34.0%
24,164	OTSEGO	11,356	6,903	4,064	389	2,839 R	60.8%	35.8%	62.9%	37.1%
263,801	OTTAWA	128,588	77,691	47,380	3,517	30,311 R	60.4%	36.8%	62.1%	37.9%
13,376	PRESQUE ISLE	6,677	3,751	2,704	222	1,047 R	56.2%	40.5%	58.1%	41.9%
24,449	ROSCOMMON	11,800	6,859	4,561	380	2,298 R	58.1%	38.7%	60.1%	39.9%
200,169	SAGINAW	80,998	36,306	42,693	1,999	6,387 D	44.8%	52.7%	46.0%	54.0%
43,114	SANILAC	16,402	10,443	5,383	576	5,060 R	63.7%	32.8%	66.0%	34.0%
8,485	SCHOOLCRAFT	3,743	2,094	1,533	116	561 R	55.9%	41.0%	57.7%	42.3%
70,648	SHIAWASSEE	29,790	14,943	13,834	1,013	1,109 R	50.2%	46.4%	51.9%	48.1%
163,040	ST. CLAIR	67,434	36,840	28,089	2,505	8,751 R	54.6%	41.7%	56.7%	43.3%
61,295	ST. JOSEPH	20,438	11,962	7,611	865	4,351 R	58.5%	37.2%	61.1%	38.9%
55,729	TUSCOLA	22,291	13,286	8,272	733	5,014 R	59.6%	37.1%	61.6%	38.4%
76,258	VAN BUREN	29,544	14,824	13,580	1,140	1,244 R	50.2%	46.0%	52.2%	47.8%
344,791	WASHTENAW	173,508	44,850	124,910	3,748	80,060 D	25.8%	72.0%	26.4%	73.6%
1,820,584	WAYNE	659,859	180,057	463,703	16,099	283,646 D	27.3%	70.3%	28.0%	72.0%
32,735	WEXFORD	13,976	8,419	4,995	562	3,424 R	60.2%	35.7%	62.8%	37.2%
9,883,640	*TOTAL*	*4,250,585*	*1,859,534*	*2,266,193*	*124,858*	*406,659 D*	*43.7%*	*53.3%*	*45.1%*	*54.9%*

MICHIGAN

SENATOR 2018

2010 Census Population	County	Total Vote	Republican (James)	Democratic (Stabenow)	Other	Rep.-Dem. Plurality	Percentage Total Vote Rep.	Total Vote Dem.	Major Vote Rep.	Major Vote Dem.
10,942	ALCONA	5,555	3,541	1,915	99	1,626 R	63.7%	34.5%	64.9%	35.1%
9,601	ALGER	4,162	2,162	1,911	89	251 R	51.9%	45.9%	53.1%	46.9%
111,408	ALLEGAN	49,762	29,834	18,890	1,038	10,944 R	60.0%	38.0%	61.2%	38.8%
29,598	ALPENA	13,083	7,380	5,412	291	1,968 R	56.4%	41.4%	57.7%	42.3%
23,580	ANTRIM	12,866	7,629	4,953	284	2,676 R	59.3%	38.5%	60.6%	39.4%
15,899	ARENAC	6,735	3,995	2,582	158	1,413 R	59.3%	38.3%	60.7%	39.3%
8,860	BARAGA	3,250	1,825	1,344	81	481 R	56.2%	41.4%	57.6%	42.4%
59,173	BARRY	26,737	16,260	9,857	620	6,403 R	60.8%	36.9%	62.3%	37.7%
107,771	BAY	46,333	22,752	22,502	1,079	250 R	49.1%	48.6%	50.3%	49.7%
17,525	BENZIE	9,773	5,080	4,484	209	596 R	52.0%	45.9%	53.1%	46.9%
156,813	BERRIEN	61,986	33,229	27,345	1,412	5,884 R	53.6%	44.1%	54.9%	45.1%
45,248	BRANCH	15,199	9,666	5,144	389	4,522 R	63.6%	33.8%	65.3%	34.7%
136,146	CALHOUN	50,045	25,950	22,739	1,356	3,211 R	51.9%	45.4%	53.3%	46.7%
52,293	CASS	19,445	11,811	7,079	555	4,732 R	60.7%	36.4%	62.5%	37.5%
25,949	CHARLEVOIX	13,662	7,783	5,596	283	2,187 R	57.0%	41.0%	58.2%	41.8%
26,152	CHEBOYGAN	12,525	7,384	4,825	316	2,559 R	59.0%	38.5%	60.5%	39.5%
38,520	CHIPPEWA	13,978	7,767	5,901	310	1,866 R	55.6%	42.2%	56.8%	43.2%
30,926	CLARE	11,851	7,048	4,513	290	2,535 R	59.5%	38.1%	61.0%	39.0%
75,382	CLINTON	37,074	18,946	17,564	564	1,382 R	51.1%	47.4%	51.9%	48.1%
14,074	CRAWFORD	6,253	3,751	2,306	196	1,445 R	60.0%	36.9%	61.9%	38.1%

MICHIGAN

SENATOR 2018

2010 Census Population	County	Total Vote	Republican (James)	Democratic (Stabenow)	Other	Rep.-Dem. Plurality	Percentage Total Vote Rep.	Percentage Total Vote Dem.	Percentage Major Vote Rep.	Percentage Major Vote Dem.
37,069	DELTA	16,416	9,197	6,932	287	2,265 R	56.0%	42.2%	57.0%	43.0%
26,168	DICKINSON	11,363	6,982	4,162	219	2,820 R	61.4%	36.6%	62.7%	37.3%
107,759	EATON	50,952	23,771	26,147	1,034	2,376 D	46.7%	51.3%	47.6%	52.4%
32,694	EMMET	17,891	9,875	7,620	396	2,255 R	55.2%	42.6%	56.4%	43.6%
425,790	GENESEE	168,278	68,648	95,903	3,727	27,255 D	40.8%	57.0%	41.7%	58.3%
25,692	GLADWIN	11,005	6,604	4,160	241	2,444 R	60.0%	37.8%	61.4%	38.6%
16,427	GOGEBIC	6,527	3,078	3,311	138	233 D	47.2%	50.7%	48.2%	51.8%
86,986	GRAND TRAVERSE	48,728	24,903	22,757	1,068	2,146 R	51.1%	46.7%	52.3%	47.7%
42,476	GRATIOT	14,299	8,180	5,764	355	2,416 R	57.2%	40.3%	58.7%	41.3%
46,688	HILLSDALE	16,800	11,310	5,079	411	6,231 R	67.3%	30.2%	69.0%	31.0%
36,628	HOUGHTON	14,321	7,503	6,533	285	970 R	52.4%	45.6%	53.5%	46.5%
33,118	HURON	13,673	8,312	5,087	274	3,225 R	60.8%	37.2%	62.0%	38.0%
280,895	INGHAM	119,163	38,870	78,012	2,281	39,142 D	32.6%	65.5%	33.3%	66.7%
63,905	IONIA	23,730	13,834	9,259	637	4,575 R	58.3%	39.0%	59.9%	40.1%
25,887	IOSCO	11,699	6,694	4,752	253	1,942 R	57.2%	40.6%	58.5%	41.5%
11,817	IRON	5,410	3,000	2,259	151	741 R	55.5%	41.8%	57.0%	43.0%
70,311	ISABELLA	22,418	10,536	11,304	578	768 D	47.0%	50.4%	48.2%	51.8%
160,248	JACKSON	60,782	33,490	25,858	1,434	7,632 R	55.1%	42.5%	56.4%	43.6%
250,331	KALAMAZOO	114,648	46,243	65,686	2,719	19,443 D	40.3%	57.3%	41.3%	58.7%
17,153	KALKASKA	8,328	5,340	2,737	251	2,603 R	64.1%	32.9%	66.1%	33.9%
602,622	KENT	279,474	136,227	137,089	6,158	862 D	48.7%	49.1%	49.8%	50.2%
2,156	KEWEENAW	1,323	704	598	21	106 R	53.2%	45.2%	54.1%	45.9%
11,539	LAKE	4,708	2,633	1,936	139	697 R	55.9%	41.1%	57.6%	42.4%
88,319	LAPEER	39,420	24,206	14,396	818	9,810 R	61.4%	36.5%	62.7%	37.3%
21,708	LEELANAU	14,192	6,775	7,216	201	441 D	47.7%	50.8%	48.4%	51.6%
99,892	LENAWEE	39,960	21,981	17,084	895	4,897 R	55.0%	42.8%	56.3%	43.7%
180,967	LIVINGSTON	96,982	58,020	37,450	1,512	20,570 R	59.8%	38.6%	60.8%	39.2%
6,631	LUCE	2,402	1,524	811	67	713 R	63.4%	33.8%	65.3%	34.7%
11,113	MACKINAC	5,713	3,298	2,325	90	973 R	57.7%	40.7%	58.7%	41.3%
840,978	MACOMB	359,469	173,369	179,975	6,125	6,606 D	48.2%	50.1%	49.1%	50.9%
24,733	MANISTEE	11,712	6,183	5,242	287	941 R	52.8%	44.8%	54.1%	45.9%
67,077	MARQUETTE	29,985	12,348	16,977	660	4,629 D	41.2%	56.6%	42.1%	57.9%
28,705	MASON	13,677	7,625	5,708	344	1,917 R	55.8%	41.7%	57.2%	42.8%
42,798	MECOSTA	15,594	8,857	6,317	420	2,540 R	56.8%	40.5%	58.4%	41.6%
24,029	MENOMINEE	8,809	4,982	3,653	174	1,329 R	56.6%	41.5%	57.7%	42.3%
83,629	MIDLAND	38,344	21,696	15,959	689	5,737 R	56.6%	41.6%	57.6%	42.4%
14,849	MISSAUKEE	6,555	4,650	1,783	122	2,867 R	70.9%	27.2%	72.3%	27.7%
152,021	MONROE	61,423	33,607	26,651	1,165	6,956 R	54.7%	43.4%	55.8%	44.2%
63,342	MONTCALM	23,317	13,878	8,758	681	5,120 R	59.5%	37.6%	61.3%	38.7%
9,765	MONTMORENCY	4,610	2,978	1,537	95	1,441 R	64.6%	33.3%	66.0%	34.0%
172,188	MUSKEGON	68,765	30,831	35,957	1,977	5,126 D	44.8%	52.3%	46.2%	53.8%
48,460	NEWAYGO	20,259	12,870	6,858	531	6,012 R	63.5%	33.9%	65.2%	34.8%
1,202,362	OAKLAND	603,819	256,017	338,986	8,816	82,969 D	42.4%	56.1%	43.0%	57.0%
26,570	OCEANA	10,757	6,263	4,213	281	2,050 R	58.2%	39.2%	59.8%	40.2%
21,699	OGEMAW	9,109	5,592	3,280	237	2,312 R	61.4%	36.0%	63.0%	37.0%
6,780	ONTONAGON	3,129	1,752	1,313	64	439 R	56.0%	42.0%	57.2%	42.8%
23,528	OSCEOLA	9,392	6,186	2,934	272	3,252 R	65.9%	31.2%	67.8%	32.2%
8,640	OSCODA	3,717	2,410	1,221	86	1,189 R	64.8%	32.8%	66.4%	33.6%
24,164	OTSEGO	11,334	7,092	3,969	273	3,123 R	62.6%	35.0%	64.1%	35.9%
263,801	OTTAWA	128,198	80,318	45,696	2,184	34,622 R	62.7%	35.6%	63.7%	36.3%
13,376	PRESQUE ISLE	6,686	3,788	2,760	138	1,028 R	56.7%	41.3%	57.8%	42.2%
24,449	ROSCOMMON	11,807	6,864	4,643	300	2,221 R	58.1%	39.3%	59.7%	40.3%
200,169	SAGINAW	80,814	37,809	41,472	1,533	3,663 D	46.8%	51.3%	47.7%	52.3%
43,114	SANILAC	16,443	10,657	5,418	368	5,239 R	64.8%	33.0%	66.3%	33.7%
8,485	SCHOOLCRAFT	3,737	2,099	1,547	91	552 R	56.2%	41.4%	57.6%	42.4%
70,648	SHIAWASSEE	29,720	15,865	13,043	812	2,822 R	53.4%	43.9%	54.9%	45.1%
163,040	ST. CLAIR	67,505	38,329	27,540	1,636	10,789 R	56.8%	40.8%	58.2%	41.8%
61,295	ST. JOSEPH	20,403	12,489	7,278	636	5,211 R	61.2%	35.7%	63.2%	36.8%
55,729	TUSCOLA	22,260	13,495	8,197	568	5,298 R	60.6%	36.8%	62.2%	37.8%
76,258	VAN BUREN	29,443	15,379	13,191	873	2,188 R	52.2%	44.8%	53.8%	46.2%

MICHIGAN

SENATOR 2018

2010 Census Population	County	Total Vote	Republican (James)	Democratic (Stabenow)	Other	Rep.-Dem. Plurality	Percentage Total Vote Rep.	Total Vote Dem.	Major Vote Rep.	Major Vote Dem.
344,791	WASHTENAW	173,226	47,380	123,305	2,541	75,925 D	27.4%	71.2%	27.8%	72.2%
1,820,584	WAYNE	658,391	190,884	455,176	12,331	264,292 D	29.0%	69.1%	29.5%	70.5%
32,735	WEXFORD	13,983	8,745	4,832	406	3,913 R	62.5%	34.6%	64.4%	35.6%
9,883,640	*TOTAL*	*4,237,271*	*1,938,818*	*2,214,478*	*83,975*	*275,660 D*	*45.8%*	*52.3%*	*46.7%*	*53.3%*

MICHIGAN

HOUSE OF REPRESENTATIVES

CD	Year	Total Vote	Republican Vote	Republican Candidate	Democratic Vote	Democratic Candidate	Other Vote	Rep.-Dem. Plurality	Percentage Total Vote Rep.	Total Vote Dem.	Major Vote Rep.	Major Vote Dem.
1	2018	332,497	187,251	BERGMAN, JACK*	145,246	MORGAN, MATTHEW		42,005 R	56.3%	43.7%	56.3%	43.7%
1	2016	360,271	197,777	BERGMAN, JACK	144,334	JOHNSON, LONNIE BARTON "LON"	18,160	53,443 R	54.9%	40.1%	57.8%	42.2%
1	2014	250,131	130,414	BENISHEK, DAN*	113,263	CANNON, JERRY	6,454	17,151 R	52.1%	45.3%	53.5%	46.5%
1	2012	347,037	167,060	BENISHEK, DAN*	165,179	MCDOWELL, GARY	14,798	1,881 R	48.1%	47.6%	50.3%	49.7%
2	2018	305,463	168,970	HUIZENGA, BILL*	131,254	DAVIDSON, ROB	5,239	37,716 R	55.3%	43.0%	56.3%	43.7%
2	2016	339,328	212,508	HUIZENGA, BILL*	110,391	MURPHY, DENNIS B.	16,429	102,117 R	62.6%	32.5%	65.8%	34.2%
2	2014	213,072	135,568	HUIZENGA, BILL*	70,851	VANDERSTELT, DEAN	6,653	64,717 R	63.6%	33.3%	65.7%	34.3%
2	2012	318,267	194,653	HUIZENGA, BILL*	108,973	GERMAN, WILLIE JR.	14,641	85,680 R	61.2%	34.2%	64.1%	35.9%
3**	2018	310,740	169,107	AMASH, JUSTIN*	134,185	ALBRO, CATHY	7,448	34,922 R	54.4%	43.2%	55.8%	44.2%
3	2016	342,365	203,545	AMASH, JUSTIN*	128,400	SMITH, DOUGLAS	10,420	75,145 R	59.5%	37.5%	61.3%	38.7%
3	2014	217,165	125,754	AMASH, JUSTIN*	84,720	GOODRICH, BOB	6,691	41,034 R	57.9%	39.0%	59.7%	40.3%
3	2012	326,283	171,675	AMASH, JUSTIN*	144,108	PESTKA, STEVE	10,500	27,567 R	52.6%	44.2%	54.4%	45.6%
4	2018	285,050	178,510	MOOLENAAR, JOHN*	106,540	HILLIARD, JEROME "JERRY"		71,970 R	62.6%	37.4%	62.6%	37.4%
4	2016	315,751	194,572	MOOLENAAR, JOHN*	101,277	WIRTH, DEBRA FREIDELL	19,902	93,295 R	61.6%	32.1%	65.8%	34.2%
4	2014	219,423	123,962	MOOLENAAR, JOHN	85,777	HOLMES, JEFF	9,684	38,185 R	56.5%	39.1%	59.1%	40.9%
4	2012	312,949	197,386	CAMP, DAVE*	104,996	WIRTH, DEBRA FREIDELL	10,567	92,390 R	63.1%	33.6%	65.3%	34.7%
5	2018	276,413	99,265	WINES, TRAVIS	164,502	KILDEE, DANIEL*	12,646	65,237 D	35.9%	59.5%	37.6%	62.4%
5	2016	319,291	112,102	HARDWICK, ALLEN	195,279	KILDEE, DANIEL*	11,910	83,177 D	35.1%	61.2%	36.5%	63.5%
5	2014	222,138	69,222	HARDWICK, ALLEN	148,182	KILDEE, DANIEL*	4,734	78,960 D	31.2%	66.7%	31.8%	68.2%
5	2012	330,146	103,931	SLEZAK, JIM	214,531	KILDEE, DANIEL	11,684	110,600 D	31.5%	65.0%	32.6%	67.4%
6	2018	293,438	147,436	UPTON, FRED*	134,082	LONGJOHN, MATT	11,920	13,354 R	50.2%	45.7%	52.4%	47.6%
6	2016	329,565	193,259	UPTON, FRED*	119,980	CLEMENTS, PAUL C.	16,326	73,279 R	58.6%	36.4%	61.7%	38.3%
6	2014	208,976	116,801	UPTON, FRED*	84,391	CLEMENTS, PAUL C.	7,784	32,410 R	55.9%	40.4%	58.1%	41.9%
6	2012	320,475	174,955	UPTON, FRED*	136,563	O'BRIEN, MIKE	8,957	38,392 R	54.6%	42.6%	56.2%	43.8%
7	2018	295,060	158,730	WALBERG, TIMOTHY*	136,330	DRISKELL, GRETCHEN D.		22,400 R	53.8%	46.2%	53.8%	46.2%
7	2016	334,807	184,321	WALBERG, TIMOTHY*	134,010	DRISKELL, GRETCHEN D.	16,476	50,311 R	55.1%	40.0%	57.9%	42.1%
7	2014	223,685	119,564	WALBERG, TIMOTHY*	92,083	BYRNES, PAM	12,038	27,481 R	53.5%	41.2%	56.5%	43.5%
7	2012	318,069	169,668	WALBERG, TIMOTHY*	136,849	HASKELL, KURT R.	11,552	32,819 R	53.3%	43.0%	55.4%	44.6%
8	2018	341,593	159,782	BISHOP, MIKE*	172,880	SLOTKIN, ELISSA	8,931	13,098 D	46.8%	50.6%	48.0%	52.0%
8	2016	366,968	205,629	BISHOP, MIKE*	143,791	SHKRELI, SUZANNA	17,548	61,838 R	56.0%	39.2%	58.8%	41.2%
8	2014	243,125	132,739	BISHOP, MIKE	102,269	SCHERTZING, ERIC	8,117	30,470 R	54.6%	42.1%	56.5%	43.5%
8	2012	345,054	202,217	ROGERS, MIKE*	128,657	ENDERLE, LANCE	14,180	73,560 R	58.6%	37.3%	61.1%	38.9%
9	2018	304,563	112,123	STEARNS, CANDIUS	181,734	LEVIN, ANDY	10,706	69,611 D	36.8%	59.7%	38.2%	61.8%
9	2016	344,775	128,937	MORSE, CHRISTOPHER R.	199,661	LEVIN, SANDER M.*	16,177	70,724 D	37.4%	57.9%	39.2%	60.8%
9	2014	225,757	81,470	BRIKHO, GEORGE	136,342	LEVIN, SANDER M.*	7,945	54,872 D	36.1%	60.4%	37.4%	62.6%
9	2012	337,316	114,760	VOLARIC, DON	208,846	LEVIN, SANDER M.*	13,710	94,086 D	34.0%	61.9%	35.5%	64.5%
10	2018	303,064	182,808	MITCHELL, PAUL*	106,061	BIZON, KIMBERLY	14,195	76,747 R	60.3%	35.0%	63.3%	36.7%
10	2016	340,983	215,132	MITCHELL, PAUL	110,112	ACCAVITTI, FRANK JR.	15,739	105,020 R	63.1%	32.3%	66.1%	33.9%
10	2014	228,692	157,069	MILLER, CANDICE S.*	67,143	STADLER, CHUCK	4,480	89,926 R	68.7%	29.4%	70.1%	29.9%
10	2012	328,612	226,075	MILLER, CANDICE S.*	97,734	STADLER, CHUCK	4,803	128,341 R	68.8%	29.7%	69.8%	30.2%

MICHIGAN

HOUSE OF REPRESENTATIVES

CD	Year	Total Vote	Republican Vote	Republican Candidate	Democratic Vote	Democratic Candidate	Other Vote	Rep.-Dem. Plurality	Percentage: Total Vote Rep.	Total Vote Dem.	Major Vote Rep.	Major Vote Dem.
11	2018	350,901	158,463	EPSTEIN, LENA	181,912	STEVENS, HALEY	10,526	23,449 D	45.2%	51.8%	46.6%	53.4%
11	2016	379,488	200,872	TROTT, DAVE A.*	152,461	KUMAR, ANIL	26,155	48,411 R	52.9%	40.2%	56.9%	43.1%
11	2014	251,238	140,435	TROTT, DAVE A.	101,681	MCKENZIE, BOBBY	9,122	38,754 R	55.9%	40.5%	58.0%	42.0%
11	2012	358,139	181,788	BENTIVOLIO, KERRY	158,879	TAJ, SYED	17,472	22,909 R	50.8%	44.4%	53.4%	46.6%
12	2018	294,628	85,115	JONES, JEFF	200,588	DINGELL, DEBBIE*	8,925	115,473 D	28.9%	68.1%	29.8%	70.2%
12	2016	328,542	96,104	JONES, JEFF	211,378	DINGELL, DEBBIE*	21,060	115,274 D	29.3%	64.3%	31.3%	68.7%
12	2014	206,660	64,716	BOWMAN, TERRENCE "TERRY"	134,346	DINGELL, DEBBIE	7,598	69,630 D	31.3%	65.0%	32.5%	67.5%
12	2012	319,223	92,472	KALLGREN, CYNTHIA	216,884	DINGELL, JOHN D. JR.*	9,867	124,412 D	29.0%	67.9%	29.9%	70.1%
13	2018	196,299			165,355	TLAIB, RASHIDA	30,944	165,355 D		84.2%		100.0%
13	2016	257,797	40,541	GORMAN, JEFF	198,771	CONYERS, JOHN JR.*	18,485	158,230 D	15.7%	77.1%	16.9%	83.1%
13	2014	166,947	27,234	GORMAN, JEFF	132,710	CONYERS, JOHN JR.*	7,003	105,476 D	16.3%	79.5%	17.0%	83.0%
13	2012	284,270	38,769	SAWICKI, HARRY	235,336	CONYERS, JOHN JR.*	10,165	196,567 D	13.6%	82.8%	14.1%	85.9%
14	2018	264,994	45,899	HERSCHFUS, MARC S.	214,334	LAWRENCE, BRENDA*	4,761	168,435 D	17.3%	80.9%	17.6%	82.4%
14	2016	310,974	58,103	KLAUSNER, HOWARD	244,135	LAWRENCE, BRENDA*	8,736	186,032 D	18.7%	78.5%	19.2%	80.8%
14	2014	212,468	41,801	BARR, CHRISTINA	165,272	LAWRENCE, BRENDA	5,395	123,471 D	19.7%	77.8%	20.2%	79.8%
14	2012	328,792	51,395	HAULER, JOHN	270,450	PETERS, GARY C.*	6,947	219,055 D	15.6%	82.3%	16.0%	84.0%
TOTAL	*2018*	*4,154,703*	*1,853,459*		*2,175,003*		*126,241*	*321,544 D*	*44.6%*	*52.4%*	*46.0%*	*54.0%*
TOTAL	*2016*	*4,670,905*	*2,243,402*		*2,193,980*		*233,523*	*49,422 R*	*48.0%*	*47.0%*	*50.6%*	*49.4%*
TOTAL	*2014*	*3,089,477*	*1,466,749*		*1,519,030*		*103,698*	*52,281 D*	*47.5%*	*49.2%*	*49.1%*	*50.9%*
TOTAL	*2012*	*4,574,632*	*2,086,804*		*2,327,985*		*159,843*	*241,181 D*	*45.6%*	*50.9%*	*47.3%*	*52.7%*

Note: An asterisk (*) denotes incumbent. **On July 4, 2019, Justin Amash switched party affiliation from Republican to Independent.

MICHIGAN

GENERAL AND PRIMARY ELECTIONS

2018 GENERAL ELECTIONS: OTHER VOTES

Governor Other vote was 56,606 Libertarian (Bill Gelineau), 29,219 U.S. Taxpayers (Todd Schleiger), 28,799 Green (Jennifer Kurland), 10,202 Natural Law (Keith Butkovich), 11 Write-in (Francis Rowley), 8 Write-in (Evan Space), 4 Write-in (Lance Herman), 3 Write-in (William Cobbs), 2 Write-in (Robin Sanders), 1 Write-in (Chaneika Penny), 1 Write-in (Clyde Lynch), 1 Write-in (Henry Lester), 1 Write-in (Patrick Burney)

Senate Other vote was 40,204 Green (Marcia Squier), 27,251 U.S. Taxpayers (George Huffman), 16,502 Natural Law (John Wilhelm), 10 Write-in (Tom Bagwell), 5 Write-in (Valerie Willis), 3 Write-in (Tim Yow)

House Other vote was:

CD 2 5,239 U.S. Taxpayers (Ronald Graeser)
CD 3 7,445 U.S. Taxpayers (Ted Gerrard), 3 Write-in (Joe Farrington)
CD 5 12,646 Working Class (Kathy Goodwin)
CD 6 11,920 U.S. Taxpayers (Stephen Young)
CD 8 6,302 Libertarian (Brian Ellison), 2,629 U.S. Taxpayers (David Lillis)
CD 9 6,797 Working Class (Andrea Kirby), 3,909 Green (John McDermott)
CD 10 11,344 Independent (Jeremy Peruski), 2,851 Green (Harley Mikkelson)
CD 11 5,799 Libertarian (Leonard Schwartz), 4,727 Independent (Cooper Nye)
CD 12 6,712 Working Class (Gary Walkowicz), 2,213 Socialist Equality (Niles Niemuth)
CD 13 22,186 Working Class (Sam Johnson), 7,980 Green (D. Wilcoxon), 633 Write-in (Brenda Jones), 75 Write-in (David Dudenhoefer), 61 Write-in (Jonathan Pommerville), 3 Write-in (DaNetta Simpson), 2 Write-in (John Conyers), 2 Write-in (Royce Kinniebrew), 1 Write-in (James Casha), 1 Write-in (Kimberly Knott)
CD 14 4,761 Working Class (Philip Kolody)

MICHIGAN

GENERAL AND PRIMARY ELECTIONS

2018 PRIMARY ELECTIONS: SUPPLEMENTARY INFORMATION

Primary	August 7, 2018	**Registration** (as of July 2018 — includes 1,005,505 inactive registrants)	7,387,060	No Party Registration

Primary Type Open—Any registered voter could participate in the primary of either party.

	REPUBLICAN PRIMARIES			DEMOCRATIC PRIMARIES		
Senator	James, John	518,564	54.7%	Stabenow, Debbie*	1,045,450	100.0%
	Pensler, Sandy	429,885	45.3%			
	White, William F. (Write-in)	57				
	TOTAL	*948,506*		*TOTAL*	*1,045,450*	
Governor	Schuette, Bill	501,959	50.7%	Whitmer, Gretchen	588,436	52.0%
	Calley, Brian	249,185	25.2%	El-Sayed, Abdul	342,179	30.2%
	Colbeck, Patrick	129,646	13.1%	Thanedar, Shri	200,645	17.7%
	Hines, Jim	108,735	11.0%	Cobbs, William (Write-in)	187	
	Space, Evan (Write-in)	51				
	TOTAL	*989,576*		*TOTAL*	*1,131,447*	
Congressional District 1	Bergman, Jack*	83,272	100.0%	Morgan, Matthew (Write-in)	29,293	100.0%
	TOTAL	*83,272*		*TOTAL*	*29,293*	
Congressional District 2	Huizenga, Bill*	79,620	100.0%	Davidson, Rob	52,221	100.0%
	TOTAL	*79,620*		*TOTAL*	*52,221*	
Congressional District 3	Amash, Justin*	69,817	99.9%	Albro, Cathy	42,619	68.2%
	Farrington, Joe (Write-in)	52	0.1%	Wooden, Fred	19,903	31.8%
	TOTAL	*69,869*		*TOTAL*	*62,522*	
Congressional District 4	Moolenaar, John*	80,290	100.0%	Hilliard, Jerome "Jerry"	32,263	66.5%
				Kozicki, Zigmond	16,261	33.5%
	TOTAL	*80,290*		*TOTAL*	*48,524*	
Congressional District 5	Wines, Travis	44,405	100.0%	Kildee, Daniel*	73,996	100.0%
	TOTAL	*44,405*		*TOTAL*	*73,996*	
Congressional District 6	Upton, Fred*	64,512	100.0%	Longjohn, Matt	22,412	37.1%
				Franklin, George	17,493	28.9%
				Benac, David	12,867	21.3%
				Eichholz, Rich	7,719	12.8%
	TOTAL	*64,512*		*TOTAL*	*60,491*	
Congressional District 7	Walberg, Timothy*	69,248	100.0%	Driskell, Gretchen D.	52,430	85.2%
				Friday, Steven	9,083	14.8%
	TOTAL	*69,248*		*TOTAL*	*61,513*	
Congressional District 8	Bishop, Mike*	75,403	92.3%	Slotkin, Elissa	57,819	70.7%
	Kumar, Lokesh	6,254	7.7%	Smith, Chris	23,996	29.3%
	TOTAL	*81,657*		*TOTAL*	*81,815*	
Congressional District 9	Stearns, Candius	47,410	100.0%	Levin, Andy	49,612	52.4%
				Lipton, Ellen	40,174	42.4%
				Brook, Martin	4,865	5.1%
	TOTAL	*47,410*		*TOTAL*	*94,651*	

MICHIGAN

GENERAL AND PRIMARY ELECTIONS

	REPUBLICAN PRIMARIES			DEMOCRATIC PRIMARIES		
Congressional District 10	Mitchell, Paul*	81,867	100.0%	Bizon, Kimberly	21,944	41.1%
				Accavitti, Frank Jr.	17,047	32.0%
				McCarthy, Michael	14,353	26.9%
	TOTAL	*81,867*		*TOTAL*	*53,344*	
Congressional District 11	Epstein, Lena	26,925	30.9%	Stevens, Haley	24,309	27.0%
	Raczkowski, Rocky	22,216	25.5%	Greimel, Tim	19,673	21.8%
	Kowall, Mike	16,011	18.4%	Gupta, Suneel	19,250	21.4%
	Kesto, Klint	12,213	14.0%	Saad, Fayrouz	17,499	19.4%
	Bentivolio, Kerry	9,831	11.3%	Skinner, Nancy	9,407	10.4%
	TOTAL	*87,196*		*TOTAL*	*90,138*	
Congressional District 12	Jones, Jeff	33,839	100.0%	Dingell, Debbie*	103,278	100.0%
	TOTAL	*33,839*		*TOTAL*	*103,278*	
Congressional District 13	Dudenhoefer, David Anthony (Write-in)	419	100.0%	Tlaib, Rashida	27,841	31.2%
				Jones, Brenda	26,941	30.2%
				Wild, Bill	12,613	14.1%
				Young II, Coleman A.	11,172	12.5%
				Conyers, Ian	5,866	6.6%
				Jackson, Shanelle	4,853	5.4%
				Knott, Kimberly (Write-in)	33	
				Kinniebrew, Royce (Write-in)	2	
	TOTAL	*419*		*TOTAL*	*89,321*	
Congressional District 14	Herschfus, Marc S.	18,546	100.0%	Lawrence, Brenda*	106,464	100.0%
	TOTAL	*18,546*		*TOTAL*	*106,464*	

Note: An asterisk (*) denotes incumbent.

MINNESOTA

Congressional districts first established for elections held in 2012

8 members

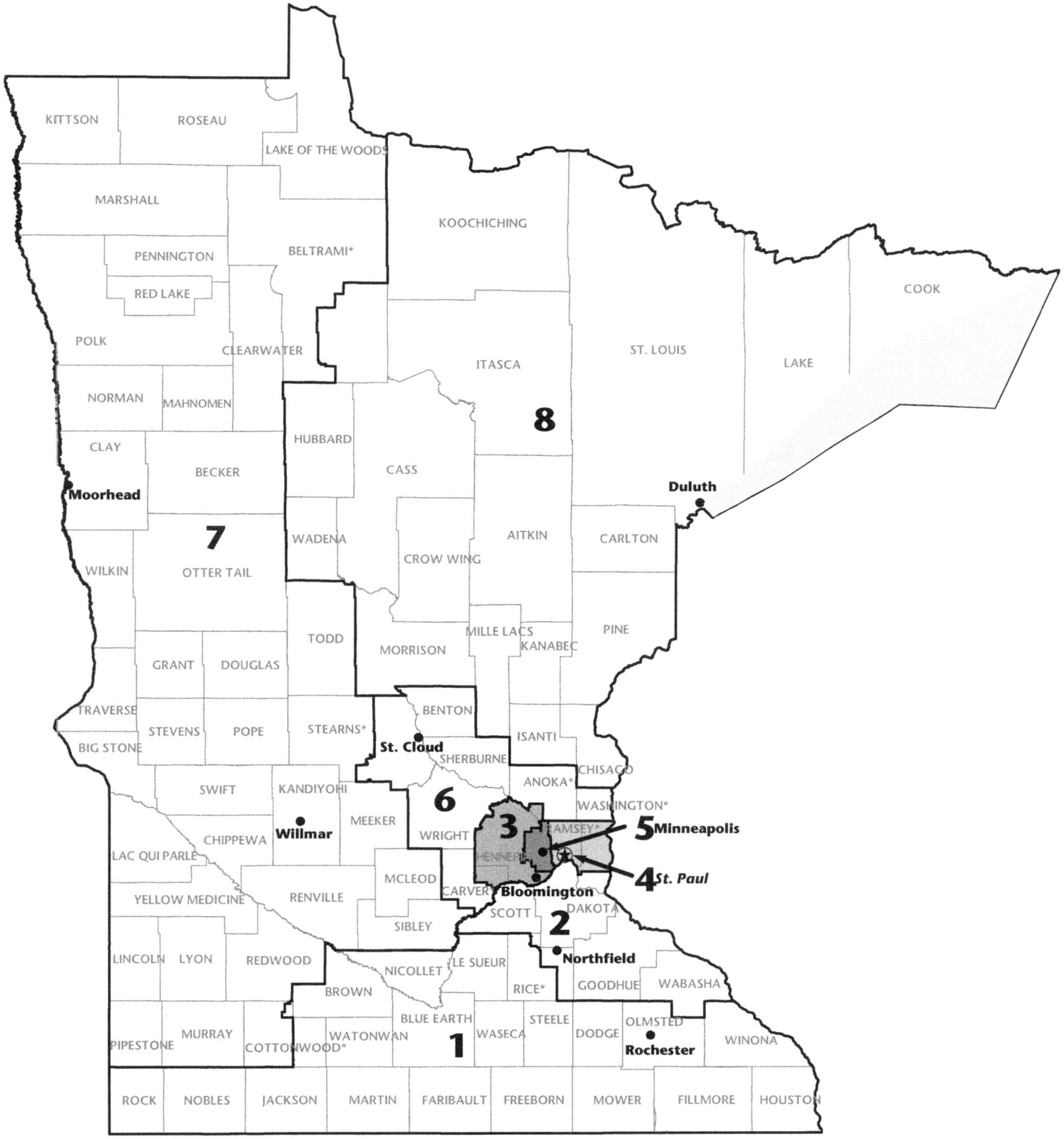

* Asterisk indicates a county whose boundaries include parts of two or more congressional districts.

MINNESOTA

Minneapolis–St. Paul Area

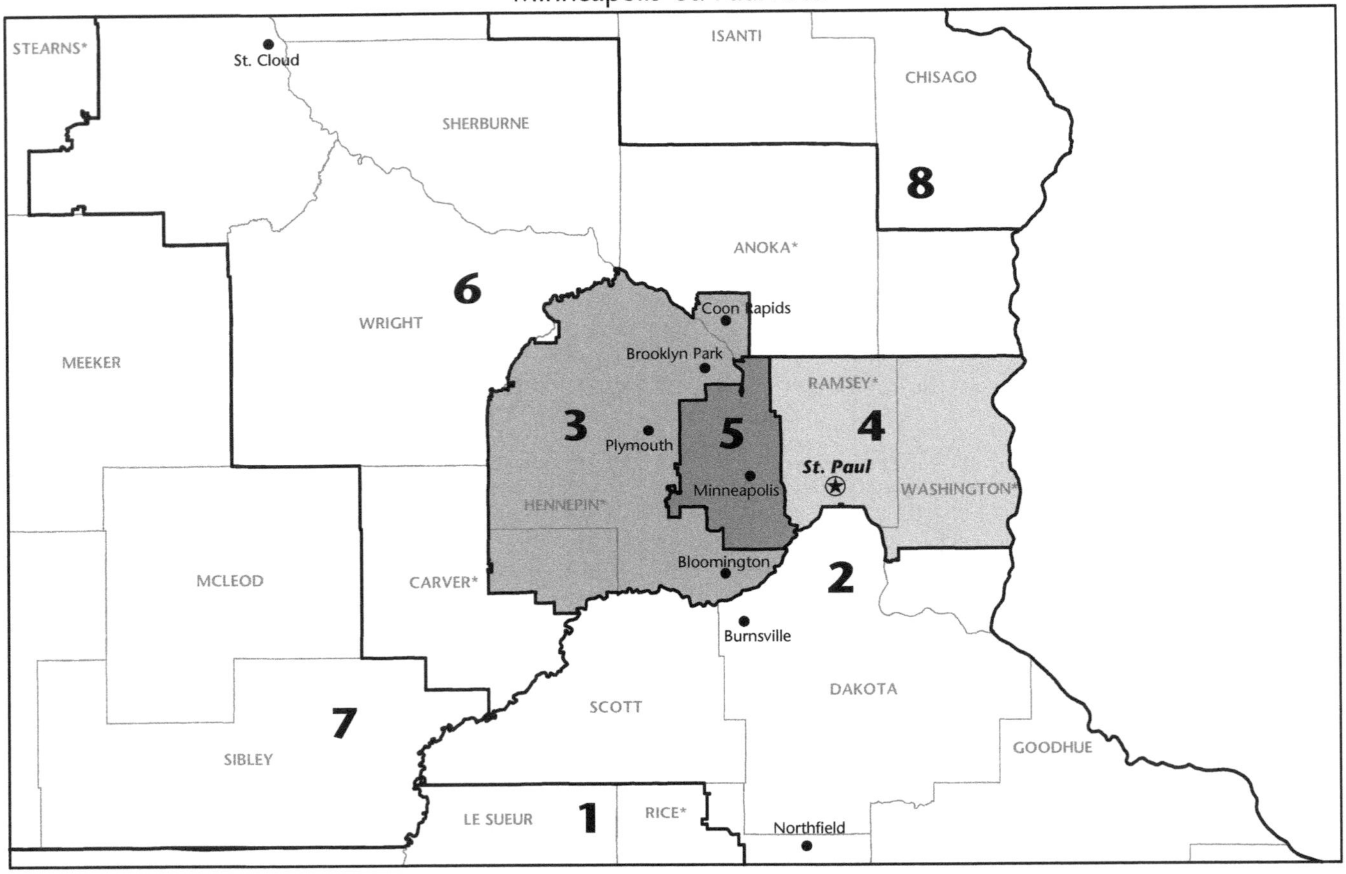

* Asterisk indicates a county whose boundaries include parts of two or more congressional districts.

MINNESOTA

GOVERNOR

Timothy J. Walz (D). Elected 2018 to a four-year term.

SENATORS (2 Democrats)

Tina Smith (D). Appointed January 3, 2018, to complete the term vacated by Al Franken (D), who resigned January 2, 2018, following sexual assault allegations against him. Smith was elected to the last two years of Franken's term in the November 6, 2018, special election.

Amy Klobuchar (D). Re-elected 2018 to a six-year term. Previously elected 2012, 2006.

REPRESENTATIVES (3 Republicans, 5 Democrats)

1. James "Jim" Hagedorn (R)
2. Angie Craig (D)
3. Dean Phillips (D)
4. Betty McCollum (D)
5. Ilhan Omar (D)
6. Tom Emmer (R)
7. Collin C. Peterson (D)
8. Pete Stauber (R)

POSTWAR VOTE FOR PRESIDENT

		Republican		Democratic				Percentage			
								Total Vote		Major Vote	
Year	Total Vote	Vote	Candidate	Vote	Candidate	Other Vote	Rep.-Dem. Plurality	Rep.	Dem.	Rep.	Dem.
2016**	2,944,813	1,322,951	Trump, Donald J.	1,367,716	Clinton, Hillary Rodham	254,146	44,765 D	44.9%	46.4%	49.2%	50.8%
2012	2,936,561	1,320,225	Romney, W. Mitt	1,546,167	Obama, Barack H.*	70,169	225,942 D	45.0%	52.7%	46.1%	53.9%
2008	2,910,369	1,275,409	McCain, John S. III	1,573,354	Obama, Barack H.	61,606	297,945 D	43.8%	54.1%	44.8%	55.2%
2004	2,828,387	1,346,695	Bush, George W.*	1,445,014	Kerry, John F.	36,678	98,319 D	47.6%	51.1%	48.2%	51.8%
2000**	2,438,685	1,109,659	Bush, George W.	1,168,266	Gore, Albert Jr.	160,760	58,607 D	45.5%	47.9%	48.7%	51.3%
1996**	2,192,640	766,476	Dole, Robert "Bob"	1,120,438	Clinton, Bill*	305,726	353,962 D	35.0%	51.1%	40.6%	59.4%
1992**	2,347,948	747,841	Bush, George H.*	1,020,997	Clinton, Bill	579,110	273,156 D	31.9%	43.5%	42.3%	57.7%
1988	2,096,790	962,337	Bush, George H.	1,109,471	Dukakis, Michael S.	24,982	147,134 D	45.9%	52.9%	46.4%	53.6%
1984	2,084,449	1,032,603	Reagan, Ronald*	1,036,364	Mondale, Walter F.	15,482	3,761 D	49.5%	49.7%	49.9%	50.1%
1980**	2,051,980	873,268	Reagan, Ronald	954,174	Carter, Jimmy*	224,538	80,906 D	42.6%	46.5%	47.8%	52.2%
1976	1,949,931	819,395	Ford, Gerald R.*	1,070,440	Carter, Jimmy	60,096	251,045 D	42.0%	54.9%	43.4%	56.6%
1972	1,741,652	898,269	Nixon, Richard M.*	802,346	McGovern, George S.	41,037	95,923 R	51.6%	46.1%	52.8%	47.2%
1968**	1,588,506	658,643	Nixon, Richard M.	857,738	Humphrey, Hubert Horatio Jr.	72,125	199,095 D	41.5%	54.0%	43.4%	56.6%
1964	1,554,462	559,624	Goldwater, Barry M. Sr.	991,117	Johnson, Lyndon B.*	3,721	431,493 D	36.0%	63.8%	36.1%	63.9%
1960	1,541,887	757,915	Nixon, Richard M.	779,933	Kennedy, John F.	4,039	22,018 D	49.2%	50.6%	49.3%	50.7%
1956	1,340,005	719,302	Eisenhower, Dwight D.*	617,525	Stevenson, Adlai E. II	3,178	101,777 R	53.7%	46.1%	53.8%	46.2%
1952	1,379,483	763,211	Eisenhower, Dwight D.	608,458	Stevenson, Adlai E. II	7,814	154,753 R	55.3%	44.1%	55.6%	44.4%
1948	1,212,226	483,617	Dewey, Thomas E.	692,966	Truman, Harry S.*	35,643	209,349 D	39.9%	57.2%	41.1%	58.9%

Note: An asterisk (*) denotes incumbent. **In past elections, the other vote included: 2016 - 112,972 Libertarian (Gary Johnson); 2000 - 126,696 Green (Nader); 1996 - 257,704 Reform (Ross Perot); 1992 - 562,506 Independent (Perot); 1980 - 174,990 Independent (John Anderson); 1968 - 68,931 American Independent (George Wallace).

MINNESOTA

POSTWAR VOTE FOR GOVERNOR

								Percentage			
		Republican		Democratic				Total Vote		Major Vote	
Year	Total Vote	Vote	Candidate	Vote	Candidate	Other Vote	Rep.-Dem. Plurality	Rep.	Dem.	Rep.	Dem.
2018	2,587,287	1,097,705	Johnson, Jeff	1,393,096	Walz, Timothy J.	96,486	295,391 D	42.4%	53.8%	44.1%	55.9%
2014	1,975,406	879,257	Johnson, Jeff	989,113	Dayton, Mark*	107,036	109,856 D	44.5%	50.1%	47.1%	52.9%
2010**	2,107,021	910,462	Emmer, Tom	919,232	Dayton, Mark	277,327	8,770 D	43.2%	43.6%	49.8%	50.2%
2006	2,202,937	1,028,568	Pawlenty, Tim*	1,007,460	Hatch, Mike	166,909	21,108 R	46.7%	45.7%	50.5%	49.5%
2002**	2,252,473	999,473	Pawlenty, Tim	821,268	Moe, Roger D.	431,732	178,205 R	44.4%	36.5%	54.9%	45.1%
1998**	2,090,518	716,880	Coleman, Norm	587,060	Humphrey, Hubert Horatio "Skip" III	786,578	129,820 R#	34.3%	28.1%	55.0%	45.0%
1994	1,765,590	1,094,165	Carlson, Arne*	589,344	Marty, John	82,081	504,821 R	62.0%	33.4%	65.0%	35.0%
1990	1,806,777	895,988	Carlson, Arne	836,218	Perpich, Rudy*	74,571	59,770 R	49.6%	46.3%	51.7%	48.3%
1986	1,415,989	606,755	Ludeman, Cal R.	790,138	Perpich, Rudy*	19,096	183,383 D	42.9%	55.8%	43.4%	56.6%
1982	1,789,539	715,796	Whitney, Wheelock	1,049,104	Perpich, Rudy*	24,639	333,308 D	40.0%	58.6%	40.6%	59.4%
1978	1,585,702	830,019	Quie, Albert H.	718,244	Perpich, Rudy*	37,439	111,775 R	52.3%	45.3%	53.6%	46.4%
1974	1,252,898	367,722	Johnson, John W.	786,787	Anderson, Wendell R.*	98,389	419,065 D	29.3%	62.8%	31.9%	68.1%
1970	1,365,443	621,780	Head, Douglas M.	737,921	Anderson, Wendell R.	5,742	116,141 D	45.5%	54.0%	45.7%	54.3%
1966	1,295,058	680,593	Levander, Harold	607,943	Rolvaag, Karl F.*	6,522	72,650 R	52.6%	46.9%	52.8%	47.2%
1962**	1,246,904	619,751	Andersen, Elmer L.*	619,842	Rolvaag, Karl F.	7,311	91 D	49.7%	49.7%	50.0%	50.0%
1960	1,550,265	783,813	Andersen, Elmer L.	760,934	Freeman, Orville L.	5,518	22,879 R	50.6%	49.1%	50.7%	49.3%
1958	1,159,915	490,731	MacKinnon, George	658,326	Freeman, Orville L.*	10,858	167,595 D	42.3%	56.8%	42.7%	57.3%
1956	1,422,161	685,196	Nelsen, Ancher	731,180	Freeman, Orville L.*	5,785	45,984 D	48.2%	51.4%	48.4%	51.6%
1954	1,151,417	538,865	Anderson, C. Elmer*	607,099	Freeman, Orville L.	5,453	68,234 D	46.8%	52.7%	47.0%	53.0%
1952	1,418,869	785,125	Anderson, C. Elmer	624,480	Freeman, Orville L.	9,264	160,645 R	55.3%	44.0%	55.7%	44.3%
1950	1,046,632	635,800	Youngdahl, Luther W.*	400,637	Peterson, Harry H.	10,195	235,163 R	60.7%	38.3%	61.3%	38.7%
1948	1,210,874	643,572	Youngdahl, Luther W.*	545,746	Halsted, Charles L.	21,556	97,826 R	53.1%	45.1%	54.1%	45.9%
1946	880,348	519,067	Youngdahl, Luther W.	349,565	Barker, Harold H.	11,716	169,502 R	59.0%	39.7%	59.8%	40.2%

Note: An asterisk (*) denotes incumbent. A pound sign (#) in the plurality column indicates that the winner in 1998 ran on the Reform Party line. **In past elections, the other vote included: 2010 - 251,487 Independence (Tom Horner); 2002 - 364,534 Independence (Timothy J. Penny); 1998 - 773,403 Reform (Jesse Ventura, who was elected with 37.0 percent of the total vote and a plurality of 56,523 votes). The term of office of Minnesota's Governor was increased from two to four years effective with the 1962 election.

POSTWAR VOTE FOR SENATOR

								Percentage			
		Republican		Democratic				Total Vote		Major Vote	
Year	Total Vote	Vote	Candidate	Vote	Candidate	Other Vote	Rep.-Dem. Plurality	Rep.	Dem.	Rep.	Dem.
2018S**	2,587,356	1,095,777	Housley, Karin	1,370,540	Smith, Tina*	121,039	274,763 D	42.4%	53.0%	44.4%	55.6%
2018	2,596,879	940,437	Newberger, James	1,566,174	Klobuchar, Amy*	90,268	625,737 D	36.2%	60.3%	37.5%	62.5%
2014	1,981,528	850,227	McFadden, Mike	1,053,205	Franken, Al*	78,096	202,978 D	42.9%	53.2%	44.7%	55.3%
2012	2,843,207	867,974	Bills, Kurt	1,854,595	Klobuchar, Amy*	120,638	986,621 D	30.5%	65.2%	31.9%	68.1%
2008**	2,887,646	1,212,317	Coleman, Norm*	1,212,629	Franken, Al	462,700	312 D	42.0%	42.0%	50.0%	50.0%
2006	2,202,772	835,653	Kennedy, Mark	1,278,849	Klobuchar, Amy	88,270	443,196 D	37.9%	58.1%	39.5%	60.5%
2002**	2,254,639	1,116,697	Coleman, Norm	1,067,246	Mondale, Walter F.	70,696	49,451 R	49.5%	47.3%	51.1%	48.9%
2000	2,419,520	1,047,474	Grams, Rod*	1,181,553	Dayton, Mark	190,493	134,079 D	43.3%	48.8%	47.0%	53.0%
1996	2,183,062	901,282	Boschwitz, Rudy	1,098,493	Wellstone, Paul D.*	183,287	197,211 D	41.3%	50.3%	45.1%	54.9%
1994	1,772,929	869,653	Grams, Rod	781,860	Wynia, Ann	121,416	87,793 R	49.1%	44.1%	52.7%	47.3%
1990	1,808,045	864,375	Boschwitz, Rudy*	911,999	Wellstone, Paul D.	31,671	47,624 D	47.8%	50.4%	48.7%	51.3%
1988	2,093,953	1,176,210	Durenberger, David*	856,694	Humphrey, Hubert Horatio "Skip" III	61,049	319,516 R	56.2%	40.9%	57.9%	42.1%
1984	2,066,143	1,199,926	Boschwitz, Rudy*	852,844	Growe, Joan Anderson	13,373	347,082 R	58.1%	41.3%	58.5%	41.5%
1982	1,804,676	949,207	Durenberger, David*	840,401	Dayton, Mark	15,068	108,806 R	52.6%	46.6%	53.0%	47.0%
1978	1,580,778	894,092	Boschwitz, Rudy	638,375	Anderson, Wendell R.*	48,311	255,717 R	56.6%	40.4%	58.3%	41.7%
1978S**	1,560,724	957,908	Durenberger, David	538,675	Short, Robert E.	64,141	419,233 R	61.4%	34.5%	64.0%	36.0%
1976	1,912,068	478,611	Brekke, Gerald W.	1,290,736	Humphrey, Hubert Horatio Jr.*	142,721	812,125 D	25.0%	67.5%	27.1%	72.9%
1972	1,731,653	742,121	Hansen, Philip	981,340	Mondale, Walter F.*	8,192	239,219 D	42.9%	56.7%	43.1%	56.9%
1970	1,364,887	568,025	MacGregor, Clark	788,256	Humphrey, Hubert Horatio Jr.	8,606	220,231 D	41.6%	57.8%	41.9%	58.1%
1966	1,271,426	574,868	Forsythe, Robert A.	685,840	Mondale, Walter F.	10,718	110,972 D	45.2%	53.9%	45.6%	54.4%
1964	1,543,600	605,933	Whitney, Wheelock	931,363	McCarthy, Eugene J.*	6,304	325,430 D	39.3%	60.3%	39.4%	60.6%
1960	1,536,839	648,586	Peterson, P. Kenneth	884,168	Humphrey, Hubert Horatio Jr.*	4,085	235,582 D	42.2%	57.5%	42.3%	57.7%
1958	1,150,883	536,629	Thye, Edward J.	608,847	McCarthy, Eugene J.	5,407	72,218 D	46.6%	52.9%	46.8%	53.2%
1954	1,138,952	479,619	Bjornson, Val	642,193	Humphrey, Hubert Horatio Jr.*	17,140	162,574 D	42.1%	56.4%	42.8%	57.2%
1952	1,387,419	785,649	Thye, Edward J.*	590,011	Carlson, William E.	11,759	195,638 R	56.6%	42.5%	57.1%	42.9%
1948	1,217,250	482,801	Ball, Joseph H.*	729,494	Humphrey, Hubert Horatio Jr.	4,955	246,693 D	39.7%	59.9%	39.8%	60.2%
1946	878,731	517,775	Thye, Edward J.	349,520	Jorgenson, Theodore	11,436	168,255 R	58.9%	39.8%	59.7%	40.3%

Note: An asterisk (*) denotes incumbent. **In past elections, the other vote included: 2008 - 437,505 Independence (Dean Barkley). In October 2002 the Democratic incumbent, Paul Wellstone, was killed in an airplane crash. Walter F. Mondale was named to replace him on the general election ballot. One of the 1978 elections and one of the 2018 elections was for a short term to fill a vacancy.

MINNESOTA

GOVERNOR 2018

2010 Census Population	County	Total Vote	Republican (Johnson)	Democratic (Walz)	Other	Rep.-Dem. Plurality	Percentage			
							Total Vote		Major Vote	
							Rep.	Dem.	Rep.	Dem.
16,202	AITKIN	8,144	4,481	3,360	303	1,121 R	55.0%	41.3%	57.1%	42.9%
330,844	ANOKA	159,286	75,957	76,239	7,090	282 D	47.7%	47.9%	49.9%	50.1%
32,504	BECKER	14,727	8,784	5,400	543	3,384 R	59.6%	36.7%	61.9%	38.1%
44,442	BELTRAMI	17,954	8,328	8,848	778	520 D	46.4%	49.3%	48.5%	51.5%
38,451	BENTON	16,048	9,405	6,020	623	3,385 R	58.6%	37.5%	61.0%	39.0%
5,269	BIG STONE	2,573	1,353	1,111	109	242 R	52.6%	43.2%	54.9%	45.1%
64,013	BLUE EARTH	28,135	10,806	16,317	1,012	5,511 D	38.4%	58.0%	39.8%	60.2%
25,893	BROWN	11,809	6,461	4,932	416	1,529 R	54.7%	41.8%	56.7%	43.3%
35,386	CARLTON	16,312	6,621	9,051	640	2,430 D	40.6%	55.5%	42.2%	57.8%
91,042	CARVER	50,856	26,822	22,334	1,700	4,488 R	52.7%	43.9%	54.6%	45.4%
28,567	CASS	13,981	8,145	5,319	517	2,826 R	58.3%	38.0%	60.5%	39.5%
12,441	CHIPPEWA	5,507	3,008	2,261	238	747 R	54.6%	41.1%	57.1%	42.9%
53,887	CHISAGO	25,774	14,556	10,091	1,127	4,465 R	56.5%	39.2%	59.1%	40.9%
58,999	CLAY	24,219	10,301	12,748	1,170	2,447 D	42.5%	52.6%	44.7%	55.3%
8,695	CLEARWATER	3,467	2,239	1,125	103	1,114 R	64.6%	32.4%	66.6%	33.4%
5,176	COOK	3,191	1,009	2,054	128	1,045 D	31.6%	64.4%	32.9%	67.1%
11,687	COTTONWOOD	5,019	2,843	2,045	131	798 R	56.6%	40.7%	58.2%	41.8%
62,500	CROW WING	31,310	18,176	11,866	1,268	6,310 R	58.1%	37.9%	60.5%	39.5%
398,552	DAKOTA	206,771	87,266	111,429	8,076	24,163 D	42.2%	53.9%	43.9%	56.1%
20,087	DODGE	9,128	5,037	3,773	318	1,264 R	55.2%	41.3%	57.2%	42.8%
36,009	DOUGLAS	18,045	10,901	6,643	501	4,258 R	60.4%	36.8%	62.1%	37.9%
14,553	FARIBAULT	6,364	3,495	2,627	242	868 R	54.9%	41.3%	57.1%	42.9%
20,866	FILLMORE	9,704	4,797	4,607	300	190 R	49.4%	47.5%	51.0%	49.0%
31,255	FREEBORN	13,970	6,651	6,846	473	195 D	47.6%	49.0%	49.3%	50.7%
46,183	GOODHUE	23,091	11,668	10,471	952	1,197 R	50.5%	45.3%	52.7%	47.3%
6,018	GRANT	3,115	1,710	1,287	118	423 R	54.9%	41.3%	57.1%	42.9%
1,152,425	HENNEPIN	626,662	182,128	422,618	21,916	240,490 D	29.1%	67.4%	30.1%	69.9%
19,027	HOUSTON	8,956	4,269	4,416	271	147 D	47.7%	49.3%	49.2%	50.8%
20,428	HUBBARD	10,130	5,885	3,883	362	2,002 R	58.1%	38.3%	60.2%	39.8%
37,816	ISANTI	17,351	10,483	6,084	784	4,399 R	60.4%	35.1%	63.3%	36.7%
45,058	ITASCA	21,562	10,470	10,130	962	340 R	48.6%	47.0%	50.8%	49.2%
10,266	JACKSON	4,661	2,594	1,879	188	715 R	55.7%	40.3%	58.0%	42.0%
16,239	KANABEC	6,702	3,853	2,547	302	1,306 R	57.5%	38.0%	60.2%	39.8%
42,239	KANDIYOHI	18,604	10,438	7,490	676	2,948 R	56.1%	40.3%	58.2%	41.8%
4,552	KITTSON	2,334	1,149	1,085	100	64 R	49.2%	46.5%	51.4%	48.6%
13,311	KOOCHICHING	5,218	2,512	2,541	165	29 D	48.1%	48.7%	49.7%	50.3%
7,259	LAC QUI PARLE	3,351	1,776	1,461	114	315 R	53.0%	43.6%	54.9%	45.1%
10,866	LAKE	5,896	2,432	3,264	200	832 D	41.2%	55.4%	42.7%	57.3%
4,045	LAKE OF THE WOODS	1,833	1,171	601	61	570 R	63.9%	32.8%	66.1%	33.9%
27,703	LE SUEUR	12,804	6,827	5,533	444	1,294 R	53.3%	43.2%	55.2%	44.8%
5,896	LINCOLN	2,431	1,326	1,049	56	277 R	54.5%	43.2%	55.8%	44.2%
25,857	LYON	9,956	5,468	4,143	345	1,325 R	54.9%	41.6%	56.9%	43.1%
5,413	MAHNOMEN	1,907	823	992	92	169 D	43.2%	52.0%	45.3%	54.7%
9,439	MARSHALL	4,088	2,512	1,436	140	1,076 R	61.4%	35.1%	63.6%	36.4%
20,840	MARTIN	8,729	5,190	3,232	307	1,958 R	59.5%	37.0%	61.6%	38.4%
36,651	MCLEOD	14,902	9,065	5,241	596	3,824 R	60.8%	35.2%	63.4%	36.6%
23,300	MEEKER	10,307	6,325	3,584	398	2,741 R	61.4%	34.8%	63.8%	36.2%
26,097	MILLE LACS	10,717	6,292	3,927	498	2,365 R	58.7%	36.6%	61.6%	38.4%
33,198	MORRISON	14,286	9,711	4,123	452	5,588 R	68.0%	28.9%	70.2%	29.8%
39,163	MOWER	14,672	6,464	7,690	518	1,226 D	44.1%	52.4%	45.7%	54.3%
8,725	MURRAY	4,122	2,323	1,676	123	647 R	56.4%	40.7%	58.1%	41.9%
32,727	NICOLLET	15,733	6,132	9,156	445	3,024 D	39.0%	58.2%	40.1%	59.9%
21,378	NOBLES	6,971	3,734	3,000	237	734 R	53.6%	43.0%	55.4%	44.6%
6,852	NORMAN	2,682	1,280	1,280	122	R	47.7%	47.7%	50.0%	50.0%
144,248	OLMSTED	71,145	30,517	38,613	2,015	8,096 D	42.9%	54.3%	44.1%	55.9%
57,303	OTTER TAIL	27,365	16,622	9,873	870	6,749 R	60.7%	36.1%	62.7%	37.3%
13,930	PENNINGTON	5,359	2,949	2,183	227	766 R	55.0%	40.7%	57.5%	42.5%
29,750	PINE	11,557	6,240	4,793	524	1,447 R	54.0%	41.5%	56.6%	43.4%
9,596	PIPESTONE	3,711	2,379	1,228	104	1,151 R	64.1%	33.1%	66.0%	34.0%
31,600	POLK	11,796	6,736	4,642	418	2,094 R	57.1%	39.4%	59.2%	40.8%

MINNESOTA

GOVERNOR 2018

2010 Census Population	County	Total Vote	Republican (Johnson)	Democratic (Walz)	Other	Rep.-Dem. Plurality	Percentage Total Vote Rep.	Total Vote Dem.	Major Vote Rep.	Major Vote Dem.
10,995	POPE	5,441	3,014	2,276	151	738 R	55.4%	41.8%	57.0%	43.0%
508,640	RAMSEY	244,036	63,685	170,553	9,798	106,868 D	26.1%	69.9%	27.2%	72.8%
4,089	RED LAKE	1,643	855	724	64	131 R	52.0%	44.1%	54.1%	45.9%
16,059	REDWOOD	6,206	3,855	2,154	197	1,701 R	62.1%	34.7%	64.2%	35.8%
15,730	RENVILLE	6,270	3,562	2,470	238	1,092 R	56.8%	39.4%	59.1%	40.9%
64,142	RICE	28,380	12,353	14,910	1,117	2,557 D	43.5%	52.5%	45.3%	54.7%
9,687	ROCK	3,765	2,288	1,390	87	898 R	60.8%	36.9%	62.2%	37.8%
15,629	ROSEAU	6,442	4,335	1,915	192	2,420 R	67.3%	29.7%	69.4%	30.6%
129,928	SCOTT	66,040	34,201	29,223	2,616	4,978 R	51.8%	44.3%	53.9%	46.1%
88,499	SHERBURNE	39,231	23,721	13,851	1,659	9,870 R	60.5%	35.3%	63.1%	36.9%
15,226	SIBLEY	6,563	3,936	2,387	240	1,549 R	60.0%	36.4%	62.2%	37.8%
200,226	ST. LOUIS	99,447	35,212	60,383	3,852	25,171 D	35.4%	60.7%	36.8%	63.2%
150,642	STEARNS	65,925	36,830	26,707	2,388	10,123 R	55.9%	40.5%	58.0%	42.0%
36,576	STEELE	16,326	8,733	6,991	602	1,742 R	53.5%	42.8%	55.5%	44.5%
9,726	STEVENS	4,378	2,306	1,916	156	390 R	52.7%	43.8%	54.6%	45.4%
9,783	SWIFT	4,041	2,179	1,751	111	428 R	53.9%	43.3%	55.4%	44.6%
24,895	TODD	9,602	6,244	3,058	300	3,186 R	65.0%	31.8%	67.1%	32.9%
3,558	TRAVERSE	1,511	806	649	56	157 R	53.3%	43.0%	55.4%	44.6%
21,676	WABASHA	9,987	5,324	4,311	352	1,013 R	53.3%	43.2%	55.3%	44.7%
13,843	WADENA	5,544	3,667	1,731	146	1,936 R	66.1%	31.2%	67.9%	32.1%
19,136	WASECA	8,153	4,406	3,500	247	906 R	54.0%	42.9%	55.7%	44.3%
238,136	WASHINGTON	129,753	57,537	67,751	4,465	10,214 D	44.3%	52.2%	45.9%	54.1%
11,211	WATONWAN	4,130	2,018	2,005	107	13 R	48.9%	48.5%	50.2%	49.8%
6,576	WILKIN	2,557	1,528	925	104	603 R	59.8%	36.2%	62.3%	37.7%
51,461	WINONA	21,361	8,679	11,893	789	3,214 D	40.6%	55.7%	42.2%	57.8%
124,700	WRIGHT	59,243	34,992	21,834	2,417	13,158 R	59.1%	36.9%	61.6%	38.4%
10,438	YELLOW MEDICINE	4,312	2,544	1,641	127	903 R	59.0%	38.1%	60.8%	39.2%
5,303,925	*TOTAL*	*2,587,287*	*1,097,705*	*1,393,096*	*96,486*	*295,391 D*	*42.4%*	*53.8%*	*44.1%*	*55.9%*

Note: Democratic candidates in Minnesota appear on the ballot for the Democratic-Farmer-Labor (DFL) party.

MINNESOTA

SENATOR 2018

2010 Census Population	County	Total Vote	Republican (Newberger)	Democratic (Klobuchar)	Other	Rep.-Dem. Plurality	Percentage Total Vote Rep.	Total Vote Dem.	Major Vote Rep.	Major Vote Dem.
16,202	AITKIN	8,187	3,808	4,118	261	310 D	46.5%	50.3%	48.0%	52.0%
330,844	ANOKA	159,628	65,707	87,756	6,165	22,049 D	41.2%	55.0%	42.8%	57.2%
32,504	BECKER	14,770	7,520	6,699	551	821 R	50.9%	45.4%	52.9%	47.1%
44,442	BELTRAMI	18,009	7,562	9,711	736	2,149 D	42.0%	53.9%	43.8%	56.2%
38,451	BENTON	16,088	8,290	7,131	667	1,159 R	51.5%	44.3%	53.8%	46.2%
5,269	BIG STONE	2,594	1,127	1,368	99	241 D	43.4%	52.7%	45.2%	54.8%
64,013	BLUE EARTH	28,138	9,984	16,776	1,378	6,792 D	35.5%	59.6%	37.3%	62.7%
25,893	BROWN	11,831	5,816	5,614	401	202 R	49.2%	47.5%	50.9%	49.1%
35,386	CARLTON	16,405	5,682	10,200	523	4,518 D	34.6%	62.2%	35.8%	64.2%
91,042	CARVER	51,054	22,540	27,168	1,346	4,628 D	44.1%	53.2%	45.3%	54.7%
28,567	CASS	14,024	7,332	6,243	449	1,089 R	52.3%	44.5%	54.0%	46.0%
12,441	CHIPPEWA	5,532	2,422	2,925	185	503 D	43.8%	52.9%	45.3%	54.7%
53,887	CHISAGO	25,839	12,663	12,138	1,038	525 R	49.0%	47.0%	51.1%	48.9%
58,999	CLAY	24,403	8,480	14,950	973	6,470 D	34.7%	61.3%	36.2%	63.8%
8,695	CLEARWATER	3,487	2,080	1,302	105	778 R	59.7%	37.3%	61.5%	38.5%

MINNESOTA

SENATOR 2018

2010 Census Population	County	Total Vote	Republican (Newberger)	Democratic (Klobuchar)	Other	Rep.-Dem. Plurality	Percentage: Total Vote Rep.	Percentage: Total Vote Dem.	Percentage: Major Vote Rep.	Percentage: Major Vote Dem.
5,176	COOK	3,215	911	2,178	126	1,267 D	28.3%	67.7%	29.5%	70.5%
11,687	COTTONWOOD	5,047	2,488	2,413	146	75 R	49.3%	47.8%	50.8%	49.2%
62,500	CROW WING	31,436	16,132	14,206	1,098	1,926 R	51.3%	45.2%	53.2%	46.8%
398,552	DAKOTA	207,324	73,462	127,016	6,846	53,554 D	35.4%	61.3%	36.6%	63.4%
20,087	DODGE	9,133	4,527	4,278	328	249 R	49.6%	46.8%	51.4%	48.6%
36,009	DOUGLAS	18,084	9,113	8,504	467	609 R	50.4%	47.0%	51.7%	48.3%
14,553	FARIBAULT	6,377	3,103	3,031	243	72 R	48.7%	47.5%	50.6%	49.4%
20,866	FILLMORE	9,732	4,263	5,128	341	865 D	43.8%	52.7%	45.4%	54.6%
31,255	FREEBORN	14,001	5,779	7,675	547	1,896 D	41.3%	54.8%	43.0%	57.0%
46,183	GOODHUE	23,177	9,940	12,379	858	2,439 D	42.9%	53.4%	44.5%	55.5%
6,018	GRANT	3,140	1,402	1,637	101	235 D	44.6%	52.1%	46.1%	53.9%
1,152,425	HENNEPIN	629,534	149,297	459,729	20,508	310,432 D	23.7%	73.0%	24.5%	75.5%
19,027	HOUSTON	8,949	4,149	4,425	375	276 D	46.4%	49.4%	48.4%	51.6%
20,428	HUBBARD	10,145	5,312	4,494	339	818 R	52.4%	44.3%	54.2%	45.8%
37,816	ISANTI	17,420	9,226	7,440	754	1,786 R	53.0%	42.7%	55.4%	44.6%
45,058	ITASCA	21,655	9,203	11,585	867	2,382 D	42.5%	53.5%	44.3%	55.7%
10,266	JACKSON	4,683	2,341	2,174	168	167 R	50.0%	46.4%	51.8%	48.2%
16,239	KANABEC	6,719	3,363	3,138	218	225 R	50.1%	46.7%	51.7%	48.3%
42,239	KANDIYOHI	18,669	8,596	9,378	695	782 D	46.0%	50.2%	47.8%	52.2%
4,552	KITTSON	2,365	943	1,325	97	382 D	39.9%	56.0%	41.6%	58.4%
13,311	KOOCHICHING	5,256	2,238	2,886	132	648 D	42.6%	54.9%	43.7%	56.3%
7,259	LAC QUI PARLE	3,362	1,404	1,866	92	462 D	41.8%	55.5%	42.9%	57.1%
10,866	LAKE	5,916	2,196	3,539	181	1,343 D	37.1%	59.8%	38.3%	61.7%
4,045	LAKE OF THE WOODS	1,852	1,072	729	51	343 R	57.9%	39.4%	59.5%	40.5%
27,703	LE SUEUR	12,880	5,979	6,444	457	465 D	46.4%	50.0%	48.1%	51.9%
5,896	LINCOLN	2,428	1,213	1,164	51	49 R	50.0%	47.9%	51.0%	49.0%
25,857	LYON	9,986	4,700	4,973	313	273 D	47.1%	49.8%	48.6%	51.4%
5,413	MAHNOMEN	1,922	708	1,098	116	390 D	36.8%	57.1%	39.2%	60.8%
9,439	MARSHALL	4,110	2,120	1,864	126	256 R	51.6%	45.4%	53.2%	46.8%
20,840	MARTIN	8,739	4,664	3,770	305	894 R	53.4%	43.1%	55.3%	44.7%
36,651	MCLEOD	14,965	7,684	6,825	456	859 R	51.3%	45.6%	53.0%	47.0%
23,300	MEEKER	10,338	5,363	4,677	298	686 R	51.9%	45.2%	53.4%	46.6%
26,097	MILLE LACS	10,730	5,492	4,771	467	721 R	51.2%	44.5%	53.5%	46.5%
33,198	MORRISON	14,323	8,678	5,246	399	3,432 R	60.6%	36.6%	62.3%	37.7%
39,163	MOWER	14,693	5,705	8,396	592	2,691 D	38.8%	57.1%	40.5%	59.5%
8,725	MURRAY	4,131	2,070	1,925	136	145 R	50.1%	46.6%	51.8%	48.2%
32,727	NICOLLET	15,729	5,517	9,632	580	4,115 D	35.1%	61.2%	36.4%	63.6%
21,378	NOBLES	7,011	3,523	3,185	303	338 R	50.2%	45.4%	52.5%	47.5%
6,852	NORMAN	2,719	1,049	1,588	82	539 D	38.6%	58.4%	39.8%	60.2%
144,248	OLMSTED	71,246	27,291	41,769	2,186	14,478 D	38.3%	58.6%	39.5%	60.5%
57,303	OTTER TAIL	27,466	14,688	12,002	776	2,686 R	53.5%	43.7%	55.0%	45.0%
13,930	PENNINGTON	5,371	2,573	2,582	216	9 D	47.9%	48.1%	49.9%	50.1%
29,750	PINE	11,599	5,528	5,648	423	120 D	47.7%	48.7%	49.5%	50.5%
9,596	PIPESTONE	3,725	2,266	1,321	138	945 R	60.8%	35.5%	63.2%	36.8%
31,600	POLK	11,877	5,785	5,729	363	56 R	48.7%	48.2%	50.2%	49.8%
10,995	POPE	5,452	2,443	2,851	158	408 D	44.8%	52.3%	46.1%	53.9%
508,640	RAMSEY	245,570	53,101	182,445	10,024	129,344 D	21.6%	74.3%	22.5%	77.5%
4,089	RED LAKE	1,668	709	900	59	191 D	42.5%	54.0%	44.1%	55.9%
16,059	REDWOOD	6,221	3,334	2,688	199	646 R	53.6%	43.2%	55.4%	44.6%
15,730	RENVILLE	6,299	2,888	3,194	217	306 D	45.8%	50.7%	47.5%	52.5%
64,142	RICE	28,500	10,604	16,881	1,015	6,277 D	37.2%	59.2%	38.6%	61.4%
9,687	ROCK	3,770	2,217	1,452	101	765 R	58.8%	38.5%	60.4%	39.6%
15,629	ROSEAU	6,474	3,771	2,517	186	1,254 R	58.2%	38.9%	60.0%	40.0%
129,928	SCOTT	66,274	29,308	34,624	2,342	5,316 D	44.2%	52.2%	45.8%	54.2%
88,499	SHERBURNE	39,347	21,437	16,491	1,419	4,946 R	54.5%	41.9%	56.5%	43.5%
15,226	SIBLEY	6,587	3,337	3,050	200	287 R	50.7%	46.3%	52.2%	47.8%
200,226	ST. LOUIS	99,814	30,293	66,056	3,465	35,763 D	30.3%	66.2%	31.4%	68.6%
150,642	STEARNS	66,117	31,821	31,970	2,326	149 D	48.1%	48.4%	49.9%	50.1%
36,576	STEELE	16,351	7,490	8,192	669	702 D	45.8%	50.1%	47.8%	52.2%
9,726	STEVENS	4,394	1,969	2,290	135	321 D	44.8%	52.1%	46.2%	53.8%

MINNESOTA

SENATOR 2018

2010 Census Population	County	Total Vote	Republican (Newberger)	Democratic (Klobuchar)	Other	Rep.-Dem. Plurality	Percentage Total Vote Rep.	Total Vote Dem.	Major Vote Rep.	Major Vote Dem.
9,783	SWIFT	4,051	1,793	2,147	111	354 D	44.3%	53.0%	45.5%	54.5%
24,895	TODD	9,636	5,516	3,863	257	1,653 R	57.2%	40.1%	58.8%	41.2%
3,558	TRAVERSE	1,530	665	825	40	160 D	43.5%	53.9%	44.6%	55.4%
21,676	WABASHA	10,006	4,695	4,961	350	266 D	46.9%	49.6%	48.6%	51.4%
13,843	WADENA	5,550	3,379	2,044	127	1,335 R	60.9%	36.8%	62.3%	37.7%
19,136	WASECA	8,155	3,872	4,035	248	163 D	47.5%	49.5%	49.0%	51.0%
238,136	WASHINGTON	130,088	47,785	78,364	3,939	30,579 D	36.7%	60.2%	37.9%	62.1%
11,211	WATONWAN	4,127	1,819	2,200	108	381 D	44.1%	53.3%	45.3%	54.7%
6,576	WILKIN	2,587	1,243	1,251	93	8 D	48.0%	48.4%	49.8%	50.2%
51,461	WINONA	21,387	8,236	12,090	1,061	3,854 D	38.5%	56.5%	40.5%	59.5%
124,700	WRIGHT	59,442	30,572	26,821	2,049	3,751 R	51.4%	45.1%	53.3%	46.7%
10,438	YELLOW MEDICINE	4,314	2,071	2,111	132	40 D	48.0%	48.9%	49.5%	50.5%
5,303,925	*TOTAL*	*2,596,879*	*940,437*	*1,566,174*	*90,268*	*625,737 D*	*36.2%*	*60.3%*	*37.5%*	*62.5%*

Note: Democratic candidates in Minnesota appear on the ballot for the Democratic-Farmer-Labor (DFL) party.

MINNESOTA

SENATOR SPECIAL 2018

2010 Census Population	County	Total Vote	Republican (Housley)	Democratic (Smith)	Other	Rep.-Dem. Plurality	Percentage Total Vote Rep.	Total Vote Dem.	Major Vote Rep.	Major Vote Dem.
16,202	AITKIN	8,141	4,412	3,316	413	1,096 R	54.2%	40.7%	57.1%	42.9%
330,844	ANOKA	159,028	75,720	74,806	8,502	914 R	47.6%	47.0%	50.3%	49.7%
32,504	BECKER	14,691	8,265	5,721	705	2,544 R	56.3%	38.9%	59.1%	40.9%
44,442	BELTRAMI	17,971	8,275	8,702	994	427 D	46.0%	48.4%	48.7%	51.3%
38,451	BENTON	16,003	9,124	5,999	880	3,125 R	57.0%	37.5%	60.3%	39.7%
5,269	BIG STONE	2,575	1,290	1,130	155	160 R	50.1%	43.9%	53.3%	46.7%
64,013	BLUE EARTH	27,966	11,461	14,614	1,891	3,153 D	41.0%	52.3%	44.0%	56.0%
25,893	BROWN	11,759	6,751	4,414	594	2,337 R	57.4%	37.5%	60.5%	39.5%
35,386	CARLTON	16,340	6,393	9,161	786	2,768 D	39.1%	56.1%	41.1%	58.9%
91,042	CARVER	50,832	26,872	22,078	1,882	4,794 R	52.9%	43.4%	54.9%	45.1%
28,567	CASS	13,990	8,081	5,280	629	2,801 R	57.8%	37.7%	60.5%	39.5%
12,441	CHIPPEWA	5,503	2,900	2,289	314	611 R	52.7%	41.6%	55.9%	44.1%
53,887	CHISAGO	25,756	14,487	9,836	1,433	4,651 R	56.2%	38.2%	59.6%	40.4%
58,999	CLAY	24,211	9,702	13,219	1,290	3,517 D	40.1%	54.6%	42.3%	57.7%
8,695	CLEARWATER	3,471	2,168	1,159	144	1,009 R	62.5%	33.4%	65.2%	34.8%
5,176	COOK	3,204	1,034	2,024	146	990 D	32.3%	63.2%	33.8%	66.2%
11,687	COTTONWOOD	4,993	2,882	1,887	224	995 R	57.7%	37.8%	60.4%	39.6%
62,500	CROW WING	31,289	18,094	11,648	1,547	6,446 R	57.8%	37.2%	60.8%	39.2%
398,552	DAKOTA	206,720	88,150	109,391	9,179	21,241 D	42.6%	52.9%	44.6%	55.4%
20,087	DODGE	9,098	5,183	3,472	443	1,711 R	57.0%	38.2%	59.9%	40.1%
36,009	DOUGLAS	18,043	10,754	6,633	656	4,121 R	59.6%	36.8%	61.9%	38.1%
14,553	FARIBAULT	6,355	3,590	2,425	340	1,165 R	56.5%	38.2%	59.7%	40.3%
20,866	FILLMORE	9,657	4,882	4,331	444	551 R	50.6%	44.8%	53.0%	47.0%
31,255	FREEBORN	13,897	6,689	6,393	815	296 R	48.1%	46.0%	51.1%	48.9%
46,183	GOODHUE	23,071	11,761	10,168	1,142	1,593 R	51.0%	44.1%	53.6%	46.4%
6,018	GRANT	3,128	1,645	1,339	144	306 R	52.6%	42.8%	55.1%	44.9%
1,152,425	HENNEPIN	627,763	182,439	419,462	25,862	237,023 D	29.1%	66.8%	30.3%	69.7%
19,027	HOUSTON	8,900	4,430	4,042	428	388 R	49.8%	45.4%	52.3%	47.7%
20,428	HUBBARD	10,127	5,870	3,769	488	2,101 R	58.0%	37.2%	60.9%	39.1%
37,816	ISANTI	17,347	10,364	6,003	980	4,361 R	59.7%	34.6%	63.3%	36.7%

MINNESOTA

SENATOR SPECIAL 2018

2010 Census Population	County	Total Vote	Republican (Housley)	Democratic (Smith)	Other	Rep.-Dem. Plurality	Percentage: Total Vote Rep.	Total Vote Dem.	Major Vote Rep.	Major Vote Dem.
45,058	ITASCA	21,545	10,201	10,141	1,203	60 R	47.3%	47.1%	50.1%	49.9%
10,266	JACKSON	4,658	2,657	1,752	249	905 R	57.0%	37.6%	60.3%	39.7%
16,239	KANABEC	6,686	3,801	2,550	335	1,251 R	56.9%	38.1%	59.8%	40.2%
42,239	KANDIYOHI	18,584	10,095	7,539	950	2,556 R	54.3%	40.6%	57.2%	42.8%
4,552	KITTSON	2,336	1,080	1,128	128	48 D	46.2%	48.3%	48.9%	51.1%
13,311	KOOCHICHING	5,235	2,450	2,581	204	131 D	46.8%	49.3%	48.7%	51.3%
7,259	LAC QUI PARLE	3,341	1,716	1,471	154	245 R	51.4%	44.0%	53.8%	46.2%
10,866	LAKE	5,896	2,432	3,209	255	777 D	41.2%	54.4%	43.1%	56.9%
4,045	LAKE OF THE WOODS	1,849	1,173	608	68	565 R	63.4%	32.9%	65.9%	34.1%
27,703	LE SUEUR	12,803	6,980	5,133	690	1,847 R	54.5%	40.1%	57.6%	42.4%
5,896	LINCOLN	2,425	1,354	964	107	390 R	55.8%	39.8%	58.4%	41.6%
25,857	LYON	9,948	5,472	4,027	449	1,445 R	55.0%	40.5%	57.6%	42.4%
5,413	MAHNOMEN	1,897	759	984	154	225 D	40.0%	51.9%	43.5%	56.5%
9,439	MARSHALL	4,082	2,349	1,570	163	779 R	57.5%	38.5%	59.9%	40.1%
20,840	MARTIN	8,701	5,251	3,004	446	2,247 R	60.3%	34.5%	63.6%	36.4%
36,651	MCLEOD	14,918	8,948	5,235	735	3,713 R	60.0%	35.1%	63.1%	36.9%
23,300	MEEKER	10,294	6,207	3,606	481	2,601 R	60.3%	35.0%	63.3%	36.7%
26,097	MILLE LACS	10,695	6,165	3,899	631	2,266 R	57.6%	36.5%	61.3%	38.7%
33,198	MORRISON	14,275	9,521	4,181	573	5,340 R	66.7%	29.3%	69.5%	30.5%
39,163	MOWER	14,632	6,478	7,316	838	838 D	44.3%	50.0%	47.0%	53.0%
8,725	MURRAY	4,093	2,293	1,595	205	698 R	56.0%	39.0%	59.0%	41.0%
32,727	NICOLLET	15,671	6,609	8,198	864	1,589 D	42.2%	52.3%	44.6%	55.4%
21,378	NOBLES	6,922	3,760	2,774	388	986 R	54.3%	40.1%	57.5%	42.5%
6,852	NORMAN	2,692	1,171	1,399	122	228 D	43.5%	52.0%	45.6%	54.4%
144,248	OLMSTED	71,083	31,314	37,088	2,681	5,774 D	44.1%	52.2%	45.8%	54.2%
57,303	OTTER TAIL	27,355	15,971	10,401	983	5,570 R	58.4%	38.0%	60.6%	39.4%
13,930	PENNINGTON	5,339	2,816	2,263	260	553 R	52.7%	42.4%	55.4%	44.6%
29,750	PINE	11,568	6,234	4,714	620	1,520 R	53.9%	40.8%	56.9%	43.1%
9,596	PIPESTONE	3,703	2,432	1,121	150	1,311 R	65.7%	30.3%	68.4%	31.6%
31,600	POLK	11,798	6,366	4,939	493	1,427 R	54.0%	41.9%	56.3%	43.7%
10,995	POPE	5,430	2,907	2,272	251	635 R	53.5%	41.8%	56.1%	43.9%
508,640	RAMSEY	244,591	63,925	167,610	13,056	103,685 D	26.1%	68.5%	27.6%	72.4%
4,089	RED LAKE	1,643	803	743	97	60 R	48.9%	45.2%	51.9%	48.1%
16,059	REDWOOD	6,192	3,847	2,038	307	1,809 R	62.1%	32.9%	65.4%	34.6%
15,730	RENVILLE	6,276	3,519	2,439	318	1,080 R	56.1%	38.9%	59.1%	40.9%
64,142	RICE	28,401	12,321	14,719	1,361	2,398 D	43.4%	51.8%	45.6%	54.4%
9,687	ROCK	3,749	2,342	1,259	148	1,083 R	62.5%	33.6%	65.0%	35.0%
15,629	ROSEAU	6,439	4,126	2,086	227	2,040 R	64.1%	32.4%	66.4%	33.6%
129,928	SCOTT	66,027	34,158	28,722	3,147	5,436 R	51.7%	43.5%	54.3%	45.7%
88,499	SHERBURNE	39,215	23,611	13,589	2,015	10,022 R	60.2%	34.7%	63.5%	36.5%
15,226	SIBLEY	6,540	3,934	2,308	298	1,626 R	60.2%	35.3%	63.0%	37.0%
200,226	ST. LOUIS	99,406	34,478	60,187	4,741	25,709 D	34.7%	60.5%	36.4%	63.6%
150,642	STEARNS	65,895	36,195	26,643	3,057	9,552 R	54.9%	40.4%	57.6%	42.4%
36,576	STEELE	16,283	8,831	6,511	941	2,320 R	54.2%	40.0%	57.6%	42.4%
9,726	STEVENS	4,380	2,260	1,926	194	334 R	51.6%	44.0%	54.0%	46.0%
9,783	SWIFT	4,036	2,086	1,787	163	299 R	51.7%	44.3%	53.9%	46.1%
24,895	TODD	9,591	6,149	3,095	347	3,054 R	64.1%	32.3%	66.5%	33.5%
3,558	TRAVERSE	1,516	778	678	60	100 R	51.3%	44.7%	53.4%	46.6%
21,676	WABASHA	9,962	5,392	4,128	442	1,264 R	54.1%	41.4%	56.6%	43.4%
13,843	WADENA	5,543	3,645	1,693	205	1,952 R	65.8%	30.5%	68.3%	31.7%
19,136	WASECA	8,111	4,537	3,222	352	1,315 R	55.9%	39.7%	58.5%	41.5%
238,136	WASHINGTON	129,855	58,429	65,900	5,526	7,471 D	45.0%	50.7%	47.0%	53.0%
11,211	WATONWAN	4,115	2,105	1,827	183	278 R	51.2%	44.4%	53.5%	46.5%
6,576	WILKIN	2,559	1,376	1,050	133	326 R	53.8%	41.0%	56.7%	43.3%
51,461	WINONA	21,278	8,998	11,078	1,202	2,080 D	42.3%	52.1%	44.8%	55.2%
124,700	WRIGHT	59,166	34,821	21,294	3,051	13,527 R	58.9%	36.0%	62.1%	37.9%
10,438	YELLOW MEDICINE	4,304	2,481	1,635	188	846 R	57.6%	38.0%	60.3%	39.7%
5,303,925	*TOTAL*	*2,587,356*	*1,095,777*	*1,370,540*	*121,039*	*274,763 D*	*42.4%*	*53.0%*	*44.4%*	*55.6%*

Note: Democratic candidates in Minnesota appear on the ballot for the Democratic-Farmer-Labor (DFL) party.

MINNESOTA

HOUSE OF REPRESENTATIVES

CD	Year	Total Vote	Republican Vote	Republican Candidate	Democratic Vote	Democratic Candidate	Other Vote	Rep.-Dem. Plurality	Percentage Total Vote Rep.	Percentage Total Vote Dem.	Percentage Major Vote Rep.	Percentage Major Vote Dem.
1	2018	291,661	146,200	HAGEDORN, JAMES "JIM"	144,885	FEEHAN, DAN	576	1,315 R	50.1%	49.7%	50.2%	49.8%
1	2016	335,877	166,526	HAGEDORN, JAMES "JIM"	169,074	WALZ, TIMOTHY J.*	277	2,548 D	49.6%	50.3%	49.6%	50.4%
1	2014	226,695	103,536	HAGEDORN, JAMES "JIM"	122,851	WALZ, TIMOTHY J.*	308	19,315 D	45.7%	54.2%	45.7%	54.3%
1	2012	335,880	142,164	QUIST, ALLEN	193,211	WALZ, TIMOTHY J.*	505	51,047 D	42.3%	57.5%	42.4%	57.6%
2	2018	337,968	159,344	LEWIS, JASON*	177,958	CRAIG, ANGIE	666	18,614 D	47.1%	52.7%	47.2%	52.8%
2	2016	370,514	173,970	LEWIS, JASON	167,315	CRAIG, ANGIE	29,229	6,655 R	47.0%	45.2%	51.0%	49.0%
2	2014	245,848	137,778	KLINE, JOHN*	95,565	OBERMUELLER, MIKE	12,505	42,213 R	56.0%	38.9%	59.0%	41.0%
2	2012	358,446	193,587	KLINE, JOHN*	164,338	OBERMUELLER, MIKE	521	29,249 R	54.0%	45.8%	54.1%	45.9%
3	2018	363,949	160,839	PAULSEN, ERIK*	202,404	PHILLIPS, DEAN	706	41,565 D	44.2%	55.6%	44.3%	55.7%
3	2016	393,464	223,077	PAULSEN, ERIK*	169,243	BONOFF, TERRI E.	1,144	53,834 R	56.7%	43.0%	56.9%	43.1%
3	2014	269,585	167,515	PAULSEN, ERIK*	101,846	SUND, SHARON	224	65,669 R	62.1%	37.8%	62.2%	37.8%
3	2012	382,705	222,335	PAULSEN, ERIK*	159,937	BARNES, BRIAN	433	62,398 R	58.1%	41.8%	58.2%	41.8%
4	2018	328,614	97,747	RYAN, GREG	216,865	MCCOLLUM, BETTY*	14,002	119,118 D	29.7%	66.0%	31.1%	68.9%
4	2016	351,944	121,032	RYAN, GREG	203,299	MCCOLLUM, BETTY*	27,613	82,267 D	34.4%	57.8%	37.3%	62.7%
4	2014	241,637	79,492	WAHLGREN, SHARNA	147,857	MCCOLLUM, BETTY*	14,288	68,365 D	32.9%	61.2%	35.0%	65.0%
4	2012	347,991	109,659	HERNANDEZ, TONY	216,685	MCCOLLUM, BETTY*	21,647	107,026 D	31.5%	62.3%	33.6%	66.4%
5	2018	343,358	74,440	ZIELINSKI, JENNIFER	267,703	OMAR, ILHAN	1,215	193,263 D	21.7%	78.0%	21.8%	78.2%
5	2016	361,882	80,660	DRAKE, FRANK NELSON	249,964	ELLISON, KEITH*	31,258	169,304 D	22.3%	69.1%	24.4%	75.6%
5	2014	236,010	56,577	DAGGETT, DOUG J.	167,079	ELLISON, KEITH*	12,354	110,502 D	24.0%	70.8%	25.3%	74.7%
5	2012	351,969	88,753	FIELDS, CHRIS	262,102	ELLISON, KEITH*	1,114	173,349 D	25.2%	74.5%	25.3%	74.7%
6	2018	315,726	192,931	EMMER, TOM*	122,332	TODD, IAN	463	70,599 R	61.1%	38.7%	61.2%	38.8%
6	2016	358,924	235,380	EMMER, TOM*	123,008	SNYDER, DAVID	536	112,372 R	65.6%	34.3%	65.7%	34.3%
6	2014	236,846	133,328	EMMER, TOM	90,926	PERSKE, JOE	12,592	42,402 R	56.3%	38.4%	59.5%	40.5%
6	2012	355,153	179,240	BACHMANN, MICHELE*	174,944	GRAVES, JIM	969	4,296 R	50.5%	49.3%	50.6%	49.4%
7	2018	281,509	134,668	HUGHES, DAVE	146,672	PETERSON, COLLIN C.*	169	12,004 D	47.8%	52.1%	47.9%	52.1%
7	2016	330,848	156,952	HUGHES, DAVE	173,589	PETERSON, COLLIN C.*	307	16,637 D	47.4%	52.5%	47.5%	52.5%
7	2014	240,835	109,955	WESTROM, TORREY NORMAN	130,546	PETERSON, COLLIN C.*	334	20,591 D	45.7%	54.2%	45.7%	54.3%
7	2012	327,576	114,151	BYBERG, LEE	197,791	PETERSON, COLLIN C.*	15,634	83,640 D	34.8%	60.4%	36.6%	63.4%
8	2018	314,211	159,364	STAUBER, PETE	141,950	RADINOVICH, JOSEPH "JOE"	12,897	17,414 R	50.7%	45.2%	52.9%	47.1%
8	2016	356,979	177,089	MILLS, STEWART	179,098	NOLAN, RICHARD M.*	792	2,009 D	49.6%	50.2%	49.7%	50.3%
8	2014	266,083	125,358	MILLS, STEWART	129,090	NOLAN, RICHARD M.*	11,635	3,732 D	47.1%	48.5%	49.3%	50.7%
8	2012	353,663	160,520	CRAVAACK, CHIP*	191,976	NOLAN, RICHARD M.	1,167	31,456 D	45.4%	54.3%	45.5%	54.5%
TOTAL	*2018*	*2,576,996*	*1,125,533*		*1,420,769*		*30,694*	*295,236 D*	*43.7%*	*55.1%*	*44.2%*	*55.8%*
TOTAL	*2016*	*2,860,432*	*1,334,686*		*1,434,590*		*91,156*	*99,904 D*	*46.7%*	*50.2%*	*48.2%*	*51.8%*
TOTAL	*2014*	*1,963,539*	*913,539*		*985,760*		*64,240*	*72,221 D*	*46.5%*	*50.2%*	*48.1%*	*51.9%*
TOTAL	*2012*	*2,813,383*	*1,210,409*		*1,560,984*		*41,990*	*350,575 D*	*43.0%*	*55.5%*	*43.7%*	*56.3%*

Note: An asterisk (*) denotes incumbent.

MINNESOTA

GENERAL AND PRIMARY ELECTIONS

2018 GENERAL ELECTIONS: OTHER VOTES

Governor	Other vote was 68,667 Grassroots-Legalize Cannabis (Chris Wright), 26,735 Libertarian (Josh Welter), 1,084 Write-in (Write-In)
Senate (full term)	66,236 Legal Marijuana Now (Dennis Schuller), 23,101 Green (Paula Overby), 931 Write-in (Write-In)
Senate (short term)	Other vote was 95,614 Legal Marijuana Now (Sarah Wellington), 24,324 Unaffiliated (Jerry Trooien), 1,101 Write-in (Write-in)
House	Other vote was:
CD 1	576 Write-in (Write-in)
CD 2	666 Write-in (Write-in)
CD 3	706 Write-in (Write-in)
CD 4	13,776 Legal Marijuana Now (Susan Sindt), 226 Write-in (Write-in)
CD 5	1,215 Write-in (Write-in)
CD 6	463 Write-in (Write-in)
CD 7	169 Write-in (Write-in)
CD 8	12,741 Independence (Ray Sandman), 156 Write-in (Write-in)

2018 PRIMARY ELECTIONS: SUPPLEMENTARY INFORMATION

Primary	August 14, 2018	**Registration** (as of May 1, 2018)	3,246,893	No Party Registration

Primary Type Open—Any registered voter could participate in the party primary of their choice.

	REPUBLICAN PRIMARIES			DEMOCRATIC PRIMARIES		
Senator (full term)	Newberger, James	201,531	69.5%	Klobuchar, Amy*	557,306	95.7%
	Anderson, Merrill	45,492	15.7%	Carlson, Steve	9,934	1.7%
	Anderson, Rae Hart	25,883	8.9%	Emery, Stephen A.	7,047	1.2%
	De La Fuente, Roque "Rocky"	17,051	5.9%	Groves, David Robert	4,511	0.8%
				Richards, Leonard J.	3,552	0.6%
	TOTAL	*289,957*		*TOTAL*	*582,350*	
Senator (short term)	Housley, Karin	186,384	62.0%	Smith, Tina*	433,705	76.1%
	Anderson, Bob	107,102	35.6%	Painter, Richard W.	78,193	13.7%
	Bey, Nikolay Nikolayevich	7,375	2.5%	Ali, Ali Chehem	18,897	3.3%
				Iverson, Gregg A.	17,825	3.1%
				Leonard, Nick	16,529	2.9%
				Seymore, Christopher Lovell Sr.	5,041	0.9%
	TOTAL	*300,861*		*TOTAL*	*570,190*	
Governor	Johnson, Jeff	168,841	52.6%	Walz, Timothy J.	242,832	41.6%
	Pawlenty, Tim	140,743	43.9%	Murphy, Erin	186,969	32.0%
	Kruse, Mathew "Matt"	11,330	3.5%	Swanson, Lori	143,517	24.6%
				Holden, Tim	6,398	1.1%
				Savior, Olé	4,019	0.7%
	TOTAL	*320,914*		*TOTAL*	*583,735*	
Congressional District 1	Hagedorn, James "Jim"	25,431	60.1%	Feehan, Dan	39,252	83.1%
	Nelson, Carla	13,631	32.2%	Minehart, Colin "Coke"	7,979	16.9%
	Williams, Steve	2,144	5.1%			
	Candler, Andrew	1,107	2.6%			
	TOTAL	*42,313*		*TOTAL*	*47,231*	

MINNESOTA

GENERAL AND PRIMARY ELECTIONS

	REPUBLICAN PRIMARIES			DEMOCRATIC PRIMARIES		
Congressional District 2	Lewis, Jason*	Unopposed		Craig, Angie	Unopposed	
Congressional District 3	Paulsen, Erik*	39,077	100.0%	Phillips, Dean	56,677	81.6%
				Young, Cole	12,784	18.4%
	TOTAL	*39,077*		*TOTAL*	*69,461*	
Congressional District 4	Ryan, Greg	23,021	100.0%	McCollum, Betty*	86,842	91.0%
				Hassan, Muad	5,398	5.7%
				Rossell, Reid	3,156	3.3%
	TOTAL	*23,021*		*TOTAL*	*95,396*	
Congressional District 5	Zielinski, Jennifer	8,680	56.5%	Omar, Ilhan	65,237	48.2%
	Chamberlin, Christopher	4,999	32.5%	Anderson Kelliher, Margaret	41,156	30.4%
	Carney, Bob Jr.	1,688	11.0%	Ray, Patricia Torres	17,629	13.0%
				Abdulahi, Jamal	4,984	3.7%
				Champion, Bobby Joe	3,831	2.8%
				Drake, Frank Nelson	2,480	1.8%
	TOTAL	*15,367*		*TOTAL*	*135,317*	
Congressional District 6	Emmer, Tom*	34,250	76.6%	Todd, Ian	33,853	100.0%
	Kern, Aliena Jeanene "A.J."	7,897	17.7%			
	Munro, Patrick	2,575	5.8%			
	TOTAL	*44,722*		*TOTAL*	*33,853*	
Congressional District 7	Hughes, Dave	30,783	72.6%	Peterson, Collin C.*	39,990	100.0%
	Prosch, Matt	11,616	27.4%			
	TOTAL	*42,399*		*TOTAL*	*39,990*	
Congressional District 8	Stauber, Pete	45,391	90.0%	Radinovich, Joseph "Joe"	30,732	44.1%
	Welty, Harry Robb	5,047	10.0%	Lee, Michelle	19,182	27.5%
				Metsa, Jason	9,229	13.2%
				Kennedy, Kirsten	8,133	11.7%
				Sorensen, Soren Christian	2,415	3.5%
	TOTAL	*50,438*		*TOTAL*	*69,691*	

Note: An asterisk (*) denotes incumbent.

MISSISSIPPI

Congressional districts first established for elections held in 2012

4 members

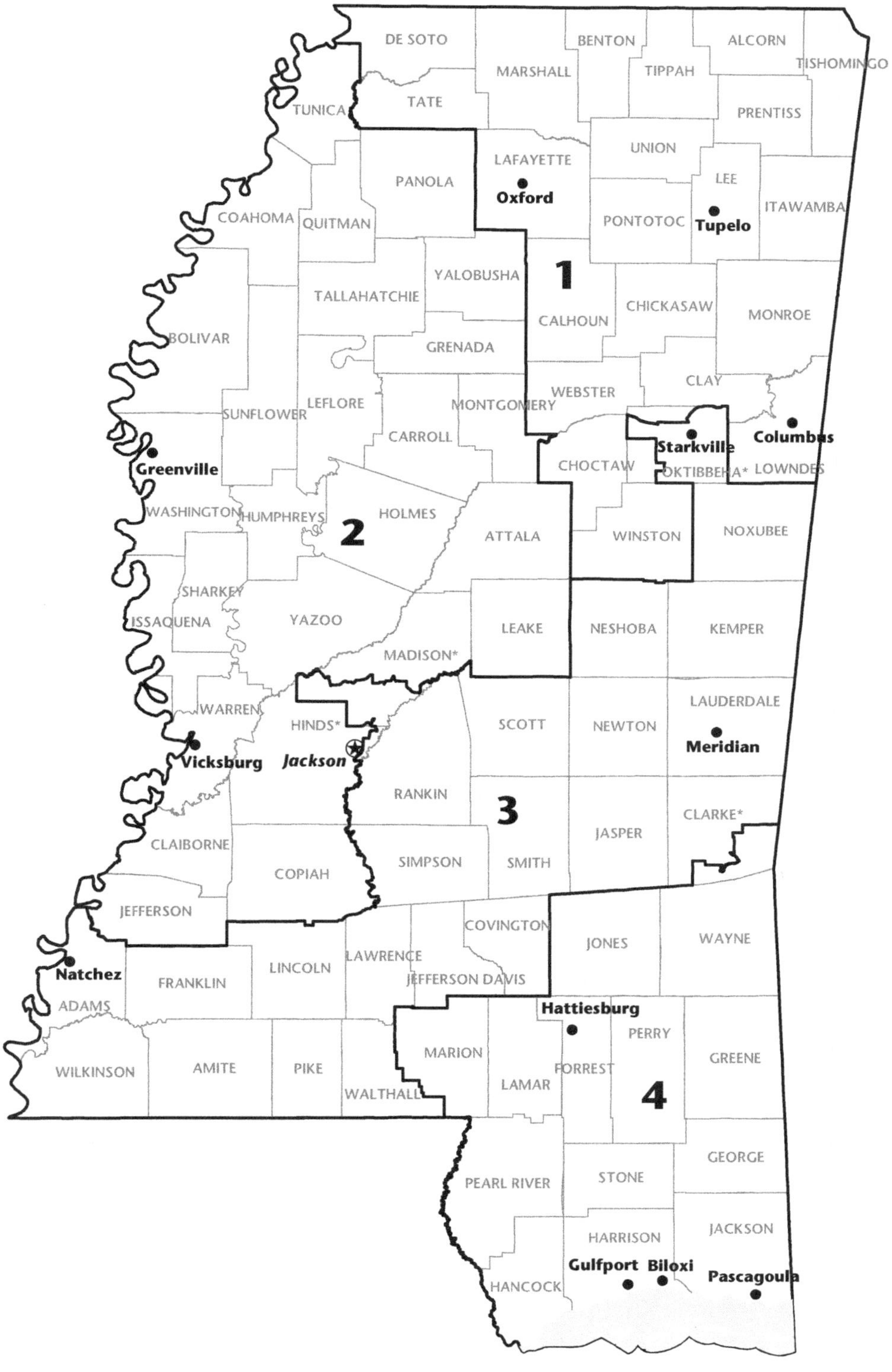

* Asterisk indicates a county whose boundaries include parts of two or more congressional districts.

MISSISSIPPI

GOVERNOR

Phil Bryant (R). Re-elected 2015 to a four-year term. Previously elected 2011.

SENATORS (2 Republicans)

Cindy Hyde-Smith (R). Appointed by the governor as interim senator following the resignation April 1, 2018, of W. Thad Cochran (R) due to health issues. Hyde-Smith was sworn in April 9, 2018, and was elected to fill the final two years of Cochran's term in the November 27, 2018, special election runoff.

Roger F. Wicker (R). Re-elected 2018 to a six-year term. Previously elected 2012 and 2008 to fill the final four years of the term vacated by the December 2007 resignation of C. Trent Lott. Wicker had been appointed to fill the vacancy and was sworn in as senator on December 31, 2007.

REPRESENTATIVES (3 Republicans, 1 Democrat)

1. Trent Kelly (R)
2. Bennie Thompson (D)
3. Michael Guest (R)
4. Steven Palazzo (R)

POSTWAR VOTE FOR PRESIDENT

		Republican		Democratic				Percentage			
								Total Vote		Major Vote	
Year	Total Vote	Vote	Candidate	Vote	Candidate	Other Vote	Rep.-Dem. Plurality	Rep.	Dem.	Rep.	Dem.
2016**	1,209,357	700,714	Trump, Donald J.	485,131	Clinton, Hillary Rodham	23,512	215,583 R	57.9%	40.1%	59.1%	40.9%
2012	1,285,584	710,746	Romney, W. Mitt	562,949	Obama, Barack H.*	11,889	147,797 R	55.3%	43.8%	55.8%	44.2%
2008	1,289,865	724,597	McCain, John S. III	554,662	Obama, Barack H.	10,606	169,935 R	56.2%	43.0%	56.6%	43.4%
2004	1,152,145	684,981	Bush, George W.*	458,094	Kerry, John F.	9,070	226,887 R	59.5%	39.8%	59.9%	40.1%
2000**	994,184	572,844	Bush, George W.	404,614	Gore, Albert Jr.	16,726	168,230 R	57.6%	40.7%	58.6%	41.4%
1996**	893,857	439,838	Dole, Robert "Bob"	394,022	Clinton, Bill*	59,997	45,816 R	49.2%	44.1%	52.7%	47.3%
1992**	981,793	487,793	Bush, George H.*	400,258	Clinton, Bill	93,742	87,535 R	49.7%	40.8%	54.9%	45.1%
1988	931,527	557,890	Bush, George H.	363,921	Dukakis, Michael S.	9,716	193,969 R	59.9%	39.1%	60.5%	39.5%
1984	941,104	582,377	Reagan, Ronald*	352,192	Mondale, Walter F.	6,535	230,185 R	61.9%	37.4%	62.3%	37.7%
1980**	892,620	441,089	Reagan, Ronald	429,281	Carter, Jimmy*	22,250	11,808 R	49.4%	48.1%	50.7%	49.3%
1976	769,361	366,846	Ford, Gerald R.*	381,309	Carter, Jimmy	21,206	14,463 D	47.7%	49.6%	49.0%	51.0%
1972	645,963	505,125	Nixon, Richard M.*	126,782	McGovern, George S.	14,056	378,343 R	78.2%	19.6%	79.9%	20.1%
1968**	654,509	88,516	Nixon, Richard M.	150,644	Humphrey, Hubert Horatio Jr.	415,349	62,128 D#	13.5%	23.0%	37.0%	63.0%
1964	409,146	356,528	Goldwater, Barry M. Sr.	52,618	Johnson, Lyndon B.*		303,910 R	87.1%	12.9%	87.1%	12.9%
1960**	298,171	73,561	Nixon, Richard M.	108,362	Kennedy, John F.	116,248	34,801 D#	24.7%	36.3%	40.4%	59.6%
1956	248,104	60,685	Eisenhower, Dwight D.*	144,453	Stevenson, Adlai E. II	42,966	83,768 D	24.5%	58.2%	29.6%	70.4%
1952	285,532	112,966	Eisenhower, Dwight D.	172,566	Stevenson, Adlai E. II		59,600 D	39.6%	60.4%	39.6%	60.4%
1948**	192,190	5,043	Dewey, Thomas E.	19,384	Truman, Harry S.*	167,763	14,341 D#	2.6%	10.1%	20.6%	79.4%

Note: An asterisk (*) denotes incumbent. A pound sign (#) indicates that the state was carried by a third party candidate or independent electoral state. **In past elections, the other vote included: 2016 - 14,435 Libertarian (Gary Johnson); 2000 - 8,122 Green (Ralph Nader); 1996 - 52,222 Reform (Ross Perot); 1992 - 85,626 Independent (Perot); 1980 - 12,036 Independent (John Anderson); 1968 - 415,349 American Independent (George Wallace); 1960 - 116,248 Unpledged Independent Democratic electors; 1948 - 167,538 States' Rights (Strom Thurmond). Thurmond won Mississippi in 1948 with 87.2 percent of the vote. The slate of Unpledged Independent Democratic electors carried the state in 1960 with 39.0 percent. Wallace won Mississippi in 1968 with 63.5 percent of the vote.

MISSISSIPPI

POSTWAR VOTE FOR GOVERNOR

		Republican		Democratic				Percentage			
								Total Vote		Major Vote	
Year	Total Vote	Vote	Candidate	Vote	Candidate	Other Vote	Rep.-Dem. Plurality	Rep.	Dem.	Rep.	Dem.
2015	725,207	480,399	Bryant, Phil*	234,858	Gray, Robert	9,950	245,541 R	66.2%	32.4%	67.2%	32.8%
2011	893,468	544,851	Bryant, Phil	348,617	DuPree, Johnny L.		196,234 R	61.0%	39.0%	61.0%	39.0%
2007	744,039	430,807	Barbour, Haley*	313,232	Eaves, John Arthur Jr.		117,575 R	57.9%	42.1%	57.9%	42.1%
2003	894,487	470,404	Barbour, Haley	409,787	Musgrove, Ronnie*	14,296	60,617 R	52.6%	45.8%	53.4%	46.6%
1999**	763,938	370,691	Parker, Mike	379,034	Musgrove, Ronnie	14,213	8,343 D	48.5%	49.6%	49.4%	50.6%
1995	819,471	455,261	Fordice, Kirk*	364,210	Molpus, Dick		91,051 R	55.6%	44.4%	55.6%	44.4%
1991	711,188	361,500	Fordice, Kirk	338,435	Mabus, Ray*	11,253	23,065 R	50.8%	47.6%	51.6%	48.4%
1987	721,695	336,006	Reed, Jack R.	385,689	Mabus, Ray		49,683 D	46.6%	53.4%	46.6%	53.4%
1983	742,737	288,764	Bramlett, Leon	409,209	Allain, William A.	44,764	120,445 D	38.9%	55.1%	41.4%	58.6%
1979	677,322	263,702	Carmichael, Gil	413,620	Winter, William		149,918 D	38.9%	61.1%	38.9%	61.1%
1975	708,033	319,632	Carmichael, Gil	369,568	Finch, Cliff	18,833	49,936 D	45.1%	52.2%	46.4%	53.6%
1971**	780,537			601,122	Waller, William L.	179,415	601,122 D		77.0%		100.0%
1967	448,696	133,378	Phillips, Rubel L.	315,318	Williams, John Bell		181,940 D	29.7%	70.3%	29.7%	70.3%
1963	363,971	138,515	Phillips, Rubel L.	225,456	Johnson, Paul B. Jr.		86,941 D	38.1%	61.9%	38.1%	61.9%
1959	57,671			57,671	Barnett, Ross R.		57,671 D		100.0%		100.0%
1955	40,707			40,707	Coleman, James P.		40,707 D		100.0%		100.0%
1951	43,422			43,422	White, Hugh L.		43,422 D		100.0%		100.0%
1947	166,095			161,993	Wright, Fielding L.	4,102	161,993 D		97.5%		100.0%

Note: An asterisk (*) denotes incumbent. **In past elections, the other vote included: 1971 - 172,762 Independent (Charles Evers), who finished second. In 1999 no candidate received a majority of the vote. Democrat Ronnie Musgrove was elected in January 2000 by the Mississippi House of Representatives. The Republican Party did not run a gubernatorial candidate in 1947, 1951, 1955, 1959, and 1971.

POSTWAR VOTE FOR SENATOR

		Republican		Democratic				Percentage			
								Total Vote		Major Vote	
Year	Total Vote	Vote	Candidate	Vote	Candidate	Other Vote	Rep.-Dem. Plurality	Rep.	Dem.	Rep.	Dem.
2018	936,215	547,619	Wicker, Roger F.*	369,567	Baria, David	19,029	178,052 R	58.5%	39.5%	59.7%	40.3%
2018S**	907,588	486,769	Hyde-Smith, Cindy*	420,819	Espy, Mike		65,950 R	53.6%	46.4%	53.6%	46.4%
2014	631,858	378,481	Cochran, W. Thad*	239,439	Childers, Travis	13,938	139,042 R	59.9%	37.9%	61.3%	38.7%
2012	1,241,568	709,626	Wicker, Roger F.*	503,467	Gore, Albert N. Jr.	28,475	206,159 R	57.2%	40.6%	58.5%	41.5%
2008S	1,243,473	683,409	Wicker, Roger F.*	560,064	Musgrove, Ronnie		123,345 R	55.0%	45.0%	55.0%	45.0%
2008	1,247,026	766,111	Cochran, W. Thad*	480,915	Fleming, Erik R.		285,196 R	61.4%	38.6%	61.4%	38.6%
2006	610,921	388,399	Lott, C. Trent*	213,000	Fleming, Erik R.	9,522	175,399 R	63.6%	34.9%	64.6%	35.4%
2002**	630,495	533,269	Cochran, W. Thad*			97,226	533,269 R	84.6%		100.0%	
2000	994,144	654,941	Lott, C. Trent*	314,090	Brown, Troy	25,113	340,851 R	65.9%	31.6%	67.6%	32.4%
1996	878,662	624,154	Cochran, W. Thad*	240,647	Hunt, James W. "Bootie"	13,861	383,507 R	71.0%	27.4%	72.2%	27.8%
1994	608,085	418,333	Lott, C. Trent*	189,752	Harper, Ken		228,581 R	68.8%	31.2%	68.8%	31.2%
1990	274,244	274,244	Cochran, W. Thad*				274,244 R	100.0%		100.0%	
1988	946,719	510,380	Lott, C. Trent	436,339	Dowdy, Wayne		74,041 R	53.9%	46.1%	53.9%	46.1%
1984	952,240	580,314	Cochran, W. Thad*	371,926	Winter, William		208,388 R	60.9%	39.1%	60.9%	39.1%
1982	645,026	230,927	Barbour, Haley	414,099	Stennis, John*		183,172 D	35.8%	64.2%	35.8%	64.2%
1978**	583,936	263,089	Cochran, W. Thad	185,454	Dantin, Maurice	135,393	77,635 R	45.1%	31.8%	58.7%	41.3%
1976	554,433			554,433	Stennis, John*		554,433 D		100.0%		100.0%
1972	645,746	249,779	Carmichael, Gil	375,102	Eastland, James O.*	20,865	125,323 D	38.7%	58.1%	40.0%	60.0%
1970**	324,215			286,622	Stennis, John*	37,593	286,622 D		88.4%		100.0%
1966	394,541	105,652	Walker, Prentiss	258,248	Eastland, James O.*	30,641	152,596 D	26.8%	65.5%	29.0%	71.0%
1964	343,364			343,364	Stennis, John*		343,364 D		100.0%		100.0%
1960	266,148	21,807	Moore, Joe A.	244,341	Eastland, James O.*		222,534 D	8.2%	91.8%	8.2%	91.8%
1958	61,039			61,039	Stennis, John*		61,039 D		100.0%		100.0%
1954	105,526	4,678	White, James A.	100,848	Eastland, James O.*		96,170 D	4.4%	95.6%	4.4%	95.6%
1952	233,919			233,919	Stennis, John*		233,919 D		100.0%		100.0%
1948	151,478			151,478	Eastland, James O.*		151,478 D		100.0%		100.0%
1947S**	193,086					193,086					
1946	46,747			46,747	Bilbo, Theodore G.*		46,747 D		100.0%		100.0%

Note: An asterisk (*) denotes incumbent. **In past elections, the other vote included: 2002 - 97,226 Reform (Shawn O'Hara), who finished second; 1978 - 133,646 Independent (Charles Evers). The 1947 election and one each of the 2008 and 2018 elections were for short terms to fill a vacancy. The results from the latter two elections reflect the outcomes of runoffs. In 1947, John Stennis received 52,068 votes (26.9 percent of the total vote) and won the election with a plurality of 6,343 votes. Other candidates that year included: 45,725 W. M. Colmer; 43,642 Forrest B. Jackson; 27,159 Paul B. Johnson; 24,492 John E. Rankin. The Republican Party did not run a candidate in Senate elections in 1946, 1948, 1952, 1958, 1964, 1970, and 1976. The Democratic Party did not run a candidate in Senate elections in 1990 and 2002.

MISSISSIPPI

SENATOR 2018

2010 Census Population	County	Total Vote	Republican (Wicker)	Democratic (Baria)	Other	Rep.-Dem. Plurality	Percentage Total Vote Rep.	Total Vote Dem.	Major Vote Rep.	Major Vote Dem.
32,297	ADAMS	10,760	4,487	6,097	176	1,610 D	41.7%	56.7%	42.4%	57.6%
37,057	ALCORN	10,166	8,167	1,780	219	6,387 R	80.3%	17.5%	82.1%	17.9%
13,131	AMITE	5,363	3,246	1,966	151	1,280 R	60.5%	36.7%	62.3%	37.7%
19,564	ATTALA	6,130	3,728	2,291	111	1,437 R	60.8%	37.4%	61.9%	38.1%
8,729	BENTON	2,784	1,645	1,091	48	554 R	59.1%	39.2%	60.1%	39.9%
34,145	BOLIVAR	10,612	3,938	6,469	205	2,531 D	37.1%	61.0%	37.8%	62.2%
14,962	CALHOUN	4,599	3,296	1,230	73	2,066 R	71.7%	26.7%	72.8%	27.2%
10,597	CARROLL	4,238	2,936	1,212	90	1,724 R	69.3%	28.6%	70.8%	29.2%
17,392	CHICKASAW	5,926	3,317	2,512	97	805 R	56.0%	42.4%	56.9%	43.1%
8,547	CHOCTAW	2,953	2,101	791	61	1,310 R	71.1%	26.8%	72.6%	27.4%
9,604	CLAIBORNE	3,240	653	2,468	119	1,815 D	20.2%	76.2%	20.9%	79.1%
16,732	CLARKE	5,990	3,944	1,933	113	2,011 R	65.8%	32.3%	67.1%	32.9%
20,634	CLAY	7,610	3,411	4,091	108	680 D	44.8%	53.8%	45.5%	54.5%
26,151	COAHOMA	6,214	2,178	3,858	178	1,680 D	35.0%	62.1%	36.1%	63.9%
29,449	COPIAH	10,180	5,052	4,867	261	185 R	49.6%	47.8%	50.9%	49.1%
19,568	COVINGTON	6,788	4,242	2,382	164	1,860 R	62.5%	35.1%	64.0%	36.0%
161,252	DE SOTO	50,879	32,750	16,858	1,271	15,892 R	64.4%	33.1%	66.0%	34.0%
74,934	FORREST	22,303	12,539	9,134	630	3,405 R	56.2%	41.0%	57.9%	42.1%
8,118	FRANKLIN	3,145	1,999	1,050	96	949 R	63.6%	33.4%	65.6%	34.4%
22,578	GEORGE	7,141	6,060	866	215	5,194 R	84.9%	12.1%	87.5%	12.5%
14,400	GREENE	3,733	2,923	703	107	2,220 R	78.3%	18.8%	80.6%	19.4%
21,906	GRENADA	7,645	4,348	3,176	121	1,172 R	56.9%	41.5%	57.8%	42.2%
43,929	HANCOCK	13,899	9,989	3,692	218	6,297 R	71.9%	26.6%	73.0%	27.0%
187,105	HARRISON	51,723	32,414	18,391	918	14,023 R	62.7%	35.6%	63.8%	36.2%
245,285	HINDS	78,706	21,644	55,780	1,282	34,136 D	27.5%	70.9%	28.0%	72.0%
19,198	HOLMES	5,375	1,068	4,222	85	3,154 D	19.9%	78.5%	20.2%	79.8%
9,375	HUMPHREYS	3,144	961	2,082	101	1,121 D	30.6%	66.2%	31.6%	68.4%
1,406	ISSAQUENA	532	258	261	13	3 D	48.5%	49.1%	49.7%	50.3%
23,401	ITAWAMBA	6,794	5,858	783	153	5,075 R	86.2%	11.5%	88.2%	11.8%
139,668	JACKSON	39,507	26,544	12,179	784	14,365 R	67.2%	30.8%	68.5%	31.5%
17,062	JASPER	6,267	2,988	3,149	130	161 D	47.7%	50.2%	48.7%	51.3%
7,726	JEFFERSON	3,060	562	2,398	100	1,836 D	18.4%	78.4%	19.0%	81.0%
12,487	JEFFERSON DAVIS	4,701	1,958	2,640	103	682 D	41.7%	56.2%	42.6%	57.4%
67,761	JONES	21,687	14,852	6,143	692	8,709 R	68.5%	28.3%	70.7%	29.3%
10,456	KEMPER	3,431	1,432	1,955	44	523 D	41.7%	57.0%	42.3%	57.7%
47,351	LAFAYETTE	16,490	9,256	6,981	253	2,275 R	56.1%	42.3%	57.0%	43.0%
55,658	LAMAR	19,711	14,777	4,437	497	10,340 R	75.0%	22.5%	76.9%	23.1%
80,261	LAUDERDALE	23,136	14,217	8,610	309	5,607 R	61.4%	37.2%	62.3%	37.7%
12,929	LAWRENCE	4,861	3,196	1,558	107	1,638 R	65.7%	32.1%	67.2%	32.8%
23,805	LEAKE	6,268	3,666	2,470	132	1,196 R	58.5%	39.4%	59.7%	40.3%
82,910	LEE	25,661	17,413	7,654	594	9,759 R	67.9%	29.8%	69.5%	30.5%
32,317	LEFLORE	8,364	2,850	5,352	162	2,502 D	34.1%	64.0%	34.7%	65.3%
34,869	LINCOLN	12,223	8,576	3,453	194	5,123 R	70.2%	28.3%	71.3%	28.7%
59,779	LOWNDES	19,646	10,720	8,638	288	2,082 R	54.6%	44.0%	55.4%	44.6%
95,203	MADISON	40,553	23,632	16,283	638	7,349 R	58.3%	40.2%	59.2%	40.8%
27,088	MARION	8,801	5,867	2,734	200	3,133 R	66.7%	31.1%	68.2%	31.8%
37,144	MARSHALL	11,313	5,415	5,692	206	277 D	47.9%	50.3%	48.8%	51.2%
36,989	MONROE	11,695	7,739	3,802	154	3,937 R	66.2%	32.5%	67.1%	32.9%
10,925	MONTGOMERY	3,840	2,254	1,526	60	728 R	58.7%	39.7%	59.6%	40.4%
29,676	NESHOBA	7,946	5,861	1,961	124	3,900 R	73.8%	24.7%	74.9%	25.1%
21,720	NEWTON	7,104	4,965	1,986	153	2,979 R	69.9%	28.0%	71.4%	28.6%
11,545	NOXUBEE	3,919	1,085	2,788	46	1,703 D	27.7%	71.1%	28.0%	72.0%
47,671	OKTIBBEHA	14,219	7,134	6,798	287	336 R	50.2%	47.8%	51.2%	48.8%
34,707	PANOLA	11,205	5,804	5,212	189	592 R	51.8%	46.5%	52.7%	47.3%
55,834	PEARL RIVER	15,704	12,373	2,899	432	9,474 R	78.8%	18.5%	81.0%	19.0%
12,250	PERRY	3,864	2,913	853	98	2,060 R	75.4%	22.1%	77.3%	22.7%
40,404	PIKE	12,598	6,502	5,857	239	645 R	51.6%	46.5%	52.6%	47.4%
29,957	PONTOTOC	9,593	7,588	1,693	312	5,895 R	79.1%	17.6%	81.8%	18.2%
25,276	PRENTISS	7,173	5,597	1,450	126	4,147 R	78.0%	20.2%	79.4%	20.6%
8,223	QUITMAN	2,389	872	1,460	57	588 D	36.5%	61.1%	37.4%	62.6%

MISSISSIPPI

SENATOR 2018

2010 Census Population	County	Total Vote	Republican (Wicker)	Democratic (Baria)	Other	Rep.-Dem. Plurality	Percentage Total Vote Rep.	Percentage Total Vote Dem.	Percentage Major Vote Rep.	Percentage Major Vote Dem.
141,617	RANKIN	51,630	37,913	12,523	1,194	25,390 R	73.4%	24.3%	75.2%	24.8%
28,264	SCOTT	7,642	4,600	2,926	116	1,674 R	60.2%	38.3%	61.1%	38.9%
4,916	SHARKEY	1,678	596	1,046	36	450 D	35.5%	62.3%	36.3%	63.7%
27,503	SIMPSON	8,733	5,697	2,855	181	2,842 R	65.2%	32.7%	66.6%	33.4%
16,491	SMITH	5,844	4,394	1,298	152	3,096 R	75.2%	22.2%	77.2%	22.8%
17,786	STONE	5,309	4,052	1,142	115	2,910 R	76.3%	21.5%	78.0%	22.0%
29,450	SUNFLOWER	7,189	2,457	4,579	153	2,122 D	34.2%	63.7%	34.9%	65.1%
15,378	TALLAHATCHIE	4,136	1,950	2,095	91	145 D	47.1%	50.7%	48.2%	51.8%
28,886	TATE	8,531	5,680	2,638	213	3,042 R	66.6%	30.9%	68.3%	31.7%
22,232	TIPPAH	6,906	5,536	1,229	141	4,307 R	80.2%	17.8%	81.8%	18.2%
19,593	TISHOMINGO	6,066	5,125	788	153	4,337 R	84.5%	13.0%	86.7%	13.3%
10,778	TUNICA	2,480	779	1,630	71	851 D	31.4%	65.7%	32.3%	67.7%
27,134	UNION	8,239	6,779	1,297	163	5,482 R	82.3%	15.7%	83.9%	16.1%
15,443	WALTHALL	5,038	3,008	1,919	111	1,089 R	59.7%	38.1%	61.1%	38.9%
48,773	WARREN	15,185	8,206	6,706	273	1,500 R	54.0%	44.2%	55.0%	45.0%
51,137	WASHINGTON	13,582	4,519	8,893	170	4,374 D	33.3%	65.5%	33.7%	66.3%
20,747	WAYNE	7,183	4,376	2,638	169	1,738 R	60.9%	36.7%	62.4%	37.6%
10,253	WEBSTER	3,917	3,114	733	70	2,381 R	79.5%	18.7%	80.9%	19.1%
9,878	WILKINSON	2,831	950	1,823	58	873 D	33.6%	64.4%	34.3%	65.7%
19,198	WINSTON	6,981	3,976	2,900	105	1,076 R	57.0%	41.5%	57.8%	42.2%
12,678	YALOBUSHA	4,654	2,574	2,011	69	563 R	55.3%	43.2%	56.1%	43.9%
28,065	YAZOO	6,960	3,578	3,251	131	327 R	51.4%	46.7%	52.4%	47.6%
2,967,297	*TOTAL*	*936,215*	*547,619*	*369,567*	*19,029*	*178,052 R*	*58.5%*	*39.5%*	*59.7%*	*40.3%*

MISSISSIPPI

SENATOR SPECIAL FIRST ROUND 2018

2010 Census Population	County	Total Vote	Republican (Hyde-Smith)	Republican (McDaniel)	Democratic (Espy)	Other	Plurality	Percentage Total Vote Hyde-Smith	Percentage Total Vote McDaniel	Percentage Total Vote Espy
32,297	ADAMS	10,826	3,406	1,273	5,947	200	2,541 E	31.5%	11.8%	54.9%
37,057	ALCORN	9,999	5,795	2,052	2,039	113	3,743 HS	58.0%	20.5%	20.4%
13,131	AMITE	5,286	2,098	1,201	1,873	114	225 HS	39.7%	22.7%	35.4%
19,564	ATTALA	6,305	2,733	970	2,524	78	209 HS	43.3%	15.4%	40.0%
8,729	BENTON	2,741	1,142	458	1,082	59	60 HS	41.7%	16.7%	39.5%
34,145	BOLIVAR	11,062	3,066	731	7,146	119	4,080 E	27.7%	6.6%	64.6%
14,962	CALHOUN	4,641	2,427	772	1,382	60	1,045 HS	52.3%	16.6%	29.8%
10,597	CARROLL	4,326	2,157	737	1,391	41	766 HS	49.9%	17.0%	32.2%
17,392	CHICKASAW	6,004	2,261	947	2,725	71	464 E	37.7%	15.8%	45.4%
8,547	CHOCTAW	3,023	1,550	573	852	48	698 HS	51.3%	19.0%	28.2%
9,604	CLAIBORNE	3,403	472	115	2,756	60	2,284 E	13.9%	3.4%	81.0%
16,732	CLARKE	6,096	2,386	1,446	1,387	877	940 HS	39.1%	23.7%	22.8%
20,634	CLAY	7,697	2,652	674	4,223	148	1,571 E	34.5%	8.8%	54.9%
26,151	COAHOMA	6,627	1,509	468	4,576	74	3,067 E	22.8%	7.1%	69.1%
29,449	COPIAH	10,525	4,336	799	5,230	160	894 E	41.2%	7.6%	49.7%
19,568	COVINGTON	6,968	2,502	1,825	2,557	84	55 E	35.9%	26.2%	36.7%
161,252	DE SOTO	50,093	20,634	11,864	16,922	673	3,712 HS	41.2%	23.7%	33.8%
74,934	FORREST	22,850	8,272	4,434	9,725	419	1,453 E	36.2%	19.4%	42.6%
8,118	FRANKLIN	3,223	1,542	550	1,084	47	458 HS	47.8%	17.1%	33.6%
22,578	GEORGE	6,979	2,973	2,866	1,001	139	107 HS	42.6%	41.1%	14.3%
14,400	GREENE	3,656	1,425	1,438	729	64	13 M	39.0%	39.3%	19.9%
21,906	GRENADA	7,721	3,199	1,027	3,394	101	195 E	41.4%	13.3%	44.0%
43,929	HANCOCK	13,527	6,918	3,063	3,256	290	3,662 HS	51.1%	22.6%	24.1%
187,105	HARRISON	51,490	24,784	7,255	18,710	741	6,074 HS	48.1%	14.1%	36.3%
245,285	HINDS	79,366	17,244	3,960	57,514	648	40,270 E	21.7%	5.0%	72.5%

MISSISSIPPI

SENATOR SPECIAL FIRST ROUND 2018

2010 Census Population	County	Total Vote	Republican (Hyde-Smith)	Republican (McDaniel)	Democratic (Espy)	Other	Plurality	Percentage Total Vote Hyde-Smith	McDaniel	Espy
19,198	HOLMES	5,640	794	196	4,574	76	3,780 E	14.1%	3.5%	81.1%
9,375	HUMPHREYS	3,227	747	150	2,282	48	1,535 E	23.1%	4.6%	70.7%
1,406	ISSAQUENA	560	217	33	305	5	88 E	38.8%	5.9%	54.5%
23,401	ITAWAMBA	6,827	4,049	1,766	953	59	2,283 HS	59.3%	25.9%	14.0%
139,668	JACKSON	39,436	19,294	6,895	12,460	787	6,834 HS	48.9%	17.5%	31.6%
17,062	JASPER	6,451	1,468	1,670	3,145	168	1,475 E	22.8%	25.9%	48.8%
7,726	JEFFERSON	3,215	407	132	2,614	62	2,207 E	12.7%	4.1%	81.3%
12,487	JEFFERSON DAVIS	4,885	1,467	515	2,830	73	1,363 E	30.0%	10.5%	57.9%
67,761	JONES	22,365	4,843	11,027	6,279	216	4,748 M	21.7%	49.3%	28.1%
10,456	KEMPER	3,421	1,086	389	1,853	93	767 E	31.7%	11.4%	54.2%
47,351	LAFAYETTE	16,322	6,858	1,929	7,294	241	436 E	42.0%	11.8%	44.7%
55,658	LAMAR	19,879	10,190	4,909	4,486	294	5,281 HS	51.3%	24.7%	22.6%
80,261	LAUDERDALE	23,093	10,138	4,116	8,273	566	1,865 HS	43.9%	17.8%	35.8%
12,929	LAWRENCE	5,174	3,035	368	1,741	30	1,294 HS	58.7%	7.1%	33.6%
23,805	LEAKE	6,561	2,748	934	2,815	64	67 E	41.9%	14.2%	42.9%
82,910	LEE	25,717	12,240	5,068	8,164	245	4,076 HS	47.6%	19.7%	31.7%
32,317	LEFLORE	8,740	2,199	493	5,863	185	3,664 E	25.2%	5.6%	67.1%
34,869	LINCOLN	12,629	7,870	1,068	3,604	87	4,266 HS	62.3%	8.5%	28.5%
59,779	LOWNDES	19,789	8,012	2,487	8,981	309	969 E	40.5%	12.6%	45.4%
95,203	MADISON	40,801	19,899	3,494	17,125	283	2,774 HS	48.8%	8.6%	42.0%
27,088	MARION	8,932	4,198	1,811	2,788	135	1,410 HS	47.0%	20.3%	31.2%
37,144	MARSHALL	11,314	3,533	1,555	5,992	234	2,459 E	31.2%	13.7%	53.0%
36,989	MONROE	11,811	5,699	1,863	4,080	169	1,619 HS	48.3%	15.8%	34.5%
10,925	MONTGOMERY	3,898	1,846	415	1,582	55	264 HS	47.4%	10.6%	40.6%
29,676	NESHOBA	8,008	4,308	1,465	2,139	96	2,169 HS	53.8%	18.3%	26.7%
21,720	NEWTON	7,224	3,285	1,695	2,141	103	1,144 HS	45.5%	23.5%	29.6%
11,545	NOXUBEE	3,973	891	180	2,799	103	1,908 E	22.4%	4.5%	70.5%
47,671	OKTIBBEHA	14,363	5,543	1,480	7,091	249	1,548 E	38.6%	10.3%	49.4%
34,707	PANOLA	11,232	4,022	1,565	5,447	198	1,425 E	35.8%	13.9%	48.5%
55,834	PEARL RIVER	15,421	6,751	5,532	2,831	307	1,219 HS	43.8%	35.9%	18.4%
12,250	PERRY	3,998	1,803	1,193	960	42	610 HS	45.1%	29.8%	24.0%
40,404	PIKE	12,746	4,887	1,727	5,909	223	1,022 E	38.3%	13.5%	46.4%
29,957	PONTOTOC	9,686	4,988	2,683	1,925	90	2,305 HS	51.5%	27.7%	19.9%
25,276	PRENTISS	7,241	4,038	1,441	1,703	59	2,335 HS	55.8%	19.9%	23.5%
8,223	QUITMAN	2,440	601	141	1,643	55	1,042 E	24.6%	5.8%	67.3%
141,617	RANKIN	51,777	29,055	9,294	13,035	393	16,020 HS	56.1%	18.0%	25.2%
28,264	SCOTT	7,879	3,517	1,078	3,208	76	309 HS	44.6%	13.7%	40.7%
4,916	SHARKEY	1,773	515	68	1,171	19	656 E	29.0%	3.8%	66.0%
27,503	SIMPSON	9,030	4,577	1,257	3,097	99	1,480 HS	50.7%	13.9%	34.3%
16,491	SMITH	6,024	2,706	1,905	1,370	43	801 HS	44.9%	31.6%	22.7%
17,786	STONE	5,367	2,836	1,239	1,230	62	1,597 HS	52.8%	23.1%	22.9%
29,450	SUNFLOWER	7,468	1,904	374	5,090	100	3,186 E	25.5%	5.0%	68.2%
15,378	TALLAHATCHIE	4,303	1,395	387	2,460	61	1,065 E	32.4%	9.0%	57.2%
28,886	TATE	8,610	3,622	2,058	2,760	170	862 HS	42.1%	23.9%	32.1%
22,232	TIPPAH	6,882	3,926	1,416	1,451	89	2,475 HS	57.0%	20.6%	21.1%
19,593	TISHOMINGO	6,006	3,529	1,502	895	80	2,027 HS	58.8%	25.0%	14.9%
10,778	TUNICA	2,542	586	143	1,725	88	1,139 E	23.1%	5.6%	67.9%
27,134	UNION	8,327	4,738	2,049	1,473	67	2,689 HS	56.9%	24.6%	17.7%
15,443	WALTHALL	5,152	2,382	705	2,006	59	376 HS	46.2%	13.7%	38.9%
48,773	WARREN	15,648	6,159	1,802	7,505	182	1,346 E	39.4%	11.5%	48.0%
51,137	WASHINGTON	14,034	3,577	593	9,667	197	6,090 E	25.5%	4.2%	68.9%
20,747	WAYNE	7,351	2,576	1,946	2,607	222	31 E	35.0%	26.5%	35.5%
10,253	WEBSTER	3,919	2,390	731	756	42	1,634 HS	61.0%	18.7%	19.3%
9,878	WILKINSON	2,743	600	406	1,597	140	997 E	21.9%	14.8%	58.2%
19,198	WINSTON	6,997	3,039	855	2,996	107	43 HS	43.4%	12.2%	42.8%
12,678	YALOBUSHA	4,668	2,004	561	2,028	75	24 E	42.9%	12.0%	43.4%
28,065	YAZOO	7,514	2,925	626	3,919	44	994 E	38.9%	8.3%	52.2%
2,967,297	*TOTAL*	*945,467*	*389,995*	*154,878*	*386,742*	*13,852*	*3,253 HS*	*41.2%*	*16.4%*	*40.9%*

Note: With the resignation of Mississippi Republican W. Thad Cochran from the Senate on April 1, 2018, a special election took place in the fall to fill the final two years of his term. The first round vote was held November 6, 2018, and since no candidate received a majority of the vote, a runoff between the top two vote-getters was held November 27, 2018. The plurality column features the vote differential between the first and second place finishers in each county.

MISSISSIPPI

SENATOR SPECIAL RUNOFF 2018

2010 Census Population	County	Total Vote	Republican (Hyde-Smith)	Democratic (Espy)	Rep.-Dem. Plurality	Percentage: Total Vote Rep.	Total Vote Dem.	Major Vote Rep.	Major Vote Dem.
32,297	ADAMS	10,601	4,113	6,488	2,375 D	38.8%	61.2%	38.8%	61.2%
37,057	ALCORN	9,204	7,120	2,084	5,036 R	77.4%	22.6%	77.4%	22.6%
13,131	AMITE	5,011	2,912	2,099	813 R	58.1%	41.9%	58.1%	41.9%
19,564	ATTALA	6,277	3,473	2,804	669 R	55.3%	44.7%	55.3%	44.7%
8,729	BENTON	2,611	1,387	1,224	163 R	53.1%	46.9%	53.1%	46.9%
34,145	BOLIVAR	10,885	3,331	7,554	4,223 D	30.6%	69.4%	30.6%	69.4%
14,962	CALHOUN	4,561	3,046	1,515	1,531 R	66.8%	33.2%	66.8%	33.2%
10,597	CARROLL	4,039	2,612	1,427	1,185 R	64.7%	35.3%	64.7%	35.3%
17,392	CHICKASAW	6,165	2,955	3,210	255 D	47.9%	52.1%	47.9%	52.1%
8,547	CHOCTAW	2,932	1,932	1,000	932 R	65.9%	34.1%	65.9%	34.1%
9,604	CLAIBORNE	3,548	453	3,095	2,642 D	12.8%	87.2%	12.8%	87.2%
16,732	CLARKE	5,642	3,486	2,156	1,330 R	61.8%	38.2%	61.8%	38.2%
20,634	CLAY	8,001	3,036	4,965	1,929 D	37.9%	62.1%	37.9%	62.1%
26,151	COAHOMA	6,859	1,748	5,111	3,363 D	25.5%	74.5%	25.5%	74.5%
29,449	COPIAH	10,585	4,694	5,891	1,197 D	44.3%	55.7%	44.3%	55.7%
19,568	COVINGTON	6,683	3,828	2,855	973 R	57.3%	42.7%	57.3%	42.7%
161,252	DE SOTO	42,884	25,326	17,558	7,768 R	59.1%	40.9%	59.1%	40.9%
74,934	FORREST	21,541	10,933	10,608	325 R	50.8%	49.2%	50.8%	49.2%
8,118	FRANKLIN	3,201	1,957	1,244	713 R	61.1%	38.9%	61.1%	38.9%
22,578	GEORGE	5,789	4,900	889	4,011 R	84.6%	15.4%	84.6%	15.4%
14,400	GREENE	3,083	2,422	661	1,761 R	78.6%	21.4%	78.6%	21.4%
21,906	GRENADA	7,486	3,943	3,543	400 R	52.7%	47.3%	52.7%	47.3%
43,929	HANCOCK	11,767	8,716	3,051	5,665 R	74.1%	25.9%	74.1%	25.9%
187,105	HARRISON	47,506	28,167	19,339	8,828 R	59.3%	40.7%	59.3%	40.7%
245,285	HINDS	80,356	18,464	61,892	43,428 D	23.0%	77.0%	23.0%	77.0%
19,198	HOLMES	6,788	974	5,814	4,840 D	14.3%	85.7%	14.3%	85.7%
9,375	HUMPHREYS	3,547	851	2,696	1,845 D	24.0%	76.0%	24.0%	76.0%
1,406	ISSAQUENA	532	227	305	78 D	42.7%	57.3%	42.7%	57.3%
23,401	ITAWAMBA	6,644	5,714	930	4,784 R	86.0%	14.0%	86.0%	14.0%
139,668	JACKSON	35,940	23,119	12,821	10,298 R	64.3%	35.7%	64.3%	35.7%
17,062	JASPER	6,476	2,796	3,680	884 D	43.2%	56.8%	43.2%	56.8%
7,726	JEFFERSON	3,192	385	2,807	2,422 D	12.1%	87.9%	12.1%	87.9%
12,487	JEFFERSON DAVIS	4,997	1,792	3,205	1,413 D	35.9%	64.1%	35.9%	64.1%
67,761	JONES	20,366	13,420	6,946	6,474 R	65.9%	34.1%	65.9%	34.1%
10,456	KEMPER	3,477	1,270	2,207	937 D	36.5%	63.5%	36.5%	63.5%
47,351	LAFAYETTE	15,218	7,702	7,516	186 R	50.6%	49.4%	50.6%	49.4%
55,658	LAMAR	18,136	13,200	4,936	8,264 R	72.8%	27.2%	72.8%	27.2%
80,261	LAUDERDALE	21,404	12,224	9,180	3,044 R	57.1%	42.9%	57.1%	42.9%
12,929	LAWRENCE	5,137	3,222	1,915	1,307 R	62.7%	37.3%	62.7%	37.3%
23,805	LEAKE	6,633	3,534	3,099	435 R	53.3%	46.7%	53.3%	46.7%
82,910	LEE	25,946	16,493	9,453	7,040 R	63.6%	36.4%	63.6%	36.4%
32,317	LEFLORE	8,733	2,499	6,234	3,735 D	28.6%	71.4%	28.6%	71.4%
34,869	LINCOLN	12,544	8,536	4,008	4,528 R	68.0%	32.0%	68.0%	32.0%
59,779	LOWNDES	19,049	9,263	9,786	523 D	48.6%	51.4%	48.6%	51.4%
95,203	MADISON	42,965	23,558	19,407	4,151 R	54.8%	45.2%	54.8%	45.2%
27,088	MARION	8,632	5,496	3,136	2,360 R	63.7%	36.3%	63.7%	36.3%
37,144	MARSHALL	10,796	4,462	6,334	1,872 D	41.3%	58.7%	41.3%	58.7%
36,989	MONROE	11,869	7,127	4,742	2,385 R	60.0%	40.0%	60.0%	40.0%
10,925	MONTGOMERY	3,745	2,036	1,709	327 R	54.4%	45.6%	54.4%	45.6%
29,676	NESHOBA	7,386	5,222	2,164	3,058 R	70.7%	29.3%	70.7%	29.3%
21,720	NEWTON	6,943	4,645	2,298	2,347 R	66.9%	33.1%	66.9%	33.1%
11,545	NOXUBEE	4,117	900	3,217	2,317 D	21.9%	78.1%	21.9%	78.1%
47,671	OKTIBBEHA	13,745	6,028	7,717	1,689 D	43.9%	56.1%	43.9%	56.1%
34,707	PANOLA	11,006	4,929	6,077	1,148 D	44.8%	55.2%	44.8%	55.2%
55,834	PEARL RIVER	13,152	10,322	2,830	7,492 R	78.5%	21.5%	78.5%	21.5%
12,250	PERRY	3,813	2,754	1,059	1,695 R	72.2%	27.8%	72.2%	27.8%
40,404	PIKE	12,472	5,795	6,677	882 D	46.5%	53.5%	46.5%	53.5%
29,957	PONTOTOC	9,366	7,304	2,062	5,242 R	78.0%	22.0%	78.0%	22.0%
25,276	PRENTISS	7,042	5,206	1,836	3,370 R	73.9%	26.1%	73.9%	26.1%
8,223	QUITMAN	2,472	684	1,788	1,104 D	27.7%	72.3%	27.7%	72.3%

MISSISSIPPI

SENATOR SPECIAL RUNOFF 2018

						Percentage			
						Total Vote		Major Vote	
2010 Census Population	County	Total Vote	Republican (Hyde-Smith)	Democratic (Espy)	Rep.-Dem. Plurality	Rep.	Dem.	Rep.	Dem.
141,617	RANKIN	48,159	34,333	13,826	20,507 R	71.3%	28.7%	71.3%	28.7%
28,264	SCOTT	8,075	4,429	3,646	783 R	54.8%	45.2%	54.8%	45.2%
4,916	SHARKEY	1,688	496	1,192	696 D	29.4%	70.6%	29.4%	70.6%
27,503	SIMPSON	8,837	5,404	3,433	1,971 R	61.2%	38.8%	61.2%	38.8%
16,491	SMITH	5,676	4,180	1,496	2,684 R	73.6%	26.4%	73.6%	26.4%
17,786	STONE	5,077	3,724	1,353	2,371 R	73.4%	26.6%	73.4%	26.6%
29,450	SUNFLOWER	7,335	2,034	5,301	3,267 D	27.7%	72.3%	27.7%	72.3%
15,378	TALLAHATCHIE	4,382	1,691	2,691	1,000 D	38.6%	61.4%	38.6%	61.4%
28,886	TATE	8,158	4,935	3,223	1,712 R	60.5%	39.5%	60.5%	39.5%
22,232	TIPPAH	6,430	4,868	1,562	3,306 R	75.7%	24.3%	75.7%	24.3%
19,593	TISHOMINGO	5,447	4,552	895	3,657 R	83.6%	16.4%	83.6%	16.4%
10,778	TUNICA	2,515	578	1,937	1,359 D	23.0%	77.0%	23.0%	77.0%
27,134	UNION	8,013	6,409	1,604	4,805 R	80.0%	20.0%	80.0%	20.0%
15,443	WALTHALL	5,045	2,716	2,329	387 R	53.8%	46.2%	53.8%	46.2%
48,773	WARREN	15,039	7,082	7,957	875 D	47.1%	52.9%	47.1%	52.9%
51,137	WASHINGTON	13,212	3,583	9,629	6,046 D	27.1%	72.9%	27.1%	72.9%
20,747	WAYNE	7,078	4,036	3,042	994 R	57.0%	43.0%	57.0%	43.0%
10,253	WEBSTER	3,782	2,937	845	2,092 R	77.7%	22.3%	77.7%	22.3%
9,878	WILKINSON	2,817	851	1,966	1,115 D	30.2%	69.8%	30.2%	69.8%
19,198	WINSTON	6,806	3,559	3,247	312 R	52.3%	47.7%	52.3%	47.7%
12,678	YALOBUSHA	4,465	2,281	2,184	97 R	51.1%	48.9%	51.1%	48.9%
28,065	YAZOO	8,055	3,448	4,607	1,159 D	42.8%	57.2%	42.8%	57.2%
2,967,297	*TOTAL*	*907,588*	*486,769*	*420,819*	*65,950 R*	*53.6%*	*46.4%*	*53.6%*	*46.4%*

MISSISSIPPI

HOUSE OF REPRESENTATIVES

									Percentage			
			Republican		Democratic				Total Vote		Major Vote	
CD	Year	Total Vote	Vote	Candidate	Vote	Candidate	Other Vote	Rep.-Dem. Plurality	Rep.	Dem.	Rep.	Dem.
1	2018	236,521	158,245	KELLY, TRENT*	76,601	WADKINS, RANDY	1,675	81,644 R	66.9%	32.4%	67.4%	32.6%
1	2016	300,423	206,455	KELLY, TRENT*	83,947	OWENS, JACOB	10,021	122,508 R	68.7%	27.9%	71.1%	28.9%
1	2014	151,111	102,622	NUNNELEE, ALAN*	43,713	DICKEY, RON E.	4,776	58,909 R	67.9%	28.9%	70.1%	29.9%
1	2012	309,177	186,760	NUNNELEE, ALAN*	114,076	MORRIS, BRAD	8,341	72,684 R	60.4%	36.9%	62.1%	37.9%
2	2018	221,379			158,921	THOMPSON, BENNIE*	62,458	158,921 D		71.8%		100.0%
2	2016	286,626	83,542	BOUIE, JOHN II	192,343	THOMPSON, BENNIE*	10,741	108,801 D	29.1%	67.1%	30.3%	69.7%
2	2014	148,646			100,688	THOMPSON, BENNIE*	47,958	100,688 D		67.7%		100.0%
2	2012	320,244	99,160	MARCY, BILL	214,978	THOMPSON, BENNIE*	6,106	115,818 D	31.0%	67.1%	31.6%	68.4%
3	2018	259,271	160,284	GUEST, MICHAEL	94,461	EVANS, MICHAEL	2,526	65,823 R	62.3%	36.7%	62.9%	37.1%
3	2016	316,445	209,490	HARPER, GREGG*	96,101	QUINN, DENNIS C.	10,854	113,389 R	66.2%	30.4%	68.6%	31.4%
3	2014	170,946	117,771	HARPER, GREGG*	47,744	MAGEE, DOUGLAS MACARTHUR "DOUG"	5,431	70,027 R	68.9%	27.9%	71.2%	28.8%
3	2012	293,322	234,717	HARPER, GREGG*			58,605	234,717 R	80.0%		100.0%	
4	2018	223,732	152,633	PALAZZO, STEVEN*	68,787	ANDERSON, JERAMEY	2,312	83,846 R	68.2%	30.7%	68.9%	31.1%
4	2016	278,779	181,323	PALAZZO, STEVEN*	77,505	GLADNEY, MARK	19,951	103,818 R	65.0%	27.8%	70.1%	29.9%
4	2014	155,576	108,776	PALAZZO, STEVEN*	37,869	MOORE, MATT	8,931	70,907 R	69.9%	24.3%	74.2%	25.8%
4	2012	285,432	182,998	PALAZZO, STEVEN*	82,344	MOORE, MATT	20,090	100,654 R	64.1%	28.8%	69.0%	31.0%
TOTAL	*2018*	*938,903*	*471,162*		*398,770*		*68,971*	*72,392 R*	*50.2%*	*42.5%*	*54.2%*	*45.8%*
TOTAL	*2016*	*1,182,273*	*680,810*		*449,896*		*51,567*	*230,914 R*	*57.6%*	*38.1%*	*60.2%*	*39.8%*
TOTAL	*2014*	*626,279*	*329,169*		*230,014*		*67,096*	*99,155 R*	*52.6%*	*36.7%*	*58.9%*	*41.1%*
TOTAL	*2012*	*1,208,175*	*703,635*		*411,398*		*93,142*	*292,237 R*	*58.2%*	*34.1%*	*63.1%*	*36.9%*

Note: An asterisk (*) denotes incumbent.

MISSISSIPPI

GENERAL AND PRIMARY ELECTIONS

2018 GENERAL ELECTIONS: OTHER VOTES

Senate Other vote was 12,981 Libertarian (Danny Bedwell), 6,048 Reform (Shawn O'Hara)

House Other vote was:

CD 1	1,675 Reform (Tracella Hill)
CD 2	48,104 Independent (Troy Ray), 14,354 Reform (Irving Harris)
CD 3	2,526 Reform (Matthew Holland)
CD 4	2,312 Reform (Lajena Sheets)

2018 PRIMARY ELECTIONS: SUPPLEMENTARY INFORMATION

Primary June 5, 2018 **Registration** (as of May 7, 2019) 1,830,250 No Party Registration

Primary Type Open—Any registered voter could participate in the party primary of his or her choice. But any voter who cast a ballot in the primary of one party could not vote in the runoff of the other party.

	REPUBLICAN PRIMARIES			DEMOCRATIC PRIMARIES		
Senator	Wicker, Roger F.*	130,118	82.8%	Sherman, Howard	27,957	31.8%
	Boyanton, Richard	27,052	17.2%	Baria, David	27,244	31.0%
				Scott, Omeria	21,278	24.2%
				Maurice, Victor Jr.	4,361	5.0%
				Garland, Jerone	4,266	4.9%
				Bohren, Jensen	2,825	3.2%
	TOTAL	*157,170*		*TOTAL*	*87,931*	
Congressional District 1	Kelly, Trent*	30,151	100.0%	Wadkins, Randy	11,692	100.0%
	TOTAL	*30,151*		*TOTAL*	*11,692*	
Congressional District 2				Thompson, Bennie*	31,203	100.0%
				TOTAL	*31,203*	
Congressional District 3	Guest, Michael	29,157	44.8%	Evans, Michael	17,016	69.3%
	Hughes, Whit	14,464	22.2%	Aycox, Michael	7,525	30.7%
	Parker, Perry	10,562	16.2%			
	Doty, Sally	6,608	10.2%			
	Dunn, Morgan	3,820	5.9%			
	Tate, Katherine "Bitzi"	416	0.6%			
	TOTAL	*65,027*		*TOTAL*	*24,541*	
	PRIMARY RUNOFF					
	Guest, Michael	31,572	65.1%			
	Hughes, Whit	16,950	34.9%			
	TOTAL	*48,522*				
Congressional District 4	Palazzo, Steven*	30,270	70.5%	Anderson, Jeramey	14,560	100.0%
	Rose, E. Brian	12,664	29.5%			
	TOTAL	*42,934*		*TOTAL*	*14,560*	

Note: An asterisk (*) denotes incumbent.

MISSOURI

Congressional districts first established for elections held in 2012

8 members

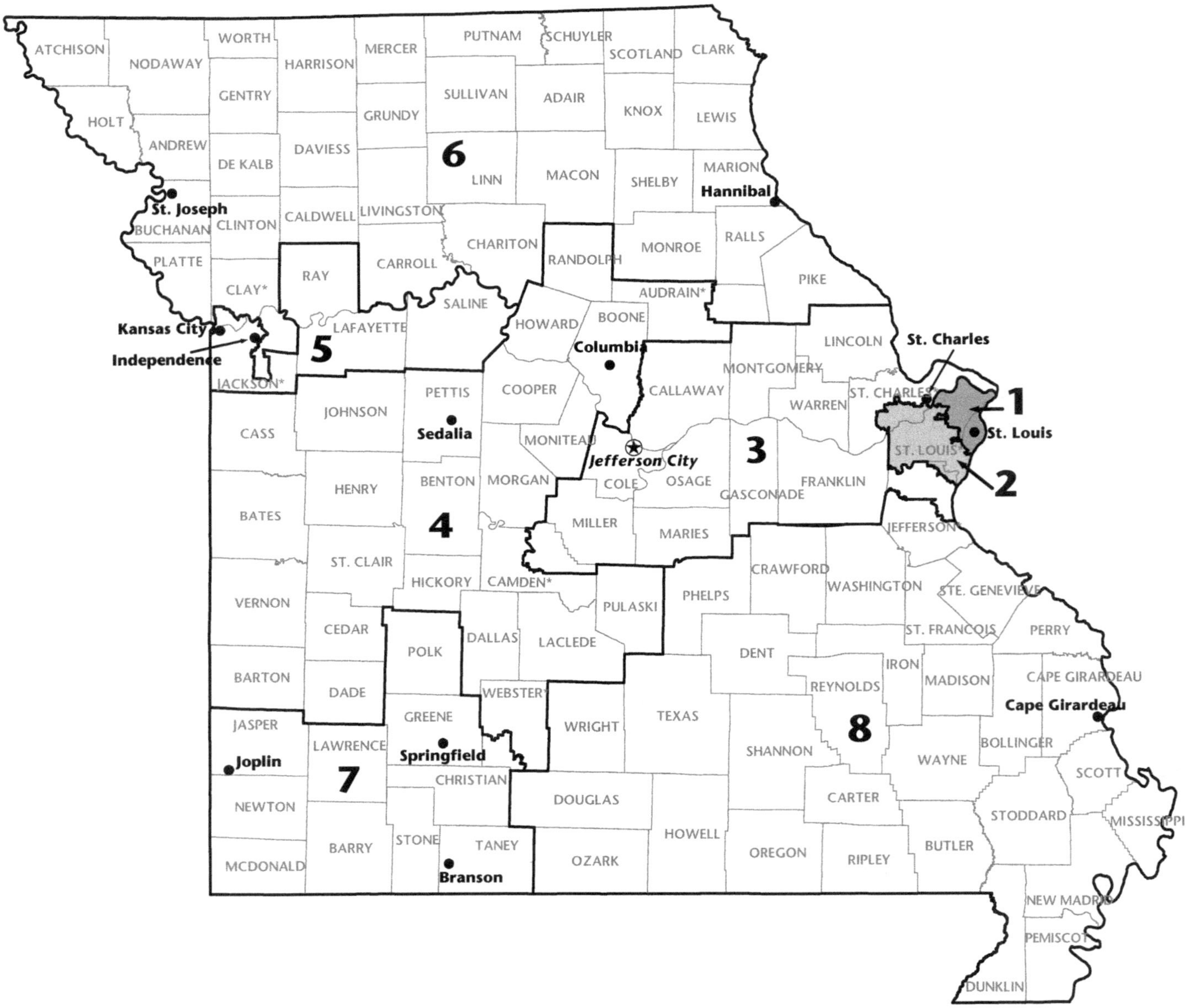

The city of St. Louis is an independent city that is treated as a county equivalent; so is Kansas City for voting purposes.

* Asterisk indicates a county whose boundaries include parts of two or more congressional districts.

MISSOURI

GOVERNOR

Mike Parson (R). Sworn in June 1, 2018, to fill the seat vacated by Eric Greitens (R), who resigned May 29, 2018, due to allegations of sexual misconduct and misuse of voter data during the 2016 election.

SENATORS (2 Republicans)

Roy Blunt (R). Re-elected 2016 to a six-year term. Previously elected 2010.

Josh Hawley (R). Elected 2018 to a six-year term.

REPRESENTATIVES (6 Republicans, 2 Democrats)

1. William Lacy Clay Jr. (D)
2. Ann Wagner (R)
3. Blaine Luetkemeyer (R)
4. Vicky Hartzler (R)
5. Emanuel Cleaver II (D)
6. Samuel B. Graves Jr. (R)
7. Billy Long (R)
8. Jason Smith (R)

POSTWAR VOTE FOR PRESIDENT

		Republican		Democratic				Percentage			
								Total Vote		Major Vote	
Year	Total Vote	Vote	Candidate	Vote	Candidate	Other Vote	Rep.-Dem. Plurality	Rep.	Dem.	Rep.	Dem.
2016	2,808,605	1,594,511	Trump, Donald J.	1,071,068	Clinton, Hillary Rodham	143,026	523,443 R	56.8%	38.1%	59.8%	40.2%
2012	2,757,323	1,482,440	Romney, W. Mitt	1,223,796	Obama, Barack H.*	51,087	258,644 R	53.8%	44.4%	54.8%	45.2%
2008	2,925,205	1,445,814	McCain, John S. III	1,441,911	Obama, Barack H.	37,480	3,903 R	49.4%	49.3%	50.1%	49.9%
2004	2,731,364	1,455,713	Bush, George W.*	1,259,171	Kerry, John F.	16,480	196,542 R	53.3%	46.1%	53.6%	46.4%
2000**	2,359,892	1,189,924	Bush, George W.	1,111,138	Gore, Albert Jr.	58,830	78,786 R	50.4%	47.1%	51.7%	48.3%
1996**	2,158,065	890,016	Dole, Robert "Bob"	1,025,935	Clinton, Bill*	242,114	135,919 D	41.2%	47.5%	46.5%	53.5%
1992**	2,391,565	811,159	Bush, George H.*	1,053,873	Clinton, Bill	526,533	242,714 D	33.9%	44.1%	43.5%	56.5%
1988	2,093,713	1,084,953	Bush, George H.	1,001,619	Dukakis, Michael S.	7,141	83,334 R	51.8%	47.8%	52.0%	48.0%
1984	2,122,783	1,274,188	Reagan, Ronald*	848,583	Mondale, Walter F.	12	425,605 R	60.0%	40.0%	60.0%	40.0%
1980**	2,099,824	1,074,181	Reagan, Ronald	931,182	Carter, Jimmy*	94,461	142,999 R	51.2%	44.3%	53.6%	46.4%
1976	1,953,600	927,443	Ford, Gerald R.*	998,387	Carter, Jimmy	27,770	70,944 D	47.5%	51.1%	48.2%	51.8%
1972	1,855,803	1,153,852	Nixon, Richard M.*	697,147	McGovern, George S.	4,804	456,705 R	62.2%	37.6%	62.3%	37.7%
1968**	1,809,502	811,932	Nixon, Richard M.	791,444	Humphrey, Hubert Horatio Jr.	206,126	20,488 R	44.9%	43.7%	50.6%	49.4%
1964	1,817,879	653,535	Goldwater, Barry M. Sr.	1,164,344	Johnson, Lyndon B.*		510,809 D	36.0%	64.0%	36.0%	64.0%
1960	1,934,422	962,221	Nixon, Richard M.	972,201	Kennedy, John F.		9,980 D	49.7%	50.3%	49.7%	50.3%
1956	1,832,562	914,289	Eisenhower, Dwight D,*	918,273	Stevenson, Adlai E. II		3,984 D	49.9%	50.1%	49.9%	50.1%
1952	1,892,062	959,429	Eisenhower, Dwight D.	929,830	Stevenson, Adlai E. II	2,803	29,599 R	50.7%	49.1%	50.8%	49.2%
1948	1,578,628	655,039	Dewey, Thomas E.	917,315	Truman, Harry S.*	6,274	262,276 D	41.5%	58.1%	41.7%	58.3%

Note: An asterisk (*) denotes incumbent. **In past elections, the other vote included: 2000 - 38,515 Green (Ralph Nader); 1996 - 217,188 Reform (Ross Perot); 1992 - 518,741 Independent (Perot); 1980 - 77,920 Independent (John Anderson); 1968 - 206,126 American Independent (George Wallace).

MISSOURI

POSTWAR VOTE FOR GOVERNOR

		Republican		Democratic				Percentage			
								Total Vote		Major Vote	
Year	Total Vote	Vote	Candidate	Vote	Candidate	Other Vote	Rep.-Dem. Plurality	Rep.	Dem.	Rep.	Dem.
2016	2,803,046	1,433,397	Greitens, Eric	1,277,360	Koster, Chris	92,289	156,037 R	51.1%	45.6%	52.9%	47.1%
2012	2,727,883	1,160,265	Spence, David "Dave"	1,494,056	Nixon, Jay W.*	73,562	333,791 D	42.5%	54.8%	43.7%	56.3%
2008	2,877,778	1,136,364	Hulshof, Kenny	1,680,611	Nixon, Jay W.	60,803	544,247 D	39.5%	58.4%	40.3%	59.7%
2004	2,719,599	1,382,419	Blunt, Matt	1,301,442	McCaskill, Claire	35,738	80,977 R	50.8%	47.9%	51.5%	48.5%
2000	2,346,830	1,131,307	Talent, James M.	1,152,752	Holden, Bob	62,771	21,445 D	48.2%	49.1%	49.5%	50.5%
1996	2,142,518	866,268	Kelly, Margaret	1,224,801	Carnahan, Mel*	51,449	358,533 D	40.4%	57.2%	41.4%	58.6%
1992	2,343,999	968,574	Webster, William L.	1,375,425	Carnahan, Mel		406,851 D	41.3%	58.7%	41.3%	58.7%
1988	2,085,928	1,339,531	Ashcroft, John*	724,919	Hearnes, Betty C.	21,478	614,612 R	64.2%	34.8%	64.9%	35.1%
1984	2,108,210	1,194,506	Ashcroft, John	913,700	Rothman, Kenneth J.	4	280,806 R	56.7%	43.3%	56.7%	43.3%
1980	2,088,028	1,098,950	Bond, Kit	981,884	Teasdale, Joseph P.*	7,194	117,066 R	52.6%	47.0%	52.8%	47.2%
1976	1,933,575	958,110	Bond, Kit*	971,184	Teasdale, Joseph P.	4,281	13,074 D	49.6%	50.2%	49.7%	50.3%
1972	1,865,683	1,029,451	Bond, Kit	832,751	Dowd, Edward L.	3,481	196,700 R	55.2%	44.6%	55.3%	44.7%
1968	1,764,602	691,797	Roos, Lawrence K.	1,072,805	Hearnes, Warren E.*		381,008 D	39.2%	60.8%	39.2%	60.8%
1964	1,789,600	678,949	Shepley, Ethan A.H.	1,110,651	Hearnes, Warren E.		431,702 D	37.9%	62.1%	37.9%	62.1%
1960	1,887,326	792,131	Farmer, Edward G.	1,095,195	Dalton, John M.		303,064 D	42.0%	58.0%	42.0%	58.0%
1956	1,808,338	866,810	Hocker, Lon	941,528	Blair, James T. Jr.		74,718 D	47.9%	52.1%	47.9%	52.1%
1952	1,870,998	886,270	Elliott, Howard	983,169	Donnelly, Phil M.	1,559	96,899 D	47.4%	52.5%	47.4%	52.6%
1948	1,567,338	670,064	Thompson, Murray E.	893,092	Smith, Forrest	4,182	223,028 D	42.8%	57.0%	42.9%	57.1%

Note: An asterisk (*) denotes incumbent.

POSTWAR VOTE FOR SENATOR

		Republican		Democratic				Percentage			
								Total Vote		Major Vote	
Year	Total Vote	Vote	Candidate	Vote	Candidate	Other Vote	Rep.-Dem. Plurality	Rep.	Dem.	Rep.	Dem.
2018	2,442,289	1,254,927	Hawley, Josh	1,112,935	McCaskill, Claire*	74,427	141,992 R	51.4%	45.6%	53.0%	47.0%
2016	2,802,641	1,378,458	Blunt, Roy*	1,300,200	Kander, Jason	123,983	78,258 R	49.2%	46.4%	51.5%	48.5%
2012	2,725,793	1,066,159	Akin, Todd	1,494,125	McCaskill, Claire*	165,509	427,966 D	39.1%	54.8%	41.6%	58.4%
2010	1,943,899	1,054,160	Blunt, Roy	789,736	Carnahan, Robin	100,003	264,424 R	54.2%	40.6%	57.2%	42.8%
2006	2,128,459	1,006,941	Talent, James M.*	1,055,255	McCaskill, Claire	66,263	48,314 D	47.3%	49.6%	48.8%	51.2%
2004	2,706,402	1,518,089	Bond, Kit*	1,158,261	Farmer, Nancy	30,052	359,828 R	56.1%	42.8%	56.7%	43.3%
2002S**	1,877,620	935,032	Talent, James M.	913,778	Carnahan, Jean*	28,810	21,254 R	49.8%	48.7%	50.6%	49.4%
2000**	2,361,586	1,142,852	Ashcroft, John*	1,191,812	Carnahan, Mel	26,922	48,960 D	48.4%	50.5%	49.0%	51.0%
1998	1,576,857	830,625	Bond, Kit*	690,208	Nixon, Jay W.	56,024	140,417 R	52.7%	43.8%	54.6%	45.4%
1994	1,775,116	1,060,149	Ashcroft, John	633,697	Wheat, Alan	81,270	426,452 R	59.7%	35.7%	62.6%	37.4%
1992	2,354,925	1,221,901	Bond, Kit*	1,057,967	Rothman-Serot, Geri	75,057	163,934 R	51.9%	44.9%	53.6%	46.4%
1988	2,078,875	1,407,416	Danforth, John C.*	660,045	Nixon, Jay W.	11,414	747,371 R	67.7%	31.8%	68.1%	31.9%
1986	1,477,327	777,612	Bond, Kit	699,624	Woods, Harriett	91	77,988 R	52.6%	47.4%	52.6%	47.4%
1982	1,543,521	784,876	Danforth, John C.*	758,629	Woods, Harriett	16	26,247 R	50.8%	49.1%	50.9%	49.1%
1980	2,066,965	985,399	McNary, Gene	1,074,859	Eagleton, Thomas F.*	6,707	89,460 D	47.7%	52.0%	47.8%	52.2%
1976	1,914,777	1,090,067	Danforth, John C.	813,571	Hearnes, Warren E.	11,139	276,496 R	56.9%	42.5%	57.3%	42.7%
1974	1,224,303	480,900	Curtis, Thomas B.	735,433	Eagleton, Thomas F.*	7,970	254,533 D	39.3%	60.1%	39.5%	60.5%
1970	1,283,912	617,903	Danforth, John C.	655,431	Symington, Stuart*	10,578	37,528 D	48.1%	51.0%	48.5%	51.5%
1968	1,737,958	850,544	Curtis, Thomas B.	887,414	Eagleton, Thomas F.		36,870 D	48.9%	51.1%	48.9%	51.1%
1964	1,783,043	596,377	Bradshaw, Jean Paul	1,186,666	Symington, Stuart*		590,289 D	33.4%	66.6%	33.4%	66.6%
1962	1,222,259	555,330	Kemper, Crosby	666,929	Long, Edward V.*		111,599 D	45.4%	54.6%	45.4%	54.6%
1960S**	1,880,232	880,576	Hocker, Lon	999,656	Long, Edward V.		119,080 D	46.8%	53.2%	46.8%	53.2%
1958	1,173,930	393,847	Palmer, Hazel	780,083	Symington, Stuart*		386,236 D	33.5%	66.5%	33.5%	66.5%
1956	1,800,984	785,048	Douglas, Herbert	1,015,936	Hennings, Thomas Carey Jr.*		230,888 D	43.6%	56.4%	43.6%	56.4%
1952	1,868,083	858,170	Kem, James P.*	1,008,523	Symington, Stuart	1,390	150,353 D	45.9%	54.0%	46.0%	54.0%
1950	1,279,631	593,139	Donnell, Forrest C.*	685,732	Hennings, Thomas Carey Jr.	760	92,593 D	46.4%	53.6%	46.4%	53.6%
1946	1,084,100	572,556	Kem, James P.	511,544	Briggs, Frank		61,012 R	52.8%	47.2%	52.8%	47.2%

Note: An asterisk (*) denotes incumbent. **In 2000, the Democratic candidate, Mel Carnahan, was killed in an airplane crash in October but his name remained on the ballot and he won the election in November. Subsequently, his widow, Jean Carnahan, was appointed to fill the seat until an election could be held in 2002 for the remaining four years of the term. The 1960 and 2002 elections were for short terms to fill a vacancy.

MISSOURI

SENATOR 2018

2010 Census Population	County	Total Vote	Republican (Hawley)	Democratic (McCaskill)	Other	Rep.-Dem. Plurality	Percentage: Total Vote Rep.	Percentage: Total Vote Dem.	Percentage: Major Vote Rep.	Percentage: Major Vote Dem.
25,607	ADAIR	8,695	4,939	3,494	262	1,445 R	56.8%	40.2%	58.6%	41.4%
17,291	ANDREW	7,590	4,919	2,372	299	2,547 R	64.8%	31.3%	67.5%	32.5%
5,685	ATCHISON	2,227	1,619	542	66	1,077 R	72.7%	24.3%	74.9%	25.1%
25,529	AUDRAIN	8,731	5,651	2,727	353	2,924 R	64.7%	31.2%	67.5%	32.5%
35,597	BARRY	12,295	9,019	2,822	454	6,197 R	73.4%	23.0%	76.2%	23.8%
12,402	BARTON	5,021	4,064	783	174	3,281 R	80.9%	15.6%	83.8%	16.2%
17,049	BATES	6,685	4,467	1,906	312	2,561 R	66.8%	28.5%	70.1%	29.9%
19,056	BENTON	8,354	5,685	2,318	351	3,367 R	68.1%	27.7%	71.0%	29.0%
12,363	BOLLINGER	4,822	3,846	886	90	2,960 R	79.8%	18.4%	81.3%	18.7%
162,642	BOONE	75,192	30,710	42,315	2,167	11,605 D	40.8%	56.3%	42.1%	57.9%
89,201	BUCHANAN	30,117	15,912	12,889	1,316	3,023 R	52.8%	42.8%	55.2%	44.8%
42,794	BUTLER	14,028	10,727	2,961	340	7,766 R	76.5%	21.1%	78.4%	21.6%
9,424	CALDWELL	3,778	2,558	1,022	198	1,536 R	67.7%	27.1%	71.5%	28.5%
44,332	CALLAWAY	17,075	10,661	5,705	709	4,956 R	62.4%	33.4%	65.1%	34.9%
44,002	CAMDEN	20,010	13,995	5,425	590	8,570 R	69.9%	27.1%	72.1%	27.9%
75,674	CAPE GIRARDEAU	32,503	22,964	8,886	653	14,078 R	70.7%	27.3%	72.1%	27.9%
9,295	CARROLL	3,744	2,761	870	113	1,891 R	73.7%	23.2%	76.0%	24.0%
6,265	CARTER	2,352	1,799	489	64	1,310 R	76.5%	20.8%	78.6%	21.4%
99,478	CASS	43,816	25,861	16,340	1,615	9,521 R	59.0%	37.3%	61.3%	38.7%
13,982	CEDAR	5,467	4,092	1,181	194	2,911 R	74.8%	21.6%	77.6%	22.4%
7,831	CHARITON	3,362	2,195	1,043	124	1,152 R	65.3%	31.0%	67.8%	32.2%
77,422	CHRISTIAN	36,384	25,384	9,882	1,118	15,502 R	69.8%	27.2%	72.0%	28.0%
7,139	CLARK	2,691	1,903	692	96	1,211 R	70.7%	25.7%	73.3%	26.7%
221,939	CLAY	97,196	45,947	48,096	3,153	2,149 D	47.3%	49.5%	48.9%	51.1%
20,743	CLINTON	8,641	5,320	2,956	365	2,364 R	61.6%	34.2%	64.3%	35.7%
75,990	COLE	33,442	20,738	11,718	986	9,020 R	62.0%	35.0%	63.9%	36.1%
17,601	COOPER	7,042	4,618	2,195	229	2,423 R	65.6%	31.2%	67.8%	32.2%
24,696	CRAWFORD	8,544	5,867	2,361	316	3,506 R	68.7%	27.6%	71.3%	28.7%
7,883	DADE	3,371	2,533	718	120	1,815 R	75.1%	21.3%	77.9%	22.1%
16,777	DALLAS	6,493	4,682	1,594	217	3,088 R	72.1%	24.5%	74.6%	25.4%
8,433	DAVIESS	3,018	2,074	820	124	1,254 R	68.7%	27.2%	71.7%	28.3%
12,892	DEKALB	3,771	2,584	1,011	176	1,573 R	68.5%	26.8%	71.9%	28.1%
15,657	DENT	6,020	4,541	1,250	229	3,291 R	75.4%	20.8%	78.4%	21.6%
13,684	DOUGLAS	5,588	4,334	1,099	155	3,235 R	77.6%	19.7%	79.8%	20.2%
31,953	DUNKLIN	7,977	5,802	1,988	187	3,814 R	72.7%	24.9%	74.5%	25.5%
101,492	FRANKLIN	42,931	25,651	15,642	1,638	10,009 R	59.7%	36.4%	62.1%	37.9%
15,222	GASCONADE	6,371	4,351	1,799	221	2,552 R	68.3%	28.2%	70.7%	29.3%
6,738	GENTRY	2,547	1,689	734	124	955 R	66.3%	28.8%	69.7%	30.3%
275,174	GREENE	116,145	63,977	47,992	4,176	15,985 R	55.1%	41.3%	57.1%	42.9%
10,261	GRUNDY	3,634	2,641	871	122	1,770 R	72.7%	24.0%	75.2%	24.8%
8,957	HARRISON	2,876	2,155	611	110	1,544 R	74.9%	21.2%	77.9%	22.1%
22,272	HENRY	8,624	5,517	2,769	338	2,748 R	64.0%	32.1%	66.6%	33.4%
9,627	HICKORY	4,131	2,753	1,227	151	1,526 R	66.6%	29.7%	69.2%	30.8%
4,912	HOLT	1,913	1,457	398	58	1,059 R	76.2%	20.8%	78.5%	21.5%
10,144	HOWARD	4,193	2,629	1,403	161	1,226 R	62.7%	33.5%	65.2%	34.8%
40,400	HOWELL	14,582	10,966	3,195	421	7,771 R	75.2%	21.9%	77.4%	22.6%
10,630	IRON	3,574	2,236	1,231	107	1,005 R	62.6%	34.4%	64.5%	35.5%
674,158	JACKSON	151,029	72,004	74,073	4,952	2,069 D	47.7%	49.0%	49.3%	50.7%
117,404	JASPER	40,388	27,743	10,745	1,900	16,998 R	68.7%	26.6%	72.1%	27.9%
218,733	JEFFERSON	90,447	49,142	37,915	3,390	11,227 R	54.3%	41.9%	56.4%	43.6%
52,595	JOHNSON	17,724	10,465	6,476	783	3,989 R	59.0%	36.5%	61.8%	38.2%
	KANSAS CITY	113,185	20,739	89,944	2,502	69,205 D	18.3%	79.5%	18.7%	81.3%
4,131	KNOX	1,578	1,097	409	72	688 R	69.5%	25.9%	72.8%	27.2%
35,571	LACLEDE	13,515	10,125	2,971	419	7,154 R	74.9%	22.0%	77.3%	22.7%
33,381	LAFAYETTE	13,421	8,429	4,506	486	3,923 R	62.8%	33.6%	65.2%	34.8%
38,634	LAWRENCE	14,034	10,311	3,188	535	7,123 R	73.5%	22.7%	76.4%	23.6%
10,211	LEWIS	3,551	2,307	872	372	1,435 R	65.0%	24.6%	72.6%	27.4%
52,566	LINCOLN	21,502	13,140	7,391	971	5,749 R	61.1%	34.4%	64.0%	36.0%
12,761	LINN	4,660	3,066	1,412	182	1,654 R	65.8%	30.3%	68.5%	31.5%
15,195	LIVINGSTON	5,188	3,565	1,445	178	2,120 R	68.7%	27.9%	71.2%	28.8%

MISSOURI

SENATOR 2018

2010 Census Population	County	Total Vote	Republican (Hawley)	Democratic (McCaskill)	Other	Rep.-Dem. Plurality	Percentage Total Vote Rep.	Percentage Total Vote Dem.	Percentage Major Vote Rep.	Percentage Major Vote Dem.
15,566	MACON	6,591	4,618	1,781	192	2,837 R	70.1%	27.0%	72.2%	27.8%
12,226	MADISON	4,442	3,119	1,166	157	1,953 R	70.2%	26.2%	72.8%	27.2%
9,176	MARIES	3,937	2,848	966	123	1,882 R	72.3%	24.5%	74.7%	25.3%
28,781	MARION	10,737	7,325	3,029	383	4,296 R	68.2%	28.2%	70.7%	29.3%
23,083	MCDONALD	6,572	5,062	1,217	293	3,845 R	77.0%	18.5%	80.6%	19.4%
3,785	MERCER	1,368	1,102	223	43	879 R	80.6%	16.3%	83.2%	16.8%
24,748	MILLER	9,898	7,513	2,097	288	5,416 R	75.9%	21.2%	78.2%	21.8%
14,358	MISSISSIPPI	3,820	2,516	1,193	111	1,323 R	65.9%	31.2%	67.8%	32.2%
15,607	MONITEAU	5,957	4,297	1,462	198	2,835 R	72.1%	24.5%	74.6%	25.4%
8,840	MONROE	3,714	2,559	1,017	138	1,542 R	68.9%	27.4%	71.6%	28.4%
12,236	MONTGOMERY	4,720	3,188	1,363	169	1,825 R	67.5%	28.9%	70.1%	29.9%
20,565	MORGAN	7,866	5,553	2,013	300	3,540 R	70.6%	25.6%	73.4%	26.6%
18,956	NEW MADRID	5,742	3,967	1,663	112	2,304 R	69.1%	29.0%	70.5%	29.5%
58,114	NEWTON	22,571	16,550	4,985	1,036	11,565 R	73.3%	22.1%	76.9%	23.1%
23,370	NODAWAY	7,697	4,661	2,712	324	1,949 R	60.6%	35.2%	63.2%	36.8%
10,881	OREGON	3,822	2,738	964	120	1,774 R	71.6%	25.2%	74.0%	26.0%
13,878	OSAGE	6,033	4,626	1,255	152	3,371 R	76.7%	20.8%	78.7%	21.3%
9,723	OZARK	4,039	3,000	915	124	2,085 R	74.3%	22.7%	76.6%	23.4%
18,296	PEMISCOT	4,532	2,968	1,458	106	1,510 R	65.5%	32.2%	67.1%	32.9%
18,971	PERRY	7,283	5,245	1,854	184	3,391 R	72.0%	25.5%	73.9%	26.1%
42,201	PETTIS	15,102	10,063	4,452	587	5,611 R	66.6%	29.5%	69.3%	30.7%
45,156	PHELPS	16,072	10,124	5,363	585	4,761 R	63.0%	33.4%	65.4%	34.6%
18,516	PIKE	6,299	3,909	2,127	263	1,782 R	62.1%	33.8%	64.8%	35.2%
89,322	PLATTE	44,464	21,618	21,477	1,369	141 R	48.6%	48.3%	50.2%	49.8%
31,137	POLK	11,725	8,268	3,028	429	5,240 R	70.5%	25.8%	73.2%	26.8%
52,274	PULASKI	10,813	7,324	3,065	424	4,259 R	67.7%	28.3%	70.5%	29.5%
4,979	PUTNAM	1,910	1,508	357	45	1,151 R	79.0%	18.7%	80.9%	19.1%
10,167	RALLS	4,406	3,095	1,192	119	1,903 R	70.2%	27.1%	72.2%	27.8%
25,414	RANDOLPH	8,903	5,986	2,555	362	3,431 R	67.2%	28.7%	70.1%	29.9%
23,494	RAY	9,466	5,479	3,522	465	1,957 R	57.9%	37.2%	60.9%	39.1%
6,696	REYNOLDS	2,535	1,795	673	67	1,122 R	70.8%	26.5%	72.7%	27.3%
14,100	RIPLEY	4,467	3,384	941	142	2,443 R	75.8%	21.1%	78.2%	21.8%
23,370	SALINE	7,842	4,570	2,897	375	1,673 R	58.3%	36.9%	61.2%	38.8%
4,431	SCHUYLER	1,615	1,149	398	68	751 R	71.1%	24.6%	74.3%	25.7%
4,843	SCOTLAND	1,616	1,163	399	54	764 R	72.0%	24.7%	74.5%	25.5%
39,191	SCOTT	14,412	10,594	3,568	250	7,026 R	73.5%	24.8%	74.8%	25.2%
8,441	SHANNON	3,233	2,254	896	83	1,358 R	69.7%	27.7%	71.6%	28.4%
6,373	SHELBY	2,736	1,935	709	92	1,226 R	70.7%	25.9%	73.2%	26.8%
360,485	ST. CHARLES	176,105	93,172	77,973	4,960	15,199 R	52.9%	44.3%	54.4%	45.6%
9,805	ST. CLAIR	4,108	2,772	1,149	187	1,623 R	67.5%	28.0%	70.7%	29.3%
65,359	ST. FRANCOIS	21,827	13,111	7,770	946	5,341 R	60.1%	35.6%	62.8%	37.2%
998,954	ST. LOUIS	457,609	163,972	284,015	9,622	120,043 D	35.8%	62.1%	36.6%	63.4%
319,294	ST. LOUIS CITY	115,146	15,937	96,828	2,381	80,891 D	13.8%	84.1%	14.1%	85.9%
18,145	STE. GENEVIEVE	7,518	3,903	3,348	267	555 R	51.9%	44.5%	53.8%	46.2%
29,968	STODDARD	10,874	8,683	1,970	221	6,713 R	79.9%	18.1%	81.5%	18.5%
32,202	STONE	14,808	11,128	3,314	366	7,814 R	75.1%	22.4%	77.1%	22.9%
6,714	SULLIVAN	1,974	1,439	482	53	957 R	72.9%	24.4%	74.9%	25.1%
51,675	TANEY	20,632	15,137	4,908	587	10,229 R	73.4%	23.8%	75.5%	24.5%
26,008	TEXAS	9,323	6,989	2,062	272	4,927 R	75.0%	22.1%	77.2%	22.8%
21,159	VERNON	7,190	5,083	1,782	325	3,301 R	70.7%	24.8%	74.0%	26.0%
32,513	WARREN	14,011	8,519	4,945	547	3,574 R	60.8%	35.3%	63.3%	36.7%
25,195	WASHINGTON	7,341	4,646	2,432	263	2,214 R	63.3%	33.1%	65.6%	34.4%
13,521	WAYNE	4,737	3,567	1,036	134	2,531 R	75.3%	21.9%	77.5%	22.5%
36,202	WEBSTER	14,572	10,338	3,783	451	6,555 R	70.9%	26.0%	73.2%	26.8%
2,171	WORTH	923	660	238	25	422 R	71.5%	25.8%	73.5%	26.5%
18,815	WRIGHT	6,849	5,272	1,373	204	3,899 R	77.0%	20.0%	79.3%	20.7%
5,988,927	*TOTAL*	*2,442,289*	*1,254,927*	*1,112,935*	*74,427*	*141,992 R*	*51.4%*	*45.6%*	*53.0%*	*47.0%*

Note: Although Kansas City is part of Jackson County, its results are listed separately.

MISSOURI

HOUSE OF REPRESENTATIVES

			Republican		Democratic				Percentage			
									Total Vote		Major Vote	
CD	Year	Total Vote	Vote	Candidate	Vote	Candidate	Other Vote	Rep.-Dem. Plurality	Rep.	Dem.	Rep.	Dem.
1	2018	274,375	45,867	VROMAN, ROBERT	219,781	CLAY, WILLIAM LACY JR.*	8,727	173,914 D	16.7%	80.1%	17.3%	82.7%
1	2016	314,024	62,714	BAILEY, STEVEN G.	236,993	CLAY, WILLIAM LACY JR.*	14,317	174,279 D	20.0%	75.5%	20.9%	79.1%
1	2014	163,494	35,273	ELDER, DANIEL J.	119,315	CLAY, WILLIAM LACY JR.*	8,906	84,042 D	21.6%	73.0%	22.8%	77.2%
1	2012	340,583	60,832	HAMLIN, ROBYN	267,927	CLAY, WILLIAM LACY JR.*	11,824	207,095 D	17.9%	78.7%	18.5%	81.5%
2	2018	376,066	192,477	WAGNER, ANN*	177,611	VANOSTRAN, CORT	5,978	14,866 R	51.2%	47.2%	52.0%	48.0%
2	2016	413,296	241,954	WAGNER, ANN*	155,689	OTTO, BILL	15,653	86,265 R	58.5%	37.7%	60.8%	39.2%
2	2014	231,117	148,191	WAGNER, ANN*	75,384	LIEBER, ARTHUR	7,542	72,807 R	64.1%	32.6%	66.3%	33.7%
2	2012	394,448	236,971	WAGNER, ANN	146,272	KOENEN, GLENN	11,205	90,699 R	60.1%	37.1%	61.8%	38.2%
3	2018	324,608	211,243	LUETKEMEYER, BLAINE*	106,589	GEPPERT, KATY	6,776	104,654 R	65.1%	32.8%	66.5%	33.5%
3	2016	368,333	249,865	LUETKEMEYER, BLAINE*	102,891	MILLER, KEVIN	15,577	146,974 R	67.8%	27.9%	70.8%	29.2%
3	2014	191,620	130,940	LUETKEMEYER, BLAINE*	52,021	DENTON, COURTNEY	8,659	78,919 R	68.3%	27.1%	71.6%	28.4%
3	2012	338,385	214,843	LUETKEMEYER, BLAINE*	111,189	MAYER, ERIC C.	12,353	103,654 R	63.5%	32.9%	65.9%	34.1%
4	2018	293,316	190,138	HARTZLER, VICKY*	95,968	HOAGENSON, RENEE	7,210	94,170 R	64.8%	32.7%	66.5%	33.5%
4	2016	332,234	225,348	HARTZLER, VICKY*	92,510	CHRISTENSEN, GORDON	14,376	132,838 R	67.8%	27.8%	70.9%	29.1%
4	2014	176,286	120,014	HARTZLER, VICKY*	46,464	IRVIN, NATE A.	9,808	73,550 R	68.1%	26.4%	72.1%	27.9%
4	2012	318,723	192,237	HARTZLER, VICKY*	113,120	HENSLEY, TERESA	13,366	79,117 R	60.3%	35.5%	63.0%	37.0%
5	2018	283,785	101,069	TURK, JACOB	175,019	CLEAVER, EMANUEL II*	7,697	73,950 D	35.6%	61.7%	36.6%	63.4%
5	2016	324,270	123,771	TURK, JACOB	190,766	CLEAVER, EMANUEL II*	9,733	66,995 D	38.2%	58.8%	39.4%	60.6%
5	2014	153,635	69,071	TURK, JACOB	79,256	CLEAVER, EMANUEL II*	5,308	10,185 D	45.0%	51.6%	46.6%	53.4%
5	2012	330,942	122,149	TURK, JACOB	200,290	CLEAVER, EMANUEL II*	8,503	78,141 D	36.9%	60.5%	37.9%	62.1%
6	2018	305,409	199,796	GRAVES, SAMUEL B. JR.*	97,660	MARTIN, HENRY	7,953	102,136 R	65.4%	32.0%	67.2%	32.8%
6	2016	350,444	238,388	GRAVES, SAMUEL B. JR.*	99,692	BLACKWELL, DAVID M.	12,364	138,696 R	68.0%	28.4%	70.5%	29.5%
6	2014	186,970	124,616	GRAVES, SAMUEL B. JR.*	55,157	HEDGE, W.A. "BILL"	7,197	69,459 R	66.7%	29.5%	69.3%	30.7%
6	2012	333,688	216,906	GRAVES, SAMUEL B. JR.*	108,503	YARBER, KYLE	8,279	108,403 R	65.0%	32.5%	66.7%	33.3%
7	2018	296,455	196,343	LONG, BILLY*	89,190	SCHOOLCRAFT, JAMIE	10,922	107,153 R	66.2%	30.1%	68.8%	31.2%
7	2016	338,607	228,692	LONG, BILLY*	92,756	WILLIAMS, GENEVIEVE	17,159	135,936 R	67.5%	27.4%	71.1%	28.9%
7	2014	163,957	104,054	LONG, BILLY*	47,282	EVANS, JIM	12,621	56,772 R	63.5%	28.8%	68.8%	31.2%
7	2012	318,740	203,565	LONG, BILLY*	98,498	EVANS, JIM	16,677	105,067 R	63.9%	30.9%	67.4%	32.6%
8	2018	264,399	194,042	SMITH, JASON*	66,151	ELLIS, KATHY	4,206	127,891 R	73.4%	25.0%	74.6%	25.4%
8	2016	308,871	229,792	SMITH, JASON*	70,009	COWELL, DAVE	9,070	159,783 R	74.4%	22.7%	76.6%	23.4%
8	2014	159,224	106,124	SMITH, JASON*	38,721	STOCKER, BARBARA HAMILL	14,379	67,403 R	66.7%	24.3%	73.3%	26.7%
8	2012	300,391	216,083	EMERSON, JO ANN*	73,755	RUSHIN, JACK	10,553	142,328 R	71.9%	24.6%	74.6%	25.4%
TOTAL	*2018*	*2,418,413*	*1,330,975*		*1,027,969*		*59,469*	*303,006 R*	*55.0%*	*42.5%*	*56.4%*	*43.6%*
TOTAL	*2016*	*2,750,079*	*1,600,524*		*1,041,306*		*108,249*	*559,218 R*	*58.2%*	*37.9%*	*60.6%*	*39.4%*
TOTAL	*2014*	*1,426,303*	*838,283*		*513,600*		*74,420*	*324,683 R*	*58.8%*	*36.0%*	*62.0%*	*38.0%*
TOTAL	*2012*	*2,675,900*	*1,463,586*		*1,119,554*		*92,760*	*344,032 R*	*54.7%*	*41.8%*	*56.7%*	*43.3%*

Note: An asterisk (*) denotes incumbent.

MISSOURI

GENERAL AND PRIMARY ELECTIONS

2018 GENERAL ELECTIONS: OTHER VOTES

Senate Other vote was 34,398 Independent (Craig O'Dear), 27,316 Libertarian (Japheth Campbell), 12,706 Green (Jo Crain), 4 Write-in (Gina Bufe), 2 Write-in (Martin Lindstedt), 1 Write-in (Rodney Stock)

House Other vote was:

CD 1	8,727 Libertarian (Robb Cunningham)
CD 2	4,229 Libertarian (Larry Kirk), 1,740 Green (David Arnold), 9 Write-in (Ken Newhouse)
CD 3	6,776 Libertarian (Donald Stolle)
CD 4	7,210 Libertarian (Mark Bliss)
CD 5	4,725 Libertarian (Alexander Howell), 2,091 Green (Maurice Copeland), 876 Constitution (E. Fredland), 5 Write-in (Patrick Marshall)
CD 6	7,953 Libertarian (Dan Hogan)
CD 7	10,920 Libertarian (Benjamin Brixey), 2 Write-in (Shawn Deines)
CD 8	4,206 Libertarian (Jonathan Shell)

2018 PRIMARY ELECTIONS: SUPPLEMENTARY INFORMATION

Primary August 7, 2018 **Registration** (as of August 1, 2018) 4,143,106 No Party Registration

Primary Type Open—Any registered voter could participate in the party primary of his or her choice.

	REPUBLICAN PRIMARIES			DEMOCRATIC PRIMARIES		
Senator	Hawley, Josh	389,878	58.6%	McCaskill, Claire*	501,872	82.6%
	Monetti, Antonio "Tony"	64,834	9.8%	Wright, Carla "Coffee"	41,126	6.8%
	Petersen, Austin	54,916	8.3%	Hogan, John	15,984	2.6%
	Nichols, Kristi	49,640	7.5%	Faust, David	15,958	2.6%
	Smith, Christina	35,024	5.3%	Earl, Angelica	15,500	2.6%
	Patterson, Ken	19,579	2.9%	Gonzalez, Travis	9,480	1.6%
	Pfeifer, Peter	16,594	2.5%	Steinman, Leonard II	7,657	1.3%
	Sykes, Courtland	13,870	2.1%			
	Ryman, Fred	8,781	1.3%			
	Hagg, Brian	6,871	1.0%			
	Krembs, Bradley	4,902	0.7%			
	TOTAL	*664,889*		*TOTAL*	*607,577*	
Congressional District 1	Vroman, Robert	5,101	34.5%	Clay, William Lacy Jr.*	81,812	56.7%
	Van Deventer, Ed	4,876	32.9%	Bush, Cori	53,250	36.9%
	Lombardi-Olive, Camille	4,829	32.6%	Shipp, Joshua	4,974	3.4%
				Davidson, DeMarco	4,243	2.9%
	TOTAL	*14,806*		*TOTAL*	*144,279*	
Congressional District 2	Wagner, Ann*	72,692	89.9%	VanOstran, Cort	45,568	41.6%
	Sachs, Noga	8,166	10.1%	Osmack, Mark	27,616	25.2%
				Haas, Bill	21,331	19.5%
				Messmer, John	10,586	9.7%
				Hazel, Robert	4,358	4.0%
	TOTAL	*80,858*		*TOTAL*	*109,459*	
Congressional District 3	Luetkemeyer, Blaine*	95,449	79.9%	Geppert, Katy	55,847	100.0%
	Bicknell, Chadwick	24,019	20.1%			
	TOTAL	*119,468*		*TOTAL*	*55,847*	
Congressional District 4	Hartzler, Vicky*	75,274	73.7%	Hoagenson, Renee	24,150	51.9%
	Webb, John	26,813	26.3%	Thompson, Hallie	22,413	48.1%
	TOTAL	*102,087*		*TOTAL*	*46,563*	

MISSOURI

GENERAL AND PRIMARY ELECTIONS

	REPUBLICAN PRIMARIES			DEMOCRATIC PRIMARIES		
Congressional District 5	Turk, Jacob	35,901	75.1%	Cleaver, Emanuel II*	87,584	100.0%
	Cambers, Kress	8,427	17.6%			
	Oaks, Richonda	3,476	7.3%			
	TOTAL	*47,804*		*TOTAL*	*87,584*	
Congressional District 6	Graves, Samuel B. Jr.*	89,675	100.0%	Martin, Henry	21,691	41.5%
				Apple, Winston	16,094	30.8%
				Andres, Ed	14,466	27.7%
	TOTAL	*89,675*		*TOTAL*	*52,251*	
Congressional District 7	Long, Billy*	68,826	65.1%	Schoolcraft, Jamie	12,609	40.6%
	Evans, Jim	18,470	17.5%	Hatfield, Kenneth	6,906	22.3%
	Norris, Lance	10,922	10.3%	de la Torre, John Farmer	6,732	21.7%
	Holcomb, Benjamin	7,451	7.1%	Jennings, Vincent	4,781	15.4%
	TOTAL	*105,669*		*TOTAL*	*31,028*	
Congressional District 8	Smith, Jason*	91,840	100.0%	Ellis, Kathy	33,823	100.0%
	TOTAL	*91,840*		*TOTAL*	*33,823*	

Note: An asterisk (*) denotes incumbent.

MONTANA

One member At Large

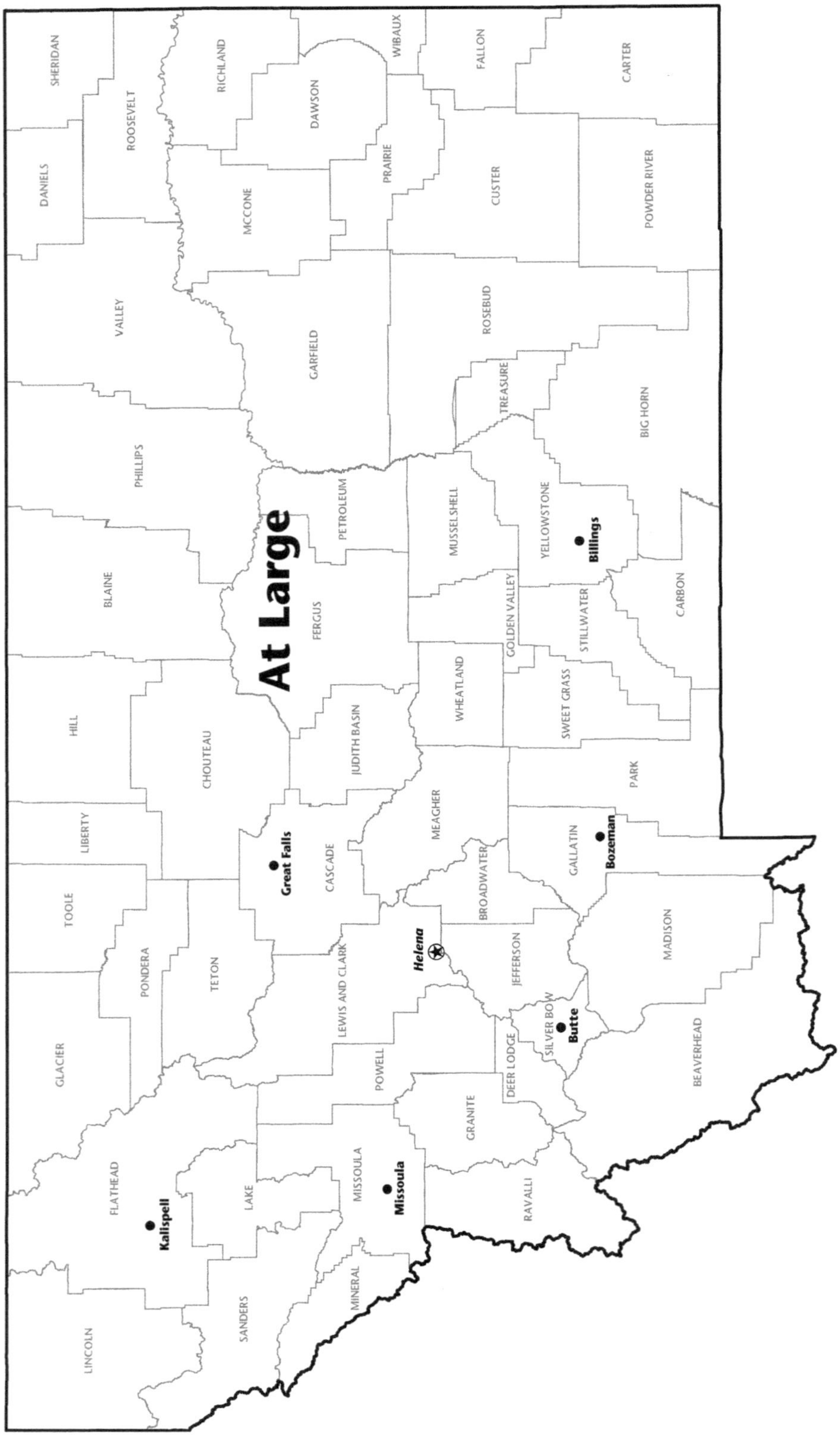

MONTANA

GOVERNOR

Steve Bullock (D). Re-elected 2016 to a four-year term. Previously elected 2012.

SENATORS (1 Democrat, 1 Republican)

Steve Daines (R). Elected 2014 to a six-year term.

Jon Tester (D). Re-elected 2018 to a six-year term. Previously elected 2012, 2006.

REPRESENTATIVE (1 Republican)

At Large. Greg Gianforte (R)

POSTWAR VOTE FOR PRESIDENT

		Republican		Democratic				Percentage			
								Total Vote		Major Vote	
Year	Total Vote	Vote	Candidate	Vote	Candidate	Other Vote	Rep.-Dem. Plurality	Rep.	Dem.	Rep.	Dem.
2016**	497,147	279,240	Trump, Donald J.	177,709	Clinton, Hillary Rodham	40,198	101,531 R	56.2%	35.7%	61.1%	38.9%
2012	484,048	267,928	Romney, W. Mitt	201,839	Obama, Barack H.*	14,281	66,089 R	55.4%	41.7%	57.0%	43.0%
2008	490,302	242,763	McCain, John S. III	231,667	Obama, Barack H.	15,872	11,096 R	49.5%	47.2%	51.2%	48.8%
2004	450,445	266,063	Bush, George W.*	173,710	Kerry, John F.	10,672	92,353 R	59.1%	38.6%	60.5%	39.5%
2000**	410,997	240,178	Bush, George W.	137,126	Gore, Albert Jr.	33,693	103,052 R	58.4%	33.4%	63.7%	36.3%
1996**	407,261	179,652	Dole, Robert "Bob"	167,922	Clinton, Bill*	59,687	11,730 R	44.1%	41.2%	51.7%	48.3%
1992**	410,611	144,207	Bush, George H.*	154,507	Clinton, Bill	111,897	10,300 D	35.1%	37.6%	48.3%	51.7%
1988	365,674	190,412	Bush, George H.	168,936	Dukakis, Michael S.	6,326	21,476 R	52.1%	46.2%	53.0%	47.0%
1984	384,377	232,450	Reagan, Ronald*	146,742	Mondale, Walter F.	5,185	85,708 R	60.5%	38.2%	61.3%	38.7%
1980**	363,952	206,814	Reagan, Ronald	118,032	Carter, Jimmy*	39,106	88,782 R	56.8%	32.4%	63.7%	36.3%
1976	328,734	173,703	Ford, Gerald R.*	149,259	Carter, Jimmy	5,772	24,444 R	52.8%	45.4%	53.8%	46.2%
1972	317,603	183,976	Nixon, Richard M.*	120,197	McGovern, George S.	13,430	63,779 R	57.9%	37.8%	60.5%	39.5%
1968**	274,404	138,835	Nixon, Richard M.	114,117	Humphrey, Hubert Horatio Jr.	21,452	24,718 R	50.6%	41.6%	54.9%	45.1%
1964	278,628	113,032	Goldwater, Barry M. Sr.	164,246	Johnson, Lyndon B.*	1,350	51,214 D	40.6%	58.9%	40.8%	59.2%
1960	277,579	141,841	Nixon, Richard M.	134,891	Kennedy, John F.	847	6,950 R	51.1%	48.6%	51.3%	48.7%
1956	271,171	154,933	Eisenhower, Dwight D.*	116,238	Stevenson, Adlai E. II		38,695 R	57.1%	42.9%	57.1%	42.9%
1952	265,037	157,394	Eisenhower, Dwight D.	106,213	Stevenson, Adlai E. II	1,430	51,181 R	59.4%	40.1%	59.7%	40.3%
1948	224,278	96,770	Dewey, Thomas E.	119,071	Truman, Harry S.*	8,437	22,301 D	43.1%	53.1%	44.8%	55.2%

Note: An asterisk (*) denotes incumbent. **In past elections, the other vote included: 2016 - 28,037 Libertarian (Gary Johnson); 2000 - 24,437 Green (Ralph Nader); 1996 - 55,229 Reform (Ross Perot); 1992 - 107,225 Independent (Perot); 1980 - 29,281 Independent (John Anderson); 1968 - 20,015 American Independent (George Wallace).

MONTANA

POSTWAR VOTE FOR GOVERNOR

		Republican		Democratic				Percentage			
								Total Vote		Major Vote	
Year	Total Vote	Vote	Candidate	Vote	Candidate	Other Vote	Rep.-Dem. Plurality	Rep.	Dem.	Rep.	Dem.
2016	509,360	236,115	Gianforte, Greg	255,933	Bullock, Steve*	17,312	19,818 D	46.4%	50.2%	48.0%	52.0%
2012	483,489	228,879	Hill, Rick	236,450	Bullock, Steve	18,160	7,571 D	47.3%	48.9%	49.2%	50.8%
2008	486,734	158,268	Brown, Roy	318,670	Schweitzer, Brian*	9,796	160,402 D	32.5%	65.5%	33.2%	66.8%
2004	446,146	205,313	Brown, Bob	225,016	Schweitzer, Brian	15,817	19,703 D	46.0%	50.4%	47.7%	52.3%
2000	410,192	209,135	Martz, Judy	193,131	O'Keefe, Mark	7,926	16,004 R	51.0%	47.1%	52.0%	48.0%
1996**	405,175	320,768	Racicot, Marc*	84,407	Jacobson, Judy		236,361 R	79.2%	20.8%	79.2%	20.8%
1992	407,842	209,401	Racicot, Marc	198,421	Bradley, Dorothy	20	10,980 R	51.3%	48.7%	51.3%	48.7%
1988	367,021	190,604	Stephens, Stan	169,313	Judge, Thomas L.	7,104	21,291 R	51.9%	46.1%	53.0%	47.0%
1984	378,970	100,070	Goodover, Pat M.	266,578	Schwinden, Ted*	12,322	166,508 D	26.4%	70.3%	27.3%	72.7%
1980	360,470	160,896	Ramirez, Jack	199,574	Schwinden, Ted		38,678 D	44.6%	55.4%	44.6%	55.4%
1976	316,720	115,848	Woodahi, Robert	195,420	Judge, Thomas L.*	5,452	79,572 D	36.6%	61.7%	37.2%	62.8%
1972	318,754	146,231	Smith, Ed	172,523	Judge, Thomas L.		26,292 D	45.9%	54.1%	45.9%	54.1%
1968	278,112	116,432	Babcock, Tim M.*	150,481	Anderson, Forrest H.	11,199	34,049 D	41.9%	54.1%	43.6%	56.4%
1964	280,975	144,113	Babcock, Tim M.	136,862	Renne, Roland		7,251 R	51.3%	48.7%	51.3%	48.7%
1960	279,881	154,230	Nutter, Donald G.	125,651	Cannon, Paul		28,579 R	55.1%	44.9%	55.1%	44.9%
1956	270,366	138,878	Aronson, John Hugo*	131,488	Olsen, Arnold		7,390 R	51.4%	48.6%	51.4%	48.6%
1952	263,792	134,423	Aronson, John Hugo	129,369	Bonner, John W.*		5,054 R	51.0%	49.0%	51.0%	49.0%
1948	222,964	97,792	Ford, Samuel C.*	124,267	Bonner, John W.	905	26,475 D	43.9%	55.7%	44.0%	56.0%

Note: An asterisk (*) denotes incumbent. **In 1996 the Democratic vote total included 7,936 absentee ballots cast for the party's initial gubernatorial candidate, Chet Blaylock, who died that October.

POSTWAR VOTE FOR SENATOR

		Republican		Democratic				Percentage			
								Total Vote		Major Vote	
Year	Total Vote	Vote	Candidate	Vote	Candidate	Other Vote	Rep.-Dem. Plurality	Rep.	Dem.	Rep.	Dem.
2018	504,384	235,963	Rosendale, Matt	253,876	Tester, Jon*	14,545	17,913 D	46.8%	50.3%	48.2%	51.8%
2014	369,826	213,709	Daines, Steve	148,184	Curtis, Amanda	7,933	65,525 R	57.8%	40.1%	59.1%	40.9%
2012	486,066	218,051	Rehberg, Dennis "Denny"	236,123	Tester, Jon*	31,892	18,072 D	44.9%	48.6%	48.0%	52.0%
2008	477,658	129,369	Kelleher, Bob	348,289	Baucus, Max S.*		218,920 D	27.1%	72.9%	27.1%	72.9%
2006	406,505	196,283	Burns, Conrad*	199,845	Tester, Jon	10,377	3,562 D	48.3%	49.2%	49.6%	50.4%
2002	326,537	103,611	Taylor, Mike	204,853	Baucus, Max S.*	18,073	101,242 D	31.7%	62.7%	33.6%	66.4%
2000	411,601	208,082	Burns, Conrad*	194,430	Schweitzer, Brian	9,089	13,652 R	50.6%	47.2%	51.7%	48.3%
1996	407,490	182,111	Rehberg, Dennis "Denny"	201,935	Baucus, Max S.*	23,444	19,824 D	44.7%	49.6%	47.4%	52.6%
1994	350,409	218,542	Burns, Conrad*	131,845	Mudd, Jack	22	86,697 R	62.4%	37.6%	62.4%	37.6%
1990	319,336	93,836	Kolstad, Allen C.	217,563	Baucus, Max S.*	7,937	123,727 D	29.4%	68.1%	30.1%	69.9%
1988	365,254	189,445	Burns, Conrad	175,809	Melcher, John*		13,636 R	51.9%	48.1%	51.9%	48.1%
1984	379,155	154,308	Cozzens, Chuck	215,704	Baucus, Max S.*	9,143	61,396 D	40.7%	56.9%	41.7%	58.3%
1982	321,062	133,789	Williams, Larry	174,861	Melcher, John*	12,412	41,072 D	41.7%	54.5%	43.3%	56.7%
1978	287,942	127,589	Williams, Larry	160,353	Baucus, Max S.		32,764 D	44.3%	55.7%	44.3%	55.7%
1976	321,445	115,213	Burger, Stanley C.	206,232	Melcher, John		91,019 D	35.8%	64.2%	35.8%	64.2%
1972	314,925	151,316	Hibbard, Henry S.	163,609	Metcalf, Lee*		12,293 D	48.0%	52.0%	48.0%	52.0%
1970	247,869	97,809	Wallace, Harold E.	150,060	Mansfield, Mike*		52,251 D	39.5%	60.5%	39.5%	60.5%
1966	259,863	121,697	Babcock, Tim M.	138,166	Metcalf, Lee*		16,469 D	46.8%	53.2%	46.8%	53.2%
1964	280,010	99,367	Blewett, Alex	180,643	Mansfield, Mike*		81,276 D	35.5%	64.5%	35.5%	64.5%
1960	276,612	136,281	Fjare, Orvin B.	140,331	Metcalf, Lee		4,050 D	49.3%	50.7%	49.3%	50.7%
1958	229,483	54,573	Welch, Lou W.	174,910	Mansfield, Mike*		120,337 D	23.8%	76.2%	23.8%	76.2%
1954	227,454	112,863	D'Ewart, Wesley A.	114,591	Murray, James E.*		1,728 D	49.6%	50.4%	49.6%	50.4%
1952	262,297	127,360	Ecton, Zales N.*	133,109	Mansfield, Mike	1,828	5,749 D	48.6%	50.7%	48.9%	51.1%
1948	221,003	94,458	Davis, Tom J.	125,193	Murray, James E.*	1,352	30,735 D	42.7%	56.6%	43.0%	57.0%
1946	190,566	101,901	Ecton, Zales N.	86,476	Erickson, Leif	2,189	15,425 R	53.5%	45.4%	54.1%	45.9%

Note: An asterisk (*) denotes incumbent.

MONTANA

SENATOR 2018

2010 Census Population	County	Total Vote	Republican (Rosendale)	Democratic (Tester)	Other	Rep.-Dem. Plurality	Percentage Total Vote Rep.	Total Vote Dem.	Major Vote Rep.	Major Vote Dem.
9,246	BEAVERHEAD	4,897	2,866	1,876	155	990 R	58.5%	38.3%	60.4%	39.6%
12,865	BIG HORN	4,676	1,558	3,027	91	1,469 D	33.3%	64.7%	34.0%	66.0%
6,491	BLAINE	3,019	982	1,961	76	979 D	32.5%	65.0%	33.4%	66.6%
5,612	BROADWATER	3,261	2,086	1,071	104	1,015 R	64.0%	32.8%	66.1%	33.9%
10,078	CARBON	6,067	3,209	2,680	178	529 R	52.9%	44.2%	54.5%	45.5%
1,160	CARTER	752	602	128	22	474 R	80.1%	17.0%	82.5%	17.5%
81,327	CASCADE	34,009	15,566	17,435	1,008	1,869 D	45.8%	51.3%	47.2%	52.8%
5,813	CHOUTEAU	2,657	1,312	1,275	70	37 R	49.4%	48.0%	50.7%	49.3%
11,699	CUSTER	4,883	2,762	1,942	179	820 R	56.6%	39.8%	58.7%	41.3%
1,751	DANIELS	941	631	281	29	350 R	67.1%	29.9%	69.2%	30.8%
8,966	DAWSON	4,073	2,700	1,233	140	1,467 R	66.3%	30.3%	68.6%	31.4%
9,298	DEER LODGE	4,236	1,208	2,892	136	1,684 D	28.5%	68.3%	29.5%	70.5%
2,890	FALLON	1,289	951	281	57	670 R	73.8%	21.8%	77.2%	22.8%
11,586	FERGUS	5,793	3,640	1,964	189	1,676 R	62.8%	33.9%	65.0%	35.0%
90,928	FLATHEAD	47,760	26,759	19,652	1,349	7,107 R	56.0%	41.1%	57.7%	42.3%
89,513	GALLATIN	55,933	21,248	33,251	1,434	12,003 D	38.0%	59.4%	39.0%	61.0%
1,206	GARFIELD	682	571	81	30	490 R	83.7%	11.9%	87.6%	12.4%
13,399	GLACIER	4,996	1,153	3,754	89	2,601 D	23.1%	75.1%	23.5%	76.5%
884	GOLDEN VALLEY	454	303	130	21	173 R	66.7%	28.6%	70.0%	30.0%
3,079	GRANITE	1,793	1,046	695	52	351 R	58.3%	38.8%	60.1%	39.9%
16,096	HILL	6,390	2,434	3,729	227	1,295 D	38.1%	58.4%	39.5%	60.5%
11,406	JEFFERSON	6,833	3,653	2,954	226	699 R	53.5%	43.2%	55.3%	44.7%
2,072	JUDITH BASIN	1,191	752	388	51	364 R	63.1%	32.6%	66.0%	34.0%
28,746	LAKE	13,772	6,491	6,916	365	425 D	47.1%	50.2%	48.4%	51.6%
63,395	LEWIS AND CLARK	35,539	14,106	20,506	927	6,400 D	39.7%	57.7%	40.8%	59.2%
2,339	LIBERTY	981	586	365	30	221 R	59.7%	37.2%	61.6%	38.4%
19,687	LINCOLN	9,337	6,137	2,902	298	3,235 R	65.7%	31.1%	67.9%	32.1%
7,691	MADISON	4,959	2,898	1,890	171	1,008 R	58.4%	38.1%	60.5%	39.5%
1,734	MCCONE	1,029	773	227	29	546 R	75.1%	22.1%	77.3%	22.7%
1,891	MEAGHER	976	629	319	28	310 R	64.4%	32.7%	66.4%	33.6%
4,223	MINERAL	2,058	1,181	785	92	396 R	57.4%	38.1%	60.1%	39.9%
109,299	MISSOULA	61,651	18,631	41,688	1,332	23,057 D	30.2%	67.6%	30.9%	69.1%
4,538	MUSSELSHELL	2,432	1,743	573	116	1,170 R	71.7%	23.6%	75.3%	24.7%
15,636	PARK	9,724	4,357	5,114	253	757 D	44.8%	52.6%	46.0%	54.0%
494	PETROLEUM	312	248	58	6	190 R	79.5%	18.6%	81.0%	19.0%
4,253	PHILLIPS	2,082	1,426	577	79	849 R	68.5%	27.7%	71.2%	28.8%
6,153	PONDERA	2,685	1,413	1,176	96	237 R	52.6%	43.8%	54.6%	45.4%
1,743	POWDER RIVER	973	748	203	22	545 R	76.9%	20.9%	78.7%	21.3%
7,027	POWELL	2,760	1,641	1,026	93	615 R	59.5%	37.2%	61.5%	38.5%
1,179	PRAIRIE	653	450	177	26	273 R	68.9%	27.1%	71.8%	28.2%
40,212	RAVALLI	23,401	13,622	9,156	623	4,466 R	58.2%	39.1%	59.8%	40.2%
9,746	RICHLAND	4,332	3,017	1,136	179	1,881 R	69.6%	26.2%	72.6%	27.4%
10,425	ROOSEVELT	3,447	1,346	2,013	88	667 D	39.0%	58.4%	40.1%	59.9%
9,233	ROSEBUD	3,367	1,765	1,511	91	254 R	52.4%	44.9%	53.9%	46.1%
11,413	SANDERS	6,154	3,856	2,071	227	1,785 R	62.7%	33.7%	65.1%	34.9%
3,384	SHERIDAN	1,812	1,017	712	83	305 R	56.1%	39.3%	58.8%	41.2%
34,200	SILVER BOW	16,312	4,246	11,672	394	7,426 D	26.0%	71.6%	26.7%	73.3%
9,117	STILLWATER	4,864	3,206	1,501	157	1,705 R	65.9%	30.9%	68.1%	31.9%
3,651	SWEET GRASS	2,098	1,372	652	74	720 R	65.4%	31.1%	67.8%	32.2%
6,073	TETON	3,157	1,784	1,290	83	494 R	56.5%	40.9%	58.0%	42.0%
5,324	TOOLE	1,903	1,208	626	69	582 R	63.5%	32.9%	65.9%	34.1%
718	TREASURE	414	279	129	6	150 R	67.4%	31.2%	68.4%	31.6%
7,369	VALLEY	3,882	2,137	1,545	200	592 R	55.0%	39.8%	58.0%	42.0%
2,168	WHEATLAND	933	586	315	32	271 R	62.8%	33.8%	65.0%	35.0%
1,017	WIBAUX	542	390	140	12	250 R	72.0%	25.8%	73.6%	26.4%
147,972	YELLOWSTONE	69,258	34,682	32,225	2,351	2,457 R	50.1%	46.5%	51.8%	48.2%
989,415	*TOTAL*	*504,384*	*235,963*	*253,876*	*14,545*	*17,913 D*	*46.8%*	*50.3%*	*48.2%*	*51.8%*

MONTANA

HOUSE OF REPRESENTATIVES

			Republican		Democratic				Percentage			
									Total Vote		Major Vote	
CD	Year	Total Vote	Vote	Candidate	Vote	Candidate	Other Vote	Rep.-Dem. Plurality	Rep.	Dem.	Rep.	Dem.
At Large	2018	504,421	256,661	GIANFORTE, GREG*	233,284	WILLIAMS, KATHLEEN	14,476	23,377 R	50.9%	46.2%	52.4%	47.6%
At Large	2016	507,831	285,358	ZINKE, RYAN*	205,919	JUNEAU, DENISE	16,554	79,439 R	56.2%	40.5%	58.1%	41.9%
At Large	2014	367,963	203,871	ZINKE, RYAN	148,690	LEWIS, JOHN	15,402	55,181 R	55.4%	40.4%	57.8%	42.2%
At Large	2012	479,740	255,468	DAINES, STEVE	204,939	GILLAN, KIM	19,333	50,529 R	53.3%	42.7%	55.5%	44.5%
At Large	2010	360,341	217,696	REHBERG, DENNIS "DENNY"*	121,954	MCDONALD, DENNIS	20,691	95,742 R	60.4%	33.8%	64.1%	35.9%
At Large	2008	480,900	308,470	REHBERG, DENNIS "DENNY"*	155,930	DRISCOLL, JOHN	16,500	152,540 R	64.1%	32.4%	66.4%	33.6%
At Large	2006	406,134	239,124	REHBERG, DENNIS "DENNY"*	158,916	LINDEEN, MONICA	8,094	80,208 R	58.9%	39.1%	60.1%	39.9%
At Large	2004	444,230	286,076	REHBERG, DENNIS "DENNY"*	145,606	VELAZQUEZ, TRACY E.	12,548	140,470 R	64.4%	32.8%	66.3%	33.7%
At Large	2002	331,321	214,100	REHBERG, DENNIS "DENNY"*	108,233	KELLY, STEVE	8,988	105,867 R	64.6%	32.7%	66.4%	33.6%
At Large	2000	410,523	211,418	REHBERG, DENNIS "DENNY"	189,971	KEENAN, NANCY	9,134	21,447 R	51.5%	46.3%	52.7%	47.3%
At Large	1998	331,551	175,748	HILL, RICK*	147,073	DESCHAMPS, DUSTY	8,730	28,675 R	53.0%	44.4%	54.4%	45.6%
At Large	1996	404,426	211,975	HILL, RICK	174,516	YELLOWTAIL, BILL	17,935	37,459 R	52.4%	43.2%	54.8%	45.2%
At Large	1994	352,133	148,715	JAMISON, CY	171,372	WILLIAMS, JOHN PATRICK "PAT"*	32,046	22,657 D	42.2%	48.7%	46.5%	53.5%
At Large	1992	403,735	189,570	MARLENEE, RON*	203,711	WILLIAMS, JOHN PATRICK "PAT"*	10,454	14,141 D	47.0%	50.5%	48.2%	51.8%

Note: An asterisk (*) denotes incumbent.

MONTANA

GENERAL AND PRIMARY ELECTIONS

2018 GENERAL ELECTIONS: OTHER VOTES

Senate Other vote was 14,545 Libertarian (Rick Breckenridge)

House Other vote was:

At Large 14,476 Libertarian (Elinor Swanson)

2018 PRIMARY ELECTIONS: SUPPLEMENTARY INFORMATION

Primary June 5, 2018 **Registration** (as of March 19, 2018) 679,333 No Party Registration

Primary Type Open–Any registered voter could participate in the party primary of his or her choice.

	REPUBLICAN PRIMARIES			DEMOCRATIC PRIMARIES		
Senator	Rosendale, Matt	51,859	33.8%	Tester, Jon*	114,948	100.0%
	Fagg, Russell	43,465	28.3%			
	Downing, Troy	29,341	19.1%			
	Olszewski, Albert	28,681	18.7%			
	TOTAL	*153,346*		*TOTAL*	*114,948*	
Governor						
Congressional At Large	Gianforte, Greg*	136,372	100.0%	Williams, Kathleen	37,513	33.5%
				Heenan, John	35,480	31.7%
				Kier, Grant	27,025	24.2%
				Moss, Lynda	5,667	5.1%
				Meyer, John	3,740	3.3%
				Pettinato, Jared	2,472	2.2%
	TOTAL	*136,372*		*TOTAL*	*111,897*	

Note: An asterisk (*) denotes incumbent.

NEBRASKA

Congressional districts first established for elections held in 2012
3 members

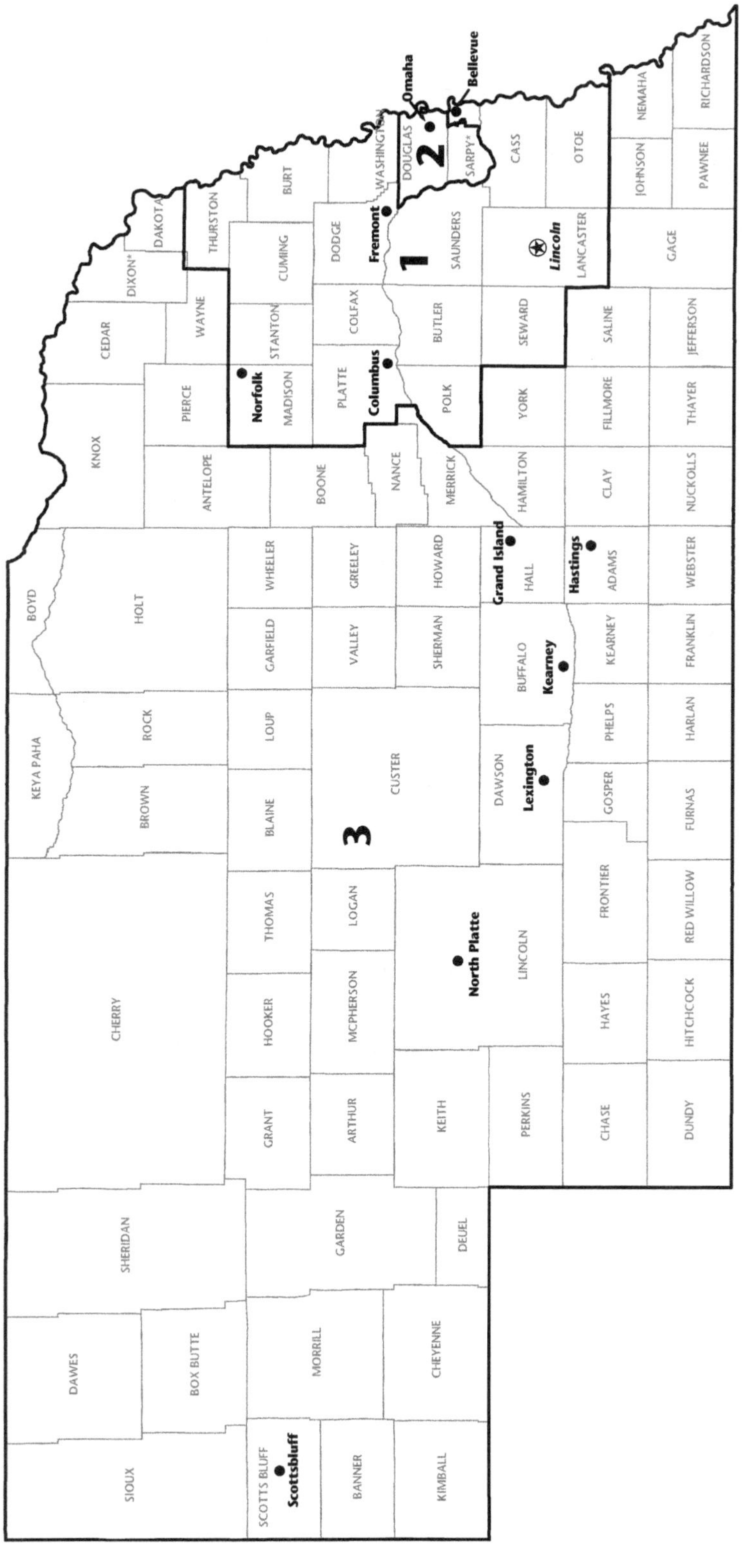

*Asterisk indicates a county whose boundaries include parts of two or more congressional districts.

NEBRASKA

GOVERNOR

Pete Ricketts (R). Re-elected 2018 to a four-year term. Previously elected 2014.

SENATORS (2 Republicans)

Deb Fischer (R). Re-elected 2018 to a six-year term. Previously elected 2012.

Ben Sasse (R). Elected 2014 to a six-year term.

REPRESENTATIVES (3 Republicans)

1. Jeff Fortenberry (R)
2. Don Bacon (R)
3. Adrian Smith (R)

POSTWAR VOTE FOR PRESIDENT

		Republican		Democratic				Percentage			
								Total Vote		Major Vote	
Year	Total Vote	Vote	Candidate	Vote	Candidate	Other Vote	Rep.-Dem. Plurality	Rep.	Dem.	Rep.	Dem.
2016**	844,227	495,961	Trump, Donald J.	284,494	Clinton, Hillary Rodham	63,772	211,467 R	58.7%	33.7%	63.5%	36.5%
2012	794,379	475,064	Romney, W. Mitt	302,081	Obama, Barack H.*	17,234	172,983 R	59.8%	38.0%	61.1%	38.9%
2008	801,281	452,979	McCain, John S. III	333,319	Obama, Barack H.	14,983	119,660 R	56.5%	41.6%	57.6%	42.4%
2004	778,186	512,814	Bush, George W.*	254,328	Kerry, John F.	11,044	258,486 R	65.9%	32.7%	66.8%	33.2%
2000**	697,019	433,862	Bush, George W.	231,780	Gore, Albert Jr.	31,377	202,082 R	62.2%	33.3%	65.2%	34.8%
1996**	677,415	363,467	Dole, Robert "Bob"	236,761	Clinton, Bill*	77,187	126,706 R	53.7%	35.0%	60.6%	39.4%
1992**	737,546	343,678	Bush, George H.*	216,864	Clinton, Bill	177,004	126,814 R	46.6%	29.4%	61.3%	38.7%
1988	661,465	397,956	Bush, George H.	259,235	Dukakis, Michael S.	4,274	138,721 R	60.2%	39.2%	60.6%	39.4%
1984	652,090	460,054	Reagan, Ronald*	187,866	Mondale, Walter F.	4,170	272,188 R	70.6%	28.8%	71.0%	29.0%
1980**	640,854	419,937	Reagan, Ronald	166,851	Carter, Jimmy*	54,066	253,086 R	65.5%	26.0%	71.6%	28.4%
1976	607,668	359,705	Ford, Gerald R.*	233,692	Carter, Jimmy	14,271	126,013 R	59.2%	38.5%	60.6%	39.4%
1972	576,289	406,298	Nixon, Richard M.*	169,991	McGovern, George S.		236,307 R	70.5%	29.5%	70.5%	29.5%
1968**	536,851	321,163	Nixon, Richard M.	170,784	Humphrey, Hubert Horatio Jr.	44,904	150,379 R	59.8%	31.8%	65.3%	34.7%
1964	584,154	276,847	Goldwater, Barry M. Sr.	307,307	Johnson, Lyndon B.*		30,460 D	47.4%	52.6%	47.4%	52.6%
1960	613,095	380,553	Nixon, Richard M.	232,542	Kennedy, John F.		148,011 R	62.1%	37.9%	62.1%	37.9%
1956	577,137	378,108	Eisenhower, Dwight D.*	199,029	Stevenson, Adlai E. II		179,079 R	65.5%	34.5%	65.5%	34.5%
1952	609,660	421,603	Eisenhower, Dwight D.	188,057	Stevenson, Adlai E. II		233,546 R	69.2%	30.8%	69.2%	30.8%
1948	488,940	264,774	Dewey, Thomas E.	224,165	Truman, Harry S.*	1	40,609 R	54.2%	45.8%	54.2%	45.8%

Note: An asterisk (*) denotes incumbent. **In past elections, the other vote included: 2016 - 38,946 Libertarian (Gary Johnson); 2000 - 24,540 Green (Ralph Nader); 1996 - 71,278 Reform (Ross Perot); 1992 - 174,104 Independent (Perot); 1980 - 44,993 Independent (John Anderson); 1968 - 44,904 American Independent (George Wallace).

NEBRASKA

POSTWAR VOTE FOR GOVERNOR

		Republican		Democratic				Percentage			
								Total Vote		Major Vote	
Year	Total Vote	Vote	Candidate	Vote	Candidate	Other Vote	Rep.-Dem. Plurality	Rep.	Dem.	Rep.	Dem.
2018	697,981	411,812	Ricketts, Pete*	286,169	Krist, Bob		125,643 R	59.0%	41.0%	59.0%	41.0%
2014	540,202	308,751	Ricketts, Pete	211,905	Hassebrook, Chuck	19,546	96,846 R	57.2%	39.2%	59.3%	40.7%
2010	487,988	360,645	Heineman, Dave*	127,343	Meister, Mike		233,302 R	73.9%	26.1%	73.9%	26.1%
2006	593,357	435,507	Heineman, Dave*	145,115	Hahn, David	12,735	290,392 R	73.4%	24.5%	75.0%	25.0%
2002	480,991	330,349	Johanns, Mike*	132,348	Dean, Stormy	18,294	198,001 R	68.7%	27.5%	71.4%	28.6%
1998	545,238	293,910	Johanns, Mike	250,678	Hoppner, Bill	650	43,232 R	53.9%	46.0%	54.0%	46.0%
1994	579,561	148,230	Spence, Gene	423,270	Nelson, Earl "Ben"*	8,061	275,040 D	25.6%	73.0%	25.9%	74.1%
1990	586,542	288,741	Orr, Kay*	292,771	Nelson, Earl "Ben"	5,030	4,030 D	49.2%	49.9%	49.7%	50.3%
1986	564,422	298,325	Orr, Kay	265,156	Boosalis, Helen	941	33,169 R	52.9%	47.0%	52.9%	47.1%
1982	547,902	270,203	Thone, Charles*	277,436	Kerrey, Bob	263	7,233 D	49.3%	50.6%	49.3%	50.7%
1978	492,423	275,473	Thone, Charles	216,754	Whelan, Gerald T.	196	58,719 R	55.9%	44.0%	56.0%	44.0%
1974	451,306	159,780	Marvel, Richard D.	267,012	Exon, J. James*	24,514	107,232 D	35.4%	59.2%	37.4%	62.6%
1970	461,619	201,994	Tiemann, Norbert T.*	248,552	Exon, J. James	11,073	46,558 D	43.8%	53.8%	44.8%	55.2%
1966**	486,396	299,245	Tiemann, Norbert T.	186,985	Sorensen, Philip C.	166	112,260 R	61.5%	38.4%	61.5%	38.5%
1964	578,090	231,029	Burney, Dwight W.	347,026	Morrison, Frank B.*	35	115,997 D	40.0%	60.0%	40.0%	60.0%
1962	464,585	221,885	Seaton, Fred A.	242,669	Morrison, Frank B.*	31	20,784 D	47.8%	52.2%	47.8%	52.2%
1960	598,971	287,302	Cooper, John R.	311,344	Morrison, Frank B.	325	24,042 D	48.0%	52.0%	48.0%	52.0%
1958	421,067	209,705	Anderson, Victor E.*	211,345	Brooks, Ralph G.	17	1,640 D	49.8%	50.2%	49.8%	50.2%
1956	567,916	308,285	Anderson, Victor E.*	228,048	Sorrell, Frank	31,583	80,237 R	54.3%	40.2%	57.5%	42.5%
1954	414,841	250,080	Anderson, Victor E.	164,753	Ritchie, William	8	85,327 R	60.3%	39.7%	60.3%	39.7%
1952	594,814	365,409	Crosby, Robert B.	229,400	Raecke, Walter R.	5	136,009 R	61.4%	38.6%	61.4%	38.6%
1950	449,728	247,089	Peterson, Val*	202,638	Raecke, Walter R.	1	44,451 R	54.9%	45.1%	54.9%	45.1%
1948	476,352	286,119	Peterson, Val*	190,214	Sorrell, Frank	19	95,905 R	60.1%	39.9%	60.1%	39.9%
1946	380,835	249,468	Peterson, Val	131,367	Sorrell, Frank		118,101 R	65.5%	34.5%	65.5%	34.5%

Note: An asterisk (*) denotes incumbent. **The term of office of Nebraska's governor was increased from two to four years effective with the 1966 election.

POSTWAR VOTE FOR SENATOR

		Republican		Democratic				Percentage			
								Total Vote		Major Vote	
Year	Total Vote	Vote	Candidate	Vote	Candidate	Other Vote	Rep.-Dem. Plurality	Rep.	Dem.	Rep.	Dem.
2018	698,883	403,151	Fischer, Deb*	269,917	Raybould, Jane	25,815	133,234 R	57.7%	38.6%	59.9%	40.1%
2014	540,337	347,636	Sasse, Ben	170,127	Domina, David A.	22,574	177,509 R	64.3%	31.5%	67.1%	32.9%
2012	788,572	455,593	Fischer, Deb	332,979	Kerrey, Bob		122,614 R	57.8%	42.2%	57.8%	42.2%
2008	792,511	455,854	Johanns, Mike	317,456	Kleeb, Scott	19,201	138,398 R	57.5%	40.1%	58.9%	41.1%
2006	592,316	213,928	Ricketts, Pete	378,388	Nelson, Earl "Ben"*		164,460 D	36.1%	63.9%	36.1%	63.9%
2002	480,217	397,438	Hagel, Chuck*	70,290	Matulka, Charlie A.	12,489	327,148 R	82.8%	14.6%	85.0%	15.0%
2000	692,344	337,967	Stenberg, Don	353,097	Nelson, Earl "Ben"	1,280	15,130 D	48.8%	51.0%	48.9%	51.1%
1996	676,789	379,933	Hagel, Chuck	281,904	Nelson, Earl "Ben"	14,952	98,029 R	56.1%	41.7%	57.4%	42.6%
1994	579,205	260,668	Stoney, Jan	317,297	Kerrey, Bob*	1,240	56,629 D	45.0%	54.8%	45.1%	54.9%
1990	593,828	243,013	Daub, Harold J.	349,779	Exon, J. James*	1,036	106,766 D	40.9%	58.9%	41.0%	59.0%
1988	667,860	278,250	Karnes, David*	378,717	Kerrey, Bob	10,893	100,467 D	41.7%	56.7%	42.4%	57.6%
1984	639,668	307,147	Hoch, Nancy	332,217	Exon, J. James*	304	25,070 D	48.0%	51.9%	48.0%	52.0%
1982	545,647	155,760	Keck, Jim	363,350	Zorinsky, Edward*	26,537	207,590 D	28.5%	66.6%	30.0%	70.0%
1978	494,368	159,806	Shasteen, Donald	334,276	Exon, J. James	286	174,470 D	32.3%	67.6%	32.3%	67.7%
1976	598,314	284,284	McCollister, John Y.	313,809	Zorinsky, Edward	221	29,525 D	47.5%	52.4%	47.5%	52.5%
1972	568,580	301,841	Curtis, Carl T.*	265,922	Carpenter, Terry	817	35,919 R	53.1%	46.8%	53.2%	46.8%
1970	458,966	240,894	Hruska, Roman L.*	217,681	Morrison, Frank B.	391	23,213 R	52.5%	47.4%	52.5%	47.5%
1966	485,101	296,116	Curtis, Carl T.*	187,950	Morrison, Frank B.	1,035	108,166 R	61.0%	38.7%	61.2%	38.8%
1964	563,401	345,772	Hruska, Roman L.*	217,605	Arndt, Raymond W.	24	128,167 R	61.4%	38.6%	61.4%	38.6%
1960	598,743	352,748	Curtis, Carl T.*	245,837	Conrad, Robert B.	158	106,911 R	58.9%	41.1%	58.9%	41.1%
1958	417,385	232,227	Hruska, Roman L.*	185,152	Morrison, Frank B.	6	47,075 R	55.6%	44.4%	55.6%	44.4%
1954	418,691	255,695	Curtis, Carl T.	162,990	Neville, Keith	6	92,705 R	61.1%	38.9%	61.1%	38.9%
1954S**	411,225	250,341	Hruska, Roman L.	160,881	Green, James F.	3	89,460 R	60.9%	39.1%	60.9%	39.1%
1952	591,749	408,971	Butler, Hugh*	164,660	Long, Stanley D.	18,118	244,311 R	69.1%	27.8%	71.3%	28.7%
1952S**	581,750	369,841	Griswold, Dwight	211,898	Ritchie, William	11	157,943 R	63.6%	36.4%	63.6%	36.4%
1948	471,895	267,575	Wherry, Kenneth S.*	204,320	Carpenter, Terry		63,255 R	56.7%	43.3%	56.7%	43.3%
1946	382,959	271,208	Butler, Hugh*	111,751	Mekota, John E.		159,457 R	70.8%	29.2%	70.8%	29.2%

Note: An asterisk (*) denotes incumbent. **One each of the 1952 and 1954 elections was for a short term to fill a vacancy.

NEBRASKA

GOVERNOR 2018

2010 Census Population	County	Total Vote	Republican (Ricketts)	Democratic (Krist)	Rep.-Dem. Plurality	Percentage Total Vote Rep.	Percentage Total Vote Dem.	Percentage Major Vote Rep.	Percentage Major Vote Dem.
31,364	ADAMS	10,219	7,067	3,152	3,915 R	69.2%	30.8%	69.2%	30.8%
6,685	ANTELOPE	2,543	2,103	440	1,663 R	82.7%	17.3%	82.7%	17.3%
460	ARTHUR	227	196	31	165 R	86.3%	13.7%	86.3%	13.7%
690	BANNER	316	254	62	192 R	80.4%	19.6%	80.4%	19.6%
478	BLAINE	264	215	49	166 R	81.4%	18.6%	81.4%	18.6%
5,505	BOONE	2,312	1,872	440	1,432 R	81.0%	19.0%	81.0%	19.0%
11,308	BOX BUTTE	3,621	2,525	1,096	1,429 R	69.7%	30.3%	69.7%	30.3%
2,099	BOYD	961	809	152	657 R	84.2%	15.8%	84.2%	15.8%
3,145	BROWN	1,365	1,151	214	937 R	84.3%	15.7%	84.3%	15.7%
46,102	BUFFALO	16,322	11,168	5,154	6,014 R	68.4%	31.6%	68.4%	31.6%
6,858	BURT	2,949	1,973	976	997 R	66.9%	33.1%	66.9%	33.1%
8,395	BUTLER	3,502	2,632	870	1,762 R	75.2%	24.8%	75.2%	24.8%
25,241	CASS	10,632	6,923	3,709	3,214 R	65.1%	34.9%	65.1%	34.9%
8,852	CEDAR	3,530	2,775	755	2,020 R	78.6%	21.4%	78.6%	21.4%
3,966	CHASE	1,559	1,354	205	1,149 R	86.9%	13.1%	86.9%	13.1%
5,713	CHERRY	2,405	1,979	426	1,553 R	82.3%	17.7%	82.3%	17.7%
9,998	CHEYENNE	3,249	2,534	715	1,819 R	78.0%	22.0%	78.0%	22.0%
6,542	CLAY	2,686	2,122	564	1,558 R	79.0%	21.0%	79.0%	21.0%
10,515	COLFAX	2,503	1,765	738	1,027 R	70.5%	29.5%	70.5%	29.5%
9,139	CUMING	3,379	2,682	697	1,985 R	79.4%	20.6%	79.4%	20.6%
10,939	CUSTER	4,639	3,861	778	3,083 R	83.2%	16.8%	83.2%	16.8%
21,006	DAKOTA	4,542	2,701	1,841	860 R	59.5%	40.5%	59.5%	40.5%
9,182	DAWES	3,367	2,179	1,188	991 R	64.7%	35.3%	64.7%	35.3%
24,326	DAWSON	6,264	4,558	1,706	2,852 R	72.8%	27.2%	72.8%	27.2%
1,941	DEUEL	712	585	127	458 R	82.2%	17.8%	82.2%	17.8%
6,000	DIXON	2,247	1,666	581	1,085 R	74.1%	25.9%	74.1%	25.9%
36,691	DODGE	12,090	7,457	4,633	2,824 R	61.7%	38.3%	61.7%	38.3%
517,110	DOUGLAS	204,355	96,120	108,235	12,115 D	47.0%	53.0%	47.0%	53.0%
2,008	DUNDY	773	654	119	535 R	84.6%	15.4%	84.6%	15.4%
5,890	FILLMORE	2,542	1,790	752	1,038 R	70.4%	29.6%	70.4%	29.6%
3,225	FRANKLIN	1,363	1,109	254	855 R	81.4%	18.6%	81.4%	18.6%
2,756	FRONTIER	1,048	857	191	666 R	81.8%	18.2%	81.8%	18.2%
4,959	FURNAS	2,138	1,767	371	1,396 R	82.6%	17.4%	82.6%	17.4%
22,311	GAGE	8,342	5,250	3,092	2,158 R	62.9%	37.1%	62.9%	37.1%
2,057	GARDEN	1,004	818	186	632 R	81.5%	18.5%	81.5%	18.5%
2,049	GARFIELD	797	666	131	535 R	83.6%	16.4%	83.6%	16.4%
2,044	GOSPER	835	685	150	535 R	82.0%	18.0%	82.0%	18.0%
614	GRANT	302	260	42	218 R	86.1%	13.9%	86.1%	13.9%
2,538	GREELEY	1,003	752	251	501 R	75.0%	25.0%	75.0%	25.0%
58,607	HALL	16,730	11,069	5,661	5,408 R	66.2%	33.8%	66.2%	33.8%
9,124	HAMILTON	4,118	3,214	904	2,310 R	78.0%	22.0%	78.0%	22.0%
3,423	HARLAN	1,504	1,231	273	958 R	81.8%	18.2%	81.8%	18.2%
967	HAYES	395	353	42	311 R	89.4%	10.6%	89.4%	10.6%
2,908	HITCHCOCK	1,077	886	191	695 R	82.3%	17.7%	82.3%	17.7%
10,435	HOLT	4,162	3,339	823	2,516 R	80.2%	19.8%	80.2%	19.8%
736	HOOKER	317	259	58	201 R	81.7%	18.3%	81.7%	18.3%
6,274	HOWARD	2,426	1,793	633	1,160 R	73.9%	26.1%	73.9%	26.1%
7,547	JEFFERSON	2,986	2,042	944	1,098 R	68.4%	31.6%	68.4%	31.6%
5,217	JOHNSON	1,796	1,124	672	452 R	62.6%	37.4%	62.6%	37.4%
6,489	KEARNEY	2,625	2,020	605	1,415 R	77.0%	23.0%	77.0%	23.0%
8,368	KEITH	3,200	2,516	684	1,832 R	78.6%	21.4%	78.6%	21.4%
824	KEYA PAHA	390	347	43	304 R	89.0%	11.0%	89.0%	11.0%
3,821	KIMBALL	1,380	1,117	263	854 R	80.9%	19.1%	80.9%	19.1%
8,701	KNOX	3,599	2,781	818	1,963 R	77.3%	22.7%	77.3%	22.7%
285,407	LANCASTER	116,506	51,560	64,946	13,386 D	44.3%	55.7%	44.3%	55.7%
36,288	LINCOLN	12,519	9,345	3,174	6,171 R	74.6%	25.4%	74.6%	25.4%
763	LOGAN	335	307	28	279 R	91.6%	8.4%	91.6%	8.4%
632	LOUP	307	250	57	193 R	81.4%	18.6%	81.4%	18.6%
34,876	MADISON	10,465	7,906	2,559	5,347 R	75.5%	24.5%	75.5%	24.5%
539	MCPHERSON	256	211	45	166 R	82.4%	17.6%	82.4%	17.6%

NEBRASKA

GOVERNOR 2018

2010 Census Population	County	Total Vote	Republican (Ricketts)	Democratic (Krist)	Rep.-Dem. Plurality	Percentage Total Vote Rep.	Percentage Total Vote Dem.	Percentage Major Vote Rep.	Percentage Major Vote Dem.
7,845	MERRICK	3,377	2,695	682	2,013 R	79.8%	20.2%	79.8%	20.2%
5,042	MORRILL	2,115	1,641	474	1,167 R	77.6%	22.4%	77.6%	22.4%
3,735	NANCE	1,246	928	318	610 R	74.5%	25.5%	74.5%	25.5%
7,248	NEMAHA	2,616	1,825	791	1,034 R	69.8%	30.2%	69.8%	30.2%
4,500	NUCKOLLS	1,765	1,425	340	1,085 R	80.7%	19.3%	80.7%	19.3%
15,740	OTOE	6,371	4,264	2,107	2,157 R	66.9%	33.1%	66.9%	33.1%
2,773	PAWNEE	1,154	804	350	454 R	69.7%	30.3%	69.7%	30.3%
2,970	PERKINS	1,224	1,029	195	834 R	84.1%	15.9%	84.1%	15.9%
9,188	PHELPS	3,855	3,162	693	2,469 R	82.0%	18.0%	82.0%	18.0%
7,266	PIERCE	2,775	2,377	398	1,979 R	85.7%	14.3%	85.7%	14.3%
32,237	PLATTE	11,043	8,570	2,473	6,097 R	77.6%	22.4%	77.6%	22.4%
5,406	POLK	2,088	1,650	438	1,212 R	79.0%	21.0%	79.0%	21.0%
11,055	RED WILLOW	3,889	3,161	728	2,433 R	81.3%	18.7%	81.3%	18.7%
8,363	RICHARDSON	3,091	2,262	829	1,433 R	73.2%	26.8%	73.2%	26.8%
1,526	ROCK	667	573	94	479 R	85.9%	14.1%	85.9%	14.1%
14,200	SALINE	4,221	2,406	1,815	591 R	57.0%	43.0%	57.0%	43.0%
158,840	SARPY	67,560	39,928	27,632	12,296 R	59.1%	40.9%	59.1%	40.9%
20,780	SAUNDERS	9,524	6,508	3,016	3,492 R	68.3%	31.7%	68.3%	31.7%
36,970	SCOTTS BLUFF	10,680	7,241	3,439	3,802 R	67.8%	32.2%	67.8%	32.2%
16,750	SEWARD	7,059	4,812	2,247	2,565 R	68.2%	31.8%	68.2%	31.8%
5,469	SHERIDAN	2,011	1,513	498	1,015 R	75.2%	24.8%	75.2%	24.8%
3,152	SHERMAN	1,294	948	346	602 R	73.3%	26.7%	73.3%	26.7%
1,311	SIOUX	537	441	96	345 R	82.1%	17.9%	82.1%	17.9%
6,129	STANTON	2,264	1,829	435	1,394 R	80.8%	19.2%	80.8%	19.2%
5,228	THAYER	2,256	1,715	541	1,174 R	76.0%	24.0%	76.0%	24.0%
647	THOMAS	344	300	44	256 R	87.2%	12.8%	87.2%	12.8%
6,940	THURSTON	1,839	963	876	87 R	52.4%	47.6%	52.4%	47.6%
4,260	VALLEY	1,799	1,444	355	1,089 R	80.3%	19.7%	80.3%	19.7%
20,234	WASHINGTON	9,209	6,457	2,752	3,705 R	70.1%	29.9%	70.1%	29.9%
9,595	WAYNE	3,218	2,296	922	1,374 R	71.3%	28.7%	71.3%	28.7%
3,812	WEBSTER	1,370	1,079	291	788 R	78.8%	21.2%	78.8%	21.2%
818	WHEELER	399	319	80	239 R	79.9%	20.1%	79.9%	20.1%
13,665	YORK	5,121	3,743	1,378	2,365 R	73.1%	26.9%	73.1%	26.9%
1,826,341	*TOTAL*	*697,981*	*411,812*	*286,169*	*125,643 R*	*59.0%*	*41.0%*	*59.0%*	*41.0%*

NEBRASKA

SENATOR 2018

2010 Census Population	County	Total Vote	Republican (Fischer)	Democratic (Raybould)	Other	Rep.-Dem. Plurality	Percentage Total Vote Rep.	Percentage Total Vote Dem.	Percentage Major Vote Rep.	Percentage Major Vote Dem.
31,364	ADAMS	10,225	6,487	3,334	404	3,153 R	63.4%	32.6%	66.1%	33.9%
6,685	ANTELOPE	2,527	2,061	396	70	1,665 R	81.6%	15.7%	83.9%	16.1%
460	ARTHUR	232	202	24	6	178 R	87.1%	10.3%	89.4%	10.6%
690	BANNER	314	263	39	12	224 R	83.8%	12.4%	87.1%	12.9%
478	BLAINE	263	223	34	6	189 R	84.8%	12.9%	86.8%	13.2%
5,505	BOONE	2,295	1,757	457	81	1,300 R	76.6%	19.9%	79.4%	20.6%
11,308	BOX BUTTE	3,630	2,632	835	163	1,797 R	72.5%	23.0%	75.9%	24.1%
2,099	BOYD	959	797	128	34	669 R	83.1%	13.3%	86.2%	13.8%
3,145	BROWN	1,385	1,153	190	42	963 R	83.2%	13.7%	85.9%	14.1%
46,102	BUFFALO	16,361	10,939	4,765	657	6,174 R	66.9%	29.1%	69.7%	30.3%

NEBRASKA

SENATOR 2018

2010 Census Population	County	Total Vote	Republican (Fischer)	Democratic (Raybould)	Other	Rep.-Dem. Plurality	Percentage: Total Vote		Percentage: Major Vote	
							Rep.	Dem.	Rep.	Dem.
6,858	BURT	2,937	1,995	836	106	1,159 R	67.9%	28.5%	70.5%	29.5%
8,395	BUTLER	3,479	2,470	871	138	1,599 R	71.0%	25.0%	73.9%	26.1%
25,241	CASS	10,609	6,787	3,393	429	3,394 R	64.0%	32.0%	66.7%	33.3%
8,852	CEDAR	3,514	2,866	537	111	2,329 R	81.6%	15.3%	84.2%	15.8%
3,966	CHASE	1,563	1,340	184	39	1,156 R	85.7%	11.8%	87.9%	12.1%
5,713	CHERRY	2,386	1,913	314	159	1,599 R	80.2%	13.2%	85.9%	14.1%
9,998	CHEYENNE	3,258	2,566	579	113	1,987 R	78.8%	17.8%	81.6%	18.4%
6,542	CLAY	2,679	1,979	592	108	1,387 R	73.9%	22.1%	77.0%	23.0%
10,515	COLFAX	2,499	1,731	693	75	1,038 R	69.3%	27.7%	71.4%	28.6%
9,139	CUMING	3,363	2,672	604	87	2,068 R	79.5%	18.0%	81.6%	18.4%
10,939	CUSTER	4,643	3,797	687	159	3,110 R	81.8%	14.8%	84.7%	15.3%
21,006	DAKOTA	4,536	2,677	1,691	168	986 R	59.0%	37.3%	61.3%	38.7%
9,182	DAWES	3,393	2,334	914	145	1,420 R	68.8%	26.9%	71.9%	28.1%
24,326	DAWSON	6,253	4,363	1,657	233	2,706 R	69.8%	26.5%	72.5%	27.5%
1,941	DEUEL	717	578	109	30	469 R	80.6%	15.2%	84.1%	15.9%
6,000	DIXON	2,225	1,655	488	82	1,167 R	74.4%	21.9%	77.2%	22.8%
36,691	DODGE	12,060	7,827	3,824	409	4,003 R	64.9%	31.7%	67.2%	32.8%
517,110	DOUGLAS	204,707	94,777	103,070	6,860	8,293 D	46.3%	50.4%	47.9%	52.1%
2,008	DUNDY	772	649	99	24	550 R	84.1%	12.8%	86.8%	13.2%
5,890	FILLMORE	2,527	1,718	690	119	1,028 R	68.0%	27.3%	71.3%	28.7%
3,225	FRANKLIN	1,349	1,044	255	50	789 R	77.4%	18.9%	80.4%	19.6%
2,756	FRONTIER	1,040	831	173	36	658 R	79.9%	16.6%	82.8%	17.2%
4,959	FURNAS	2,139	1,719	334	86	1,385 R	80.4%	15.6%	83.7%	16.3%
22,311	GAGE	8,335	4,896	3,024	415	1,872 R	58.7%	36.3%	61.8%	38.2%
2,057	GARDEN	1,001	816	139	46	677 R	81.5%	13.9%	85.4%	14.6%
2,049	GARFIELD	799	667	113	19	554 R	83.5%	14.1%	85.5%	14.5%
2,044	GOSPER	837	667	147	23	520 R	79.7%	17.6%	81.9%	18.1%
614	GRANT	301	282	14	5	268 R	93.7%	4.7%	95.3%	4.7%
2,538	GREELEY	995	732	238	25	494 R	73.6%	23.9%	75.5%	24.5%
58,607	HALL	16,787	10,483	5,624	680	4,859 R	62.4%	33.5%	65.1%	34.9%
9,124	HAMILTON	4,108	3,076	896	136	2,180 R	74.9%	21.8%	77.4%	22.6%
3,423	HARLAN	1,490	1,149	287	54	862 R	77.1%	19.3%	80.0%	20.0%
967	HAYES	393	350	32	11	318 R	89.1%	8.1%	91.6%	8.4%
2,908	HITCHCOCK	1,079	890	154	35	736 R	82.5%	14.3%	85.2%	14.8%
10,435	HOLT	4,149	3,226	725	198	2,501 R	77.8%	17.5%	81.7%	18.3%
736	HOOKER	311	258	49	4	209 R	83.0%	15.8%	84.0%	16.0%
6,274	HOWARD	2,416	1,696	610	110	1,086 R	70.2%	25.2%	73.5%	26.5%
7,547	JEFFERSON	2,979	1,913	924	142	989 R	64.2%	31.0%	67.4%	32.6%
5,217	JOHNSON	1,774	1,101	581	92	520 R	62.1%	32.8%	65.5%	34.5%
6,489	KEARNEY	2,630	1,952	592	86	1,360 R	74.2%	22.5%	76.7%	23.3%
8,368	KEITH	3,210	2,542	567	101	1,975 R	79.2%	17.7%	81.8%	18.2%
824	KEYA PAHA	386	336	42	8	294 R	87.0%	10.9%	88.9%	11.1%
3,821	KIMBALL	1,380	1,122	202	56	920 R	81.3%	14.6%	84.7%	15.3%
8,701	KNOX	3,588	2,812	669	107	2,143 R	78.4%	18.6%	80.8%	19.2%
285,407	LANCASTER	117,131	49,449	63,175	4,507	13,726 D	42.2%	53.9%	43.9%	56.1%
36,288	LINCOLN	12,500	8,999	2,886	615	6,113 R	72.0%	23.1%	75.7%	24.3%
763	LOGAN	337	306	23	8	283 R	90.8%	6.8%	93.0%	7.0%
632	LOUP	307	247	51	9	196 R	80.5%	16.6%	82.9%	17.1%
34,876	MADISON	10,513	7,949	2,236	328	5,713 R	75.6%	21.3%	78.0%	22.0%
539	MCPHERSON	262	228	22	12	206 R	87.0%	8.4%	91.2%	8.8%
7,845	MERRICK	3,363	2,563	647	153	1,916 R	76.2%	19.2%	79.8%	20.2%
5,042	MORRILL	2,115	1,699	308	108	1,391 R	80.3%	14.6%	84.7%	15.3%
3,735	NANCE	1,237	885	315	37	570 R	71.5%	25.5%	73.8%	26.2%
7,248	NEMAHA	2,611	1,788	727	96	1,061 R	68.5%	27.8%	71.1%	28.9%
4,500	NUCKOLLS	1,752	1,321	365	66	956 R	75.4%	20.8%	78.4%	21.6%
15,740	OTOE	6,342	4,098	1,977	267	2,121 R	64.6%	31.2%	67.5%	32.5%
2,773	PAWNEE	1,153	774	332	47	442 R	67.1%	28.8%	70.0%	30.0%
2,970	PERKINS	1,224	1,011	180	33	831 R	82.6%	14.7%	84.9%	15.1%
9,188	PHELPS	3,859	3,068	671	120	2,397 R	79.5%	17.4%	82.1%	17.9%
7,266	PIERCE	2,765	2,339	341	85	1,998 R	84.6%	12.3%	87.3%	12.7%

NEBRASKA

SENATOR 2018

2010 Census Population	County	Total Vote	Republican (Fischer)	Democratic (Raybould)	Other	Rep.-Dem. Plurality	Percentage Total Vote Rep.	Total Vote Dem.	Major Vote Rep.	Major Vote Dem.
32,237	PLATTE	11,037	8,372	2,343	322	6,029 R	75.9%	21.2%	78.1%	21.9%
5,406	POLK	2,093	1,574	448	71	1,126 R	75.2%	21.4%	77.8%	22.2%
11,055	RED WILLOW	3,887	3,051	696	140	2,355 R	78.5%	17.9%	81.4%	18.6%
8,363	RICHARDSON	3,084	2,137	858	89	1,279 R	69.3%	27.8%	71.4%	28.6%
1,526	ROCK	665	569	79	17	490 R	85.6%	11.9%	87.8%	12.2%
14,200	SALINE	4,218	2,255	1,732	231	523 R	53.5%	41.1%	56.6%	43.4%
158,840	SARPY	67,673	39,306	25,706	2,661	13,600 R	58.1%	38.0%	60.5%	39.5%
20,780	SAUNDERS	9,519	6,479	2,664	376	3,815 R	68.1%	28.0%	70.9%	29.1%
36,970	SCOTTS BLUFF	10,746	7,398	2,887	461	4,511 R	68.8%	26.9%	71.9%	28.1%
16,750	SEWARD	7,065	4,607	2,174	284	2,433 R	65.2%	30.8%	67.9%	32.1%
5,469	SHERIDAN	2,037	1,670	275	92	1,395 R	82.0%	13.5%	85.9%	14.1%
3,152	SHERMAN	1,290	873	370	47	503 R	67.7%	28.7%	70.2%	29.8%
1,311	SIOUX	537	447	69	21	378 R	83.2%	12.8%	86.6%	13.4%
6,129	STANTON	2,261	1,817	363	81	1,454 R	80.4%	16.1%	83.3%	16.7%
5,228	THAYER	2,234	1,606	539	89	1,067 R	71.9%	24.1%	74.9%	25.1%
647	THOMAS	338	291	36	11	255 R	86.1%	10.7%	89.0%	11.0%
6,940	THURSTON	1,829	970	817	42	153 R	53.0%	44.7%	54.3%	45.7%
4,260	VALLEY	1,798	1,388	359	51	1,029 R	77.2%	20.0%	79.5%	20.5%
20,234	WASHINGTON	9,194	6,462	2,438	294	4,024 R	70.3%	26.5%	72.6%	27.4%
9,595	WAYNE	3,218	2,388	724	106	1,664 R	74.2%	22.5%	76.7%	23.3%
3,812	WEBSTER	1,364	997	318	49	679 R	73.1%	23.3%	75.8%	24.2%
818	WHEELER	414	343	60	11	283 R	82.9%	14.5%	85.1%	14.9%
13,665	YORK	5,124	3,659	1,281	184	2,378 R	71.4%	25.0%	74.1%	25.9%
1,826,341	*TOTAL*	*698,883*	*403,151*	*269,917*	*25,815*	*133,234 R*	*57.7%*	*38.6%*	*59.9%*	*40.1%*

NEBRASKA

HOUSE OF REPRESENTATIVES

CD	Year	Total Vote	Republican Vote	Republican Candidate	Democratic Vote	Democratic Candidate	Other Vote	Rep.-Dem. Plurality	Percentage Total Vote Rep.	Total Vote Dem.	Major Vote Rep.	Major Vote Dem.
1	2018	234,781	141,712	FORTENBERRY, JEFF*	93,069	MCCLURE, JESSICA		48,643 R	60.4%	39.6%	60.4%	39.6%
1	2016	273,238	189,771	FORTENBERRY, JEFF*	83,467	WIK, DANIEL M.		106,304 R	69.5%	30.5%	69.5%	30.5%
1	2014	179,057	123,219	FORTENBERRY, JEFF*	55,838	CRAWFORD, DENNIS P.		67,381 R	68.8%	31.2%	68.8%	31.2%
1	2012	256,095	174,889	FORTENBERRY, JEFF*	81,206	REIMAN, KOREY L.		93,683 R	68.3%	31.7%	68.3%	31.7%
2	2018	248,485	126,715	BACON, DON*	121,770	EASTMAN, KARA		4,945 R	51.0%	49.0%	51.0%	49.0%
2	2016	288,308	141,066	BACON, DON	137,602	ASHFORD, BRAD*	9,640	3,464 R	48.9%	47.7%	50.6%	49.4%
2	2014	171,509	78,157	TERRY, LEE*	83,872	ASHFORD, BRAD	9,480	5,715 D	45.6%	48.9%	48.2%	51.8%
2	2012	263,731	133,964	TERRY, LEE*	129,767	EWING, JOHN W. JR.		4,197 R	50.8%	49.2%	50.8%	49.2%
3	2018	213,304	163,650	SMITH, ADRIAN*	49,654	THEOBALD, PAUL		113,996 R	76.7%	23.3%	76.7%	23.3%
3	2016	226,907	226,907	SMITH, ADRIAN*				226,907 R	100.0%		100.0%	
3	2014	184,964	139,440	SMITH, ADRIAN*	45,524	SULLIVAN, MARK		93,916 R	75.4%	24.6%	75.4%	24.6%
3	2012	252,689	187,423	SMITH, ADRIAN*	65,266	SULLIVAN, MARK		122,157 R	74.2%	25.8%	74.2%	25.8%
TOTAL	*2018*	*696,570*	*432,077*		*264,493*			*167,584 R*	*62.0%*	*38.0%*	*62.0%*	*38.0%*
TOTAL	*2016*	*788,453*	*557,744*		*221,069*		*9,640*	*336,675 R*	*70.7%*	*28.0%*	*71.6%*	*28.4%*
TOTAL	*2014*	*535,530*	*340,816*		*185,234*		*9,480*	*155,582 R*	*63.6%*	*34.6%*	*64.8%*	*35.2%*
TOTAL	*2012*	*772,515*	*496,276*		*276,239*			*220,037 R*	*64.2%*	*35.8%*	*64.2%*	*35.8%*

Note: An asterisk (*) denotes incumbent.

NEBRASKA

GENERAL AND PRIMARY ELECTIONS

2018 GENERAL ELECTIONS: OTHER VOTES

Senate Other vote was 25,349 Libertarian (Jim Schultz), 466 Write-in (Scattered Write-in)

2018 PRIMARY ELECTIONS: SUPPLEMENTARY INFORMATION

Primary	May 15, 2018	**Registration** (as of May 15, 2018)	1,199,474	Republican	577,390
				Democratic	355,691
				Libertarian	13,495
				Nonpartisan	252,898

Primary Type Closed—Registered Democrats and Republicans could vote only in their party's primary. Voters registered as Nonpartisan could participate in either party's primary for the Senate and House (but not for governor).

	REPUBLICAN PRIMARIES			DEMOCRATIC PRIMARIES		
Senator	Fischer, Deb*	128,157	75.8%	Raybould, Jane	59,067	63.7%
	Watson, Todd F.	19,661	11.6%	Janicek, Chris	18,752	20.2%
	Heidel, Jack	9,413	5.6%	Svoboda, Frank	10,548	11.4%
	Stein, Jeffrey Lynn	6,380	3.8%	Marvin, Larry	4,393	4.7%
	Macek, Dennis	5,483	3.2%			
	TOTAL	*169,094*		*TOTAL*	*92,760*	
Governor	Ricketts, Pete*	138,292	81.4%	Krist, Bob	54,992	59.8%
	Gabel, Krystal	31,568	18.6%	Ward, Vanessa	26,478	28.8%
				Davis, Tyler	10,472	11.4%
	TOTAL	*169,860*		*TOTAL*	*91,942*	
Congressional District 1	Fortenberry, Jeff*	51,809	100.0%	McClure, Jessica	22,199	65.7%
				Crawford, Dennis P.	11,386	33.7%
				Scattered Write-ins	185	0.5%
	TOTAL	*51,809*		*TOTAL*	*33,770*	
Congressional District 2	Bacon, Don*	33,852	100.0%	Eastman, Kara	21,357	51.6%
				Ashford, Brad	19,998	48.4%
	TOTAL	*33,852*		*TOTAL*	*41,355*	
Congressional District 3	Smith, Adrian*	50,878	65.7%	Theobald, Paul	16,395	100.0%
	Penner, Kirk	20,116	26.0%			
	Kowalski, Arron	4,461	5.8%			
	Bolinger, Larry	1,935	2.5%			
	TOTAL	*77,390*		*TOTAL*	*16,395*	

Note: An asterisk (*) denotes incumbent.

NEVADA

Congressional districts first established for elections held in 2012

4 members

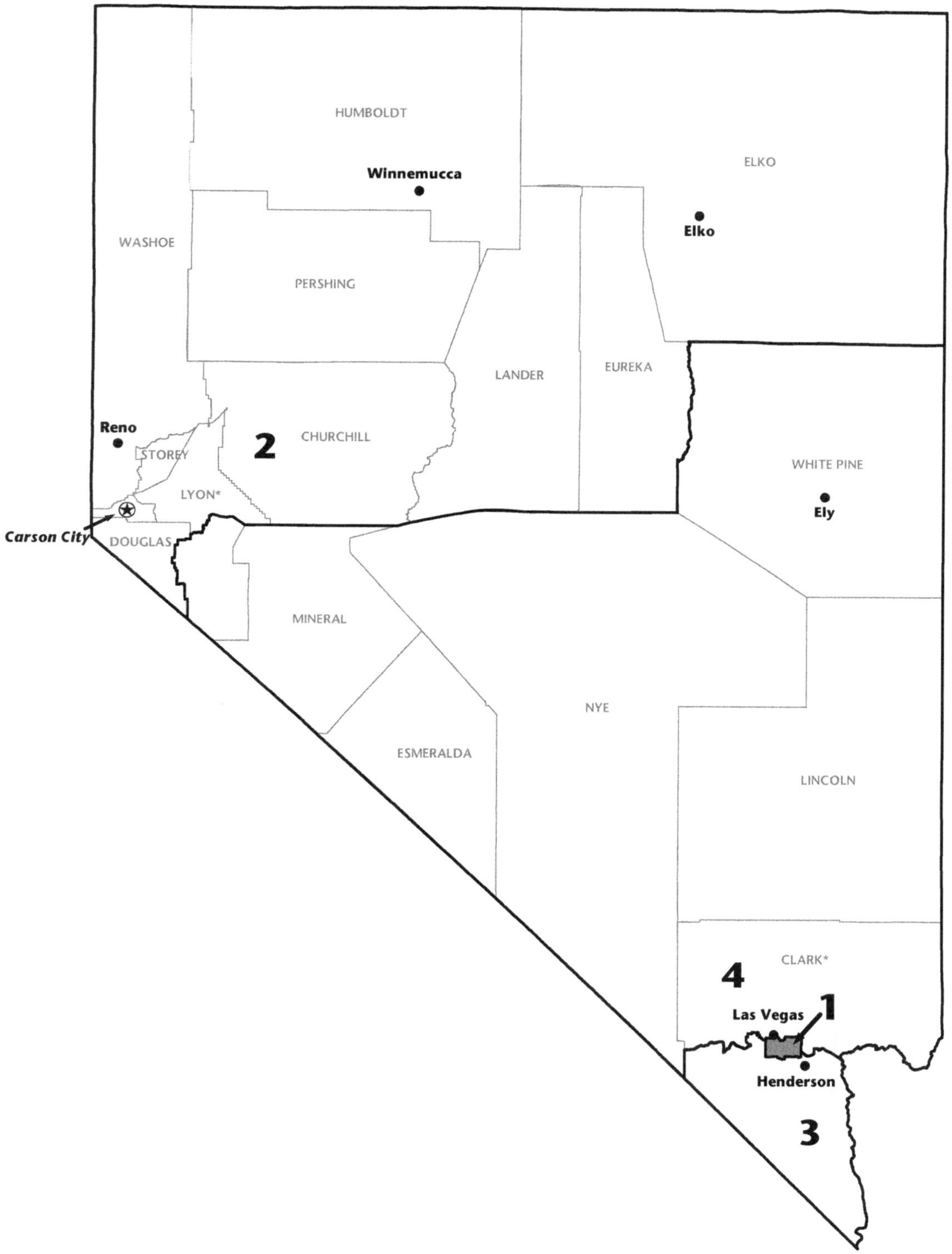

The city of Carson City is an independent city that is treated as a county equivalent; the label is included only for the city.

* Asterisk indicates a county whose boundaries include parts of two or more congressional districts.

NEVADA

Greater Las Vegas Area

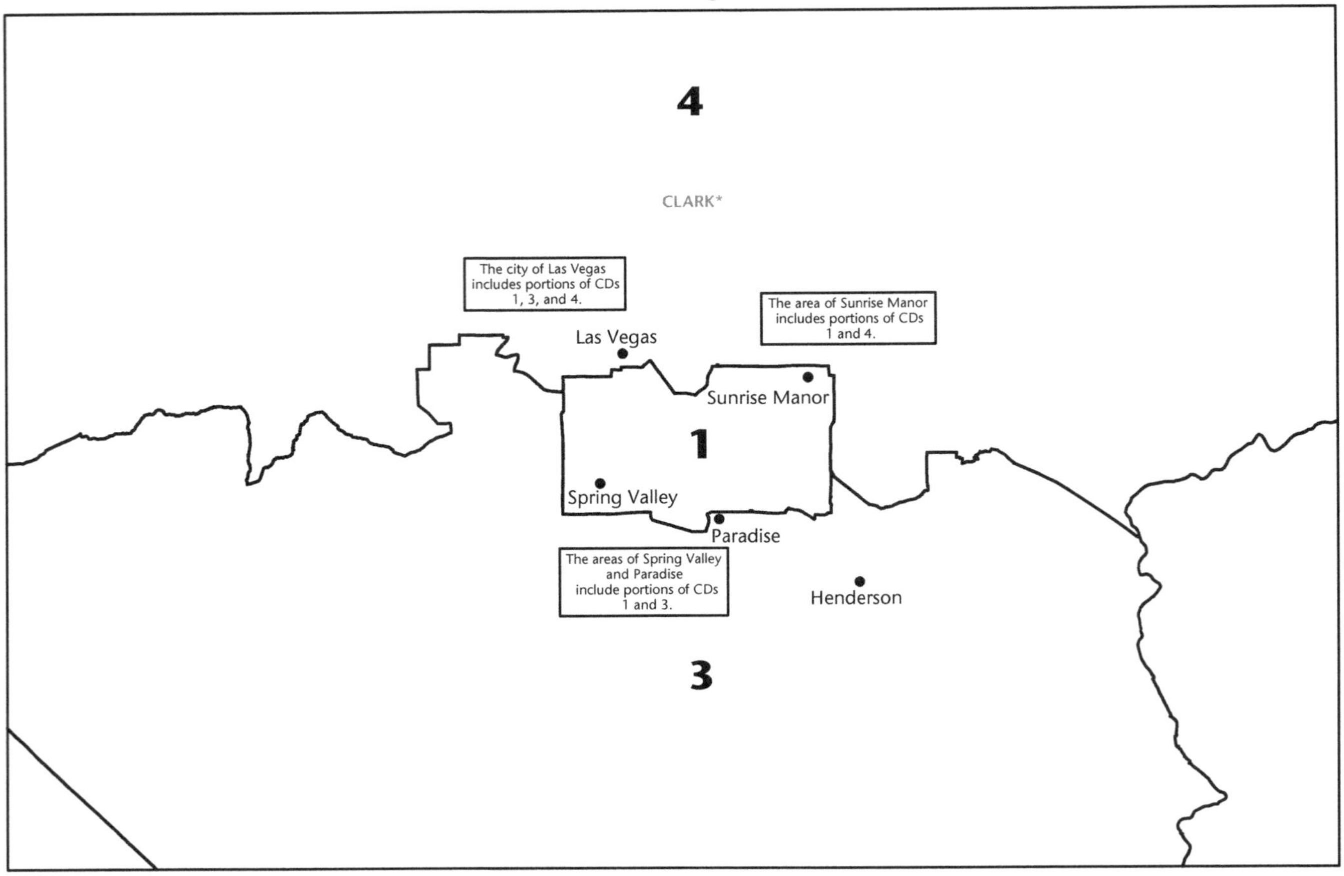

* Asterisk indicates a county whose boundaries include parts of two or more congressional districts.

NEVADA

GOVERNOR

Steve Sisolak (D). Elected 2018 to a four-year term.

SENATORS (2 Democrats)

Jacky Rosen (D). Elected 2018 to a six-year term.

Catherine Cortez Masto (D). Elected 2016 to a six-year term.

REPRESENTATIVES (1 Republican, 3 Democrats)

1. Dina Titus (D)
2. Mark Amodei (R)
3. Susie Lee (D)
4. Steven A. Horsford (D)

POSTWAR VOTE FOR PRESIDENT

		Republican		Democratic				Percentage			
								Total Vote		Major Vote	
Year	Total Vote	Vote	Candidate	Vote	Candidate	Other Vote	Rep.-Dem. Plurality	Rep.	Dem.	Rep.	Dem.
2016**	1,125,385	512,058	Trump, Donald J.	539,260	Clinton, Hillary Rodham	74,067	27,202 D	45.5%	47.9%	48.7%	51.3%
2012	1,014,918	463,567	Romney, W. Mitt	531,373	Obama, Barack H.*	19,978	67,806 D	45.7%	52.4%	46.6%	53.4%
2008	967,848	412,827	McCain, John S. III	533,736	Obama, Barack H.	21,285	120,909 D	42.7%	55.1%	43.6%	56.4%
2004	829,587	418,690	Bush, George W.*	397,190	Kerry, John F.	13,707	21,500 R	50.5%	47.9%	51.3%	48.7%
2000**	608,970	301,575	Bush, George W.	279,978	Gore, Albert Jr.	27,417	21,597 R	49.5%	46.0%	51.9%	48.1%
1996**	464,279	199,244	Dole, Robert "Bob"	203,974	Clinton, Bill*	61,061	4,730 D	42.9%	43.9%	49.4%	50.6%
1992**	506,318	175,828	Bush, George H.*	189,148	Clinton, Bill	141,342	13,320 D	34.7%	37.4%	48.2%	51.8%
1988	350,067	206,040	Bush, George H.	132,738	Dukakis, Michael S.	11,289	73,302 R	58.9%	37.9%	60.8%	39.2%
1984	286,667	188,770	Reagan, Ronald*	91,655	Mondale, Walter F.	6,242	97,115 R	65.8%	32.0%	67.3%	32.7%
1980**	247,885	155,017	Reagan, Ronald	66,666	Carter, Jimmy*	26,202	88,351 R	62.5%	26.9%	69.9%	30.1%
1976	201,876	101,273	Ford, Gerald R.*	92,479	Carter, Jimmy	8,124	8,794 R	50.2%	45.8%	52.3%	47.7%
1972	181,766	115,750	Nixon, Richard M.*	66,016	McGovern, George S.		49,734 R	63.7%	36.3%	63.7%	36.3%
1968**	154,218	73,188	Nixon, Richard M.	60,598	Humphrey, Hubert Horatio Jr.	20,432	12,590 R	47.5%	39.3%	54.7%	45.3%
1964	135,433	56,094	Goldwater, Barry M. Sr.	79,339	Johnson, Lyndon B.*		23,245 D	41.4%	58.6%	41.4%	58.6%
1960	107,267	52,387	Nixon, Richard M.	54,880	Kennedy, John F.		2,493 D	48.8%	51.2%	48.8%	51.2%
1956	96,689	56,049	Eisenhower, Dwight D.*	40,640	Stevenson, Adlai E. II		15,409 R	58.0%	42.0%	58.0%	42.0%
1952	82,190	50,502	Eisenhower, Dwight D.	31,688	Stevenson, Adlai E. II		18,814 R	61.4%	38.6%	61.4%	38.6%
1948	62,117	29,357	Dewey, Thomas E.	31,291	Truman, Harry S.*	1,469	1,934 D	47.3%	50.4%	48.4%	51.6%

Note: An asterisk (*) denotes incumbent. **In past elections, the other vote included: 2016 - 37,384 Libertarian (Gary Johnson); 2000 - 15,008 Green (Ralph Nader); 1996 - 43,986 Reform (Ross Perot); 1992 - 132,580 Independent (Perot); 1980 - 17,651 Independent (John Anderson); 1968 - 20,432 American Independent (George Wallace).

NEVADA

POSTWAR VOTE FOR GOVERNOR

		Republican		Democratic				Percentage			
								Total Vote		Major Vote	
Year	Total Vote	Vote	Candidate	Vote	Candidate	Other Vote	Rep.-Dem. Plurality	Rep.	Dem.	Rep.	Dem.
2018	971,799	440,320	Laxalt, Adam	480,007	Sisolak, Steve	51,472	39,687 D	45.3%	49.4%	47.8%	52.2%
2014	547,349	386,340	Sandoval, Brian*	130,722	Goodman, Robert "Bob"	30,287	255,618 R	70.6%	23.9%	74.7%	25.3%
2010	716,529	382,350	Sandoval, Brian	298,171	Reid, Rory	36,008	84,179 R	53.4%	41.6%	56.2%	43.8%
2006	582,158	279,003	Gibbons, James A. "Jim"	255,684	Titus, Dina	47,471	23,319 R	47.9%	43.9%	52.2%	47.8%
2002	504,079	344,001	Guinn, Kenny*	110,935	Neal, Joe	49,143	233,066 R	68.2%	22.0%	75.6%	24.4%
1998	433,630	223,892	Guinn, Kenny	182,281	Jones, Jan Laverty	27,457	41,611 R	51.6%	42.0%	55.1%	44.9%
1994	379,676	156,875	Gibbons, James A. "Jim"	200,026	Miller, Robert J.*	22,775	43,151 D	41.3%	52.7%	44.0%	56.0%
1990	320,743	95,789	Gallaway, Jim	207,878	Miller, Robert J.*	17,076	112,089 D	29.9%	64.8%	31.5%	68.5%
1986	260,375	65,081	Cafferata, Patty	187,268	Bryan, Richard H.*	8,026	122,187 D	25.0%	71.9%	25.8%	74.2%
1982	239,751	100,104	List, Robert F.*	128,132	Bryan, Richard H.	11,515	28,028 D	41.8%	53.4%	43.9%	56.1%
1978	192,445	108,097	List, Robert F.	76,361	Rose, Robert E.	7,987	31,736 R	56.2%	39.7%	58.6%	41.4%
1974**	169,358	28,959	Crumpler, Shirley	114,114	O'Callaghan, Mike*	26,285	85,155 D	17.1%	67.4%	20.2%	79.8%
1970	146,991	64,400	Fike, Ed	70,697	O'Callaghan, Mike	11,894	6,297 D	43.8%	48.1%	47.7%	52.3%
1966	137,677	71,807	Laxalt, Paul	65,870	Sawyer, Grant*		5,937 R	52.2%	47.8%	52.2%	47.8%
1962	96,929	32,145	Gragson, Oran K.	64,784	Sawyer, Grant*		32,639 D	33.2%	66.8%	33.2%	66.8%
1958	84,889	34,025	Russell, Charles H.*	50,864	Sawyer, Grant		16,839 D	40.1%	59.9%	40.1%	59.9%
1954	78,462	41,665	Russell, Charles H.*	36,797	Pittman, Vail		4,868 R	53.1%	46.9%	53.1%	46.9%
1950	61,773	35,609	Russell, Charles H.	26,164	Pittman, Vail*		9,445 R	57.6%	42.4%	57.6%	42.4%
1946	49,902	21,247	Jepson, Melvin E.	28,655	Pittman, Vail		7,408 D	42.6%	57.4%	42.6%	57.4%

Note: An asterisk (*) denotes incumbent. **In past elections, the other vote included: 1974 - 26,285 Independent American (James Ray Houston).

POSTWAR VOTE FOR SENATOR

		Republican		Democratic				Percentage			
								Total Vote		Major Vote	
Year	Total Vote	Vote	Candidate	Vote	Candidate	Other Vote	Rep.-Dem. Plurality	Rep.	Dem.	Rep.	Dem.
2018	972,132	441,202	Heller, Dean*	490,071	Rosen, Jacky	40,859	48,869 D	45.4%	50.4%	47.4%	52.6%
2016	1,108,294	495,079	Heck, Joe	521,994	Masto, Catherine Cortez	91,221	26,915 D	44.7%	47.1%	48.7%	51.3%
2012	997,805	457,656	Heller, Dean*	446,080	Berkley, Shelley	94,069	11,576 R	45.9%	44.7%	50.6%	49.4%
2010	721,404	321,361	Angle, Sharron E.	362,785	Reid, Harry*	37,258	41,424 D	44.5%	50.3%	47.0%	53.0%
2006	582,572	322,501	Ensign, John*	238,796	Carter, Jack	21,275	83,705 R	55.4%	41.0%	57.5%	42.5%
2004	810,068	284,640	Ziser, Richard	494,805	Reid, Harry*	30,623	210,165 D	35.1%	61.1%	36.5%	63.5%
2000	600,250	330,687	Ensign, John	238,260	Bernstein, Ed	31,303	92,427 R	55.1%	39.7%	58.1%	41.9%
1998	435,790	208,222	Ensign, John	208,650	Reid, Harry*	18,918	428 D	47.8%	47.9%	49.9%	50.1%
1994	380,530	156,020	Furman, Hal	193,804	Bryan, Richard H.*	30,706	37,784 D	41.0%	50.9%	44.6%	55.4%
1992	495,887	199,413	Dahl, Demar	253,150	Reid, Harry*	43,324	53,737 D	40.2%	51.0%	44.1%	55.9%
1988	349,649	161,336	Hecht, Jacob Chic*	175,548	Bryan, Richard H.	12,765	14,212 D	46.1%	50.2%	47.9%	52.1%
1986	261,932	116,606	Santini, James	130,955	Reid, Harry	14,371	14,349 D	44.5%	50.0%	47.1%	52.9%
1982	240,394	120,377	Hecht, Jacob Chic	114,720	Cannon, Howard W.*	5,297	5,657 R	50.1%	47.7%	51.2%	48.8%
1980	246,436	144,224	Laxalt, Paul*	92,129	Gojack, Mary	10,083	52,095 R	58.5%	37.4%	61.0%	39.0%
1976	201,980	63,471	Towell, David	127,295	Cannon, Howard W.*	11,214	63,824 D	31.4%	63.0%	33.3%	66.7%
1974	169,473	79,605	Laxalt, Paul	78,981	Reid, Harry	10,887	624 R	47.0%	46.6%	50.2%	49.8%
1970	147,768	60,838	Raggio, William J.	85,187	Cannon, Howard W.*	1,743	24,349 D	41.2%	57.6%	41.7%	58.3%
1968	152,690	69,068	Fike, Ed	83,622	Bible, Alan Harvey*		14,554 D	45.2%	54.8%	45.2%	54.8%
1964	134,624	67,288	Laxalt, Paul	67,336	Cannon, Howard W.*		48 D	50.0%	50.0%	50.0%	50.0%
1962	97,192	33,749	Wright, William B.	63,443	Bible, Alan Harvey*		29,694 D	34.7%	65.3%	34.7%	65.3%
1958	84,492	35,760	Malone, George W.*	48,732	Cannon, Howard W.		12,972 D	42.3%	57.7%	42.3%	57.7%
1956	96,389	45,712	Young, Cliff	50,677	Bible, Alan Harvey*		4,965 D	47.4%	52.6%	47.4%	52.6%
1954S**	77,513	32,470	Brown, Ernest S.	45,043	Bible, Alan Harvey		12,573 D	41.9%	58.1%	41.9%	58.1%
1952	81,090	41,906	Malone, George W.*	39,184	Mechling, Thomas B.		2,722 R	51.7%	48.3%	51.7%	48.3%
1950	61,762	25,933	Marshall, George E.	35,829	McCarran, Patrick A.*		9,896 D	42.0%	58.0%	42.0%	58.0%
1946	50,354	27,801	Malone, George W.	22,553	Bunker, Berkeley L.		5,248 R	55.2%	44.8%	55.2%	44.8%

Note: An asterisk (*) denotes incumbent. **The 1954 election was for a short term to fill a vacancy.

NEVADA

GOVERNOR 2018

2010 Census Population	County	Total Vote	Republican (Laxalt)	Democratic (Sisolak)	Other	Rep.-Dem. Plurality	Percentage Total Vote Rep.	Percentage Total Vote Dem.	Percentage Major Vote Rep.	Percentage Major Vote Dem.
55,274	CARSON CITY	22,681	12,080	9,249	1,352	2,831 R	53.3%	40.8%	56.6%	43.4%
24,877	CHURCHILL	9,607	7,033	1,869	705	5,164 R	73.2%	19.5%	79.0%	21.0%
1,951,269	CLARK	651,901	266,216	352,814	32,871	86,598 D	40.8%	54.1%	43.0%	57.0%
46,997	DOUGLAS	26,045	16,897	7,962	1,186	8,935 R	64.9%	30.6%	68.0%	32.0%
48,818	ELKO	15,170	11,444	2,604	1,122	8,840 R	75.4%	17.2%	81.5%	18.5%
783	ESMERALDA	371	273	51	47	222 R	73.6%	13.7%	84.3%	15.7%
1,987	EUREKA	757	609	61	87	548 R	80.4%	8.1%	90.9%	9.1%
16,528	HUMBOLDT	5,543	4,061	1,067	415	2,994 R	73.3%	19.2%	79.2%	20.8%
5,775	LANDER	2,091	1,571	316	204	1,255 R	75.1%	15.1%	83.3%	16.7%
5,345	LINCOLN	1,952	1,440	266	246	1,174 R	73.8%	13.6%	84.4%	15.6%
51,980	LYON	20,913	14,211	5,267	1,435	8,944 R	68.0%	25.2%	73.0%	27.0%
4,772	MINERAL	1,809	1,067	540	202	527 R	59.0%	29.9%	66.4%	33.6%
43,946	NYE	17,494	11,103	4,607	1,784	6,496 R	63.5%	26.3%	70.7%	29.3%
6,753	PERSHING	1,764	1,255	360	149	895 R	71.1%	20.4%	77.7%	22.3%
4,010	STOREY	2,359	1,476	721	162	755 R	62.6%	30.6%	67.2%	32.8%
421,407	WASHOE	188,098	87,226	91,684	9,188	4,458 D	46.4%	48.7%	48.8%	51.2%
10,030	WHITE PINE	3,244	2,358	569	317	1,789 R	72.7%	17.5%	80.6%	19.4%
2,700,551	*TOTAL*	*971,799*	*440,320*	*480,007*	*51,472*	*39,687 D*	*45.3%*	*49.4%*	*47.8%*	*52.2%*

NEVADA

SENATOR 2018

2010 Census Population	County	Total Vote	Republican (Heller)	Democratic (Rosen)	Other	Rep.-Dem. Plurality	Percentage Total Vote Rep.	Percentage Total Vote Dem.	Percentage Major Vote Rep.	Percentage Major Vote Dem.
55,274	CARSON CITY	22,694	12,328	9,321	1,045	3,007 R	54.3%	41.1%	56.9%	43.1%
24,877	CHURCHILL	9,612	7,042	1,999	571	5,043 R	73.3%	20.8%	77.9%	22.1%
1,951,269	CLARK	652,044	266,675	359,028	26,341	92,353 D	40.9%	55.1%	42.6%	57.4%
46,997	DOUGLAS	26,057	16,742	8,303	1,012	8,439 R	64.3%	31.9%	66.8%	33.2%
48,818	ELKO	15,174	11,491	2,904	779	8,587 R	75.7%	19.1%	79.8%	20.2%
783	ESMERALDA	371	280	52	39	228 R	75.5%	14.0%	84.3%	15.7%
1,987	EUREKA	758	633	74	51	559 R	83.5%	9.8%	89.5%	10.5%
16,528	HUMBOLDT	5,549	4,022	1,188	339	2,834 R	72.5%	21.4%	77.2%	22.8%
5,775	LANDER	2,093	1,588	350	155	1,238 R	75.9%	16.7%	81.9%	18.1%
5,345	LINCOLN	1,950	1,547	283	120	1,264 R	79.3%	14.5%	84.5%	15.5%
51,980	LYON	20,924	14,296	5,526	1,102	8,770 R	68.3%	26.4%	72.1%	27.9%
4,772	MINERAL	1,810	1,056	570	184	486 R	58.3%	31.5%	64.9%	35.1%
43,946	NYE	17,503	11,397	4,888	1,218	6,509 R	65.1%	27.9%	70.0%	30.0%
6,753	PERSHING	1,764	1,271	398	95	873 R	72.1%	22.6%	76.2%	23.8%
4,010	STOREY	2,360	1,495	724	141	771 R	63.3%	30.7%	67.4%	32.6%
421,407	WASHOE	188,227	86,988	93,828	7,411	6,840 D	46.2%	49.8%	48.1%	51.9%
10,030	WHITE PINE	3,242	2,351	635	256	1,716 R	72.5%	19.6%	78.7%	21.3%
2,700,551	*TOTAL*	*972,132*	*441,202*	*490,071*	*40,859*	*48,869 D*	*45.4%*	*50.4%*	*47.4%*	*52.6%*

NEVADA

HOUSE OF REPRESENTATIVES

			Republican		Democratic				Percentage			
									Total Vote		Major Vote	
CD	Year	Total Vote	Vote	Candidate	Vote	Candidate	Other Vote	Rep.-Dem. Plurality	Rep.	Dem.	Rep.	Dem.
1	2018	152,201	46,978	BENTLEY, JOYCE	100,707	TITUS, DINA*	4,516	53,729 D	30.9%	66.2%	31.8%	68.2%
1	2016	188,352	54,174	PERRY, MARY	116,537	TITUS, DINA*	17,641	62,363 D	28.8%	61.9%	31.7%	68.3%
1	2014	80,299	30,413	TEIJEIRO, ANNETTE	45,643	TITUS, DINA*	4,243	15,230 D	37.9%	56.8%	40.0%	60.0%
1	2012	179,278	56,521	EDWARDS, CHRIS	113,967	TITUS, DINA	8,790	57,446 D	31.5%	63.6%	33.2%	66.8%
2	2018	287,537	167,435	AMODEI, MARK*	120,102	KOBLE, CLINT		47,333 R	58.2%	41.8%	58.2%	41.8%
2	2016	313,336	182,676	AMODEI, MARK*	115,722	EVANS, H.D. "CHIP"	14,938	66,954 R	58.3%	36.9%	61.2%	38.8%
2	2014	186,210	122,402	AMODEI, MARK*	52,016	SPEES, KRISTEN	11,792	70,386 R	65.7%	27.9%	70.2%	29.8%
2	2012	281,449	162,213	AMODEI, MARK*	102,019	KOEPNICK, SAMUEL	17,217	60,194 R	57.6%	36.2%	61.4%	38.6%
3	2018	286,168	122,566	TARKANIAN, DANNY	148,501	LEE, SUSIE	15,101	25,935 D	42.8%	51.9%	45.2%	54.8%
3	2016	310,963	142,926	TARKANIAN, DANNY	146,869	ROSEN, JACKY	21,168	3,943 D	46.0%	47.2%	49.3%	50.7%
3	2014	145,719	88,528	HECK, JOE*	52,644	BILBRAY, ERIN	4,547	35,884 R	60.8%	36.1%	62.7%	37.3%
3	2012	272,523	137,244	HECK, JOE*	116,823	OCEGUERA, JOHN	18,456	20,421 R	50.4%	42.9%	54.0%	46.0%
4	2018	234,868	102,748	HARDY, CRESENT	121,962	HORSFORD, STEVEN A.	10,158	19,214 D	43.7%	51.9%	45.7%	54.3%
4	2016	265,846	118,328	HARDY, CRESENT*	128,985	KIHUEN, RUBEN	18,533	10,657 D	44.5%	48.5%	47.8%	52.2%
4	2014	130,781	63,466	HARDY, CRESENT	59,844	HORSFORD, STEVEN A.*	7,471	3,622 R	48.5%	45.8%	51.5%	48.5%
4	2012	240,492	101,261	TARKANIAN, DANNY	120,501	HORSFORD, STEVEN A.	18,730	19,240 D	42.1%	50.1%	45.7%	54.3%
TOTAL	*2018*	*960,774*	*439,727*		*491,272*		*29,775*	*51,545 D*	*45.8%*	*51.1%*	*47.2%*	*52.8%*
TOTAL	*2016*	*1,078,497*	*498,104*		*508,113*		*72,280*	*10,009 D*	*46.2%*	*47.1%*	*49.5%*	*50.5%*
TOTAL	*2014*	*543,009*	*304,809*		*210,147*		*28,053*	*94,662 R*	*56.1%*	*38.7%*	*59.2%*	*40.8%*
TOTAL	*2012*	*973,742*	*457,239*		*453,310*		*63,193*	*3,929 R*	*47.0%*	*46.6%*	*50.2%*	*49.8%*

Note: An asterisk (*) denotes incumbent.

NEVADA

GENERAL AND PRIMARY ELECTIONS

2018 GENERAL ELECTIONS: OTHER VOTES

Governor Other vote was 18,865 Other ("None Of These Candidates"), 13,891 No Party (Ryan Bundy), 10,076 Independent American (Russell Best), 8,640 Libertarian (Jared Lord)

Senate Other vote was 15,303 Other ("None Of These Candidates"), 9,269 No Party (Barry Michaels), 9,196 Libertarian (Tim Hagan), 7,091 Independent American (Kamau Bakari)

House Other vote was:

CD 1 2,454 Independent American (Dan Garfield), 2,062 Libertarian (Robert Strawder)

CD 3 4,555 Libertarian (Steve Brown), 3,627 No Party (David Goossen), 3,481 Independent American (Harry Vickers), 1,887 No Party (Gil Eisner), 1,551 No Party (Tony Gumina)

CD 4 3,180 Independent American (Warren Markowitz), 2,733 No Party (Rodney Smith), 2,213 Libertarian (Gregg Luckner), 2,032 No Party (Dean McGonigle)

2018 PRIMARY ELECTIONS: SUPPLEMENTARY INFORMATION

Primary	June 12, 2018	**Registration** (as of June 2018 – includes 231,317 inactive registrants)	1,695,450	Democratic	655,016
				Republican	556,612
				Independent American	76,293
				Libertarian	17,200
				Other	18,505
				Nonpartisan	371,824

Primary Type Closed—Only registered Democrats and Republicans could vote in their party's primary.

NEVADA

GENERAL AND PRIMARY ELECTIONS

	REPUBLICAN PRIMARIES			DEMOCRATIC PRIMARIES		
Senator	Heller, Dean*	99,509	70.0%	Rosen, Jacky	110,567	77.1%
	Heck, Thomas "Tom"	26,296	18.5%	"None Of These Candidates"	10,078	7.0%
	"None Of These Candidates"	5,978	4.2%	Knight, David	6,346	4.4%
	Brooks, Sherry	5,145	3.6%	Rheinhart, Allen	4,782	3.3%
	Gazala, Sarah	4,011	2.8%	Sbaih, Jesse	4,540	3.2%
	Harrell, Vic	1,282	0.9%	Mahendra, Bobby	3,835	2.7%
				Burleigh, Daniel	3,244	2.3%
	TOTAL	*142,221*		*TOTAL*	*143,392*	
Governor	Laxalt, Adam	101,651	71.5%	Sisolak, Steve	72,749	50.0%
	Schwartz, Dan	12,919	9.1%	Giunchigliani, Chris	56,511	38.9%
	Fisher, Jared	6,696	4.7%	"None Of These Candidates"	5,069	3.5%
	Carlisle, Stephanie	6,401	4.5%	Bonaventura, John	4,351	3.0%
	"None Of These Candidates"	6,136	4.3%	Thorns, Henry	2,761	1.9%
	Boyd, Bill	6,028	4.2%	Jones, David	2,511	1.7%
	Lusak, Stanleigh Harold	1,011	0.7%	Dewan, Asheesh	1,468	1.0%
	Conquest, Frederick L.	766	0.5%			
	Dundas, Edward	576	0.4%			
	TOTAL	*142,184*		*TOTAL*	*145,420*	
Congressional District 1	Bentley, Joyce	6,444	55.2%	Titus, Dina*	20,898	78.7%
	Horne, Fred	5,235	44.8%	D'Silva, Reuben	5,659	21.3%
	TOTAL	*11,679*		*TOTAL*	*26,557*	
Congressional District 2	Amodei, Mark*	42,351	71.7%	Koble, Clint	9,453	26.1%
	Angle, Sharron E.	10,837	18.3%	Fogarty, Patrick	8,619	23.8%
	Beck, Joel	5,006	8.5%	Shepherd, Rick	7,699	21.3%
	Luetkehans, Ian	882	1.5%	Alm, Vance	4,784	13.2%
				Hurley, Jesse	2,907	8.0%
				Schofield, Jack Jr.	2,713	7.5%
	TOTAL	*59,076*		*TOTAL*	*36,175*	
Congressional District 3	Tarkanian, Danny	15,257	44.1%	Lee, Susie	25,475	66.9%
	Mortensen, Michelle	8,491	24.6%	Weiss, Michael	3,115	8.2%
	Hammond, Scott	5,804	16.8%	Stoltz, Eric	2,759	7.2%
	McKeon, David	1,698	4.9%	Love, Jack	2,208	5.8%
	Teijeiro, Annette	1,225	3.5%	Hart, Richard	1,847	4.9%
	Carter, Patrick	942	2.7%	Schiffman, Steven M.	1,338	3.5%
	Jones, Stephanie	450	1.3%	Pinjuv, Guy	1,331	3.5%
	Hamilton, Eddie	360	1.0%			
	La Croix, Thomas	345	1.0%			
	TOTAL	*34,572*		*TOTAL*	*38,073*	
Congressional District 4	Hardy, Cresent	15,257	47.4%	Horsford, Steven A.	22,730	61.7%
	Gibbs, David	6,102	19.0%	Spearman, Patricia	5,613	15.2%
	Townsend, Bill	3,659	11.4%	Vilela, Amy	3,388	9.2%
	Wegner, Kenneth	3,626	11.3%	Stephens, Allison	2,216	6.0%
	Miller, Jeff	2,563	8.0%	Anzalone, John	2,134	5.8%
	Monroe, Mike A.	973	3.0%	Zeller, Sid	736	2.0%
	TOTAL	*32,180*		*TOTAL*	*36,817*	

Note: An asterisk (*) denotes incumbent.

NEW HAMPSHIRE

Congressional districts first established for elections held in 2012

2 members

* Asterisk indicates a county whose boundaries include parts of two or more congressional districts.

NEW HAMPSHIRE

GOVERNOR

Chris Sununu (R). Re-elected 2018 to a two-year term. Previously elected 2016.

SENATORS (2 Democrats)

Jeanne Shaheen (D). Re-elected 2014 to a six-year term. Previously elected 2008.

Maggie Hassan (D). Elected 2016 to a six-year term.

REPRESENTATIVES (2 Democrats)

1. Chris Pappas (D)
2. Ann McLane Kuster (D)

POSTWAR VOTE FOR PRESIDENT

		Republican		Democratic				Percentage			
								Total Vote		Major Vote	
Year	Total Vote	Vote	Candidate	Vote	Candidate	Other Vote	Rep.-Dem. Plurality	Rep.	Dem.	Rep.	Dem.
2016**	744,296	345,790	Trump, Donald J.	348,526	Clinton, Hillary Rodham	49,980	2,736 D	46.5%	46.8%	49.8%	50.2%
2012	710,972	329,918	Romney, W. Mitt	369,561	Obama, Barack H.*	11,493	39,643 D	46.4%	52.0%	47.2%	52.8%
2008	710,970	316,534	McCain, John S. III	384,826	Obama, Barack H.	9,610	68,292 D	44.5%	54.1%	45.1%	54.9%
2004	677,738	331,237	Bush, George W.*	340,511	Kerry, John F.	5,990	9,274 D	48.9%	50.2%	49.3%	50.7%
2000**	569,081	273,559	Bush, George W.	266,348	Gore, Albert Jr.	29,174	7,211 R	48.1%	46.8%	50.7%	49.3%
1996**	499,175	196,532	Dole, Robert "Bob"	246,214	Clinton, Bill*	56,429	49,682 D	39.4%	49.3%	44.4%	55.6%
1992**	537,943	202,484	Bush, George H.*	209,040	Clinton, Bill	126,419	6,556 D	37.6%	38.9%	49.2%	50.8%
1988	451,074	281,537	Bush, George H.	163,696	Dukakis, Michael S.	5,841	117,841 R	62.4%	36.3%	63.2%	36.8%
1984	389,066	267,051	Reagan, Ronald*	120,395	Mondale, Walter F.	1,620	146,656 R	68.6%	30.9%	68.9%	31.1%
1980**	383,990	221,705	Reagan, Ronald	108,864	Carter, Jimmy*	53,421	112,841 R	57.7%	28.4%	67.1%	32.9%
1976	339,618	185,935	Ford, Gerald R.*	147,635	Carter, Jimmy	6,048	38,300 R	54.7%	43.5%	55.7%	44.3%
1972	334,055	213,724	Nixon, Richard M.*	116,435	McGovern, George S.	3,896	97,289 R	64.0%	34.9%	64.7%	35.3%
1968**	297,298	154,903	Nixon, Richard M.	130,589	Humphrey, Hubert Horatio Jr.	11,806	24,314 R	52.1%	43.9%	54.3%	45.7%
1964	288,093	104,029	Goldwater, Barry M. Sr.	184,064	Johnson, Lyndon B.*		80,035 D	36.1%	63.9%	36.1%	63.9%
1960	295,761	157,989	Nixon, Richard M.	137,772	Kennedy, John F.		20,217 R	53.4%	46.6%	53.4%	46.6%
1956	266,994	176,519	Eisenhower, Dwight D.*	90,364	Stevenson, Adlai E. II	111	86,155 R	66.1%	33.8%	66.1%	33.9%
1952	272,950	166,287	Eisenhower, Dwight D.	106,663	Stevenson, Adlai E. II		59,624 R	60.9%	39.1%	60.9%	39.1%
1948	231,440	121,299	Dewey, Thomas E.	107,995	Truman, Harry S.*	2,146	13,304 R	52.4%	46.7%	52.9%	47.1%

Note: An asterisk (*) denotes incumbent. **In past elections, the other vote included: 2016 - 30,777 Libertarian (Gary Johnson); 2000 - 22,198 Green (Ralph Nader); 1996 - 48,390 Reform (Ross Perot); 1992 - 121,337 Independent (Perot); 1980 - 49,693 Independent (John Anderson); 1968 - 11,173 American Independent (George Wallace).

NEW HAMPSHIRE

POSTWAR VOTE FOR GOVERNOR

		Republican		Democratic				Percentage			
								Total Vote		Major Vote	
Year	Total Vote	Vote	Candidate	Vote	Candidate	Other Vote	Rep.-Dem. Plurality	Rep.	Dem.	Rep.	Dem.
2018	573,602	302,764	Sununu, Chris*	262,359	Kelly, Molly	8,479	40,405 R	52.8%	45.7%	53.6%	46.4%
2016	724,863	354,040	Sununu, Chris	337,589	Van Ostern, Colin	33,234	16,451 R	48.8%	46.6%	51.2%	48.8%
2014	486,183	230,610	Havenstein, Walter "Walt"	254,666	Hassan, Maggie*	907	24,056 D	47.4%	52.4%	47.5%	52.5%
2012	693,877	295,026	Lamontagne, Ovide M.	378,934	Hassan, Maggie	19,917	83,908 D	42.5%	54.6%	43.8%	56.2%
2010	456,588	205,616	Stephen, John A.	240,346	Lynch, John*	10,626	34,730 D	45.0%	52.6%	46.1%	53.9%
2008	682,910	188,555	Kenney, Joseph D.	479,042	Lynch, John*	15,313	290,487 D	27.6%	70.1%	28.2%	71.8%
2006	403,679	104,288	Coburn, Jim	298,760	Lynch, John*	631	194,472 D	25.8%	74.0%	25.9%	74.1%
2004	667,020	325,981	Benson, Craig*	340,299	Lynch, John	740	14,318 D	48.9%	51.0%	48.9%	51.1%
2002	442,976	259,663	Benson, Craig	169,277	Fernald, Mark D.	14,036	90,386 R	58.6%	38.2%	60.5%	39.5%
2000	564,953	246,952	Humphrey, Gordon John	275,038	Shaheen, Jeanne*	42,963	28,086 D	43.7%	48.7%	47.3%	52.7%
1998	318,940	98,473	Lucas, Jay	210,769	Shaheen, Jeanne*	9,698	112,296 D	30.9%	66.1%	31.8%	68.2%
1996	497,040	196,321	Lamontagne, Ovide M.	284,175	Shaheen, Jeanne	16,544	87,854 D	39.5%	57.2%	40.9%	59.1%
1994	311,882	218,134	Merrill, Steve*	79,686	King, Wayne D.	14,062	138,448 R	69.9%	25.6%	73.2%	26.8%
1992	516,170	289,170	Merrill, Steve	206,232	Arnesen, Deborah A.	20,768	82,938 R	56.0%	40.0%	58.4%	41.6%
1990	295,018	177,773	Gregg, Judd*	101,923	Grandmaison, J. Joseph	15,322	75,850 R	60.3%	34.5%	63.6%	36.4%
1988	441,923	267,064	Gregg, Judd	172,543	McEachern, Paul	2,316	94,521 R	60.4%	39.0%	60.8%	39.2%
1986	251,107	134,824	Sununu, John H.*	116,142	McEachern, Paul	141	18,682 R	53.7%	46.3%	53.7%	46.3%
1984	383,910	256,574	Sununu, John H.*	127,156	Spirou, Chris	180	129,418 R	66.8%	33.1%	66.9%	33.1%
1982	282,588	145,389	Sununu, John H.	132,317	Gallen, Hugh J.*	4,882	13,072 R	51.4%	46.8%	52.4%	47.6%
1980	384,031	156,178	Thomson, Meldrim Jr.	226,436	Gallen, Hugh J.*	1,417	70,258 D	40.7%	59.0%	40.8%	59.2%
1978	269,587	122,464	Thomson, Meldrim Jr.*	133,133	Gallen, Hugh J.	13,990	10,669 D	45.4%	49.4%	47.9%	52.1%
1976	342,669	197,589	Thomson, Meldrim Jr.*	145,015	Spanos, Harry V.	65	52,574 R	57.7%	42.3%	57.7%	42.3%
1974	226,665	115,933	Thomson, Meldrim Jr.*	110,591	Leonard, Richard W.	141	5,342 R	51.1%	48.8%	51.2%	48.8%
1972**	323,102	133,702	Thomson, Meldrim Jr.	126,107	Crowley, Roger J.	63,293	7,595 R	41.4%	39.0%	51.5%	48.5%
1970	222,441	102,298	Peterson, Walter R.*	98,098	Crowley, Roger J.	22,045	4,200 R	46.0%	44.1%	51.0%	49.0%
1968	285,342	149,902	Peterson, Walter R.	135,378	Bussiere, Emile R.	62	14,524 R	52.5%	47.4%	52.5%	47.5%
1966	233,642	107,259	Gregg, Hugh	125,882	King, John W.*	501	18,623 D	45.9%	53.9%	46.0%	54.0%
1964	285,863	94,824	Pillsbury, John	190,863	King, John W.*	176	96,039 D	33.2%	66.8%	33.2%	66.8%
1962	230,048	94,567	Pillsbury, John	135,481	King, John W.		40,914 D	41.1%	58.9%	41.1%	58.9%
1960	290,527	161,123	Powell, Wesley*	129,404	Boutin, Bernard L.		31,719 R	55.5%	44.5%	55.5%	44.5%
1958	206,745	106,790	Powell, Wesley	99,955	Boutin, Bernard L.		6,835 R	51.7%	48.3%	51.7%	48.3%
1956	258,695	141,578	Dwinell, Lane*	117,117	Shaw, John		24,461 R	54.7%	45.3%	54.7%	45.3%
1954	194,631	107,287	Dwinell, Lane	87,344	Shaw, John		19,943 R	55.1%	44.9%	55.1%	44.9%
1952	265,715	167,791	Gregg, Hugh	97,924	Craig, William H.		69,867 R	63.1%	36.9%	63.1%	36.9%
1950	191,239	108,907	Adams, Sherman*	82,258	Bingham, Robert P.	74	26,649 R	56.9%	43.0%	57.0%	43.0%
1948	222,571	116,212	Adams, Sherman	105,207	Hill, Herbert W.	1,152	11,005 R	52.2%	47.3%	52.5%	47.5%
1946	163,451	103,204	Dale, Charles M.	60,247	Keefe, F. Clyde		42,957 R	63.1%	36.9%	63.1%	36.9%

Note: An asterisk (*) denotes incumbent. **In past elections, the other vote included: 1972 - 63,199 Independent (Malcolm McLane).

NEW HAMPSHIRE

POSTWAR VOTE FOR SENATOR

		Republican		Democratic				Percentage			
								Total Vote		Major Vote	
Year	Total Vote	Vote	Candidate	Vote	Candidate	Other Vote	Rep.-Dem. Plurality	Rep.	Dem.	Rep.	Dem.
2016	739,140	353,632	Ayotte, Kelly*	354,649	Hassan, Maggie	30,859	1,017 D	47.8%	48.0%	49.9%	50.1%
2014	488,159	235,347	Brown, Scott P.	251,184	Shaheen, Jeanne*	1,628	15,837 D	48.2%	51.5%	48.4%	51.6%
2010	455,149	273,218	Ayotte, Kelly	167,545	Hodes, Paul W.	14,386	105,673 R	60.0%	36.8%	62.0%	38.0%
2008	694,787	314,403	Sununu, John E.*	358,438	Shaheen, Jeanne	21,946	44,035 D	45.3%	51.6%	46.7%	53.3%
2004	657,086	434,847	Gregg, Judd*	221,549	Haddock, Dorris R. "Granny D"	690	213,298 R	66.2%	33.7%	66.2%	33.8%
2002	447,135	227,229	Sununu, John E.	207,478	Shaheen, Jeanne	12,428	19,751 R	50.8%	46.4%	52.3%	47.7%
1998	314,956	213,477	Gregg, Judd*	88,883	Condodemetraky, George	12,596	124,594 R	67.8%	28.2%	70.6%	29.4%
1996	491,966	242,304	Smith, Robert C.*	227,397	Swett, Dick	22,265	14,907 R	49.3%	46.2%	51.6%	48.4%
1992	518,416	249,591	Gregg, Judd	234,982	Rauh, John	33,843	14,609 R	48.1%	45.3%	51.5%	48.5%
1990	291,393	189,792	Smith, Robert C.	91,299	Durkin, John A.	10,302	98,493 R	65.1%	31.3%	67.5%	32.5%
1986	244,797	154,090	Rudman, Warren B.*	79,225	Peabody, Endicott	11,482	74,865 R	62.9%	32.4%	66.0%	34.0%
1984	384,406	225,828	Humphrey, Gordon John*	157,447	D'Amours, Norman E.	1,131	68,381 R	58.7%	41.0%	58.9%	41.1%
1980	375,060	195,559	Rudman, Warren B.	179,455	Durkin, John A.*	46	16,104 R	52.1%	47.8%	52.1%	47.9%
1978	263,779	133,745	Humphrey, Gordon John	127,945	McIntyre, Thomas J.*	2,089	5,800 R	50.7%	48.5%	51.1%	48.9%
1975S**	262,682	113,007	Wyman, Louis C.	140,778	Durkin, John A.	8,897	27,771 D	43.0%	53.6%	44.5%	55.5%
1974**	223,363	110,926	Wyman, Louis C.	110,924	Durkin, John A.	1,513	2 R	49.7%	49.7%	50.0%	50.0%
1972	324,354	139,852	Powell, Wesley	184,495	McIntyre, Thomas J.*	7	44,643 D	43.1%	56.9%	43.1%	56.9%
1968	286,989	170,163	Cotton, Norris R.*	116,816	King, John W.	10	53,347 R	59.3%	40.7%	59.3%	40.7%
1966	229,305	105,241	Thyng, Harrison R.	123,888	McIntyre, Thomas J.*	176	18,647 D	45.9%	54.0%	45.9%	54.1%
1962	224,479	134,035	Cotton, Norris R.*	90,444	Catalfo, Alfred Jr.		43,591 R	59.7%	40.3%	59.7%	40.3%
1962S**	224,811	107,199	Bass, Perkins	117,612	McIntyre, Thomas J.		10,413 D	47.7%	52.3%	47.7%	52.3%
1960	287,545	173,521	Bridges, Styles*	114,024	Hill, Herbert W.		59,497 R	60.3%	39.7%	60.3%	39.7%
1956	251,943	161,424	Cotton, Norris R.*	90,519	Pickett, Laurence M.		70,905 R	64.1%	35.9%	64.1%	35.9%
1954	194,536	117,150	Bridges, Styles*	77,386	Morin, Gerard L.		39,764 R	60.2%	39.8%	60.2%	39.8%
1954S**	189,558	114,068	Cotton, Norris R.	75,490	Betley, Stanley J.		38,578 R	60.2%	39.8%	60.2%	39.8%
1950	190,573	106,142	Tobey, Charles W.*	72,473	Kelley, Emmet J.	11,958	33,669 R	55.7%	38.0%	59.4%	40.6%
1948	222,898	129,600	Bridges, Styles*	91,760	Fortin, Alfred E.	1,538	37,840 R	58.1%	41.2%	58.5%	41.5%

Note: An asterisk (*) denotes incumbent. **Following the closely contested 1974 election, neither candidate was seated and the 1975 special election was held for the remaining years of that term. One each of the 1954 and 1962 elections was for a short term to fill a vacancy.

NEW HAMPSHIRE

GOVERNOR 2018

							Percentage			
							Total Vote		Major Vote	
2010 Census Population	County	Total Vote	Republican (Sununu)	Democratic (Kelly)	Other	Rep.-Dem. Plurality	Rep.	Dem.	Rep.	Dem.
60,088	BELKNAP	26,920	16,856	9,690	374	7,166 R	62.6%	36.0%	63.5%	36.5%
47,818	CARROLL	24,005	13,308	10,432	265	2,876 R	55.4%	43.5%	56.1%	43.9%
77,117	CHESHIRE	32,542	13,875	18,158	509	4,283 D	42.6%	55.8%	43.3%	56.7%
33,055	COOS	11,610	6,397	4,988	225	1,409 R	55.1%	43.0%	56.2%	43.8%
89,118	GRAFTON	40,308	16,734	22,932	642	6,198 D	41.5%	56.9%	42.2%	57.8%
400,721	HILLSBOROUGH	162,468	87,846	72,033	2,589	15,813 R	54.1%	44.3%	54.9%	45.1%
146,445	MERRIMACK	65,025	33,513	30,540	972	2,973 R	51.5%	47.0%	52.3%	47.7%
295,223	ROCKINGHAM	140,163	79,195	59,269	1,699	19,926 R	56.5%	42.3%	57.2%	42.8%
123,143	STRAFFORD	53,306	25,782	26,593	931	811 D	48.4%	49.9%	49.2%	50.8%
43,742	SULLIVAN	17,255	9,258	7,724	273	1,534 R	53.7%	44.8%	54.5%	45.5%
1,316,470	*TOTAL*	*573,602*	*302,764*	*262,359*	*8,479*	*40,405 R*	*52.8%*	*45.7%*	*53.6%*	*46.4%*

NEW HAMPSHIRE

GOVERNOR 2018

2010 Census Population	City/Town	Total Vote	Republican (Sununu)	Democratic (Kelly)	Other	Rep.-Dem. Plurality	Percentage Total Vote Rep.	Percentage Total Vote Dem.	Percentage Major Vote Rep.	Percentage Major Vote Dem.
11,201	AMHERST	6,287	3,269	2,941	77	328 R	52.0%	46.8%	52.6%	47.4%
6,751	ATKINSON	3,550	2,279	1,229	42	1,050 R	64.2%	34.6%	65.0%	35.0%
8,576	BARRINGTON	4,322	2,331	1,904	87	427 R	53.9%	44.1%	55.0%	45.0%
21,203	BEDFORD	10,973	6,815	4,075	83	2,740 R	62.1%	37.1%	62.6%	37.4%
7,356	BELMONT	2,710	1,818	858	34	960 R	67.1%	31.7%	67.9%	32.1%
10,051	BERLIN	2,846	1,420	1,360	66	60 R	49.9%	47.8%	51.1%	48.9%
7,519	BOW	4,253	2,175	2,045	33	130 R	51.1%	48.1%	51.5%	48.5%
13,355	CLAREMONT	3,945	2,117	1,766	62	351 R	53.7%	44.8%	54.5%	45.5%
42,695	CONCORD	17,685	7,244	10,176	265	2,932 D	41.0%	57.5%	41.6%	58.4%
10,115	CONWAY	4,039	1,871	2,117	51	246 D	46.3%	52.4%	46.9%	53.1%
33,109	DERRY	11,431	6,632	4,605	194	2,027 R	58.0%	40.3%	59.0%	41.0%
29,987	DOVER	14,154	5,878	8,054	222	2,176 D	41.5%	56.9%	42.2%	57.8%
14,638	DURHAM	6,552	1,618	4,806	128	3,188 D	24.7%	73.4%	25.2%	74.8%
6,411	EPPING	3,145	1,862	1,238	45	624 R	59.2%	39.4%	60.1%	39.9%
14,306	EXETER	7,821	3,344	4,405	72	1,061 D	42.8%	56.3%	43.2%	56.8%
6,786	FARMINGTON	2,245	1,410	784	51	626 R	62.8%	34.9%	64.3%	35.7%
8,477	FRANKLIN	2,791	1,657	1,085	49	572 R	59.4%	38.9%	60.4%	39.6%
7,126	GILFORD	3,733	2,299	1,399	35	900 R	61.6%	37.5%	62.2%	37.8%
17,651	GOFFSTOWN	7,215	4,183	2,932	100	1,251 R	58.0%	40.6%	58.8%	41.2%
8,523	HAMPSTEAD	4,144	2,693	1,420	31	1,273 R	65.0%	34.3%	65.5%	34.5%
15,430	HAMPTON	8,403	4,593	3,737	73	856 R	54.7%	44.5%	55.1%	44.9%
11,260	HANOVER	6,133	1,066	5,032	35	3,966 D	17.4%	82.0%	17.5%	82.5%
7,684	HOLLIS	4,305	2,288	1,953	64	335 R	53.1%	45.4%	53.9%	46.1%
13,451	HOOKSETT	5,954	3,613	2,263	78	1,350 R	60.7%	38.0%	61.5%	38.5%
24,467	HUDSON	9,367	5,682	3,531	154	2,151 R	60.7%	37.7%	61.7%	38.3%
5,457	JAFFREY	2,218	1,155	1,043	20	112 R	52.1%	47.0%	52.5%	47.5%
23,409	KEENE	9,580	2,900	6,539	141	3,639 D	30.3%	68.3%	30.7%	69.3%
6,025	KINGSTON	2,836	1,751	1,049	36	702 R	61.7%	37.0%	62.5%	37.5%
15,951	LACONIA	6,196	3,726	2,381	89	1,345 R	60.1%	38.4%	61.0%	39.0%
13,151	LEBANON	6,055	1,908	4,070	77	2,162 D	31.5%	67.2%	31.9%	68.1%
8,271	LITCHFIELD	3,650	2,346	1,269	35	1,077 R	64.3%	34.8%	64.9%	35.1%
5,928	LITTLETON	2,235	1,206	975	54	231 R	54.0%	43.6%	55.3%	44.7%
24,129	LONDONDERRY	10,769	6,354	4,300	115	2,054 R	59.0%	39.9%	59.6%	40.4%
109,565	MANCHESTER	36,957	19,147	17,130	680	2,017 R	51.8%	46.4%	52.8%	47.2%
25,494	MERRIMACK TOWN	11,576	6,535	4,885	156	1,650 R	56.5%	42.2%	57.2%	42.8%
15,115	MILFORD	6,403	3,447	2,816	140	631 R	53.8%	44.0%	55.0%	45.0%
86,494	NASHUA	31,417	14,847	16,093	477	1,246 D	47.3%	51.2%	48.0%	52.0%
8,936	NEWMARKET	4,455	1,821	2,572	62	751 D	40.9%	57.7%	41.5%	58.5%
6,507	NEWPORT	2,081	1,296	742	43	554 R	62.3%	35.7%	63.6%	36.4%
12,897	PELHAM	5,557	3,563	1,897	97	1,666 R	64.1%	34.1%	65.3%	34.7%
7,115	PEMBROKE	2,922	1,582	1,304	36	278 R	54.1%	44.6%	54.8%	45.2%
6,284	PETERBOROUGH	3,390	1,168	2,167	55	999 D	34.5%	63.9%	35.0%	65.0%
7,609	PLAISTOW	3,097	1,872	1,171	54	701 R	60.4%	37.8%	61.5%	38.5%
6,990	PLYMOUTH	2,573	829	1,672	72	843 D	32.2%	65.0%	33.1%	66.9%
20,779	PORTSMOUTH	11,209	3,864	7,226	119	3,362 D	34.5%	64.5%	34.8%	65.2%
10,138	RAYMOND	3,890	2,514	1,318	58	1,196 R	64.6%	33.9%	65.6%	34.4%
29,752	ROCHESTER	11,572	6,799	4,560	213	2,239 R	58.8%	39.4%	59.9%	40.1%
28,776	SALEM	11,466	7,293	4,036	137	3,257 R	63.6%	35.2%	64.4%	35.6%
8,693	SEABROOK	3,141	1,993	1,114	34	879 R	63.5%	35.5%	64.1%	35.9%
11,766	SOMERSWORTH	4,072	2,069	1,929	74	140 R	50.8%	47.4%	51.8%	48.2%
7,230	SWANZEY	2,919	1,484	1,393	42	91 R	50.8%	47.7%	51.6%	48.4%
8,785	WEARE	3,713	2,366	1,266	81	1,100 R	63.7%	34.1%	65.1%	34.9%
13,592	WINDHAM	6,673	4,218	2,384	71	1,834 R	63.2%	35.7%	63.9%	36.1%
6,269	WOLFEBORO	3,669	2,125	1,515	29	610 R	57.9%	41.3%	58.4%	41.6%

NEW HAMPSHIRE

HOUSE OF REPRESENTATIVES

			Republican		Democratic				Percentage			
									Total Vote		Major Vote	
CD	Year	Total Vote	Vote	Candidate	Vote	Candidate	Other Vote	Rep.-Dem. Plurality	Rep.	Dem.	Rep.	Dem.
1	2018	291,039	130,996	EDWARDS, EDDIE	155,884	PAPPAS, CHRIS	4,159	24,888 D	45.0%	53.6%	45.7%	54.3%
1	2016	365,984	157,176	GUINTA, FRANK C.*	162,080	SHEA-PORTER, CAROL	46,728	4,904 D	42.9%	44.3%	49.2%	50.8%
1	2014	242,736	125,508	GUINTA, FRANK C.	116,769	SHEA-PORTER, CAROL*	459	8,739 R	51.7%	48.1%	51.8%	48.2%
1	2012	345,022	158,659	GUINTA, FRANK C.*	171,650	SHEA-PORTER, CAROL	14,713	12,991 D	46.0%	49.8%	48.0%	52.0%
2	2018	279,705	117,990	NEGRON, STEVEN	155,358	KUSTER, ANN MCLANE*	6,357	37,368 D	42.2%	55.5%	43.2%	56.8%
2	2016	350,793	158,973	LAWRENCE, JAMES "JIM"	174,495	KUSTER, ANN MCLANE*	17,325	15,522 D	45.3%	49.7%	47.7%	52.3%
2	2014	238,184	106,871	GARCIA, MARILINDA	130,700	KUSTER, ANN MCLANE*	613	23,829 D	44.9%	54.9%	45.0%	55.0%
2	2012	337,394	152,977	BASS, CHARLES*	169,275	KUSTER, ANN MCLANE	15,142	16,298 D	45.3%	50.2%	47.5%	52.5%
TOTAL	*2018*	*570,744*	*248,986*		*311,242*		*10,516*	*62,256 D*	*43.6%*	*54.5%*	*44.4%*	*55.6%*
TOTAL	*2016*	*716,777*	*316,149*		*336,575*		*64,053*	*20,426 D*	*44.1%*	*47.0%*	*48.4%*	*51.6%*
TOTAL	*2014*	*480,920*	*232,379*		*247,469*		*1,072*	*15,090 D*	*48.3%*	*51.5%*	*48.4%*	*51.6%*
TOTAL	*2012*	*682,416*	*311,636*		*340,925*		*29,855*	*29,289 D*	*45.7%*	*50.0%*	*47.8%*	*52.2%*

Note: An asterisk (*) denotes incumbent.

NEW HAMPSHIRE

GENERAL AND PRIMARY ELECTIONS

2018 GENERAL ELECTIONS: OTHER VOTES

Governor	Other vote was 8,197 Libertarian (Jilletta Jarvis), 282 Write-in (Scattered Write-in)
House	Other vote was:
CD 1	4,048 Libertarian (Dan Belforti), 111 Write-in (Scattered Write-in)
CD 2	6,206 Libertarian (Justin O'Donnell), 151 Write-in (Scattered Write-in)

2018 PRIMARY ELECTIONS: SUPPLEMENTARY INFORMATION

Primary	September 11, 2018	**Registration** (as of September 11, 2018)	962,396	Republican	296,553
				Democratic	278,764
				Libertarian	689
				Undeclared	386,390

Primary Type Semi-open—Registered Democrats and Republicans could vote only in their party's primary. "Undeclared" voters could participate in either party's primary, but must declare affiliation at the polls.

	REPUBLICAN PRIMARIES			DEMOCRATIC PRIMARIES		
Governor	Sununu, Chris*	91,025	98.3%	Kelly, Molly	80,599	65.5%
	Scattered Write-In	692	0.7%	Marchand, Steve	41,612	33.8%
	Kelly, Molly (Write-in)	577	0.6%	Sununu, Chris (Write-in)	563	0.5%
	Marchand, Steve (Write-in)	160	0.2%	Scattered Write-In	167	0.1%
	Day, Aaron (Write-in)	90	0.1%	Jarvis, Jilletta (Write-in)	17	
	Jarvis, Jilletta (Write-in)	39		Day, Aaron (Write-in)	8	
	TOTAL	*92,583*		*TOTAL*	*122,966*	

NEW HAMPSHIRE

GENERAL AND PRIMARY ELECTIONS

	REPUBLICAN PRIMARIES			DEMOCRATIC PRIMARIES		
Congressional District 1	Edwards, Eddie	23,763	47.4%	Pappas, Chris	27,350	42.4%
	Sanborn, Andy	20,852	41.6%	Sullivan, Maura Corby	19,560	30.3%
	Martin, Andy	2,126	4.2%	Messmer, Mindi	6,143	9.5%
	Callis, Michael	1,272	2.5%	Andrews, Naomi	4,546	7.0%
	Denaro, Jeffory W.	983	2.0%	Soldati, Lincoln T.	2,003	3.1%
	Crochetiere, Bruce	780	1.6%	McEachern, Deaglan	1,686	2.6%
	Pappas, Chris (Write-in)	175	0.3%	Sanders, Levi	1,160	1.8%
	Sullivan, Maura Corby (Write-in)	74	0.1%	MacKenzie, Mark S.	765	1.2%
	Messmer, Mindi (Write-in)	19		O'Rourke, Terence Murphy	667	1.0%
	Soldati, Lincoln T. (Write-in)	18		Cardinal, Paul	328	0.5%
	Andrews, Naomi (Write-in)	15		Martin, William	235	0.4%
	O'Rourke, Terence Murphy (Write-in)	7		Edwards, Eddie (Write-in)	53	0.1%
	Belforti, Dan (Write-in)	5		Scattered Write-In	36	0.1%
	Sanders, Levi (Write-in)	3		Sanborn, Andy (Write-in)	30	
	Cardinal, Paul (Write-in)	2		Martin, Andy (Write-in)	7	
	MacKenzie, Mark S. (Write-in)	2		Callis, Michael (Write-in)	2	
	McEachern, Deaglan (Write-in)	1		Belforti, Dan (Write-in)	1	
				Denaro, Jeffory W. (Write-in)	1	
	TOTAL	*50,097*		*TOTAL*	*64,573*	
Congressional District 2	Negron, Steven	11,195	25.9%	Kuster, Ann McLane*	55,955	99.1%
	Levenson, Stewart I.	10,952	25.3%	Scattered Write-In	412	0.7%
	Blankenbeker, Lynne	9,858	22.8%	Negron, Steven (Write-in)	27	
	Burns, Robert	6,802	15.7%	Levenson, Stewart I. (Write-in)	26	
	Belanger, Brian	2,421	5.6%	Blankenbeker, Lynne (Write-in)	19	
	Mercer, Jay	1,234	2.9%	Burns, Robert (Write-in)	19	
	Beloin, Gerard	630	1.5%	Mercer, Jay (Write-in)	6	
	Kuster, Ann McLane (Write-in)	121	0.3%	O'Donnell, Justin Francis (Write-in)	3	
	O'Donnell, Justin Francis (Write-in)	11		Belanger, Brian (Write-in)	1	
	Alciere, Tom (Write-in)	5				
	TOTAL	*43,229*		*TOTAL*	*56,468*	

Note: An asterisk (*) denotes incumbent.

NEW JERSEY

Congressional districts first established for elections held in 2012

12 members

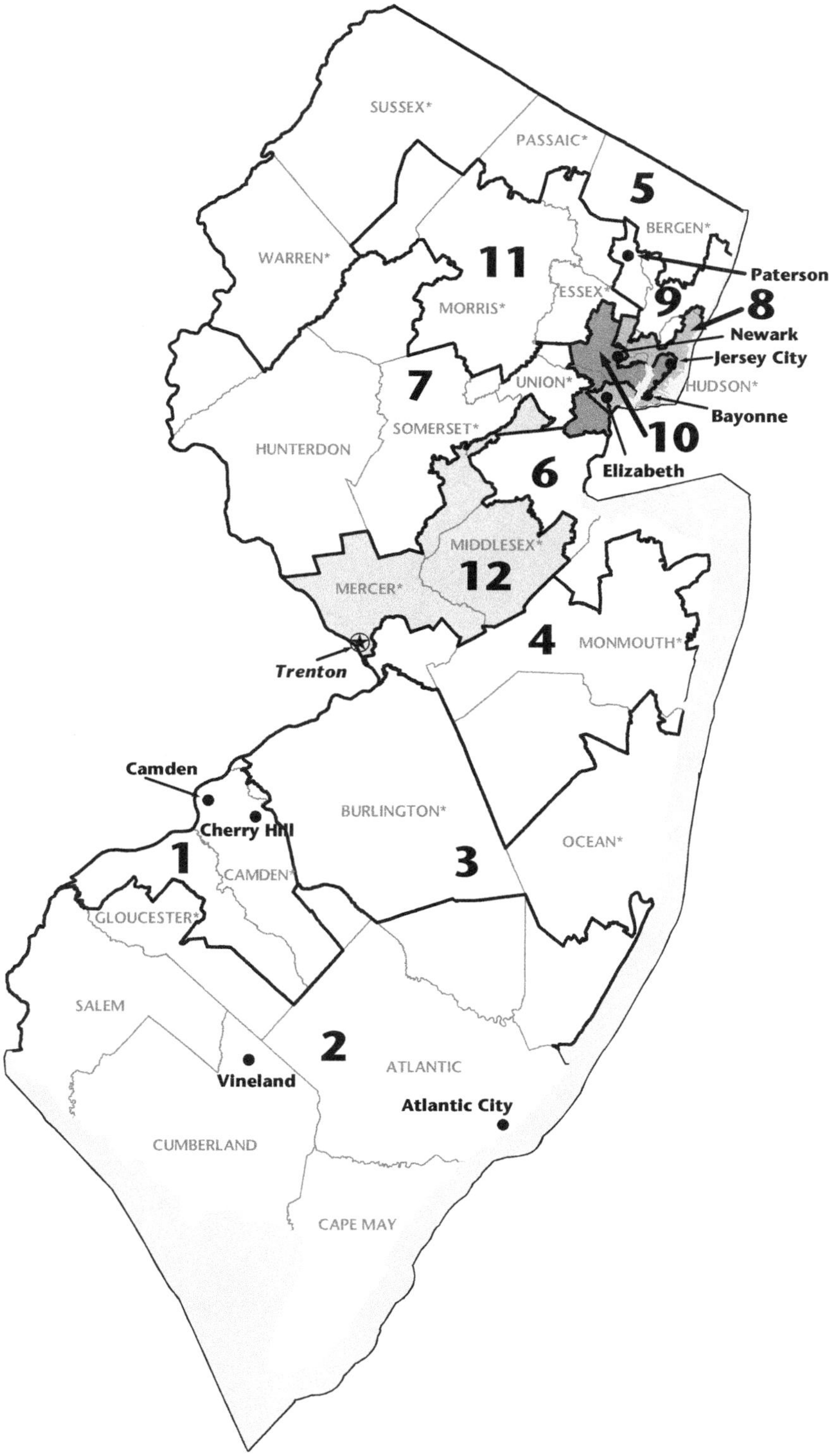

* Asterisk indicates a county whose boundaries include parts of two or more congressional districts.

NEW JERSEY

Northern New Jersey Gateway Area

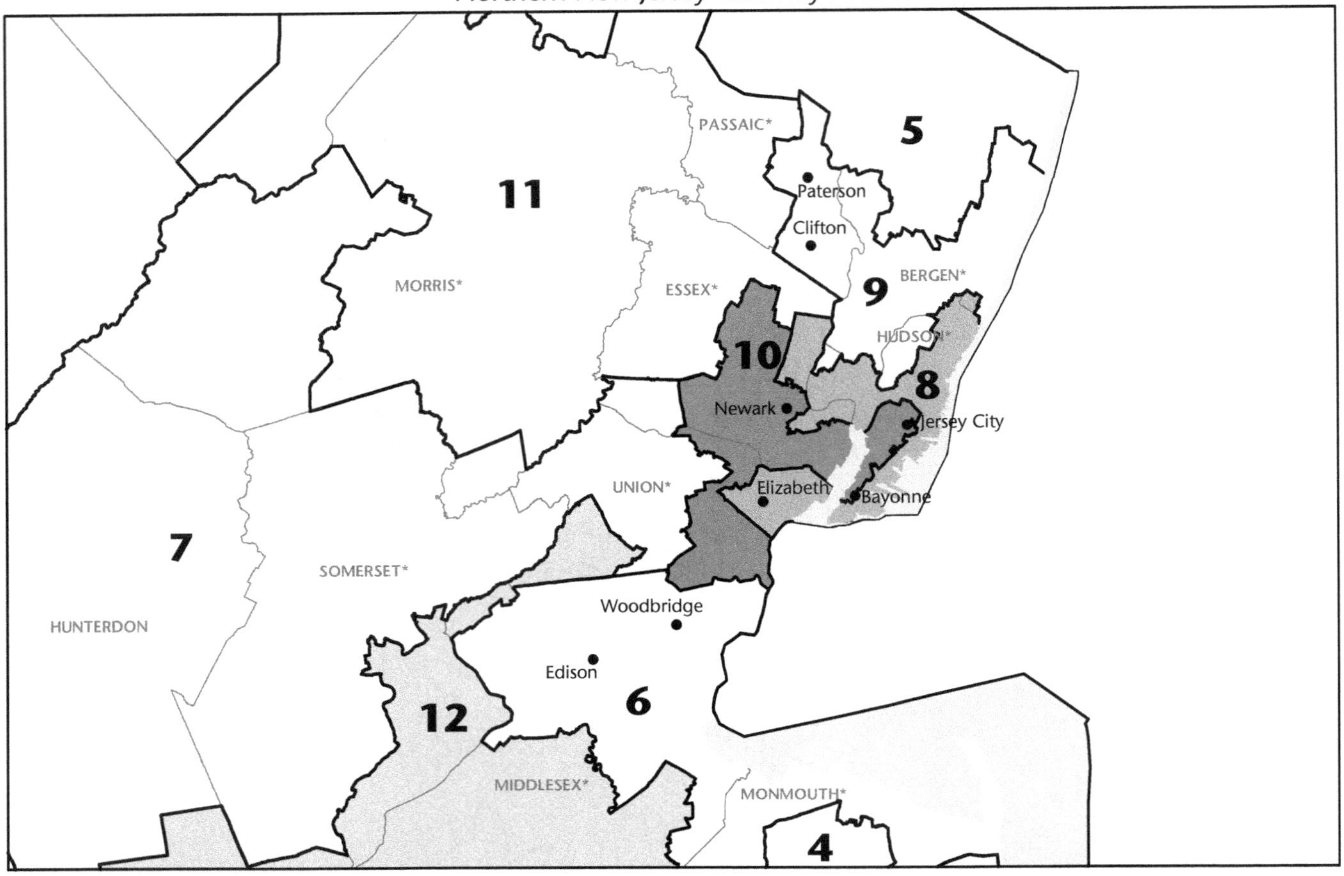

* Asterisk indicates a county whose boundaries include parts of two or more congressional districts.

NEW JERSEY

GOVERNOR

Philip Murphy (D). Elected 2017 to a four-year term.

SENATORS (2 Democrats)

Cory Booker (D). Re-elected 2014 to a six-year term. Previously elected October 16, 2013, to serve the remainder of the term vacated by the June 2013 death of Frank Lautenberg (D). Jeff Chiesa (R) had been appointed June 6, 2013, to fill the vacant seat until the October 2013 special election.

Robert Menendez (D). Re-elected 2018 to a six-year term. Previously elected 2012, 2006.

REPRESENTATIVES (1 Republicans, 11 Democrats)

1. Donald Norcross (D)
2. Jeff Van Drew (D)
3. Andy Kim (D)
4. Christopher H. Smith (R)
5. Joshua S. Gottheimer (D)
6. Frank Pallone (D)
7. Tom Malinowski (D)
8. Albio Sires (D)
9. William J. Pascrell Jr. (D)
10. Donald M. Payne Jr. (D)
11. Mikie Sherrill (D)
12. Bonnie Watson Coleman (D)

POSTWAR VOTE FOR PRESIDENT

		Republican		Democratic				Percentage			
								Total Vote		Major Vote	
Year	Total Vote	Vote	Candidate	Vote	Candidate	Other Vote	Rep.-Dem. Plurality	Rep.	Dem.	Rep.	Dem.
2016**	3,874,046	1,601,933	Trump, Donald J.	2,148,278	Clinton, Hillary Rodham	123,835	546,345 D	41.4%	55.5%	42.7%	57.3%
2012	3,640,292	1,477,568	Romney, W. Mitt	2,125,101	Obama, Barack H.*	37,623	647,533 D	40.6%	58.4%	41.0%	59.0%
2008	3,868,237	1,613,207	McCain, John S. III	2,215,422	Obama, Barack H.	39,608	602,215 D	41.7%	57.3%	42.1%	57.9%
2004	3,611,691	1,670,003	Bush, George W.*	1,911,430	Kerry, John F.	30,258	241,427 D	46.2%	52.9%	46.6%	53.4%
2000**	3,187,226	1,284,173	Bush, George W.	1,788,850	Gore, Albert Jr.	114,203	504,677 D	40.3%	56.1%	41.8%	58.2%
1996**	3,075,807	1,103,078	Dole, Robert "Bob"	1,652,329	Clinton, Bill*	320,400	549,251 D	35.9%	53.7%	40.0%	60.0%
1992**	3,343,594	1,356,865	Bush, George H.*	1,436,206	Clinton, Bill	550,523	79,341 D	40.6%	43.0%	48.6%	51.4%
1988	3,099,553	1,743,192	Bush, George H.	1,320,352	Dukakis, Michael S.	36,009	422,840 R	56.2%	42.6%	56.9%	43.1%
1984	3,217,862	1,933,630	Reagan, Ronald*	1,261,323	Mondale, Walter F.	22,909	672,307 R	60.1%	39.2%	60.5%	39.5%
1980**	2,975,684	1,546,557	Reagan, Ronald	1,147,364	Carter, Jimmy*	281,763	399,193 R	52.0%	38.6%	57.4%	42.6%
1976	3,014,472	1,509,688	Ford, Gerald R.*	1,444,653	Carter, Jimmy	60,131	65,035 R	50.1%	47.9%	51.1%	48.9%
1972	2,997,229	1,845,502	Nixon, Richard M.*	1,102,211	McGovern, George S.	49,516	743,291 R	61.6%	36.8%	62.6%	37.4%
1968**	2,875,395	1,325,467	Nixon, Richard M.	1,264,206	Humphrey, Hubert Horatio Jr.	285,722	61,261 R	46.1%	44.0%	51.2%	48.8%
1964	2,847,663	964,174	Goldwater, Barry M. Sr.	1,868,231	Johnson, Lyndon B.*	15,258	904,057 D	33.9%	65.6%	34.0%	66.0%
1960	2,773,111	1,363,324	Nixon, Richard M.	1,385,415	Kennedy, John F.	24,372	22,091 D	49.2%	50.0%	49.6%	50.4%
1956	2,484,312	1,606,942	Eisenhower, Dwight D.*	850,337	Stevenson, Adlai E. II	27,033	756,605 R	64.7%	34.2%	65.4%	34.6%
1952	2,418,554	1,373,613	Eisenhower, Dwight D.	1,015,902	Stevenson, Adlai E. II	29,039	357,711 R	56.8%	42.0%	57.5%	42.5%
1948	1,949,555	981,124	Dewey, Thomas E.	895,455	Truman, Harry S.*	72,976	85,669 R	50.3%	45.9%	52.3%	47.7%

Note: An asterisk (*) denotes incumbent. **In past elections, the other vote included: 2016 - 72,477 Libertarian (Gary Johnson); 2000 - 94,554 Green (Ralph Nader); 1996 - 262,134 Reform (Ross Perot); 1992 - 521,829 Independent (Perot); 1980 - 234,632 Independent (John Anderson); 1968 - 262,187 American Independent (George Wallace).

NEW JERSEY

POSTWAR VOTE FOR GOVERNOR

		Republican		Democratic				Percentage			
								Total Vote		Major Vote	
Year	Total Vote	Vote	Candidate	Vote	Candidate	Other Vote	Rep.-Dem. Plurality	Rep.	Dem.	Rep.	Dem.
2017	2,147,415	899,583	Guadagno, Kim	1,203,110	Murphy, Philip	44,722	303,527 D	41.9%	56.0%	42.8%	57.2%
2013	2,120,866	1,278,932	Christie, Chris*	809,978	Buono, Barbara	31,956	468,954 R	60.3%	38.2%	61.2%	38.8%
2009	2,423,792	1,174,445	Christie, Chris	1,087,731	Corzine, Jon S.*	161,616	86,714 R	48.5%	44.9%	51.9%	48.1%
2005	2,290,099	985,271	Forrester, Doug	1,224,551	Corzine, Jon S.	80,277	239,280 D	43.0%	53.5%	44.6%	55.4%
2001	2,227,165	928,174	Schundler, Bret	1,256,853	McGreevey, James	42,138	328,679 D	41.7%	56.4%	42.5%	57.5%
1997	2,418,344	1,133,394	Whitman, Christine T.*	1,107,968	McGreevey, James	176,982	25,426 R	46.9%	45.8%	50.6%	49.4%
1993	2,505,964	1,236,124	Whitman, Christine T.	1,210,031	Florio, James J.*	59,809	26,093 R	49.3%	48.3%	50.5%	49.5%
1989	2,253,800	838,553	Courter, James A.	1,379,973	Florio, James J.	35,274	541,420 D	37.2%	61.2%	37.8%	62.2%
1985	1,972,624	1,372,631	Kean, Thomas H.*	578,402	Shapiro, Peter	21,591	794,229 R	69.6%	29.3%	70.4%	29.6%
1981	2,317,239	1,145,999	Kean, Thomas H.	1,144,202	Florio, James J.	27,038	1,797 R	49.5%	49.4%	50.0%	50.0%
1977	2,126,264	888,880	Bateman, Raymond H.	1,184,564	Byrne, Brendan T.*	52,820	295,684 D	41.8%	55.7%	42.9%	57.1%
1973	2,122,010	676,235	Sandman, Charles W.	1,414,613	Byrne, Brendan T.	31,162	738,378 D	31.9%	66.7%	32.3%	67.7%
1969	2,366,606	1,411,905	Cahill, William T.	911,003	Meyner, Robert B.	43,698	500,902 R	59.7%	38.5%	60.8%	39.2%
1965	2,229,583	915,996	Dumont, Wayne Jr.	1,279,568	Hughes, Richard J.*	34,019	363,572 D	41.1%	57.4%	41.7%	58.3%
1961	2,152,662	1,049,274	Mitchell, James P.	1,084,194	Hughes, Richard J.	19,194	34,920 D	48.7%	50.4%	49.2%	50.8%
1957	2,018,488	897,321	Forbes, Malcolm Stevenson Sr.	1,101,130	Meyner, Robert B.*	20,037	203,809 D	44.5%	54.6%	44.9%	55.1%
1953	1,810,812	809,068	Troast, Paul L.	962,710	Meyner, Robert B.	39,034	153,642 D	44.7%	53.2%	45.7%	54.3%
1949**	1,718,788	885,882	Driscoll, Alfred Eastlack*	810,022	Wene, Elmer H.	22,884	75,860 R	51.5%	47.1%	52.2%	47.8%
1946	1,414,527	807,378	Driscoll, Alfred Eastlack	585,960	Hansen, Lewis G.	21,189	221,418 R	57.1%	41.4%	57.9%	42.1%

Note: An asterisk (*) denotes incumbent. **The term of office of New Jersey's Governor was increased from three to four years effective with the 1949 election.

POSTWAR VOTE FOR SENATOR

		Republican		Democratic				Percentage			
								Total Vote		Major Vote	
Year	Total Vote	Vote	Candidate	Vote	Candidate	Other Vote	Rep.-Dem. Plurality	Rep.	Dem.	Rep.	Dem.
2018	3,169,310	1,357,355	Hugin, Robert "Bob"	1,711,654	Menendez, Robert*	100,301	354,299 D	42.8%	54.0%	44.2%	55.8%
2014	1,869,535	791,297	Bell, Jeffrey	1,043,866	Booker, Cory*	34,372	252,569 D	42.3%	55.8%	43.1%	56.9%
2013S**	1,348,659	593,684	Lonegan, Steven M.	740,742	Booker, Cory	14,233	147,058 D	44.0%	54.9%	44.5%	55.5%
2012	3,374,668	1,329,405	Kyrillos, Joe	1,985,783	Menendez, Robert*	59,480	656,378 D	39.4%	58.8%	40.1%	59.9%
2008	3,482,445	1,461,025	Zimmer, Dick	1,951,218	Lautenberg, Frank R.*	70,202	490,193 D	42.0%	56.0%	42.8%	57.2%
2006	2,250,070	997,775	Kean, Tom Jr.	1,200,843	Menendez, Robert*	51,452	203,068 D	44.3%	53.4%	45.4%	54.6%
2002	2,112,604	928,439	Forrester, Douglas R.	1,138,193	Lautenberg, Frank R.	45,972	209,754 D	43.9%	53.9%	44.9%	55.1%
2000	3,015,662	1,420,267	Franks, Bob	1,511,237	Corzine, Jon S.	84,158	90,970 D	47.1%	50.1%	48.4%	51.6%
1996	2,884,106	1,227,817	Zimmer, Dick	1,519,328	Torricelli, Robert G.	136,961	291,511 D	42.6%	52.7%	44.7%	55.3%
1994	2,054,887	966,244	Haytaian, Garabed	1,033,487	Lautenberg, Frank R.*	55,156	67,243 D	47.0%	50.3%	48.3%	51.7%
1990	1,938,454	918,874	Whitman, Christine T.	977,810	Bradley, Bill Warren*	41,770	58,936 D	47.4%	50.4%	48.4%	51.6%
1988	2,987,634	1,349,937	Dawkins, Peter M.	1,599,905	Lautenberg, Frank R.*	37,792	249,968 D	45.2%	53.6%	45.8%	54.2%
1984	3,096,456	1,080,100	Mochary, Mary V.	1,986,644	Bradley, Bill Warren*	29,712	906,544 D	34.9%	64.2%	35.2%	64.8%
1982	2,193,945	1,047,626	Fenwick, Millicent	1,117,549	Lautenberg, Frank R.	28,770	69,923 D	47.8%	50.9%	48.4%	51.6%
1978	1,957,515	844,200	Bell, Jeffrey	1,082,960	Bradley, Bill Warren	30,355	238,760 D	43.1%	55.3%	43.8%	56.2%
1976	2,771,387	1,054,505	Norcross, David F.	1,681,140	Williams, Harrison A. Jr.*	35,742	626,635 D	38.0%	60.7%	38.5%	61.5%
1972	2,791,907	1,743,854	Case, Clifford P.*	963,573	Kerbs, Paul J.	84,480	780,281 R	62.5%	34.5%	64.4%	35.6%
1970	2,142,105	903,026	Gross, Nelson G.	1,157,074	Williams, Harrison A. Jr.*	82,005	254,048 D	42.2%	54.0%	43.8%	56.2%
1966	2,130,688	1,278,843	Case, Clifford P.*	788,021	Wilentz, Warren W.	63,824	490,822 R	60.0%	37.0%	61.9%	38.1%
1964	2,709,575	1,011,280	Shanley, Bernard M.	1,677,515	Williams, Harrison A. Jr.*	20,780	666,235 D	37.3%	61.9%	37.6%	62.4%
1960	2,664,556	1,483,832	Case, Clifford*	1,151,385	Lord, Thorn	29,339	332,447 R	55.7%	43.2%	56.3%	43.7%
1958	1,881,329	882,287	Kean, Robert Winthrop	966,832	Williams, Harrison A. Jr.	32,210	84,545 D	46.9%	51.4%	47.7%	52.3%
1954	1,770,557	861,528	Case, Clifford P.*	858,158	Howell, Charles R.	50,871	3,370 R	48.7%	48.5%	50.1%	49.9%
1952	2,318,232	1,286,782	Smith, H. Alexander*	1,011,187	Alexander, Archibald S.	20,263	275,595 R	55.5%	43.6%	56.0%	44.0%
1948	1,869,882	934,720	Hendrickson, Robert C.	884,414	Alexander, Archibald S.	50,748	50,306 R	50.0%	47.3%	51.4%	48.6%
1946	1,367,155	799,808	Smith, H. Alexander*	548,458	Brunner, George E.	18,889	251,350 R	58.5%	40.1%	59.3%	40.7%

Note: An asterisk (*) denotes incumbent. **The 2013 election was for a short term to fill a vacancy.

NEW JERSEY

GOVERNOR 2017

2010 Census Population	County	Total Vote	Republican (Guadagno)	Democratic (Murphy)	Other	Rep.-Dem. Plurality	Percentage: Total Vote Rep.	Total Vote Dem.	Major Vote Rep.	Major Vote Dem.
274,549	ATLANTIC	67,015	28,456	36,952	1,607	8,496 D	42.5%	55.1%	43.5%	56.5%
905,116	BERGEN	227,929	94,904	129,265	3,760	34,361 D	41.6%	56.7%	42.3%	57.7%
448,734	BURLINGTON	124,714	52,191	70,453	2,070	18,262 D	41.8%	56.5%	42.6%	57.4%
513,657	CAMDEN	120,915	37,113	81,268	2,534	44,155 D	30.7%	67.2%	31.4%	68.6%
97,265	CAPE MAY	30,284	16,118	13,566	600	2,552 R	53.2%	44.8%	54.3%	45.7%
156,898	CUMBERLAND	28,390	11,876	15,686	828	3,810 D	41.8%	55.3%	43.1%	56.9%
783,969	ESSEX	162,701	30,633	129,470	2,598	98,837 D	18.8%	79.6%	19.1%	80.9%
288,288	GLOUCESTER	76,695	32,448	42,349	1,898	9,901 D	42.3%	55.2%	43.4%	56.6%
634,266	HUDSON	109,677	19,236	88,271	2,170	69,035 D	17.5%	80.5%	17.9%	82.1%
128,349	HUNTERDON	45,350	26,708	17,697	945	9,011 R	58.9%	39.0%	60.1%	39.9%
366,513	MERCER	92,483	30,645	59,992	1,846	29,347 D	33.1%	64.9%	33.8%	66.2%
809,858	MIDDLESEX	176,205	70,940	100,847	4,418	29,907 D	40.3%	57.2%	41.3%	58.7%
630,380	MONMOUTH	184,529	101,525	79,432	3,572	22,093 R	55.0%	43.0%	56.1%	43.9%
492,276	MORRIS	145,327	77,203	65,507	2,617	11,696 R	53.1%	45.1%	54.1%	45.9%
576,567	OCEAN	157,996	98,135	56,582	3,279	41,553 R	62.1%	35.8%	63.4%	36.6%
501,226	PASSAIC	95,455	36,230	57,415	1,810	21,185 D	38.0%	60.1%	38.7%	61.3%
66,083	SALEM	17,237	8,629	7,814	794	815 R	50.1%	45.3%	52.5%	47.5%
323,444	SOMERSET	92,273	44,231	45,935	2,107	1,704 D	47.9%	49.8%	49.1%	50.9%
149,265	SUSSEX	42,549	25,401	15,431	1,717	9,970 R	59.7%	36.3%	62.2%	37.8%
536,499	UNION	121,259	39,552	79,113	2,594	39,561 D	32.6%	65.2%	33.3%	66.7%
108,692	WARREN	28,432	17,409	10,065	958	7,344 R	61.2%	35.4%	63.4%	36.6%
8,791,894	*TOTAL*	*2,147,415*	*899,583*	*1,203,110*	*44,722*	*303,527 D*	*41.9%*	*56.0%*	*42.8%*	*57.2%*

NEW JERSEY

SENATOR 2018

2010 Census Population	County	Total Vote	Republican (Hugin)	Democratic (Menendez)	Other	Rep.-Dem. Plurality	Percentage: Total Vote Rep.	Total Vote Dem.	Major Vote Rep.	Major Vote Dem.
274,549	ATLANTIC	94,073	45,954	44,617	3,502	1,337 R	48.8%	47.4%	50.7%	49.3%
905,116	BERGEN	344,183	146,406	188,235	9,542	41,829 D	42.5%	54.7%	43.8%	56.2%
448,734	BURLINGTON	187,100	82,240	98,749	6,111	16,509 D	44.0%	52.8%	45.4%	54.6%
513,657	CAMDEN	183,016	63,279	113,137	6,600	49,858 D	34.6%	61.8%	35.9%	64.1%
97,265	CAPE MAY	40,677	24,823	14,555	1,299	10,268 R	61.0%	35.8%	63.0%	37.0%
156,898	CUMBERLAND	40,147	19,244	19,386	1,517	142 D	47.9%	48.3%	49.8%	50.2%
783,969	ESSEX	253,633	53,537	194,068	6,028	140,531 D	21.1%	76.5%	21.6%	78.4%
288,288	GLOUCESTER	112,702	56,090	52,303	4,309	3,787 R	49.8%	46.4%	51.7%	48.3%
634,266	HUDSON	173,130	36,087	132,180	4,863	96,093 D	20.8%	76.3%	21.4%	78.6%
128,349	HUNTERDON	63,134	36,116	24,823	2,195	11,293 R	57.2%	39.3%	59.3%	40.7%
366,513	MERCER	126,783	41,225	80,773	4,785	39,548 D	32.5%	63.7%	33.8%	66.2%
809,858	MIDDLESEX	255,621	98,764	148,806	8,051	50,042 D	38.6%	58.2%	39.9%	60.1%
630,380	MONMOUTH	261,419	140,628	112,383	8,408	28,245 R	53.8%	43.0%	55.6%	44.4%
492,276	MORRIS	215,038	114,783	93,763	6,492	21,020 R	53.4%	43.6%	55.0%	45.0%
576,567	OCEAN	224,222	141,902	75,597	6,723	66,305 R	63.3%	33.7%	65.2%	34.8%
501,226	PASSAIC	149,324	58,382	86,242	4,700	27,860 D	39.1%	57.8%	40.4%	59.6%
66,083	SALEM	23,815	13,687	9,060	1,068	4,627 R	57.5%	38.0%	60.2%	39.8%
323,444	SOMERSET	136,182	61,373	70,359	4,450	8,986 D	45.1%	51.7%	46.6%	53.4%
149,265	SUSSEX	60,875	37,720	20,229	2,926	17,491 R	62.0%	33.2%	65.1%	34.9%
536,499	UNION	183,633	60,758	117,937	4,938	57,179 D	33.1%	64.2%	34.0%	66.0%
108,692	WARREN	40,603	24,357	14,452	1,794	9,905 R	60.0%	35.6%	62.8%	37.2%
8,791,894	*TOTAL*	*3,169,310*	*1,357,355*	*1,711,654*	*100,301*	*354,299 D*	*42.8%*	*54.0%*	*44.2%*	*55.8%*

NEW JERSEY

HOUSE OF REPRESENTATIVES

			Republican		Democratic				Percentage			
									Total Vote		Major Vote	
CD	Year	Total Vote	Vote	Candidate	Vote	Candidate	Other Vote	Rep.-Dem. Plurality	Rep.	Dem.	Rep.	Dem.
1	2018	263,418	87,617	DILKS, PAUL	169,628	NORCROSS, DONALD*	6,173	82,011 D	33.3%	64.4%	34.1%	65.9%
1	2016	305,473	112,388	PATTERSON, BOB	183,231	NORCROSS, DONALD*	9,854	70,843 D	36.8%	60.0%	38.0%	62.0%
1	2014	162,492	64,073	COBB, GARRY W.	93,315	NORCROSS, DONALD	5,104	29,242 D	39.4%	57.4%	40.7%	59.3%
1	2012	308,519	92,459	HORTON, GREGORY W.	210,470	ANDREWS, ROBERT E.*	5,590	118,011 D	30.0%	68.2%	30.5%	69.5%
2	2018	258,363	116,866	GROSSMAN, SETH	136,685	VAN DREW, JEFF	4,812	19,819 D	45.2%	52.9%	46.1%	53.9%
2	2016	297,795	176,338	LOBIONDO, FRANK A.*	110,838	COLE, DAVID H.	10,619	65,500 R	59.2%	37.2%	61.4%	38.6%
2	2014	177,148	108,875	LOBIONDO, FRANK A.*	66,026	HUGHES, WILLIAM J. JR.	2,247	42,849 R	61.5%	37.3%	62.2%	37.8%
2	2012	289,072	166,679	LOBIONDO, FRANK A.*	116,463	SHOBER, CASSANDRA	5,930	50,216 R	57.7%	40.3%	58.9%	41.1%
3	2018	306,875	149,500	MACARTHUR, TOM*	153,473	KIM, ANDY	3,902	3,973 D	48.7%	50.0%	49.3%	50.7%
3	2016	328,060	194,596	MACARTHUR, TOM*	127,526	LAVERGNE, FREDERICK JOHN	5,938	67,070 R	59.3%	38.9%	60.4%	39.6%
3	2014	186,103	100,471	MACARTHUR, TOM	82,537	BELGARD, AIMEE	3,095	17,934 R	54.0%	44.4%	54.9%	45.1%
3	2012	324,406	174,257	RUNYAN, JON*	145,509	ADLER, SHELLEY	4,640	28,748 R	53.7%	44.9%	54.5%	45.5%
4	2018	294,348	163,065	SMITH, CHRISTOPHER H.*	126,766	WELLE, JOSH	4,517	36,299 R	55.4%	43.1%	56.3%	43.7%
4	2016	332,684	211,992	SMITH, CHRISTOPHER H.*	111,532	PHILLIPSON, LORNA	9,160	100,460 R	63.7%	33.5%	65.5%	34.5%
4	2014	174,849	118,826	SMITH, CHRISTOPHER H.*	54,415	SCOLAVINO, RUBEN	1,608	64,411 R	68.0%	31.1%	68.6%	31.4%
4	2012	306,249	195,146	SMITH, CHRISTOPHER H.*	107,992	FROELICH, BRIAN P.	3,111	87,154 R	63.7%	35.3%	64.4%	35.6%
5	2018	301,823	128,255	MCCANN, JOHN J. JR.	169,546	GOTTHEIMER, JOSHUA S.*	4,022	41,291 D	42.5%	56.2%	43.1%	56.9%
5	2016	337,701	157,690	GARRETT, SCOTT*	172,587	GOTTHEIMER, JOSHUA S.	7,424	14,897 D	46.7%	51.1%	47.7%	52.3%
5	2014	188,921	104,678	GARRETT, SCOTT*	81,808	CHO, ROY	2,435	22,870 R	55.4%	43.3%	56.1%	43.9%
5	2012	304,377	167,503	GARRETT, SCOTT*	130,102	GUSSEN, ADAM	6,772	37,401 R	55.0%	42.7%	56.3%	43.7%
6	2018	221,195	80,443	PEZZULLO, RICHARD J.	140,752	PALLONE, FRANK*		60,309 D	36.4%	63.6%	36.4%	63.6%
6	2016	263,435	91,908	SONNEK-SCHMELZ, BRENT	167,895	PALLONE, FRANK*	3,632	75,987 D	34.9%	63.7%	35.4%	64.6%
6	2014	120,457	46,891	WILKINSON, ANTHONY E.	72,190	PALLONE, FRANK*	1,376	25,299 D	38.9%	59.9%	39.4%	60.6%
6	2012	239,638	84,360	LITTLE, ANNA C.	151,782	PALLONE, FRANK*	3,496	67,422 D	35.2%	63.3%	35.7%	64.3%
7	2018	322,742	150,785	LANCE, LEONARD*	166,985	MALINOWSKI, TOM	4,972	16,200 D	46.7%	51.7%	47.5%	52.5%
7	2016	343,635	185,850	LANCE, LEONARD*	148,188	JACOB, PETER	9,597	37,662 R	54.1%	43.1%	55.6%	44.4%
7	2014	175,997	104,287	LANCE, LEONARD*	68,232	KOVACH, JANICE	3,478	36,055 R	59.3%	38.8%	60.4%	39.6%
7	2012	307,395	175,704	LANCE, LEONARD*	123,090	CHIVUKULA, UPENDRA J.	8,601	52,614 R	57.2%	40.0%	58.8%	41.2%
8	2018	153,455	28,725	MUNIZ, JOHN	119,881	SIRES, ALBIO*	4,849	91,156 D	18.7%	78.1%	19.3%	80.7%
8	2016	174,889	32,337	KHAN, AGHA	134,733	SIRES, ALBIO*	7,819	102,396 D	18.5%	77.0%	19.4%	80.6%
8	2014	79,518	15,141	TISCORNIA, JUDE ANTHONY	61,510	SIRES, ALBIO*	2,867	46,369 D	19.0%	77.4%	19.8%	80.2%
8	2012	167,800	31,767	KARCZEWSKI, MARIA	130,857	SIRES, ALBIO*	5,176	99,090 D	18.9%	78.0%	19.5%	80.5%
9	2018	200,416	57,854	FISHER, ERIC	140,832	PASCRELL, WILLIAM J. JR.*	1,730	82,978 D	28.9%	70.3%	29.1%	70.9%
9	2016	233,242	65,376	CASTILLO, HECTOR L.	162,642	PASCRELL, WILLIAM J. JR.*	5,224	97,266 D	28.0%	69.7%	28.7%	71.3%
9	2014	120,459	36,246	PAUL, DIERDRE	82,498	PASCRELL, WILLIAM J. JR.*	1,715	46,252 D	30.1%	68.5%	30.5%	69.5%
9	2012	220,148	55,094	BOTEACH, SHMULEY	162,834	PASCRELL, WILLIAM J. JR.*	2,220	107,740 D	25.0%	74.0%	25.3%	74.7%
10	2018	200,159	20,191	KHAN, AGHA	175,253	PAYNE, DONALD M. JR.*	4,715	155,062 D	10.1%	87.6%	10.3%	89.7%
10	2016	222,771	26,450	PINCKNEY, DAVID H.	190,856	PAYNE, DONALD M. JR.*	5,465	164,406 D	11.9%	85.7%	12.2%	87.8%
10	2014	112,123	14,154	DENTLEY, YOLANDA	95,734	PAYNE, DONALD M. JR.*	2,235	81,580 D	12.6%	85.4%	12.9%	87.1%
10	2012	230,060	24,271	KELEMEN, BRIAN C.	201,435	PAYNE, DONALD M. JR.	4,354	177,164 D	10.5%	87.6%	10.8%	89.2%
11	2018	323,574	136,322	WEBBER, JAY	183,684	SHERRILL, MIKIE	3,568	47,362 D	42.1%	56.8%	42.6%	57.4%
11	2016	334,992	194,299	FRELINGHUYSEN, RODNEY*	130,162	WENZEL, JOSEPH M.	10,531	64,137 R	58.0%	38.9%	59.9%	40.1%
11	2014	174,932	109,455	FRELINGHUYSEN, RODNEY*	65,477	DUNEC, MARK S.		43,978 R	62.6%	37.4%	62.6%	37.4%
11	2012	309,899	182,239	FRELINGHUYSEN, RODNEY*	123,935	ARVANITES, JOHN	3,725	58,304 R	58.8%	40.0%	59.5%	40.5%
12	2018	252,375	79,041	KIPNIS, DARYL	173,334	COLEMAN, BONNIE WATSON*		94,293 D	31.3%	68.7%	31.3%	68.7%
12	2016	288,634	92,407	UCCIO, STEVEN J.	181,430	COLEMAN, BONNIE WATSON*	14,797	89,023 D	32.0%	62.9%	33.7%	66.3%
12	2014	148,366	54,168	ECK, ALIETA	90,430	COLEMAN, BONNIE WATSON	3,768	36,262 D	36.5%	61.0%	37.5%	62.5%
12	2012	274,391	80,907	BECK, ERIC A.	189,938	HOLT, RUSH D.*	3,546	109,031 D	29.5%	69.2%	29.9%	70.1%
TOTAL	*2018*	*3,098,743*	*1,198,664*		*1,856,819*		*43,260*	*658,155 D*	*38.7%*	*59.9%*	*39.2%*	*60.8%*
TOTAL	*2016*	*3,463,311*	*1,541,631*		*1,821,620*		*100,060*	*279,989 D*	*44.5%*	*52.6%*	*45.8%*	*54.2%*
TOTAL	*2014*	*1,821,365*	*877,265*		*914,172*		*29,928*	*36,907 D*	*48.2%*	*50.2%*	*49.0%*	*51.0%*
TOTAL	*2012*	*3,281,954*	*1,430,386*		*1,794,407*		*57,161*	*364,021 D*	*43.6%*	*54.7%*	*44.4%*	*55.6%*

Note: An asterisk (*) denotes incumbent.

NEW JERSEY

GENERAL AND PRIMARY ELECTIONS

2018 GENERAL ELECTIONS: OTHER VOTES

Governor (2017) Other vote was 12,294 Reduce Property Taxes (Gina Genovese), 10,531 Libertarian (Peter Rohrman), 10,053 Green (Seth Kaper-Dale), 6,864 Constitution (Matthew Riccardi), 4,980 We the People (Vincent Ross)

Senate Other vote was 25,150 Green (Madelyn Hoffman), 21,212 Libertarian (Murray Sabrin), 19,897 For the People (Natalie Rivera), 16,101 New Day NJ (Tricia Flanagan), 9,087 Make it Simple (Kevin Kimple), 8,854 Economic Growth (Hank Schroeder)

House Other vote was:

CD 1	2,821 Libertarian (Robert Shapiro), 2,368 We Deserve Better (Paul Hamlin), 984 Your Voice Hard (Mohammad Kabir)
CD 2	1,726 Libertarian (John Ordille), 1,154 Time for Truth (Steven Fenichel), 1,064 Cannot be Bought (Anthony Sanchez), 868 Other (William Benfer)
CD 3	3,902 Constitution (Lawrence Berlinski)
CD 4	1,387 Libertarian (Michael Rufo), 1,064 Ed the Barber (Edward Stackhouse), 851 Check this column (Brian Reynolds), 844 The Inclusion Candidate (Felicia Stoler), 371 Time for Change (Allen Yusufov)
CD 5	2,115 Libertarian (James Tosone), 1,907 Trade, Health, Environment (Wendy Goetz)
CD 7	2,676 Green (Diane Moxley), 2,296 Freedom, Responsibility, Action (Gregg Mele)
CD 8	3,658 New Way Forward (Mahmoud Mahmoud), 1,191 Libertarian (Dan Delaney)
CD 9	1,730 Libertarian (Claudio Belusic)
CD 10	2,070 C4C 2018 (Cynthia Johnson), 2,038 Never Give Up (Joanne Miller), 607 Libertarian (Scott Diroma)
CD 11	2,182 Honesty, Integrity, Compassion (Robert Crook), 1,386 Libertarian (Ryan Martinez)

2018 PRIMARY ELECTIONS: SUPPLEMENTARY INFORMATION

Primary	June 5, 2018	**Registration** (as of May 31, 2018)	5,827,760	Democratic	2,148,565
				Republican	1,251,264
				Libertarian	9,804
				Conservative	8,091
				U.S. Constitution	7,793
				Green	6,407
				Socialist	3,459
				Natural Law	3,082
				Reform	952
				Unaffiliated	2,388,343

Primary Type Semi-open—Registered Democrats and Republicans could vote only in their party's primary. "Unaffiliated" voters could participate in either party's primary if they were willing to become a member of that party.

	REPUBLICAN PRIMARIES			DEMOCRATIC PRIMARIES		
Senator	Hugin, Robert "Bob"	168,052	75.1%	Menendez, Robert*	262,477	62.3%
	Goldberg, Brian D.	55,624	24.9%	McCormick, Lisa A.	158,998	37.7%
	TOTAL	*223,676*		*TOTAL*	*421,475*	
Governor (2017)	Guadagno, Kim	113,846	46.87%	Murphy, Philip	243,643	48.4%
	Ciattarelli, Jack	75,556	31.1%	Johnson, Jim	110,250	21.9%
	Singh, Hirsch	23,728	9.8%	Wisniewski, John S.	108,532	21.6%
	Rullo, Joe Rudy	15,816	6.5%	Lesniak, Raymond J.	24,318	4.8%
	Rogers, Steven	14,187	5.8%	Brennan, William	11,263	2.2%
				Zinna, Mark	5,213	1.0%
	TOTAL	*243,133*		*TOTAL*	*503,219*	

NEW JERSEY

GENERAL AND PRIMARY ELECTIONS

	REPUBLICAN PRIMARIES			DEMOCRATIC PRIMARIES		
Congressional District 1	Dilks, Paul	12,363	100.0%	Norcross, Donald*	39,788	84.1%
				Carlson, Robert	4,570	9.7%
				Tomaszewski, Scot John	2,953	6.2%
	TOTAL	*12,363*		*TOTAL*	*47,311*	
Congressional District 2	Grossman, Seth	10,215	39.0%	Van Drew, Jeff	16,901	57.0%
	Singh, Hirsh	7,983	30.5%	Youngblood, Tanzie	5,495	18.5%
	Fiocchi, Samuel	6,107	23.3%	Cunningham, Will	4,795	16.2%
	Turkavage, Robert "Turk"	1,854	7.1%	Kleinman, Nathan	2,467	8.3%
	TOTAL	*26,159*		*TOTAL*	*29,658*	
Congressional District 3	MacArthur, Tom*	25,612	100.0%	Kim, Andy	28,514	100.0%
	TOTAL	*25,612*		*TOTAL*	*28,514*	
Congressional District 4	Smith, Christopher H.*	25,930	100.0%	Welle, Josh	16,905	57.1%
				Keady, Jim	12,682	42.9%
	TOTAL	*25,930*		*TOTAL*	*29,587*	
Congressional District 5	McCann, John J. Jr.	16,685	53.0%	Gottheimer, Joshua S.*	27,486	100.0%
	Lonegan, Steven M.	14,767	47.0%			
	TOTAL	*31,452*		*TOTAL*	*27,486*	
Congressional District 6	Pezzullo, Richard J.	9,827	100.0%	Pallone, Frank*	23,621	86.2%
				Walker, Javahn	3,770	13.8%
	TOTAL	*9,827*		*TOTAL*	*27,391*	
Congressional District 7	Lance, Leonard*	24,934	74.9%	Malinowski, Tom	26,172	66.8%
	Brown, Lindsay	4,795	14.4%	Jacob, Peter	7,503	19.1%
	Barsoom, Raafat	3,556	10.7%	Jois, Goutam	5,507	14.1%
	TOTAL	*33,285*		*TOTAL*	*39,182*	
Congressional District 8	Muniz, John	3,052	100.0%	Sires, Albio*	31,583	100.0%
	TOTAL	*3,052*		*TOTAL*	*31,583*	
Congressional District 9	Fisher, Eric	5,142	100.0%	Pascrell, William J. Jr.*	23,365	85.7%
				Henry, William	3,911	14.3%
	TOTAL	*5,142*		*TOTAL*	*27,276*	
Congressional District 10	Khan, Agha	2,292	100.0%	Payne, Donald M. Jr.*	38,206	91.7%
				Fraser, Aaron	3,442	8.3%
	TOTAL	*2,292*		*TOTAL*	*41,648*	
Congressional District 11	Webber, Jay	16,417	40.0%	Sherrill, Mikie	35,338	77.4%
	De Neufville, Peter	12,487	30.5%	Harris, Tamara	6,615	14.5%
	Ghee, Antony	8,991	21.9%	Washburne, Mark	1,538	3.4%
	Allocco, Patrick	1,680	4.1%	Heslin, Alison	1,253	2.7%
	Hewitt, Martin	1,428	3.5%	Cobert, Mitchell	885	1.9%
	TOTAL	*41,003*		*TOTAL*	*45,629*	
Congressional District 12	Kipnis, Daryl	9,776	100.0%	Coleman, Bonnie Watson*	35,430	100.0%
	TOTAL	*9,776*		*TOTAL*	*35,430*	

Note: An asterisk (*) denotes incumbent.

NEW MEXICO

Congressional districts first established for elections held in 2012

3 members

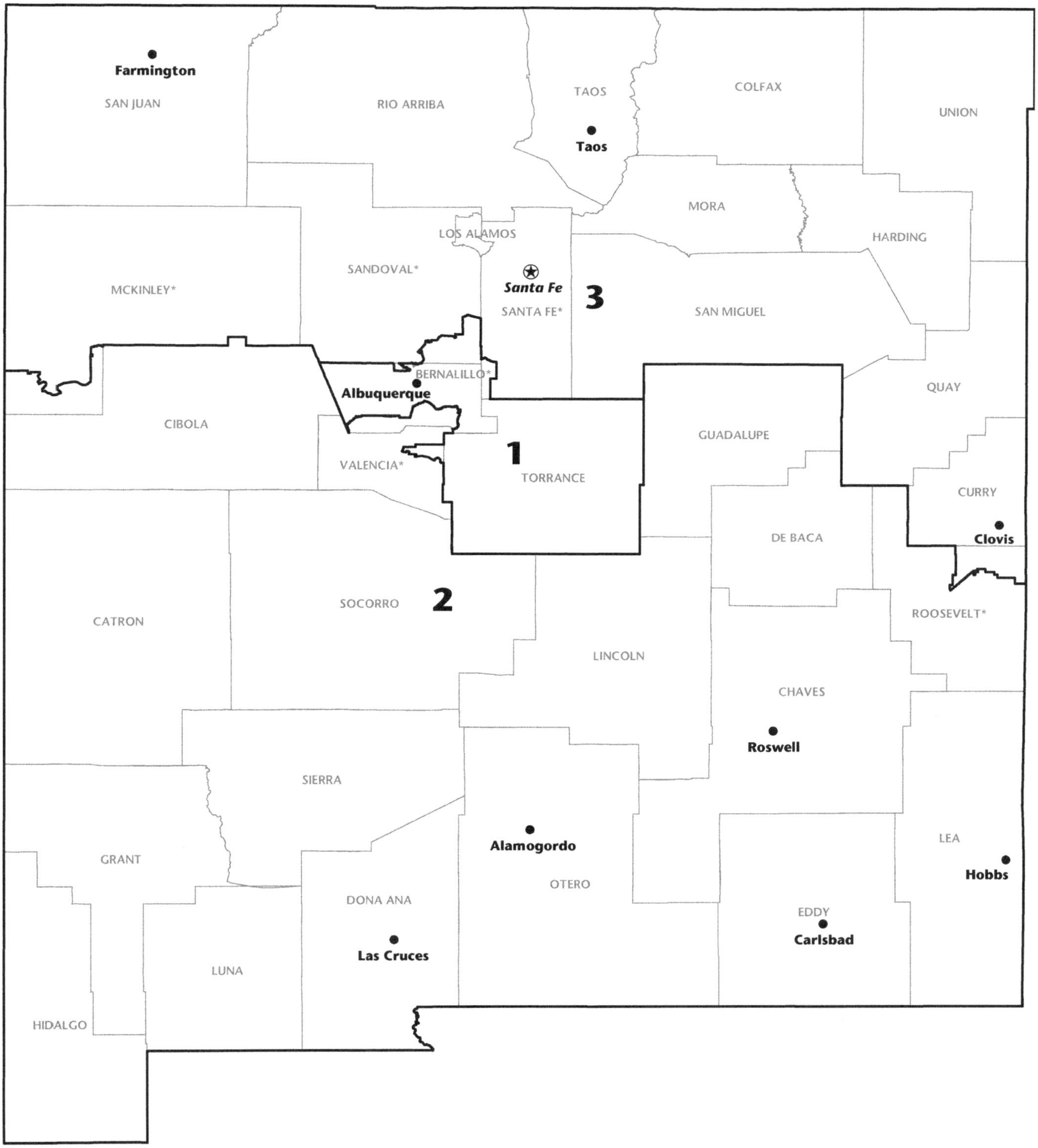

* Asterisk indicates a county whose boundaries include parts of two or more congressional districts.

NEW MEXICO

GOVERNOR

Michelle Lujan Grisham (D). Elected 2018 to a four-year term.

SENATORS (2 Democrats)

Martin Heinrich (D). Re-elected 2018 to a six-year term. Previously elected 2012.

Tom Udall (D). Re-elected 2014 to a six-year term. Previously elected 2008.

REPRESENTATIVES (3 Democrats)

1. Debra Haaland (D)
2. Xochitl Torres Small (D)
3. Ben Ray Lujan (D)

POSTWAR VOTE FOR PRESIDENT

		Republican		Democratic				Percentage			
								Total Vote		Major Vote	
Year	Total Vote	Vote	Candidate	Vote	Candidate	Other Vote	Rep.-Dem. Plurality	Rep.	Dem.	Rep.	Dem.
2016**	798,319	319,667	Trump, Donald J.	385,234	Clinton, Hillary Rodham	93,418	65,567 D	40.0%	48.3%	45.3%	54.7%
2012	783,757	335,788	Romney, W. Mitt	415,335	Obama, Barack H.*	32,634	79,547 D	42.8%	53.0%	44.7%	55.3%
2008	830,158	346,832	McCain, John S. III	472,422	Obama, Barack H.	10,904	125,590 D	41.8%	56.9%	42.3%	57.7%
2004	756,304	376,930	Bush, George W.*	370,942	Kerry, John F.	8,432	5,988 R	49.8%	49.0%	50.4%	49.6%
2000**	598,605	286,417	Bush, George W.	286,783	Gore, Albert Jr.	25,405	366 D	47.8%	47.9%	50.0%	50.0%
1996**	556,074	232,751	Dole, Robert "Bob"	273,495	Clinton, Bill*	49,828	40,744 D	41.9%	49.2%	46.0%	54.0%
1992**	569,986	212,824	Bush, George H.*	261,617	Clinton, Bill	95,545	48,793 D	37.3%	45.9%	44.9%	55.1%
1988	521,287	270,341	Bush, George H.	244,497	Dukakis, Michael S.	6,449	25,844 R	51.9%	46.9%	52.5%	47.5%
1984	514,370	307,101	Reagan, Ronald*	201,769	Mondale, Walter F.	5,500	105,332 R	59.7%	39.2%	60.3%	39.7%
1980**	456,971	250,779	Reagan, Ronald	167,826	Carter, Jimmy*	38,366	82,953 R	54.9%	36.7%	59.9%	40.1%
1976	418,409	211,419	Ford, Gerald R.*	201,148	Carter, Jimmy	5,842	10,271 R	50.5%	48.1%	51.2%	48.8%
1972	386,241	235,606	Nixon, Richard M.*	141,084	McGovern, George S.	9,551	94,522 R	61.0%	36.5%	62.5%	37.5%
1968**	327,350	169,692	Nixon, Richard M.	130,081	Humphrey, Hubert Horatio Jr.	27,577	39,611 R	51.8%	39.7%	56.6%	43.4%
1964	328,645	132,838	Goldwater, Barry M. Sr.	194,015	Johnson, Lyndon B.*	1,792	61,177 D	40.4%	59.0%	40.6%	59.4%
1960	311,107	153,733	Nixon, Richard M.	156,027	Kennedy, John F.	1,347	2,294 D	49.4%	50.2%	49.6%	50.4%
1956	253,926	146,788	Eisenhower, Dwight D.*	106,098	Stevenson, Adlai E. II	1,040	40,690 R	57.8%	41.8%	58.0%	42.0%
1952	238,608	132,170	Eisenhower, Dwight D.	105,661	Stevenson, Adlai E. II	777	26,509 R	55.4%	44.3%	55.6%	44.4%
1948	187,063	80,303	Dewey, Thomas E.	105,464	Truman, Harry S.*	1,296	25,161 D	42.9%	56.4%	43.2%	56.8%

Note: An asterisk (*) denotes incumbent. **In past elections, the other vote included: 2016 - 74,541 Libertarian (Gary Johnson); 2000 - 21,251 Green (Ralph Nader); 1996 - 32,257 Reform (Ross Perot); 1992 - 91,895 Independent (Perot); 1980 - 29,459 Independent (John Anderson); 1968 - 25,737 American Independent (George Wallace).

NEW MEXICO

POSTWAR VOTE FOR GOVERNOR

Year	Total Vote	Republican Vote	Republican Candidate	Democratic Vote	Democratic Candidate	Other Vote	Rep.-Dem. Plurality	Total Vote Rep. (%)	Total Vote Dem. (%)	Major Vote Rep. (%)	Major Vote Dem. (%)
2018	696,459	298,091	Pearce, Steve	398,368	Grisham, Michelle Lujan		100,277 D	42.8%	57.2%	42.8%	57.2%
2014	512,805	293,443	Martinez, Susana*	219,362	King, Gary K.		74,081 R	57.2%	42.8%	57.2%	42.8%
2010	602,827	321,219	Martinez, Susana	280,614	Denish, Diane D.	994	40,605 R	53.3%	46.5%	53.4%	46.6%
2006	559,170	174,364	Dendahl, John	384,806	Richardson, Bill*		210,442 D	31.2%	68.8%	31.2%	68.8%
2002	484,233	189,074	Sanchez, John A.	268,693	Richardson, Bill	26,466	79,619 D	39.0%	55.5%	41.3%	58.7%
1998	498,703	271,948	Johnson, Gary E.*	226,755	Chavez, Martin J.		45,193 R	54.5%	45.5%	54.5%	45.5%
1994**	467,621	232,945	Johnson, Gary E.	186,686	King, Bruce*	47,990	46,259 R	49.8%	39.9%	55.5%	44.5%
1990	411,232	185,692	Bond, Frank	224,564	King, Bruce	976	38,872 D	45.2%	54.6%	45.3%	54.7%
1986	394,833	209,455	Carruthers, Garrey E.	185,378	Powell, Ray B.		24,077 R	53.0%	47.0%	53.0%	47.0%
1982	407,466	191,626	Irick, John B.	215,840	Anaya, Toney		24,214 D	47.0%	53.0%	47.0%	53.0%
1978	345,577	170,848	Skeen, Joseph R.	174,631	King, Bruce	98	3,783 D	49.4%	50.5%	49.5%	50.5%
1974	328,742	160,430	Skeen, Joseph R.	164,172	Apodaca, Jerry	4,140	3,742 D	48.8%	49.9%	49.4%	50.6%
1970**	290,375	134,640	Domenici, Peter V.	148,835	King, Bruce	6,900	14,195 D	46.4%	51.3%	47.5%	52.5%
1968	318,975	160,140	Cargo, David F.*	157,230	Chavez, Fabian	1,605	2,910 R	50.2%	49.3%	50.5%	49.5%
1966	260,232	134,625	Cargo, David F.	125,587	Lusk, T. E.	20	9,038 R	51.7%	48.3%	51.7%	48.3%
1964	318,042	126,540	Tucker, Merle H.	191,497	Campbell, Jack M.*	5	64,957 D	39.8%	60.2%	39.8%	60.2%
1962	247,135	116,184	Mechem, Edwin L.*	130,933	Campbell, Jack M.	18	14,749 D	47.0%	53.0%	47.0%	53.0%
1960	305,542	153,765	Mechem, Edwin L.	151,777	Burroughs, John*		1,988 R	50.3%	49.7%	50.3%	49.7%
1958	205,048	101,567	Mechem, Edwin L.*	103,481	Burroughs, John		1,914 D	49.5%	50.5%	49.5%	50.5%
1956	251,751	131,488	Mechem, Edwin L.	120,263	Simms, John F. Jr.*		11,225 R	52.2%	47.8%	52.2%	47.8%
1954	193,956	83,373	Stockton, Alvin	110,583	Simms, John F. Jr.		27,210 D	43.0%	57.0%	43.0%	57.0%
1952	240,150	129,116	Mechem, Edwin L.*	111,034	Grantham, Everett		18,082 R	53.8%	46.2%	53.8%	46.2%
1950	180,205	96,846	Mechem, Edwin L.	83,359	Miles, John E.		13,487 R	53.7%	46.3%	53.7%	46.3%
1948	189,992	86,023	Lujan, Manuel	103,969	Mabry, Thomas J.*		17,946 D	45.3%	54.7%	45.3%	54.7%
1946	132,630	62,575	Safford, Edward L.	70,055	Mabry, Thomas J.		7,480 D	47.2%	52.8%	47.2%	52.8%

Note: An asterisk (*) denotes incumbent. **In past elections, the other vote included: 1994 - 47,990 Green (Roberto Mondragon). The term of New Mexico's Governor was increased from two to four years effective with the 1970 election.

POSTWAR VOTE FOR SENATOR

Year	Total Vote	Republican Vote	Republican Candidate	Democratic Vote	Democratic Candidate	Other Vote	Rep.-Dem. Plurality	Total Vote Rep. (%)	Total Vote Dem. (%)	Major Vote Rep. (%)	Major Vote Dem. (%)
2018**	697,012	212,813	Rich, Mick	376,998	Heinrich, Martin*	107,201	164,185 D	30.5%	54.1%	36.1%	63.9%
2014	515,506	229,097	Weh, Allen	286,409	Udall, Tom*		57,312 D	44.4%	55.6%	44.4%	55.6%
2012	775,792	351,259	Wilson, Heather A.	395,717	Heinrich, Martin	28,816	44,458 D	45.3%	51.0%	47.0%	53.0%
2008	823,650	318,522	Pearce, Steve	505,128	Udall, Tom		186,606 D	38.7%	61.3%	38.7%	61.3%
2006	558,550	163,826	McCulloch, Allen	394,365	Bingaman, Jeff*	359	230,539 D	29.3%	70.6%	29.3%	70.7%
2002	483,340	314,301	Domenici, Peter V.*	169,039	Tristani, Gloria		145,262 R	65.0%	35.0%	65.0%	35.0%
2000	589,526	225,517	Redmond, Bill	363,744	Bingaman, Jeff*	265	138,227 D	38.3%	61.7%	38.3%	61.7%
1996	551,821	357,171	Domenici, Peter V.*	164,356	Trujillo, Art	30,294	192,815 R	64.7%	29.8%	68.5%	31.5%
1994	463,196	213,025	McMillan, Colin R.	249,989	Bingaman, Jeff*	182	36,964 D	46.0%	54.0%	46.0%	54.0%
1990	406,938	296,712	Domenici, Peter V.*	110,033	Benavides, Tom R.	193	186,679 R	72.9%	27.0%	72.9%	27.1%
1988	508,598	186,579	Valentine, William	321,983	Bingaman, Jeff*	36	135,404 D	36.7%	63.3%	36.7%	63.3%
1984	502,634	361,371	Domenici, Peter V.*	141,253	Pratt, Judith A.	10	220,118 R	71.9%	28.1%	71.9%	28.1%
1982	404,810	187,128	Schmitt, Harrison*	217,682	Bingaman, Jeff		30,554 D	46.2%	53.8%	46.2%	53.8%
1978	343,554	183,442	Domenici, Peter V.*	160,045	Anaya, Toney	67	23,397 R	53.4%	46.6%	53.4%	46.6%
1976	413,141	234,681	Schmitt, Harrison	176,382	Montoya, Joseph M.*	2,078	58,299 R	56.8%	42.7%	57.1%	42.9%
1972	378,330	204,253	Domenici, Peter V.	173,815	Daniels, Jack	262	30,438 R	54.0%	45.9%	54.0%	46.0%
1970	289,906	135,004	Carter, Anderson	151,486	Montoya, Joseph M.*	3,416	16,482 D	46.6%	52.3%	47.1%	52.9%
1966	258,203	120,988	Carter, Anderson	137,205	Anderson, Clinton P.*	10	16,217 D	46.9%	53.1%	46.9%	53.1%
1964	325,774	147,562	Mechem, Edwin L.	178,209	Montoya, Joseph M.	3	30,647 D	45.3%	54.7%	45.3%	54.7%
1960	300,551	109,897	Colwes, William	190,654	Anderson, Clinton P.*		80,757 D	36.6%	63.4%	36.6%	63.4%
1958	203,323	75,827	Atchley, Forrest S.	127,496	Chavez, Dennis*		51,669 D	37.3%	62.7%	37.3%	62.7%
1954	194,422	83,071	Mechem, Edwin L.	111,351	Anderson, Clinton P.*		28,280 D	42.7%	57.3%	42.7%	57.3%
1952	239,711	117,168	Hurley, Patrick J.	122,543	Chavez, Dennis*		5,375 D	48.9%	51.1%	48.9%	51.1%
1948	188,495	80,226	Hurley, Patrick J.	108,269	Anderson, Clinton P.		28,043 D	42.6%	57.4%	42.6%	57.4%
1946	133,282	64,632	Hurley, Patrick J.	68,650	Chavez, Dennis*		4,018 D	48.5%	51.5%	48.5%	51.5%

Note: An asterisk (*) denotes incumbent. **In past elections, the other vote included: 2018 - Libertarian 107,201 (Gary Johnson).

NEW MEXICO

GOVERNOR 2018

2010 Census Population	County	Total Vote	Republican (Pearce)	Democratic (Grisham)	Rep.-Dem. Plurality	Percentage Total Vote Rep.	Percentage Total Vote Dem.	Percentage Major Vote Rep.	Percentage Major Vote Dem.
662,564	BERNALILLO	240,701	91,221	149,480	58,259 D	37.9%	62.1%	37.9%	62.1%
3,725	CATRON	1,843	1,332	511	821 R	72.3%	27.7%	72.3%	27.7%
65,645	CHAVES	16,700	11,352	5,348	6,004 R	68.0%	32.0%	68.0%	32.0%
27,213	CIBOLA	7,129	3,141	3,988	847 D	44.1%	55.9%	44.1%	55.9%
13,750	COLFAX	4,662	2,335	2,327	8 R	50.1%	49.9%	50.1%	49.9%
48,376	CURRY	10,213	7,107	3,106	4,001 R	69.6%	30.4%	69.6%	30.4%
2,022	DE BACA	816	587	229	358 R	71.9%	28.1%	71.9%	28.1%
209,233	DONA ANA	60,939	23,985	36,954	12,969 D	39.4%	60.6%	39.4%	60.6%
53,829	EDDY	15,809	11,178	4,631	6,547 R	70.7%	29.3%	70.7%	29.3%
29,514	GRANT	11,793	4,750	7,043	2,293 D	40.3%	59.7%	40.3%	59.7%
4,687	GUADALUPE	1,694	673	1,021	348 D	39.7%	60.3%	39.7%	60.3%
695	HARDING	478	300	178	122 R	62.8%	37.2%	62.8%	37.2%
4,894	HIDALGO	1,627	842	785	57 R	51.8%	48.2%	51.8%	48.2%
64,727	LEA	13,931	10,845	3,086	7,759 R	77.8%	22.2%	77.8%	22.2%
20,497	LINCOLN	7,841	5,216	2,625	2,591 R	66.5%	33.5%	66.5%	33.5%
17,950	LOS ALAMOS	10,245	4,240	6,005	1,765 D	41.4%	58.6%	41.4%	58.6%
25,095	LUNA	6,143	3,176	2,967	209 R	51.7%	48.3%	51.7%	48.3%
71,492	MCKINLEY	18,355	5,238	13,117	7,879 D	28.5%	71.5%	28.5%	71.5%
4,881	MORA	2,342	678	1,664	986 D	28.9%	71.1%	28.9%	71.1%
63,797	OTERO	17,094	10,644	6,450	4,194 R	62.3%	37.7%	62.3%	37.7%
9,041	QUAY	3,089	1,945	1,144	801 R	63.0%	37.0%	63.0%	37.0%
40,246	RIO ARRIBA	12,811	3,459	9,352	5,893 D	27.0%	73.0%	27.0%	73.0%
19,846	ROOSEVELT	4,652	3,222	1,430	1,792 R	69.3%	30.7%	69.3%	30.7%
130,044	SAN JUAN	37,308	23,961	13,347	10,614 R	64.2%	35.8%	64.2%	35.8%
29,393	SAN MIGUEL	9,239	2,238	7,001	4,763 D	24.2%	75.8%	24.2%	75.8%
131,561	SANDOVAL	55,228	24,803	30,425	5,622 D	44.9%	55.1%	44.9%	55.1%
144,170	SANTA FE	67,086	14,394	52,692	38,298 D	21.5%	78.5%	21.5%	78.5%
11,988	SIERRA	4,723	2,843	1,880	963 R	60.2%	39.8%	60.2%	39.8%
17,866	SOCORRO	6,260	2,664	3,596	932 D	42.6%	57.4%	42.6%	57.4%
32,937	TAOS	14,493	2,687	11,806	9,119 D	18.5%	81.5%	18.5%	81.5%
16,383	TORRANCE	5,365	3,317	2,048	1,269 R	61.8%	38.2%	61.8%	38.2%
4,549	UNION	1,474	1,059	415	644 R	71.8%	28.2%	71.8%	28.2%
76,569	VALENCIA	24,376	12,659	11,717	942 R	51.9%	48.1%	51.9%	48.1%
2,059,179	*TOTAL*	*696,459*	*298,091*	*398,368*	*100,277 D*	*42.8%*	*57.2%*	*42.8%*	*57.2%*

NEW MEXICO

SENATOR 2018

2010 Census Population	County	Total Vote	Republican (Rich)	Democratic (Heinrich)	Libertarian (Johnson)	Rep.-Dem. Plurality	Percentage Total Vote Rep.	Percentage Total Vote Dem.	Percentage Total Vote Libertarian
662,564	BERNALILLO	241,288	61,932	140,082	39,274	78,150 D	25.7%	36.4%	16.3%
3,725	CATRON	1,842	1,075	550	217	525 R	58.4%	49.4%	11.8%
65,645	CHAVES	16,672	8,727	5,279	2,666	3448 R	52.3%	25.4%	16.0%
27,213	CIBOLA	7,121	1,842	3,924	1,355	2082 D	25.9%	26.2%	19.0%
13,750	COLFAX	4,679	1,615	2,333	731	718 D	34.5%	34.0%	15.6%
48,376	CURRY	10,187	5,896	2,793	1,498	3,103 R	57.9%	21.1%	14.7%
2,022	DE BACA	805	342	267	196	75 R	42.5%	39.8%	24.3%
209,233	DONA ANA	60,781	18,101	34,651	8,029	16550 D	29.8%	29.0%	13.2%
53,829	EDDY	15,755	8,826	4,834	2,095	3992 R	56.0%	29.3%	13.3%
29,514	GRANT	11,803	3,598	6,763	1,442	3165 D	30.5%	40.0%	12.2%
4,687	GUADALUPE	1,678	292	1,094	292	802 D	17.4%	35.8%	17.4%
695	HARDING	481	199	198	84	1 R	41.4%	69.2%	17.5%
4,894	HIDALGO	1,595	607	790	198	183 D	38.1%	32.6%	12.4%
64,727	LEA	13,841	8,882	3,331	1,628	5,551 R	64.2%	21.4%	11.8%
20,497	LINCOLN	7,850	4,122	2,617	1,111	1505 R	52.5%	38.3%	14.2%

NEW MEXICO

SENATOR 2018

2010 Census Population	County	Total Vote	Republican (Rich)	Democratic (Heinrich)	Libertarian (Johnson)	Rep.-Dem. Plurality	Percentage Total Vote Rep.	Dem.	Libertarian
17,950	LOS ALAMOS	10,300	2,576	5,798	1,926	3,222 D	25.0%	57.4%	18.7%
25,095	LUNA	6,141	2,313	3,005	823	692 D	37.7%	24.5%	13.4%
71,492	MCKINLEY	18,373	2,915	12,409	3,049	9,360 D	15.9%	25.7%	16.6%
4,881	MORA	2,322	372	1,564	386	1,178 D	16.0%	47.6%	16.6%
63,797	OTERO	17,121	8,460	6,370	2,291	2,090 R	49.4%	26.8%	13.4%
9,041	QUAY	3,087	1,534	1,016	537	518 R	49.7%	34.1%	17.4%
40,246	RIO ARRIBA	12,753	1,945	8,773	2,035	6,738 D	15.3%	31.7%	16.0%
19,846	ROOSEVELT	4,633	2,606	1,277	750	1,329 R	56.2%	23.3%	16.2%
130,044	SAN JUAN	37,363	18,002	12,485	6,876	5,517 R	48.2%	28.7%	18.4%
29,393	SAN MIGUEL	9,230	1,298	6,609	1,323	5,286 D	14.1%	31.4%	14.3%
131,561	SANDOVAL	55,380	17,785	28,198	9,397	10,413 D	32.1%	42.1%	17.0%
144,170	SANTA FE	67,182	9,546	49,994	7,642	40,448 D	14.2%	46.6%	11.4%
11,988	SIERRA	4,732	2,048	1,917	767	131 R	43.3%	39.5%	16.2%
17,866	SOCORRO	6,238	1,700	3,409	1,129	1,709 D	27.3%	34.9%	18.1%
32,937	TAOS	14,506	1,556	10,838	2,112	8,726 D	10.7%	44.0%	14.6%
16,383	TORRANCE	5,366	2,433	1,982	951	451 R	45.3%	32.8%	17.7%
4,549	UNION	1,464	878	334	252	544 R	60.0%	32.2%	17.2%
76,569	VALENCIA	24,443	8,790	11,514	4,139	2,724 D	36.0%	31.9%	16.9%
2,059,179	*TOTAL*	*697,012*	*212,813*	*376,998*	*107,201*	*164,185 D*	*30.5%*	*54.1%*	*15.4%*

Note: The plurality column features the vote differential between the first and second place finishers in each county.

NEW MEXICO

HOUSE OF REPRESENTATIVES

CD	Year	Total Vote	Republican Vote	Republican Candidate	Democratic Vote	Democratic Candidate	Other Vote	Rep.-Dem. Plurality	Total Vote Rep.	Total Vote Dem.	Major Vote Rep.	Major Vote Dem.
1	2018	249,162	90,507	ARNOLD-JONES, JANICE E.	147,336	HAALAND, DEBRA	11,319	56,829 D	36.3%	59.1%	38.1%	61.9%
1	2016	277,967	96,879	PRIEM, RICHARD G.	181,088	GRISHAM, MICHELLE LUJAN*		84,209 D	34.9%	65.1%	34.9%	65.1%
1	2014	180,032	74,558	FRESE, MICHAEL H.	105,474	GRISHAM, MICHELLE LUJAN*		30,916 D	41.4%	58.6%	41.4%	58.6%
1	2012	275,856	112,473	ARNOLD-JONES, JANICE E.	162,924	GRISHAM, MICHELLE LUJAN	459	50,451 D	40.8%	59.1%	40.8%	59.2%
2	2018	199,256	97,767	HERRELL, YVETTE	101,489	TORRES SMALL, XOCHITL		3,722 D	49.1%	50.9%	49.1%	50.9%
2	2016	228,817	143,515	PEARCE, STEVE*	85,232	SOULES, MERRIE LEE	70	58,283 R	62.7%	37.2%	62.7%	37.3%
2	2014	147,777	95,209	PEARCE, STEVE*	52,499	LARA, ROXANNE "ROCKY"	69	42,710 R	64.4%	35.5%	64.5%	35.5%
2	2012	225,515	133,180	PEARCE, STEVE*	92,162	ERHARD, EVELYN MADRID	173	41,018 R	59.1%	40.9%	59.1%	40.9%
3	2018	244,893	76,427	MCFALL, JERALD	155,201	LUJAN, BEN RAY*	13,265	78,774 D	31.2%	63.4%	33.0%	67.0%
3	2016	273,342	102,730	ROMERO, MICHAEL H.	170,612	LUJAN, BEN RAY*		67,882 D	37.6%	62.4%	37.6%	62.4%
3	2014	184,076	70,775	BYRD, JEFFERSON L.	113,249	LUJAN, BEN RAY*	52	42,474 D	38.4%	61.5%	38.5%	61.5%
3	2012	264,719	97,616	BYRD, JEFFERSON L.	167,103	LUJAN, BEN RAY*		69,487 D	36.9%	63.1%	36.9%	63.1%
TOTAL	*2018*	*693,311*	*264,701*		*404,026*		*24,584*	*139,325 D*	*38.2%*	*58.3%*	*39.6%*	*60.4%*
TOTAL	*2016*	*780,126*	*343,124*		*436,932*		*70*	*93,808 D*	*44.0%*	*56.0%*	*44.0%*	*56.0%*
TOTAL	*2014*	*511,885*	*240,542*		*271,222*		*121*	*30,680 D*	*47.0%*	*53.0%*	*47.0%*	*53.0%*
TOTAL	*2012*	*766,090*	*343,269*		*422,189*		*632*	*78,920 D*	*44.8%*	*55.1%*	*44.8%*	*55.2%*

Note: An asterisk (*) denotes incumbent.

NEW MEXICO

GENERAL AND PRIMARY ELECTIONS

2018 GENERAL ELECTIONS: OTHER VOTES

House	Other vote was:
CD 1	11,319 Libertarian (Lloyd Princeton)
CD 2	13,265 Libertarian (Christopher Manning)

2018 PRIMARY ELECTIONS: SUPPLEMENTARY INFORMATION

Primary	June 5, 2018	**Registration** (as of May 31, 2018)	1,233,210	Democratic	565,507
				Republican	375,922
				Other	13,315
				Libertarian	8,318
				No Party, Independent, Declined to State	270,148

Primary Type Closed—Only registered Democrats and Republicans could vote in their party's primary.

	REPUBLICAN PRIMARIES			DEMOCRATIC PRIMARIES		
Senator	Rich, Mick	67,502	100.0%	Heinrich, Martin*	152,145	100.0%
	TOTAL	*67,502*		*TOTAL*	*152,145*	
Governor	Pearce, Steve	75,162	100.0%	Grisham, Michelle Lujan	116,754	66.4%
				Apodaca, Jeff	38,975	22.2%
				Cervantes, Joseph	20,169	11.5%
	TOTAL	*75,162*		*TOTAL*	*175,898*	
Congressional District 1	Arnold-Jones, Janice E.	19,316	100.0%	Haaland, Debra	25,444	40.6%
				Martinez, Damon	16,182	25.8%
				Lopez, Antoinette	12,919	20.6%
				Moya, Paul	3,691	5.9%
				Davis, Patrick	2,385	3.8%
				Lara, Damian	2,063	3.3%
				Heitner, Jesse Andrew (Write-in)	3	
	TOTAL	*19,316*		*TOTAL*	*62,687*	
Congressional District 2	Herrell, Yvette	16,023	49.0%	Torres Small, Xochitl	25,395	72.6%
	Newman, Monty	10,474	32.0%	Hildebrandt, Madeline	9,577	27.4%
	Clarkson, Gavin	4,060	12.4%			
	Griffin, Clayburn	2,143	6.6%			
	TOTAL	*32,700*		*TOTAL*	*34,972*	
Congressional District 3	McFall, Jerald	20,480	100.0%	Lujan, Ben Ray*	63,909	100.0%
	TOTAL	*20,480*		*TOTAL*	*63,909*	

Note: An asterisk (*) denotes incumbent.

NEW YORK

Congressional districts first established for elections held in 2012
27 members

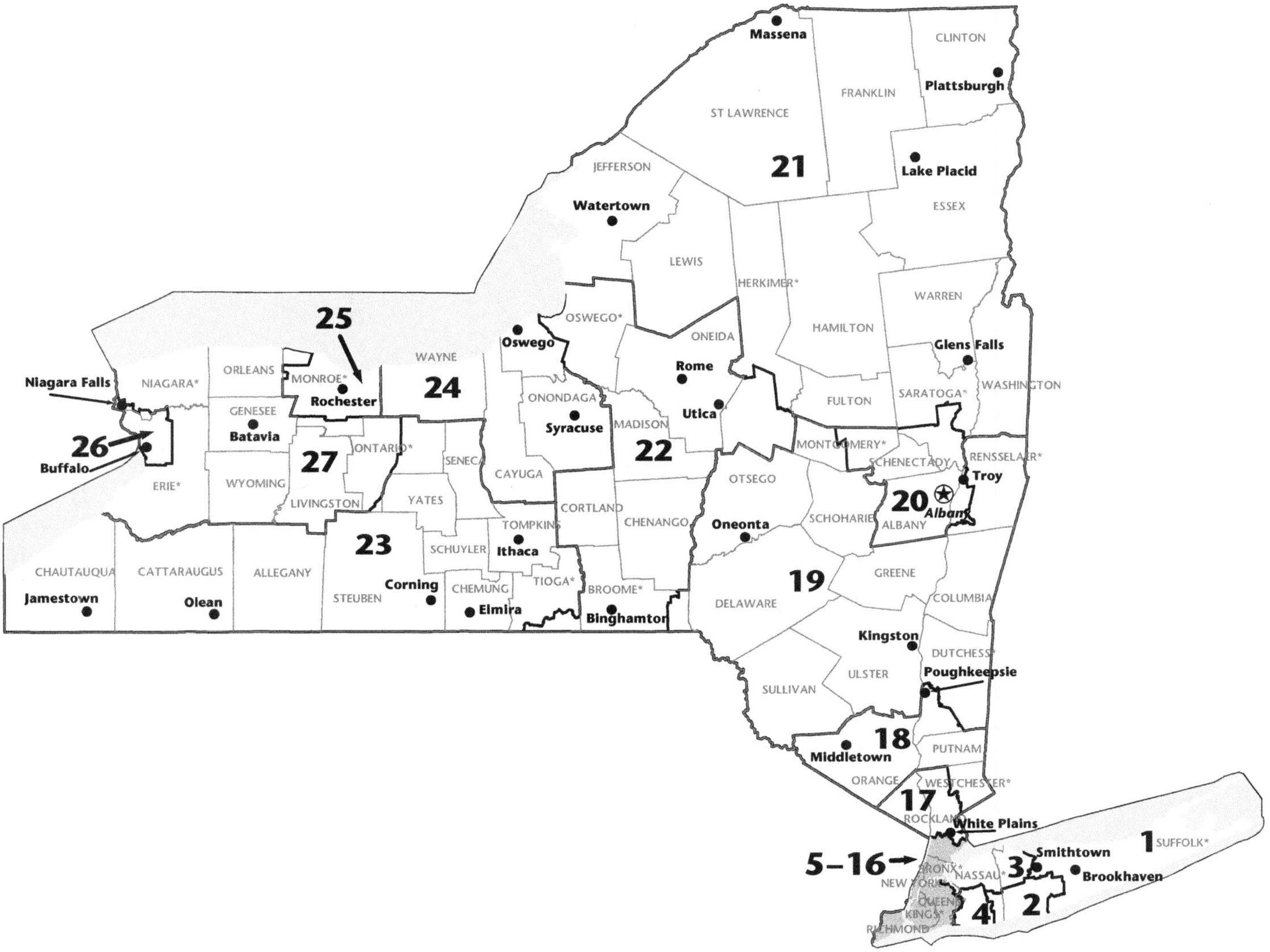

* Asterisk indicates a county whose boundaries include parts of two or more congressional districts.

NEW YORK

New York City Area

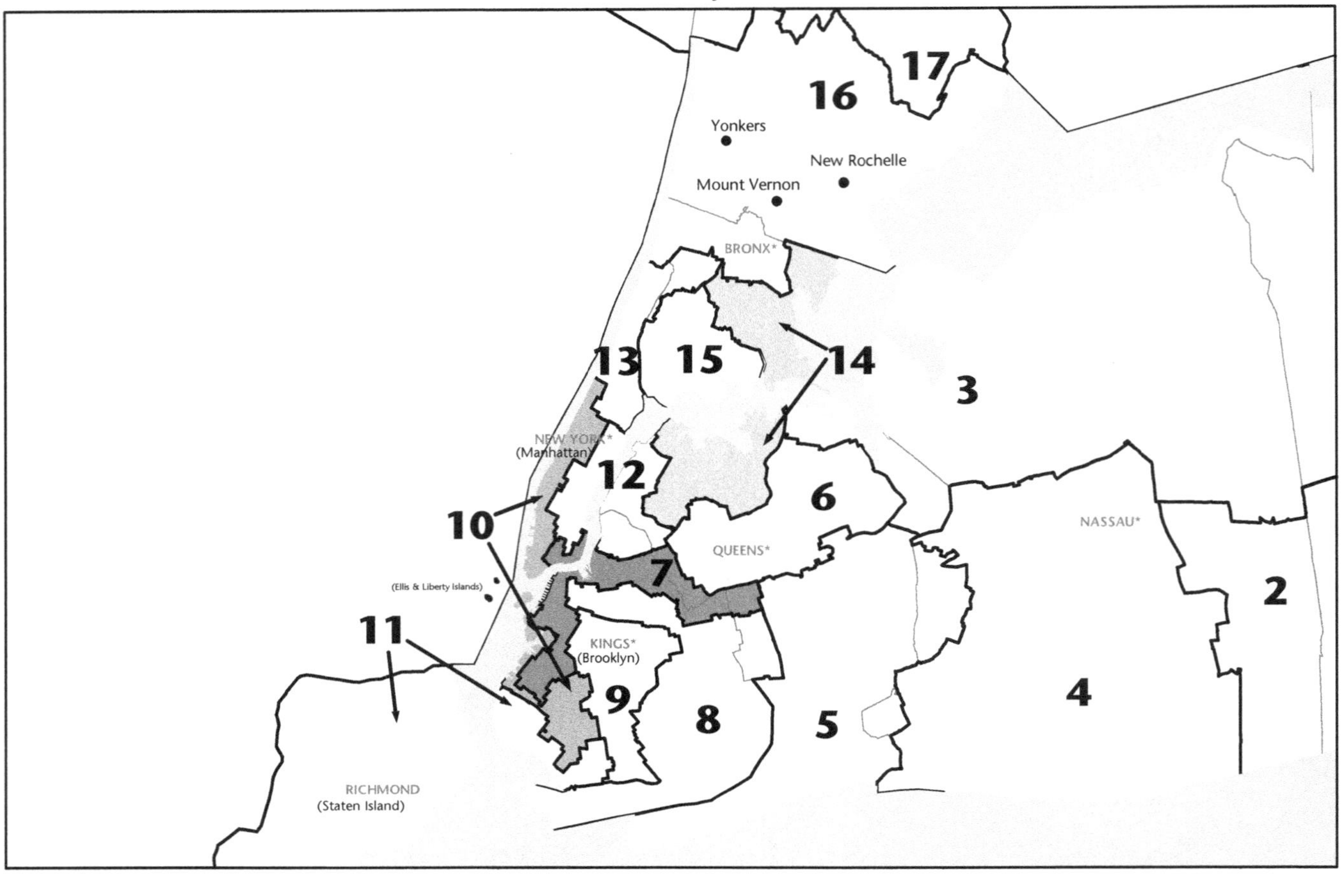

* Asterisk indicates a county whose boundaries include parts of two or more congressional districts.

NEW YORK

GOVERNOR

Andrew M. Cuomo (D). Re-elected 2018 to a four-year term. Previously elected 2014, 2010.

SENATORS (2 Democrats)

Kirsten E. Gillibrand (D). Re-elected 2018 to a six-year term. Previously elected 2012 and the remaining two years of the term vacated by Hillary Rodham Clinton (D), who resigned in January 2009 to become U.S. secretary of state. Gillibrand sworn in as senator January 27, 2009, shortly after the vacancy occurred.

Charles E. Schumer (D). Re-elected 2016 to a six-year term. Previously elected 2010, 2004, 1998.

REPRESENTATIVES (6 Republicans, 21 Democrats)

1. Lee M. Zeldin (R)
2. Peter T. King (R)
3. Thomas R. Suozzi (D)
4. Kathleen M. Rice (D)
5. Gregory W. Meeks (D)
6. Grace Meng (D)
7. Nydia Velazquez (D)
8. Hakeem Jeffries (D)
9. Yvette D. Clarke (D)
10. Jerrold Nadler (D)
11. Max Rose (D)
12. Carolyn B. Maloney (D)
13. Adriano Espaillat (D)
14. Alexandria Ocasio-Cortez (D)
15. Jose E. Serrano (D)
16. Eliot L. Engel (D)
17. Nita M. Lowey (D)
18. Sean Maloney (D)
19. Antonio Delgado (D)
20. Paul D. Tonko (D)
21. Elise Stefanik (R)
22. Anthony Brindisi (D)
23. Thomas W. Reed II (R)
24. John M. Katko (R)
25. Joseph D. Morelle (D)
26. Brian M. Higgins (D)
27. Chris Collins (R)

POSTWAR VOTE FOR PRESIDENT

		Republican		Democratic				Percentage: Total Vote		Percentage: Major Vote	
Year	Total Vote	Vote	Candidate	Vote	Candidate	Other Vote	Rep.-Dem. Plurality	Rep.	Dem.	Rep.	Dem.
2016**	7,721,442	2,819,533	Trump, Donald J.	4,556,118	Clinton, Hillary Rodham	345,791	1,736,585 D	36.5%	59.0%	38.2%	61.8%
2012	7,081,159	2,490,431	Romney, W. Mitt	4,485,741	Obama, Barack H.*	104,987	1,995,310 D	35.2%	63.3%	35.7%	64.3%
2008	7,640,931	2,752,771	McCain, John S. III	4,804,945	Obama, Barack H.	83,215	2,052,174 D	36.0%	62.9%	36.4%	63.6%
2004	7,391,036	2,962,567	Bush, George W.*	4,314,280	Kerry, John F.	114,189	1,351,713 D	40.1%	58.4%	40.7%	59.3%
2000**	6,821,999	2,403,374	Bush, George W.	4,107,697	Gore, Albert Jr.	310,928	1,704,323 D	35.2%	60.2%	36.9%	63.1%
1996**	6,316,129	1,933,492	Dole, Robert "Bob"	3,756,177	Clinton, Bill*	626,460	1,822,685 D	30.6%	59.5%	34.0%	66.0%
1992**	6,926,925	2,346,649	Bush, George H.*	3,444,450	Clinton, Bill	1,135,826	1,097,801 D	33.9%	49.7%	40.5%	59.5%
1988	6,485,683	3,081,871	Bush, George H.	3,347,882	Dukakis, Michael S.	55,930	266,011 D	47.5%	51.6%	47.9%	52.1%
1984	6,806,810	3,664,763	Reagan, Ronald*	3,119,609	Mondale, Walter F.	22,438	545,154 R	53.8%	45.8%	54.0%	46.0%
1980**	6,201,959	2,893,831	Reagan, Ronald	2,728,372	Carter, Jimmy*	579,756	165,459 R	46.7%	44.0%	51.5%	48.5%
1976	6,534,170	3,100,791	Ford, Gerald R.*	3,389,558	Carter, Jimmy	43,821	288,767 D	47.5%	51.9%	47.8%	52.2%
1972	7,165,919	4,192,778	Nixon, Richard M.*	2,951,084	McGovern, George S.	22,057	1,241,694 R	58.5%	41.2%	58.7%	41.3%
1968**	6,791,688	3,007,932	Nixon, Richard M.	3,378,470	Humphrey, Hubert Horatio Jr.	405,286	370,538 D	44.3%	49.7%	47.1%	52.9%
1964	7,166,275	2,243,559	Goldwater, Barry M. Sr.	4,913,102	Johnson, Lyndon B.*	9,614	2,669,543 D	31.3%	68.6%	31.3%	68.7%
1960	7,291,079	3,446,419	Nixon, Richard M.	3,830,085	Kennedy, John F.	14,575	383,666 D	47.3%	52.5%	47.4%	52.6%
1956	7,095,971	4,345,506	Eisenhower, Dwight D.*	2,747,944	Stevenson, Adlai E. II	2,521	1,597,562 R	61.2%	38.7%	61.3%	38.7%
1952	7,128,239	3,952,813	Eisenhower, Dwight D.	3,104,601	Stevenson, Adlai E. II	70,825	848,212 R	55.5%	43.6%	56.0%	44.0%
1948**	6,177,337	2,841,163	Dewey, Thomas E.	2,780,204	Truman, Harry S.*	555,970	60,959 R	46.0%	45.0%	50.5%	49.5%

Note: An asterisk (*) denotes incumbent. **In past elections, the other vote included: 2016 - 176,598 Libertarian (Gary Johnson); 2000 - 244,030 Green (Ralph Nader); 1996 - 503,458 Reform (Ross Perot); 1992 - 1,090,721 Independent (Perot); 1980 - 467,801 Independent (John Anderson); 1968 - 358,864 American Independent (George Wallace); 1948 - 509,559 Progressive (Henry Wallace).

NEW YORK

POSTWAR VOTE FOR GOVERNOR

		Republican		Democratic				Percentage			
								Total Vote		Major Vote	
Year	Total Vote	Vote	Candidate	Vote	Candidate	Other Vote	Rep.-Dem. Plurality	Rep.	Dem.	Rep.	Dem.
2018	6,104,477	2,207,602	Molinaro, Marcus	3,635,340	Cuomo, Andrew M.*	261,535	1,427,738 D	36.2%	59.6%	37.8%	62.2%
2014	3,819,086	1,537,077	Astorino, Rob	2,069,480	Cuomo, Andrew M.*	212,529	532,403 D	40.2%	54.2%	42.6%	57.4%
2010	4,658,825	1,548,184	Paladino, Carl	2,911,721	Cuomo, Andrew M.	198,920	1,363,537 D	33.2%	62.5%	34.7%	65.3%
2006	4,437,220	1,274,335	Faso, John	3,086,709	Spitzer, Eliot	76,176	1,812,374 D	28.7%	69.6%	29.2%	70.8%
2002**	4,579,078	2,262,255	Pataki, George E.*	1,534,064	McCall, H. Carl	782,759	728,191 R	49.4%	33.5%	59.6%	40.4%
1998	4,735,236	2,571,991	Pataki, George E.*	1,570,317	Vallone, Peter F.	592,928	1,001,674 R	54.3%	33.2%	62.1%	37.9%
1994	5,208,762	2,538,702	Pataki, George E.	2,364,904	Cuomo, Mario M.*	305,156	173,798 R	48.7%	45.4%	51.8%	48.2%
1990**	4,056,896	865,948	Rinfret, Pierre A.	2,157,087	Cuomo, Mario M.*	1,033,861	1,291,139 D	21.3%	53.2%	28.6%	71.4%
1986	4,294,124	1,363,810	O'Rourke, Andrew P.	2,775,229	Cuomo, Mario M.*	155,085	1,411,419 D	31.8%	64.6%	32.9%	67.1%
1982	5,254,891	2,494,827	Lehrman, Lew	2,675,213	Cuomo, Mario M.	84,851	180,386 D	47.5%	50.9%	48.3%	51.7%
1978	4,768,820	2,156,404	Duryea, Perry B.	2,429,272	Carey, Hugh L.*	183,144	272,868 D	45.2%	50.9%	47.0%	53.0%
1974	5,293,176	2,219,667	Wilson, Malcolm*	3,028,503	Carey, Hugh L.	45,006	808,836 D	41.9%	57.2%	42.3%	57.7%
1970	6,013,064	3,151,432	Rockefeller, Nelson A.*	2,421,426	Goldberg, Arthur J.	440,206	730,006 R	52.4%	40.3%	56.5%	43.5%
1966**	6,006,246	2,690,626	Rockefeller, Nelson A.*	2,298,363	O'Connor, Frank	1,017,257	392,263 R	44.8%	38.3%	53.9%	46.1%
1962	5,805,631	3,081,587	Rockefeller, Nelson A.*	2,552,418	Morgenthau, Robert M.	171,626	529,169 R	53.1%	44.0%	54.7%	45.3%
1958	5,712,665	3,126,929	Rockefeller, Nelson A.	2,553,895	Harriman, Averell*	31,841	573,034 R	54.7%	44.7%	55.0%	45.0%
1954	5,161,942	2,549,613	Ives, Irving M.	2,560,738	Harriman, Averell	51,591	11,125 D	49.4%	49.6%	49.9%	50.1%
1950	5,308,889	2,819,523	Dewey, Thomas E.*	2,246,855	Lynch, Walter A.	242,511	572,668 R	53.1%	42.3%	55.7%	44.3%
1946	4,964,552	2,825,633	Dewey, Thomas E.*	2,138,482	Mead, James M.	437	687,151 R	56.9%	43.1%	56.9%	43.1%

Note: An asterisk (*) denotes incumbent. **In past elections, the other vote included: 2002 - 654,016 Independence (B. Thomas Golisano); 1990 - 827,614 Conservative (Herbert I. London); 1966 - 510,023 Conservative (Paul L. Adams), 507,234 Liberal (Franklin Roosevelt Jr.).

POSTWAR VOTE FOR SENATOR

		Republican		Democratic				Percentage			
								Total Vote		Major Vote	
Year	Total Vote	Vote	Candidate	Vote	Candidate	Other Vote	Rep.-Dem. Plurality	Rep.	Dem.	Rep.	Dem.
2018	6,059,023	1,998,220	Farley, Chele C.	4,056,931	Gillibrand, Kirsten E.*	3,872	2,058,711 D	33.0%	67.0%	33.0%	67.0%
2016	7,396,305	2,009,355	Long, Wendy	5,221,945	Schumer, Charles E.*	165,005	3,212,590 D	27.2%	70.6%	27.8%	72.2%
2012	6,679,678	1,758,702	Long, Wendy	4,822,330	Gillibrand, Kirsten E.*	98,646	3,063,628 D	26.3%	72.2%	26.7%	73.3%
2010	4,596,796	1,480,423	Townsend, Jay	3,047,880	Schumer, Charles E.*	68,493	1,567,457 D	32.2%	66.3%	32.7%	67.3%
2010S**	4,508,771	1,582,693	DioGuardi, Joseph J.	2,837,684	Gillibrand, Kirsten E.*	88,394	1,254,991 D	35.1%	62.9%	35.8%	64.2%
2006	4,490,053	1,392,189	Spencer, John	3,008,428	Clinton, Hillary Rodham*	89,436	1,616,239 D	31.0%	67.0%	31.6%	68.4%
2004	6,702,875	1,625,069	Mills, Howard D.	4,769,824	Schumer, Charles E.*	307,982	3,144,755 D	24.2%	71.2%	25.4%	74.6%
2000	6,779,839	2,915,730	Lazio, Rick A.	3,747,310	Clinton, Hillary Rodham	116,799	831,580 D	43.0%	55.3%	43.8%	56.2%
1998	4,670,805	2,058,988	D'Amato, Alfonse M.*	2,551,065	Schumer, Charles E.	60,752	492,077 D	44.1%	54.6%	44.7%	55.3%
1994	4,794,601	1,988,308	Castro, Bernadette	2,646,541	Moynihan, Daniel Patrick*	159,752	658,233 D	41.5%	55.2%	42.9%	57.1%
1992	6,458,826	3,166,994	D'Amato, Alfonse M.*	3,086,200	Abrams, Robert	205,632	80,794 R	49.0%	47.8%	50.6%	49.4%
1988	6,040,980	1,875,784	McMillan, Robert	4,048,649	Moynihan, Daniel Patrick*	116,547	2,172,865 D	31.1%	67.0%	31.7%	68.3%
1986	4,179,447	2,378,197	D'Amato, Alfonse M.*	1,723,216	Green, Mark J.	78,034	654,981 R	56.9%	41.2%	58.0%	42.0%
1982	4,967,729	1,696,766	Sullivan, Florence M.	3,232,146	Moynihan, Daniel Patrick*	38,817	1,535,380 D	34.2%	65.1%	34.4%	65.6%
1980**	6,014,914	2,699,652	D'Amato, Alfonse M.	2,618,661	Holtzman, Elizabeth	696,601	80,991 R	44.9%	43.5%	50.8%	49.2%
1976	6,319,755	2,836,633	Buckley, James L.*	3,422,594	Moynihan, Daniel Patrick	60,528	585,961 D	44.9%	54.2%	45.3%	54.7%
1974	5,163,600	2,340,188	Javits, Jacob K.*	1,973,781	Clark, Ramsey	849,631	366,407 R	45.3%	38.2%	54.2%	45.8%
1970**	5,904,782	1,434,472	Goodell, Charles E.*	2,171,232	Ottinger, Richard L.	2,299,078	736,760 D#	24.3%	36.8%	39.8%	60.2%
1968**	6,574,415	3,269,772	Javits, Jacob K.*	2,150,695	O'Dwyer, Paul	1,153,948	1,119,077 R	49.7%	32.7%	60.3%	39.7%
1964	7,151,686	3,104,056	Keating, Kenneth B.*	3,823,749	Kennedy, Robert F.	223,881	719,693 D	43.4%	53.5%	44.8%	55.2%
1962	5,703,168	3,272,417	Javits, Jacob K.*	2,289,323	Donovan, James B.	141,428	983,094 R	57.4%	40.1%	58.8%	41.2%
1958	5,602,088	2,842,942	Keating, Kenneth B.	2,709,950	Hogan, Frank S.	49,196	132,992 R	50.7%	48.4%	51.2%	48.8%
1956	6,991,136	3,723,933	Javits, Jacob K.	3,265,159	Wagner, Robert Ferdinand	2,044	458,774 R	53.3%	46.7%	53.3%	46.7%
1952	6,980,259	3,853,934	Ives, Irving M.*	2,521,736	Cashmore, John	604,589	1,332,198 R	55.2%	36.1%	60.4%	39.6%
1950	5,228,403	2,367,353	Hanley, Joe R.	2,632,313	Lehman, Herbert H.*	228,737	264,960 D	45.3%	50.3%	47.4%	52.6%
1949S**	4,966,878	2,384,381	Dulles, John Foster	2,582,438	Lehman, Herbert H.	59	198,057 D	48.0%	52.0%	48.0%	52.0%
1946	4,867,564	2,559,365	Ives, Irving M.	2,308,112	Lehman, Herbert H.	87	251,253 R	52.6%	47.4%	52.6%	47.4%

Note: An asterisk (*) denotes incumbent. A pound sign (#) in the plurality column indicates that the winner in 1970 did not run under the banner of either major party. **In past elections, the other vote included: 1980 - 664,544 Liberal (Jacob K. Javits); 1970 - 2,288,190 Conservative (James L. Buckley); 1968 - 1,139,402 Conservative (Buckley). Buckley won the 1970 election with 38.8 percent of the total vote and a plurality of 116,958 votes. The 1949 election and one of the 2010 elections were for short terms to fill a vacancy.

NEW YORK

GOVERNOR 2018

2010 Census Population	County	Total Vote	Republican (Molinaro)	Democratic (Cuomo)	Other	Rep.-Dem. Plurality	Percentage: Total Vote Rep.	Percentage: Total Vote Dem.	Percentage: Major Vote Rep.	Percentage: Major Vote Dem.
304,204	ALBANY	114,221	45,917	59,692	8,612	13,775 D	40.2%	52.3%	43.5%	56.5%
48,946	ALLEGANY	14,888	10,132	3,486	1,270	6,646 R	68.1%	23.4%	74.4%	25.6%
1,385,108	BRONX	288,356	23,079	260,556	4,721	237,477 D	8.0%	90.4%	8.1%	91.9%
200,600	BROOME	72,274	36,583	31,519	4,172	5,064 R	50.6%	43.6%	53.7%	46.3%
80,317	CATTARAUGUS	23,625	15,028	7,034	1,563	7,994 R	63.6%	29.8%	68.1%	31.9%
80,026	CAYUGA	26,840	14,706	9,783	2,351	4,923 R	54.8%	36.4%	60.1%	39.9%
134,905	CHAUTAUQUA	43,488	25,823	15,447	2,218	10,376 R	59.4%	35.5%	62.6%	37.4%
88,830	CHEMUNG	29,723	17,294	10,191	2,238	7,103 R	58.2%	34.3%	62.9%	37.1%
50,477	CHENANGO	16,596	10,259	5,069	1,268	5,190 R	61.8%	30.5%	66.9%	33.1%
82,128	CLINTON	26,134	13,227	11,485	1,422	1,742 R	50.6%	43.9%	53.5%	46.5%
63,096	COLUMBIA	29,269	14,253	13,665	1,351	588 R	48.7%	46.7%	51.1%	48.9%
49,336	CORTLAND	16,244	7,953	6,383	1,908	1,570 R	49.0%	39.3%	55.5%	44.5%
47,980	DELAWARE	17,126	9,934	5,796	1,396	4,138 R	58.0%	33.8%	63.2%	36.8%
297,488	DUTCHESS	113,335	59,131	51,179	3,025	7,952 R	52.2%	45.2%	53.6%	46.4%
919,040	ERIE	339,767	150,679	174,766	14,322	24,087 D	44.3%	51.4%	46.3%	53.7%
39,370	ESSEX	13,881	6,705	6,489	687	216 R	48.3%	46.7%	50.8%	49.2%
51,599	FRANKLIN	14,030	7,007	5,472	1,551	1,535 R	49.9%	39.0%	56.2%	43.8%
55,531	FULTON	16,826	11,901	4,080	845	7,821 R	70.7%	24.2%	74.5%	25.5%
60,079	GENESEE	21,081	13,967	5,400	1,714	8,567 R	66.3%	25.6%	72.1%	27.9%
49,221	GREENE	19,170	12,088	6,113	969	5,975 R	63.1%	31.9%	66.4%	33.6%
4,836	HAMILTON	2,778	1,792	722	264	1,070 R	64.5%	26.0%	71.3%	28.7%
64,519	HERKIMER	21,753	14,374	5,924	1,455	8,450 R	66.1%	27.2%	70.8%	29.2%
116,229	JEFFERSON	29,817	19,064	8,862	1,891	10,202 R	63.9%	29.7%	68.3%	31.7%
2,504,700	KINGS	635,083	84,648	524,080	26,355	439,432 D	13.3%	82.5%	13.9%	86.1%
27,087	LEWIS	9,056	6,553	1,854	649	4,699 R	72.4%	20.5%	77.9%	22.1%
65,393	LIVINGSTON	24,346	14,627	7,637	2,082	6,990 R	60.1%	31.4%	65.7%	34.3%
73,442	MADISON	25,908	14,616	9,006	2,286	5,610 R	56.4%	34.8%	61.9%	38.1%
744,344	MONROE	280,266	118,909	143,110	18,247	24,201 D	42.4%	51.1%	45.4%	54.6%
50,219	MONTGOMERY	15,341	10,153	4,384	804	5,769 R	66.2%	28.6%	69.8%	30.2%
1,339,532	NASSAU	495,317	204,399	281,730	9,188	77,331 D	41.3%	56.9%	42.0%	58.0%
1,585,873	NEW YORK	533,999	52,677	460,368	20,954	407,691 D	9.9%	86.2%	10.3%	89.7%
216,469	NIAGARA	72,333	41,242	27,951	3,140	13,291 R	57.0%	38.6%	59.6%	40.4%
234,878	ONEIDA	78,665	44,938	27,931	5,796	17,007 R	57.1%	35.5%	61.7%	38.3%
467,026	ONONDAGA	175,619	74,523	85,182	15,914	10,659 D	42.4%	48.5%	46.7%	53.3%
107,931	ONTARIO	43,663	23,975	16,618	3,070	7,357 R	54.9%	38.1%	59.1%	40.9%
372,813	ORANGE	122,581	60,901	56,882	4,798	4,019 R	49.7%	46.4%	51.7%	48.3%
42,883	ORLEANS	12,899	8,893	3,082	924	5,811 R	68.9%	23.9%	74.3%	25.7%
122,109	OSWEGO	38,664	23,129	11,844	3,691	11,285 R	59.8%	30.6%	66.1%	33.9%
62,259	OTSEGO	21,203	11,592	8,151	1,460	3,441 R	54.7%	38.4%	58.7%	41.3%
99,710	PUTNAM	38,535	20,914	16,556	1,065	4,358 R	54.3%	43.0%	55.8%	44.2%
2,230,722	QUEENS	495,931	90,533	391,190	14,208	300,657 D	18.3%	78.9%	18.8%	81.2%
159,429	RENSSELAER	60,500	32,362	23,633	4,505	8,729 R	53.5%	39.1%	57.8%	42.2%
468,730	RICHMOND	138,886	67,063	69,116	2,707	2,053 D	48.3%	49.8%	49.2%	50.8%
311,687	ROCKLAND	101,205	44,020	54,436	2,749	10,416 D	43.5%	53.8%	44.7%	55.3%
219,607	SARATOGA	95,330	52,337	37,133	5,860	15,204 R	54.9%	39.0%	58.5%	41.5%
154,727	SCHENECTADY	54,926	27,474	23,961	3,491	3,513 R	50.0%	43.6%	53.4%	46.6%
32,749	SCHOHARIE	12,218	8,190	3,099	929	5,091 R	67.0%	25.4%	72.5%	27.5%
18,343	SCHUYLER	7,381	4,024	2,414	943	1,610 R	54.5%	32.7%	62.5%	37.5%
35,251	SENECA	11,657	6,408	4,164	1,085	2,244 R	55.0%	35.7%	60.6%	39.4%
111,944	ST. LAWRENCE	32,499	18,632	11,376	2,491	7,256 R	57.3%	35.0%	62.1%	37.9%
98,990	STEUBEN	33,885	21,035	9,310	3,540	11,725 R	62.1%	27.5%	69.3%	30.7%
1,493,350	SUFFOLK	533,756	247,169	274,518	12,069	27,349 D	46.3%	51.4%	47.4%	52.6%
77,547	SULLIVAN	24,555	12,991	10,486	1,078	2,505 R	52.9%	42.7%	55.3%	44.7%
51,125	TIOGA	18,287	11,045	5,978	1,264	5,067 R	60.4%	32.7%	64.9%	35.1%
101,564	TOMPKINS	37,160	8,859	24,325	3,976	15,466 D	23.8%	65.5%	26.7%	73.3%
182,493	ULSTER	78,661	33,509	41,400	3,752	7,891 D	42.6%	52.6%	44.7%	55.3%
65,707	WARREN	26,108	14,745	9,815	1,548	4,930 R	56.5%	37.6%	60.0%	40.0%
63,216	WASHINGTON	20,522	12,879	6,411	1,232	6,468 R	62.8%	31.2%	66.8%	33.2%
93,772	WAYNE	31,369	19,574	9,241	2,554	10,333 R	62.4%	29.5%	67.9%	32.1%
949,113	WESTCHESTER	333,402	102,180	222,685	8,537	120,505 D	30.6%	66.8%	31.5%	68.5%

NEW YORK

GOVERNOR 2018

2010 Census Population	County	Total Vote	Republican (Molinaro)	Democratic (Cuomo)	Other	Rep.-Dem. Plurality	Percentage Total Vote Rep.	Total Vote Dem.	Major Vote Rep.	Major Vote Dem.
42,155	WYOMING	13,372	9,997	2,612	763	7,385 R	74.8%	19.5%	79.3%	20.7%
25,348	YATES	8,167	4,991	2,558	618	2,433 R	61.1%	31.3%	66.1%	33.9%
19,378,102	*TOTAL*	*6,104,477*	*2,207,602*	*3,635,340*	*261,535*	*1,427,738 D*	*36.2%*	*59.6%*	*37.8%*	*62.2%*

Note: Candidates in New York can appear on the ballot line of more than one party. In the 2018 gubernatorial election, the candidates received the following votes per party: Andrew M. Cuomo - 3,424,416 (Democrat), 114,478 (Working Families), 68,713 (Independence), 27,733 (Women's Equality); Marcus Molinaro - 1,926,485 (Republican), 253,624 (Conservative), 27,493 (Reform). New York City is composed of five boroughs (or counties): Bronx, Kings, New York, Queens, and Richmond. The aggregate 2018 gubernatorial vote in New York City was as follows: 2,092,255 TOTAL; 1,705,310 (81.5%) Democratic (Cuomo); 318,000 (15.2%) Republican (Molinaro); 68,945 (3.3%) Other.

NEW YORK

SENATOR 2018

2010 Census Population	County	Total Vote	Republican (Farley)	Democratic (Gillibrand)	Other	Rep.-Dem. Plurality	Percentage Total Vote Rep.	Total Vote Dem.	Major Vote Rep.	Major Vote Dem.
304,204	ALBANY	114,695	36,456	78,115	124	41,659 D	31.8%	68.1%	31.8%	68.2%
48,946	ALLEGANY	14,724	9,261	5,460	3	3,801 R	62.9%	37.1%	62.9%	37.1%
1,385,108	BRONX	280,924	23,033	257,723	168	234,690 D	8.2%	91.7%	8.2%	91.8%
200,600	BROOME	72,090	30,897	41,145	48	10,248 D	42.9%	57.1%	42.9%	57.1%
80,317	CATTARAUGUS	23,692	13,256	10,431	5	2,825 R	56.0%	44.0%	56.0%	44.0%
80,026	CAYUGA	27,064	13,232	13,823	9	591 D	48.9%	51.1%	48.9%	51.1%
134,905	CHAUTAUQUA	43,184	22,361	20,810	13	1,551 R	51.8%	48.2%	51.8%	48.2%
88,830	CHEMUNG	29,263	14,902	14,347	14	555 R	50.9%	49.0%	50.9%	49.1%
50,477	CHENANGO	16,292	8,996	7,286	10	1,710 R	55.2%	44.7%	55.3%	44.7%
82,128	CLINTON	25,944	10,012	15,930	2	5,918 D	38.6%	61.4%	38.6%	61.4%
63,096	COLUMBIA	29,213	11,055	18,137	21	7,082 D	37.8%	62.1%	37.9%	62.1%
49,336	CORTLAND	16,223	7,099	9,113	11	2,014 D	43.8%	56.2%	43.8%	56.2%
47,980	DELAWARE	16,946	9,066	7,871	9	1,195 R	53.5%	46.4%	53.5%	46.5%
297,488	DUTCHESS	110,991	47,268	63,675	48	16,407 D	42.6%	57.4%	42.6%	57.4%
919,040	ERIE	333,884	127,860	206,024		78,164 D	38.3%	61.7%	38.3%	61.7%
39,370	ESSEX	13,892	5,591	8,294	7	2,703 D	40.2%	59.7%	40.3%	59.7%
51,599	FRANKLIN	13,823	5,576	8,245	2	2,669 D	40.3%	59.6%	40.3%	59.7%
55,531	FULTON	16,690	9,790	6,896	4	2,894 R	58.7%	41.3%	58.7%	41.3%
60,079	GENESEE	20,711	12,552	8,149	10	4,403 R	60.6%	39.3%	60.6%	39.4%
49,221	GREENE	19,251	10,293	8,944	14	1,349 R	53.5%	46.5%	53.5%	46.5%
4,836	HAMILTON	2,742	1,662	1,078	2	584 R	60.6%	39.3%	60.7%	39.3%
64,519	HERKIMER	21,146	11,742	9,395	9	2,347 R	55.5%	44.4%	55.6%	44.4%
116,229	JEFFERSON	29,640	14,884	14,741	15	143 R	50.2%	49.7%	50.2%	49.8%
2,504,700	KINGS	629,372	85,973	542,736	663	456,763 D	13.7%	86.2%	13.7%	86.3%
27,087	LEWIS	8,830	5,120	3,707	3	1,413 R	58.0%	42.0%	58.0%	42.0%
65,393	LIVINGSTON	24,100	12,782	11,311	7	1,471 R	53.0%	46.9%	53.1%	46.9%
73,442	MADISON	25,735	12,894	12,817	24	77 R	50.1%	49.8%	50.1%	49.9%
744,344	MONROE	280,097	105,198	174,788	111	69,590 D	37.6%	62.4%	37.6%	62.4%
50,219	MONTGOMERY	15,161	8,131	7,024	6	1,107 R	53.6%	46.3%	53.7%	46.3%
1,339,532	NASSAU	499,245	204,875	294,186	184	89,311 D	41.0%	58.9%	41.1%	58.9%
1,585,873	NEW YORK	536,360	53,813	481,779	768	427,966 D	10.0%	89.8%	10.0%	90.0%
216,469	NIAGARA	71,342	36,088	35,225	29	863 R	50.6%	49.4%	50.6%	49.4%
234,878	ONEIDA	76,087	37,446	38,613	28	1,167 D	49.2%	50.7%	49.2%	50.8%
467,026	ONONDAGA	175,945	66,599	109,201	145	42,602 D	37.9%	62.1%	37.9%	62.1%
107,931	ONTARIO	43,683	20,543	23,126	14	2,583 D	47.0%	52.9%	47.0%	53.0%

NEW YORK

SENATOR 2018

2010 Census Population	County	Total Vote	Republican (Farley)	Democratic (Gillibrand)	Other	Rep.-Dem. Plurality	Percentage Total Vote Rep.	Total Vote Dem.	Major Vote Rep.	Major Vote Dem.
372,813	ORANGE	120,377	52,640	67,701	36	15,061 D	43.7%	56.2%	43.7%	56.3%
42,883	ORLEANS	12,548	7,999	4,545	4	3,454 R	63.7%	36.2%	63.8%	36.2%
122,109	OSWEGO	38,230	20,499	17,717	14	2,782 R	53.6%	46.3%	53.6%	46.4%
62,259	OTSEGO	21,429	9,969	11,453	7	1,484 D	46.5%	53.4%	46.5%	53.5%
99,710	PUTNAM	38,333	19,222	19,103	8	119 R	50.1%	49.8%	50.2%	49.8%
2,230,722	QUEENS	488,639	89,810	398,414	415	308,604 D	18.4%	81.5%	18.4%	81.6%
159,429	RENSSELAER	60,668	25,964	34,680	24	8,716 D	42.8%	57.2%	42.8%	57.2%
468,730	RICHMOND	136,666	65,375	71,175	116	5,800 D	47.8%	52.1%	47.9%	52.1%
311,687	ROCKLAND	99,174	39,730	59,386	58	19,656 D	40.1%	59.9%	40.1%	59.9%
219,607	SARATOGA	95,649	43,114	52,523	12	9,409 D	45.1%	54.9%	45.1%	54.9%
154,727	SCHENECTADY	54,777	22,005	32,735	37	10,730 D	40.2%	59.8%	40.2%	59.8%
32,749	SCHOHARIE	12,086	6,726	5,355	5	1,371 R	55.7%	44.3%	55.7%	44.3%
18,343	SCHUYLER	7,314	3,868	3,440	6	428 R	52.9%	47.0%	52.9%	47.1%
35,251	SENECA	11,491	5,484	5,997	10	513 D	47.7%	52.2%	47.8%	52.2%
111,944	ST. LAWRENCE	32,176	14,201	17,970	5	3,769 D	44.1%	55.8%	44.1%	55.9%
98,990	STEUBEN	33,650	19,776	13,868	6	5,908 R	58.8%	41.2%	58.8%	41.2%
1,493,350	SUFFOLK	529,150	239,477	289,528	145	50,051 D	45.3%	54.7%	45.3%	54.7%
77,547	SULLIVAN	24,270	11,319	12,937	14	1,618 D	46.6%	53.3%	46.7%	53.3%
51,125	TIOGA	18,198	10,188	8,002	8	2,186 R	56.0%	44.0%	56.0%	44.0%
101,564	TOMPKINS	37,328	8,399	28,818	111	20,419 D	22.5%	77.2%	22.6%	77.4%
182,493	ULSTER	77,618	27,410	50,163	45	22,753 D	35.3%	64.6%	35.3%	64.7%
65,707	WARREN	25,759	11,118	14,634	7	3,516 D	43.2%	56.8%	43.2%	56.8%
63,216	WASHINGTON	20,410	9,940	10,465	5	525 D	48.7%	51.3%	48.7%	51.3%
93,772	WAYNE	31,465	17,522	13,931	12	3,591 R	55.7%	44.3%	55.7%	44.3%
949,113	WESTCHESTER	331,377	96,978	234,173	226	137,195 D	29.3%	70.7%	29.3%	70.7%
42,155	WYOMING	13,170	8,837	4,330	3	4,507 R	67.1%	32.9%	67.1%	32.9%
25,348	YATES	8,090	4,344	3,743	3	601 R	53.7%	46.3%	53.7%	46.3%
19,378,102	*TOTAL*	*6,059,023*	*1,998,220*	*4,056,931*	*3,872*	*2,058,711 D*	*33.0%*	*67.0%*	*33.0%*	*67.0%*

Note: Candidates in New York can appear on the ballot line of more than one party. In the 2018 gubernatorial election, the candidates received the following votes per party: Kirsten E. Gillibrand - 3,755,489 (Democrat), 160,128 (Working Families), 99,325 (Independence), 41,989 (Women's Equality); Chele C. Farley - 1,730,439 (Republican), 246,171 (Conservative), 21,610 (Reform). New York City is composed of five boroughs (or counties): Bronx, Kings, New York, Queens, and Richmond. The aggregate 2018 gubernatorial vote in New York City was as follows: 2,071,961 TOTAL; 1,751,827 (84.5%) Democratic (Gillibrand); 318,004 (15.3%) Republican (Farley); 2,130 (0.1%) Other.

NEW YORK

HOUSE OF REPRESENTATIVES

CD	Year	Total Vote	Republican Vote	Republican Candidate	Democratic Vote	Democratic Candidate	Other Vote	Rep.-Dem. Plurality	Percentage Total Vote Rep.	Total Vote Dem.	Major Vote Rep.	Major Vote Dem.
1	2018	270,053	139,027	ZELDIN, LEE M.*	127,991	GERSHON, PERRY	3,035	11,036 R	51.5%	47.4%	52.1%	47.9%
1	2016	323,890	188,499	ZELDIN, LEE M.*	135,278	THRONE-HOLST, ANNA	113	53,221 R	58.2%	41.8%	58.2%	41.8%
1	2014	172,865	94,035	ZELDIN, LEE M.	78,722	BISHOP, TIMOTHY H.*	108	15,313 R	54.4%	45.5%	54.4%	45.6%
1	2012	278,659	132,304	ALTSCHULER, RANDY	146,179	BISHOP, TIMOTHY H.*	176	13,875 D	47.5%	52.5%	47.5%	52.5%
2	2018	241,217	128,078	KING, PETER T.*	113,074	GRECHEN SHIRLEY, LIUBA	65	15,004 R	53.1%	46.9%	53.1%	46.9%
2	2016	292,595	181,506	KING, PETER T.*	110,938	GREGORY, DUWAYNE	151	70,568 R	62.0%	37.9%	62.1%	37.9%
2	2014	139,330	95,177	KING, PETER T.*	41,814	MAHER, PATRICIA M.	2,339	53,363 R	68.3%	30.0%	69.5%	30.5%
2	2012	242,943	142,309	KING, PETER T.*	100,545	FALCONE, VIVIANNE	89	41,764 R	58.6%	41.4%	58.6%	41.4%
3	2018	267,062	109,514	DEBONO, DAN	157,456	SUOZZI, THOMAS R.*	92	47,942 D	41.0%	59.0%	41.0%	59.0%
3	2016	324,254	152,304	MARTINS, JACK M.	171,775	SUOZZI, THOMAS R.	175	19,471 D	47.0%	53.0%	47.0%	53.0%
3	2014	164,375	74,269	LALLY, GRANT M.	90,032	ISRAEL, STEVE J.*	74	15,763 D	45.2%	54.8%	45.2%	54.8%
3	2012	273,171	113,203	LABATE, STEPHEN	157,880	ISRAEL, STEVE J.*	2,088	44,677 D	41.4%	57.8%	41.8%	58.2%

NEW YORK

HOUSE OF REPRESENTATIVES

			Republican		Democratic				Percentage			
									Total Vote		Major Vote	
CD	Year	Total Vote	Vote	Candidate	Vote	Candidate	Other Vote	Rep.-Dem. Plurality	Rep.	Dem.	Rep.	Dem.
4	2018	260,206	100,571	BENNO, AMEER	159,535	RICE, KATHLEEN M.*	100	58,964 D	38.7%	61.3%	38.7%	61.3%
4	2016	313,000	126,438	GURFEIN, DAVID	186,423	RICE, KATHLEEN M.*	139	59,985 D	40.4%	59.6%	40.4%	59.6%
4	2014	170,099	80,127	BLAKEMAN, BRUCE	89,793	RICE, KATHLEEN M.	179	9,666 D	47.1%	52.8%	47.2%	52.8%
4	2012	265,300	85,693	BECKER, FRANCIS X. JR.	163,955	MCCARTHY, CAROLYN*	15,652	78,262 D	32.3%	61.8%	34.3%	65.7%
5	2018	161,471			160,500	MEEKS, GREGORY W.*	971	160,500 D		99.4%		100.0%
5	2016	233,853	30,312	O'REILLY, MICHAEL	199,815	MEEKS, GREGORY W.*	3,726	169,503 D	13.0%	85.4%	13.2%	86.8%
5	2014	79,821			75,712	MEEKS, GREGORY W.*	4,109	75,712 D		94.9%		100.0%
5	2012	187,141	17,875	JENNINGS, ALLAN JR.	167,836	MEEKS, GREGORY W.*	1,430	149,961 D	9.6%	89.7%	9.6%	90.4%
6	2018	123,421			111,646	MENG, GRACE*	11,775	111,646 D		90.5%		100.0%
6	2016	189,433	50,617	MAIO, DANNIEL	136,506	MENG, GRACE*	2,310	85,889 D	26.7%	72.1%	27.1%	72.9%
6	2014	55,963			55,368	MENG, GRACE*	595	55,368 D		98.9%		100.0%
6	2012	164,374	50,846	HALLORAN, DANIEL	111,501	MENG, GRACE	2,027	60,655 D	30.9%	67.8%	31.3%	68.7%
7	2018	157,302			146,687	VELAZQUEZ, NYDIA*	10,615	146,687 D		93.3%		100.0%
7	2016	189,890	17,478	ROMAGUERA, ALLAN E.	172,146	VELAZQUEZ, NYDIA*	266	154,668 D	9.2%	90.7%	9.2%	90.8%
7	2014	63,812	5,713	FERNANDEZ, JOSE LUIS	56,593	VELAZQUEZ, NYDIA*	1,506	50,880 D	9.0%	88.7%	9.2%	90.8%
7	2012	152,111			143,930	VELAZQUEZ, NYDIA*	8,181	143,930 D		94.6%		100.0%
8	2018	191,567			180,376	JEFFRIES, HAKEEM*	11,191	180,376 D		94.2%		100.0%
8	2016	230,203			214,595	JEFFRIES, HAKEEM*	15,608	214,595 D		93.2%		100.0%
8	2014	83,999			77,255	JEFFRIES, HAKEEM*	6,744	77,255 D		92.0%		100.0%
8	2012	204,207	17,650	BELLONE, ALAN	184,039	JEFFRIES, HAKEEM	2,518	166,389 D	8.6%	90.1%	8.8%	91.2%
9	2018	203,423	20,901	GAYOT, LUTCHI	181,455	CLARKE, YVETTE D.*	1,067	160,554 D	10.3%	89.2%	10.3%	89.7%
9	2016	232,094			214,189	CLARKE, YVETTE D.*	17,905	214,189 D		92.3%		100.0%
9	2014	92,569			82,659	CLARKE, YVETTE D.*	9,910	82,659 D		89.3%		100.0%
9	2012	213,431	24,164	CAVANAGH, DANIEL	186,141	CLARKE, YVETTE D.*	3,126	161,977 D	11.3%	87.2%	11.5%	88.5%
10	2018	210,958	37,619	LEVIN, NAOMI	173,095	NADLER, JERROLD*	244	135,476 D	17.8%	82.1%	17.9%	82.1%
10	2016	246,525	53,857	ROSENTHAL, PHILIP	192,371	NADLER, JERROLD*	297	138,514 D	21.8%	78.0%	21.9%	78.1%
10	2014	101,881			89,080	NADLER, JERROLD*	12,801	89,080 D		87.4%		100.0%
10	2012	205,349	39,413	CHAN, MICHAEL	165,743	NADLER, JERROLD*	193	126,330 D	19.2%	80.7%	19.2%	80.8%
11	2018	192,173	89,441	DONOVAN, DANIEL M. JR.*	101,823	ROSE, MAX	909	12,382 D	46.5%	53.0%	46.8%	53.2%
11	2016	232,317	142,934	DONOVAN, DANIEL M. JR.*	85,257	REICHARD, RICHARD	4,126	57,677 R	61.5%	36.7%	62.6%	37.4%
11	2014	107,363	58,886	GRIMM, MICHAEL G.*	45,244	RECCHIA JR., DOMENIC M.	3,233	13,642 R	54.8%	42.1%	56.6%	43.4%
11	2012	197,635	103,118	GRIMM, MICHAEL G.*	92,430	MURPHY, MARK	2,087	10,688 R	52.2%	46.8%	52.7%	47.3%
12	2018	251,877	30,446	RABIN, ELIOT	217,430	MALONEY, CAROLYN B.*	4,001	186,984 D	12.1%	86.3%	12.3%	87.7%
12	2016	294,071	49,399	ARDINI, ROBERT	244,358	MALONEY, CAROLYN B.*	314	194,959 D	16.8%	83.1%	16.8%	83.2%
12	2014	113,429	22,731	DI IORIO, NICHOLAS S. "NICK"	90,603	MALONEY, CAROLYN B.*	95	67,872 D	20.0%	79.9%	20.1%	79.9%
12	2012	241,426	46,841	WIGHT, CHRISTOPHER	194,370	MALONEY, CAROLYN B.*	215	147,529 D	19.4%	80.5%	19.4%	80.6%
13	2018	190,688	10,268	BUTLER, JINEEA	180,035	ESPAILLAT, ADRIANO*	385	169,767 D	5.4%	94.4%	5.4%	94.6%
13	2016	233,737	16,089	EVANS, TONY	207,194	ESPAILLAT, ADRIANO	10,454	191,105 D	6.9%	88.6%	7.2%	92.8%
13	2014	78,353			68,396	RANGEL, CHARLES B.*	9,957	68,396 D		87.3%		100.0%
13	2012	192,913	12,147	SCHLEY, CRAIG	175,016	RANGEL, CHARLES B.*	5,750	162,869 D	6.3%	90.7%	6.5%	93.5%
14	2018	141,204	19,202	PAPPAS, ANTHONY	110,318	OCASIO-CORTEZ, ALEXANDRIA	11,684	91,116 D	13.6%	78.1%	14.8%	85.2%
14	2016	178,323	30,545	SPOTORNO, FRANK	147,587	CROWLEY, JOSEPH*	191	117,042 D	17.1%	82.8%	17.1%	82.9%
14	2014	57,204			50,352	CROWLEY, JOSEPH*	6,852	50,352 D		88.0%		100.0%
14	2012	145,190	21,755	GIBBONS, WILLIAM JR.	120,761	CROWLEY, JOSEPH*	2,674	99,006 D	15.0%	83.2%	15.3%	84.7%
15	2018	129,751	5,205	GONZALEZ, JASON	124,469	SERRANO, JOSE E.*	77	119,264 D	4.0%	95.9%	4.0%	96.0%
15	2016	174,036	6,129	VEGA, ALEJANDRO	165,688	SERRANO, JOSE E.*	2,219	159,559 D	3.5%	95.2%	3.6%	96.4%
15	2014	56,563			54,906	SERRANO, JOSE E.*	1,657	54,906 D		97.1%		100.0%
15	2012	157,115	4,427	DELLA VALLE, FRANK	152,661	SERRANO, JOSE E.*	27	148,234 D	2.8%	97.2%	2.8%	97.2%
16	2018	183,356			182,044	ENGEL, ELIOT L.*	1,312	182,044 D		99.3%		100.0%
16	2016	222,230			209,857	ENGEL, ELIOT L.*	12,373	209,857 D		94.4%		100.0%
16	2014	100,391			99,658	ENGEL, ELIOT L.*	733	99,658 D		99.3%		100.0%
16	2012	236,553	53,935	MCLAUGHLIN, JOSEPH	179,562	ENGEL, ELIOT L.*	3,056	125,627 D	22.8%	75.9%	23.1%	76.9%
17	2018	193,841			170,168	LOWEY, NITA M.*	23,673	170,168 D		87.8%		100.0%
17	2016	216,585			214,530	LOWEY, NITA M.*	2,055	214,530 D		99.1%		100.0%
17	2014	174,054	75,781	DAY, CHRIS	98,150	LOWEY, NITA M.*	123	22,369 D	43.5%	56.4%	43.6%	56.4%
17	2012	266,205	91,899	CARVIN, JOE	171,417	LOWEY, NITA M.*	2,889	79,518 D	34.5%	64.4%	34.9%	65.1%

NEW YORK

HOUSE OF REPRESENTATIVES

			Republican		Democratic				Percentage			
									Total Vote		Major Vote	
CD	Year	Total Vote	Vote	Candidate	Vote	Candidate	Other Vote	Rep.-Dem. Plurality	Rep.	Dem.	Rep.	Dem.
18	2018	251,690	112,035	O'DONNELL, JAMES	139,564	MALONEY, SEAN*	91	27,529 D	44.5%	55.5%	44.5%	55.5%
18	2016	291,527	129,369	OLIVA, PHIL	162,060	MALONEY, SEAN*	98	32,691 D	44.4%	55.6%	44.4%	55.6%
18	2014	179,091	85,660	HAYWORTH, NAN	88,993	MALONEY, SEAN*	4,438	3,333 D	47.8%	49.7%	49.0%	51.0%
18	2012	277,063	133,049	HAYWORTH, NAN*	143,845	MALONEY, SEAN	169	10,796 D	48.0%	51.9%	48.1%	51.9%
19	2018	287,986	132,873	FASO, JOHN*	147,873	DELGADO, ANTONIO	7,240	15,000 D	46.1%	51.3%	47.3%	52.7%
19	2016	307,614	166,171	FASO, JOHN	141,224	TEACHOUT, ZEPHYR	219	24,947 R	54.0%	45.9%	54.1%	45.9%
19	2014	204,173	131,594	GIBSON, CHRISTOPHER P.*	72,470	ELDRIDGE, SEAN	109	59,124 R	64.5%	35.5%	64.5%	35.5%
19	2012	284,679	150,245	GIBSON, CHRISTOPHER P.*	134,295	SCHREIBMAN, JULIAN	139	15,950 R	52.8%	47.2%	52.8%	47.2%
20	2018	266,014	89,058	VITOLLO, FRANCIS JOSEPH	176,811	TONKO, PAUL D.*	145	87,753 D	33.5%	66.5%	33.5%	66.5%
20	2016	313,939	100,740	VITOLLO, FRANCIS JOSEPH	213,018	TONKO, PAUL D.*	181	112,278 D	32.1%	67.9%	32.1%	67.9%
20	2014	204,329	79,104	FISCHER, JIM	125,111	TONKO, PAUL D.*	114	46,007 D	38.7%	61.2%	38.7%	61.3%
20	2012	297,314	93,778	DIETERICH, ROBERT	203,401	TONKO, PAUL D.*	135	109,623 D	31.5%	68.4%	31.6%	68.4%
21	2018	235,267	131,981	STEFANIK, ELISE*	99,791	COBB, TEDRA LYNN	3,495	32,190 R	56.1%	42.4%	56.9%	43.1%
21	2016	272,606	177,886	STEFANIK, ELISE*	82,161	DERRICK, MIKE	12,559	95,725 R	65.3%	30.1%	68.4%	31.6%
21	2014	174,668	96,226	STEFANIK, ELISE	59,063	WOOLF, AARON	19,379	37,163 R	55.1%	33.8%	62.0%	38.0%
21	2012	252,556	121,646	DOHENY, MATTHEW A.	126,631	OWENS, WILLIAM L. "BILL"*	4,279	4,985 D	48.2%	50.1%	49.0%	51.0%
22	2018	251,212	123,242	TENNEY, CLAUDIA*	127,715	BRINDISI, ANTHONY	255	4,473 D	49.1%	50.8%	49.1%	50.9%
22	2016	278,531	129,444	TENNEY, CLAUDIA	114,266	MYERS, KIM	34,821	15,178 R	46.5%	41.0%	53.1%	46.9%
22	2014	131,932	129,851	HANNA, RICHARD L.*			2,081	129,851 R	98.4%		100.0%	
22	2012	260,863	157,941	HANNA, RICHARD L.*	102,080	LAMB, DAN	842	55,861 R	60.5%	39.1%	60.7%	39.3%
23	2018	240,374	130,323	REED, THOMAS W. II*	109,932	MITRANO, TRACY	119	20,391 R	54.2%	45.7%	54.2%	45.8%
23	2016	279,735	161,050	REED, THOMAS W. II*	118,584	PLUMB, JOHN	101	42,466 R	57.6%	42.4%	57.6%	42.4%
23	2014	183,481	113,130	REED, THOMAS W. II*	70,242	ROBERTSON, MARTHA	109	42,888 R	61.7%	38.3%	61.7%	38.3%
23	2012	265,282	137,669	REED, THOMAS W. II*	127,535	SHINAGAWA, NATE	78	10,134 R	51.9%	48.1%	51.9%	48.1%
24	2018	260,477	136,920	KATKO, JOHN M.*	123,226	BALTER, DANA	331	13,694 R	52.6%	47.3%	52.6%	47.4%
24	2016	302,115	182,761	KATKO, JOHN M.*	119,040	DEACON, COLLEEN	314	63,721 R	60.5%	39.4%	60.6%	39.4%
24	2014	199,222	118,474	KATKO, JOHN M.	80,304	MAFFEI, DANIEL B.*	444	38,170 R	59.5%	40.3%	59.6%	40.4%
24	2012	292,988	127,054	BUERKLE, ANN MARIE*	143,044	MAFFEI, DANIEL B.	22,890	15,990 D	43.4%	48.8%	47.0%	53.0%
25	2018	270,120	110,736	MAXWELL, JIM	159,244	MORELLE, JOSEPH D.	140	48,508 D	41.0%	59.0%	41.0%	59.0%
25	2016	325,831	142,650	ASSINI, MARK W.	182,950	SLAUGHTER, LOUISE M.*	231	40,300 D	43.8%	56.1%	43.8%	56.2%
25	2014	192,971	95,932	ASSINI, MARK W.	96,803	SLAUGHTER, LOUISE M.*	236	871 D	49.7%	50.2%	49.8%	50.2%
25	2012	313,452	133,389	BROOKS, MAGGIE	179,810	SLAUGHTER, LOUISE M.*	253	46,421 D	42.6%	57.4%	42.6%	57.4%
26	2018	230,663	61,488	ZENO, RENEE MARIE	169,166	HIGGINS, BRIAN M.*	9	107,678 D	26.7%	73.3%	26.7%	73.3%
26	2016	288,679	73,377	SCHRATZ, SHELLY	215,289	HIGGINS, BRIAN M.*	13	141,912 D	25.4%	74.6%	25.4%	74.6%
26	2014	166,124	52,909	WEPPNER, KATHLEEN "KATHY"	113,210	HIGGINS, BRIAN M.*	5	60,301 D	31.8%	68.1%	31.9%	68.1%
26	2012	284,271	71,666	MADIGAN, MICHAEL H.	212,588	HIGGINS, BRIAN M.*	17	140,922 D	25.2%	74.8%	25.2%	74.8%
27	2018	285,300	140,146	COLLINS, CHRIS*	139,059	MCMURRAY, NATHAN D.	6,095	1,087 R	49.1%	48.7%	50.2%	49.8%
27	2016	328,809	220,885	COLLINS, CHRIS*	107,832	KASTENBAUM, DIANA	92	113,053 R	67.2%	32.8%	67.2%	32.8%
27	2014	203,645	144,675	COLLINS, CHRIS*	58,911	O'DONNELL, JIM	59	85,764 R	71.0%	28.9%	71.1%	28.9%
27	2012	317,534	161,220	COLLINS, CHRIS	156,219	HOCHUL, KATHY COURTNEY*	95	5,001 R	50.8%	49.2%	50.8%	49.2%
TOTAL	*2018*	*5,948,673*	*1,859,074*		*3,990,483*		*99,116*	*2,131,409 D*	*31.3%*	*67.1%*	*31.8%*	*68.2%*
TOTAL	*2016*	*7,116,422*	*2,530,440*		*4,464,931*		*121,051*	*1,934,491 D*	*35.6%*	*62.7%*	*36.2%*	*63.8%*
TOTAL	*2014*	*3,651,707*	*1,554,274*		*2,009,444*		*87,989*	*455,170 D*	*42.6%*	*55.0%*	*43.6%*	*56.4%*
TOTAL	*2012*	*6,469,725*	*2,245,236*		*4,143,414*		*81,075*	*1,898,178 D*	*34.7%*	*64.0%*	*35.1%*	*64.9%*

Note: An asterisk (*) denotes incumbent. New York allows cross-endorsements, where third parties could endorse candidates of the major parties. All such votes are credited to the major parties with which the candidates identified.

NEW YORK

GENERAL AND PRIMARY ELECTIONS

2018 GENERAL ELECTIONS: OTHER VOTES

Governor	Other vote was 103,946 Green (Howie Hawkins), 95,033 Libertarian (Larry Sharpe), 55,441 Serve America Movement (Stephanie Miner), 7,115 Write-in (Scattered Write-in)
Senate	Other vote was 3,872 Write-in (Scattered Write-in)
House	Other vote was:
CD 1	2,988 Women's Equality Party (Kate Browning), 47 Write-in (Scattered Write-in)
CD 2	65 Write-in (Scattered Write-in)
CD 3	92 Write-in (Scattered Write-in)
CD 4	100 Write-in (Scattered Write-in)
CD 5	971 Write-in (Scattered Write-in)
CD 6	11,209 Green (Thomas Hillgardner), 566 Write-in (Scattered Write-in)
CD 7	8,670 Conservative (Joseph Lieberman), 1,740 Reform (Jeff Kurzon), 205 Write-in (Scattered Write-in)
CD 8	9,997 Conservative (Ernest Johnson), 1,031 Reform (Jessica White), 163 Write-in (Scattered Write-in)
CD 9	779 Reform (Joel Anabilah-Azumah), 288 Write-in (Scattered Write-in)
CD 10	244 Write-in (Scattered Write-in)
CD 11	774 Green (Henry Bardel), 135 Write-in (Scattered Write-in)
CD 12	3,728 Green (Scott Hutchins), 273 Write-in (Scattered Write-in)
CD 13	385 Write-in (Scattered Write-in)
CD 14	9,348 Working Families (Joseph Crowley), 2,254 Conservative (Elizabeth Perri), 82 Write-in (Scattered Write-in)
CD 15	77 Write-in (Scattered Write-in)
CD 16	1,312 Write-in (Scattered Write-in)
CD 17	23,150 Reform (Joseph Ciardullo), 523 Write-in (Scattered Write-in)
CD 18	91 Write-in (Scattered Write-in)
CD 19	4,313 Green (Steven Greenfield), 2,835 Independent (Diane Neal), 92 Write-in (Scattered Write-in)
CD 20	145 Write-in (Scattered Write-in)
CD 21	3,437 Green (Lynn Kahn), 58 Write-in (Scattered Write-in)
CD 22	255 Write-in (Scattered Write-in)
CD 23	119 Write-in (Scattered Write-in)
CD 24	331 Write-in (Scattered Write-in)
CD 25	140 Write-in (Scattered Write-in)
CD 26	152 Write-in (Scattered Write-in)
CD 27	9 Write-in (Scattered Write-in)

2018 PRIMARY ELECTIONS: SUPPLEMENTARY INFORMATION

Primary	June 28, 2018	**Registration** (as of April 1, 2018 – includes 1,092,955 inactive registrants)	12,396,403	Democratic	6,201,033
				Republican	2,823,758
				Independence	481,831
				Conservative	155,500
				Working Families	46,453
				Green	29,787
				Other Parties	7,329
				Women's Equality	4,675
				Reform	1,882
				Unaffiliated	2,644,155

Primary Type Closed—Only registered Democrats and Republicans could vote in their party's primary.

NEW YORK

GENERAL AND PRIMARY ELECTIONS

	REPUBLICAN PRIMARIES			DEMOCRATIC PRIMARIES		
Senator	Farley, Chele C.	Unopposed		Gillibrand, Kirsten E.*	Unopposed	
Governor	Molinaro, Marcus	Unopposed		Cuomo, Andrew*	964,883	65.3%
				Nixon, Cynthia	508,125	34.4%
				Write-in	5,431	0.4%
				TOTAL	*1,478,439*	
Congressional District 1	Zeldin, Lee M.*	Unopposed		Gershon, Perry	7,902	35.5%
				Browning, Kate M.	6,813	30.6%
				Viloria-Fisher, Vivian	3,616	16.3%
				Pechefsky, David	2,565	11.5%
				DiMasi, Elaine	1,344	6.0%
				TOTAL	*22,240*	
Congressional District 2	King, Peter T.*	Unopposed		Grechen Shirley, Liuba	7,315	57.3%
				Gregory, DuWayne	5,456	42.7%
				TOTAL	*12,771*	
Congressional District 3	DeBono, Dan	Unopposed		Suozzi, Thomas R.*	Unopposed	
Congressional District 4	Benno, Ameer	Unopposed		Rice, Kathleen M.*	Unopposed	
Congressional District 5				Meeks, Gregory W.*	11,060	81.6%
				Achille, Carl H.	1,288	9.5%
				Choudhury, Mizanur "Mizan"	1,200	8.9%
				TOTAL	*13,548*	
Congressional District 6				Meng, Grace*	Unopposed	
Congressional District 7				Velazquez, Nydia*	Unopposed	
Congressional District 8				Jeffries, Hakeem*	Unopposed	
Congressional District 9	Gayot, Lutchi	Unopposed		Clarke, Yvette D.*	16,202	53.0%
				Bunkeddeko, Adem	14,350	47.0%
				TOTAL	*30,552*	
Congressional District 10	Levin, Naomi	Unopposed		Nadler, Jerrold*	Unopposed	
Congressional District 11	Donovan, Daniel Jr.*	13,515	62.9%	Rose, Max	11,539	63.3%
	Grimm, Michael	7,957	37.1%	DeVito, Michael Jr.	3,642	20.0%
				Vaid, Omar M.	1,589	8.7%
				Mohan, Radhakrishna	719	3.9%
				Sperling, Paul	486	2.7%
				Emig, Zach	249	1.4%
	TOTAL	*21,472*		*TOTAL*	*18,224*	
Congressional District 12	Rabin, Eliot	Unopposed		Maloney, Carolyn B.*	26,742	59.6%
				Patel, Suraj	18,098	40.4%
				TOTAL	*44,840*	
Congressional District 13	Butler, Jineea	Unopposed		Espaillat, Adriano*	Unopposed	
Congressional District 14	Pappas, Anthony	Unopposed		Ocasio-Cortez, Alexandria	16,898	56.7%
				Crowley, Joseph*	12,880	43.3%
				TOTAL	*29,778*	

NEW YORK

GENERAL AND PRIMARY ELECTIONS

	REPUBLICAN PRIMARIES		DEMOCRATIC PRIMARIES		
Congressional District 15	Gonzalez, Jason	Unopposed	Serrano, Jose E.*	Unopposed	
Congressional District 16			Engel, Eliot L.*	22,160	73.7%
			Lewis, Jonathan	4,866	16.2%
			Briscoe, Joyce	1,772	5.9%
			Lawrence, Derickson K.	1,280	4.3%
			TOTAL	*30,078*	
Congressional District 17			Lowey, Nita M.*	Unopposed	
Congressional District 18	O'Donnell, James	Unopposed	Maloney, Sean*	Unopposed	
Congressional District 19	Faso, John*	Unopposed	Delgado, Antonio	8,576	22.1%
			Ryan, Patrick	6,941	17.9%
			Rhodes, Gareth T.	6,890	17.8%
			Flynn, Brian	5,245	13.5%
			Beals, Jeffrey "Jeff"	4,991	12.9%
			Clegg, David J.	4,257	11.0%
			Collier, Erin	1,908	4.9%
			TOTAL	*38,808*	
Congressional District 20	Vitollo, Francis Joseph	Unopposed	Tonko, Paul D.*	Unopposed	
Congressional District 21	Stefanik, Elise*	Unopposed	Cobb, Tedra Lynn	10,853	55.3%
			Wilson, Katie	2,356	12.0%
			Ratigan, Dylan	2,313	11.8%
			Martz, Emily	2,165	11.0%
			Nelson, Patrick F.	1,802	9.2%
			Boyajian, Don	129	0.7%
			TOTAL	*19,618*	
Congressional District 22	Tenney, Claudia*	Unopposed	Brindisi, Anthony	Unopposed	
Congressional District 23	Reed, Thomas W. II*	Unopposed	Mitrano, Tracy	7,724	32.9%
			Della Pia, Max H.	7,494	31.9%
			Andrei, Linda	3,603	15.3%
			Golden, Ian	3,142	13.4%
			Sundquist, Edward A.	1,538	6.5%
			TOTAL	*23,501*	
Congressional District 24	Katko, John M.*	Unopposed	Balter, Dana	14,897	62.4%
			Perez Williams, Juanita	8,958	37.6%
			TOTAL	*23,855*	
Congressional District 25	Maxwell, Jim	Unopposed	Morelle, Joseph D.	16,245	45.7%
			Barnhart, Rachel	7,003	19.7%
			Wilt, Robin	6,158	17.3%
			Mcfadden, Adam	6,103	17.2%
			TOTAL	*35,509*	
Congressional District 26	Zeno, Renee Marie	Unopposed	Higgins, Brian M.*	Unopposed	
Congressional District 27	Collins, Chris*	Unopposed	McMurray, Nathan D.	Unopposed	

Note: An asterisk (*) denotes incumbent.

NORTH CAROLINA

Congressional districts first established for elections held in 2016

13 members

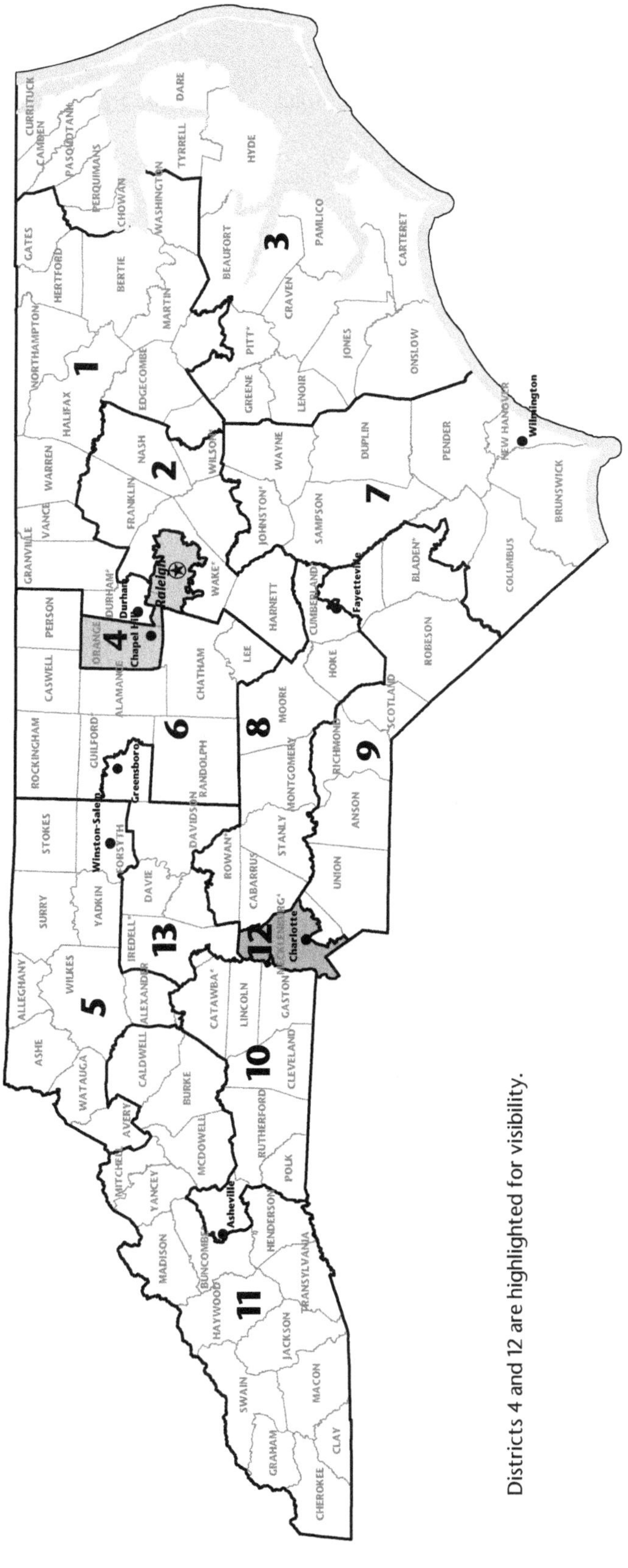

Districts 4 and 12 are highlighted for visibility.

NORTH CAROLINA

GOVERNOR

Roy Cooper (D). Elected 2016 to a four-year term.

SENATORS (2 Republicans)

Richard Burr (R). Re-elected 2016 to a six-year term. Previously elected 2010, 2004.

Thom Tillis (R). Elected 2014 to a six-year term.

REPRESENTATIVES (10 Republicans, 3 Democrats)

1. George K. "G. K." Butterfield (D)
2. George Holding (R)
3. Greg Murphy (R)*
4. David E. Price (D)
5. Virginia Ann Foxx (R)
6. Mark Walker (R)
7. David Rouzer (R)
8. Richard Hudson (R)
9. Dan Bishop (R)**
10. Patrick T. McHenry (R)
11. Mark Meadows (R)
12. Alma S. Adams (D)
13. Ted Budd (R)

*The CD 3 seat became vacant following the death of Walter B. Jones Jr. (R) on February 10, 2019. A special election to fill the seat was scheduled September 10, 2019. Republican Greg Murphy was declared the winner.

**The CD 9 seat remained vacant following the November 6, 2018, general election and the results were not certified following allegations of absentee ballot election fraud by Republican operatives. A special election was scheduled September 10, 2019.

POSTWAR VOTE FOR PRESIDENT

		Republican		Democratic				Percentage			
								Total Vote		Major Vote	
Year	Total Vote	Vote	Candidate	Vote	Candidate	Other Vote	Rep.-Dem. Plurality	Rep.	Dem.	Rep.	Dem.
2016**	4,741,564	2,362,631	Trump, Donald J.	2,189,316	Clinton, Hillary Rodham	189,617	173,315 R	49.8%	46.2%	51.9%	48.1%
2012	4,505,372	2,270,395	Romney, W. Mitt	2,178,391	Obama, Barack H.*	56,586	92,004 R	50.4%	48.4%	51.0%	49.0%
2008	4,310,789	2,128,474	McCain, John S. III	2,142,651	Obama, Barack H.	39,664	14,177 D	49.4%	49.7%	49.8%	50.2%
2004	3,501,007	1,961,166	Bush, George W.*	1,525,849	Kerry, John F.	13,992	435,317 R	56.0%	43.6%	56.2%	43.8%
2000	2,911,262	1,631,163	Bush, George W.	1,257,692	Gore, Albert Jr.	22,407	373,471 R	56.0%	43.2%	56.5%	43.5%
1996**	2,515,807	1,225,938	Dole, Robert "Bob"	1,107,849	Clinton, Bill*	182,020	118,089 R	48.7%	44.0%	52.5%	47.5%
1992**	2,611,850	1,134,661	Bush, George H.*	1,114,042	Clinton, Bill	363,147	20,619 R	43.4%	42.7%	50.5%	49.5%
1988	2,134,370	1,237,258	Bush, George H.	890,167	Dukakis, Michael S.	6,945	347,091 R	58.0%	41.7%	58.2%	41.8%
1984	2,175,361	1,346,481	Reagan, Ronald*	824,287	Mondale, Walter F.	4,593	522,194 R	61.9%	37.9%	62.0%	38.0%
1980**	1,855,833	915,018	Reagan, Ronald	875,635	Carter, Jimmy*	65,180	39,383 R	49.3%	47.2%	51.1%	48.9%
1976	1,677,914	741,960	Ford, Gerald R.*	926,365	Carter, Jimmy	9,589	184,405 D	44.2%	55.2%	44.5%	55.5%
1972	1,518,612	1,054,889	Nixon, Richard M.*	438,705	McGovern, George S.	25,018	616,184 R	69.5%	28.9%	70.6%	29.4%
1968**	1,587,493	627,192	Nixon, Richard M.	464,113	Humphrey, Hubert Horatio Jr.	496,188	163,079 R	39.5%	29.2%	57.5%	42.5%
1964	1,424,983	624,844	Goldwater, Barry M. Sr.	800,139	Johnson, Lyndon B.*		175,295 D	43.8%	56.2%	43.8%	56.2%
1960	1,368,556	655,420	Nixon, Richard M.	713,136	Kennedy, John F.		57,716 D	47.9%	52.1%	47.9%	52.1%
1956	1,165,592	575,062	Eisenhower, Dwight D.*	590,530	Stevenson, Adlai E. II		15,468 D	49.3%	50.7%	49.3%	50.7%
1952	1,210,910	558,107	Eisenhower, Dwight D.	652,803	Stevenson, Adlai E. II		94,696 D	46.1%	53.9%	46.1%	53.9%
1948**	791,209	258,572	Dewey, Thomas E.	459,070	Truman, Harry S.*	73,567	200,498 D	32.7%	58.0%	36.0%	64.0%

Note: An asterisk (*) denotes incumbent. **In past elections, the other vote included: 2016 - 130,126 Libertarian (Gary Johnson); 1996 - 168,059 Reform (Ross Perot); 1992 - 357,864 Independent (Perot); 1980 - 52,800 Independent (John Anderson); 1968 - 496,188 American Independent (George Wallace, who finished second); 1948 - 69,652 States' Rights (Strom Thurmond).

NORTH CAROLINA

POSTWAR VOTE FOR GOVERNOR

		Republican		Democratic				Percentage			
								Total Vote		Major Vote	
Year	Total Vote	Vote	Candidate	Vote	Candidate	Other Vote	Rep.-Dem. Plurality	Rep.	Dem.	Rep.	Dem.
2016	4,711,014	2,298,880	McCrory, Pat*	2,309,157	Cooper, Roy	102,977	10,277 D	48.8%	49.0%	49.9%	50.1%
2012	4,468,295	2,440,707	McCrory, Pat	1,931,580	Dalton, Walter H.	96,008	509,127 R	54.6%	43.2%	55.8%	44.2%
2008	4,268,941	2,001,168	McCrory, Pat	2,146,189	Perdue, Bev	121,584	145,021 D	46.9%	50.3%	48.3%	51.7%
2004	3,486,688	1,495,021	Ballantine, Patrick J.	1,939,154	Easley, Mike*	52,513	444,133 D	42.9%	55.6%	43.5%	56.5%
2000	2,942,062	1,360,960	Vinroot, Richard	1,530,324	Easley, Mike	50,778	169,364 D	46.3%	52.0%	47.1%	52.9%
1996	2,566,185	1,097,053	Hayes, Robert "Robin"	1,436,638	Hunt, James B. Jr.*	32,494	339,585 D	42.8%	56.0%	43.3%	56.7%
1992	2,595,184	1,121,955	Gardner, James C.	1,368,246	Hunt, James B. Jr.	104,983	246,291 D	43.2%	52.7%	45.1%	54.9%
1988	2,180,205	1,222,338	Martin, James G.*	957,867	Jordan, Robert B.		264,471 R	56.1%	43.9%	56.1%	43.9%
1984	2,226,727	1,208,167	Martin, James G.	1,011,209	Edmisten, Rufus	7,351	196,958 R	54.3%	45.4%	54.4%	45.6%
1980	1,847,432	691,449	Lake, Beverly	1,143,145	Hunt, James B. Jr.*	12,838	451,696 D	37.4%	61.9%	37.7%	62.3%
1976	1,663,814	564,092	Flaherty, David T.	1,081,293	Hunt, James B. Jr.	18,429	517,201 D	33.9%	65.0%	34.3%	65.7%
1972	1,504,785	767,470	Holshouser, James E. Jr.	729,104	Bowles, Hargrove Skipper Jr.	8,211	38,366 R	51.0%	48.5%	51.3%	48.7%
1968	1,558,308	737,075	Gardner, James C.	821,233	Scott, Robert W.		84,158 D	47.3%	52.7%	47.3%	52.7%
1964	1,396,508	606,165	Gavin, Robert L.	790,343	Moore, Dan K.		184,178 D	43.4%	56.6%	43.4%	56.6%
1960	1,350,360	613,975	Gavin, Robert L.	735,248	Sanford, Terry	1,137	121,273 D	45.5%	54.4%	45.5%	54.5%
1956	1,135,859	375,379	Hayes, Kyle	760,480	Hodges, Luther H.		385,101 D	33.0%	67.0%	33.0%	67.0%
1952	1,179,635	383,329	Seawell, Herbert F. Jr.	796,306	Umstead, William B.		412,977 D	32.5%	67.5%	32.5%	67.5%
1948	780,525	206,166	Pritchard, George M.	570,995	Scott, W. Kerr	3,364	364,829 D	26.4%	73.2%	26.5%	73.5%

Note: An asterisk (*) denotes incumbent.

POSTWAR VOTE FOR SENATOR

		Republican		Democratic				Percentage			
								Total Vote		Major Vote	
Year	Total Vote	Vote	Candidate	Vote	Candidate	Other Vote	Rep.-Dem. Plurality	Rep.	Dem.	Rep.	Dem.
2016	4,691,133	2,395,376	Burr, Richard M.*	2,128,165	Ross, Deborah K.	167,592	267,211 R	51.1%	45.4%	53.0%	47.0%
2014	2,915,281	1,423,259	Tillis, Thom	1,377,651	Hagan, Kay*	114,371	45,608 R	48.8%	47.3%	50.8%	49.2%
2010	2,660,079	1,458,046	Burr, Richard M.*	1,145,074	Marshall, Elaine	56,959	312,972 R	54.8%	43.0%	56.0%	44.0%
2008	4,271,970	1,887,510	Dole, Elizabeth*	2,249,311	Hagan, Kay	135,149	361,801 D	44.2%	52.7%	45.6%	54.4%
2004	3,472,082	1,791,450	Burr, Richard M.	1,632,527	Bowles, Erskine B.	48,105	158,923 R	51.6%	47.0%	52.3%	47.7%
2002	2,331,181	1,248,664	Dole, Elizabeth	1,047,983	Bowles, Erskine B.	34,534	200,681 R	53.6%	45.0%	54.4%	45.6%
1998	2,012,143	945,943	Faircloth, Lauch*	1,029,237	Edwards, John	36,963	83,294 D	47.0%	51.2%	47.9%	52.1%
1996	2,556,456	1,345,833	Helms, Jesse*	1,173,875	Gantt, Harvey B.	36,748	171,958 R	52.6%	45.9%	53.4%	46.6%
1992	2,577,891	1,297,892	Faircloth, Lauch	1,194,015	Sanford, Terry*	85,984	103,877 R	50.3%	46.3%	52.1%	47.9%
1990	2,069,585	1,087,331	Helms, Jesse*	981,573	Gantt, Harvey B.	681	105,758 R	52.5%	47.4%	52.6%	47.4%
1986	1,591,330	767,668	Broyhill, James Thomas*	823,662	Sanford, Terry		55,994 D	48.2%	51.8%	48.2%	51.8%
1984	2,239,051	1,156,768	Helms, Jesse*	1,070,488	Hunt, James B. Jr.	11,795	86,280 R	51.7%	47.8%	51.9%	48.1%
1980	1,797,665	898,064	East, John P.	887,653	Morgan, Robert*	11,948	10,411 R	50.0%	49.4%	50.3%	49.7%
1978	1,135,814	619,151	Helms, Jesse*	516,663	Ingram, John		102,488 R	54.5%	45.5%	54.5%	45.5%
1974	1,020,367	377,618	Stevens, William E.	633,775	Morgan, Robert	8,974	256,157 D	37.0%	62.1%	37.3%	62.7%
1972	1,472,541	795,248	Helms, Jesse	677,293	Galifianakis, Nick		117,955 R	54.0%	46.0%	54.0%	46.0%
1968	1,437,340	566,934	Somers, Robert V.	870,406	Ervin, Sam James Jr.*		303,472 D	39.4%	60.6%	39.4%	60.6%
1966	901,978	400,502	Shallcross, John S.	501,440	Jordan, B. Everett*	36	100,938 D	44.4%	55.6%	44.4%	55.6%
1962	813,155	321,635	Greene, Claude L. Jr.	491,520	Ervin, Sam James Jr.*		169,885 D	39.6%	60.4%	39.6%	60.4%
1960	1,291,485	497,964	Hayes, Kyle	793,521	Jordan, B. Everett*		295,557 D	38.6%	61.4%	38.6%	61.4%
1958S**	616,469	184,977	Clarke, Richard C. Jr.	431,492	Jordan, B. Everett*		246,515 D	30.0%	70.0%	30.0%	70.0%
1956	1,098,828	367,475	Johnson, Joel A.	731,353	Ervin, Sam James Jr.*		363,878 D	33.4%	66.6%	33.4%	66.6%
1954	619,634	211,322	West, Paul C.	408,312	Scott, W. Kerr		196,990 D	34.1%	65.9%	34.1%	65.9%
1954S**	410,574			410,574	Ervin, Sam James Jr.*		410,574 D		100.0%		100.0%
1950	548,277	171,804	Leavitt, Halsey B.	376,473	Hoey, Clyde R.*		204,669 D	31.3%	68.7%	31.3%	68.7%
1950S**	544,924	177,753	Gavin, E. L.	364,912	Smith, Willis	2,259	187,159 D	32.6%	67.0%	32.8%	67.2%
1948	764,559	220,307	Wilkinson, John A.	540,762	Broughton, J. Melville*	3,490	320,455 D	28.8%	70.7%	28.9%	71.1%

Note: An asterisk (*) denotes incumbent. **One each of the 1950 and 1954 elections as well as the 1958 election were for short terms to fill vacancies. The Republican Party did not run a Senate candidate in the 1954 election for the short term.

NORTH CAROLINA

HOUSE OF REPRESENTATIVES

			Republican		Democratic				Percentage: Total Vote		Percentage: Major Vote	
CD	Year	Total Vote	Vote	Candidate	Vote	Candidate	Other Vote	Rep.-Dem. Plurality	Rep.	Dem.	Rep.	Dem.
1**	2018	272,675	82,218	ALLISON, ROGER	190,457	BUTTERFIELD, GEORGE K. "G.K."*		108,239 D	30.2%	69.8%	30.2%	69.8%
1**	2016	350,699	101,567	DEW, H. POWELL JR.	240,661	BUTTERFIELD, GEORGE K. "G.K."*	8,471	139,094 D	29.0%	68.6%	29.7%	70.3%
1	2014	210,323	55,990	RICH, ARTHUR	154,333	BUTTERFIELD, GEORGE K. "G.K."*		98,343 D	26.6%	73.4%	26.6%	73.4%
1	2012	338,066	77,288	DILAURO, PETE	254,644	BUTTERFIELD, GEORGE K. "G.K."*	6,134	177,356 D	22.9%	75.3%	23.3%	76.7%
2**	2018	331,704	170,072	HOLDING, GEORGE*	151,977	COLEMAN, LINDA	9,655	18,095 R	51.3%	45.8%	52.8%	47.2%
2**	2016	390,567	221,485	HOLDING, GEORGE*	169,082	MCNEIL, JOHN P.		52,403 R	56.7%	43.3%	56.7%	43.3%
2	2014	207,607	122,128	ELLMERS, RENEE*	85,479	AIKEN, CLAY		36,649 R	58.8%	41.2%	58.8%	41.2%
2	2012	311,397	174,066	ELLMERS, RENEE*	128,973	WILKINS, STEVE	8,358	45,093 R	55.9%	41.4%	57.4%	42.6%
3**	2018	187,901	187,901	JONES, WALTER B. JR.*					100.0%		100.0%	
3**	2016	323,701	217,531	JONES, WALTER B. JR.*	106,170	REEVES, ERNEST TYRONE		111,361 R	67.2%	32.8%	67.2%	32.8%
3	2014	205,597	139,415	JONES, WALTER B. JR.*	66,182	ADAME, MARSHALL		73,233 R	67.8%	32.2%	67.8%	32.2%
3	2012	309,885	195,571	JONES, WALTER B. JR.*	114,314	ANDERSON, ERIK		81,257 R	63.1%	36.9%	63.1%	36.9%
4**	2018	341,403	82,052	LOOR, STEVE VON	247,067	PRICE, DAVID E.*	12,284	165,015 D	24.0%	72.4%	24.9%	75.1%
4**	2016	409,541	130,161	GOOGE, SUE	279,380	PRICE, DAVID E.*		149,219 D	31.8%	68.2%	31.8%	68.2%
4	2014	227,362	57,416	WRIGHT, PAUL	169,946	PRICE, DAVID E.*		112,530 D	25.3%	74.7%	25.3%	74.7%
4	2012	348,485	88,951	D'ANNUNZIO, TIM	259,534	PRICE, DAVID E.*		170,583 D	25.5%	74.5%	25.5%	74.5%
5**	2018	280,385	159,917	FOXX, VIRGINIA ANN*	120,468	ADAMS, DENISE "DD"		39,449 R	57.0%	43.0%	57.0%	43.0%
5**	2016	355,512	207,625	FOXX, VIRGINIA ANN*	147,887	BRANNON, JOSHUA "JOSH"		59,738 R	58.4%	41.6%	58.4%	41.6%
5	2014	228,252	139,279	FOXX, VIRGINIA ANN*	88,973	BRANNON, JOSHUA "JOSH"		50,306 R	61.0%	39.0%	61.0%	39.0%
5	2012	349,197	200,945	FOXX, VIRGINIA ANN*	148,252	MOTSINGER, ELISABETH		52,693 R	57.5%	42.5%	57.5%	42.5%
6**	2018	284,360	160,709	WALKER, MARK*	123,651	WATTS, RYAN		37,058 R	56.5%	43.5%	56.5%	43.5%
6**	2016	351,150	207,983	WALKER, MARK*	143,167	GLIDEWELL, POWELL WATKINS "PETE" III		64,816 R	59.2%	40.8%	59.2%	40.8%
6	2014	251,070	147,312	WALKER, MARK	103,758	FJELD, LAURA		43,554 R	58.7%	41.3%	58.7%	41.3%
6	2012	364,583	222,116	COBLE, HOWARD*	142,467	FORIEST, TONY		79,649 R	60.9%	39.1%	60.9%	39.1%
7**	2018	282,312	156,809	ROUZER, DAVID*	120,838	HORTON, KYLE	4,665	35,971 R	55.5%	42.8%	56.5%	43.5%
7**	2016	347,706	211,801	ROUZER, DAVID*	135,905	CASTEEN, J. WESLEY		75,896 R	60.9%	39.1%	60.9%	39.1%
7	2014	226,504	134,431	ROUZER, DAVID	84,054	BARFIELD JR., JONATHAN	8,019	50,377 R	59.4%	37.1%	61.5%	38.5%
7	2012	336,736	168,041	ROUZER, DAVID	168,695	MCINTYRE, MIKE*		654 D	49.9%	50.1%	49.9%	50.1%
8**	2018	255,521	141,402	HUDSON, RICHARD*	114,119	MCNEILL, FRANK		27,283 R	55.3%	44.7%	55.3%	44.7%
8**	2016	323,045	189,863	HUDSON, RICHARD*	133,182	MILLS, THOMAS		56,681 R	58.8%	41.2%	58.8%	41.2%
8	2014	187,422	121,568	HUDSON, RICHARD*	65,854	BLUE, ANTONIO		55,714 R	64.9%	35.1%	64.9%	35.1%
8	2012	302,280	160,695	HUDSON, RICHARD	137,139	KISSELL, LARRY*	4,446	23,556 R	53.2%	45.4%	54.0%	46.0%
9#**	2018	282,717	139,246	HARRIS, MARK	138,341	MCCREADY, DANIEL "DAN"	5,130	905 R	49.3%	48.9%	50.2%	49.8%
9**	2016	332,493	193,452	PITTENGER, ROBERT*	139,041	CANO, CHRISTIAN		54,411 R	58.2%	41.8%	58.2%	41.8%
9	2014	173,668	163,080	PITTENGER, ROBERT*			10,588	163,080 R	93.9%		100.0%	
9	2012	375,690	194,537	PITTENGER, ROBERT	171,503	ROBERTS, JENNIFER	9,650	23,034 R	51.8%	45.7%	53.1%	46.9%
10**	2018	278,228	164,969	MCHENRY, PATRICK T.*	113,259	BROWN, DAVID WILSON		51,710 R	59.3%	40.7%	59.3%	40.7%
10**	2016	349,744	220,825	MCHENRY, PATRICK T.*	128,919	MILLARD, ANDY		91,906 R	63.1%	36.9%	63.1%	36.9%
10	2014	218,796	133,504	MCHENRY, PATRICK T.*	85,292	MACQUEEN IV, TATE		48,212 R	61.0%	39.0%	61.0%	39.0%
10	2012	334,849	190,826	MCHENRY, PATRICK T.*	144,023	KEEVER, PATRICIA R. "PATSY"		46,803 R	57.0%	43.0%	57.0%	43.0%
11**	2018	300,666	178,012	MEADOWS, MARK*	116,508	PRICE, PHILLIP G.	6,146	61,504 R	59.2%	38.7%	60.4%	39.6%
11**	2016	359,508	230,405	MEADOWS, MARK*	129,103	BRYSON, FREDERICK "RICK"		101,302 R	64.1%	35.9%	64.1%	35.9%
11	2014	230,024	144,682	MEADOWS, MARK*	85,342	HILL, THOMAS		59,340 R	62.9%	37.1%	62.9%	37.1%
11	2012	331,426	190,319	MEADOWS, MARK	141,107	ROGERS, HAYDEN		49,212 R	57.4%	42.6%	57.4%	42.6%
12**	2018	279,138	75,164	WRIGHT, PAUL	203,974	ADAMS, ALMA S.*		128,810 D	26.9%	73.1%	26.9%	73.1%
12**	2016	349,300	115,185	THREATT, LEON	234,115	ADAMS, ALMA S.*		118,930 D	33.0%	67.0%	33.0%	67.0%
12	2014	172,664	42,568	COAKLEY, VINCE	130,096	ADAMS, ALMA S.		87,528 D	24.7%	75.3%	24.7%	75.3%
12	2012	310,908	63,317	BROSCH, JACK	247,591	WATT, MELVIN*		184,274 D	20.4%	79.6%	20.4%	79.6%
13**	2018	286,316	147,570	BUDD, TED*	130,402	MANNING, KATHY	8,344	17,168 R	51.5%	45.5%	53.1%	46.9%
13**	2016	355,492	199,443	BUDD, TED	156,049	DAVIS, BRUCE		43,394 R	56.1%	43.9%	56.1%	43.9%
13	2014	268,709	153,991	HOLDING, GEORGE*	114,718	CLEARY, BRENDA		39,273 R	57.3%	42.7%	57.3%	42.7%
13	2012	370,610	210,495	HOLDING, GEORGE	160,115	MALONE, CHARLES		50,380 R	56.8%	43.2%	56.8%	43.2%
TOTAL	*2018*	*3,663,326*	*1,846,041*		*1,771,061*		*46,224*	*74,980 R*	*50.4%*	*48.3%*	*51.0%*	*49.0%*
TOTAL	*2016*	*4,598,458*	*2,447,326*		*2,142,661*		*8,471*	*304,665 R*	*53.2%*	*46.6%*	*53.3%*	*46.7%*
TOTAL	*2014*	*2,807,998*	*1,555,364*		*1,234,027*		*18,607*	*321,337 R*	*55.4%*	*43.9%*	*55.8%*	*44.2%*
TOTAL	*2012*	*4,384,112*	*2,137,167*		*2,218,357*		*28,588*	*81,190 D*	*48.7%*	*50.6%*	*49.1%*	*50.9%*

Note: An asterisk (*) denotes incumbent. #The CD 9 seat remained vacant following the November 6, 2018, general election and the results were not certified following allegations of absentee ballot election fraud by Republican operatives. The CD 9 results are included in the House tally for North Carolina. **Due to mid-decade redistricting, boundaries for all districts are not comparable to those used in the 2012 and 2014 races.

NORTH CAROLINA

GENERAL AND PRIMARY ELECTIONS

2018 GENERAL ELECTIONS: OTHER VOTES

House	Other vote was:
CD 2	9,655 Libertarian (Jeff Matemu)
CD 4	12,284 Libertarian (Barbara Howe)
CD 7	4,665 Constitution (David Fallin)
CD 9	5,130 Libertarian (Jeff Scott)
CD 11	6,146 Libertarian (Clifton Ingram)
CD 13	5,513 Libertarian (Tom Bailey), 2,831 Green (Robert Corriher)

2018 PRIMARY ELECTIONS: SUPPLEMENTARY INFORMATION

Primary	May 8, 2018	**Registration** (as of May 8, 2018)	6,915,043	Democratic	2,654,250
				Republican	2,077,546
				Green	67
				Libertarian	35,297
				Unaffiliated	2,147,883

Primary Type Semi-open—Registered Democrats and Republicans could vote only in their party's primary. Unaffiliated voters could participate in the primary of any recognized party. However, if a voter cast a ballot in one party's primary, he or she could not participate in the runoff of another party.

	REPUBLICAN PRIMARIES			DEMOCRATIC PRIMARIES		
Congressional District 1	Allison, Roger	Unopposed		Butterfield, George K. "G.K."*	Unopposed	
Congressional District 2	Holding, George*	17,979	76.2%	Coleman, Linda	18,650	56.0%
	Chesser, Allen	5,612	23.8%	Romley, Ken	10,742	32.3%
				May, Wendy Ella	3,895	11.7%
	TOTAL	*23,591*		*TOTAL*	*33,287*	
Congressional District 3	Jones, Walter B. Jr.*	20,963	43.0%			
	Law, Phil	14,343	29.4%			
	Dacey, Scott	13,421	27.5%			
	TOTAL	*48,727*				
Congressional District 4	Loor, Steve Von	Unopposed		Price, David E.*	52,203	77.1%
				Laws, Michelle	11,120	16.4%
				Watkins, Richard L.	4,391	6.5%
				TOTAL	*67,714*	
Congressional District 5	Foxx, Virginia Ann*	32,654	80.8%	Adams, Denise "DD"	15,509	54.4%
	Gentry, Dillon	5,703	14.1%	Marshall, Jennifer "Jenny"	12,987	45.6%
	Meader, Cortland J. Jr.	2,063	5.1%			
	TOTAL	*40,420*		*TOTAL*	*28,496*	
Congressional District 6	Walker, Mark*	Unopposed		Watts, Ryan	26,072	77.2%
				Wong, Gerald	7,719	22.8%
				TOTAL	*33,791*	
Congressional District 7	Rouzer, David*	Unopposed		Horton, Kyle	21,499	67.0%
				Parker, Grayson	10,587	33.0%
				TOTAL	*32,086*	

NORTH CAROLINA

GENERAL AND PRIMARY ELECTIONS

	REPUBLICAN PRIMARIES			DEMOCRATIC PRIMARIES		
Congressional District 8	Hudson, Richard*	Unopposed		McNeill, Frank	16,019	56.0%
				Huffman, Scott	6,581	23.0%
				Tiegel, Marc	5,997	21.0%
				TOTAL	*28,597*	
Congressional District 9	Harris, Mark	17,302	48.5%	McCready, Daniel "Dan"	38,098	82.8%
	Pittenger, Robert*	16,474	46.2%	Cano, Christian	7,922	17.2%
	Goins, Clarence W. Jr.	1,867	5.2%			
	TOTAL	*35,643*		*TOTAL*	*46,020*	
Congressional District 10	McHenry, Patrick T.*	34,173	70.7%	Brown, David Wilson	Unopposed	
	Collias, Gina	6,664	13.8%			
	Gregory, Jeff	3,724	7.7%			
	Roberts, Ira	1,701	3.5%			
	Blankenship, Seth	1,443	3.0%			
	Wiley, Albert Lee Jr.	616	1.3%			
	TOTAL	*48,321*				
Congressional District 11	Meadows, Mark*	35,665	86.3%	Price, Phillip G.	13,499	40.6%
	Archerd, Chuck	5,639	13.7%	Woodsmall, Steve	10,356	31.1%
				Donaldson, D. Scott	9,402	28.3%
	TOTAL	*41,304*		*TOTAL*	*33,257*	
Congressional District 12	Wright, Paul	3,221	43.2%	Adams, Alma S.*	38,849	85.5%
	Bonham, Paul	2,349	31.5%	Young, Keith	2,549	5.6%
	Persson, Carl	1,885	25.3%	Register, Patrick	2,074	4.6%
				Ortiz, Gabriel "Gabe"	1,959	4.3%
	TOTAL	*7,455*		*TOTAL*	*45,431*	
Congressional District 13	Budd, Ted*	Unopposed		Manning, Kathy	19,554	70.1%
				Coker, Adam	8,324	29.9%
				TOTAL	*27,878*	

Note: An asterisk (*) denotes incumbent.

NORTH DAKOTA

One member At Large

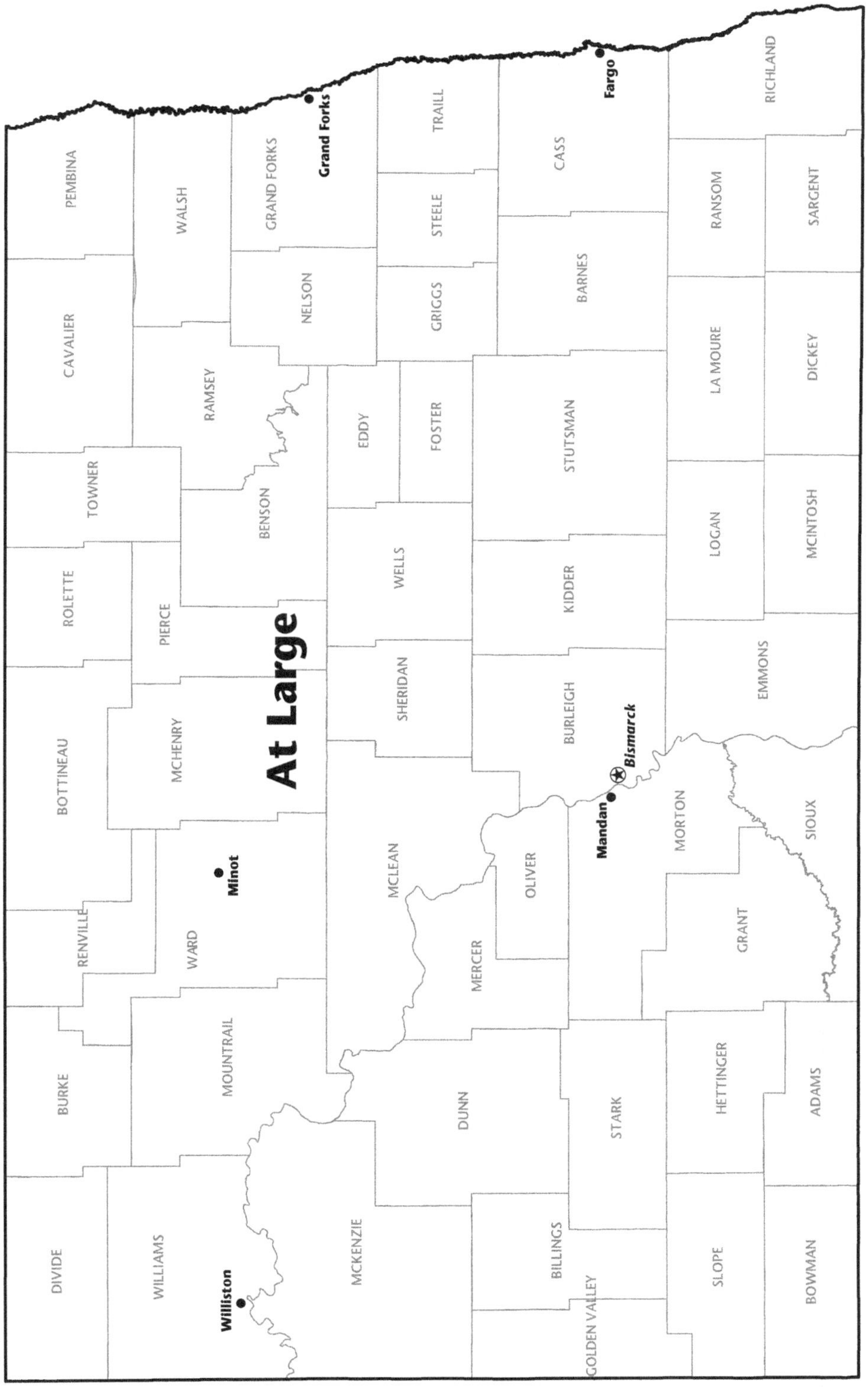

NORTH DAKOTA

GOVERNOR

Doug Burgum (R). Elected 2016 to a four-year term.

SENATORS (2 Republicans)

Kevin Cramer (R). Elected 2018 to a six-year term.

John Hoeven (R). Re-elected 2016 to a six-year term. Previously elected 2010.

REPRESENTATIVES (1 Republican)

At Large. Kelly Armstrong (R)

POSTWAR VOTE FOR PRESIDENT

		Republican		Democratic				Percentage			
								Total Vote		Major Vote	
Year	Total Vote	Vote	Candidate	Vote	Candidate	Other Vote	Rep.-Dem. Plurality	Rep.	Dem.	Rep.	Dem.
2016**	344,360	216,794	Trump, Donald J.	93,758	Clinton, Hillary Rodham	33,808	123,036 R	63.0%	27.2%	69.8%	30.2%
2012	322,627	188,163	Romney, W. Mitt	124,827	Obama, Barack H.*	9,637	63,336 R	58.3%	38.7%	60.1%	39.9%
2008	316,621	168,601	McCain, John S. III	141,278	Obama, Barack H.	6,742	27,323 R	53.3%	44.6%	54.4%	45.6%
2004	312,833	196,651	Bush, George W.*	111,052	Kerry, John F.	5,130	85,599 R	62.9%	35.5%	63.9%	36.1%
2000**	288,256	174,852	Bush, George W.	95,284	Gore, Albert Jr.	18,120	79,568 R	60.7%	33.1%	64.7%	35.3%
1996**	266,411	125,050	Dole, Robert "Bob"	106,905	Clinton, Bill*	34,456	18,145 R	46.9%	40.1%	53.9%	46.1%
1992**	308,133	136,244	Bush, George H.*	99,168	Clinton, Bill	72,721	37,076 R	44.2%	32.2%	57.9%	42.1%
1988	297,261	166,559	Bush, George H.	127,739	Dukakis, Michael S.	2,963	38,820 R	56.0%	43.0%	56.6%	43.4%
1984	308,971	200,336	Reagan, Ronald*	104,429	Mondale, Walter F.	4,206	95,907 R	64.8%	33.8%	65.7%	34.3%
1980**	301,545	193,695	Reagan, Ronald	79,189	Carter, Jimmy*	28,661	114,506 R	64.2%	26.3%	71.0%	29.0%
1976	297,188	153,470	Ford, Gerald R.*	136,078	Carter, Jimmy	7,640	17,392 R	51.6%	45.8%	53.0%	47.0%
1972	280,514	174,109	Nixon, Richard M.*	100,384	McGovern, George S.	6,021	73,725 R	62.1%	35.8%	63.4%	36.6%
1968**	247,882	138,669	Nixon, Richard M.	94,769	Humphrey, Hubert Horatio Jr.	14,444	43,900 R	55.9%	38.2%	59.4%	40.6%
1964	258,389	108,207	Goldwater, Barry M. Sr.	149,784	Johnson, Lyndon B.*	398	41,577 D	41.9%	58.0%	41.9%	58.1%
1960	278,431	154,310	Nixon, Richard M.	123,963	Kennedy, John F.	158	30,347 R	55.4%	44.5%	55.5%	44.5%
1956	253,991	156,766	Eisenhower, Dwight D.*	96,742	Stevenson, Adlai E. II	483	60,024 R	61.7%	38.1%	61.8%	38.2%
1952	270,127	191,712	Eisenhower, Dwight D.	76,694	Stevenson, Adlai E. II	1,721	115,018 R	71.0%	28.4%	71.4%	28.6%
1948	220,716	115,139	Dewey, Thomas E.	95,812	Truman, Harry S.*	9,765	19,327 R	52.2%	43.4%	54.6%	45.4%

Note: An asterisk (*) denotes incumbent. **In past elections, the other vote included: 2016 - 21,434 Libertarian (Gary Johnson); 2000 - 9,486 Green (Ralph Nader); 1996 - 32,515 Reform (Ross Perot); 1992 - 71,084 Independent (Perot); 1980 - 23,640 Independent (John Anderson); 1968 - 14,244 American Independent (George Wallace).

NORTH DAKOTA

POSTWAR VOTE FOR GOVERNOR

		Republican		Democratic				Percentage			
								Total Vote		Major Vote	
Year	Total Vote	Vote	Candidate	Vote	Candidate	Other Vote	Rep.-Dem. Plurality	Rep.	Dem.	Rep.	Dem.
2016	339,601	259,863	Burgum, Doug	65,855	Nelson, Marvin E.	13,883	194,008 R	76.5%	19.4%	79.8%	20.2%
2012	317,812	200,526	Dalrymple, Jack*	109,047	Taylor, Ryan M.	8,239	91,479 R	63.1%	34.3%	64.8%	35.2%
2008	315,692	235,009	Hoeven, John*	74,279	Mathern, Tim	6,404	160,730 R	74.4%	23.5%	76.0%	24.0%
2004	309,873	220,803	Hoeven, John*	84,877	Satrom, Joe	4,193	135,926 R	71.3%	27.4%	72.2%	27.8%
2000	289,412	159,255	Hoeven, John	130,144	Heitkamp, Heidi	13	29,111 R	55.0%	45.0%	55.0%	45.0%
1996	264,298	174,937	Schafer, Edward T.*	89,349	Kaldor, Lee	12	85,588 R	66.2%	33.8%	66.2%	33.8%
1992	304,861	176,398	Schafer, Edward T.	123,845	Spaeth, Nicholas	4,618	52,553 R	57.9%	40.6%	58.8%	41.2%
1988	299,080	119,986	Mallberg, Leon L.	179,094	Sinner, George A.*		59,108 D	40.1%	59.9%	40.1%	59.9%
1984	314,382	140,460	Olson, Allen I.*	173,922	Sinner, George A.		33,462 D	44.7%	55.3%	44.7%	55.3%
1980	302,621	162,230	Olson, Allen I.	140,391	Link, Arthur A.*		21,839 R	53.6%	46.4%	53.6%	46.4%
1976	297,249	138,321	Elkin, Richard	153,309	Link, Arthur A.*	5,619	14,988 D	46.5%	51.6%	47.4%	52.6%
1972	281,931	138,032	Davis, John E.	143,899	Link, Arthur A.		5,867 D	49.0%	51.0%	49.0%	51.0%
1968	247,998	108,380	McCarney, Robert P.	135,955	Guy, William L.*	3,663	27,575 D	43.7%	54.8%	44.4%	55.6%
1964**	262,661	116,247	Halcrow, Don	146,414	Guy, William L.*		30,167 D	44.3%	55.7%	44.3%	55.7%
1962	228,509	113,251	Andrews, Mark	115,258	Guy, William L.*		2,007 D	49.6%	50.4%	49.6%	50.4%
1960	275,375	122,486	Dahl, C. P.	136,148	Guy, William L.	16,741	13,662 D	44.5%	49.4%	47.4%	52.6%
1958	210,599	111,836	Davis, John E.*	98,763	Lord, John F.		13,073 R	53.1%	46.9%	53.1%	46.9%
1956	252,435	147,566	Davis, John E.	104,869	Warner, Wallace E.		42,697 R	58.5%	41.5%	58.5%	41.5%
1954	193,501	124,253	Brunsdale, Norman*	69,248	Bymers, Cornelius		55,005 R	64.2%	35.8%	64.2%	35.8%
1952	253,934	199,944	Brunsdale, Norman*	53,990	Johnson, Ole S.		145,954 R	78.7%	21.3%	78.7%	21.3%
1950	183,772	121,822	Brunsdale, Norman	61,950	Byerly, Clyde G.		59,872 R	66.3%	33.7%	66.3%	33.7%
1948	214,958	131,764	Aandahl, Fred G.*	80,655	Henry, Howard	2,539	51,109 R	61.3%	37.5%	62.0%	38.0%
1946	169,391	116,672	Aandahl, Fred G.*	52,719	Burdick, Quentin N.		63,953 R	68.9%	31.1%	68.9%	31.1%

Note: An asterisk (*) denotes incumbent. **The term of office of North Dakota's Governor was increased from two to four years effective with the 1964 election.

POSTWAR VOTE FOR SENATOR

		Republican		Democratic				Percentage			
								Total Vote		Major Vote	
Year	Total Vote	Vote	Candidate	Vote	Candidate	Other Vote	Rep.-Dem. Plurality	Rep.	Dem.	Rep.	Dem.
2018	326,138	179,720	Cramer, Kevin	144,376	Heitkamp, Heidi*	2,042	35,344 R	55.1%	44.3%	55.5%	44.5%
2016	342,501	268,788	Hoeven, John*	58,116	Glassheim, Eliot	15,597	210,672 R	78.5%	17.0%	82.2%	17.8%
2012	320,851	158,282	Berg, Rick	161,163	Heitkamp, Heidi	1,406	2,881 D	49.3%	50.2%	49.5%	50.5%
2010	238,812	181,689	Hoeven, John	52,955	Potter, Tracy	4,168	128,734 R	76.1%	22.2%	77.4%	22.6%
2006	218,152	64,417	Grotberg, Dwight	150,146	Conrad, Kent*	3,589	85,729 D	29.5%	68.8%	30.0%	70.0%
2004	310,696	98,553	Liffrig, Mike G.	212,143	Dorgan, Byron L.*		113,590 D	31.7%	68.3%	31.7%	68.3%
2000	287,539	111,069	Sand, Duane	176,470	Conrad, Kent*		65,401 D	38.6%	61.4%	38.6%	61.4%
1998	213,358	75,013	Nalewaja, Donna	134,747	Dorgan, Byron L.*	3,598	59,734 D	35.2%	63.2%	35.8%	64.2%
1994	236,547	99,390	Clayburg, Ben	137,157	Conrad, Kent*		37,767 D	42.0%	58.0%	42.0%	58.0%
1992	303,957	118,162	Sydness, Steve	179,347	Dorgan, Byron L.	6,448	61,185 D	38.9%	59.0%	39.7%	60.3%
1992S**	163,311	55,194	Dalrymple, Jack	103,246	Conrad, Kent*	4,871	48,052 D	33.8%	63.2%	34.8%	65.2%
1988	289,170	112,937	Striden, Earl	171,899	Burdick, Quentin N.*	4,334	58,962 D	39.1%	59.4%	39.6%	60.4%
1986	288,998	141,797	Andrews, Mark*	143,932	Conrad, Kent	3,269	2,135 D	49.1%	49.8%	49.6%	50.4%
1982	262,465	89,304	Knorr, Gene	164,873	Burdick, Quentin N.*	8,288	75,569 D	34.0%	62.8%	35.1%	64.9%
1980	299,272	210,347	Andrews, Mark	86,658	Johanneson, Kent	2,267	123,689 R	70.3%	29.0%	70.8%	29.2%
1976	283,062	103,466	Stroup, Richard	175,772	Burdick, Quentin N.*	3,824	72,306 D	36.6%	62.1%	37.1%	62.9%
1974	235,661	114,117	Young, Milton R.*	113,931	Guy, William L.	7,613	186 R	48.4%	48.3%	50.0%	50.0%
1970	219,560	82,996	Kleppe, Tom	134,519	Burdick, Quentin N.*	2,045	51,523 D	37.8%	61.3%	38.2%	61.8%
1968	239,776	154,968	Young, Milton R.*	80,815	Lashkowitz, Herschel	3,993	74,153 R	64.6%	33.7%	65.7%	34.3%
1964	258,945	109,681	Kleppe, Tom	149,264	Burdick, Quentin N.*		39,583 D	42.4%	57.6%	42.4%	57.6%
1962	223,737	135,705	Young, Milton R.*	88,032	Lanier, William		47,673 R	60.7%	39.3%	60.7%	39.3%
1960S**	210,349	103,475	Davis, John E.	104,593	Burdick, Quentin N.	2,281	1,118 D	49.2%	49.7%	49.7%	50.3%
1958	204,635	117,070	Langer, William*	84,892	Vendsel, Raymond	2,673	32,178 R	57.2%	41.5%	58.0%	42.0%
1956	244,161	155,305	Young, Milton R.*	87,919	Burdick, Quentin N.	937	67,386 R	63.6%	36.0%	63.9%	36.1%
1952**	237,995	157,907	Langer, William*	55,347	Morrison, Harold A.	24,741	102,560 R	66.3%	23.3%	74.0%	26.0%
1950	186,716	126,209	Young, Milton R.*	60,507	O'Brien, Harry		65,702 R	67.6%	32.4%	67.6%	32.4%
1946**	165,382	88,210	Langer, William*	38,368	Larson, Abner B.	38,804	49,842 R	53.3%	23.2%	69.7%	30.3%
1946S**	136,852	75,998	Young, Milton R.*	37,507	Lanier, William	23,347	38,491 R	55.5%	27.4%	67.0%	33.0%

Note: An asterisk (*) denotes incumbent. **In past elections, the other vote included: 1952 - 24,741 Independent (Fred G. Aandahl); 1946 - 38,804 Independent (Arthur E. Thompson), who finished second; 1946 Special - 20,848 Independent (Gerald P. Nye). One of the 1992 elections was for a short term to fill a vacancy and the special election was held in December. The 1946 and 1960 special elections were held in June for short terms to fill vacancies.

NORTH DAKOTA

SENATOR 2018

2010 Census Population	County	Total Vote	Republican (Cramer)	Democratic (Heitkamp)	Other	Rep.-Dem. Plurality	Percentage Total Vote Rep.	Total Vote Dem.	Major Vote Rep.	Major Vote Dem.
2,343	ADAMS	1,164	796	364	4	432 R	68.4%	31.3%	68.6%	31.4%
11,066	BARNES	5,043	2,507	2,517	19	10 D	49.7%	49.9%	49.9%	50.1%
6,660	BENSON	2,267	828	1,427	12	599 D	36.5%	62.9%	36.7%	63.3%
783	BILLINGS	565	450	115		335 R	79.6%	20.4%	79.6%	20.4%
6,429	BOTTINEAU	3,271	2,147	1,110	14	1,037 R	65.6%	33.9%	65.9%	34.1%
3,151	BOWMAN	1,649	1,233	404	12	829 R	74.8%	24.5%	75.3%	24.7%
1,968	BURKE	964	729	228	7	501 R	75.6%	23.7%	76.2%	23.8%
81,308	BURLEIGH	46,209	28,494	17,357	358	11,137 R	61.7%	37.6%	62.1%	37.9%
149,778	CASS	77,427	32,217	44,723	487	12,506 D	41.6%	57.8%	41.9%	58.1%
3,993	CAVALIER	1,958	1,181	765	12	416 R	60.3%	39.1%	60.7%	39.3%
5,289	DICKEY	2,170	1,253	911	6	342 R	57.7%	42.0%	57.9%	42.1%
2,071	DIVIDE	1,197	720	469	8	251 R	60.2%	39.2%	60.6%	39.4%
3,536	DUNN	2,034	1,499	525	10	974 R	73.7%	25.8%	74.1%	25.9%
2,385	EDDY	1,234	675	555	4	120 R	54.7%	45.0%	54.9%	45.1%
3,550	EMMONS	1,835	1,433	391	11	1,042 R	78.1%	21.3%	78.6%	21.4%
3,343	FOSTER	1,654	1,052	588	14	464 R	63.6%	35.6%	64.1%	35.9%
1,680	GOLDEN VALLEY	880	704	171	5	533 R	80.0%	19.4%	80.5%	19.5%
66,861	GRAND FORKS	27,936	12,952	14,827	157	1,875 D	46.4%	53.1%	46.6%	53.4%
2,394	GRANT	1,268	925	337	6	588 R	72.9%	26.6%	73.3%	26.7%
2,420	GRIGGS	1,226	688	534	4	154 R	56.1%	43.6%	56.3%	43.7%
2,477	HETTINGER	1,269	988	274	7	714 R	77.9%	21.6%	78.3%	21.7%
2,435	KIDDER	1,280	911	364	5	547 R	71.2%	28.4%	71.5%	28.5%
4,139	LA MOURE	2,069	1,203	857	9	346 R	58.1%	41.4%	58.4%	41.6%
1,990	LOGAN	977	741	228	8	513 R	75.8%	23.3%	76.5%	23.5%
5,395	MCHENRY	2,553	1,659	879	15	780 R	65.0%	34.4%	65.4%	34.6%
2,809	MCINTOSH	1,455	982	467	6	515 R	67.5%	32.1%	67.8%	32.2%
6,360	MCKENZIE	4,193	3,012	1,167	14	1,845 R	71.8%	27.8%	72.1%	27.9%
8,962	MCLEAN	5,050	3,320	1,701	29	1,619 R	65.7%	33.7%	66.1%	33.9%
8,424	MERCER	4,024	2,941	1,061	22	1,880 R	73.1%	26.4%	73.5%	26.5%
27,471	MORTON	14,896	9,583	5,175	138	4,408 R	64.3%	34.7%	64.9%	35.1%
7,673	MOUNTRAIL	3,820	2,208	1,605	7	603 R	57.8%	42.0%	57.9%	42.1%
3,126	NELSON	1,647	770	866	11	96 D	46.8%	52.6%	47.1%	52.9%
1,846	OLIVER	972	717	250	5	467 R	73.8%	25.7%	74.1%	25.9%
7,413	PEMBINA	2,962	1,814	1,132	16	682 R	61.2%	38.2%	61.6%	38.4%
4,357	PIERCE	1,888	1,168	711	9	457 R	61.9%	37.7%	62.2%	37.8%
11,451	RAMSEY	5,057	2,668	2,336	53	332 R	52.8%	46.2%	53.3%	46.7%
5,457	RANSOM	2,310	890	1,399	21	509 D	38.5%	60.6%	38.9%	61.1%
2,470	RENVILLE	1,193	832	356	5	476 R	69.7%	29.8%	70.0%	30.0%
16,321	RICHLAND	7,307	3,316	3,943	48	627 D	45.4%	54.0%	45.7%	54.3%
13,937	ROLETTE	5,045	993	4,042	10	3,049 D	19.7%	80.1%	19.7%	80.3%
3,829	SARGENT	2,002	821	1,171	10	350 D	41.0%	58.5%	41.2%	58.8%
1,321	SHERIDAN	789	607	179	3	428 R	76.9%	22.7%	77.2%	22.8%
4,153	SIOUX	1,446	221	1,211	14	990 D	15.3%	83.7%	15.4%	84.6%
727	SLOPE	381	307	73	1	234 R	80.6%	19.2%	80.8%	19.2%
24,199	STARK	12,166	8,945	3,151	70	5,794 R	73.5%	25.9%	74.0%	26.0%
1,975	STEELE	960	399	557	4	158 D	41.6%	58.0%	41.7%	58.3%
21,100	STUTSMAN	9,583	5,489	4,027	67	1,462 R	57.3%	42.0%	57.7%	42.3%
2,246	TOWNER	1,127	624	497	6	127 R	55.4%	44.1%	55.7%	44.3%
8,121	TRAILL	3,742	1,735	1,988	19	253 D	46.4%	53.1%	46.6%	53.4%
11,119	WALSH	4,512	2,550	1,937	25	613 R	56.5%	42.9%	56.8%	43.2%
61,675	WARD	24,128	15,105	8,856	167	6,249 R	62.6%	36.7%	63.0%	37.0%
4,207	WELLS	2,233	1,601	622	10	979 R	71.7%	27.9%	72.0%	28.0%
22,398	WILLIAMS	11,151	8,117	2,976	58	5,141 R	72.8%	26.7%	73.2%	26.8%
672,591	*TOTAL*	*326,138*	*179,720*	*144,376*	*2,042*	*35,344 R*	*55.1%*	*44.3%*	*55.5%*	*44.5%*

Note: Democratic candidates in North Dakota appear on the ballot for the Democratic-Nonpartisan League Party.

NORTH DAKOTA

HOUSE OF REPRESENTATIVES

			Republican		Democratic				Percentage			
									Total Vote		Major Vote	
CD	Year	Total Vote	Vote	Candidate	Vote	Candidate	Other Vote	Rep.-Dem. Plurality	Rep.	Dem.	Rep.	Dem.
At Large	2018	321,532	193,568	ARMSTRONG, KELLY	114,377	SCHNEIDER, MAC	13,587	79,191 R	60.2%	35.6%	62.9%	37.1%
At Large	2016	338,459	233,980	CRAMER, KEVIN*	80,377	IRON EYES, CHASE	24,102	153,603 R	69.1%	23.7%	74.4%	25.6%
At Large	2014	248,670	138,100	CRAMER, KEVIN*	95,678	SINNER, GEORGE	14,892	42,422 R	55.5%	38.5%	59.1%	40.9%
At Large	2012	316,071	173,433	CRAMER, KEVIN	131,869	GULLESON, PAM	10,769	41,564 R	54.9%	41.7%	56.8%	43.2%
At Large	2010	237,137	129,802	BERG, RICK	106,542	POMEROY, EARL*	793	23,260 R	54.7%	44.9%	54.9%	45.1%
At Large	2008	313,965	119,388	SAND, DUANE	194,577	POMEROY, EARL*		75,189 D	38.0%	62.0%	38.0%	62.0%
At Large	2006	217,621	74,687	MECHTEL, MATT	142,934	POMEROY, EARL*		68,247 D	34.3%	65.7%	34.3%	65.7%
At Large	2004	310,814	125,684	SAND, DUANE	185,130	POMEROY, EARL*		59,446 D	40.4%	59.6%	40.4%	59.6%
At Large	2002	231,030	109,957	CLAYBURGH, RICK	121,073	POMEROY, EARL*		11,116 D	47.6%	52.4%	47.6%	52.4%
At Large	2000	285,658	127,251	DORSO, JOHN	151,173	POMEROY, EARL*	7,234	23,922 D	44.5%	52.9%	45.7%	54.3%
At Large	1998	212,888	87,511	CRAMER, KEVIN	119,668	POMEROY, EARL*	5,709	32,157 D	41.1%	56.2%	42.2%	57.8%
At Large	1996	263,010	113,684	CRAMER, KEVIN	144,833	POMEROY, EARL*	4,493	31,149 D	43.2%	55.1%	44.0%	56.0%
At Large	1994	235,389	105,988	PORTER, GARY	123,134	POMEROY, EARL*	6,267	17,146 D	45.0%	52.3%	46.3%	53.7%
At Large	1992	297,898	117,442	KORSMO, JOHN T.	169,273	POMEROY, EARL	11,183	51,831 D	39.4%	56.8%	41.0%	59.0%
At Large	1990	233,979	81,443	SCHAFER, EDWARD T.	152,530	DORGAN, BYRON L.*	6	71,087 D	34.8%	65.2%	34.8%	65.2%
At Large	1988	299,982	84,475	SYDNESS, STEVE	212,583	DORGAN, BYRON L.*	2,924	128,108 D	28.2%	70.9%	28.4%	71.6%
At Large	1986	286,361	66,989	VINJE, SYVER	216,258	DORGAN, BYRON L.*	3,114	149,269 D	23.4%	75.5%	23.7%	76.3%
At Large	1984	308,729	65,761	ALTENBURG, LOIS I.	242,968	DORGAN, BYRON L.*		177,207 D	21.3%	78.7%	21.3%	78.7%
At Large	1982	260,499	72,241	JONES, KENT	186,534	DORGAN, BYRON L.*	1,724	114,293 D	27.7%	71.6%	27.9%	72.1%
At Large	1980	293,076	124,707	SMYKOWSKI, JIM	166,437	DORGAN, BYRON L.	1,932	41,730 D	42.6%	56.8%	42.8%	57.2%
At Large	1978	220,348	147,746	ANDREWS, MARK*	68,016	HAGEN, BRUCE	4,586	79,730 R	67.1%	30.9%	68.5%	31.5%
At Large	1976	289,881	181,018	ANDREWS, MARK*	104,263	OMDAHL, LLOYD B.	4,600	76,755 R	62.4%	36.0%	63.5%	36.5%
At Large	1974	233,688	130,184	ANDREWS, MARK*	103,504	DORGAN, BYRON L.		26,680 R	55.7%	44.3%	55.7%	44.3%
At Large	1972	268,721	195,360	ANDREWS, MARK*	72,850	ISTA, RICHARD	511	122,510 R	72.7%	27.1%	72.8%	27.2%

Note: An asterisk (*) denotes incumbent. Democratic candidates in North Dakota appear on the ballot for the Democratic-Nonpartisan League Party. North Dakota had two House seats prior to 1972.

NORTH DAKOTA

GENERAL AND PRIMARY ELECTIONS

2018 GENERAL ELECTIONS: OTHER VOTES

Senate Other vote was 2,042 Write-in (Scattered Write-in)

House Other vote was:

At Large 13,066 Independent (Charles Tuttle), 521 Write-in (Scattered Write-in)

2018 PRIMARY ELECTIONS: SUPPLEMENTARY INFORMATION

Primary June 12, 2018

Registration (No Formal Registration) No Party Registration

Primary Type Open—Any person of voting age (18 years old at the time of the primary election) could participate in the primary of either party. As of June 12, 2018, North Dakota's estimated voting-age population was 581,641.

NORTH DAKOTA

GENERAL AND PRIMARY ELECTIONS

	REPUBLICAN PRIMARIES			DEMOCRATIC PRIMARIES		
Senator	Cramer, Kevin	61,529	87.7%	Heitkamp, Heidi*	36,729	99.6%
	O'Neill, Thomas	8,509	12.1%	Write-In	154	0.4%
	Write-In	95	0.1%			
	TOTAL	*70,133*		*TOTAL*	*36,883*	
Congressional At Large	Armstrong, Kelly	37,364	56.2%	Schneider, Mac	33,727	99.8%
	Campbell, Tom	17,861	26.9%	Write-In	74	0.2%
	Abentroth, Tiffany	5,921	8.9%			
	Schaffner, Paul	5,243	7.9%			
	Write-In	76	0.1%			
	TOTAL	*66,465*		*TOTAL*	*33,801*	

Note: An asterisk (*) denotes incumbent.

OHIO

Congressional districts first established for elections held in 2012

16 members

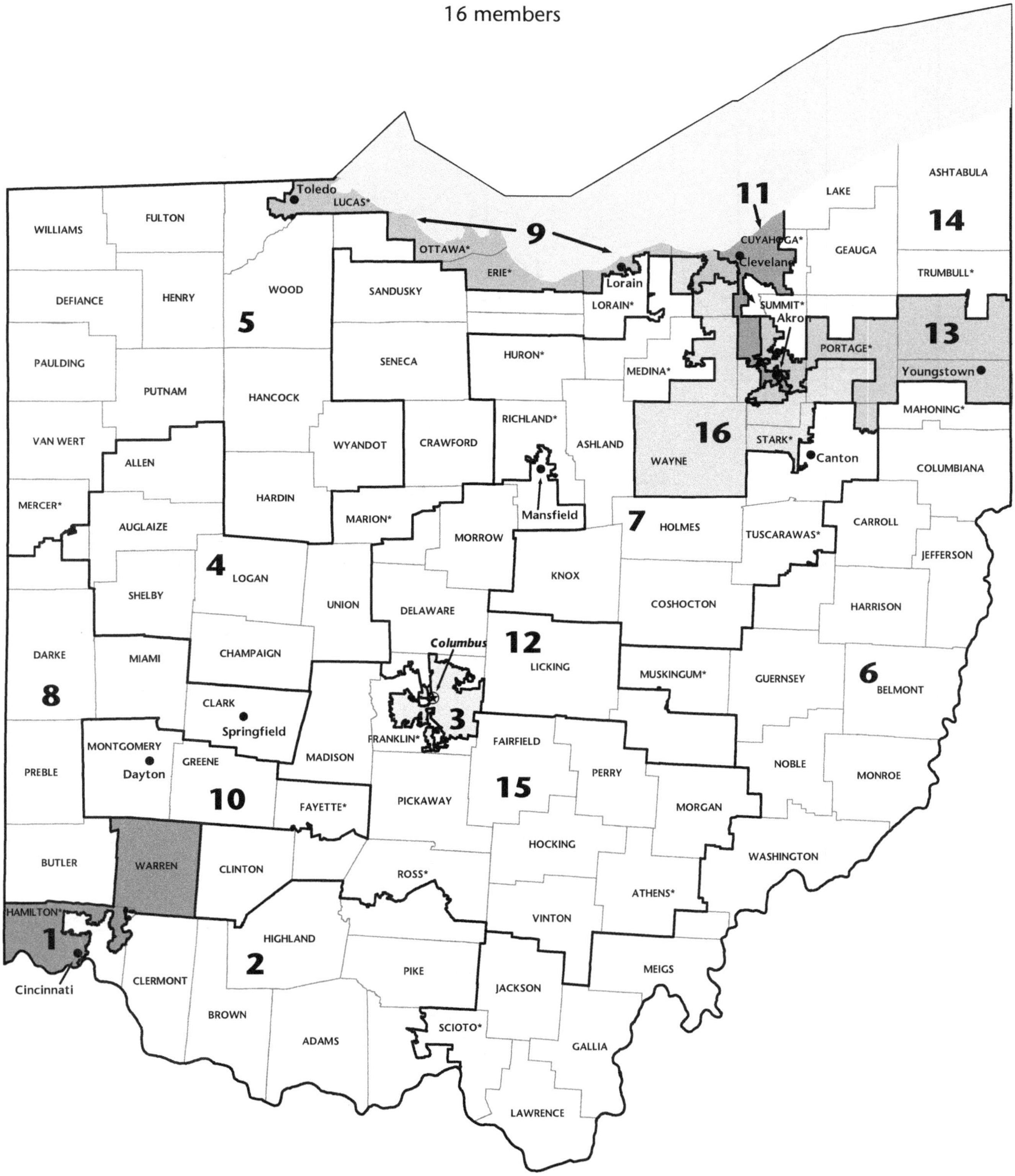

* Asterisk indicates a county whose boundaries include parts of two or more congressional districts.

OHIO

Cleveland Area

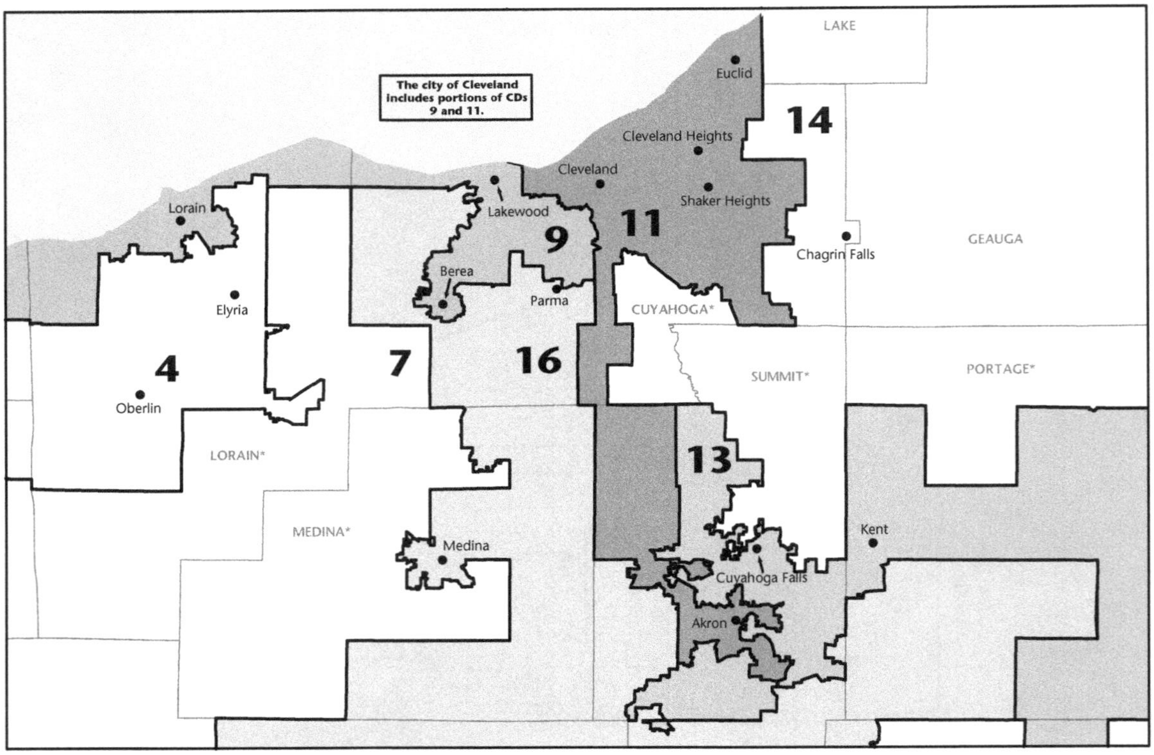

Columbus Area

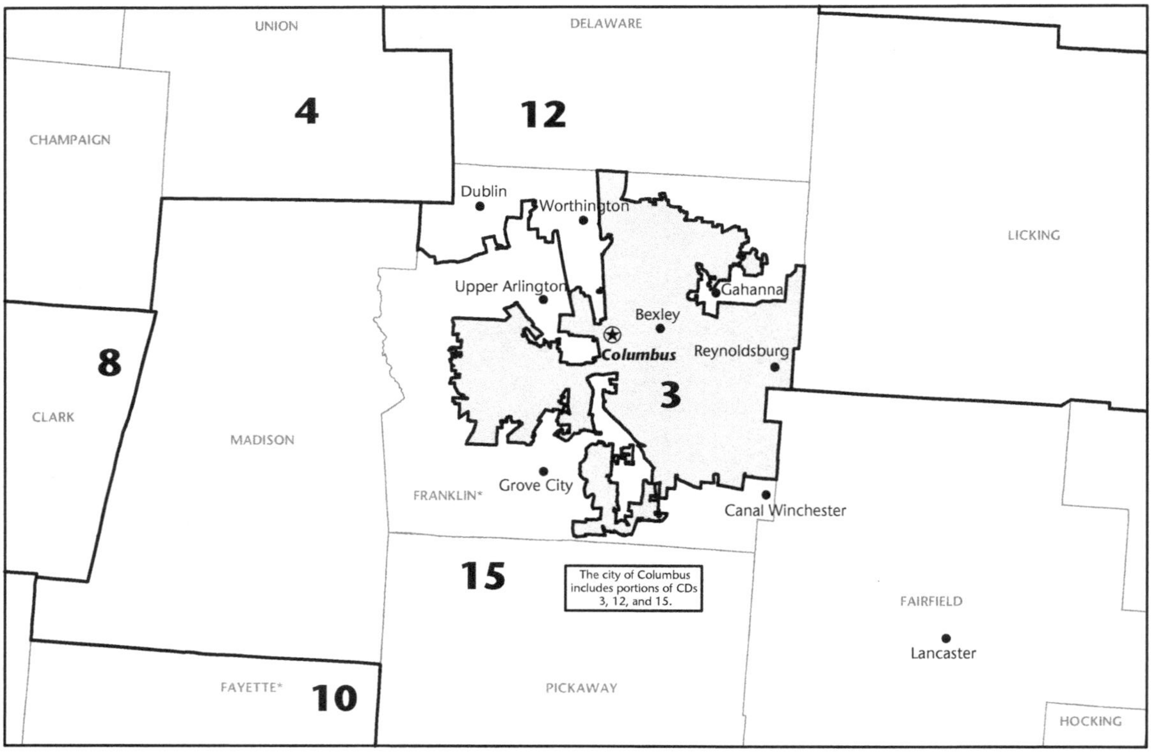

* Asterisk indicates a county whose boundaries include parts of two or more congressional districts.

OHIO

GOVERNOR

Michael "Mike" Dewine (R). Elected 2018 to a four-year term.

SENATORS (1 Republican, 1 Democrat)

Sherrod Brown (D). Re-elected 2018 to a six-year term. Previously elected 2012, 2006.

Rob Portman (R). Re-elected 2016 to a six-year term. Previously elected 2010.

REPRESENTATIVES (12 Republicans, 4 Democrats)

1. Steve Chabot (R)
2. Brad Wenstrup (R)
3. Joyce Beatty (D)
4. Jim Jordan (R)
5. Bob Latta (R)
6. Bill Johnson (R)
7. Bob Gibbs (R)
8. Warren Davidson (R)
9. Marcy Kaptur (D)
10. Michael R. Turner (R)
11. Marcia L. Fudge (D)
12. Troy Balderson (R)
13. Tim Ryan (D)
14. David Joyce (R)
15. Steve Stivers (R)
16. Anthony Gonzalez (R)

POSTWAR VOTE FOR PRESIDENT

		Republican		Democratic					Percentage			
									Total Vote		Major Vote	
Year	Total Vote	Vote	Candidate	Vote	Candidate	Other Vote	Rep.-Dem. Plurality		Rep.	Dem.	Rep.	Dem.
2016**	5,496,487	2,841,005	Trump, Donald J.	2,394,164	Clinton, Hillary Rodham	261,318	446,841	R	51.7%	43.6%	54.3%	45.7%
2012	5,580,840	2,661,433	Romney, W. Mitt	2,827,710	Obama, Barack H.*	91,697	166,277	D	47.7%	50.7%	48.5%	51.5%
2008	5,708,350	2,677,820	McCain, John S. III	2,940,044	Obama, Barack H.	90,486	262,224	D	46.9%	51.5%	47.7%	52.3%
2004	5,627,908	2,859,768	Bush, George W.*	2,741,167	Kerry, John F.	26,973	118,601	R	50.8%	48.7%	51.1%	48.9%
2000**	4,701,998	2,350,363	Bush, George W.	2,183,628	Gore, Albert Jr.	168,007	166,735	R	50.0%	46.4%	51.8%	48.2%
1996**	4,534,434	1,859,883	Dole, Robert "Bob"	2,148,222	Clinton, Bill*	526,329	288,339	D	41.0%	47.4%	46.4%	53.6%
1992**	4,939,967	1,894,310	Bush, George H.*	1,984,942	Clinton, Bill	1,060,715	90,632	D	38.3%	40.2%	48.8%	51.2%
1988	4,393,699	2,416,549	Bush, George H.	1,939,629	Dukakis, Michael S.	37,521	476,920	R	55.0%	44.1%	55.5%	44.5%
1984	4,547,619	2,678,560	Reagan, Ronald*	1,825,440	Mondale, Walter F.	43,619	853,120	R	58.9%	40.1%	59.5%	40.5%
1980**	4,283,603	2,206,545	Reagan, Ronald	1,752,414	Carter, Jimmy*	324,644	454,131	R	51.5%	40.9%	55.7%	44.3%
1976	4,111,873	2,000,505	Ford, Gerald R.*	2,011,621	Carter, Jimmy	99,747	11,116	D	48.7%	48.9%	49.9%	50.1%
1972	4,094,787	2,441,827	Nixon, Richard M.*	1,558,889	McGovern, George S.	94,071	882,938	R	59.6%	38.1%	61.0%	39.0%
1968**	3,959,698	1,791,014	Nixon, Richard M.	1,700,586	Humphrey, Hubert Horatio Jr.	468,098	90,428	R	45.2%	42.9%	51.3%	48.7%
1964	3,969,196	1,470,865	Goldwater, Barry M. Sr.	2,498,331	Johnson, Lyndon B.*		1,027,466	D	37.1%	62.9%	37.1%	62.9%
1960	4,161,859	2,217,611	Nixon, Richard M.	1,944,248	Kennedy, John F.		273,363	R	53.3%	46.7%	53.3%	46.7%
1956	3,702,265	2,262,610	Eisenhower, Dwight D.*	1,439,655	Stevenson, Adlai E. II		822,955	R	61.1%	38.9%	61.1%	38.9%
1952	3,700,758	2,100,391	Eisenhower, Dwight D.	1,600,367	Stevenson, Adlai E. II		500,024	R	56.8%	43.2%	56.8%	43.2%
1948	2,936,071	1,445,684	Dewey, Thomas E.	1,452,791	Truman, Harry S.*	37,596	7,107	D	49.2%	49.5%	49.9%	50.1%

Note: An asterisk (*) denotes incumbent. **In past elections, the other vote included: 2016 - 174,498 Libertarian (Gary Johnson); 2000 - 117,799 Green (Ralph Nader); 1996 - 483,207 Reform (Ross Perot); 1992 - 1,036,426 Independent (Perot); 1980 - 254,472 Independent (John Anderson); 1968 - 467,495 American Independent (George Wallace).

OHIO

POSTWAR VOTE FOR GOVERNOR

		Republican		Democratic				Percentage			
								Total Vote		Major Vote	
Year	Total Vote	Vote	Candidate	Vote	Candidate	Other Vote	Rep.-Dem. Plurality	Rep.	Dem.	Rep.	Dem.
2018	4,429,582	2,231,917	DeWine, Michael "Mike"	2,067,847	Cordray, Richard	129,818	164,070 R	50.4%	46.7%	51.9%	48.1%
2014	3,055,913	1,944,848	Kasich, John R.*	1,009,359	FitzGerald, Ed	101,706	935,489 R	63.6%	33.0%	65.8%	34.2%
2010	3,852,469	1,889,186	Kasich, John R.	1,812,059	Strickland, Ted*	151,224	77,127 R	49.0%	47.0%	51.0%	49.0%
2006	4,022,754	1,474,285	Blackwell, J. Kenneth	2,435,384	Strickland, Ted	113,085	961,099 D	36.6%	60.5%	37.7%	62.3%
2002	3,228,992	1,865,007	Taft, Robert Alphonso*	1,236,924	Hagan, Timothy	127,061	628,083 R	57.8%	38.3%	60.1%	39.9%
1998	3,354,213	1,678,721	Taft, Robert Alphonso	1,498,956	Fisher, Lee	176,536	179,765 R	50.0%	44.7%	52.8%	47.2%
1994	3,346,238	2,401,572	Voinovich, George*	835,849	Burch, Robert L.	108,817	1,565,723 R	71.8%	25.0%	74.2%	25.8%
1990	3,482,650	1,938,103	Voinovich, George	1,544,416	Celebrezze, Anthony J.	131	393,687 R	55.7%	44.3%	55.7%	44.3%
1986	3,066,611	1,207,264	Rhodes, James A.	1,858,372	Celeste, Richard F.*	975	651,108 D	39.4%	60.6%	39.4%	60.6%
1982	3,356,791	1,303,962	Brown, Clarence J. Jr.	1,981,952	Celeste, Richard F.	70,877	677,990 D	38.8%	59.0%	39.7%	60.3%
1978	2,843,351	1,402,167	Rhodes, James A.*	1,354,631	Celeste, Richard F.	86,553	47,536 R	49.3%	47.6%	50.9%	49.1%
1974	3,072,010	1,493,679	Rhodes, James A.	1,482,191	Gilligan, John J.*	96,140	11,488 R	48.6%	48.2%	50.2%	49.8%
1970	3,184,131	1,382,657	Cloud, Roger	1,725,560	Gilligan, John J.	75,914	342,903 D	43.4%	54.2%	44.5%	55.5%
1966	2,887,331	1,795,277	Rhodes, James A.*	1,092,054	Reams, Henry Frazier "Frazier" Jr.		703,223 R	62.2%	37.8%	62.2%	37.8%
1962	3,116,953	1,836,432	Rhodes, James A.	1,280,521	Disalle, Michael V.*		555,911 R	58.9%	41.1%	58.9%	41.1%
1958**	3,284,134	1,414,874	O'Neill, C. William*	1,869,260	Disalle, Michael V.		454,386 D	43.1%	56.9%	43.1%	56.9%
1956	3,542,091	1,984,988	O'Neill, C. William	1,557,103	Disalle, Michael V.		427,885 R	56.0%	44.0%	56.0%	44.0%
1954	2,597,790	1,192,528	Rhodes, James A.	1,405,262	Lausche, Frank J.*		212,734 D	45.9%	54.1%	45.9%	54.1%
1952	3,605,168	1,590,058	Taft, Charles P.	2,015,110	Lausche, Frank J.*		425,052 D	44.1%	55.9%	44.1%	55.9%
1950	2,892,819	1,370,570	Ebright, Don H.	1,522,249	Lausche, Frank J.*		151,679 D	47.4%	52.6%	47.4%	52.6%
1948	3,018,289	1,398,514	Herbert, Thomas J.*	1,619,775	Lausche, Frank J.		221,261 D	46.3%	53.7%	46.3%	53.7%
1946	2,303,750	1,166,550	Herbert, Thomas J.	1,125,997	Lausche, Frank J.*	11,203	40,553 R	50.6%	48.9%	50.9%	49.1%

Note: An asterisk (*) denotes incumbent. **The term of office of Ohio's Governor was increased from two to four years effective with the 1958 election.

POSTWAR VOTE FOR SENATOR

		Republican		Democratic				Percentage			
								Total Vote		Major Vote	
Year	Total Vote	Vote	Candidate	Vote	Candidate	Other Vote	Rep.-Dem. Plurality	Rep.	Dem.	Rep.	Dem.
2018	4,410,898	2,053,963	Renacci, Jim	2,355,923	Brown, Sherrod*	1,012	301,960 D	46.6%	53.4%	46.6%	53.4%
2016	5,374,164	3,118,567	Portman, Rob*	1,996,908	Strickland, Ted	258,689	1,121,659 R	58.0%	37.2%	61.0%	39.0%
2012	5,449,114	2,435,740	Mandel, Josh	2,762,757	Brown, Sherrod*	250,617	327,017 D	44.7%	50.7%	46.9%	53.1%
2010	3,815,098	2,168,742	Portman, Rob	1,503,297	Fisher, Lee	143,059	665,445 R	56.8%	39.4%	59.1%	40.9%
2006	4,019,236	1,761,037	DeWine, Michael "Mike"*	2,257,369	Brown, Sherrod	830	496,332 D	43.8%	56.2%	43.8%	56.2%
2004	5,426,196	3,464,651	Voinovich, George*	1,961,249	Fingerhut, Eric D.	296	1,503,402 R	63.9%	36.1%	63.9%	36.1%
2000	4,448,801	2,665,512	DeWine, Michael "Mike"*	1,595,066	Celeste, Theodore S.	188,223	1,070,446 R	59.9%	35.9%	62.6%	37.4%
1998	3,404,351	1,922,087	Voinovich, George	1,482,054	Boyle, Mary O.	210	440,033 R	56.5%	43.5%	56.5%	43.5%
1994	3,436,884	1,836,556	DeWine, Michael "Mike"	1,348,213	Hyatt, Joel	252,115	488,343 R	53.4%	39.2%	57.7%	42.3%
1992	4,793,953	2,028,300	DeWine, Michael "Mike"	2,444,419	Glenn, John H.*	321,234	416,119 D	42.3%	51.0%	45.3%	54.7%
1988	4,352,905	1,872,716	Voinovich, George	2,480,038	Metzenbaum, Howard M.*	151	607,322 D	43.0%	57.0%	43.0%	57.0%
1986	3,121,188	1,171,893	Kindness, Thomas N.	1,949,208	Glenn, John H.*	87	777,315 D	37.5%	62.5%	37.5%	62.5%
1982	3,395,463	1,396,790	Pfeifer, Paul E.	1,923,767	Metzenbaum, Howard M.*	74,906	526,977 D	41.1%	56.7%	42.1%	57.9%
1980	4,027,303	1,137,695	Betts, James E.	2,770,786	Glenn, John H.*	118,822	1,633,091 D	28.2%	68.8%	29.1%	70.9%
1976	3,920,613	1,823,774	Taft, Robert Alphonso*	1,941,113	Metzenbaum, Howard M.	155,726	117,339 D	46.5%	49.5%	48.4%	51.6%
1974	2,987,951	918,133	Perk, Ralph J.	1,930,670	Glenn, John H.	139,148	1,012,537 D	30.7%	64.6%	32.2%	67.8%
1970	3,151,274	1,565,682	Taft, Robert Alphonso	1,495,262	Metzenbaum, Howard M.	90,330	70,420 R	49.7%	47.4%	51.2%	48.8%
1968	3,743,121	1,928,964	Saxbe, William B.	1,814,152	Gilligan, John J.	5	114,812 R	51.5%	48.5%	51.5%	48.5%
1964	3,830,389	1,906,781	Taft, Robert Alphonso	1,923,608	Young, Stephen M.*		16,827 D	49.8%	50.2%	49.8%	50.2%
1962	2,995,105	1,151,292	Briley, John Marshall	1,843,813	Lausche, Frank J.*		692,521 D	38.4%	61.6%	38.4%	61.6%
1958	3,149,410	1,497,199	Bricker, John W.*	1,652,211	Young, Stephen M.		155,012 D	47.5%	52.5%	47.5%	52.5%
1956	3,525,499	1,660,910	Bender, George H.*	1,864,589	Lausche, Frank J.		203,679 D	47.1%	52.9%	47.1%	52.9%
1954S**	2,512,773	1,257,874	Bender, George H.	1,254,899	Burke, Thomas A.		2,975 R	50.1%	49.9%	50.1%	49.9%
1952	3,442,291	1,878,961	Bricker, John W.*	1,563,330	Disalle, Michael V.		315,631 R	54.6%	45.4%	54.6%	45.4%
1950	2,860,102	1,645,643	Taft, Robert Alphonso*	1,214,459	Ferguson, Joseph T.		431,184 R	57.5%	42.5%	57.5%	42.5%
1946	2,237,269	1,275,774	Bricker, John W.	947,610	Huffman, James W.	13,885	328,164 R	57.0%	42.4%	57.4%	42.6%
1946S**	2,123,526	1,193,942	Taft, Kingsley A.	929,584	Webber, Henry P.		264,358 R	56.2%	43.8%	56.2%	43.8%

Note: An asterisk (*) denotes incumbent. **One of the 1946 elections and the 1954 election were for short terms to fill a vacancy.

OHIO

GOVERNOR 2018

2010 Census Population	County	Total Vote	Republican (DeWine)	Democratic (Cordray)	Other	Rep.-Dem. Plurality	Percentage Total Vote		Percentage Major Vote	
							Rep.	Dem.	Rep.	Dem.
28,550	ADAMS	8,749	6,302	2,184	263	4,118 R	72.0%	25.0%	74.3%	25.7%
106,331	ALLEN	35,966	24,200	10,825	941	13,375 R	67.3%	30.1%	69.1%	30.9%
53,139	ASHLAND	18,717	12,846	5,157	714	7,689 R	68.6%	27.6%	71.4%	28.6%
101,497	ASHTABULA	32,234	17,184	13,668	1,382	3,516 R	53.3%	42.4%	55.7%	44.3%
64,757	ATHENS	22,643	7,566	14,261	816	6,695 D	33.4%	63.0%	34.7%	65.3%
45,949	AUGLAIZE	19,160	14,902	3,676	582	11,226 R	77.8%	19.2%	80.2%	19.8%
70,400	BELMONT	24,888	15,614	8,686	588	6,928 R	62.7%	34.9%	64.3%	35.7%
44,846	BROWN	14,850	10,668	3,683	499	6,985 R	71.8%	24.8%	74.3%	25.7%
368,130	BUTLER	135,540	82,771	48,890	3,879	33,881 R	61.1%	36.1%	62.9%	37.1%
28,836	CARROLL	10,302	6,772	3,114	416	3,658 R	65.7%	30.2%	68.5%	31.5%
40,097	CHAMPAIGN	14,839	10,023	4,197	619	5,826 R	67.5%	28.3%	70.5%	29.5%
138,333	CLARK	48,117	27,967	18,537	1,613	9,430 R	58.1%	38.5%	60.1%	39.9%
197,363	CLERMONT	80,143	53,508	23,847	2,788	29,661 R	66.8%	29.8%	69.2%	30.8%
42,040	CLINTON	15,054	10,884	3,647	523	7,237 R	72.3%	24.2%	74.9%	25.1%
107,841	COLUMBIANA	35,630	22,846	11,625	1,159	11,221 R	64.1%	32.6%	66.3%	33.7%
36,901	COSHOCTON	11,920	7,768	3,738	414	4,030 R	65.2%	31.4%	67.5%	32.5%
43,784	CRAWFORD	14,508	9,786	4,202	520	5,584 R	67.5%	29.0%	70.0%	30.0%
1,280,122	CUYAHOGA	485,634	150,848	323,276	11,510	172,428 D	31.1%	66.6%	31.8%	68.2%
52,959	DARKE	19,652	15,161	3,820	671	11,341 R	77.1%	19.4%	79.9%	20.1%
39,037	DEFIANCE	13,953	8,834	4,649	470	4,185 R	63.3%	33.3%	65.5%	34.5%
174,214	DELAWARE	95,244	53,674	39,655	1,915	14,019 R	56.4%	41.6%	57.5%	42.5%
77,079	ERIE	30,278	14,577	14,494	1,207	83 R	48.1%	47.9%	50.1%	49.9%
146,156	FAIRFIELD	59,759	35,445	22,702	1,612	12,743 R	59.3%	38.0%	61.0%	39.0%
29,030	FAYETTE	8,541	5,955	2,381	205	3,574 R	69.7%	27.9%	71.4%	28.6%
1,163,414	FRANKLIN	487,351	166,057	310,205	11,089	144,148 D	34.1%	63.7%	34.9%	65.1%
42,698	FULTON	16,307	10,467	5,275	565	5,192 R	64.2%	32.3%	66.5%	33.5%
30,934	GALLIA	9,727	6,820	2,707	200	4,113 R	70.1%	27.8%	71.6%	28.4%
93,389	GEAUGA	42,573	25,468	15,887	1,218	9,581 R	59.8%	37.3%	61.6%	38.4%
161,573	GREENE	68,914	42,173	24,557	2,184	17,616 R	61.2%	35.6%	63.2%	36.8%
40,087	GUERNSEY	12,642	8,242	3,965	435	4,277 R	65.2%	31.4%	67.5%	32.5%
802,374	HAMILTON	339,684	148,272	181,979	9,433	33,707 D	43.6%	53.6%	44.9%	55.1%
74,782	HANCOCK	28,426	19,112	8,427	887	10,685 R	67.2%	29.6%	69.4%	30.6%
32,058	HARDIN	9,414	6,309	2,714	391	3,595 R	67.0%	28.8%	69.9%	30.1%
15,864	HARRISON	5,825	3,851	1,780	194	2,071 R	66.1%	30.6%	68.4%	31.6%
28,215	HENRY	10,735	7,255	3,091	389	4,164 R	67.6%	28.8%	70.1%	29.9%
43,589	HIGHLAND	13,600	9,942	3,222	436	6,720 R	73.1%	23.7%	75.5%	24.5%
29,380	HOCKING	9,954	5,988	3,604	362	2,384 R	60.2%	36.2%	62.4%	37.6%
42,366	HOLMES	8,882	7,031	1,595	256	5,436 R	79.2%	18.0%	81.5%	18.5%
59,626	HURON	18,934	11,536	6,517	881	5,019 R	60.9%	34.4%	63.9%	36.1%
33,225	JACKSON	10,212	6,913	3,047	252	3,866 R	67.7%	29.8%	69.4%	30.6%
69,709	JEFFERSON	24,559	14,863	8,890	806	5,973 R	60.5%	36.2%	62.6%	37.4%
60,921	KNOX	22,571	14,726	7,126	719	7,600 R	65.2%	31.6%	67.4%	32.6%
230,041	LAKE	95,085	50,783	41,355	2,947	9,428 R	53.4%	43.5%	55.1%	44.9%
62,450	LAWRENCE	20,549	13,510	6,557	482	6,953 R	65.7%	31.9%	67.3%	32.7%
166,492	LICKING	68,708	41,647	25,168	1,893	16,479 R	60.6%	36.6%	62.3%	37.7%
45,858	LOGAN	16,480	11,823	3,989	668	7,834 R	71.7%	24.2%	74.8%	25.2%
301,356	LORAIN	114,558	52,268	58,846	3,444	6,578 D	45.6%	51.4%	47.0%	53.0%
441,815	LUCAS	152,530	57,004	90,232	5,294	33,228 D	37.4%	59.2%	38.7%	61.3%
43,435	MADISON	13,862	9,084	4,371	407	4,713 R	65.5%	31.5%	67.5%	32.5%
238,823	MAHONING	90,719	38,689	49,740	2,290	11,051 D	42.6%	54.8%	43.8%	56.2%
66,501	MARION	20,592	12,631	7,176	785	5,455 R	61.3%	34.8%	63.8%	36.2%
172,332	MEDINA	75,361	43,650	29,529	2,182	14,121 R	57.9%	39.2%	59.6%	40.4%
23,770	MEIGS	7,865	5,383	2,290	192	3,093 R	68.4%	29.1%	70.2%	29.8%
40,814	MERCER	17,334	13,697	3,161	476	10,536 R	79.0%	18.2%	81.2%	18.8%
102,506	MIAMI	35,592	25,106	9,115	1,371	15,991 R	70.5%	25.6%	73.4%	26.6%
14,642	MONROE	5,136	3,219	1,760	157	1,459 R	62.7%	34.3%	64.7%	35.3%
535,153	MONTGOMERY	206,030	100,021	99,812	6,197	209 R	48.5%	48.4%	50.1%	49.9%
15,054	MORGAN	5,106	3,297	1,663	146	1,634 R	64.6%	32.6%	66.5%	33.5%
34,827	MORROW	13,208	9,127	3,601	480	5,526 R	69.1%	27.3%	71.7%	28.3%
86,074	MUSKINGUM	29,135	18,622	9,653	860	8,969 R	63.9%	33.1%	65.9%	34.1%

OHIO

GOVERNOR 2018

2010 Census Population	County	Total Vote	Republican (DeWine)	Democratic (Cordray)	Other	Rep.-Dem. Plurality	Percentage Total Vote Rep.	Percentage Total Vote Dem.	Percentage Major Vote Rep.	Percentage Major Vote Dem.
14,645	NOBLE	4,634	3,146	1,338	150	1,808 R	67.9%	28.9%	70.2%	29.8%
41,428	OTTAWA	18,262	9,880	7,695	687	2,185 R	54.1%	42.1%	56.2%	43.8%
19,614	PAULDING	6,885	4,705	1,965	215	2,740 R	68.3%	28.5%	70.5%	29.5%
36,058	PERRY	11,592	7,418	3,754	420	3,664 R	64.0%	32.4%	66.4%	33.6%
55,698	PICKAWAY	19,990	13,230	6,219	541	7,011 R	66.2%	31.1%	68.0%	32.0%
28,709	PIKE	8,866	5,360	3,237	269	2,123 R	60.5%	36.5%	62.3%	37.7%
161,419	PORTAGE	60,669	29,563	28,679	2,427	884 R	48.7%	47.3%	50.8%	49.2%
42,270	PREBLE	15,823	11,389	3,678	756	7,711 R	72.0%	23.2%	75.6%	24.4%
34,499	PUTNAM	14,879	11,875	2,672	332	9,203 R	79.8%	18.0%	81.6%	18.4%
124,475	RICHLAND	44,684	28,381	14,827	1,476	13,554 R	63.5%	33.2%	65.7%	34.3%
78,064	ROSS	23,447	13,987	8,760	700	5,227 R	59.7%	37.4%	61.5%	38.5%
60,944	SANDUSKY	22,113	12,373	8,721	1,019	3,652 R	56.0%	39.4%	58.7%	41.3%
79,499	SCIOTO	23,845	14,499	8,806	540	5,693 R	60.8%	36.9%	62.2%	37.8%
56,745	SENECA	18,750	11,521	6,457	772	5,064 R	61.4%	34.4%	64.1%	35.9%
49,423	SHELBY	18,584	13,924	4,032	628	9,892 R	74.9%	21.7%	77.5%	22.5%
375,586	STARK	139,764	75,121	59,949	4,694	15,172 R	53.7%	42.9%	55.6%	44.4%
541,781	SUMMIT	211,938	88,088	117,744	6,106	29,656 D	41.6%	55.6%	42.8%	57.2%
210,312	TRUMBULL	74,780	34,139	38,522	2,119	4,383 D	45.7%	51.5%	47.0%	53.0%
92,582	TUSCARAWAS	32,268	19,394	11,649	1,225	7,745 R	60.1%	36.1%	62.5%	37.5%
52,300	UNION	23,911	15,526	7,598	787	7,928 R	64.9%	31.8%	67.1%	32.9%
28,744	VAN WERT	10,714	8,112	2,293	309	5,819 R	75.7%	21.4%	78.0%	22.0%
13,435	VINTON	4,060	2,561	1,380	119	1,181 R	63.1%	34.0%	65.0%	35.0%
212,693	WARREN	99,521	66,190	30,720	2,611	35,470 R	66.5%	30.9%	68.3%	31.7%
61,778	WASHINGTON	23,387	15,497	7,221	669	8,276 R	66.3%	30.9%	68.2%	31.8%
114,520	WAYNE	40,060	25,270	13,470	1,320	11,800 R	63.1%	33.6%	65.2%	34.8%
37,642	WILLIAMS	13,415	9,323	3,604	488	5,719 R	69.5%	26.9%	72.1%	27.9%
125,488	WOOD	50,097	25,193	23,051	1,853	2,142 R	50.3%	46.0%	52.2%	47.8%
22,615	WYANDOT	8,163	5,565	2,286	312	3,279 R	68.2%	28.0%	70.9%	29.1%
11,536,504	*TOTAL*	*4,429,582*	*2,231,917*	*2,067,847*	*129,818*	*164,070 R*	*50.4%*	*46.7%*	*51.9%*	*48.1%*

OHIO

SENATOR 2018

2010 Census Population	County	Total Vote	Republican (Renacci)	Democratic (Brown)	Other	Rep.-Dem. Plurality	Percentage Total Vote Rep.	Percentage Total Vote Dem.	Percentage Major Vote Rep.	Percentage Major Vote Dem.
28,550	ADAMS	8,643	6,000	2,635	8	3,365 R	69.4%	30.5%	69.5%	30.5%
106,331	ALLEN	35,929	21,492	14,429	8	7,063 R	59.8%	40.2%	59.8%	40.2%
53,139	ASHLAND	18,523	12,048	6,472	3	5,576 R	65.0%	34.9%	65.1%	34.9%
101,497	ASHTABULA	32,267	15,794	16,473		679 D	48.9%	51.1%	48.9%	51.1%
64,757	ATHENS	22,602	7,126	15,472	4	8,346 D	31.5%	68.5%	31.5%	68.5%
45,949	AUGLAIZE	19,161	13,603	5,557	1	8,046 R	71.0%	29.0%	71.0%	29.0%
70,400	BELMONT	24,769	13,159	11,603	7	1,556 R	53.1%	46.8%	53.1%	46.9%
44,846	BROWN	14,838	10,184	4,651	3	5,533 R	68.6%	31.3%	68.6%	31.4%
368,130	BUTLER	135,736	80,106	55,604	26	24,502 R	59.0%	41.0%	59.0%	41.0%
28,836	CARROLL	10,293	6,503	3,788	2	2,715 R	63.2%	36.8%	63.2%	36.8%
40,097	CHAMPAIGN	14,815	9,372	5,443		3,929 R	63.3%	36.7%	63.3%	36.7%
138,333	CLARK	47,980	24,446	23,525	9	921 R	51.0%	49.0%	51.0%	49.0%
197,363	CLERMONT	79,730	51,918	27,803	9	24,115 R	65.1%	34.9%	65.1%	34.9%
42,040	CLINTON	15,002	10,356	4,645	1	5,711 R	69.0%	31.0%	69.0%	31.0%
107,841	COLUMBIANA	35,847	21,849	13,995	3	7,854 R	61.0%	39.0%	61.0%	39.0%

OHIO

SENATOR 2018

2010 Census Population	County	Total Vote	Republican (Renacci)	Democratic (Brown)	Other	Rep.-Dem. Plurality	Percentage Total Vote Rep.	Percentage Total Vote Dem.	Percentage Major Vote Rep.	Percentage Major Vote Dem.
36,901	COSHOCTON	11,844	7,163	4,680	1	2,483 R	60.5%	39.5%	60.5%	39.5%
43,784	CRAWFORD	14,496	9,149	5,345	2	3,804 R	63.1%	36.9%	63.1%	36.9%
1,280,122	CUYAHOGA	483,364	132,948	350,362	54	217,414 D	27.5%	72.5%	27.5%	72.5%
52,959	DARKE	19,492	13,921	5,569	2	8,352 R	71.4%	28.6%	71.4%	28.6%
39,037	DEFIANCE	13,820	8,003	5,812	5	2,191 R	57.9%	42.1%	57.9%	42.1%
174,214	DELAWARE	94,336	49,587	44,743	6	4,844 R	52.6%	47.4%	52.6%	47.4%
77,079	ERIE	30,298	13,633	16,659	6	3,026 D	45.0%	55.0%	45.0%	55.0%
146,156	FAIRFIELD	59,246	32,707	26,518	21	6,189 R	55.2%	44.8%	55.2%	44.8%
29,030	FAYETTE	8,481	5,566	2,914	1	2,652 R	65.6%	34.4%	65.6%	34.4%
1,163,414	FRANKLIN	484,509	151,588	332,825	96	181,237 D	31.3%	68.7%	31.3%	68.7%
42,698	FULTON	16,164	9,454	6,707	3	2,747 R	58.5%	41.5%	58.5%	41.5%
30,934	GALLIA	9,630	6,275	3,355		2,920 R	65.2%	34.8%	65.2%	34.8%
93,389	GEAUGA	42,507	23,397	19,104	6	4,293 R	55.0%	44.9%	55.1%	44.9%
161,573	GREENE	68,377	38,102	30,243	32	7,859 R	55.7%	44.2%	55.7%	44.3%
40,087	GUERNSEY	12,545	7,529	5,014	2	2,515 R	60.0%	40.0%	60.0%	40.0%
802,374	HAMILTON	337,713	137,116	200,404	193	63,288 D	40.6%	59.3%	40.6%	59.4%
74,782	HANCOCK	28,061	17,123	10,929	9	6,194 R	61.0%	38.9%	61.0%	39.0%
32,058	HARDIN	9,402	5,899	3,497	6	2,402 R	62.7%	37.2%	62.8%	37.2%
15,864	HARRISON	5,808	3,327	2,480	1	847 R	57.3%	42.7%	57.3%	42.7%
28,215	HENRY	10,577	6,109	4,468		1,641 R	57.8%	42.2%	57.8%	42.2%
43,589	HIGHLAND	13,465	9,526	3,939		5,587 R	70.7%	29.3%	70.7%	29.3%
29,380	HOCKING	9,883	5,474	4,408	1	1,066 R	55.4%	44.6%	55.4%	44.6%
42,366	HOLMES	8,817	6,755	2,059	3	4,696 R	76.6%	23.4%	76.6%	23.4%
59,626	HURON	18,796	10,522	8,274		2,248 R	56.0%	44.0%	56.0%	44.0%
33,225	JACKSON	10,070	6,255	3,815		2,440 R	62.1%	37.9%	62.1%	37.9%
69,709	JEFFERSON	24,562	13,180	11,376	6	1,804 R	53.7%	46.3%	53.7%	46.3%
60,921	KNOX	22,707	14,290	8,413	4	5,877 R	62.9%	37.1%	62.9%	37.1%
230,041	LAKE	94,607	45,313	49,276	18	3,963 D	47.9%	52.1%	47.9%	52.1%
62,450	LAWRENCE	20,360	12,292	8,064	4	4,228 R	60.4%	39.6%	60.4%	39.6%
166,492	LICKING	68,622	39,142	29,469	11	9,673 R	57.0%	42.9%	57.0%	43.0%
45,858	LOGAN	16,479	11,243	5,235	1	6,008 R	68.2%	31.8%	68.2%	31.8%
301,356	LORAIN	113,876	46,403	67,452	21	21,049 D	40.7%	59.2%	40.8%	59.2%
441,815	LUCAS	151,048	50,223	100,807	18	50,584 D	33.2%	66.7%	33.3%	66.7%
43,435	MADISON	13,734	8,617	5,116	1	3,501 R	62.7%	37.3%	62.7%	37.3%
238,823	MAHONING	90,256	35,654	54,594	8	18,940 D	39.5%	60.5%	39.5%	60.5%
66,501	MARION	20,546	11,850	8,677	19	3,173 R	57.7%	42.2%	57.7%	42.3%
172,332	MEDINA	74,986	40,478	34,493	15	5,985 R	54.0%	46.0%	54.0%	46.0%
23,770	MEIGS	7,825	4,926	2,898	1	2,028 R	63.0%	37.0%	63.0%	37.0%
40,814	MERCER	17,143	12,637	4,504	2	8,133 R	73.7%	26.3%	73.7%	26.3%
102,506	MIAMI	35,283	23,219	12,064		11,155 R	65.8%	34.2%	65.8%	34.2%
14,642	MONROE	5,283	2,765	2,518		247 R	52.3%	47.7%	52.3%	47.7%
535,153	MONTGOMERY	205,482	90,242	115,200	40	24,958 D	43.9%	56.1%	43.9%	56.1%
15,054	MORGAN	5,031	2,916	2,115		801 R	58.0%	42.0%	58.0%	42.0%
34,827	MORROW	13,123	8,761	4,361	1	4,400 R	66.8%	33.2%	66.8%	33.2%
86,074	MUSKINGUM	28,903	16,504	12,395	4	4,109 R	57.1%	42.9%	57.1%	42.9%
14,645	NOBLE	4,667	2,958	1,709		1,249 R	63.4%	36.6%	63.4%	36.6%
41,428	OTTAWA	18,279	8,799	9,477	3	678 D	48.1%	51.8%	48.1%	51.9%
19,614	PAULDING	6,889	4,656	2,232	1	2,424 R	67.6%	32.4%	67.6%	32.4%
36,058	PERRY	11,495	6,895	4,599	1	2,296 R	60.0%	40.0%	60.0%	40.0%
55,698	PICKAWAY	19,785	12,302	7,481	2	4,821 R	62.2%	37.8%	62.2%	37.8%
28,709	PIKE	8,797	4,897	3,900		997 R	55.7%	44.3%	55.7%	44.3%
161,419	PORTAGE	60,556	28,231	32,303	22	4,072 D	46.6%	53.3%	46.6%	53.4%
42,270	PREBLE	15,784	10,838	4,942	4	5,896 R	68.7%	31.3%	68.7%	31.3%
34,499	PUTNAM	14,781	10,408	4,369	4	6,039 R	70.4%	29.6%	70.4%	29.6%
124,475	RICHLAND	44,499	26,499	17,984	16	8,515 R	59.5%	40.4%	59.6%	40.4%
78,064	ROSS	23,342	12,738	10,602	2	2,136 R	54.6%	45.4%	54.6%	45.4%
60,944	SANDUSKY	22,130	11,141	10,987	2	154 R	50.3%	49.6%	50.3%	49.7%
79,499	SCIOTO	23,641	13,014	10,627		2,387 R	55.0%	45.0%	55.0%	45.0%
56,745	SENECA	18,692	9,945	8,741	6	1,204 R	53.2%	46.8%	53.2%	46.8%
49,423	SHELBY	18,616	13,433	5,183		8,250 R	72.2%	27.8%	72.2%	27.8%

OHIO

SENATOR 2018

2010 Census Population	County	Total Vote	Republican (Renacci)	Democratic (Brown)	Other	Rep.-Dem. Plurality	Percentage Total Vote Rep.	Total Vote Dem.	Major Vote Rep.	Major Vote Dem.
375,586	STARK	139,163	70,588	68,526	49	2,062 R	50.7%	49.2%	50.7%	49.3%
541,781	SUMMIT	212,745	83,149	129,479	117	46,330 D	39.1%	60.9%	39.1%	60.9%
210,312	TRUMBULL	74,882	31,482	43,381	19	11,899 D	42.0%	57.9%	42.1%	57.9%
92,582	TUSCARAWAS	32,335	18,244	14,088	3	4,156 R	56.4%	43.6%	56.4%	43.6%
52,300	UNION	23,711	14,747	8,964		5,783 R	62.2%	37.8%	62.2%	37.8%
28,744	VAN WERT	10,741	7,721	3,020		4,701 R	71.9%	28.1%	71.9%	28.1%
13,435	VINTON	4,108	2,467	1,641		826 R	60.1%	39.9%	60.1%	39.9%
212,693	WARREN	99,592	63,757	35,815	20	27,942 R	64.0%	36.0%	64.0%	36.0%
61,778	WASHINGTON	23,170	13,908	9,259	3	4,649 R	60.0%	40.0%	60.0%	40.0%
114,520	WAYNE	39,830	24,324	15,495	11	8,829 R	61.1%	38.9%	61.1%	38.9%
37,642	WILLIAMS	13,200	7,927	5,272	1	2,655 R	60.1%	39.9%	60.1%	39.9%
125,488	WOOD	49,663	22,105	27,540	18	5,435 D	44.5%	55.5%	44.5%	55.5%
22,615	WYANDOT	8,113	5,051	3,062		1,989 R	62.3%	37.7%	62.3%	37.7%
11,536,504	*TOTAL*	*4,410,898*	*2,053,963*	*2,355,923*	*1,012*	*301,960 D*	*46.6%*	*53.4%*	*46.6%*	*53.4%*

OHIO

HOUSE OF REPRESENTATIVES

CD	Year	Total Vote	Republican Vote	Republican Candidate	Democratic Vote	Democratic Candidate	Other Vote	Rep.-Dem. Plurality	Percentage Total Vote Rep.	Total Vote Dem.	Major Vote Rep.	Major Vote Dem.
1	2018	300,871	154,409	CHABOT, STEVE*	141,118	PUREVAL, AFTAB	5,344	13,291 R	51.3%	46.9%	52.2%	47.8%
1	2016	354,788	210,014	CHABOT, STEVE*	144,644	YOUNG, MICHELE	130	65,370 R	59.2%	40.8%	59.2%	40.8%
1	2014	197,383	124,779	CHABOT, STEVE*	72,604	KUNDRATA, FRED		52,175 R	63.2%	36.8%	63.2%	36.8%
1	2012	349,716	201,907	CHABOT, STEVE*	131,490	SINNARD, JEFF	16,319	70,417 R	57.7%	37.6%	60.6%	39.4%
2	2018	289,661	166,714	WENSTRUP, BRAD*	119,333	SCHILLER, JILL	3,614	47,381 R	57.6%	41.2%	58.3%	41.7%
2	2016	340,279	221,193	WENSTRUP, BRAD*	111,694	SMITH, WILLIAM	7,392	109,499 R	65.0%	32.8%	66.4%	33.6%
2	2014	201,111	132,658	WENSTRUP, BRAD*	68,453	TYSZKIEWICZ, MAREK		64,205 R	66.0%	34.0%	66.0%	34.0%
2	2012	331,381	194,299	WENSTRUP, BRAD	137,082	SMITH, WILLIAM		57,217 R	58.6%	41.4%	58.6%	41.4%
3	2018	246,677	65,040	BURGESS, JAMES	181,575	BEATTY, JOYCE*	62	116,535 D	26.4%	73.6%	26.4%	73.6%
3	2016	291,351	91,560	ADAMS, JOHN	199,791	BEATTY, JOYCE*		108,231 D	31.4%	68.6%	31.4%	68.6%
3	2014	143,261	51,475	ADAMS, JOHN	91,769	BEATTY, JOYCE*	17	40,294 D	35.9%	64.1%	35.9%	64.1%
3	2012	295,938	77,903	LONG, CHRIS	201,921	BEATTY, JOYCE	16,114	124,018 D	26.3%	68.2%	27.8%	72.2%
4	2018	257,405	167,993	JORDAN, JIM*	89,412	GARRETT, JANET		78,581 R	65.3%	34.7%	65.3%	34.7%
4	2016	309,208	210,227	JORDAN, JIM*	98,981	GARRETT, JANET		111,246 R	68.0%	32.0%	68.0%	32.0%
4	2014	186,072	125,907	JORDAN, JIM*	60,165	GARRETT, JANET		65,742 R	67.7%	32.3%	67.7%	32.3%
4	2012	312,998	182,643	JORDAN, JIM*	114,214	SLONE, JIM	16,141	68,429 R	58.4%	36.5%	61.5%	38.5%
5	2018	283,617	176,569	LATTA, BOB*	99,655	GALBRAITH, JOHN MICHAEL	7,393	76,914 R	62.3%	35.1%	63.9%	36.1%
5	2016	344,991	244,599	LATTA, BOB*	100,392	NEU, JAMES JR.		144,207 R	70.9%	29.1%	70.9%	29.1%
5	2014	202,300	134,449	LATTA, BOB*	58,507	FRY, ROBERT	9,344	75,942 R	66.5%	28.9%	69.7%	30.3%
5	2012	351,878	201,514	LATTA, BOB*	137,806	ZIMMANN, ANGELA	12,558	63,708 R	57.3%	39.2%	59.4%	40.6%
6	2018	249,490	172,774	JOHNSON, BILL*	76,716	ROBERTS, SHAWNA		96,058 R	69.3%	30.7%	69.3%	30.7%
6	2016	302,755	213,975	JOHNSON, BILL*	88,780	LORENTZ, MICHAEL L.		125,195 R	70.7%	29.3%	70.7%	29.3%
6	2014	190,652	111,026	JOHNSON, BILL*	73,561	GARRISON, JENNIFER	6,065	37,465 R	58.2%	38.6%	60.1%	39.9%
6	2012	308,980	164,536	JOHNSON, BILL*	144,444	WILSON, CHARLES A. JR.		20,092 R	53.3%	46.7%	53.3%	46.7%
7	2018	260,653	153,117	GIBBS, BOB*	107,536	HARBAUGH, KEN		45,581 R	58.7%	41.3%	58.7%	41.3%
7	2016	309,553	198,221	GIBBS, BOB*	89,638	RICH, ROY	21,694	108,583 R	64.0%	29.0%	68.9%	31.1%
7	2014	143,959	143,959	GIBBS, BOB*				143,959 R	100.0%		100.0%	
7	2012	315,812	178,104	GIBBS, BOB*	137,708	HEALY-ABRAMS, JOYCE		40,396 R	56.4%	43.6%	56.4%	43.6%
8	2018	261,133	173,852	DAVIDSON, WARREN*	87,281	ENOCH, VANESSA		86,571 R	66.6%	33.4%	66.6%	33.4%
8	2016	325,506	223,833	DAVIDSON, WARREN*	87,794	FOUGHT, STEVEN	13,879	136,039 R	68.8%	27.0%	71.8%	28.2%
8	2014	188,330	126,539	BOEHNER, JOHN A.*	51,534	POETTER, TOM	10,257	75,005 R	67.2%	27.4%	71.1%	28.9%
8	2012	246,442	246,380	BOEHNER, JOHN A.*			62	246,380 R	100.0%		100.0%	

OHIO

HOUSE OF REPRESENTATIVES

			Republican		Democratic				Percentage			
									Total Vote		Major Vote	
CD	Year	Total Vote	Vote	Candidate	Vote	Candidate	Other Vote	Rep.-Dem. Plurality	Rep.	Dem.	Rep.	Dem.
9	2018	231,937	74,670	KRAUS, STEVEN W.	157,219	KAPTUR, MARCY*	48	82,549 D	32.2%	67.8%	32.2%	67.8%
9	2016	282,398	88,427	LARSON, DONALD P.	193,966	KAPTUR, MARCY*	5	105,539 D	31.3%	68.7%	31.3%	68.7%
9	2014	160,715	51,704	MAY, RICHARD	108,870	KAPTUR, MARCY*	141	57,166 D	32.2%	67.7%	32.2%	67.8%
9	2012	298,166	68,666	WURZELBACHER, SAMUEL	217,775	KAPTUR, MARCY*	11,725	149,109 D	23.0%	73.0%	24.0%	76.0%
10	2018	281,726	157,554	TURNER, MICHAEL R.*	118,785	GASPER, THERESA	5,387	38,769 R	55.9%	42.2%	57.0%	43.0%
10	2016	336,602	215,724	TURNER, MICHAEL R.*	109,981	KLEPINGER, ROBERT	10,897	105,743 R	64.1%	32.7%	66.2%	33.8%
10	2014	200,606	130,752	TURNER, MICHAEL R.*	63,249	KLEPINGER, ROBERT	6,605	67,503 R	65.2%	31.5%	67.4%	32.6%
10	2012	349,671	208,201	TURNER, MICHAEL R.*	131,097	NEUHARDT, SHAREN SWARTZ	10,373	77,104 R	59.5%	37.5%	61.4%	38.6%
11	2018	250,660	44,486	GOLDSTEIN, BEVERLY A.	206,138	FUDGE, MARCIA L.*	36	161,652 D	17.7%	82.2%	17.8%	82.2%
11	2016	302,686	59,769	GOLDSTEIN, BEVERLY A.	242,917	FUDGE, MARCIA L.*		183,148 D	19.7%	80.3%	19.7%	80.3%
11	2014	172,566	35,461	ZETZER, MARK	137,105	FUDGE, MARCIA L.*		101,644 D	20.5%	79.5%	20.5%	79.5%
11	2012	258,378			258,378	FUDGE, MARCIA L.*		258,378 D		100.0%		100.0%
12	2018	341,647	175,677	BALDERSON, TROY*	161,251	O'CONNOR, DANNY	4,719	14,426 R	51.4%	47.2%	52.1%	47.9%
12	2016	377,534	251,266	TIBERI, PAT*	112,638	ALBERTSON, ED	13,630	138,628 R	66.6%	29.8%	69.0%	31.0%
12	2014	221,081	150,573	TIBERI, PAT*	61,360	TIBBS, DAVID ARTHUR	9,148	89,213 R	68.1%	27.8%	71.0%	29.0%
12	2012	368,488	233,874	TIBERI, PAT*	134,614	REESE, JIM		99,260 R	63.5%	36.5%	63.5%	36.5%
13	2018	251,370	98,047	DEPIZZO, CHRISTOPHER	153,323	RYAN, TIM*		55,276 D	39.0%	61.0%	39.0%	61.0%
13	2016	308,004	99,377	MORCKEL, RICHARD A.	208,610	RYAN, TIM*	17	109,233 D	32.3%	67.7%	32.3%	67.7%
13	2014	175,549	55,233	PEKAREK, THOMAS	120,230	RYAN, TIM*	86	64,997 D	31.5%	68.5%	31.5%	68.5%
13	2012	323,612	88,120	AGANA, MARISHA	235,492	RYAN, TIM*		147,372 D	27.2%	72.8%	27.2%	72.8%
14	2018	307,358	169,809	JOYCE, DAVID*	137,549	RADER, ELIZABETH "BETSY"		32,260 R	55.2%	44.8%	55.2%	44.8%
14	2016	350,269	219,191	JOYCE, DAVID*	130,907	WAGER, MICHAEL	171	88,284 R	62.6%	37.4%	62.6%	37.4%
14	2014	214,580	135,736	JOYCE, DAVID*	70,856	WAGER, MICHAEL	7,988	64,880 R	63.3%	33.0%	65.7%	34.3%
14	2012	339,884	183,660	JOYCE, DAVID	131,638	BLANCHARD, DALE VIRGIL	24,586	52,022 R	54.0%	38.7%	58.2%	41.8%
15	2018	292,443	170,593	STIVERS, STEVE*	116,112	NEAL, RICK	5,738	54,481 R	58.3%	39.7%	59.5%	40.5%
15	2016	336,807	222,847	STIVERS, STEVE*	113,960	WHARTON, SCOTT		108,887 R	66.2%	33.8%	66.2%	33.8%
15	2014	194,621	128,496	STIVERS, STEVE*	66,125	WHARTON, SCOTT		62,371 R	66.0%	34.0%	66.0%	34.0%
15	2012	333,465	205,277	STIVERS, STEVE*	128,188	LANG, PAT		77,089 R	61.6%	38.4%	61.6%	38.4%
16	2018	299,710	170,029	GONZALEZ, ANTHONY	129,681	PALMER, SUSAN MORAN		40,348 R	56.7%	43.3%	56.7%	43.3%
16	2016	345,624	225,794	RENACCI, JIM*	119,830	MUNDY, KEITH		105,964 R	65.3%	34.7%	65.3%	34.7%
16	2014	207,375	132,176	RENACCI, JIM*	75,199	CROSSLAND, PETE		56,977 R	63.7%	36.3%	63.7%	36.3%
16	2012	355,771	185,167	RENACCI, JIM*	170,604	SUTTON, BETTY		14,563 R	52.0%	48.0%	52.0%	48.0%
TOTAL	*2018*	*4,406,358*	*2,291,333*		*2,082,684*		*32,341*	*208,649 R*	*52.0%*	*47.3%*	*52.4%*	*47.6%*
TOTAL	*2016*	*5,218,355*	*2,996,017*		*2,154,523*		*67,815*	*841,494 R*	*57.4%*	*41.3%*	*58.2%*	*41.8%*
TOTAL	*2014*	*3,000,161*	*1,770,923*		*1,179,587*		*49,651*	*591,336 R*	*59.0%*	*39.3%*	*60.0%*	*40.0%*
TOTAL	*2012*	*5,140,580*	*2,620,251*		*2,412,451*		*107,878*	*207,800 R*	*51.0%*	*46.9%*	*52.1%*	*47.9%*

Note: An asterisk (*) denotes incumbent.

OHIO

GENERAL AND PRIMARY ELECTIONS

2018 GENERAL ELECTIONS: OTHER VOTES

Governor Other vote was 79,985 Libertarian (Travis Irvine), 49,475 Green (Constance Gadell-Newton), 185 Write-in (Renea Turner), 132 Write-in (Richard Duncan), 41 Write-in (Rebecca Ayres)

Senate Other vote was 1,012 Write-in (Stephen Faris)

House Other vote was:

CD 1	5,339 Libertarian (Dirk Kubala), 5 Write-in (Kiumars Kiani)
CD 2	3,606 Green (Jim Condit), 8 Write-in (David Baker)
CD 3	62 Write-in (Millie Milam)
CD 5	7,393 Libertarian (Don Kissick)
CD 9	48 Write-in (McKenzie Levindofske)
CD 10	5,387 Libertarian (David Harlow)
CD 11	36 Write-in (James Bell)
CD 12	4,718 Green (Joe Manchik), 1 Write-in (Marc Fagin)
CD 15	5,738 Libertarian (Johnathan Miller)

2018 PRIMARY ELECTIONS: SUPPLEMENTARY INFORMATION

Primary	May 8, 2018	**Registration** (as of May 8, 2018)	7,941,921	No Party Registration

Primary Type Open—Any registered voter could participate in the primary of either party. However, records are kept of voter participation in recent primaries, and voters who cast a ballot in one party's primary could be challenged if they attempted to participate in the other party's primary. They could be asked to sign an affidavit affirming the fact that they were voting in the opposing party's primary and would become identified with that party because of their primary ballot cast.

	REPUBLICAN PRIMARIES			DEMOCRATIC PRIMARIES		
Senator	Renacci, Jim	363,622	47.3%	Brown, Sherrod*	613,373	100.0%
	Gibbons, Michael	243,426	31.7%			
	Ackison, Melissa	100,543	13.1%			
	Kiley, Dan	30,684	4.0%			
	Eckhart, Don Elijah	29,796	3.9%			
	Pinion, Timothy A. (Write-in)	78				
	TOTAL	*768,149*		*TOTAL*	*613,373*	
Governor	DeWine, Michael "Mike"	499,639	59.8%	Corday, Richard	428,159	62.2%
	Taylor, Mary	335,328	40.2%	Kucinich, Dennis J.	158,284	23.0%
				Schiavoni, Joseph	63,131	9.2%
				O'Neill, Bill	22,667	3.3%
				Ray, Paul	9,536	1.4%
				Ealy, Larry	7,011	1.0%
	TOTAL	*834,967*		*TOTAL*	*688,788*	
Congressional District 1	Chabot, Steve*	41,298	83.2%	Pureval, Aftab	28,068	100.0%
	Ronan, Samuel	8,324	16.8%			
	TOTAL	*49,622*		*TOTAL*	*28,068*	
Congressional District 2	Wenstrup, Brad*	45,508	100.0%	Schiller, Jill	18,110	54.2%
				Everhard, Janet	11,505	34.4%
				Smith, William	3,791	11.3%
	TOTAL	*45,508*		*TOTAL*	*33,406*	

OHIO

GENERAL AND PRIMARY ELECTIONS

	REPUBLICAN PRIMARIES			DEMOCRATIC PRIMARIES		
Congressional District 3	Burgess, James	19,559	93.1%	Beatty, Joyce*	46,338	100.0%
	Haji, Abdulkadi	1,450	6.9%			
	TOTAL	*21,009*		*TOTAL*	*46,338*	
Congressional District 4	Jordan, Jim*	56,191	85.3%	Garrett, Janet	17,715	83.8%
	Miller, Joseph	9,646	14.7%	Slatzer-Rose, Cody	3,413	16.2%
	TOTAL	*65,837*		*TOTAL*	*21,128*	
Congressional District 5	Latta, Bob*	45,732	73.7%	Galbraith, John Michael	19,317	73.2%
	Wolfrum, Todd	10,385	16.7%	Neu, James Jr.	7,070	26.8%
	Kreienkamp, Bob	5,897	9.5%			
	TOTAL	*62,014*		*TOTAL*	*26,387*	
Congressional District 6	Johnson, Bill*	50,271	84.1%	Roberts, Shawna	22,024	74.5%
	Blazek, Robert	9,501	15.9%	Lange, Werner	7,534	25.5%
	TOTAL	*59,772*		*TOTAL*	*29,558*	
Congressional District 7	Gibbs, Bob*	42,274	77.9%	Harbaugh, Ken	24,042	80.2%
	Quinn, Patrick	6,211	11.4%	Pikus, Patrick	5,937	19.8%
	Robertson, Terry	5,765	10.6%			
	TOTAL	*54,250*		*TOTAL*	*29,979*	
Congressional District 8	Davidson, Warren*	52,351	100.0%	Enoch, Vanessa	11,587	57.9%
				Jones, Ted	3,258	16.3%
				Guyette, Matthew J.	2,728	13.6%
				Ebben, Bill	2,437	12.2%
	TOTAL	*52,351*		*TOTAL*	*20,010*	
Congressional District 9	Kraus, Steven W.	10,373	49.4%	Kaptur, Marcy*	41,502	85.5%
	Colton, Keith	6,263	29.9%	Garcia, Joshua	7,029	14.5%
	Franklin, W. Benjamin	4,342	20.7%			
	TOTAL	*20,978*		*TOTAL*	*48,531*	
Congressional District 10	Turner, Michael R.*	43,047	79.8%	Gasper, Theresa	23,077	67.0%
	Anderson, John	6,192	11.5%	Klepinger, Robert	8,814	25.6%
	Mitchel, John	4,693	8.7%	Milisits, Michael	2,544	7.4%
	TOTAL	*53,932*		*TOTAL*	*34,435*	
Congressional District 11	Goldstein, Beverly A.	7,017	52.5%	Fudge, Marcia L.*	65,905	99.9%
	Dunham, Gregory	6,336	47.5%	Washington Ross, Felicia (Write-in)	64	0.1%
	TOTAL	*13,353*		*TOTAL*	*65,969*	
Congressional District 12	Balderson, Troy	19,552	28.7%	O'Connor, Danny	18,211	40.5%
	Leneghan, Melanie	18,777	27.6%	Russell, John	7,310	16.3%
	Kane, Tim	11,491	16.9%	Scott, Zach	7,236	16.1%
	Bacon, Kevin	9,711	14.3%	Patton, Jackie	6,299	14.0%
	O'Brien, Carol	4,415	6.5%	Albertson, Ed	3,531	7.9%
	Halverstadt, Jonathan "Jon"	1,130	1.7%	Wilson, Douglas "Doug"	1,683	3.7%
	Shoemaker Jr., Mick	802	1.2%	Peters, John	670	1.5%
	Cohen, Lawrence "Larry"	798	1.2%			
	Manley, Patrick	788	1.2%			
	Adams, John	618	0.9%			
	TOTAL	*68,082*		*TOTAL*	*44,940*	
Congressional District 13	DePizzo, Christopher	24,296	100.0%	Ryan, Tim*	54,967	87.2%
				Luchansky, John Stephen	4,908	7.8%
				Crow, Robert	3,195	5.1%
	TOTAL	*24,296*		*TOTAL*	*63,070*	
Congressional District 14	Joyce, David*	50,317	100.0%	Rader, Elizabeth "Betsy"	36,077	100.0%
	TOTAL	*50,317*		*TOTAL*	*36,077*	

OHIO

GENERAL AND PRIMARY ELECTIONS

	REPUBLICAN PRIMARIES			DEMOCRATIC PRIMARIES		
Congressional District 15	Stivers, Steve*	49,549	100.0%	Neal, Rick	22,343	63.5%
				Jarvis, Rob	12,820	36.5%
	TOTAL	*49,549*		*TOTAL*	*35,163*	
Congressional District 16	Gonzalez, Anthony	34,327	53.1%	Palmer, Susan Moran	14,507	34.6%
	Hagan, Christina	26,380	40.8%	Goodrich, Grant	11,758	28.1%
	Grusenmeyer, Michael	3,977	6.1%	Mulloy, "T.J."	6,511	15.5%
				Dent, Mark	3,932	9.4%
				Godfrey, Aaron	3,313	7.9%
				Wilson, John	1,876	4.5%
	TOTAL	*64,684*		*TOTAL*	*41,897*	

Note: An asterisk (*) denotes incumbent.

OKLAHOMA

Congressional districts first established for elections held in 2012
5 members

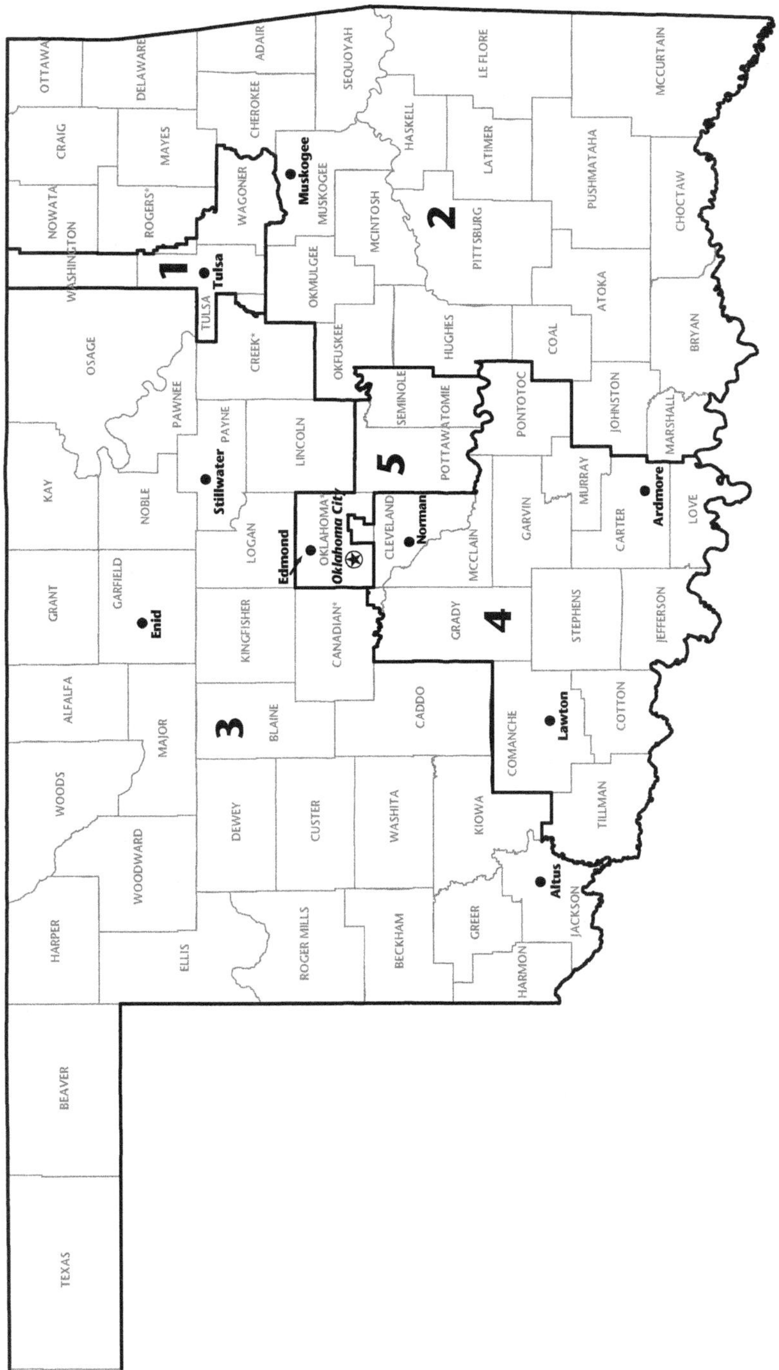

* Asterisk indicates a county whose boundaries include parts of two or more congressional districts.

OKLAHOMA

GOVERNOR

Kevin Stitt (R). Elected 2018 to a four-year term.

SENATORS (2 Republicans)

James M. Inhofe (R). Re-elected 2014 to a six-year term. Previously elected 2008, 2002, 1996, and 1994 to fill out the remaining two years of the term vacated when David L. Boren (D) resigned in November 1994 to become president of the University of Oklahoma.

James Lankford (R). Re-elected 2016 to a six-year term. Previously elected 2014 to complete the final two years of the term vacated by Tom Coburn (R), who resigned January 3, 2015, after the recurrence of prostate cancer.

REPRESENTATIVES (4 Republicans, 1 Democrat)

1. Kevin Hern (R)
2. Markwayne Mullin (R)
3. Frank D. Lucas (R)
4. Thomas J. Cole (R)
5. Kendra Horn (D)

POSTWAR VOTE FOR PRESIDENT

		Republican		Democratic				Percentage			
								Total Vote		Major Vote	
Year	Total Vote	Vote	Candidate	Vote	Candidate	Other Vote	Rep.-Dem. Plurality	Rep.	Dem.	Rep.	Dem.
2016**	1,452,992	949,136	Trump, Donald J.	420,375	Clinton, Hillary Rodham	83,481	528,761 R	65.3%	28.9%	69.3%	30.7%
2012	1,334,872	891,325	Romney, W. Mitt	443,547	Obama, Barack H.*		447,778 R	66.8%	33.2%	66.8%	33.2%
2008	1,462,661	960,165	McCain, John S. III	502,496	Obama, Barack H.		457,669 R	65.6%	34.4%	65.6%	34.4%
2004	1,463,758	959,792	Bush, George W.*	503,966	Kerry, John F.		455,826 R	65.6%	34.4%	65.6%	34.4%
2000	1,234,229	744,337	Bush, George W.	474,276	Gore, Albert Jr.	15,616	270,061 R	60.3%	38.4%	61.1%	38.9%
1996**	1,206,713	582,315	Dole, Robert "Bob"	488,105	Clinton, Bill*	136,293	94,210 R	48.3%	40.4%	54.4%	45.6%
1992**	1,390,359	592,929	Bush, George H.*	473,066	Clinton, Bill	324,364	119,863 R	42.6%	34.0%	55.6%	44.4%
1988	1,171,036	678,367	Bush, George H.	483,423	Dukakis, Michael S.	9,246	194,944 R	57.9%	41.3%	58.4%	41.6%
1984	1,255,676	861,530	Reagan, Ronald*	385,080	Mondale, Walter F.	9,066	476,450 R	68.6%	30.7%	69.1%	30.9%
1980**	1,149,708	695,570	Reagan, Ronald	402,026	Carter, Jimmy*	52,112	293,544 R	60.5%	35.0%	63.4%	36.6%
1976	1,092,251	545,708	Ford, Gerald R.*	532,442	Carter, Jimmy	14,101	13,266 R	50.0%	48.7%	50.6%	49.4%
1972	1,029,900	759,025	Nixon, Richard M.*	247,147	McGovern, George S.	23,728	511,878 R	73.7%	24.0%	75.4%	24.6%
1968**	943,086	449,697	Nixon, Richard M.	301,658	Humphrey, Hubert Horatio Jr.	191,731	148,039 R	47.7%	32.0%	59.9%	40.1%
1964	932,499	412,665	Goldwater, Barry M. Sr.	519,834	Johnson, Lyndon B.*		107,169 D	44.3%	55.7%	44.3%	55.7%
1960	903,150	533,039	Nixon, Richard M.	370,111	Kennedy, John F.		162,928 R	59.0%	41.0%	59.0%	41.0%
1956	859,350	473,769	Eisenhower, Dwight D.*	385,581	Stevenson, Adlai E. II		88,188 R	55.1%	44.9%	55.1%	44.9%
1952	948,984	518,045	Eisenhower, Dwight D.	430,939	Stevenson, Adlai E. II		87,106 R	54.6%	45.4%	54.6%	45.4%
1948	721,599	268,817	Dewey, Thomas E.	452,782	Truman, Harry S.*		183,965 D	37.3%	62.7%	37.3%	62.7%

Note: An asterisk (*) denotes incumbent. **In past elections, the other vote included: 2016 - 83,481 Libertarian (Gary Johnson); 1996 - 130,788 Reform (Ross Perot); 1992 - 319,878 Independent (Perot); 1980 - 38,284 Independent (John Anderson); 1968 - 191,731 American Independent (George Wallace).

OKLAHOMA

POSTWAR VOTE FOR GOVERNOR

		Republican		Democratic				Percentage			
								Total Vote		Major Vote	
Year	Total Vote	Vote	Candidate	Vote	Candidate	Other Vote	Rep.-Dem. Plurality	Rep.	Dem.	Rep.	Dem.
2018	1,186,385	644,579	Stitt, Kevin	500,973	Edmondson, Drew	40,833	143,606 R	54.3%	42.2%	56.3%	43.7%
2014	824,831	460,298	Fallin, Mary*	338,239	Dorman, Joe	26,294	122,059 R	55.8%	41.0%	57.6%	42.4%
2010	1,034,767	625,506	Fallin, Mary	409,261	Askins, Jari		216,245 R	60.4%	39.6%	60.4%	39.6%
2006	926,462	310,327	Istook, Ernest J.	616,135	Henry, Brad*		305,808 D	33.5%	66.5%	33.5%	66.5%
2002**	1,035,620	441,277	Largent, Steve	448,143	Henry, Brad	146,200	6,866 D	42.6%	43.3%	49.6%	50.4%
1998	873,585	505,498	Keating, Frank*	357,552	Boyd, Laura	10,535	147,946 R	57.9%	40.9%	58.6%	41.4%
1994**	995,012	466,740	Keating, Frank	294,936	Mildren, Jack	233,336	171,804 R	46.9%	29.6%	61.3%	38.7%
1990	911,314	297,584	Price, Bill	523,196	Walters, David	90,534	225,612 D	32.7%	57.4%	36.3%	63.7%
1986	909,925	431,762	Bellmon, Henry Louis	405,295	Walters, David	72,868	26,467 R	47.5%	44.5%	51.6%	48.4%
1982	883,130	332,207	Daxon, Tom	548,159	Nigh, George*	2,764	215,952 D	37.6%	62.1%	37.7%	62.3%
1978	777,414	367,055	Shotts, Ron	402,240	Nigh, George	8,119	35,185 D	47.2%	51.7%	47.7%	52.3%
1974	804,842	290,459	Inhofe, James M.	514,383	Boren, David L.		223,924 D	36.1%	63.9%	36.1%	63.9%
1970	698,790	336,157	Bartlett, Dewey F.*	338,338	Hall, David	24,295	2,181 D	48.1%	48.4%	49.8%	50.2%
1966	677,258	377,078	Bartlett, Dewey F.	296,328	Moore, Preston J.	3,852	80,750 R	55.7%	43.8%	56.0%	44.0%
1962	709,763	392,316	Bellmon, Henry Louis	315,357	Atkinson, W. P.	2,090	76,959 R	55.3%	44.4%	55.4%	44.6%
1958	538,839	107,495	Ferguson, Phil	399,504	Edmondson, J. Howard	31,840	292,009 D	19.9%	74.1%	21.2%	78.8%
1954	609,194	251,808	Sparks, Reuben K.	357,386	Gary, Raymond		105,578 D	41.3%	58.7%	41.3%	58.7%
1950	644,276	313,205	Ferguson, Jo O.	329,308	Murray, Johnston	1,763	16,103 D	48.6%	51.1%	48.7%	51.3%
1946	494,599	227,426	Flynn, Olney F.	259,491	Turner, Roy J.	7,682	32,065 D	46.0%	52.5%	46.7%	53.3%

Note: An asterisk (*) denotes incumbent. **In past elections, the other vote included: 2002 - 146,200 Independent (Gary L. Richardson); 1994 - 233,336 Independent (Wes Watkins).

POSTWAR VOTE FOR SENATOR

		Republican		Democratic				Percentage			
								Total Vote		Major Vote	
Year	Total Vote	Vote	Candidate	Vote	Candidate	Other Vote	Rep.-Dem. Plurality	Rep.	Dem.	Rep.	Dem.
2016	1,448,047	980,892	Lankford, James*	355,911	Workman, Mike	111,244	624,981 R	67.7%	24.6%	73.4%	26.6%
2014	820,733	558,166	Inhofe, James M.*	234,307	Silverstein, Matthew Benjamin "Matt"	28,260	323,859 R	68.0%	28.5%	70.4%	29.6%
2014S**	820,890	557,002	Lankford, James	237,923	Johnson, Connie	25,965	319,079 R	67.9%	29.0%	70.1%	29.9%
2010	1,017,151	718,482	Coburn, Tom*	265,814	Rogers, Jim	32,855	452,668 R	70.6%	26.1%	73.0%	27.0%
2008	1,346,819	763,375	Inhofe, James M.*	527,736	Rice, Andrew	55,708	235,639 R	56.7%	39.2%	59.1%	40.9%
2004	1,446,846	763,433	Coburn, Tom	596,750	Carson, Brad	86,663	166,683 R	52.8%	41.2%	56.1%	43.9%
2002	1,018,424	583,579	Inhofe, James M.*	369,789	Walters, David	65,056	213,790 R	57.3%	36.3%	61.2%	38.8%
1998	859,713	570,682	Nickles, Don*	268,898	Carroll, Don E.	20,133	301,784 R	66.4%	31.3%	68.0%	32.0%
1996	1,183,150	670,610	Inhofe, James M.*	474,162	Boren, Jim	38,378	196,448 R	56.7%	40.1%	58.6%	41.4%
1994S**	982,430	542,390	Inhofe, James M.	392,488	McCurdy, Dave	47,552	149,902 R	55.2%	40.0%	58.0%	42.0%
1992	1,294,423	757,876	Nickles, Don*	494,350	Lewis, Steve	42,197	263,526 R	58.5%	38.2%	60.5%	39.5%
1990	884,498	148,814	Jones, Stephen	735,684	Boren, David L.*		586,870 D	16.8%	83.2%	16.8%	83.2%
1986	893,666	493,436	Nickles, Don*	400,230	Jones, James R.		93,206 R	55.2%	44.8%	55.2%	44.8%
1984	1,197,937	280,638	Crozier, Will E. Bill	906,131	Boren, David L.*	11,168	625,493 D	23.4%	75.6%	23.6%	76.4%
1980	1,098,294	587,252	Nickles, Don	478,283	Coats, Andrew	32,759	108,969 R	53.5%	43.5%	55.1%	44.9%
1978	754,264	247,857	Kamm, Robert B.	493,953	Boren, David L.	12,454	246,096 D	32.9%	65.5%	33.4%	66.6%
1974	791,809	390,997	Bellmon, Henry Louis*	387,162	Edmondson, Ed	13,650	3,835 R	49.4%	48.9%	50.2%	49.8%
1972	1,005,148	516,934	Bartlett, Dewey F.	478,212	Edmondson, Ed	10,002	38,722 R	51.4%	47.6%	51.9%	48.1%
1968	909,119	470,120	Bellmon, Henry Louis	419,658	Monroney, Almer Stillwell Mike*	19,341	50,462 R	51.7%	46.2%	52.8%	47.2%
1966	638,742	295,585	Patterson, Pat J.	343,157	Harris, Fred R.*		47,572 D	46.3%	53.7%	46.3%	53.7%
1964S**	912,174	445,392	Wilkinson, Bud	466,782	Harris, Fred R.		21,390 D	48.8%	51.2%	48.8%	51.2%
1962	664,712	307,966	Crawford, B. Hayden	353,890	Monroney, Almer Stillwell Mike*	2,856	45,924 D	46.3%	53.2%	46.5%	53.5%
1960	864,475	385,646	Crawford, B. Hayden	474,116	Kerr, Robert Samuel Sr.*	4,713	88,470 D	44.6%	54.8%	44.9%	55.1%
1956	831,142	371,146	McKeever, Douglas	459,996	Monroney, Almer Stillwell Mike*		88,850 D	44.7%	55.3%	44.7%	55.3%
1954	600,120	262,013	Mock, Fred M.	335,127	Kerr, Robert Samuel Sr.*	2,980	73,114 D	43.7%	55.8%	43.9%	56.1%
1950	631,177	285,224	Alexander, W. H.	345,953	Monroney, Almer Stillwell Mike		60,729 D	45.2%	54.8%	45.2%	54.8%
1948	708,931	265,169	Rizley, Ross	441,654	Kerr, Robert Samuel Sr.	2,108	176,485 D	37.4%	62.3%	37.5%	62.5%

Note: An asterisk (*) denotes incumbent. **The 1964, 1994, and 2014 elections were for short terms to fill vacancies.

OKLAHOMA

GOVERNOR 2018

2010 Census Population	County	Total Vote	Republican (Stitt)	Democratic (Edmondson)	Other	Rep.-Dem. Plurality	Percentage Total Vote Rep.	Percentage Total Vote Dem.	Percentage Major Vote Rep.	Percentage Major Vote Dem.
22,683	ADAIR	5,173	3,187	1,745	241	1,442 R	61.6%	33.7%	64.6%	35.4%
5,642	ALFALFA	1,801	1,333	391	77	942 R	74.0%	21.7%	77.3%	22.7%
14,182	ATOKA	4,039	2,789	1,155	95	1,634 R	69.1%	28.6%	70.7%	29.3%
5,636	BEAVER	1,799	1,454	272	73	1,182 R	80.8%	15.1%	84.2%	15.8%
22,119	BECKHAM	5,705	4,061	1,396	248	2,665 R	71.2%	24.5%	74.4%	25.6%
11,943	BLAINE	2,953	1,941	889	123	1,052 R	65.7%	30.1%	68.6%	31.4%
42,416	BRYAN	11,349	7,301	3,746	302	3,555 R	64.3%	33.0%	66.1%	33.9%
29,600	CADDO	7,362	4,047	3,043	272	1,004 R	55.0%	41.3%	57.1%	42.9%
115,541	CANADIAN	45,951	27,410	16,744	1,797	10,666 R	59.7%	36.4%	62.1%	37.9%
47,557	CARTER	14,004	9,090	4,445	469	4,645 R	64.9%	31.7%	67.2%	32.8%
46,987	CHEROKEE	13,901	6,336	6,970	595	634 D	45.6%	50.1%	47.6%	52.4%
15,205	CHOCTAW	4,035	2,634	1,286	115	1,348 R	65.3%	31.9%	67.2%	32.8%
2,475	CIMARRON	799	682	98	19	584 R	85.4%	12.3%	87.4%	12.6%
255,755	CLEVELAND	92,147	42,268	46,648	3,231	4,380 D	45.9%	50.6%	47.5%	52.5%
5,925	COAL	1,846	1,127	659	60	468 R	61.1%	35.7%	63.1%	36.9%
124,098	COMANCHE	26,543	13,180	12,336	1,027	844 R	49.7%	46.5%	51.7%	48.3%
6,193	COTTON	2,005	1,312	598	95	714 R	65.4%	29.8%	68.7%	31.3%
15,029	CRAIG	4,740	2,863	1,713	164	1,150 R	60.4%	36.1%	62.6%	37.4%
69,967	CREEK	22,693	14,870	7,048	775	7,822 R	65.5%	31.1%	67.8%	32.2%
27,469	CUSTER	8,288	5,239	2,715	334	2,524 R	63.2%	32.8%	65.9%	34.1%
41,487	DELAWARE	13,101	8,543	4,114	444	4,429 R	65.2%	31.4%	67.5%	32.5%
4,810	DEWEY	1,768	1,404	315	49	1,089 R	79.4%	17.8%	81.7%	18.3%
4,151	ELLIS	1,477	1,186	236	55	950 R	80.3%	16.0%	83.4%	16.6%
60,580	GARFIELD	17,375	11,008	5,613	754	5,395 R	63.4%	32.3%	66.2%	33.8%
27,576	GARVIN	7,919	5,140	2,510	269	2,630 R	64.9%	31.7%	67.2%	32.8%
52,431	GRADY	17,148	11,173	5,281	694	5,892 R	65.2%	30.8%	67.9%	32.1%
4,527	GRANT	1,704	1,250	378	76	872 R	73.4%	22.2%	76.8%	23.2%
6,239	GREER	1,473	946	469	58	477 R	64.2%	31.8%	66.9%	33.1%
2,922	HARMON	746	443	277	26	166 R	59.4%	37.1%	61.5%	38.5%
3,685	HARPER	1,210	948	214	48	734 R	78.3%	17.7%	81.6%	18.4%
12,769	HASKELL	3,701	2,348	1,246	107	1,102 R	63.4%	33.7%	65.3%	34.7%
14,003	HUGHES	3,825	2,323	1,336	166	987 R	60.7%	34.9%	63.5%	36.5%
26,446	JACKSON	6,486	4,301	1,989	196	2,312 R	66.3%	30.7%	68.4%	31.6%
6,472	JEFFERSON	1,569	1,099	424	46	675 R	70.0%	27.0%	72.2%	27.8%
10,957	JOHNSTON	3,019	1,976	962	81	1,014 R	65.5%	31.9%	67.3%	32.7%
46,562	KAY	12,989	7,859	4,582	548	3,277 R	60.5%	35.3%	63.2%	36.8%
15,034	KINGFISHER	5,112	3,846	1,064	202	2,782 R	75.2%	20.8%	78.3%	21.7%
9,446	KIOWA	2,714	1,645	972	97	673 R	60.6%	35.8%	62.9%	37.1%
11,154	LATIMER	3,017	1,774	1,125	118	649 R	58.8%	37.3%	61.2%	38.8%
50,384	LE FLORE	12,803	8,009	4,467	327	3,542 R	62.6%	34.9%	64.2%	35.8%
34,273	LINCOLN	11,276	7,323	3,418	535	3,905 R	64.9%	30.3%	68.2%	31.8%
41,848	LOGAN	15,859	9,847	5,371	641	4,476 R	62.1%	33.9%	64.7%	35.3%
9,423	LOVE	2,769	1,902	808	59	1,094 R	68.7%	29.2%	70.2%	29.8%
7,527	MAJOR	2,746	2,177	470	99	1,707 R	79.3%	17.1%	82.2%	17.8%
15,840	MARSHALL	4,415	2,943	1,351	121	1,592 R	66.7%	30.6%	68.5%	31.5%
41,259	MAYES	12,927	7,837	4,604	486	3,233 R	60.6%	35.6%	63.0%	37.0%
34,506	MCCLAIN	13,804	9,021	4,286	497	4,735 R	65.4%	31.0%	67.8%	32.2%
33,151	MCCURTAIN	7,567	5,178	2,211	178	2,967 R	68.4%	29.2%	70.1%	29.9%
20,252	MCINTOSH	6,620	3,612	2,785	223	827 R	54.6%	42.1%	56.5%	43.5%
13,488	MURRAY	4,369	2,751	1,443	175	1,308 R	63.0%	33.0%	65.6%	34.4%
70,990	MUSKOGEE	19,699	9,515	9,516	668	1 D	48.3%	48.3%	50.0%	50.0%
11,561	NOBLE	3,984	2,543	1,252	189	1,291 R	63.8%	31.4%	67.0%	33.0%
10,536	NOWATA	3,506	2,319	1,016	171	1,303 R	66.1%	29.0%	69.5%	30.5%
12,191	OKFUSKEE	3,104	1,752	1,241	111	511 R	56.4%	40.0%	58.5%	41.5%
718,633	OKLAHOMA	233,599	98,994	126,667	7,938	27,673 D	42.4%	54.2%	43.9%	56.1%
40,069	OKMULGEE	11,038	5,846	4,849	343	997 R	53.0%	43.9%	54.7%	45.3%
47,472	OSAGE	15,355	8,629	6,202	524	2,427 R	56.2%	40.4%	58.2%	41.8%
31,848	OTTAWA	8,525	4,752	3,502	271	1,250 R	55.7%	41.1%	57.6%	42.4%
16,577	PAWNEE	4,928	3,076	1,645	207	1,431 R	62.4%	33.4%	65.2%	34.8%
77,350	PAYNE	22,757	11,193	10,650	914	543 R	49.2%	46.8%	51.2%	48.8%

OKLAHOMA

GOVERNOR 2018

2010 Census Population	County	Total Vote	Republican (Stitt)	Democratic (Edmondson)	Other	Rep.-Dem. Plurality	Percentage Total Vote Rep.	Percentage Total Vote Dem.	Percentage Major Vote Rep.	Percentage Major Vote Dem.
45,837	PITTSBURG	13,385	7,986	4,842	557	3,144 R	59.7%	36.2%	62.3%	37.7%
37,492	PONTOTOC	11,889	6,233	5,293	363	940 R	52.4%	44.5%	54.1%	45.9%
69,442	POTTAWATOMIE	21,022	11,996	8,093	933	3,903 R	57.1%	38.5%	59.7%	40.3%
11,572	PUSHMATAHA	3,333	2,102	1,106	125	996 R	63.1%	33.2%	65.5%	34.5%
3,647	ROGER MILLS	1,500	1,157	283	60	874 R	77.1%	18.9%	80.3%	19.7%
86,905	ROGERS	33,124	21,450	10,605	1,069	10,845 R	64.8%	32.0%	66.9%	33.1%
25,482	SEMINOLE	6,574	3,681	2,607	286	1,074 R	56.0%	39.7%	58.5%	41.5%
42,391	SEQUOYAH	11,482	6,695	4,480	307	2,215 R	58.3%	39.0%	59.9%	40.1%
45,048	STEPHENS	13,802	9,314	4,081	407	5,233 R	67.5%	29.6%	69.5%	30.5%
20,640	TEXAS	4,138	3,097	894	147	2,203 R	74.8%	21.6%	77.6%	22.4%
7,992	TILLMAN	2,091	1,315	716	60	599 R	62.9%	34.2%	64.7%	35.3%
603,403	TULSA	202,584	101,518	95,350	5,716	6,168 R	50.1%	47.1%	51.6%	48.4%
73,085	WAGONER	25,947	16,346	8,700	901	7,646 R	63.0%	33.5%	65.3%	34.7%
50,976	WASHINGTON	17,831	11,226	6,017	588	5,209 R	63.0%	33.7%	65.1%	34.9%
11,629	WASHITA	3,805	2,653	963	189	1,690 R	69.7%	25.3%	73.4%	26.6%
8,878	WOODS	2,844	1,929	797	118	1,132 R	67.8%	28.0%	70.8%	29.2%
20,081	WOODWARD	5,898	4,326	1,388	184	2,938 R	73.3%	23.5%	75.7%	24.3%
3,751,351	*TOTAL*	*1,186,385*	*644,579*	*500,973*	*40,833*	*143,606 R*	*54.3%*	*42.2%*	*56.3%*	*43.7%*

OKLAHOMA

HOUSE OF REPRESENTATIVES

CD	Year	Total Vote	Republican Vote	Republican Candidate	Democratic Vote	Democratic Candidate	Other Vote	Rep.-Dem. Plurality	Percentage Total Vote Rep.	Percentage Total Vote Dem.	Percentage Major Vote Rep.	Percentage Major Vote Dem.
1	2018	253,171	150,129	HERN, KEVIN	103,042	GILPIN, TIM		47,087 R	59.3%	40.7%	59.3%	40.7%
1	2016		Unopposed	BRIDENSTINE, JIM*				R				
1	2014		Unopposed	BRIDENSTINE, JIM*				R				
1	2012	285,312	181,084	BRIDENSTINE, JIM	91,421	OLSON, JOHN	12,807	89,663 R	63.5%	32.0%	66.5%	33.5%
2	2018	216,002	140,451	MULLIN, MARKWAYNE*	65,021	NICHOLS, JASON	10,530	75,430 R	65.0%	30.1%	68.4%	31.6%
2	2016	268,870	189,839	MULLIN, MARKWAYNE*	62,387	HARRIS-TILL, JOSHUA	16,644	127,452 R	70.6%	23.2%	75.3%	24.7%
2	2014	158,407	110,925	MULLIN, MARKWAYNE*	38,964	EVERETT, EARL E.	8,518	71,961 R	70.0%	24.6%	74.0%	26.0%
2	2012	250,612	143,701	MULLIN, MARKWAYNE	96,081	WALLACE, ROB	10,830	47,620 R	57.3%	38.3%	59.9%	40.1%
3	2018	234,065	172,913	LUCAS, FRANK D.*	61,152	ROBBINS, FRANKIE		111,761 R	73.9%	26.1%	73.9%	26.1%
3	2016	290,615	227,525	LUCAS, FRANK D.*	63,090	ROBBINS, FRANKIE		164,435 R	78.3%	21.7%	78.3%	21.7%
3	2014	169,605	133,335	LUCAS, FRANK D.*	36,270	ROBBINS, FRANKIE		97,065 R	78.6%	21.4%	78.6%	21.4%
3	2012	268,003	201,744	LUCAS, FRANK D.*	53,472	MURRAY, TIMOTHY RAY	12,787	148,272 R	75.3%	20.0%	79.0%	21.0%
4	2018	236,638	149,227	COLE, TOM*	78,088	BRANNON, MARY	9,323	71,139 R	63.1%	33.0%	65.6%	34.4%
4	2016	293,189	204,143	COLE, TOM*	76,472	OWEN, CHRISTINA	12,574	127,671 R	69.6%	26.1%	72.7%	27.3%
4	2014	166,268	117,721	COLE, TOM*	40,998	SMITH, BERT	7,549	76,723 R	70.8%	24.7%	74.2%	25.8%
4	2012	260,331	176,740	COLE, TOM*	71,846	BEBO, DONNA MARIE	11,745	104,894 R	67.9%	27.6%	71.1%	28.9%
5	2018	238,960	117,811	RUSSELL, STEVE D.*	121,149	HORN, KENDRA		3,338 D	49.3%	50.7%	49.3%	50.7%
5	2016	280,570	160,184	RUSSELL, STEVE D.*	103,273	MCAFFREY, AL	17,113	56,911 R	57.1%	36.8%	60.8%	39.2%
5	2014	159,133	95,632	RUSSELL, STEVE D.	57,790	MCAFFREY, AL	5,711	37,842 R	60.1%	36.3%	62.3%	37.7%
5	2012	261,677	153,603	LANKFORD, JAMES*	97,504	GUILD, TOM	10,570	56,099 R	58.7%	37.3%	61.2%	38.8%
TOTAL	*2018*	*1,178,836*	*730,531*		*428,452*		*19,853*	*302,079 R*	*62.0%*	*36.3%*	*63.0%*	*37.0%*
TOTAL	*2016*	*1,133,244*	*781,691*		*305,222*		*46,331*	*476,469 R*	*69.0%*	*26.9%*	*71.9%*	*28.1%*
TOTAL	*2014*	*653,413*	*457,613*		*174,022*		*21,778*	*283,591 R*	*70.0%*	*26.6%*	*72.4%*	*27.6%*
TOTAL	*2012*	*1,325,935*	*856,872*		*410,324*		*58,739*	*446,548 R*	*64.6%*	*30.9%*	*67.6%*	*32.4%*

Note: An asterisk (*) denotes incumbent.

OKLAHOMA

GENERAL AND PRIMARY ELECTIONS

2018 GENERAL ELECTIONS: OTHER VOTES

Governor Other vote was 40,833 Libertarian (Chris Powell)

House Other vote was:

CD 2 6,390 Independent (John Foreman), 4,140 Libertarian (Richard Castaldo)
CD 4 9,323 Independent (Ruby Peters)

2018 PRIMARY ELECTIONS: SUPPLEMENTARY INFORMATION

Primary June 26, 2018

Primary Runoff August 28, 2018

Registration (as of January 15, 2018) 2,016,157

Republican	942,621
Democratic	769,772
Libertarian	4,897
Independent	298,867

Primary Type Semi-Open—Only registered Democrats and Republicans could vote in their party's primary. Independent voters could vote in the Democratic primary.

	REPUBLICAN PRIMARIES			DEMOCRATIC PRIMARIES		
Governor	Cornett, Mick	132,806	29.3%	Edmondson, Drew	242,764	61.4%
	Stitt, Kevin	110,479	24.4%	Johnson, Constance "Connie"	152,730	38.6%
	Lamb, Todd G.	107,985	23.9%			
	Fisher, Dan	35,818	7.9%			
	Jones, Gary A.	25,243	5.6%			
	Richardson, Gary	18,185	4.0%			
	Stephens, Blake "Cowboy"	12,211	2.7%			
	Barnett, Christopher	5,240	1.2%			
	Gowdy, Barry	2,347	0.5%			
	Foutch, Eric	2,292	0.5%			
	TOTAL	*452,606*		*TOTAL*	*395,494*	
Congressional District 1	Harris, Tim	28,431	27.5%	Gilpin, Tim	24,567	34.5%
	Hern, Kevin	23,466	22.7%	Douglas, Amanda	23,093	32.4%
	Coleman, Andy	22,608	21.8%	Fields, Gwendolyn	13,980	19.6%
	Dahm, Nathan	20,868	20.2%	Keeter, Mark A.	6,025	8.5%
	Stockstill, Danny	8,100	7.8%	Hullum, David Matthew	3,580	5.0%
	TOTAL	*103,473*		*TOTAL*	*71,245*	
	PRIMARY RUNOFF			**PRIMARY RUNOFF**		
	Hern, Kevin	40,401	54.9%	Gilpin, Tim	16,995	59.4%
	Harris, Tim	33,155	45.1%	Douglas, Amanda	11,628	40.6%
	TOTAL	*73,556*		*TOTAL*	*28,623*	
Congressional District 2	Mullin, Markwayne*	32,654	54.1%	Nichols, Jason	32,576	37.9%
	Jackson, Jarrin	15,204	25.2%	Padgett, Clay	20,833	24.2%
	Jackson, Brian	6,907	11.5%	McIntosh, Elijah	16,359	19.0%
	McCarthy, John	5,549	9.2%	Jenner, Virginia D. "Blue Jeans"	16,222	18.9%
	TOTAL	*60,314*		*TOTAL*	*85,990*	
				PRIMARY RUNOFF		
				Nichols, Jason	19,562	56.8%
				Padgett, Clay	14,850	43.2%
				TOTAL	*34,412*	
Congressional District 3	Lucas, Frank D.*	Unopposed		Robins, Frankie Lee	38,767	64.8%
				Thibodeaux, Murray Mark	21,024	35.2%
				TOTAL	*59,791*	

OKLAHOMA

GENERAL AND PRIMARY ELECTIONS

	REPUBLICAN PRIMARIES			DEMOCRATIC PRIMARIES		
Congressional District 4	Cole, Tom*	55,929	64.7%	Brannon, Mary	25,757	34.4%
	Taylor, James	30,461	35.3%	Gipson, Fred Allen	22,756	30.4%
				Varner, Mallory	13,953	18.6%
				Klutts, Roxann	12,493	16.7%
	TOTAL	*86,390*		*TOTAL*	*74,959*	
				PRIMARY RUNOFF		
				Brannon, Mary	15,251	57.5%
				Gipson, Fred Allen	11,268	42.5%
				TOTAL	*26,519*	
Congressional District 5	Russell, Steve D.*	66,030	83.6%	Horn, Kendra	34,892	43.8%
	Dunson, Gregory	7,642	9.7%	Guild, Tom	14,251	17.9%
	Edwards, DeJuan	5,290	6.7%	Britt, Elysabeth	10,752	13.5%
				Porter, Eddie	8,459	10.6%
				Kelley-Leonard, Leona	6,697	8.4%
				Meade, Tyson Todd	4,530	5.7%
	TOTAL	*78,962*		*TOTAL*	*79,581*	
				PRIMARY RUNOFF		
				Horn, Kendra	22,067	75.8%
				Guild, Tom	7,043	24.2%
				TOTAL	*29,110*	

Note: An asterisk (*) denotes incumbent. A runoff was triggered if the leading candidate received less than 50 percent of the primary vote.

OREGON

Congressional districts first established for elections held in 2012
5 members

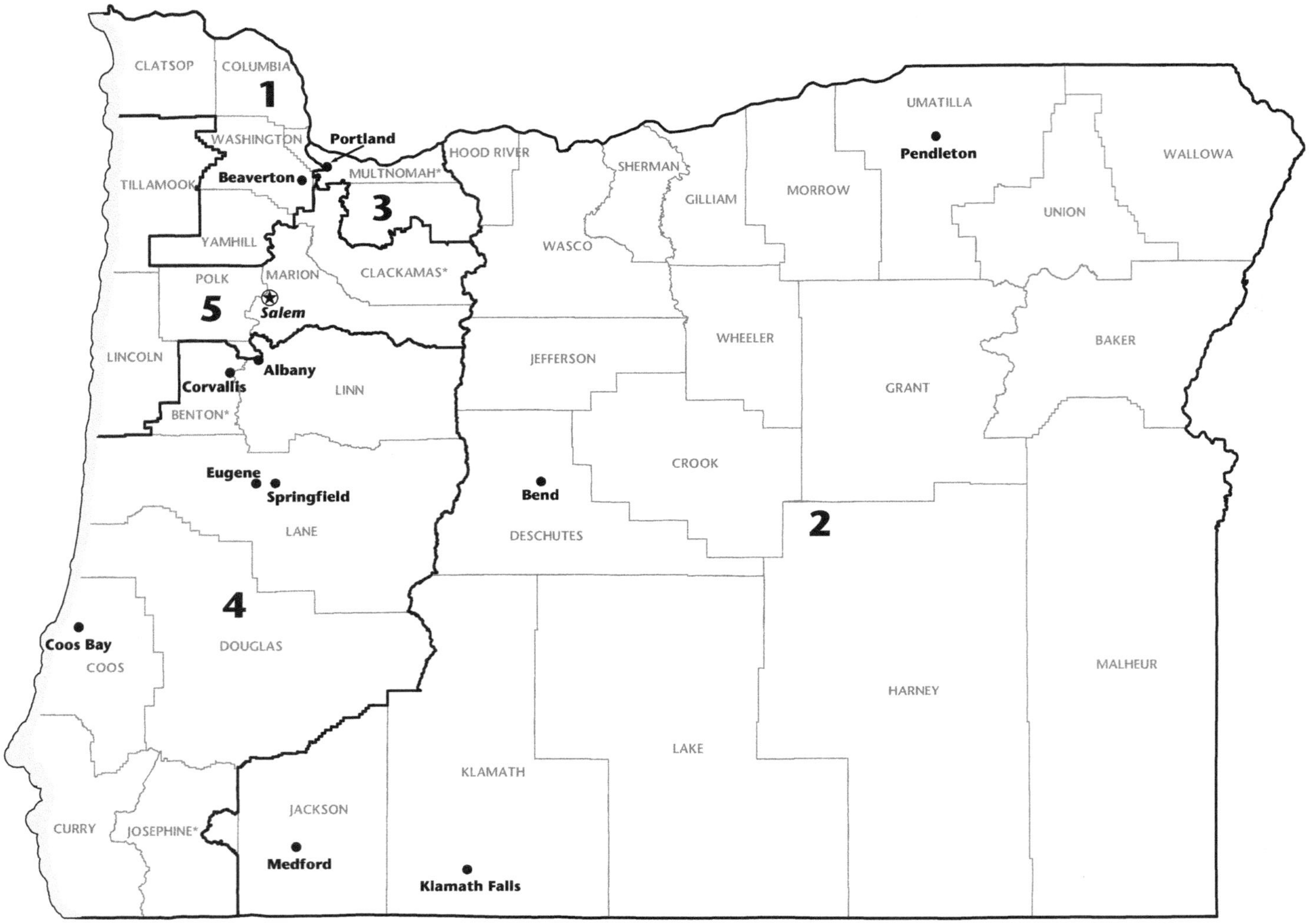

* Asterisk indicates a county whose boundaries include parts of two or more congressional districts.

OREGON

GOVERNOR

Kate Brown (D). Re-elected 2018 to a four-year term. Elected 2016, in a special election after having assumed the governorship, to complete the remaining two years of the term vacated by the resignation February 18, 2015, of John Kitzhaber (D). He left office under an ethics cloud involving conflict of interest charges spawned by his fiancée.

SENATORS (2 Democrats)

Jeff Merkley (D). Re-elected 2014 to a six-year term. Previously elected 2008.

Ron Wyden (D). Re-elected 2016 to a six-year term. Previously elected 2010, 2004, 1998, and in a special election January 30, 1996, to serve the remaining three years of the term vacated when Senator Robert W. Packwood (R) resigned in October 1995.

REPRESENTATIVES (1 Republican, 4 Democrats)

1. Suzanne Bonamici (D)
2. Greg Walden (R)
3. Earl Blumenauer (D)
4. Peter A. DeFazio (D)
5. Kurt Schrader (D)

POSTWAR VOTE FOR PRESIDENT

		Republican		Democratic				Percentage: Total Vote		Percentage: Major Vote	
Year	Total Vote	Vote	Candidate	Vote	Candidate	Other Vote	Rep.-Dem. Plurality	Rep.	Dem.	Rep.	Dem.
2016**	2,001,336	782,403	Trump, Donald J.	1,002,106	Clinton, Hillary Rodham	216,827	219,703 D	39.1%	50.1%	43.8%	56.2%
2012	1,789,270	754,175	Romney, W. Mitt	970,488	Obama, Barack H.*	64,607	216,313 D	42.1%	54.2%	43.7%	56.3%
2008	1,827,864	738,475	McCain, John S. III	1,037,291	Obama, Barack H.	52,098	298,816 D	40.4%	56.7%	41.6%	58.4%
2004	1,836,782	866,831	Bush, George W.*	943,163	Kerry, John F.	26,788	76,332 D	47.2%	51.3%	47.9%	52.1%
2000**	1,533,968	713,577	Bush, George W.	720,342	Gore, Albert Jr.	100,049	6,765 D	46.5%	47.0%	49.8%	50.2%
1996**	1,377,760	538,152	Dole, Robert "Bob"	649,641	Clinton, Bill*	189,967	111,489 D	39.1%	47.2%	45.3%	54.7%
1992**	1,462,643	475,757	Bush, George H.*	621,314	Clinton, Bill	365,572	145,557 D	32.5%	42.5%	43.4%	56.6%
1988	1,201,694	560,126	Bush, George H.	616,206	Dukakis, Michael S.	25,362	56,080 D	46.6%	51.3%	47.6%	52.4%
1984	1,226,527	685,700	Reagan, Ronald*	536,479	Mondale, Walter F.	4,348	149,221 R	55.9%	43.7%	56.1%	43.9%
1980**	1,181,516	571,044	Reagan, Ronald	456,890	Carter, Jimmy*	153,582	114,154 R	48.3%	38.7%	55.6%	44.4%
1976	1,029,876	492,120	Ford, Gerald R.*	490,407	Carter, Jimmy	47,349	1,713 R	47.8%	47.6%	50.1%	49.9%
1972	927,946	486,686	Nixon, Richard M.*	392,760	McGovern, George S.	48,500	93,926 R	52.4%	42.3%	55.3%	44.7%
1968**	819,622	408,433	Nixon, Richard M.	358,866	Humphrey, Hubert Horatio Jr.	52,323	49,567 R	49.8%	43.8%	53.2%	46.8%
1964	786,305	282,779	Goldwater, Barry M. Sr.	501,017	Johnson, Lyndon B.*	2,509	218,238 D	36.0%	63.7%	36.1%	63.9%
1960	776,421	408,060	Nixon, Richard M.	367,402	Kennedy, John F.	959	40,658 R	52.6%	47.3%	52.6%	47.4%
1956	736,132	406,393	Eisenhower, Dwight D.*	329,204	Stevenson, Adlai E. II	535	77,189 R	55.2%	44.7%	55.2%	44.8%
1952	695,059	420,815	Eisenhower, Dwight D.	270,579	Stevenson, Adlai E. II	3,665	150,236 R	60.5%	38.9%	60.9%	39.1%
1948	524,080	260,904	Dewey, Thomas E.	243,147	Truman, Harry S.*	20,029	17,757 R	49.8%	46.4%	51.8%	48.2%

Note: An asterisk (*) denotes incumbent. **In past elections, the other vote included: 2016 - 94,231 Libertarian (Gary Johnson); 2000 - 77,357 Green (Ralph Nader); 1996 - 121,221 Reform (Ross Perot); 1992 - 354,091 Independent (Perot); 1980 - 112,389 Independent (John Anderson); 1968 - 49,683 American Independent (George Wallace).

OREGON

POSTWAR VOTE FOR GOVERNOR

		Republican		Democratic				Percentage			
								Total Vote		Major Vote	
Year	Total Vote	Vote	Candidate	Vote	Candidate	Other Vote	Rep.-Dem. Plurality	Rep.	Dem.	Rep.	Dem.
2018	1,866,997	814,988	Buehler, Knute	934,498	Brown, Kate*	117,511	119,510 D	43.7%	50.1%	46.6%	53.4%
2016S**	1,944,807	844,372	Pierce, Bud	985,022	Brown, Kate*	115,413	140,650 D	43.4%	50.6%	46.2%	53.8%
2014	1,469,717	648,542	Richardson, Dennis	733,230	Kitzhaber, John*	87,945	84,688 D	44.1%	49.9%	46.9%	53.1%
2010	1,453,548	694,287	Dudley, Chris	716,525	Kitzhaber, John	42,736	22,238 D	47.8%	49.3%	49.2%	50.8%
2006	1,379,475	589,748	Saxton, Ron	699,786	Kulongoski, Ted*	89,941	110,038 D	42.8%	50.7%	45.7%	54.3%
2002	1,260,497	581,785	Mannix, Kevin L.	618,004	Kulongoski, Ted	60,708	36,219 D	46.2%	49.0%	48.5%	51.5%
1998	1,113,098	334,001	Sizemore, Bill	717,061	Kitzhaber, John*	62,036	383,060 D	30.0%	64.4%	31.8%	68.2%
1994	1,221,010	517,874	Smith, Denny	622,083	Kitzhaber, John	81,053	104,209 D	42.4%	50.9%	45.4%	54.6%
1990**	1,112,847	444,646	Frohnmayer, Dave	508,749	Roberts, Barbara	159,452	64,103 D	40.0%	45.7%	46.6%	53.4%
1986	1,059,630	506,986	Paulus, Norma	549,456	Goldschmidt, Neil	3,188	42,470 D	47.8%	51.9%	48.0%	52.0%
1982	1,042,009	639,841	Atiyeh, Victor*	374,316	Kulongoski, Ted	27,852	265,525 R	61.4%	35.9%	63.1%	36.9%
1978	911,143	498,452	Atiyeh, Victor	409,411	Straub, Robert W.*	3,280	89,041 R	54.7%	44.9%	54.9%	45.1%
1974	770,574	324,751	Atiyeh, Victor	444,812	Straub, Robert W.	1,011	120,061 D	42.1%	57.7%	42.2%	57.8%
1970	666,394	369,964	McCall, Tom*	293,892	Straub, Robert W.	2,538	76,072 R	55.5%	44.1%	55.7%	44.3%
1966	682,862	377,346	McCall, Tom	305,008	Straub, Robert W.	508	72,338 R	55.3%	44.7%	55.3%	44.7%
1962	637,407	345,497	Hatfield, Mark O.*	265,359	Thornton, Robert Y.	26,551	80,138 R	54.2%	41.6%	56.6%	43.4%
1958	599,994	331,900	Hatfield, Mark O.	267,934	Holmes, Robert D.*	160	63,966 R	55.3%	44.7%	55.3%	44.7%
1956S**	731,279	361,840	Smith, Elmo E.	369,439	Holmes, Robert D.		7,599 D	49.5%	50.5%	49.5%	50.5%
1954	566,701	322,522	Patterson, Paul	244,179	Carson, Joseph K. Jr.		78,343 R	56.9%	43.1%	56.9%	43.1%
1950	505,910	334,160	McKay, Douglas*	171,750	Flegal, Austin F.		162,410 R	66.1%	33.9%	66.1%	33.9%
1948S**	509,624	271,295	McKay, Douglas	226,949	Wallace, Lew	11,380	44,346 R	53.2%	44.5%	54.5%	45.5%
1946	344,155	237,681	Snell, Earl*	106,474	Donaugh, Carl C.		131,207 R	69.1%	30.9%	69.1%	30.9%

Note: An asterisk (*) denotes incumbent. **In past elections, the other vote included: 1990 - 144,062 Independent (Al Mobley). The 1948, 1956, and 2016 elections were for short terms to fill a vacancy.

POSTWAR VOTE FOR SENATOR

		Republican		Democratic				Percentage			
								Total Vote		Major Vote	
Year	Total Vote	Vote	Candidate	Vote	Candidate	Other Vote	Rep.-Dem. Plurality	Rep.	Dem.	Rep.	Dem.
2016	1,952,478	651,106	Callahan, Mark	1,105,119	Wyden, Ron*	196,253	454,013 D	33.3%	56.6%	37.1%	62.9%
2014	1,461,618	538,847	Wehby, Monica	814,537	Merkley, Jeff*	108,234	275,690 D	36.9%	55.7%	39.8%	60.2%
2010	1,442,588	566,199	Huffman, Jim	825,507	Wyden, Ron*	50,882	259,308 D	39.2%	57.2%	40.7%	59.3%
2008	1,767,504	805,159	Smith, Gordon H.*	864,392	Merkley, Jeff	97,953	59,233 D	45.6%	48.9%	48.2%	51.8%
2004	1,780,550	565,254	King, Al	1,128,728	Wyden, Ron*	86,568	563,474 D	31.7%	63.4%	33.4%	66.6%
2002	1,267,221	712,287	Smith, Gordon H.*	501,898	Bradbury, Bill	53,036	210,389 R	56.2%	39.6%	58.7%	41.3%
1998	1,117,747	377,739	Lim, John	682,425	Wyden, Ron*	57,583	304,686 D	33.8%	61.1%	35.6%	64.4%
1996	1,360,230	677,336	Smith, Gordon H.*	624,370	Bruggere, Tom	58,524	52,966 R	49.8%	45.9%	52.0%	48.0%
1996S**	1,196,608	553,519	Smith, Gordon H.	571,739	Wyden, Ron	71,350	18,220 D	46.3%	47.8%	49.2%	50.8%
1992	1,376,033	717,455	Packwood, Robert W.*	639,851	Aucoin, Les	18,727	77,604 R	52.1%	46.5%	52.9%	47.1%
1990	1,099,255	590,095	Hatfield, Mark O.*	507,743	Lonsdale, Harry	1,417	82,352 R	53.7%	46.2%	53.8%	46.2%
1986	1,042,555	656,317	Packwood, Robert W.*	375,735	Bauman, Rick	10,503	280,582 R	63.0%	36.0%	63.6%	36.4%
1984	1,214,735	808,152	Hatfield, Mark O.*	406,122	Hendriksen, Margie	461	402,030 R	66.5%	33.4%	66.6%	33.4%
1980	1,140,494	594,290	Packwood, Robert W.*	501,963	Kulongoski, Ted	44,241	92,327 R	52.1%	44.0%	54.2%	45.8%
1978	892,518	550,165	Hatfield, Mark O.*	341,616	Cook, Vernon	737	208,549 R	61.6%	38.3%	61.7%	38.3%
1974	766,414	420,984	Packwood, Robert W.*	338,591	Roberts, Betty	6,839	82,393 R	54.9%	44.2%	55.4%	44.6%
1972	920,833	494,671	Hatfield, Mark O.*	425,036	Morse, Wayne L.	1,126	69,635 R	53.7%	46.2%	53.8%	46.2%
1968	814,176	408,646	Packwood, Robert W.	405,353	Morse, Wayne L.*	177	3,293 R	50.2%	49.8%	50.2%	49.8%
1966	685,067	354,391	Hatfield, Mark O.	330,374	Duncan, Robert B.	302	24,017 R	51.7%	48.2%	51.8%	48.2%
1962	636,558	291,587	Unander, Sig	344,716	Morse, Wayne L.*	255	53,129 D	45.8%	54.2%	45.8%	54.2%
1960	755,875	343,009	Smith, Elmo E.	412,757	Neuberger, Maurine B.*	109	69,748 D	45.4%	54.6%	45.4%	54.6%
1956	732,254	335,405	McKay, Douglas	396,849	Morse, Wayne L.*		61,444 D	45.8%	54.2%	45.8%	54.2%
1954	569,088	283,313	Cordon, Guy*	285,775	Neuberger, Richard L.		2,462 D	49.8%	50.2%	49.8%	50.2%
1950	503,455	376,510	Morse, Wayne L.*	116,780	Latourette, Howard	10,165	259,730 R	74.8%	23.2%	76.3%	23.7%
1948	498,570	299,295	Cordon, Guy*	199,275	Wilson, Manley J.		100,020 R	60.0%	40.0%	60.0%	40.0%

Note: An asterisk (*) denotes incumbent. **The January 1996 election was for a short term to fill a vacancy.

OREGON

GOVERNOR 2018

2010 Census Population	County	Total Vote	Republican (Buehler)	Democratic (Brown)	Other	Rep.-Dem. Plurality	Total Vote Rep.	Total Vote Dem.	Major Vote Rep.	Major Vote Dem.
16,134	BAKER	8,264	6,023	1,572	669	4,451 R	72.9%	19.0%	79.3%	20.7%
85,579	BENTON	44,231	14,990	26,592	2,649	11,602 D	33.9%	60.1%	36.0%	64.0%
375,992	CLACKAMAS	200,266	98,468	91,088	10,710	7,380 R	49.2%	45.5%	51.9%	48.1%
37,039	CLATSOP	18,558	8,294	8,909	1,355	615 D	44.7%	48.0%	48.2%	51.8%
49,351	COLUMBIA	24,617	12,953	9,519	2,145	3,434 R	52.6%	38.7%	57.6%	42.4%
63,043	COOS	28,727	16,520	9,622	2,585	6,898 R	57.5%	33.5%	63.2%	36.8%
20,978	CROOK	11,536	8,516	2,285	735	6,231 R	73.8%	19.8%	78.8%	21.2%
22,364	CURRY	11,533	6,474	4,141	918	2,333 R	56.1%	35.9%	61.0%	39.0%
157,733	DESCHUTES	96,099	49,983	40,676	5,440	9,307 R	52.0%	42.3%	55.1%	44.9%
107,667	DOUGLAS	49,238	32,413	11,824	5,001	20,589 R	65.8%	24.0%	73.3%	26.7%
1,871	GILLIAM	993	691	218	84	473 R	69.6%	22.0%	76.0%	24.0%
7,445	GRANT	3,853	2,923	649	281	2,274 R	75.9%	16.8%	81.8%	18.2%
7,422	HARNEY	3,547	2,722	584	241	2,138 R	76.7%	16.5%	82.3%	17.7%
22,346	HOOD RIVER	10,828	3,789	6,485	554	2,696 D	35.0%	59.9%	36.9%	63.1%
203,206	JACKSON	101,907	51,623	42,207	8,077	9,416 R	50.7%	41.4%	55.0%	45.0%
21,720	JEFFERSON	8,852	5,518	2,635	699	2,883 R	62.3%	29.8%	67.7%	32.3%
82,713	JOSEPHINE	40,470	24,499	12,214	3,757	12,285 R	60.5%	30.2%	66.7%	33.3%
66,380	KLAMATH	28,256	19,134	6,301	2,821	12,833 R	67.7%	22.3%	75.2%	24.8%
7,895	LAKE	3,557	2,774	476	307	2,298 R	78.0%	13.4%	85.4%	14.6%
351,715	LANE	177,172	67,737	96,841	12,594	29,104 D	38.2%	54.7%	41.2%	58.8%
46,034	LINCOLN	24,219	9,884	12,610	1,725	2,726 D	40.8%	52.1%	43.9%	56.1%
116,672	LINN	54,662	33,051	16,461	5,150	16,590 R	60.5%	30.1%	66.8%	33.2%
31,313	MALHEUR	8,970	6,000	2,159	811	3,841 R	66.9%	24.1%	73.5%	26.5%
315,335	MARION	126,978	63,323	55,238	8,417	8,085 R	49.9%	43.5%	53.4%	46.6%
11,173	MORROW	3,754	2,534	844	376	1,690 R	67.5%	22.5%	75.0%	25.0%
735,334	MULTNOMAH	378,098	83,507	279,384	15,207	195,877 D	22.1%	73.9%	23.0%	77.0%
75,403	POLK	37,315	19,341	15,529	2,445	3,812 R	51.8%	41.6%	55.5%	44.5%
1,765	SHERMAN	985	736	190	59	546 R	74.7%	19.3%	79.5%	20.5%
25,250	TILLAMOOK	13,142	6,606	5,616	920	990 R	50.3%	42.7%	54.1%	45.9%
75,889	UMATILLA	24,108	15,178	7,085	1,845	8,093 R	63.0%	29.4%	68.2%	31.8%
25,748	UNION	11,756	7,983	2,877	896	5,106 R	67.9%	24.5%	73.5%	26.5%
7,008	WALLOWA	4,032	2,668	1,088	276	1,580 R	66.2%	27.0%	71.0%	29.0%
25,213	WASCO	11,357	5,841	4,604	912	1,237 R	51.4%	40.5%	55.9%	44.1%
529,710	WASHINGTON	248,479	97,286	137,886	13,307	40,600 D	39.2%	55.5%	41.4%	58.6%
1,441	WHEELER	818	594	158	66	436 R	72.6%	19.3%	79.0%	21.0%
99,193	YAMHILL	45,820	24,412	17,931	3,477	6,481 R	53.3%	39.1%	57.7%	42.3%
3,831,074	*TOTAL*	*1,866,997*	*814,988*	*934,498*	*117,511*	*119,510 D*	*43.7%*	*50.1%*	*46.6%*	*53.4%*

OREGON

HOUSE OF REPRESENTATIVES

CD	Year	Total Vote	Republican Vote	Republican Candidate	Democratic Vote	Democratic Candidate	Other Vote	Rep.-Dem. Plurality	Total Vote Rep.	Total Vote Dem.	Major Vote Rep.	Major Vote Dem.
1	2018	363,249	116,446	VERBEEK, JOHN	231,198	BONAMICI, SUZANNE*	15,605	114,752 D	32.1%	63.6%	33.5%	66.5%
1	2016	378,095	139,756	HEINRICH, BRIAN J.	225,391	BONAMICI, SUZANNE*	12,948	85,635 D	37.0%	59.6%	38.3%	61.7%
1	2014	279,253	96,245	YATES, JASON	160,038	BONAMICI, SUZANNE*	22,970	63,793 D	34.5%	57.3%	37.6%	62.4%
1	2012	331,980	109,699	MORGAN, DELINDA	197,845	BONAMICI, SUZANNE*	24,436	88,146 D	33.0%	59.6%	35.7%	64.3%
2	2018	368,709	207,597	WALDEN, GREG*	145,298	MCLEOD-SKINNER, JAMIE	15,814	62,299 R	56.3%	39.4%	58.8%	41.2%
2	2016	380,739	272,952	WALDEN, GREG*	106,640	CRARY, JAMES "JIM"	1,147	166,312 R	71.7%	28.0%	71.9%	28.1%
2	2014	287,425	202,374	WALDEN, GREG*	73,785	CHRISTOFFERSON, AELEA	11,266	128,589 R	70.4%	25.7%	73.3%	26.7%
2	2012	332,255	228,043	WALDEN, GREG*	96,741	SEGERS, JOYCE B.	7,471	131,302 R	68.6%	29.1%	70.2%	29.8%

OREGON

HOUSE OF REPRESENTATIVES

									Percentage			
			Republican		Democratic				Total Vote		Major Vote	
CD	Year	Total Vote	Vote	Candidate	Vote	Candidate	Other Vote	Rep.-Dem. Plurality	Rep.	Dem.	Rep.	Dem.
3	2018	384,326	76,187	HARRISON, THOMAS S. IV	279,019	BLUMENAUER, EARL*	29,120	202,832 D	19.8%	72.6%	21.4%	78.6%
3	2016	382,355			274,687	BLUMENAUER, EARL*	107,668	274,687 D		71.8%		100.0%
3	2014	292,757	57,424	BUCHAL, JAMES	211,748	BLUMENAUER, EARL*	23,585	154,324 D	19.6%	72.3%	21.3%	78.7%
3	2012	355,875	70,325	GREEN, RONALD	264,979	BLUMENAUER, EARL*	20,571	194,654 D	19.8%	74.5%	21.0%	79.0%
4	2018	372,893	152,414	ROBINSON, ART	208,710	DEFAZIO, PETER A.*	11,769	56,296 D	40.9%	56.0%	42.2%	57.8%
4	2016	397,568	157,743	ROBINSON, ART	220,628	DEFAZIO, PETER A.*	19,197	62,885 D	39.7%	55.5%	41.7%	58.3%
4	2014	310,179	116,534	ROBINSON, ART	181,624	DEFAZIO, PETER A.*	12,021	65,090 D	37.6%	58.6%	39.1%	60.9%
4	2012	360,088	140,549	ROBINSON, ART	212,866	DEFAZIO, PETER A.*	6,673	72,317 D	39.0%	59.1%	39.8%	60.2%
5	2018	358,469	149,887	CALLAHAN, MARK	197,187	SCHRADER, KURT*	11,395	47,300 D	41.8%	55.0%	43.2%	56.8%
5	2016	373,108	160,443	WILLIS, COLM	199,505	SCHRADER, KURT*	13,160	39,062 D	43.0%	53.5%	44.6%	55.4%
5	2014	281,088	110,332	SMITH, TOOTIE	150,944	SCHRADER, KURT*	19,812	40,612 D	39.3%	53.7%	42.2%	57.8%
5	2012	327,970	139,223	THOMPSON, FRED	177,229	SCHRADER, KURT*	11,518	38,006 D	42.4%	54.0%	44.0%	56.0%
TOTAL	*2018*	*1,847,646*	*702,531*		*1,061,412*		*83,703*	*358,881 D*	*38.0%*	*57.4%*	*39.8%*	*60.2%*
TOTAL	*2016*	*1,911,865*	*730,894*		*1,026,851*		*154,120*	*295,957 D*	*38.2%*	*53.7%*	*41.6%*	*58.4%*
TOTAL	*2014*	*1,450,702*	*582,909*		*778,139*		*89,654*	*195,230 D*	*40.2%*	*53.6%*	*42.8%*	*57.2%*
TOTAL	*2012*	*1,708,168*	*687,839*		*949,660*		*70,669*	*261,821 D*	*40.3%*	*55.6%*	*42.0%*	*58.0%*

Note: An asterisk (*) denotes incumbent.

OREGON

GENERAL AND PRIMARY ELECTIONS

2018 GENERAL ELECTIONS: OTHER VOTES

Governor Other vote was 53,392 Independent (Patrick Starnes), 28,927 Libertarian (Nick Chen), 21,145 Constitution (Aaron Auer), 11,013 Progressive (Chris Henry), 3,034 Write-in (Scattered Write-in)

House Other vote was:

CD 1 15,121 Libertarian (Drew Layda), 484 Write-in (Scattered Write-in)

CD 2 15,536 Independent (Mark Roberts), 278 Write-in (Scattered Write-in)

CD 3 21,352 Independent (Marc Koller), 5,767 Libertarian (Gary Dye), 1,487 Constitution (Michael Marsh), 514 Write-in (Scattered Write-in)

CD 4 5,956 Pacific Green (Michael Beilstein), 5,370 Libertarian (Richard Jacobson), 443 Write-in (Scattered Write-in)

CD 5 6,054 Libertarian (Daniel Souza), 4,802 Pacific Green (Marvin Sandnes), 539 Write-in (Scattered Write-in)

2018 PRIMARY ELECTIONS: SUPPLEMENTARY INFORMATION

Primary	May 15, 2018	**Registration** (as of May 1 2018)	2,678,515	Democratic	956,279
				Republican	700,177
				Independent	120,174
				Libertarian	18,997
				Working Families	9,986
				Pacific Green	9,708
				Constitution	3,732
				Progressive	2,054
				Other	18,890
				Non-Affiliated	838,518

Primary Type Closed—Only registered Democrats and Republicans could vote in their party's primary.

OREGON

GENERAL AND PRIMARY ELECTIONS

	REPUBLICAN PRIMARIES			DEMOCRATIC PRIMARIES		
Governor	Buehler, Knute	144,103	45.9%	Brown, Kate*	324,451	81.9%
	Carpenter, Sam	90,572	28.8%	Jones, Ed	33,464	8.5%
	Wooldridge, Greg	63,049	20.1%	Neville, Candace	29,110	7.4%
	Cuff, Bruce A.	4,857	1.5%	Scattered Write-in	8,912	2.3%
	Smith, Jeff	4,691	1.5%			
	Stauffer, David	2,096	0.7%			
	Scatterd Write-in	1,701	0.5%			
	Edwards, Jonathan III	861	0.3%			
	Bohach, Keenan	787	0.3%			
	Hyland, Brett	755	0.2%			
	Tacy, Jack	512	0.2%			
	TOTAL	*313,984*		*TOTAL*	*395,937*	
Congressional District 1	Verbeek, John	21,191	50.6%	Bonamici, Suzanne*	69,774	91.7%
	Griffith, George	17,049	40.7%	Barajas, Ricky	2,945	3.9%
	Miller, Preston	3,228	7.7%	Stansfield, Michael	2,936	3.9%
	Scattered Write-in	402	1.0%	Scattered Write-in	424	0.6%
	TOTAL	*41,870*		*TOTAL*	*76,079*	
Congressional District 2	Walden, Greg*	71,543	77.3%	McLeod-Skinner, Jamie	25,351	42.8%
	Romero, Paul J. Jr.	15,181	16.4%	Neahring, Jennifer "Jenni"	14,020	23.7%
	Pollock, Randy	5,514	6.0%	Crary, James "Jim"	6,774	11.4%
	Scattered Write-in	280	0.3%	White, Timothy	3,469	5.9%
				Mason, Raz	3,137	5.3%
				Burnette, Eric	2,734	4.6%
				Byrne, Michael	2,546	4.3%
				Scattered Write-in	1,173	2.0%
	TOTAL	*92,518*		*TOTAL*	*59,204*	
Congressional District 3	Scattered Write-in	1,470	93.4%	Blumenauer, Earl*	91,226	90.8%
	Harrison, Thomas S. IV (Write-in)	104	6.6%	Lavine, Ben	6,008	6.0%
				Barnett, Charles	1,586	1.6%
				Hafner, Eric	1,377	1.4%
				Scattered Write-in	291	0.3%
	TOTAL	*1,574*		*TOTAL*	*100,488*	
Congressional District 4	Robinson, Art	30,384	45.5%	DeFazio, Peter A.*	78,575	91.4%
	Boice, Court	15,773	23.6%	Arcangel, Daniel	6,672	7.8%
	Perkins, Jo Rae	13,892	20.8%	Scattered Write-in	717	0.8%
	Polen, Michael	3,970	5.9%			
	Strek, Stefan	2,244	3.4%			
	Scattered Write-in	503	0.8%			
	TOTAL	*66,766*		*TOTAL*	*85,964*	
Congressional District 5	Callahan, Mark	33,933	61.9%	Schrader, Kurt*	59,196	86.1%
	Nations, Joey	11,300	20.6%	Wright, Peter	9,002	13.1%
	Reynolds, Robert	9,120	16.6%	Scattered Write-in	549	0.8%
	Scattered Write-in	465	0.8%			
	TOTAL	*54,818*		*TOTAL*	*68,747*	

Note: An asterisk (*) denotes incumbent.

PENNSYLVANIA

Congressional districts first established for elections held in 2018
18 members

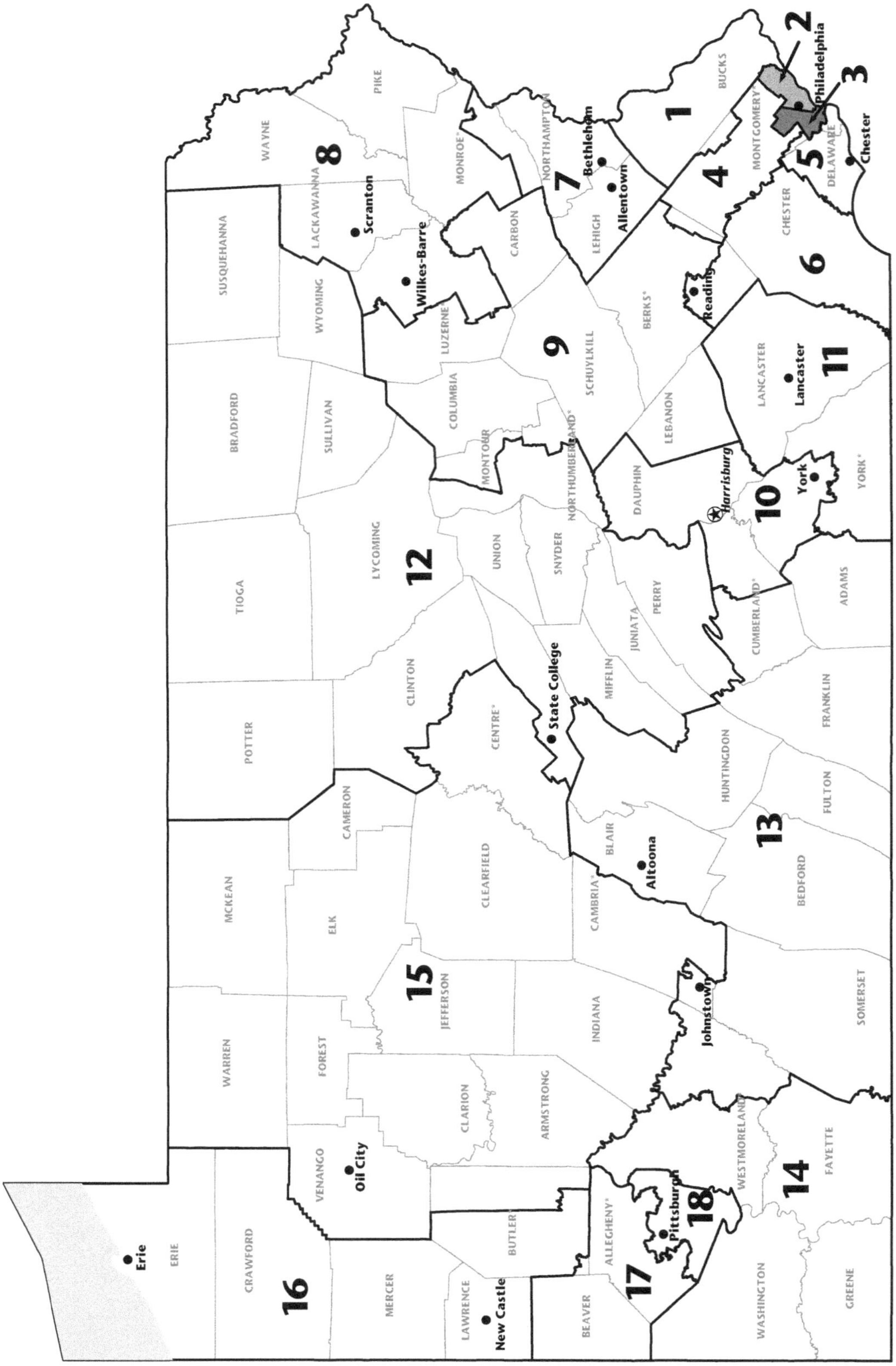

The city of Philadelphia is coextensive with the county of Philadelphia; and includes all of CDs 2 and 3 and a portion ot CD 5.

The city of Pittsburgh is entirely within CD 18.

PENNSYLVANIA

GOVERNOR

Thomas W. Wolf (D). Re-elected 2018 to a four-year term. Previously elected 2014.

SENATORS (1 Republican, 1 Democrat)

Bob Casey Jr. (D). Re-elected 2018 to a six-year term. Previously elected 2012, 2006.

Pat Toomey (R). Re-elected 2016 to a six-year term. Previously elected 2010.

REPRESENTATIVES (9 Republicans, 9 Democrats)

1. Brian K. Fitzpatrick (R)
2. Brendan F. Boyle (D)
3. Dwight Evans (D)
4. Madeleine Dean (D)
5. Mary Gay Scanlon (D)
6. Chrissy Houlahan (D)
7. Susan Wild (D)
8. Matt Cartwright (D)
9. Dan Meuser (R)
10. Scott Perry (R)
11. Lloyd K. Smucker (R)
12. Fred Keller (R)
13. John Joyce (R)
14. Guy Reschenthaler (R)
15. Glenn Thompson (R)
16. Mike Kelly (R)
17. Conor Lamb (D)
18. Mike Doyle (D)

POSTWAR VOTE FOR PRESIDENT

		Republican		Democratic				Percentage			
								Total Vote		Major Vote	
Year	Total Vote	Vote	Candidate	Vote	Candidate	Other Vote	Rep.-Dem. Plurality	Rep.	Dem.	Rep.	Dem.
2016**	6,165,478	2,970,733	Trump, Donald J.	2,926,441	Clinton, Hillary Rodham	268,304	44,292 R	48.2%	47.5%	50.4%	49.6%
2012	5,753,670	2,680,434	Romney, W. Mitt	2,990,274	Obama, Barack H.*	82,962	309,840 D	46.6%	52.0%	47.3%	52.7%
2008	6,013,272	2,655,885	McCain, John S. III	3,276,363	Obama, Barack H.	81,024	620,478 D	44.2%	54.5%	44.8%	55.2%
2004	5,769,590	2,793,847	Bush, George W.*	2,938,095	Kerry, John F.	37,648	144,248 D	48.4%	50.9%	48.7%	51.3%
2000**	4,913,119	2,281,127	Bush, George W.	2,485,967	Gore, Albert Jr.	146,025	204,840 D	46.4%	50.6%	47.9%	52.1%
1996**	4,506,118	1,801,169	Dole, Robert "Bob"	2,215,819	Clinton, Bill*	489,130	414,650 D	40.0%	49.2%	44.8%	55.2%
1992**	4,959,810	1,791,841	Bush, George H.*	2,239,164	Clinton, Bill	928,805	447,323 D	36.1%	45.1%	44.5%	55.5%
1988	4,536,251	2,300,087	Bush, George H.	2,194,944	Dukakis, Michael S.	41,220	105,143 R	50.7%	48.4%	51.2%	48.8%
1984	4,844,903	2,584,323	Reagan, Ronald*	2,228,131	Mondale, Walter F.	32,449	356,192 R	53.3%	46.0%	53.7%	46.3%
1980**	4,561,501	2,261,872	Reagan, Ronald	1,937,540	Carter, Jimmy*	362,089	324,332 R	49.6%	42.5%	53.9%	46.1%
1976	4,620,787	2,205,604	Ford, Gerald R.*	2,328,677	Carter, Jimmy	86,506	123,073 D	47.7%	50.4%	48.6%	51.4%
1972	4,592,106	2,714,521	Nixon, Richard M.*	1,796,951	McGovern, George S.	80,634	917,570 R	59.1%	39.1%	60.2%	39.8%
1968**	4,747,928	2,090,017	Nixon, Richard M.	2,259,405	Humphrey, Hubert Horatio Jr.	398,506	169,388 D	44.0%	47.6%	48.1%	51.9%
1964	4,822,690	1,673,657	Goldwater, Barry M. Sr.	3,130,954	Johnson, Lyndon B.*	18,079	1,457,297 D	34.7%	64.9%	34.8%	65.2%
1960	5,006,541	2,439,956	Nixon, Richard M.	2,556,282	Kennedy, John F.	10,303	116,326 D	48.7%	51.1%	48.8%	51.2%
1956	4,576,503	2,585,252	Eisenhower, Dwight D.*	1,981,769	Stevenson, Adlai E. II	9,482	603,483 R	56.5%	43.3%	56.6%	43.4%
1952	4,580,969	2,415,789	Eisenhower, Dwight D.	2,146,269	Stevenson, Adlai E. II	18,911	269,520 R	52.7%	46.9%	53.0%	47.0%
1948	3,735,348	1,902,197	Dewey, Thomas E.	1,752,426	Truman, Harry S.*	80,725	149,771 R	50.9%	46.9%	52.0%	48.0%

Note: An asterisk (*) denotes incumbent. **In past elections, the other vote included: 2016 - 146,715 Libertarian (Gary Johnson); 2000 - 103,392 Green (Ralph Nader); 1996 - 430,984 Reform (Ross Perot); 1992 - 902,667 Independent (Perot); 1980 - 292,921 Independent (John Anderson); 1968 - 378,582 American Independent (George Wallace).

PENNSYLVANIA

POSTWAR VOTE FOR GOVERNOR

		Republican		Democratic				Percentage			
								Total Vote		Major Vote	
Year	Total Vote	Vote	Candidate	Vote	Candidate	Other Vote	Rep.-Dem. Plurality	Rep.	Dem.	Rep.	Dem.
2018	5,012,555	2,039,882	Wagner, Scott	2,895,652	Wolf, Thomas W.*	77,021	855,770 D	40.7%	57.8%	41.3%	58.7%
2014	3,495,866	1,575,511	Corbett, Tom*	1,920,355	Wolf, Thomas W.		344,844 D	45.1%	54.9%	45.1%	54.9%
2010	3,989,102	2,172,763	Corbett, Tom	1,814,788	Onorato, Dan	1,551	357,975 R	54.5%	45.5%	54.5%	45.5%
2006	4,096,077	1,622,135	Swann, Lynn	2,470,517	Rendell, Edward G.*	3,425	848,382 D	39.6%	60.3%	39.6%	60.4%
2002	3,583,179	1,589,408	Fisher, Mike	1,913,235	Rendell, Edward G.	80,536	323,827 D	44.4%	53.4%	45.4%	54.6%
1998**	3,025,152	1,736,844	Ridge, Thomas J.*	938,745	Itkin, Ivan	349,563	798,099 R	57.4%	31.0%	64.9%	35.1%
1994**	3,588,526	1,627,976	Ridge, Thomas J.	1,433,099	Singel, Mark S.	527,451	194,877 R	45.4%	39.9%	53.2%	46.8%
1990	3,052,760	987,516	Hafer, Barbara	2,065,244	Casey, Robert*		1,077,728 D	32.3%	67.7%	32.3%	67.7%
1986	3,388,275	1,638,268	Scranton, William III	1,717,484	Casey, Robert	32,523	79,216 D	48.4%	50.7%	48.8%	51.2%
1982	3,683,985	1,872,784	Thornburgh, Richard*	1,772,353	Ertel, Allen E.	38,848	100,431 R	50.8%	48.1%	51.4%	48.6%
1978	3,741,969	1,966,042	Thornburgh, Richard	1,737,888	Flaherty, Peter	38,039	228,154 R	52.5%	46.4%	53.1%	46.9%
1974	3,491,234	1,578,917	Lewis, Andrew L.	1,878,252	Shapp, Milton J.*	34,065	299,335 D	45.2%	53.8%	45.7%	54.3%
1970	3,700,060	1,542,854	Broderick, Raymond	2,043,029	Shapp, Milton J.*	114,177	500,175 D	41.7%	55.2%	43.0%	57.0%
1966	4,050,668	2,110,349	Shafer, Raymond P.	1,868,719	Shapp, Milton J.	71,600	241,630 R	52.1%	46.1%	53.0%	47.0%
1962	4,378,042	2,424,918	Scranton, William W.	1,938,627	Dilworth, Richardson	14,497	486,291 R	55.4%	44.3%	55.6%	44.4%
1958	3,986,918	1,948,769	McGonigle, Arthur T.	2,024,852	Lawrence, David L.	13,297	76,083 D	48.9%	50.8%	49.0%	51.0%
1954	3,720,457	1,717,070	Wood, Lloyd H.	1,996,266	Leader, George M.	7,121	279,196 D	46.2%	53.7%	46.2%	53.8%
1950	3,540,059	1,796,119	Fine, John S.	1,710,355	Dilworth, Richardson	33,585	85,764 R	50.7%	48.3%	51.2%	48.8%
1946	3,123,994	1,828,462	Duff, James H.	1,270,947	Rice, John S.	24,585	557,515 R	58.5%	40.7%	59.0%	41.0%

Note: An asterisk (*) denotes incumbent. **In past elections, the other vote included: 1998 - 315,761 Constitutional (Peg Luksik); 1994 - 460,269 Constitutional (Luksik).

POSTWAR VOTE FOR SENATOR

		Republican		Democratic				Percentage			
								Total Vote		Major Vote	
Year	Total Vote	Vote	Candidate	Vote	Candidate	Other Vote	Rep.-Dem. Plurality	Rep.	Dem.	Rep.	Dem.
2018	5,009,400	2,134,848	Barletta, Lou	2,792,437	Casey, Bob Jr.*	82,115	657,589 D	42.6%	55.7%	43.3%	56.7%
2016	6,051,856	2,951,702	Toomey, Pat*	2,865,012	McGinty, Katie A.	235,142	86,690 R	48.8%	47.3%	50.7%	49.3%
2012	5,629,491	2,509,132	Smith, Tom	3,021,364	Casey, Bob Jr.*	98,995	512,232 D	44.6%	53.7%	45.4%	54.6%
2010	3,977,661	2,028,945	Toomey, Pat	1,948,716	Sestak, Joe		80,229 R	51.0%	49.0%	51.0%	49.0%
2006	4,081,043	1,684,778	Santorum, Rick*	2,392,984	Casey, Bob Jr.	3,281	708,206 D	41.3%	58.6%	41.3%	58.7%
2004	5,559,105	2,925,080	Specter, Arlen*	2,334,126	Hoeffel, Joseph M.	299,899	590,954 R	52.6%	42.0%	55.6%	44.4%
2000	4,735,504	2,481,962	Santorum, Rick*	2,154,908	Klink, Ron	98,634	327,054 R	52.4%	45.5%	53.5%	46.5%
1998	2,957,772	1,814,180	Specter, Arlen*	1,028,839	Lloyd, Bill	114,753	785,341 R	61.3%	34.8%	63.8%	36.2%
1994	3,513,361	1,735,691	Santorum, Rick	1,648,481	Wofford, Harris*	129,189	87,210 R	49.4%	46.9%	51.3%	48.7%
1992	4,802,410	2,358,125	Specter, Arlen*	2,224,966	Yeakel, Lynn	219,319	133,159 R	49.1%	46.3%	51.5%	48.5%
1991S**	3,382,746	1,521,986	Thornburgh, Richard	1,860,760	Wofford, Harris*		338,774 D	45.0%	55.0%	45.0%	55.0%
1988	4,366,598	2,901,715	Heinz, Henry John III*	1,416,764	Vignola, Joseph C.	48,119	1,484,951 R	66.5%	32.4%	67.2%	32.8%
1986	3,378,226	1,906,537	Specter, Arlen*	1,448,219	Edgar, Robert W.	23,470	458,318 R	56.4%	42.9%	56.8%	43.2%
1982	3,604,108	2,136,418	Heinz, Henry John III*	1,412,965	Wecht, Cyril H.	54,725	723,453 R	59.3%	39.2%	60.2%	39.8%
1980	4,418,042	2,230,404	Specter, Arlen	2,122,391	Flaherty, Peter	65,247	108,013 R	50.5%	48.0%	51.2%	48.8%
1976	4,546,353	2,381,891	Heinz, Henry John III	2,126,977	Green, William J. III	37,485	254,914 R	52.4%	46.8%	52.8%	47.2%
1974	3,477,812	1,843,317	Schweiker, Richard S.*	1,596,121	Flaherty, Peter	38,374	247,196 R	53.0%	45.9%	53.6%	46.4%
1970	3,644,305	1,874,106	Scott, Hugh*	1,653,774	Sesler, William G.	116,425	220,332 R	51.4%	45.4%	53.1%	46.9%
1968	4,624,218	2,399,762	Schweiker, Richard S.	2,117,662	Clark, Joseph S.*	106,794	282,100 R	51.9%	45.8%	53.1%	46.9%
1964	4,803,835	2,429,858	Scott, Hugh*	2,359,223	Blatt, Genevieve	14,754	70,635 R	50.6%	49.1%	50.7%	49.3%
1962	4,383,475	2,134,649	Van Zandt, James E.	2,238,383	Clark, Joseph S.*	10,443	103,734 D	48.7%	51.1%	48.8%	51.2%
1958	3,988,622	2,042,586	Scott, Hugh	1,929,821	Leader, George M.	16,215	112,765 R	51.2%	48.4%	51.4%	48.6%
1956	4,529,874	2,250,671	Duff, James H.*	2,268,641	Clark, Joseph S.	10,562	17,970 D	49.7%	50.1%	49.8%	50.2%
1952	4,519,761	2,331,034	Martin, Edward*	2,168,546	Bard, Guy Kurtz	20,181	162,488 R	51.6%	48.0%	51.8%	48.2%
1950	3,548,703	1,820,400	Duff, James H.	1,694,076	Myers, Francis J.*	34,227	126,324 R	51.3%	47.7%	51.8%	48.2%
1946	3,127,860	1,853,458	Martin, Edward	1,245,338	Guffey, Joseph F.*	29,064	608,120 R	59.3%	39.8%	59.8%	40.2%

Note: An asterisk (*) denotes incumbent. **The 1991 election was for a short term to fill a vacancy.

PENNSYLVANIA

GOVERNOR 2018

							Percentage			
							Total Vote		Major Vote	
2010 Census Population	County	Total Vote	Republican (Wagner)	Democratic (Wolf)	Other	Rep.-Dem. Plurality	Rep.	Dem.	Rep.	Dem.
101,407	ADAMS	39,053	22,501	15,862	690	6,639 R	57.6%	40.6%	58.7%	41.3%
1,223,348	ALLEGHENY	541,305	168,893	364,710	7,702	195,817 D	31.2%	67.4%	31.7%	68.3%
68,941	ARMSTRONG	24,643	15,373	8,839	431	6,534 R	62.4%	35.9%	63.5%	36.5%
170,539	BEAVER	67,876	30,593	36,166	1,117	5,573 D	45.1%	53.3%	45.8%	54.2%
49,762	BEDFORD	18,863	14,261	4,408	194	9,853 R	75.6%	23.4%	76.4%	23.6%
411,442	BERKS	144,426	65,756	76,136	2,534	10,380 D	45.5%	52.7%	46.3%	53.7%
127,089	BLAIR	43,522	28,175	14,622	725	13,553 R	64.7%	33.6%	65.8%	34.2%
62,622	BRADFORD	20,420	13,068	6,852	500	6,216 R	64.0%	33.6%	65.6%	34.4%
625,249	BUCKS	294,329	117,912	172,302	4,115	54,390 D	40.1%	58.5%	40.6%	59.4%
183,862	BUTLER	79,711	45,242	32,891	1,578	12,351 R	56.8%	41.3%	57.9%	42.1%
143,679	CAMBRIA	49,894	27,530	21,639	725	5,891 R	55.2%	43.4%	56.0%	44.0%
5,085	CAMERON	1,773	1,127	619	27	508 R	63.6%	34.9%	64.5%	35.5%
65,249	CARBON	22,542	12,476	9,659	407	2,817 R	55.3%	42.8%	56.4%	43.6%
153,990	CENTRE	60,678	24,353	34,961	1,364	10,608 D	40.1%	57.6%	41.1%	58.9%
498,886	CHESTER	236,775	87,873	145,212	3,690	57,339 D	37.1%	61.3%	37.7%	62.3%
39,988	CLARION	14,094	8,594	5,191	309	3,403 R	61.0%	36.8%	62.3%	37.7%
81,642	CLEARFIELD	26,892	17,241	9,235	416	8,006 R	64.1%	34.3%	65.1%	34.9%
39,238	CLINTON	12,476	6,727	5,517	232	1,210 R	53.9%	44.2%	54.9%	45.1%
67,295	COLUMBIA	22,638	12,424	9,822	392	2,602 R	54.9%	43.4%	55.8%	44.2%
88,765	CRAWFORD	30,544	17,859	12,137	548	5,722 R	58.5%	39.7%	59.5%	40.5%
235,406	CUMBERLAND	104,478	49,496	52,807	2,175	3,311 D	47.4%	50.5%	48.4%	51.6%
268,100	DAUPHIN	108,549	42,436	64,045	2,068	21,609 D	39.1%	59.0%	39.9%	60.1%
558,979	DELAWARE	250,643	80,576	167,211	2,856	86,635 D	32.1%	66.7%	32.5%	67.5%
31,946	ELK	11,301	6,918	4,206	177	2,712 R	61.2%	37.2%	62.2%	37.8%
280,566	ERIE	101,711	39,387	60,790	1,534	21,403 D	38.7%	59.8%	39.3%	60.7%
136,606	FAYETTE	40,909	20,471	19,791	647	680 R	50.0%	48.4%	50.8%	49.2%
7,716	FOREST	1,938	1,159	746	33	413 R	59.8%	38.5%	60.8%	39.2%
149,618	FRANKLIN	54,922	35,634	18,447	841	17,187 R	64.9%	33.6%	65.9%	34.1%
14,845	FULTON	5,296	4,202	1,037	57	3,165 R	79.3%	19.6%	80.2%	19.8%
38,686	GREENE	12,448	6,381	5,844	223	537 R	51.3%	46.9%	52.2%	47.8%
45,913	HUNTINGDON	15,901	10,586	5,037	278	5,549 R	66.6%	31.7%	67.8%	32.2%
88,880	INDIANA	29,396	16,179	12,715	502	3,464 R	55.0%	43.3%	56.0%	44.0%
45,200	JEFFERSON	15,574	11,036	4,277	261	6,759 R	70.9%	27.5%	72.1%	27.9%
24,636	JUNIATA	8,493	5,780	2,550	163	3,230 R	68.1%	30.0%	69.4%	30.6%
214,437	LACKAWANNA	83,913	28,616	54,237	1,060	25,621 D	34.1%	64.6%	34.5%	65.5%
519,445	LANCASTER	202,224	102,229	96,040	3,955	6,189 R	50.6%	47.5%	51.6%	48.4%
91,108	LAWRENCE	32,241	16,714	15,035	492	1,679 R	51.8%	46.6%	52.6%	47.4%
133,568	LEBANON	49,108	28,096	20,159	853	7,937 R	57.2%	41.1%	58.2%	41.8%
349,497	LEHIGH	128,606	49,071	77,248	2,287	28,177 D	38.2%	60.1%	38.8%	61.2%
320,918	LUZERNE	107,823	50,701	55,734	1,388	5,033 D	47.0%	51.7%	47.6%	52.4%
116,111	LYCOMING	41,025	25,570	14,727	728	10,843 R	62.3%	35.9%	63.5%	36.5%
43,450	MCKEAN	12,593	8,512	3,899	182	4,613 R	67.6%	31.0%	68.6%	31.4%
116,638	MERCER	41,100	22,211	18,200	689	4,011 R	54.0%	44.3%	55.0%	45.0%
46,682	MIFFLIN	13,745	9,408	4,127	210	5,281 R	68.4%	30.0%	69.5%	30.5%
169,842	MONROE	55,437	22,530	32,064	843	9,534 D	40.6%	57.8%	41.3%	58.7%
799,874	MONTGOMERY	381,446	120,206	256,252	4,988	136,046 D	31.5%	67.2%	31.9%	68.1%
18,267	MONTOUR	7,015	3,642	3,228	145	414 R	51.9%	46.0%	53.0%	47.0%
297,735	NORTHAMPTON	115,122	47,527	65,749	1,846	18,222 D	41.3%	57.1%	42.0%	58.0%
94,528	NORTHUMBERLAND	28,821	16,122	12,135	564	3,987 R	55.9%	42.1%	57.1%	42.9%
45,969	PERRY	17,196	10,915	5,905	376	5,010 R	63.5%	34.3%	64.9%	35.1%
1,526,006	PHILADELPHIA	554,175	64,514	484,124	5,537	419,610 D	11.6%	87.4%	11.8%	88.2%
57,369	PIKE	20,800	11,408	9,074	318	2,334 R	54.8%	43.6%	55.7%	44.3%
17,457	POTTER	6,248	4,687	1,452	109	3,235 R	75.0%	23.2%	76.3%	23.7%
148,289	SCHUYLKILL	48,718	26,640	21,179	899	5,461 R	54.7%	43.5%	55.7%	44.3%
39,702	SNYDER	13,332	8,283	4,833	216	3,450 R	62.1%	36.3%	63.2%	36.8%
77,742	SOMERSET	28,728	19,020	9,138	570	9,882 R	66.2%	31.8%	67.5%	32.5%
6,428	SULLIVAN	2,699	1,661	977	61	684 R	61.5%	36.2%	63.0%	37.0%
43,356	SUSQUEHANNA	15,719	10,137	5,273	309	4,864 R	64.5%	33.5%	65.8%	34.2%
41,981	TIOGA	14,778	10,472	3,991	315	6,481 R	70.9%	27.0%	72.4%	27.6%
44,947	UNION	14,396	7,676	6,426	294	1,250 R	53.3%	44.6%	54.4%	45.6%

PENNSYLVANIA

GOVERNOR 2018

2010 Census Population	County	Total Vote	Republican (Wagner)	Democratic (Wolf)	Other	Rep.-Dem. Plurality	Percentage: Total Vote Rep.	Percentage: Total Vote Dem.	Percentage: Major Vote Rep.	Percentage: Major Vote Dem.
54,984	VENANGO	18,625	10,856	7,431	338	3,425 R	58.3%	39.9%	59.4%	40.6%
41,815	WARREN	14,483	8,766	5,447	270	3,319 R	60.5%	37.6%	61.7%	38.3%
207,820	WASHINGTON	82,418	40,662	39,898	1,858	764 R	49.3%	48.4%	50.5%	49.5%
52,822	WAYNE	20,086	11,751	8,023	312	3,728 R	58.5%	39.9%	59.4%	40.6%
365,169	WESTMORELAND	146,295	76,126	67,950	2,219	8,176 R	52.0%	46.4%	52.8%	47.2%
28,276	WYOMING	10,649	6,344	4,101	204	2,243 R	59.6%	38.5%	60.7%	39.3%
434,972	YORK	168,978	90,590	75,313	3,075	15,277 R	53.6%	44.6%	54.6%	45.4%
12,702,379	*TOTAL*	*5,012,555*	*2,039,882*	*2,895,652*	*77,021*	*855,770 D*	*40.7%*	*57.8%*	*41.3%*	*58.7%*

PENNSYLVANIA

SENATOR 2018

2010 Census Population	County	Total Vote	Republican (Barletta)	Democratic (Casey)	Other	Rep.-Dem. Plurality	Percentage: Total Vote Rep.	Percentage: Total Vote Dem.	Percentage: Major Vote Rep.	Percentage: Major Vote Dem.
101,407	ADAMS	39,102	23,419	14,880	803	8,539 R	59.9%	38.1%	61.1%	38.9%
1,223,348	ALLEGHENY	541,703	176,351	355,907	9,445	179,556 D	32.6%	65.7%	33.1%	66.9%
68,941	ARMSTRONG	24,488	15,449	8,570	469	6,879 R	63.1%	35.0%	64.3%	35.7%
170,539	BEAVER	67,642	31,916	34,442	1,284	2,526 D	47.2%	50.9%	48.1%	51.9%
49,762	BEDFORD	18,823	14,044	4,567	212	9,477 R	74.6%	24.3%	75.5%	24.5%
411,442	BERKS	144,533	68,159	73,714	2,660	5,555 D	47.2%	51.0%	48.0%	52.0%
127,089	BLAIR	43,165	27,826	14,599	740	13,227 R	64.5%	33.8%	65.6%	34.4%
62,622	BRADFORD	20,328	13,032	6,926	370	6,106 R	64.1%	34.1%	65.3%	34.7%
625,249	BUCKS	294,317	124,133	165,408	4,776	41,275 D	42.2%	56.2%	42.9%	57.1%
183,862	BUTLER	79,495	46,875	31,010	1,610	15,865 R	59.0%	39.0%	60.2%	39.8%
143,679	CAMBRIA	49,607	27,367	21,590	650	5,777 R	55.2%	43.5%	55.9%	44.1%
5,085	CAMERON	1,765	1,080	653	32	427 R	61.2%	37.0%	62.3%	37.7%
65,249	CARBON	22,574	13,519	8,739	316	4,780 R	59.9%	38.7%	60.7%	39.3%
153,990	CENTRE	60,664	24,332	34,778	1,554	10,446 D	40.1%	57.3%	41.2%	58.8%
498,886	CHESTER	236,718	92,380	140,138	4,200	47,758 D	39.0%	59.2%	39.7%	60.3%
39,988	CLARION	14,031	8,838	4,924	269	3,914 R	63.0%	35.1%	64.2%	35.8%
81,642	CLEARFIELD	26,803	16,852	9,540	411	7,312 R	62.9%	35.6%	63.9%	36.1%
39,238	CLINTON	12,378	6,869	5,289	220	1,580 R	55.5%	42.7%	56.5%	43.5%
67,295	COLUMBIA	22,638	13,437	8,837	364	4,600 R	59.4%	39.0%	60.3%	39.7%
88,765	CRAWFORD	30,035	17,813	11,720	502	6,093 R	59.3%	39.0%	60.3%	39.7%
235,406	CUMBERLAND	104,400	54,525	47,738	2,137	6,787 R	52.2%	45.7%	53.3%	46.7%
268,100	DAUPHIN	108,708	47,152	59,533	2,023	12,381 D	43.4%	54.8%	44.2%	55.8%
558,979	DELAWARE	251,002	84,423	163,216	3,363	78,793 D	33.6%	65.0%	34.1%	65.9%
31,946	ELK	11,282	6,610	4,498	174	2,112 R	58.6%	39.9%	59.5%	40.5%
280,566	ERIE	100,889	40,348	58,906	1,635	18,558 D	40.0%	58.4%	40.7%	59.3%
136,606	FAYETTE	40,705	20,514	19,563	628	951 R	50.4%	48.1%	51.2%	48.8%
7,716	FOREST	1,932	1,201	693	38	508 R	62.2%	35.9%	63.4%	36.6%
149,618	FRANKLIN	55,027	36,735	17,385	907	19,350 R	66.8%	31.6%	67.9%	32.1%
14,845	FULTON	5,304	4,173	1,061	70	3,112 R	78.7%	20.0%	79.7%	20.3%
38,686	GREENE	12,428	6,422	5,819	187	603 R	51.7%	46.8%	52.5%	47.5%
45,913	HUNTINGDON	15,911	10,491	5,126	294	5,365 R	65.9%	32.2%	67.2%	32.8%
88,880	INDIANA	29,543	16,314	12,702	527	3,612 R	55.2%	43.0%	56.2%	43.8%
45,200	JEFFERSON	15,576	10,872	4,437	267	6,435 R	69.8%	28.5%	71.0%	29.0%
24,636	JUNIATA	8,468	5,853	2,412	203	3,441 R	69.1%	28.5%	70.8%	29.2%
214,437	LACKAWANNA	84,256	31,922	51,444	890	19,522 D	37.9%	61.1%	38.3%	61.7%

PENNSYLVANIA

SENATOR 2018

2010 Census Population	County	Total Vote	Republican (Barletta)	Democratic (Casey)	Other	Rep.-Dem. Plurality	Percentage Total Vote Rep.	Total Vote Dem.	Major Vote Rep.	Major Vote Dem.
519,445	LANCASTER	202,364	107,454	90,521	4,389	16,933 R	53.1%	44.7%	54.3%	45.7%
91,108	LAWRENCE	32,147	17,375	14,324	448	3,051 R	54.0%	44.6%	54.8%	45.2%
133,568	LEBANON	49,149	29,836	18,368	945	11,468 R	60.7%	37.4%	61.9%	38.1%
349,497	LEHIGH	128,438	52,576	73,632	2,230	21,056 D	40.9%	57.3%	41.7%	58.3%
320,918	LUZERNE	108,296	58,040	49,200	1,056	8,840 R	53.6%	45.4%	54.1%	45.9%
116,111	LYCOMING	41,080	26,488	13,893	699	12,595 R	64.5%	33.8%	65.6%	34.4%
43,450	MCKEAN	12,454	8,285	3,972	197	4,313 R	66.5%	31.9%	67.6%	32.4%
116,638	MERCER	41,097	22,290	18,136	671	4,154 R	54.2%	44.1%	55.1%	44.9%
46,682	MIFFLIN	13,752	9,564	3,934	254	5,630 R	69.5%	28.6%	70.9%	29.1%
169,842	MONROE	55,412	23,968	30,626	818	6,658 D	43.3%	55.3%	43.9%	56.1%
799,874	MONTGOMERY	380,865	126,666	248,454	5,745	121,788 D	33.3%	65.2%	33.8%	66.2%
18,267	MONTOUR	7,034	3,943	2,966	125	977 R	56.1%	42.2%	57.1%	42.9%
297,735	NORTHAMPTON	114,616	50,385	62,275	1,956	11,890 D	44.0%	54.3%	44.7%	55.3%
94,528	NORTHUMBERLAND	28,875	17,926	10,524	425	7,402 R	62.1%	36.4%	63.0%	37.0%
45,969	PERRY	17,178	11,607	5,186	385	6,421 R	67.6%	30.2%	69.1%	30.9%
1,526,006	PHILADELPHIA	554,507	66,653	481,467	6,387	414,814 D	12.0%	86.8%	12.2%	87.8%
57,369	PIKE	20,794	11,772	8,696	326	3,076 R	56.6%	41.8%	57.5%	42.5%
17,457	POTTER	6,202	4,564	1,537	101	3,027 R	73.6%	24.8%	74.8%	25.2%
148,289	SCHUYLKILL	48,842	30,452	17,691	699	12,761 R	62.3%	36.2%	63.3%	36.7%
39,702	SNYDER	13,393	8,826	4,322	245	4,504 R	65.9%	32.3%	67.1%	32.9%
77,742	SOMERSET	28,637	18,896	9,322	419	9,574 R	66.0%	32.6%	67.0%	33.0%
6,428	SULLIVAN	2,730	1,720	962	48	758 R	63.0%	35.2%	64.1%	35.9%
43,356	SUSQUEHANNA	15,916	10,112	5,521	283	4,591 R	63.5%	34.7%	64.7%	35.3%
41,981	TIOGA	14,704	10,242	4,145	317	6,097 R	69.7%	28.2%	71.2%	28.8%
44,947	UNION	14,441	8,317	5,901	223	2,416 R	57.6%	40.9%	58.5%	41.5%
54,984	VENANGO	18,512	11,210	6,945	357	4,265 R	60.6%	37.5%	61.7%	38.3%
41,815	WARREN	14,369	8,734	5,390	245	3,344 R	60.8%	37.5%	61.8%	38.2%
207,820	WASHINGTON	82,496	41,958	39,220	1,318	2,738 R	50.9%	47.5%	51.7%	48.3%
52,822	WAYNE	20,162	12,269	7,625	268	4,644 R	60.9%	37.8%	61.7%	38.3%
365,169	WESTMORELAND	145,258	79,078	63,778	2,402	15,300 R	54.4%	43.9%	55.4%	44.6%
28,276	WYOMING	10,628	6,582	3,868	178	2,714 R	61.9%	36.4%	63.0%	37.0%
434,972	YORK	168,812	95,814	69,272	3,726	26,542 R	56.8%	41.0%	58.0%	42.0%
12,702,379	*TOTAL*	*5,009,400*	*2,134,848*	*2,792,437*	*82,115*	*657,589 D*	*42.6%*	*55.7%*	*43.3%*	*56.7%*

PENNSYLVANIA

HOUSE OF REPRESENTATIVES

CD	Year	Total Vote	Republican Vote	Republican Candidate	Democratic Vote	Democratic Candidate	Other Vote	Rep.-Dem. Plurality	Percentage Total Vote Rep.	Total Vote Dem.	Major Vote Rep.	Major Vote Dem.
1**	2018	329,798	169,053	FITZPATRICK, BRIAN K.*	160,745	WALLACE, SCOTT		8,308 R	51.3%	48.7%	51.3%	48.7%
1	2016	299,010	53,219	WILLIAMS, DEBORAH L.	245,791	BRADY, ROBERT A.*		192,572 D	17.8%	82.2%	17.8%	82.2%
1	2014	158,441	27,193	RATH, MEGAN ANN	131,248	BRADY, ROBERT A.*		104,055 D	17.2%	82.8%	17.2%	82.8%
1	2012	277,102	41,708	FEATHERMAN, JOHN J.	235,394	BRADY, ROBERT A.*		193,686 D	15.1%	84.9%	15.1%	84.9%
2**	2018	201,982	42,382	TORRES, DAVID	159,600	BOYLE, BRENDAN F.*		117,218 D	21.0%	79.0%	21.0%	79.0%
2	2016	357,645	35,131	JONES, JAMES A.	322,514	EVANS, DWIGHT		287,383 D	9.8%	90.2%	9.8%	90.2%
2	2014	206,538	25,397	JAMES, ARMOND	181,141	FATTAH, CHAKA*		155,744 D	12.3%	87.7%	12.3%	87.7%
2	2012	356,386	33,381	MANSFIELD, ROBERT	318,176	FATTAH, CHAKA*	4,829	284,795 D	9.4%	89.3%	9.5%	90.5%
3**	2018	307,997	20,387	LEIB, BRYAN	287,610	EVANS, DWIGHT*		267,223 D	6.6%	93.4%	6.6%	93.4%
3	2016	244,893	244,893	KELLY, MIKE*				244,893 R	100.0%		100.0%	
3	2014	187,790	113,859	KELLY, MIKE*	73,931	LAVALLEE, DANIEL		39,928 R	60.6%	39.4%	60.6%	39.4%
3	2012	302,514	165,826	KELLY, MIKE*	123,933	EATON, MISSA	12,755	41,893 R	54.8%	41.0%	57.2%	42.8%

PENNSYLVANIA

HOUSE OF REPRESENTATIVES

			Republican		Democratic				Percentage			
									Total Vote		Major Vote	
CD	Year	Total Vote	Vote	Candidate	Vote	Candidate	Other Vote	Rep.-Dem. Plurality	Rep.	Dem.	Rep.	Dem.
4**	2018	332,991	121,467	DAVID, DANIEL "DAN"	211,524	DEAN, MADELEINE		90,057 D	36.5%	63.5%	36.5%	63.5%
4	2016	334,000	220,628	PERRY, SCOTT*	113,372	BURKHOLDER, JOSHUA T.		107,256 R	66.1%	33.9%	66.1%	33.9%
4	2014	197,340	147,090	PERRY, SCOTT*	50,250	THOMPSON, LINDA DELIAH		96,840 R	74.5%	25.5%	74.5%	25.5%
4	2012	303,980	181,603	PERRY, SCOTT	104,643	PERKINSON, HARRY	17,734	76,960 R	59.7%	34.4%	63.4%	36.6%
5**	2018	304,714	106,075	KIM, PEARL	198,639	SCANLON, MARY GAY		92,564 D	34.8%	65.2%	34.8%	65.2%
5	2016	307,843	206,761	THOMPSON, GLENN*	101,082	TAYLOR, KERITH STRANO		105,679 R	67.2%	32.8%	67.2%	32.8%
5	2014	180,857	115,018	THOMPSON, GLENN*	65,839	TAYLOR, KERITH STRANO		49,179 R	63.6%	36.4%	63.6%	36.4%
5	2012	282,465	177,740	THOMPSON, GLENN*	104,725	DUMAS, CHARLES		73,015 R	62.9%	37.1%	62.9%	37.1%
6**	2018	301,828	124,124	MCCAULEY, GREG	177,704	HOULAHAN, CHRISSY		53,580 D	41.1%	58.9%	41.1%	58.9%
6	2016	362,469	207,469	COSTELLO, RYAN A.*	155,000	PARRISH, MICHAEL D.		52,469 R	57.2%	42.8%	57.2%	42.8%
6	2014	212,544	119,643	COSTELLO, RYAN A.	92,901	TRIVEDI, MANAN		26,742 R	56.3%	43.7%	56.3%	43.7%
6	2012	335,528	191,725	GERLACH, JAMES W.*	143,803	TRIVEDI, MANAN		47,922 R	57.1%	42.9%	57.1%	42.9%
7**	2018	263,261	114,437	NOTHSTEIN, MARTY	140,813	WILD, SUSAN	8,011	26,376 D	43.5%	53.5%	44.8%	55.2%
7	2016	379,502	225,678	MEEHAN, PATRICK*	153,824	BALCHUNIS, MARY ELLEN		71,854 R	59.5%	40.5%	59.5%	40.5%
7	2014	235,125	145,869	MEEHAN, PATRICK*	89,256	BALCHUNIS, MARY ELLEN		56,613 R	62.0%	38.0%	62.0%	38.0%
7	2012	353,451	209,942	MEEHAN, PATRICK*	143,509	BADEY, GEORGE		66,433 R	59.4%	40.6%	59.4%	40.6%
8**	2018	248,166	112,563	CHRIN, JOHN	135,603	CARTWRIGHT, MATT*		23,040 D	45.4%	54.6%	45.4%	54.6%
8	2016	380,818	207,263	FITZPATRICK, BRIAN K.	173,555	SANTARSIERO, STEVEN J.		33,708 R	54.4%	45.6%	54.4%	45.6%
8	2014	222,498	137,731	FITZPATRICK, MICHAEL G.*	84,767	STROUSE, KEVIN		52,964 R	61.9%	38.1%	61.9%	38.1%
8	2012	352,238	199,379	FITZPATRICK, MICHAEL G.*	152,859	BOOCKVAR, KATHY		46,520 R	56.6%	43.4%	56.6%	43.4%
9**	2018	248,927	148,723	MEUSER, DAN	100,204	WOLFF, DENNY		48,519 R	59.7%	40.3%	59.7%	40.3%
9	2016	294,565	186,580	SHUSTER, BILL*	107,985	HALVORSON, ARTHUR		78,595 R	63.3%	36.7%	63.3%	36.7%
9	2014	173,317	110,094	SHUSTER, BILL*	63,223	HARTZOK, ALANNA K.		46,871 R	63.5%	36.5%	63.5%	36.5%
9	2012	274,305	169,177	SHUSTER, BILL*	105,128	RAMSBURG, KAREN		64,049 R	61.7%	38.3%	61.7%	38.3%
10**	2018	291,033	149,365	PERRY, SCOTT*	141,668	SCOTT, GEORGE		7,697 R	51.3%	48.7%	51.3%	48.7%
10	2016	301,105	211,282	MARINO, THOMAS A.*	89,823	MOLESEVICH, MICHAEL M.		121,459 R	70.2%	29.8%	70.2%	29.8%
10	2014	180,322	112,851	MARINO, THOMAS A.*	44,737	BRION, SCOTT F.	22,734	68,114 R	62.6%	24.8%	71.6%	28.4%
10	2012	273,790	179,563	MARINO, THOMAS A.*	94,227	SCOLLO, PHILLIP		85,336 R	65.6%	34.4%	65.6%	34.4%
11**	2018	277,584	163,708	SMUCKER, LLOYD K.*	113,876	KING, JESSICA		49,832 R	59.0%	41.0%	59.0%	41.0%
11	2016	313,221	199,421	BARLETTA, LOU*	113,800	MARSICANO, MICHAEL PAUL		85,621 R	63.7%	36.3%	63.7%	36.3%
11	2014	184,692	122,464	BARLETTA, LOU*	62,228	OSTROWSKI, ANDY J.		60,236 R	66.3%	33.7%	66.3%	33.7%
11	2012	285,198	166,967	BARLETTA, LOU*	118,231	STILP, GENE		48,736 R	58.5%	41.5%	58.5%	41.5%
12**	2018	243,872	161,047	MARINO, THOMAS A.*	82,825	FRIEDENBERG, MARC		78,222 R	66.0%	34.0%	66.0%	34.0%
12	2016	359,204	221,851	ROTHFUS, KEITH*	137,353	MCCLELLAND, ERIN		84,498 R	61.8%	38.2%	61.8%	38.2%
12	2014	215,921	127,993	ROTHFUS, KEITH*	87,928	MCCLELLAND, ERIN		40,065 R	59.3%	40.7%	59.3%	40.7%
12	2012	338,941	175,352	ROTHFUS, KEITH	163,589	CRITZ, MARK S.*		11,763 R	51.7%	48.3%	51.7%	48.3%
13**	2018	253,266	178,533	JOYCE, JOHN	74,733	OTTAWAY, BRENT		103,800 R	70.5%	29.5%	70.5%	29.5%
13	2016	239,316			239,316	BOYLE, BRENDAN F.*		239,316 D		100.0%		100.0%
13	2014	184,150	60,549	ADCOCK, CARSON DEE	123,601	BOYLE, BRENDAN F.		63,052 D	32.9%	67.1%	32.9%	67.1%
13	2012	303,819	93,918	ROONEY, JOE	209,901	SCHWARTZ, ALLYSON Y.*		115,983 D	30.9%	69.1%	30.9%	69.1%
14**	2018	261,437	151,386	RESCHENTHALER, GUY	110,051	BOERIO, BIBIANA		41,335 R	57.9%	42.1%	57.9%	42.1%
14	2016	343,292	87,999	MCALLISTER, LEONARD FRANCIS JR.	255,293	DOYLE, MIKE*		167,294 D	25.6%	74.4%	25.6%	74.4%
14	2014	148,351			148,351	DOYLE, MIKE*		148,351 D		100.0%		100.0%
14	2012	327,634	75,702	LESSMANN, HANS	251,932	DOYLE, MIKE*		176,230 D	23.1%	76.9%	23.1%	76.9%
15**	2018	243,572	165,245	THOMPSON, GLENN*	78,327	BOSER, SUSAN		86,918 R	67.8%	32.2%	67.8%	32.2%
15	2016	326,474	190,618	DENT, CHARLIE W.*	124,129	DAUGHERTY, RICK	11,727	66,489 R	58.4%	38.0%	60.6%	39.4%
15	2014	128,285	128,285	DENT, CHARLIE W.*				128,285 R	100.0%		100.0%	
15	2012	297,724	168,960	DENT, CHARLIE W.*	128,764	DAUGHERTY, RICK		40,196 R	56.8%	43.2%	56.8%	43.2%
16**	2018	262,396	135,348	KELLY, MIKE*	124,109	DINICOLA, RONALD	2,939	11,239 R	51.6%	47.3%	52.2%	47.8%
16	2016	313,773	168,669	SMUCKER, LLOYD K.	134,586	HARTMAN, CHRISTINA M.	10,518	34,083 R	53.8%	42.9%	55.6%	44.4%
16	2014	176,235	101,722	PITTS, JOSEPH R.*	74,513	HOUGHTON, THOMAS D.		27,209 R	57.7%	42.3%	57.7%	42.3%
16	2012	284,781	156,192	PITTS, JOSEPH R.*	111,185	STRADER, ARYANNA	17,404	45,007 R	54.8%	39.0%	58.4%	41.6%
17**	2018	325,579	142,417	ROTHFUS, KEITH*	183,162	LAMB, CONOR*		40,745 D	43.7%	56.3%	43.7%	56.3%
17	2016	293,164	135,430	CONNOLLY, MATTHEW DONALD "MATT"	157,734	CARTWRIGHT, MATT*		22,304 D	46.2%	53.8%	46.2%	53.8%
17	2014	165,051	71,371	MOYLAN III, DAVID J.	93,680	CARTWRIGHT, MATT*		22,309 D	43.2%	56.8%	43.2%	56.8%
17	2012	267,601	106,208	CUMMINGS, LAUREEN	161,393	CARTWRIGHT, MATT		55,185 D	39.7%	60.3%	39.7%	60.3%

PENNSYLVANIA

HOUSE OF REPRESENTATIVES

			Republican		Democratic				Percentage			
									Total Vote		Major Vote	
CD	Year	Total Vote	Vote	Candidate	Vote	Candidate	Other Vote	Rep.-Dem. Plurality	Rep.	Dem.	Rep.	Dem.
18**	2018	231,472			231,472	DOYLE, MIKE*		231,472 D		100.0%		100.0%
18	2016	293,684	293,684	MURPHY, TIMOTHY*				293,684 R	100.0%		100.0%	
18	2014	166,076	166,076	MURPHY, TIMOTHY*				166,076 R	100.0%		100.0%	
18	2012	338,873	216,727	MURPHY, TIMOTHY*	122,146	MAGGI, LARRY		94,581 R	64.0%	36.0%	64.0%	36.0%
TOTAL	*2018*	*4,929,875*	*2,206,260*		*2,712,665*		*10,950*	*506,405 D*	*44.8%*	*55.0%*	*44.9%*	*55.1%*
TOTAL	*2016*	*5,743,978*	*3,096,576*		*2,625,157*		*22,245*	*471,419 R*	*53.9%*	*45.7%*	*54.1%*	*45.9%*
TOTAL	*2014*	*3,323,533*	*1,833,205*		*1,467,594*		*22,734*	*365,611 R*	*55.2%*	*44.2%*	*55.5%*	*44.5%*
TOTAL	*2012*	*5,556,330*	*2,710,070*		*2,793,538*		*52,722*	*83,468 D*	*48.8%*	*50.3%*	*49.2%*	*50.8%*

Note: An asterisk (*) denotes incumbent. **Due to court-ordered redistricting, boundaries for all districts are not comparable to those used in the 2012, 2014, and 2016 races. Incumbents in their newly drawn districts are indicated.

PENNSYLVANIA

GENERAL AND PRIMARY ELECTIONS

2018 GENERAL ELECTIONS: OTHER VOTES

Governor	Other vote was 49,229 Libertarian (Ken Krawchuk), 27,792 Green (Paul Glover)
Senate	Other vote was 50,907 Libertarian (Dale Kerns), 31,208 Green (Neal Gale)
House	Other vote was:
CD 7	8,011 Libertarian (Tim Silfies)
CD 16	2,939 Libertarian (Ebert Beeman)

2018 PRIMARY ELECTIONS: SUPPLEMENTARY INFORMATION

Primary	May 15, 2018	**Registration** (as of May 15, 2018)	8,460,068	Democratic	4,042,928
				Republican	3,227,611
				Libertarian	44,399
				Green	11,548
				Other	1,133,582

Primary Type Closed—Only registered Democrats and Republicans could vote in their party's primary.

	REPUBLICAN PRIMARIES			DEMOCRATIC PRIMARIES		
Senator	Barletta, Lou	433,312	63.0%	Casey, Bob Jr.*	752,008	100.0%
	Christiana, James "Jim" III	254,118	37.0%			
	TOTAL	*687,430*		*TOTAL*	*752,008*	
Governor	Wagner, Scott	326,612	44.3%	Wolf, Thomas W.*	749,812	100.0%
	Mango, Paul	271,857	36.9%			
	Ellsworth, Laura	138,843	18.8%			
	TOTAL	*737,312*		*TOTAL*	*749,812*	

PENNSYLVANIA

GENERAL AND PRIMARY ELECTIONS

	REPUBLICAN PRIMARIES			DEMOCRATIC PRIMARIES		
Congressional District 1	Fitzpatrick, Brian K.*	31,394	67.0%	Wallace, Scott	27,676	56.5%
	Malik, Dean	15,461	33.0%	Reddick, Rachel	17,313	35.3%
				Bacher, Steve	4,014	8.2%
	TOTAL	*46,855*		*TOTAL*	*49,003*	
Congressional District 2	Torres, David	7,523	100.0%	Boyle, Brendan F.*	23,641	64.6%
				Lawrence, Michele	12,974	35.4%
	TOTAL	*7,523*		*TOTAL*	*36,615*	
Congressional District 3	Leib, Bryan	3,430	100.0%	Evans, Dwight*	73,800	80.8%
				Johnson, Kevin	17,548	19.2%
	TOTAL	*3,430*		*TOTAL*	*91,348*	
Congressional District 4	David, Daniel "Dan"	29,032	100.0%	Dean, Madeleine	42,749	72.6%
				Goodman, Shira	9,714	16.5%
				Hoeffel, Joseph M.	6,456	11.0%
	TOTAL	*29,032*		*TOTAL*	*58,919*	
Congressional District 5	Kim, Pearl	34,352	100.0%	Scanlon, Mary Gay	17,220	28.4%
				Lunkenheimer, Ashley	9,291	15.3%
				Lazer, Richard "Rich"	9,095	15.0%
				Sheehan, Molly	6,216	10.2%
				Vitali, Greg	5,726	9.4%
				Li, Lindy	4,236	7.0%
				Wright, Theresa	3,149	5.2%
				Kirkland, Thaddeus	2,420	4.0%
				Davidson, Margo	2,413	4.0%
				Arata, Larry III	925	1.5%
	TOTAL	*34,352*		*TOTAL*	*60,691*	
Congressional District 6	McCauley, Greg	32,375	100.0%	Houlahan, Chrissy	35,636	100.0%
	TOTAL	*32,375*		*TOTAL*	*35,636*	
Congressional District 7	Nothstein, Marty	16,241	50.5%	Wild, Susan	15,262	33.5%
	Browning, Dean	15,923	49.5%	Morganelli, John	13,754	30.1%
				Edwards, Greg	11,602	25.4%
				Ruggles, Roger	2,467	5.4%
				Daugherty, Rick	1,760	3.9%
				Clark, David	777	1.7%
	TOTAL	*32,164*		*TOTAL*	*45,622*	
Congressional District 8	Chrin, John	15,221	48.5%	Cartwright, Matt*	36,189	100.0%
	Peters, Joe	10,951	34.9%			
	Kuniegel, Robert	5,233	16.7%			
	TOTAL	*31,405*		*TOTAL*	*36,189*	
Congressional District 9	Meuser, Dan	26,866	52.9%	Wolff, Denny	11,205	40.5%
	Halcovage, George	12,162	24.0%	Wegman, Gary	8,647	31.3%
	Uehlinger, Scott	11,721	23.1%	Quick, Laura	7,782	28.2%
	TOTAL	*50,749*		*TOTAL*	*27,634*	
Congressional District 10	Perry, Scott*	57,504	100.0%	Scott, George	13,977	36.3%
				Corbin-Johnson, Shavonnia	13,413	34.9%
				Ding, Eric	6,921	18.0%
				Howe, Alan	4,160	10.8%
	TOTAL	*57,504*		*TOTAL*	*38,471*	
Congressional District 11	Smucker, Lloyd K.*	34,232	58.5%	King, Jessica	22,892	100.0%
	Beiler, Chester Omar "Chet"	24,241	41.5%			
	TOTAL	*58,473*		*TOTAL*	*22,892*	
Congressional District 12	Marino, Thomas A.*	39,967	67.0%	Friedenberg, Marc	12,802	50.4%
	McLinko, Doug	19,662	33.0%	Herschel, Judith "Judy"	12,606	49.6%
	TOTAL	*59,629*		*TOTAL*	*25,408*	

PENNSYLVANIA

GENERAL AND PRIMARY ELECTIONS

	REPUBLICAN PRIMARIES			DEMOCRATIC PRIMARIES		
Congressional District 13	Joyce, John	14,828	22.0%	Ottaway, Brent	21,362	100.0%
	Eichelberger, John	13,311	19.8%			
	Bloom, Stephen	12,231	18.2%			
	Mastriano, Douglas	10,509	15.6%			
	Halvorson, Arthur L. "Art"	10,323	15.3%			
	Schooley, Travis	3,036	4.5%			
	Washabaugh, Bernard	1,913	2.8%			
	Hornberger, Benjamin Dayton	1,195	1.8%			
	TOTAL	*67,346*		*TOTAL*	*21,362*	
Congressional District 14	Reschenthaler, Guy	23,737	55.2%	Boerio, Bibiana	18,308	43.2%
	Saccone, Rick	19,274	44.8%	Sedlock, Adam	10,119	23.9%
				Solomon, Robert	8,068	19.0%
				Prigg, Tom	5,888	13.9%
	TOTAL	*43,011*		*TOTAL*	*42,383*	
Congressional District 15	Thompson, Glenn*	45,322	100.0%	Boser, Susan	20,411	74.6%
				Jodun, Wade	6,965	25.4%
	TOTAL	*45,322*		*TOTAL*	*27,376*	
Congressional District 16	Kelly, Mike*	39,412	100.0%	DiNicola, Ronald	23,480	60.0%
				Rieger, Chris	9,758	24.9%
				Multari, Robert	5,914	15.1%
	TOTAL	*39,412*		*TOTAL*	*39,152*	
Congressional District 17	Rothfus, Keith*	38,513	100.0%	Lamb, Conor*	52,590	100.0%
	TOTAL	*38,513*		*TOTAL*	*52,590*	
Congressional District 18				Doyle, Mike*	52,080	75.9%
				Brooks, Janis C.	16,549	24.1%
				TOTAL	*68,629*	

Note: An asterisk (*) denotes incumbent.

RHODE ISLAND

Congressional districts first established for elections held in 2012

2 members

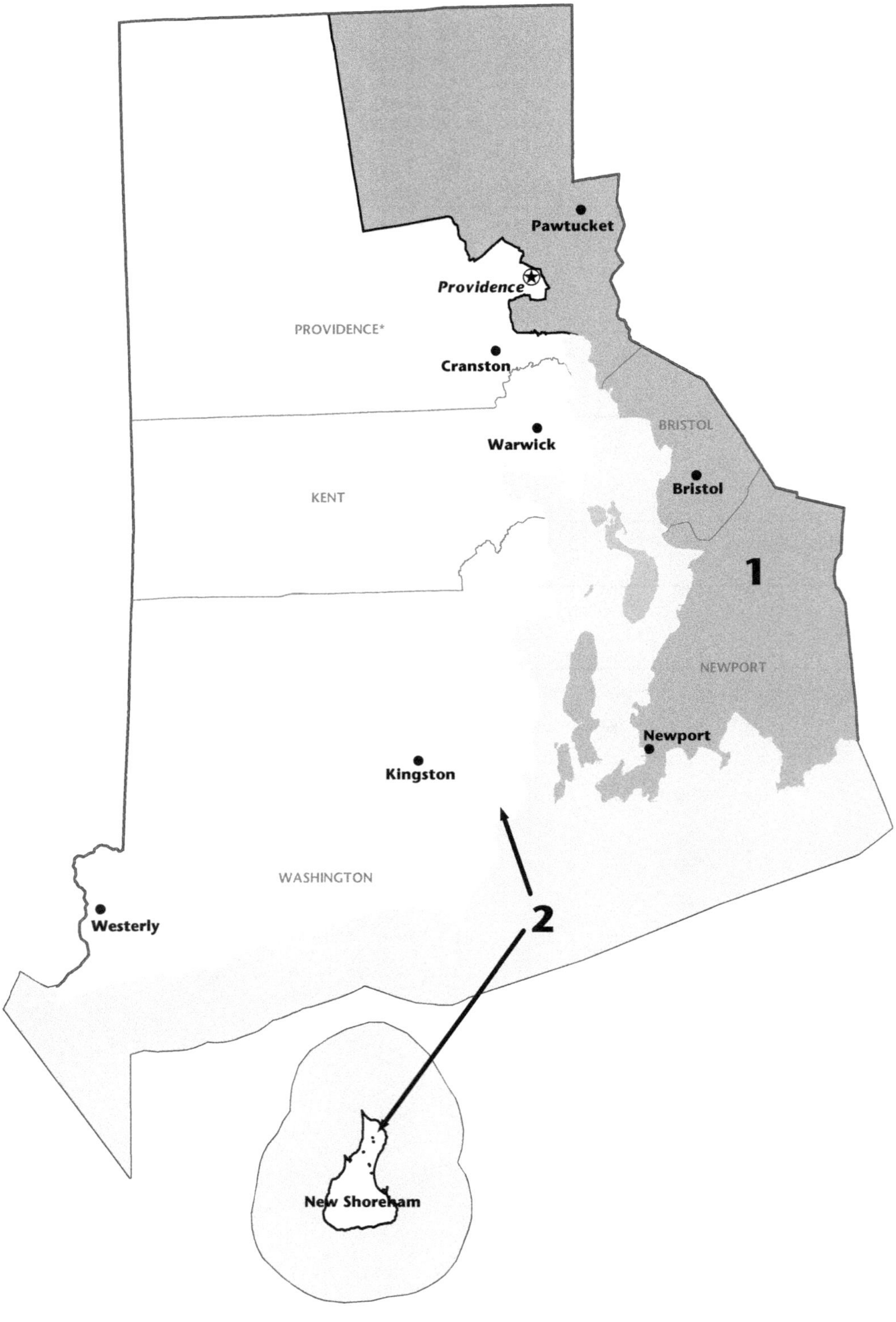

* Asterisk indicates a county whose boundaries include parts of two or more congressional districts.

RHODE ISLAND

GOVERNOR

Gina Raimondo (D). Re-elected 2018 to a four-year term. Previously elected 2014.

SENATORS (2 Democrats)

Jack F. Reed (D). Re-elected 2014 to a six-year term. Previously elected 2008, 2002, 1996.

Sheldon Whitehouse (D). Re-elected 2018 to a six-year term. Previously elected 2012, 2006.

REPRESENTATIVES (2 Democrats)

1. David N. Cicilline (D)
2. James R. Langevin (D)

POSTWAR VOTE FOR PRESIDENT

		Republican		Democratic				Percentage			
								Total Vote		Major Vote	
Year	Total Vote	Vote	Candidate	Vote	Candidate	Other Vote	Rep.-Dem. Plurality	Rep.	Dem.	Rep.	Dem.
2016**	464,144	180,543	Trump, Donald J.	252,525	Clinton, Hillary Rodham	31,076	71,982 D	38.9%	54.4%	41.7%	58.3%
2012	446,049	157,204	Romney, W. Mitt	279,677	Obama, Barack H.*	9,168	122,473 D	35.2%	62.7%	36.0%	64.0%
2008	471,766	165,391	McCain, John S. III	296,571	Obama, Barack H.	9,804	131,180 D	35.1%	62.9%	35.8%	64.2%
2004	437,134	169,046	Bush, George W.*	259,760	Kerry, John F.	8,328	90,714 D	38.7%	59.4%	39.4%	60.6%
2000**	409,047	130,555	Bush, George W.	249,508	Gore, Albert Jr.	28,984	118,953 D	31.9%	61.0%	34.4%	65.6%
1996**	390,284	104,683	Dole, Robert "Bob"	233,050	Clinton, Bill*	52,551	128,367 D	26.8%	59.7%	31.0%	69.0%
1992**	453,477	131,601	Bush, George H.*	213,299	Clinton, Bill	108,577	81,698 D	29.0%	47.0%	38.2%	61.8%
1988	404,620	177,761	Bush, George H.	225,123	Dukakis, Michael S.	1,736	47,362 D	43.9%	55.6%	44.1%	55.9%
1984	410,492	212,080	Reagan, Ronald*	197,106	Mondale, Walter F.	1,306	14,974 R	51.7%	48.0%	51.8%	48.2%
1980**	416,072	154,793	Reagan, Ronald	198,342	Carter, Jimmy*	62,937	43,549 D	37.2%	47.7%	43.8%	56.2%
1976	411,170	181,249	Ford, Gerald R.*	227,636	Carter, Jimmy	2,285	46,387 D	44.1%	55.4%	44.3%	55.7%
1972	415,808	220,383	Nixon, Richard M.*	194,645	McGovern, George S.	780	25,738 R	53.0%	46.8%	53.1%	46.9%
1968**	385,000	122,359	Nixon, Richard M.	246,518	Humphrey, Hubert Horatio Jr.	16,123	124,159 D	31.8%	64.0%	33.2%	66.8%
1964	390,091	74,615	Goldwater, Barry M. Sr.	315,463	Johnson, Lyndon B.*	13	240,848 D	19.1%	80.9%	19.1%	80.9%
1960	405,535	147,502	Nixon, Richard M.	258,032	Kennedy, John F.	1	110,530 D	36.4%	63.6%	36.4%	63.6%
1956	387,609	225,819	Eisenhower, Dwight D.*	161,790	Stevenson, Adlai E. II		64,029 R	58.3%	41.7%	58.3%	41.7%
1952	414,498	210,935	Eisenhower, Dwight D.	203,293	Stevenson, Adlai E. II	270	7,642 R	50.9%	49.0%	50.9%	49.1%
1948	327,702	135,787	Dewey, Thomas E.	188,736	Truman, Harry S.*	3,179	52,949 D	41.4%	57.6%	41.8%	58.2%

Note: An asterisk (*) denotes incumbent. **In past elections, the other vote included: 2016 - 14,746 Libertarian (Gary Johnson); 2000 - 25,052 Green (Ralph Nader); 1996 - 43,723 Reform (Ross Perot); 1992 - 105,045 Independent (Perot); 1980 - 59,819 Independent (John Anderson); 1968 - 15,678 American Independent (George Wallace).

RHODE ISLAND

POSTWAR VOTE FOR GOVERNOR

		Republican		Democratic				Percentage			
								Total Vote		Major Vote	
Year	Total Vote	Vote	Candidate	Vote	Candidate	Other Vote	Rep.-Dem. Plurality	Rep.	Dem.	Rep.	Dem.
2018	376,401	139,932	Fung, Allan	198,122	Raimondo, Gina*	38,347	58,190 D	37.2%	52.6%	41.4%	58.6%
2014**	324,055	117,428	Fung, Allan	131,899	Raimondo, Gina	74,728	14,471 D	36.2%	40.7%	47.1%	52.9%
2010**	342,545	114,911	Robitaille, John F.	78,896	Caprio, Frank T.	148,738	36,015 R#	33.5%	23.0%	59.3%	40.7%
2006	387,010	197,366	Carcieri, Donald L.*	189,562	Fogarty, Charles J.	82	7,804 R	51.0%	49.0%	51.0%	49.0%
2002	332,655	181,827	Carcieri, Donald L.	150,229	York, Myrth	599	31,598 R	54.7%	45.2%	54.8%	45.2%
1998	306,383	156,180	Almond, Lincoln C.*	129,105	York, Myrth	21,098	27,075 R	51.0%	42.1%	54.7%	45.3%
1994**	361,377	171,194	Almond, Lincoln C.	157,361	York, Myrth	32,822	13,833 R	47.4%	43.5%	52.1%	47.9%
1992	424,818	145,590	Leonard, Elizabeth Ann	261,484	Sundlun, Bruce G.*	17,744	115,894 D	34.3%	61.6%	35.8%	64.2%
1990	356,672	92,177	Diprete, Edward*	264,411	Sundlun, Bruce G.	84	172,234 D	25.8%	74.1%	25.8%	74.2%
1988	400,516	203,550	Diprete, Edward*	196,936	Sundlun, Bruce G.	30	6,614 R	50.8%	49.2%	50.8%	49.2%
1986	322,724	208,822	Diprete, Edward*	104,508	Sundlun, Bruce G.	9,394	104,314 R	64.7%	32.4%	66.6%	33.4%
1984	408,375	245,059	Diprete, Edward	163,311	Solomon, Anthony J.	5	81,748 R	60.0%	40.0%	60.0%	40.0%
1982	337,259	79,602	Marzullo, Vincent	247,208	Garrahy, J. Joseph*	10,449	167,606 D	23.6%	73.3%	24.4%	75.6%
1980	405,916	106,729	Cianci, Vincent A.	299,174	Garrahy, J. Joseph*	13	192,445 D	26.3%	73.7%	26.3%	73.7%
1978	314,363	96,596	Almond, Lincoln C.	197,386	Garrahy, J. Joseph*	20,381	100,790 D	30.7%	62.8%	32.9%	67.1%
1976	398,683	178,254	Taft, James L.	218,561	Garrahy, J. Joseph	1,868	40,307 D	44.7%	54.8%	44.9%	55.1%
1974	321,660	69,224	Nugent, James W.	252,436	Noel, Philip W.*		183,212 D	21.5%	78.5%	21.5%	78.5%
1972	412,866	194,315	DeSimone, Herbert F.	216,953	Noel, Philip W.	1,598	22,638 D	47.1%	52.5%	47.2%	52.8%
1970	346,342	171,549	DeSimone, Herbert F.	173,420	Licht, Frank*	1,373	1,871 D	49.5%	50.1%	49.7%	50.3%
1968	383,725	187,958	Chafee, John H.*	195,766	Licht, Frank	1	7,808 D	49.0%	51.0%	49.0%	51.0%
1966	332,064	210,202	Chafee, John H.*	121,862	Hobbs, Horace E.		88,340 R	63.3%	36.7%	63.3%	36.7%
1964	391,668	239,501	Chafee, John H.*	152,165	Gallogly, Edward P.	2	87,336 R	61.1%	38.9%	61.1%	38.9%
1962	327,506	163,952	Chafee, John H.	163,554	Notte, John A. Jr.*		398 R	50.1%	49.9%	50.1%	49.9%
1960	401,362	174,044	Del Sesto, Christopher*	227,318	Notte, John A. Jr.		53,274 D	43.4%	56.6%	43.4%	56.6%
1958	346,780	176,505	Del Sesto, Christopher	170,275	Roberts, Dennis J.*		6,230 R	50.9%	49.1%	50.9%	49.1%
1956	383,919	191,604	Del Sesto, Christopher	192,315	Roberts, Dennis J.*		711 D	49.9%	50.1%	49.9%	50.1%
1954	328,670	137,131	Lewis, Dean J.	189,595	Roberts, Dennis J.*	1,944	52,464 D	41.7%	57.7%	42.0%	58.0%
1952	409,689	194,102	Archambault, Raoul	215,587	Roberts, Dennis J.*		21,485 D	47.4%	52.6%	47.4%	52.6%
1950	296,808	120,683	Lachapelle, Eugene J.	176,125	Roberts, Dennis J.		55,442 D	40.7%	59.3%	40.7%	59.3%
1948	323,863	124,441	Ruerat, Albert P.	198,056	Pastore, John O.*	1,366	73,615 D	38.4%	61.2%	38.6%	61.4%
1946	275,341	126,456	Murphy, John G.	148,885	Pastore, John O.*		22,429 D	45.9%	54.1%	45.9%	54.1%

Note: An asterisk (*) denotes incumbent. A pound sign (#) in the plurality column indicates that the winner in 2010 did not run under the banner of either major party. **In past elections, the other vote included: 2014 - 69,278 Moderate (Robert J. Healey Jr.); 2010 - 123,571 Independent (Lincoln Chafee), who was elected with 36.1 percent of the total vote and a plurality of 8,660 votes. The term of office of Rhode Island's Governor was increased from two to four years effective with the 1994 election.

RHODE ISLAND

POSTWAR VOTE FOR SENATOR

		Republican		Democratic				Percentage			
								Total Vote		Major Vote	
Year	Total Vote	Vote	Candidate	Vote	Candidate	Other Vote	Rep.-Dem. Plurality	Rep.	Dem.	Rep.	Dem.
2018	376,738	144,421	Flanders , Robert Jr.	231,477	Whitehouse, Sheldon*	840	87,056 D	38.3%	61.4%	38.4%	61.6%
2014	316,898	92,684	Zaccaria, Mark S.	223,675	Reed, Jack F.*	539	130,991 D	29.2%	70.6%	29.3%	70.7%
2012	418,189	146,222	Hinckley, Barry	271,034	Whitehouse, Sheldon*	933	124,812 D	35.0%	64.8%	35.0%	65.0%
2008	438,812	116,174	Tingle, Robert G.	320,644	Reed, Jack F.*	1,994	204,470 D	26.5%	73.1%	26.6%	73.4%
2006	385,451	179,001	Chafee, Lincoln D.*	206,110	Whitehouse, Sheldon	340	27,109 D	46.4%	53.5%	46.5%	53.5%
2002	323,912	69,881	Tingle, Robert G.	253,922	Reed, Jack F.*	109	184,041 D	21.6%	78.4%	21.6%	78.4%
2000	391,537	222,588	Chafee, Lincoln D.*	161,023	Weygand, Robert A.	7,926	61,565 R	56.8%	41.1%	58.0%	42.0%
1996	363,371	127,368	Mayer, Nancy J.	230,676	Reed, Jack F.	5,327	103,308 D	35.1%	63.5%	35.6%	64.4%
1994	345,388	222,856	Chafee, John H.*	122,532	Kushner, Linda J.		100,324 R	64.5%	35.5%	64.5%	35.5%
1990	364,062	138,947	Schneider, Claudine	225,105	Pell, Claiborne*	10	86,158 D	38.2%	61.8%	38.2%	61.8%
1988	397,996	217,273	Chafee, John H.*	180,717	Licht, Richard A.	6	36,556 R	54.6%	45.4%	54.6%	45.4%
1984	395,285	108,492	Leonard, Barbara	286,780	Pell, Claiborne*	13	178,288 D	27.4%	72.6%	27.4%	72.6%
1982	342,779	175,495	Chafee, John H.*	167,283	Michaelson, Julius C.	1	8,212 R	51.2%	48.8%	51.2%	48.8%
1978	305,618	76,061	Reynolds, James G.	229,557	Pell, Claiborne*		153,496 D	24.9%	75.1%	24.9%	75.1%
1976	398,906	230,329	Chafee, John H.	167,665	Lorber, Richard P.	912	62,664 R	57.7%	42.0%	57.9%	42.1%
1972	413,432	188,990	Chafee, John H.	221,942	Pell, Claiborne*	2,500	32,952 D	45.7%	53.7%	46.0%	54.0%
1970	341,222	107,351	McLaughlin, John	230,469	Pastore, John O.*	3,402	123,118 D	31.5%	67.5%	31.8%	68.2%
1966	324,173	104,838	Briggs, Ruth M.	219,331	Pell, Claiborne*	4	114,493 D	32.3%	67.7%	32.3%	67.7%
1964	386,322	66,715	Lagueux, Ronald R.	319,607	Pastore, John O.*		252,892 D	17.3%	82.7%	17.3%	82.7%
1960	399,983	124,408	Archambault, Raoul	275,575	Pell, Claiborne		151,167 D	31.1%	68.9%	31.1%	68.9%
1958	344,519	122,353	Ewing, Bayard	222,166	Pastore, John O.*		99,813 D	35.5%	64.5%	35.5%	64.5%
1954	326,624	132,970	Sundlun, Walter I.	193,654	Green, Theodore Francis*		60,684 D	40.7%	59.3%	40.7%	59.3%
1952	410,978	185,850	Ewing, Bayard	225,128	Pastore, John O.*		39,278 D	45.2%	54.8%	45.2%	54.8%
1950S**	299,410	114,890	Levy, Austin T.	184,520	Pastore, John O.		69,630 D	38.4%	61.6%	38.4%	61.6%
1948	320,952	130,668	Hazard, Thomas P.	190,284	Green, Theodore Francis*		59,616 D	40.7%	59.3%	40.7%	59.3%
1946	273,528	122,780	Dyer, W. Gurnee	150,748	McGrath, J. Howard		27,968 D	44.9%	55.1%	44.9%	55.1%

Note: An asterisk (*) denotes incumbent. **The 1950 election was for a short term to fill a vacancy.

RHODE ISLAND

GOVERNOR 2018

							Percentage			
							Total Vote		Major Vote	
2010 Census Population	County	Total Vote	Republican (Fung)	Democratic (Raimondo)	Other	Rep.-Dem. Plurality	Rep.	Dem.	Rep.	Dem.
49,875	BRISTOL	21,179	6,772	12,316	2,091	5,544 D	32.0%	58.2%	35.5%	64.5%
166,158	KENT	67,429	29,921	29,673	7,835	248 R	44.4%	44.0%	50.2%	49.8%
82,888	NEWPORT	33,571	10,346	20,014	3,211	9,668 D	30.8%	59.6%	34.1%	65.9%
626,667	PROVIDENCE	198,124	72,247	106,688	19,189	34,441 D	36.5%	53.8%	40.4%	59.6%
126,979	WASHINGTON	56,098	20,646	29,431	6,021	8,785 D	36.8%	52.5%	41.2%	58.8%
1,052,567	*TOTAL*	*376,401*	*139,932*	*198,122*	*38,347*	*58,190 D*	*37.2%*	*52.6%*	*41.4%*	*58.6%*

RHODE ISLAND

GOVERNOR 2018

2010 Census Population	City/Town	Total Vote	Republican (Fung)	Democratic (Raimondo)	Other	Rep.-Dem. Plurality	Percentage: Total Vote Rep.	Percentage: Total Vote Dem.	Percentage: Major Vote Rep.	Percentage: Major Vote Dem.
16,310	BARRINGTON	8,268	2,270	5,376	622	3,106 D	27.5%	65.0%	29.7%	70.3%
22,954	BRISTOL TOWN	8,922	3,115	4,778	1,029	1,663 D	34.9%	53.6%	39.5%	60.5%
15,955	BURRILLVILLE	6,025	3,364	1,880	781	1,484 R	55.8%	31.2%	64.1%	35.9%
19,376	CENTRAL FALLS	2,561	363	1,936	262	1,573 D	14.2%	75.6%	15.8%	84.2%
7,827	CHARLESTOWN	3,768	1,361	2,003	404	642 D	36.1%	53.2%	40.5%	59.5%
35,014	COVENTRY	14,103	7,003	5,467	1,633	1,536 R	49.7%	38.8%	56.2%	43.8%
80,387	CRANSTON	31,390	16,651	12,687	2,052	3,964 R	53.0%	40.4%	56.8%	43.2%
33,506	CUMBERLAND	13,993	5,349	7,033	1,611	1,684 D	38.2%	50.3%	43.2%	56.8%
13,146	EAST GREENWICH	6,663	2,657	3,447	559	790 D	39.9%	51.7%	43.5%	56.5%
47,037	EAST PROVIDENCE	17,052	5,084	9,974	1,994	4,890 D	29.8%	58.5%	33.8%	66.2%
6,425	EXETER	2,976	1,420	1,213	343	207 R	47.7%	40.8%	53.9%	46.1%
4,606	FOSTER	2,125	1,091	781	253	310 R	51.3%	36.8%	58.3%	41.7%
9,746	GLOCESTER	4,327	2,302	1,514	511	788 R	53.2%	35.0%	60.3%	39.7%
8,188	HOPKINTON	3,423	1,434	1,552	437	118 D	41.9%	45.3%	48.0%	52.0%
5,405	JAMESTOWN	3,234	972	1,971	291	999 D	30.1%	60.9%	33.0%	67.0%
28,769	JOHNSTON	10,804	5,571	4,205	1,028	1,366 R	51.6%	38.9%	57.0%	43.0%
21,105	LINCOLN	9,191	4,002	4,193	996	191 D	43.5%	45.6%	48.8%	51.2%
3,492	LITTLE COMPTON	1,940	658	1,098	184	440 D	33.9%	56.6%	37.5%	62.5%
16,150	MIDDLETOWN	6,125	1,918	3,589	618	1,671 D	31.3%	58.6%	34.8%	65.2%
15,868	NARRAGANSETT	7,029	2,724	3,560	745	836 D	38.8%	50.6%	43.3%	56.7%
1,051	NEW SHOREHAM	772	140	569	63	429 D	18.1%	73.7%	19.7%	80.3%
24,672	NEWPORT CITY	7,879	1,754	5,413	712	3,659 D	22.3%	68.7%	24.5%	75.5%
26,486	NORTH KINGSTOWN	13,140	5,092	6,605	1,443	1,513 D	38.8%	50.3%	43.5%	56.5%
32,078	NORTH PROVIDENCE	12,158	5,129	5,708	1,321	579 D	42.2%	46.9%	47.3%	52.7%
11,967	NORTH SMITHFIELD	5,006	2,338	2,112	556	226 R	46.7%	42.2%	52.5%	47.5%
71,148	PAWTUCKET	17,051	3,940	11,087	2,024	7,147 D	23.1%	65.0%	26.2%	73.8%
17,389	PORTSMOUTH	7,896	2,674	4,427	795	1,753 D	33.9%	56.1%	37.7%	62.3%
178,042	PROVIDENCE CITY	42,830	6,027	33,527	3,276	27,500 D	14.1%	78.3%	15.2%	84.8%
7,708	RICHMOND	3,287	1,488	1,373	426	115 R	45.3%	41.8%	52.0%	48.0%
10,329	SCITUATE	5,249	3,053	1,657	539	1,396 R	58.2%	31.6%	64.8%	35.2%
21,430	SMITHFIELD	8,893	4,282	3,604	1,007	678 R	48.2%	40.5%	54.3%	45.7%
30,639	SOUTH KINGSTOWN	12,616	3,830	7,452	1,334	3,622 D	30.4%	59.1%	33.9%	66.1%
15,780	TIVERTON	6,497	2,370	3,516	611	1,146 D	36.5%	54.1%	40.3%	59.7%
10,611	WARREN	3,989	1,387	2,162	440	775 D	34.8%	54.2%	39.1%	60.9%
82,672	WARWICK	34,330	14,511	15,713	4,106	1,202 D	42.3%	45.8%	48.0%	52.0%
6,135	WEST GREENWICH	2,841	1,559	962	320	597 R	54.9%	33.9%	61.8%	38.2%
29,191	WEST WARWICK	9,492	4,191	4,084	1,217	107 R	44.2%	43.0%	50.6%	49.4%
22,787	WESTERLY	9,087	3,157	5,104	826	1,947 D	34.7%	56.2%	38.2%	61.8%
41,186	WOONSOCKET	9,469	3,701	4,790	978	1,089 D	39.1%	50.6%	43.6%	56.4%
1,052,567	*TOTAL*	*376,401*	*139,932*	*198,122*	*38,347*	*58,190 D*	*37.2%*	*52.6%*	*41.4%*	*58.6%*

RHODE ISLAND

SENATOR 2018

2010 Census Population	County	Total Vote	Republican (Flanders)	Democratic (Whitehouse)	Other	Rep.-Dem. Plurality	Percentage: Total Vote Rep.	Percentage: Total Vote Dem.	Percentage: Major Vote Rep.	Percentage: Major Vote Dem.
49,875	BRISTOL	21,246	7,757	13,441	48	5,684 D	36.5%	63.3%	36.6%	63.4%
166,158	KENT	67,598	30,749	36,704	145	5,955 D	45.5%	54.3%	45.6%	54.4%
82,888	NEWPORT	33,742	12,228	21,453	61	9,225 D	36.2%	63.6%	36.3%	63.7%
626,667	PROVIDENCE	197,640	70,495	126,669	476	56,174 D	35.7%	64.1%	35.8%	64.2%
126,979	WASHINGTON	56,370	23,189	33,071	110	9,882 D	41.1%	58.7%	41.2%	58.8%
	Votes Not Reported by County	142	3	139		136 D	2.1%	97.9%	2.1%	97.9%
1,052,567	*TOTAL*	*376,738*	*144,421*	*231,477*	*840*	*87,056 D*	*38.3%*	*61.4%*	*38.4%*	*61.6%*

RHODE ISLAND

SENATE 2018

2010 Census Population	City/Town	Total Vote	Republican (Flanders)	Democratic (Whitehouse)	Other	Rep.-Dem. Plurality	Percentage Total Vote Rep.	Total Vote Dem.	Major Vote Rep.	Major Vote Dem.
16,310	BARRINGTON	8,285	2,696	5,568	21	2,872 D	32.5%	67.2%	32.6%	67.4%
22,954	BRISTOL TOWN	8,956	3,527	5,410	19	1,883 D	39.4%	60.4%	39.5%	60.5%
15,955	BURRILLVILLE	6,033	3,366	2,656	11	710 R	55.8%	44.0%	55.9%	44.1%
19,376	CENTRAL FALLS	2,524	377	2,135	12	1,758 D	14.9%	84.6%	15.0%	85.0%
7,827	CHARLESTOWN	3,773	1,566	2,198	9	632 D	41.5%	58.3%	41.6%	58.4%
35,014	COVENTRY	14,140	7,157	6,940	43	217 R	50.6%	49.1%	50.8%	49.2%
80,387	CRANSTON	31,242	13,274	17,896	72	4,622 D	42.5%	57.3%	42.6%	57.4%
33,506	CUMBERLAND	13,984	5,907	8,050	27	2,143 D	42.2%	57.6%	42.3%	57.7%
13,146	EAST GREENWICH	6,669	2,884	3,775	10	891 D	43.2%	56.6%	43.3%	56.7%
47,037	EAST PROVIDENCE	17,042	5,547	11,441	54	5,894 D	32.5%	67.1%	32.7%	67.3%
6,425	EXETER	2,986	1,529	1,450	7	79 R	51.2%	48.6%	51.3%	48.7%
4,606	FOSTER	2,128	1,129	995	4	134 R	53.1%	46.8%	53.2%	46.8%
9,746	GLOCESTER	4,324	2,345	1,972	7	373 R	54.2%	45.6%	54.3%	45.7%
8,188	HOPKINTON	3,420	1,631	1,779	10	148 D	47.7%	52.0%	47.8%	52.2%
5,405	JAMESTOWN	3,265	1,086	2,173	6	1,087 D	33.3%	66.6%	33.3%	66.7%
28,769	JOHNSTON	10,804	5,427	5,359	18	68 R	50.2%	49.6%	50.3%	49.7%
21,105	LINCOLN	9,196	4,201	4,973	22	772 D	45.7%	54.1%	45.8%	54.2%
3,492	LITTLE COMPTON	1,962	796	1,159	7	363 D	40.6%	59.1%	40.7%	59.3%
16,150	MIDDLETOWN	6,123	2,204	3,907	12	1,703 D	36.0%	63.8%	36.1%	63.9%
15,868	NARRAGANSETT	7,077	3,020	4,042	15	1,022 D	42.7%	57.1%	42.8%	57.2%
1,051	NEW SHOREHAM	772	167	604	1	437 D	21.6%	78.2%	21.7%	78.3%
24,672	NEWPORT CITY	7,951	2,095	5,845	11	3,750 D	26.3%	73.5%	26.4%	73.6%
26,486	NORTH KINGSTOWN	13,222	5,594	7,610	18	2,016 D	42.3%	57.6%	42.4%	57.6%
32,078	NORTH PROVIDENCE	12,160	4,946	7,186	28	2,240 D	40.7%	59.1%	40.8%	59.2%
11,967	NORTH SMITHFIELD	5,020	2,511	2,503	6	8 R	50.0%	49.9%	50.1%	49.9%
71,148	PAWTUCKET	17,031	4,273	12,710	48	8,437 D	25.1%	74.6%	25.2%	74.8%
17,389	PORTSMOUTH	7,941	3,232	4,694	15	1,462 D	40.7%	59.1%	40.8%	59.2%
178,042	PROVIDENCE CITY	42,587	5,835	36,629	123	30,794 D	13.7%	86.0%	13.7%	86.3%
7,708	RICHMOND	3,301	1,638	1,657	6	19 D	49.6%	50.2%	49.7%	50.3%
10,329	SCITUATE	5,215	3,067	2,138	10	929 R	58.8%	41.0%	58.9%	41.1%
21,430	SMITHFIELD	8,905	4,434	4,457	14	23 D	49.8%	50.1%	49.9%	50.1%
30,639	SOUTH KINGSTOWN	12,733	4,289	8,411	33	4,122 D	33.7%	66.1%	33.8%	66.2%
15,780	TIVERTON	6,500	2,815	3,675	10	860 D	43.3%	56.5%	43.4%	56.6%
10,611	WARREN	4,005	1,534	2,463	8	929 D	38.3%	61.5%	38.4%	61.6%
82,672	WARWICK	34,449	14,872	19,504	73	4,632 D	43.2%	56.6%	43.3%	56.7%
6,135	WEST GREENWICH	2,843	1,597	1,240	6	357 R	56.2%	43.6%	56.3%	43.7%
29,191	WEST WARWICK	9,497	4,239	5,245	13	1,006 D	44.6%	55.2%	44.7%	55.3%
22,787	WESTERLY	9,086	3,755	5,320	11	1,565 D	41.3%	58.6%	41.4%	58.6%
41,186	WOONSOCKET	9,445	3,856	5,569	20	1,713 D	40.8%	59.0%	40.9%	59.1%
1,052,567	*TOTAL*	*376,596*	*144,418*	*231,338*	*840*	*86,920 D*	*38.3%*	*61.4%*	*38.4%*	*61.6%*

Note: There were 142 votes not reported by city/town: 139 for Sheldon Whitehouse (D) and 3 for Robert Flanders Jr. (R).

RHODE ISLAND

HOUSE OF REPRESENTATIVES

CD	Year	Total Vote	Republican Vote	Republican Candidate	Democratic Vote	Democratic Candidate	Other Vote	Rep.-Dem. Plurality	Percentage Total Vote Rep.	Total Vote Dem.	Major Vote Rep.	Major Vote Dem.
1	2018	174,083	57,567	DONOVAN, PATRICK J.	116,099	CICILLINE, DAVID N.*	417	58,532 D	33.1%	66.7%	33.1%	66.9%
1	2016	202,371	71,023	TAUB, H. RUSSELL	130,534	CICILLINE, DAVID N.*	814	59,511 D	35.1%	64.5%	35.2%	64.8%
1	2014	146,353	58,877	LYNCH, CORMICK	87,060	CICILLINE, DAVID N.*	416	28,183 D	40.2%	59.5%	40.3%	59.7%
1	2012	205,115	83,737	DOHERTY, BRENDAN P.	108,612	CICILLINE, DAVID N.*	12,766	24,875 D	40.8%	53.0%	43.5%	56.5%

RHODE ISLAND

HOUSE OF REPRESENTATIVES

			Republican		Democratic				Percentage			
									Total Vote		Major Vote	
CD	Year	Total Vote	Vote	Candidate	Vote	Candidate	Other Vote	Rep.-Dem. Plurality	Rep.	Dem.	Rep.	Dem.
2	2018	199,197	72,271	CAIOZZO, SALVATORE	126,476	LANGEVIN, JAMES R.*	450	54,205 D	36.3%	63.5%	36.4%	63.6%
2	2016	229,148	70,301	REIS, RHUE	133,108	LANGEVIN, JAMES R.*	25,739	62,807 D	30.7%	58.1%	34.6%	65.4%
2	2014	169,904	63,844	REIS, RHUE	105,716	LANGEVIN, JAMES R.*	344	41,872 D	37.6%	62.2%	37.7%	62.3%
2	2012	222,660	78,189	RILEY, MICHAEL G.	124,067	LANGEVIN, JAMES R.*	20,404	45,878 D	35.1%	55.7%	38.7%	61.3%
TOTAL	*2018*	*373,280*	*129,838*		*242,575*		*867*	*112,737 D*	*34.8%*	*65.0%*	*34.9%*	*65.1%*
TOTAL	*2016*	*431,519*	*141,324*		*263,642*		*26,553*	*122,318 D*	*32.8%*	*61.1%*	*34.9%*	*65.1%*
TOTAL	*2014*	*316,257*	*122,721*		*192,776*		*760*	*70,055 D*	*38.8%*	*61.0%*	*38.9%*	*61.1%*
TOTAL	*2012*	*427,775*	*161,926*		*232,679*		*33,170*	*70,753 D*	*37.9%*	*54.4%*	*41.0%*	*59.0%*

Note: An asterisk (*) denotes incumbent.

RHODE ISLAND

GENERAL AND PRIMARY ELECTIONS

2018 GENERAL ELECTIONS: OTHER VOTES

Governor Other vote was 16,532 Independent (Joseph Trillo), 10,155 Moderate (William Gilbert), 6,223 Independent (Luis Munoz), 4,191 Compassion (Anne Armstrong), 1,246 Write-in (Write-in)

Senate 840 Write-in (Write-in)

House Other vote was:

CD 1 417 Write-in (Write-in)
CD 2 450 Write-in (Write-in)

2018 PRIMARY ELECTIONS: SUPPLEMENTARY INFORMATION

Primary September 12, 2018

Registration (as of September 1, 2018) 781,960

Democratic	307,963
Republican	92,021
Moderate	3,307
Unaffiliated	378,669

Primary Type Semi-open—Registered Democrats and Republicans could vote only in their party's primary. Unaffiliated voters could participate in either party's primary.

	REPUBLICAN PRIMARIES			DEMOCRATIC PRIMARIES		
Senator	Flanders, Robert Jr.	26,543	87.7%	Whitehouse, Sheldon*	89,140	76.8%
	De La Fuente, Roque "Rocky"	3,722	12.3%	Fontes, Patricia J.	26,947	23.2%
	TOTAL	*30,265*		*TOTAL*	*116,087*	
Governor	Fung, Allan	18,661	56.4%	Raimondo, Gina*	67,370	57.2%
	Morgan, Patricia	13,267	40.1%	Brown, Matthew "Matt"	39,518	33.5%
	Feroce, Giovanni	1,159	3.5%	Dickinson, Spencer	10,987	9.3%
	TOTAL	*33,087*		*TOTAL*	*117,875*	
Congressional District 1	Donovan, Patrick J.	7,574	78.3%	Cicilline, David N.*	47,762	78.0%
	Wysocki, Frederick	2,093	21.7%	Young, Christopher	13,474	22.0%
	TOTAL	*9,667*		*TOTAL*	*61,236*	
Congressional District 2	Caiozzo, Salvatore	15,398	100.0%	Langevin, James R.*	44,634	100.0%
	TOTAL	*15,398*		*TOTAL*	*44,634*	

Note: An asterisk (*) denotes incumbent.

SOUTH CAROLINA

Congressional districts first established for elections held in 2012

7 members

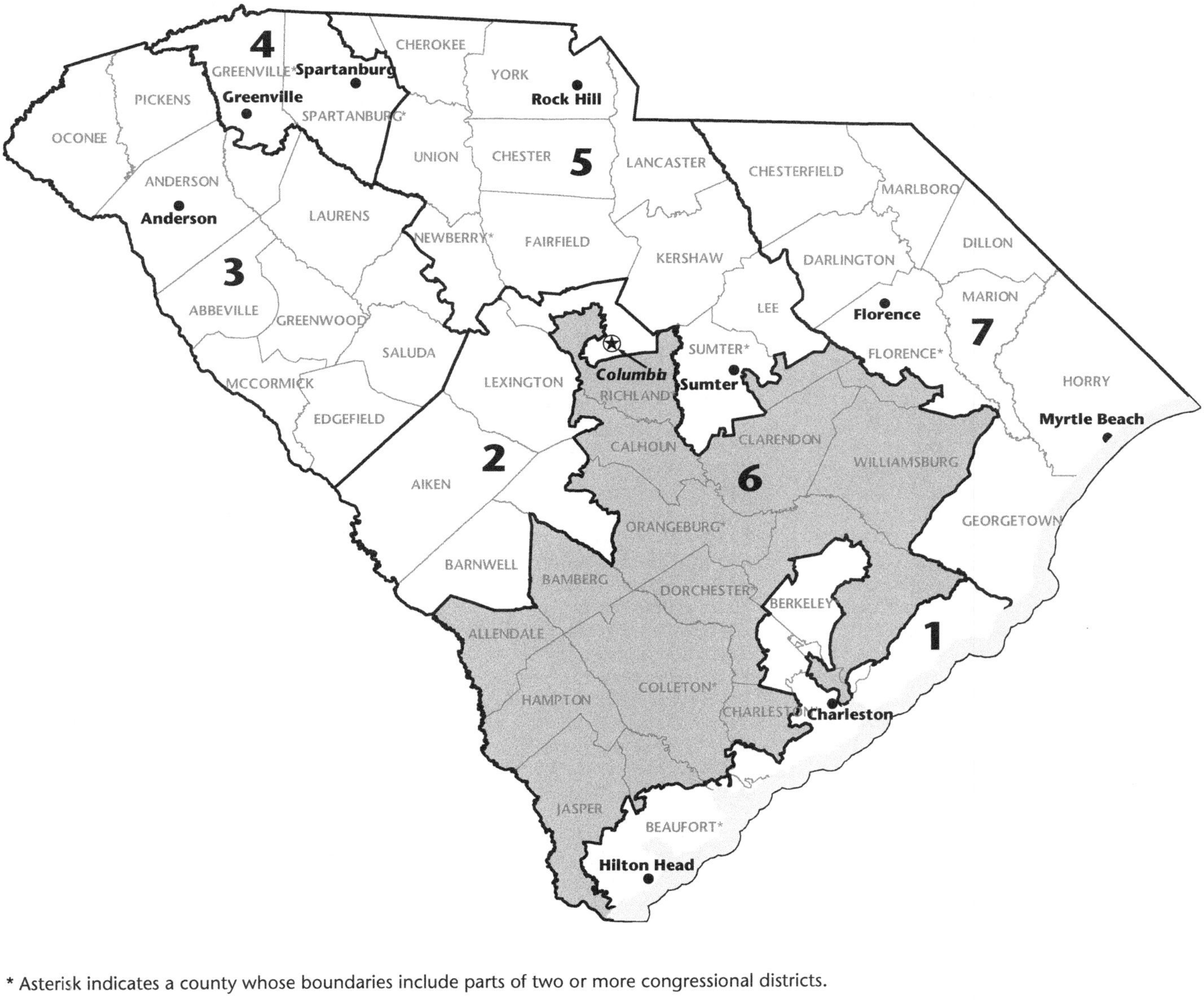

* Asterisk indicates a county whose boundaries include parts of two or more congressional districts.

SOUTH CAROLINA

GOVERNOR

Henry D. McMaster (R). Assumed office January 25, 2017, to complete the remainder of the term vacated by the January 24, 2017, resignation of Nikki R. Haley to become U.S. ambassador to the United Nations. McMaster won a full four-year term in 2018.

SENATORS (2 Republicans)

Lindsey Graham (R). Re-elected 2014 to a six-year term. Previously elected 2008, 2002.

Tim Scott (R). Elected 2016 to a six-year term. Previously elected 2014 to fill out a short term. Initially sworn in on January 3, 2013, to fill the vacancy created by the resignation of Jim DeMint (R), who resigned two days earlier to become president of the Heritage Foundation.

REPRESENTATIVES (5 Republicans, 2 Democrats)

1. Joe Cunningham (D)
2. Joe Wilson (R)
3. Jeff Duncan (R)
4. William Timmons (R)
5. Ralph Norman (R)
6. James E. Clyburn (D)
7. Tom Rice (R)

POSTWAR VOTE FOR PRESIDENT

		Republican		Democratic				Percentage			
								Total Vote		Major Vote	
Year	Total Vote	Vote	Candidate	Vote	Candidate	Other Vote	Rep.-Dem. Plurality	Rep.	Dem.	Rep.	Dem.
2016**	2,103,027	1,155,389	Trump, Donald J.	855,373	Clinton, Hillary Rodham	92,265	300,016 R	54.9%	40.7%	57.5%	42.5%
2012	1,964,118	1,071,645	Romney, W. Mitt	865,941	Obama, Barack H.*	26,532	205,704 R	54.6%	44.1%	55.3%	44.7%
2008	1,920,969	1,034,896	McCain, John S. III	862,449	Obama, Barack H.	23,624	172,447 R	53.9%	44.9%	54.5%	45.5%
2004	1,617,730	937,974	Bush, George W.*	661,699	Kerry, John F.	18,057	276,275 R	58.0%	40.9%	58.6%	41.4%
2000**	1,382,717	785,937	Bush, George W.	565,561	Gore, Albert Jr.	31,219	220,376 R	56.8%	40.9%	58.2%	41.8%
1996**	1,151,689	573,458	Dole, Robert "Bob"	506,283	Clinton, Bill*	71,948	67,175 R	49.8%	44.0%	53.1%	46.9%
1992**	1,202,527	577,507	Bush, George H.*	479,514	Clinton, Bill	145,506	97,993 R	48.0%	39.9%	54.6%	45.4%
1988	986,009	606,443	Bush, George H.	370,554	Dukakis, Michael S.	9,012	235,889 R	61.5%	37.6%	62.1%	37.9%
1984	968,529	615,539	Reagan, Ronald*	344,459	Mondale, Walter F.	8,531	271,080 R	63.6%	35.6%	64.1%	35.9%
1980**	894,071	441,841	Reagan, Ronald	430,385	Carter, Jimmy*	21,845	11,456 R	49.4%	48.1%	50.7%	49.3%
1976	802,583	346,149	Ford, Gerald R.*	450,807	Carter, Jimmy	5,627	104,658 D	43.1%	56.2%	43.4%	56.6%
1972	673,960	477,044	Nixon, Richard M.*	186,824	McGovern, George S.	10,092	290,220 R	70.8%	27.7%	71.9%	28.1%
1968**	666,978	254,062	Nixon, Richard M.	197,486	Humphrey, Hubert Horatio Jr.	215,430	56,576 R	38.1%	29.6%	56.3%	43.7%
1964	524,779	309,048	Goldwater, Barry M. Sr.	215,723	Johnson, Lyndon B.*	8	93,325 R	58.9%	41.1%	58.9%	41.1%
1960	386,688	188,558	Nixon, Richard M.	198,129	Kennedy, John F.	1	9,571 D	48.8%	51.2%	48.8%	51.2%
1956**	300,583	75,700	Eisenhower, Dwight D.*	136,372	Stevenson, Adlai E. II	88,511	60,672 D	25.2%	45.4%	35.7%	64.3%
1952	341,087	168,082	Eisenhower, Dwight D.	173,004	Stevenson, Adlai E. II	1	4,922 D	49.3%	50.7%	49.3%	50.7%
1948**	142,571	5,386	Dewey, Thomas E.	34,423	Truman, Harry S.*	102,762	29,037 D#	3.8%	24.1%	13.5%	86.5%

Note: An asterisk (*) denotes incumbent. A pound sign (#) in the plurality column indicates that the winner in 1948 did not run under the banner of either major party. **In past elections, the other vote included: 2016 - 49,204 Libertarian (Gary Johnson); 2000 - 20,200 Green (Ralph Nader); 1996 - 64,386 Reform (Ross Perot); 1992 - 138,872 Independent (Perot); 1980 - 14,153 Independent (John Anderson); 1968 - 215,430 American Independent (George Wallace), who finished second; 1956 - 88,509 Uncommitted States' Rights electors, which placed second; 1948 - 102,607 States' Rights (Strom Thurmond), who won South Carolina with 72.0 percent of the total vote and a plurality of 68,184 votes.

SOUTH CAROLINA

POSTWAR VOTE FOR GOVERNOR

		Republican		Democratic				Percentage			
								Total Vote		Major Vote	
Year	Total Vote	Vote	Candidate	Vote	Candidate	Other Vote	Rep.-Dem. Plurality	Rep.	Dem.	Rep.	Dem.
2018	1,707,569	921,342	McMaster, Henry D.*	784,182	Smith, James	2,045	137,160 R	54.0%	45.9%	54.0%	46.0%
2014	1,246,301	696,645	Haley, Nikki R.*	516,166	Sheheen, Vincent A.	33,490	180,479 R	55.9%	41.4%	57.4%	42.6%
2010	1,344,198	690,525	Haley, Nikki R.	630,534	Sheheen, Vincent A.	23,139	59,991 R	51.4%	46.9%	52.3%	47.7%
2006	1,091,952	601,868	Sanford, Marshall Clement "Mark" Jr.*	489,076	Moore, Tommy	1,008	112,792 R	55.1%	44.8%	55.2%	44.8%
2002	1,107,725	585,422	Sanford, Marshall Clement "Mark" Jr.	521,140	Hodges, James H.*	1,163	64,282 R	52.8%	47.0%	52.9%	47.1%
1998	1,070,869	484,088	Beasley, David*	570,070	Hodges, James H.	16,711	85,982 D	45.2%	53.2%	45.9%	54.1%
1994	933,850	470,756	Beasley, David	447,002	Theodore, Nick A.	16,092	23,754 R	50.4%	47.9%	51.3%	48.7%
1990	760,965	528,831	Campbell, Carroll*	212,034	Mitchell, Theo	20,100	316,797 R	69.5%	27.9%	71.4%	28.6%
1986	753,751	384,565	Campbell, Carroll	361,325	Daniel, Mike	7,861	23,240 R	51.0%	47.9%	51.6%	48.4%
1982	671,625	202,806	Workman, W. D. III	468,819	Riley, Richard W.*		266,013 D	30.2%	69.8%	30.2%	69.8%
1978	627,182	236,946	Young, Edward L.	384,898	Riley, Richard W.	5,338	147,952 D	37.8%	61.4%	38.1%	61.9%
1974	523,199	266,109	Edwards, James B.	248,938	Dorn, W.J. Bryan	8,152	17,171 R	50.9%	47.6%	51.7%	48.3%
1970	484,257	221,233	Watson, Albert W.	249,951	West, John C.	13,073	28,718 D	45.7%	51.6%	47.0%	53.0%
1966	439,942	184,088	Rogers, Joseph O. Jr.	255,854	McNair, Robert E.*		71,766 D	41.8%	58.2%	41.8%	58.2%
1962	253,721			253,704	Russell, Donald S.	17	253,704 D		100.0%		100.0%
1958	77,740			77,714	Hollings, Ernest F.	26	77,714 D		100.0%		100.0%
1954	214,212			214,204	Timmerman, George Bell	8	214,204 D		100.0%		100.0%
1950	50,642			50,633	Byrnes, James F.	9	50,633 D		100.0%		100.0%
1946	26,520			26,520	Thurmond, James Strom		26,520 D		100.0%		100.0%

Note: An asterisk (*) denotes incumbent. The Republican Party did not run a candidate in the gubernatorial elections of 1946, 1950, 1954, 1958, and 1962.

POSTWAR VOTE FOR SENATOR

		Republican		Democratic				Percentage			
								Total Vote		Major Vote	
Year	Total Vote	Vote	Candidate	Vote	Candidate	Other Vote	Rep.-Dem. Plurality	Rep.	Dem.	Rep.	Dem.
2016	2,049,893	1,241,609	Scott, Tim*	757,022	Dixon, Thomas	51,262	484,587 R	60.6%	36.9%	62.1%	37.9%
2014	1,240,075	672,941	Graham, Lindsey*	480,933	Hutto, C. Bradley "Brad"	86,201	192,008 R	54.3%	38.8%	58.3%	41.7%
2014S**	1,238,982	757,215	Scott, Tim*	459,583	Dickerson, Joyce	22,184	297,632 R	61.1%	37.1%	62.2%	37.8%
2010	1,318,794	810,771	DeMint, James W. "Jim"*	364,598	Greene, Alvin M.	143,425	446,173 R	61.5%	27.6%	69.0%	31.0%
2008	1,871,431	1,076,534	Graham, Lindsey*	790,621	Conley, Bob	4,276	285,913 R	57.5%	42.2%	57.7%	42.3%
2004	1,597,221	857,167	DeMint, James W. "Jim"	704,384	Tenenbaum, Inez M.	35,670	152,783 R	53.7%	44.1%	54.9%	45.1%
2002	1,102,948	600,010	Graham, Lindsey	487,359	Sanders, Alex	15,579	112,651 R	54.4%	44.2%	55.2%	44.8%
1998	1,068,367	488,132	Inglis, Robert D.	562,791	Hollings, Ernest F.*	17,444	74,659 D	45.7%	52.7%	46.4%	53.6%
1996	1,161,372	619,859	Thurmond, James Strom*	510,951	Close, Elliott	30,562	108,908 R	53.4%	44.0%	54.8%	45.2%
1992	1,180,438	554,175	Hartnett, Thomas F.	591,030	Hollings, Ernest F.*	35,233	36,855 D	46.9%	50.1%	48.4%	51.6%
1990	750,716	482,032	Thurmond, James Strom*	244,112	Cunningham, Bob	24,572	237,920 R	64.2%	32.5%	66.4%	33.6%
1986	737,962	262,886	McMaster, Henry D.	465,500	Hollings, Ernest F.*	9,576	202,614 D	35.6%	63.1%	36.1%	63.9%
1984	965,130	644,815	Thurmond, James Strom*	306,982	Purvis, Melvin	13,333	337,833 R	66.8%	31.8%	67.7%	32.3%
1980	870,594	257,946	Mays, Marshall T.	612,554	Hollings, Ernest F.*	94	354,608 D	29.6%	70.4%	29.6%	70.4%
1978	632,852	351,733	Thurmond, James Strom*	281,119	Ravenel, Charles D.		70,614 R	55.6%	44.4%	55.6%	44.4%
1974	512,397	146,645	Bush, Gwenfred	356,126	Hollings, Ernest F.*	9,626	209,481 D	28.6%	69.5%	29.2%	70.8%
1972	672,246	426,601	Thurmond, James Strom*	245,457	Zeigler, Eugene N.	188	181,144 R	63.5%	36.5%	63.5%	36.5%
1968	652,855	248,780	Parker, Marshall	404,060	Hollings, Ernest F.*	15	155,280 D	38.1%	61.9%	38.1%	61.9%
1966	436,252	271,297	Thurmond, James Strom*	164,955	Morrah, Bradley		106,342 R	62.2%	37.8%	62.2%	37.8%
1966S**		212,032	Parker, Marshall	223,790	Hollings, Ernest F.		11,758 D			48.7%	51.3%
1962	312,647	133,930	Workman, W. D. III	178,712	Johnston, Olin D.*	5	44,782 D	42.8%	57.2%	42.8%	57.2%
1960	330,266			330,164	Thurmond, James Strom*	102	330,164 D		100.0%		100.0%
1956	279,845	49,695	Crawford, L. P.	230,150	Johnston, Olin D.*		180,455 D	17.8%	82.2%	17.8%	82.2%
1956S**				245,371	Thurmond, James Strom*		245,371 D				100.0%
1954**	226,967			83,525	Brown, Edgar A.	143,442	83,525 D#		36.8%		100.0%
1950	50,277			50,240	Johnston, Olin D.*	37	50,240 D		99.9%		100.0%
1948	135,998			135,998	Maybank, Burnet R.*		135,998 D		100.0%		100.0%

Note: An asterisk (*) denotes incumbent. A pound sign (#) in the plurality column indicates that the winner in 1954 was an Independent Democrat. **In past elections, the other vote included: 1954 - 143,442 Independent Democratic (Strom Thurmond). Thurmond ran as a write-in candidate and won with 63.1 percent of the total vote and a plurality of 59,917 votes. One each of the 1956, 1966, and 2014 elections was for a short term to fill a vacancy. The Republican Party did not run a Senate candidate in 1948, 1950, 1954, 1956 (for the short term), and 1960.

SOUTH CAROLINA

GOVERNOR 2018

2010 Census Population	County	Total Vote	Republican (McMaster)	Democratic (Smith)	Other	Rep.-Dem. Plurality	Percentage Total Vote Rep.	Percentage Total Vote Dem.	Percentage Major Vote Rep.	Percentage Major Vote Dem.
25,417	ABBEVILLE	8,572	5,451	3,113	8	2,338 R	63.6%	36.3%	63.7%	36.3%
160,099	AIKEN	59,612	36,801	22,754	57	14,047 R	61.7%	38.2%	61.8%	38.2%
10,419	ALLENDALE	2,898	608	2,289	1	1,681 D	21.0%	79.0%	21.0%	79.0%
187,126	ANDERSON	62,893	43,412	19,386	95	24,026 R	69.0%	30.8%	69.1%	30.9%
15,987	BAMBERG	4,382	1,552	2,828	2	1,276 D	35.4%	64.5%	35.4%	64.6%
22,621	BARNWELL	7,289	3,734	3,549	6	185 R	51.2%	48.7%	51.3%	48.7%
162,233	BEAUFORT	70,433	38,399	31,971	63	6,428 R	54.5%	45.4%	54.6%	45.4%
177,843	BERKELEY	65,669	35,107	30,452	110	4,655 R	53.5%	46.4%	53.6%	46.4%
15,175	CALHOUN	5,948	2,952	2,990	6	38 D	49.6%	50.3%	49.7%	50.3%
350,209	CHARLESTON	147,451	62,642	84,634	175	21,992 D	42.5%	57.4%	42.5%	57.5%
55,342	CHEROKEE	16,711	11,730	4,964	17	6,766 R	70.2%	29.7%	70.3%	29.7%
33,140	CHESTER	10,863	5,665	5,195	3	470 R	52.1%	47.8%	52.2%	47.8%
46,734	CHESTERFIELD	11,977	6,730	5,241	6	1,489 R	56.2%	43.8%	56.2%	43.8%
34,971	CLARENDON	12,090	5,722	6,365	3	643 D	47.3%	52.6%	47.3%	52.7%
38,892	COLLETON	13,226	6,891	6,321	14	570 R	52.1%	47.8%	52.2%	47.8%
68,681	DARLINGTON	23,315	11,871	11,436	8	435 R	50.9%	49.0%	50.9%	49.1%
32,062	DILLON	8,194	4,052	4,141	1	89 D	49.5%	50.5%	49.5%	50.5%
136,555	DORCHESTER	50,896	27,563	23,275	58	4,288 R	54.2%	45.7%	54.2%	45.8%
26,985	EDGEFIELD	9,392	5,636	3,747	9	1,889 R	60.0%	39.9%	60.1%	39.9%
23,956	FAIRFIELD	9,279	3,409	5,865	5	2,456 D	36.7%	63.2%	36.8%	63.2%
136,885	FLORENCE	45,516	22,947	22,533	36	414 R	50.4%	49.5%	50.5%	49.5%
60,158	GEORGETOWN	25,858	14,083	11,760	15	2,323 R	54.5%	45.5%	54.5%	45.5%
451,225	GREENVILLE	176,571	102,195	74,007	369	28,188 R	57.9%	41.9%	58.0%	42.0%
69,661	GREENWOOD	23,147	13,973	9,140	34	4,833 R	60.4%	39.5%	60.5%	39.5%
21,090	HAMPTON	6,624	2,558	4,051	15	1,493 D	38.6%	61.2%	38.7%	61.3%
269,291	HORRY	110,638	71,985	38,574	79	33,411 R	65.1%	34.9%	65.1%	34.9%
24,777	JASPER	9,360	4,346	5,002	12	656 D	46.4%	53.4%	46.5%	53.5%
61,697	KERSHAW	23,497	13,881	9,588	28	4,293 R	59.1%	40.8%	59.1%	40.9%
76,652	LANCASTER	32,872	19,554	13,297	21	6,257 R	59.5%	40.5%	59.5%	40.5%
66,537	LAURENS	20,348	12,899	7,415	34	5,484 R	63.4%	36.4%	63.5%	36.5%
19,220	LEE	6,368	2,174	4,190	4	2,016 D	34.1%	65.8%	34.2%	65.8%
262,391	LEXINGTON	99,551	62,544	36,854	153	25,690 R	62.8%	37.0%	62.9%	37.1%
33,062	MARION	10,421	3,963	6,450	8	2,487 D	38.0%	61.9%	38.1%	61.9%
28,933	MARLBORO	7,767	3,166	4,594	7	1,428 D	40.8%	59.1%	40.8%	59.2%
10,233	MCCORMICK	4,431	2,327	2,103	1	224 R	52.5%	47.5%	52.5%	47.5%
37,508	NEWBERRY	13,030	7,644	5,374	12	2,270 R	58.7%	41.2%	58.7%	41.3%
74,273	OCONEE	27,582	19,599	7,945	38	11,654 R	71.1%	28.8%	71.2%	28.8%
92,501	ORANGEBURG	30,643	9,222	21,402	19	12,180 D	30.1%	69.8%	30.1%	69.9%
119,224	PICKENS	38,614	28,139	10,393	82	17,746 R	72.9%	26.9%	73.0%	27.0%
384,504	RICHLAND	141,438	41,793	99,476	169	57,683 D	29.5%	70.3%	29.6%	70.4%
19,875	SALUDA	6,876	4,516	2,356	4	2,160 R	65.7%	34.3%	65.7%	34.3%
284,307	SPARTANBURG	94,874	58,442	36,264	168	22,178 R	61.6%	38.2%	61.7%	38.3%
107,456	SUMTER	34,426	14,578	19,830	18	5,252 D	42.3%	57.6%	42.4%	57.6%
28,961	UNION	8,943	5,208	3,728	7	1,480 R	58.2%	41.7%	58.3%	41.7%
34,423	WILLIAMSBURG	11,554	3,774	7,769	11	3,995 D	32.7%	67.2%	32.7%	67.3%
226,073	YORK	95,530	55,905	39,571	54	16,334 R	58.5%	41.4%	58.6%	41.4%
4,625,364	*TOTAL*	*1,707,569*	*921,342*	*784,182*	*2,045*	*137,160 R*	*54.0%*	*45.9%*	*54.0%*	*46.0%*

SOUTH CAROLINA

HOUSE OF REPRESENTATIVES

			Republican		Democratic				Percentage			
									Total Vote		Major Vote	
CD	Year	Total Vote	Vote	Candidate	Vote	Candidate	Other Vote	Rep.-Dem. Plurality	Rep.	Dem.	Rep.	Dem.
1	2018	287,433	141,473	ARRINGTON, KATIE	145,455	CUNNINGHAM, JOE	505	3,982 D	49.2%	50.6%	49.3%	50.7%
1	2016	325,170	190,410	SANFORD, MARK*	119,779	CHERNY, DIMITRI	14,981	70,631 R	58.6%	36.8%	61.4%	38.6%
1	2014	127,815	119,392	SANFORD, MARK*			8,423	119,392 R	93.4%		100.0%	
1	2012	290,013	179,908	SCOTT, TIM*	103,557	ROSE, BOBBIE G.	6,548	76,351 R	62.0%	35.7%	63.5%	36.5%
2	2018	257,139	144,642	WILSON, JOE*	109,199	CARRIGAN, SEAN	3,298	35,443 R	56.3%	42.5%	57.0%	43.0%
2	2016	304,996	183,746	WILSON, JOE*	109,452	BJORN, ARIK	11,798	74,294 R	60.2%	35.9%	62.7%	37.3%
2	2014	194,808	121,649	WILSON, JOE*	68,719	BLACK, PHIL	4,440	52,930 R	62.4%	35.3%	63.9%	36.1%
2	2012	203,718	196,116	WILSON, JOE*			7,602	196,116 R	96.3%		100.0%	
3	2018	226,204	153,338	DUNCAN, JEFF*	70,046	GEREN, MARY	2,820	83,292 R	67.8%	31.0%	68.6%	31.4%
3	2016	272,481	198,431	DUNCAN, JEFF*	73,766	CLEVELAND, HOSEA	284	124,665 R	72.8%	27.1%	72.9%	27.1%
3	2014	164,009	116,741	DUNCAN, JEFF*	47,181	MULLIS, BARBARA JO	87	69,560 R	71.2%	28.8%	71.2%	28.8%
3	2012	254,763	169,512	DUNCAN, JEFF*	84,735	DOYLE, BRIAN RYAN B.	516	84,777 R	66.5%	33.3%	66.7%	33.3%
4	2018	243,950	145,321	TIMMONS, WILLIAM	89,182	BROWN, BRANDON P.	9,447	56,139 R	59.6%	36.6%	62.0%	38.0%
4	2016	295,670	198,648	GOWDY, TREY*	91,676	FEDALEI, CHRISTOPHER	5,346	106,972 R	67.2%	31.0%	68.4%	31.6%
4	2014	149,049	126,452	GOWDY, TREY*			22,597	126,452 R	84.8%		100.0%	
4	2012	266,884	173,201	GOWDY, TREY*	89,964	MORROW, DEB	3,719	83,237 R	64.9%	33.7%	65.8%	34.2%
5	2018	248,579	141,757	NORMAN, RALPH*	103,129	PARNELL, ARCHIE	3,693	38,628 R	57.0%	41.5%	57.9%	42.1%
5	2016	297,781	175,909	MULVANEY, MICK*	115,437	PERSON, FRANCIS "FRAN"	6,435	60,472 R	59.1%	38.8%	60.4%	39.6%
5	2014	175,145	103,078	MULVANEY, MICK*	71,985	ADAMS, TOM A.	82	31,093 R	58.9%	41.1%	58.9%	41.1%
5	2012	278,003	154,324	MULVANEY, MICK*	123,443	KNOTT, JOYCE	236	30,881 R	55.5%	44.4%	55.6%	44.4%
6	2018	206,433	58,282	GRESSMANN, GERHARD	144,765	CLYBURN, JAMES E.*	3,386	86,483 D	28.2%	70.1%	28.7%	71.3%
6	2016	253,901	70,099	STERLING, LAURA	177,947	CLYBURN, JAMES E.*	5,855	107,848 D	27.6%	70.1%	28.3%	71.7%
6	2014	173,432	44,311	CULLER, ANTHONY	125,747	CLYBURN, JAMES E.*	3,374	81,436 D	25.5%	72.5%	26.1%	73.9%
6	2012	233,615			218,717	CLYBURN, JAMES E.*	14,898	218,717 D		93.6%		100.0%
7	2018	239,554	142,681	RICE, TOM*	96,564	WILLIAMS, ROBERT	309	46,117 R	59.6%	40.3%	59.6%	40.4%
7	2016	289,463	176,468	RICE, TOM*	112,744	HYMAN, MAL	251	63,724 R	61.0%	38.9%	61.0%	39.0%
7	2014	171,524	102,833	RICE, TOM*	68,576	TINUBU, GLORIA BROMELL	115	34,257 R	60.0%	40.0%	60.0%	40.0%
7	2012	275,738	153,068	RICE, TOM	122,389	TINUBU, GLORIA BROMELL	281	30,679 R	55.5%	44.4%	55.6%	44.4%
TOTAL	*2018*	*1,709,292*	*927,494*		*758,340*		*23,458*	*169,154 R*	*54.3%*	*44.4%*	*55.0%*	*45.0%*
TOTAL	*2016*	*2,039,462*	*1,193,711*		*800,801*		*44,950*	*392,910 R*	*58.5%*	*39.3%*	*59.8%*	*40.2%*
TOTAL	*2014*	*1,155,782*	*734,456*		*382,208*		*39,118*	*352,248 R*	*63.5%*	*33.1%*	*65.8%*	*34.2%*
TOTAL	*2012*	*1,802,734*	*1,026,129*		*742,805*		*33,800*	*283,324 R*	*56.9%*	*41.2%*	*58.0%*	*42.0%*

Note: An asterisk (*) denotes incumbent. Some Democratic candidates received votes on additional ballot lines for the Working Families Party and the Green Party. These votes are included in their totals above.

SOUTH CAROLINA

GENERAL AND PRIMARY ELECTIONS

2018 GENERAL ELECTIONS: OTHER VOTES

Governor Other vote was 2,045 Write-in (Write-in)

House Other vote was:

CD 1 505 Write-in (Write-in)
CD 2 3,111 American and Republican (Sonny Narang), 187 Write-in (Write-in)
CD 3 2,697 American and Republican (Dave Moore), 123 Write-in (Write-in)
CD 4 9,203 American and Republican (Guy Furay), 244 Write-in (Write-in)
CD 5 3,443 Constitution (Michael Chandler), 250 Write-in (Write-in)
CD 6 319 American (Josh Thornton), 273 Libertarian (Victor Kocher), 242 Green (David Kulma), 65 Write-in (Write-in)
CD 7 3,214 Green (Bryan Pugh), 172 Write-in (Write-in)

SOUTH CAROLINA

GENERAL AND PRIMARY ELECTIONS

2018 PRIMARY ELECTIONS: SUPPLEMENTARY INFORMATION

Primary	June 12, 2018	**Registration** (as of June 12, 2018)	3,061,670	No Party Registration
Primary Runoff	June 26, 2018			
Primary Type	Open—Any registered voter could participate in either the Democratic or Republican primary, although any voter who participated in one party's primary could not vote in a runoff of the other party.			

	REPUBLICAN PRIMARIES			DEMOCRATIC PRIMARIES		
Governor	McMaster, Henry D.*	155,723	42.3%	Smith, James	148,633	61.8%
	Warren, John	102,390	27.8%	Willis, Marguerite	66,248	27.5%
	Templeton, Catherine	78,705	21.4%	Noble, Phil	25,587	10.6%
	Bryant, Kevin	24,790	6.7%			
	McGill, Yancey	6,375	1.7%			
	TOTAL	*367,983*		*TOTAL*	*240,468*	
	PRIMARY RUNOFF					
	McMaster, Henry D.*	184,286	53,6%			
	Warren, John	159,349	46.4%			
	TOTAL	*343,635*				
Congressional District 1	Arrington, Katie	33,153	50.6%	Cunningham, Joe	23,493	71.5%
	Sanford, Mark*	30,496	46.5%	Smith, Toby	9,366	28.5%
	Cherny, Dimitri	1,932	2.9%			
	TOTAL	*65,581*		*TOTAL*	*32,859*	
Congressional District 2	Wilson, Joe*	Unopposed		Robertson, Annabelle	14,168	41.8%
				Carrigan, Sean	13,496	39.8%
				Black, Phil	6,225	18.4%
				TOTAL	*33,889*	
				PRIMARY RUNOFF		
				Carrigan, Sean	5,733	53.3%
				Robertson, Annabelle	5,016	46.7%
				TOTAL	*10,749*	
Congressional District 3	Duncan, Jeff*	Unopposed		Geren, Mary	12,971	69.7%
				Cleveland, Hosea	5,630	30.3%
				TOTAL	*18,601*	
Congressional District 4	Bright, Lee	16,742	25.0%	Turner, Doris	7,070	29.5%
	Timmons, William	12,885	19.2%	Brown, Brandon P.	6,833	28.5%
	Hamilton, Daniel	12,494	18.6%	Graben, Eric	6,174	25.7%
	Kimbrell, Joshua	7,465	11.1%	Morin, Will	2,192	9.1%
	Epley, James	5,386	8.0%	Davis, John "J.T."	1,733	7.2%
	Brown, Stephen	5,078	7.6%			
	Pierce, Shannon	2,442	3.6%			
	Burns, Mark	1,662	2.5%			
	Schmid, Claude	1,415	2.1%			
	Albert, Dan	510	0.8%			
	Mosser, John	457	0.7%			
	Sanders, Justin	354	0.5%			
	Bell, Barry	200	0.3%			
	TOTAL	*67,090*		*TOTAL*	*24,002*	
	PRIMARY RUNOFF			**PRIMARY RUNOFF**		
	Timmons, William	37,096	54.3%	Brown, Brandon P.	7,097	62.1%
	Bright, Lee	31,236	45.7%	Turner, Doris	4,340	37.9%
	TOTAL	*68,332*		*TOTAL*	*11,437*	

SOUTH CAROLINA

GENERAL AND PRIMARY ELECTIONS

	REPUBLICAN PRIMARIES			DEMOCRATIC PRIMARIES		
Congressional District 5	Norman, Ralph*	Unopposed		Parnell, Archie	16,648	60.0%
				Moore, Sidney	4,766	17.2%
				Ali, Mark	3,722	13.4%
				Lough, Steve	2,627	9.5%
				TOTAL	*27,763*	
Congressional District 6	Gressmann, Gerhard	Unopposed		Clyburn, James E.*	Unopposed	
Congressional District 7	Rice, Tom*	38,346	83.6%	Williams, Robert	14,222	41.3%
	Hammond, Larry Guy	7,532	16.4%	Hyman, Mal	10,225	29.7%
				Hopkins, Bill	6,122	17.8%
				Fischer, Bruce	3,863	11.2%
	TOTAL	*45,878*		*TOTAL*	*34,432*	
				PRIMARY RUNOFF		
				Williams, Robert	7,729	51.4%
				Hyman, Mal	7,309	48.6%
				TOTAL	*15,038*	

Note: An asterisk (*) denotes incumbent.

SOUTH DAKOTA

One member At Large

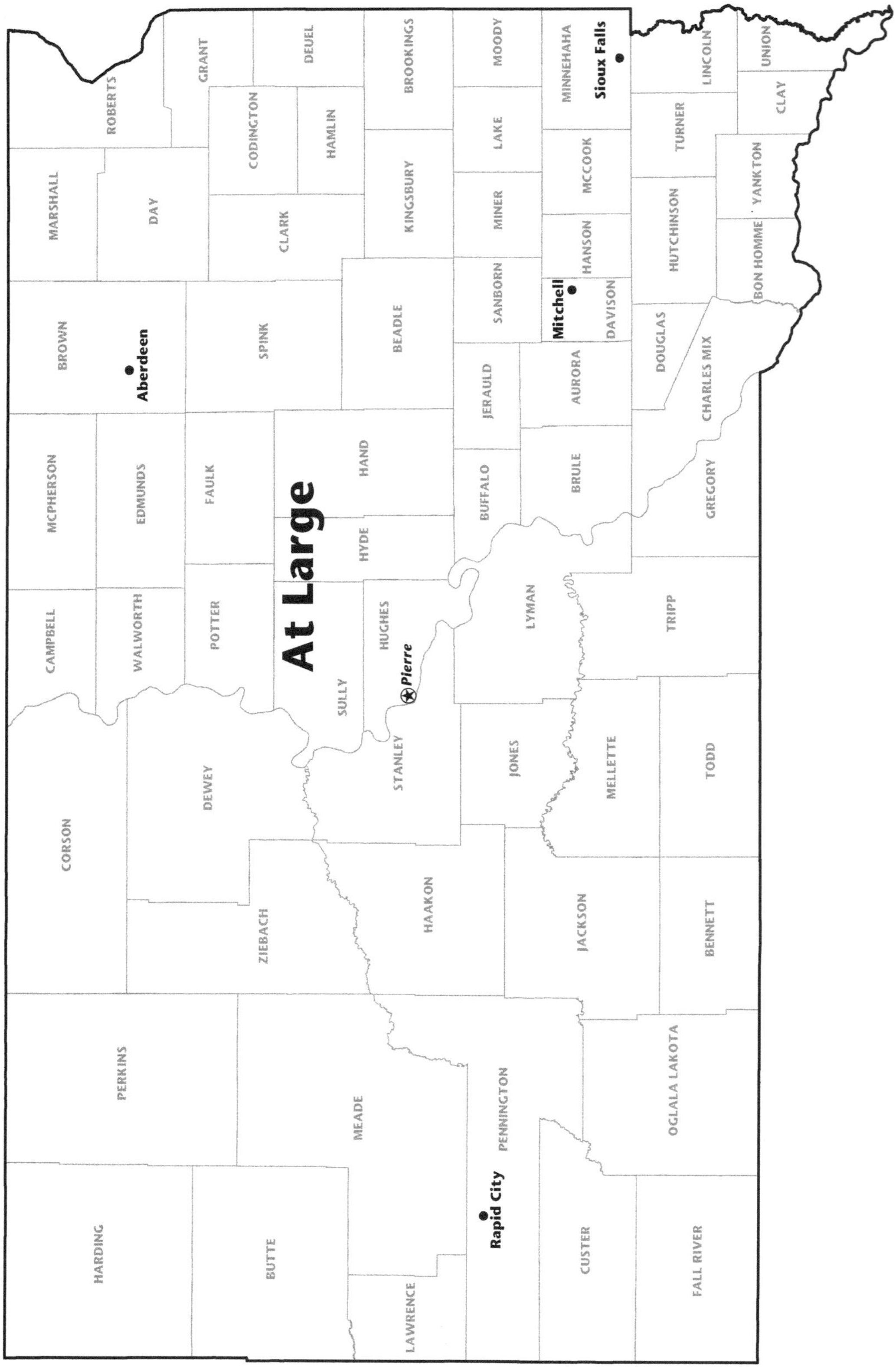

SOUTH DAKOTA

GOVERNOR

Kristi Noem (R). Elected 2018 to a four-year term.

SENATORS (2 Republicans)

Mike Rounds (R). Elected 2014 to a six-year term.

John Thune (R). Re-elected 2016 to a six-year term. Previously elected 2010, 2004.

REPRESENTATIVE (1 Republican)

At Large. Dusty Johnson (R)

POSTWAR VOTE FOR PRESIDENT

		Republican		Democratic				Percentage			
								Total Vote		Major Vote	
Year	Total Vote	Vote	Candidate	Vote	Candidate	Other Vote	Rep.-Dem. Plurality	Rep.	Dem.	Rep.	Dem.
2016**	370,093	227,721	Trump, Donald J.	117,458	Clinton, Hillary Rodham	24,914	110,263 R	61.5%	31.7%	66.0%	34.0%
2012	363,815	210,610	Romney, W. Mitt	145,039	Obama, Barack H.*	8,166	65,571 R	57.9%	39.9%	59.2%	40.8%
2008	381,975	203,054	McCain, John S. III	170,924	Obama, Barack H.	7,997	32,130 R	53.2%	44.7%	54.3%	45.7%
2004	388,215	232,584	Bush, George W.*	149,244	Kerry, John F.	6,387	83,340 R	59.9%	38.4%	60.9%	39.1%
2000	316,269	190,700	Bush, George W.	118,804	Gore, Albert Jr.	6,765	71,896 R	60.3%	37.6%	61.6%	38.4%
1996**	323,826	150,543	Dole, Robert "Bob"	139,333	Clinton, Bill*	33,950	11,210 R	46.5%	43.0%	51.9%	48.1%
1992**	336,254	136,718	Bush, George H.*	124,888	Clinton, Bill	74,648	11,830 R	40.7%	37.1%	52.3%	47.7%
1988	312,991	165,415	Bush, George H.	145,560	Dukakis, Michael S.	2,016	19,855 R	52.8%	46.5%	53.2%	46.8%
1984	317,867	200,267	Reagan, Ronald*	116,113	Mondale, Walter F.	1,487	84,154 R	63.0%	36.5%	63.3%	36.7%
1980**	327,703	198,343	Reagan, Ronald	103,855	Carter, Jimmy*	25,505	94,488 R	60.5%	31.7%	65.6%	34.4%
1976	300,678	151,505	Ford, Gerald R.*	147,068	Carter, Jimmy	2,105	4,437 R	50.4%	48.9%	50.7%	49.3%
1972	307,415	166,476	Nixon, Richard M.*	139,945	McGovern, George S.	994	26,531 R	54.2%	45.5%	54.3%	45.7%
1968**	281,264	149,841	Nixon, Richard M.	118,023	Humphrey, Hubert Horatio Jr.	13,400	31,818 R	53.3%	42.0%	55.9%	44.1%
1964	293,118	130,108	Goldwater, Barry M. Sr.	163,010	Johnson, Lyndon B.*		32,902 D	44.4%	55.6%	44.4%	55.6%
1960	306,487	178,417	Nixon, Richard M.	128,070	Kennedy, John F.		50,347 R	58.2%	41.8%	58.2%	41.8%
1956	293,857	171,569	Eisenhower, Dwight D.*	122,288	Stevenson, Adlai E. II		49,281 R	58.4%	41.6%	58.4%	41.6%
1952	294,283	203,857	Eisenhower, Dwight D.	90,426	Stevenson, Adlai E. II		113,431 R	69.3%	30.7%	69.3%	30.7%
1948	250,105	129,651	Dewey, Thomas E.	117,653	Truman, Harry S.*	2,801	11,998 R	51.8%	47.0%	52.4%	47.6%

Note: An asterisk (*) denotes incumbent. **In past elections, the other vote included: 2016 - 20,850 Libertarian (Gary Johnson); 1996 - 31,250 Reform (Ross Perot); 1992 - 73,295 Independent (Perot); 1980 - 21,431 Independent (John Anderson); 1968 - 13,400 American Independent (George Wallace).

SOUTH DAKOTA

POSTWAR VOTE FOR GOVERNOR

		Republican		Democratic				Percentage			
								Total Vote		Major Vote	
Year	Total Vote	Vote	Candidate	Vote	Candidate	Other Vote	Rep.-Dem. Plurality	Rep.	Dem.	Rep.	Dem.
2018	339,214	172,912	Noem, Kristi	161,454	Sutton, Billie	4,848	11,458 R	51.0%	47.6%	51.7%	48.3%
2014	277,403	195,477	Daugaard, Dennis*	70,549	Wismer, Susan	11,377	124,928 R	70.5%	25.4%	73.5%	26.5%
2010	317,083	195,046	Daugaard, Dennis	122,037	Heidepriem, Scott		73,009 R	61.5%	38.5%	61.5%	38.5%
2006	335,508	206,990	Rounds, Mike*	121,226	Billion, Jack	7,292	85,764 R	61.7%	36.1%	63.1%	36.9%
2002	334,559	189,920	Rounds, Mike	140,263	Abbott, Jim	4,376	49,657 R	56.8%	41.9%	57.5%	42.5%
1998	260,187	166,621	Janklow, William J.*	85,473	Hunhoff, Bernie	8,093	81,148 R	64.0%	32.9%	66.1%	33.9%
1994	311,613	172,515	Janklow, William J.	126,273	Beddow, Jim	12,825	46,242 R	55.4%	40.5%	57.7%	42.3%
1990	256,723	151,198	Mickelson, George S.*	105,525	Samuelson, Bob L.		45,673 R	58.9%	41.1%	58.9%	41.1%
1986	294,441	152,543	Mickelson, George S.	141,898	Herseth, R. Lars		10,645 R	51.8%	48.2%	51.8%	48.2%
1982	278,565	197,429	Janklow, William J.*	81,136	O'Connor, Michael J.		116,293 R	70.9%	29.1%	70.9%	29.1%
1978	259,795	147,116	Janklow, William J.	112,679	McKellips, Roger		34,437 R	56.6%	43.4%	56.6%	43.4%
1974	278,228	129,077	Olson, John E.	149,151	Kneip, Richard F.*		20,074 D	46.4%	53.6%	46.4%	53.6%
1972	308,177	123,165	Thompson, Carveth	185,012	Kneip, Richard F.*		61,847 D	40.0%	60.0%	40.0%	60.0%
1970	239,963	108,347	Farrar, Frank*	131,616	Kneip, Richard F.		23,269 D	45.2%	54.8%	45.2%	54.8%
1968	276,906	159,646	Farrar, Frank	117,260	Chamerlin, Robert		42,386 R	57.7%	42.3%	57.7%	42.3%
1966	228,214	131,710	Boe, Nils A.*	96,504	Chamerlin, Robert		35,206 R	57.7%	42.3%	57.7%	42.3%
1964	290,570	150,151	Boe, Nils A.	140,419	Lindley, John F.		9,732 R	51.7%	48.3%	51.7%	48.3%
1962	256,120	143,682	Gubbrud, Archie M.*	112,438	Herseth, Ralph		31,244 R	56.1%	43.9%	56.1%	43.9%
1960	304,625	154,530	Gubbrud, Archie M.	150,095	Herseth, Ralph*		4,435 R	50.7%	49.3%	50.7%	49.3%
1958	258,281	125,520	Saunders, Phil	132,761	Herseth, Ralph		7,241 D	48.6%	51.4%	48.6%	51.4%
1956	292,017	158,819	Foss, Joe*	133,198	Herseth, Ralph		25,621 R	54.4%	45.6%	54.4%	45.6%
1954	236,255	133,878	Foss, Joe	102,377	Martin, Ed C.		31,501 R	56.7%	43.3%	56.7%	43.3%
1952	289,514	203,102	Anderson, Sigurd*	86,412	Iverson, Sherman A.		116,690 R	70.2%	29.8%	70.2%	29.8%
1950	253,316	154,254	Anderson, Sigurd	99,062	Robbie, Joe		55,192 R	60.9%	39.1%	60.9%	39.1%
1948	245,372	149,883	Mickelson, George T.*	95,489	Volz, Harold J.		54,394 R	61.1%	38.9%	61.1%	38.9%
1946	162,292	108,998	Mickelson, George T.	53,294	Haeder, Richard		55,704 R	67.2%	32.8%	67.2%	32.8%

Note: An asterisk (*) denotes incumbent. The term of office of South Dakota's governor was increased from two to four years effective with the 1974 election.

POSTWAR VOTE FOR SENATOR

		Republican		Democratic				Percentage			
								Total Vote		Major Vote	
Year	Total Vote	Vote	Candidate	Vote	Candidate	Other Vote	Rep.-Dem. Plurality	Rep.	Dem.	Rep.	Dem.
2016	369,656	265,516	Thune, John*	104,140	Williams, Jay		161,376 R	71.8%	28.2%	71.8%	28.2%
2014**	279,412	140,741	Rounds, Mike	82,456	Weiland, Rick	56,215	58,285 R	50.4%	29.5%	63.1%	36.9%
2010	227,947	227,947	Thune, John*				227,947 R	100.0%		100.0%	
2008	380,673	142,784	Dykstra, Joel	237,889	Johnson, Timothy P.*		95,105 D	37.5%	62.5%	37.5%	62.5%
2004	391,188	197,848	Thune, John	193,340	Daschle, Thomas A.*		4,508 R	50.6%	49.4%	50.6%	49.4%
2002	337,508	166,957	Thune, John	167,481	Johnson, Timothy P.*	3,070	524 D	49.5%	49.6%	49.9%	50.1%
1998	262,111	95,431	Schmidt, Ron	162,884	Daschle, Thomas A.*	3,796	67,453 D	36.4%	62.1%	36.9%	63.1%
1996	324,487	157,954	Pressler, Larry*	166,533	Johnson, Timothy P.		8,579 D	48.7%	51.3%	48.7%	51.3%
1992	334,495	108,733	Haar, Charlene	217,095	Daschle, Thomas A.*	8,667	108,362 D	32.5%	64.9%	33.4%	66.6%
1990	258,976	135,682	Pressler, Larry*	116,727	Muenster, Ted	6,567	18,955 R	52.4%	45.1%	53.8%	46.2%
1986	295,830	143,173	Abdnor, James*	152,657	Daschle, Thomas A.		9,484 D	48.4%	51.6%	48.4%	51.6%
1984	315,713	235,176	Pressler, Larry*	80,537	Cunningham, George V.		154,639 R	74.5%	25.5%	74.5%	25.5%
1980	327,478	190,594	Abdnor, James	129,018	McGovern, George S.*	7,866	61,576 R	58.2%	39.4%	59.6%	40.4%
1978	255,599	170,832	Pressler, Larry	84,767	Barnett, Don		86,065 R	66.8%	33.2%	66.8%	33.2%
1974	278,884	130,955	Thorsness, Leo K.	147,929	McGovern, George S.*		16,974 D	47.0%	53.0%	47.0%	53.0%
1972	306,386	131,613	Hirsch, Robert W.	174,773	Abourezk, James George*		43,160 D	43.0%	57.0%	43.0%	57.0%
1968	279,912	120,951	Gubbrud, Archie M.	158,961	McGovern, George S.*		38,010 D	43.2%	56.8%	43.2%	56.8%
1966	227,080	150,517	Mundt, Karl E.*	76,563	Wright, Donn H.		73,954 R	66.3%	33.7%	66.3%	33.7%
1962	254,319	126,861	Bottum, Joe*	127,458	McGovern, George S.		597 D	49.9%	50.1%	49.9%	50.1%
1960	305,442	160,181	Mundt, Karl E.*	145,261	McGovern, George S.		14,920 R	52.4%	47.6%	52.4%	47.6%
1956	290,622	147,621	Case, Francis*	143,001	Holum, Kenneth		4,620 R	50.8%	49.2%	50.8%	49.2%
1954	235,745	135,071	Mundt, Karl E.*	100,674	Holum, Kenneth		34,397 R	57.3%	42.7%	57.3%	42.7%
1950	251,362	160,670	Case, Francis	90,692	Engel, John A.		69,978 R	63.9%	36.1%	63.9%	36.1%
1948	242,833	144,084	Mundt, Karl E.	98,749	Engel, John A.		45,335 R	59.3%	40.7%	59.3%	40.7%

Note: An asterisk (*) denotes incumbent. ** In past elections, the other vote included: 2014 - 47,741 Independent (Larry Pressler). The Democratic Party did not run a Senate candidate in the 2010 election.

SOUTH DAKOTA

GOVERNOR 2018

2010 Census Population	County	Total Vote	Republican (Noem)	Democratic (Sutton)	Other	Rep.-Dem. Plurality	Percentage: Total Vote Rep.	Percentage: Total Vote Dem.	Percentage: Major Vote Rep.	Percentage: Major Vote Dem.
2,710	AURORA	1,280	644	607	29	37 R	50.3%	47.4%	51.5%	48.5%
17,398	BEADLE	6,108	3,182	2,832	94	350 R	52.1%	46.4%	52.9%	47.1%
3,431	BENNETT	1,102	553	523	26	30 R	50.2%	47.5%	51.4%	48.6%
7,070	BON HOMME	2,747	1,303	1,408	36	105 D	47.4%	51.3%	48.1%	51.9%
31,965	BROOKINGS	11,780	5,225	6,372	183	1,147 D	44.4%	54.1%	45.1%	54.9%
36,531	BROWN	14,365	6,821	7,338	206	517 D	47.5%	51.1%	48.2%	51.8%
5,255	BRULE	2,130	1,103	991	36	112 R	51.8%	46.5%	52.7%	47.3%
1,912	BUFFALO	548	138	403	7	265 D	25.2%	73.5%	25.5%	74.5%
10,110	BUTTE	3,808	2,505	1,234	69	1,271 R	65.8%	32.4%	67.0%	33.0%
1,466	CAMPBELL	732	550	173	9	377 R	75.1%	23.6%	76.1%	23.9%
9,129	CHARLES MIX	3,552	1,661	1,853	38	192 D	46.8%	52.2%	47.3%	52.7%
3,691	CLARK	1,664	879	768	17	111 R	52.8%	46.2%	53.4%	46.6%
13,864	CLAY	4,644	1,552	3,039	53	1,487 D	33.4%	65.4%	33.8%	66.2%
27,227	CODINGTON	10,693	5,865	4,697	131	1,168 R	54.8%	43.9%	55.5%	44.5%
4,050	CORSON	1,110	426	667	17	241 D	38.4%	60.1%	39.0%	61.0%
8,216	CUSTER	4,409	2,789	1,547	73	1,242 R	63.3%	35.1%	64.3%	35.7%
19,504	DAVISON	7,274	3,779	3,398	97	381 R	52.0%	46.7%	52.7%	47.3%
5,710	DAY	2,777	1,207	1,531	39	324 D	43.5%	55.1%	44.1%	55.9%
4,364	DEUEL	1,989	1,053	893	43	160 R	52.9%	44.9%	54.1%	45.9%
5,301	DEWEY	1,841	393	1,430	18	1,037 D	21.3%	77.7%	21.6%	78.4%
3,002	DOUGLAS	1,496	1,120	363	13	757 R	74.9%	24.3%	75.5%	24.5%
4,071	EDMUNDS	1,708	1,018	671	19	347 R	59.6%	39.3%	60.3%	39.7%
7,094	FALL RIVER	3,192	2,059	1,065	68	994 R	64.5%	33.4%	65.9%	34.1%
2,364	FAULK	1,075	674	388	13	286 R	62.7%	36.1%	63.5%	36.5%
7,356	GRANT	3,220	1,780	1,388	52	392 R	55.3%	43.1%	56.2%	43.8%
4,271	GREGORY	2,153	1,107	1,029	17	78 R	51.4%	47.8%	51.8%	48.2%
1,937	HAAKON	945	734	196	15	538 R	77.7%	20.7%	78.9%	21.1%
5,903	HAMLIN	2,716	1,764	923	29	841 R	64.9%	34.0%	65.6%	34.4%
3,431	HAND	1,662	950	683	29	267 R	57.2%	41.1%	58.2%	41.8%
3,331	HANSON	1,610	945	647	18	298 R	58.7%	40.2%	59.4%	40.6%
1,255	HARDING	686	505	174	7	331 R	73.6%	25.4%	74.4%	25.6%
17,022	HUGHES	8,007	3,749	4,144	114	395 D	46.8%	51.8%	47.5%	52.5%
7,343	HUTCHINSON	3,290	2,082	1,180	28	902 R	63.3%	35.9%	63.8%	36.2%
1,420	HYDE	660	407	248	5	159 R	61.7%	37.6%	62.1%	37.9%
3,031	JACKSON	987	513	454	20	59 R	52.0%	46.0%	53.1%	46.9%
2,071	JERAULD	663	478	173	12	305 R	72.1%	26.1%	73.4%	26.6%
1,006	JONES	373	361	0	12	349 R	96.8%	0.0%	100.0%	0.0%
5,148	KINGSBURY	2,455	1,303	1,111	41	192 R	53.1%	45.3%	54.0%	46.0%
11,200	LAKE	5,207	2,483	2,669	55	186 D	47.7%	51.3%	48.2%	51.8%
24,097	LAWRENCE	10,898	5,984	4,675	239	1,309 R	54.9%	42.9%	56.1%	43.9%
44,828	LINCOLN	24,206	12,894	11,109	203	1,785 R	53.3%	45.9%	53.7%	46.3%
3,755	LYMAN	1,400	691	682	27	9 R	49.4%	48.7%	50.3%	49.7%
4,656	MARSHALL	1,977	853	1,093	31	240 D	43.1%	55.3%	43.8%	56.2%
5,618	MCCOOK	2,497	1,375	1,083	39	292 R	55.1%	43.4%	55.9%	44.1%
2,459	MCPHERSON	1,054	729	309	16	420 R	69.2%	29.3%	70.2%	29.8%
25,434	MEADE	10,228	6,413	3,559	256	2,854 R	62.7%	34.8%	64.3%	35.7%
2,048	MELLETTE	711	299	395	17	96 D	42.1%	55.6%	43.1%	56.9%
2,389	MINER	1,105	523	570	12	47 D	47.3%	51.6%	47.8%	52.2%
169,468	MINNEHAHA	70,681	32,355	37,450	876	5,095 D	45.8%	53.0%	46.4%	53.6%
6,486	MOODY	2,853	1,340	1,469	44	129 D	47.0%	51.5%	47.7%	52.3%
13,586	OGLALA LAKOTA	3,036	214	2,778	44	2,564 D	7.0%	91.5%	7.2%	92.8%
100,948	PENNINGTON	41,670	22,944	17,988	738	4,956 R	55.1%	43.2%	56.1%	43.9%
2,982	PERKINS	1,344	953	368	23	585 R	70.9%	27.4%	72.1%	27.9%
2,329	POTTER	1,209	821	373	15	448 R	67.9%	30.9%	68.8%	31.2%
10,149	ROBERTS	3,745	1,643	2,062	40	419 D	43.9%	55.1%	44.3%	55.7%
2,355	SANBORN	1,028	593	419	16	174 R	57.7%	40.8%	58.6%	41.4%
6,415	SPINK	2,807	1,376	1,394	37	18 D	49.0%	49.7%	49.7%	50.3%
2,966	STANLEY	1,487	762	704	21	58 R	51.2%	47.3%	52.0%	48.0%
1,373	SULLY	812	500	296	16	204 R	61.6%	36.5%	62.8%	37.2%
9,612	TODD	2,241	390	1,831	20	1,441 D	17.4%	81.7%	17.6%	82.4%
5,644	TRIPP	2,489	1,430	1,023	36	407 R	57.5%	41.1%	58.3%	41.7%
8,347	TURNER	3,867	2,272	1,556	39	716 R	58.8%	40.2%	59.4%	40.6%

SOUTH DAKOTA

GOVERNOR 2018

2010 Census Population	County	Total Vote	Republican (Noem)	Democratic (Sutton)	Other	Rep.-Dem. Plurality	Percentage Total Vote Rep.	Total Vote Dem.	Major Vote Rep.	Major Vote Dem.
14,399	UNION	6,685	4,068	2,544	73	1,524 R	60.9%	38.1%	61.5%	38.5%
5,438	WALWORTH	2,259	1,468	752	39	716 R	65.0%	33.3%	66.1%	33.9%
22,438	YANKTON	9,012	4,121	4,757	134	636 D	45.7%	52.8%	46.4%	53.6%
2,801	ZIEBACH	822	241	572	9	331 D	29.3%	69.6%	29.6%	70.4%
814,180	*TOTAL*	*339,214*	*172,912*	*161,454*	*4,848*	*11,458 R*	*51.0%*	*47.6%*	*51.7%*	*48.3%*

SOUTH DAKOTA

HOUSE OF REPRESENTATIVES

CD	Year	Total Vote	Republican Vote	Republican Candidate	Democratic Vote	Democratic Candidate	Other Vote	Rep.-Dem. Plurality	Percentage Total Vote Rep.	Total Vote Dem.	Major Vote Rep.	Major Vote Dem.
At Large	2018	335,965	202,695	JOHNSON, DUSTIN "DUSTY"	121,033	BJORKMAN, TIMOTHY	12,237	81,662 R	60.3%	36.0%	62.6%	37.4%
At Large	2016	369,973	237,163	NOEM, KRISTI*	132,810	HAWKS, PAULA		104,353 R	64.1%	35.9%	64.1%	35.9%
At Large	2014	276,319	183,834	NOEM, KRISTI*	92,485	ROBINSON, CORINNA		91,349 R	66.5%	33.5%	66.5%	33.5%
At Large	2012	361,429	207,640	NOEM, KRISTI*	153,789	VARILEK, MATT		53,851 R	57.4%	42.6%	57.4%	42.6%
At Large	2010	319,426	153,703	NOEM, KRISTI	146,589	SANDLIN, STEPHANIE HERSETH*	19,134	7,114 R	48.1%	45.9%	51.2%	48.8%
At Large	2008	379,007	122,966	LIEN, CHRIS	256,041	SANDLIN, STEPHANIE HERSETH*		133,075 D	32.4%	67.6%	32.4%	67.6%
At Large	2006	333,562	97,864	WHALEN, BRUCE W.	230,468	SANDLIN, STEPHANIE HERSETH*	5,230	132,604 D	29.3%	69.1%	29.8%	70.2%
At Large	2004	389,468	178,823	DIEDRICH, LARRY W.	207,837	SANDLIN, STEPHANIE HERSETH*	2,808	29,014 D	45.9%	53.4%	46.2%	53.8%
At Large	2002	336,807	180,023	JANKLOW, WILLIAM J.	153,656	SANDLIN, STEPHANIE HERSETH	3,128	26,367 R	53.4%	45.6%	54.0%	46.0%
At Large	2000	314,761	231,083	THUNE, JOHN*	78,321	HOHN, CURT	5,357	152,762 R	73.4%	24.9%	74.7%	25.3%
At Large	1998	258,590	194,157	THUNE, JOHN*	64,433	MOSER, JEFF		129,724 R	75.1%	24.9%	75.1%	24.9%
At Large	1996	323,203	186,393	THUNE, JOHN	119,547	WEILAND, RICK	17,263	66,846 R	57.7%	37.0%	60.9%	39.1%
At Large	1994	305,922	112,054	BERKHOUT, JAN	183,036	JOHNSON, TIMOTHY P.*	10,832	70,982 D	36.6%	59.8%	38.0%	62.0%
At Large	1992	332,902	89,375	TIMMER, JOHN	230,070	JOHNSON, TIMOTHY P.*	13,457	140,695 D	26.8%	69.1%	28.0%	72.0%
At Large	1990	257,298	83,484	FRANKENFELD, DON	173,814	JOHNSON, TIMOTHY P.*		90,330 D	32.4%	67.6%	32.4%	67.6%
At Large	1988	311,916	88,157	VOLK, DAVID	223,759	JOHNSON, TIMOTHY P.*		135,602 D	28.3%	71.7%	28.3%	71.7%
At Large	1986	289,723	118,261	BELL, DALE	171,462	JOHNSON, TIMOTHY P.		53,201 D	40.8%	59.2%	40.8%	59.2%
At Large	1984	316,222	134,821	BELL, DALE	181,401	DASCHLE, THOMAS A.*		46,580 D	42.6%	57.4%	42.6%	57.4%
At Large	1982	275,652	133,530	ROBERTS, CLINT*	142,122	DASCHLE, THOMAS A.*		8,592 D	48.4%	51.6%	48.4%	51.6%

Note: An asterisk (*) denotes incumbent. Prior to 1982, South Dakota had two congressional districts.

SOUTH DAKOTA

GENERAL AND PRIMARY ELECTIONS

2018 GENERAL ELECTIONS: OTHER VOTES

Governor Other vote was 4,848 Libertarian (Kurt Evans)

House Other vote was:

At Large 7,323 Independent (Ronald Wieczorek), 4,914 Libertarian (George Hendrickson)

SOUTH DAKOTA

GENERAL AND PRIMARY ELECTIONS

2018 PRIMARY ELECTIONS: SUPPLEMENTARY INFORMATION

Primary	June 5, 2018	**Registration** (as of June 5, 2018 — excluding 57,110 inactive registrants)	530,890	Republican	249,986
				Democratic	156,354
				Libertarian	1,719
				Other	791
				Constitution	470
				No Party Affiliation/ Independent	121,570

Primary Type Republicans held a "closed" primary, with only registered Republicans allowed to vote in it. Democrats held a "semi-open" primary, with registered Democrats, independents, and other voters not affiliated with a recognized political party eligible to cast a Democratic primary ballot.

	REPUBLICAN PRIMARIES			DEMOCRATIC PRIMARIES	
Governor	Noem, Kristi	57,598	56.0%	Sutton, Billie	Unopposed
	Jackley, Marty	45,174	44.0%		
	TOTAL	*102,772*			
Congressional At Large	Johnson, Dusty	47,120	46.8%	Bjorkman, Timothy	Unopposed
	Krebs, Shantel	29,551	29.3%		
	Tapio, Neal	24,040	23.9%		
	TOTAL	*100,711*			

TENNESSEE

Congressional districts first established for elections held in 2012
9 members

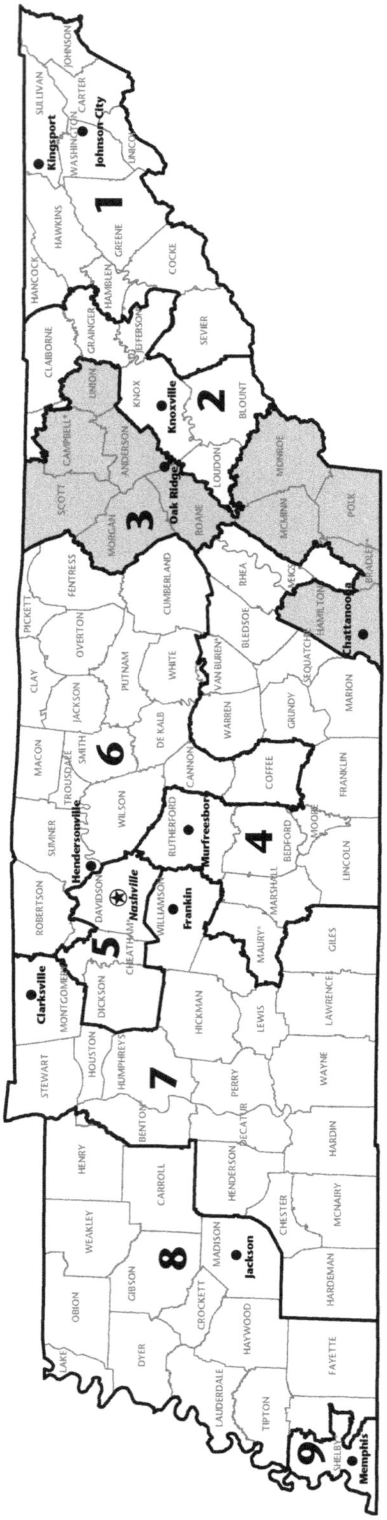

* Asterisk indicates a county whose boundaries include parts of two or more congressional districts.

TENNESSEE

GOVERNOR

Bill Lee (R). Elected 2018 to a four-year term.

SENATORS (2 Republicans)

Lamar Alexander (R). Re-elected 2014 to a six-year term. Previously elected 2008, 2002.

Marsha Blackburn (R). Elected 2018 to a six-year term.

REPRESENTATIVES (7 Republicans, 2 Democrats)

1. Phil Roe (R)
2. Tim Burchett (R)
3. Chuck Fleischmann (R)
4. Scott DesJarlais (R)
5. Jim Cooper (D)
6. John Rose (R)
7. Mark Green (R)
8. David Kustoff (R)
9. Steven I. Cohen (D)

POSTWAR VOTE FOR PRESIDENT

		Republican		Democratic				Percentage			
								Total Vote		Major Vote	
Year	Total Vote	Vote	Candidate	Vote	Candidate	Other Vote	Rep.-Dem. Plurality	Rep.	Dem.	Rep.	Dem.
2016**	2,508,027	1,522,925	Trump, Donald J.	870,695	Clinton, Hillary Rodham	114,407	652,230 R	60.7%	34.7%	63.6%	36.4%
2012	2,458,577	1,462,330	Romney, W. Mitt	960,709	Obama, Barack H.*	35,538	501,621 R	59.5%	39.1%	60.4%	39.6%
2008	2,599,749	1,479,178	McCain, John S. III	1,087,437	Obama, Barack H.	33,134	391,741 R	56.9%	41.8%	57.6%	42.4%
2004	2,437,319	1,384,375	Bush, George W.*	1,036,477	Kerry, John F.	16,467	347,898 R	56.8%	42.5%	57.2%	42.8%
2000**	2,076,181	1,061,949	Bush, George W.	981,720	Gore, Albert Jr.	32,512	80,229 R	51.1%	47.3%	52.0%	48.0%
1996**	1,894,105	863,530	Dole, Robert "Bob"	909,146	Clinton, Bill*	121,429	45,616 D	45.6%	48.0%	48.7%	51.3%
1992**	1,982,638	841,300	Bush, George H.*	933,521	Clinton, Bill	207,817	92,221 D	42.4%	47.1%	47.4%	52.6%
1988	1,636,250	947,233	Bush, George H.	679,794	Dukakis, Michael S.	9,223	267,439 R	57.9%	41.5%	58.2%	41.8%
1984	1,711,994	990,212	Reagan, Ronald*	711,714	Mondale, Walter F.	10,068	278,498 R	57.8%	41.6%	58.2%	41.8%
1980**	1,617,616	787,761	Reagan, Ronald	783,051	Carter, Jimmy*	46,804	4,710 R	48.7%	48.4%	50.1%	49.9%
1976	1,476,345	633,969	Ford, Gerald R.*	825,879	Carter, Jimmy	16,497	191,910 D	42.9%	55.9%	43.4%	56.6%
1972	1,201,182	813,147	Nixon, Richard M.*	357,293	McGovern, George S.	30,742	455,854 R	67.7%	29.7%	69.5%	30.5%
1968**	1,248,617	472,592	Nixon, Richard M.	351,233	Humphrey, Hubert Horatio Jr.	424,792	121,359 R	37.8%	28.1%	57.4%	42.6%
1964	1,143,946	508,965	Goldwater, Barry M. Sr.	634,947	Johnson, Lyndon B.*	34	125,982 D	44.5%	55.5%	44.5%	55.5%
1960	1,051,792	556,577	Nixon, Richard M.	481,453	Kennedy, John F.	13,762	75,124 R	52.9%	45.8%	53.6%	46.4%
1956	939,404	462,288	Eisenhower, Dwight D.*	456,507	Stevenson, Adlai E. II	20,609	5,781 R	49.2%	48.6%	50.3%	49.7%
1952	892,553	446,147	Eisenhower, Dwight D.	443,710	Stevenson, Adlai E. II	2,696	2,437 R	50.0%	49.7%	50.1%	49.9%
1948**	550,283	202,914	Dewey, Thomas E.	270,402	Truman, Harry S.*	76,967	67,488 D	36.9%	49.1%	42.9%	57.1%

Note: An asterisk (*) denotes incumbent. **In past elections, the other vote included: 2016 - 70,397 Libertarian (Gary Johnson); 2000 - 19,781 Green (Ralph Nader); 1996 - 105,918 Reform (Ross Perot); 1992 - 199,968 Independent (Perot); 1980 - 35,991 Independent (John Anderson); 1968 - 424,792 American Independent (George Wallace), who finished second; 1948 - 73,815 States' Rights (Strom Thurmond).

TENNESSEE

POSTWAR VOTE FOR GOVERNOR

		Republican		Democratic				Percentage			
								Total Vote		Major Vote	
Year	Total Vote	Vote	Candidate	Vote	Candidate	Other Vote	Rep.-Dem. Plurality	Rep.	Dem.	Rep.	Dem.
2018	2,243,294	1,336,106	Lee, Bill	864,863	Dean, Karl	42,325	471,243 R	59.6%	38.6%	60.7%	39.3%
2014	1,353,728	951,796	Haslam, Bill*	309,237	Brown, Charles V. "Charlie"	92,695	642,559 R	70.3%	22.8%	75.5%	24.5%
2010	1,601,549	1,041,545	Haslam, Bill	529,851	McWherter, Mike	30,153	511,694 R	65.0%	33.1%	66.3%	33.7%
2006	1,818,549	540,853	Bryson, Jim	1,247,491	Bredesen, Phil*	30,205	706,638 D	29.7%	68.6%	30.2%	69.8%
2002	1,653,167	786,803	Hilleary, Van	837,284	Bredesen, Phil	29,080	50,481 D	47.6%	50.6%	48.4%	51.6%
1998	976,236	669,973	Sundquist, Don*	287,750	Hooker, John Jay Jr.	18,513	382,223 R	68.6%	29.5%	70.0%	30.0%
1994	1,487,124	807,107	Sundquist, Don	664,243	Bredesen, Phil	15,774	142,864 R	54.3%	44.7%	54.9%	45.1%
1990	790,441	289,348	Henry, Dwight	480,885	McWherter, Ned*	20,208	191,537 D	36.6%	60.8%	37.6%	62.4%
1986	1,210,339	553,449	Dunn, Winfield	656,602	McWherter, Ned	288	103,153 D	45.7%	54.2%	45.7%	54.3%
1982	1,238,927	737,963	Alexander, Lamar*	500,937	Tyree, Randy	27	237,026 R	59.6%	40.4%	59.6%	40.4%
1978	1,189,695	661,959	Alexander, Lamar	523,495	Butcher, Jake	4,241	138,464 R	55.6%	44.0%	55.8%	44.2%
1974	1,040,714	455,467	Alexander, Lamar	576,833	Blanton, L. Ray	8,414	121,366 D	43.8%	55.4%	44.1%	55.9%
1970	1,108,247	575,777	Dunn, Winfield	509,521	Hooker, John Jay Jr.	22,949	66,256 R	52.0%	46.0%	53.1%	46.9%
1966	656,566			532,998	Ellington, Buford	123,568	532,998 D		81.2%		100.0%
1962**	620,758	99,884	Patty, Hubert D.	315,648	Clement, Frank G.	205,226	215,764 D	16.1%	50.8%	24.0%	76.0%
1958**	432,545	35,938	Wall, Thomas P.	248,874	Ellington, Buford	147,733	212,936 D	8.3%	57.5%	12.6%	87.4%
1954**	322,586			281,291	Clement, Frank G.*	41,295	281,291 D		87.2%		100.0%
1952	806,771	166,377	Witt, R. Beecher	640,290	Clement, Frank G.	104	473,913 D	20.6%	79.4%	20.6%	79.4%
1950**	236,194			184,437	Browning, Gordon*	51,757	184,437 D		78.1%		100.0%
1948	543,881	179,957	Acuff, Roy	363,903	Browning, Gordon	21	183,946 D	33.1%	66.9%	33.1%	66.9%
1946	229,456	73,222	Lowe, W. O.	149,937	McCord, James N.*	6,297	76,715 D	31.9%	65.3%	32.8%	67.2%

Note: An asterisk (*) denotes incumbent. **In past elections, the other vote included: 1962 - 203,765 Independent (William R. Anderson), who finished second; 1958 - 136,399 Independent (Jim Nance McCord), who finished second; 1954 - 39,574 Independent (John R. Neal), who finished second; 1950 - 51,757 Independent (Neal), who finished second. The Republican Party did not run a gubernatorial candidate in 1950, 1954, and 1966. The term of office of Tennessee's governor was increased from two to four years effective with the 1954 election.

POSTWAR VOTE FOR SENATOR

		Republican		Democratic				Percentage			
								Total Vote		Major Vote	
Year	Total Vote	Vote	Candidate	Vote	Candidate	Other Vote	Rep.-Dem. Plurality	Rep.	Dem.	Rep.	Dem.
2018	2,243,740	1,227,483	Blackburn, Marsha	985,450	Bredesen, Phil	30,807	242,033 R	54.7%	43.9%	55.5%	44.5%
2014	1,366,628	850,087	Alexander, Lamar*	437,848	Ball, Gordon	78,693	412,239 R	62.2%	32.0%	66.0%	34.0%
2012	2,321,477	1,506,443	Corker, Bob*	705,882	Clayton, Mark E.	109,152	800,561 R	64.9%	30.4%	68.1%	31.9%
2008	2,424,585	1,579,477	Alexander, Lamar*	767,236	Tuke, Robert D.	77,872	812,241 R	65.1%	31.6%	67.3%	32.7%
2006	1,833,695	929,911	Corker, Bøb	879,976	Ford, Harold E. Jr.	23,808	49,935 R	50.7%	48.0%	51.4%	48.6%
2002	1,642,421	891,420	Alexander, Lamar	728,295	Clement, Robert Nelson	22,706	163,125 R	54.3%	44.3%	55.0%	45.0%
2000	1,928,613	1,255,444	Frist, William H.*	621,152	Clark, Jeff	52,017	634,292 R	65.1%	32.2%	66.9%	33.1%
1996	1,778,664	1,091,554	Thompson, Fred*	654,937	Houston, Gordon J.	32,173	436,617 R	61.4%	36.8%	62.5%	37.5%
1994	1,480,391	834,226	Frist, William H.	623,164	Sasser, James R.*	23,001	211,062 R	56.4%	42.1%	57.2%	42.8%
1994S**	1,465,862	885,998	Thompson, Fred	565,930	Cooper, Jim	13,934	320,068 R	60.4%	38.6%	61.0%	39.0%
1990	783,922	233,703	Hawkins, William R.	530,898	Gore, Albert Jr.*	19,321	297,195 D	29.8%	67.7%	30.6%	69.4%
1988	1,567,181	541,033	Anderson, Bill	1,020,061	Sasser, James R.*	6,087	479,028 D	34.5%	65.1%	34.7%	65.3%
1984	1,648,036	557,016	Ashe, Victor	1,000,607	Gore, Albert Jr.	90,413	443,591 D	33.8%	60.7%	35.8%	64.2%
1982	1,259,785	479,642	Beard, Robin L.	780,113	Sasser, James R.*	30	300,471 D	38.1%	61.9%	38.1%	61.9%
1978	1,157,094	642,644	Baker, Howard H. Jr.*	466,228	Eskind, Jane	48,222	176,416 R	55.5%	40.3%	58.0%	42.0%
1976	1,432,046	673,231	Brock, William E.*	751,180	Sasser, James R.	7,635	77,949 D	47.0%	52.5%	47.3%	52.7%
1972	1,164,195	716,539	Baker, Howard H. Jr.*	440,599	Blanton, L. Ray	7,057	275,940 R	61.5%	37.8%	61.9%	38.1%
1970	1,097,041	562,645	Brock, William E.	519,858	Gore, Albert Sr.*	14,538	42,787 R	51.3%	47.4%	52.0%	48.0%
1966	866,961	483,063	Baker, Howard H. Jr.*	383,843	Clement, Frank G.	55	99,220 R	55.7%	44.3%	55.7%	44.3%
1964	1,064,018	493,475	Kuykendall, Daniel H.	570,542	Gore, Albert Sr.*	1	77,067 D	46.4%	53.6%	46.4%	53.6%
1964S**	1,091,093	517,330	Baker, Howard H. Jr.	568,905	Bass, Ross	4,858	51,575 D	47.4%	52.1%	47.6%	52.4%
1960	828,519	234,053	Frazier, A. Bradley	594,460	Kefauver, Estes*	6	360,407 D	28.2%	71.7%	28.2%	71.8%
1958	401,666	76,371	Atkins, Hobart F.	317,324	Gore, Albert Sr.*	7,971	240,953 D	19.0%	79.0%	19.4%	80.6%
1954	356,094	106,971	Wall, Tom	249,121	Kefauver, Estes*	2	142,150 D	30.0%	70.0%	30.0%	70.0%
1952	735,219	153,479	Atkins, Hobart F.	545,432	Gore, Albert Sr.	36,308	391,953 D	20.9%	74.2%	22.0%	78.0%
1948	499,138	166,947	Reece, B. Carroll	326,062	Kefauver, Estes	6,129	159,115 D	33.4%	65.3%	33.9%	66.1%
1946	218,713	57,237	Ladd, W. B.	145,654	McKellar, Kenneth D.*	15,822	88,417 D	26.2%	66.6%	28.2%	71.8%

Note: An asterisk (*) denotes incumbent. **One each of the 1964 and 1994 elections was for a short term to fill a vacancy.

TENNESSEE

GOVERNOR 2018

2010 Census Population	County	Total Vote	Republican (Lee)	Democratic (Dean)	Other	Rep.-Dem. Plurality	Percentage Total Vote Rep.	Total Vote Dem.	Major Vote Rep.	Major Vote Dem.
75,129	ANDERSON	26,040	16,265	9,462	313	6,803 R	62.5%	36.3%	63.2%	36.8%
45,058	BEDFORD	13,049	9,489	3,447	113	6,042 R	72.7%	26.4%	73.4%	26.6%
16,489	BENTON	5,346	3,696	1,599	51	2,097 R	69.1%	29.9%	69.8%	30.2%
12,876	BLEDSOE	4,072	3,102	923	47	2,179 R	76.2%	22.7%	77.1%	22.9%
123,010	BLOUNT	46,775	32,958	13,362	455	19,596 R	70.5%	28.6%	71.2%	28.8%
98,963	BRADLEY	33,765	26,123	7,287	355	18,836 R	77.4%	21.6%	78.2%	21.8%
40,716	CAMPBELL	10,154	7,820	2,189	145	5,631 R	77.0%	21.6%	78.1%	21.9%
13,801	CANNON	4,657	3,473	1,157	27	2,316 R	74.6%	24.8%	75.0%	25.0%
28,522	CARROLL	8,788	6,451	2,247	90	4,204 R	73.4%	25.6%	74.2%	25.8%
57,424	CARTER	18,617	14,922	3,525	170	11,397 R	80.2%	18.9%	80.9%	19.1%
39,105	CHEATHAM	14,459	9,966	4,417	76	5,549 R	68.9%	30.5%	69.3%	30.7%
17,131	CHESTER	5,387	4,161	1,131	95	3,030 R	77.2%	21.0%	78.6%	21.4%
32,213	CLAIBORNE	8,487	6,514	1,871	102	4,643 R	76.8%	22.0%	77.7%	22.3%
7,861	CLAY	2,571	1,773	778	20	995 R	69.0%	30.3%	69.5%	30.5%
35,662	COCKE	10,362	8,139	2,080	143	6,059 R	78.5%	20.1%	79.6%	20.4%
52,796	COFFEE	17,008	11,828	4,867	313	6,961 R	69.5%	28.6%	70.8%	29.2%
14,586	CROCKETT	4,484	3,274	1,173	37	2,101 R	73.0%	26.2%	73.6%	26.4%
56,053	CUMBERLAND	23,829	18,217	5,396	216	12,821 R	76.4%	22.6%	77.1%	22.9%
626,681	DAVIDSON	244,528	78,286	152,441	13,801	74,155 D	32.0%	62.3%	33.9%	66.1%
11,757	DECATUR	3,864	2,844	937	83	1,907 R	73.6%	24.2%	75.2%	24.8%
18,723	DEKALB	5,957	4,176	1,737	44	2,439 R	70.1%	29.2%	70.6%	29.4%
49,666	DICKSON	16,706	11,413	5,202	91	6,211 R	68.3%	31.1%	68.7%	31.3%
38,335	DYER	11,107	8,515	2,431	161	6,084 R	76.7%	21.9%	77.8%	22.2%
38,413	FAYETTE	17,074	11,883	4,943	248	6,940 R	69.6%	29.0%	70.6%	29.4%
17,959	FENTRESS	6,389	5,043	1,255	91	3,788 R	78.9%	19.6%	80.1%	19.9%
41,052	FRANKLIN	13,933	9,432	4,413	88	5,019 R	67.7%	31.7%	68.1%	31.9%
49,683	GIBSON	16,091	11,402	4,474	215	6,928 R	70.9%	27.8%	71.8%	28.2%
29,485	GILES	9,601	6,730	2,750	121	3,980 R	70.1%	28.6%	71.0%	29.0%
22,657	GRAINGER	6,838	5,476	1,285	77	4,191 R	80.1%	18.8%	81.0%	19.0%
68,831	GREENE	20,570	16,196	4,169	205	12,027 R	78.7%	20.3%	79.5%	20.5%
13,703	GRUNDY	3,755	2,699	1,007	49	1,692 R	71.9%	26.8%	72.8%	27.2%
62,544	HAMBLEN	17,393	13,197	4,063	133	9,134 R	75.9%	23.4%	76.5%	23.5%
336,463	HAMILTON	133,433	74,437	57,794	1,202	16,643 R	55.8%	43.3%	56.3%	43.7%
6,819	HANCOCK	1,800	1,447	331	22	1,116 R	80.4%	18.4%	81.4%	18.6%
27,253	HARDEMAN	7,512	4,060	3,336	116	724 R	54.0%	44.4%	54.9%	45.1%
26,026	HARDIN	8,200	6,410	1,603	187	4,807 R	78.2%	19.5%	80.0%	20.0%
56,833	HAWKINS	17,444	14,069	3,202	173	10,867 R	80.7%	18.4%	81.5%	18.5%
18,787	HAYWOOD	5,861	2,522	3,269	70	747 D	43.0%	55.8%	43.6%	56.4%
27,769	HENDERSON	8,640	6,922	1,642	76	5,280 R	80.1%	19.0%	80.8%	19.2%
32,330	HENRY	10,841	7,698	3,031	112	4,667 R	71.0%	28.0%	71.7%	28.3%
24,690	HICKMAN	6,989	4,894	2,025	70	2,869 R	70.0%	29.0%	70.7%	29.3%
8,426	HOUSTON	2,755	1,738	990	27	748 R	63.1%	35.9%	63.7%	36.3%
18,538	HUMPHREYS	5,896	3,813	2,037	46	1,776 R	64.7%	34.5%	65.2%	34.8%
11,638	JACKSON	3,927	2,647	1,242	38	1,405 R	67.4%	31.6%	68.1%	31.9%
51,407	JEFFERSON	16,147	12,411	3,581	155	8,830 R	76.9%	22.2%	77.6%	22.4%
18,244	JOHNSON	5,892	4,809	1,013	70	3,796 R	81.6%	17.2%	82.6%	17.4%
432,226	KNOX	166,443	96,006	68,437	2,000	27,569 R	57.7%	41.1%	58.4%	41.6%
7,832	LAKE	1,462	951	337	174	614 R	65.0%	23.1%	73.8%	26.2%
27,815	LAUDERDALE	6,668	4,026	2,543	99	1,483 R	60.4%	38.1%	61.3%	38.7%
41,869	LAWRENCE	12,954	9,834	3,048	72	6,786 R	75.9%	23.5%	76.3%	23.7%
12,161	LEWIS	4,045	2,969	1,048	28	1,921 R	73.4%	25.9%	73.9%	26.1%
33,361	LINCOLN	10,488	8,110	2,105	273	6,005 R	77.3%	20.1%	79.4%	20.6%
48,556	LOUDON	21,647	16,245	5,181	221	11,064 R	75.0%	23.9%	75.8%	24.2%
22,248	MACON	6,373	5,078	1,246	49	3,832 R	79.7%	19.6%	80.3%	19.7%
98,294	MADISON	32,853	18,722	13,759	372	4,963 R	57.0%	41.9%	57.6%	42.4%
28,237	MARION	9,231	6,327	2,806	98	3,521 R	68.5%	30.4%	69.3%	30.7%
30,617	MARSHALL	10,031	7,074	2,891	66	4,183 R	70.5%	28.8%	71.0%	29.0%
80,956	MAURY	32,730	21,297	11,149	284	10,148 R	65.1%	34.1%	65.6%	34.4%
52,266	MCMINN	15,824	12,268	3,382	174	8,886 R	77.5%	21.4%	78.4%	21.6%
26,075	MCNAIRY	8,174	6,201	1,825	148	4,376 R	75.9%	22.3%	77.3%	22.7%

TENNESSEE

GOVERNOR 2018

2010 Census Population	County	Total Vote	Republican (Lee)	Democratic (Dean)	Other	Rep.-Dem. Plurality	Percentage Total Vote Rep.	Total Vote Dem.	Major Vote Rep.	Major Vote Dem.
11,753	MEIGS	3,806	2,920	846	40	2,074 R	76.7%	22.2%	77.5%	22.5%
44,519	MONROE	14,495	11,146	3,206	143	7,940 R	76.9%	22.1%	77.7%	22.3%
172,331	MONTGOMERY	51,724	27,920	22,664	1,140	5,256 R	54.0%	43.8%	55.2%	44.8%
6,362	MOORE	2,506	1,944	524	38	1,420 R	77.6%	20.9%	78.8%	21.2%
21,987	MORGAN	5,633	4,331	1,243	59	3,088 R	76.9%	22.1%	77.7%	22.3%
31,807	OBION	9,578	7,425	2,053	100	5,372 R	77.5%	21.4%	78.3%	21.7%
22,083	OVERTON	7,224	4,951	2,213	60	2,738 R	68.5%	30.6%	69.1%	30.9%
7,915	PERRY	2,447	1,771	654	22	1,117 R	72.4%	26.7%	73.0%	27.0%
5,077	PICKETT	2,284	1,689	586	9	1,103 R	73.9%	25.7%	74.2%	25.8%
16,825	POLK	5,833	4,359	1,422	52	2,937 R	74.7%	24.4%	75.4%	24.6%
72,321	PUTNAM	24,369	16,407	7,710	252	8,697 R	67.3%	31.6%	68.0%	32.0%
31,809	RHEA	9,394	7,382	1,926	86	5,456 R	78.6%	20.5%	79.3%	20.7%
54,181	ROANE	19,284	13,868	5,207	209	8,661 R	71.9%	27.0%	72.7%	27.3%
66,283	ROBERTSON	24,158	16,816	7,177	165	9,639 R	69.6%	29.7%	70.1%	29.9%
262,604	RUTHERFORD	98,973	56,957	41,108	908	15,849 R	57.5%	41.5%	58.1%	41.9%
22,228	SCOTT	5,485	4,472	961	52	3,511 R	81.5%	17.5%	82.3%	17.7%
14,112	SEQUATCHIE	5,005	3,766	1,185	54	2,581 R	75.2%	23.7%	76.1%	23.9%
89,889	SEVIER	30,054	23,059	6,442	553	16,617 R	76.7%	21.4%	78.2%	21.8%
927,644	SHELBY	290,148	106,594	175,478	8,076	68,884 D	36.7%	60.5%	37.8%	62.2%
19,166	SMITH	6,556	4,745	1,756	55	2,989 R	72.4%	26.8%	73.0%	27.0%
13,324	STEWART	4,480	3,102	1,329	49	1,773 R	69.2%	29.7%	70.0%	30.0%
156,823	SULLIVAN	54,370	41,548	12,373	449	29,175 R	76.4%	22.8%	77.1%	22.9%
160,645	SUMNER	65,576	44,149	20,914	513	23,235 R	67.3%	31.9%	67.9%	32.1%
61,081	TIPTON	19,318	14,074	4,908	336	9,166 R	72.9%	25.4%	74.1%	25.9%
7,870	TROUSDALE	2,651	1,739	881	31	858 R	65.6%	33.2%	66.4%	33.6%
18,313	UNICOI	6,294	5,008	1,228	58	3,780 R	79.6%	19.5%	80.3%	19.7%
19,109	UNION	5,224	4,028	1,133	63	2,895 R	77.1%	21.7%	78.0%	22.0%
5,548	VAN BUREN	2,213	1,555	624	34	931 R	70.3%	28.2%	71.4%	28.6%
39,839	WARREN	11,472	7,737	3,643	92	4,094 R	67.4%	31.8%	68.0%	32.0%
122,979	WASHINGTON	45,036	31,066	13,584	386	17,482 R	69.0%	30.2%	69.6%	30.4%
17,021	WAYNE	4,731	3,876	818	37	3,058 R	81.9%	17.3%	82.6%	17.4%
35,021	WEAKLEY	9,892	7,203	2,557	132	4,646 R	72.8%	25.8%	73.8%	26.2%
25,841	WHITE	8,444	6,374	2,005	65	4,369 R	75.5%	23.7%	76.1%	23.9%
183,182	WILLIAMSON	105,654	68,189	34,647	2,818	33,542 R	64.5%	32.8%	66.3%	33.7%
113,993	WILSON	53,067	35,488	16,987	592	18,501 R	66.9%	32.0%	67.6%	32.4%
6,346,105	*TOTAL*	*2,243,294*	*1,336,106*	*864,863*	*42,325*	*471,243 R*	*59.6%*	*38.6%*	*60.7%*	*39.3%*

TENNESSEE

SENATOR 2018

2010 Census Population	County	Total Vote	Republican (Blackburn)	Democratic (Bredesen)	Other	Rep.-Dem. Plurality	Percentage Total Vote Rep.	Total Vote Dem.	Major Vote Rep.	Major Vote Dem.
75,129	ANDERSON	26,008	14,720	10,818	470	3,902 R	56.6%	41.6%	57.6%	42.4%
45,058	BEDFORD	13,033	8,942	3,929	162	5,013 R	68.6%	30.1%	69.5%	30.5%
16,489	BENTON	5,298	3,489	1,722	87	1,767 R	65.9%	32.5%	67.0%	33.0%
12,876	BLEDSOE	4,076	2,908	1,096	72	1,812 R	71.3%	26.9%	72.6%	27.4%
123,010	BLOUNT	46,782	29,928	16,040	814	13,888 R	64.0%	34.3%	65.1%	34.9%
98,963	BRADLEY	33,954	24,433	9,030	491	15,403 R	72.0%	26.6%	73.0%	27.0%
40,716	CAMPBELL	10,147	7,208	2,712	227	4,496 R	71.0%	26.7%	72.7%	27.3%
13,801	CANNON	4,646	3,198	1,381	67	1,817 R	68.8%	29.7%	69.8%	30.2%
28,522	CARROLL	8,779	6,044	2,606	129	3,438 R	68.8%	29.7%	69.9%	30.1%
57,424	CARTER	18,693	13,946	4,547	200	9,399 R	74.6%	24.3%	75.4%	24.6%

TENNESSEE

SENATOR 2018

2010 Census Population	County	Total Vote	Republican (Blackburn)	Democratic (Bredesen)	Other	Rep.-Dem. Plurality	Percentage Total Vote Rep.	Total Vote Dem.	Major Vote Rep.	Major Vote Dem.
39,105	CHEATHAM	14,452	9,135	5,150	167	3,985 R	63.2%	35.6%	63.9%	36.1%
17,131	CHESTER	5,395	3,902	1,344	149	2,558 R	72.3%	24.9%	74.4%	25.6%
32,213	CLAIBORNE	8,496	6,083	2,245	168	3,838 R	71.6%	26.4%	73.0%	27.0%
7,861	CLAY	2,559	1,643	871	45	772 R	64.2%	34.0%	65.4%	34.6%
35,662	COCKE	10,382	7,528	2,621	233	4,907 R	72.5%	25.2%	74.2%	25.8%
52,796	COFFEE	17,026	11,115	5,572	339	5,543 R	65.3%	32.7%	66.6%	33.4%
14,586	CROCKETT	4,491	2,984	1,418	89	1,566 R	66.4%	31.6%	67.8%	32.2%
56,053	CUMBERLAND	23,808	16,966	6,321	521	10,645 R	71.3%	26.5%	72.9%	27.1%
626,681	DAVIDSON	243,639	69,338	172,137	2,164	102,799 D	28.5%	70.7%	28.7%	71.3%
11,757	DECATUR	3,878	2,718	1,080	80	1,638 R	70.1%	27.8%	71.6%	28.4%
18,723	DEKALB	5,954	3,906	1,984	64	1,922 R	65.6%	33.3%	66.3%	33.7%
49,666	DICKSON	16,700	10,465	5,992	243	4,473 R	62.7%	35.9%	63.6%	36.4%
38,335	DYER	11,114	8,013	2,898	203	5,115 R	72.1%	26.1%	73.4%	26.6%
38,413	FAYETTE	17,224	11,371	5,639	214	5,732 R	66.0%	32.7%	66.8%	33.2%
17,959	FENTRESS	6,337	4,745	1,440	152	3,305 R	74.9%	22.7%	76.7%	23.3%
41,052	FRANKLIN	13,927	8,981	4,776	170	4,205 R	64.5%	34.3%	65.3%	34.7%
49,683	GIBSON	16,174	10,407	5,353	414	5,054 R	64.3%	33.1%	66.0%	34.0%
29,485	GILES	9,610	6,403	3,082	125	3,321 R	66.6%	32.1%	67.5%	32.5%
22,657	GRAINGER	6,810	5,039	1,658	113	3,381 R	74.0%	24.3%	75.2%	24.8%
68,831	GREENE	20,490	14,844	5,398	248	9,446 R	72.4%	26.3%	73.3%	26.7%
13,703	GRUNDY	3,758	2,587	1,101	70	1,486 R	68.8%	29.3%	70.1%	29.9%
62,544	HAMBLEN	17,407	12,134	4,972	301	7,162 R	69.7%	28.6%	70.9%	29.1%
336,463	HAMILTON	133,708	67,152	65,119	1,437	2,033 R	50.2%	48.7%	50.8%	49.2%
6,819	HANCOCK	1,780	1,327	422	31	905 R	74.6%	23.7%	75.9%	24.1%
27,253	HARDEMAN	7,535	3,869	3,560	106	309 R	51.3%	47.2%	52.1%	47.9%
26,026	HARDIN	8,246	6,181	1,917	148	4,264 R	75.0%	23.2%	76.3%	23.7%
56,833	HAWKINS	17,471	13,058	4,222	191	8,836 R	74.7%	24.2%	75.6%	24.4%
18,787	HAYWOOD	5,886	2,364	3,449	73	1,085 D	40.2%	58.6%	40.7%	59.3%
27,769	HENDERSON	8,651	6,514	2,024	113	4,490 R	75.3%	23.4%	76.3%	23.7%
32,330	HENRY	10,848	7,190	3,497	161	3,693 R	66.3%	32.2%	67.3%	32.7%
24,690	HICKMAN	6,982	4,563	2,286	133	2,277 R	65.4%	32.7%	66.6%	33.4%
8,426	HOUSTON	2,736	1,613	1,078	45	535 R	59.0%	39.4%	59.9%	40.1%
18,538	HUMPHREYS	5,892	3,549	2,264	79	1,285 R	60.2%	38.4%	61.1%	38.9%
11,638	JACKSON	3,923	2,514	1,361	48	1,153 R	64.1%	34.7%	64.9%	35.1%
51,407	JEFFERSON	16,114	11,435	4,347	332	7,088 R	71.0%	27.0%	72.5%	27.5%
18,244	JOHNSON	5,898	4,520	1,301	77	3,219 R	76.6%	22.1%	77.6%	22.4%
432,226	KNOX	166,162	84,407	79,283	2,472	5,124 R	50.8%	47.7%	51.6%	48.4%
7,832	LAKE	1,451	930	490	31	440 R	64.1%	33.8%	65.5%	34.5%
27,815	LAUDERDALE	6,671	3,745	2,810	116	935 R	56.1%	42.1%	57.1%	42.9%
41,869	LAWRENCE	12,968	9,365	3,439	164	5,926 R	72.2%	26.5%	73.1%	26.9%
12,161	LEWIS	4,054	2,836	1,177	41	1,659 R	70.0%	29.0%	70.7%	29.3%
33,361	LINCOLN	10,542	7,949	2,437	156	5,512 R	75.4%	23.1%	76.5%	23.5%
48,556	LOUDON	21,605	14,834	6,371	400	8,463 R	68.7%	29.5%	70.0%	30.0%
22,248	MACON	6,348	4,768	1,483	97	3,285 R	75.1%	23.4%	76.3%	23.7%
98,294	MADISON	32,907	17,127	15,316	464	1,811 R	52.0%	46.5%	52.8%	47.2%
28,237	MARION	9,173	5,839	3,166	168	2,673 R	63.7%	34.5%	64.8%	35.2%
30,617	MARSHALL	10,041	6,543	3,380	118	3,163 R	65.2%	33.7%	65.9%	34.1%
80,956	MAURY	32,559	19,569	12,560	430	7,009 R	60.1%	38.6%	60.9%	39.1%
52,266	MCMINN	15,819	11,434	4,122	263	7,312 R	72.3%	26.1%	73.5%	26.5%
26,075	MCNAIRY	8,188	6,007	2,036	145	3,971 R	73.4%	24.9%	74.7%	25.3%
11,753	MEIGS	3,795	2,694	1,040	61	1,654 R	71.0%	27.4%	72.1%	27.9%
44,519	MONROE	14,460	10,274	3,838	348	6,436 R	71.1%	26.5%	72.8%	27.2%
172,331	MONTGOMERY	51,887	25,932	24,807	1,148	1,125 R	50.0%	47.8%	51.1%	48.9%
6,362	MOORE	2,504	1,856	611	37	1,245 R	74.1%	24.4%	75.2%	24.8%
21,987	MORGAN	5,640	4,083	1,436	121	2,647 R	72.4%	25.5%	74.0%	26.0%
31,807	OBION	9,559	7,118	2,326	115	4,792 R	74.5%	24.3%	75.4%	24.6%
22,083	OVERTON	7,195	4,640	2,452	103	2,188 R	64.5%	34.1%	65.4%	34.6%
7,915	PERRY	2,432	1,644	724	64	920 R	67.6%	29.8%	69.4%	30.6%
5,077	PICKETT	2,270	1,599	646	25	953 R	70.4%	28.5%	71.2%	28.8%
16,825	POLK	5,819	4,127	1,585	107	2,542 R	70.9%	27.2%	72.3%	27.7%

TENNESSEE

SENATOR 2018

2010 Census Population	County	Total Vote	Republican (Blackburn)	Democratic (Bredesen)	Other	Rep.-Dem. Plurality	Percentage Total Vote Rep.	Percentage Total Vote Dem.	Percentage Major Vote Rep.	Percentage Major Vote Dem.
72,321	PUTNAM	24,333	15,230	8,750	353	6,480 R	62.6%	36.0%	63.5%	36.5%
31,809	RHEA	9,412	6,866	2,371	175	4,495 R	72.9%	25.2%	74.3%	25.7%
54,181	ROANE	19,340	12,727	6,242	371	6,485 R	65.8%	32.3%	67.1%	32.9%
66,283	ROBERTSON	24,109	15,501	8,311	297	7,190 R	64.3%	34.5%	65.1%	34.9%
262,604	RUTHERFORD	99,125	52,254	45,692	1,179	6,562 R	52.7%	46.1%	53.3%	46.7%
22,228	SCOTT	5,501	4,232	1,176	93	3,056 R	76.9%	21.4%	78.3%	21.7%
14,112	SEQUATCHIE	5,017	3,564	1,367	86	2,197 R	71.0%	27.2%	72.3%	27.7%
89,889	SEVIER	30,084	21,541	7,769	774	13,772 R	71.6%	25.8%	73.5%	26.5%
927,644	SHELBY	291,145	96,493	190,885	3,767	94,392 D	33.1%	65.6%	33.6%	66.4%
19,166	SMITH	6,516	4,317	2,111	88	2,206 R	66.3%	32.4%	67.2%	32.8%
13,324	STEWART	4,495	2,938	1,492	65	1,446 R	65.4%	33.2%	66.3%	33.7%
156,823	SULLIVAN	54,493	38,753	15,183	557	23,570 R	71.1%	27.9%	71.8%	28.2%
160,645	SUMNER	65,565	41,099	23,762	704	17,337 R	62.7%	36.2%	63.4%	36.6%
61,081	TIPTON	19,393	13,390	5,625	378	7,765 R	69.0%	29.0%	70.4%	29.6%
7,870	TROUSDALE	2,628	1,586	1,002	40	584 R	60.4%	38.1%	61.3%	38.7%
18,313	UNICOI	6,280	4,659	1,554	67	3,105 R	74.2%	24.7%	75.0%	25.0%
19,109	UNION	5,228	3,739	1,382	107	2,357 R	71.5%	26.4%	73.0%	27.0%
5,548	VAN BUREN	2,207	1,451	711	45	740 R	65.7%	32.2%	67.1%	32.9%
39,839	WARREN	11,419	7,018	4,200	201	2,818 R	61.5%	36.8%	62.6%	37.4%
122,979	WASHINGTON	45,201	28,514	16,246	441	12,268 R	63.1%	35.9%	63.7%	36.3%
17,021	WAYNE	4,736	3,787	906	43	2,881 R	80.0%	19.1%	80.7%	19.3%
35,021	WEAKLEY	9,901	6,704	3,047	150	3,657 R	67.7%	30.8%	68.8%	31.2%
25,841	WHITE	8,423	5,979	2,293	151	3,686 R	71.0%	27.2%	72.3%	27.7%
183,182	WILLIAMSON	105,369	62,039	42,611	719	19,428 R	58.9%	40.4%	59.3%	40.7%
113,993	WILSON	53,054	32,810	19,447	797	13,363 R	61.8%	36.7%	62.8%	37.2%
6,346,105	*TOTAL*	*2,243,740*	*1,227,483*	*985,450*	*30,807*	*242,033 R*	*54.7%*	*43.9%*	*55.5%*	*44.5%*

TENNESSEE

HOUSE OF REPRESENTATIVES

CD	Year	Total Vote	Republican Vote	Republican Candidate	Democratic Vote	Democratic Candidate	Other Vote	Rep.-Dem. Plurality	Percentage Total Vote Rep.	Percentage Total Vote Dem.	Percentage Major Vote Rep.	Percentage Major Vote Dem.
1	2018	224,282	172,835	ROE, PHIL*	47,138	OLSEN, MARTIN	4,309	125,697 R	77.1%	21.0%	78.6%	21.4%
1	2016	253,025	198,293	ROE, PHIL*	39,024	BOHMS, ALAN	15,708	159,269 R	78.4%	15.4%	83.6%	16.4%
1	2014	139,470	115,533	ROE, PHIL*			23,937	115,533 R	82.8%		100.0%	
1	2012	239,672	182,252	ROE, PHIL*	47,663	WOODRUFF, ALAN	9,757	134,589 R	76.0%	19.9%	79.3%	20.7%
2	2018	262,134	172,856	BURCHETT, TIM	86,668	HOYOS, RENEE	2,610	86,188 R	65.9%	33.1%	66.6%	33.4%
2	2016	280,856	212,455	DUNCAN, JOHN J. JR.*	68,401	STARR, STUART		144,054 R	75.6%	24.4%	75.6%	24.4%
2	2014	166,751	120,883	DUNCAN, JOHN J. JR.*	37,612	SCOTT, BOB	8,256	83,271 R	72.5%	22.6%	76.3%	23.7%
2	2012	264,505	196,894	DUNCAN, JOHN J. JR.*	54,522	GOODALE, TROY	13,089	142,372 R	74.4%	20.6%	78.3%	21.7%
3	2018	245,765	156,512	FLEISCHMANN, CHUCK*	84,731	MITCHELL, DANIELLE	4,522	71,781 R	63.7%	34.5%	64.9%	35.1%
3	2016	266,006	176,613	FLEISCHMANN, CHUCK*	76,727	SHEKARI, MELODY	12,666	99,886 R	66.4%	28.8%	69.7%	30.3%
3	2014	156,097	97,344	FLEISCHMANN, CHUCK*	53,983	HEADRICK, MARY M.	4,770	43,361 R	62.4%	34.6%	64.3%	35.7%
3	2012	256,909	157,830	FLEISCHMANN, CHUCK*	91,094	HEADRICK, MARY M.	7,985	66,736 R	61.4%	35.5%	63.4%	36.6%
4	2018	232,451	147,323	DESJARLAIS, SCOTT*	78,065	PHILLIPS, MARIAH	7,063	69,258 R	63.4%	33.6%	65.4%	34.6%
4	2016	254,937	165,796	DESJARLAIS, SCOTT*	89,141	REYNOLDS, STEVEN		76,655 R	65.0%	35.0%	65.0%	35.0%
4	2014	145,418	84,815	DESJARLAIS, SCOTT*	51,357	SHERRELL, LENDA	9,246	33,458 R	58.3%	35.3%	62.3%	37.7%
4	2012	230,590	128,568	DESJARLAIS, SCOTT*	102,022	STEWART, ERIC		26,546 R	55.8%	44.2%	55.8%	44.2%
5	2018	262,248	84,317	BALL, JODY	177,923	COOPER, JIM*	8	93,606 D	32.2%	67.8%	32.2%	67.8%
5	2016	273,544	102,433	SNYDER, STACY RIES	171,111	COOPER, JIM*		68,678 D	37.4%	62.6%	37.4%	62.6%
5	2014	154,276	55,078	RIES, BOB	96,148	COOPER, JIM*	3,050	41,070 D	35.7%	62.3%	36.4%	63.6%
5	2012	263,095	86,240	STAATS, BRAD	171,621	COOPER, JIM*	5,234	85,381 D	32.8%	65.2%	33.4%	66.6%

TENNESSEE

HOUSE OF REPRESENTATIVES

			Republican		Democratic				Percentage			
									Total Vote		Major Vote	
CD	Year	Total Vote	Vote	Candidate	Vote	Candidate	Other Vote	Rep.-Dem. Plurality	Rep.	Dem.	Rep.	Dem.
6	2018	248,740	172,810	ROSE, JOHN	70,370	BARLOW, DAWN	5,560	102,440 R	69.5%	28.3%	71.1%	28.9%
6	2016	284,490	202,234	BLACK, DIANE*	61,995	KENT, DAVID W.	20,261	140,239 R	71.1%	21.8%	76.5%	23.5%
6	2014	162,097	115,231	BLACK, DIANE*	37,232	POWERS, AMOS SCOTT	9,634	77,999 R	71.1%	23.0%	75.6%	24.4%
6	2012	241,241	184,383	BLACK, DIANE*			56,858	184,383 R	76.4%		100.0%	
7	2018	254,384	170,071	GREEN, MARK	81,661	KANEW, JUSTIN	2,652	88,410 R	66.9%	32.1%	67.6%	32.4%
7	2016	277,513	200,407	BLACKBURN, MARSHA*	65,226	CHANDLER, THARON	11,880	135,181 R	72.2%	23.5%	75.4%	24.6%
7	2014	157,907	110,534	BLACKBURN, MARSHA*	42,280	CRAMER, DANIEL N.	5,093	68,254 R	70.0%	26.8%	72.3%	27.7%
7	2012	257,306	182,730	BLACKBURN, MARSHA*	61,679	AMOUZOUVIK, CREDO	12,897	121,051 R	71.0%	24.0%	74.8%	25.2%
8	2018	248,345	168,030	KUSTOFF, DAVID*	74,755	PEARSON, ERIKA	5,560	93,275 R	67.7%	30.1%	69.2%	30.8%
8	2016	282,733	194,386	KUSTOFF, DAVID	70,925	HOBSON, RICKEY	17,422	123,461 R	68.8%	25.1%	73.3%	26.7%
8	2014	172,595	122,255	FINCHER, STEPHEN LEE*	42,433	BRADLEY, WES	7,907	79,822 R	70.8%	24.6%	74.2%	25.8%
8	2012	279,422	190,923	FINCHER, STEPHEN LEE*	79,490	DIXON, TIMOTHY	9,009	111,433 R	68.3%	28.4%	70.6%	29.4%
9	2018	181,476	34,901	BERGMANN, CHARLOTTE	145,139	COHEN, STEPHEN I.*	1,436	110,238 D	19.2%	80.0%	19.4%	80.6%
9	2016	217,957	41,123	ALBERSON, FLOYD WAYNE	171,631	COHEN, STEPHEN I.*	5,203	130,508 D	18.9%	78.7%	19.3%	80.7%
9	2014	116,550	27,173	BERGMANN, CHARLOTTE	87,376	COHEN, STEPHEN I.*	2,001	60,203 D	23.3%	75.0%	23.7%	76.3%
9	2012	250,987	59,742	FLINN, GEORGE S. "JR."	188,422	COHEN, STEPHEN I.*	2,823	128,680 D	23.8%	75.1%	24.1%	75.9%
TOTAL	*2018*	*2,159,825*	*1,279,655*		*846,450*		*33,720*	*433,205 R*	*59.2%*	*39.2%*	*60.2%*	*39.8%*
TOTAL	*2016*	*2,391,061*	*1,493,740*		*814,181*		*83,140*	*679,559 R*	*62.5%*	*34.1%*	*64.7%*	*35.3%*
TOTAL	*2014*	*1,371,161*	*848,846*		*448,421*		*73,894*	*400,425 R*	*61.9%*	*32.7%*	*65.4%*	*34.6%*
TOTAL	*2012*	*2,283,727*	*1,369,562*		*796,513*		*117,652*	*573,049 R*	*60.0%*	*34.9%*	*63.2%*	*36.8%*

Note: An asterisk (*) denotes incumbent.

TENNESSEE

GENERAL AND PRIMARY ELECTIONS

2018 GENERAL ELECTIONS: OTHER VOTES

Governor Other vote was 5,198 Independent (Sherry Clark), 4,687 Independent (Mark Wright), 3,631 Independent (Patrick Whitlock), 3,070 Independent (Yvonne Neubert), 2,969 Independent (Heather Scott), 2,841 Independent (Mark Brown), 2,444 Independent (Joe Wilmoth), 1,550 Independent (George Smith), 1,502 Independent (Cory King), 1,396 Independent (Tracy Tisdale), 1,217 Independent (Justin Cornett), 1,096 Independent (Chad Riden), 1,059 Independent (Robert Sawyers), 1,012 Independent (Vinnie Vineyard), 981 Independent (Rick Tyler), 869 Independent (Gabriel Fancher), 814 Independent (Sean Fleming), 800 Independent (Alfred Rapoza), 755 Independent (Jessie McDonald), 739 Independent (Toney Mitchell), 726 Independent (Mike Toews), 652 Independent (Matthew Koch), 613 Independent (Jeremy Stephenson), 609 Independent (Tommy McAnally), 588 Independent (Jaron Weidner), 496 Independent (William Helmstetter), 11 Write-in (Eddie Murphy)

Senate Other vote was 9,455 Independent (Trudy Austin), 8,717 Independent (Dean Hill), 5,084 Independent (Kris Todd), 3,398 Independent (John Carico), 2,226 Independent (Breton Phillips), 1,927 Independent (Kevin McCants)

House Other vote was:

CD 1 4,309 Independent (Michael Salyer)

CD 2 967 Independent (Greg Samples), 657 Independent (Jeffrey Grunau), 637 Independent (Marc Whitmire), 349 Independent (Keith Latorre)

CD 3 4,522 Independent (Rick Tyler)

CD 4 7,056 Independent (Michael Shupe), 7 Write-in (Russell Steele)

CD 5 8 Write-in (Marshal Weaver)

CD 6 3,426 Independent (David Ross), 2,134 Independent (Lloyd Dunn)

CD 7 1,582 Independent (Leonard Ladner), 1,070 Independent (Brent Legendre)

CD 8 5,560 Independent (James Hart)

CD 9 1,436 Independent (Leo AwGoWhat)

TENNESSEE

GENERAL AND PRIMARY ELECTIONS

2018 PRIMARY ELECTIONS: SUPPLEMENTARY INFORMATION

Primary	August 2, 2018	**Registration** (as of June 30, 2018 – includes 435,800 inactive registrants)	4,000,662	No Party Registration

Primary Type Open—Any registered voter could participate in either the Democratic or the Republican primary, but must declare affiliation with that party at the polls.

	REPUBLICAN PRIMARIES			DEMOCRATIC PRIMARIES		
Senator	Blackburn, Marsha	613,513	84.5%	Bredesen, Phil	349,718	91.5%
	Pettigrew, Aaron	112,705	15.5%	Davis, Gary G.	20,170	5.3%
	Hay, Tommy N. (Write-in)	11		Wolfe, John	12,269	3.2%
	Emerson, Tom Jr. (Write-in)	2				
	TOTAL	*726,231*		*TOTAL*	*382,157*	
Governor	Lee, Bill	291,414	36.8%	Dean, Karl	280,553	75.1%
	Boyd, Randy	193,054	24.3%	Fitzhugh, Craig	72,553	19.4%
	Black, Diane	182,457	23.0%	Payne, Mezianne	20,284	5.4%
	Harwell, Beth	121,484	15.3%			
	White, Kay C.	3,215	0.4%			
	Marceaux, Basil Sr.	1,264	0.2%			
	TOTAL	*792,888*		*TOTAL*	*373,390*	
Congressional District 1	Roe, Phil*	71,556	73.7%	Olsen, Martin	13,313	100.0%
	McKinley, Todd	16,175	16.7%			
	Brooks, James	5,058	5.2%			
	Banyas, Mickie	4,253	4.4%			
	TOTAL	*97,042*		*TOTAL*	*13,313*	
Congressional District 2	Burchett, Tim	47,875	48.2%	Hoyos, Renee	22,220	72.4%
	Matlock, James	35,855	36.1%	Williams, Joshua	7,077	23.1%
	Nickloes, Sarah	10,961	11.0%	Schenkenfelder, Joseph	1,383	4.5%
	Emert, Jason	2,305	2.3%			
	Hamblin, Hank	855	0.9%			
	Sagliano, Vito	844	0.8%			
	Stansberry, David	657	0.7%			
	TOTAL	*99,352*		*TOTAL*	*30,680*	
Congressional District 3	Fleischmann, Charles*	67,830	79.4%	Mitchell, Danielle	30,927	100.0%
	Massengale, Jeremy	10,219	12.0%			
	Spurlock, William	5,359	6.3%			
	Shevlin, Harold	2,055	2.4%			
	TOTAL	*85,463*		*TOTAL*	*30,927*	
Congressional District 4	DesJarlais, Scott*	61,994	70.0%	Phillips, Mariah	15,474	47.5%
	Maddux, David "Jack"	26,580	30.0%	Hale, Christopher	11,309	34.7%
				Reynolds, Steven	5,788	17.8%
	TOTAL	*88,574*		*TOTAL*	*32,571*	
Congressional District 5	Ball, Jody	20,321	55.8%	Cooper, Jim*	70,480	100.0%
	Dean, Glen	16,107	44.2%			
	Williams, Christopher "Kit" (Write-in)	13				
	TOTAL	*36,441*		*TOTAL*	*70,480*	
Congressional District 6	Rose, John	43,797	41.3%	Barlow, Dawn	16,881	54.5%
	Corlew, Bob	33,091	31.2%	Wineinger, Merrilee	6,827	22.1%
	Matheny, Judd	16,758	15.8%	Finley, Christopher	4,654	15.0%
	Vivio, Lavern	9,462	8.9%	Heffernan, Peter	2,584	8.4%
	Monday, Christopher	3,026	2.9%			
	TOTAL	*106,134*		*TOTAL*	*30,946*	

TENNESSEE

GENERAL AND PRIMARY ELECTIONS

	REPUBLICAN PRIMARIES			DEMOCRATIC PRIMARIES		
Congressional District 7	Green, Mark	83,314	100.0%	Kanew, Justin	21,315	62.1%
				Reel, Matt	13,006	37.9%
	TOTAL	*83,314*		*TOTAL*	*34,321*	
Congressional District 8	Kustoff, David*	57,741	56.0%	Pearson, Erika	17,137	50.4%
	Flinn, George S. Jr.	40,903	39.7%	Boatner, John	16,847	49.6%
	Owens, Colleen	4,460	4.3%			
	TOTAL	*103,104*		*TOTAL*	*33,984*	
Congressional District 9	Bergmann, Charlotte	17,971	100.0%	Cohen, Stephen*	67,433	90.9%
				Smith, Kasandra	4,734	6.4%
				Richmond, Isaac	1,976	2.7%
	TOTAL	*17,971*		*TOTAL*	*74,143*	

Note: An asterisk (*) denotes incumbent.

TEXAS

Congressional districts first established for elections held in 2012
36 members

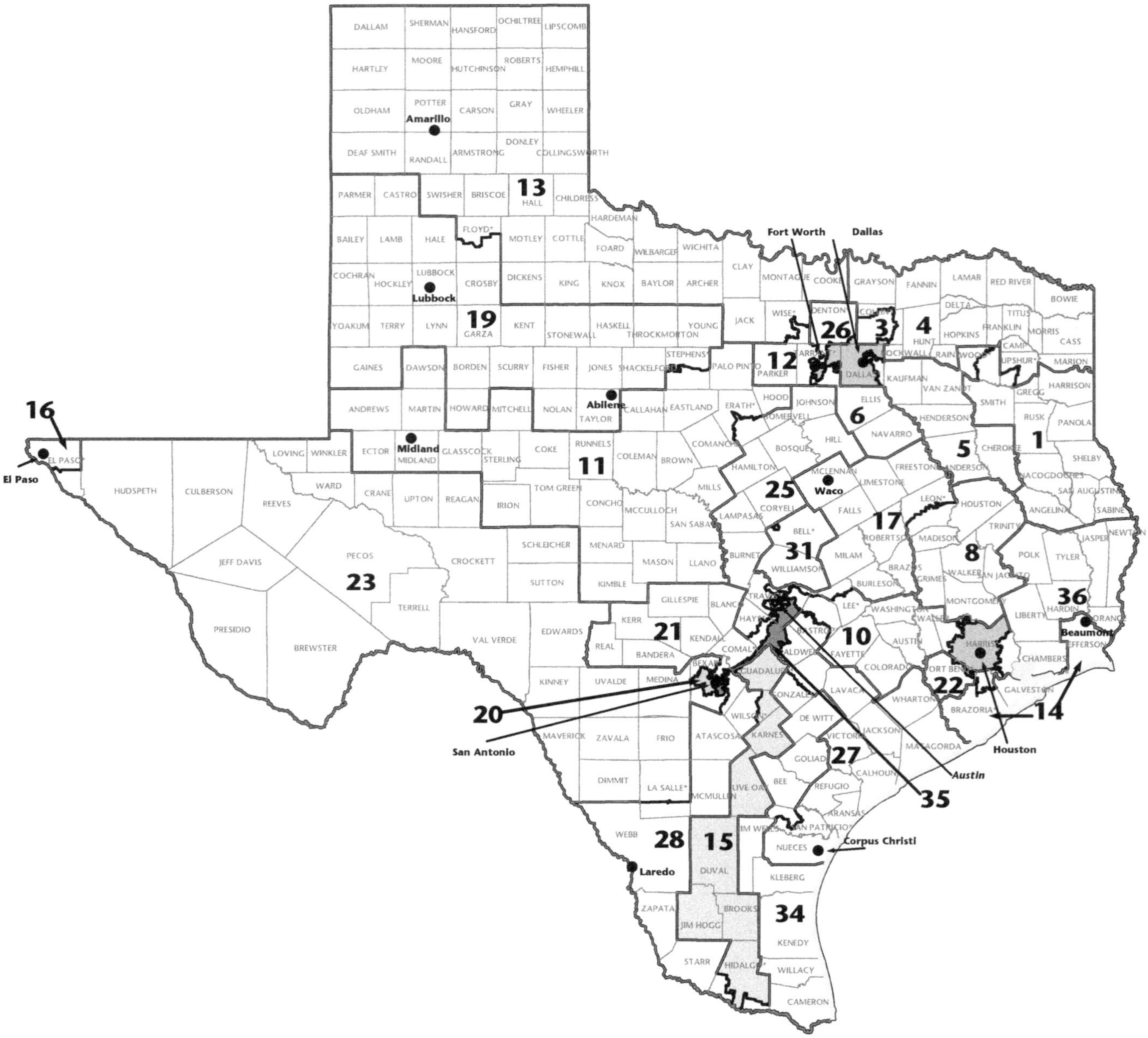

* Asterisk indicates a county whose boundaries include parts of two or more congressional districts.

TEXAS

Greater Dallas–Fort Worth Area

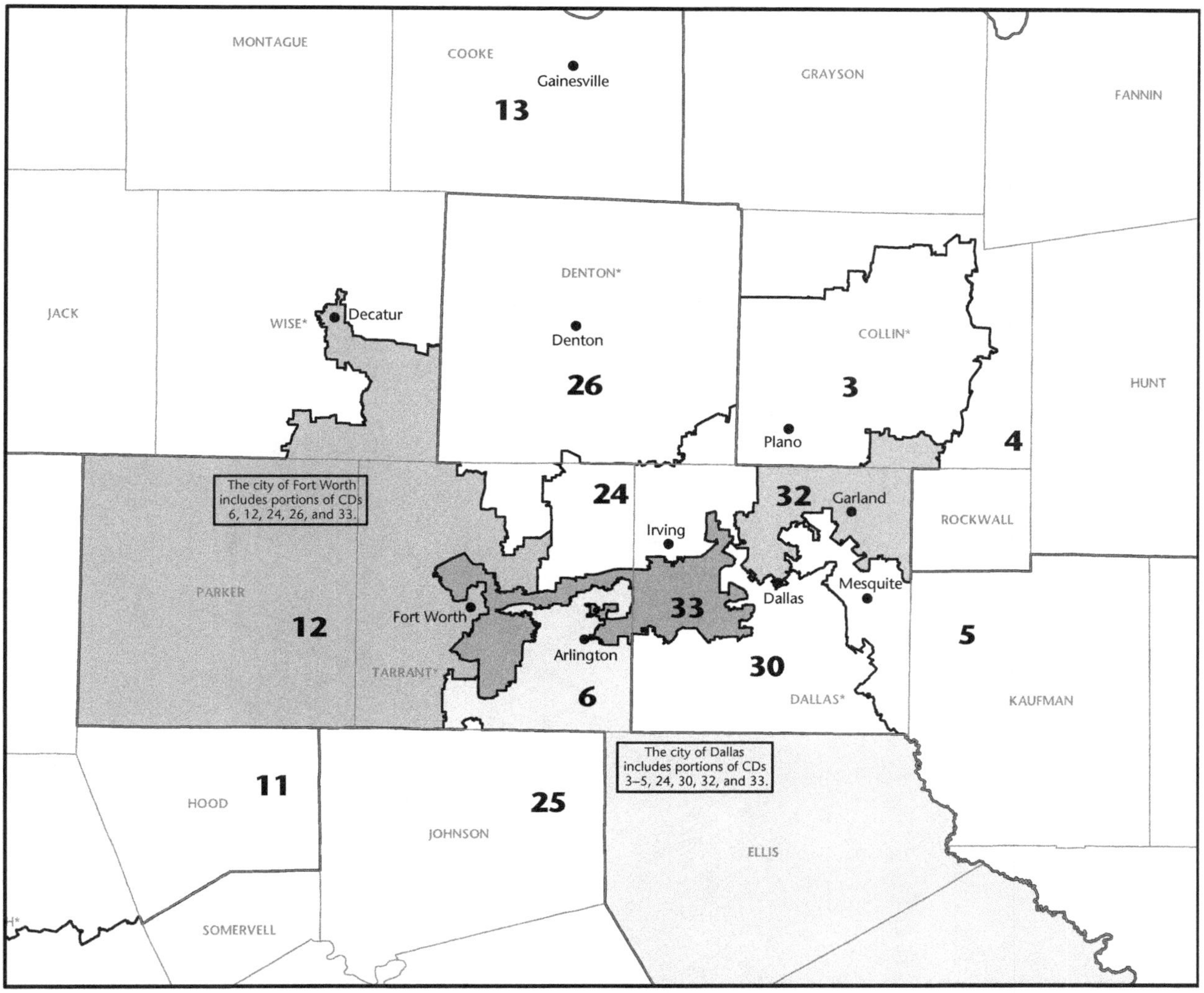

* Asterisk indicates a county whose boundaries include parts of two or more congressional districts.

TEXAS

Greater Houston Area

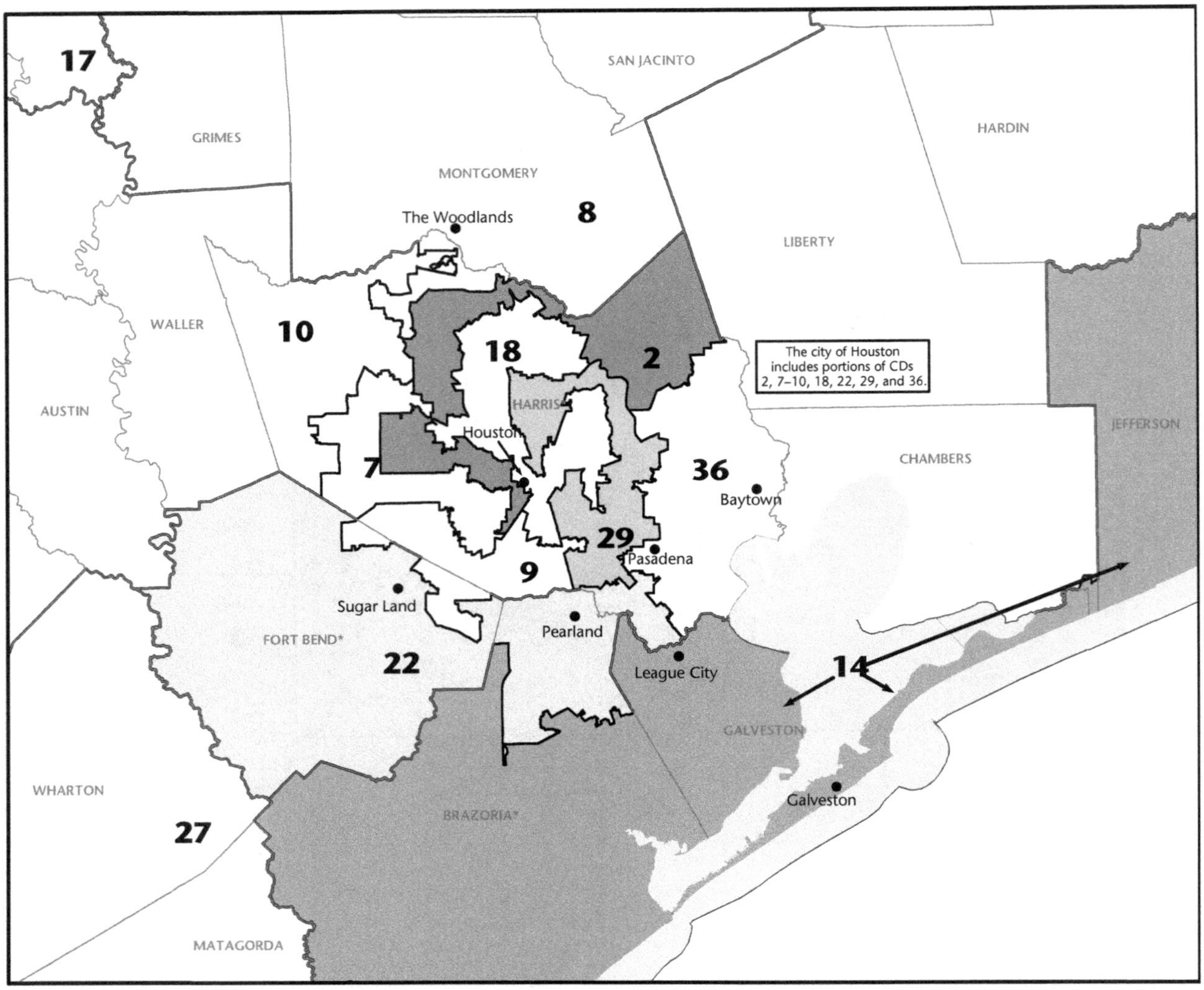

* Asterisk indicates a county whose boundaries include parts of two or more congressional districts.

TEXAS

Greater San Antonio, Austin Areas

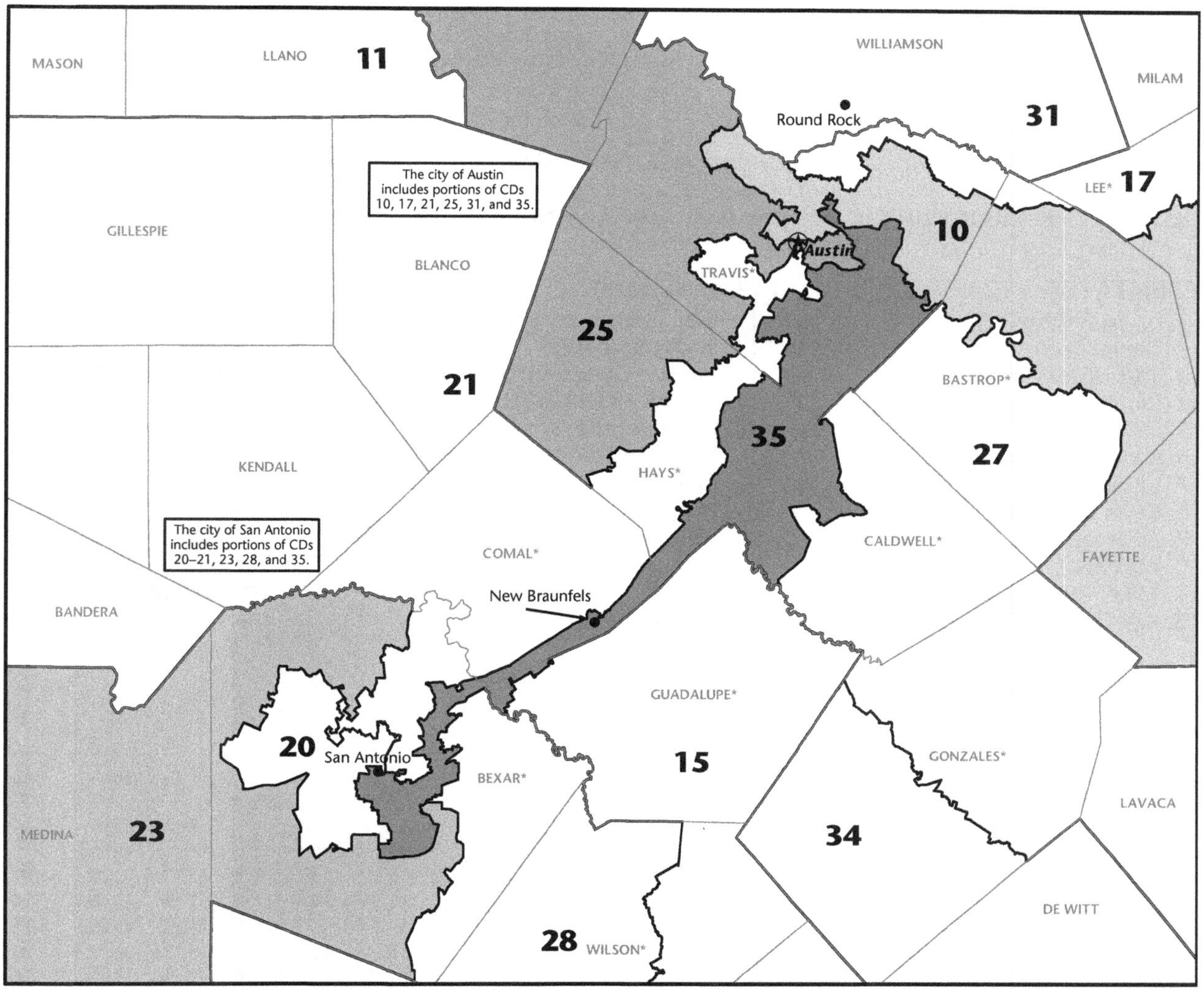

* Asterisk indicates a county whose boundaries include parts of two or more congressional districts.

TEXAS

GOVERNOR

Greg Abbott (R). Re-elected 2018 to a four-year term. Previously elected 2014.

SENATORS (2 Republicans)

John Cornyn (R). Re-elected 2014 to a six-year term. Previously elected 2008, 2002.

Ted Cruz (R). Re-elected 2018 to a six-year term. Previously elected 2012.

REPRESENTATIVES (23 Republicans, 13 Democrats)

1. Louie Gohmert (R)
2. Daniel Crenshaw (R)
3. Van Taylor (R)
4. John Ratcliffe (R)
5. Lance Gooden (R)
6. Ronald Wright (R)
7. Lizzie Pannill Fletcher (D)
8. Kevin Brady (R)
9. Al Green (D)
10. Michael T. McCaul (R)
11. Mike Conaway (R)
12. Kay Granger (R)
13. Mac Thornberry (R)
14. Randy Weber (R)
15. Vicente Gonzalez (D)
16. Veronica Escobar (D)
17. Bill Flores (R)
18. Sheila Jackson Lee (D)
19. Jodey Arrington (R)
20. Joaquin Castro (D)
21. Chip Roy (R)
22. Pete Olson (R)
23. Will Hurd (R)
24. Kenny E. Marchant (R)
25. Roger Williams (R)
26. Michael C. Burgess (R)
27. Michael Cloud (R)
28. Henry Cuellar (D)
29. Sylvia R. Garcia (D)
30. Eddie Bernice Johnson (D)
31. John Carter (R)
32. Colin Allred (D)
33. Marc Veasey (D)
34. Filemon Vela (D)
35. Lloyd Doggett (D)
36. Brian Babin (R)

POSTWAR VOTE FOR PRESIDENT

		Republican		Democratic				Percentage			
								Total Vote		Major Vote	
Year	Total Vote	Vote	Candidate	Vote	Candidate	Other Vote	Rep.-Dem. Plurality	Rep.	Dem.	Rep.	Dem.
2016**	8,969,226	4,685,047	Trump, Donald J.	3,877,868	Clinton, Hillary Rodham	406,311	807,179 R	52.2%	43.2%	54.7%	45.3%
2012	7,993,851	4,569,843	Romney, W. Mitt	3,308,124	Obama, Barack H.*	115,884	1,261,719 R	57.2%	41.4%	58.0%	42.0%
2008	8,077,795	4,479,328	McCain, John S. III	3,528,633	Obama, Barack H.	69,834	950,695 R	55.5%	43.7%	55.9%	44.1%
2004	7,410,765	4,526,917	Bush, George W.*	2,832,704	Kerry, John F.	51,144	1,694,213 R	61.1%	38.2%	61.5%	38.5%
2000**	6,407,637	3,799,639	Bush, George W.	2,433,746	Gore, Albert Jr.	174,252	1,365,893 R	59.3%	38.0%	61.0%	39.0%
1996**	5,611,644	2,736,167	Dole, Robert "Bob"	2,459,683	Clinton, Bill*	415,794	276,484 R	48.8%	43.8%	52.7%	47.3%
1992**	6,154,018	2,496,071	Bush, George H.*	2,281,815	Clinton, Bill	1,376,132	214,256 R	40.6%	37.1%	52.2%	47.8%
1988	5,427,410	3,036,829	Bush, George H.	2,352,748	Dukakis, Michael S.	37,833	684,081 R	56.0%	43.3%	56.3%	43.7%
1984	5,397,571	3,433,428	Reagan, Ronald*	1,949,276	Mondale, Walter F.	14,867	1,484,152 R	63.6%	36.1%	63.8%	36.2%
1980**	4,541,636	2,510,705	Reagan, Ronald	1,881,147	Carter, Jimmy*	149,784	629,558 R	55.3%	41.4%	57.2%	42.8%
1976	4,071,884	1,953,300	Ford, Gerald R.*	2,082,319	Carter, Jimmy	36,265	129,019 D	48.0%	51.1%	48.4%	51.6%
1972	3,471,285	2,298,896	Nixon, Richard M.*	1,154,293	McGovern, George S.	18,096	1,144,603 R	66.2%	33.3%	66.6%	33.4%
1968**	3,079,216	1,227,844	Nixon, Richard M.	1,266,804	Humphrey, Hubert Horatio Jr.	584,568	38,960 D	39.9%	41.1%	49.2%	50.8%
1964	2,626,811	958,566	Goldwater, Barry M. Sr.	1,663,185	Johnson, Lyndon B.*	5,060	704,619 D	36.5%	63.3%	36.6%	63.4%
1960	2,311,084	1,121,310	Nixon, Richard M.	1,167,567	Kennedy, John F.	22,207	46,257 D	48.5%	50.5%	49.0%	51.0%
1956	1,955,168	1,080,619	Eisenhower, Dwight D.*	859,958	Stevenson, Adlai E. II	14,591	220,661 R	55.3%	44.0%	55.7%	44.3%
1952	2,075,946	1,102,878	Eisenhower, Dwight D.	969,228	Stevenson, Adlai E. II	3,840	133,650 R	53.1%	46.7%	53.2%	46.8%
1948**	1,249,577	303,467	Dewey, Thomas E.	824,235	Truman, Harry S.*	121,875	520,768 D	24.3%	66.0%	26.9%	73.1%

Note: An asterisk (*) denotes incumbent. **In past elections, the other vote included: 2016 - 283,492 Libertarian (Gary Johnson); 2000 - 137,994 Green (Ralph Nader); 1996 - 378,537 Reform (Ross Perot); 1992 - 1,354,781 Independent (Perot); 1980 - 111,613 Independent (John Anderson); 1968 - 584,269 American Independent (George Wallace); 1948 - 113,920 States' Rights (Strom Thurmond).

TEXAS

POSTWAR VOTE FOR GOVERNOR

		Republican		Democratic				Percentage			
								Total Vote		Major Vote	
Year	Total Vote	Vote	Candidate	Vote	Candidate	Other Vote	Rep.-Dem. Plurality	Rep.	Dem.	Rep.	Dem.
2018	8,343,443	4,656,196	Abbott, Greg*	3,546,615	Valdez, Lupe	140,632	1,109,581 R	55.8%	42.5%	56.8%	43.2%
2014	4,718,268	2,796,547	Abbott, Greg	1,835,596	Davis, Wendy R.	86,125	960,951 R	59.3%	38.9%	60.4%	39.6%
2010	4,979,870	2,737,481	Perry, Rick*	2,106,395	White, Bill	135,994	631,086 R	55.0%	42.3%	56.5%	43.5%
2006**	4,399,116	1,716,792	Perry, Rick*	1,310,337	Bell, Chris	1,371,987	406,455 R	39.0%	29.8%	56.7%	43.3%
2002	4,553,987	2,632,591	Perry, Rick*	1,819,798	Sanchez, Tony	101,598	812,793 R	57.8%	40.0%	59.1%	40.9%
1998	3,738,483	2,551,454	Bush, George W.*	1,165,444	Mauro, Garry	21,585	1,386,010 R	68.2%	31.2%	68.6%	31.4%
1994	4,396,242	2,350,994	Bush, George W.	2,016,928	Richards, Ann*	28,320	334,066 R	53.5%	45.9%	53.8%	46.2%
1990	3,892,487	1,826,231	Williams, Clayton	1,925,670	Richards, Ann	140,586	99,439 D	46.9%	49.5%	48.7%	51.3%
1986	3,441,460	1,813,779	Clements, William P.	1,584,515	White, Mark*	43,166	229,264 R	52.7%	46.0%	53.4%	46.6%
1982	3,191,091	1,465,937	Clements, William P.*	1,697,870	White, Mark	27,284	231,933 D	45.9%	53.2%	46.3%	53.7%
1978	2,369,764	1,183,839	Clements, William P.	1,166,979	Hill, John	18,946	16,860 R	50.0%	49.2%	50.4%	49.6%
1974**	1,654,957	514,725	Granberry, Jim	1,016,334	Briscoe, Dolph*	123,898	501,609 D	31.1%	61.4%	33.6%	66.4%
1972	3,410,071	1,534,060	Grover, Henry C.	1,633,913	Briscoe, Dolph	242,098	99,853 D	45.0%	47.9%	48.4%	51.6%
1970	2,235,855	1,037,723	Eggers, Paul W.	1,197,736	Smith, Preston*	396	160,013 D	46.4%	53.6%	46.4%	53.6%
1968	2,916,508	1,254,331	Eggers, Paul W.	1,662,019	Smith, Preston	158	407,688 D	43.0%	57.0%	43.0%	57.0%
1966	1,425,861	368,025	Kennerly, T. E.	1,037,517	Connally, John B.*	20,319	669,492 D	25.8%	72.8%	26.2%	73.8%
1964	2,544,753	661,675	Crichton, Jack	1,877,793	Connally, John B.*	5,285	1,216,118 D	26.0%	73.8%	26.1%	73.9%
1962	1,569,181	715,025	Cox, Jack	847,036	Connally, John B.	7,120	132,011 D	45.6%	54.0%	45.8%	54.2%
1960	2,250,718	612,963	Steger, William	1,637,755	Daniel, Price*		1,024,792 D	27.2%	72.8%	27.2%	72.8%
1958	789,133	94,098	Mayer, Edwin S.	695,035	Daniel, Price*		600,937 D	11.9%	88.1%	11.9%	88.1%
1956	1,826,242	271,088	Bryant, William R.	1,433,051	Daniel, Price	122,103	1,161,963 D	14.8%	78.5%	15.9%	84.1%
1954	636,892	66,154	Adams, Tod R.	569,533	Shivers, Allan*	1,205	503,379 D	10.4%	89.4%	10.4%	89.6%
1952	1,890,535			1,853,863	Shivers, Allan*	36,672	1,853,863 D		98.1%		100.0%
1950	407,138	39,793	Currie, Ralph W.	367,345	Shivers, Allan*		327,552 D	9.8%	90.2%	9.8%	90.2%
1948	1,208,860	177,399	Lane, Alvin H.	1,024,160	Jester, Beauford H.*	7,301	846,761 D	14.7%	84.7%	14.8%	85.2%
1946	378,784	33,277	Nolte, Eugene Jr.	345,507	Jester, Beauford H.		312,230 D	8.8%	91.2%	8.8%	91.2%

Note: An asterisk (*) denotes incumbent. **In past elections, the other vote included: 2006 - 796,851 Independent (Carole Keeton Strayhorn); 547,674 Independent (Richard "Kinky" Friedman). The term of office of Texas's governor was increased from two to four years effective with the 1974 election. The Republican Party did not run a candidate in the 1952 gubernatorial election.

TEXAS

POSTWAR VOTE FOR SENATOR

Year	Total Vote	Republican		Democratic		Other Vote	Rep.-Dem. Plurality	Percentage: Total Vote		Percentage: Major Vote	
		Vote	Candidate	Vote	Candidate			Rep.	Dem.	Rep.	Dem.
2018	8,371,655	4,260,553	Cruz, Ted*	4,045,632	O'Rourke, Beto	65,470	214,921 R	50.9%	48.3%	51.3%	48.7%
2014	4,648,358	2,861,531	Cornyn, John*	1,597,387	Alameel, David	189,440	1,264,144 R	61.6%	34.4%	64.2%	35.8%
2012	7,864,822	4,440,137	Cruz, Ted	3,194,927	Sadler, Paul	229,758	1,245,210 R	56.5%	40.6%	58.2%	41.8%
2008	7,912,075	4,337,469	Cornyn, John*	3,389,365	Noriega, Richard J. "Rick"	185,241	948,104 R	54.8%	42.8%	56.1%	43.9%
2006	4,314,663	2,661,789	Hutchison, Kay Bailey*	1,555,202	Radnofsky, Barbara Ann	97,672	1,106,587 R	61.7%	36.0%	63.1%	36.9%
2002	4,514,012	2,496,243	Cornyn, John	1,955,758	Kirk, Ron	62,011	540,485 R	55.3%	43.3%	56.1%	43.9%
2000	6,276,652	4,082,091	Hutchison, Kay Bailey*	2,030,315	Kelly, Gene	164,246	2,051,776 R	65.0%	32.3%	66.8%	33.2%
1996	5,527,441	3,027,680	Gramm, W. Phil*	2,428,776	Morales, Victor M.	70,985	598,904 R	54.8%	43.9%	55.5%	44.5%
1994	4,279,940	2,604,218	Hutchison, Kay Bailey*	1,639,615	Mattox, Jim	36,107	964,603 R	60.8%	38.3%	61.4%	38.6%
1993S**	1,765,254	1,188,716	Hutchison, Kay Bailey	576,538	Krueger, Robert*		612,178 R	67.3%	32.7%	67.3%	32.7%
1990	3,822,157	2,302,357	Gramm, W. Phil*	1,429,986	Parmer, Hugh	89,814	872,371 R	60.2%	37.4%	61.7%	38.3%
1988	5,323,606	2,129,228	Boulter, E. Beau	3,149,806	Bentsen, Lloyd M. Jr.*	44,572	1,020,578 D	40.0%	59.2%	40.3%	59.7%
1984	5,319,178	3,116,348	Gramm, W. Phil	2,202,557	Doggett, Lloyd	273	913,791 R	58.6%	41.4%	58.6%	41.4%
1982	3,103,167	1,256,759	Collins, James M.	1,818,223	Bentsen, Lloyd M. Jr.*	28,185	561,464 D	40.5%	58.6%	40.9%	59.1%
1978	2,312,540	1,151,376	Tower, John G.*	1,139,149	Krueger, Robert	22,015	12,227 R	49.8%	49.3%	50.3%	49.7%
1976	3,874,516	1,636,370	Steelman, Alan	2,199,956	Bentsen, Lloyd M. Jr.*	38,190	563,586 D	42.2%	56.8%	42.7%	57.3%
1972	3,413,918	1,822,877	Tower, John G.*	1,511,985	Sanders, Barefoot	79,056	310,892 R	53.4%	44.3%	54.7%	45.3%
1970	2,231,671	1,035,794	Bush, George H.	1,194,069	Bentsen, Lloyd M. Jr.	1,808	158,275 D	46.4%	53.5%	46.5%	53.5%
1966	1,493,182	842,501	Tower, John G.*	643,855	Carr, Waggoner	6,826	198,646 R	56.4%	43.1%	56.7%	43.3%
1964	2,603,856	1,134,337	Bush, George H.	1,463,958	Yarborough, Ralph*	5,561	329,621 D	43.6%	56.2%	43.7%	56.3%
1961S**		448,217	Tower, John G.	437,874	Blakley, William A.*	886,091	10,343 R			50.6%	49.4%
1960	2,253,764	926,653	Tower, John G.	1,306,605	Johnson, Lyndon B.*	20,506	379,952 D	41.1%	58.0%	41.5%	58.5%
1958	787,128	185,926	Whittenburg, Roy	587,030	Yarborough, Ralph*	14,172	401,104 D	23.6%	74.6%	24.1%	75.9%
1957S**	874,899	219,591	Hutcheson, Thad	364,605	Yarborough, Ralph	290,803	655,408 R	25.1%	74.9%	25.1%	74.9%
1954	636,475	94,131	Watson, Carlos G.	539,319	Johnson, Lyndon B.*	3,025	445,188 D	14.8%	84.7%	14.9%	85.1%
1952**	1,894,671			1,894,671	Daniel, Price		1,894,671 D		100.0%		100.0%
1948	1,061,363	349,665	Porter, Jack	702,785	Johnson, Lyndon B.	8,913	353,120 D	32.9%	66.2%	33.2%	66.8%
1946	380,550	43,619	Sells, Murray C.	336,931	Connally, Tom T.*		293,312 D	11.5%	88.5%	11.5%	88.5%

Note: An asterisk (*) denotes incumbent. **The June 1993 election was for a short term to fill a vacancy; the vote above was for the special election runoff. The April 1957 and May 1961 elections were also for short terms to fill vacancies. Although neither vote was held with official party designations, the 1961 vote above reflected the result of a runoff between unofficial party candidates. In 1957 there was a single ballot without a runoff and Democrat Ralph Yarborough polled 364,605 votes (38.1 percent of the total vote) and won the election with a 73,802-vote plurality over Democrat Martin Dies, and the plurality listed takes into account the Democratic votes for both Yarborough and Dies. The Republican Party did not run a candidate in the 1952 Senate election.

TEXAS

GOVERNOR 2018

2010 Census Population	County	Total Vote	Republican (Abbott)	Democratic (Valdez)	Other	Rep.-Dem. Plurality	Percentage Total Vote Rep.	Percentage Total Vote Dem.	Percentage Major Vote Rep.	Percentage Major Vote Dem.
58,458	ANDERSON	14,751	11,732	2,868	151	8,864 R	79.5%	19.4%	80.4%	19.6%
14,786	ANDREWS	4,125	3,400	687	38	2,713 R	82.4%	16.7%	83.2%	16.8%
86,771	ANGELINA	26,351	19,701	6,406	244	13,295 R	74.8%	24.3%	75.5%	24.5%
23,158	ARANSAS	8,980	7,075	1,797	108	5,278 R	78.8%	20.0%	79.7%	20.3%
9,054	ARCHER	3,610	3,259	323	28	2,936 R	90.3%	8.9%	91.0%	9.0%
1,901	ARMSTRONG	895	822	59	14	763 R	91.8%	6.6%	93.3%	6.7%
44,911	ATASCOSA	12,174	8,361	3,655	158	4,706 R	68.7%	30.0%	69.6%	30.4%
28,417	AUSTIN	11,029	9,009	1,897	123	7,112 R	81.7%	17.2%	82.6%	17.4%
7,165	BAILEY	1,606	1,241	348	17	893 R	77.3%	21.7%	78.1%	21.9%
20,485	BANDERA	9,588	7,866	1,602	120	6,264 R	82.0%	16.7%	83.1%	16.9%
74,171	BASTROP	27,398	16,351	10,407	640	5,944 R	59.7%	38.0%	61.1%	38.9%
3,726	BAYLOR	1,234	1,090	129	15	961 R	88.3%	10.5%	89.4%	10.6%
31,861	BEE	7,178	4,827	2,261	90	2,566 R	67.2%	31.5%	68.1%	31.9%
310,235	BELL	86,398	51,157	33,803	1,438	17,354 R	59.2%	39.1%	60.2%	39.8%
1,714,773	BEXAR	546,397	251,043	285,502	9,852	34,459 D	45.9%	52.3%	46.8%	53.2%
10,497	BLANCO	5,795	4,329	1,351	115	2,978 R	74.7%	23.3%	76.2%	23.8%
641	BORDEN	339	321	17	1	304 R	94.7%	5.0%	95.0%	5.0%
18,212	BOSQUE	7,158	5,948	1,104	106	4,844 R	83.1%	15.4%	84.3%	15.7%
92,565	BOWIE	28,289	20,651	7,357	281	13,294 R	73.0%	26.0%	73.7%	26.3%
313,166	BRAZORIA	111,546	70,373	39,536	1,637	30,837 R	63.1%	35.4%	64.0%	36.0%
194,851	BRAZOS	64,168	39,424	23,361	1,383	16,063 R	61.4%	36.4%	62.8%	37.2%
9,232	BREWSTER	4,062	2,033	1,933	96	100 R	50.0%	47.6%	51.3%	48.7%
1,637	BRISCOE	623	556	58	9	498 R	89.2%	9.3%	90.6%	9.4%
7,223	BROOKS	1,868	658	1,198	12	540 D	35.2%	64.1%	35.5%	64.5%
38,106	BROWN	12,240	10,640	1,458	142	9,182 R	86.9%	11.9%	87.9%	12.1%
17,187	BURLESON	6,599	5,254	1,277	68	3,977 R	79.6%	19.4%	80.4%	19.6%
42,750	BURNET	18,549	14,497	3,712	340	10,785 R	78.2%	20.0%	79.6%	20.4%
38,066	CALDWELL	11,457	6,723	4,509	225	2,214 R	58.7%	39.4%	59.9%	40.1%
21,381	CALHOUN	6,118	4,409	1,627	82	2,782 R	72.1%	26.6%	73.0%	27.0%
13,544	CALLAHAN	5,015	4,475	486	54	3,989 R	89.2%	9.7%	90.2%	9.8%
406,220	CAMERON	77,511	34,407	41,991	1,113	7,584 D	44.4%	54.2%	45.0%	55.0%
12,401	CAMP	3,885	2,816	1,028	41	1,788 R	72.5%	26.5%	73.3%	26.7%
6,182	CARSON	2,453	2,209	208	36	2,001 R	90.1%	8.5%	91.4%	8.6%
30,464	CASS	10,289	8,323	1,890	76	6,433 R	80.9%	18.4%	81.5%	18.5%
8,062	CASTRO	1,615	1,226	371	18	855 R	75.9%	23.0%	76.8%	23.2%
35,096	CHAMBERS	15,168	12,505	2,460	203	10,045 R	82.4%	16.2%	83.6%	16.4%
50,845	CHEROKEE	15,035	11,943	2,938	154	9,005 R	79.4%	19.5%	80.3%	19.7%
7,041	CHILDRESS	1,765	1,546	206	13	1,340 R	87.6%	11.7%	88.2%	11.8%
10,752	CLAY	4,286	3,807	449	30	3,358 R	88.8%	10.5%	89.5%	10.5%
3,127	COCHRAN	679	550	122	7	428 R	81.0%	18.0%	81.8%	18.2%
3,320	COKE	1,320	1,187	118	15	1,069 R	89.9%	8.9%	91.0%	9.0%
8,895	COLEMAN	3,130	2,774	328	28	2,446 R	88.6%	10.5%	89.4%	10.6%
782,341	COLLIN	353,694	208,075	139,175	6,444	68,900 R	58.8%	39.3%	59.9%	40.1%
3,057	COLLINGSWORTH	939	827	101	11	726 R	88.1%	10.8%	89.1%	10.9%
20,874	COLORADO	7,613	5,992	1,558	63	4,434 R	78.7%	20.5%	79.4%	20.6%
108,472	COMAL	61,795	46,635	14,145	1,015	32,490 R	75.5%	22.9%	76.7%	23.3%
13,974	COMANCHE	4,613	3,906	657	50	3,249 R	84.7%	14.2%	85.6%	14.4%
4,087	CONCHO	983	825	145	13	680 R	83.9%	14.8%	85.1%	14.9%
38,437	COOKE	14,512	12,294	2,054	164	10,240 R	84.7%	14.2%	85.7%	14.3%
75,388	CORYELL	15,931	11,281	4,392	258	6,889 R	70.8%	27.6%	72.0%	28.0%
1,505	COTTLE	559	468	88	3	380 R	83.7%	15.7%	84.2%	15.8%
4,375	CRANE	1,047	842	197	8	645 R	80.4%	18.8%	81.0%	19.0%
3,719	CROCKETT	1,266	921	333	12	588 R	72.7%	26.3%	73.4%	26.6%
6,059	CROSBY	1,417	1,005	392	20	613 R	70.9%	27.7%	71.9%	28.1%
2,398	CULBERSON	757	324	422	11	98 D	42.8%	55.7%	43.4%	56.6%
6,703	DALLAM	1,122	985	129	8	856 R	87.8%	11.5%	88.4%	11.6%
2,368,139	DALLAS	723,897	283,659	425,208	15,030	141,549 D	39.2%	58.7%	40.0%	60.0%
13,833	DAWSON	3,009	2,240	739	30	1,501 R	74.4%	24.6%	75.2%	24.8%
20,097	DE WITT	6,119	5,115	942	62	4,173 R	83.6%	15.4%	84.4%	15.6%
19,372	DEAF SMITH	3,773	2,788	957	28	1,831 R	73.9%	25.4%	74.4%	25.6%

TEXAS

GOVERNOR 2018

2010 Census Population	County	Total Vote	Republican (Abbott)	Democratic (Valdez)	Other	Rep.-Dem. Plurality	Percentage: Total Vote		Percentage: Major Vote	
							Rep.	Dem.	Rep.	Dem.
5,231	DELTA	1,936	1,606	301	29	1,305 R	83.0%	15.5%	84.2%	15.8%
662,614	DENTON	294,474	174,472	113,808	6,194	60,664 R	59.2%	38.6%	60.5%	39.5%
2,444	DICKENS	758	656	96	6	560 R	86.5%	12.7%	87.2%	12.8%
9,996	DIMMIT	2,851	1,042	1,787	22	745 D	36.5%	62.7%	36.8%	63.2%
3,677	DONLEY	1,284	1,130	134	20	996 R	88.0%	10.4%	89.4%	10.6%
11,782	DUVAL	3,958	1,479	2,457	22	978 D	37.4%	62.1%	37.6%	62.4%
18,583	EASTLAND	6,199	5,434	708	57	4,726 R	87.7%	11.4%	88.5%	11.5%
137,130	ECTOR	30,557	21,934	8,211	412	13,723 R	71.8%	26.9%	72.8%	27.2%
2,002	EDWARDS	742	635	100	7	535 R	85.6%	13.5%	86.4%	13.6%
800,647	EL PASO	200,629	62,749	134,181	3,699	71,432 D	31.3%	66.9%	31.9%	68.1%
149,610	ELLIS	60,501	43,647	15,879	975	27,768 R	72.1%	26.2%	73.3%	26.7%
37,890	ERATH	12,596	10,356	2,073	167	8,283 R	82.2%	16.5%	83.3%	16.7%
17,866	FALLS	4,669	3,344	1,286	39	2,058 R	71.6%	27.5%	72.2%	27.8%
33,915	FANNIN	10,754	8,856	1,767	131	7,089 R	82.4%	16.4%	83.4%	16.6%
24,554	FAYETTE	10,461	8,576	1,777	108	6,799 R	82.0%	17.0%	82.8%	17.2%
3,974	FISHER	1,488	1,161	310	17	851 R	78.0%	20.8%	78.9%	21.1%
6,446	FLOYD	1,877	1,448	412	17	1,036 R	77.1%	21.9%	77.8%	22.2%
1,336	FOARD	436	331	101	4	230 R	75.9%	23.2%	76.6%	23.4%
585,375	FORT BEND	254,854	125,867	125,374	3,613	493 R	49.4%	49.2%	50.1%	49.9%
10,605	FRANKLIN	3,955	3,359	537	59	2,822 R	84.9%	13.6%	86.2%	13.8%
19,816	FREESTONE	6,539	5,336	1,143	60	4,193 R	81.6%	17.5%	82.4%	17.6%
17,217	FRIO	3,634	1,844	1,739	51	105 R	50.7%	47.9%	51.5%	48.5%
17,526	GAINES	3,833	3,305	475	53	2,830 R	86.2%	12.4%	87.4%	12.6%
291,309	GALVESTON	113,435	72,104	39,314	2,017	32,790 R	63.6%	34.7%	64.7%	35.3%
6,461	GARZA	1,277	1,078	186	13	892 R	84.4%	14.6%	85.3%	14.7%
24,837	GILLESPIE	12,545	10,351	2,030	164	8,321 R	82.5%	16.2%	83.6%	16.4%
1,226	GLASSCOCK	553	515	36	2	479 R	93.1%	6.5%	93.5%	6.5%
7,210	GOLIAD	3,062	2,397	617	48	1,780 R	78.3%	20.2%	79.5%	20.5%
19,807	GONZALES	5,615	4,393	1,170	52	3,223 R	78.2%	20.8%	79.0%	21.0%
22,535	GRAY	5,948	5,330	551	67	4,779 R	89.6%	9.3%	90.6%	9.4%
120,877	GRAYSON	43,027	32,562	9,857	608	22,705 R	75.7%	22.9%	76.8%	23.2%
121,730	GREGG	35,981	25,558	10,015	408	15,543 R	71.0%	27.8%	71.8%	28.2%
26,604	GRIMES	8,644	6,684	1,858	102	4,826 R	77.3%	21.5%	78.2%	21.8%
131,533	GUADALUPE	54,403	36,284	17,265	854	19,019 R	66.7%	31.7%	67.8%	32.2%
36,273	HALE	7,373	5,532	1,727	114	3,805 R	75.0%	23.4%	76.2%	23.8%
3,353	HALL	964	815	142	7	673 R	84.5%	14.7%	85.2%	14.8%
8,517	HAMILTON	3,338	2,903	405	30	2,498 R	87.0%	12.1%	87.8%	12.2%
5,613	HANSFORD	1,691	1,548	118	25	1,430 R	91.5%	7.0%	92.9%	7.1%
4,139	HARDEMAN	1,157	997	154	6	843 R	86.2%	13.3%	86.6%	13.4%
54,635	HARDIN	20,010	17,528	2,327	155	15,201 R	87.6%	11.6%	88.3%	11.7%
4,092,459	HARRIS	1,206,717	559,819	628,804	18,094	68,985 D	46.4%	52.1%	47.1%	52.9%
65,631	HARRISON	22,566	16,747	5,562	257	11,185 R	74.2%	24.6%	75.1%	24.9%
6,062	HARTLEY	1,623	1,491	125	7	1,366 R	91.9%	7.7%	92.3%	7.7%
5,899	HASKELL	1,668	1,387	267	14	1,120 R	83.2%	16.0%	83.9%	16.1%
157,107	HAYS	79,525	37,895	39,486	2,144	1,591 D	47.7%	49.7%	49.0%	51.0%
3,807	HEMPHILL	1,365	1,199	152	14	1,047 R	87.8%	11.1%	88.7%	11.3%
78,532	HENDERSON	26,703	21,775	4,622	306	17,153 R	81.5%	17.3%	82.5%	17.5%
774,769	HIDALGO	151,026	55,421	93,935	1,670	38,514 D	36.7%	62.2%	37.1%	62.9%
35,089	HILL	11,430	9,262	2,052	116	7,210 R	81.0%	18.0%	81.9%	18.1%
22,935	HOCKLEY	6,072	4,947	1,030	95	3,917 R	81.5%	17.0%	82.8%	17.2%
51,182	HOOD	24,940	20,865	3,765	310	17,100 R	83.7%	15.1%	84.7%	15.3%
35,161	HOPKINS	11,880	9,533	2,218	129	7,315 R	80.2%	18.7%	81.1%	18.9%
23,732	HOUSTON	7,350	5,659	1,641	50	4,018 R	77.0%	22.3%	77.5%	22.5%
35,012	HOWARD	7,371	5,737	1,542	92	4,195 R	77.8%	20.9%	78.8%	21.2%
3,476	HUDSPETH	886	538	335	13	203 R	60.7%	37.8%	61.6%	38.4%
86,129	HUNT	28,413	22,078	5,946	389	16,132 R	77.7%	20.9%	78.8%	21.2%
22,150	HUTCHINSON	6,640	5,874	687	79	5,187 R	88.5%	10.3%	89.5%	10.5%
1,599	IRION	737	641	87	9	554 R	87.0%	11.8%	88.0%	12.0%
9,044	JACK	2,811	2,539	246	26	2,293 R	90.3%	8.8%	91.2%	8.8%
14,075	JACKSON	4,758	4,016	715	27	3,301 R	84.4%	15.0%	84.9%	15.1%

TEXAS

GOVERNOR 2018

2010 Census Population	County	Total Vote	Republican (Abbott)	Democratic (Valdez)	Other	Rep.-Dem. Plurality	Percentage Total Vote Rep.	Percentage Total Vote Dem.	Percentage Major Vote Rep.	Percentage Major Vote Dem.
35,710	JASPER	11,808	9,732	1,990	86	7,742 R	82.4%	16.9%	83.0%	17.0%
2,342	JEFF DAVIS	1,165	719	407	39	312 R	61.7%	34.9%	63.9%	36.1%
252,273	JEFFERSON	74,266	38,999	34,516	751	4,483 R	52.5%	46.5%	53.0%	47.0%
5,300	JIM HOGG	1,455	509	938	8	429 D	35.0%	64.5%	35.2%	64.8%
40,838	JIM WELLS	9,781	5,088	4,616	77	472 R	52.0%	47.2%	52.4%	47.6%
150,934	JOHNSON	52,364	41,485	10,105	774	31,380 R	79.2%	19.3%	80.4%	19.6%
20,202	JONES	4,981	4,167	757	57	3,410 R	83.7%	15.2%	84.6%	15.4%
14,824	KARNES	4,123	3,023	1,054	46	1,969 R	73.3%	25.6%	74.1%	25.9%
103,350	KAUFMAN	38,344	27,491	10,294	559	17,197 R	71.7%	26.8%	72.8%	27.2%
33,410	KENDALL	19,744	16,076	3,382	286	12,694 R	81.4%	17.1%	82.6%	17.4%
416	KENEDY	171	111	57	3	54 R	64.9%	33.3%	66.1%	33.9%
808	KENT	337	299	34	4	265 R	88.7%	10.1%	89.8%	10.2%
49,625	KERR	22,132	17,566	4,268	298	13,298 R	79.4%	19.3%	80.5%	19.5%
4,607	KIMBLE	1,713	1,529	161	23	1,368 R	89.3%	9.4%	90.5%	9.5%
286	KING	127	120	6	1	114 R	94.5%	4.7%	95.2%	4.8%
3,598	KINNEY	1,191	890	290	11	600 R	74.7%	24.3%	75.4%	24.6%
32,061	KLEBERG	8,559	4,831	3,629	99	1,202 R	56.4%	42.4%	57.1%	42.9%
3,719	KNOX	1,094	866	217	11	649 R	79.2%	19.8%	80.0%	20.0%
6,886	LA SALLE	1,460	728	725	7	3 R	49.9%	49.7%	50.1%	49.9%
49,793	LAMAR	16,534	13,103	3,231	200	9,872 R	79.2%	19.5%	80.2%	19.8%
13,977	LAMB	3,449	2,785	629	35	2,156 R	80.7%	18.2%	81.6%	18.4%
19,677	LAMPASAS	7,517	6,073	1,343	101	4,730 R	80.8%	17.9%	81.9%	18.1%
19,263	LAVACA	7,731	6,856	830	45	6,026 R	88.7%	10.7%	89.2%	10.8%
16,612	LEE	5,836	4,650	1,129	57	3,521 R	79.7%	19.3%	80.5%	19.5%
16,801	LEON	6,583	5,781	751	51	5,030 R	87.8%	11.4%	88.5%	11.5%
75,643	LIBERTY	20,546	16,527	3,816	203	12,711 R	80.4%	18.6%	81.2%	18.8%
23,384	LIMESTONE	6,917	5,330	1,535	52	3,795 R	77.1%	22.2%	77.6%	22.4%
3,302	LIPSCOMB	1,064	947	109	8	838 R	89.0%	10.2%	89.7%	10.3%
11,531	LIVE OAK	3,647	3,114	504	29	2,610 R	85.4%	13.8%	86.1%	13.9%
19,301	LLANO	10,176	8,287	1,751	138	6,536 R	81.4%	17.2%	82.6%	17.4%
82	LOVING	56	47	9		38 R	83.9%	16.1%	83.9%	16.1%
278,831	LUBBOCK	91,174	61,775	27,266	2,133	34,509 R	67.8%	29.9%	69.4%	30.6%
5,915	LYNN	1,696	1,380	302	14	1,078 R	81.4%	17.8%	82.0%	18.0%
13,664	MADISON	3,832	3,081	722	29	2,359 R	80.4%	18.8%	81.0%	19.0%
10,546	MARION	3,525	2,553	939	33	1,614 R	72.4%	26.6%	73.1%	26.9%
4,799	MARTIN	1,546	1,303	229	14	1,074 R	84.3%	14.8%	85.1%	14.9%
4,012	MASON	1,959	1,605	333	21	1,272 R	81.9%	17.0%	82.8%	17.2%
36,702	MATAGORDA	10,484	7,705	2,673	106	5,032 R	73.5%	25.5%	74.2%	25.8%
54,258	MAVERICK	10,561	3,495	6,940	126	3,445 D	33.1%	65.7%	33.5%	66.5%
8,283	MCCULLOCH	2,676	2,275	368	33	1,907 R	85.0%	13.8%	86.1%	13.9%
234,906	MCLENNAN	75,008	49,195	24,734	1,079	24,461 R	65.6%	33.0%	66.5%	33.5%
707	MCMULLEN	429	395	33	1	362 R	92.1%	7.7%	92.3%	7.7%
46,006	MEDINA	16,187	12,057	3,964	166	8,093 R	74.5%	24.5%	75.3%	24.7%
2,242	MENARD	780	646	130	4	516 R	82.8%	16.7%	83.2%	16.8%
136,872	MIDLAND	42,842	34,049	8,101	692	25,948 R	79.5%	18.9%	80.8%	19.2%
24,757	MILAM	7,990	6,080	1,795	115	4,285 R	76.1%	22.5%	77.2%	22.8%
4,936	MILLS	2,014	1,790	206	18	1,584 R	88.9%	10.2%	89.7%	10.3%
9,403	MITCHELL	1,907	1,595	298	14	1,297 R	83.6%	15.6%	84.3%	15.7%
19,719	MONTAGUE	7,408	6,563	765	80	5,798 R	88.6%	10.3%	89.6%	10.4%
455,746	MONTGOMERY	190,310	144,664	43,044	2,602	101,620 R	76.0%	22.6%	77.1%	22.9%
21,904	MOORE	4,058	3,268	750	40	2,518 R	80.5%	18.5%	81.3%	18.7%
12,934	MORRIS	4,221	3,018	1,159	44	1,859 R	71.5%	27.5%	72.3%	27.7%
1,210	MOTLEY	497	458	35	4	423 R	92.2%	7.0%	92.9%	7.1%
64,524	NACOGDOCHES	21,518	14,411	6,843	264	7,568 R	67.0%	31.8%	67.8%	32.2%
47,735	NAVARRO	14,408	10,818	3,411	179	7,407 R	75.1%	23.7%	76.0%	24.0%
14,445	NEWTON	4,670	3,771	870	29	2,901 R	80.7%	18.6%	81.3%	18.7%
15,216	NOLAN	4,058	3,200	807	51	2,393 R	78.9%	19.9%	79.9%	20.1%
340,223	NUECES	93,950	52,918	39,720	1,312	13,198 R	56.3%	42.3%	57.1%	42.9%
10,223	OCHILTREE	2,407	2,169	212	26	1,957 R	90.1%	8.8%	91.1%	8.9%
2,052	OLDHAM	809	742	62	5	680 R	91.7%	7.7%	92.3%	7.7%

TEXAS

GOVERNOR 2018

2010 Census Population	County	Total Vote	Republican (Abbott)	Democratic (Valdez)	Other	Rep.-Dem. Plurality	Percentage: Total Vote Rep.	Percentage: Total Vote Dem.	Percentage: Major Vote Rep.	Percentage: Major Vote Dem.
81,837	ORANGE	26,286	21,724	4,348	214	17,376 R	82.6%	16.5%	83.3%	16.7%
28,111	PALO PINTO	9,430	7,811	1,529	90	6,282 R	82.8%	16.2%	83.6%	16.4%
23,796	PANOLA	8,737	7,182	1,494	61	5,688 R	82.2%	17.1%	82.8%	17.2%
116,927	PARKER	54,825	45,981	8,099	745	37,882 R	83.9%	14.8%	85.0%	15.0%
10,269	PARMER	2,046	1,680	352	14	1,328 R	82.1%	17.2%	82.7%	17.3%
15,507	PECOS	3,503	2,299	1,167	37	1,132 R	65.6%	33.3%	66.3%	33.7%
45,413	POLK	16,728	13,130	3,378	220	9,752 R	78.5%	20.2%	79.5%	20.5%
121,073	POTTER	24,362	17,299	6,674	389	10,625 R	71.0%	27.4%	72.2%	27.8%
7,818	PRESIDIO	1,652	465	1,157	30	692 D	28.1%	70.0%	28.7%	71.3%
10,914	RAINS	4,407	3,810	566	31	3,244 R	86.5%	12.8%	87.1%	12.9%
120,725	RANDALL	48,368	39,586	8,065	717	31,521 R	81.8%	16.7%	83.1%	16.9%
3,367	REAGAN	836	697	127	12	570 R	83.4%	15.2%	84.6%	15.4%
3,309	REAL	1,566	1,341	213	12	1,128 R	85.6%	13.6%	86.3%	13.7%
12,860	RED RIVER	4,406	3,476	904	26	2,572 R	78.9%	20.5%	79.4%	20.6%
13,783	REEVES	2,357	1,210	1,123	24	87 R	51.3%	47.6%	51.9%	48.1%
7,383	REFUGIO	2,496	1,726	751	19	975 R	69.2%	30.1%	69.7%	30.3%
929	ROBERTS	469	448	16	5	432 R	95.5%	3.4%	96.6%	3.4%
16,622	ROBERTSON	6,253	4,448	1,753	52	2,695 R	71.1%	28.0%	71.7%	28.3%
78,337	ROCKWALL	38,636	28,582	9,432	622	19,150 R	74.0%	24.4%	75.2%	24.8%
10,501	RUNNELS	3,258	2,885	345	28	2,540 R	88.6%	10.6%	89.3%	10.7%
53,330	RUSK	16,244	12,864	3,233	147	9,631 R	79.2%	19.9%	79.9%	20.1%
10,834	SABINE	3,958	3,477	458	23	3,019 R	87.8%	11.6%	88.4%	11.6%
8,865	SAN AUGUSTINE	3,000	2,296	684	20	1,612 R	76.5%	22.8%	77.0%	23.0%
26,384	SAN JACINTO	9,335	7,722	1,529	84	6,193 R	82.7%	16.4%	83.5%	16.5%
64,804	SAN PATRICIO	18,216	12,173	5,842	201	6,331 R	66.8%	32.1%	67.6%	32.4%
6,131	SAN SABA	2,059	1,835	211	13	1,624 R	89.1%	10.2%	89.7%	10.3%
3,461	SCHLEICHER	957	758	187	12	571 R	79.2%	19.5%	80.2%	19.8%
16,921	SCURRY	4,368	3,750	577	41	3,173 R	85.9%	13.2%	86.7%	13.3%
3,378	SHACKELFORD	1,285	1,190	87	8	1,103 R	92.6%	6.8%	93.2%	6.8%
25,448	SHELBY	7,542	6,132	1,366	44	4,766 R	81.3%	18.1%	81.8%	18.2%
3,034	SHERMAN	817	701	74	42	627 R	85.8%	9.1%	90.5%	9.5%
209,714	SMITH	77,229	55,708	20,623	898	35,085 R	72.1%	26.7%	73.0%	27.0%
8,490	SOMERVELL	3,684	3,143	499	42	2,644 R	85.3%	13.5%	86.3%	13.7%
60,968	STARR	10,280	3,217	6,968	95	3,751 D	31.3%	67.8%	31.6%	68.4%
9,630	STEPHENS	2,968	2,653	291	24	2,362 R	89.4%	9.8%	90.1%	9.9%
1,143	STERLING	488	445	39	4	406 R	91.2%	8.0%	91.9%	8.1%
1,490	STONEWALL	610	503	96	11	407 R	82.5%	15.7%	84.0%	16.0%
4,128	SUTTON	1,199	939	248	12	691 R	78.3%	20.7%	79.1%	20.9%
7,854	SWISHER	1,885	1,491	368	26	1,123 R	79.1%	19.5%	80.2%	19.8%
1,809,034	TARRANT	625,894	340,404	273,814	11,676	66,590 R	54.4%	43.7%	55.4%	44.6%
131,506	TAYLOR	40,705	31,152	8,880	673	22,272 R	76.5%	21.8%	77.8%	22.2%
984	TERRELL	455	316	136	3	180 R	69.5%	29.9%	69.9%	30.1%
12,651	TERRY	2,802	2,221	552	29	1,669 R	79.3%	19.7%	80.1%	19.9%
1,641	THROCKMORTON	697	625	63	9	562 R	89.7%	9.0%	90.8%	9.2%
32,334	TITUS	7,976	5,861	2,017	98	3,844 R	73.5%	25.3%	74.4%	25.6%
110,224	TOM GREEN	34,653	25,792	8,373	488	17,419 R	74.4%	24.2%	75.5%	24.5%
1,024,266	TRAVIS	479,820	145,910	320,550	13,360	174,640 D	30.4%	66.8%	31.3%	68.7%
14,585	TRINITY	5,169	4,293	835	41	3,458 R	83.1%	16.2%	83.7%	16.3%
21,766	TYLER	7,119	6,079	973	67	5,106 R	85.4%	13.7%	86.2%	13.8%
39,309	UPSHUR	14,009	11,638	2,177	194	9,461 R	83.1%	15.5%	84.2%	15.8%
3,355	UPTON	1,016	860	148	8	712 R	84.6%	14.6%	85.3%	14.7%
26,405	UVALDE	7,905	4,755	3,070	80	1,685 R	60.2%	38.8%	60.8%	39.2%
48,879	VAL VERDE	11,365	5,993	5,241	131	752 R	52.7%	46.1%	53.3%	46.7%
52,579	VAN ZANDT	17,949	15,609	2,150	190	13,459 R	87.0%	12.0%	87.9%	12.1%
86,793	VICTORIA	27,147	19,599	7,245	303	12,354 R	72.2%	26.7%	73.0%	27.0%
67,861	WALKER	17,796	12,199	5,331	266	6,868 R	68.5%	30.0%	69.6%	30.4%
43,205	WALLER	16,600	10,639	5,791	170	4,848 R	64.1%	34.9%	64.8%	35.2%
10,658	WARD	2,926	2,201	690	35	1,511 R	75.2%	23.6%	76.1%	23.9%
33,718	WASHINGTON	13,470	10,532	2,730	208	7,802 R	78.2%	20.3%	79.4%	20.6%
250,304	WEBB	48,911	16,287	32,055	569	15,768 D	33.3%	65.5%	33.7%	66.3%

TEXAS

GOVERNOR 2018

2010 Census Population	County	Total Vote	Republican (Abbott)	Democratic (Valdez)	Other	Rep.-Dem. Plurality	Percentage Total Vote Rep.	Percentage Total Vote Dem.	Percentage Major Vote Rep.	Percentage Major Vote Dem.
41,280	WHARTON	12,911	9,472	3,332	107	6,140 R	73.4%	25.8%	74.0%	26.0%
5,410	WHEELER	1,821	1,682	126	13	1,556 R	92.4%	6.9%	93.0%	7.0%
131,500	WICHITA	33,920	24,817	8,614	489	16,203 R	73.2%	25.4%	74.2%	25.8%
13,535	WILBARGER	3,457	2,722	685	50	2,037 R	78.7%	19.8%	79.9%	20.1%
22,134	WILLACY	4,226	1,931	2,257	38	326 D	45.7%	53.4%	46.1%	53.9%
422,679	WILLIAMSON	207,513	112,214	90,002	5,297	22,212 R	54.1%	43.4%	55.5%	44.5%
42,918	WILSON	17,703	13,704	3,800	199	9,904 R	77.4%	21.5%	78.3%	21.7%
7,110	WINKLER	1,453	1,150	284	19	866 R	79.1%	19.5%	80.2%	19.8%
59,127	WISE	23,120	19,633	3,184	303	16,449 R	84.9%	13.8%	86.0%	14.0%
41,964	WOOD	16,881	14,406	2,324	151	12,082 R	85.3%	13.8%	86.1%	13.9%
7,879	YOAKUM	1,893	1,558	303	32	1,255 R	82.3%	16.0%	83.7%	16.3%
18,550	YOUNG	6,392	5,579	726	87	4,853 R	87.3%	11.4%	88.5%	11.5%
14,018	ZAPATA	2,168	861	1,292	15	431 D	39.7%	59.6%	40.0%	60.0%
11,677	ZAVALA	2,850	748	2,082	20	1,334 D	26.2%	73.1%	26.4%	73.6%
25,145,561	*TOTAL*	*8,343,443*	*4,656,196*	*3,546,615*	*140,632*	*1,109,581 R*	*55.8%*	*42.5%*	*56.8%*	*43.2%*

TEXAS

SENATOR 2018

2010 Census Population	County	Total Vote	Republican (Cruz)	Democratic (O'Rourke)	Other	Rep.-Dem. Plurality	Percentage Total Vote Rep.	Percentage Total Vote Dem.	Percentage Major Vote Rep.	Percentage Major Vote Dem.
58,458	ANDERSON	14,736	11,335	3,307	94	8,028 R	76.9%	22.4%	77.4%	22.6%
14,786	ANDREWS	4,131	3,338	776	17	2,562 R	80.8%	18.8%	81.1%	18.9%
86,771	ANGELINA	26,449	19,166	7,130	153	12,036 R	72.5%	27.0%	72.9%	27.1%
23,158	ARANSAS	8,980	6,677	2,247	56	4,430 R	74.4%	25.0%	74.8%	25.2%
9,054	ARCHER	3,602	3,208	376	18	2,832 R	89.1%	10.4%	89.5%	10.5%
1,901	ARMSTRONG	899	819	74	6	745 R	91.1%	8.2%	91.7%	8.3%
44,911	ATASCOSA	12,204	7,753	4,332	119	3,421 R	63.5%	35.5%	64.2%	35.8%
28,417	AUSTIN	11,047	8,722	2,241	84	6,481 R	79.0%	20.3%	79.6%	20.4%
7,165	BAILEY	1,616	1,204	405	7	799 R	74.5%	25.1%	74.8%	25.2%
20,485	BANDERA	9,584	7,643	1,865	76	5,778 R	79.7%	19.5%	80.4%	19.6%
74,171	BASTROP	27,461	15,067	12,082	312	2,985 R	54.9%	44.0%	55.5%	44.5%
3,726	BAYLOR	1,235	1,070	156	9	914 R	86.6%	12.6%	87.3%	12.7%
31,861	BEE	7,217	4,342	2,811	64	1,531 R	60.2%	38.9%	60.7%	39.3%
310,235	BELL	86,577	47,437	38,417	723	9,020 R	54.8%	44.4%	55.3%	44.7%
1,714,773	BEXAR	549,570	217,600	326,946	5,024	109,346 D	39.6%	59.5%	40.0%	60.0%
10,497	BLANCO	5,808	4,181	1,570	57	2,611 R	72.0%	27.0%	72.7%	27.3%
641	BORDEN	343	320	22	1	298 R	93.3%	6.4%	93.6%	6.4%
18,212	BOSQUE	7,155	5,718	1,374	63	4,344 R	79.9%	19.2%	80.6%	19.4%
92,565	BOWIE	28,321	20,157	7,982	182	12,175 R	71.2%	28.2%	71.6%	28.4%
313,166	BRAZORIA	111,753	65,693	45,228	832	20,465 R	58.8%	40.5%	59.2%	40.8%
194,851	BRAZOS	64,487	35,971	27,876	640	8,095 R	55.8%	43.2%	56.3%	43.7%
9,232	BREWSTER	4,086	1,879	2,147	60	268 D	46.0%	52.5%	46.7%	53.3%
1,637	BRISCOE	624	553	69	2	484 R	88.6%	11.1%	88.9%	11.1%
7,223	BROOKS	1,923	543	1,376	4	833 D	28.2%	71.6%	28.3%	71.7%
38,106	BROWN	12,132	10,391	1,670	71	8,721 R	85.6%	13.8%	86.2%	13.8%
17,187	BURLESON	6,551	5,079	1,427	45	3,652 R	77.5%	21.8%	78.1%	21.9%
42,750	BURNET	18,490	13,859	4,444	187	9,415 R	75.0%	24.0%	75.7%	24.3%
38,066	CALDWELL	11,481	6,147	5,227	107	920 R	53.5%	45.5%	54.0%	46.0%
21,381	CALHOUN	6,119	4,198	1,874	47	2,324 R	68.6%	30.6%	69.1%	30.9%
13,544	CALLAHAN	5,023	4,373	610	40	3,763 R	87.1%	12.1%	87.8%	12.2%

TEXAS

SENATOR 2018

2010 Census Population	County	Total Vote	Republican (Cruz)	Democratic (O'Rourke)	Other	Rep.-Dem. Plurality	Percentage Total Vote Rep.	Percentage Total Vote Dem.	Percentage Major Vote Rep.	Percentage Major Vote Dem.
406,220	CAMERON	77,912	28,574	48,770	568	20,196 D	36.7%	62.6%	36.9%	63.1%
12,401	CAMP	3,892	2,749	1,119	24	1,630 R	70.6%	28.8%	71.1%	28.9%
6,182	CARSON	2,459	2,192	245	22	1,947 R	89.1%	10.0%	89.9%	10.1%
30,464	CASS	10,217	8,148	2,024	45	6,124 R	79.7%	19.8%	80.1%	19.9%
8,062	CASTRO	1,623	1,219	394	10	825 R	75.1%	24.3%	75.6%	24.4%
35,096	CHAMBERS	15,181	12,146	2,926	109	9,220 R	80.0%	19.3%	80.6%	19.4%
50,845	CHEROKEE	14,941	11,631	3,207	103	8,424 R	77.8%	21.5%	78.4%	21.6%
7,041	CHILDRESS	1,770	1,526	236	8	1,290 R	86.2%	13.3%	86.6%	13.4%
10,752	CLAY	4,288	3,710	547	31	3,163 R	86.5%	12.8%	87.2%	12.8%
3,127	COCHRAN	686	541	140	5	401 R	78.9%	20.4%	79.4%	20.6%
3,320	COKE	1,297	1,150	137	10	1,013 R	88.7%	10.6%	89.4%	10.6%
8,895	COLEMAN	3,126	2,759	351	16	2,408 R	88.3%	11.2%	88.7%	11.3%
782,341	COLLIN	355,966	187,425	165,614	2,927	21,811 R	52.7%	46.5%	53.1%	46.9%
3,057	COLLINGSWORTH	928	810	113	5	697 R	87.3%	12.2%	87.8%	12.2%
20,874	COLORADO	7,637	5,779	1,825	33	3,954 R	75.7%	23.9%	76.0%	24.0%
108,472	COMAL	61,495	44,079	16,830	586	27,249 R	71.7%	27.4%	72.4%	27.6%
13,974	COMANCHE	4,610	3,799	781	30	3,018 R	82.4%	16.9%	82.9%	17.1%
4,087	CONCHO	980	803	163	14	640 R	81.9%	16.6%	83.1%	16.9%
38,437	COOKE	14,540	11,879	2,550	111	9,329 R	81.7%	17.5%	82.3%	17.7%
75,388	CORYELL	15,863	10,626	5,067	170	5,559 R	67.0%	31.9%	67.7%	32.3%
1,505	COTTLE	557	458	97	2	361 R	82.2%	17.4%	82.5%	17.5%
4,375	CRANE	1,055	836	213	6	623 R	79.2%	20.2%	79.7%	20.3%
3,719	CROCKETT	1,276	928	340	8	588 R	72.7%	26.6%	73.2%	26.8%
6,059	CROSBY	1,422	978	437	7	541 R	68.8%	30.7%	69.1%	30.9%
2,398	CULBERSON	827	297	521	9	224 D	35.9%	63.0%	36.3%	63.7%
6,703	DALLAM	1,115	970	139	6	831 R	87.0%	12.5%	87.5%	12.5%
2,368,139	DALLAS	727,889	241,126	481,395	5,368	240,269 D	33.1%	66.1%	33.4%	66.6%
13,833	DAWSON	3,015	2,192	811	12	1,381 R	72.7%	26.9%	73.0%	27.0%
20,097	DE WITT	6,131	4,974	1,128	29	3,846 R	81.1%	18.4%	81.5%	18.5%
19,372	DEAF SMITH	3,775	2,680	1,067	28	1,613 R	71.0%	28.3%	71.5%	28.5%
5,231	DELTA	1,932	1,562	354	16	1,208 R	80.8%	18.3%	81.5%	18.5%
662,614	DENTON	295,802	158,744	134,649	2,409	24,095 R	53.7%	45.5%	54.1%	45.9%
2,444	DICKENS	754	635	113	6	522 R	84.2%	15.0%	84.9%	15.1%
9,996	DIMMIT	2,894	840	2,042	12	1,202 D	29.0%	70.6%	29.1%	70.9%
3,677	DONLEY	1,279	1,110	161	8	949 R	86.8%	12.6%	87.3%	12.7%
11,782	DUVAL	4,113	1,330	2,765	18	1,435 D	32.3%	67.2%	32.5%	67.5%
18,583	EASTLAND	6,205	5,377	800	28	4,577 R	86.7%	12.9%	87.0%	13.0%
137,130	ECTOR	30,474	20,996	9,230	248	11,766 R	68.9%	30.3%	69.5%	30.5%
2,002	EDWARDS	757	604	145	8	459 R	79.8%	19.2%	80.6%	19.4%
800,647	EL PASO	203,614	50,943	151,482	1,189	100,539 D	25.0%	74.4%	25.2%	74.8%
149,610	ELLIS	60,589	41,022	19,106	461	21,916 R	67.7%	31.5%	68.2%	31.8%
37,890	ERATH	12,625	10,055	2,486	84	7,569 R	79.6%	19.7%	80.2%	19.8%
17,866	FALLS	4,680	3,215	1,445	20	1,770 R	68.7%	30.9%	69.0%	31.0%
33,915	FANNIN	10,750	8,569	2,107	74	6,462 R	79.7%	19.6%	80.3%	19.7%
24,554	FAYETTE	10,479	8,228	2,198	53	6,030 R	78.5%	21.0%	78.9%	21.1%
3,974	FISHER	1,494	1,139	340	15	799 R	76.2%	22.8%	77.0%	23.0%
6,446	FLOYD	1,879	1,394	476	9	918 R	74.2%	25.3%	74.5%	25.5%
1,336	FOARD	435	321	113	1	208 R	73.8%	26.0%	74.0%	26.0%
585,375	FORT BEND	255,438	111,423	142,399	1,616	30,976 D	43.6%	55.7%	43.9%	56.1%
10,605	FRANKLIN	3,974	3,300	639	35	2,661 R	83.0%	16.1%	83.8%	16.2%
19,816	FREESTONE	6,562	5,243	1,279	40	3,964 R	79.9%	19.5%	80.4%	19.6%
17,217	FRIO	3,680	1,636	2,016	28	380 D	44.5%	54.8%	44.8%	55.2%
17,526	GAINES	3,849	3,317	513	19	2,804 R	86.2%	13.3%	86.6%	13.4%
291,309	GALVESTON	113,622	67,641	45,065	916	22,576 R	59.5%	39.7%	60.0%	40.0%
6,461	GARZA	1,287	1,068	203	16	865 R	83.0%	15.8%	84.0%	16.0%
24,837	GILLESPIE	12,543	9,890	2,572	81	7,318 R	78.8%	20.5%	79.4%	20.6%
1,226	GLASSCOCK	554	513	37	4	476 R	92.6%	6.7%	93.3%	6.7%
7,210	GOLIAD	3,072	2,326	717	29	1,609 R	75.7%	23.3%	76.4%	23.6%
19,807	GONZALES	5,625	4,173	1,421	31	2,752 R	74.2%	25.3%	74.6%	25.4%
22,535	GRAY	5,901	5,246	615	40	4,631 R	88.9%	10.4%	89.5%	10.5%

TEXAS

SENATOR 2018

2010 Census Population	County	Total Vote	Republican (Cruz)	Democratic (O'Rourke)	Other	Rep.-Dem. Plurality	Percentage Total Vote Rep.	Total Vote Dem.	Major Vote Rep.	Major Vote Dem.
120,877	GRAYSON	43,144	31,655	11,157	332	20,498 R	73.4%	25.9%	73.9%	26.1%
121,730	GREGG	35,936	24,569	11,133	234	13,436 R	68.4%	31.0%	68.8%	31.2%
26,604	GRIMES	8,607	6,499	2,037	71	4,462 R	75.5%	23.7%	76.1%	23.9%
131,533	GUADALUPE	54,571	33,938	20,079	554	13,859 R	62.2%	36.8%	62.8%	37.2%
36,273	HALE	7,392	5,360	1,970	62	3,390 R	72.5%	26.7%	73.1%	26.9%
3,353	HALL	971	807	161	3	646 R	83.1%	16.6%	83.4%	16.6%
8,517	HAMILTON	3,330	2,795	507	28	2,288 R	83.9%	15.2%	84.6%	15.4%
5,613	HANSFORD	1,710	1,552	138	20	1,414 R	90.8%	8.1%	91.8%	8.2%
4,139	HARDEMAN	1,162	973	185	4	788 R	83.7%	15.9%	84.0%	16.0%
54,635	HARDIN	20,098	17,391	2,636	71	14,755 R	86.5%	13.1%	86.8%	13.2%
4,092,459	HARRIS	1,207,754	498,902	700,200	8,652	201,298 D	41.3%	58.0%	41.6%	58.4%
65,631	HARRISON	22,593	16,226	6,245	122	9,981 R	71.8%	27.6%	72.2%	27.8%
6,062	HARTLEY	1,624	1,467	153	4	1,314 R	90.3%	9.4%	90.6%	9.4%
5,899	HASKELL	1,674	1,362	302	10	1,060 R	81.4%	18.0%	81.9%	18.1%
157,107	HAYS	79,746	33,308	45,584	854	12,276 D	41.8%	57.2%	42.2%	57.8%
3,807	HEMPHILL	1,375	1,209	157	9	1,052 R	87.9%	11.4%	88.5%	11.5%
78,532	HENDERSON	26,511	20,891	5,415	205	15,476 R	78.8%	20.4%	79.4%	20.6%
774,769	HIDALGO	151,755	46,505	104,416	834	57,911 D	30.6%	68.8%	30.8%	69.2%
35,089	HILL	11,433	8,927	2,443	63	6,484 R	78.1%	21.4%	78.5%	21.5%
22,935	HOCKLEY	6,094	4,844	1,211	39	3,633 R	79.5%	19.9%	80.0%	20.0%
51,182	HOOD	25,005	20,090	4,720	195	15,370 R	80.3%	18.9%	81.0%	19.0%
35,161	HOPKINS	11,920	9,306	2,545	69	6,761 R	78.1%	21.4%	78.5%	21.5%
23,732	HOUSTON	7,360	5,552	1,772	36	3,780 R	75.4%	24.1%	75.8%	24.2%
35,012	HOWARD	7,404	5,651	1,693	60	3,958 R	76.3%	22.9%	76.9%	23.1%
3,476	HUDSPETH	933	509	407	17	102 R	54.6%	43.6%	55.6%	44.4%
86,129	HUNT	28,488	21,115	7,151	222	13,964 R	74.1%	25.1%	74.7%	25.3%
22,150	HUTCHINSON	6,642	5,854	753	35	5,101 R	88.1%	11.3%	88.6%	11.4%
1,599	IRION	738	636	96	6	540 R	86.2%	13.0%	86.9%	13.1%
9,044	JACK	2,813	2,498	296	19	2,202 R	88.8%	10.5%	89.4%	10.6%
14,075	JACKSON	4,840	3,991	832	17	3,159 R	82.5%	17.2%	82.7%	17.3%
35,710	JASPER	11,833	9,504	2,282	47	7,222 R	80.3%	19.3%	80.6%	19.4%
2,342	JEFF DAVIS	1,177	683	466	28	217 R	58.0%	39.6%	59.4%	40.6%
252,273	JEFFERSON	74,239	36,731	37,128	380	397 D	49.5%	50.0%	49.7%	50.3%
5,300	JIM HOGG	1,478	410	1,060	8	650 D	27.7%	71.7%	27.9%	72.1%
40,838	JIM WELLS	9,900	4,520	5,331	49	811 D	45.7%	53.8%	45.9%	54.1%
150,934	JOHNSON	52,436	39,571	12,411	454	27,160 R	75.5%	23.7%	76.1%	23.9%
20,202	JONES	4,984	4,115	832	37	3,283 R	82.6%	16.7%	83.2%	16.8%
14,824	KARNES	4,136	2,900	1,203	33	1,697 R	70.1%	29.1%	70.7%	29.3%
103,350	KAUFMAN	38,372	26,118	12,002	252	14,116 R	68.1%	31.3%	68.5%	31.5%
33,410	KENDALL	19,796	15,292	4,340	164	10,952 R	77.2%	21.9%	77.9%	22.1%
416	KENEDY	180	100	77	3	23 R	55.6%	42.8%	56.5%	43.5%
808	KENT	337	288	44	5	244 R	85.5%	13.1%	86.7%	13.3%
49,625	KERR	22,205	16,822	5,198	185	11,624 R	75.8%	23.4%	76.4%	23.6%
4,607	KIMBLE	1,704	1,495	195	14	1,300 R	87.7%	11.4%	88.5%	11.5%
286	KING	131	124	6	1	118 R	94.7%	4.6%	95.4%	4.6%
3,598	KINNEY	1,199	827	358	14	469 R	69.0%	29.9%	69.8%	30.2%
32,061	KLEBERG	8,596	4,081	4,456	59	375 D	47.5%	51.8%	47.8%	52.2%
3,719	KNOX	1,093	855	229	9	626 R	78.2%	21.0%	78.9%	21.1%
6,886	LA SALLE	1,489	673	813	3	140 D	45.2%	54.6%	45.3%	54.7%
49,793	LAMAR	16,568	12,711	3,731	126	8,980 R	76.7%	22.5%	77.3%	22.7%
13,977	LAMB	3,457	2,741	699	17	2,042 R	79.3%	20.2%	79.7%	20.3%
19,677	LAMPASAS	7,470	5,836	1,569	65	4,267 R	78.1%	21.0%	78.8%	21.2%
19,263	LAVACA	7,737	6,688	1,019	30	5,669 R	86.4%	13.2%	86.8%	13.2%
16,612	LEE	5,847	4,487	1,322	38	3,165 R	76.7%	22.6%	77.2%	22.8%
16,801	LEON	6,589	5,711	855	23	4,856 R	86.7%	13.0%	87.0%	13.0%
75,643	LIBERTY	20,576	16,041	4,421	114	11,620 R	78.0%	21.5%	78.4%	21.6%
23,384	LIMESTONE	6,916	5,211	1,672	33	3,539 R	75.3%	24.2%	75.7%	24.3%
3,302	LIPSCOMB	1,067	942	116	9	826 R	88.3%	10.9%	89.0%	11.0%
11,531	LIVE OAK	3,651	3,029	601	21	2,428 R	83.0%	16.5%	83.4%	16.6%
19,301	LLANO	10,154	7,954	2,124	76	5,830 R	78.3%	20.9%	78.9%	21.1%

TEXAS

SENATOR 2018

2010 Census Population	County	Total Vote	Republican (Cruz)	Democratic (O'Rourke)	Other	Rep.-Dem. Plurality	Percentage: Total Vote Rep.	Percentage: Total Vote Dem.	Percentage: Major Vote Rep.	Percentage: Major Vote Dem.
82	LOVING	54	47	6	1	41 R	87.0%	11.1%	88.7%	11.3%
278,831	LUBBOCK	91,579	58,780	32,068	731	26,712 R	64.2%	35.0%	64.7%	35.3%
5,915	LYNN	1,697	1,369	323	5	1,046 R	80.7%	19.0%	80.9%	19.1%
13,664	MADISON	3,831	3,033	780	18	2,253 R	79.2%	20.4%	79.5%	20.5%
10,546	MARION	3,497	2,448	1,018	31	1,430 R	70.0%	29.1%	70.6%	29.4%
4,799	MARTIN	1,554	1,297	243	14	1,054 R	83.5%	15.6%	84.2%	15.8%
4,012	MASON	1,967	1,560	402	5	1,158 R	79.3%	20.4%	79.5%	20.5%
36,702	MATAGORDA	10,457	7,330	3,049	78	4,281 R	70.1%	29.2%	70.6%	29.4%
54,258	MAVERICK	10,776	2,951	7,727	98	4,776 D	27.4%	71.7%	27.6%	72.4%
8,283	MCCULLOCH	2,671	2,245	400	26	1,845 R	84.1%	15.0%	84.9%	15.1%
234,906	MCLENNAN	74,875	45,855	28,452	568	17,403 R	61.2%	38.0%	61.7%	38.3%
707	MCMULLEN	430	387	41	2	346 R	90.0%	9.5%	90.4%	9.6%
46,006	MEDINA	16,179	11,444	4,621	114	6,823 R	70.7%	28.6%	71.2%	28.8%
2,242	MENARD	783	632	145	6	487 R	80.7%	18.5%	81.3%	18.7%
136,872	MIDLAND	42,955	32,867	9,723	365	23,144 R	76.5%	22.6%	77.2%	22.8%
24,757	MILAM	7,987	5,922	1,997	68	3,925 R	74.1%	25.0%	74.8%	25.2%
4,936	MILLS	2,004	1,764	229	11	1,535 R	88.0%	11.4%	88.5%	11.5%
9,403	MITCHELL	1,913	1,585	323	5	1,262 R	82.9%	16.9%	83.1%	16.9%
19,719	MONTAGUE	7,421	6,424	941	56	5,483 R	86.6%	12.7%	87.2%	12.8%
455,746	MONTGOMERY	190,096	137,395	51,268	1,433	86,127 R	72.3%	27.0%	72.8%	27.2%
21,904	MOORE	4,060	3,248	787	25	2,461 R	80.0%	19.4%	80.5%	19.5%
12,934	MORRIS	4,234	2,953	1,260	21	1,693 R	69.7%	29.8%	70.1%	29.9%
1,210	MOTLEY	527	483	40	4	443 R	91.7%	7.6%	92.4%	7.6%
64,524	NACOGDOCHES	21,633	13,775	7,732	126	6,043 R	63.7%	35.7%	64.0%	36.0%
47,735	NAVARRO	14,416	10,391	3,918	107	6,473 R	72.1%	27.2%	72.6%	27.4%
14,445	NEWTON	4,676	3,660	993	23	2,667 R	78.3%	21.2%	78.7%	21.3%
15,216	NOLAN	4,074	3,120	928	26	2,192 R	76.6%	22.8%	77.1%	22.9%
340,223	NUECES	94,067	45,956	47,392	719	1,436 D	48.9%	50.4%	49.2%	50.8%
10,223	OCHILTREE	2,415	2,160	230	25	1,930 R	89.4%	9.5%	90.4%	9.6%
2,052	OLDHAM	816	732	82	2	650 R	89.7%	10.0%	89.9%	10.1%
81,837	ORANGE	26,332	21,164	5,050	118	16,114 R	80.4%	19.2%	80.7%	19.3%
28,111	PALO PINTO	9,430	7,547	1,837	46	5,710 R	80.0%	19.5%	80.4%	19.6%
23,796	PANOLA	8,749	7,120	1,598	31	5,522 R	81.4%	18.3%	81.7%	18.3%
116,927	PARKER	54,495	44,071	9,956	468	34,115 R	80.9%	18.3%	81.6%	18.4%
10,269	PARMER	2,057	1,675	372	10	1,303 R	81.4%	18.1%	81.8%	18.2%
15,507	PECOS	3,520	2,161	1,339	20	822 R	61.4%	38.0%	61.7%	38.3%
45,413	POLK	16,750	12,794	3,850	106	8,944 R	76.4%	23.0%	76.9%	23.1%
121,073	POTTER	24,424	16,689	7,521	214	9,168 R	68.3%	30.8%	68.9%	31.1%
7,818	PRESIDIO	1,667	436	1,221	10	785 D	26.2%	73.2%	26.3%	73.7%
10,914	RAINS	4,406	3,702	681	23	3,021 R	84.0%	15.5%	84.5%	15.5%
120,725	RANDALL	48,455	38,479	9,613	363	28,866 R	79.4%	19.8%	80.0%	20.0%
3,367	REAGAN	834	692	136	6	556 R	83.0%	16.3%	83.6%	16.4%
3,309	REAL	1,564	1,311	245	8	1,066 R	83.8%	15.7%	84.3%	15.7%
12,860	RED RIVER	4,418	3,427	973	18	2,454 R	77.6%	22.0%	77.9%	22.1%
13,783	REEVES	2,398	1,128	1,255	15	127 D	47.0%	52.3%	47.3%	52.7%
7,383	REFUGIO	2,492	1,636	847	9	789 R	65.7%	34.0%	65.9%	34.1%
929	ROBERTS	460	441	19		422 R	95.9%	4.1%	95.9%	4.1%
16,622	ROBERTSON	6,268	4,295	1,942	31	2,353 R	68.5%	31.0%	68.9%	31.1%
78,337	ROCKWALL	38,699	26,615	11,754	330	14,861 R	68.8%	30.4%	69.4%	30.6%
10,501	RUNNELS	3,234	2,842	385	7	2,457 R	87.9%	11.9%	88.1%	11.9%
53,330	RUSK	16,282	12,597	3,609	76	8,988 R	77.4%	22.2%	77.7%	22.3%
10,834	SABINE	3,967	3,456	496	15	2,960 R	87.1%	12.5%	87.4%	12.6%
8,865	SAN AUGUSTINE	3,016	2,266	734	16	1,532 R	75.1%	24.3%	75.5%	24.5%
26,384	SAN JACINTO	9,339	7,499	1,785	55	5,714 R	80.3%	19.1%	80.8%	19.2%
64,804	SAN PATRICIO	18,219	11,335	6,777	107	4,558 R	62.2%	37.2%	62.6%	37.4%
6,131	SAN SABA	2,069	1,811	247	11	1,564 R	87.5%	11.9%	88.0%	12.0%
3,461	SCHLEICHER	952	735	209	8	526 R	77.2%	22.0%	77.9%	22.1%
16,921	SCURRY	4,363	3,705	642	16	3,063 R	84.9%	14.7%	85.2%	14.8%
3,378	SHACKELFORD	1,281	1,174	103	4	1,071 R	91.6%	8.0%	91.9%	8.1%
25,448	SHELBY	7,561	6,008	1,521	32	4,487 R	79.5%	20.1%	79.8%	20.2%

TEXAS

SENATOR 2018

2010 Census Population	County	Total Vote	Republican (Cruz)	Democratic (O'Rourke)	Other	Rep.-Dem. Plurality	Percentage Total Vote Rep.	Total Vote Dem.	Major Vote Rep.	Major Vote Dem.
3,034	SHERMAN	822	692	87	43	605 R	84.2%	10.6%	88.8%	11.2%
209,714	SMITH	77,400	53,760	23,182	458	30,578 R	69.5%	30.0%	69.9%	30.1%
8,490	SOMERVELL	3,691	3,033	633	25	2,400 R	82.2%	17.1%	82.7%	17.3%
60,968	STARR	10,784	2,443	8,273	68	5,830 D	22.7%	76.7%	22.8%	77.2%
9,630	STEPHENS	2,968	2,631	324	13	2,307 R	88.6%	10.9%	89.0%	11.0%
1,143	STERLING	486	442	44		398 R	90.9%	9.1%	90.9%	9.1%
1,490	STONEWALL	614	497	112	5	385 R	80.9%	18.2%	81.6%	18.4%
4,128	SUTTON	1,206	934	265	7	669 R	77.4%	22.0%	77.9%	22.1%
7,854	SWISHER	1,895	1,461	420	14	1,041 R	77.1%	22.2%	77.7%	22.3%
1,809,034	TARRANT	627,894	309,189	313,497	5,208	4,308 D	49.2%	49.9%	49.7%	50.3%
131,506	TAYLOR	40,657	29,811	10,489	357	19,322 R	73.3%	25.8%	74.0%	26.0%
984	TERRELL	467	323	139	5	184 R	69.2%	29.8%	69.9%	30.1%
12,651	TERRY	2,813	2,169	629	15	1,540 R	77.1%	22.4%	77.5%	22.5%
1,641	THROCKMORTON	703	617	77	9	540 R	87.8%	11.0%	88.9%	11.1%
32,334	TITUS	8,005	5,685	2,265	55	3,420 R	71.0%	28.3%	71.5%	28.5%
110,224	TOM GREEN	34,630	24,648	9,690	292	14,958 R	71.2%	28.0%	71.8%	28.2%
1,024,266	TRAVIS	484,204	119,278	359,772	5,154	240,494 D	24.6%	74.3%	24.9%	75.1%
14,585	TRINITY	5,175	4,146	998	31	3,148 R	80.1%	19.3%	80.6%	19.4%
21,766	TYLER	7,139	5,919	1,185	35	4,734 R	82.9%	16.6%	83.3%	16.7%
39,309	UPSHUR	13,984	11,529	2,364	91	9,165 R	82.4%	16.9%	83.0%	17.0%
3,355	UPTON	1,031	854	169	8	685 R	82.8%	16.4%	83.5%	16.5%
26,405	UVALDE	7,935	4,348	3,528	59	820 R	54.8%	44.5%	55.2%	44.8%
48,879	VAL VERDE	11,405	5,345	5,955	105	610 D	46.9%	52.2%	47.3%	52.7%
52,579	VAN ZANDT	17,932	15,182	2,634	116	12,548 R	84.7%	14.7%	85.2%	14.8%
86,793	VICTORIA	27,208	19,005	8,046	157	10,959 R	69.9%	29.6%	70.3%	29.7%
67,861	WALKER	17,853	11,535	6,186	132	5,349 R	64.6%	34.6%	65.1%	34.9%
43,205	WALLER	16,603	10,167	6,335	101	3,832 R	61.2%	38.2%	61.6%	38.4%
10,658	WARD	2,920	2,096	800	24	1,296 R	71.8%	27.4%	72.4%	27.6%
33,718	WASHINGTON	13,492	10,134	3,263	95	6,871 R	75.1%	24.2%	75.6%	24.4%
250,304	WEBB	49,381	13,814	35,159	408	21,345 D	28.0%	71.2%	28.2%	71.8%
41,280	WHARTON	12,942	9,094	3,793	55	5,301 R	70.3%	29.3%	70.6%	29.4%
5,410	WHEELER	1,810	1,679	125	6	1,554 R	92.8%	6.9%	93.1%	6.9%
131,500	WICHITA	33,918	23,648	9,971	299	13,677 R	69.7%	29.4%	70.3%	29.7%
13,535	WILBARGER	3,439	2,639	776	24	1,863 R	76.7%	22.6%	77.3%	22.7%
22,134	WILLACY	4,325	1,527	2,773	25	1,246 D	35.3%	64.1%	35.5%	64.5%
422,679	WILLIAMSON	208,221	99,857	105,850	2,514	5,993 D	48.0%	50.8%	48.5%	51.5%
42,918	WILSON	17,719	13,025	4,567	127	8,458 R	73.5%	25.8%	74.0%	26.0%
7,110	WINKLER	1,455	1,123	321	11	802 R	77.2%	22.1%	77.8%	22.2%
59,127	WISE	23,117	19,023	3,915	179	15,108 R	82.3%	16.9%	82.9%	17.1%
41,964	WOOD	16,740	13,987	2,635	118	11,352 R	83.6%	15.7%	84.1%	15.9%
7,879	YOAKUM	1,903	1,558	335	10	1,223 R	81.9%	17.6%	82.3%	17.7%
18,550	YOUNG	6,405	5,543	821	41	4,722 R	86.5%	12.8%	87.1%	12.9%
14,018	ZAPATA	2,223	821	1,392	10	571 D	36.9%	62.6%	37.1%	62.9%
11,677	ZAVALA	2,917	589	2,313	15	1,724 D	20.2%	79.3%	20.3%	79.7%
25,145,561	*TOTAL*	*8,371,655*	*4,260,553*	*4,045,632*	*65,470*	*214,921 R*	*50.9%*	*48.3%*	*51.3%*	*48.7%*

TEXAS

HOUSE OF REPRESENTATIVES

			Republican		Democratic				Percentage			
									Total Vote		Major Vote	
CD	Year	Total Vote	Vote	Candidate	Vote	Candidate	Other Vote	Rep.-Dem. Plurality	Rep.	Dem.	Rep.	Dem.
1	2018	232,720	168,165	GOHMERT, LOUIE*	61,263	MCKELLAR, SHIRLEY J.	3,292	106,902 R	72.3%	26.3%	73.3%	26.7%
1	2016	260,409	192,434	GOHMERT, LOUIE*	62,847	MCKELLAR, SHIRLEY J.	5,128	129,587 R	73.9%	24.1%	75.4%	24.6%
1	2014	148,560	115,084	GOHMERT, LOUIE*	33,476	MCKELLAR, SHIRLEY J.		81,608 R	77.5%	22.5%	77.5%	22.5%
1	2012	249,658	178,322	GOHMERT, LOUIE*	67,222	MCKELLAR, SHIRLEY J.	4,114	111,100 R	71.4%	26.9%	72.6%	27.4%
2	2018	263,392	139,188	CRENSHAW, DANIEL	119,992	LITTON, TODD	4,212	19,196 R	52.8%	45.6%	53.7%	46.3%
2	2016	278,236	168,692	POE, TED*	100,231	BRYAN, PAT	9,313	68,461 R	60.6%	36.0%	62.7%	37.3%
2	2014	150,026	101,936	POE, TED*	44,462	LETSOS, NIKO	3,628	57,474 R	67.9%	29.6%	69.6%	30.4%
2	2012	246,328	159,664	POE, TED*	80,512	DOUGHERTY, JIM	6,152	79,152 R	64.8%	32.7%	66.5%	33.5%
3	2018	312,511	169,520	TAYLOR, VAN	138,234	BURCH, LORIE	4,757	31,286 R	54.2%	44.2%	55.1%	44.9%
3	2016	316,467	193,684	JOHNSON, SAM*	109,420	BELL, ADAM P.	13,363	84,264 R	61.2%	34.6%	63.9%	36.1%
3	2014	138,280	113,404	JOHNSON, SAM*			24,876	113,404 R	82.0%		100.0%	
3	2012	187,180	187,180	JOHNSON, SAM*				187,180 R	100.0%		100.0%	
4	2018	249,245	188,667	RATCLIFFE, JOHN*	57,400	KRANTZ, CATHERINE	3,178	131,267 R	75.7%	23.0%	76.7%	23.3%
4	2016	246,220	216,643	RATCLIFFE, JOHN*			29,577	216,643 R	88.0%		100.0%	
4	2014	115,085	115,085	RATCLIFFE, JOHN				115,085 R	100.0%		100.0%	
4	2012	250,343	182,679	HALL, RALPH M.*	60,214	HATHCOX, VALINDA	7,450	122,465 R	73.0%	24.1%	75.2%	24.8%
5	2018	209,507	130,617	GOODEN, LANCE	78,666	WOOD, DAN	224	51,951 R	62.3%	37.5%	62.4%	37.6%
5	2016	192,875	155,469	HENSARLING, JEB*			37,406	155,469 R	80.6%		100.0%	
5	2014	104,262	88,998	HENSARLING, JEB*			15,264	88,998 R	85.4%		100.0%	
5	2012	208,230	134,091	HENSARLING, JEB*	69,178	MROSKO, LINDA S.	4,961	64,913 R	64.4%	33.2%	66.0%	34.0%
6	2018	256,042	135,961	WRIGHT, RONALD	116,350	SANCHEZ, JANA LYNNE	3,731	19,611 R	53.1%	45.4%	53.9%	46.1%
6	2016	273,296	159,444	BARTON, JOE L.*	106,667	WOOLRIDGE, RUBY FAYE	7,185	52,777 R	58.3%	39.0%	59.9%	40.1%
6	2014	150,996	92,334	BARTON, JOE L.*	55,027	COZAD, DAVID E.	3,635	37,307 R	61.1%	36.4%	62.7%	37.3%
6	2012	249,936	145,019	BARTON, JOE L.*	98,053	SANDERS, KENNETH	6,864	46,966 R	58.0%	39.2%	59.7%	40.3%
7	2018	243,601	115,642	CULBERSON, JOHN*	127,959	FLETCHER, LIZZIE PANNILL		12,317 D	47.5%	52.5%	47.5%	52.5%
7	2016	255,533	143,542	CULBERSON, JOHN*	111,991	CARGAS, JAMES		31,551 R	56.2%	43.8%	56.2%	43.8%
7	2014	143,219	90,606	CULBERSON, JOHN*	49,478	CARGAS, JAMES	3,135	41,128 R	63.3%	34.5%	64.7%	35.3%
7	2012	234,837	142,793	CULBERSON, JOHN*	85,553	CARGAS, JAMES	6,491	57,240 R	60.8%	36.4%	62.5%	37.5%
8	2018	273,170	200,619	BRADY, KEVIN*	67,930	DAVID, STEVEN	4,621	132,689 R	73.4%	24.9%	74.7%	25.3%
8	2016	236,379	236,379	BRADY, KEVIN*				236,379 R	100.0%		100.0%	
8	2014	140,013	125,066	BRADY, KEVIN*			14,947	125,066 R	89.3%		100.0%	
8	2012	251,052	194,043	BRADY, KEVIN*	51,051	BURNS, NEIL	5,958	142,992 R	77.3%	20.3%	79.2%	20.8%
9	2018	153,001			136,256	GREEN, AL*	16,745	136,256 D		89.1%		100.0%
9	2016	188,523	36,491	MARTIN, JEFF	152,032	GREEN, AL*		115,541 D	19.4%	80.6%	19.4%	80.6%
9	2014	86,003			78,109	GREEN, AL*	7,894	78,109 D		90.8%		100.0%
9	2012	183,566	36,139	MUELLER, STEVE	144,075	GREEN, AL*	3,352	107,936 D	19.7%	78.5%	20.1%	79.9%
10	2018	307,827	157,166	MCCAUL, MICHAEL T.*	144,034	SIEGEL, MIKE	6,627	13,132 R	51.1%	46.8%	52.2%	47.8%
10	2016	312,600	179,221	MCCAUL, MICHAEL T.*	120,170	WALTER-CADIEN, TAWANA	13,209	59,051 R	57.3%	38.4%	59.9%	40.1%
10	2014	176,460	109,726	MCCAUL, MICHAEL T.*	60,243	WALTER-CADIEN, TAWANA	6,491	49,483 R	62.2%	34.1%	64.6%	35.4%
10	2012	264,019	159,783	MCCAUL, MICHAEL T.*	95,710	WALTER-CADIEN, TAWANA	8,526	64,073 R	60.5%	36.3%	62.5%	37.5%
11	2018	220,377	176,603	CONAWAY, MIKE*	40,631	LEEDER, JENNIE LOU	3,143	135,972 R	80.1%	18.4%	81.3%	18.7%
11	2016	225,548	201,871	CONAWAY, MIKE*			23,677	201,871 R	89.5%		100.0%	
11	2014	119,574	107,939	CONAWAY, MIKE*			11,635	107,939 R	90.3%		100.0%	
11	2012	226,023	177,742	CONAWAY, MIKE*	41,970	RILEY, JIM	6,311	135,772 R	78.6%	18.6%	80.9%	19.1%
12	2018	268,491	172,557	GRANGER, KAY*	90,994	ADIA, VANESSA	4,940	81,563 R	64.3%	33.9%	65.5%	34.5%
12	2016	283,115	196,482	GRANGER, KAY*	76,029	BRADSHAW, BILL	10,604	120,453 R	69.4%	26.9%	72.1%	27.9%
12	2014	158,730	113,186	GRANGER, KAY*	41,757	GREENE, MARK	3,787	71,429 R	71.3%	26.3%	73.1%	26.9%
12	2012	247,712	175,649	GRANGER, KAY*	66,080	ROBINSON, DAVE	5,983	109,569 R	70.9%	26.7%	72.7%	27.3%
13	2018	207,285	169,027	THORNBERRY, MAC*	35,083	SAGAN, GREG	3,175	133,944 R	81.5%	16.9%	82.8%	17.2%
13	2016	221,242	199,050	THORNBERRY, MAC*			22,192	199,050 R	90.0%		100.0%	
13	2014	131,451	110,842	THORNBERRY, MAC*	16,822	MINTER, MIKE G.	3,787	94,020 R	84.3%	12.8%	86.8%	13.2%
13	2012	206,388	187,775	THORNBERRY, MAC*			18,613	187,775 R	91.0%		100.0%	
14	2018	234,528	138,942	WEBER, RANDY*	92,212	BELL, ADRIENNE	3,374	46,730 R	59.2%	39.3%	60.1%	39.9%
14	2016	259,685	160,631	WEBER, RANDY*	99,054	COLE, MICHAEL K.		61,577 R	61.9%	38.1%	61.9%	38.1%
14	2014	145,698	90,116	WEBER, RANDY*	52,545	BROWN, DONALD G.	3,037	37,571 R	61.9%	36.1%	63.2%	36.8%
14	2012	245,839	131,460	WEBER, RANDY	109,697	LAMPSON, NICK	4,682	21,763 R	53.5%	44.6%	54.5%	45.5%

TEXAS

HOUSE OF REPRESENTATIVES

			Republican		Democratic				Percentage			
									Total Vote		Major Vote	
CD	Year	Total Vote	Vote	Candidate	Vote	Candidate	Other Vote	Rep.-Dem. Plurality	Rep.	Dem.	Rep.	Dem.
15	2018	164,802	63,862	WESTLEY, TIM	98,333	GONZALEZ, VICENTE*	2,607	34,471 D	38.8%	59.7%	39.4%	60.6%
15	2016	177,479	66,877	WESTLEY, TIM	101,712	GONZALEZ, VICENTE	8,890	34,835 D	37.7%	57.3%	39.7%	60.3%
15	2014	90,184	39,016	ZAMORA, EDDIE	48,708	HINOJOSA, RUBÉN*	2,460	9,692 D	43.3%	54.0%	44.5%	55.5%
15	2012	146,661	54,056	BRUEGGEMANN, DALE A.	89,296	HINOJOSA, RUBÉN*	3,309	35,240 D	36.9%	60.9%	37.7%	62.3%
16	2018	181,754	49,127	SEEBERGER, RICK	124,437	ESCOBAR, VERONICA	8,190	75,310 D	27.0%	68.5%	28.3%	71.7%
16	2016	175,229			150,228	O'ROURKE, BETO*	25,001	150,228 D		85.7%		100.0%
16	2014	73,105	21,324	ROEN, COREY DEAN	49,338	O'ROURKE, BETO*	2,443	28,014 D	29.2%	67.5%	30.2%	69.8%
16	2012	155,005	51,043	CARRASCO, BARBARA	101,403	O'ROURKE, BETO	2,559	50,360 D	32.9%	65.4%	33.5%	66.5%
17	2018	237,351	134,841	FLORES, BILL*	98,070	KENNEDY, RICK	4,440	36,771 R	56.8%	41.3%	57.9%	42.1%
17	2016	245,728	149,417	FLORES, BILL*	86,603	MATTA, WILLIAM	9,708	62,814 R	60.8%	35.2%	63.3%	36.7%
17	2014	132,865	85,807	FLORES, BILL*	43,049	HAYNES, NICK	4,009	42,758 R	64.6%	32.4%	66.6%	33.4%
17	2012	179,262	143,284	FLORES, BILL*			35,978	143,284 R	79.9%		100.0%	
18	2018	184,332	38,368	PATE, AVA REYNERO	138,704	JACKSON LEE, SHEILA*	7,260	100,336 D	20.8%	75.2%	21.7%	78.3%
18	2016	204,308	48,306	BARTLEY, LORI	150,157	JACKSON LEE, SHEILA*	5,845	101,851 D	23.6%	73.5%	24.3%	75.7%
18	2014	106,010	26,249	SEIBERT, SEAN	76,097	JACKSON LEE, SHEILA*	3,664	49,848 D	24.8%	71.8%	25.6%	74.4%
18	2012	194,932	44,015	SEIBERT, SEAN	146,223	JACKSON LEE, SHEILA*	4,694	102,208 D	22.6%	75.0%	23.1%	76.9%
19	2018	201,985	151,946	ARRINGTON, JODEY*	50,039	LEVARIO, MIGUEL		101,907 R	75.2%	24.8%	75.2%	24.8%
19	2016	203,475	176,314	ARRINGTON, JODEY			27,161	176,314 R	86.7%		100.0%	
19	2014	116,818	90,160	NEUGEBAUER, RANDY*	21,458	MARCHBANKS, JAMES NEAL	5,200	68,702 R	77.2%	18.4%	80.8%	19.2%
19	2012	192,063	163,239	NEUGEBAUER, RANDY*			28,824	163,239 R	85.0%		100.0%	
20	2018	171,963			139,038	CASTRO, JOAQUIN*	32,925	139,038 D		80.9%		100.0%
20	2016	187,669			149,640	CASTRO, JOAQUIN*	38,029	149,640 D		79.7%		100.0%
20	2014	87,964			66,554	CASTRO, JOAQUIN*	21,410	66,554 D		75.7%		100.0%
20	2012	186,177	62,376	ROSA, DAVID	119,032	CASTRO, JOAQUIN	4,769	56,656 D	33.5%	63.9%	34.4%	65.6%
21	2018	353,617	177,654	ROY, CHIP	168,421	KOPSER, JOSEPH	7,542	9,233 R	50.2%	47.6%	51.3%	48.7%
21	2016	356,031	202,967	SMITH, LAMAR*	129,765	WAKELY, TOM	23,299	73,202 R	57.0%	36.4%	61.0%	39.0%
21	2014	188,996	135,660	SMITH, LAMAR*			53,336	135,660 R	71.8%		100.0%	
21	2012	308,865	187,015	SMITH, LAMAR*	109,326	DUVAL, CANDACE E.	12,524	77,689 R	60.5%	35.4%	63.1%	36.9%
22	2018	297,405	152,750	OLSON, PETE*	138,153	KULKARNI, SRI PRESTON	6,502	14,597 R	51.4%	46.5%	52.5%	47.5%
22	2016	305,543	181,864	OLSON, PETE*	123,679	GIBSON, MARK		58,185 R	59.5%	40.5%	59.5%	40.5%
22	2014	151,566	100,861	OLSON, PETE*	47,844	BRISCOE, FRANK	2,861	53,017 R	66.5%	31.6%	67.8%	32.2%
22	2012	250,911	160,668	OLSON, PETE*	80,203	ROGERS, KESHA	10,040	80,465 R	64.0%	32.0%	66.7%	33.3%
23	2018	210,069	103,285	HURD, WILL*	102,359	JONES, GINA ORTIZ	4,425	926 R	49.2%	48.7%	50.2%	49.8%
23	2016	228,965	110,577	HURD, WILL*	107,526	GALLEGO, PETE P.	10,862	3,051 R	48.3%	47.0%	50.7%	49.3%
23	2014	115,429	57,459	HURD, WILL	55,037	GALLEGO, PETE P.*	2,933	2,422 R	49.8%	47.7%	51.1%	48.9%
23	2012	192,169	87,547	CANSECO, FRANCISCO "QUICO"*	96,676	GALLEGO, PETE P.	7,946	9,129 D	45.6%	50.3%	47.5%	52.5%
24	2018	263,418	133,317	MARCHANT, KENNY E.*	125,231	MCDOWELL, JAN	4,870	8,086 R	50.6%	47.5%	51.6%	48.4%
24	2016	275,635	154,845	MARCHANT, KENNY E.*	108,389	MCDOWELL, JAN	12,401	46,456 R	56.2%	39.3%	58.8%	41.2%
24	2014	144,073	93,712	MARCHANT, KENNY E.*	46,548	MCGEHEARTY, PATRICK F.	3,813	47,164 R	65.0%	32.3%	66.8%	33.2%
24	2012	243,489	148,586	MARCHANT, KENNY E.*	87,645	RUSK, TIM	7,258	60,941 R	61.0%	36.0%	62.9%	37.1%
25	2018	304,553	163,023	WILLIAMS, ROGER*	136,385	OLIVER, JULIE	5,145	26,638 R	53.5%	44.8%	54.4%	45.6%
25	2016	310,196	180,988	WILLIAMS, ROGER*	117,073	THOMAS, KATHI	12,135	63,915 R	58.3%	37.7%	60.7%	39.3%
25	2014	177,883	107,120	WILLIAMS, ROGER*	64,463	MONTOYA, MARCO	6,300	42,657 R	60.2%	36.2%	62.4%	37.6%
25	2012	263,932	154,245	WILLIAMS, ROGER	98,827	HENDERSON, ELAINE M.	10,860	55,418 R	58.4%	37.4%	60.9%	39.1%
26	2018	312,505	185,551	BURGESS, MICHAEL C.*	121,938	FAGAN, LINSEY	5,016	63,613 R	59.4%	39.0%	60.3%	39.7%
26	2016	319,080	211,730	BURGESS, MICHAEL C.*	94,507	MAUCK, ERIC	12,843	117,223 R	66.4%	29.6%	69.1%	30.9%
26	2014	141,470	116,944	BURGESS, MICHAEL C.*			24,526	116,944 R	82.7%		100.0%	
26	2012	258,723	176,642	BURGESS, MICHAEL C.*	74,237	SANCHEZ, DAVID	7,844	102,405 R	68.3%	28.7%	70.4%	29.6%
27	2018	207,421	125,118	CLOUD, MICHAEL*	75,929	HOLGUIN, ERIC	6,374	49,189 R	60.3%	36.6%	62.2%	37.8%
27	2016	230,580	142,251	FARENTHOLD, R. BLAKE*	88,329	BARRERA, RAUL "ROY"		53,922 R	61.7%	38.3%	61.7%	38.3%
27	2014	131,047	83,342	FARENTHOLD, R. BLAKE*	44,152	REED, WESLEY C.	3,553	39,190 R	63.6%	33.7%	65.4%	34.6%
27	2012	212,651	120,684	FARENTHOLD, R. BLAKE*	83,395	HARRISON, ROSE MEZA	8,572	37,289 R	56.8%	39.2%	59.1%	40.9%
28	2018	139,226			117,494	CUELLAR, HENRY*	21,732	117,494 D		84.4%		100.0%
28	2016	184,442	57,740	HARDIN, ZEFFEN	122,086	CUELLAR, HENRY*	4,616	64,346 D	31.3%	66.2%	32.1%	67.9%
28	2014	76,136			62,508	CUELLAR, HENRY*	13,628	62,508 D		82.1%		100.0%
28	2012	165,645	49,309	HAYWARD, WILLIAM R.	112,456	CUELLAR, HENRY*	3,880	63,147 D	29.8%	67.9%	30.5%	69.5%

TEXAS

HOUSE OF REPRESENTATIVES

CD	Year	Total Vote	Republican Vote	Republican Candidate	Democratic Vote	Democratic Candidate	Other Vote	Rep.-Dem. Plurality	Percentage Total Vote Rep.	Percentage Total Vote Dem.	Percentage Major Vote Rep.	Percentage Major Vote Dem.
29	2018	117,494	28,098	ARONOFF, PHILLIP	88,188	GARCIA, SYLVIA R.	1,208	60,090 D	23.9%	75.1%	24.2%	75.8%
29	2016	131,982	31,646	GARZA, JULIO	95,649	GREEN, GENE*	4,687	64,003 D	24.0%	72.5%	24.9%	75.1%
29	2014	46,143			41,321	GREEN, GENE*	4,822	41,321 D		89.5%		100.0%
29	2012	95,611			86,053	GREEN, GENE*	9,558	86,053 D		90.0%		100.0%
30	2018	183,174			166,784	JOHNSON, EDDIE BERNICE*	16,390	166,784 D		91.1%		100.0%
30	2016	218,826	41,518	LINGERFELT, CHARLES	170,502	JOHNSON, EDDIE BERNICE*	6,806	128,984 D	19.0%	77.9%	19.6%	80.4%
30	2014	105,793			93,041	JOHNSON, EDDIE BERNICE*	12,752	93,041 D		87.9%		100.0%
30	2012	217,014	41,222	WASHINGTON, TRAVIS	171,059	JOHNSON, EDDIE BERNICE*	4,733	129,837 D	19.0%	78.8%	19.4%	80.6%
31	2018	286,007	144,680	CARTER, JOHN*	136,362	HEGAR, MARY JENNINGS "MJ"	4,965	8,318 R	50.6%	47.7%	51.5%	48.5%
31	2016	284,588	166,060	CARTER, JOHN*	103,852	CLARK, MIKE	14,676	62,208 R	58.4%	36.5%	61.5%	38.5%
31	2014	143,028	91,607	CARTER, JOHN*	45,715	MINOR, LOUIE	5,706	45,892 R	64.0%	32.0%	66.7%	33.3%
31	2012	237,187	145,348	CARTER, JOHN*	82,977	WYMAN, STEPHEN M.	8,862	62,371 R	61.3%	35.0%	63.7%	36.3%
32	2018	275,620	126,101	SESSIONS, PETE*	144,067	ALLRED, COLIN	5,452	17,966 D	45.8%	52.3%	46.7%	53.3%
32	2016	229,171	162,868	SESSIONS, PETE*			66,303	162,868 R	71.1%		100.0%	
32	2014	156,096	96,495	SESSIONS, PETE*	55,325	PEREZ, FRANK	4,276	41,170 R	61.8%	35.4%	63.6%	36.4%
32	2012	251,636	146,653	SESSIONS, PETE*	99,288	MCGOVERN, KATHERINE SAVERS	5,695	47,365 R	58.3%	39.5%	59.6%	40.4%
33	2018	119,224	26,120	BILLUPS, WILLIE	90,805	VEASEY, MARC*	2,299	64,685 D	21.9%	76.2%	22.3%	77.7%
33	2016	126,369	33,222	MITCHELL, M. MARK	93,147	VEASEY, MARC*		59,925 D	26.3%	73.7%	26.3%	73.7%
33	2014	50,592			43,769	VEASEY, MARC*	6,823	43,769 D		86.5%		100.0%
33	2012	117,375	30,252	BRADLEY, CHUCK	85,114	VEASEY, MARC	2,009	54,862 D	25.8%	72.5%	26.2%	73.8%
34	2018	143,068	57,243	GONZALEZ, REY JR.	85,825	VELA, FILEMON*		28,582 D	40.0%	60.0%	40.0%	60.0%
34	2016	166,961	62,323	GONZALEZ, REY JR.	104,638	VELA, FILEMON*		42,315 D	37.3%	62.7%	37.3%	62.7%
34	2014	79,877	30,811	SMITH, LARRY S.	47,503	VELA, FILEMON*	1,563	16,692 D	38.6%	59.5%	39.3%	60.7%
34	2012	144,778	52,448	BRADSHAW, JESSICA PUENTE	89,606	VELA, FILEMON	2,724	37,158 D	36.2%	61.9%	36.9%	63.1%
35	2018	194,067	50,553	SMALLING, DAVID	138,278	DOGGETT, LLOYD*	5,236	87,725 D	26.0%	71.3%	26.8%	73.2%
35	2016	197,576	62,384	NARVAIZ, SUSAN	124,612	DOGGETT, LLOYD*	10,580	62,228 D	31.6%	63.1%	33.4%	66.6%
35	2014	96,225	32,040	NARVAIZ, SUSAN	60,124	DOGGETT, LLOYD*	4,061	28,084 D	33.3%	62.5%	34.8%	65.2%
35	2012	165,179	52,894	NARVAIZ, SUSAN	105,626	DOGGETT, LLOYD*	6,659	52,732 D	32.0%	63.9%	33.4%	66.6%
36	2018	221,956	161,048	BABIN, BRIAN*	60,908	STEELE, DAYNA		100,140 R	72.6%	27.4%	72.6%	27.4%
36	2016	218,565	193,675	BABIN, BRIAN*			24,890	193,675 R	88.6%		100.0%	
36	2014	133,842	101,663	BABIN, BRIAN	29,543	COLE, MICHAEL K.	2,636	72,120 R	76.0%	22.1%	77.5%	22.5%
36	2012	233,832	165,405	STOCKMAN, STEVE	62,143	MARTIN, MAX	6,284	103,262 R	70.7%	26.6%	72.7%	27.3%
TOTAL	*2018*	*8,202,708*	*4,135,359*		*3,852,752*		*214,597*	*282,607 R*	*50.4%*	*47.0%*	*51.8%*	*48.2%*
TOTAL	*2016*	*8,528,526*	*4,877,605*		*3,160,535*		*490,386*	*1,717,070 R*	*57.2%*	*37.1%*	*60.7%*	*39.3%*
TOTAL	*2014*	*4,453,499*	*2,684,592*		*1,474,016*		*294,891*	*1,210,576 R*	*60.3%*	*33.1%*	*64.6%*	*35.4%*
TOTAL	*2012*	*7,664,208*	*4,429,270*		*2,949,900*		*285,038*	*1,479,370 R*	*57.8%*	*38.5%*	*60.0%*	*40.0%*

Note: An asterisk (*) denotes incumbent.

TEXAS

GENERAL AND PRIMARY ELECTIONS

2018 GENERAL ELECTIONS: OTHER VOTES

Governor	Other vote was 140,632 Libertarian (Mark Tippetts)
Senate	Other vote was 65,470 Libertarian (Neal Dikeman)
House	Other vote was:
CD 1	3,292 Libertarian (Jeff Callaway)
CD 2	2,373 Libertarian (Patrick Gunnels), 1,839 Independent Party (Scott Cubbler)
CD 3	4,604 Libertarian (Christopher Claytor), 153 Write-in (Jeff Simmons)
CD 4	3,178 Libertarian (Ken Ashby)
CD 5	224 Write-in (Phil Gray)

TEXAS

GENERAL AND PRIMARY ELECTIONS

House	Other vote was:
CD 6	3,731 Libertarian (Jason Harber)
CD 8	4,621 Libertarian (Chris Duncan)
CD 9	5,940 Libertarian (Phil Kurtz), 5,774 Independent Party (Benjamin Hernandez), 5,031 Independent Party (Kesha Rogers)
CD 10	6,627 Libertarian (Mike Ryan)
CD 11	3,143 Libertarian (Rhett Smith)
CD 12	4,940 Libertarian (Jacob Leddy)
CD 13	3,175 Libertarian (Calvin DeWeese)
CD 15	3,374 Libertarian (Don Conley)
CD 16	2,607 Libertarian (Anthony Cristo)
CD 17	8,147 Independent (Ben Mendoza), 43 Write-in (Sam Williams)
CD 18	4,440 Libertarian (Peter Churchman)
CD 20	32,925 Libertarian (Jeffrey Blunt)
CD 21	7,542 Libertarian (Lee Santos)
CD 22	3,261 Libertarian (John McElligott), 3,241 Independent (Kellen Sweny)
CD 23	4,425 Libertarian (Ruben Corvalan)
CD 24	4,870 Libertarian (Mike Kolls)
CD 25	5,145 Libertarian (Desarae Lindsey)
CD 26	5,016 Libertarian (Mark Boler)
CD 28	4,274 Independent (James Duerr), 2,100 Libertarian (Daniel Tinus)
CD 29	172 Independent (Judith Cutright), 144 Libertarian (Daniel Tinus), 51 Independent (Christopher Suprun)
CD 30	16,390 Libertarian (Shawn Jones)
CD 31	4,965 Libertarian (Jason Hope)
CD 32	5,452 Libertarian (Melina Baker)
	2,299 Libertarian (Jason Reeves)
CD 35	5,236 Libertarian (Clark Patterson)

2018 PRIMARY ELECTIONS: SUPPLEMENTARY INFORMATION

Primary	March 6, 2018	**Registration** (as of March 6, 2018)	15,249,541	No Party Registration
Primary Runoff	May 22, 2018			

Primary Type Open—Any registered voter could participate in the Democratic or Republican primary, although if he or she voted in the primary of one party, he or she could not vote in the runoff of the other party.

	REPUBLICAN PRIMARIES			DEMOCRATIC PRIMARIES		
Senator	Cruz, Ted*	1,322,724	85.4%	O'Rourke, Beto	644,632	61.8%
	Miller, Mary	94,715	6.1%	Hernandez, Sema	247,424	23.7%
	Jacobson, Bruce Jr.	64,791	4.2%	Kimbrough, Edward	150,858	14.5%
	Stefano, Stefano de	44,456	2.9%			
	Sam, Geraldine	22,887	1.5%			
	TOTAL	*1,549,573*		*TOTAL*	*1,042,914*	

TEXAS

GENERAL AND PRIMARY ELECTIONS

	REPUBLICAN PRIMARIES			DEMOCRATIC PRIMARIES		
Governor	Abbott, Greg*	1,400,647	90.4%	Valdez, Lupe	438,820	42.9%
	Krueger, Barbara	127,858	8.3%	White, Andrew	280,200	27.4%
	Kilgore, Larry	20,501	1.3%	Davis, Cedric Jr.	84,215	8.2%
				Yarbrough, Grady	54,935	5.4%
				Payne, Jeffrey	48,590	4.8%
				Ocegueda, Adrian	45,020	4.4%
				Wakely, Thomas	34,834	3.4%
				Clark, James Jolly	21,994	2.2%
				Mumbach, Joe	13,950	1.4%
	TOTAL	*1,549,006*		*TOTAL*	*1,022,558*	
				PRIMARY RUNOFF		
				Valdez, Lupe	232,020	53.4%
				White, Andrew	202,869	46.6%
				TOTAL	*434,889*	
Congressional District 1	Gohmert, Louie*	64,241	88.3%	McKellar, Shirley J.	9,234	61.0%
	Culler, Anthony	6,526	9.0%	Beal, Brent	5,895	39.0%
	Rowjee, Roshin	1,962	2.7%			
	TOTAL	*72,729*		*TOTAL*	*15,129*	
Congressional District 2	Roberts, Kevin	15,273	33.0%	Litton, Todd	15,152	52.8%
	Crenshaw, Daniel	12,679	27.4%	Jones, J. Darnell	6,336	22.1%
	Wall, Kathaleen	12,524	27.1%	Malik, Silky	2,783	9.7%
	Walker, Rick	3,320	7.2%	Parvizian, H. P.	2,269	7.9%
	Havens, Jonny	936	2.0%	Khorasani, Ali A.	2,152	7.5%
	Lurie, Justin L.	425	0.9%			
	Spiers, Jon	418	0.9%			
	Balat, David	348	0.8%			
	Whittaker, Malcolm	322	0.7%			
	TOTAL	*46,245*		*TOTAL*	*28,692*	
	PRIMARY RUNOFF					
	Crenshaw, Daniel	20,392	69.8%			
	Roberts, Kevin	8,808	30.2%			
	TOTAL	*29,200*				
Congressional District 3	Taylor, Van	45,650	84.7%	Burch, Lorie	15,519	49.6%
	Niederkorn, David	5,065	9.4%	Johnson, Sam	8,971	28.7%
	Donkervoet, Alex	3,197	5.9%	Bell, Adam P.	5,617	18.0%
				Yhap, Medrick	1,175	3.8%
	TOTAL	*53,912*		*TOTAL*	*31,282*	
				PRIMARY RUNOFF		
				Burch, Lorie	9,377	75.0%
				Johnson, Sam	3,123	25.0%
				TOTAL	*12,500*	
Congressional District 4	Ratcliffe, John*	63,275	85.5%	Krantz, Catherine	9,040	68.6%
	Cooper, John	10,735	14.5%	Bethel, Lander	4,134	31.4%
	TOTAL	*74,010*		*TOTAL*	*13,174*	
Congressional District 5	Gooden, Lance	17,551	30.0%	Wood, Dan	16,923	100.0%
	Pounds, Bunni	12,851	21.9%			
	Deen, Sam	10,051	17.2%			
	Sheets, Kenneth	7,024	12.0%			
	Wright, Jason	6,690	11.4%			
	Campbell, Danny	1,770	3.0%			
	Williams, David	1,601	2.7%			
	Lingerfelt, Charles	1,022	1.7%			
	TOTAL	*58,560*		*TOTAL*	*16,923*	
	PRIMARY RUNOFF					
	Gooden, Lance	18,364	54.0%			
	Pounds, Bunni	15,634	46.0%			
	TOTAL	*33,998*				

TEXAS

GENERAL AND PRIMARY ELECTIONS

	REPUBLICAN PRIMARIES			DEMOCRATIC PRIMARIES		
Congressional District 6	Wright, Ronald	20,750	45.1%	Woolridge, Ruby Faye	10,895	36.9%
	Ellzey, J.K. "Jake"	9,999	21.8%	Sanchez, Jana Lynne	10,880	36.9%
	Cope, Ken	3,540	7.7%	Duncan, John W.	3,987	13.5%
	Dubberly, Shannon	2,884	6.3%	Snider, Justin	2,021	6.9%
	Mitchell, Mark	2,152	4.7%	Shocklee, Levii R.	1,704	5.8%
	Ratterree, Troy	1,858	4.0%			
	Harrison, Kevin	1,771	3.9%			
	Gagliardi, Deborah	1,676	3.6%			
	Dillingham, Thomas	544	1.2%			
	Dandridge, Shawn	518	1.1%			
	Hassell, Mel	268	0.6%			
	TOTAL	*45,960*		*TOTAL*	*29,487*	
	PRIMARY RUNOFF			**PRIMARY RUNOFF**		
	Wright, Ronald	12,775	52.2%	Sanchez, Jana Lynne	6,117	53.1%
	Ellzey, J.K. "Jake"	11,711	47.8%	Woolridge, Ruby Faye	5,398	46.9%
	TOTAL	*24,486*		*TOTAL*	*11,515*	
Congressional District 7	Culberson, John*	29,052	76.1%	Fletcher, Lizzie Pannill	9,768	29.4%
	Ziegler, Edward	9,117	23.9%	Moser, Laura	8,099	24.3%
				Westin, Jason	6,375	19.2%
				Triantaphyllis, Alex	5,234	15.7%
				Sanchez, Ivan	1,895	5.7%
				Butler, Joshua A.	1,253	3.8%
				Cargas, James	651	2.0%
	TOTAL	*38,169*		*TOTAL*	*33,275*	
				PRIMARY RUNOFF		
				Fletcher, Lizzie Pannill	11,506	67.1%
				Moser, Laura	5,637	32.9%
				TOTAL	*17,143*	
Congressional District 8	Brady, Kevin*	67,593	100.0%	David, Steven	13,183	100.0%
	TOTAL	*67,593*		*TOTAL*	*13,183*	
Congressional District 9				Green, Al*	32,881	100.0%
				TOTAL	*32,881*	
Congressional District 10	McCaul, Michael T.*	42,088	80.1%	Siegel, Mike	15,511	40.0%
	Cook, John W.	10,458	19.9%	Walter-Cadien, Tawana	6,963	18.0%
				Walker, Tami	6,033	15.6%
				Eden, Madeline K.	5,532	14.3%
				Harris, Matt	2,838	7.3%
				Nelson, Kevin	1,597	4.1%
				Degrow, Richie	302	0.8%
	TOTAL	*52,546*		*TOTAL*	*38,776*	
				PRIMARY RUNOFF		
				Siegel, Mike	12,333	69.8%
				Walter-Cadien, Tawana	5,330	30.2%
				TOTAL	*17,663*	
Congressional District 11	Conaway, Mike*	63,526	83.0%	Leeder, Jennie Lou	7,273	82.9%
	Myers, Paul	13,049	17.0%	Pfalzgraf, Eric	1,499	17.1%
	TOTAL	*76,575*		*TOTAL*	*8,772*	
Congressional District 12	Granger, Kay*	49,385	100.0%	Adia, Vanessa	21,018	100.0%
	TOTAL	*49,385*		*TOTAL*	*21,018*	
Congressional District 13	Thornberry, Mac*	71,018	100.0%	Sagan, Greg	7,322	100.0%
	TOTAL	*71,018*		*TOTAL*	*7,322*	

TEXAS

GENERAL AND PRIMARY ELECTIONS

	REPUBLICAN PRIMARIES			DEMOCRATIC PRIMARIES		
Congressional District 14	Weber, Randy*	33,720	75.3%	Bell, Adrienne	19,600	79.8%
	Sargent, Bill "Sarge"	8,770	19.6%	Barnes, Levy Q. Jr.	4,951	20.2%
	Casey, Keith	2,298	5.1%			
	TOTAL	*44,788*		*TOTAL*	*24,551*	
Congressional District 15	Westley, Tim	14,794	100.0%	Gonzalez, Vicente*	33,549	100.0%
	TOTAL	*14,794*		*TOTAL*	*33,549*	
Congressional District 16	Seeberger, Rick	7,328	69.4%	Escobar, Veronica	31,009	61.5%
	Garcia-Ureste, Alia	3,238	30.6%	Fenenbock, Dori	11,071	22.0%
				Chavez, Norma	3,357	6.7%
				Garcia, Enrique	2,684	5.3%
				Tilghman, Jerome	1,495	3.0%
				Carrillo, John	780	1.5%
	TOTAL	*10,566*		*TOTAL*	*50,396*	
Congressional District 17	Flores, Bill*	44,388	100.0%	Kennedy, Rick	14,424	63.4%
				Mantey, Dale	8,326	36.6%
	TOTAL	*44,388*		*TOTAL*	*22,750*	
Congressional District 18	Pate, Ava Reynero	7,634	100.0%	Jackson Lee, Sheila*	32,625	85.3%
				Johnson, Richard A.	5,622	14.7%
	TOTAL	*7,634*		*TOTAL*	*38,247*	
Congressional District 19	Arrington, Jodey*	55,433	100.0%	Levario, Miguel	9,648	100.0%
	TOTAL	*55,433*		*TOTAL*	*9,648*	
Congressional District 20				Castro, Joaquin*	32,189	100.0%
				TOTAL	*32,189*	
Congressional District 21	Roy, Chip	19,428	27.1%	Wilson, Mary Street	15,736	30.9%
	McCall, Matt	12,152	16.9%	Kopser, Joseph	14,787	29.0%
	Negley, William	11,163	15.5%	Crowe, Derrick	11,742	23.1%
	Isaac, Jason	7,208	10.0%	McFadden, Elliott	8,667	17.0%
	Sarver, Jenifer	4,027	5.6%			
	Stovall, Robert	3,414	4.8%			
	Narvaiz, Susan	2,720	3.8%			
	Canseco, Francisco "Quico"	2,489	3.5%			
	Krause, Ryan	2,300	3.2%			
	Poteet, Al M.	1,300	1.8%			
	Wardlaw, Peggy	1,285	1.8%			
	Temple, Samuel	1,020	1.4%			
	White, Anthony J.	952	1.3%			
	Burkhart, Eric	723	1.0%			
	Garza, Mauro	663	0.9%			
	Pruitt, Autry J.	455	0.6%			
	Hagen, Foster	394	0.5%			
	Andaraz, Ivan A.	96	0.1%			
	TOTAL	*71,789*		*TOTAL*	*50,932*	
	PRIMARY RUNOFF			**PRIMARY RUNOFF**		
	Roy, Chip	18,088	52.7%	Kopser, Joseph	14,765	57.9%
	McCall, Matt	16,243	47.3%	Wilson, Mary Street	10,722	42.1%
	TOTAL	*34,331*		*TOTAL*	*25,487*	

TEXAS

GENERAL AND PRIMARY ELECTIONS

	REPUBLICAN PRIMARIES			DEMOCRATIC PRIMARIES		
Congressional District 22	Olson, Pete*	35,918	78.4%	Kulkarni, Sri Preston	9,515	31.8%
	Nguyen, Danny	6,181	13.5%	Plummer, Letitia	7,258	24.3%
	Green, James	2,531	5.5%	Brown, Steve	6,269	21.0%
	Zmrhal, Eric	1,177	2.6%	Johnson, Margarita Ruiz	3,776	12.6%
				Gibson, Mark	3,060	10.2%
	TOTAL	*45,807*		*TOTAL*	*29,878*	
				PRIMARY RUNOFF		
				Kulkarni, Sri Preston	9,517	62.1%
				Plummer, Letitia	5,805	37.9%
				TOTAL	*15,322*	
Congressional District 23	Hurd, Will*	25,001	80.3%	Jones, Gina Ortiz	18,443	41.6%
	Arredondo-Lynch, Alma	6,144	19.7%	Trevino, Rick	7,710	17.4%
				Canales, Judy	7,538	17.0%
				Hulings, Jay	6,649	15.0%
				Villescaz, Angela “Angie”	4,032	9.1%
	TOTAL	*31,145*		*TOTAL*	*44,372*	
				PRIMARY RUNOFF		
				Jones, Gina Ortiz	17,570	67.9%
				Trevino, Rick	8,296	32.1%
				TOTAL	*25,866*	
Congressional District 24	Marchant, Kenny E.*	30,310	74.4%	McDowell, Jan	14,626	52.5%
	Davidson, Johnathan Kyle	10,425	25.6%	Biggan, John	5,998	21.5%
				Allen, Edward “Todd”	5,574	20.0%
				Imhoff, Josh	1,678	6.0%
	TOTAL	*40,735*		*TOTAL*	*27,876*	
Congressional District 25	Williams, Roger*	51,122	100.0%	Perri, Chris	13,984	32.8%
				Oliver, Julie	11,274	26.4%
				Thomas, Kathi	9,024	21.2%
				Hansen, West	4,508	10.6%
				Panda, Chetan	3,853	9.0%
	TOTAL	*51,122*		*TOTAL*	*42,643*	
				PRIMARY RUNOFF		
				Oliver, Julie	12,052	52.2%
				Perri, Chris	11,043	47.8%
				TOTAL	*23,095*	
Congressional District 26	Burgess, Michael C.*	42,556	77.0%	Fagan, Linsey	13,895	52.7%
Birkenstock, Veronica	12,720	23.0%	Fisher, Will	12,489	47.3%	
	TOTAL	*55,276*		*TOTAL*	*26,384*	
Congressional District 27	Bruun, Bech	15,919	36.1%	Barrera, Raul “Roy”	8,766	41.2%
	Cloud, Michael	14,920	33.8%	Holguin, Eric	4,953	23.3%
	Mapp, Christopher K.	5,356	12.1%	Foster, Vanessa Edwards	4,057	19.1%
	Hall, Jerry Ray	3,649	8.3%	McDonald, Ronnie C.	3,484	16.4%
	Grunwald, John	3,027	6.9%			
	Gassman, Eddie	1,237	2.8%			
	TOTAL	*44,108*		*TOTAL*	*21,260*	
	PRIMARY RUNOFF			**PRIMARY RUNOFF**		
	Cloud, Michael	15,249	61.0%	Holguin, Eric	6,448	61.9%
	Bruun, Bech	9,741	39.0%	Barrera, Raul “Roy”	3,964	38.1%
	TOTAL	*24,990*		*TOTAL*	*10,412*	
Congressional District 28				Cuellar, Henry*	39,221	100.0%
				TOTAL	*39,221*	

TEXAS

GENERAL AND PRIMARY ELECTIONS

	REPUBLICAN PRIMARIES			DEMOCRATIC PRIMARIES		
Congressional District 29	Aronoff, Phillip	2,406	38.6%	Garcia, Sylvia R.	11,727	63.3%
	Montiel, Carmen Maria	1,470	23.6%	Javed, Tahir	3,831	20.7%
	Blanco, Jaimy Z.	1,314	21.1%	Garcia, Roel	1,221	6.6%
	Schafranek, Robert	1,043	16.7%	Morales, Hector	563	3.0%
				Reyes, Augustine H.	525	2.8%
				Garcia, Dominique Michelle	478	2.6%
				Valencia, Pedro	193	1.0%
	TOTAL	*6,233*		*TOTAL*	*18,538*	
	PRIMARY RUNOFF					
	Aronoff, Phillip	1,153	51.8%			
	Montiel, Carmen Maria	1,072	48.2%			
	TOTAL	*2,225*				
Congressional District 30				Johnson, Eddie Bernice*	32,669	63.6%
				Caraway, Barbara Mallory	11,723	22.8%
				Williams, Eric	6,971	13.6%
				TOTAL	*51,363*	
Congressional District 31	Carter, John*	34,623	65.5%	Hegar, Mary Jennings "MJ"	13,900	44.9%
	Sweeney, Mike	18,236	34.5%	Mann, Christine Eady	10,368	33.5%
				Clark, Mike	3,475	11.2%
				Lester, Kent	3,193	10.3%
	TOTAL	*52,859*		*TOTAL*	*30,936*	
				PRIMARY RUNOFF		
				Hegar, Mary Jennings "MJ"	8,879	62.3%
				Mann, Christine Eady	5,380	37.7%
				TOTAL	*14,259*	
Congressional District 32	Sessions, Pete*	32,929	79.3%	Allred, Colin	15,498	38.4%
	Brown, Paul	8,599	20.7%	Salerno, Lillian	7,400	18.3%
				Shipp, Brett	6,589	16.3%
				Meier, Ed	5,525	13.7%
				Rodriguez, George	3,062	7.6%
				Marshall, Ron	1,306	3.2%
				Maternowski, Todd	952	2.4%
	TOTAL	*41,528*		*TOTAL*	*40,332*	
				PRIMARY RUNOFF		
				Allred, Colin	15,823	69.4%
				Salerno, Lillian	6,992	30.6%
				TOTAL	*22,815*	
Congressional District 33	Billups, Willie	5,254	100.0%	Veasey, Marc*	15,175	70.3%
				Quintanilla, Carlos	6,405	29.7%
	TOTAL	*5,254*		*TOTAL*	*21,580*	
Congressional District 34	Gonzalez, Rey Jr.	10,227	100.0%	Vela, Filemon*	25,344	100.0%
	TOTAL	*10,227*		*TOTAL*	*25,344*	
Congressional District 35	Smalling, David	7,148	53.3%	Doggett, Lloyd*	32,101	100.0%
	Alexander, Sherrill Kenneth "SK"	6,264	46.7%			
	TOTAL	*13,412*		*TOTAL*	*32,101*	
Congressional District 36	Babin, Brian*	50,317	100.0%	Steele, Dayna	9,891	72.0%
				Powell, Jon	3,847	28.0%
	TOTAL	*50,317*		*TOTAL*	*13,738*	

Note: An asterisk (*) denotes incumbent.

UTAH

Congressional districts first established for elections held in 2012

4 members

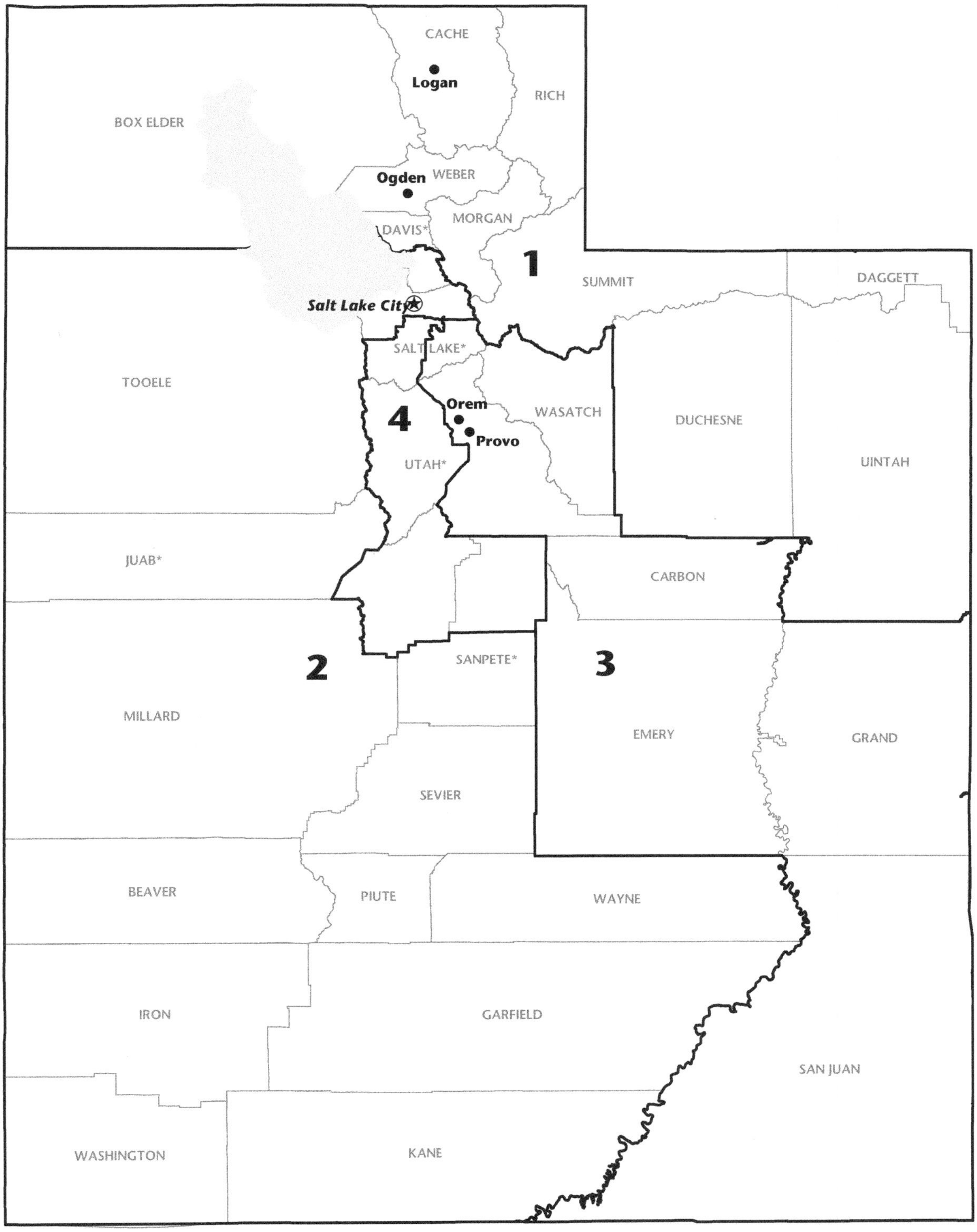

* Asterisk indicates a county whose boundaries include parts of two or more congressional districts.

UTAH

GOVERNOR

Gary R. Herbert (R). Re-elected 2016 to a four-year term. Previously elected 2014, and 2010 to remaining two years of term vacated by resignation of Jon Huntsman Jr. (R) to become ambassador to China. Herbert sworn in as governor August 11, 2009.

SENATORS (2 Republicans)

Mitt Romney (R). Elected 2018 to a six-year term.

Mike Lee (R). Re-elected 2016 to a six-year term. Previously elected 2010.

REPRESENTATIVES (3 Republicans, 1 Democrat)

1. Robert "Rob" Bishop (R)
2. Chris Stewart (R)
3. John Curtis (R)
4. Ben McAdams (D)

POSTWAR VOTE FOR PRESIDENT

		Republican		Democratic				Percentage			
								Total Vote		Major Vote	
Year	Total Vote	Vote	Candidate	Vote	Candidate	Other Vote	Rep.-Dem. Plurality	Rep.	Dem.	Rep.	Dem.
2016**	1,131,430	515,231	Trump, Donald J.	310,676	Clinton, Hillary Rodham	305,523	204,555 R	45.5%	27.5%	62.4%	37.6%
2012	1,017,440	740,600	Romney, W. Mitt	251,813	Obama, Barack H.*	25,027	488,787 R	72.8%	24.7%	74.6%	25.4%
2008	952,370	596,030	McCain, John S. III	327,670	Obama, Barack H.	28,670	268,360 R	62.6%	34.4%	64.5%	35.5%
2004	927,844	663,742	Bush, George W.*	241,199	Kerry, John F.	22,903	422,543 R	71.5%	26.0%	73.3%	26.7%
2000**	770,754	515,096	Bush, George W.	203,053	Gore, Albert Jr.	52,605	312,043 R	66.8%	26.3%	71.7%	28.3%
1996**	665,629	361,911	Dole, Robert "Bob"	221,633	Clinton, Bill*	82,085	140,278 R	54.4%	33.3%	62.0%	38.0%
1992**	743,999	322,632	Bush, George H.*	183,429	Clinton, Bill	237,938	139,203 R	43.4%	24.7%	63.8%	36.2%
1988	647,008	428,442	Bush, George H.	207,343	Dukakis, Michael S.	11,223	221,099 R	66.2%	32.0%	67.4%	32.6%
1984	629,656	469,105	Reagan, Ronald*	155,369	Mondale, Walter F.	5,182	313,736 R	74.5%	24.7%	75.1%	24.9%
1980**	604,222	439,687	Reagan, Ronald	124,266	Carter, Jimmy*	40,269	315,421 R	72.8%	20.6%	78.0%	22.0%
1976	541,198	337,908	Ford, Gerald R.*	182,110	Carter, Jimmy	21,180	155,798 R	62.4%	33.6%	65.0%	35.0%
1972	478,476	323,643	Nixon, Richard M.*	126,284	McGovern, George S.	28,549	197,359 R	67.6%	26.4%	71.9%	28.1%
1968**	422,568	238,728	Nixon, Richard M.	156,665	Humphrey, Hubert Horatio Jr.	27,175	82,063 R	56.5%	37.1%	60.4%	39.6%
1964	401,413	181,785	Goldwater, Barry M. Sr.	219,628	Johnson, Lyndon B.*		37,843 D	45.3%	54.7%	45.3%	54.7%
1960	374,709	205,361	Nixon, Richard M.	169,248	Kennedy, John F.	100	36,113 R	54.8%	45.2%	54.8%	45.2%
1956	333,995	215,631	Eisenhower, Dwight D.*	118,364	Stevenson, Adlai E. II		97,267 R	64.6%	35.4%	64.6%	35.4%
1952	329,554	194,190	Eisenhower, Dwight D.	135,364	Stevenson, Adlai E. II		58,826 R	58.9%	41.1%	58.9%	41.1%
1948	276,306	124,402	Dewey, Thomas E.	149,151	Truman, Harry S.*	2,753	24,749 D	45.0%	54.0%	45.5%	54.5%

Note: An asterisk (*) denotes incumbent. **In past elections, the other vote included: 2016 - 243,690 Unaffiliated (Evan McMullin); 39,608 Libertarian (Gary Johnson); 2000 - 35,850 Green (Ralph Nader); 1996 - 66,461 Reform (Ross Perot); 1992 - 203,400 Independent (Perot), who finished second; 1980 - 30,284 Independent (John Anderson); 1968 - 26,906 American Independent (George Wallace).

UTAH

POSTWAR VOTE FOR GOVERNOR

		Republican		Democratic				Percentage			
								Total Vote		Major Vote	
Year	Total Vote	Vote	Candidate	Vote	Candidate	Other Vote	Rep.-Dem. Plurality	Rep.	Dem.	Rep.	Dem.
2016	1,125,035	750,850	Herbert, Gary R.*	323,349	Weinholtz, Mike	50,836	427,501 R	66.7%	28.7%	69.9%	30.1%
2012	1,006,524	688,592	Herbert, Gary R.*	277,622	Cooke, Peter S.	40,310	410,970 R	68.4%	27.6%	71.3%	28.7%
2010S**	643,307	412,151	Herbert, Gary R.*	205,246	Corroon, Peter	25,910	206,905 R	64.1%	31.9%	66.8%	33.2%
2008	945,525	734,049	Huntsman, Jon Jr.*	186,503	Springmeyer, Bob	24,973	547,546 R	77.6%	19.7%	79.7%	20.3%
2004	919,960	531,190	Huntsman, Jon Jr.	380,359	Matheson, Scot Jr.	8,411	150,831 R	57.7%	41.3%	58.3%	41.7%
2000	761,806	424,837	Leavitt, Mike O.*	321,979	Orton, Bill	14,990	102,858 R	55.8%	42.3%	56.9%	43.1%
1996	671,879	503,693	Leavitt, Mike O.*	156,616	Bradley, Jim	11,570	347,077 R	75.0%	23.3%	76.3%	23.7%
1992**	762,549	321,713	Leavitt, Mike O.	177,181	Hanson, Stewart	263,655	144,532 R	42.2%	23.2%	64.5%	35.5%
1988**	649,114	260,462	Bangerter, Norman H.*	249,321	Wilson, Ted	139,331	11,141 R	40.1%	38.4%	51.1%	48.9%
1984	629,619	351,792	Bangerter, Norman H.	275,669	Owens, Wayne	2,158	76,123 R	55.9%	43.8%	56.1%	43.9%
1980	600,019	266,578	Wright, Bob	330,974	Matheson, Scott M.*	2,467	64,396 D	44.4%	55.2%	44.6%	55.4%
1976	539,649	248,027	Romney, Vernon B.	280,706	Matheson, Scott M.	10,916	32,679 D	46.0%	52.0%	46.9%	53.1%
1972	476,447	144,449	Strike, Nicholas L.	331,998	Rampton, Calvin L.*		187,549 D	30.3%	69.7%	30.3%	69.7%
1968	421,012	131,729	Buehner, Carl W.	289,283	Rampton, Calvin L.*		157,554 D	31.3%	68.7%	31.3%	68.7%
1964	398,256	171,300	Melich, Mitchell	226,956	Rampton, Calvin L.		55,656 D	43.0%	57.0%	43.0%	57.0%
1960	371,489	195,634	Clyde, George Dewey*	175,855	Barlocker, William A.		19,779 R	52.7%	47.3%	52.7%	47.3%
1956**	332,889	127,164	Clyde, George Dewey	111,297	Romney, L. C.	94,428	15,867 R	38.2%	33.4%	53.3%	46.7%
1952	327,704	180,516	Lee, J. Bracken*	147,188	Glade, Earl J.		33,328 R	55.1%	44.9%	55.1%	44.9%
1948	275,067	151,253	Lee, J. Bracken	123,814	Maw, Herbert B.*		27,439 R	55.0%	45.0%	55.0%	45.0%

Note: An asterisk (*) denotes incumbent. **In past elections, the other vote included: 1992 - 255,753 Independent (Merrill Cook), who finished second; 1988 - 136,651 Independent (Cook); 1956 - 94,428 Independent (J. Bracken Lee). The 2010 election was for a short term to fill a vacancy.

POSTWAR VOTE FOR SENATOR

		Republican		Democratic				Percentage			
								Total Vote		Major Vote	
Year	Total Vote	Vote	Candidate	Vote	Candidate	Other Vote	Rep.-Dem. Plurality	Rep.	Dem.	Rep.	Dem.
2018	1,062,897	665,215	Romney, Mitt	328,541	Wilson, Jenny	69,141	336,674 R	62.6%	30.9%	66.9%	33.1%
2016	1,115,608	760,241	Lee, Mike*	301,860	Snow, Misty K.	53,507	458,381 R	68.1%	27.1%	71.6%	28.4%
2012	1,006,901	657,608	Hatch, Orrin G.*	301,873	Howell, Scott N.	47,420	355,735 R	65.3%	30.0%	68.5%	31.5%
2010	633,829	390,179	Lee, Mike	207,685	Granato, Sam	35,965	182,494 R	61.6%	32.8%	65.3%	34.7%
2006	571,252	356,238	Hatch, Orrin G.*	177,459	Ashdown, Pete	37,555	178,779 R	62.4%	31.1%	66.7%	33.3%
2004	911,726	626,640	Bennett, Robert F.*	258,955	Van Dam, R. Paul	26,131	367,685 R	68.7%	28.4%	70.8%	29.2%
2000	769,704	504,803	Hatch, Orrin G.*	242,569	Howell, Scott N.	22,332	262,234 R	65.6%	31.5%	67.5%	32.5%
1998	494,909	316,652	Bennett, Robert F.*	163,172	Leckman, Scott	15,085	153,480 R	64.0%	33.0%	66.0%	34.0%
1994	519,323	357,297	Hatch, Orrin G.*	146,938	Shea, Patrick A.	15,088	210,359 R	68.8%	28.3%	70.9%	29.1%
1992	758,479	420,069	Bennett, Robert F.	301,228	Owens, Wayne	37,182	118,841 R	55.4%	39.7%	58.2%	41.8%
1988	640,702	430,089	Hatch, Orrin G.*	203,364	Moss, Brian	7,249	226,725 R	67.1%	31.7%	67.9%	32.1%
1986	435,111	314,608	Garn, E. J.*	115,523	Oliver, Craig	4,980	199,085 R	72.3%	26.6%	73.1%	26.9%
1982	530,802	309,332	Hatch, Orrin G.*	219,482	Wilson, Ted	1,988	89,850 R	58.3%	41.3%	58.5%	41.5%
1980	594,298	437,675	Garn, E. J.*	151,454	Berman, Dan	5,169	286,221 R	73.6%	25.5%	74.3%	25.7%
1976	540,108	290,221	Hatch, Orrin G.	241,948	Moss, Frank E.*	7,939	48,273 R	53.7%	44.8%	54.5%	45.5%
1974	420,642	210,299	Garn, E. J.	185,377	Owens, Wayne	24,966	24,922 R	50.0%	44.1%	53.1%	46.9%
1970	374,303	159,004	Burton, Laurence J.	210,207	Moss, Frank E.*	5,092	51,203 D	42.5%	56.2%	43.1%	56.9%
1968	419,262	225,075	Bennett, Wallace F.*	192,168	Weilenmann, Milton	2,019	32,907 R	53.7%	45.8%	53.9%	46.1%
1964	397,384	169,562	Wilkinson, Ernest L.	227,822	Moss, Frank E.*		58,260 D	42.7%	57.3%	42.7%	57.3%
1962	318,411	166,755	Bennett, Wallace F.*	151,656	King, David S.		15,099 R	52.4%	47.6%	52.4%	47.6%
1958**	291,311	101,471	Watkins, Arthur V.*	112,827	Moss, Frank E.	77,013	11,356 D	34.8%	38.7%	47.4%	52.6%
1956	330,381	178,261	Bennett, Wallace F.*	152,120	Hopkin, Alonzo F.		26,141 R	54.0%	46.0%	54.0%	46.0%
1952	327,033	177,435	Watkins, Arthur V.*	149,598	Granger, Walter K.		27,837 R	54.3%	45.7%	54.3%	45.7%
1950	264,440	142,427	Bennett, Wallace F.	121,198	Thomas, Elbert D.*	815	21,229 R	53.9%	45.8%	54.0%	46.0%
1946	197,399	101,142	Watkins, Arthur V.	96,257	Murdock, Abe*		4,885 R	51.2%	48.8%	51.2%	48.8%

Note: An asterisk (*) denotes incumbent. **In past elections, the other vote included: 1958 - 77,013 Independent (J. Bracken Lee).

UTAH

SENATOR 2018

2010 Census Population	County	Total Vote	Republican (Romney)	Democratic (Wilson)	Other	Rep.-Dem. Plurality	Percentage: Total Vote Rep.	Percentage: Total Vote Dem.	Percentage: Major Vote Rep.	Percentage: Major Vote Dem.
6,629	BEAVER	2,132	1,620	298	214	1,322 R	76.0%	14.0%	84.5%	15.5%
49,975	BOX ELDER	18,927	14,803	2,603	1,521	12,200 R	78.2%	13.8%	85.0%	15.0%
112,656	CACHE	39,903	28,344	8,854	2,705	19,490 R	71.0%	22.2%	76.2%	23.8%
21,403	CARBON	6,888	4,387	1,879	622	2,508 R	63.7%	27.3%	70.0%	30.0%
1,059	DAGGETT	439	335	80	24	255 R	76.3%	18.2%	80.7%	19.3%
306,479	DAVIS	124,279	86,840	29,249	8,190	57,591 R	69.9%	23.5%	74.8%	25.2%
18,607	DUCHESNE	5,771	4,522	569	680	3,953 R	78.4%	9.9%	88.8%	11.2%
10,976	EMERY	3,872	3,033	509	330	2,524 R	78.3%	13.1%	85.6%	14.4%
5,172	GARFIELD	2,140	1,626	388	126	1,238 R	76.0%	18.1%	80.7%	19.3%
9,225	GRAND	4,338	1,935	2,138	265	203 D	44.6%	49.3%	47.5%	52.5%
46,163	IRON	15,801	11,286	2,846	1,669	8,440 R	71.4%	18.0%	79.9%	20.1%
10,246	JUAB	4,154	3,320	492	342	2,828 R	79.9%	11.8%	87.1%	12.9%
7,125	KANE	3,117	2,135	746	236	1,389 R	68.5%	23.9%	74.1%	25.9%
12,503	MILLARD	4,613	3,672	512	429	3,160 R	79.6%	11.1%	87.8%	12.2%
9,469	MORGAN	5,095	4,144	600	351	3,544 R	81.3%	11.8%	87.4%	12.6%
1,556	PIUTE	692	524	77	91	447 R	75.7%	11.1%	87.2%	12.8%
2,264	RICH	1,097	911	124	62	787 R	83.0%	11.3%	88.0%	12.0%
1,029,655	SALT LAKE	415,473	207,719	186,856	20,898	20,863 R	50.0%	45.0%	52.6%	47.4%
14,746	SAN JUAN	5,393	2,934	2,096	363	838 R	54.4%	38.9%	58.3%	41.7%
27,822	SANPETE	9,252	7,367	1,139	746	6,228 R	79.6%	12.3%	86.6%	13.4%
20,802	SEVIER	7,287	5,810	771	706	5,039 R	79.7%	10.6%	88.3%	11.7%
36,324	SUMMIT	20,210	9,170	10,229	811	1,059 D	45.4%	50.6%	47.3%	52.7%
58,218	TOOELE	21,955	14,407	5,491	2,057	8,916 R	65.6%	25.0%	72.4%	27.6%
32,588	UINTAH	10,256	7,946	1,135	1,175	6,811 R	77.5%	11.1%	87.5%	12.5%
516,564	UTAH	175,568	135,240	28,856	11,472	106,384 R	77.0%	16.4%	82.4%	17.6%
23,530	WASATCH	12,188	8,126	3,467	595	4,659 R	66.7%	28.4%	70.1%	29.9%
138,115	WASHINGTON	60,509	42,602	11,757	6,150	30,845 R	70.4%	19.4%	78.4%	21.6%
2,778	WAYNE	1,357	999	267	91	732 R	73.6%	19.7%	78.9%	21.1%
231,236	WEBER	80,191	49,458	24,513	6,220	24,945 R	61.7%	30.6%	66.9%	33.1%
2,763,885	*TOTAL*	*1,062,897*	*665,215*	*328,541*	*69,141*	*336,674 R*	*62.6%*	*30.9%*	*66.9%*	*33.1%*

UTAH

HOUSE OF REPRESENTATIVES

CD	Year	Total Vote	Republican Vote	Republican Candidate	Democratic Vote	Democratic Candidate	Other Vote	Rep.-Dem. Plurality	Percentage: Total Vote Rep.	Percentage: Total Vote Dem.	Percentage: Major Vote Rep.	Percentage: Major Vote Dem.
1	2018	254,333	156,692	BISHOP, ROBERT "ROB"*	63,308	CASTILLO, LEE	34,333	93,384 R	61.6%	24.9%	71.2%	28.8%
1	2016	277,455	182,928	BISHOP, ROBERT "ROB"*	73,381	CLEMENS, PETER C.	21,146	109,547 R	65.9%	26.4%	71.4%	28.6%
1	2014	130,034	84,231	BISHOP, ROBERT "ROB"*	36,422	MCALEER, DONNA M.	9,381	47,809 R	64.8%	28.0%	69.8%	30.2%
1	2012	245,528	175,487	BISHOP, ROBERT "ROB"*	60,611	MCALEER, DONNA M.	9,430	114,876 R	71.5%	24.7%	74.3%	25.7%
2	2018	270,044	151,489	STEWART, CHRIS*	105,051	GHORBANI, SHIREEN	13,504	46,438 R	56.1%	38.9%	59.1%	40.9%
2	2016	276,841	170,542	STEWART, CHRIS*	93,780	ALBARRAN, CHARLENE	12,519	76,762 R	61.6%	33.9%	64.5%	35.5%
2	2014	146,188	88,915	STEWART, CHRIS*	47,585	ROBLES, LUZ	9,688	41,330 R	60.8%	32.6%	65.1%	34.9%
2	2012	248,545	154,523	STEWART, CHRIS	83,176	SEEGMILLER, JAY	10,846	71,347 R	62.2%	33.5%	65.0%	35.0%
3	2018	258,858	174,856	CURTIS, JOHN*	70,686	SINGER, JAMES	13,316	104,170 R	67.5%	27.3%	71.2%	28.8%
3	2016	285,305	209,589	CHAFFETZ, JASON*	75,716	TRYON, STEPHEN		133,873 R	73.5%	26.5%	73.5%	26.5%
3	2014	142,580	102,952	CHAFFETZ, JASON*	32,059	WONNACOTT, BRIAN	7,569	70,893 R	72.2%	22.5%	76.3%	23.7%
3	2012	259,547	198,828	CHAFFETZ, JASON*	60,719	SIMONSEN, SOREN D.		138,109 R	76.6%	23.4%	76.6%	23.4%

UTAH

HOUSE OF REPRESENTATIVES

			Republican		Democratic				Percentage			
									Total Vote		Major Vote	
CD	Year	Total Vote	Vote	Candidate	Vote	Candidate	Other Vote	Rep.-Dem. Plurality	Rep.	Dem.	Rep.	Dem.
4	2018	269,271	134,270	LOVE, MIA B.*	134,964	MCADAMS, BEN	37	694 D	49.9%	50.1%	49.9%	50.1%
4	2016	274,569	147,597	LOVE, MIA B.*	113,413	OWENS, DOUG	13,559	34,184 R	53.8%	41.3%	56.5%	43.5%
4	2014	147,168	74,936	LOVE, MIA B.	67,425	OWENS, DOUG	4,807	7,511 R	50.9%	45.8%	52.6%	47.4%
4	2012	245,277	119,035	LOVE, MIA B.	119,803	MATHESON, JIM*	6,439	768 D	48.5%	48.8%	49.8%	50.2%
TOTAL	*2018*	*1,052,506*	*617,307*		*374,009*		*61,190*	*243,298 R*	*58.7%*	*35.5%*	*62.3%*	*37.7%*
TOTAL	*2016*	*1,114,170*	*710,656*		*356,290*		*47,224*	*354,366 R*	*63.8%*	*32.0%*	*66.6%*	*33.4%*
TOTAL	*2014*	*565,970*	*351,034*		*183,491*		*31,445*	*167,543 R*	*62.0%*	*32.4%*	*65.7%*	*34.3%*
TOTAL	*2012*	*998,897*	*647,873*		*324,309*		*26,715*	*323,564 R*	*64.9%*	*32.5%*	*66.6%*	*33.4%*

Note: An asterisk (*) denotes incumbent.

UTAH

GENERAL AND PRIMARY ELECTIONS

2018 GENERAL ELECTIONS: OTHER VOTES

Senate Other vote was 28,774 Constitution (Tim Aalders), 27,607 Libertarian (Craig Bowden), 12,708 Independent American (Reed McCandless), 29 Write-in (Caleb Reeve), 17 Write-in (Tyrone Jensen), 3 Write-in (Ryan Jackson), 2 Write-in (Hektor Reiksthegn), 1 Write-in (Glade Fitzgerald)

House Other vote was:

CD 1 29,547 United Utah Party (Eric Eliason), 4,786 Green (Adam Davis)

CD 2 13,504 Libertarian (Jeffrey Whipple)

CD 3 6,686 Independent American (Gregory Duerden), 6,630 United Utah Party (Timothy Zeidner)

CD 4 13,745 United Utah Party (Jim Bennett), 4,550 Independent (Sean Whalen), 3,643 Libertarian (Joe Buchman), 2,286 Independent American (Jason Christensen)

2018 PRIMARY ELECTIONS: SUPPLEMENTARY INFORMATION

Primary	June 26, 2018	**Registration** (as of June 25, 2018 — includes 253,647 inactive registrants)	1,570,644	Republican	738,274
				Democratic	188,422
				Independent American	28,989
				Libertarian	14,481
				Constitution	5,817
				Green	995
				United Utah	717
				Unaffiliated	592,949

Primary Type Semi-Open—Registered Democrats and unaffiliated voters could participate in the Democratic primary. Only registered Republicans could vote in the Republican primary.

UTAH

GENERAL AND PRIMARY ELECTIONS

	REPUBLICAN PRIMARIES			DEMOCRATIC PRIMARIES		
Senator	Romney, Mitt	240,021	71.3%	Wilson, Jenny	Unopposed	
	Kennedy, Mike	96,771	28.7%			
	TOTAL	*336,792*				
Congressional District 1	Bishop, Robert "Rob"*	Unopposed		Castillo, Lee	7,273	57.2%
				Weiland, Kurt	5,439	42.8%
				TOTAL	*12,712*	
Congressional District 2	Stewart, Chris*	Unopposed		Ghorbani, Shireen	Unopposed	
Congressional District 3	Curtis, John*	66,404	73.3%	Singer, James	Unopposed	
	Herrod, Christopher	24,158	26.7%			
	TOTAL	*90,562*				
Congressional District 4	Love, Mia B.*	Unopposed		McAdams, Ben	Unopposed	

Note: An asterisk (*) denotes incumbent.

VERMONT

One member At Large

VERMONT

GOVERNOR

Phil Scott (R). Re-elected 2018 to a two-year term. Previously elected 2016.

SENATORS (1 Democrat, 1 Independent)

Patrick J. Leahy (D). Re-elected 2016 to a six-year term. Previously elected 2010, 2004, 1998, 1992, 1986, 1980, 1974.

Bernard Sanders (Ind.). Re-elected 2018 to a six-year term. Previously elected 2012, 2006.

REPRESENTATIVE (1 Democrat)

At Large. Peter Welch (D)

POSTWAR VOTE FOR PRESIDENT

		Republican		Democratic				Percentage				
								Total Vote		Major Vote		
Year	Total Vote	Vote	Candidate	Vote	Candidate	Other Vote	Rep.-Dem. Plurality	Rep.	Dem.	Rep.	Dem.
2016**	315,067	95,369	Trump, Donald J.	178,573	Clinton, Hillary Rodham	41,125	83,204 D	30.3%	56.7%	34.8%	65.2%
2012	299,290	92,698	Romney, W. Mitt	199,239	Obama, Barack H.*	7,353	106,541 D	31.0%	66.6%	31.8%	68.2%
2008	325,046	98,974	McCain, John S. III	219,262	Obama, Barack H.	6,810	120,288 D	30.4%	67.5%	31.1%	68.9%
2004	312,309	121,180	Bush, George W.*	184,067	Kerry, John F.	7,062	62,887 D	38.8%	58.9%	39.7%	60.3%
2000**	294,308	119,775	Bush, George W.	149,022	Gore, Albert Jr.	25,511	29,247 D	40.7%	50.6%	44.6%	55.4%
1996**	258,449	80,352	Dole, Robert "Bob"	137,894	Clinton, Bill*	40,203	57,542 D	31.1%	53.4%	36.8%	63.2%
1992**	289,701	88,122	Bush, George H.*	133,592	Clinton, Bill	67,987	45,470 D	30.4%	46.1%	39.7%	60.3%
1988	243,328	124,331	Bush, George H.	115,776	Dukakis, Michael S.	3,221	8,555 R	51.1%	47.6%	51.8%	48.2%
1984	234,561	135,865	Reagan, Ronald*	95,730	Mondale, Walter F.	2,966	40,135 R	57.9%	40.8%	58.7%	41.3%
1980**	213,299	94,628	Reagan, Ronald	81,952	Carter, Jimmy*	36,719	12,676 R	44.4%	38.4%	53.6%	46.4%
1976	187,765	102,085	Ford, Gerald R.*	80,954	Carter, Jimmy	4,726	21,131 R	54.4%	43.1%	55.8%	44.2%
1972	186,947	117,149	Nixon, Richard M.*	68,174	McGovern, George S.	1,624	48,975 R	62.7%	36.5%	63.2%	36.8%
1968**	161,404	85,142	Nixon, Richard M.	70,255	Humphrey, Hubert Horatio Jr.	6,007	14,887 R	52.8%	43.5%	54.8%	45.2%
1964	163,089	54,942	Goldwater, Barry M. Sr.	108,127	Johnson, Lyndon B.*	20	53,185 D	33.7%	66.3%	33.7%	66.3%
1960	167,324	98,131	Nixon, Richard M.	69,186	Kennedy, John F.	7	28,945 R	58.6%	41.3%	58.6%	41.4%
1956	152,978	110,390	Eisenhower, Dwight D.*	42,549	Stevenson, Adlai E. II	39	67,841 R	72.2%	27.8%	72.2%	27.8%
1952	153,557	109,717	Eisenhower, Dwight D.	43,355	Stevenson, Adlai E. II	485	66,362 R	71.5%	28.2%	71.7%	28.3%
1948	123,382	75,926	Dewey, Thomas E.	45,557	Truman, Harry S.*	1,899	30,369 R	61.5%	36.9%	62.5%	37.5%

Note: An asterisk (*) denotes incumbent. **In past elections, the other vote included: 2016 - 10,078 Libertarian (Gary Johnson); 2000 - 20,374 Green (Ralph Nader); 1996 - 31,024 Reform (Ross Perot); 1992 - 65,991 Independent (Perot); 1980 - 31,761 Independent (John Anderson); 1968 - 5,104 American Independent (George Wallace).

VERMONT

POSTWAR VOTE FOR GOVERNOR

		Republican		Democratic				Percentage			
								Total Vote		Major Vote	
Year	Total Vote	Vote	Candidate	Vote	Candidate	Other Vote	Rep.-Dem. Plurality	Rep.	Dem.	Rep.	Dem.
2018	274,087	151,261	Scott, Phil*	110,335	Hallquist, Christine	12,491	40,926 R	55.2%	40.3%	57.8%	42.2%
2016	315,295	166,817	Scott, Phil	139,253	Minter, Sue	9,225	27,564 R	52.9%	44.2%	54.5%	45.5%
2014**	193,087	87,075	Milne, Scott	89,509	Shumlin, Peter*	16,503	2,434 D	45.1%	46.4%	49.3%	50.7%
2012	295,261	110,940	Brock, Randy	170,598	Shumlin, Peter*	13,723	59,658 D	37.6%	57.8%	39.4%	60.6%
2010**	241,605	115,212	Dubie, Brian E.	119,543	Shumlin, Peter	6,850	4,331 D	47.7%	49.5%	49.1%	50.9%
2008**	319,085	170,492	Douglas, Jim*	69,534	Symington, Gaye	79,059	100,958 R	53.4%	21.8%	71.0%	29.0%
2006	262,524	148,014	Douglas, Jim*	108,090	Parker, Scudder	6,420	39,924 R	56.4%	41.2%	57.8%	42.2%
2004	309,285	181,540	Douglas, Jim*	117,327	Clavell, Peter	10,418	64,213 R	58.7%	37.9%	60.7%	39.3%
2002**	230,161	103,436	Douglas, Jim	97,565	Racine, Doug	29,160	5,871 R	44.9%	42.4%	51.5%	48.5%
2000	293,473	111,359	Dwyer, Ruth	148,059	Dean, Howard B.*	34,055	36,700 D	37.9%	50.5%	42.9%	57.1%
1998	218,120	89,726	Dwyer, Ruth	121,425	Dean, Howard B.*	6,969	31,699 D	41.1%	55.7%	42.5%	57.5%
1996	254,648	57,161	Gropper, John L.	179,544	Dean, Howard B.*	17,943	122,383 D	22.4%	70.5%	24.1%	75.9%
1994	212,046	40,292	Kelley, David F.	145,661	Dean, Howard B.*	26,093	105,369 D	19.0%	68.7%	21.7%	78.3%
1992	285,728	65,837	McClaughry, John	213,523	Dean, Howard B.*	6,368	147,686 D	23.0%	74.7%	23.6%	76.4%
1990	211,422	109,540	Snelling, Richard A.	97,321	Welch, Peter	4,561	12,219 R	51.8%	46.0%	53.0%	47.0%
1988	242,879	105,191	Bernhardt, Michael	134,438	Kunin, Madeline*	3,250	29,247 D	43.3%	55.4%	43.9%	56.1%
1986**	196,716	75,162	Smith, Peter	92,379	Kunin, Madeline*	29,175	17,217 D	38.2%	47.0%	44.9%	55.1%
1984	233,753	113,264	Easton, John J.	116,938	Kunin, Madeline	3,551	3,674 D	48.5%	50.0%	49.2%	50.8%
1982	169,251	93,111	Snelling, Richard A.*	74,394	Kunin, Madeline	1,746	18,717 R	55.0%	44.0%	55.6%	44.4%
1980	210,381	123,229	Snelling, Richard A.*	77,363	Diamond, M. Jerome	9,789	45,866 R	58.6%	36.8%	61.4%	38.6%
1978	124,482	78,181	Snelling, Richard A.*	42,482	Granai, Edwin C.	3,819	35,699 R	62.8%	34.1%	64.8%	35.2%
1976	185,929	99,268	Snelling, Richard A.	75,262	Hackel, Stella B.	11,399	24,006 R	53.4%	40.5%	56.9%	43.1%
1974	141,156	53,672	Kennedy, Walter L.	79,842	Salmon, Thomas P.*	7,642	26,170 D	38.0%	56.6%	40.2%	59.8%
1972	189,237	82,491	Hackett, Luther F.	104,533	Salmon, Thomas P.	2,213	22,042 D	43.6%	55.2%	44.1%	55.9%
1970	153,528	87,458	Davis, Deane C.*	66,028	O'Brien, Leo	42	21,430 R	57.0%	43.0%	57.0%	43.0%
1968	161,089	89,387	Davis, Deane C.	71,656	Daley, John J.	46	17,731 R	55.5%	44.5%	55.5%	44.5%
1966	136,262	57,577	Snelling, Richard A.	78,669	Hoff, Philip H.*	16	21,092 D	42.3%	57.7%	42.3%	57.7%
1964	164,199	57,576	Foote, Ralph A.	106,611	Hoff, Philip H.*	12	49,035 D	35.1%	64.9%	35.1%	64.9%
1962	121,422	60,035	Keyser, F. Ray Jr.*	61,383	Hoff, Philip H.	4	1,348 D	49.4%	50.6%	49.4%	50.6%
1960	164,632	92,861	Keyser, F. Ray Jr.	71,755	Niquette, Russell F.	16	21,106 R	56.4%	43.6%	56.4%	43.6%
1958	123,728	62,222	Stafford, Robert T.	61,503	Leddy, Bernard J.	3	719 R	50.3%	49.7%	50.3%	49.7%
1956	153,809	88,379	Johnson, Joseph B.*	65,420	Branon, E. Frank	10	22,959 R	57.5%	42.5%	57.5%	42.5%
1954	114,360	59,778	Johnson, Joseph B.	54,554	Branon, E. Frank	28	5,224 R	52.3%	47.7%	52.3%	47.7%
1952	150,836	78,338	Emerson, Lee Earl*	60,051	Larrow, Robert W.	12,447	18,287 R	51.9%	39.8%	56.6%	43.4%
1950	87,155	64,915	Emerson, Lee Earl	22,227	Moran, J. Edward	13	42,688 R	74.5%	25.5%	74.5%	25.5%
1948	120,183	86,394	Gibson, Ernest Willard Jr.*	33,588	Ryan, Charles F.	201	52,806 R	71.9%	27.9%	72.0%	28.0%
1946	72,044	57,849	Gibson, Ernest Willard Jr.	14,096	Coburn, Berthold C.	99	43,753 R	80.3%	19.6%	80.4%	19.6%

Note: An asterisk (*) denotes incumbent. **In past elections, the other vote included: 2008 - 69,791 Independent (Anthony Pollina), who finished second; 1986 - 28,430 Independent (Bernard Sanders). In 1986, 2002, 2010, and 2014 in the absence of a majority of the total vote for any candidate, the State Legislature elected the governor — Democrat Madeleine M. Kunin in January 1987, Republican Jim Douglas in January 2003, and Democrat Peter Shumlin in January 2011 and January 2015.

VERMONT

POSTWAR VOTE FOR SENATOR

		Republican		Democratic				Percentage			
								Total Vote		Major Vote	
Year	Total Vote	Vote	Candidate	Vote	Candidate	Other Vote	Rep.-Dem. Plurality	Rep.	Dem.	Rep.	Dem.
2018	272,624	74,815	Zupan, Lawrence			197,809	74,815 R#	27.4%		100.0%	
2016	313,809	103,637	Milne, Scott	192,243	Leahy, Patrick J.*	17,929	88,606 D	33.0%	61.3%	35.0%	65.0%
2012**	294,267	73,198	MacGovern, John			221,069	73,798 R#	24.9%		100.0%	
2010	235,178	72,699	Britton, Len	151,281	Leahy, Patrick J.*	11,198	78,582 D	30.9%	64.3%	32.5%	67.5%
2006**	262,419	84,924	Tarrant, Richard			177,495	84,924 R#	32.4%		100.0%	
2004	307,208	75,398	McMullen, Jack	216,972	Leahy, Patrick J.*	14,838	141,574 D	24.5%	70.6%	25.8%	74.2%
2000	288,500	189,133	Jeffords, James M.*	73,352	Flanagan, Ed	26,015	115,781 R	65.6%	25.4%	72.1%	27.9%
1998	214,036	48,051	Tuttle, Fred	154,567	Leahy, Patrick J.*	11,418	106,516 D	22.4%	72.2%	23.7%	76.3%
1994	211,672	106,505	Jeffords, James M.*	85,868	Backus, Jan	19,299	20,637 R	50.3%	40.6%	55.4%	44.6%
1992	285,739	123,854	Douglas, Jim	154,762	Leahy, Patrick J.*	7,123	30,908 D	43.3%	54.2%	44.5%	55.5%
1988	240,108	163,183	Jeffords, James M.	71,460	Gray, William	5,465	91,723 R	68.0%	29.8%	69.5%	30.5%
1986	196,532	67,798	Snelling, Richard A.	124,123	Leahy, Patrick J.*	4,611	56,325 D	34.5%	63.2%	35.3%	64.7%
1982	168,003	84,450	Stafford, Robert T.*	79,340	Guest, James A.	4,213	5,110 R	50.3%	47.2%	51.6%	48.4%
1980	209,124	101,421	Ledbetter, Stewart M.	104,176	Leahy, Patrick J.*	3,527	2,755 D	48.5%	49.8%	49.3%	50.7%
1976	189,046	94,481	Stafford, Robert T.*	85,682	Salmon, Thomas P.	8,883	8,799 R	50.0%	45.3%	52.4%	47.6%
1974	142,772	66,223	Mallary, Richard W.	70,629	Leahy, Patrick J.	5,920	4,406 D	46.4%	49.5%	48.4%	51.6%
1972S**	71,348	45,888	Stafford, Robert T.*	23,842	Major, Randolph T.	1,618	22,046 R	64.3%	33.4%	65.8%	34.2%
1970	154,899	91,198	Prouty, Winston L.*	62,271	Hoff, Philip H.	1,430	28,927 R	58.9%	40.2%	59.4%	40.6%
1968**	157,375	157,154	Aiken, George David*			221	157,154 R	99.9%		100.0%	
1964	164,350	87,879	Prouty, Winston L.*	76,457	Fayette, Frederick J.	14	11,422 R	53.5%	46.5%	53.5%	46.5%
1962	121,571	81,241	Aiken, George David*	40,134	Johnson, W. Robert	196	41,107 R	66.8%	33.0%	66.9%	33.1%
1958	124,442	64,900	Prouty, Winston L.	59,536	Fayette, Frederick J.	6	5,364 R	52.2%	47.8%	52.2%	47.8%
1956	155,289	103,101	Aiken, George David*	52,184	O'Shea, Bernard G.	4	50,917 R	66.4%	33.6%	66.4%	33.6%
1952	154,052	111,406	Flanders, Ralph E.*	42,630	Johnston, Allan R.	16	68,776 R	72.3%	27.7%	72.3%	27.7%
1950	89,171	69,543	Aiken, George David*	19,608	Bigelow, James E.	20	49,935 R	78.0%	22.0%	78.0%	22.0%
1946	73,340	54,729	Flanders, Ralph E.	18,594	McDevitt, Charles P.	17	36,135 R	74.6%	25.4%	74.6%	25.4%

Note: An asterisk (*) denotes incumbent. A pound sign (#) indicates that the winner was an independent. **In past elections, the other vote included: 2018 - 183,649 Independent (Bernard Sanders), who received 67.4 percent of the total vote and was re-elected with a plurality of 108,834 votes; 2012 - 209,053 Independent (Bernard Sanders), who received 71.0 percent of the total vote and was re-elected with a plurality of 135,855 votes; 2006 - 171,638 Independent (Bernard Sanders), who received 65.4 percent of the total vote and was elected with a plurality of 86,714 votes. Sanders also won the Democratic primary in 2006, 2012, and 2018, but declined the nomination each time in order to run as an independent. The Democratic Party did not run a candidate in the 2006, 2012, and 2018 Senate elections. The January 1972 election was for a short term to fill a vacancy. In 1968 the Republican candidate (George D. Aiken) won both major party nominations.

VERMONT

GOVERNOR 2018

							Percentage			
							Total Vote		Major Vote	
2010 Census Population	County	Total Vote	Republican (Scott)	Democratic (Hallquist)	Other	Rep.-Dem. Plurality	Rep.	Dem.	Rep.	Dem.
36,821	ADDISON	17,339	9,514	7,203	622	2,311 R	54.9%	41.5%	56.9%	43.1%
37,125	BENNINGTON	14,686	7,351	6,152	1,183	1,199 R	50.1%	41.9%	54.4%	45.6%
31,227	CALEDONIA	11,751	7,427	3,850	474	3,577 R	63.2%	32.8%	65.9%	34.1%
156,545	CHITTENDEN	75,935	38,443	35,121	2,371	3,322 R	50.6%	46.3%	52.3%	47.7%
6,306	ESSEX	2,216	1,573	506	137	1,067 R	71.0%	22.8%	75.7%	24.3%
47,746	FRANKLIN	18,302	12,592	4,991	719	7,601 R	68.8%	27.3%	71.6%	28.4%
6,970	GRAND ISLE	3,709	2,429	1,138	142	1,291 R	65.5%	30.7%	68.1%	31.9%
24,475	LAMOILLE	11,460	6,571	4,548	341	2,023 R	57.3%	39.7%	59.1%	40.9%
28,936	ORANGE	12,582	7,492	4,469	621	3,023 R	59.5%	35.5%	62.6%	37.4%
27,231	ORLEANS	9,950	6,538	3,010	402	3,528 R	65.7%	30.3%	68.5%	31.5%

VERMONT

GOVERNOR 2018

2010 Census Population	County	Total Vote	Republican (Scott)	Democratic (Hallquist)	Other	Rep.-Dem. Plurality	Percentage Total Vote Rep.	Percentage Total Vote Dem.	Percentage Major Vote Rep.	Percentage Major Vote Dem.
61,642	RUTLAND	24,473	15,630	7,038	1,805	8,592 R	63.9%	28.8%	69.0%	31.0%
59,534	WASHINGTON	27,412	15,182	11,340	890	3,842 R	55.4%	41.4%	57.2%	42.8%
44,513	WINDHAM	19,068	7,193	10,708	1,167	3,515 D	37.7%	56.2%	40.2%	59.8%
56,670	WINDSOR	25,204	13,326	10,261	1,617	3,065 R	52.9%	40.7%	56.5%	43.5%
625,741	*TOTAL*	*274,087*	*151,261*	*110,335*	*12,491*	*40,926 R*	*55.2%*	*40.3%*	*57.8%*	*42.2%*

2010 Census Population	City/Town	Total Vote	Republican (Scott)	Democratic (Hallquist)	Other	Rep.-Dem. Plurality	Percentage Total Vote Rep.	Percentage Total Vote Dem.	Percentage Major Vote Rep.	Percentage Major Vote Dem.
9,052	BARRE CITY	2,630	1,681	861	88	820 R	63.9%	32.7%	66.1%	33.9%
7,924	BARRE TOWN	3,553	2,767	690	96	2,077 R	77.9%	19.4%	80.0%	20.0%
15,764	BENNINGTON	4,955	2,243	2,259	453	16 D	45.3%	45.6%	49.8%	50.2%
12,046	BRATTLEBORO	5,085	1,408	3,391	286	1,983 D	27.7%	66.7%	29.3%	70.7%
42,417	BURLINGTON	18,455	5,793	11,948	714	6,155 D	31.4%	64.7%	32.7%	67.3%
17,067	COLCHESTER	6,661	4,188	2,284	189	1,904 R	62.9%	34.3%	64.7%	35.3%
4,621	DERBY	1,789	1,251	483	55	768 R	69.9%	27.0%	72.1%	27.9%
19,587	ESSEX	9,806	5,828	3,729	249	2,099 R	59.4%	38.0%	61.0%	39.0%
9,952	HARTFORD	4,341	2,133	2,006	202	127 R	49.1%	46.2%	51.5%	48.5%
5,009	JERICHO	2,881	1,632	1,180	69	452 R	56.6%	41.0%	58.0%	42.0%
5,981	LYNDON	1,679	1,172	439	68	733 R	69.8%	26.1%	72.7%	27.3%
4,391	MANCHESTER	2,095	1,122	880	93	242 R	53.6%	42.0%	56.0%	44.0%
8,496	MIDDLEBURY	3,485	1,453	1,944	88	491 D	41.7%	55.8%	42.8%	57.2%
10,352	MILTON	4,474	3,267	1,086	121	2,181 R	73.0%	24.3%	75.1%	24.9%
7,855	MONTPELIER	4,476	1,596	2,758	122	1,162 D	35.7%	61.6%	36.7%	63.3%
5,227	MORRISTOWN	2,429	1,427	951	51	476 R	58.7%	39.2%	60.0%	40.0%
6,207	NORTHFIELD	1,832	1,217	564	51	653 R	66.4%	30.8%	68.3%	31.7%
4,778	RANDOLPH	2,002	1,218	701	83	517 R	60.8%	35.0%	63.5%	36.5%
4,081	RICHMOND	2,330	1,177	1,103	50	74 R	50.5%	47.3%	51.6%	48.4%
5,282	ROCKINGHAM	1,650	697	834	119	137 D	42.2%	50.5%	45.5%	54.5%
16,495	RUTLAND CITY	5,554	3,524	1,718	312	1,806 R	63.4%	30.9%	67.2%	32.8%
4,054	RUTLAND TOWN	1,928	1,357	486	85	871 R	70.4%	25.2%	73.6%	26.4%
7,144	SHELBURNE	4,275	2,369	1,828	78	541 R	55.4%	42.8%	56.4%	43.6%
17,904	SOUTH BURLINGTON	9,455	4,865	4,341	249	524 R	51.5%	45.9%	52.8%	47.2%
9,373	SPRINGFIELD	2,918	1,661	961	296	700 R	56.9%	32.9%	63.3%	36.7%
6,918	ST. ALBANS CITY	2,086	1,263	754	69	509 R	60.5%	36.1%	62.6%	37.4%
5,999	ST. ALBANS TOWN	2,790	1,998	701	91	1,297 R	71.6%	25.1%	74.0%	26.0%
7,603	ST. JOHNSBURY	2,449	1,486	885	78	601 R	60.7%	36.1%	62.7%	37.3%
4,314	STOWE	2,633	1,476	1,097	60	379 R	56.1%	41.7%	57.4%	42.6%
6,427	SWANTON	2,157	1,609	473	75	1,136 R	74.6%	21.9%	77.3%	22.7%
5,064	WATERBURY	2,696	1,496	1,133	67	363 R	55.5%	42.0%	56.9%	43.1%
8,698	WILLISTON	4,986	3,092	1,788	106	1,304 R	62.0%	35.9%	63.4%	36.6%
7,267	WINOOSKI	2,808	1,062	1,637	109	575 D	37.8%	58.3%	39.3%	60.7%
3,048	WOODSTOCK	1,666	854	752	60	102 R	51.3%	45.1%	53.2%	46.8%

VERMONT

SENATOR 2018

2010 Census Population	City	Total Vote	Republican (Zupan)	Independent (Sanders)	Other	Rep.-Ind. Plurality	Percentage Total Vote Rep.	Total Vote Ind.	Major Vote Rep.	Major Vote Ind.
36,821	ADDISON	17,202	4,439	11,965	798	7,526 I	25.8%	69.6%	27.1%	72.9%
37,125	BENNINGTON	14,732	3,910	8,971	1,851	5,061 I	26.5%	60.9%	30.4%	69.6%
31,227	CALEDONIA	11,666	4,296	6,803	567	2,507 I	36.8%	58.3%	38.7%	61.3%
156,545	CHITTENDEN	75,490	16,441	55,669	3,380	39,228 I	21.8%	73.7%	22.8%	77.2%
6,306	ESSEX	2,176	976	1,059	141	83 I	44.9%	48.7%	48.0%	52.0%
47,746	FRANKLIN	18,214	6,782	10,492	940	3,710 I	37.2%	57.6%	39.3%	60.7%
6,970	GRAND ISLE	3,685	1,229	2,307	149	1,078 I	33.4%	62.6%	34.8%	65.2%
24,475	LAMOILLE	11,355	2,931	7,989	435	5,058 I	25.8%	70.4%	26.8%	73.2%
28,936	ORANGE	12,538	3,790	8,099	649	4,309 I	30.2%	64.6%	31.9%	68.1%
27,231	ORLEANS	9,876	3,853	5,571	452	1,718 I	39.0%	56.4%	40.9%	59.1%
61,642	RUTLAND	24,359	9,576	13,587	1,196	4,011 I	39.3%	55.8%	41.3%	58.7%
59,534	WASHINGTON	27,265	6,517	19,395	1,353	12,878 I	23.9%	71.1%	25.2%	74.8%
44,513	WINDHAM	19,014	3,673	14,386	955	10,713 I	19.3%	75.7%	20.3%	79.7%
56,670	WINDSOR	25,052	6,402	17,356	1,294	10,954 I	25.6%	69.3%	26.9%	73.1%
625,741	*TOTAL*	*272,624*	*74,815*	*183,649*	*14,160*	*108,834 I*	*27.4%*	*67.4%*	*28.9%*	*71.1%*

2010 Census Population	City/Town	Total Vote	Republican (Zupan)	Independent (Sanders)	Other	Rep.-Ind. Plurality	Percentage Total Vote Rep.	Total Vote Ind.	Major Vote Rep.	Major Vote Ind.
9,052	BARRE CITY	2,643	797	1,646	851	849 I	30.2%	62.3%	32.6%	67.4%
7,924	BARRE TOWN	3,581	1,461	1,845	386	384 I	40.8%	51.5%	44.2%	55.8%
15,764	BENNINGTON	5,009	1,172	3,128	1,958	1,956 I	23.4%	62.4%	27.3%	72.7%
12,046	BRATTLEBORO	5,082	588	4,284	3,698	3,696 I	11.6%	84.3%	12.1%	87.9%
42,417	BURLINGTON	18,446	1,813	15,716	13,905	13,903 I	9.8%	85.2%	10.3%	89.7%
17,067	COLCHESTER	6,630	2,012	4,363	2,353	2,351 I	30.3%	65.8%	31.6%	68.4%
4,621	DERBY	1,775	735	958	225	223 I	41.4%	54.0%	43.4%	56.6%
19,587	ESSEX	9,788	2,683	6,715	4,034	4,032 I	27.4%	68.6%	28.5%	71.5%
9,952	HARTFORD	4,310	912	3,141	2,231	2,229 I	21.2%	72.9%	22.5%	77.5%
5,009	JERICHO	2,885	781	1,991	1,212	1,210 I	27.1%	69.0%	28.2%	71.8%
5,981	LYNDON	1,677	721	876	157	155 I	43.0%	52.2%	45.1%	54.9%
4,391	MANCHESTER	2,077	604	1,319	717	715 I	29.1%	63.5%	31.4%	68.6%
8,496	MIDDLEBURY	3,485	526	2,797	2,273	2,271 I	15.1%	80.3%	15.8%	84.2%
10,352	MILTON	4,438	1,797	2,408	613	611 I	40.5%	54.3%	42.7%	57.3%
7,855	MONTPELIER	4,439	457	3,832	3,377	3,375 I	10.3%	86.3%	10.7%	89.3%
5,227	MORRISTOWN	2,423	605	1,739	1,136	1,134 I	25.0%	71.8%	25.8%	74.2%
6,207	NORTHFIELD	1,823	594	1,138	546	544 I	32.6%	62.4%	34.3%	65.7%
4,778	RANDOLPH	2,004	579	1,327	750	748 I	28.9%	66.2%	30.4%	69.6%
4,081	RICHMOND	2,319	495	1,753	1,260	1,258 I	21.3%	75.6%	22.0%	78.0%
5,282	ROCKINGHAM	1,653	349	1,207	860	858 I	21.1%	73.0%	22.4%	77.6%
16,495	RUTLAND CITY	5,546	2,032	3,228	1,198	1,196 I	36.6%	58.2%	38.6%	61.4%
4,054	RUTLAND TOWN	1,915	800	1,034	236	234 I	41.8%	54.0%	43.6%	56.4%
7,144	SHELBURNE	4,199	918	3,075	2,159	2,157 I	21.9%	73.2%	23.0%	77.0%
17,904	SOUTH BURLINGTON	9,397	1,909	7,050	5,143	5,141 I	20.3%	75.0%	21.3%	78.7%
9,373	SPRINGFIELD	2,930	1,037	1,748	713	711 I	35.4%	59.7%	37.2%	62.8%
6,918	ST. ALBANS CITY	2,105	596	1,397	803	801 I	28.3%	66.4%	29.9%	70.1%
5,999	ST. ALBANS TOWN	2,762	1,037	1,585	550	548 I	37.5%	57.4%	39.5%	60.5%
7,603	ST. JOHNSBURY	2,436	831	1,483	654	652 I	34.1%	60.9%	35.9%	64.1%
4,314	STOWE	2,575	574	1,896	1,324	1,322 I	22.3%	73.6%	23.2%	76.8%
6,427	SWANTON	2,139	865	1,152	289	287 I	40.4%	53.9%	42.9%	57.1%
5,064	WATERBURY	2,696	512	2,066	1,556	1,554 I	19.0%	76.6%	19.9%	80.1%
8,698	TON	4,964	1,378	3,380	2,004	2,002 I	27.8%	68.1%	29.0%	71.0%
7,267	WINOOSKI	2,797	383	2,252	1,871	1,869 I	13.7%	80.5%	14.5%	85.5%
3,048	WOODSTOCK	1,657	323	1,273	952	950 I	19.5%	76.8%	20.2%	79.8%

VERMONT

HOUSE OF REPRESENTATIVES

			Republican		Democratic				Percentage			
									Total Vote		Major Vote	
CD	Year	Total Vote	Vote	Candidate	Vote	Candidate	Other Vote	Rep.-Dem. Plurality	Rep.	Dem.	Rep.	Dem.
At Large	2018	272,451	70,705	TYNIO, ANYA	188,547	WELCH, PETER*	13,199	117,842 D	26.0%	69.2%	27.3%	72.7%
At Large	2016	295,334			264,414	WELCH, PETER*	30,920	264,414 D		89.5%		100.0%
At Large	2014	191,504	59,432	DONKA, MARK	123,349	WELCH, PETER*	8,723	63,917 D	31.0%	64.4%	32.5%	67.5%
At Large	2012	289,931	67,543	DONKA, MARK	208,600	WELCH, PETER*	13,788	141,057 D	23.3%	71.9%	24.5%	75.5%
At Large	2010	238,521	76,403	BEAUDRY, PAUL D.	154,006	WELCH, PETER*	8,112	77,603 D	32.0%	64.6%	33.2%	66.8%
At Large	2008	298,151			248,203	WELCH, PETER*	49,948	248,203 D		83.2%		100.0%
At Large	2006	262,726	117,023	RAINVILLE, MARTHA	139,815	WELCH, PETER	5,888	22,792 D	44.5%	53.2%	45.6%	54.4%
At Large	2004	305,008	74,271	PARKE, GREG	21,684	DROWN, LARRY	209,053	52,587 R#	24.4%	7.1%	77.4%	22.6%
At Large	2002	225,476	72,813	MEUB, WILLIAM			152,663	72,813 R#	32.3%		100.0%	
At Large	2000	283,366	51,977	KERIN, KAREN ANN	14,918	DIAMONDSTONE, PETE	216,471	37,059 R#	18.3%	5.3%	77.7%	22.3%
At Large	1998	215,133	70,740	CANDON, MARK			144,393	70,740 R#	32.9%		100.0%	
At Large	1996	254,706	83,021	SWEETSER, SUSAN W.	23,830	LONG, JACK	147,855	59,191 R#	32.6%	9.4%	77.7%	22.3%
At Large	1994	211,449	98,523	CARROLL, JOHN			112,926	98,523 R#	46.6%		100.0%	
At Large	1992	281,626	86,901	PHILBIN, TIMOTHY	22,279	YOUNG, LEWIS E.	172,446	64,622 R#	30.9%	7.9%	79.6%	20.4%
At Large	1990	209,856	82,938	SMITH, PETER*	6,315	SANDOVAL, DOLORES	120,603	76,623 R#	39.5%	3.0%	92.9%	7.1%
At Large	1988	240,131	98,937	SMITH, PETER	45,330	POIRIER, PAUL N.	95,864	53,607 R	41.2%	18.9%	68.6%	31.4%
At Large	1986	188,954	168,403	JEFFORDS, JAMES M.*			20,551	168,403 R	89.1%		100.0%	
At Large	1984	226,297	148,025	JEFFORDS, JAMES M.*	60,360	POLLINA, ANTHONY	17,912	87,665 R	65.4%	26.7%	71.0%	29.0%
At Large	1982	164,951	114,191	JEFFORDS, JAMES M.*	38,296	KAPLAN, MARK A.	12,464	75,895 R	69.2%	23.2%	74.9%	25.1%
At Large	1980	194,697	154,274	JEFFORDS, JAMES M.*			40,423	154,274 R	79.2%		100.0%	
At Large	1978	120,502	90,688	JEFFORDS, JAMES M.*	23,228	DIETZ, S. MARIE	6,586	67,460 R	75.3%	19.3%	79.6%	20.4%
At Large	1976	184,783	124,458	JEFFORDS, JAMES M.*	60,202	BURGESS, JOHN A.	123	64,256 R	67.4%	32.6%	67.4%	32.6%
At Large	1974	140,899	74,561	JEFFORDS, JAMES M.	56,342	CAIN, FRANCIS J.	9,996	18,219 R	52.9%	40.0%	57.0%	43.0%
At Large	1972	186,028	120,924	MALLARY, RICHARD W.	65,062	MEYER, WILLIAM H.	42	55,862 R	65.0%	35.0%	65.0%	35.0%
At Large	1970	152,557	103,806	STAFFORD, ROBERT T.*	44,415	O'SHEA, BERNARD G.	4,336	59,391 R	68.0%	29.1%	70.0%	30.0%
At Large	1968	157,133	156,956	STAFFORD, ROBERT T.*			177	156,956 R	99.9%		100.0%	
At Large	1966	135,748	89,097	STAFFORD, ROBERT T.*	46,643	RYAN, WILLIAM J.	8	42,454 R	65.6%	34.4%	65.6%	34.4%
At Large	1964	163,452	92,252	STAFFORD, ROBERT T.*	71,193	O'SHEA, BERNARD G.	7	21,059 R	56.4%	43.6%	56.4%	43.6%
At Large	1962	121,381	68,822	STAFFORD, ROBERT T.*	52,535	REYNOLDS, HAROLD	24	16,287 R	56.7%	43.3%	56.7%	43.3%
At Large	1960	166,035	94,905	STAFFORD, ROBERT T.	71,111	MEYER, WILLIAM H.*	19	23,794 R	57.2%	42.8%	57.2%	42.8%
At Large	1958	122,702	59,536	ARTHUR, HAROLD J.	63,131	MEYER, WILLIAM H.	35	3,595 D	48.5%	51.5%	48.5%	51.5%
At Large	1956	154,536	103,736	PROUTY, WINSTON L.*	50,797	ST. AMOUR, CAMILLE	3	52,939 R	67.1%	32.9%	67.1%	32.9%
At Large	1954	114,289	70,143	PROUTY, WINSTON L.*	44,141	BOYLAN, JOHN J.	5	26,002 R	61.4%	38.6%	61.4%	38.6%
At Large	1952	153,060	109,871	PROUTY, WINSTON L.*	43,187	COMINGS, HERBERT B.	2	66,684 R	71.8%	28.2%	71.8%	28.2%
At Large	1950	88,851	65,248	PROUTY, WINSTON L.	22,709	COMINGS, HERBERT B.	894	42,539 R	73.4%	25.6%	74.2%	25.8%
At Large	1948	121,968	74,076	PLUMLEY, CHARLES A.*	47,767	READY, ROBERT W.	125	26,309 R	60.7%	39.2%	60.8%	39.2%
At Large	1946	73,066	46,985	PLUMLEY, CHARLES A.*	26,056	CALDBECK, MATTHEW J.	25	20,929 R	64.3%	35.7%	64.3%	35.7%

Note: An asterisk (*) denotes incumbent. A pound sign (#) indicates that the winner was an independent (Bernard Sanders).

VERMONT

GENERAL AND PRIMARY ELECTIONS

2018 GENERAL ELECTIONS: OTHER VOTES

Governor Other vote was 3,266 Independent (Trevor Barlow), 2,287 Independent (Charles Laramie), 2,129 Independent (Cris Ericson), 1,855 Earth Rights (Stephen Marx), 1,839 Liberty Union (Emily Peyton), 1,115 Write-in (Write-in)

Senate Other vote was 3,665 Independent Non-Partisan (Brad Peacock), 2,763 Independent Non-Partisan (Russell Beste), 2,244 Independent Non-Partisan (Edward Gilbert), 1,979 Independent Non-Partisan (Folasade Adeluola), 1,171 Liberty Union (Reid Kane), 1,130 Independent Non-Partisan (Jon Svitavsky), 914 Independent Non-Partisan (Bruce Busa), 294 Write-in (Write-in)

House Other vote was:

At Large 9,110 Independent (Cris Ericson), 3,924 Liberty Union (Laura Potter), 165 Write-in (Write-in)

VERMONT

GENERAL AND PRIMARY ELECTIONS

2018 PRIMARY ELECTIONS: SUPPLEMENTARY INFORMATION

Primary August 14, 2018 **Registration** (as of August 14, 2018) 475,820 No Party Registration

Primary Type Open—Any registered voter could participate in the primary of any recognized party.

	REPUBLICAN PRIMARIES			DEMOCRATIC PRIMARIES		
Senator	Paige, H. Brooke	9,805	37.5%	Sanders, Bernard*	63,683	94.0%
	Zupan, Lawrence	9,383	35.9%	Adeluola, Folasade	3,766	5.6%
	Pannu, Jasdeep	4,527	17.3%	Write-in	281	0.4%
	Write-in	1,394	5.3%			
	De La Fuente, Roque "Rocky"	1,057	4.0%	(See note below)		
	TOTAL	*26,166*		*TOTAL*	*67,730*	
Governor	Scott, Phil*	24,142	66.7%	Hallquist, Christine	27,622	45.0%
	Stern, Keith M.	11,669	32.2%	Ehlers, James	12,668	20.6%
	Write-in	404	1.1%	Siegel, Brenda	12,262	20.0%
				Sonneborn, Ethan	4,696	7.6%
				Write-in	4,143	6.7%
	TOTAL	*36,215*		*TOTAL*	*61,391*	
Congressional At Large	Paige, H. Brooke	14,703	59.8%	Welch, Peter*	56,041	84.0%
	Tynio, Anya	8,481	34.5%	Freilich, Daniel	7,889	11.8%
	Write-in	1,393	5.7%	Mitchell, Benjamin	2,680	4.0%
				Write-in	134	0.2%
	TOTAL	*24,577*		*TOTAL*	*66,744*	

Note: An asterisk (*) denotes incumbent. After winning the Democratic primary, Bernard Sanders declined the party's nomination in order to run as an Independent.

VIRGINIA

Congressional districts first established for elections held in 2016
11 members

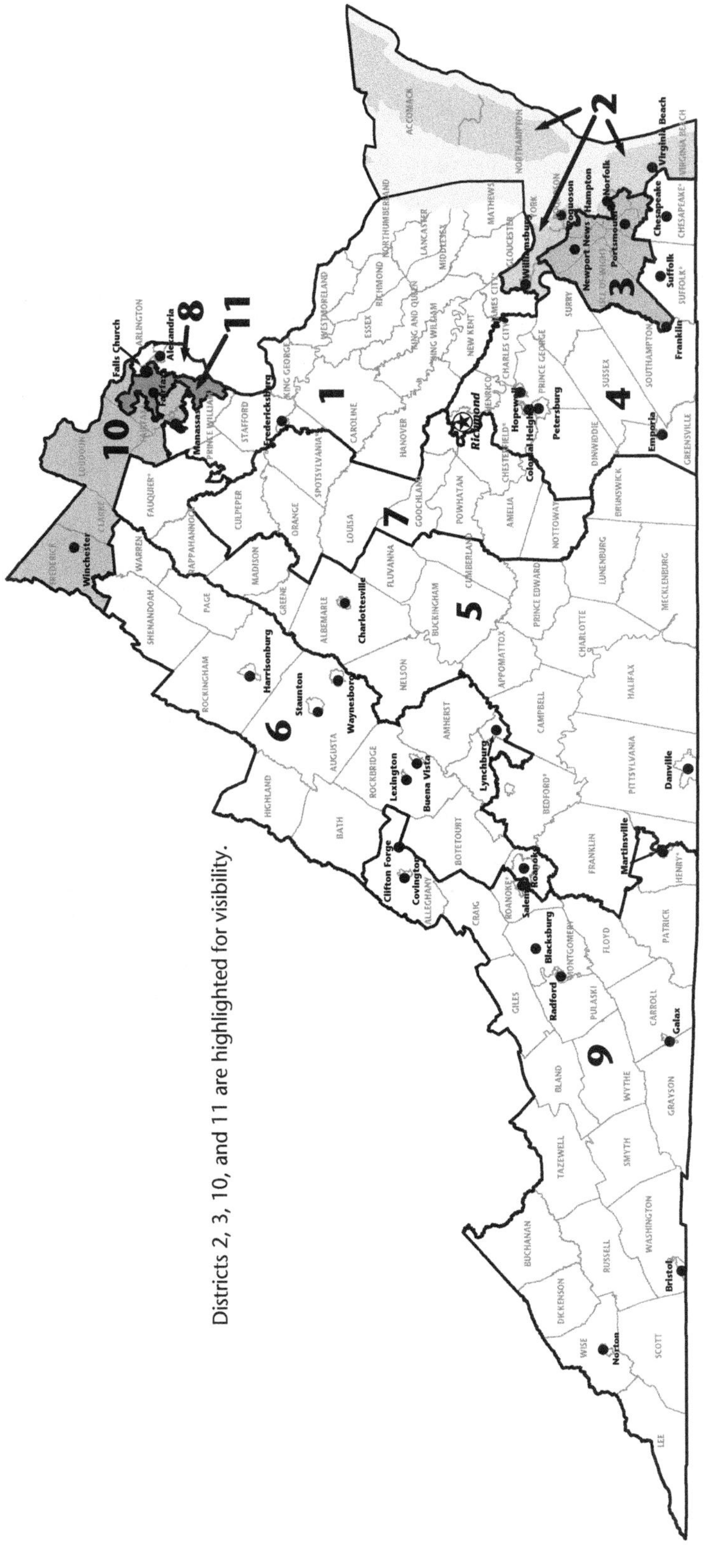

Districts 2, 3, 10, and 11 are highlighted for visibility.

Independent cities are treated as county equivalents; in most cases labels are included only for the city.
* Asterisk indicates a county whose boundaries include parts of two or more congressional districts.

VIRGINIA

GOVERNOR

Ralph S. Northam (D). Elected 2017 to a four-year term.

SENATORS (2 Democrats)

Tim Kaine (D). Re-elected 2018 to a six-year term. Previously elected 2012.

Mark R. Warner (D). Re-elected 2014 to a six-year term. Previously elected 2008.

REPRESENTATIVES (4 Republicans, 7 Democrats)

1. Robert J. "Rob" Wittman (R)
2. Elaine Luria (D)
3. Robert C. "Bobby" Scott (D)
4. Donald A. McEachin (D)
5. Denver Riggleman (R)
6. Benjamin Cline (R)
7. Abigail Spanberger (D)
8. Donald S. Beyer Jr. (D)
9. H. Morgan Griffith (R)
10. Jennifer Wexton (D)
11. Gerald E. "Gerry" Connolly (D)

POSTWAR VOTE FOR PRESIDENT

		Republican		Democratic				Percentage			
								Total Vote		Major Vote	
Year	Total Vote	Vote	Candidate	Vote	Candidate	Other Vote	Rep.-Dem. Plurality	Rep.	Dem.	Rep.	Dem.
2016**	3,982,752	1,769,443	Trump, Donald J.	1,981,473	Clinton, Hillary Rodham	231,836	212,030 D	44.4%	49.8%	47.2%	52.8%
2012	3,854,489	1,822,522	Romney, W. Mitt	1,971,820	Obama, Barack H.*	60,147	149,298 D	47.3%	51.2%	48.0%	52.0%
2008	3,723,260	1,725,005	McCain, John S. III	1,959,532	Obama, Barack H.	38,723	234,527 D	46.3%	52.6%	46.8%	53.2%
2004	3,198,367	1,716,959	Bush, George W.*	1,454,742	Kerry, John F.	26,666	262,217 R	53.7%	45.5%	54.1%	45.9%
2000**	2,739,447	1,437,490	Bush, George W.	1,217,290	Gore, Albert Jr.	84,667	220,200 R	52.5%	44.4%	54.1%	45.9%
1996**	2,416,642	1,138,350	Dole, Robert "Bob"	1,091,060	Clinton, Bill*	187,232	47,290 R	47.1%	45.1%	51.1%	48.9%
1992**	2,558,665	1,150,517	Bush, George H.*	1,038,650	Clinton, Bill	369,498	111,867 R	45.0%	40.6%	52.6%	47.4%
1988	2,191,609	1,309,162	Bush, George H.	859,799	Dukakis, Michael S.	22,648	449,363 R	59.7%	39.2%	60.4%	39.6%
1984	2,146,635	1,337,078	Reagan, Ronald*	796,250	Mondale, Walter F.	13,307	540,828 R	62.3%	37.1%	62.7%	37.3%
1980**	1,866,032	989,609	Reagan, Ronald	752,174	Carter, Jimmy*	124,249	237,435 R	53.0%	40.3%	56.8%	43.2%
1976	1,697,094	836,554	Ford, Gerald R.*	813,896	Carter, Jimmy	46,644	22,658 R	49.3%	48.0%	50.7%	49.3%
1972	1,457,019	988,493	Nixon, Richard M.*	438,887	McGovern, George S.	29,639	549,606 R	67.8%	30.1%	69.3%	30.7%
1968**	1,361,491	590,319	Nixon, Richard M.	442,387	Humphrey, Hubert Horatio Jr.	328,785	147,932 R	43.4%	32.5%	57.2%	42.8%
1964	1,042,267	481,334	Goldwater, Barry M. Sr.	558,038	Johnson, Lyndon B.*	2,895	76,704 D	46.2%	53.5%	46.3%	53.7%
1960	771,449	404,521	Nixon, Richard M.	362,327	Kennedy, John F.	4,601	42,194 R	52.4%	47.0%	52.8%	47.2%
1956	697,978	386,459	Eisenhower, Dwight D.*	267,760	Stevenson, Adlai E. II	43,759	118,699 R	55.4%	38.4%	59.1%	40.9%
1952	619,689	349,037	Eisenhower, Dwight D.	268,677	Stevenson, Adlai E. II	1,975	80,360 R	56.3%	43.4%	56.5%	43.5%
1948**	419,256	172,070	Dewey, Thomas E.	200,786	Truman, Harry S.*	46,400	28,716 D	41.0%	47.9%	46.1%	53.9%

Note: An asterisk (*) denotes incumbent. **In past elections, the other vote included: 2016 - 118,274 Libertarian (Gary Johnson); 2000 - 59,398 Green (Ralph Nader); 1996 - 159,861 Reform (Ross Perot); 1992 - 348,639 Independent (Perot); 1980 - 95,418 Independent (John Anderson); 1968 - 321,833 American Independent (George Wallace); 1948 - 43,393 States' Rights (Strom Thurmond).

VIRGINIA

POSTWAR VOTE FOR GOVERNOR

		Republican		Democratic				Percentage			
								Total Vote		Major Vote	
Year	Total Vote	Vote	Candidate	Vote	Candidate	Other Vote	Rep.-Dem. Plurality	Rep.	Dem.	Rep.	Dem.
2017	2,614,282	1,175,731	Gillespie, Edward W. "Ed"	1,409,175	Northam, Ralph S.	29,376	233,444 D	45.0%	53.9%	45.5%	54.5%
2013	2,241,071	1,013,354	Cuccinelli, Ken	1,069,789	McAuliffe, Terry R.	157,928	56,435 D	45.2%	47.7%	48.6%	51.4%
2009	1,985,103	1,163,651	McDonnell, Robert F.	818,950	Deeds, R. Creigh	2,502	344,701 R	58.6%	41.3%	58.7%	41.3%
2005	1,983,778	912,327	Kilgore, Jerry W.	1,025,942	Kaine, Tim	45,509	113,615 D	46.0%	51.7%	47.1%	52.9%
2001	1,886,721	887,234	Earley, Mark	984,177	Warner, Mark R.	15,310	96,943 D	47.0%	52.2%	47.4%	52.6%
1997	1,736,314	969,062	Gilmore, James S. III	738,971	Beyer, Donald S. Jr.	28,281	230,091 R	55.8%	42.6%	56.7%	43.3%
1993	1,793,916	1,045,319	Allen, George F.	733,527	Terry, Mary Sue	15,070	311,792 R	58.3%	40.9%	58.8%	41.2%
1989	1,789,078	890,195	Coleman, J. Marshall	896,936	Wilder, L. Douglas	1,947	6,741 D	49.8%	50.1%	49.8%	50.2%
1985	1,343,240	601,649	Durrette, Wyatt B.	741,438	Baliles, Gerald L.	153	139,789 D	44.8%	55.2%	44.8%	55.2%
1981	1,420,638	659,398	Coleman, J. Marshall	760,384	Robb, Charles S.	856	100,986 D	46.4%	53.5%	46.4%	53.6%
1977	1,250,940	699,302	Dalton, John N.	541,319	Howell, Henry	10,319	157,983 R	55.9%	43.3%	56.4%	43.6%
1973**	1,035,495	525,075	Godwin, Mills E. Jr.			510,420	525,075 R	50.7%		100.0%	
1969	915,764	480,869	Holton, Linwood	415,695	Battle, William C.	19,200	65,174 R	52.5%	45.4%	53.6%	46.4%
1965**	562,789	212,207	Holton, Linwood	269,526	Godwin, Mills E. Jr.	81,056	57,319 D	37.7%	47.9%	44.1%	55.9%
1961	394,490	142,567	Pearson, H. Clyde	251,861	Harrison, Albertis S. Jr.	62	109,294 D	36.1%	63.8%	36.1%	63.9%
1957	517,655	188,628	Dalton, Ted	326,921	Almond, J. Lindsay Jr.	2,106	138,293 D	36.4%	63.2%	36.6%	63.4%
1953	414,025	183,328	Dalton, Ted	226,998	Stanley, Thomas B.	3,699	43,670 D	44.3%	54.8%	44.7%	55.3%
1949	262,350	71,991	Johnson, Walter	184,772	Battle, John S.	5,587	112,781 D	27.4%	70.4%	28.0%	72.0%
1945	164,741	52,386	Landreth, S. Lloyd	112,355	Tuck, William M.		59,969 D	31.8%	68.2%	31.8%	68.2%

Note: An asterisk (*) denotes incumbent. **In past elections, the other vote included: 1973 - 510,103 Independent (Henry Howell); 1965 - 75,307 Conservative (William J. Story Jr.). The plurality is the difference between the Republican and Democratic vote. The Democratic Party did not run a candidate in the 1973 gubernatorial election. In past elections, the other vote included: 1973 - 510,103 Independent (Henry Howell), who finished second; 1965 - 75,307 Conservative (William J. Story Jr.). The Democratic Party did not run a candidate in the 1973 gubernatorial election.

POSTWAR VOTE FOR SENATOR

		Republican		Democratic				Percentage			
								Total Vote		Major Vote	
Year	Total Vote	Vote	Candidate	Vote	Candidate	Other Vote	Rep.-Dem. Plurality	Rep.	Dem.	Rep.	Dem.
2018	3,351,373	1,374,313	Stewart, Corey A.	1,910,370	Kaine, Tim*	66,690	536,057 D	41.0%	57.0%	41.8%	58.2%
2014	2,184,473	1,055,940	Gillespie, Edward W. "Ed"	1,073,667	Warner, Mark R.*	54,866	17,727 D	48.3%	49.1%	49.6%	50.4%
2012	3,802,196	1,785,542	Allen, George F.	2,010,067	Kaine, Tim	6,587	224,525 D	47.0%	52.9%	47.0%	53.0%
2008	3,643,294	1,228,830	Gilmore, James S. III	2,369,327	Warner, Mark R.	45,137	1,140,497 D	33.7%	65.0%	34.2%	65.8%
2006	2,370,445	1,166,277	Allen, George F.*	1,175,606	Webb, Jim H. Jr.	28,562	9,329 D	49.2%	49.6%	49.8%	50.2%
2002	1,489,422	1,229,894	Warner, John W.*			259,528	1,229,894 R	82.6%		100.0%	
2000	2,718,301	1,420,460	Allen, George F.	1,296,093	Robb, Charles S.*	1,748	124,367 R	52.3%	47.7%	52.3%	47.7%
1996	2,354,715	1,235,744	Warner, John W.*	1,115,982	Warner, Mark R.	2,989	119,762 R	52.5%	47.4%	52.5%	47.5%
1994**	2,057,463	882,213	North, Oliver L.	938,376	Robb, Charles S.*	236,874	56,163 D	42.9%	45.6%	48.5%	51.5%
1990**	1,083,660	876,782	Warner, John W.*			206,878	876,782 R	80.9%		100.0%	
1988	2,068,897	593,652	Dawkins, Maurice A.	1,474,086	Robb, Charles S.	1,159	880,434 D	28.7%	71.2%	28.7%	71.3%
1984	2,007,487	1,406,194	Warner, John W.*	601,142	Harrison, Edythe C.	151	805,052 R	70.0%	29.9%	70.1%	29.9%
1982	1,415,622	724,571	Trible, Paul	690,839	Davis, Richard	212	33,732 R	51.2%	48.8%	51.2%	48.8%
1978	1,222,256	613,232	Warner, John W.	608,511	Miller, Andrew P.	513	4,721 R	50.2%	49.8%	50.2%	49.8%
1976**	1,557,500			596,009	Zumwalt, Elmo R.	961,491	596,009 D#		38.3%		100.0%
1972	1,396,268	718,337	Scott, William L.	643,963	Spong, William B.*	33,968	74,374 R	51.4%	46.1%	52.7%	47.3%
1970**	946,751	145,031	Garland, Ray L.	295,057	Rawlings, George C.	506,663	150,026 D#	15.3%	31.2%	33.0%	67.0%
1966	733,879	245,681	Ould, James P. Jr.	429,855	Spong, William B.	58,343	184,174 D	33.5%	58.6%	36.4%	63.6%
1966S**	729,839	272,804	Traylor, Lawrence M.	389,028	Byrd, Harry Flood Jr.*	68,007	116,224 D	37.4%	53.3%	41.2%	58.8%
1964**	928,363	176,624	May, Richard A.	592,260	Byrd, Harry F.*	159,479	415,636 D	19.0%	63.8%	23.0%	77.0%
1960**	622,820			506,169	Robertson, A. Willis*	116,651	506,169 D		81.3%		100.0%
1958**	457,640			317,221	Byrd, Harry F.*	140,419	317,221 D		69.3%		100.0%
1954**	306,447			244,844	Robertson, A. Willis*	61,603	244,844 D		79.9%		100.0%
1952**	543,516			398,677	Byrd, Harry F.*	144,839	398,677 D		73.4%		100.0%
1948	386,998	119,366	Woods, Robert H.	253,865	Robertson, A. Willis*	13,767	134,499 D	30.8%	65.6%	32.0%	68.0%
1946	252,863	77,005	Parsons, Lester S.	163,960	Byrd, Harry F.*	11,898	86,955 D	30.5%	64.8%	32.0%	68.0%
1946S**	248,962	72,253	Woods, Robert H.	169,680	Robertson, A. Willis	7,029	97,427 D	29.0%	68.2%	29.9%	70.1%

Note: An asterisk (*) denotes incumbent. A pound sign (#) indicates that winner was an independent. **In past elections, the other vote included: 1994 - 235,324 Independent (J. Marshall Coleman); 1990 - 196,755 Independent (Nancy Spannaus), who finished second; 1976 - 890,778 Independent (Harry Flood Byrd Jr.), who won the election with 57.2 percent of the total vote and a plurality of 294,769 votes; 1970 - 506,633 Independent (Harry Flood Byrd Jr.), who won the election with 53.5 percent of the total vote and a plurality of 211,576 votes; 1964 - 95,526 Independent (James W. Respess); 1960 - 88,718 Independent Democrat (Stuart D. Baker), who finished second; 1958 - 120,224 Independent (Louis Wensel), who finished second; 1954 - 32,681 Independent Democrat (Charles William Lewis Jr.), who finished second; 1952 - 69,133 Independent Democrat (H. M. Vise Sr.), who finished second; 67,281 Social Democrat (Clarke T. Robb). One each of the 1946 and 1966 elections was for a short term to fill a vacancy. The Democratic Party did not run a candidate in the Senate elections of 1990 and 2002. The Republican Party did not run a candidate in the Senate elections of 1952, 1954, 1958, 1960, and 1976.

VIRGINIA

GOVERNOR 2017

2010 Census Population	County/City	Total Vote	Republican (Gillespie)	Democratic (Northam)	Other	Rep.-Dem. Plurality	Percentage Total Vote Rep.	Percentage Total Vote Dem.	Percentage Major Vote Rep.	Percentage Major Vote Dem.
33,164	ACCOMACK	10,666	5,736	4,876	54	860 R	53.8%	45.7%	54.1%	45.9%
98,970	ALBEMARLE	42,308	14,857	26,969	482	12,112 D	35.1%	63.7%	35.5%	64.5%
139,966	ALEXANDRIA	52,187	10,822	40,896	469	30,074 D	20.7%	78.4%	20.9%	79.1%
16,250	ALLEGHANY	4,403	2,888	1,478	37	1,410 R	65.6%	33.6%	66.1%	33.9%
12,690	AMELIA	4,614	3,170	1,403	41	1,767 R	68.7%	30.4%	69.3%	30.7%
32,353	AMHERST	10,144	6,431	3,616	97	2,815 R	63.4%	35.6%	64.0%	36.0%
14,973	APPOMATTOX	5,171	3,894	1,227	50	2,667 R	75.3%	23.7%	76.0%	24.0%
207,627	ARLINGTON	85,214	16,268	68,093	853	51,825 D	19.1%	79.9%	19.3%	80.7%
73,750	AUGUSTA	23,574	17,217	6,030	327	11,187 R	73.0%	25.6%	74.1%	25.9%
4,731	BATH	1,481	1,013	450	18	563 R	68.4%	30.4%	69.2%	30.8%
68,676	BEDFORD	27,807	20,573	6,985	249	13,588 R	74.0%	25.1%	74.7%	25.3%
6,824	BLAND	2,084	1,676	388	20	1,288 R	80.4%	18.6%	81.2%	18.8%
33,148	BOTETOURT	12,501	8,965	3,409	127	5,556 R	71.7%	27.3%	72.5%	27.5%
17,835	BRISTOL	4,294	3,006	1,242	46	1,764 R	70.0%	28.9%	70.8%	29.2%
17,434	BRUNSWICK	4,757	2,010	2,728	19	718 D	42.3%	57.3%	42.4%	57.6%
24,098	BUCHANAN	4,542	3,449	1,062	31	2,387 R	75.9%	23.4%	76.5%	23.5%
17,146	BUCKINGHAM	4,602	2,638	1,924	40	714 R	57.3%	41.8%	57.8%	42.2%
6,650	BUENA VISTA	1,655	1,090	529	36	561 R	65.9%	32.0%	67.3%	32.7%
54,842	CAMPBELL	17,372	12,791	4,415	166	8,376 R	73.6%	25.4%	74.3%	25.7%
28,545	CAROLINE	8,360	4,135	4,126	99	9 R	49.5%	49.4%	50.1%	49.9%
30,042	CARROLL	8,275	6,363	1,838	74	4,525 R	76.9%	22.2%	77.6%	22.4%
7,256	CHARLES CITY	2,716	1,000	1,699	17	699 D	36.8%	62.6%	37.1%	62.9%
12,586	CHARLOTTE	4,014	2,559	1,419	36	1,140 R	63.8%	35.4%	64.3%	35.7%
43,475	CHARLOTTESVILLE	16,445	2,315	13,943	187	11,628 D	14.1%	84.8%	14.2%	85.8%
222,209	CHESAPEAKE	72,444	33,108	38,459	877	5,351 D	45.7%	53.1%	46.3%	53.7%
316,236	CHESTERFIELD	118,663	58,297	58,991	1,375	694 D	49.1%	49.7%	49.7%	50.3%
14,034	CLARKE	5,572	3,102	2,400	70	702 R	55.7%	43.1%	56.4%	43.6%
17,411	COLONIAL HEIGHTS	5,164	3,710	1,389	65	2,321 R	71.8%	26.9%	72.8%	27.2%
5,961	COVINGTON	1,342	784	545	13	239 R	58.4%	40.6%	59.0%	41.0%
5,190	CRAIG	1,841	1,398	413	30	985 R	75.9%	22.4%	77.2%	22.8%
46,689	CULPEPER	13,583	8,423	4,990	170	3,433 R	62.0%	36.7%	62.8%	37.2%
10,052	CUMBERLAND	3,135	1,810	1,292	33	518 R	57.7%	41.2%	58.3%	41.7%
43,055	DANVILLE	11,027	4,664	6,304	59	1,640 D	42.3%	57.2%	42.5%	57.5%
15,903	DICKENSON	3,444	2,458	959	27	1,499 R	71.4%	27.8%	71.9%	28.1%
28,001	DINWIDDIE	8,335	4,565	3,712	58	853 R	54.8%	44.5%	55.2%	44.8%
5,927	EMPORIA	1,633	702	909	22	207 D	43.0%	55.7%	43.6%	56.4%
11,151	ESSEX	3,723	1,963	1,730	30	233 R	52.7%	46.5%	53.2%	46.8%
1,081,726	FAIRFAX	376,004	117,141	255,200	3,663	138,059 D	31.2%	67.9%	31.5%	68.5%
22,565	FAIRFAX CITY	8,300	2,822	5,380	98	2,558 D	34.0%	64.8%	34.4%	65.6%
12,332	FALLS CHURCH	6,054	1,195	4,781	78	3,586 D	19.7%	79.0%	20.0%	80.0%
65,203	FAUQUIER	24,039	14,332	9,430	277	4,902 R	59.6%	39.2%	60.3%	39.7%
15,279	FLOYD	5,491	3,468	1,946	77	1,522 R	63.2%	35.4%	64.1%	35.9%
25,691	FLUVANNA	9,225	4,864	4,267	94	597 R	52.7%	46.3%	53.3%	46.7%
56,159	FRANKLIN	17,588	12,062	5,315	211	6,747 R	68.6%	30.2%	69.4%	30.6%
8,582	FRANKLIN CITY	2,556	1,002	1,539	15	537 D	39.2%	60.2%	39.4%	60.6%
78,305	FREDERICK	24,315	15,656	8,363	296	7,293 R	64.4%	34.4%	65.2%	34.8%
24,286	FREDERICKSBURG	7,221	2,463	4,649	109	2,186 D	34.1%	64.4%	34.6%	65.4%
7,042	GALAX	1,355	930	409	16	521 R	68.6%	30.2%	69.5%	30.5%
17,286	GILES	5,834	4,161	1,604	69	2,557 R	71.3%	27.5%	72.2%	27.8%
36,858	GLOUCESTER	12,659	8,159	4,356	144	3,803 R	64.5%	34.4%	65.2%	34.8%
21,717	GOOCHLAND	10,541	6,520	3,911	110	2,609 R	61.9%	37.1%	62.5%	37.5%
15,533	GRAYSON	4,537	3,478	1,029	30	2,449 R	76.7%	22.7%	77.2%	22.8%
18,403	GREENE	6,309	4,000	2,219	90	1,781 R	63.4%	35.2%	64.3%	35.7%
12,243	GREENSVILLE	2,893	1,232	1,643	18	411 D	42.6%	56.8%	42.9%	57.1%
36,241	HALIFAX	10,414	6,291	4,037	86	2,254 R	60.4%	38.8%	60.9%	39.1%
137,436	HAMPTON	40,378	11,050	28,906	422	17,856 D	27.4%	71.6%	27.7%	72.3%
99,863	HANOVER	43,149	27,779	14,755	615	13,024 R	64.4%	34.2%	65.3%	34.7%
48,914	HARRISONBURG	10,312	3,596	6,555	161	2,959 D	34.9%	63.6%	35.4%	64.6%
306,935	HENRICO	115,036	43,747	69,969	1,320	26,222 D	38.0%	60.8%	38.5%	61.5%
54,151	HENRY	14,057	9,046	4,895	116	4,151 R	64.4%	34.8%	64.9%	35.1%

VIRGINIA

GOVERNOR 2017

2010 Census Population	County/City	Total Vote	Republican (Gillespie)	Democratic (Northam)	Other	Rep.-Dem. Plurality	Percentage Total Vote Rep.	Percentage Total Vote Dem.	Percentage Major Vote Rep.	Percentage Major Vote Dem.
2,321	HIGHLAND	1,034	699	317	18	382 R	67.6%	30.7%	68.8%	31.2%
22,591	HOPEWELL	5,456	2,641	2,728	87	87 D	48.4%	50.0%	49.2%	50.8%
35,270	ISLE OF WIGHT	14,123	8,039	5,957	127	2,082 R	56.9%	42.2%	57.4%	42.6%
67,009	JAMES CITY	31,801	15,937	15,561	303	376 R	50.1%	48.9%	50.6%	49.4%
6,945	KING AND QUEEN	2,471	1,404	1,039	28	365 R	56.8%	42.0%	57.5%	42.5%
23,584	KING GEORGE	7,149	4,396	2,658	95	1,738 R	61.5%	37.2%	62.3%	37.7%
15,935	KING WILLIAM	5,975	3,889	2,017	69	1,872 R	65.1%	33.8%	65.8%	34.2%
11,391	LANCASTER	4,808	2,680	2,098	30	582 R	55.7%	43.6%	56.1%	43.9%
25,587	LEE	6,678	5,289	1,304	85	3,985 R	79.2%	19.5%	80.2%	19.8%
7,042	LEXINGTON	1,747	572	1,161	14	589 D	32.7%	66.5%	33.0%	67.0%
312,311	LOUDOUN	117,477	46,396	69,778	1,303	23,382 D	39.5%	59.4%	39.9%	60.1%
33,153	LOUISA	11,803	7,153	4,481	169	2,672 R	60.6%	38.0%	61.5%	38.5%
12,914	LUNENBURG	3,649	2,158	1,468	23	690 R	59.1%	40.2%	59.5%	40.5%
75,568	LYNCHBURG	21,306	10,959	10,047	300	912 R	51.4%	47.2%	52.2%	47.8%
13,308	MADISON	4,931	3,082	1,789	60	1,293 R	62.5%	36.3%	63.3%	36.7%
37,821	MANASSAS	9,312	3,899	5,295	118	1,396 D	41.9%	56.9%	42.4%	57.6%
14,273	MANASSAS PARK	3,076	1,064	1,958	54	894 D	34.6%	63.7%	35.2%	64.8%
13,821	MARTINSVILLE	3,735	1,489	2,187	59	698 D	39.9%	58.6%	40.5%	59.5%
8,978	MATHEWS	3,950	2,531	1,386	33	1,145 R	64.1%	35.1%	64.6%	35.4%
32,727	MECKLENBURG	8,561	5,125	3,399	37	1,726 R	59.9%	39.7%	60.1%	39.9%
10,959	MIDDLESEX	4,320	2,673	1,606	41	1,067 R	61.9%	37.2%	62.5%	37.5%
94,392	MONTGOMERY	28,133	12,500	15,115	518	2,615 D	44.4%	53.7%	45.3%	54.7%
15,020	NELSON	6,172	3,019	3,014	139	5 R	48.9%	48.8%	50.0%	50.0%
18,429	NEW KENT	8,551	5,711	2,729	111	2,982 R	66.8%	31.9%	67.7%	32.3%
180,719	NEWPORT NEWS	46,960	15,986	30,367	607	14,381 D	34.0%	64.7%	34.5%	65.5%
242,803	NORFOLK CITY	53,653	13,490	39,453	710	25,963 D	25.1%	73.5%	25.5%	74.5%
12,389	NORTHAMPTON	4,378	1,855	2,492	31	637 D	42.4%	56.9%	42.7%	57.3%
12,330	NORTHUMBERLAND	5,345	3,285	2,022	38	1,263 R	61.5%	37.8%	61.9%	38.1%
3,958	NORTON	860	561	287	12	274 R	65.2%	33.4%	66.2%	33.8%
15,853	NOTTOWAY	4,250	2,408	1,812	30	596 R	56.7%	42.6%	57.1%	42.9%
33,481	ORANGE	10,915	6,653	4,160	102	2,493 R	61.0%	38.1%	61.5%	38.5%
24,042	PAGE	6,726	4,850	1,809	67	3,041 R	72.1%	26.9%	72.8%	27.2%
18,490	PATRICK	5,633	4,320	1,259	54	3,061 R	76.7%	22.4%	77.4%	22.6%
32,420	PETERSBURG	8,167	938	7,164	65	6,226 D	11.5%	87.7%	11.6%	88.4%
63,506	PITTSYLVANIA	19,573	13,701	5,759	113	7,942 R	70.0%	29.4%	70.4%	29.6%
12,150	POQUOSON	4,830	3,473	1,298	59	2,175 R	71.9%	26.9%	72.8%	27.2%
95,535	PORTSMOUTH	28,710	8,167	20,156	387	11,989 D	28.4%	70.2%	28.8%	71.2%
28,046	POWHATAN	11,505	8,256	3,109	140	5,147 R	71.8%	27.0%	72.6%	27.4%
23,368	PRINCE EDWARD	5,654	2,708	2,881	65	173 D	47.9%	51.0%	48.5%	51.5%
35,725	PRINCE GEORGE	10,305	6,044	4,150	111	1,894 R	58.7%	40.3%	59.3%	40.7%
402,002	PRINCE WILLIAM	122,714	46,454	74,932	1,328	28,478 D	37.9%	61.1%	38.3%	61.7%
34,872	PULASKI	11,778	8,081	3,533	164	4,548 R	68.6%	30.0%	69.6%	30.4%
16,408	RADFORD	3,940	1,707	2,163	70	456 D	43.3%	54.9%	44.1%	55.9%
7,373	RAPPAHANNOCK	3,287	1,772	1,488	27	284 R	53.9%	45.3%	54.4%	45.6%
9,254	RICHMOND	2,371	1,479	876	16	603 R	62.4%	36.9%	62.8%	37.2%
204,214	RICHMOND CITY	71,258	12,262	58,047	949	45,785 D	17.2%	81.5%	17.4%	82.6%
92,376	ROANOKE	33,722	20,648	12,650	424	7,998 R	61.2%	37.5%	62.0%	38.0%
97,032	ROANOKE CITY	24,344	8,890	15,099	355	6,209 D	36.5%	62.0%	37.1%	62.9%
22,307	ROCKBRIDGE	7,933	4,873	2,974	86	1,899 R	61.4%	37.5%	62.1%	37.9%
76,314	ROCKINGHAM	25,270	17,880	7,061	329	10,819 R	70.8%	27.9%	71.7%	28.3%
28,897	RUSSELL	6,711	5,144	1,506	61	3,638 R	76.7%	22.4%	77.4%	22.6%
24,802	SALEM	8,196	4,946	3,134	116	1,812 R	60.3%	38.2%	61.2%	38.8%
23,177	SCOTT	6,139	4,997	1,089	53	3,908 R	81.4%	17.7%	82.1%	17.9%
41,993	SHENANDOAH	13,314	9,220	3,932	162	5,288 R	69.3%	29.5%	70.1%	29.9%
32,208	SMYTH	7,939	6,107	1,747	85	4,360 R	76.9%	22.0%	77.8%	22.2%
18,570	SOUTHAMPTON	6,155	3,564	2,529	62	1,035 R	57.9%	41.1%	58.5%	41.5%
122,397	SPOTSYLVANIA	36,798	20,481	15,869	448	4,612 R	55.7%	43.1%	56.3%	43.7%
128,961	STAFFORD	40,644	21,123	19,011	510	2,112 R	52.0%	46.8%	52.6%	47.4%
23,746	STAUNTON	7,589	3,406	4,047	136	641 D	44.9%	53.3%	45.7%	54.3%
84,585	SUFFOLK	28,532	11,623	16,621	288	4,998 D	40.7%	58.3%	41.2%	58.8%

VIRGINIA

GOVERNOR 2017

2010 Census Population	County/City	Total Vote	Republican (Gillespie)	Democratic (Northam)	Other	Rep.-Dem. Plurality	Percentage Total Vote Rep.	Total Vote Dem.	Major Vote Rep.	Major Vote Dem.
7,058	SURRY	2,959	1,268	1,658	33	390 D	42.9%	56.0%	43.3%	56.7%
12,087	SUSSEX	3,284	1,429	1,829	26	400 D	43.5%	55.7%	43.9%	56.1%
45,078	TAZEWELL	10,093	8,373	1,657	63	6,716 R	83.0%	16.4%	83.5%	16.5%
437,994	VIRGINIA BEACH	128,120	60,073	66,442	1,605	6,369 D	46.9%	51.9%	47.5%	52.5%
37,575	WARREN	10,373	6,711	3,531	131	3,180 R	64.7%	34.0%	65.5%	34.5%
54,876	WASHINGTON	16,404	12,247	4,003	154	8,244 R	74.7%	24.4%	75.4%	24.6%
21,006	WAYNESBORO	5,895	3,144	2,653	98	491 R	53.3%	45.0%	54.2%	45.8%
17,454	WESTMORELAND	5,360	2,865	2,442	53	423 R	53.5%	45.6%	54.0%	46.0%
14,068	WILLIAMSBURG	5,273	1,492	3,725	56	2,233 D	28.3%	70.6%	28.6%	71.4%
26,203	WINCHESTER	6,648	2,969	3,569	110	600 D	44.7%	53.7%	45.4%	54.6%
41,452	WISE	8,628	6,630	1,910	88	4,720 R	76.8%	22.1%	77.6%	22.4%
29,235	WYTHE	8,511	6,321	2,114	76	4,207 R	74.3%	24.8%	74.9%	25.1%
65,464	YORK	23,059	12,708	10,068	283	2,640 R	55.1%	43.7%	55.8%	44.2%
7,994,802	*TOTAL*	*2,614,282*	*1,175,731*	*1,409,175*	*29,376*	*233,444 D*	*45.0%*	*53.9%*	*45.5%*	*54.5%*

VIRGINIA

SENATOR 2018

2010 Census Population	County/City	Total Vote	Republican (Stewart)	Democratic (Kaine)	Other	Rep.-Dem. Plurality	Percentage Total Vote Rep.	Total Vote Dem.	Major Vote Rep.	Major Vote Dem.
33,164	ACCOMACK	12,745	6,605	5,997	143	608 R	51.8%	47.1%	52.4%	47.6%
98,970	ALBEMARLE	53,326	16,371	35,701	1,254	19,330 D	30.7%	66.9%	31.4%	68.6%
16,250	ALLEGHANY	5,453	3,433	1,952	68	1,481 R	63.0%	35.8%	63.8%	36.2%
12,690	AMELIA	5,849	3,823	1,938	88	1,885 R	65.4%	33.1%	66.4%	33.6%
32,353	AMHERST	12,545	7,779	4,541	225	3,238 R	62.0%	36.2%	63.1%	36.9%
14,973	APPOMATTOX	6,681	4,751	1,828	102	2,923 R	71.1%	27.4%	72.2%	27.8%
207,627	ARLINGTON	106,910	16,495	87,258	3,157	70,763 D	15.4%	81.6%	15.9%	84.1%
73,750	AUGUSTA	29,807	20,796	8,427	584	12,369 R	69.8%	28.3%	71.2%	28.8%
4,731	BATH	1,742	1,142	576	24	566 R	65.6%	33.1%	66.5%	33.5%
68,676	BEDFORD	35,548	25,301	9,632	615	15,669 R	71.2%	27.1%	72.4%	27.6%
6,824	BLAND	2,453	1,916	504	33	1,412 R	78.1%	20.5%	79.2%	20.8%
33,148	BOTETOURT	15,521	10,720	4,543	258	6,177 R	69.1%	29.3%	70.2%	29.8%
17,434	BRUNSWICK	6,156	2,394	3,717	45	1,323 D	38.9%	60.4%	39.2%	60.8%
24,098	BUCHANAN	5,933	4,095	1,785	53	2,310 R	69.0%	30.1%	69.6%	30.4%
17,146	BUCKINGHAM	6,138	3,249	2,802	87	447 R	52.9%	45.7%	53.7%	46.3%
54,842	CAMPBELL	21,979	15,239	6,305	435	8,934 R	69.3%	28.7%	70.7%	29.3%
28,545	CAROLINE	11,353	5,323	5,838	192	515 D	46.9%	51.4%	47.7%	52.3%
30,042	CARROLL	10,620	8,042	2,459	119	5,583 R	75.7%	23.2%	76.6%	23.4%
7,256	CHARLES CITY	3,337	1,168	2,131	38	963 D	35.0%	63.9%	35.4%	64.6%
12,586	CHARLOTTE	4,719	2,792	1,871	56	921 R	59.2%	39.6%	59.9%	40.1%
316,236	CHESTERFIELD	153,797	67,835	83,091	2,871	15,256 D	44.1%	54.0%	44.9%	55.1%
14,034	CLARKE	7,186	3,845	3,210	131	635 R	53.5%	44.7%	54.5%	45.5%
5,190	CRAIG	2,193	1,615	544	34	1,071 R	73.6%	24.8%	74.8%	25.2%
46,689	CULPEPER	19,400	10,913	8,093	394	2,820 R	56.3%	41.7%	57.4%	42.6%
10,052	CUMBERLAND	4,194	2,270	1,849	75	421 R	54.1%	44.1%	55.1%	44.9%
15,903	DICKENSON	4,475	2,926	1,524	25	1,402 R	65.4%	34.1%	65.8%	34.2%
28,001	DINWIDDIE	10,576	5,626	4,865	85	761 R	53.2%	46.0%	53.6%	46.4%
11,151	ESSEX	4,418	2,115	2,266	37	151 D	47.9%	51.3%	48.3%	51.7%
1,081,726	FAIRFAX	480,485	129,095	340,740	10,650	211,645 D	26.9%	70.9%	27.5%	72.5%
65,203	FAUQUIER	32,214	17,801	13,735	678	4,066 R	55.3%	42.6%	56.4%	43.6%

VIRGINIA

SENATOR 2018

2010 Census Population	County/City	Total Vote	Republican (Stewart)	Democratic (Kaine)	Other	Rep.-Dem. Plurality	Percentage Total Vote Rep.	Total Vote Dem.	Major Vote Rep.	Major Vote Dem.
15,279	FLOYD	6,746	4,180	2,480	86	1,700 R	62.0%	36.8%	62.8%	37.2%
25,691	FLUVANNA	12,001	5,793	5,981	227	188 D	48.3%	49.8%	49.2%	50.8%
56,159	FRANKLIN	22,181	14,849	6,995	337	7,854 R	66.9%	31.5%	68.0%	32.0%
78,305	FREDERICK	34,213	20,640	12,885	688	7,755 R	60.3%	37.7%	61.6%	38.4%
17,286	GILES	6,638	4,500	2,036	102	2,464 R	67.8%	30.7%	68.8%	31.2%
36,858	GLOUCESTER	15,637	9,816	5,529	292	4,287 R	62.8%	35.4%	64.0%	36.0%
21,717	GOOCHLAND	13,225	7,472	5,443	310	2,029 R	56.5%	41.2%	57.9%	42.1%
15,533	GRAYSON	5,733	4,249	1,412	72	2,837 R	74.1%	24.6%	75.1%	24.9%
18,403	GREENE	8,130	4,749	3,183	198	1,566 R	58.4%	39.2%	59.9%	40.1%
12,243	GREENSVILLE	3,491	1,363	2,109	19	746 D	39.0%	60.4%	39.3%	60.7%
36,241	HALIFAX	13,686	7,691	5,869	126	1,822 R	56.2%	42.9%	56.7%	43.3%
99,863	HANOVER	53,722	32,333	20,228	1,161	12,105 R	60.2%	37.7%	61.5%	38.5%
306,935	HENRICO	145,518	47,786	94,826	2,906	47,040 D	32.8%	65.2%	33.5%	66.5%
54,151	HENRY	18,728	11,471	7,061	196	4,410 R	61.3%	37.7%	61.9%	38.1%
2,321	HIGHLAND	1,184	772	400	12	372 R	65.2%	33.8%	65.9%	34.1%
35,270	ISLE OF WIGHT	16,809	9,171	7,357	281	1,814 R	54.6%	43.8%	55.5%	44.5%
67,009	JAMES CITY	38,818	17,955	20,146	717	2,191 D	46.3%	51.9%	47.1%	52.9%
6,945	KING AND QUEEN	2,972	1,615	1,318	39	297 R	54.3%	44.3%	55.1%	44.9%
23,584	KING GEORGE	9,747	5,546	3,976	225	1,570 R	56.9%	40.8%	58.2%	41.8%
15,935	KING WILLIAM	7,510	4,707	2,675	128	2,032 R	62.7%	35.6%	63.8%	36.2%
11,391	LANCASTER	5,706	2,947	2,683	76	264 R	51.6%	47.0%	52.3%	47.7%
25,587	LEE	6,821	5,096	1,671	54	3,425 R	74.7%	24.5%	75.3%	24.7%
312,311	LOUDOUN	168,008	58,369	106,064	3,575	47,695 D	34.7%	63.1%	35.5%	64.5%
33,153	LOUISA	15,428	8,790	6,384	254	2,406 R	57.0%	41.4%	57.9%	42.1%
12,914	LUNENBURG	4,475	2,480	1,943	52	537 R	55.4%	43.4%	56.1%	43.9%
13,308	MADISON	6,029	3,655	2,273	101	1,382 R	60.6%	37.7%	61.7%	38.3%
8,978	MATHEWS	4,416	2,791	1,566	59	1,225 R	63.2%	35.5%	64.1%	35.9%
32,727	MECKLENBURG	11,805	6,533	5,149	123	1,384 R	55.3%	43.6%	55.9%	44.1%
10,959	MIDDLESEX	5,130	3,014	2,031	85	983 R	58.8%	39.6%	59.7%	40.3%
94,392	MONTGOMERY	35,508	14,382	20,109	1,017	5,727 D	40.5%	56.6%	41.7%	58.3%
15,020	NELSON	7,378	3,417	3,808	153	391 D	46.3%	51.6%	47.3%	52.7%
18,429	NEW KENT	10,683	6,774	3,736	173	3,038 R	63.4%	35.0%	64.5%	35.5%
12,389	NORTHAMPTON	5,113	2,124	2,924	65	800 D	41.5%	57.2%	42.1%	57.9%
12,330	NORTHUMBERLAND	6,269	3,567	2,631	71	936 R	56.9%	42.0%	57.6%	42.4%
15,853	NOTTOWAY	5,305	2,775	2,466	64	309 R	52.3%	46.5%	52.9%	47.1%
33,481	ORANGE	14,952	8,577	6,148	227	2,429 R	57.4%	41.1%	58.2%	41.8%
24,042	PAGE	8,295	5,825	2,356	114	3,469 R	70.2%	28.4%	71.2%	28.8%
18,490	PATRICK	6,689	4,999	1,633	57	3,366 R	74.7%	24.4%	75.4%	24.6%
63,506	PITTSYLVANIA	25,306	16,923	8,105	278	8,818 R	66.9%	32.0%	67.6%	32.4%
28,046	POWHATAN	14,968	10,254	4,384	330	5,870 R	68.5%	29.3%	70.1%	29.9%
23,368	PRINCE EDWARD	7,073	3,064	3,893	116	829 D	43.3%	55.0%	44.0%	56.0%
35,725	PRINCE GEORGE	12,627	7,004	5,475	148	1,529 R	55.5%	43.4%	56.1%	43.9%
402,002	PRINCE WILLIAM	163,846	54,040	106,449	3,357	52,409 D	33.0%	65.0%	33.7%	66.3%
34,872	PULASKI	12,078	7,835	4,063	180	3,772 R	64.9%	33.6%	65.9%	34.1%
7,373	RAPPAHANNOCK	3,883	1,984	1,845	54	139 R	51.1%	47.5%	51.8%	48.2%
9,254	RICHMOND	2,899	1,683	1,191	25	492 R	58.1%	41.1%	58.6%	41.4%
92,376	ROANOKE	41,966	24,194	17,012	760	7,182 R	57.7%	40.5%	58.7%	41.3%
22,307	ROCKBRIDGE	9,349	5,622	3,584	143	2,038 R	60.1%	38.3%	61.1%	38.9%
76,314	ROCKINGHAM	31,645	21,151	9,811	683	11,340 R	66.8%	31.0%	68.3%	31.7%
28,897	RUSSELL	8,951	6,379	2,471	101	3,908 R	71.3%	27.6%	72.1%	27.9%
23,177	SCOTT	7,522	5,824	1,627	71	4,197 R	77.4%	21.6%	78.2%	21.8%
41,993	SHENANDOAH	16,483	10,836	5,362	285	5,474 R	65.7%	32.5%	66.9%	33.1%
32,208	SMYTH	9,668	6,864	2,683	121	4,181 R	71.0%	27.8%	71.9%	28.1%
18,570	SOUTHAMPTON	6,989	3,869	3,047	73	822 R	55.4%	43.6%	55.9%	44.1%
122,397	SPOTSYLVANIA	51,974	26,466	24,554	954	1,912 R	50.9%	47.2%	51.9%	48.1%
128,961	STAFFORD	56,049	26,368	28,536	1,145	2,168 D	47.0%	50.9%	48.0%	52.0%
7,058	SURRY	3,475	1,436	1,997	42	561 D	41.3%	57.5%	41.8%	58.2%
12,087	SUSSEX	3,888	1,598	2,258	32	660 D	41.1%	58.1%	41.4%	58.6%
45,078	TAZEWELL	13,371	10,428	2,809	134	7,619 R	78.0%	21.0%	78.8%	21.2%
37,575	WARREN	14,259	8,875	5,060	324	3,815 R	62.2%	35.5%	63.7%	36.3%

VIRGINIA

SENATOR 2018

2010 Census Population	County/City	Total Vote	Republican (Stewart)	Democratic (Kaine)	Other	Rep.-Dem. Plurality	Percentage Total Vote Rep.	Total Vote Dem.	Major Vote Rep.	Major Vote Dem.
54,876	WASHINGTON	20,457	14,350	5,825	282	8,525 R	70.1%	28.5%	71.1%	28.9%
17,454	WESTMORELAND	6,949	3,421	3,448	80	27 D	49.2%	49.6%	49.8%	50.2%
41,452	WISE	10,955	7,991	2,860	104	5,131 R	72.9%	26.1%	73.6%	26.4%
29,235	WYTHE	10,712	7,669	2,879	164	4,790 R	71.6%	26.9%	72.7%	27.3%
65,464	YORK	29,033	14,828	13,634	571	1,194 R	51.1%	47.0%	52.1%	47.9%
	Independent Cities									
139,966	ALEXANDRIA	65,811	10,734	53,307	1,770	42,573 D	16.3%	81.0%	16.8%	83.2%
17,835	BRISTOL	5,271	3,427	1,770	74	1,657 R	65.0%	33.6%	65.9%	34.1%
6,650	BUENA VISTA	1,754	1,047	666	41	381 R	59.7%	38.0%	61.1%	38.9%
43,475	CHARLOTTESVILLE	20,485	2,346	17,641	498	15,295 D	11.5%	86.1%	11.7%	88.3%
222,209	CHESAPEAKE	90,732	39,632	49,506	1,594	9,874 D	43.7%	54.6%	44.5%	55.5%
17,411	COLONIAL HEIGHTS	6,415	4,183	2,105	127	2,078 R	65.2%	32.8%	66.5%	33.5%
5,961	COVINGTON	1,776	957	785	34	172 R	53.9%	44.2%	54.9%	45.1%
43,055	DANVILLE	15,114	5,518	9,418	178	3,900 D	36.5%	62.3%	36.9%	63.1%
5,927	EMPORIA	1,790	608	1,163	19	555 D	34.0%	65.0%	34.3%	65.7%
22,565	FAIRFAX CITY	10,589	2,988	7,330	271	4,342 D	28.2%	69.2%	29.0%	71.0%
12,332	FALLS CHURCH	7,189	1,112	5,902	175	4,790 D	15.5%	82.1%	15.9%	84.1%
8,582	FRANKLIN CITY	2,991	1,065	1,894	32	829 D	35.6%	63.3%	36.0%	64.0%
24,286	FREDERICKSBURG	9,710	2,832	6,621	257	3,789 D	29.2%	68.2%	30.0%	70.0%
7,042	GALAX	1,830	1,198	620	12	578 R	65.5%	33.9%	65.9%	34.1%
137,436	HAMPTON	50,488	12,696	37,078	714	24,382 D	25.1%	73.4%	25.5%	74.5%
48,914	HARRISONBURG	13,724	4,056	9,234	434	5,178 D	29.6%	67.3%	30.5%	69.5%
22,591	HOPEWELL	6,884	2,894	3,878	112	984 D	42.0%	56.3%	42.7%	57.3%
7,042	LEXINGTON	2,120	569	1,511	40	942 D	26.8%	71.3%	27.4%	72.6%
75,568	LYNCHBURG	26,845	12,238	13,582	1,025	1,344 D	45.6%	50.6%	47.4%	52.6%
37,821	MANASSAS	12,929	4,496	8,130	303	3,634 D	34.8%	62.9%	35.6%	64.4%
14,273	MANASSAS PARK	4,385	1,260	3,032	93	1,772 D	28.7%	69.1%	29.4%	70.6%
13,821	MARTINSVILLE	4,544	1,566	2,889	89	1,323 D	34.5%	63.6%	35.2%	64.8%
180,719	NEWPORT NEWS	58,321	17,891	39,398	1,032	21,507 D	30.7%	67.6%	31.2%	68.8%
242,803	NORFOLK CITY	67,493	15,603	50,565	1,325	34,962 D	23.1%	74.9%	23.6%	76.4%
3,958	NORTON	1,099	672	408	19	264 R	61.1%	37.1%	62.2%	37.8%
32,420	PETERSBURG	10,243	989	9,170	84	8,181 D	9.7%	89.5%	9.7%	90.3%
12,150	POQUOSON	5,995	4,105	1,737	153	2,368 R	68.5%	29.0%	70.3%	29.7%
95,535	PORTSMOUTH	33,155	8,601	23,985	569	15,384 D	25.9%	72.3%	26.4%	73.6%
16,408	RADFORD	5,078	1,958	2,979	141	1,021 D	38.6%	58.7%	39.7%	60.3%
204,214	RICHMOND CITY	89,273	11,962	75,485	1,826	63,523 D	13.4%	84.6%	13.7%	86.3%
97,032	ROANOKE CITY	31,282	10,509	20,149	624	9,640 D	33.6%	64.4%	34.3%	65.7%
24,802	SALEM	9,883	5,571	4,116	196	1,455 R	56.4%	41.6%	57.5%	42.5%
23,746	STAUNTON	9,599	3,937	5,417	245	1,480 D	41.0%	56.4%	42.1%	57.9%
84,585	SUFFOLK	35,292	13,397	21,397	498	8,000 D	38.0%	60.6%	38.5%	61.5%
437,994	VIRGINIA BEACH	169,415	73,575	91,813	4,027	18,238 D	43.4%	54.2%	44.5%	55.5%
21,006	WAYNESBORO	7,718	3,713	3,849	156	136 D	48.1%	49.9%	49.1%	50.9%
14,068	WILLIAMSBURG	6,200	1,547	4,530	123	2,983 D	25.0%	73.1%	25.5%	74.5%
26,203	WINCHESTER	9,124	3,657	5,242	225	1,585 D	40.1%	57.5%	41.1%	58.9%
	TOTAL	*3,351,373*	*1,374,313*	*1,910,370*	*66,690*	*536,057 D*	*41.0%*	*57.0%*	*41.8%*	*58.2%*

VIRGINIA

HOUSE OF REPRESENTATIVES

									Percentage			
			Republican		Democratic				Total Vote		Major Vote	
CD	Year	Total Vote	Vote	Candidate	Vote	Candidate	Other Vote	Rep.-Dem. Plurality	Rep.	Dem.	Rep.	Dem.
1**	2018	332,101	183,250	WITTMAN, ROBERT J. "ROB"*	148,464	WILLIAMS, VANGIE	387	34,786 R	55.2%	44.7%	55.2%	44.8%
1**	2016	384,655	230,213	WITTMAN, ROBERT J. "ROB"*	140,785	ROWE, MATT	13,657	89,428 R	59.8%	36.6%	62.1%	37.9%
1	2014	209,621	131,861	WITTMAN, ROBERT J. "ROB"*	72,059	MOSHER, NORMAN "NORM"	5,701	59,802 R	62.9%	34.4%	64.7%	35.3%
1	2012	356,806	200,845	WITTMAN, ROBERT J. "ROB"*	147,036	COOK, ADAM M.	8,925	53,809 R	56.3%	41.2%	57.7%	42.3%
2*	2018	273,400	133,458	TAYLOR, SCOTT W.*	139,571	LURIA, ELAINE	371	6,113 D	48.8%	51.1%	48.9%	51.1%
2**	2016	310,640	190,475	TAYLOR, SCOTT W.	119,440	BROWN, SHAUN DENISE	725	71,035 R	61.3%	38.4%	61.5%	38.5%
2	2014	173,060	101,558	RIGELL, E. SCOTT*	71,178	PATRICK, SUZANNE	324	30,380 R	58.7%	41.1%	58.8%	41.2%
2	2012	309,222	166,231	RIGELL, E. SCOTT*	142,548	HIRSCHBIEL, PAUL O. JR.	443	23,683 R	53.8%	46.1%	53.8%	46.2%
3**	2018	217,722			198,615	SCOTT, ROBERT C. "BOBBY"*	19,107	198,615 D		91.2%		100.0%
3**	2016	312,371	103,289	WILLIAMS, MARTIN "MARTY"	208,337	SCOTT, ROBERT C. "BOBBY"*	745	105,048 D	33.1%	66.7%	33.1%	66.9%
3	2014	147,402			139,197	SCOTT, ROBERT C. "BOBBY"*	8,205	139,197 D		94.4%		100.0%
3	2012	318,936	58,931	LONGO, DEAN J.	259,199	SCOTT, ROBERT C. "BOBBY"*	806	200,268 D	18.5%	81.3%	18.5%	81.5%
4**	2018	299,854	107,706	MCADAMS, RYAN	187,642	MCEACHIN, A. DONALD*	4,506	79,936 D	35.9%	62.6%	36.5%	63.5%
4**	2016	346,699	145,731	WADE, MIKE	200,136	MCEACHIN, A. DONALD	832	54,405 D	42.0%	57.7%	42.1%	57.9%
4	2014	200,638	120,684	FORBES, J. RANDY*	75,270	FAUSZ, ELLIOTT	4,684	45,414 R	60.2%	37.5%	61.6%	38.4%
4	2012	350,046	199,292	FORBES, J. RANDY*	150,190	WARD, ELLA P.	564	49,102 R	56.9%	42.9%	57.0%	43.0%
5	2018	310,926	165,339	RIGGLEMAN, DENVER III	145,040	COCKBURN, LESLIE	547	20,299 R	53.2%	46.6%	53.3%	46.7%
5	2016	356,765	207,758	GARRETT, TOM	148,339	DITTMAR, JANE	668	59,419 R	58.2%	41.6%	58.3%	41.7%
5	2014	204,945	124,735	HURT, ROBERT*	73,482	GAUGHAN, WALTER LAWRENCE "LAWRENCE"	6,728	51,253 R	60.9%	35.9%	62.9%	37.1%
5	2012	348,111	193,009	HURT, ROBERT*	149,214	DOUGLASS, JOHN WADE	5,888	43,795 R	55.4%	42.9%	56.4%	43.6%
6	2018	281,377	167,957	CLINE, BENJAMIN	113,133	LEWIS, JENNIFER	287	54,824 R	59.7%	40.2%	59.8%	40.2%
6	2016	338,456	225,471	GOODLATTE, ROBERT W. "BOB"*	112,170	DEGNER, KAI	815	113,301 R	66.6%	33.1%	66.8%	33.2%
6	2014	179,708	133,898	GOODLATTE, ROBERT W. "BOB"*			45,810		74.5%		100.0%	
6	2012	323,893	211,278	GOODLATTE, ROBERT W. "BOB"*	111,949	SCHMOOKLER, ANDY	666	99,329 R	65.2%	34.6%	65.4%	34.6%
7**	2018	349,803	169,295	BRAT, DAVID*	176,079	SPANBERGER, ABIGAIL	4,429	6,784 D	48.4%	50.3%	49.0%	51.0%
7**	2016	379,209	218,057	BRAT, DAVID*	160,159	BEDELL, EILEEN	993	57,898 R	57.5%	42.2%	57.7%	42.3%
7	2014	243,351	148,026	BRAT, DAVID	89,914	TRAMMELL, JOHN K. "JACK"	5,411	58,112 R	60.8%	36.9%	62.2%	37.8%
7	2012	381,909	222,983	CANTOR, ERIC I.*	158,012	POWELL, E. WAYNE	914	64,971 R	58.4%	41.4%	58.5%	41.5%
8	2018	324,748	76,899	OH, THOMAS	247,137	BEYER, DONALD S. JR.*	712	170,238 D	23.7%	76.1%	23.7%	76.3%
8	2016	360,687	98,387	HERNICK, CHARLES ALAN	246,653	BEYER, DONALD S. JR.*	15,647	148,266 D	27.3%	68.4%	28.5%	71.5%
8	2014	203,076	63,810	EDMOND, MICAH	128,102	BEYER, DONALD S. JR.	11,164	64,292 D	31.4%	63.1%	33.2%	66.8%
8	2012	351,187	107,370	MURRAY, J. PATRICK	226,847	MORAN, JAMES P. JR.*	16,970	119,477 D	30.6%	64.6%	32.1%	67.9%
9	2018	246,980	160,933	GRIFFITH, H. MORGAN*	85,833	FLACCAVENTO, ANTHONY J.	214	75,100 R	65.2%	34.8%	65.2%	34.8%
9	2016	310,327	212,838	GRIFFITH, H. MORGAN*	87,877	KITTS, DEREK	9,612	124,961 R	68.6%	28.3%	70.8%	29.2%
9	2014	162,815	117,465	GRIFFITH, H. MORGAN*			45,350		72.1%		100.0%	
9	2012	301,658	184,882	GRIFFITH, H. MORGAN*	116,400	FLACCAVENTO, ANTHONY J.	376	68,482 R	61.3%	38.6%	61.4%	38.6%
10	2018	367,795	160,841	COMSTOCK, BARBARA*	206,356	WEXTON, JENNIFER	598	45,515 D	43.7%	56.1%	43.8%	56.2%
10	2016	400,117	210,791	COMSTOCK, BARBARA*	187,712	BENNETT, LUANN	1,614	23,079 R	52.7%	46.9%	52.9%	47.1%
10	2014	222,910	125,914	COMSTOCK, BARBARA	89,957	FOUST, JOHN	7,039	35,957 R	56.5%	40.4%	58.3%	41.7%
10	2012	366,444	214,038	WOLF, FRANK R.*	142,024	CABRAL, KRISTIN A.	10,382	72,014 R	58.4%	38.8%	60.1%	39.9%
11	2018	308,250	83,023	DOVE, JEFFREY	219,191	CONNOLLY, GERALD E. "GERRY"*	6,036	136,168 D	26.9%	71.1%	27.5%	72.5%
11	2016	282,322			247,818	CONNOLLY, GERALD E. "GERRY"*	34,504	247,818 D		87.8%		100.0%
11	2014	187,787	75,796	SCHOLTE, SUZANNE	106,780	CONNOLLY, GERALD E. "GERRY"*	5,211	30,984 D	40.4%	56.9%	41.5%	58.5%
11	2012	332,243	117,902	PERKINS, CHRIS S.	202,606	CONNOLLY, GERALD E. "GERRY"*	11,735	84,704 D	35.5%	61.0%	36.8%	63.2%
TOTAL	*2018*	*3,312,956*	*1,408,701*		*1,867,061*		*37,194*	*458,360 D*	*42.5%*	*56.4%*	*43.0%*	*57.0%*
TOTAL	*2016*	*3,782,248*	*1,843,010*		*1,859,426*		*79,812*	*16,416 D*	*48.7%*	*49.2%*	*49.8%*	*50.2%*
TOTAL	*2014*	*2,135,313*	*1,143,747*		*845,939*		*145,627*	*297,808 R*	*53.6%*	*39.6%*	*57.5%*	*42.5%*
TOTAL	*2012*	*3,740,455*	*1,876,761*		*1,806,025*		*57,669*	*70,736 R*	*50.2%*	*48.3%*	*51.0%*	*49.0%*

Note: An asterisk (*) denotes incumbent. **Due to mid-decade redistricting, boundaries for all districts except CD 5,6,8,9,10, and 11 are not comparable to those used in the 2012 and 2014 races.

VIRGINIA

GENERAL AND PRIMARY ELECTIONS

2018 GENERAL ELECTIONS: OTHER VOTES

Governor	Other vote was 27,987 Libertarian (Clifford Hyra), 1,389 Write-in (Write-in)
Senate	Other vote was 61,565 Libertarian (Matt Waters), 5,125 Write-in (Write-in)
House	Other vote was:
CD 1	387 Write-in (Write-in)
CD 2	371 Write-in (Write-ins)
CD 3	19,107 Write-in (Write-in)
CD 4	4,233 Libertarian (Peter Wells), 273 Write-in (Write-in)
CD 5	547 Write-in (Write-ins)
CD 6	287 Write-in (Write-ins)
CD 7	4,216 Libertarian (Joseph Walton), 213 Write-in (Write-in)
CD 8	712 Write-in (Write-in)
CD 9	214 Write-in (Write-in)
CD 10	598 Write-in (Write-ins)
CD 11	5,546 Libertarian (Stevan Porter), 490 Write-in (Write-in)

2018 PRIMARY ELECTIONS: SUPPLEMENTARY INFORMATION

Primary	June 12, 2018	**Registration** (as of June 1, 2018 — includes 337,497 inactive registrants)	5,572,133	No Party Registration

Primary Type Open—Any registered voter could participate in the primary of either party.

	REPUBLICAN PRIMARIES			DEMOCRATIC PRIMARIES		
Senator	Stewart, Corey A.	136,610	44.9%	Kaine, Tim*	Unopposed	
	Freitas, Nick	131,321	43.1%			
	Jackson, Earl W	36,508	12.0%			
	TOTAL	*304,439*				
Governor (2017)	Gillespie, Edward W. "Ed"	160,003	43.7%	Northam, Ralph S.	303,531	55.9%
	Stewart, Corey A.	155,466	42.5%	Perriello, Tom S.P.	239,285	44.1%
	Wagner, Frank W.	50,313	13.8%			
	TOTAL	*365,782*		*TOTAL*	*542,816*	
Congressional District 1	Wittman, Robert J. "Rob"*	Unopposed		Williams, Vangie	11,008	40.0%
				Santana, Edwin Jr.	9,059	32.9%
				Suddarth, John	7,471	27.1%
				TOTAL	*27,538*	
Congressional District 2	Taylor, Scott W.*	28,515	76.0%	Luria, Elaine	17,552	62.3%
	Jones, Mary	8,982	24.0%	Mallard, Karen	10,610	37.7%
	TOTAL	*37,497*		*TOTAL*	*28,162*	
Congressional District 3				Scott, Robert C. "Bobby"*	Unopposed	
Congressional District 4	McAdams, Ryan	17,513	72.6%	McEachin, A. Donald*	Unopposed	
	Fenty, Shion	6,621	27.4%			
	TOTAL	*24,134*				
Congressional District 5	Riggleman, Denver III	Unopposed		Cockburn, Leslie	No Primary	

VIRGINIA

GENERAL AND PRIMARY ELECTIONS

	REPUBLICAN PRIMARIES			DEMOCRATIC PRIMARIES		
Congressional District 6	Cline, Benjamin	No Primary		Lewis, Jennifer	8,202	47.7%
				Volosin, Peter	4,678	27.2%
				Moore, Charlotte	3,175	18.5%
				Coppola, Sergio II	1,150	6.7%
				TOTAL	*17,205*	
Congressional District 7	Brat, David*	Unopposed		Spanberger, Abigail	33,210	72.7%
				Ward, Dan	12,483	27.3%
				TOTAL	*45,693*	
Congressional District 8	Oh, Thomas	Unopposed		Beyer, Donald S. Jr.*	Unopposed	
Congressional District 9	Griffith, H. Morgan*	Unopposed		Flaccavento, Anthony J.	10,756	78.6%
				Santopietro, Justin	2,921	21.4%
				TOTAL	*13,677*	
Congressional District 10	Comstock, Barbara*	28,287	60.7%	Wexton, Jennifer	22,405	41.9%
	Hill, Shak	18,311	39.3%	Friedman, Alison	12,283	23.0%
				Stover, Lindsey	8,567	16.0%
				Helmer, Daniel	6,712	12.5%
				Pelletier, Paul	2,010	3.8%
				Biggins, Julia	1,513	2.8%
	TOTAL	*46,598*		*TOTAL*	*53,490*	
Congressional District 11	Dove, Jeffrey	Unopposed		Connolly, Gerald E. "Gerry"*	Unopposed	

Note: An asterisk (*) denotes incumbent.

WASHINGTON

Congressional districts first established for elections held in 2012
10 members

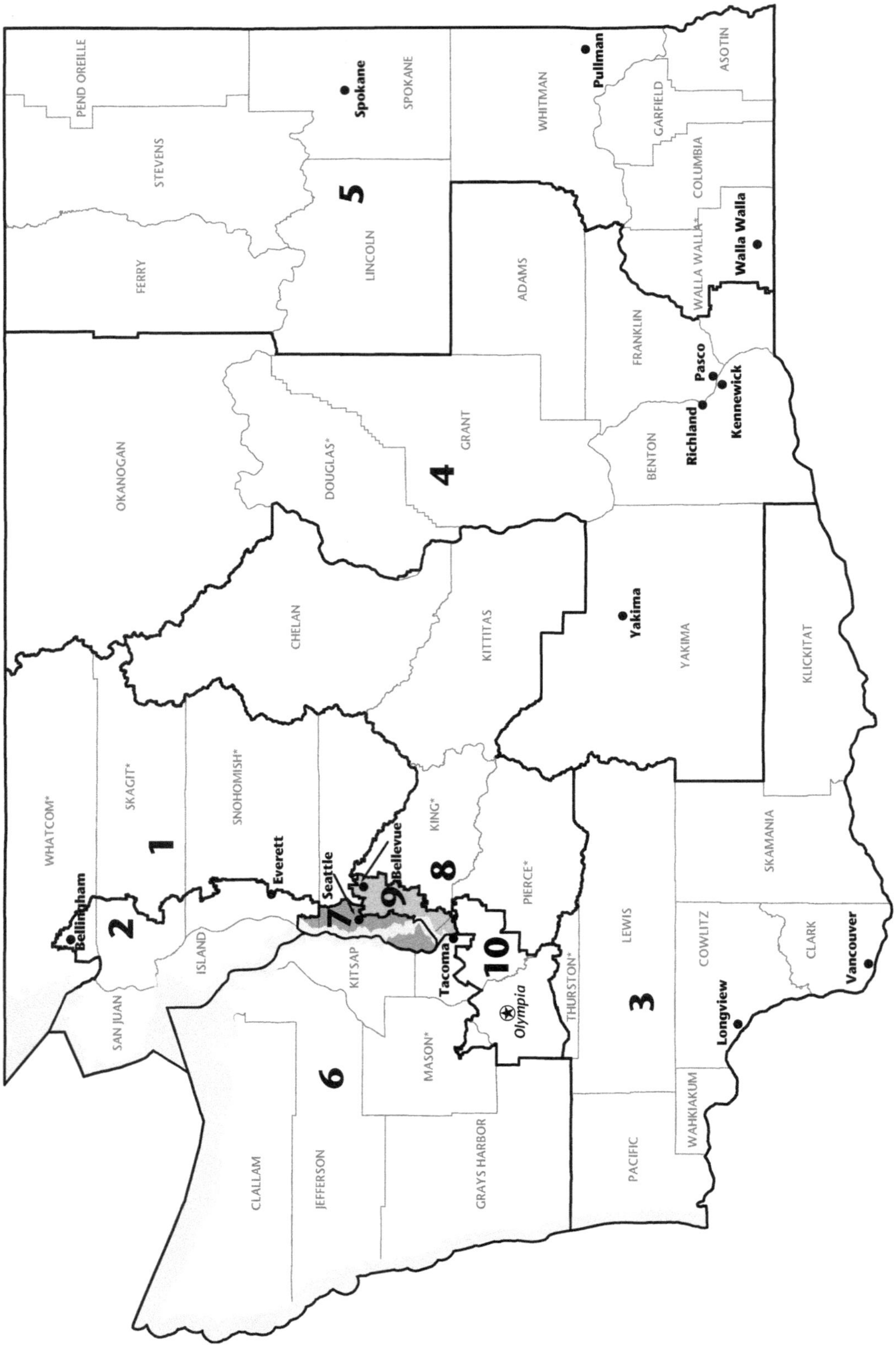

* Asterisk indicates a county whose boundaries include parts of two or more congressional districts.

WASHINGTON

Seattle Area

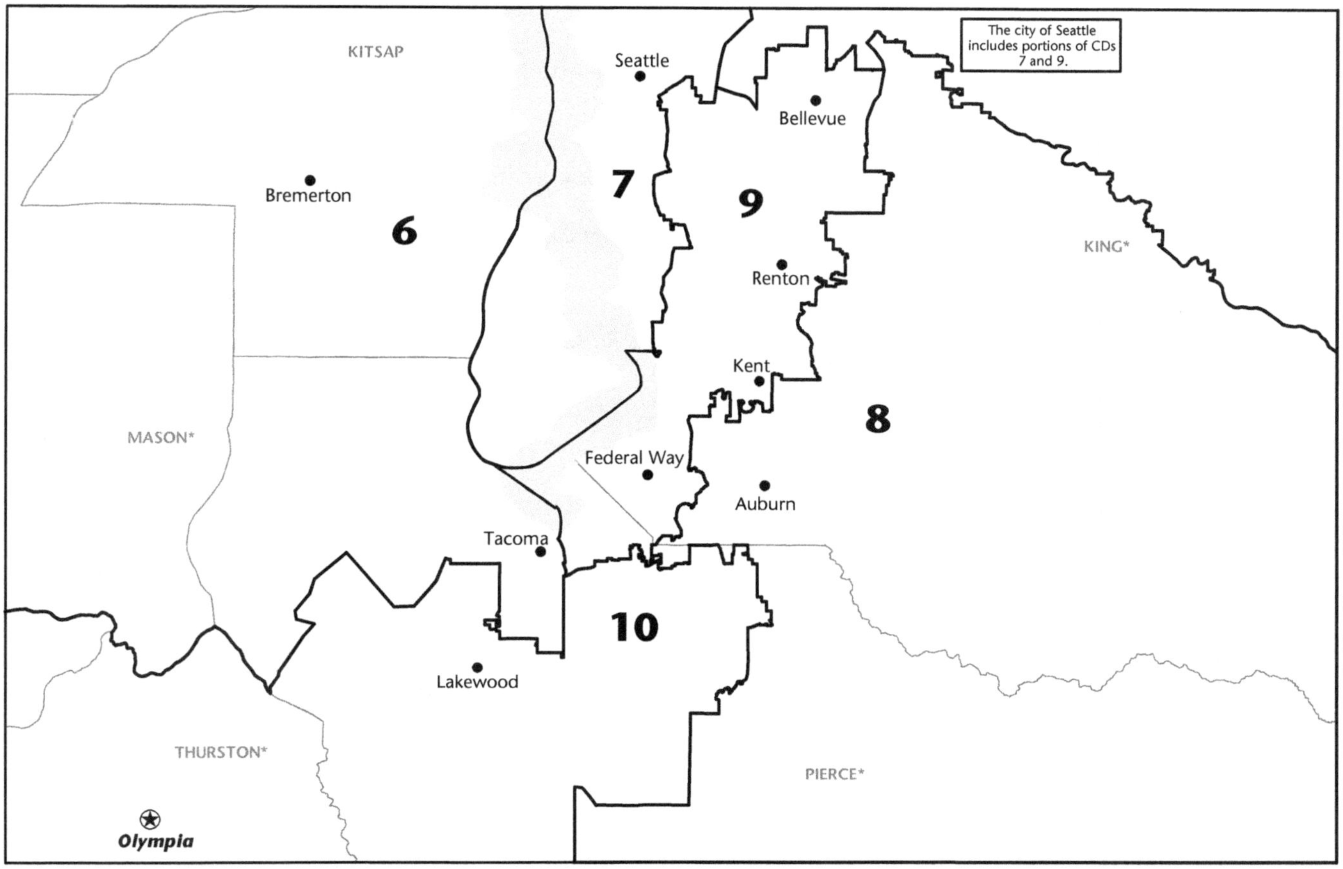

* Asterisk indicates a county whose boundaries include parts of two or more congressional districts.

WASHINGTON

GOVERNOR

Jay Inslee (D). Re-elected 2016 to a four-year term. Previously elected 2012.

SENATORS (2 Democrats)

Maria Cantwell (D). Re-elected 2018 to a six-year term. Previously elected 2012, 2006, 2000.

Patty Murray (D). Re-elected 2016 to a six-year term. Previously elected 2010, 2004, 1998, 1992.

REPRESENTATIVES (3 Republicans, 7 Democrats)

1. Suzan DelBene (D)
2. Rick Larsen (D)
3. Jaime Herrera Beutler (R)
4. Dan Newhouse (R)
5. Cathy McMorris Rodgers (R)
6. Derek Kilmer (D)
7. Pramila Jayapal (D)
8. Kim Schrier (D)
9. Adam Smith (D)
10. Denny Heck (D)

POSTWAR VOTE FOR PRESIDENT

		Republican		Democratic				Percentage			
								Total Vote		Major Vote	
Year	Total Vote	Vote	Candidate	Vote	Candidate	Other Vote	Rep.-Dem. Plurality	Rep.	Dem.	Rep.	Dem.
2016**	3,317,019	1,221,747	Trump, Donald J.	1,742,718	Clinton, Hillary Rodham	352,554	520,971 D	36.8%	52.5%	41.2%	58.8%
2012	3,125,516	1,290,670	Romney, W. Mitt	1,755,396	Obama, Barack H.*	79,450	464,726 D	41.3%	56.2%	42.4%	57.6%
2008	3,036,878	1,229,216	McCain, John S. III	1,750,848	Obama, Barack H.	56,814	521,632 D	40.5%	57.7%	41.2%	58.8%
2004	2,859,084	1,304,894	Bush, George W.*	1,510,201	Kerry, John F.	43,989	205,307 D	45.6%	52.8%	46.4%	53.6%
2000**	2,487,433	1,108,864	Bush, George W.	1,247,652	Gore, Albert Jr.	130,917	138,788 D	44.6%	50.2%	47.1%	52.9%
1996**	2,253,837	840,712	Dole, Robert "Bob"	1,123,323	Clinton, Bill*	289,802	282,611 D	37.3%	49.8%	42.8%	57.2%
1992**	2,288,230	731,234	Bush, George H.*	993,037	Clinton, Bill	563,959	261,803 D	32.0%	43.4%	42.4%	57.6%
1988	1,865,253	903,835	Bush, George H.	933,516	Dukakis, Michael S.	27,902	29,681 D	48.5%	50.0%	49.2%	50.8%
1984	1,883,910	1,051,670	Reagan, Ronald*	807,352	Mondale, Walter F.	24,888	244,318 R	55.8%	42.9%	56.6%	43.4%
1980**	1,742,394	865,244	Reagan, Ronald	650,193	Carter, Jimmy*	226,957	215,051 R	49.7%	37.3%	57.1%	42.9%
1976	1,555,534	777,732	Ford, Gerald R.*	717,323	Carter, Jimmy	60,479	60,409 R	50.0%	46.1%	52.0%	48.0%
1972	1,470,847	837,135	Nixon, Richard M.*	568,334	McGovern, George S.	65,378	268,801 R	56.9%	38.6%	59.6%	40.4%
1968**	1,304,281	588,510	Nixon, Richard M.	616,037	Humphrey, Hubert Horatio Jr.	99,734	27,527 D	45.1%	47.2%	48.9%	51.1%
1964	1,258,556	470,366	Goldwater, Barry M. Sr.	779,881	Johnson, Lyndon B.*	8,309	309,515 D	37.4%	62.0%	37.6%	62.4%
1960	1,241,572	629,273	Nixon, Richard M.	599,298	Kennedy, John F.	13,001	29,975 R	50.7%	48.3%	51.2%	48.8%
1956	1,150,889	620,430	Eisenhower, Dwight D.*	523,002	Stevenson, Adlai E. II	7,457	97,428 R	53.9%	45.4%	54.3%	45.7%
1952	1,102,708	599,107	Eisenhower, Dwight D.	492,845	Stevenson, Adlai E. II	10,756	106,262 R	54.3%	44.7%	54.9%	45.1%
1948	905,058	386,314	Dewey, Thomas E.	476,165	Truman, Harry S.*	42,579	89,851 D	42.7%	52.6%	44.8%	55.2%

Note: An asterisk (*) denotes incumbent. **In past elections, the other vote included: 2016 - 160,879 Libertarian (Gary Johnson); 2000 - 103,002 Green (Ralph Nader); 1996 - 201,003 Reform (Ross Perot); 1992 - 541,780 Independent (Perot); 1980 - 185,073 Independent (John Anderson); 1968 - 96,990 American Independent (George Wallace).

WASHINGTON

POSTWAR VOTE FOR GOVERNOR

		Republican		Democratic				Percentage			
								Total Vote		Major Vote	
Year	Total Vote	Vote	Candidate	Vote	Candidate	Other Vote	Rep.-Dem. Plurality	Rep.	Dem.	Rep.	Dem.
2016	3,245,282	1,476,346	Bryant, Bill	1,760,520	Inslee, Jay*	8,416	284,174 D	45.5%	54.2%	45.6%	54.4%
2012	3,071,047	1,488,245	McKenna, Rob	1,582,802	Inslee, Jay		94,557 D	48.5%	51.5%	48.5%	51.5%
2008	3,002,862	1,404,124	Rossi, Dino	1,598,738	Gregoire, Christine*		194,614 D	46.8%	53.2%	46.8%	53.2%
2004**	2,810,058	1,373,232	Rossi, Dino	1,373,361	Gregoire, Christine	63,465	129 D	48.9%	48.9%	50.0%	50.0%
2000	2,469,852	980,060	Carlson, John	1,441,973	Locke, Gary*	47,819	461,913 D	39.7%	58.4%	40.5%	59.5%
1996	2,237,030	940,538	Craswell, Ellen	1,296,492	Locke, Gary		355,954 D	42.0%	58.0%	42.0%	58.0%
1992	2,270,826	1,086,216	Eikenberry, Ken	1,184,315	Lowry, Mike	295	98,099 D	47.8%	52.2%	47.8%	52.2%
1988	1,874,929	708,481	Williams, Bob	1,166,448	Gardner, Booth*		457,967 D	37.8%	62.2%	37.8%	62.2%
1984	1,888,987	881,994	Spellman, John D.*	1,006,993	Gardner, Booth		124,999 D	46.7%	53.3%	46.7%	53.3%
1980	1,730,896	981,083	Spellman, John D.	749,813	McDermott, James A.		231,270 R	56.7%	43.3%	56.7%	43.3%
1976	1,546,380	687,039	Spellman, John D.	821,797	Ray, Dixy Lee	37,544	134,758 D	44.4%	53.1%	45.5%	54.5%
1972	1,472,542	747,825	Evans, Daniel J.*	630,613	Rosellini, Albert D.	94,104	117,212 R	50.8%	42.8%	54.3%	45.7%
1968	1,265,354	692,377	Evans, Daniel J.*	560,262	O'Connell, John J.	12,715	132,115 R	54.7%	44.3%	55.3%	44.7%
1964	1,250,274	697,256	Evans, Daniel J.	548,692	Rosellini, Albert D.*	4,326	148,564 R	55.8%	43.9%	56.0%	44.0%
1960	1,215,748	594,122	Andrews, Lloyd J.	611,987	Rosellini, Albert D.*	9,639	17,865 D	48.9%	50.3%	49.3%	50.7%
1956	1,128,977	508,041	Anderson, Emmett T.	616,773	Rosellini, Albert D.	4,163	108,732 D	45.0%	54.6%	45.2%	54.8%
1952	1,078,497	567,822	Langlie, Arthur B.*	510,675	Mitchell, Hugh B.		57,147 R	52.6%	47.4%	52.6%	47.4%
1948	883,141	445,958	Langlie, Arthur B.	417,035	Wallgren, Monrad C.*	20,148	28,923 R	50.5%	47.2%	51.7%	48.3%

Note: An asterisk (*) denotes incumbent. **In 2004, the initial official vote count put Republican Dino Rossi ahead by 261 votes. A machine recount reduced Rossi's margin to 42 votes. A subsequent manual recount gave Democrat Christine Gregoire the election by a margin of 129 votes (see above), and she was inaugurated governor.

POSTWAR VOTE FOR SENATOR

		Republican		Democratic				Percentage			
								Total Vote		Major Vote	
Year	Total Vote	Vote	Candidate	Vote	Candidate	Other Vote	Rep.-Dem. Plurality	Rep.	Dem.	Rep.	Dem.
2018	3,086,168	1,282,804	Hutchison, Susan	1,803,364	Cantwell, Maria*		520,560 D	41.6%	58.4%	41.6%	58.4%
2016	3,243,317	1,329,338	Vance, Chris	1,913,979	Murray, Patty*		584,641 D	41.0%	59.0%	41.0%	59.0%
2012	3,069,417	1,213,924	Baumgartner, Michael	1,855,493	Cantwell, Maria*		641,569 D	39.5%	60.5%	39.5%	60.5%
2010	2,511,094	1,196,164	Rossi, Dino	1,314,930	Murray, Patty*		118,766 D	47.6%	52.4%	47.6%	52.4%
2006	2,083,734	832,106	McGavick, Mike	1,184,659	Cantwell, Maria*	66,969	352,553 D	39.9%	56.9%	41.3%	58.7%
2004	2,818,651	1,204,584	Nethercutt, George R.	1,549,708	Murray, Patty*	64,359	345,124 D	42.7%	55.0%	43.7%	56.3%
2000	2,461,379	1,197,208	Gorton, Slade*	1,199,437	Cantwell, Maria	64,734	2,229 D	48.6%	48.7%	50.0%	50.0%
1998	1,888,561	785,377	Smith, Linda	1,103,184	Murray, Patty*		317,807 D	41.6%	58.4%	41.6%	58.4%
1994	1,700,173	947,821	Gorton, Slade*	752,352	Sims, Ron		195,469 R	55.7%	44.3%	55.7%	44.3%
1992	2,219,162	1,020,829	Chandler, Rod	1,197,973	Murray, Patty	360	177,144 D	46.0%	54.0%	46.0%	54.0%
1988	1,848,542	944,359	Gorton, Slade	904,183	Lowry, Mike		40,176 R	51.1%	48.9%	51.1%	48.9%
1986	1,337,367	650,931	Gorton, Slade*	677,471	Adams, Brock	8,965	26,540 D	48.7%	50.7%	49.0%	51.0%
1983S**	1,213,307	672,326	Evans, Daniel J.*	540,981	Lowry, Mike		131,345 R	55.4%	44.6%	55.4%	44.6%
1982	1,368,476	332,273	Jewett, Doug	943,655	Jackson, Henry M.*	92,548	611,382 D	24.3%	69.0%	26.0%	74.0%
1980	1,728,369	936,317	Gorton, Slade	792,052	Magnuson, Warren G.*		144,265 R	54.2%	45.8%	54.2%	45.8%
1976	1,491,111	361,546	Brown, George M.	1,071,219	Jackson, Henry M.*	58,346	709,673 D	24.2%	71.8%	25.2%	74.8%
1974	1,007,847	363,626	Metcalf, Jack	611,811	Magnuson, Warren G.*	32,410	248,185 D	36.1%	60.7%	37.3%	62.7%
1970	1,066,807	170,790	Elicker, Charles W.	879,385	Jackson, Henry M.*	16,632	708,595 D	16.0%	82.4%	16.3%	83.7%
1968	1,236,063	435,894	Metcalf, Jack	796,183	Magnuson, Warren G.*	3,986	360,289 D	35.3%	64.4%	35.4%	64.6%
1964	1,213,088	337,138	Andrews, Lloyd J.	875,950	Jackson, Henry M.*		538,812 D	27.8%	72.2%	27.8%	72.2%
1962	943,229	446,204	Christensen, Richard G.	491,365	Magnuson, Warren G.*	5,660	45,161 D	47.3%	52.1%	47.6%	52.4%
1958	886,822	278,271	Bantz, William B.	597,040	Jackson, Henry M.*	11,511	318,769 D	31.4%	67.3%	31.8%	68.2%
1956	1,122,217	436,652	Langlie, Arthur B.	685,565	Magnuson, Warren G.*		248,913 D	38.9%	61.1%	38.9%	61.1%
1952	1,058,735	460,884	Cain, Harry P.*	595,288	Jackson, Henry M.	2,563	134,404 D	43.5%	56.2%	43.6%	56.4%
1950	744,783	342,464	Williams, Walter	397,719	Magnuson, Warren G.*	4,600	55,255 D	46.0%	53.4%	46.3%	53.7%
1946	660,342	358,847	Cain, Harry P.	298,683	Mitchell, Hugh B.	2,812	60,164 R	54.3%	45.2%	54.6%	45.4%

Note: An asterisk (*) denotes incumbent. **The 1983 election was for a short term to fill a vacancy.

WASHINGTON

SENATOR 2018

2010 Census Population	County	Total Vote	Republican (Hutchison)	Democratic (Cantwell)	Rep.-Dem. Plurality	Percentage Total Vote Rep.	Percentage Total Vote Dem.	Percentage Major Vote Rep.	Percentage Major Vote Dem.
18,728	ADAMS	4,232	2,867	1,365	1,502 R	67.7%	32.3%	67.7%	32.3%
21,623	ASOTIN	9,107	5,298	3,809	1,489 R	58.2%	41.8%	58.2%	41.8%
175,177	BENTON	75,125	46,938	28,187	18,751 R	62.5%	37.5%	62.5%	37.5%
72,453	CHELAN	33,562	18,775	14,787	3,988 R	55.9%	44.1%	55.9%	44.1%
71,404	CLALLAM	39,540	19,504	20,036	532 D	49.3%	50.7%	49.3%	50.7%
425,363	CLARK	193,772	91,153	102,619	11,466 D	47.0%	53.0%	47.0%	53.0%
4,078	COLUMBIA	2,199	1,468	731	737 R	66.8%	33.2%	66.8%	33.2%
102,410	COWLITZ	44,258	23,773	20,485	3,288 R	53.7%	46.3%	53.7%	46.3%
38,431	DOUGLAS	14,902	9,512	5,390	4,122 R	63.8%	36.2%	63.8%	36.2%
7,551	FERRY	3,488	2,159	1,329	830 R	61.9%	38.1%	61.9%	38.1%
78,163	FRANKLIN	22,312	13,329	8,983	4,346 R	59.7%	40.3%	59.7%	40.3%
2,266	GARFIELD	1,325	880	445	435 R	66.4%	33.6%	66.4%	33.6%
89,120	GRANT	26,492	18,333	8,159	10,174 R	69.2%	30.8%	69.2%	30.8%
72,797	GRAYS HARBOR	28,456	14,851	13,605	1,246 R	52.2%	47.8%	52.2%	47.8%
78,506	ISLAND	42,013	19,672	22,341	2,669 D	46.8%	53.2%	46.8%	53.2%
29,872	JEFFERSON	20,833	6,502	14,331	7,829 D	31.2%	68.8%	31.2%	68.8%
1,931,249	KING	955,725	247,071	708,654	461,583 D	25.9%	74.1%	25.9%	74.1%
251,133	KITSAP	120,155	52,308	67,847	15,539 D	43.5%	56.5%	43.5%	56.5%
40,915	KITTITAS	19,326	10,996	8,330	2,666 R	56.9%	43.1%	56.9%	43.1%
20,318	KLICKITAT	10,665	5,776	4,889	887 R	54.2%	45.8%	54.2%	45.8%
75,455	LEWIS	33,871	22,793	11,078	11,715 R	67.3%	32.7%	67.3%	32.7%
10,570	LINCOLN	5,578	3,974	1,604	2,370 R	71.2%	28.8%	71.2%	28.8%
60,699	MASON	27,636	14,416	13,220	1,196 R	52.2%	47.8%	52.2%	47.8%
41,120	OKANOGAN	16,645	9,414	7,231	2,183 R	56.6%	43.4%	56.6%	43.4%
20,920	PACIFIC	10,859	5,332	5,527	195 D	49.1%	50.9%	49.1%	50.9%
13,001	PEND OREILLE	6,856	4,379	2,477	1,902 R	63.9%	36.1%	63.9%	36.1%
795,225	PIERCE	326,274	152,177	174,097	21,920 D	46.6%	53.4%	46.6%	53.4%
15,769	SAN JUAN	11,042	3,026	8,016	4,990 D	27.4%	72.6%	27.4%	72.6%
116,901	SKAGIT	54,620	26,498	28,122	1,624 D	48.5%	51.5%	48.5%	51.5%
11,066	SKAMANIA	5,582	2,919	2,663	256 R	52.3%	47.7%	52.3%	47.7%
713,335	SNOHOMISH	320,967	136,749	184,218	47,469 D	42.6%	57.4%	42.6%	57.4%
471,221	SPOKANE	227,508	115,508	112,000	3,508 R	50.8%	49.2%	50.8%	49.2%
43,531	STEVENS	22,570	15,296	7,274	8,022 R	67.8%	32.2%	67.8%	32.2%
252,264	THURSTON	124,149	51,472	72,677	21,205 D	41.5%	58.5%	41.5%	58.5%
3,978	WAHKIAKUM	2,423	1,341	1,082	259 R	55.3%	44.7%	55.3%	44.7%
58,781	WALLA WALLA	25,593	13,731	11,862	1,869 R	53.7%	46.3%	53.7%	46.3%
201,140	WHATCOM	108,824	43,781	65,043	21,262 D	40.2%	59.8%	40.2%	59.8%
44,776	WHITMAN	17,250	7,875	9,375	1,500 D	45.7%	54.3%	45.7%	54.3%
243,231	YAKIMA	70,434	40,958	29,476	11,482 R	58.2%	41.8%	58.2%	41.8%
6,724,540	*TOTAL*	*3,086,168*	*1,282,804*	*1,803,364*	*520,560 D*	*41.6%*	*58.4%*	*41.6%*	*58.4%*

WASHINGTON

HOUSE OF REPRESENTATIVES

CD	Year	Total Vote	Republican Vote	Republican Candidate	Democratic Vote	Democratic Candidate	Other Vote	Rep.-Dem. Plurality	Percentage Total Vote Rep.	Percentage Total Vote Dem.	Percentage Major Vote Rep.	Percentage Major Vote Dem.
1	2018	332,743	135,534	BEELER, JEFFREY	197,209	DELBENE, SUZAN*		61,675 D	40.7%	59.3%	40.7%	59.3%
1	2016	349,398	155,779	SUTHERLAND, ROBERT	193,619	DELBENE, SUZAN*		37,840 D	44.6%	55.4%	44.6%	55.4%
1	2014	225,579	101,428	CELIS, PEDRO	124,151	DELBENE, SUZAN*		22,723 D	45.0%	55.0%	45.0%	55.0%
1	2012	328,212	151,187	KOSTER, JOHN	177,025	DELBENE, SUZAN*		25,838 D	46.1%	53.9%	46.1%	53.9%
2	2018	294,833			210,187	LARSEN, RICK*	84,646	210,187 D		71.3%		100.0%
2	2016	325,408	117,094	HENNEMANN, MARC	208,314	LARSEN, RICK*		91,220 D	36.0%	64.0%	36.0%	64.0%
2	2014	201,691	79,518	GUILLOT, B.J.	122,173	LARSEN, RICK*		42,655 D	39.4%	60.6%	39.4%	60.6%
2	2012	302,291	117,465	MATTHEWS, DAN	184,826	LARSEN, RICK*		67,361 D	38.9%	61.1%	38.9%	61.1%

WASHINGTON

HOUSE OF REPRESENTATIVES

			Republican		Democratic				Percentage			
									Total Vote		Major Vote	
CD	Year	Total Vote	Vote	Candidate	Vote	Candidate	Other Vote	Rep.-Dem. Plurality	Rep.	Dem.	Rep.	Dem.
3	2018	307,226	161,819	BEUTLER, JAIME HERRERA*	145,407	LONG, CAROLYN		16,412 R	52.7%	47.3%	52.7%	47.3%
3	2016	313,277	193,457	BEUTLER, JAIME HERRERA*	119,820	MOELLER, JIM		73,637 R	61.8%	38.2%	61.8%	38.2%
3	2014	202,814	124,796	BEUTLER, JAIME HERRERA*	78,018	DINGETHAL, BOB		46,778 R	61.5%	38.5%	61.5%	38.5%
3	2012	293,884	177,446	BEUTLER, JAIME HERRERA*	116,438	HAUGEN, JON T.		61,008 R	60.4%	39.6%	60.4%	39.6%
4	2018	225,336	141,551	NEWHOUSE, DAN M.*	83,785	BROWN, CHRISTINE		57,766 R	62.8%	37.2%	62.8%	37.2%
4	2016**	229,919	132,517	NEWHOUSE, DAN M.*			97,402	132,517 R	57.6%		100.0%	
4	2014	153,079	77,772	NEWHOUSE, DAN M.			75,307	77,772 R	50.8%		100.0%	
4	2012	233,689	154,749	HASTINGS, DOC*	78,940	BAECHLER, MARY		75,809 R	66.2%	33.8%	66.2%	33.8%
5	2018	320,347	175,422	RODGERS, CATHY MCMORRIS*	144,925	BROWN, LISA		30,497 R	54.8%	45.2%	54.8%	45.2%
5	2016	323,534	192,959	RODGERS, CATHY MCMORRIS*	130,575	PAKOOTAS, JOSEPH "JOE"		62,384 R	59.6%	40.4%	59.6%	40.4%
5	2014	223,242	135,470	RODGERS, CATHY MCMORRIS*	87,772	PAKOOTAS, JOSEPH "JOE"		47,698 R	60.7%	39.3%	60.7%	39.3%
5	2012	308,578	191,066	RODGERS, CATHY MCMORRIS*	117,512	COWAN, RICH		73,554 R	61.9%	38.1%	61.9%	38.1%
6	2018	323,086	116,677	DIGHTMAN, DOUGLAS	206,409	KILMER, DEREK*		89,732 D	36.1%	63.9%	36.1%	63.9%
6	2016	327,834	126,116	BLOOM, TODD	201,718	KILMER, DEREK*		75,602 D	38.5%	61.5%	38.5%	61.5%
6	2014	224,290	83,025	MCCLENDON, MARTIN "MARTY"	141,265	KILMER, DEREK*		58,240 D	37.0%	63.0%	37.0%	63.0%
6	2012	316,386	129,725	DRISCOLL, BILL	186,661	KILMER, DEREK		56,936 D	41.0%	59.0%	41.0%	59.0%
7	2018	394,681	64,881	KELLER, CRAIG	329,800	JAYAPAL, PRAMILA*		264,919 D	16.4%	83.6%	16.4%	83.6%
7	2016**	378,754			212,010	JAYAPAL, PRAMILA	166,744	212,010 D		56.0%		100.0%
7	2014	251,875	47,921	KELLER, CRAIG	203,954	MCDERMOTT, JAMES A.*		156,033 D	19.0%	81.0%	19.0%	81.0%
7	2012	374,580	76,212	BEMIS, RON	298,368	MCDERMOTT, JAMES A.*		222,156 D	20.3%	79.7%	20.3%	79.7%
8	2018	313,057	148,968	ROSSI, DINO	164,089	SCHRIER, KIM		15,121 D	47.6%	52.4%	47.6%	52.4%
8	2016	320,865	193,145	REICHERT, DAVID GEORGE "DAVE"*	127,720	VENTRELLA, TONY		65,425 R	60.2%	39.8%	60.2%	39.8%
8	2014	198,744	125,741	REICHERT, DAVID GEORGE "DAVE"*	73,003	RITCHIE, JASON		52,738 R	63.3%	36.7%	63.3%	36.7%
8	2012	302,090	180,204	REICHERT, DAVID GEORGE "DAVE"*	121,886	PORTERFIELD, KAREN		58,318 R	59.7%	40.3%	59.7%	40.3%
9	2018	240,567			163,345	SMITH, ADAM*	77,222	163,345 D		67.9%		100.0%
9	2016	281,482	76,317	BASLER, DOUG	205,165	SMITH, ADAM*		128,848 D	27.1%	72.9%	27.1%	72.9%
9	2014	166,794	48,662	BASLER, DOUG	118,132	SMITH, ADAM*		69,470 D	29.2%	70.8%	29.2%	70.8%
9	2012	268,139	76,105	POSTMA, JAMES	192,034	SMITH, ADAM*		115,929 D	28.4%	71.6%	28.4%	71.6%
10	2018	270,075	103,860	BRUMBLES, JOSEPH	166,215	HECK, DENNY*		62,355 D	38.5%	61.5%	38.5%	61.5%
10	2016	290,564	120,104	POSTMA, JAMES	170,460	HECK, DENNY*		50,356 D	41.3%	58.7%	41.3%	58.7%
10	2014	181,492	82,213	MCDONALD, JOYCE	99,279	HECK, DENNY*		17,066 D	45.3%	54.7%	45.3%	54.7%
10	2012	278,417	115,381	MURI, RICHARD	163,036	HECK, DENNY		47,655 D	41.4%	58.6%	41.4%	58.6%
TOTAL	*2018*	*3,021,951*	*1,048,712*		*1,811,371*		*161,868*	*762,659 D*	*34.7%*	*59.9%*	*36.7%*	*63.3%*
TOTAL	*2016*	*3,141,035*	*1,307,488*		*1,569,401*		*264,146*	*261,913 D*	*41.6%*	*50.0%*	*45.4%*	*54.6%*
TOTAL	*2014*	*2,029,600*	*906,546*		*1,047,747*		*75,307*	*141,201 D*	*44.7%*	*51.6%*	*46.4%*	*53.6%*
TOTAL	*2012*	*3,006,266*	*1,369,540*		*1,636,726*			*267,186 D*	*45.6%*	*54.4%*	*45.6%*	*54.4%*

Note: An asterisk (*) denotes incumbent. ** In Washington's jungle primary, the top two vote recipients in 2018 in CD 9 (Adam Smith and Sarah Smith) were both Democrats. When the vote for all Democratic candidates is aggregated, the Democratic total becomes 1,888,593, while the vote for Other becomes 84,646.

WASHINGTON

GENERAL AND PRIMARY ELECTIONS

2018 GENERAL ELECTIONS: OTHER VOTES

President Other vote was 160,879 Libertarian (Gary Johnson), 107,805 Write-in (Scattered Write-In), 58,417 Green (Jill Stein), 17,623 Constitution (Darrell Castle), 4,307 Socialist Workers (Alyson Kennedy), 3,523 Peace and Freedom (Gloria La Riva)

House Other vote was:

CD 2 84,646 Libertarian (Brian Luke)

CD 9 77,222 Democrat (Sarah Smith)

WASHINGTON

GENERAL AND PRIMARY ELECTIONS

2018 PRIMARY ELECTIONS: SUPPLEMENTARY INFORMATION

Primary	August 7, 2018	**Registration** (as of August 7, 2018)	4,299,309	No Party Registration

Primary Type Open—Any registered voter could participate in the primary, in which candidates of all parties ran together on the same ballot. The top two vote-getters advanced to the November general election.

ALL-PARTY PRIMARIES

Senator	Cantwell, Maria* (Democrat)#	929,961	54.7%
	Hutchison, Susan (Republican)#	413,317	24.3%
	Swank, Keith (Republican)	39,818	2.3%
	Gibson, Joey (Republican)	38,676	2.3%
	Tannehill, Clint R. (Democrat)	35,770	2.1%
	Bryant, Dave (Republican)	33,962	2.0%
	Coday, Art (Republican)	30,654	1.8%
	Ferguson, Jennifer (Independent)	25,224	1.5%
	Owen, Tim (Republican)	23,167	1.4%
	Hawkins, Matt (Republican)	13,324	0.8%
	Rivers, Don L. (Democrat)	12,634	0.7%
	Luke, Mike (Libertarian)	12,302	0.7%
	Stockwell, Glen R. "Stocky" (Republican)	11,611	0.7%
	Amundson, Thor (Independent)	9,393	0.6%
	Said, Mohammad (Democrat)	8,649	0.5%
	Heines, Matthew D. (Republican)	7,737	0.5%
	Hoffman, Steve (Freedom Socialist)	7,390	0.4%
	GoodSpaceGuy, (Republican)	7,057	0.4%
	Orlinski, John (Republican)	6,905	0.4%
	Strider, Dave (Independent)	6,821	0.4%
	De La Fuente, Roque "Rocky" (Republican)	5,724	0.3%
	Deal, James Robert (Green)	3,849	0.2%
	Wright, Sam (Human Rights)	3,761	0.2%
	Chase, Brad (Fuck Democrats, Fuck Republicans)	2,655	0.2%
	Kalberer, George H. (Democrat)	2,448	0.1%
	Jackson, Charlie R. (Independent)	2,411	0.1%
	Smith, RC (Republican)	2,238	0.1%
	Butler, Jon (Independent)	2,016	0.1%
	Tsimerman, Alex (Standupamerica)	1,366	0.1%
	TOTAL	*1,700,840*	
Congressional District 1	DelBene, Suzan* (Democrat)#	106,107	59.3%
	Beeler, Jeffrey (Republican)#	45,830	25.6%
	Stafne, Scott (Republican)	20,354	11.4%
	Pilskog, Adam (No Party)	5,007	2.8%
	Mair, Robert (No Party)	1,622	0.9%
	TOTAL	*178,920*	
Congressional District 2	Larsen, Rick* (Democrat)#	101,497	64.9%
	Luke, Brian (Libertarian)#	12,320	7.9%
	Franco, Gary (Independent)	12,269	7.8%
	Carlson, Collin Richard (Democrat)	12,058	7.7%
	Mover, Uncle (Moderate Republican)	11,832	7.6%
	Bird, Stonewall Jackson "Stoney" (Green)	6,525	4.2%
	TOTAL	*156,501*	

WASHINGTON

GENERAL AND PRIMARY ELECTIONS

ALL-PARTY PRIMARIES

Congressional District 3	Beutler, Jaime Herrera* (Republican)#	68,961	42.1%
	Long, Carolyn (Democrat)#	57,798	35.3%
	McDevitt, David (Democrat)	13,124	8.0%
	Bowerman, Earl (Republican)	9,018	5.5%
	Gasque, Dorothy (Democrat)	7,983	4.9%
	Cortney, Michael (Republican)	5,528	3.4%
	Hash, Martin (Democrat)	1,498	0.9%
	TOTAL	*163,910*	
Congressional District 4	Newhouse, Dan M.* (Republican)#	77,203	63.2%
	Brown, Christine (Democrat)#	44,868	36.8%
	TOTAL	*122,071*	
Congressional District 5	Rodgers, Cathy McMorris* (Republican)#	99,689	49.3%
	Brown, Lisa (Democrat)#	91,738	45.4%
	Saulibio, Dave (Trump Populist Party)	4,845	2.4%
	Bonneau, Jered (Republican)	4,453	2.2%
	Ilonummi, Kari Olavi (Republican)	1,507	0.7%
	TOTAL	*202,232*	
Congressional District 6	Kilmer, Derek* (Democrat)#	117,848	63.5%
	Dightman, Douglas (Republican)#	60,651	32.7%
	Vega, Tyler Myles (Progressive)	7,080	3.8%
	TOTAL	*185,579*	
Congressional District 7	Jayapal, Pramila* (Democrat)#	189,175	82.7%
	Keller, Craig (Republican)#	39,657	17.3%
	TOTAL	*228,832*	
Congressional District 8	Rossi, Dino (Republican)#	73,288	43.1%
	Schrier, Kim (Democrat)#	31,837	18.7%
	Rittereiser, Jason (Democrat)	30,708	18.1%
	Hader, Shannon (Democrat)	21,317	12.5%
	Hughes-Hageman, Jack (Republican)	4,270	2.5%
	Pross, Gordon Allen (Republican)	2,081	1.2%
	Cramer, Tom (Democrat)	1,468	0.9%
	Grassie, Bill (Independent)	1,163	0.7%
	Reyes, Richard Travis (Libertarian)	1,154	0.7%
	Arnold, Keith (Independent)	1,090	0.6%
	Dillon, Patrick (Independent)	898	0.5%
	Mahaffey, Todd (No Party)	673	0.4%
	TOTAL	*169,947*	
Congressional District 9	Smith, Adam* (Democrat)#	71,035	48.4%
	Smith, Sarah (Democrat)#	39,409	26.9%
	Basler, Doug (Republican)	36,254	24.7%
	TOTAL	*146,698*	
Congressional District 10	Heck, Denny* (Democrat)#	82,552	58.2%
	Brumbles, Joseph (Republican)#	45,270	31.9%
	Borrelli, Tamborine (Independent Progressive)	7,997	5.6%
	Slotnick, Nancy Dailey (Independent)	6,127	4.3%
	TOTAL	*141,946*	

Note: An asterisk (*) denotes incumbent. A pound sign (#) next to the top two candidates in each primary indicates that they qualified for the general election. For all offices, Washington held an all-party primary, in which candidates of all parties ran together on a single ballot. The top two vote-getters, regardless of party, advanced to the November general election. Candidates identified themselves on the ballot as "preferring" a particular party (or independent, non-party status), whether or not they were a member of that party or were supported by that party.

WEST VIRGINIA

Congressional districts first established for elections held in 2012

3 members

WEST VIRGINIA

GOVERNOR

Jim Justice (R). Elected 2016 to a four-year term. (Justice was elected as a Democrat in 2016 but became a Republican on August 3, 2017.)

SENATORS (1 Republican, 1 Democrat)

Shelley Moore Capito (R). Elected 2014 to a six-year term.

Joe Manchin III (D). Re-elected 2018 to a six-year term. Previously elected 2012, and 2010 to fill the remaining two years of the term vacated by the death of Robert C. Byrd (D) in June 2010. Carte Goodwin (D) was appointed to fill the vacancy until the special election could be held in November 2010.

REPRESENTATIVES (3 Republicans)

1. David B. McKinley (R)
2. Alex X. Mooney (R)
3. Carol Miller (R)

POSTWAR VOTE FOR PRESIDENT

								Percentage			
		Republican		Democratic				Total Vote		Major Vote	
Year	Total Vote	Vote	Candidate	Vote	Candidate	Other Vote	Rep.-Dem. Plurality	Rep.	Dem.	Rep.	Dem.
2016**	714,423	489,371	Trump, Donald J.	188,794	Clinton, Hillary Rodham	36,258	300,577 R	68.5%	26.4%	72.2%	27.8%
2012	670,438	417,655	Romney, W. Mitt	238,269	Obama, Barack H.*	14,514	179,386 R	62.3%	35.5%	63.7%	36.3%
2008	713,451	397,466	McCain, John S. III	303,857	Obama, Barack H.	12,128	93,609 R	55.7%	42.6%	56.7%	43.3%
2004	755,887	423,778	Bush, George W.*	326,541	Kerry, John F.	5,568	97,237 R	56.1%	43.2%	56.5%	43.5%
2000**	648,124	336,475	Bush, George W.	295,497	Gore, Albert Jr.	16,152	40,978 R	51.9%	45.6%	53.2%	46.8%
1996**	636,459	233,946	Dole, Robert "Bob"	327,812	Clinton, Bill*	74,701	93,866 D	36.8%	51.5%	41.6%	58.4%
1992**	683,762	241,974	Bush, George H.*	331,001	Clinton, Bill	110,787	89,027 D	35.4%	48.4%	42.2%	57.8%
1988	653,311	310,065	Bush, George H.	341,016	Dukakis, Michael S.	2,230	30,951 D	47.5%	52.2%	47.6%	52.4%
1984	735,742	405,483	Reagan, Ronald*	328,125	Mondale, Walter F.	2,134	77,358 R	55.1%	44.6%	55.3%	44.7%
1980**	737,715	334,206	Reagan, Ronald	367,462	Carter, Jimmy*	36,047	33,256 D	45.3%	49.8%	47.6%	52.4%
1976	750,964	314,760	Ford, Gerald R.*	435,914	Carter, Jimmy	290	121,154 D	41.9%	58.0%	41.9%	58.1%
1972	762,399	484,964	Nixon, Richard M.*	277,435	McGovern, George S.		207,529 R	63.6%	36.4%	63.6%	36.4%
1968**	754,206	307,555	Nixon, Richard M.	374,091	Humphrey, Hubert Horatio Jr.	72,560	66,536 D	40.8%	49.6%	45.1%	54.9%
1964	792,040	253,953	Goldwater, Barry M. Sr.	538,087	Johnson, Lyndon B.*		284,134 D	32.1%	67.9%	32.1%	67.9%
1960	837,781	395,995	Nixon, Richard M.	441,786	Kennedy, John F.		45,791 D	47.3%	52.7%	47.3%	52.7%
1956	830,831	449,297	Eisenhower, Dwight D.*	381,534	Stevenson, Adlai E. II		67,763 R	54.1%	45.9%	54.1%	45.9%
1952	873,548	419,970	Eisenhower, Dwight D.	453,578	Stevenson, Adlai E. II		33,608 D	48.1%	51.9%	48.1%	51.9%
1948	748,750	316,251	Dewey, Thomas E.	429,188	Truman, Harry S.*	3,311	112,937 D	42.2%	57.3%	42.4%	57.6%

Note: An asterisk (*) denotes incumbent. **In past elections, the other vote included: 2016 - 23,004 Libertarian (Gary Johnson); 2000 - 10,680 Green (Ralph Nader); 1996 - 71,639 Reform (Ross Perot); 1992 - 108,829 Independent (Perot); 1980 - 31,691 Independent (John Anderson); 1968 - 72,560 American Independent (George Wallace).

WEST VIRGINIA

POSTWAR VOTE FOR GOVERNOR

		Republican		Democratic				Percentage			
								Total Vote		Major Vote	
Year	Total Vote	Vote	Candidate	Vote	Candidate	Other Vote	Rep.-Dem. Plurality	Rep.	Dem.	Rep.	Dem.
2016	713,879	301,987	Cole, Bill	350,408	Justice, Jim	61,484	48,421 D	42.3%	49.1%	46.3%	53.7%
2012	664,455	303,291	Maloney, Bill	335,468	Tomblin, Earl Ray*	25,696	32,177 D	45.6%	50.5%	47.5%	52.5%
2011S**	301,084	141,656	Maloney, Bill	149,202	Tomblin, Earl Ray*	10,226	7,546 D	47.0%	49.6%	48.7%	51.3%
2008	706,046	181,612	Weeks, Russ	492,697	Manchin, Joe III*	31,737	311,085 D	25.7%	69.8%	26.9%	73.1%
2004	744,433	253,131	Warner, Monty	472,758	Manchin, Joe III	18,544	219,627 D	34.0%	63.5%	34.9%	65.1%
2000	648,047	305,926	Underwood, Cecil H.*	324,822	Wise, Robert Ellsworth	17,299	18,896 D	47.2%	50.1%	48.5%	51.5%
1996	628,559	324,518	Underwood, Cecil H.	287,870	Pritt, Charlotte	16,171	36,648 R	51.6%	45.8%	53.0%	47.0%
1992	657,193	240,390	Benedict, Cleveland K.	368,302	Caperton, Gaston*	48,501	127,912 D	36.6%	56.0%	39.5%	60.5%
1988	649,593	267,172	Moore, Arch A. Jr.*	382,421	Caperton, Gaston		115,249 D	41.1%	58.9%	41.1%	58.9%
1984	741,502	394,937	Moore, Arch A. Jr.	346,565	See, Clyde M.		48,372 R	53.3%	46.7%	53.3%	46.7%
1980	742,150	337,240	Moore, Arch A. Jr.	401,863	Rockefeller, John D. IV*	3,047	64,623 D	45.4%	54.1%	45.6%	54.4%
1976	749,270	253,420	Underwood, Cecil H.	495,661	Rockefeller, John D. IV	189	242,241 D	33.8%	66.2%	33.8%	66.2%
1972	774,279	423,817	Moore, Arch A. Jr.*	350,462	Rockefeller, John D. IV		73,355 R	54.7%	45.3%	54.7%	45.3%
1968	743,845	378,315	Moore, Arch A. Jr.	365,530	Sprouse, James M.		12,785 R	50.9%	49.1%	50.9%	49.1%
1964	788,582	355,559	Underwood, Cecil H.	433,023	Smith, Hulett		77,464 D	45.1%	54.9%	45.1%	54.9%
1960	827,420	380,665	Neely, Harold E.	446,755	Barron, W. W.		66,090 D	46.0%	54.0%	46.0%	54.0%
1956	817,623	440,502	Underwood, Cecil H.	377,121	Mollohan, Robert H.		63,381 R	53.9%	46.1%	53.9%	46.1%
1952	882,527	427,629	Holt, Rush D.	454,898	Marland, William C.		27,269 D	48.5%	51.5%	48.5%	51.5%
1948	768,061	329,309	Boreman, Herbert S.	438,752	Patteson, Okey L.		109,443 D	42.9%	57.1%	42.9%	57.1%

Note: An asterisk (*) denotes incumbent. **The 2011 election was for a short term to fill a vacancy.

POSTWAR VOTE FOR SENATOR

		Republican		Democratic				Percentage			
								Total Vote		Major Vote	
Year	Total Vote	Vote	Candidate	Vote	Candidate	Other Vote	Rep.-Dem. Plurality	Rep.	Dem.	Rep.	Dem.
2018	586,034	271,113	Morrisey, Patrick	290,510	Manchin, Joe III*	24,411	19,397 D	46.3%	49.6%	48.3%	51.7%
2014	453,659	281,820	Capito, Shelley Moore	156,360	Tennant, Natalie E.	15,479	125,460 R	62.1%	34.5%	64.3%	35.7%
2012	660,212	240,787	Raese, John R.	399,908	Manchin, Joe III*	19,517	159,121 D	36.5%	60.6%	37.6%	62.4%
2010S**	529,948	230,013	Raese, John R.	283,358	Manchin, Joe III	16,577	53,345 D	43.4%	53.5%	44.8%	55.2%
2008	702,308	254,629	Wolfe, Jay	447,560	Rockefeller, John D. IV*	119	192,931 D	36.3%	63.7%	36.3%	63.7%
2006	459,884	155,043	Raese, John R.	296,276	Byrd, Robert C.*	8,565	141,233 D	33.7%	64.4%	34.4%	65.6%
2002	436,183	160,902	Wolfe, M. Jay	275,281	Rockefeller, John D. IV*		114,379 D	36.9%	63.1%	36.9%	63.1%
2000	603,477	121,635	Gallaher, David T.	469,215	Byrd, Robert C.*	12,627	347,580 D	20.2%	77.8%	20.6%	79.4%
1996	595,614	139,088	Burks, Betty A.	456,526	Rockefeller, John D. IV*		317,438 D	23.4%	76.6%	23.4%	76.6%
1994	420,936	130,441	Klos, Stan	290,495	Byrd, Robert C.*		160,054 D	31.0%	69.0%	31.0%	69.0%
1990	404,305	128,071	Yoder, John	276,234	Rockefeller, John D. IV*		148,163 D	31.7%	68.3%	31.7%	68.3%
1988	634,547	223,564	Wolfe, M. Jay	410,983	Byrd, Robert C.*		187,419 D	35.2%	64.8%	35.2%	64.8%
1984	722,212	344,680	Raese, John R.	374,233	Rockefeller, John D. IV	3,299	29,553 D	47.7%	51.8%	47.9%	52.1%
1982	565,314	173,910	Benedict, Cleveland K.	387,170	Byrd, Robert C.*	4,234	213,260 D	30.8%	68.5%	31.0%	69.0%
1978	493,351	244,317	Moore, Arch A. Jr.	249,034	Randolph, Jennings*		4,717 D	49.5%	50.5%	49.5%	50.5%
1976	566,790			566,423	Byrd, Robert C.*	367	566,423 D		99.9%		100.0%
1972	731,841	245,531	Leonard, Louise	486,310	Randolph, Jennings*		240,779 D	33.5%	66.5%	33.5%	66.5%
1970	445,623	99,658	Dodson, Elmer H.	345,965	Byrd, Robert C.*		246,307 D	22.4%	77.6%	22.4%	77.6%
1966	491,216	198,891	Love, Francis J.	292,325	Randolph, Jennings*		93,434 D	40.5%	59.5%	40.5%	59.5%
1964	761,087	246,072	Benedict, Cooper P.	515,015	Byrd, Robert C.*		268,943 D	32.3%	67.7%	32.3%	67.7%
1960	828,292	369,935	Underwood, Cecil H.	458,355	Randolph, Jennings*	2	88,420 D	44.7%	55.3%	44.7%	55.3%
1958	644,917	263,172	Revercomb, Chapman*	381,745	Byrd, Robert C.		118,573 D	40.8%	59.2%	40.8%	59.2%
1958S**	630,677	256,510	Hoblitzell, John D. Jr.*	374,167	Randolph, Jennings		117,657 D	40.7%	59.3%	40.7%	59.3%
1956S**	805,174	432,123	Revercomb, Chapman	373,051	Marland, William C.		59,072 R	53.7%	46.3%	53.7%	46.3%
1954	593,329	268,066	Sweeney, Thomas	325,263	Neely, Matthew M.*		57,197 D	45.2%	54.8%	45.2%	54.8%
1952	876,573	406,554	Revercomb, Chapman	470,019	Kilgore, Harley M.*		63,465 D	46.4%	53.6%	46.4%	53.6%
1948	763,888	328,534	Revercomb, Chapman*	435,354	Neely, Matthew M.		106,820 D	43.0%	57.0%	43.0%	57.0%
1946	542,768	269,617	Sweeney, Thomas	273,151	Kilgore, Harley M.*		3,534 D	49.7%	50.3%	49.7%	50.3%

Note: An asterisk (*) denotes incumbent. **The 1956 election, one of the 1958 elections, and the 2010 election were for short terms to fill a vacancy. The Republican Party did not run a candidate in the 1976 Senate election.

WEST VIRGINIA

SENATOR 2018

2010 Census Population	County	Total Vote	Republican (Morrisey)	Democratic (Manchin)	Other	Rep.-Dem. Plurality	Percentage Total Vote Rep.	Total Vote Dem.	Major Vote Rep.	Major Vote Dem.
16,589	BARBOUR	4,935	2,562	2,121	252	441 R	51.9%	43.0%	54.7%	45.3%
104,169	BERKELEY	34,035	18,111	14,508	1,416	3,603 R	53.2%	42.6%	55.5%	44.5%
24,629	BOONE	6,817	2,710	3,894	213	1,184 D	39.8%	57.1%	41.0%	59.0%
14,523	BRAXTON	4,192	1,887	2,148	157	261 D	45.0%	51.2%	46.8%	53.2%
24,069	BROOKE	7,828	3,513	3,987	328	474 D	44.9%	50.9%	46.8%	53.2%
96,319	CABELL	29,061	11,267	16,909	885	5,642 D	38.8%	58.2%	40.0%	60.0%
7,627	CALHOUN	2,133	1,065	967	101	98 R	49.9%	45.3%	52.4%	47.6%
9,386	CLAY	2,432	1,197	1,141	94	56 R	49.2%	46.9%	51.2%	48.8%
8,202	DODDRIDGE	2,209	1,352	746	111	606 R	61.2%	33.8%	64.4%	35.6%
46,039	FAYETTE	12,223	5,160	6,502	561	1,342 D	42.2%	53.2%	44.2%	55.8%
8,693	GILMER	1,999	929	944	126	15 D	46.5%	47.2%	49.6%	50.4%
11,937	GRANT	3,890	2,820	935	135	1,885 R	72.5%	24.0%	75.1%	24.9%
35,480	GREENBRIER	12,212	5,563	6,201	448	638 D	45.6%	50.8%	47.3%	52.7%
23,964	HAMPSHIRE	6,878	4,313	2,325	240	1,988 R	62.7%	33.8%	65.0%	35.0%
30,676	HANCOCK	10,117	4,963	4,707	447	256 R	49.1%	46.5%	51.3%	48.7%
14,025	HARDY	4,540	2,467	1,880	193	587 R	54.3%	41.4%	56.8%	43.2%
69,099	HARRISON	22,511	9,512	11,491	1,508	1,979 D	42.3%	51.0%	45.3%	54.7%
29,211	JACKSON	10,211	4,964	4,890	357	74 R	48.6%	47.9%	50.4%	49.6%
53,498	JEFFERSON	20,782	9,360	10,666	756	1,306 D	45.0%	51.3%	46.7%	53.3%
193,063	KANAWHA	63,878	22,527	39,333	2,018	16,806 D	35.3%	61.6%	36.4%	63.6%
16,372	LEWIS	5,586	2,879	2,326	381	553 R	51.5%	41.6%	55.3%	44.7%
21,720	LINCOLN	5,640	2,553	2,899	188	346 D	45.3%	51.4%	46.8%	53.2%
36,743	LOGAN	9,582	4,708	4,574	300	134 R	49.1%	47.7%	50.7%	49.3%
56,418	MARION	19,366	7,280	10,889	1,197	3,609 D	37.6%	56.2%	40.1%	59.9%
33,107	MARSHALL	10,789	4,868	5,485	436	617 D	45.1%	50.8%	47.0%	53.0%
27,324	MASON	8,363	3,805	4,270	288	465 D	45.5%	51.1%	47.1%	52.9%
22,113	MCDOWELL	4,565	2,198	2,222	145	24 D	48.1%	48.7%	49.7%	50.3%
62,264	MERCER	18,040	10,033	7,430	577	2,603 R	55.6%	41.2%	57.5%	42.5%
28,212	MINERAL	8,934	5,525	3,108	301	2,417 R	61.8%	34.8%	64.0%	36.0%
26,839	MINGO	6,952	3,825	2,929	198	896 R	55.0%	42.1%	56.6%	43.4%
96,189	MONONGALIA	30,947	10,918	18,010	2,019	7,092 D	35.3%	58.2%	37.7%	62.3%
13,502	MONROE	4,932	2,644	2,125	163	519 R	53.6%	43.1%	55.4%	44.6%
17,541	MORGAN	6,204	3,783	2,143	278	1,640 R	61.0%	34.5%	63.8%	36.2%
26,233	NICHOLAS	7,843	3,948	3,588	307	360 R	50.3%	45.7%	52.4%	47.6%
44,443	OHIO	15,823	6,588	8,731	504	2,143 D	41.6%	55.2%	43.0%	57.0%
7,695	PENDLETON	2,518	1,478	948	92	530 R	58.7%	37.6%	60.9%	39.1%
7,605	PLEASANTS	2,522	1,266	1,157	99	109 R	50.2%	45.9%	52.2%	47.8%
8,719	POCAHONTAS	2,846	1,411	1,269	166	142 R	49.6%	44.6%	52.6%	47.4%
33,520	PRESTON	10,365	5,943	3,686	736	2,257 R	57.3%	35.6%	61.7%	38.3%
55,486	PUTNAM	21,319	10,090	10,513	716	423 D	47.3%	49.3%	49.0%	51.0%
78,859	RALEIGH	24,127	12,620	10,581	926	2,039 R	52.3%	43.9%	54.4%	45.6%
29,405	RANDOLPH	8,896	4,017	4,472	407	455 D	45.2%	50.3%	47.3%	52.7%
10,449	RITCHIE	3,196	1,961	1,082	153	879 R	61.4%	33.9%	64.4%	35.6%
14,926	ROANE	4,220	1,899	2,165	156	266 D	45.0%	51.3%	46.7%	53.3%
13,927	SUMMERS	4,087	1,868	2,069	150	201 D	45.7%	50.6%	47.4%	52.6%
16,895	TAYLOR	5,290	2,642	2,376	272	266 R	49.9%	44.9%	52.7%	47.3%
7,141	TUCKER	3,132	1,502	1,469	161	33 R	48.0%	46.9%	50.6%	49.4%
9,208	TYLER	2,803	1,603	1,065	135	538 R	57.2%	38.0%	60.1%	39.9%
24,254	UPSHUR	7,534	4,010	3,102	422	908 R	53.2%	41.2%	56.4%	43.6%
42,481	WAYNE	12,704	5,954	6,395	355	441 D	46.9%	50.3%	48.2%	51.8%
9,154	WEBSTER	2,294	1,120	1,033	141	87 R	48.8%	45.0%	52.0%	48.0%
16,583	WETZEL	4,946	2,135	2,518	293	383 D	43.2%	50.9%	45.9%	54.1%
5,717	WIRT	1,871	1,005	790	76	215 R	53.7%	42.2%	56.0%	44.0%
86,956	WOOD	29,026	13,696	14,189	1,141	493 D	47.2%	48.9%	49.1%	50.9%
23,796	WYOMING	5,889	3,096	2,607	186	489 R	52.6%	44.3%	54.3%	45.7%
1,852,994	*TOTAL*	*586,034*	*271,113*	*290,510*	*24,411*	*19,397 D*	*46.3%*	*49.6%*	*48.3%*	*51.7%*

WEST VIRGINIA

HOUSE OF REPRESENTATIVES

			Republican		Democratic				Percentage			
									Total Vote		Major Vote	
CD	Year	Total Vote	Vote	Candidate	Vote	Candidate	Other Vote	Rep.-Dem. Plurality	Rep.	Dem.	Rep.	Dem.
1	2018	198,214	127,997	MCKINLEY, DAVID*	70,217	FERSHEE, KENDRA		57,780 R	64.6%	35.4%	64.6%	35.4%
1	2016	237,003	163,469	MCKINLEY, DAVID*	73,534	MANYPENNY, MIKE		89,935 R	69.0%	31.0%	69.0%	31.0%
1	2014	144,600	92,491	MCKINLEY, DAVID*	52,109	GAINER, GLEN B. III		40,382 R	64.0%	36.0%	64.0%	36.0%
1	2012	214,151	133,809	MCKINLEY, DAVID*	80,342	THORN, SUE		53,467 R	62.5%	37.5%	62.5%	37.5%
2	2018	204,792	110,504	MOONEY, ALEX X.*	88,011	SERGENT, TALLEY	6,277	22,493 R	54.0%	43.0%	55.7%	44.3%
2	2016	242,014	140,807	MOONEY, ALEX X.*	101,207	HUNT, MARK		39,600 R	58.2%	41.8%	58.2%	41.8%
2	2014	154,238	72,619	MOONEY, ALEX X.	67,687	CASEY, NICK	13,932	4,932 R	47.1%	43.9%	51.8%	48.2%
2	2012	226,766	158,206	CAPITO, SHELLEY MOORE*	68,560	SWINT, HOWARD		89,646 R	69.8%	30.2%	69.8%	30.2%
3	2018	174,985	98,645	MILLER, CAROL	76,340	OJEDA, RICHARD II		22,305 R	56.4%	43.6%	56.4%	43.6%
3	2016	207,332	140,741	JENKINS, EVAN*	49,708	DETCH, MATT	16,883	91,033 R	67.9%	24.0%	73.9%	26.1%
3	2014	140,401	77,713	JENKINS, EVAN	62,688	RAHALL, NICK J. II*		15,025 R	55.4%	44.6%	55.4%	44.6%
3	2012	200,437	92,238	SNUFFER, RICK	108,199	RAHALL, NICK J. II*		15,961 D	46.0%	54.0%	46.0%	54.0%
TOTAL	*2018*	*577,991*	*337,146*		*234,568*		*6,277*	*102,578 R*	*58.3%*	*40.6%*	*59.0%*	*41.0%*
TOTAL	*2016*	*686,349*	*445,017*		*224,449*		*16,883*	*220,568 R*	*64.8%*	*32.7%*	*66.5%*	*33.5%*
TOTAL	*2014*	*439,239*	*242,823*		*182,484*		*13,932*	*60,339 R*	*55.3%*	*41.5%*	*57.1%*	*42.9%*
TOTAL	*2012*	*641,354*	*384,253*		*257,101*			*127,152 R*	*59.9%*	*40.1%*	*59.9%*	*40.1%*

Note: An asterisk (*) denotes incumbent.

WEST VIRGINIA

GENERAL AND PRIMARY ELECTIONS

2018 GENERAL ELECTIONS: OTHER VOTES

Senate Other vote was 24,411 Libertarian (Rusty Hollen)

House Other vote was:

CD 2 6,277 Mountain (Daniel Lutz)

2018 PRIMARY ELECTIONS: SUPPLEMENTARY INFORMATION

Primary	May 8, 2018	**Registration** (as of April 30, 2018)	1,242,585	Democratic	577,977
				Republican	374,931
				Libertarian	3,241
				Mountain	1,646
				Other	30,525
				No Party	254,265

Primary Type Semi-Open—Registered Democrats and registered Republicans could vote only in their party's primary. Those voters registered with no party could participate in either the Democratic or the Republican primary.

	REPUBLICAN PRIMARIES			DEMOCRATIC PRIMARIES		
Senator	Morrisey, Patrick	48,007	34.9%	Manchin, Joe III*	112,658	69.9%
	Jenkins, Evan	40,185	29.2%	Swearengin, Paula Jean	48,594	30.1%
	Blankenship, Don	27,478	20.0%			
	Willis, Thomas "Tom"	13,540	9.8%			
	Copley, Bo	4,248	3.1%			
	Newbrough, Jack	4,115	3.0%			
	TOTAL	*137,573*		*TOTAL*	*161,252*	

WEST VIRGINIA

GENERAL AND PRIMARY ELECTIONS

	REPUBLICAN PRIMARIES			DEMOCRATIC PRIMARIES		
Congressional District 1	McKinley, David*	40,330	100.0%	Fershee, Kendra	23,137	47.2%
				Baxter, Ralph	18,670	38.1%
				Payne, Tom	7,169	14.6%
	TOTAL	*40,330*		*TOTAL*	*48,976*	
Congressional District 2	Mooney, Alex X.*	36,724	100.0%	Sergent, Talley	29,457	62.6%
				Scheinberg, Aaron	17,620	37.4%
	TOTAL	*36,724*		*TOTAL*	*47,077*	
Congressional District 3	Miller, Carol	8,923	23.8%	Ojeda, Richard II	29,867	52.2%
	Philips, Rupie	7,319	19.5%	Love, Shirley	14,109	24.6%
	Gearheart, Gary M. "Marty"	6,814	18.2%	Davis, Paul E.	9,137	16.0%
	Lucas, Conrad Gale	6,771	18.1%	Hagerman, Janice "Byrd"	4,147	7.2%
	Snuffer, Rick	3,987	10.6%			
	Amjad, Ayne	2,795	7.5%			
	Payton, Philip	861	2.3%			
	TOTAL	*37,470*		*TOTAL*	*57,260*	

Note: An asterisk (*) denotes incumbent.

WISCONSIN

Congressional districts first established for elections held in 2012

8 members

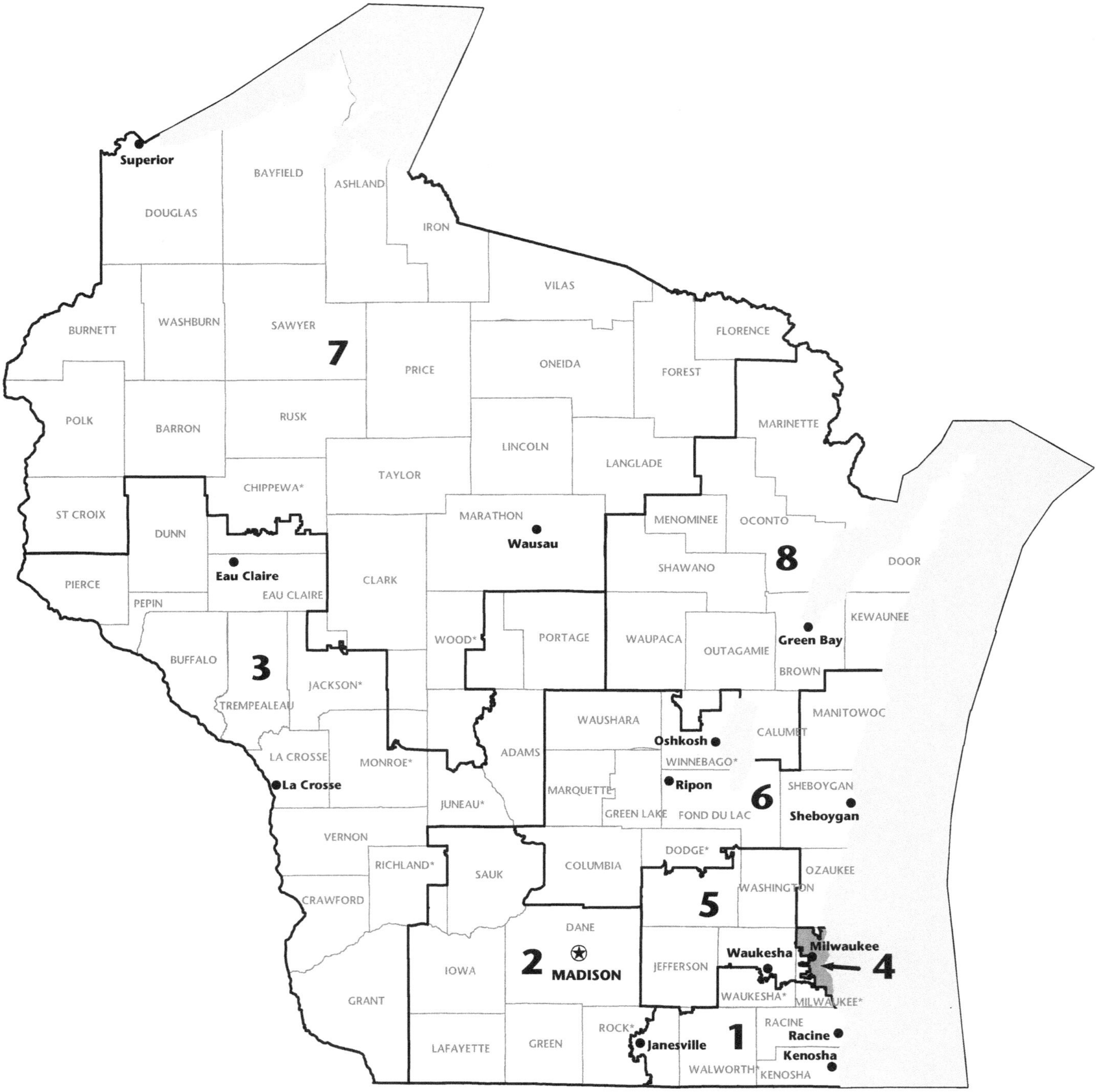

* Asterisk indicates a county whose boundaries include parts of two or more congressional districts.

WISCONSIN

GOVERNOR

Tony Evers (D). Elected 2018 to a four-year term.

SENATORS (1 Republican, 1 Democrat)

Tammy Baldwin (D). Re-elected 2018 to a six-year term. Previously elected 2012.

Ron Johnson (R). Re-elected 2016 to a six-year term. Previously elected 2010.

REPRESENTATIVES (5 Republicans, 3 Democrats)

1. Bryan Steil (R)
2. Mark Pocan (D)
3. Ron Kind (D)
4. Gwen Moore (D)
5. F. James Sensenbrenner Jr. (R)
6. Glenn S. Grothman (R)
7. Sean Duffy (R)
8. Mike Gallagher (R)

POSTWAR VOTE FOR PRESIDENT

		Republican		Democratic				Percentage			
								Total Vote		Major Vote	
Year	Total Vote	Vote	Candidate	Vote	Candidate	Other Vote	Rep.-Dem. Plurality	Rep.	Dem.	Rep.	Dem.
2016**	2,976,150	1,405,284	Trump, Donald J.	1,382,536	Clinton, Hillary Rodham	188,330	22,748 R	47.2%	46.5%	50.4%	49.6%
2012	3,068,434	1,407,966	Romney, W. Mitt	1,620,985	Obama, Barack H.*	39,483	213,019 D	45.9%	52.8%	46.5%	53.5%
2008	2,983,417	1,262,393	McCain, John S. III	1,677,211	Obama, Barack H.	43,813	414,818 D	42.3%	56.2%	42.9%	57.1%
2004	2,997,007	1,478,120	Bush, George W.*	1,489,504	Kerry, John F.	29,383	11,384 D	49.3%	49.7%	49.8%	50.2%
2000**	2,598,607	1,237,279	Bush, George W.	1,242,987	Gore, Albert Jr.	118,341	5,708 D	47.6%	47.8%	49.9%	50.1%
1996**	2,196,169	845,029	Dole, Robert "Bob"	1,071,971	Clinton, Bill*	279,169	226,942 D	38.5%	48.8%	44.1%	55.9%
1992**	2,531,114	930,855	Bush, George H.*	1,041,066	Clinton, Bill	559,193	110,211 D	36.8%	41.1%	47.2%	52.8%
1988	2,191,608	1,047,499	Bush, George H.	1,126,794	Dukakis, Michael S.	17,315	79,295 D	47.8%	51.4%	48.2%	51.8%
1984	2,211,689	1,198,584	Reagan, Ronald*	995,740	Mondale, Walter F.	17,365	202,844 R	54.2%	45.0%	54.6%	45.4%
1980**	2,273,221	1,088,845	Reagan, Ronald	981,584	Carter, Jimmy*	202,792	107,261 R	47.9%	43.2%	52.6%	47.4%
1976	2,104,175	1,004,987	Ford, Gerald R.*	1,040,232	Carter, Jimmy	58,956	35,245 D	47.8%	49.4%	49.1%	50.9%
1972	1,852,890	989,430	Nixon, Richard M.*	810,174	McGovern, George S.	53,286	179,256 R	53.4%	43.7%	55.0%	45.0%
1968**	1,691,538	809,997	Nixon, Richard M.	748,804	Humphrey, Hubert Horatio Jr.	132,737	61,193 R	47.9%	44.3%	52.0%	48.0%
1964	1,691,815	638,495	Goldwater, Barry M. Sr.	1,050,424	Johnson, Lyndon B.*	2,896	411,929 D	37.7%	62.1%	37.8%	62.2%
1960	1,729,082	895,175	Nixon, Richard M.	830,805	Kennedy, John F.	3,102	64,370 R	51.8%	48.0%	51.9%	48.1%
1956	1,550,558	954,844	Eisenhower, Dwight D.*	586,768	Stevenson, Adlai E. II	8,946	368,076 R	61.6%	37.8%	61.9%	38.1%
1952	1,607,370	979,744	Eisenhower, Dwight D.	622,175	Stevenson, Adlai E. II	5,451	357,569 R	61.0%	38.7%	61.2%	38.8%
1948	1,276,800	590,959	Dewey, Thomas E.	647,310	Truman, Harry S.*	38,531	56,351 D	46.3%	50.7%	47.7%	52.3%

Note: An asterisk (*) denotes incumbent. **In past elections, the other vote included: 2016 - 106,674 Libertarian (Gary Johnson); 2000 - 94,070 Green (Ralph Nader); 1996 - 227,339 Reform (Ross Perot); 1992 - 544,479 Independent (Perot); 1980 - 160,657 Independent (John Anderson); 1968 - 127,835 American Independent (George Wallace).

WISCONSIN

POSTWAR VOTE FOR GOVERNOR

		Republican		Democratic				Percentage			
								Total Vote		Major Vote	
Year	Total Vote	Vote	Candidate	Vote	Candidate	Other Vote	Rep.-Dem. Plurality	Rep.	Dem.	Rep.	Dem.
2018	2,673,308	1,295,080	Walker, Scott*	1,324,307	Evers, Tony	53,921	29,227 D	48.4%	49.5%	49.4%	50.6%
2014	2,410,314	1,259,706	Walker, Scott*	1,122,913	Burke, Mary	27,695	136,793 R	52.3%	46.6%	52.9%	47.1%
2012S**	2,516,065	1,335,585	Walker, Scott*	1,164,480	Barrett, Thomas M.	16,000	171,105 R	53.1%	46.3%	53.4%	46.6%
2010	2,160,832	1,128,941	Walker, Scott	1,004,303	Barrett, Thomas M.	27,588	124,638 R	52.2%	46.5%	52.9%	47.1%
2006	2,161,700	979,427	Green, Mark	1,139,115	Doyle, James E.*	43,158	159,688 D	45.3%	52.7%	46.2%	53.8%
2002**	1,775,349	734,779	McCallum, Scott*	800,515	Doyle, James E.	240,055	65,736 D	41.4%	45.1%	47.9%	52.1%
1998	1,756,014	1,047,716	Thompson, Tommy G.*	679,553	Garvey, Ed	28,745	368,163 R	59.7%	38.7%	60.7%	39.3%
1994	1,563,835	1,051,326	Thompson, Tommy G.*	482,850	Chvala, Chuck	29,659	568,476 R	67.2%	30.9%	68.5%	31.5%
1990	1,379,727	802,321	Thompson, Tommy G.*	576,280	Loftus, Thomas	1,126	226,041 R	58.2%	41.8%	58.2%	41.8%
1986	1,526,960	805,090	Thompson, Tommy G.	705,578	Earl, Anthony S.*	16,292	99,512 R	52.7%	46.2%	53.3%	46.7%
1982	1,580,344	662,838	Kohler, Terry J.	896,812	Earl, Anthony S.	20,694	233,974 D	41.9%	56.7%	42.5%	57.5%
1978	1,500,996	816,056	Dreyfus, Lee S.	673,813	Schreiber, Martin J.*	11,127	142,243 R	54.4%	44.9%	54.8%	45.2%
1974	1,181,976	497,195	Dyke, William D.	628,639	Lucey, Patrick J.*	56,142	131,444 D	42.1%	53.2%	44.2%	55.8%
1970**	1,343,160	602,617	Olson, Jack B.	728,403	Lucey, Patrick J.	12,140	125,786 D	44.9%	54.2%	45.3%	54.7%
1968	1,689,738	893,463	Knowles, Warren P.*	791,100	Lafollette, Bronson C.	5,175	102,363 R	52.9%	46.8%	53.0%	47.0%
1966	1,170,173	626,041	Knowles, Warren P.*	539,258	Lucey, Patrick J.	4,874	86,783 R	53.5%	46.1%	53.7%	46.3%
1964	1,694,887	856,779	Knowles, Warren P.	837,901	Reynolds, John W.*	207	18,878 R	50.6%	49.4%	50.6%	49.4%
1962	1,265,900	625,536	Kuehn, Philip G.	637,491	Reynolds, John W.	2,873	11,955 D	49.4%	50.4%	49.5%	50.5%
1960	1,728,009	837,123	Kuehn, Philip G.	890,868	Nelson, Gaylord Anton*	18	53,745 D	48.4%	51.6%	48.4%	51.6%
1958	1,202,219	556,391	Thomson, Vernon W.*	644,296	Nelson, Gaylord Anton	1,532	87,905 D	46.3%	53.6%	46.3%	53.7%
1956	1,557,788	808,273	Thomson, Vernon W.	749,421	Proxmire, William	94	58,852 R	51.9%	48.1%	51.9%	48.1%
1954	1,158,666	596,158	Kohler, Walter J. Jr.*	560,747	Proxmire, William	1,761	35,411 R	51.5%	48.4%	51.5%	48.5%
1952	1,615,214	1,009,171	Kohler, Walter J. Jr.*	601,844	Proxmire, William	4,199	407,327 R	62.5%	37.3%	62.6%	37.4%
1950	1,138,148	605,649	Kohler, Walter J. Jr.	525,319	Thompson, Carl W.	7,180	80,330 R	53.2%	46.2%	53.6%	46.4%
1948	1,266,139	684,839	Rennebohm, Oscar*	558,497	Thompson, Carl W.	22,803	126,342 R	54.1%	44.1%	55.1%	44.9%
1946	1,040,444	621,970	Goodland, Walter S.*	406,499	Hoan, Daniel W.	11,975	215,471 R	59.8%	39.1%	60.5%	39.5%

Note: An asterisk (*) denotes incumbent. **The 2012 Wisconsin gubernatorial contest was a special recall election held in June 2012. Governor Scott Walker retained his office. In past elections, the other vote included: 2002 - 185,455 Libertarian (Ed Thompson). The term of office of Wisconsin's Governor was increased from two to four years effective with the 1970 election.

POSTWAR VOTE FOR SENATOR

		Republican		Democratic				Percentage			
								Total Vote		Major Vote	
Year	Total Vote	Vote	Candidate	Vote	Candidate	Other Vote	Rep.-Dem. Plurality	Rep.	Dem.	Rep.	Dem.
2018	2,660,763	1,184,885	Vukmir, Leah	1,472,914	Baldwin, Tammy*	2,964	288,029 D	44.5%	55.4%	44.6%	55.4%
2016	2,948,741	1,479,471	Johnson, Ron*	1,380,335	Feingold, Russell D.	88,935	99,136 R	50.2%	46.8%	51.7%	48.3%
2012	3,009,411	1,380,126	Thompson, Tommy G.	1,547,104	Baldwin, Tammy	82,181	166,978 D	45.9%	51.4%	47.1%	52.9%
2010	2,171,331	1,125,999	Johnson, Ron	1,020,958	Feingold, Russell D.*	24,374	105,041 R	51.9%	47.0%	52.4%	47.6%
2006	2,138,297	630,299	Lorge, Robert Gerald	1,439,214	Kohl, Herbert H.*	68,784	808,915 D	29.5%	67.3%	30.5%	69.5%
2004	2,949,743	1,301,183	Michels, Tim	1,632,697	Feingold, Russell D.*	15,863	331,514 D	44.1%	55.4%	44.4%	55.6%
2000	2,540,083	940,744	Gillespie, John	1,563,238	Kohl, Herbert H.*	36,101	622,494 D	37.0%	61.5%	37.6%	62.4%
1998	1,760,836	852,272	Neumann, Mark W.	890,059	Feingold, Russell D.*	18,505	37,787 D	48.4%	50.5%	48.9%	51.1%
1994	1,565,628	636,989	Welch, Robert T.	912,662	Kohl, Herbert H.*	15,977	275,673 D	40.7%	58.3%	41.1%	58.9%
1992	2,455,124	1,129,599	Kasten, Robert W.*	1,290,662	Feingold, Russell D.	34,863	161,063 D	46.0%	52.6%	46.7%	53.3%
1988	2,168,190	1,030,440	Engeleiter, Susan	1,128,625	Kohl, Herbert H.	9,125	98,185 D	47.5%	52.1%	47.7%	52.3%
1986	1,483,174	754,573	Kasten, Robert W.*	702,963	Garvey, Ed	25,638	51,610 R	50.9%	47.4%	51.8%	48.2%
1982	1,544,981	527,355	McCallum, Scott	983,311	Proxmire, William*	34,315	455,956 D	34.1%	63.6%	34.9%	65.1%
1980	2,204,202	1,106,311	Kasten, Robert W.	1,065,487	Nelson, Gaylord Anton*	32,404	40,824 R	50.2%	48.3%	50.9%	49.1%
1976	1,935,183	521,902	York, Stanley	1,396,970	Proxmire, William*	16,311	875,068 D	27.0%	72.2%	27.2%	72.8%
1974	1,199,495	429,327	Petri, Thomas E.	740,700	Nelson, Gaylord Anton*	29,468	311,373 D	35.8%	61.8%	36.7%	63.3%
1970	1,338,967	381,297	Erickson, John E.	948,445	Proxmire, William*	9,225	567,148 D	28.5%	70.8%	28.7%	71.3%
1968	1,654,861	633,910	Leonard, Jerris	1,020,931	Nelson, Gaylord Anton*	20	387,021 D	38.3%	61.7%	38.3%	61.7%
1964	1,673,776	780,116	Renk, Wilbur N.	892,013	Proxmire, William*	1,647	111,897 D	46.6%	53.3%	46.7%	53.3%
1962	1,260,168	594,846	Wiley, Alexander*	662,342	Nelson, Gaylord Anton	2,980	67,496 D	47.2%	52.6%	47.3%	52.7%
1958	1,194,678	510,398	Steinle, Roland J.	682,440	Proxmire, William*	1,840	172,042 D	42.7%	57.1%	42.8%	57.2%
1957S**	772,620	312,931	Kohler, Walter J. Jr.	435,985	Proxmire, William	23,704	123,054 D	40.5%	56.4%	41.8%	58.2%
1956	1,523,356	892,473	Wiley, Alexander*	627,903	Maier, Henry W.	2,980	264,570 R	58.6%	41.2%	58.7%	41.3%
1952	1,605,228	870,444	McCarthy, Joseph R.*	731,402	Fairchild, Thomas E.	3,382	139,042 R	54.2%	45.6%	54.3%	45.7%
1950	1,116,135	595,283	Wiley, Alexander*	515,539	Fairchild, Thomas E.	5,313	79,744 R	53.3%	46.2%	53.6%	46.4%
1946	1,014,594	620,430	McCarthy, Joseph R.	378,772	McMurray, Howard J.	15,392	241,658 R	61.2%	37.3%	62.1%	37.9%

Note: An asterisk (*) denotes incumbent. **The August 1957 election was for a short term to fill a vacancy.

WISCONSIN

GOVERNOR 2018

2010 Census Population	County	Total Vote	Republican (Walker)	Democratic (Evers)	Other	Rep.-Dem. Plurality	Percentage Total Vote Rep.	Percentage Total Vote Dem.	Percentage Major Vote Rep.	Percentage Major Vote Dem.
20,875	ADAMS	9,291	5,209	3,892	190	1,317 R	56.1%	41.9%	57.2%	42.8%
16,157	ASHLAND	6,920	2,584	4,168	168	1,584 D	37.3%	60.2%	38.3%	61.7%
45,870	BARRON	18,568	10,655	7,623	290	3,032 R	57.4%	41.1%	58.3%	41.7%
15,014	BAYFIELD	8,797	3,458	5,152	187	1,694 D	39.3%	58.6%	40.2%	59.8%
248,007	BROWN	115,669	61,424	51,724	2,521	9,700 R	53.1%	44.7%	54.3%	45.7%
13,587	BUFFALO	5,976	3,463	2,385	128	1,078 R	57.9%	39.9%	59.2%	40.8%
15,457	BURNETT	7,588	4,664	2,742	182	1,922 R	61.5%	36.1%	63.0%	37.0%
48,971	CALUMET	23,703	14,313	8,992	398	5,321 R	60.4%	37.9%	61.4%	38.6%
62,415	CHIPPEWA	27,775	15,499	11,739	537	3,760 R	55.8%	42.3%	56.9%	43.1%
34,690	CLARK	11,714	7,469	4,015	230	3,454 R	63.8%	34.3%	65.0%	35.0%
56,833	COLUMBIA	27,034	12,363	14,124	547	1,761 D	45.7%	52.2%	46.7%	53.3%
16,644	CRAWFORD	6,604	3,117	3,354	133	237 D	47.2%	50.8%	48.2%	51.8%
488,073	DANE	294,623	69,206	220,052	5,365	150,846 D	23.5%	74.7%	23.9%	76.1%
88,759	DODGE	37,810	23,516	13,552	742	9,964 R	62.2%	35.8%	63.4%	36.6%
27,785	DOOR	16,979	8,536	8,151	292	385 R	50.3%	48.0%	51.2%	48.8%
44,159	DOUGLAS	18,759	7,251	11,034	474	3,783 D	38.7%	58.8%	39.7%	60.3%
43,857	DUNN	18,457	9,255	8,667	535	588 R	50.1%	47.0%	51.6%	48.4%
98,736	EAU CLAIRE	48,833	20,855	26,768	1,210	5,913 D	42.7%	54.8%	43.8%	56.2%
4,423	FLORENCE	2,181	1,503	643	35	860 R	68.9%	29.5%	70.0%	30.0%
101,633	FOND DU LAC	45,186	27,941	16,439	806	11,502 R	61.8%	36.4%	63.0%	37.0%
9,304	FOREST	3,982	2,421	1,486	75	935 R	60.8%	37.3%	62.0%	38.0%
51,208	GRANT	19,597	9,502	9,665	430	163 D	48.5%	49.3%	49.6%	50.4%
36,842	GREEN	17,090	7,333	9,378	379	2,045 D	42.9%	54.9%	43.9%	56.1%
19,051	GREEN LAKE	8,184	5,411	2,633	140	2,778 R	66.1%	32.2%	67.3%	32.7%
23,687	IOWA	11,176	4,289	6,674	213	2,385 D	38.4%	59.7%	39.1%	60.9%
5,916	IRON	3,092	1,785	1,264	43	521 R	57.7%	40.9%	58.5%	41.5%
20,449	JACKSON	8,016	4,129	3,713	174	416 R	51.5%	46.3%	52.7%	47.3%
83,686	JEFFERSON	38,157	21,475	16,018	664	5,457 R	56.3%	42.0%	57.3%	42.7%
26,664	JUNEAU	10,131	5,689	4,247	195	1,442 R	56.2%	41.9%	57.3%	42.7%
166,426	KENOSHA	68,074	31,512	34,481	2,081	2,969 D	46.3%	50.7%	47.8%	52.2%
20,574	KEWAUNEE	9,499	5,792	3,572	135	2,220 R	61.0%	37.6%	61.9%	38.1%
114,638	LA CROSSE	57,081	23,537	32,103	1,441	8,566 D	41.2%	56.2%	42.3%	57.7%
16,836	LAFAYETTE	6,564	3,324	3,135	105	189 R	50.6%	47.8%	51.5%	48.5%
19,977	LANGLADE	9,265	5,712	2,825	728	2,887 R	61.7%	30.5%	66.9%	33.1%
28,743	LINCOLN	13,510	7,865	5,335	310	2,530 R	58.2%	39.5%	59.6%	40.4%
81,442	MANITOWOC	35,556	21,360	13,513	683	7,847 R	60.1%	38.0%	61.3%	38.7%
134,063	MARATHON	62,144	36,886	24,057	1,201	12,829 R	59.4%	38.7%	60.5%	39.5%
41,749	MARINETTE	17,405	10,916	6,193	296	4,723 R	62.7%	35.6%	63.8%	36.2%
15,404	MARQUETTE	7,195	4,143	2,911	141	1,232 R	57.6%	40.5%	58.7%	41.3%
4,232	MENOMINEE	1,132	233	866	33	633 D	20.6%	76.5%	21.2%	78.8%
947,735	MILWAUKEE	393,877	124,055	262,124	7,698	138,069 D	31.5%	66.5%	32.1%	67.9%
44,673	MONROE	16,799	9,464	6,969	366	2,495 R	56.3%	41.5%	57.6%	42.4%
37,660	OCONTO	17,591	11,490	5,858	243	5,632 R	65.3%	33.3%	66.2%	33.8%
35,998	ONEIDA	19,600	11,248	7,850	502	3,398 R	57.4%	40.1%	58.9%	41.1%
176,695	OUTAGAMIE	83,414	45,359	36,290	1,765	9,069 R	54.4%	43.5%	55.6%	44.4%
86,395	OZAUKEE	51,176	32,069	18,394	713	13,675 R	62.7%	35.9%	63.5%	36.5%
7,469	PEPIN	3,135	1,745	1,333	57	412 R	55.7%	42.5%	56.7%	43.3%
41,019	PIERCE	17,501	8,740	8,193	568	547 R	49.9%	46.8%	51.6%	48.4%
44,205	POLK	18,603	10,866	7,333	404	3,533 R	58.4%	39.4%	59.7%	40.3%
70,019	PORTAGE	34,871	15,958	18,007	906	2,049 D	45.8%	51.6%	47.0%	53.0%
14,159	PRICE	6,679	3,996	2,585	98	1,411 R	59.8%	38.7%	60.7%	39.3%
195,408	RACINE	87,190	44,770	40,498	1,922	4,272 R	51.3%	46.4%	52.5%	47.5%
18,021	RICHLAND	7,053	3,285	3,623	145	338 D	46.6%	51.4%	47.6%	52.4%
160,331	ROCK	68,366	26,904	39,680	1,782	12,776 D	39.4%	58.0%	40.4%	59.6%
14,755	RUSK	6,099	3,797	2,184	118	1,613 R	62.3%	35.8%	63.5%	36.5%
61,976	SAUK	28,932	12,615	15,630	687	3,015 D	43.6%	54.0%	44.7%	55.3%
16,557	SAWYER	8,197	4,542	3,484	171	1,058 R	55.4%	42.5%	56.6%	43.4%
41,949	SHAWANO	18,000	11,478	6,121	401	5,357 R	63.8%	34.0%	65.2%	34.8%
115,507	SHEBOYGAN	53,247	31,520	20,801	926	10,719 R	59.2%	39.1%	60.2%	39.8%
84,345	ST. CROIX	40,070	22,108	16,690	1,272	5,418 R	55.2%	41.7%	57.0%	43.0%

WISCONSIN

GOVERNOR 2018

							Percentage			
							Total Vote		Major Vote	
2010 Census Population	County	Total Vote	Republican (Walker)	Democratic (Evers)	Other	Rep.-Dem. Plurality	Rep.	Dem.	Rep.	Dem.
20,689	TAYLOR	8,088	5,690	2,269	129	3,421 R	70.4%	28.1%	71.5%	28.5%
28,816	TREMPEALEAU	12,255	6,623	5,393	239	1,230 R	54.0%	44.0%	55.1%	44.9%
29,773	VERNON	13,066	6,276	6,550	240	274 D	48.0%	50.1%	48.9%	51.1%
21,430	VILAS	12,519	7,814	4,510	195	3,304 R	62.4%	36.0%	63.4%	36.6%
102,228	WALWORTH	45,459	27,088	17,394	977	9,694 R	59.6%	38.3%	60.9%	39.1%
15,911	WASHBURN	7,916	4,461	3,292	163	1,169 R	56.4%	41.6%	57.5%	42.5%
131,887	WASHINGTON	70,545	50,958	18,703	884	32,255 R	72.2%	26.5%	73.2%	26.8%
389,891	WAUKESHA	221,807	146,699	72,131	2,977	74,568 R	66.1%	32.5%	67.0%	33.0%
52,410	WAUPACA	22,473	13,909	8,143	421	5,766 R	61.9%	36.2%	63.1%	36.9%
24,496	WAUSHARA	10,629	6,719	3,742	168	2,977 R	63.2%	35.2%	64.2%	35.8%
166,994	WINNEBAGO	75,753	38,368	35,610	1,775	2,758 R	50.6%	47.0%	51.9%	48.1%
74,749	WOOD	33,081	18,871	13,638	572	5,233 R	57.0%	41.2%	58.0%	42.0%
5,686,986	*TOTAL*	*2,673,308*	*1,295,080*	*1,324,307*	*53,921*	*29,227 D*	*48.4%*	*49.5%*	*49.4%*	*50.6%*

WISCONSIN

SENATOR 2018

							Percentage			
							Total Vote		Major Vote	
2010 Census Population	County	Total Vote	Republican (Vukmir)	Democratic (Baldwin)	Other	Rep.-Dem. Plurality	Rep.	Dem.	Rep.	Dem.
20,875	ADAMS	9,399	4,854	4,537	8	317 R	51.6%	48.3%	51.7%	48.3%
16,157	ASHLAND	6,892	2,351	4,533	8	2,182 D	34.1%	65.8%	34.2%	65.8%
45,870	BARRON	18,493	9,911	8,571	11	1,340 R	53.6%	46.3%	53.6%	46.4%
15,014	BAYFIELD	8,775	3,233	5,541	1	2,308 D	36.8%	63.1%	36.8%	63.2%
248,007	BROWN	115,066	55,750	59,132	184	3,382 D	48.5%	51.4%	48.5%	51.5%
13,587	BUFFALO	5,917	2,968	2,945	4	23 R	50.2%	49.8%	50.2%	49.8%
15,457	BURNETT	7,528	4,289	3,239		1,050 R	57.0%	43.0%	57.0%	43.0%
48,971	CALUMET	23,563	12,822	10,741		2,081 R	54.4%	45.6%	54.4%	45.6%
62,415	CHIPPEWA	27,629	13,830	13,798	1	32 R	50.1%	49.9%	50.1%	49.9%
34,690	CLARK	11,644	6,558	5,084	2	1,474 R	56.3%	43.7%	56.3%	43.7%
56,833	COLUMBIA	26,940	11,674	15,230	36	3,556 D	43.3%	56.5%	43.4%	56.6%
16,644	CRAWFORD	6,555	2,703	3,852		1,149 D	41.2%	58.8%	41.2%	58.8%
488,073	DANE	293,979	65,515	228,050	414	162,535 D	22.3%	77.6%	22.3%	77.7%
88,759	DODGE	37,490	21,482	16,007	1	5,475 R	57.3%	42.7%	57.3%	42.7%
27,785	DOOR	16,947	7,494	9,442	11	1,948 D	44.2%	55.7%	44.2%	55.8%
44,159	DOUGLAS	18,622	6,925	11,689	8	4,764 D	37.2%	62.8%	37.2%	62.8%
43,857	DUNN	18,367	8,623	9,743	1	1,120 D	46.9%	53.0%	47.0%	53.0%
98,736	EAU CLAIRE	48,642	18,957	29,614	71	10,657 D	39.0%	60.9%	39.0%	61.0%
4,423	FLORENCE	2,167	1,438	729		709 R	66.4%	33.6%	66.4%	33.6%
101,633	FOND DU LAC	44,602	25,496	19,065	41	6,431 R	57.2%	42.7%	57.2%	42.8%
9,304	FOREST	3,944	2,062	1,879	3	183 R	52.3%	47.6%	52.3%	47.7%
51,208	GRANT	19,420	8,860	10,554	6	1,694 D	45.6%	54.3%	45.6%	54.4%
36,842	GREEN	17,037	6,732	10,294	11	3,562 D	39.5%	60.4%	39.5%	60.5%
19,051	GREEN LAKE	8,117	4,893	3,222	2	1,671 R	60.3%	39.7%	60.3%	39.7%
23,687	IOWA	11,114	3,835	7,270	9	3,435 D	34.5%	65.4%	34.5%	65.5%
5,916	IRON	3,064	1,605	1,459		146 R	52.4%	47.6%	52.4%	47.6%
20,449	JACKSON	7,981	3,611	4,370		759 D	45.2%	54.8%	45.2%	54.8%
83,686	JEFFERSON	37,911	19,809	18,055	47	1,754 R	52.3%	47.6%	52.3%	47.7%
26,664	JUNEAU	10,096	5,429	4,658	9	771 R	53.8%	46.1%	53.8%	46.2%
166,426	KENOSHA	67,589	29,181	38,296	112	9,115 D	43.2%	56.7%	43.2%	56.8%

WISCONSIN

SENATOR 2018

2010 Census Population	County	Total Vote	Republican (Vukmir)	Democratic (Baldwin)	Other	Rep.-Dem. Plurality	Percentage Total Vote Rep.	Total Vote Dem.	Major Vote Rep.	Major Vote Dem.
20,574	KEWAUNEE	9,454	5,158	4,287	9	871 R	54.6%	45.3%	54.6%	45.4%
114,638	LA CROSSE	56,891	21,160	35,731		14,571 D	37.2%	62.8%	37.2%	62.8%
16,836	LAFAYETTE	6,493	2,900	3,592	1	692 D	44.7%	55.3%	44.7%	55.3%
19,977	LANGLADE	9,128	5,239	3,889		1,350 R	57.4%	42.6%	57.4%	42.6%
28,743	LINCOLN	13,379	6,901	6,463	15	438 R	51.6%	48.3%	51.6%	48.4%
81,442	MANITOWOC	35,373	18,795	16,541	37	2,254 R	53.1%	46.8%	53.2%	46.8%
134,063	MARATHON	61,813	32,661	29,084	68	3,577 R	52.8%	47.1%	52.9%	47.1%
41,749	MARINETTE	17,252	9,731	7,520	1	2,211 R	56.4%	43.6%	56.4%	43.6%
15,404	MARQUETTE	7,134	3,791	3,337	6	454 R	53.1%	46.8%	53.2%	46.8%
4,232	MENOMINEE	1,116	220	896		676 D	19.7%	80.3%	19.7%	80.3%
947,735	MILWAUKEE	392,858	111,684	280,426	748	168,742 D	28.4%	71.4%	28.5%	71.5%
44,673	MONROE	16,731	8,559	8,151	21	408 R	51.2%	48.7%	51.2%	48.8%
37,660	OCONTO	17,449	10,392	7,042	15	3,350 R	59.6%	40.4%	59.6%	40.4%
35,998	ONEIDA	19,473	10,112	9,338	23	774 R	51.9%	48.0%	52.0%	48.0%
176,695	OUTAGAMIE	82,974	41,354	41,618	2	264 D	49.8%	50.2%	49.8%	50.2%
86,395	OZAUKEE	51,010	29,480	21,464	66	8,016 R	57.8%	42.1%	57.9%	42.1%
7,469	PEPIN	3,107	1,578	1,529		49 R	50.8%	49.2%	50.8%	49.2%
41,019	PIERCE	17,466	8,247	9,216	3	969 D	47.2%	52.8%	47.2%	52.8%
44,205	POLK	18,544	10,245	8,299		1,946 R	55.2%	44.8%	55.2%	44.8%
70,019	PORTAGE	34,725	14,510	20,170	45	5,660 D	41.8%	58.1%	41.8%	58.2%
14,159	PRICE	6,651	3,515	3,136		379 R	52.8%	47.2%	52.8%	47.2%
195,408	RACINE	86,750	41,213	45,397	140	4,184 D	47.5%	52.3%	47.6%	52.4%
18,021	RICHLAND	6,986	2,980	4,000	6	1,020 D	42.7%	57.3%	42.7%	57.3%
160,331	ROCK	68,011	25,322	42,616	73	17,294 D	37.2%	62.7%	37.3%	62.7%
14,755	RUSK	6,046	3,381	2,654	11	727 R	55.9%	43.9%	56.0%	44.0%
61,976	SAUK	28,826	11,866	16,960		5,094 D	41.2%	58.8%	41.2%	58.8%
16,557	SAWYER	8,100	4,159	3,938	3	221 R	51.3%	48.6%	51.4%	48.6%
41,949	SHAWANO	17,852	10,438	7,414		3,024 R	58.5%	41.5%	58.5%	41.5%
115,507	SHEBOYGAN	52,925	28,667	24,183	75	4,484 R	54.2%	45.7%	54.2%	45.8%
84,345	ST. CROIX	39,864	21,069	18,765	30	2,304 R	52.9%	47.1%	52.9%	47.1%
20,689	TAYLOR	8,035	5,005	3,028	2	1,977 R	62.3%	37.7%	62.3%	37.7%
28,816	TREMPEALEAU	12,168	5,633	6,526	9	893 D	46.3%	53.6%	46.3%	53.7%
29,773	VERNON	12,959	5,459	7,495	5	2,036 D	42.1%	57.8%	42.1%	57.9%
21,430	VILAS	12,491	7,166	5,308	17	1,858 R	57.4%	42.5%	57.4%	42.6%
102,228	WALWORTH	45,216	24,844	20,299	73	4,545 R	54.9%	44.9%	55.0%	45.0%
15,911	WASHBURN	7,858	4,190	3,664	4	526 R	53.3%	46.6%	53.3%	46.7%
131,887	WASHINGTON	70,175	47,102	23,072	1	24,030 R	67.1%	32.9%	67.1%	32.9%
389,891	WAUKESHA	220,630	136,190	84,147	293	52,043 R	61.7%	38.1%	61.8%	38.2%
52,410	WAUPACA	22,316	12,792	9,509	15	3,283 R	57.3%	42.6%	57.4%	42.6%
24,496	WAUSHARA	10,540	6,106	4,434		1,672 R	57.9%	42.1%	57.9%	42.1%
166,994	WINNEBAGO	75,585	35,282	40,185	118	4,903 D	46.7%	53.2%	46.8%	53.2%
74,749	WOOD	32,919	16,899	15,992	28	907 R	51.3%	48.6%	51.4%	48.6%
5,686,986	*TOTAL*	*2,660,763*	*1,184,885*	*1,472,914*	*2,964*	*288,029 D*	*44.5%*	*55.4%*	*44.6%*	*55.4%*

WISCONSIN

HOUSE OF REPRESENTATIVES

			Republican		Democratic				Percentage			
									Total Vote		Major Vote	
CD	Year	Total Vote	Vote	Candidate	Vote	Candidate	Other Vote	Rep.-Dem. Plurality	Rep.	Dem.	Rep.	Dem.
1	2018	325,317	177,492	STEIL, BRYAN	137,508	BRYCE, RANDY	10,317	39,984 R	54.6%	42.3%	56.3%	43.7%
1	2016	354,245	230,072	RYAN, PAUL D.*	107,003	SOLEN, RYAN	17,170	123,069 R	64.9%	30.2%	68.3%	31.7%
1	2014	288,170	182,316	RYAN, PAUL D.*	105,552	ZERBAN, ROB	302	76,764 R	63.3%	36.6%	63.3%	36.7%
1	2012	365,058	200,423	RYAN, PAUL D.*	158,414	ZEBRAN, ROB	6,221	42,009 R	54.9%	43.4%	55.9%	44.1%
2	2018	317,295			309,116	POCAN, MARK*	8,179	309,116 D		97.4%		100.0%
2	2016	398,060	124,044	THERON, PETER	273,537	POCAN, MARK*	479	149,493 D	31.2%	68.7%	31.2%	68.8%
2	2014	328,847	103,619	THERON, PETER	224,920	POCAN, MARK*	308	121,301 D	31.5%	68.4%	31.5%	68.5%
2	2012	390,898	124,683	LEE, CHAD	265,422	POCAN, MARK	793	140,739 D	31.9%	67.9%	32.0%	68.0%
3	2018	314,989	126,980	TOFT, STEVE	187,888	KIND, RON*	121	60,908 D	40.3%	59.6%	40.3%	59.7%
3	2016	260,370			257,401	KIND, RON*	2,969	257,401 D		98.9%		100.0%
3	2014	275,161	119,540	KURTZ, TONY	155,368	KIND, RON*	253	35,828 D	43.4%	56.5%	43.5%	56.5%
3	2012	339,764	121,713	BOLAND, RAY	217,712	KIND, RON*	339	95,999 D	35.8%	64.1%	35.9%	64.1%
4	2018	273,087	59,091	ROGERS, TIM	206,487	MOORE, GWEN*	7,509	147,396 D	21.6%	75.6%	22.2%	77.8%
4	2016	286,909			220,181	MOORE, GWEN*		220,181 D		76.7%		100.0%
4	2014	254,892	68,490	SEBRING, DAN	179,045	MOORE, GWEN*	7,357	110,555 D	26.9%	70.2%	27.7%	72.3%
4	2012	325,788	80,787	SEBRING, DAN	235,257	MOORE, GWEN*	9,744	154,470 D	24.8%	72.2%	25.6%	74.4%
5	2018	364,288	225,619	SENSENBRENNER, F. JAMES JR.*	138,385	PALZEWICZ, TOM	284	87,234 R	61.9%	38.0%	62.0%	38.0%
5	2016	390,844	260,706	SENSENBRENNER, F. JAMES JR.*	114,477	PENEBAKER, KHARY	15,661	146,229 R	66.7%	29.3%	69.5%	30.5%
5	2014	332,826	231,160	SENSENBRENNER, F. JAMES JR.*	101,190	ROCKWOOD, CHRIS B.	476	129,970 R	69.5%	30.4%	69.6%	30.4%
5	2012	369,664	250,335	SENSENBRENNER, F. JAMES JR.*	118,478	HEASTER, DAVE	851	131,857 R	67.7%	32.1%	67.9%	32.1%
6	2018	325,065	180,311	GROTHMAN, GLENN S.*	144,536	KOHL, DAN	218	35,775 R	55.5%	44.5%	55.5%	44.5%
6	2016	357,183	204,147	GROTHMAN, GLENN S.*	133,072	LLOYD, SARAH	19,964	71,075 R	57.2%	37.3%	60.5%	39.5%
6	2014	299,033	169,767	GROTHMAN, GLENN S.	122,212	HARRIS, MARK L.	7,054	47,555 R	56.8%	40.9%	58.1%	41.9%
6	2012	359,745	223,460	PETRI, THOMAS E.*	135,921	KALLAS, JOSEPH C.	364	87,539 R	62.1%	37.8%	62.2%	37.8%
7	2018	322,840	194,061	DUFFY, SEAN*	124,307	ENGEBRETSON, MARGARET	4,472	69,754 R	60.1%	38.5%	61.0%	39.0%
7	2016	362,271	223,418	DUFFY, SEAN*	138,643	HOEFT, MARY	210	84,775 R	61.7%	38.3%	61.7%	38.3%
7	2014	286,603	169,891	DUFFY, SEAN*	112,949	WESTLUND, KELLY	3,763	56,942 R	59.3%	39.4%	60.1%	39.9%
7	2012	359,669	201,720	DUFFY, SEAN*	157,524	KREITLOW, PAT	425	44,196 R	56.1%	43.8%	56.2%	43.8%
8	2018	328,774	209,410	GALLAGHER, MIKE*	119,265	LIEGEOIS, BEAU	99	90,145 R	63.7%	36.3%	63.7%	36.3%
8	2016	363,780	227,892	GALLAGHER, MIKE	135,682	NELSON, TOM	206	92,210 R	62.6%	37.3%	62.7%	37.3%
8	2014	290,048	188,553	RIBBLE, REID J.*	101,345	GRUETT, RON	150	87,208 R	65.0%	34.9%	65.0%	35.0%
8	2012	355,464	198,874	RIBBLE, REID J.*	156,287	WALL, JAMIE	303	42,587 R	55.9%	44.0%	56.0%	44.0%
TOTAL	*2018*	*2,571,655*	*1,172,964*		*1,367,492*		*31,199*	*194,528 D*	*45.6%*	*53.2%*	*46.2%*	*53.8%*
TOTAL	*2016*	*2,773,662*	*1,270,279*		*1,379,996*		*123,387*	*109,717 D*	*45.8%*	*49.8%*	*47.9%*	*52.1%*
TOTAL	*2014*	*2,355,580*	*1,233,336*		*1,102,581*		*19,663*	*130,755 R*	*52.4%*	*46.8%*	*52.8%*	*47.2%*
TOTAL	*2012*	*2,866,050*	*1,401,995*		*1,445,015*		*19,040*	*43,020 D*	*48.9%*	*50.4%*	*49.2%*	*50.8%*

Note: An asterisk (*) denotes incumbent.

WISCONSIN

GENERAL AND PRIMARY ELECTIONS

2018 GENERAL ELECTIONS: OTHER VOTES

Governor	Other vote was 20,225 Libertarian (Phillip Anderson), 18,884 Independent (Maggie Turnbull), 11,087 Green (Michael White), 2,745 Independent (Arnie Enz), 966 Write-in (Scattered Write-in), 4 Write-in (Ryan Cason), 3 Write-in (William Davis), 2 Write-in (Mark Grimek), 2 Write-in (Richard Turtenwald), 1 Write-in (Corban Gehler), 1 Write-in (Paul Boucher), 1 Write-in (Robbie Hoffman)
Senate	Other vote was 2,922 Write-in (Scattered Write-in), 28 Write-in (Mary Jo Walters), 14 Write-in (John Schiess)
House	Other vote was:
CD 1	10,006 Independent (Ken Yorgan), 304 Write-in (Scattered Write-in), 7 Write-in (Joseph Kexel)
CD 2	8,141 Write-in (Scattered Write-in), 29 Write-in (Joey Reed), 8 Write-in (Rick Cruz), 1 Write-in (Bradley Burt)
CD 3	121 Write-in (Scattered Write-in)
CD 4	7,170 Independent (Robert Raymond), 339 Write-in (Scattered Write-in)
CD 5	283 Write-in (Scattered Write-in), 1 Write-in (Ramon Garcia)
CD 6	218 Write-in (Scattered Write-in)
CD 7	4,416 Independent (Ken Driessen), 53 Write-in (Scattered Write-in), 3 Write-in (Bob Look)
CD 8	99 Write-in (Scattered Write-in)

2018 PRIMARY ELECTIONS: SUPPLEMENTARY INFORMATION

Primary	August 14, 2018	**Registration** (as of August 1, 2018)	3,112,905	No Party Registration

Primary Type Open—Any registered voter could participate in the party primary of his or her choice.

	REPUBLICAN PRIMARIES			DEMOCRATIC PRIMARIES		
Senator	Vukmir, Leah	217,230	48.9%	Baldwin, Tammy*	510,812	99.6%
	Nicholson, Kevin	191,276	43.1%	Scattering (Write-in)	1,848	0.4%
	Lucia, George C.	18,786	4.2%			
	Jones, Griffin	8,699	2.0%			
	Barman, Charles	7,959	1.8%			
	Scattering (Write-in)	303	0.1%			
	TOTAL	*444,253*		*TOTAL*	*512,660*	
Governor	Walker, Scott*	417,276	91.5%	Evers, Tony	225,082	41.8%
	Meyer, Robert	38,269	8.4%	Mitchell, Mahlon	87,926	16.3%
	Scattering (Write-in)	267	0.1%	Roys, Kelda Helen	69,086	12.8%
	Cason, Ryan (Write-in)	11		Vinehout, Kathleen	44,168	8.2%
	Paul, Adam Nicholas (Write-in)	7		McCabe, Mike	39,885	7.4%
				Flynn, Matt	31,580	5.9%
				Soglin, Paul R.	28,158	5.2%
				Gronik, Andy	6,627	1.2%
				Wachs, Dana	4,216	0.8%
				Pade, Josh	1,908	0.4%
				Scattering (Write-in)	211	
				Boucher, Paul (Write-in)	10	
	TOTAL	*455,830*		*TOTAL*	*538,857*	

WISCONSIN

GENERAL AND PRIMARY ELECTIONS

	REPUBLICAN PRIMARIES			DEMOCRATIC PRIMARIES		
Congressional District 1	Steil, Bryan	30,885	51.5%	Bryce, Randy	36,406	59.5%
	Polce, Nick	8,948	14.9%	Myers, Cathy	24,699	40.4%
	Nehlen, Paul	6,638	11.1%	Scattering (Write-in)	50	0.1%
	Steen, Kevin Adam	6,262	10.4%			
	Ryan, Jeremy	6,226	10.4%			
	Boivin, Brad	924	1.5%			
	Scattering (Write-in)	59	0.1%			
	TOTAL	*59,942*		*TOTAL*	*61,155*	
Congressional District 2	Scattering (Write-in)	886	98.4%	Pocan, Mark*	115,246	99.7%
	Reed, Joey Wayne (Write-in)	14	1.6%	Scattering (Write-in)	364	0.3%
	TOTAL	*900*		*TOTAL*	*115,610*	
Congressional District 3	Toft, Steve	35,768	99.9%	Kind, Ron*	59,643	99.8%
	Scattering (Write-in)	38	0.1%	Scattering (Write-in)	132	0.2%
	TOTAL	*35,806*		*TOTAL*	*59,775*	
Congressional District 4	Rogers, Tim	8,912	55.3%	Moore, Gwen*	76,991	88.9%
	Werner, Cindy	7,122	44.2%	George, Gary R.	9,468	10.9%
	Scattering (Write-in)	69	0.4%	Scattering (Write-in)	181	0.2%
	TOTAL	*16,103*		*TOTAL*	*86,640*	
Congressional District 5	Sensenbrenner, F. James Jr.*	73,397	81.2%	Palzewicz, Tom	43,192	99.8%
	Vipond, Jennifer Hoppe	17,011	18.8%	Scattering (Write-in)	85	0.2%
	Scattering (Write-in)	34		Garcia, Ramon (Write-in)	5	
	TOTAL	*90,442*		*TOTAL*	*43,282*	
Congressional District 6	Grothman, Glenn S.*	60,485	99.6%	Kohl, Dan	41,862	99.8%
	Scattering (Write-in)	234	0.4%	Scattering (Write-in)	72	0.2%
	TOTAL	*60,719*		*TOTAL*	*41,934*	
Congressional District 7	Duffy, Sean*	60,708	99.7%	Engebretson, Margaret	27,194	57.2%
	Scattering (Write-in)	209	0.3%	Ewert, Brian	20,285	42.7%
				Scattering (Write-in)	34	0.1%
				Look, Bob (Write-in)	11	
	TOTAL	*60,917*		*TOTAL*	*47,524*	
Congressional District 8	Gallagher, Mike*	62,524	99.9%	Liegeois, Beau	38,450	99.9%
	Scattering (Write-in)	56	0.1%	Scattering (Write-in)	48	0.1%
	TOTAL	*62,580*		*TOTAL*	*38,498*	

Note: An asterisk (*) denotes incumbent.

WYOMING

One member At Large

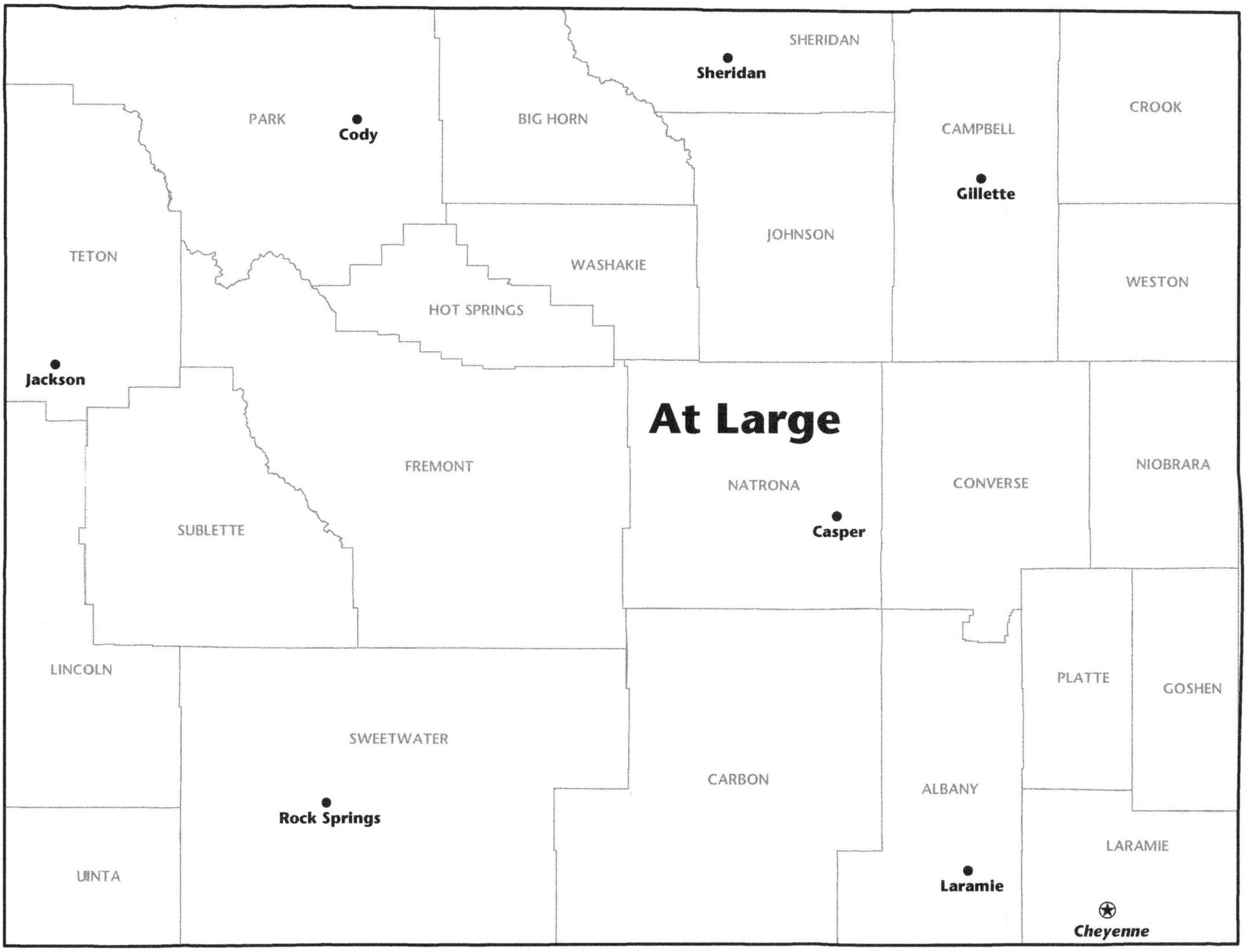

WYOMING

GOVERNOR

Mark Gordon (R). Elected 2018 to a four-year term.

SENATORS (2 Republicans)

John Barrasso (R). Re-elected 2018 to a six-year term. Previously elected 2012, and 2008 to complete the remaining four years of the term vacated by the June 2007 death of Senator Craig Thomas (R); sworn in as Thomas's successor June 25, 2007.

Michael B. Enzi (R). Re-elected 2014 to a six-year term. Previously elected 2008, 2002, 1996.

REPRESENTATIVE (1 Republican)

At Large. Elizabeth "Liz" Cheney (R)

POSTWAR VOTE FOR PRESIDENT

		Republican		Democratic				Percentage			
								Total Vote		Major Vote	
Year	Total Vote	Vote	Candidate	Vote	Candidate	Other Vote	Rep.-Dem. Plurality	Rep.	Dem.	Rep.	Dem.
2016**	255,849	174,419	Trump, Donald J.	55,973	Clinton, Hillary Rodham	25,457	118,446 R	68.2%	21.9%	75.7%	24.3%
2012	249,061	170,962	Romney, W. Mitt	69,286	Obama, Barack H.*	8,813	101,676 R	68.6%	27.8%	71.2%	28.8%
2008	254,658	164,958	McCain, John S. III	82,868	Obama, Barack H.	6,832	82,090 R	64.8%	32.5%	66.6%	33.4%
2004	243,428	167,629	Bush, George W.*	70,776	Kerry, John F.	5,023	96,853 R	68.9%	29.1%	70.3%	29.7%
2000**	218,351	147,947	Bush, George W.	60,481	Gore, Albert Jr.	9,923	87,466 R	67.8%	27.7%	71.0%	29.0%
1996**	211,571	105,388	Dole, Robert "Bob"	77,934	Clinton, Bill*	28,249	27,454 R	49.8%	36.8%	57.5%	42.5%
1992**	200,598	79,347	Bush, George H.*	68,160	Clinton, Bill	53,091	11,187 R	39.6%	34.0%	53.8%	46.2%
1988	176,551	106,867	Bush, George H.	67,113	Dukakis, Michael S.	2,571	39,754 R	60.5%	38.0%	61.4%	38.6%
1984	188,968	133,241	Reagan, Ronald*	53,370	Mondale, Walter F.	2,357	79,871 R	70.5%	28.2%	71.4%	28.6%
1980**	176,713	110,700	Reagan, Ronald	49,427	Carter, Jimmy*	16,586	61,273 R	62.6%	28.0%	69.1%	30.9%
1976	156,343	92,717	Ford, Gerald R.*	62,239	Carter, Jimmy	1,387	30,478 R	59.3%	39.8%	59.8%	40.2%
1972	145,570	100,464	Nixon, Richard M.*	44,358	McGovern, George S.	748	56,106 R	69.0%	30.5%	69.4%	30.6%
1968**	127,205	70,927	Nixon, Richard M.	45,173	Humphrey, Hubert Horatio Jr.	11,105	25,754 R	55.8%	35.5%	61.1%	38.9%
1964	142,716	61,998	Goldwater, Barry M. Sr.	80,718	Johnson, Lyndon B.*		18,720 D	43.4%	56.6%	43.4%	56.6%
1960	140,782	77,451	Nixon, Richard M.	63,331	Kennedy, John F.		14,120 R	55.0%	45.0%	55.0%	45.0%
1956	124,127	74,573	Eisenhower, Dwight D.*	49,554	Stevenson, Adlai E. II		25,019 R	60.1%	39.9%	60.1%	39.9%
1952	129,253	81,049	Eisenhower, Dwight D.	47,934	Stevenson, Adlai E. II	270	33,115 R	62.7%	37.1%	62.8%	37.2%
1948	101,425	47,947	Dewey, Thomas E.	52,354	Truman, Harry S.*	1,124	4,407 D	47.3%	51.6%	47.8%	52.2%

Note: An asterisk (*) denotes incumbent. **In past elections, the other vote included: 2016 - 13,287 Libertarian (Gary Johnson); 2000 - 4,625 Green (Ralph Nader); 1996 - 25,928 Reform (Ross Perot); 1992 - 51,263 Independent (Perot); 1980 - 12,072 Independent (John Anderson); 1968 - 11,105 American Independent (George Wallace).

WYOMING

POSTWAR VOTE FOR GOVERNOR

		Republican		Democratic				Percentage			
								Total Vote		Major Vote	
Year	Total Vote	Vote	Candidate	Vote	Candidate	Other Vote	Rep.-Dem. Plurality	Rep.	Dem.	Rep.	Dem.
2018	203,238	136,412	Gordon, Mark	55,965	Throne, Mary A.	10,861	80,447 R	67.1%	27.5%	70.9%	29.1%
2014	167,877	99,700	Mead, Matt*	45,752	Gosar, Peter	22,425	53,948 R	59.4%	27.3%	68.5%	31.5%
2010	188,463	123,780	Mead, Matt	43,240	Petersen, Leslie	21,443	80,540 R	65.7%	22.9%	74.1%	25.9%
2006	193,892	58,100	Hunkins, Ray	135,516	Freudenthal, Dave*	276	77,416 D	30.0%	69.9%	30.0%	70.0%
2002	185,459	88,873	Bebout, Eli	92,662	Freudenthal, Dave	3,924	3,789 D	47.9%	50.0%	49.0%	51.0%
1998	174,888	97,235	Geringer, Jim*	70,754	Vinich, John P.	6,899	26,481 R	55.6%	40.5%	57.9%	42.1%
1994	200,990	118,016	Geringer, Jim	80,747	Karpan, Kathy	2,227	37,269 R	58.7%	40.2%	59.4%	40.6%
1990	160,109	55,471	Mead, Mary	104,638	Sullivan, Mike*		49,167 D	34.6%	65.4%	34.6%	65.4%
1986	164,720	75,841	Simpson, Peter	88,879	Sullivan, Mike		13,038 D	46.0%	54.0%	46.0%	54.0%
1982	168,555	62,128	Morton, Warren A.	106,427	Herschler, Ed*		44,299 D	36.9%	63.1%	36.9%	63.1%
1978	137,567	67,595	Ostlund, John C.	69,972	Herschler, Ed*		2,377 D	49.1%	50.9%	49.1%	50.9%
1974	128,386	56,645	Jones, Dick	71,741	Herschler, Ed		15,096 D	44.1%	55.9%	44.1%	55.9%
1970	118,257	74,249	Hathaway, Stanley K.*	44,008	Rooney, John J.		30,241 R	62.8%	37.2%	62.8%	37.2%
1966	120,873	65,624	Hathaway, Stanley K.	55,249	Wilkerson, Ernest		10,375 R	54.3%	45.7%	54.3%	45.7%
1962	119,268	64,970	Hansen, Clifford P.	54,298	Gage, Jack R.*		10,672 R	54.5%	45.5%	54.5%	45.5%
1958	112,537	52,488	Simpson, Milward L.*	55,070	Hickey, John J.	4,979	2,582 D	46.6%	48.9%	48.8%	51.2%
1954	111,438	56,275	Simpson, Milward L.	55,163	Jack, William		1,112 R	50.5%	49.5%	50.5%	49.5%
1950	96,959	54,441	Barrett, Frank A.	42,518	McIntyre, John J.		11,923 R	56.1%	43.9%	56.1%	43.9%
1946	81,353	38,333	Wright, Earl	43,020	Hunt, Lester C.*		4,687 D	47.1%	52.9%	47.1%	52.9%

Note: An asterisk (*) denotes incumbent.

POSTWAR VOTE FOR SENATOR

		Republican		Democratic				Percentage			
								Total Vote		Major Vote	
Year	Total Vote	Vote	Candidate	Vote	Candidate	Other Vote	Rep.-Dem. Plurality	Rep.	Dem.	Rep.	Dem.
2018	203,420	136,210	Barrasso, John*	61,227	Trauner, Gary	5,983	74,983 R	67.0%	30.1%	69.0%	31.0%
2014	168,390	121,554	Enzi, Michael B.*	29,377	Hardy, Charles E. "Charlie"	17,459	92,177 R	72.2%	17.4%	80.5%	19.5%
2012	244,862	185,250	Barrasso, John*	53,019	Chestnut, Tim	6,593	132,231 R	75.7%	21.7%	77.7%	22.3%
2008	249,946	189,046	Enzi, Michael B.*	60,631	Rothfuss, Chris	269	128,415 R	75.6%	24.3%	75.7%	24.3%
2008S**	249,558	183,063	Barrasso, John*	66,202	Carter, Nick	293	116,861 R	73.4%	26.5%	73.4%	26.6%
2006	193,136	135,174	Thomas, Craig*	57,671	Groutage, Dale	291	77,503 R	70.0%	29.9%	70.1%	29.9%
2002	183,280	133,710	Enzi, Michael B.*	49,570	Corcoran, Joyce Jansa		84,140 R	73.0%	27.0%	73.0%	27.0%
2000	213,659	157,622	Thomas, Craig*	47,087	Logan, Mel	8,950	110,535 R	73.8%	22.0%	77.0%	23.0%
1996	211,077	114,116	Enzi, Michael B.	89,103	Karpan, Kathy	7,858	25,013 R	54.1%	42.2%	56.2%	43.8%
1994	201,710	118,754	Thomas, Craig	79,287	Sullivan, Mike	3,669	39,467 R	58.9%	39.3%	60.0%	40.0%
1990	157,632	100,784	Simpson, Alan K.*	56,848	Helling, Kathy		43,936 R	63.9%	36.1%	63.9%	36.1%
1988	180,964	91,143	Wallop, Malcolm*	89,821	Vinich, John P.		1,322 R	50.4%	49.6%	50.4%	49.6%
1984	186,898	146,373	Simpson, Alan K.*	40,525	Ryan, Victor A.		105,848 R	78.3%	21.7%	78.3%	21.7%
1982	167,191	94,725	Wallop, Malcolm*	72,466	McDaniel, Rodger		22,259 R	56.7%	43.3%	56.7%	43.3%
1978	133,364	82,908	Simpson, Alan K.	50,456	Whitaker, Raymond B.		32,452 R	62.2%	37.8%	62.2%	37.8%
1976	155,368	84,810	Wallop, Malcolm	70,558	McGee, Gale*		14,252 R	54.6%	45.4%	54.6%	45.4%
1972	142,067	101,314	Hansen, Clifford P.*	40,753	Vinich, Mike		60,561 R	71.3%	28.7%	71.3%	28.7%
1970	120,486	53,279	Wold, John S.	67,207	McGee, Gale*		13,928 D	44.2%	55.8%	44.2%	55.8%
1966	122,689	63,548	Hansen, Clifford P.	59,141	Roncalio, Teno		4,407 R	51.8%	48.2%	51.8%	48.2%
1964	141,670	65,185	Wold, John S.	76,485	McGee, Gale*		11,300 D	46.0%	54.0%	46.0%	54.0%
1962S**	119,372	69,043	Simpson, Milward L.	50,329	Hickey, John J.*		18,714 R	57.8%	42.2%	57.8%	42.2%
1960	138,550	78,103	Thomson, E. Keith	60,447	Whitaker, Raymond B.		17,656 R	56.4%	43.6%	56.4%	43.6%
1958	114,157	56,122	Barrett, Frank A.*	58,035	McGee, Gale		1,913 D	49.2%	50.8%	49.2%	50.8%
1954	112,252	54,407	Harrison, William Henry	57,845	O'Mahoney, Joseph C.*		3,438 D	48.5%	51.5%	48.5%	51.5%
1952	130,097	67,176	Barrett, Frank A.	62,921	O'Mahoney, Joseph C.*		4,255 R	51.6%	48.4%	51.6%	48.4%
1948	101,480	43,527	Robertson, Edward V.*	57,953	Hunt, Lester C.		14,426 D	42.9%	57.1%	42.9%	57.1%
1946	81,557	35,714	Henderson, Harry B.	45,843	O'Mahoney, Joseph C.*		10,129 D	43.8%	56.2%	43.8%	56.2%

Note: An asterisk (*) denotes incumbent. **The 1962 election and one of the 2008 elections were for short terms to fill a vacancy.

WYOMING

GOVERNOR 2018

2010 Census Population	County	Total Vote	Republican (Gordon)	Democratic (Throne)	Other	Rep.-Dem. Plurality	Percentage Total Vote Rep.	Total Vote Dem.	Major Vote Rep.	Major Vote Dem.
36,299	ALBANY	14,411	6,494	7,137	780	643 D	45.1%	49.5%	47.6%	52.4%
11,668	BIG HORN	4,314	3,391	608	315	2,783 R	78.6%	14.1%	84.8%	15.2%
46,133	CAMPBELL	13,010	10,398	1,856	756	8,542 R	79.9%	14.3%	84.9%	15.1%
15,885	CARBON	5,166	3,560	1,314	292	2,246 R	68.9%	25.4%	73.0%	27.0%
13,833	CONVERSE	4,939	3,872	757	310	3,115 R	78.4%	15.3%	83.6%	16.4%
7,083	CROOK	3,088	2,575	358	155	2,217 R	83.4%	11.6%	87.8%	12.2%
40,123	FREMONT	14,358	9,251	4,299	808	4,952 R	64.4%	29.9%	68.3%	31.7%
13,249	GOSHEN	4,805	3,568	957	280	2,611 R	74.3%	19.9%	78.9%	21.1%
4,812	HOT SPRINGS	2,251	1,682	443	126	1,239 R	74.7%	19.7%	79.2%	20.8%
8,569	JOHNSON	3,881	3,245	478	158	2,767 R	83.6%	12.3%	87.2%	12.8%
91,738	LARAMIE	32,702	20,052	11,196	1,454	8,856 R	61.3%	34.2%	64.2%	35.8%
18,106	LINCOLN	7,172	5,511	1,155	506	4,356 R	76.8%	16.1%	82.7%	17.3%
75,450	NATRONA	24,480	16,866	6,352	1,262	10,514 R	68.9%	25.9%	72.6%	27.4%
2,484	NIOBRARA	1,160	918	153	89	765 R	79.1%	13.2%	85.7%	14.3%
28,205	PARK	11,809	8,815	2,277	717	6,538 R	74.6%	19.3%	79.5%	20.5%
8,667	PLATTE	3,776	2,644	845	287	1,799 R	70.0%	22.4%	75.8%	24.2%
29,116	SHERIDAN	11,814	8,727	2,667	420	6,060 R	73.9%	22.6%	76.6%	23.4%
10,247	SUBLETTE	3,402	2,664	602	136	2,062 R	78.3%	17.7%	81.6%	18.4%
43,806	SWEETWATER	12,933	8,375	3,758	800	4,617 R	64.8%	29.1%	69.0%	31.0%
21,294	TETON	11,688	4,736	6,541	411	1,805 D	40.5%	56.0%	42.0%	58.0%
21,118	UINTA	6,263	4,547	1,296	420	3,251 R	72.6%	20.7%	77.8%	22.2%
8,533	WASHAKIE	3,112	2,396	568	148	1,828 R	77.0%	18.3%	80.8%	19.2%
7,208	WESTON	2,704	2,125	348	231	1,777 R	78.6%	12.9%	85.9%	14.1%
563,626	*TOTAL*	*203,238*	*136,412*	*55,965*	*10,861*	*80,447 R*	*67.1%*	*27.5%*	*70.9%*	*29.1%*

WYOMING

SENATOR 2018

2010 Census Population	County	Total Vote	Republican (Barrasso)	Democratic (Trauner)	Other	Rep.-Dem. Plurality	Percentage Total Vote Rep.	Total Vote Dem.	Major Vote Rep.	Major Vote Dem.
36,299	ALBANY	14,419	6,366	7,576	477	1,210 D	44.2%	52.5%	45.7%	54.3%
11,668	BIG HORN	4,317	3,564	639	114	2,925 R	82.6%	14.8%	84.8%	15.2%
46,133	CAMPBELL	13,051	11,020	1,628	403	9,392 R	84.4%	12.5%	87.1%	12.9%
15,885	CARBON	5,194	3,673	1,359	162	2,314 R	70.7%	26.2%	73.0%	27.0%
13,833	CONVERSE	4,957	3,959	834	164	3,125 R	79.9%	16.8%	82.6%	17.4%
7,083	CROOK	3,089	2,643	335	111	2,308 R	85.6%	10.8%	88.8%	11.2%
40,123	FREMONT	14,395	9,262	4,734	399	4,528 R	64.3%	32.9%	66.2%	33.8%
13,249	GOSHEN	4,798	3,658	1,020	120	2,638 R	76.2%	21.3%	78.2%	21.8%
4,812	HOT SPRINGS	2,258	1,742	455	61	1,287 R	77.1%	20.2%	79.3%	20.7%
8,569	JOHNSON	3,889	3,085	722	82	2,363 R	79.3%	18.6%	81.0%	19.0%
91,738	LARAMIE	32,608	19,473	12,167	968	7,306 R	59.7%	37.3%	61.5%	38.5%
18,106	LINCOLN	7,197	5,846	1,152	199	4,694 R	81.2%	16.0%	83.5%	16.5%
75,450	NATRONA	24,464	16,359	7,285	820	9,074 R	66.9%	29.8%	69.2%	30.8%
2,484	NIOBRARA	1,159	980	144	35	836 R	84.6%	12.4%	87.2%	12.8%
28,205	PARK	11,827	8,938	2,589	300	6,349 R	75.6%	21.9%	77.5%	22.5%
8,667	PLATTE	3,785	2,850	801	134	2,049 R	75.3%	21.2%	78.1%	21.9%
29,116	SHERIDAN	11,805	8,318	3,205	282	5,113 R	70.5%	27.1%	72.2%	27.8%
10,247	SUBLETTE	3,407	2,653	668	86	1,985 R	77.9%	19.6%	79.9%	20.1%
43,806	SWEETWATER	12,973	8,577	3,943	453	4,634 R	66.1%	30.4%	68.5%	31.5%
21,294	TETON	11,750	3,833	7,691	226	3,858 D	32.6%	65.5%	33.3%	66.7%

WYOMING

SENATOR 2018

2010 Census Population	County	Total Vote	Republican (Barrasso)	Democratic (Trauner)	Other	Rep.-Dem. Plurality	Percentage Total Vote Rep.	Total Vote Dem.	Major Vote Rep.	Major Vote Dem.
21,118	UINTA	6,280	4,713	1,371	196	3,342 R	75.0%	21.8%	77.5%	22.5%
8,533	WASHAKIE	3,110	2,423	588	99	1,835 R	77.9%	18.9%	80.5%	19.5%
7,208	WESTON	2,688	2,275	321	92	1,954 R	84.6%	11.9%	87.6%	12.4%
563,626	*TOTAL*	*203,420*	*136,210*	*61,227*	*5,983*	*74,983 R*	*67.0%*	*30.1%*	*69.0%*	*31.0%*

WYOMING

HOUSE OF REPRESENTATIVES

CD	Year	Total Vote	Republican Vote	Republican Candidate	Democratic Vote	Democratic Candidate	Other Vote	Rep.-Dem. Plurality	Percentage Total Vote Rep.	Total Vote Dem.	Major Vote Rep.	Major Vote Dem.
At Large	2018	201,245	127,963	CHENEY, ELIZABETH "LIZ"*	59,903	HUNTER, GREG	13,379	68,060 R	63.6%	29.8%	68.1%	31.9%
At Large	2016	251,776	156,176	CHENEY, ELIZABETH "LIZ"	75,466	GREENE, RYAN	20,134	80,710 R	62.0%	30.0%	67.4%	32.6%
At Large	2014	165,100	113,038	LUMMIS, CYNTHIA M.*	37,803	GRAYSON, RICHARD	14,259	75,235 R	68.5%	22.9%	74.9%	25.1%
At Large	2012	241,621	166,452	LUMMIS, CYNTHIA M.*	57,573	HENRICHSEN, CHRIS	17,596	108,879 R	68.9%	23.8%	74.3%	25.7%
At Large	2010	186,969	131,661	LUMMIS, CYNTHIA M.*	45,768	WENDT, DAVID	9,540	85,893 R	70.4%	24.5%	74.2%	25.8%
At Large	2008	249,395	131,244	LUMMIS, CYNTHIA M.	106,758	TRAUNER, GARY	11,393	24,486 R	52.6%	42.8%	55.1%	44.9%
At Large	2006	193,369	93,336	CUBIN, BARBARA*	92,324	TRAUNER, GARY	7,709	1,012 R	48.3%	47.7%	50.3%	49.7%
At Large	2004	239,034	132,107	CUBIN, BARBARA*	99,989	LADD, TED	6,938	32,118 R	55.3%	41.8%	56.9%	43.1%
At Large	2002	182,152	110,229	CUBIN, BARBARA*	65,961	AKIN, RON	5,962	44,268 R	60.5%	36.2%	62.6%	37.4%
At Large	2000	212,312	141,848	CUBIN, BARBARA*	60,638	GREEN, MICHAEL ALLEN	9,826	81,210 R	66.8%	28.6%	70.1%	29.9%
At Large	1998	174,219	100,687	CUBIN, BARBARA*	67,399	FARRIS, SCOTT	6,133	33,288 R	57.8%	38.7%	59.9%	40.1%
At Large	1996	209,983	116,004	CUBIN, BARBARA*	85,724	MAXFIELD, PETE	8,255	30,280 R	55.2%	40.8%	57.5%	42.5%
At Large	1994	196,197	104,426	CUBIN, BARBARA	81,022	SCHUSTER, BOB	10,749	23,404 R	53.2%	41.3%	56.3%	43.7%
At Large	1992	196,977	113,882	THOMAS, CRAIG*	77,418	HERSCHLER, JON	5,677	36,464 R	57.8%	39.3%	59.5%	40.5%
At Large	1990	158,055	87,078	THOMAS, CRAIG	70,977	MAXFIELD, PETE		16,101 R	55.1%	44.9%	55.1%	44.9%
At Large	1988	177,651	118,350	CHENEY, RICHARD*	56,527	SHARRATT, BRYAN	2,774	61,823 R	66.6%	31.8%	67.7%	32.3%
At Large	1986	159,787	111,007	CHENEY, RICHARD*	48,780	GILMORE, RICK		62,227 R	69.5%	30.5%	69.5%	30.5%
At Large	1984	187,904	138,234	CHENEY, RICHARD*	45,857	MCFADDEN, HUGH B.	3,813	92,377 R	73.6%	24.4%	75.1%	24.9%
At Large	1982	159,277	113,236	CHENEY, RICHARD*	46,041	HOMMEL, THEODORE H.		67,195 R	71.1%	28.9%	71.1%	28.9%
At Large	1980	169,699	116,361	CHENEY, RICHARD*	53,338	ROGERS, JIM		63,023 R	68.6%	31.4%	68.6%	31.4%
At Large	1978	129,377	75,855	CHENEY, RICHARD	53,522	BAGLEY, BILL		22,333 R	58.6%	41.4%	58.6%	41.4%
At Large	1976	151,868	66,147	HART, LARRY	85,721	RONCALIO, TENO*		19,574 D	43.6%	56.4%	43.6%	56.4%
At Large	1974	126,933	57,499	STROOCK, TOM	69,434	RONCALIO, TENO*		11,935 D	45.3%	54.7%	45.3%	54.7%
At Large	1972	146,299	70,667	KIDD, WILLIAM	75,632	RONCALIO, TENO*		4,965 D	48.3%	51.7%	48.3%	51.7%
At Large	1970	116,304	57,848	ROBERTS, HARRY	58,456	RONCALIO, TENO*		608 D	49.7%	50.3%	49.7%	50.3%
At Large	1968	123,313	77,363	WOLD, JOHN S.	45,950	LINFORD, VELMA		31,413 R	62.7%	37.3%	62.7%	37.3%
At Large	1966	120,426	62,984	HARRISON, WILLIAM HENRY	57,442	CHRISTIAN, AL		5,542 R	52.3%	47.7%	52.3%	47.7%
At Large	1964	139,175	68,482	HARRISON, WILLIAM HENRY	70,693	RONCALIO, TENO*		2,211 D	49.2%	50.8%	49.2%	50.8%
At Large	1962	116,474	71,489	HARRISON, WILLIAM HENRY*	44,985	MANKUS, LOUIS A.		26,504 R	61.4%	38.6%	61.4%	38.6%
At Large	1960	134,331	70,241	HARRISON, WILLIAM HENRY	64,090	ARMSTRONG, HEPBURN T.		6,151 R	52.3%	47.7%	52.3%	47.7%
At Large	1958	111,780	59,894	THOMSON, E. KEITH*	51,886	WHITAKER, RAYMOND B.		8,008 R	53.6%	46.4%	53.6%	46.4%
At Large	1956	120,128	69,903	THOMSON, E. KEITH*	50,225	O'CALLAGHAN, JERRY A.		19,678 R	58.2%	41.8%	58.2%	41.8%
At Large	1954	108,771	61,111	THOMSON, E. KEITH	47,660	TULLY, SAM		13,451 R	56.2%	43.8%	56.2%	43.8%
At Large	1952	126,720	76,161	HARRISON, WILLIAM HENRY*	50,559	ROSS, ROBERT R. JR.		25,602 R	60.1%	39.9%	60.1%	39.9%
At Large	1950	93,348	50,865	HARRISON, WILLIAM HENRY	42,483	CLARK, JOHN B.		8,382 R	54.5%	45.5%	54.5%	45.5%
At Large	1948	97,464	50,218	BARRETT, FRANK A.*	47,246	FLANNERY, L. G.		2,972 R	51.5%	48.5%	51.5%	48.5%
At Large	1946	79,438	44,482	BARRETT, FRANK A.*	34,956	MCINTYRE, JOHN J.		9,526 R	56.0%	44.0%	56.0%	44.0%

Note: An asterisk (*) denotes incumbent.

WYOMING

GENERAL AND PRIMARY ELECTIONS

2018 GENERAL ELECTIONS: OTHER VOTES

Governor Other vote was 6,751 Centrist (Rex Rammell), 3,010 Libertarian (Lawrence Struempf), 1,100 Write-in (Write-ins)

Senate Other vote was 5,658 Libertarian (Joseph Porambo), 325 Write-in (Write-ins)

House Other vote was:

At Large 6,918 Libertarian (Richard Brubaker), 6,070 Constitution (Daniel Cummings), 391 Write-in (Write-ins)

2018 PRIMARY ELECTIONS: SUPPLEMENTARY INFORMATION

Primary	August 21, 2018	**Registration** (as of August 21, 2018)	266,464	Republican	180,686
				Democratic	46,378
				Libertarian	2,386
				Constitution	782
				Other	127
				Unaffiliated	36,105

Primary Type Semi Open—Only registered Democrats and Republicans could vote in their party's primary, although on primary day, any new voter could register with the party of his or her choice and any previously registered voter could participate in another party's primary by changing his or her registration to that party.

	REPUBLICAN PRIMARIES			DEMOCRATIC PRIMARIES		
Senator	Barrasso, John*	74,292	64.8%	Trauner, Gary	17,562	98.9%
	Dodson, Dave	32,647	28.5%	Write-In	195	1.1%
	Holtz, John	2,981	2.6%			
	Hardy, Charlie	2,377	2.1%			
	De La Fuente, Roque "Rocky"	1,280	1.1%			
	Van Risseghem, Anthony L.	870	0.8%			
	Write-In	267	0.2%			
	TOTAL	*114,714*		*TOTAL*	*17,757*	
Governor	Gordon, Mark	38,951	33.4%	Throne, Mary A.	12,948	71.6%
	Friess, Foster	29,842	25.6%	Green, Michael Allen	2,391	13.2%
	Hageman, Harriet M.	25,052	21.5%	Casner, Kenneth R.	1,213	6.7%
	Galeotos, Sam E.	14,554	12.5%	Wilde, Rex	1,201	6.6%
	Haynes, Taylor	6,511	5.6%	Write-In	323	1.8%
	Dahlin, Bill	1,763	1.5%			
	Write-In	113	0.1%			
	TOTAL	*116,786*		*TOTAL*	*18,076*	
Congressional At Large	Cheney, Elizabeth "Liz"*	75,183	67.7%	Hunter, Greg	10,332	60.9%
	Miller, Rod	22,045	19.9%	Helm, Travis	6,527	38.5%
	Stanley, Blake E.	13,307	12.0%	Write-In	100	0.6%
	Write-In	478	0.4%			
	TOTAL	*111,013*		*TOTAL*	*16,959*	

Note: An asterisk (*) denotes incumbent.

DISTRICT OF COLUMBIA

DISTRICT OF COLUMBIA

DELEGATE

Elaine Holmes Norton (D). Re-elected 2018 to a two-year term. Previously elected 2016, 2014, 2012, 2010, 2008, 2006, 2004, 2002, 2000, 1998, 1996, 1994, 1992, 1990.

POSTWAR VOTE FOR PRESIDENT

		Republican		Democratic				Percentage			
								Total Vote		Major Vote	
Year	Total Vote	Vote	Candidate	Vote	Candidate	Other Vote	Rep.-Dem. Plurality	Rep.	Dem.	Rep.	Dem.
2016**	311,268	12,723	Trump, Donald J.	282,830	Clinton, Hillary Rodham	15,715	270,107 D	4.1%	90.9%	4.3%	95.7%
2012	293,764	21,381	Romney, W. Mitt	267,070	Obama, Barack H.*	5,313	245,689 D	7.3%	90.9%	7.4%	92.6%
2008	265,853	17,367	McCain, John S. III	245,800	Obama, Barack H.	2,686	228,433 D	6.5%	92.5%	6.6%	93.4%
2004	227,586	21,256	Bush, George W.*	202,970	Kerry, John F.	3,360	181,714 D	9.3%	89.2%	9.5%	90.5%
2000**	201,894	18,073	Bush, George W.	171,923	Gore, Albert Jr.	11,898	153,850 D	9.0%	85.2%	9.5%	90.5%
1996**	185,726	17,339	Dole, Robert "Bob"	158,220	Clinton, Bill*	10,167	140,881 D	9.3%	85.2%	9.9%	90.1%
1992**	227,572	20,698	Bush, George H.*	192,619	Clinton, Bill	14,255	171,921 D	9.1%	84.6%	9.7%	90.3%
1988	192,877	27,590	Bush, George H.	159,407	Dukakis, Michael S.	5,880	131,817 D	14.3%	82.6%	14.8%	85.2%
1984	211,288	29,009	Reagan, Ronald*	180,408	Mondale, Walter F.	1,871	151,399 D	13.7%	85.4%	13.9%	86.1%
1980**	175,237	23,545	Reagan, Ronald	131,113	Carter, Jimmy*	20,579	107,568 D	13.4%	74.8%	15.2%	84.8%
1976	168,830	27,873	Ford, Gerald R.*	137,818	Carter, Jimmy	3,139	109,945 D	16.5%	81.6%	16.8%	83.2%
1972	163,421	35,226	Nixon, Richard M.*	127,627	McGovern, George S.	568	92,401 D	21.6%	78.1%	21.6%	78.4%
1968	170,578	31,012	Nixon, Richard M.	139,566	Humphrey, Hubert Horatio Jr.		108,554 D	18.2%	81.8%	18.2%	81.8%
1964**	198,597	28,801	Goldwater, Barry M. Sr.	169,796	Johnson, Lyndon B.*		140,995 D	14.5%	85.5%	14.5%	85.5%

Note: An asterisk (*) denotes incumbent. **In past elections, the other vote included: 2016 - 4,906 Libertarian (Gary Johnson); 2000 - 10,576 Green (Ralph Nader); 1996 - 3,611 Reform (Ross Perot); 1992 - 9,681 Independent (Perot); 1980 - 16,337 Independent (John Anderson). Under the Twenty-third Amendment to the Constitution, the District of Columbia could choose presidential electors beginning with the 1964 election.

POSTWAR VOTE FOR DELEGATE

		Republican		Democratic				Percentage			
								Total Vote		Major Vote	
Year	Total Vote	Vote	Candidate	Vote	Candidate	Other Vote	Rep.-Dem. Plurality	Rep.	Dem.	Rep.	Dem.
2018	228,769	9,700	Nelson F. Rimensnyder	199,124	Norton, Eleanor Holmes*	19,945	189,424 D	4.2%	87.0%	4.6%	95.4%
2016	300,906			265,178	Norton, Eleanor Holmes*	35,728	265,178 D		88.1%		100.0%
2014	171,893	11,673	Nelson F. Rimensnyder	143,923	Norton, Eleanor Holmes*	16,297	132,250 D	6.8%	83.7%	7.5%	92.5%
2012	278,563			246,664	Norton, Eleanor Holmes*	31,899	246,664 D		88.5%		100.0%
2010	132,656	8,109	Smith, Missy Reilly	117,990	Norton, Eleanor Holmes*	6,557	109,881 D	6.1%	88.9%	6.4%	93.6%
2008	247,741			228,376	Norton, Eleanor Holmes*	19,095	228,376 D		92.3%		100.0%
2006	114,777			111,726	Norton, Eleanor Holmes*	3,051	111,726 D		97.3%		100.0%
2004	221,213	18,296	Monroe, Michael Andrew	202,027	Norton, Eleanor Holmes*	890	183,731 D	8.3%	91.3%	8.3%	91.7%
2002	128,233			119,268	Norton, Eleanor Holmes*	8,965	119,628 D		93.0%		100.0%
2000	175,631	10,258	Wolterbeek, Edward	158,824	Norton, Eleanor Holmes*	6,549	148,566 D	5.8%	90.4%	6.1%	93.9%
1998	136,359	8,610	Wolterbeek, Edward	122,228	Norton, Eleanor Holmes*	5,221	113,618 D	6.3%	89.6%	6.6%	93.4%
1996	149,998	11,306	Simonds, Sprague	134,996	Norton, Eleanor Holmes*	3,696	123,690 D	7.5%	90.0%	7.7%	92.3%
1994	173,664	13,828	Saltz, Donald	154,988	Norton, Eleanor Holmes*	4,848	141,160 D	8.0%	89.2%	8.2%	91.8%
1992	196,574	20,108	Emerson, Susan	166,808	Norton, Eleanor Holmes*	9,838	146,700 D	10.2%	84.8%	10.8%	89.2%
1990	159,627	41,999	Singleton, Harry M.	98,442	Norton, Eleanor Holmes	19,186	56,443 D	26.3%	61.7%	29.9%	70.1%
1988	170,933	22,936	Reed, William	121,817	Fauntroy, Walter E.*	26180	98,881 D	13.4%	71.3%	15.8%	84.2%
1986	126,855	17,643	King, Mary L.H.	101,604	Fauntroy, Walter E.*	7,608	83,961 D	13.9%	80.1%	14.8%	85.2%
1984	161,771			154,583	Fauntroy, Walter E.*	7,188	154,583 D		95.6%		100.0%
1982	112,543	17,242	West, John	93,422	Fauntroy, Walter E.*	1,879	76,180 D	15.3%	83.0%	15.6%	84.4%
1980	151,046	21,245	Roehr, Robert J.	112,339	Fauntroy, Walter E.*	17,462	91,094 D	14.1%	74.4%	15.9%	84.1%
1978	96,306	11,677	Champion, Jackson R.	76,557	Fauntroy, Walter E.*	8,072	64,880 D	12.1%	79.5%	13.2%	86.8%
1976	159,790	21,699	Hall, Daniel L.	123,464	Fauntroy, Walter E.*	14,627	101,765 D	13.6%	77.3%	14.9%	85.1%
1974	104,014	9,166	Phillips, William R.	66,337	Fauntroy, Walter E.*	28,511	57,171 D	8.8%	63.8%	12.1%	87.9%
1972	159,612	39,487	Chin-Lee, William	95,300	Fauntroy, Walter E.*	24,825	55,813 D	24.7%	59.7%	29.3%	70.7%
1971S**	116,635	29,249	Nevius, John A.	68,166	Fauntroy, Walter E.	19,220	38,917 D	25.1%	58.4%	30.0%	70.0%

Note: An asterisk (*) denotes incumbent. **The 1971 election was held in March for a short term until the end of the 92nd Congress.

DISTRICT OF COLUMBIA

GENERAL AND PRIMARY ELECTIONS

2018 GENERAL ELECTIONS: OTHER VOTES

Delegate Other vote was 8,636 Statehood Green (Natale "Lino" Stracuzzi), 5,509 Independent (John Cheeks), 4,034 Libertarian (Bruce Majors), 1,766 Write-in

2018 PRIMARY ELECTIONS: SUPPLEMENTARY INFORMATION

Primary	July 9, 2018	**Registration** (as of July 9, 2018)	479,723	Democratic	364,514
				Republican	29,504
				Statehood Green	3,802
				Libertarian	1,090
				No Party Affiliation	80,813

Primary Type Closed—Only registered Democrats and Republicans could vote in their party's primary.

	REPUBLICAN PRIMARIES			DEMOCRATIC PRIMARIES		
Delegate	Write-in	750	100.0%	Norton, Eleanor Holmes*	60,842	76.5%
				Ford, Kim R.	18,178	22.9%
				Write-in	515	0.1%
	TOTAL	*750*		*TOTAL*	*79,535*	

Note: An asterisk (*) denotes incumbent.